LAW AND BUSINESS OF THE ENTERTAINMENT INDUSTRIES

LAW AND BUSINESS OF THE ENTERTAINMENT INDUSTRIES

Fifth Edition

DONALD E. BIEDERMAN
Former Executive Vice President/Legal & Business Affairs and General Counsel, Warner/Chappell Music, Inc., Los Angeles, CA and Professor of Law and Director, National Institute of Entertainment & Media Law Southwestern University School of Law, Los Angeles, CA

EDWARD P. PIERSON
Executive Vice President/Legal & Business Affairs and General Counsel, Warner/Chappell Music, Inc., Los Angeles, CA and Adjunct Professor of Law Southwestern University School of Law, Los Angeles, CA

MARTIN E. SILFEN
Member of the Virginia Bar, Fulbright Senior Specialist and Adjunct Professor of Law, Intellectual Property Summer Institute at Franklin Pierce Law Center, Concord, NH

JANNA GLASSER
Vice President and General Counsel, Mona Lisa Sound, Inc.
Law Offices of Janna Glasser, Esq.
Member of the New York Bar

CHARLES J. BIEDERMAN
Counsel, Manatt, Phelps & Phillips, LLP, Los Angeles, CA,
Member of the New York, Georgia, and Tennessee Bars

KENNETH J. ABDO
Vice President, Lommen Abdo Law Firm, Minneapolis, MN
Adjunct Professor of Entertainment Law, William Mitchell College of Law, St. Paul, MN

SCOTT D. SANDERS
Scott D. Sanders, P.C., and Adjunct Professor, Emory University School of Law, Atlanta, GA
Member of the Georgia Bar

 PRAEGER

Westport, Connecticut
London

Library of Congress Cataloging-in-Publication Data

Law and business of the entertainment industries / by
Donald E. Biederman . . . [et al.]. – 5th ed.
     p. cm.
   Includes bibliographical references and index.
   ISBN 0–275–99205–5 (alk. paper)
   1. Performing arts–Law and legislation–United States. 2. Entertainers–Legal status, laws,
   etc.–United States. 3. Artists' contracts–United States. I. Biederman, Donald E.
   KF4290.L39 2007
   344.73'099–dc22   2006025317

British Library Cataloguing in Publication Data is available.

Library of Congress Catalog Card Number: 2006025317
ISBN: 0–275–99205–5

First published in 2007

Praeger Publishers, 88 Post Road West, Westport, CT 06881
An imprint of Greenwood Publishing Group, Inc.
www.praeger.com

Printed in the United States of America

The paper used in this book complies with the
Permanent Paper Standard issued by the National
Information Standards Organization (Z39.48–1984).

10 9 8 7 6 5 4

CONTENTS

ACKNOWLEDGMENTS

The help we received from those we thanked in earlier editions is still reflected in the pages of the new edition. In the Fourth Edition, we thanked the following and we continue to gratefully recognize their contributions and support: Linda Benjamin and Tom Garvin, of Garvin & Benjamin, Los Angeles; Don Engel, of Engel & Engel, Los Angeles; David Gurley, Staff Counsel, Division of Labor Standards Enforcement, California Department of Industrial Relations; Professor Sheldon H. Halpern, of Ohio State University School of Law; Rob Hassett, of Hassett, Cohen, Goldstein & Port LLP, Atlanta; Bob Kohn, of Emusic.com; Donald S. Passman, of Gang Tyre Ramer & Brown, Beverly Hills; Chip Robertson, of Paul Hastings Janofsky & Walker, Los Angeles; Carol Fein Ross and Mitchell Kinzer, of Warner Books, New York; Ira B. Selsky, of Grubman Indursky & Schindler PC, New York; Anthony J. Sylvester, of Riker, Danzig, Scherer, Hyland & Perretti LLP, Morristown, New Jersey; and our research assistants for the Fourth Edition: Kimberly Frasca, Rebecca Leithen, Pauliana Nadjarians, Bryan Sullivan, and Vito Torchia, Jr.

For this, the Fifth Edition, we would individually like to express our thanks to the following colleagues and research assistants from whom we have had the benefit of assistance, support and encouragment:

From Martin E. Silfen, Esq.

Alison S, Cohen, Esq., of Epstein, Levinson, Bodine, Hurwitz and Weinstein LLP and

Joseph J. Dapello, Esq., of Schreck, Rose, Dapello and Adams LLP for their forms and text.

Melissa Daniel, of William & Mary School of Law for her valuable research and editing assistance.

From Ed Pierson, Esq.

We gratefully acknowledge the work and assistance of Zeina Hamzeh who has made great contributions to this edition. Also many thanks to Marie Creakman. We would also like to acknowledge our appreciation for the years of support we have received from Southwestern University School of Law (including, without limitation, Doreen Heyer, Assistant Dean for Academic Support, and Professor Robert Lind)

From Janna Glasser, Esq.

Dawn Jubeck, Assistant to Jay S. Bowen, Esq., and Jay S. Bowen, Esq., Bowen Riley Warnock & Jacobson, PLC for their insight and assistance in *PolyGram, Inc. v. Legacy Entertainment Group, et al.*

Marc J. Zwillinger, Esq., and his assistants Tritina L. Johnson and Joanne C. Whitley, Sonnenschein Nath & Rosenthal LLP, for their assistance in *DirecTV v. Pepe, et al.*

From Jeff Biederman, Esq.

Jordan Bromley for his tireless research assistance and good ideas

Alan M. Brunswick, Esq. for sharing his knowledge regarding collective bargaining agreements in the entertainment industries.

Stan Soocher, Editor-in-Chief, Entertainment Law & Finance; Associate Professor of Music & Entertainment Studies at the University of Colorado at Denver

Jeffrey D. Neuburger, Brown, Raysman, Millstein, Felder & Steiner LLP, New York

Melissa Biederman and Marna Biederman for their research and organizational assistance

Anna, Will, and Alex for their love and support and for sharing me all those weekends

From Ken Abdo, Esq.

Professor Jack Sahl for contributions to Chapter 1

Melissa Clark, Esq. for research assistance to Chapters 1 and 8

Theresa Abdo Whelan for research and editing assistance Chapters 1, 4, and 8

Lon Sobel for contributions to Chapter 8

Bryan R. Feldhaus, Esq. for research assistance

Daniel M. Satorius, Esq., Lommen Abdo Law Firm, Minneapolis, for editorial assistance to Chapter 8

From Scott Sanders, Esq.

Bertis E. Downs IV, REM general counsel and Adjunct Professor at University of Georgia School of Law, Athens, GA

Stan Soocher, Editor-in-Chief, Entertainment Law & Finance; Associate Professor of Music & Entertainment Studies at the University of Colorado at Denver

Michael B. Landau, Professor and Director, Intellectual Property Law Program, Georgia State University College of Law, Atlanta; co-author of *Lindey on Entertainment, Publishing & the Arts*

John L. Simson, Executive Director, SoundExchange, Washington, D.C.

Robert "Bob" Donnelly, Esq. New York

Thanks to all of them, and to those who have been in our corner from the beginning

Lastly, our thanks to all those who gave us permission to include their writings in this volume. To paraphrase the late Casey Stengel, "We couldna done it without the players."

May 2006
The Authors

DEDICATION TO DON BIEDERMAN

My father died on August 8, 2002. In the days after he died, time seemed elastic. Big chunks seemed to fly by in an instant. In other moments, time slowed, sounds seemed muffled, and we seemed to be walking under water. I remember being amazed that the world went on in its normal rhythm, when it had so fundamentally changed. One of the first concrete things I remember doing after coming back from the hospital was calling Suzanne Staszak-Silva, our publisher's editor, to tell her Dad had died, and that our family wanted this book to continue.

My father had reason to be proud of this book and his other successes, although they seemed almost commonplace to me growing up, viewed against the backdrop of family history: My great grandfather Benjamin and his brother, as very young boys, made their way from Hungary, across Europe, and across the sea to New York. He made a life here, a world away from home, not knowing the language. Benjamin's son, William, was the first child of that generation to live beyond the age of five. Benjamin died young, leaving William's mother to raise William, and his younger siblings, Jeannie and Martin.

William earned a scholarship to Cornell University. While there, he ran cross-country, rowed crew, and was Phi Beta Kappa, while working two jobs and helping to support his mother, brother, and sister back home. William earned a Ph.D. in chemical engineering and became a professor at Columbia University. When the Great Depression began, William left Columbia and became an orthodontist, a better paying career that helped him support his growing family. He remained an academic at heart, inventing and patenting a number of orthodontic instruments.

My father, in his turn, won a New York State Regents scholarship, attended Cornell, and graduated from Harvard Law School. His early career was spent in the JAG Corps in the Army, as a staff attorney for the City of New York, and then in private practice in a small firm in Queens. As family lore tells it, late one morning, one of the name partners in my father's firm came into his office and asked if my dad could cover a deal for him. My father agreed and the partner handed over a thick document. "What is this?" My father asked. "It's a record deal. You need to be in the City this afternoon to negotiate it." "We do record deals?" My dad asked, skeptically. The partner replied that there was nothing to worry about, that my dad could read it on the train into the City. Apparently that negotiation went well, as a few months later, my father was offered a position as General Attorney at CBS Records. He worked in the music business for the next twenty-eight years.

Many years later, after he had moved on from CBS to be Vice President at ABC Records, a partner at Mitchell, Silberberg, & Knupp, and for the last 17 years of his career, Executive Vice President for Legal and Business Affairs and General Counsel for Warner/Chappel Music, I saw him speak to a group of law students. Following his talk, a student asked him, "How come you've never been the number one guy at the companies you work for? Don't you want to be the number one guy?" My dad laughed. [This talk took place during the successful run of the great Buffalo Bills teams of the early '90s.] He replied that the question was quintessentially American: Why is it that in this country we assume being number one is everything and anything less nothing? Marv Levy was a great coach, and the Bills were one of the great teams in history. The fact they hadn't been able to win "The Big One" didn't erase the fact that they had been the dominant NFL team for many years. Then he smiled, paused and said, "You know, I don't think anyone would look at my career and say it was B+; and I certainly don't feel that way. . . . I wouldn't change a single thing about my life. Not a thing. You know, the Number One Guy never makes it to a dance recital or a Little League game."

By the time the first edition of this book came out, William Biederman had died. One of the very few regrets my father ever verbalized to me was that his father had not lived to see it. My grandfather and my dad were close, but my grandfather did not fully understand why my father did not have the same singularity of purpose that he did. To my grandfather's old-world sensibilities, the fact that my dad played in a band and played and loved sports was strange and a distraction from *Work*.

My father was proud of his career, but always said his greatest achievement was his family. My grandfather would have been immensely proud of his son authoring this book and being recognized as a leader in his chosen field. Now it is my turn to try to fill William's son's very big shoes. Don Biederman is gone, but I have been given the privilege of contributing to this fifth edition of this work.

I have two sons of my own—Will and Alex. I will share with them the stories of Benjamin and William Biederman's struggles to launch this family in this country—a level of energy and effort that was always held up to me as heroic. But I think I will emphasize more the lessons that William's son taught to me: that one's greatest achievement is one's family, that one's relationships are the measure of the man, that being a hero is more than dramatic achievements, that sometimes it's the guy who just puts on his pants in the morning and goes to work who is the true hero. Every day I live, that lesson makes more sense.

"Ever the best of friends, Pip"
—*Charles Dickens' Great Expectations*

Charles J. Biederman
Santa Monica, California
March, 2006

DON BIEDERMAN REMEMBERED AND MISSED

The entertainment law community lost a great friend, mentor, and legend with the passing of Donald Biederman on August 8, 2002.

Don's law practice, writings, teachings, and reputation touched hundreds of entertainment law practitioners. For many of us he set the standard and model that one aspires to in an entertainment law practice.

Don was Executive Vice President and General Counsel of Warner/Chappell Music, Inc., where he worked for over seventeen years. He was also the Director of Southwestern Law School's National Entertainment and Media Law Institute (which later changed its name to the Donald E. Biederman Entertainment and Media Law Institute in honor of Don). He was the initial and lead co-author of every prior edition of this casebook as well as the editor of another book entitled, *Legal & Business Problems of the Music Industry.*

As we reflect back on his rich life, the common theme, recalled by those of us who had the pleasure to know and work with him, is that Don Biederman was a man of absolute integrity, a man whose word could be relied upon and who would always do what was right, fair, and just. In addition, his legal skills and intellect were unparalleled. No one could write a letter as pithy, clever, powerful, or inspired as Don. When it came to drafting contracts, Don became respected and recognized for his ability to take the long, complex, unreadable agreement and reduce it to a short and concise agreement that would state exactly what the parties intended in a way all could understand.

Don was a friend to many and his generosity was boundless. He was always incredibly generous with his time. He helped lawyers, students, musicians, and songwriters in countless ways: making recommendations when one was out of work, helping a student understand a concept after hours, helping the struggling musician or songwriter pay the rent. Scores of entertainment lawyers (this author included) can and will forever state and remember, "I would not have my job today were it not for Don Biederman."

The first Music Chair of the American Bar Association's Forum Committee on the Entertainment and Sports Industries (from 1980–1983) was Don Biederman. In that role he helped many of us learn about music law and helped us to become involved in his committee. At the time he was a partner in the Los Angeles law firm of Mitchell Silberberg & Knupp. Prior to that, he was vice president of legal affairs and administration for ABC Records, Inc. from 1977–1979 and entered the field of entertainment law as a general attorney for CBS Records Group in 1972.

As if his role as a great lawyer, executive, author, teacher, and father were not enough to secure his legacy and the respect of his peers, Don Biederman's six year battle with cancer showed us dignity, courage and bravery that was nothing short of miraculous.

We shall always miss Don: his humor, his friendship, his intellect, his heart and his inspiration.

May we all find some of that inspiration he had and shared in the students that he taught, the lawyers he mentored, the writings he left, the reputation he still has, and the standard he has set.

Ed Pierson

INTRODUCTION:
AN OVERVIEW

As the entertainment industries (which for the purposes of this work, include theatrical films, television, records, music publishing, literary publishing, and "new media") expand globally, both economically and culturally, and are ever-challenged by the new technologies of the times, interest in the legal and business considerations of these industries expands. Essentially, these are industries that deal with content and its distribution—art and technology constantly assure that the areas of law that concern these industries are forever challenged.

For some, the law and business are more fascinating, dramatic, and comical than much of the content they concern. For all of us who are or will be involved in the content and distribution of entertainment properties, legal and business issues multiply as artists create in new media, content is distributed in new formats, and entertainment becomes more global.

When the first editions of this book were "published" (in a pre-internet world utilizing substantial amounts of "magic transparent tape" and many hours at a copy machine), "entertainment law" was a new area of study taught by a handful of largely part-time professors at perhaps a dozen law schools. When the authors of this work set out to refine and expand their self-published sets of materials and to collaborate on the initial edition of this book, they had to face the same questions the reader faces at this point in the reading and the study (i.e. what is the scope and perspective of the study of entertainment law and just what is it that we call entertainment law?).
The title of the book provides the basic answer to the question.

Unlike other areas of law where "the law of" a topic was appropriate and applicable, we saw the need to include "Law and Business" in the title. We saw a set of industries that was first perpetually challenged by the clash of art and commerce and only grew and thrived by a balancing of both the legal and business aspects that it involved. If one wants to be in the business of entertainment, we believe that person should have an understanding of the art, the law and the business. Great law means little or nothing without great content and a full understanding of how the industry and its economics work. As important as it may be for an entertainment lawyer to understand digital rights from an international copyright perspective, it is an understanding of how an artist is paid (to the penny) on a digital download, a master ringtone, or the "streaming" use of a song on a subscription service that the entertainment lawyer needs to know.

Also, the title of this book denotes "industries" as being plural and, in so doing, we see and recognize that each of these industries has distinct business practices and customs. While there may be a common component of distribution involved (and a handful of multi-national companies such as Disney, Fox, or Time Warner do control much of the content being distributed), we believe a full understanding (in particular of the content [vs. distribution] side of entertainment) requires an appreciation for the nuances and practices of each of the respective industries.

Finally, we elected not to use the words "entertainment law" in the title for several reasons. If one asks lawyers who consider themselves entertainment lawyers what entertainment law is, one will receive many different answers. For some, it is a business of rights, be they copyright, trademark, privacy, or publicity. For others, it is litigation and the perspective pleadings, court and appellate practice where the emphasis is on demands, claims, defenses, and law. But most entertainment lawyers are involved in and varying degrees focus on the transaction: that is the focus of this textbook. Specifically, we try to focus on what the primary role of an entertainment lawyer is in the publication of a book or the release of a recording, DVD, the production of a television program, motion picture, or game and the transactional issues they raise.

The legal aspects of the entertainment industries involve many areas of law that include intellectual property, corporate, anti-trust, tax, labor, tort, and contract law. Entertainment law sounds sexy, but it is really an amalgam of the very basic tenets of law, applied to new fact patterns, technologies, and media. Certainly, it is more fun to say one represents Britney Spears or Brad Pitt, but as an entertainment lawyer, one should always have the emphasis on "lawyer," not entertainment. This means knowing the foundations of law, not just being up on the latest technologies.

The approach of this textbook to these areas is as follows: first, we will look at the various representatives of entertainers, including lawyers, managers, and agents, and the unique legal and regulatory issues their relationships create. Then, we will look at the two fundamental areas of any entertainment content development, acquiring talent and the complex issues of rights (both recognizing and acquiring them). In Chapters 4 and 5 we will look at some of the unique issues of contract performance, exploitation obligations, and remedies that involve entertainment. Chapters 6 though 10 focus on five of the primary entertainment industries: literary publishing, music publishing, sound recordings, film, and television. Finally, in Chapter 11 we will look at new technologies, business models, and industries.

In reading these materials we urge you to consider several overriding themes:

Everything in entertainment becomes increasingly global as technology expands without bounds.

Technology and globalization—at the same time they create new opportunities and areas for exploitation, they create new risks and dangers to owners of entertainment content.

Intellectual property protection and legislation on an international basis are essential and are forever being challenged by technology.

Entertainment properties increasingly are being released in a multitude of configurations and industries: songs become plays that become movies that become books that become Broadway plays that become video games that have action figures that will have their own TV show that will appear as characters in someone's virtual life website.

Entertainment and advertising will continue to merge and blend and in doing so, will ever-challenge rights owners and those who represent them.

There will be continued and accelerated consolidation in the entertainment industries as the various technologies converge. There are also indications of a reverse trend, as the reality that with bigness comes smallness, economics and creativity will always fuel the entry of new players in the entertainment industries.

Finally there were the entertainment industries before the Internet and digital technologies, and we see industries forever changed and changing. It is an exciting time to be an entertainment lawyer. We say "bring it on."

Part One

Chapter 1

REPRESENTING TALENT

1.1 A BUSINESS OF INTERMEDIARIES

This chapter discusses issues that arise between talent and various types of professional representatives.

As anyone who has attended the various industry conferences that have proliferated in recent years can attest to, the "newbies" who come to network, ask questions and test the water for opportunities to enter "the Business," most often ask questions regarding representation: When do I need a manager? Whom should I choose? How do I get an agent? Do I need a lawyer to look over my first contract? Who do I need to get my tape/script/CD/headshot to, in order to get a [fill in the blank]? What these questions indicate is that even the uninitiated have grasped the fact that this is an industry full of intermediaries and gatekeepers. Most people have in their mind the relationship between the characters portrayed by Cuba Gooding, Jr. and Tom Cruise in the film, *Jerry Maguire:* Everyone is looking to find (or become) someone who gets the call to "show me the money!"

Although many talented people are adept at handling their business affairs, and the general awareness and knowledge of the industry (thanks to the proliferation of books, college, business and law school programs, and conferences on the entertainment industries) has increased over time, "talent" still engages a wide range of professionals to assist them in handling their careers. An established artist will normally have a "team" of advisors that includes, among others, a personal manager, business manager, agent, and attorney. At its best, the team represents a varied skill and contact set that can be utilized to further the artist's career objectives.

The various team members are commonly paid a percentage of the entertainer's income. This makes these service providers equity participants in the artist's career, giving them an incentive to provide maximum effort, while allowing the artist to get the help she or he needs but cannot afford. Personal managers are typically paid 15%–20% of the artist's "gross income" [although "gross" is usually reduced by a number of "carve outs"], agents receive 10% of income from bookings, business managers typically receive 5% of income received by the artist. These percentages vary in relation to the relative bargaining power of the parties involved, but regardless, they represent a significant portion of an artist's overall income. It should be noted that some business managers will operate on an hourly basis, and increasingly, lawyers are operating on a percentage in the way personal and business managers have traditionally done. These arrangements normally provide for a commission rate of 5%, with some attorneys lowering that rate on income derived from touring.

An agent's job is to find work for their clients. In the film and television industries the agents wield immense power, as they are the gatekeepers to the casting directors, producers and studios, the people who place a particular actor in a film, television program, or commercial. Young people enter the agencies in the mailroom hoping to hustle their way in to an assistant position on an agents "desk," where they can make their mark. The classic case is David Geffen who, after starting in the William Morris mailroom, went on to found first Asylum Records (which he sold to Warner Communications, Inc.), Geffen Records (which he later sold to MCA Records in a deal valued at over $500 million, only to see the value of his MCA shares balloon to over $700 million when MCA was acquired by Matsushita), and to produce on Broadway (*Cats, Dreamgirls*), and for the screen (*Little Shop of Horrors* and *Beetlejuice*). Subsequently, Geffen became (along with Steven Spielberg and Jeffrey Katzenberg) a founding principal of DreamWorks SKG. In recent years, in order to increase the potential for higher compensation (by, for example, producing films one's clients are starring in), as well as the opportunity to avoid regulation, many agents have become managers, and have gone into business with their former agency clients and others. As we will see below, such activity appears to be perfectly legal in both New York and California, so long as the venture is not a subterfuge.

"Personal managers," the "quarterbacks" of the team, are a slightly different breed, at least theoretically. Although they resemble agents in their involvement with the endless dealmaking which characterizes the entertainment industries, genuine personal managers are concerned with career development and will therefore be focused on long term planning, as well as the day-to-day activities of their clients. One recent trend in personal management has been the creation of multi-office, national (and sometimes international) management firms. Management Companies like The Firm, Red Light, Q Prime and Nettwerk, manage a wide variety of talent and frequently have auxiliary businesses that assist that talent with aspects of their career like merchandise, website development, etcetera. A powerful management company can be an invaluable asset to a musical artist in today's unstable business climate. Industry critics often complain that the record labels do not have the time or inclination to develop artists any more. What these large management firms provide is the resources and reach to do artist development. In the best case scenarios, these firms become, in effect, another label, giving the artist a better chance of breaking through to success.

In addition to "*personal* managers," there are "*business* managers," usually (but by no means always) CPAs, who generally restrict themselves to *financial* aspects of their clients' careers. The business manager's functions can range from simple accounting services to paying the client's bills, advising on investments, effectively running tours, and other extremely complicated functions. A business manager has strong fiduciary obligations to the client, as is illustrated by *ABKCO Music Inc. v. Harrisongs Music, Ltd.*, which follows.

Attorneys and personal managers have for many years been the predominant dealmakers in the fields of records and music publishing. This may be due to the fact that records did not begin to develop into a truly major area of the entertainment industries until the 1950s, and did not receive a great deal of attention from the agents until the attorney/manager pattern had become established. It may also be due to the fact that each of the various entertainment industries is a "people" business—a relatively small number of participants who know and deal with each other constantly. Then, too, in California and New York, agent fees are effectively limited to 10 percent of gross receipts (while personal managers customarily receive anywhere from 15 to 25 percent, although in individual cases the fees may run higher or lower), and the California Labor Commission will not approve an agent's contract that does not require a measurable level of performance: A certain amount of work must be secured on a regular basis, or the artist can terminate the term of the agreement. These considerations may act as something of a deterrent to the involvement of agents in records and music publishing.

Because entertainment law is a highly competitive practice, the lawyer often assumes non-traditional legal roles and responsibilities. Marketing, advertising, selling (shopping), packaging, networking and deal-making are common business activities for agents, managers and lawyers. As a result, lawyers often resemble agents and managers. However, lawyers are distinguishable from agents, managers and entrepreneurs because they are governed by codes of professional behavior. Unlike agents and managers, lawyers must be highly educated and trained. They must pass a bar examination before being licensed to practice law. Their qualifications and character are scrutinized prior to entering law school and before taking the bar exam. After becoming licensed, most states require lawyers to continue legal education and training to maintain licensure.

Lawyers' achievements are often overshadowed by criticism of lawyer self-interest, greed, and incompetence. As a result, grievances and malpractice claims are filed against entertainment lawyers. A lawyer's violation of the code threatens his or her reputation, license, and livelihood. Lawyers' reputations depend on their ability to build and maintain ethical and professional relationships. Terms such as fiduciary, counselor, mediator, arbitrator and advocate reflect the critical and powerful roles that lawyers perform. Despite the jokes and jabs, the high standard of living that many lawyers enjoy reflects the significant value that society attaches to legal services.

Entertainment attorneys who aggressively represent clients often test the limits of permissible professional conduct by acquiring an ownership interest in a client's career or when they seem to become advocates of their own self-interest instead of their clients'. Given the highly competitive and entrepreneurial nature of the entertainment business, it is not surprising that entertainment lawyers are the subject of complaints before disciplinary authorities and the courts.

1.2 ATTORNEYS

Practicing law today involves significant risks, given the increase in the complexity of the law, advancements in technology, the sophistication of clients who expect competent, efficient and reasonably priced services, and the litigious nature of consumers. Entertainment lawyers must know how their insurance policies define the practice of law to insure that the policies cover their activities. It is worth noting that in recent years, legal malpractice insurers have become aware of the unique risks entertainment lawyers face. Insurance questionnaires specifically inquire whether the lawyer provides services akin to management or agent work.

Professional responsibility is one of the most rapidly changing fields in law—creating additional risk for lawyers. There have been changes to the ABA Model Rules of Professional Conduct (1983) (MRPC), a code of ethical conduct that has been adopted in some version by more than 45 states. Courts adjudicating malpractice actions, and disciplinary authorities considering grievances, often use these codes to evaluate the propriety of lawyer conduct. In 2002, the American Bar Association adopted substantial revisions to the MRPC. The name and format of the amended Rules are the same as in 1983. Although few states presently follow the MRPC as amended in 2002, many have established committees to review the changes. This section refers to the amended Model Rules, unless stated otherwise.

1.2.1 Establishing an Attorney-Client Relationship

Courts and disciplinary authorities have found that the attorney-client relationship exists as soon as the client reasonably relies on the attorney's advice. As a result, attorneys must be careful about casually offering advice on legal matters. An attorney should formally establish a professional relationship with a client and memorialize it in writing. An attorney should not give advice unless the attorney is prepared to accept responsibility for the consequences of the client's reliance thereon. Lawyers should be especially careful not to give advice at "beauty contest" interviews by parties seeking to hire lawyers, because they may be liable for incorrect advice and may also be precluded from representing the clients' opponents for conflict of interest reasons. Ideally, the attorney should inform a prospective client at the initial meeting that he or she is not providing legal advice, and should reiterate this point in a follow-up letter thanking the person for his or her interest. This follow-up letter may also include the terms of a retention agreement that should have been discussed at the initial meeting. The retention agreement should clearly outline the scope and conditions of the lawyer's representation as well as the basis for the fee if the client decides to employ the attorney. A comprehensive and precise retention agreement defines the expectations of the attorney and the client, facilitates good client relations, and protects the attorney against claims of wrongdoing based on the client's unreasonable expectations.

1.2.2 Duty of Competence

One of the most important decisions an attorney makes is the decision to represent a client. Attorneys are generally free to reject a client's offer of employment. However, once an attorney agrees to represent a client, MRPC 1.1 requires the lawyer to provide competent representation. Competence requires the legal knowledge, skill, thoroughness, and preparation reasonably necessary for the representation. The Comment to MRPC 1.1 states that in determining the competency of a lawyer to handle a matter, "relevant factors include the relative complexity and specialized nature of the matter, the lawyer's general experience, the lawyer's training and experience in the field in question, and the preparation and study" the lawyer can give to the matter. Thus, attending continuing legal education programs for entertainment lawyers is a good idea. The comment also recognizes that it may be necessary to associate or consult with a more experienced lawyer or even refer the matter to another lawyer. As a result, consultations even among more experienced entertainment lawyers are common and highly advisable. Lawyers must be careful in making referrals or associating counsel because they might be liable for incompetent referrals or associations.

1.2.3 Conflicts of Interest

Conflicts of interest in the entertainment industry have increasingly attracted significant attention. The public and the profession seem to have insatiable appetites for following lawsuits filed by famous artists against their famous lawyers. The lawsuits arc a wake-up call to many entertainment lawyers to re-examine their practices in light of the profession's codes of conduct. The unconventional culture of the entertainment business is conducive to conflicts of interest and other lawyer misconduct. The business is fast-paced, highly competitive, and intense.

It has also been described as "incestuous"; a premium is attached to "who you know." The entertainment business also tends to be dominated, at least at the corporate top, by a small number of resilient power brokers. It is not unusual for these individuals to be fired or to resign from their positions and then to resurface in a similarly powerful position in another company. Good entertainment lawyers follow the trade journals and other media to track the activities and movements of this group. Part of the purpose of keeping abreast of such developments in the entertainment business should be to avoid conflicts of interest and other potential ethical problems.

It is worth noting that many in the entertainment business feel that conflicts of interest not only are common but also may be beneficial to parties. For example, if a prominent entertainment attorney represents a successful producer and a famous actor and unites them, as some agents do, in a "package" deal, that combination may insure a "box-office hit." Although the package deal brings together clients with possibly differing interests, the combination ultimately makes the producer, actor, lawyer, and studio more successful. Everyone wins. For a less famous talent, the package is very valuable because it could launch their career towards national prominence. There is always the risk however, that attorneys may protect their special relationships with the studio and others in package deals by promoting more prominent clients at the expense of less famous clients.

1.2.3.1 Multiple Client Representation

MRPC 1.7 sets forth the general rule governing conflicts of interest:

a. *Except as provided in paragraph (b), a lawyer shall not represent a client if the representation involves a concurrent conflict of interest. A concurrent conflict of interest exists if:*

   (1) the representation of one client will be directly adverse to another client; or

   (2) *there is a significant risk that the representation of one or more clients will be materially limited by the lawyer's responsibilities to another client, a former client or a third person or by a personal interest of the lawyer.*

b. *Notwithstanding the existence of a concurrent conflict of interest under paragraph (a), a lawyer may represent a client if:*

   (1) *the lawyer reasonably believes that the lawyer will be able to provide competent and diligent representation to each affected client;*

   (2) *the representation is not prohibited by law;*

   (3) *the representation does not involve the assertion of a claim by one client against another client represented by the lawyer in the same litigation or other proceeding before a tribunal; and*

   (4) *each affected client gives informed consent, confirmed in writing.*

Under MRPC 1.7(a), an attorney's simultaneous representation of a music manager who is a prior client and an artist in negotiating their artist-management contract raises serious conflicts of interest issues.

Some commentators contend that attorneys should decline joint representation in this context because of the inherent conflict in the positions of the parties. The parties' interests with respect to certain contract provisions, such as the duration of the contract, may be directly adverse. Even if the parties' interests are not directly adverse, a concurrent conflict of interest may exist if there is a significant risk that the attorney's responsibilities to the earlier client, the manager, may materially limit the attorney's representation of the artist and violate 1.7(a). The manager's attorney should ask the artist to retain independent counsel to facilitate the negotiation of the contract, to help ensure the enforcement of an eventual agreement, and to avoid personal liability for violating the conflict of interest rules. Another, perhaps less prudent, option is for the manager's attorney to obtain written informed consent from both clients of any conflicts of interest. It is important to note that some conflicts are nonconsentable. Comment 14 to MRPC 1.7 describes a nonconsentable conflict as one in which, "the lawyer involved cannot properly ask for such agreement or provide representation on the basis of the client's consent."

1.2.3.2 The Comments to MRPC 1.7—A Better Understanding of Conflicts of Interest

The conflict of interest rules are designed to protect and advance two important values—confidentiality and undivided loyalty—in the attorney-client relationship. These two values overlap and are at the core of the lawyer's fiduciary duty to clients. Both values are disregarded by a lawyer who harms a client by sharing the client's confidences with the client's adversary—reflecting obvious disloyalty. The Comments to MRPC 1.7 provide additional insight concerning the lawyer's ethical duty of loyalty to the client.

The Comment to MRPC 1.7(a) indicates that an attorney is generally prohibited from representing a client when that representation involves a concurrent conflict of interest. "Thus, absent consent, a lawyer may not act as an advocate in one matter against a person the lawyer represents in some other matter, even when the matters are wholly unrelated. Another less obvious example involves several parties forming a partnership. The safest practice is for each partner to secure separate counsel in negotiating or reviewing the partnership agreement. Alternatively, MRPC 1.7 expressly provides that after full disclosure of the potential conflicts of interest, the parties can waive such conflicts of interest by giving their informed consent, confirmed in writing, to multiple representations. Of course, if a direct conflict of interest does arise between the parties during the negotiation of the partnership agreement, or litigation erupts among the parties, the Comment to MRPC 1.7 suggests that unless the lawyer has obtained the informed consent of the client under the conditions of 1.7(b), the attorney ordinarily must withdraw in order to safeguard the confidentiality of the parities pursuant to MRPC 1.6. It is important to note that the representation of multiple parties is not uncommon and not always impermissible in the entertainment business. For example, it may be permissible for a lawyer to negotiate a recording contract for a manager and the members of a group with a third party record label.

The Comment to MRPC 1.7(a) explains that loyalty to the client is also compromised "when there is significant risk that the representation of one or more clients will be materially limited by the lawyer's responsibilities to another client, a former client or a third person or by a personal interest of the lawyer. . . . " In such a case, the lawyer is unable to recommend or carry out an appropriate course of action for the client. For example, a lawyer representing a personal manager in an artist management contract cannot ethically acquiesce to a shorter duration of the contract because the artist's father, a builder, has promised to give the lawyer a good rate on remodeling his home.

Subdivision (b) of MRPC 1.7 permits a lawyer to represent a client notwithstanding the existence of a concurrent conflict of interest if (1) the lawyer reasonably believes that the lawyer will be able to provide competent and diligent representation to each affected client; (2) the representation is not prohibited by law; (3) the representation does not involve the assertion of a claim by one client against another client represented by the lawyer in the same litigation or other proceeding before a tribunal; and (4) each affected client gives informed consent, confirmed in writing. It is often very difficult to anticipate, and thus to inform the individuals in the group about, all of the possible future conflicts of interest that may arise among them. When a lawyer is in doubt about undertaking or continuing representation because of a conflict of interest concern, he or she should consult with other lawyers, preferably experts in professional responsibility. If the lawyer is still concerned about the representation, he or she should decline representation until the new client responsible for the conflict of interest obtains independent counsel.

The Comments to MRPC 1.7 acknowledge that conflicts of interest in contexts other than litigation may be difficult to assess. "Relevant factors in determining whether there is significant potential for material limitation include the duration and intimacy of the lawyer's relationship with the client or clients involved, the functions being performed by the lawyer, the likelihood that disagreements will arise, and the likely prejudice to the client from the conflict. The question is often one of proximity and degree." Thus, the evaluation of lawyer conduct in the entertainment industry will involve to some degree the custom and nuances involved in the business as well as the MRPC and its Comments. For example, if the lawyer represents a corporation which may "loan-out" the services of the artist or manager shareholder, the Comments warn of the potential for conflict if the lawyer also serves on the corporation's board of directors.

1.2.3.3 Other Noteworthy Conflicts of Interest Issues

Business transactions. On its face, MRPC 1.8 appears to state clearly that a lawyer shall not enter a business transaction with a client unless

(1) the transaction is fair and reasonable to the client, (2) the client is advised in writing of the desirability of seeking and is given a reasonable opportunity to seek the advice of independent legal counsel on the transaction, and (3) the client gives informed consent, in writing and signed by the client, to the essential terms of the transaction and the lawyer's role in the transaction, including whether the lawyer is representing the client in the transaction. Does entering into a shopping agreement for a contingent fee from income derived from a record contract, the sale of a book, or some similar deal constitute entering a business transaction? The attorney should disclaim in the shopping agreement that the parties are entering into a joint business venture, to help ensure that the lawyer does not violate the ethical rules concerning a business transaction with a client.

Payment for attorney fees by another. MRPC 1.8(f) permits someone other than the client to pay the lawyer for his services if the client gives informed consent and there is no interference with the lawyer's independent professional judgment and relationship with client, including the need to protect client confidences. For example, a manager could pay a lawyer to represent an artist in divorce proceedings. It is even possible, although not especially advisable, that a manager could pay a lawyer to represent an artist and negotiate a personal management agreement with the manager's lawyer. If the fee arrangement creates a conflict of interest for the lawyer, then the lawyer must comply with MRPC 1.7.2 (1.8 Comment 12 says this).

Attorney interest in literary rights. MRPC 1.8(d) precludes a lawyer from making or negotiating an agreement with the client prior to the conclusion of the representation that gives the lawyer literary or media rights to a portrayal or account based in substantial part on information relating to the representation. In the context of ongoing litigation, the conclusion of representation occurs when there is a non-appealable final judgment. It is important to note that the rule does not prohibit a lawyer representing a client in a transaction concerning literary property from accepting as his fee an ownership interest in the property.

Conflicts in representing former clients. Like practicing in small communities, the "incestuous" entertainment industry gives rise to potential conflicts of interest with respect to representing a party against a former client. MRPC Rule 1.9 and its Comments state that a conflict of interest arises with a former client when the lawyer's representation of a new client bears a "substantial relationship" to the matter of the representation that the attorney provided to a former client. Disqualification of a lawyer from the subsequent representation is for the protection of the former client. The lawyer should either withdraw from representation or seek the former client's informed consent regarding the conflict of interest, realizing that in some cases a waiver will be difficult because of the risk that the lawyer will harm the former client by using the former client's confidences. The former client's informed consent must be confirmed in writing. In this type of conflict of interest situation, the lawyer is advised to have as full and frank a discussion as possible with parties, keeping in mind the need to preserve each client's secrets and confidences.

1.2.4 Music Lawyer as Manager or Agent

Lawyers can serve as agents or managers while simultaneously practicing law. In the music industry, lawyers procure recording contracts for their clients and help manage their career by participating in career strategy and deal making. Unlike agents, lawyers usually do not regularly book personal appearances for their clients. Thus, lawyers often tend to act more like managers than agents. Personal management requires daily and detailed attention to the personal affairs and logistics of an artist. Because an experienced music lawyer may know the business better than an inexperienced manager, the attorney who has a proactive relationship with the artist and manager may find himself or herself making recommendations, facilitating relationships, creating opportunities, and advising the manager as well as the artist. By doing so, the lawyer becomes, in effect, part of the management team. In some cases, the attorney may be invited by both artist and management to take on duties that are generally the prerogative of artist management. This usually means representation on a contingent fee basis and greater involvement with the artist's daily affairs in addition to providing general legal counsel. By limiting the work a lawyer can dedicate to other legal clients, the attorney may become more like a company general counsel or "in-house" lawyer.

Lawyers are agents and it is axiomatic that an attorney's authority to represent clients creates an agency and fiduciary relationship. Attorneys who regularly (and not "incidentally") make deals on a speculative basis in return for a contingent payment may still be required to be separately licensed as an agent under the applicable statute of the state in which the attorney's principal place of business is located. This should obviate the need for the attorney/agent to register as an agent elsewhere. However, should an attorney/agent establish an office or agency in a state in which he or she is not licensed to practice law, licensing under that state's rules as an agent (and certainly as an attorney, if the intention is to practice law) will be required.

1.2.5 Special Considerations Regarding Lawyer Conduct

1.2.5.1 Merging the Roles of Various Entertainment Representatives

Lawyers' ethical obligations are extensive and often long lasting. These obligations also create challenges for entertainment lawyers who perform services often rendered by other personnel, such as agents. The general rule is that entertainment attorneys who also act as agents or managers are still subject to their states' codes of professional conduct to the extent that any of their activities involve the delivery of legal services. Lawyers cannot merely switch titles to avoid their ethical responsibilities. As a result, lawyers have taken different approaches to dealing with what is perceived as a competitive disadvantage in the entertainment business when acting in these other roles. Some attorneys argue that when they act as an agent or a manager they are not providing legal services and, therefore, are not subject to the codes of professional conduct. This approach has some risk as lawyers' professional liability policies may not cover all of their services. Other attorneys formally establish separate businesses that render financial advice, career advice, or solicit employment opportunities. The attorneys may incorporate the businesses and employ full-time personnel but they expressly do not provide legal services.

As long as attorneys are licensed to practice law, they are subject to their states' codes of professional conduct for even their non-professional activities. Lawyers must be very careful when creating separate business enterprises to make sure that these are not used to circumvent the lawyer's ethical obligations. For example, a lawyer could create a separate talent agency and then solicit in-person talent for the agency. The lawyer could not use such solicitation, however, to develop clientele for his law practice.

1.2.5.2 Advertising and Solicitations

MRPC 7.2 and 7.3 governs lawyer advertisement and solicitation. In general, lawyers can mail written advertisements and solicitations directly to prospective clients providing they are truthful and non-deceptive. Lawyers may also advertise through recorded or electronic communication, including public media. Lawyers "shall not by in-person, live telephone, or real-time electronic contact solicit professional employment from a prospective client when a significant motive for the lawyer's" contact is pecuniary gain, unless the person contacted is a lawyer or has a family, close personal, or prior professional relationship with the lawyer. Lawyers also cannot state or imply that they are specialists in a field of law, such as entertainment law, unless the lawyer has been certified as a specialist by an organization that has been approved by an appropriate state authority or that has been accredited by the American Bar Association and the name of the certifying organization is clearly identified in the communication.

Entertainment lawyers can communicate or promote their legal services in several ways in hope of developing their practice. The most effective way is to establish a strong reputation for providing competent and efficient legal work with the general public as well as the profession. Lawyers are able to create a profile in the arts and entertainment community by attending industry events, volunteering their service for arts organizations, authoring entertainment law articles, writing and lecturing for continuing legal education programs, and speaking to non-lawyer groups, which are all effective ways to network and to develop an entertainment practice.

1.2.6 Compensation for Attorney Services and Retention Agreements

Entertainment lawyers deal in the development of creative material. Their relationships with talent and entertainment companies are important to developing a successful practice. Lawyers market or "shop" talent and their creative properties to companies for purchase, license and ultimately for commercial exploitation. Shopping talent and their properties is highly speculative work—only a very small percentage of talent or their properties ever achieve commercial success. Since many entertainment clients cannot afford to retain lawyers on an hourly basis for their services, including shopping their creative work, clients and lawyers instead often agree to a contingency fee arrangement. A comprehensive retention agreement for legal services should unambiguously address scope of representation and the basis of payment. A separate shopping agreement may also be considered if this is the primary or only service provided by the attorney.

Unlike employment contracts with managers and agents, clients can terminate employment contracts with lawyers at any time. If a client terminates his or her lawyer, the lawyer is generally entitled to only quantum meruit recovery. Lawyers offer a broad range of professional services and it may be useful to have a specific contractual provision regarding the lawyer's shopping services and compensation. To help ensure that a lawyer's work is covered by his or her professional liability insurance, the retention agreement should specify that the client is retaining the lawyer primarily for law-related services. If the retention agreement provides for compensation based on an hourly rate, the rate for the lawyer's services will vary depending on a several factors, including the complexity of the representation, the lawyer's unique skills and experience, and the value for such services in a particular geographical area. Representation of a more national or international nature may generate higher hourly rates than for more local work. Lawyers' hourly rates for entertainment work generally range from between $200 to $400 per hour.

A customary contingent fee ranges from 5% to 10% of the defined compensation earned by the client and rarely exceeds 10%. The exact percentage depends, in part, on the client's record for commercial or critical success and the likelihood that the lawyer's efforts will be successful. For example, when representing musicians, it is reasonable with a superstar to be paid a lower percentage of the compensation than with a new or "baby act." Successfully shopping a new artist to a recording contract with a small, local, independent record company is a situation in which a lawyer might charge 10% of the artist's gross compensation. A lower contingency fee is expected if coupled with a reduced hourly fee. In both the hourly rate and the contingency fee arrangements, the client usually pays the out-of-pocket costs.

With contingency fee arrangements, the definition of compensation is a negotiated term. In many entertainment contracts, gross compensation is defined broadly. It may exclude, however, income that is not derived from or enhanced by the lawyer's professional services. For example, when representing a book author, it may be appropriate for the lawyer to include in gross compensation income from book publishing and also proceeds from television, a motion picture, or personal appearances. The lawyer wants to apply the contingency rate or commission to as much of the client gross compensation as is reasonable in the industry and under the MRPC. This may be justified because first, the book deal created all the other commercial opportunities for the client-author and second, the lawyer's legal services are being used in these other areas. It is worth noting that it may be in the client-author's best interests to exclude some streams of income, such as proceeds from music, theatrical, or other "unrelated" sources. Like managers, agents, and entertainment companies, lawyers are reluctant to limit the possible sources or streams of income. They usually insist on a percentage of the gross compensation from any source, whether known or yet to be discovered, especially given the trend in multimedia and the crossover nature of entertainment products in new technology. Lawyer contingency agreements, like personal management contracts, may also provide for a declining percentage rate after expiration of the term (a "sunset" provision). This provision requires the client to pay the contingency fee for the lawyer's past services even after the representation is terminated, usually for a period of six to twelve months. In addition and distinct from the sunset provision, the lawyer may negotiate and receive an ongoing commission on the client's proceeds derived from deals that the lawyer helped to procure for the client. The commission may be for a limited period or extend for so long as the artist receives royalties from that source.

Model Rule 1.5 requires hourly and contingent fees to be reasonable. Attorneys can consider the following criteria in determining a reasonable fee: "the time and labor required, the novelty and difficulty of the questions involved, the skill requisite to perform the legal service properly; . . . the fee customarily charged in the locality for similar legal services; the amount involved and the results obtained; . . . the experience, reputation, and the ability of the lawyer or lawyers performing the services required; and whether the fee is fixed or contingent." These criteria offer attorneys great flexibility and protection in charging fees. Thus, it is not unusual to find entertainment lawyers in different parts of the country charging similar fees for national or international projects because of the unique skill and experience they share in the field.

Contingent fee agreements must be in writing, signed by the client, and "state the method by which fees are to be determined, the percentage or percentages that shall accrue to the lawyer in the event of settlement, trial or appeal, litigation and other expenses to be deducted from the recovery, and whether such expenses are deducted before or after the contingent fee is calculated. The agreement must clearly notify the client of any expenses for which the client will be liable, whether or not the client is the prevailing party." Contingent fees may produce more income for attorneys than hourly fees. This is permissible, in part, because there is often a risk with contingent fees that the attorney will not be paid because the representation is unsuccessful. For many entertainment attorneys, the potential value of a deal or successful representation dictates the amount or reasonableness of a contingency fee.

Entertainment attorneys often assist in the personal management of a client. Managers frequently bill between 15% and 20% of a talent's gross income for their services. Attorneys assuming managerial responsibilities may wish to consider the customary amounts that managers are paid in setting a reasonable contingency fee.

In some entertainment fields, it is customary for the talent's services to be provided by a "loan-out" corporation, a "personal services" corporation, or some other entity, owned and controlled by the talent. Such entities include production, music touring and merchandise companies. The lawyer's Engagement Letter of Agreement should either acknowledge or anticipate the representation of these entities by including them as parties or having a contractual provision that designates the lawyer as the counsel for the entities upon their formation.

1.2.8 Sanctions

State supreme courts regulate the right to practice law even for lawyers who never appear in court. These courts establish codes of professional conduct and disciplinary systems to protect the public and the bar. Federal courts usually defer to state admission standards in admitting lawyers and admission is only necessary for those lawyers who practice in a particular federal court. Both state supreme and federal courts can discipline lawyers.

There are two principle methods by which the public can hold lawyers and judges accountable for their misconduct. The first method is filing a lawsuit against an attorney for civil liability. Most lawsuits filed against attorneys are for negligence, a fiduciary breach, breach of contract or fraud. Successful plaintiffs in lawyer liability cases are entitled to attorneys' fees and to punitive damages when the attorney's conduct involves gross negligence or malice.

The second method of holding lawyers accountable involves the states' disciplinary systems. Clients and others can file a grievance against an attorney with the state authority responsible for reviewing lawyer conduct, for example, the statewide disciplinary counsel. These authorities often rely on assistance from state and local bar associations to receive, review, investigate, prosecute, and hear grievances. Grievances and sanctions against lawyers have increased in recent years. The range of sanctions for lawyer discipline includes: disbarment, suspension, formal reprimand, informal reprimand, and a fine. One or more of these sanctions may be applied to an attorney for one significant violation or an accumulation of lesser violations of a state's professional conduct code.

NOTES _____

1. The California Labor Commissioner ruled that an attorney who owned a production company was not procuring employment as an agent for an artist/client when he hired the artist to be in one of his productions. The Commissioner held that an attorney having an ownership interest in the employment is functioning as an employer, not as an agent "with third parties" within the meaning of the Act. However, conflict of interest issues were raised but not resolved by the Commissioner.

2. Author John Grisham sued his attorney for breach of fiduciary duty and malpractice, in part, for not advising him of the conflicts of interest in the attorney's simultaneous representation of both Grisham and his agent. Grisham claimed he retained the lawyer on the advice of his agent and that the attorney failed to inform Grisham that he did not have to renew his original agreement with the agent. *See* Richard E. Flamm & Joseph B. Anderson, *Conflict of Interest in Entertainment Law Practice, Revisited,* 14 ENT. & SPORTS L. J. 3 (1996) (discussing *Grisham v. Garon-Brooke Assocs., Inc.,* Action No. 3:96 CV045-B (N.D. Miss. 1996)).

3. MRPC, Rule 1.7, Comment 14. Billy Joel sued his former New York lawyers claiming $90 million in damages. The law firm was regarded as one of the most powerful music entertainment law firms. Joel charged attorney Grubman with conflict of interest, alleging that Mr. Grubman represented the singer while also representing his manager, top executives of his recording label, CBS Records (now Sony/BMG Music), and the merchandising company that holds the franchise for t-shirts and other items. Grubman's firm alleged that any conflicts were fully disclosed. Joel's conflict of interest claims also include an allegation that Grubman paid kickbacks to Billy Joel's manager in order to retain Joel as a client. Joel also claimed breach of contract, fraud, breach of fiduciary duty, and legal malpractice against his former attorney. Grubman was hired by Billy Joel's manager (and former brother-in-law) to represent Joel in negotiations with CBS Records. In a separate action, Joel also sued his former manager. *Joel v. Grubman,* 1992, Case No. 261–55–92 N.Y. Sup. Ct.

4. A television producer sued his former law firm alleging that the firm secretly represented other clients whose interests conflicted with his. Producer Phillip DeGuere, Jr., claimed that CBS contracted with him as writer and executive producer on "The Twilight Zone" series. CBS canceled the series after taping only nine of the 22 episodes it had ordered. DeGuere claimed that, under the contract, the network owed him $900,000 but that upon counseling with his law firm, he agreed to accept $250,000 in cash and a commitment for a different 13-week series in a subsequent season. DeGuere claimed he did not know that at the same time the law firm was representing him against CBS, the firm was also representing Columbia Pictures against CBS in a deal for the purchase of the daytime drama, "The Young and The Restless." DeGuere's suit claimed that, because CBS paid a premium price for the soap opera, it was forced to cut development of new shows, including a new television project produced by DeGuere, hence limiting CBS's ability to perform under the terms of his settlement agreement with him. DeGuere's attorney stated that the law firm should not be representing studios when they are also representing talent who must negotiate deals with those studios. *Persistence of Vision, Inc. v. Ziffren, Brittenham & Branca,* 1992, L.S. Sup. Ct. Case No. BC021603.

5. *Id.* At Rule 1.7, Comment [6]; *see Cinema 5, Limited v. Cinerama, Inc.,* 528 F.2d 1384 (2d Cir 1976) (establishes the general standard in federal courts that a lawyer cannot sue an actively represented client of another firm in which the attorney is a partner). *But see Universal City Studios v. Reimerdes,* 98 F. Supp. 2d 449 (S.D.N.Y. 2000). In *Reimerdes,* Time Warner sought the disqualification of a lawyer who represented a defendant in a suit by the movie studios against the defendant who posted a computer program over the Internet that defeats the encryption

system for DVDs. *Id.* 450–51. The same lawyer represented Time Warner and other defendants in an unrelated suit involving the rights to the term, "Muggles," from the Harry Potter books. *Id.* The federal judge in the Southern District of New York denied Time Warner Entertainment's disqualification motion because Time Warner had improperly delayed the filing of its motion to unfairly prejudice the defendant. *Id.* at 455. In addition, there was no evidence that the defendant's lawyer was privy to any of Time Warner's secrets because of the lawyer's work for Time Warner involving the "Muggles" case. *Id. See also* Stan Soocher, *Bit Parts* 16 Enter. Law & Fin. 8 (May 2000) (briefly discussing *Reimerdes*).

6. The widow of the late popular songwriter and singer, Jim Croce, sued in New York Federal Court claiming unconscionability and breach of fiduciary duty against Croce's publishers, managers, and an attorney on managerial and personal services contracts. At the initial meeting, an attorney was introduced to the Croces as "the lawyer" and reviewed the contract terms. The Croces were aware that the attorney had a business relationship with the publishers and managers on the transaction. Although the attorney was clearly not the Croces' lawyer, and the Court upheld the contracts, the Court found the attorney liable for all of Croce's legal fees in challenging the contracts. The Court held that the attorney had breached a fiduciary duty to the Croces by failing to advise them to seek independent counsel. The lesson of the Croce case is that a lawyer who stands to profit from a business enterprise may find himself in a fiduciary relationship with a non-client by failing to advise independent counsel at the outset. The case has also inspired the inclusion of an acknowledgment in management contracts that the artist has been advised of the opportunity to seek independent counsel. *Croce v. Kurnit*, 565 F. Supp. 884 (S.D.N.Y. 1982), *aff'd.*, 737 F.2d 229 (2d Cir. 1984).

7. MRPC, Rule 1.9(a) & (b)(2). An action was filed by Steve Fargnoli, a former manager for the musician, Prince, alleging a conflict of interest stemming from the Ziffren firm's formerly representing Fargnoli from 1981 to 1986, then later representing Prince during a time when Fargnoli sued the musician and his corporations. The suit alleged that the Ziffren firm disclosed to Prince some of Fargnoli's confidential communications protected under the attorney/client privilege. The Ziffren firm had helped Prince and Fargnoli settle a dispute during their representation of Prince and at the invitation of Fargnoli. In granting the law firm summary judgment, the Court noted that the parties had entered into a release including conflict of interest claims after the parties settled their dispute. *Fargnoli v. Ziffren, Brittenham & Branca*, 1992, Case No. BC068280 L.A. Sup. Ct.

8. The most common action brought against attorneys is for negligence. The essential elements of a negligence claim are: "(1) the employment of the attorney or other basis for imposing a duty; (2) the failure of the attorney to exercise ordinary skill and knowledge; and (3) that such negligence was the proximate cause of damage to the plaintiff;" and (4) actual damages. *Id.* at 607–08. As part of a lawyer malpractice action, courts have traditionally required the plaintiff to show that but for the attorney's conduct the client would succeeded in the underlying claim. S*ee, Kituskie v. Corbman*, 714 A.2d 1027 (Pa. 1998) (holding that the uncollectability of a judgment in the underlying action is an affirmative defense to a malpractice claim against an attorney); see also Morgan, *supra* note 8, at 89 (discussing lawyer malpractice claims and the so-called "suit-within-a-suit" requirement).

GENERAL LEGAL REPRESENTATION SERVICES INCLUDING SHOPPING

CONTINGENCY FEE BASIS

MUSIC

FORM AGREEMENT

_____, 20__

Jane Doe

John Doe

_____

Address

_____

_____

Re: ENGAGEMENT LETTER OF AGREEMENT

Dear Jane and John:

We are delighted to work with you and thank you for selecting our firm as your attorneys in connection with ongoing general counsel services related to your recording and entertainment career. "You" or "your" herein refers to "Jane Doe and John Doe, professionally known as "The JJ Band" or any entity subsequently formed by either of you or any renaming of any entity which continues to feature you as a music artist in the Entertainment Business (as defined in paragraph 4.d). Our engagement will be covered by the terms of this letter agreement, unless we mutually provide otherwise.

1. **TERM.** The Term of this Agreement is effective as of _____, 200__ and will continue until terminated in writing by either you or us subject to continuing payments under paragraph 4 and further subject to our exclusive representation of you for "Shopping" (as defined in paragraph 2.c).

2. **SCOPE OF SERVICES PROVIDED.**

    a) We will serve as general counsel to you on legal matters which shall generally include transactional work, including negotiating and drafting contracts and advising on the following matters: intellectual property (including trademark and copyright filings); Shopping and securing music recording, music publishing, personal management and business management contracts, which decision to enter shall be in your sole judgment; public appearances; literary; books; film and telefilm rights; the formation or maintenance of corporations or partnerships, corporate; labor; coordination and general supervision or engagement of other lawyers or experts; and other reasonably related services related to the Entertainment Business ("Services"). _____ will be your primary lawyer. We shall work in the interest of forwarding your career in the Entertainment and Literary Fields. We shall be directly accountable to you.

    b) The Contingent Fees (as provided in paragraph 4. herein), do not include compensation for our rendering legal advice on matters such as securities, investments, money management, tax, litigation, arbitration, and other matters that are not set forth in paragraph 2(a) hereof. It also does not include rendering Services in states, countries or jurisdictions in which the matter requires that we must be admitted to practice law. For those matters not covered by the contingent fees, we will advise you of the current hourly billing rates and you can decide whether you would like us to provide needed legal services or not.

c) *Shopping.* _____ shall be the principal lawyer responsible for your matters including efforts to secure the Recording and Publishing Agreements (as defined in paragraph 4(b)(ii)) with companies and upon terms to be approved at your sole discretion ("Shopping"). We shall be your exclusive Shopping representative for one (1) year ("Shopping Period") and will diligently present your music and assist you with identifying and corresponding with recording and publishing companies with the goal of finding a company with which you would like to enter an agreement for your services.

3. **TERMINATION.** Subject to the conditions set forth in paragraph 1., you can terminate this Agreement at any time for any reason. We can terminate this Agreement at any time, if we feel we can no longer properly represent you for any reason. Upon termination, you will pay us: (1) any undisputed hourly fees and charges due through the date of termination; (2) Contingent Fees as they come due and any costs incurred, including copying charges for any files in connection with any transfer thereof. If you and we agree, we shall provide Services through whatever project benchmark or assignment you want us to complete. Disputed fees and charges will be resolved by arbitration (see paragraph 8 below). Unless you and we otherwise agree in writing, we shall have no obligation to retain your files beyond one year after our Services conclude.

4. **CONTINGENT FEES AND COSTS.**

a) *Contingent Fees.* For Services to be rendered for the matters set forth in paragraph 2(a) hereof you shall pay us as "Contingent Fees" on "Gross Compensation" (as defined in paragraph 4(e) herein) from all sources in the Entertainment Business as follows:

   (i) Five percent (5%) of Gross Compensation and upon the termination of this Agreement, this amount shall be paid on Gross Compensation earned during one (1) year following termination. This amount shall exclude Contingent Fees for shopping.

   (ii) With respect to any recording agreement or music publishing agreement entered into or negotiated during the Term or Shopping Period, as a result of our Shopping efforts ("Recording and Publishing Agreements"), we shall be paid ten percent (10%) herein, on any money advances payable to you under the Recording and Publishing Agreements. The advances payable to you shall include any artist personal advance and any balance remaining to which you are entitled from a recording budget and/or recording fund ("Advances"). The Contingent Fees shall apply to Advances payable to you applicable to the first album under any Recording and Publishing Agreements.

   (iii) After the Term, we shall be paid Contingent Fees of five percent (5%) in perpetuity of all royalties payable to you or earned by you after repayment by you of any recoupable amounts payable against royalties applicable to the First Album limited to your recordings and compositions written by you which are released and exploited under the Recording and Publishing Agreements.

b) *Costs.* In addition to Contingent Fees, you will also be responsible for advancing or reimbursing us for costs and expenses we incur on your behalf. Such costs and expenses will be billed to you and will include photocopy charges (_____¢ per page), computerized legal research, staff overtime if required to meet deadlines imposed by you, travel expenses, filing fees, registration fees for copyrights and trademarks, messenger fees, long-distance telephone charges, outgoing and incoming fax (_____¢ per page), Federal Express or overnight delivery charges, secretarial overtime which is due to special needs of your matter, and miscellaneous expenses. To the extent we advance those costs on your behalf, you agree to reimburse us for them; and from time to time we may request that you make an advance payment for an unusual cost item. We will get your prior permission before incurring large client cost disbursements. No single expense of $100 or more will be expended without your consent.

c) "Entertainment Business" shall mean and include any and all branches of the entertainment, literary, broadcasting, merchandising, and/or commercial exploitation fields now existing or hereafter developed, direct or ancillary, including without limitation, all forms of motion pictures, personal appearances, personal endorsements, touring, radio, records, music, music publishing, recording, electrical transcriptions, books and printed material, television, telefilm, videodiscs and videocassettes.

d) "Gross Compensation" shall mean and include, without limitation, salaries, advances, earnings, fees, royalties, residuals, repeat and/or rerun fees, gifts (but only if such gifts are in lieu of partial or full compensation to you), and any form of payment in kind or bartered or exchanged services, bonuses, shares of profit, shares of stock, partnership interests, percentages and the total amount paid to you for any record package, television or radio program (live or recorded), motion picture or other entertainment packages, and/or which are earned and received directly or indirectly by you or your heirs, executors, administrators or assigns, or by any other person, firm or corporation as your compensation for activities in the Entertainment and Literary Fields. With respect to stock, or the right to buy stock, in any corporation, our percentage shall apply to said stock, or the right to buy stock, and we shall be entitled to our percentage share thereof. If any corporation, partnership, trust, joint venture, association, proprietorship or other business entity in which you have a direct or indirect interest shall receive any revenues or compensation for permitting or contracting for the use of your services, name, likeness, or endorsement, then your proportionate share of such revenues or compensation shall be deemed to be Gross Compensation received by you for the purposes of this Agreement.

e) Notwithstanding the foregoing, with respect to your personal appearances, for purposes of computing commissions hereunder, there shall be deducted from "Gross Compensation" earned by you in respect thereof, when applicable, the amount, if any, which shall be payable by you or on your behalf in respect of so called "Sound and Lights" (generally the direct cost to you for third-party-provided sound and lighting reinforcement for live performances) for such engagements.

Regarding personal appearances, agency fees, directly related transportation fees, equipment rental fees and lodging expenses shall also be deducted from Gross Income. In addition, the term "Gross Compensation" shall specifically not include actual recording costs (records and videos) paid by you or on your behalf to third parties, except with respect to a recording fund or recording budget on the first album; monies payable to you by any entity which monies are contractually required to be paid by you and are in fact paid by you to another record company (i.e., an "override"); payments paid by you, or paid on your behalf, to third parties in the nature of deficit tour support; and bona fide loans.

5. **REVIEW BY INDEPENDENT COUNSEL.** We hereby advise you to seek outside counsel in connection with this Agreement and your execution hereof. We cannot represent you in connection with any agreement with us and we give you no advice.

6. **BILLING LOGISTICS.**

a) For those matters that may be billed on an hourly basis, payment is due upon receipt of the invoice. A Statement of Account will be forwarded to you automatically each month if you have any outstanding invoices to be paid promptly. Regardless of how your payment is designated to be applied, all payments received will first be applied against accrued late payment charges, then to costs or expenses advanced or incurred, and last to fees. We add a late payment charge to accounts not paid within thirty days of the invoice date. The late payment charge is currently assessed at a rate of 1% per month on any unpaid balance for corporations and .66% per month for individuals or, if less, the maximum legal rate. In the event that an account becomes delinquent, the firm employs prudent collection procedures and the firm may discontinue representation. If an account goes unpaid for 120 days after the services are rendered, the account is referred to an attorney for collection. By entering this Agreement, you also agree to pay all costs incurred by this firm in collecting on your delinquent account, including reasonable attorneys' fees. Our minimum billing increment on hourly matters is currently one-quarter of one hour. At your request, from time to time, we would be happy to estimate our anticipated hourly fees on particular matters not covered by the Contingent Fee arrangement, but we cannot warrant that our estimates will be met, since legal costs cannot be predicted and are subject to many variables that neither we, nor you, can control.

b) Our Contingent Fees are payable immediately upon payment to you of Gross Compensation to which such Fees pertain. In that regard, we may include in any agreement which we negotiate on your behalf, as to which Contingent Fees apply, a provision irrevocably requiring the remitter to directly pay to us the Contingent Fees on your behalf simultaneously with payment to you of Gross Compensation. You shall render an accounting to us within fifteen (15) days of the end of each month, and with each payment you make to us showing the basis of such payment.

c) We, our accountants, attorneys or agents shall have the right to review your determination or calculation of Gross Compensation and the financial figures supporting the computation of your payments from Gross Compensation and any and all other relevant or supporting documents on which any Contingent Fee due us was or could be made. These shall include all tax returns, bank records and individual tax returns of shareholders or board members. In the reports presented to us from you, you shall explain the basis for the computation of Contingent Fees. If we shall so request, we shall be given the opportunity, upon reasonable advance written notice, and in a manner calculated to provide the least disruption to your business operations, review and audit the underlying figures giving rise to the Contingent Fee computations. Any such audit shall be conducted at our sole expense, except that, if the audit discloses that Contingent Fees paid to us were understated by an amount in excess of 10% for any Term Year, then you shall reimburse us for the reasonable expense of such audit.

7. **AVOIDING DISAPPOINTED EXPECTATIONS AND RESOLVING DISPUTES.** We want to serve you well. We believe that the best way to avoid disappointments and misunderstandings is for there to be frequent and open communication between us. You understand that we make no promises or guarantees about the outcome of any matter. If a dispute between us should arise, we want to settle it quickly and fairly. We will try to do so through discussion. If we are not successful in doing so, then both parties agree to settle any dispute arising between us by prompt, confidential and binding arbitration under the auspices and pursuant to the rules of the American Arbitration Association in Minneapolis, Minnesota.

8. **CONFLICTS OF INTEREST.** You understand that we represent other parties in the field of entertainment (and may have certain ownership or participation interests in entertainment ventures), and that from time to time conflicts of interest may arise between you and other clients of the firm. If a conflict arises of which we are aware we shall promptly advise you and we will try to assist in resolving such conflicts. If such conflict cannot be overcome, we will have the right to represent you, to represent others, or to withdraw completely. In any such case, it may be necessary for you to engage separate counsel.

9. **MISCELLANEOUS PROVISION.** This Agreement represents the entire agreement between the parties concerned and the subject matter hereof and supersedes all prior agreements with respect thereto between the parties hereto and any of them. This Agreement shall be binding upon and inure to the benefit of the parties hereto and their respective successors, assigns, heirs and personal representatives. This Agreement shall be subject to and governed by the laws of the State of Minnesota and all questions concerning the meaning and intention of the terms of this Agreement and concerning the validity hereof and questions relating to the performance hereunder shall be adjudged and resolved in accordance with the laws of said state. Whenever possible, each provision of this Agreement and each related document shall be interpreted in such manner as to be effective and valid under applicable law, but if any provision of this Agreement or any related document shall be prohibited by or invalid under applicable law, such provision shall be ineffective only to the extent of such prohibition or invalidity without invalidating the remainder of such provision or

the remaining provisions of this Agreement or such related documents. This Agreement may not be and shall not be deemed or construed to be modified, amended, rescinded, cancelled or waived in whole or in part except by written instrument signed by the parties hereto.

10. **SIGNING.** If you agree, sign and return. Please indicate your approval and agreement to the scope and terms of our engagement by executing the enclosed copy of this letter and returning it to me.

We look forward to working with you.

Yours very truly,

By:_____

ATTORNEY

Approved and agreed.

Dated:_____, 200_

Signed:_____

Signed:_____

[Artist(s) individually, professionally known as The JJ Band and doing business as (loan-out or services company)]

1.3 AGENTS AND PERSONAL MANAGERS

1.3.1 Union Regulation of Agents

In theatre, films and television, the activities of agents and unions are closely interrelated. Although the collective bargaining agreements by which employment in these industries are governed are negotiated directly between the unions and the producers, the overwhelming majority of working performers in these industries are represented by agents, who (with one major exception), in turn, are heavily regulated by the unions through their "franchising" systems, i.e., licenses under which agents agree to abide by specific union regulations. If an agent lacks a union "franchise," the members of the subject union are not permitted to engage that agent to represent them. One of the principal points upon which a union will insist is that the agent not commission minimum salaries, i.e., "scale" payments, or amounts received by way of reimbursement for such items as travel expenses in connection with work. Consequently, agents will seek a rate of scale plus ten percent (i.e. the amount of agent commission allowed under most franchise agreements). As of the time of this writing, there is no contract in place between the Screen Actors Guild (SAG) and the Association of Talent Agents (ATA). [ATA is a nonprofit trade association including over 100 talent agencies primarily located in Los Angeles and New York, representing artist clients in the areas of film, stage, television, radio, commercials and literary work.] Most of the major agencies have continued to operate under the parameters of the prior agreement, but smaller agencies (which, not coincidentally, are the agencies most available to new talent—i.e. those with the least amount of bargaining power) have been more aggressive regarding what funds are commissionable.

1.3.2 State Regulation of Agents

When examining state regulation of agents, the focus naturally starts with New York and California—the two states with the lion's share of the entertainment business in this country. Both require the licensing of agents, and serving as an agent without registering and being licensed can carry severe penalties, as the statutes set forth in this section reveal. Both licensed and unlicensed agents are affected by the legislation in these two jurisdictions.

Increasingly, other states are beginning to regulate agents. Rising costs for most elements of music, film and television production and increased competition from other states and territories for this lucrative "clean" industry have caused a diffusion of the entertainment business. [A good example would be the success of North Carolina in luring increased film-making to that state in the 1990s and migration of significant film work to Vancouver, British Columbia, the "Hollywood of the North".]

Who is an agent remains the fundamental question, as demonstrated in the seminal New York cases *Pine* and *Mandel.* In *Pine,* a "one-shot" effort at securing a recording contract resulted in a decision that the "finder" was an agent, whereas in *Mandel,* a non-practicing attorney, acting as a manager under a management contract that provided he not required in any to procure" employment, was found to be a manager rather than an unlicensed agent.

The pertinent portions of the New York and California statutes are provided below, along with cases interpreting the statutes. At the end of this section, we have provided a "typical" management contract for review.

1.3.2.1 New York General Business Law

§ 170. Application of article

This article shall apply to all employment agencies in the state.

§ 171. Definitions

Whenever used in this article:

1. "Commissioner" means the industrial commissioner of the state of New York, except that in the application of this article to the city of New York the term "commissioner" means the commissioner of licenses of such city.
2.a. "Employment agency" means any person (as hereinafter defined) who, for a fee, procures or attempts to procure:
(1) employment or engagements for persons seeking employment.
     . . . .
3. "Fee" means anything of value, including any money or other valuable consideration charged, collected, received, paid or promised for any service, or act rendered or to be rendered by an employment agency.
     . . . .
7. "Person" means any individual, company, society, association, corporation, manager, contractor, subcontractor, partnership, bureau, agency, service, office or the agent or employee of the foregoing.

8. "Theatrical employment agency" means any person . . . who procures or attempts to procure employment or engagements for circus, vaudeville, the variety field, the legitimate theater, motion pictures, radio, television, phonograph recordings, transcriptions, opera, concert, ballet, modeling or other entertainments or exhibitions or performances, but such term does not include the business of managing such entertainments, exhibitions or performances, or the artists or attractions constituting the same, where such business only incidentally involves the seeking of employment therefor.

9. "Theatrical engagement" means any engagement or employment of a person as an actor, performer or entertainer in employment. . . .

§ 172. License required

No person shall open, keep, maintain, own, operate or carry on any employment agency unless such person shall have first procured a license therefore as provided in this article. Such license shall be issued by the commissioner of labor, except that if the employment agency is to be conducted in the city of New York such license shall be issued by the commissioner of consumer affairs of such city. Such license shall be posted in a conspicuous place in said agency.

§ 174. Procedure upon application; grant of license

. . . .

2. Any person may file, within one week after such application is so posted in the said office, a written protest against the issuance of such license. Such protest shall be in writing and signed by the person filing the same or his authorized agent or attorney, and shall state reasons why the said license should not be granted. Upon the filing of such protest the commissioner shall appoint a time and place for the hearing of such application, and shall give at least five days' notice of such time and place to the applicant and the person filing such protest. . . . If it shall appear upon such hearing or from the inspection, examination or investigation made by the commissioner that the applicant or agency manager is not a person of good character or responsibility; or that he or the agency manager has not had at least two years experience as a placement employee, vocational counsellor or in related activities, or other satisfactory business experience which similarly tend to establish the competence of such individual to direct and operate the placement activities of the agency; or that the place where such agency is to be conducted is not a suitable place therefor; or that the applicant has not complied with the provisions of this article; the said application shall be denied and a license shall not be granted. Each application should be granted or refused within thirty days from the date of its filing.

§ 176. Assignment or transfer of license; change of location; additional locations

A license granted as provided in this article shall not be valid for any person other than the person to whom it is issued or any place other than that designated in the license and shall not be assigned or transferred without the consent of the commissioner. . . . The location of an employment agency shall not be changed without the consent of the commissioner, and such change of location shall be indorsed upon the license. . . .

§ 181. Contracts, receipts.

It shall be the duty of every employment agency to give to each applicant for employment:

1. A true copy of every contract executed between such agency and such applicant, which shall have printed on it or attached to it a statement setting forth in a clear and concise manner the provisions of sections one hundred eighty-five, and one hundred eighty-six of this article.
. . . .

3. A receipt for any fee, deposit, consideration, or payment which such agency receives from such applicant, which shall have printed or written on it the name of the applicant, the name and address of the employment agency, the date and amount of such fee, deposit, consideration or payment or portion thereof for which the receipt is given, the purpose for which it was paid, and the signature of the person receiving such payment. If the applicant for employment has been recruited from outside the state for domestic or house-hold employment the receipt shall have printed on it, or attached to it, a copy of section one hundred eighty-four of this article.

§ 185. Fees

1. Circumstances permitting fee. An employment agency shall not charge or accept a fee or other consideration unless in accordance with the terms of a written contract with a job applicant. . . . The maximum fees provided for herein for all types of placements or employment may be charged to the job applicant and a similar fee may be charged to the employer. . . .
2. Size of fee; payment schedule. The gross fee charged to the job applicant and the gross fee charged to the employer each shall not exceed the amounts enumerated in the schedules set forth in this section, for any single employment or engagement, except as hereinabove provided; and such fees shall be subject to the provisions of section one hundred eighty-six of this article.
. . . .

4. Types of employment. For the purpose of placing a ceiling over the fees charged by persons conducting employment agencies, types of employment shall be classified as follows: . . . Class "C"—theatrical engagements;
. . . .

8. Fee ceiling: For a placement in class "C" employment the gross fee shall not exceed, for a single engagement, ten per cent of the compensation payable to the applicant, except that for employment or engagements for orchestras and for employment or engagements in the opera and concert fields such fees shall not exceed twenty per cent of the compensation.

§ 187. Additional prohibitions

An employment agency shall not engage in any of the following activities or conduct:

(1) Induce or attempt to induce any employee to terminate his employment in order to obtain other employment through such agency; . . . or

procure or attempt to procure the discharge of any person from his employment.

(2) Publish or cause to be published any false, fraudulent or misleading information, representation, promise, notice or advertisement.
. . . .

(5) Send or cause to be sent any person to any employer where the employment agency knows, or reasonably should have known, that the prospective employment is or would be in violation of state or federal laws governing minimum wages or child labor, or in violation of article sixty-five of the education law relating to compulsory education or article four of the labor law, or, that a labor dispute is in progress, without notifying the applicant of such fact, and delivering to him a clear written statement that a labor dispute exists at the place of such employment, or make any referral to an employment or occupation prohibited by law.

(6) Send or cause to be sent any person to any place which the employment agency knows or reasonably should have known is maintained for immoral or illicit purposes; nor knowingly permit persons of bad character, prostitutes, gamblers, procurers or intoxicated persons to frequent such agency.
. . . .

(8) Engage in any business on the premises of the employment agency other than the business of operating an employment agency, except as owner, manager, employee or agent, the business of furnishing services to employers through the employment of temporary employees. . . .

§ 189. Enforcement of provisions of this article

1. This article shall be enforced by the commissioner of labor, except that in the city of New York this article and such sections shall be enforced by the commissioner of consumer affairs of such city.

2. To effectuate the purposes of this article, the commissioner or any duly authorized agent or inspector designated by such commissioner, shall have authority to inspect the premises, registers, contract forms, receipt books, application forms, referral forms, reference forms, reference reports and financial records of fees charged and refunds made of each employment agency, which are essential to the operation of such agency, and of each applicant for an employment agency license, as frequently as necessary to insure compliance with this article and such sections; but in no event shall any employment agency be inspected less frequently than once every eighteen months. The commissioner shall also have authority to subpoena records and witnesses or otherwise to conduct investigations of any employer or other person where he has reasonable grounds for believing that such employer or person is violating or has conspired or is conspiring with an employment agency to violate this article or such sections.

3. To effectuate the purposes of this article, the commissioner may make reasonable administrative rules within the standards set in this article. . . .

4. Complaints against any such licensed person shall be made orally or in writing to the commissioner, or be sent in an affidavit form without

appearing in person, and may be made by recognized employment agencies, trade associations, or others. The commissioner may hold a hearing on a complaint with the powers provided by section one hundred seventy-four of this article. . . . A daily calendar of all hearings shall be kept by the commissioner and shall be posted in a conspicuous place in his public office for at least one day before the date of such hearings. The commissioner shall render his decision within thirty days from the time the matter is finally submitted to him. The commissioner shall keep a record of all such complaints and hearings.

5. Following such hearing if it has been shown that the licensed person or his agent, employee or anyone acting on his behalf is guilty of violating any provision of this article or is not a person of good character and responsibility, the commissioner may suspend or revoke the license of such licensed person and/or levy a fine against such licensed person for each violation not to exceed $500. Whenever such commissioner shall suspend or revoke the license of any employment agency, or shall levy a fine against such agency, said determination shall be subject to judicial review in proceedings brought pursuant to article seventy-eight of the civil practice law and rules. Whenever such license is revoked, another license or agency manager permit shall not be issued within three years from the date of such revocation to said licensed person or his agency manager or to any person with whom the licensee has been associated in the business of furnishing employment or engagements. . . .

§ 190. Penalties for violations

Any person who violates and the officers of a corporation and stockholders holding ten percent or more of the stock of a corporation which is not publicly traded, who knowingly permit the corporation to violate sections one hundred seventy-two, one hundred seventy-three, one hundred seventy-six, one hundred eighty-four, one hundred eighty-four-a, one hundred eighty-five, one hundred eighty-five-a, one hundred eighty-six, or one hundred eighty-seven of this article shall be guilty of a misdemeanor and upon conviction shall be subject to a fine not to exceed one thousand dollars, or imprisonment for not more than one year, or both, by any court of competent jurisdiction. The violation of any other provision of this article shall be punishable by a fine not to exceed one hundred dollars or imprisonment for not more than thirty days. Criminal proceedings based upon violations of these sections shall be instituted by the commissioner and may be instituted by any persons aggrieved by such violations.

Pine v. Laine, 321 N.Y.S.2d 303 (N.Y. App. D.V. 1st Dep't. 1971)

Order of the Supreme Court, New York County, entered on September 30, 1970, denying defendant's motion for summary judgment, unanimously reversed, on the law, the motion granted, and the complaint dismissed. The Clerk is directed to enter judgment in favor of defendant dismissing the complaint, with costs. Appellant shall recover of respondent $50 costs and disbursements of this appeal.

Plaintiff sues for $35,000 for work, labor, and services performed in arranging a recording contract between the defendant and ABC Records. The Court at Special Term determined that there was an issue of fact "as to whether the plaintiff was acting as an employment agency or as the personal manager of the defendant when he performed the alleged services for the defendant. . . . "

Inasmuch as the plaintiff was not licensed as an employment agency pursuant to Article 11 of the General Business Law, unless he comes within the exception of § [171 (8)] as a personal manager where the seeking of employment is only incidental to the business of managing, he may not recover. See *Mandel v. Liebman*, 303 N.Y. 88, 100 N.E.2d 149 (1951).

It is clear that the defendant had a manager, and that the only service performed by the plaintiff, although he sought to become the manager of the defendant, was this one procurement of a recording contract.

Under the circumstances, plaintiff cannot come within the exception.

NOTES _____

1. It has been observed that while New York law has been interpreted to provide only a single exemption to licensing under the statute (that permitted for "incidental bookings"), the statute's language appears to contemplate two exceptions: First, there is the "business of managing . . . artists or attractions." In addition, it has been argued that the statute's language ("but such term does not include the business of managing") could be held to apply to nonmanagers such as producers, directors, or others who actually manage the *entertainment or performance* (as distinguished from managing, the *actual performer*). See Donald S. Zakarin, "Litigation Between Artists and Managers," in *Entertainment Litigation* (1988) (ABA Forum Committee on the Entertainment and Sports Industries, 750 No. Lakeshore Dr., Chicago, Ill. 60611).

2. Although, as will be seen below, California provides exclusive original jurisdiction over talent agency disputes to the Labor Commission, New York has no such statutory procedure and such questions must be resolved via the court system. However, if a licensed talent agent is involved, revocation of the agent's license can be a powerful lever for the complaining client. Since revocation of a license by an administrative agency is a quasi-judicial act, *Matter of 125 Bar Corp. v. State Liquor Authority*, 24 N.Y.2d 174 (1969), the "substantial evidence" test applies, *Matter of Older v. Board of Education*, 27 N.Y.2d 333, 337 (1941).

Mandel v. Liebman, 100 N.E.2d 149 (N.Y. 1951)

[Max Liebman began his career staging weekend musical revues at a summer camp in the Poconos. He moved on to produce "Your Show of Shows," 90 minutes live every Saturday night, certainly the preeminent variety show in the early years of TV and, arguably, still the best ever. In 1946, prior to his immense success in TV, Liebman signed a contract with Mandel, a nonpracticing attorney engaged in the business of personal management. The contract provided that Mandel would act as Liebman's "personal representative and manager" for five years for compensation of 10 percent of gross receipts from contracts entered into during the term as well as those extending beyond the term.

The agreement also provided that any income which might accrue to Liebman from the entertainment business thereafter "shall be due to the opportunities now procured for him" by Mandel.

Mandel had no express duties under the agreement. While the agreement stated that Liebman "hereby employs" Mandel "to use his ability and experience as such manager and personal representative in the guidance and furtherance" of Liebman's career, and "to advise him in connection with all offers of employment and contracts for services, and conclude for him such contracts," the contract went on to state that Mandel "shall only devote as much time and attention to the activities and affairs" of Liebman as Mandel's "opinion and judgment . . . deems necessary."

Two years later, the parties argued, and Mandel brought an action to recover unpaid commissions. The lower court dismissed his complaint on the grounds that the contract was an attorney's retainer agreement, and that a client has the right to discharge his attorney at any time, with or without cause, subject to payment of quantum merit for services rendered. The appellate division upheld the dismissal on the grounds that the agreement was unconscionable and therefore void as against public policy, because "the plaintiff was not required to render any services to defendant . . . and yet defendant was required to pay plaintiff 'what might be called a tribute in perpetuity.'"

The Court of Appeals reversed and ordered a new trial.

Conway, J.

It is commonplace, of course, that adult persons, suffering from no disabilities, have complete freedom of contract and that the courts will not inquire into the adequacy of the consideration. . . .

Despite the general rule, courts sometimes look to the adequacy of the consideration in order to determine whether the bargain provided for is so grossly unreasonable in the light of the mores and business practices of the time and place as to be unenforceable according to its literal terms. . . . It has been suggested that an unconscionable contract is one "such as no man in his senses and not under a delusion would make on the one hand, and as no honest or fair man would accept on the other." . . .

There might be some force to the claim of unconscionability in the case at bar if the contract could properly be construed as was done by the majority in the Appellate Division. . . . We do not think that that is a permissible construction under our decisions. See *Wood v. Lucy, Lady Duff-Gordon,* 222 N.Y. 88, 90–91. . . . Even if the contract had merely provided that plaintiff was employed "as personal representative and manager," with no further description of his duties, that would have been sufficient, for it could be shown that to these parties, in a specialized field with its own peculiar customs and usages, that phrase was enough to measure the entire extent of plaintiff's required services. . . .

The further provision . . . that plaintiff "shall only devote so much time and attention to [defendant's] activities and affairs . . . as the opinion and judgment [of plaintiff] deems necessary" must be given a reasonable interpretation consonant with the purpose of the contract. . . . The provision seems merely to constitute an attempt on the part of plaintiff to protect himself from excessive and unreasonable demands upon his time. See *Meyers v. Nolan,* . . . 18 Cal. App. 2d at page 323, 63 p. 2d at page 1217, where it was said: "The fact that the contract provided that the managers could devote as much time to defendant's affairs as they deemed necessary does not destroy its mutuality. The very nature of the business of the parties was such that representation of other actors was to be expected. The clause was evidently inserted to avoid any misunderstanding on the subject and to more clearly define the rights and obligations of the managers." Of course, as defendant urges, it is theoretically possible that plaintiff, under this provision, could deem it necessary to devote no time to the activities and affairs of defendant, but in that event, it is clear that plaintiff would not be performing the contract but would be breaching it and foregoing his right to compensation.

Since plaintiff, as we hold, was required to render some service to defendant under the contract, it cannot be said that the contract was unconscionable. . . . It is not for the court to decide whether defendant made a good or bad bargain. We fail to see how the contract can be described as one "such as no man in his senses . . . would make" and "no honest or fair man would accept" . . . or one which would "shock the conscience and confound the judgment of any man of common sense" . . . or even one which is "so extreme as to appear unconscionable according to the mores and business practices of the time and place" (1 *Corbin on Contracts,* sec. 128, p. 400), particularly since, as we are told, without denial the contract of May 8, 1946, is similar in most respects to contracts in current and general use in the entertainment industry. . . .

There is thus no need at this time to discuss the measure of compensation provided in the contract which the Appellate Division characterized as "a tribute in perpetuity." We note only, without passing upon the matter, that a question may be raised as to the validity or enforceability of one provision relating to compensation. Defendant agreed that any future earning of his in the entertainment world "shall be due to the opportunities now procured for him" by plaintiff. This provision would seem to create a conclusive presumption that any employments obtained by defendant during the term of the contract, and any continuance or renewal thereof thereafter, shall be deemed to have been due to the efforts of plaintiff, entitling the latter to the agreed percentage thereon. Somewhat comparable provisions have been held unenforceable. . . . The question, however, is not presented on this record for, while defendant did testify as to the amount of his earnings for the year in question and the different sources thereof, there was no evidence as to which sources were referable to plaintiff's advice, guidance and assistance, and which were not. . . .

Finally, we do not think that the contract of May 8, 1946, at least upon its face, may be held to be a retainer agreement between attorney and client with respect to some matter in controversy under which the client may discharge the attorney at any time. . . . Here, plaintiff was employed as defendant's personal representative and manager, a position which might well have been filled by a nonlawyer. As a lawyer, plaintiff might be called upon to use his legal training in handling defendant's affairs, but that is not sufficient, as a matter of law, to transform an otherwise binding contract of employment into a contract at will on the part of the employer. . . .

Likewise, it cannot be said as a matter of law that the contract was illegal and void for the reason that plaintiff, in violation of section 172 of the General Business Law, Consol. Laws, c. 20, was conducting a theatrical employment agency without a license therefor. By express exemption in subdivision 4 of section 171 of the General Business Law, a person engaged in the business of managing "entertainments, exhibitions or performances, or the artists or attractions constituting the same, where such business only incidentally involves the seeking of employment therefor" is not required to be licensed. . . . It was specifically provided that "this contract does not in any way contemplate that [Mandel] shall act as agent for the purpose of procuring further contracts or work for [Liebman]," that [Mandel] was "not required in any way to procure" such contracts or work, and that in the event [Liebman] "needs additional employment or work then an agent shall be employed by [Liebman] to procure such employment, and the services of said agent shall be separately paid for" by defendant. . . .

NOTES

The issue of unconscionability in management agreements was revisited in *Reznor v. J. Artist Management, Inc. et al.,* 365 F.Supp. 2d 565 (S.D.N.Y. 2005). In *Reznor,* Trent Reznor, lead singer of the band *Nine Inch Nails* ("NIN"), filed suit against his manager of fifteen years, alleging fraud, breach of contract, breach of fiduciary duty, and various other claims. At the time they met in 1988, Reznor was "a 'bit' player in a Cleveland band called the 'Exotic Birds' and his manager "worked in his family's machine equipment business by day and by night was a part-time promoter of local music acts. . . ." *Id.* at 568. By 1985, NIN had been approached for a recording agreement and the manager wanted a written contract. The manager asked an attorney, whom the management company had retained to negotiate the band's recording agreement, to prepare a written management contract. The manager testified that the attorney simply forwarded a standard form agreement for review, while the attorney testified that the manager supplied the attorney with the material terms of the deal. Both Reznor and the manager testified to the fact that the terms of the management agreement were not discussed prior to it being presented to Reznor in 1989. *Id.* at 5. "Reznor says that he may have glanced through [the Management Agreement], but because of his trust in [the manager] he signed the contract right there." *Id.* at 570. Granting the manager's request for summary judgment on the issue on unconscionability, the court noted that "at a minimum an unconscionability claim requires proof that a contract 'was both procedurally and substantively unconscionable when made— i.e. some showing of an absence of meaningful choice on the part of one of the parties together with contract terms which are unreasonable favorable to the other party'" *Id.* at 576 (citations omitted). The court noted that there was no allegation that, at the time management agreement was signed, Reznor lacked bargaining power relative to the manager, nor was there evidence that the terms of the deal [a five year term and 20% commission rate on contracts signed during the term of the contract] were so unfavorable or unusual as to violate public policy.

In *Reznor*, the manager wanted a written contract as his band's career began to "heat up." Would a signed deal memo have been sufficient? In *Gurley v. King*, 183 S.W. 3d 30 (Tenn. Ct. App. 2005), artist Matt King entered into a management contract with In House Inc. in 1995. Relations between King and In House soured, and In House brought in Cathy Gurley to assist in managing King. In March 1999, King and Gurley agreed that following the expiration of the In House/King agreement, King would engage Gurley as his manager, for three years, with a commission rate of 15% of gross income, the same rate provided for in the In House/King agreement. King and Gurley signed a memorandum of their agreement that provided: "*This letter will serve to state that I will sign an exclusive management agreement with Cathy Gurley for a period of three years. This will begin either when my agreement with In House ends (December 1999) or earlier if Cathy is able to persuade In-House to relinquish their contract. . . . The details of the agreement will be worked out later but will basically follow the same arrangement currently in place with In House.*"

In December of 1999, King and Gurley met and King suggested that they terminate their business relationship. Gurley eventually sued for breach of contract to enforce the memorandum, and King argued that it was only an "agreement to agree." The trial court granted summary judgment to King on the grounds that the memorandum was too uncertain and indefinite to be enforced. The Tennessee Court of Appeals reinstated the case for trial. The court noted the Court of Appeals of Texas discussion regarding the "governing principles of law": "It is only when an essential term is left open for future negotiation that there is nothing more than an unenforceable agreement to agree. . . . Under some circumstances, a binding contract may be formed if the parties agree on material terms, even thought they leave open other provisions for later negotiation. . . . Similarly, a letter of intent may be binding even though it refers to the drafting of a future, more formal agreement." *Id.* at 35. The *Gurley* court went on to state "[i]n the case at bar, we are dealing with [a case where] it is alleged that all material provisions of the Gurley/King Contract had been agreed to and the parties intended to formalize that agreement by a later writing. No "good faith" negotiation of essential elements of contract is involved." *Id.* at 41.

1.3.2.2 California Labor Code

(as amended by AB 1901, enacted September 1994)

Article 1: Scope and Definitions

§ 1700.1. Definitions—Engagements

As used in this chapter:

(a) "Theatrical engagement" means any engagement or employment of a person as an actor, performer, or entertainer in a circus, vaudeville, theatrical, or other entertainment, exhibition, or performance.

(b) "Motion picture engagement" means any engagement or employment of a person as an actor, actress, director, scenario, or continuity writer, camera man, or in any capacity concerned with the making of motion pictures.

(c) "Emergency engagement" means an engagement which has to be performed within 24 hours from the time when the contract for such engagement is made.

§1700.2. Fee Defined

(a) As used in this chapter, "fee" means any of the following:

(1) Any money or other valuable consideration paid or promised to be paid for services rendered or to be rendered by any person conducting the business of a talent agency under this chapter.

(2) Any money received by any person in excess of that which has been paid out by him for transportation, transfer of baggage, or board and lodging for any applicant for employment.

(3) The difference between the amount of money received by any person who furnished employees, performers, or entertainers for circus, vaudeville, theatrical, or other entertainments, exhibitions, or performances, and the amount paid by him to such employee, performer, or entertainer. . . .

§ 1700.3. License, Licensee—Defined

As used in this chapter:

(a) "License" means a license issued by the Labor Commissioner to carry on the business of a talent agency under this chapter.

(b) "Licensee" means a talent agency which holds a valid, unrevoked, and unforfeited license under this chapter.

§ 1700.4. Talent Agency, Artists—Defined

(a) "Talent agency" means a person or corporation who engages in the occupation of procuring, offering, promising, or attempting to procure employment or engagements for an artist or artists, except that the activities of procuring, offering, or promising to procure recording contracts for an artist or artists shall not of itself subject a person or corporation to regulation and licensing under this chapter. Talent agencies may, in addition, counsel or direct artists in the development of their professional careers.

"Artists" means actors and actresses rendering services on the legitimate stage and in the production of motion pictures, radio artists, musical artists, musical organizations, directors of legitimate stage, motion picture and radio productions, musical directors, writers, cinematographers, composers, lyricists, arrangers, and other artists and persons rendering professional services in motion picture, theatrical, radio, television and other entertainment enterprises.

Article 2: Licenses

§ 1700.5. Talent Agency—Must Obtain License

No person shall engage in or carry on the occupation of a talent agency without first procuring a license therefor from the Labor Commissioner. Such license shall be posted in a conspicuous place in the office of the licensee. . . .

§ 1700.6. License Application—Contents

The application must be accompanied by two sets of fingerprints of the applicant and affidavits of at least two reputable residents, who have known, or been associated with, the applicant for two years, of the city or county in which the business of the talent agency is to be conducted that the applicant is a person of good moral character or, in the case of a corporation, has a reputation for fair dealing.

§ 1700.7. License Applicants—Investigation

Upon receipt of an application for a license the Labor Commissioner may cause an investigation to be made as to the character and responsibility of the applicant and of the premises designated in such application as the place in which it is proposed to conduct the business of the talent agency. . . .

§1700.9. No license shall be granted to conduct the business of a talent agency:

(a) In a place that would endanger the health, safety, or welfare of the artist.
(b) To a person whose license has been revoked within three years from the date of application.

§ 1700.21. Revocation, Suspension of License—Grounds

The Labor Commissioner may revoke or suspend any license when it is shown that any of the following occur:

(a) The licensee or his or her agent has violated or failed to comply with any of the provisions of this chapter, or
(b) The licensee has ceased to be of good moral character, or
(c) The conditions under which the license was issued have changed or no longer exist.
(d) the licensee has made any material misrepresentation or false statement in his or her application for a license.

§ 1700.22. Revocation, Suspension of License—Hearing, Procedure

Before revoking or suspending any license, the Labor Commissioner shall afford the holder of such license an opportunity to be heard in person or by counsel. The proceedings shall be conducted in accordance with Chapter 5 (commencing at Section 11500) of Part I of Division 3 of Title 2 of the Government Code, and the commissioner shall have all the powers granted therein.

Article 3: Operation and Management

§ 1700.23. Contract Forms—Approval

Every talent agency shall submit to the Labor Commissioner a form or forms of contract to be utilized by such talent agency in entering into written contracts with artists for the employment of the services of such talent agency by such artists, and secure the approval of the Labor Commissioner thereof. Such approval shall not be withheld as to any proposed form of contract unless such proposed form of contract is unfair, unjust and oppressive to the artist. Each such form of contract, except under the conditions specified in Section 1700.45, shall contain an agreement by the talent agency to refer any controversy between the artist and the talent agency relating to the terms of the contract to the Labor Commissioner for adjustment. There shall be printed on the face of the contract in prominent type the following: "This talent agency is licensed by the Labor Commissioner of the State of California." . . .

§ 1700.24. Fee schedules of talent agency; Filing; Posting; Changes

Every talent agency shall file with the Labor Commissioner a schedule of fees to be charged and collected in the conduct of that occupation, and shall also keep a copy of the schedule posted in a conspicuous place in the office of the talent agency. Changes in the schedule may be made from time to time, but no fee or change of fee shall become effective until seven days after the date of filing thereof with the Labor Commissioner and until posted for not less than seven days in a conspicuous place in the office of the talent agency.

§ 1700.25. Trust Funds Accounts; Disbursement of Funds; Recordkeeping Requirements

(a) A licensee who receives any payment of funds on behalf of an artist shall immediately deposit that amount in a trust fund maintained by him or her in a bank or other recognized depository. The funds, less the licensee's commission, shall be disbursed to the artist within 30 days after receipt. However, notwithstanding the preceding sentence, the licensee may retain the funds beyond 30 days of receipt in either of the following instances:

   (1) To the extent necessary to offset an obligation of the artist to the talent agency that is then due and owing.

   (2) When the funds are the subject of a controversy pending before the Labor Commissioner under Section 1700.44 concerning a fee alleged to be owed by the artist to the licensee.

(b) A separate record shall be maintained of all funds received on behalf of an artist and the record shall further indicate the disposition of the funds.

(c) If disputed by the artist and the dispute is referred to the Labor Commissioner, the failure of a licensee to disburse funds to an artist within 30 days of receipt shall constitute a "controversy" within the meaning of Section 1700.44.

(d) Any funds specified in subdivision (a) that are the subject of a controversy pending before the Labor Commissioner under Section 1700.44 shall be retained in the trust fund account specified in subdivision (a) and shall not be used by the licensee for any purpose until the controversy is determined by the Labor Commissioner or settled by the parties.

(e) If the Labor Commissioner finds, in proceedings under Section 1700.44, that the licensee's failure to disburse funds to an artist within the time required by subdivision (a) was a willful violation, the Labor Commissioner may, in addition to other relief under Section 1700.44, order the following:

   (1) Award reasonable attorney's fees to the prevailing artist.

   (2) Award interest to the prevailing artist on the funds wrongfully withheld at the rate of 10 percent per annum during the period of the violation.

(f) Nothing in subdivision (c), (d) or (e) shall be deemed to supersede Section 1700.45 or to affect the enforceability of a contractual arbitration provision meeting the criteria of Section 1700.45.

§ 1700.26. Records Required

Every talent agency shall keep records in a form approved by the Labor Commissioner, in which shall be entered the following:

   (1) The name and address of each artist employing such talent agency;

   (2) The amount of fee received from the artist;

(3) The employment secured by the artist during the term of the contract between the artist and the agency, and the amount of compensation received by the artist pursuant thereto;

(4) Other information which the Labor Commissioner requires.

No talent agency, its agent or employees, shall make any false entry in any such records. . . .

§ 1700.30. Sale or transfer of interest in an agency without official consent

No talent agency shall sell, transfer, or give away to any person other than a director, officer, manager, employee, or shareholder of the talent agency any interest in or the right to participate in the profits of the talent agency without the written consent of the Labor Commissioner.

§ 1700.32. Publication of Information, Advertisements

No talent agency shall publish or cause to be published any false, fraudulent, or misleading information, representation, notice, or advertisement. All advertisements of a talent agency by means of cards, circulars, or signs, and in newspapers and other publications, and all letterheads, receipts, and blanks shall be printed and contain the licensed name and address of the talent agency and the words "talent agency." No talent agency shall give any false information or make any false promises or representations concerning an engagement or employment to any applicant who applies for an engagement or employment.

§ 1700.33. Sending Artist to Unsafe Place; Duty of Reasonable Inquiry

No talent agency shall send or cause to be sent, any artist to any place where the health, safety or welfare of the artist could be adversely affected, the character of which place the talent agency could have ascertained upon reasonable inquiry.

§ 1700.34. Minors—Sending to Saloons Prohibited

No talent agency shall send any minor to any saloon or place where intoxicating liquors are sold to be consumed on the premises.

§ 1700.35. Persons of Bad Character

No talent agency shall knowingly permit any persons of bad character, prostitutes, gamblers, intoxicated persons, or procurers to frequent, or be employed in, the place of business of the talent agency.

§ 1700.36. Applications from Children—Prohibited

No talent agency shall accept any application for employment made by or on behalf of any minor, as defined by subdivision (c) of Section 1286, or shall place or assist in placing any such minor in any employment whatever in violation of Part 4 (commencing with Section 1171).

§ 1700.37. Contracts with Minors—Disaffirmance

A minor cannot disaffirm a contract, otherwise valid, entered into during minority, either during the actual minority of the minor entering into such contract or at any time thereafter, with a duly licensed talent agency as defined in Section 1700.4 to secure him engagements to render artistic or creative services in motion pictures, television, the production of phonograph records, the legitimate or living stage, or otherwise in the entertainment field including, but without being limited to, services as an actor, actress, dancer, musician, comedian, singer, or other performer or entertainer, or as a writer, director, producer, production executive, choreographer, composer, conductor or designer, the blank form of which has been approved by the Labor Commissioner pursuant to Section 1700.23, where such contract has been approved by the superior court of the county where such minor resides or is employed.

Such approval may be given by the superior court on the petition of either party to the contract after such reasonable notice to the other party thereto as may be fixed by said court, with opportunity to such other party to appear and be heard.

§ 1700.38. Employment under Strike Conditions

No talent agency shall knowingly secure employment for an artist in any place where a strike, lockout, or other labor trouble exists, without notifying the artist of such conditions.

§ 1700.39. Fee Division with Employer—Prohibited

No talent agency shall divide fees with an employer, an agent or other employee of an employer.

§ 1700.40. Fees—Repayment

(a) No talent agency shall collect a registration fee. In the event that a talent agency shall collect from an artist a fee or expenses for obtaining employment for the artist, and the artist shall fail to procure such employment, or the artist shall fail to be paid for such employment, such talent agency shall, upon demand therefor, repay to the artist the fee and expenses so collected. Unless repayment thereof is made within 48 hours after demand therefor, the talent agency shall pay to the artist an additional sum equal to the amount of the fee.

(b) No talent agency may refer an artist to any person, firm or corporation in which the talent agency has a direct or indirect financial interest for other services to be rendered to the artist, including, but not limited to, photography, audition tapes, demonstration reels or similar materials, business management, personal management, coaching, dramatic school, casting or talent brochures, agency-client directories, or other printing.

(c) No talent agency may accept any referral fee or similar compensation from any person, association, or corporation, providing services of any type expressly set forth in subdivision (b) to an artist under contract with the talent agency. . . .

§ 1700.41. Reimbursement of artist for expenses incurred in going outside city in unsuccessful effort to obtain employment

In cases where an artist is sent by a talent agency beyond the limits of the city in which the office of such talent agency is located upon the representation of such talent agency that employment of a particular type will there be available for the artist and the artist does not find such employment available, such talent agency shall reimburse the artist for any actual expenses incurred in going to and returning from the place where the artist has been so sent unless the artist has been otherwise so reimbursed.

§ 1700.44. Dispute Determination by Commissioner; Appeal

(a) In cases of controversy arising under this chapter the parties involved shall refer the matters in dispute to the Labor Commissioner, who shall hear and determine the same, subject to an appeal within 10 days after determination, to the superior court where the same shall be heard de novo. . . .

(b) Notwithstanding any other provision of law to the contrary, failure of any person to obtain a license from the Labor Commissioners pursuant to this chapter shall not be considered a criminal act under any law of this state.

(c) No action or proceeding shall be brought pursuant to this chapter with respect to any violation which is alleged to have occurred more than one year prior to the commencement of the action or proceeding.

(d) It is not unlawful for a person or corporation which is not licensed pursuant to this chapter to act in conjunction with, and at the request of, a licensed talent agency in the negotiation of an employment contract.

§ 1700.45. Contractual Arbitration Provisions—Validity

Notwithstanding Section 1700.44, a provision in a contract providing for the decision by arbitration of any controversy under the contract or as to its existence, validity, construction, performance, nonperformance, breach, operation, continuance, or termination, shall be valid:

(a) If the provision is contained in a contract between a talent agency and a person for whom such talent agency under the contract undertakes to endeavor to secure employment, or

(b) If the provision is inserted in the contract pursuant to any rule, regulation, or contract of a bona fide labor union regulating the relations of its members to a talent agency, and

(c) If the contract provides for reasonable notice to the Labor Commissioner of the time and place of all arbitration hearings, and

(d) If the contract provides that the Labor Commissioner or his authorized representative has the right to attend all arbitration hearings.

Except as otherwise provided in this section, any such arbitration shall be governed by the provisions of Title 9 (commencing with Section 1280) of Part 3 of the Code of Civil Procedure. If there is such an arbitration provision in such a contract, the contract need not provide that the talent agency agrees to refer any controversy between the applicant and the talent agency regarding the terms of the contract to the Labor Commissioner for adjustment, and Section 1700.44 shall not apply to controversies pertaining to the contract.

A provision in a contract providing for the decision by arbitration of any controversy arising under this chapter which does not meet the requirements of this section is not made valid by Section 1281 of the Code of Civil Procedure.

Buchwald v. Superior Court of San Francisco, 62 Cal.Rptr. 364 (Cal.Ct.App. 1967)

ELKINGTON, J.

[Matthew Katz signed the members of the band Jefferson Airplane to management, recording and music publishing agreements. Disputes were to be resolved by arbitration under the rules of the American Arbitration Association. The band, however, sought to have the matter referred to the Labor Commissioner under the legislative antecedent of the Talent Agency Act. Katz objected, because he did not possess an agency license.]

The Act is a remedial statute. Statutes such as the Act are designed to correct abuses that have long been recognized and which have been the subject of both legislative action and judicial decision. . . . Such statutes are enacted for the protection of those seeking employment. . . .

Since the clear object of the Act is to prevent improper persons from becoming [agents] and to regulate such activity for the protection of the public, a contract between an unlicensed [agent] and an artist is void. . . . And as to such contracts, artists, being of the class for whose benefit the Act was passed, are not to be ordinarily considered as being *in pari delicto*. . . .

[Under the management agreement form, Katz,] for a percentage of each petitioner's earnings undertook, among other things, to act as "exclusive personal representative, advisor and manager in the entertainment field." The contract contained a provision reading: "It is clearly understood that you [Katz] are not an employment agent or theatrical agent, that you have not offered or attempted to promise to obtain employment or engagements for me, and you are not obligated, authorized or expected to do so." . . .

[Despite the contractual arbitration clause, the band] filed with the Labor Commissioner a "Petition to Determine Controversy," alleging among other things: "Complainants complain that in September of 1965, defendant [Matthew Katz] acting as an [agent] and through false and fraudulent statements and by duress, caused complainants to sign with defendant as an [agent]; that defendant, prior to the time of signing said contracts, promised the complainants and each of them that he would procure bookings for them; that defendant thereafter procured bookings for them; that defendant thereafter procured bookings for the complainants and insisted that the complainants perform the bookings procured by him; that complainants sought to procure their own bookings, and that defendant refused them the right to procure their own bookings; that at the time that said contracts were negotiated, defendant Matthew Katz was not licensed as an [agent] . . . ; that the contract presented to each complainant was not submitted to the Labor Commissioner, State of California . . . ; that Matthew Katz has not performed in accordance with [various sections] of the Labor Code ; that Matthew Katz never rendered an accounting to the complainants for thousands of dollars received by

Mr. Katz for their services; that Matthew Katz has not allowed complainants to inspect the books and records maintained by Matthew Katz with respect to fees earned by the complainants and has cashed checks intended for one or more of the above complainants for his own use and benefit."

Katz appeared and filed his answer to the petition in which he objected to the jurisdiction of the Labor Commissioner. . . .

Admittedly, Katz was not licensed as an [agent].

The Act . . . defines "licensee" as an "[agent] which holds a valid, unrevoked, and unforfeited license. . . ."

Certain sections . . . refer to "licensee" in such context that the word can reasonably apply only to a licensed artists' manager. Other sections, including those which are the subject of the Petition to Determine Controversy, refer to [agents] in such manner that they apply reasonably to both licensed and unlicensed [agents]. . . .

Remedial statutes should be liberally construed to effect their objects and suppress the mischief at which they are directed. . . . It would be unreasonable to construe the Act as applying only to licensed artists' managers, thus allowing an artists' manager, by nonsubmission to the licensing provisions of the Act, to exclude himself from its restrictions and regulations enacted in the public interest. "Statutes must be given a reasonable and common sense construction in accordance with the apparent purpose and intention of the lawmakers—one that is practical rather than technical, and that will lead to wise policy rather than to mischief or absurdity." (45 Cal. Jur.2d, Statutes, § 116, pp. 625–626.)

We conclude that [agents] (as defined by the Act), whether they be licensed or unlicensed, are bound and regulated by the Artists' Managers Act. . . .

The Act gives the Labor Commissioner jurisdiction over those who are [agents] in fact. The petition filed with the Labor Commissioner alleges facts which if true indicate that the written contracts were but subterfuges and that Katz had agreed to, and did, act as an [agent]. Clearly the Act may not be circumvented by allowing language of the written contract to control—if Katz had in fact agreed to, and had acted as an [agent]. The form of the transaction, rather than its substance would control. . . .

The court, or as here, the Labor Commissioner, is free to search out illegality lying behind the form in which a transaction has been cast for the purpose of concealing such illegality. (*Lewis & Queen v. N.M. Ball Sons, supra*, 48 Cal.2d 141, 148.) "The court will look through provisions, valid on their face, and with the aid of payroll evidence, determine that the contract is actually illegal or is part of an illegal transaction." (1 Witkin, Summary of Cal. Law (1960) Contracts, § 157, p. 169.)

In support of his position that as a matter of law he is not an [agent] Katz cites *Raden v. Laurie*, 120 Cal. App. 2d 778 [262 P.2d 61]. That case, decided in 1953, concerned the Private Employment Agencies

Act, sections 1550–1650 (also found in part 2, div. 6 relating to "Employment Agencies") which at that time regulated persons doing business as artists' managers. . . .

The inapplicability of *Raden v. Laurie* to the instant controversy is obvious. There, on a motion for summary judgment, no showing, prima facie or otherwise, was made (as regards the contract sued upon or its subject matter) that Raden had agreed to act, or had acted as an [agent] (or employment agency). The District Court of Appeal found no evidence which would support a conclusion that the contract was a sham or pretext designed to conceal the true agreement or to evade the law. On the uncontroverted facts the court had jurisdiction over the controversy and the Labor Commissioner did not. In the proceedings before us a prima *facie* showing was made to the Labor Commissioner as to matters over which he had jurisdiction. . . .

Applying to the [Talent Agency] Act the construction given to its sister and parent statutes the following appears: The Act is broad and comprehensive. The Labor Commissioner is empowered to hear and determine disputes under it, *including the validity of the [agent]-artist contract* and the liability, if any, of the parties thereunder. (See *Garson v. Division of Labor Law Enforcement*, 33 Cal.2d 861, 866 [206 P.2d 368].) He may be compelled to assume this power. (*Bollatin v. Workman Service Co.*, 128 Cal. App. 2d 339, 341 [275 P.2d 599].) In the settlement of disputes the jurisdiction of the Labor Commissioner is similar to, but broader, than the power of an arbitrator under Code of Civil Procedure sections 1280–1294.2. . . . The Labor Commissioner's awards are enforceable in the same manner as awards of private arbitrators under Code of Civil Procedure sections 1285–1288.8. . . .

Section 1700.44 of the Act is mandatory. It provides that the parties involved, artists and [agent], in any controversy arising under the Act, *shall* refer the matters in dispute to the commissioner. . . .

Since the instant controversy was pending before, and was properly within the jurisdiction of, the Labor Commissioner, the doctrine of "exhaustion of administrative remedies" applies. . . . This well known concept is expressed in *Abelleira v. District Court of Appeal*, 17 Cal.2d 280, 292–293 [109 P.2d 942, 132 A.L.R. 715], as "where an administrative remedy is provided by statute, relief must be sought from the administrative body and this remedy exhausted before the courts will act. . . . It is not a matter of judicial discretion, but is a fundamental rule of procedure laid down by courts of last resort, followed under the doctrine of *stare decisis,* and binding upon all courts." . . .

We hold as to cases of controversies arising under the [Talent Agency] Act that the Labor Commissioner has original jurisdiction to hear and determine the same to the exclusion of the superior court, subject to an appeal within 10 days after determination, to the superior court where the same shall be heard de novo. (See § 1700.44.) . . . [Katz argued that the contractual provision for private arbitration prevented application to the Labor Commissioner.]

This argument overlooks the basic contention of petitioners that their agreement with Katz is wholly invalid because of his noncompliance with the Act. If the agreement is void no rights, including the claimed right to private arbitration, can be derived from it.

Loving & Evans v. Blick, supra, 33 Cal.2d 603, 610, states: "It seems clear that the power of the arbitrator to determine the rights of the parties is dependent upon the existence of a valid contract under which such rights might arise." [Citations ommitted.]. . .

We conclude that petitioners are entitled, by way of certiorari, to the relief sought by them. The orders of the superior court dated January 17, 1967 are annulled. . . .

NOTES _____

1. In *Raden v. Laurie,* 262 P.2d. 61 (Cal. 1953), the alleged agent confined his activities to working to develop the poise and skills of a young actress and to taking her around to auditions where she might obtain work, without ever directly seeking to obtain employment for her.
2. Although the *Buchwald* court stressed substance over form, an agreement which on its face indicates unlicensed agent activity will be held void regardless of the actual activities undertaken by the representative, according to the decision of the Special Hearing Officer in *Ivy v. Howard,* Labor Commission Case No. TAC 18–94 (1994).

The *Buchwald* and *Raden* cases served to establish parameters for determining who was and who was not an "agent" in California. In *Pryor,* below, we see the draconian punishments which can befall one who falls on the wrong side of the line.

Pryor v. Franklin, Case No. TAC 17 MP114 Labor Commissioner, State of California Division of Labor Standards Enforcement (August 18, 1982)

C. G. JOSEPH, SPECIAL HEARING OFFICER

[Franklin managed Richard Pryor from 1975 until 1980. In 1981 Pryor and his "loan-out" corporation filed a Petition to Determine Controversy pursuant to Labor Code § 1700.44. After the hearing the special hearing officer determined that Franklin had acted as an unlicensed talent agency and that the agreement between Franklin and Pryor was void and unenforceable as to Pryor. In addition, the hearing officer ordered Franklin to repay $3,110,918 to Pryor.

Franklin had admittedly negotiated numerous agreements on behalf on Pryor. In addition, testimony established that Franklin had promised to procure employment for Pryor and to negotiate the agreements therefor, in all fields of entertainment. Franklin held himself out to third parties as Pryor's "agent" and resisted attempts by other agents to render agency services to Pryor on the ground that he was already doing so. In addition, promptly after commencing his duties on Pryor's behalf, Franklin terminated Pryor's attorney, accountant, and other professional representatives.

Franklin was extremely active. He procured and attempted to procure employment for Pryor with Universal Studios, Paramount Pictures, 20th Century-Fox, Columbia Pictures, Tandem Productions, Steven Krantz Productions, Rastar Productions, Warner Bros. Records, NBC, and others. He also set up a U.S. live concert tour of some 75 dates. Among the films in which Pryor appeared were *Silver Streak, California Suite, The Wiz, Car Wash,* and *Richard Pryor Live in Concert.* At all times, Franklin served as Pryor's "sole and exclusive negotiator."

In his defense, Franklin asserted that he had not solicited or initiated the contacts which led to Pryor's employment, but had merely reacted to the approaches of third parties. However, said the hearing officer, even if this were true, " . . . the furthering of an offer constitutes a significant aspect of procurement prohibited by law since the process of procurement includes the entire process of reaching an agreement." If it were otherwise, the act would be gutted, particularly as to "the most sought after artists whose services are in the greatest demand."

However, the hearing officer found that Franklin had, in fact, initiated contacts which led to the formation of contracts and that he had "often initiated requests to amend and sometimes significantly change or replace an employment agreement."]

. . . Further, respondent's both conceiving and implementing an "overall strategy" concerning Pryor's employment and career, represents an illustration of Respondent's dual activities in both advising, counseling or directing Pryor in the development or advancement of his professional career, while at the same time Respondent was engaged in procuring and attempting to procure employment for Pryor in various entertainment fields. . . .

[The hearing officer then characterized as a "blatant subterfuge" Franklin's assertion that he had served as Pryor's attorney. Franklin was not licensed to practice law either in Georgia (he had his office in Atlanta) or in California, where Pryor resided and where Franklin performed many of his services. His contention could therefore "invite both civil and criminal proceedings; . . . any underlying contract for such services would be void and unenforceable." However, because of a failure of evidence on this point, the hearing officer stated:]

. . . we do not need to reach the question as to whether Respondent's conduct would have constituted a violation of the Act if he had been licensed to practice law in the State of California—a professional status which would have rendered him subject to another panoply of regulatory statutes, rules and judicial decisions. . . .

[Franklin did handle some purely business and corporate matters, and as to these business-management functions, no violation was seen. Further, Franklin did not violate the act by referring legal and corporate matters to be handled by attorneys. However, these were incidental activities, not the heart of the relationship between Pryor and

Franklin. To decide otherwise, "we would have to elevate form over substance, which would emasculate the Act and permit wide ranging abuses through subterfuge and artifice."

Franklin also used the leverage which accrued to him as Pryor's representative to secure employment for other entertainment clients, as well as employment opportunities and consideration for himself. He was paid (and received credit) as executive producer on some of Pryor's films, although he was not required to perform any services, evidencing "conflict of interest and blatant self-dealing."

There was also evidence that Franklin did not account to Pryor for, or return, some $1,850,000 of Pryor's funds.

Therefore, according to the hearing officer:]

. . . In view of the unconscionable and continuing wrongful conduct by Respondent, including numerous acts of embezzlement, fraud and defalcation while acting in a fiduciary capacity, and in view of Respondent's numerous violations of the Act, we hold that this [sic] an appropriate case for the exercise of the broadest remedy of restitution. . . .

[In an attempt to avoid this result, Franklin argued that Pryor was in *pari delicto,* but the hearing officer rejected this argument and held that Franklin was "solely culpable for the numerous violations of law" and that Pryor shared none of the blame or guilt. In support, the hearing officer cited a 1975 memorandum of law prepared at Franklin's request discussing the act, which showed that the violations were not innocent. Therefore, Franklin was ordered to repay his commission from inception, amounting to $753,217, as well as his executive producer fees (which, the hearing officer reasoned, would have gone to Pryor if not diverted to Franklin), together with interest of $506,000 on the three amounts (including the $1,850,000).

However, the hearing officer determined he had no jurisdiction over Pryor's investment funds which might have been misappropriated by Franklin subsequent to being invested, since these were not "related to the artist's employment or the talent agency's unlawful procurement activities."]

Although the Pryor case might be read to indicate that a true manager cannot participate in the negotiation process, this is not always the case, as the following decisions illustrate.

Barr v. Rothberg, Case No. TAC 14–90 Labor Commissioner, State of California Division of Labor Standards Enforcement (April 30, 1992)

S. M. KAYE, SPECIAL HEARING OFFICER

INTRODUCTION

Barr filed a petition to determine controversy against Rothberg . . . pursuant to section 1700.44. Barr alleged that the parties had entered into an oral management agreement in April of 1988; that pursuant to the terms of that oral agreement Rothberg rendered services for Barr; that on or about November of 1989, Rothberg made false and fraudulent representations in order to induce Barr to execute a written management agreement; that as a result of the false and fraudulent representations, Barr executed the written agreement; that during the period of early 1988 through February of 1990, Rothberg acted as a talent agency, procuring, offering, promising or attempting to procure employment for Barr; that Rothberg was not licensed as a talent agency pursuant to the provisions of sections 1700 et seq. and that Rothberg attempted to use the written and oral agreement as a subterfuge to circumvent and evade the licensing requirements.

Barr prayed for the following relief:

1. An order determining that [Rothberg had] violated section 1700 et seq. of the Labor Code;
2. A determination that the oral and written agreements were void and unenforceable and that petitioners had no liability thereon and respondents had no rights or privileges thereunder;
3. An accounting from [Rothberg] with regard to that received by [Rothberg] in connection with services rendered by petitioner; . . . [and other relief, including]
5. An order requiring [Rothberg to refund commissions] in an amount not less than $265,000. . . .

Respondents filed an answer to the petition essentially denying the allegations, while raising affirmative defenses and subsequently filed an amended answer seeking affirmative relief.

DISCUSSION

. . . To conclude that Rothberg acted as a talent agent during the relevant period requires a finding from all the evidence presented that Rothberg . . . engaged in the procuring, offering, promising or attempting to procure employment or engagements for Barr. . . .

[I]t is important to this discussion to understand what the parties intended [their] relationship to be, and what it was. We note that Barr was represented by a licensed talent agency [when the Barr-Rothberg relationship began,] the Triad Agency.

It was clear from their first meeting, that Rothberg liked Barr, "was crazy about her," saw her as a movie star and wanted to see Barr achieve her desire to be a "female Woody Allen." Their testimony revealed that much of their discussions revolved around Barr's career goals, as well as Barr's work and personal problems.

Shortly after her relationship with Rothberg began, Barr terminated the Triad Agency as her talent agent. Barr subsequently, but prior to the period at issue here, hired the William Morris Agency as her talent agent. The William Morris Agency continued to represent Barr through the period at issue here.

The William Morris Agency received a commission on Barr's work, with one exception, that of the "Roseanne" television show. [It was the Triad Agency that "procured" the "Roseanne" television show for Barr. Barr was involved in the show at the time she hired the William Morris Agency and the William Morris Agency elected not to receive commissions on the "Roseanne" television show—Eds.] We come now to the crux of this entire matter, the "Roseanne" show, the renegotiation of the contract on that show and Rothberg's role in the renegotiation of that contract.

A number of meetings were held regarding the renegotiation of the "Roseanne" television show. Those who attended the meetings included representatives of the William Morris Agency, the Carsey-Werner Company as the producer of the series, Arlyne Rothberg and Barry Hirsch who is an attorney with the firm of Armstrong & Hirsch, specializing in entertainment law, particularly motion pictures and television.

Although representatives of the William Morris Agency were present at the meetings, Mr. Hirsch acted as the lead negotiator at these meetings. That someone other than the talent agency would take the lead in negotiations, is not unusual. It is an accepted practice in the industry when considering the various relationships, that of the client, the lawyer and the production company.

That Rothberg participated at the meetings is clear. That her efforts on Barr's behalf were goal oriented is also clear. Rothberg concentrated on the "creative" issues, the writers, the producers, the "created by" credit and Barr being afforded her due as a result of the success of the show.

What emerges from all of this is the conclusion that renegotiation meetings were a joint effort on the part of Rothberg, Hirsch and the William Morris Agency, collectively working on Barr's behalf, not for the purpose of "procuring" employment, but rather, to aid Barr in the achievement of the goals she desired.

Therefore, it is this hearing officer's conclusion that the relationship . . . was one of artist and personal manager and that was in fact what Rothberg and Barr intended that relationship to be. Rothberg acted as a personal manager and not as a talent agent. . . .

In light of the resolution of this issue, any further discussion relating to the parties' relationship is unnecessary. All other issues are moot. Accordingly, the petition is dismissed. The relief requested by the parties is denied.

NOTES _____

It is not essential that the licensed members of the artist's "team" be present at all times in order for a manager to participate safely in the process of securing employment and negotiating the terms thereof. In *Snipes v. Dolores Robinson Entertainment,* Labor Commission Case No. TAC 36–96 (1998), a manager whose involvement was pursuant to a written request from a licensed agent (one of the statutory exceptions) was allowed to conduct direct negotiations.

Shortly before the decision of the Labor Commissioner in *Barr v. Rothberg, supra*, the Commissioner decided *Arsenio Hall v. X Management, Inc.*, TAC No. 19–90 (Jack Allen, Special Hearing Officer) (April 24, 1992), invalidating the management agreement between Hall and X Management *ab initio* and ordering X Management to repay commissions of more than $2 million. While that proceeding was pending, Robert Wachs, one of the principals of X Management, brought an action challenging the constitutionality of the licensing provisions of the Talent Agency Act. The Superior Court granted summary judgment to the Labor Commissioner, which was affirmed in *Wachs v. Curry*, 13 Cal. App. 4th 616, 16 Cal. Rptr. 2d 496 (Ct. App. 2d Dist. 1993), which appeared to prescribe a "center of gravity" test to be applied to the representative's entire business. If the representative's overall business was not within the ambit of the Act, the representative would not be considered an unlicensed agent even though performing activities covered by the Act in a specific instance. However, a different panel of the same court subsequently expounded a "bright line" theory—*any* unlicensed activity was covered by the Act—in *Waisbren v. Peppercorn Productions, Inc.*, 48 Cal.Rptr.2d 437 (Ct. App. 2d Dist. 1995). The "bright line" rule was underscored in the decision which follows.

Park v. Deftones, 71 Cal. App. 4th 1465, 84 Cal. Rptr. 2d 616 (Ct. App. 2d Dist.), *reh. denied*, 1999 Cal. LEXIS 5248 (1999)

NOTT, ACTING P. J.

Dave Park appeals from the summary judgment entered against him in his action for breach of contract and intentional interference with contractual relations. His action arises from the termination of his personal manager contract by the Deftones, a music act . . . without paying him commissions which he asserts are due him. In addition, Park alleges that after he secured a recording contract for the Deftones with Maverick Records (Maverick), the record company and one of its agents, Guy Oseary, purposefully interfered with Park's contractual relationship with the Deftones. The trial court granted summary judgment on the ground that the management contract between the Deftones and Park was void, Park having violated the Talent Agencies Act (the Act) by securing performance engagements for the Deftones without being licensed as a talent agency. We affirm on that ground.

PROCEDURAL AND FACTUAL BACKGROUND

Park filed this action in October 1996. . . . In February 1997, the Deftones filed a petition before the Labor Commissioner, seeking to void the management agreements. Park unsuccessfully sought dismissal of the petition as untimely filed. The Labor Commissioner determined that Park had violated the Act by obtaining performance engagements for the Deftones on 84 occasions without a license. He issued an order stating that the personal management agreements entered into in 1992, 1993, and 1994 were "null, void and unenforceable." Park demanded a trial de novo in the administrative proceeding. [Defendants] filed a motion for summary judgment on the grounds that the undisputed facts showed that . . . between September 1991 and September 1994,

Park procured numerous performances for the Deftones, and . . . was not a licensed talent agency during that period. . . .

Park opposed the motions [although he] admitted that he had obtained more than 80 engagements for the Deftones. He asserted that the Deftones' petition before the Labor Commission was untimely filed and that his services did not require a talent agency license because they were rendered without a commission and were undertaken in order to obtain a recording agreement. The trial court entered summary judgment in favor of all defendants.

DISCUSSION

I. Timeliness

Park contends that the Deftones' petition before the Labor Commissioner and the defense based upon the Act are barred by the one-year statute of limitations [prescribed in § 1700. 44, subd. (c) of the Talent Agency Act, because] the last time he booked a concert for the Deftones was in August 1994 [and] that the Deftones' petition, filed in February 1997, was therefore not timely. Park concludes that the Deftones may not rely upon the Act as a defense because Park's own action was filed more than one year after he last booked a concert for the Deftones.

The Labor Commissioner, who is statutorily charged with enforcing the Act (§ 1700.44, subd. (a)), found that the Deftones' petition was timely because it was brought within one year of Park's filing an action to collect commissions under the challenged [management agreement, for procuring the recording agreement]. The Commissioner stated that the attempt to collect commissions allegedly due under the agreements was itself a violation of the Act. (*Moreno v. Park* (Jan. 20, 1998, Lab.Comr.) No. 9–97, p. 4.)

In construing a statute, the court gives considerable weight to the interpretation placed on the statute by the administrative agency charged with enforcing it. (*Robinson v. Fair Employment & Housing Com.* (1992) 2 Cal.4th 226, 234, 5 Cal.Rptr.2d 782, 825 P.2d 767.) The Labor Commissioner's interpretation avoids the encouragement of preemptive proceedings before it. It also assures that the party who has engaged in illegal activity may not avoid its consequences through the timing of his own collection action.

We conclude that the Labor Commissioner's interpretation is reasonable, and that the Deftones' petition was timely filed.

II. Incidental procurement of employment

The Act provides that "No person shall engage in or carry on the occupation of a talent agency without first procuring a license therefor from the Labor Commissioner." (§ 1700.5.) A talent agency is "a person or corporation who engages in the occupation of procuring, offering, promising, or attempting to procure employment or engagements for an artist or artists, except that the activities of procuring, offering, or promising to procure recording contracts for an artist or artists shall not of itself subject a person or corporation to regulation and licensing under this chapter. . . . " (§ 1700.4, subd. (a).)

Unlike talent agents, personal managers are not covered by the Act. Personal managers primarily advise, counsel, direct, and coordinate the development of the artist's career. They advise in both business and personal matters, frequently lend money to young artists, and serve as spokespersons for the artists. (See *Waisbren v. Peppercorn Productions, Inc.* (1995) 41 Cal. App. 4th 246, 252–253, 48 Cal.Rptr.2d 437.)

Park argues that as a personal manager his goal in procuring engagements for the Deftones was to obtain a recording agreement. He contends that his actions were therefore exempt from regulation. That position was rejected in *Waisbren, supra,* 41 Cal. App. 4th at p. 259, 48 Cal.Rptr.2d 437. In *Waisbren,* a promoter brought an action for breach of contract against a company engaged in designing and creating puppets. The defendant moved for summary judgment on the ground the parties' agreement for the plaintiff's services was void because he had performed the duties of a talent agent without obtaining a license. The plaintiff asserted that a license was unnecessary because his procurement activities were minimal and incidental. He had also assisted in project development, managed certain business affairs, supervised client relations and publicity, performed casting duties, coordinated production, and handled office functions. In return, he was to receive 15 percent of the company's profits. *Waisbren* holds that even incidental activity in procuring employment for an artist is subject to regulation under the Act.

The reasoning of *Waisbren* is convincing. It relies upon the remedial purpose of the Act and the statutory goal of protecting artists from long recognized abuses. The decision is also based upon the Labor Commissioner's long held position that a license is required for incidental procurement activities. The court in Waisbren found the Labor Commissioner's position to be supported by legislative history and, in particular, by the recommendations contained in the Report of the California Entertainment Commission, which were adopted by the Legislature in amending the Act in 1986. *Wachs v. Curry* (1993) 13 Cal. App. 4th 616, 16 Cal.Rptr.2d 496, relied upon by Park, does not further his cause. In *Wachs,* the personal manager plaintiffs brought a declaratory relief action challenging the constitutionality of the Act on its face. They took the position that the Act's exemption for procurement activities involving recording contracts violated the equal protection clause and that the Act's use of the term "procure" was so vague as to violate due process. *Wachs* rejected both of those positions. It also interpreted the Act, which applies to persons engaged in the occupation of procuring employment for artists, as applying only where a person's procurement activities constitute a significant part of his business.

(*Id.* at pp. 627–628, 16 Cal.Rptr.2d 496.) The court did not define "significant part." The court acknowledged that " . . . the only question before us is whether the word 'procure' in the context of the Act is so lacking in objective content that it provides no standard at all by which to measure an agent's conduct" (*id.* at p. 628, 16 Cal.Rptr.2d 496, italics omitted). We agree with *Waisbren* that the interpretation stated in *Wachs* is dictum and that even incidental procurement is regulated.

III. Absence of a commission

Park also contends that his procuring employment for the Deftones is not regulated by the Act because he was not compensated for that work. We disagree. Park's 1993 and 1994 agreements with the Deftones expressly provided that Park was to receive a 20 percent commission on all income earned from employment that Park secured. Although Park stated in declaration testimony that he received no commission for procuring engagements for the Deftones, the contracts appear to provide for compensation. [Note in original: The agreements acknowledge that Park is not a licensed talent agent and is under no obligation to procure employment for the Deftones.] In addition, Park would receive compensation for his services ultimately from commissions for obtaining a recording contract for the Deftones. Thus, it is not clear that Park should be treated as one who was not compensated for his services.

Park's position, moreover, is not supported by the language of the Act. The Act regulates those who engage in the occupation of procuring engagements for artists. (§ 1700.4 subd. (a).) The Act does not expressly include or exempt procurement where no compensation is made. *Waisbren* states at footnote 6: "By using [the term 'occupation'], the Legislature intended to cover those who are compensated for their procurement efforts." (41 Cal. App. 4th at p. 254, 48 Cal.Rptr.2d 437.) The issue of compensation, however, was not before the court in *Waisbren*. The language in footnote 6 is dictum which we conclude is not supported by the purpose and legislative history of the Act. One may engage in an occupation which includes procuring engagements without receiving direct compensation for that activity.

As explained in *Waisbren,* the purpose of the Act is remedial, and its aim goes beyond regulating the amount of fees which can be charged for booking acts. For example, an agent must have his form of contract approved by the Labor Commissioner, maintain his client's funds in a trust fund account, record and retain certain information about his client, and refrain from giving false information to an artist concerning potential employment. (See §§ 1700.23, 1700.25, 1700.26, 1700.32, and 1700.41.) Because the Act is remedial, it should be liberally construed to promote its general object. (See *Buchwald v. Superior Court* (1967) 254 Cal. App. 2d 347, 354, 62 Cal. Rptr. 364.) The abuses at which these requirements are aimed apply equally where the personal manager procures work for the artist without a commission, but rather for the deferred benefits from obtaining a recording contract.

In 1982, the Legislature created the California Entertainment Commission (the Commission) to study the laws and practices of this and other states relating to the licensing of agents and representatives of artists in the entertainment industry in order to recommend to the Legislature a model bill regarding licensing. (See *Waisbren, supra,* 41 Cal. App. 4th at p. 256, 48 Cal.Rptr.2d 437.) In 1985, the Commission submitted its report to the Governor and the Legislature (the Report). The Legislature followed the Commission's recommendations in enacting the 1986 amendments to the Act. (See *Waisbren, supra,* 41 Cal. App. 4th at p. 258, 48 Cal.Rptr.2d 437.) The Report [as to which the court took judicial notice, under Evidence Code § 452 subd. (c)] states that the Commission reviewed and rejected a proposal which would have exempted from the Act anyone who does not charge a fee or commission for procuring employment for an artist. The Commission concluded: "It is the majority view of the Commission that personal managers or anyone not licensed as a talent agent should not, under any condition or circumstances, be allowed to procure employment for an artist without being licensed as a talent agent, except in accordance with the present provisions of the Act." (Report, p. 6.)

The Legislature accepted the Report and codified the Commission's recommendations, approving the Commission's view that no exemption should be created for those who do not charge a fee for procuring employment for an artist. We conclude that the Act requires a license to engage in procurement activities even if no commission is received for the service.

ZEBROWSKI, J., and MALLANO, J. [Judge of the Los Angeles Superior Court, assigned by the Chief Justice pursuant to article VI, section 6 of the California Constitution], concur.

NOTES _____

1. The one-year statute of limitations set out in §1700.44(c) does not apply to "pure defenses" raised under the Talent Agencies Act. *Styne v. Stevens,* 26 Cal. 4th 42, 109 Cal.Rptr.2d 14 (2001).

2. The "bright-line" rule was most recently revisited in *Yoo v. Robi,* 126 Cal. App. 4th 1089, 24 Cal. Rptr 3d 740 (Cal. App. 2 Dist. Feb 14, 2005) (NO. B165843), as modified on denial of rehearing (Mar 09, 2005), review denied (May 11, 2005). One further interesting aspect of the *Yoo* decision is the court's rejection in dicta of the manager's contention that sending out promotional packages and negotiating performance contracts did not constitute "procuring" or "attempting to procure" employment as provided in §1700.4(a):

   If promoting an artist requires a talent agency license, [Manager] argues, then public relations firms, publicists and advertising agencies all would have to be licensed as talent agencies. [Manager] further maintains when personal managers negotiate performance contracts on behalf of their artist clients they are merely acting as spokespersons for the artists so the artists can concentrate on their artistry and not have to spend their time conversing with booking agents.

We need not decide in this case whether public relations firms, publicists and advertising agencies should be required to register as talent agencies because [Manager] does not contend he is any of these. We note, however, a rational distinction can be drawn between promoting an artist to the public generally and "[t]he talent agent's primary function [of marketing] the artist's talent to buyers within the entertainment industry." Furthermore, the Act was intended to remedy abuse of persons seeking employment in the entertainment industry as shown by its provisions requiring the fingerprinting of license applicants, investigations into their character, posting of bonds, and labor commission approval of talent agency contracts as well as prohibiting a talent agent from sending an artist to an unsafe place, sending a minor to a saloon and allowing prostitutes, gamblers, drunks and pimps to frequent or be employed in a talent agent's place of business. . . .

There is also a distinction between being the spokesperson for a client on a contract and being the negotiator for a client on a contract. The spokesperson merely passes on the client's desires or demands to the person who is contemplating engaging the client. But the function of a negotiator is not merely to pass messages back and forth between the principals. Negotiators use their understanding of their clients' values, desires and demands, the other parties' values, desires and demands and their own discretion and intuition to bring about through give-and-take a deal acceptable to the principals.

While personal managers often serve "as spokespersons for the artists" talent agents typically serve as negotiators "negotiating the particulars of employment." Obviously, a talent agent might act as a spokesperson for a client just as a personal manager might act as a negotiator for a client. The role a personal manager played with respect to any given contract is a question of fact. Here the evidence showed with respect to Robi's appearances in Santa Clara and Bristol Connecticut that [Manager] negotiated the terms of the engagements . . . and presented the completed agreements to Robi for his signature. We concur in the trial court's findings that in these and numerous other matters Wolf acted in the role of a talent agency.

Id. at 1101–1102.

Chinn v. Tobin, Labor Commission Case No. TAC 17–96

MILES E. LOCKER, SPECIAL HEARING OFFICER

BACKGROUND

[Petitioners Chinn and Wampole signed an "Artist Agreement" and a "Personal Management Agreement" with Respondent Tobin,] the owner of a business that engaged in the recording and publishing of music. . . .

Under the "Artist Agreement," petitioners agreed to render their "exclusive recording services" to [Tobin, who] would be the sole owner of all master recordings [with] exclusive rights to manufacture records from those master recordings [or license others to do so], and to permit the public performance of these recordings; [and] would hold the publishing rights to any compositions recorded by [Chinn and Wampole], and [Tobin] could subsequently assign all or part of these rights to a publishing company. In return, Respondent agreed to commercially exploit and finance the production of petitioner's recordings, and to pay various recording costs, advances to petitioners, and royalties. The Artist Agreement also provided that Respondent could produce, at his discretion, music videos [which he would then own], with petitioners entitled to royalties based on any profits that may result from the commercial exploitation of such videos.

Pursuant to the Artist Agreement, Tobin arranged for Petitioners' use of a professional recording studio and sound engineer, and secured and paid for the services of session musicians to record with Petitioners. Tobin also undertook efforts to promote Petitioners' recordings with record industry executives and with radio programmers through meetings and the distribution of promotional CD recordings. Respondent paid over $43,000 for recording studio time [and related services, equipment and materials.]

Under the "Personal Management Agreement," [the term of which was coterminous with that of the Artist Agreement] petitioners agreed that Respondent would serve [for a commission of 20% of their gross income from sources *other than* the Artist Agreement] as their "exclusive personal manager" and "adviser" [sic] . . . in connection with all matters relating to their careers, and, with their approval] "[to] prepare, negotiate [and] consummate . . . any and all agreements, documents, and contracts for Artist's services [but that] Artist understands that Manager is not an employment agent, theatrical agent, or artist's manager, and that Manager has not offered, attempted or promised to obtain employment or engagements for Artist, and that Manager is not permitted, obligated, authorized or expected to do so . . ."

[When Tobin sued Chinn and Wampole for breach of contract, they petitioned the Labor Commissioner under Labor Code §1700.44, claiming that Tobin was an unlicensed agent.]

LEGAL ANALYSIS

. . . In essence, petitioners' case boils down to the allegation that respondent "procured employment" for Big Soul, within the meaning of Labor Code section 1700.4(a), by obtaining their songwriting services for his own music publishing business [and that this constituted unlicensed agency activity.] . . . No evidence of any sort was presented to indicate that Respondent procured, offered, attempted or promised to secure employment for Petitioners, with respect to Petitioners' song writing services, for any person or entity other than the Respondent himself and Respondent's music publishing business. We do not believe that this would establish a violation . . . [Note: Although Labor Code section 1700.4(a) exempts "procuring, offering, or promising to procure *recording contracts* for an artist" from the scope of activities for which a talent agency license is required, this exemption does not expressly extend to the procurement of *music publishing* contracts. As with all remedial legislation, exemptions must be strictly construed—Eds]. Respondent argues, however, that the rights granted to him under the music publishing provision of the Artist Agreement are expressly defined to include only those musical compositions that are "recorded by [Petitioners] under this [Artist] Agreement," that these music publishing rights fall within the statutory exemption for recording contracts. This argument ignores the fact that music publishing and recording are two separate endeavors . . . [and] music publishing and songwriting does not fall within the recording contract exemption, regardless of whether the right to publish an artist's music is limited only to compositions that are contained on that artist's record . . . [A] person or entity who employs an artist does not "procure employment" for that artist, within the meaning of Labor Code section 1700.04(a), by directly engaging the services of that Artist . . . [Unlike] the role an agent plays when acting as an intermediary between the artist whom the agent represents and the third-party employer who seeks to engage the artist's services.

Petitioners' novel argument would mean that every television or film production company that directly hires an actor, and that every concert producer that directly engages the services of a musical group, without undertaking any communications or negotiations with the actor's or musical group's talent agent, would itself need to be licensed. . . . To suggest that any person who engages the services of an artist for himself is [acting as an agent] is to radically expand the reach of the Talent Agencies Act beyond recognition. . . . We can find nothing in the legislative history of the Talent Agencies Act that would even remotely indicate any legislative intent to require the licensing of employers who directly offer employment to artists, and to construe the Act in such a manner would lead to absurd results.

[The test, the SO stated, citing *Hums v. Margie Ventures, Inc.*, 174 Cal. App. 3d 486 (1985) was] the substantive reality behind the contractual language. [In the *Margie* case, the respondent] merely functioned as a loan-out company for providing Hums' services to third party producers. [Here, petitioners] failed to present any evidence, or offer of proof, that respondent ever procured or promised or offered or attempted to procure employment for petitioners with any third party. [Note: Petitioners did present evidence that Tobin "made several attempts to obtain [major] label distribution for Big Soul and had contacts with at least one European "subpublisher." These activities were consistent with Tobin's rights under the Artist Agreement, with respect to his ownership of Big Soul's recordings and compositions. Tobin was not negotiating with these record companies and subpublishers to employ Big Soul, but, rather, to secure distribution. In this respect, Tobin's role was analogous to an independent television production company that hires actors and other necessary employees for the production, that bears the expenses incurred in completing the production, that owns the movie or television series that it produced, and that has the right to enter into distribution agreements with networks for this movie or series. The Talent Agencies Act does not require that an independent television producer be licensed to engage in such activities. There is no reason to treat an independent music producer any differently. And the evidence presented here leaves no doubt that Tobin is a bona fide music producer, in contrast to the fictitious "theatrical production" company that was created in *Margie* for the purpose of "loaning out" the artist's services to third party producers as a means of evading the Act's licensing requirements—Eds.]

[Nor was the arrangement disabled by the fact that Tobin had the right to negotiate and consummate agreements under the Personal Management Agreement, because the subject paragraph] grants this authority to Respondent "in accordance with" another paragraph of the Agreement that states that Tobin "is not permitted, obligated, authorized or expected" to obtain employment or engagements for Big Soul, and that Tobin shall consult with Big Soul in the selection or engagement of any talent agent. . . . It was the parties' intent that these contract provisions be construed in a manner that complies with the Talent Agencies Act.

It is a basic principle of contract law that a contract must be given such an interpretation as will make it lawful, if it can be done without violating the intentions of the parties. (Civil Code section 1643.) [Because of the exemption provided under Labor Code section 1700.44(d), Tobin could work with, and at the request of, a licensed agent, and the Barr decision, above, we] therefore construe paragraphs 3(c) and 7 of the Personal Management Agreement as allowing Tobin to engage in only those procurement activities, and only under those circumstances that are permitted by Labor Code section 1700.44(d).

NOTE

So Locker's observation concerning music publishing agreements should be of considerable interest to attorneys, who regularly "shop" and negotiate such agreements: "Although Labor Code section 1700.44(a) exempts 'procuring, offering or promising to procure *recording contracts* for an artist' from the scope of activities for which a talent agency license is required, this exemption does not expressly extend to the procurement of *music publishing* contract . . . As with all remedial legislation, exemptions must be strictly construed. . . . Music publishing and recording are two separate endeavors . . . Music publishing and songwriting does not fall within the recording contract exemption" (emphasis in original). Although the decision in *Pryor v. Franklin,* above, suggests that the existence of an elaborate legislative licensing procedure for attorneys would immunize them from the necessity to obtain licenses under the Talent Agencies Act, the Labor Commissioner takes the position that attorneys are subject to the Act when negotiating music publishing agreements. See Donald E. Biederman, "Agents v. Managers Revisited," 1 Vand. J. of Ent. L. and Prac. No. 1, p. 5 (Spring 1999).

1.4 BUSINESS MANAGERS

The business manager can act in the simple role of paymaster, taking care of the client's bills, tax returns, and similar matters. Some business managers perform the additional role of investment adviser, handling tax shelters, pension plans, and other matters not directly related to the artist's day-to-day financial functions. Inevitably, the business manager is privy to the most intimate details of the client's economic life. As the following case indicates, a very high level of fiduciary duty attaches to the role of business manager.

ABKCO Music, Inc. v. Harrisongs Music, Ltd., 722 F.2d 990
(2d Cir. 1983)

Pierce, J.

[Bright Tunes Music Corporation sued George Harrison, ("GH") and related entities ("Harrison Interests"), claiming that GH's song "My Sweet Lord" ("MSL") infringed Bright Tunes' "He's So Fine" ("HSF").]

When this action was commenced, the business affairs of The Beatles, including Harrison Interests, were handled by ABKCO Music, Inc. (ABKCO) and Allen B. Klein, its President and "moving spirit." *ABKCO Music, Inc. v. Harrisongs Music, Ltd.*, 508 F. Supp. 798, 799 (S.D.N.Y. 1981). ABKCO was Harrison's business manager during the initial stages of the copyright liability action herein, at which time the litigation was handled for Harrison by ABKCO's General Counsel.

The following events preceded the instant appeal. Shortly after this action was commenced in February 1971, Klein (representing Harrisongs Music, Inc. and George Harrison) met with Seymour Barash (President and major stockholder of Bright Tunes) to discuss possible settlement of this lawsuit. Although Klein, at trial, denied having specific knowledge of the details of this discussion, he testified that he had suggested to Barash, around February of 1971, a purchase of the entire stock of Bright Tunes as a way to dispose of this lawsuit. Thus, in 1971, Klein was acting on behalf of Harrison Interests in an effort to settle this copyright infringement claim brought by Bright Tunes, although no settlement resulted.

Subsequent to the Klein-Barash meeting, Bright Tunes went into "judicial dissolution proceedings." This infringement action was placed on the district court's suspense calendar on March 3, 1972, and was resumed by Bright Tunes (in receivership) in early 1973. Also in early 1973 (March 31), ABKCO's management contract with The Beatles expired. Bitter and protracted litigation ensued between The Beatles and ABKCO over the winding down of management affairs—a dispute that ended in 1977 with The Beatles paying ABKCO $4.2 million in settlement.

There is some disagreement as to whether further settlement negotiations took place between Harrison Interests and Bright Tunes between 1973 and mid-1975. It appears undisputed, however, that Harrison Interests' attorney at least initiated settlement talks in the late summer of 1975; that in the period October 1975 through February 1976, settlement discussions took place between Bright Tunes' counsel and counsel for Harrison Interests regarding settlement of this infringement action (an offer by Harrison Interests based on United States royalties); and that those discussions were in the 50%/50% or 60%/40% range. These discussions culminated in a $148,000 offer by Harrison Interests in January of 1976 (representing 40% of the United States royalties).

At about the same time (1975), apparently unknown to George Harrison, Klein had been negotiating with Bright Tunes to purchase all of Bright Tunes' stock. That such negotiations were taking place was confirmed as early as October 30, 1975, in a letter from Seymour Barash (Bright Tunes' former President) to Howard Sheldon (Bright Tunes' Receiver), in which Barash reported that there had been an offer from Klein for a substantial sum of money. The same letter observed that "[Klein] would not be interested in purchasing all of the stock of Bright Tunes . . . if there was any doubt as to the outcome of this litigation."

In late November 1975, Klein (on behalf of ABKCO) offered to pay Bright Tunes $100,000 for a call on all Bright Tunes' stock, exercisable for an additional $160,000 upon a judicial determination as to copyright infringement. In connection with this offer, Klein furnished to Bright Tunes three schedules summarizing the following financial information concerning "My Sweet Lord": (1) domestic royalty income of Harrisongs Music, Inc. on MSL; (2) an updated version of that first schedule; and (3) Klein's own estimated value of the copyright, including an estimate of foreign royalties (performance and mechanical) and his assessment of the total worldwide future earnings.

Barash considered the Klein offer only a starting point. He thought that a value of $600,000 was more accurate and recommended a $200,000 call, based on a $600,000 gross sales price. Also in December 1975, Barash noted, in a letter to counsel for the Peter Maurice Co., that Harrison Interests' counsel had never furnished a certified statement of worldwide royalties of MSL, but that from conversations between Stephen Tenenbaum (accountant for several Bright Tunes stockholders) and Klein, Bright Tunes had been given that information by Klein.

Shortly thereafter, on January 19, 1976, Barash informed Howard Sheldon (Bright Tunes' Receiver) of the Klein offer and of the Bright Tunes stockholders' unanimous decision to reject it. Barash noted that "[s]ince Mr. Klein is in a position to know the true earnings of 'My Sweet Lord,' his offer should give all of us an indication of the true value of this copyright and litigation." Sheldon responded in a letter dated January 21, 1976, noting, *inter alia,* that Harrison's attorneys were informed that no settlement would be considered by Bright Tunes until total sales of MSL were determined after appropriate figures were checked.

On January 30, 1976, the eve of the liability trial, a meeting was held by Bright Tunes' attorney for all of Bright Tunes' stockholders (or their counsel) and representatives of Ronald Mack. The purpose of the meeting was to present Bright Tunes with an offer by Harrison Interests of $148,000, representing 40% of the writers' and publishers' royalties earned in the United States (but without relinquishment by Harrison of the MSL copyright). At the time, Bright Tunes' attorney regarded the offer as "a good one." 508 F. Supp. at 802. The Harrison offer was not accepted, however. Bright Tunes raised its demand from 50% of the United States royalties, to 75% worldwide, plus surrender of the MSL copyright. The parties were unable to reach agreement and the matter proceeded to trial.

A three-day bench trial on liability was held before Judge Owen on February 23–25, 1976. On August 31, 1976 (amended September 1, 1976), the district judge rendered a decision for the plaintiff as to liability, based on his finding that "My Sweet Lord" was substantially similar to "He's So Fine" and that Harrison had had access to the latter. *Bright Tunes Music Corp. v. Harrisongs Music, Ltd.*, 420 F. Supp. 177 (S.D.N.Y. 1976). The issue of damages and other relief was scheduled for trial at a later date.

Following the liability trial, Klein, still acting for ABKCO, continued to discuss with Bright Tunes the purchase of the rights to HSF. During 1977, no serious settlement discussions were held between Bright Tunes and Harrison Interests. Indeed, the record indicates that throughout 1977 Bright Tunes did not authorize its attorneys to give Harrison a specific settlement figure. By November 30, 1977, Bright Tunes' counsel noted that Klein had made an offer on behalf of ABKCO that "far exceeds any proposal that has been made by the defendants."

On February 8, 1978, another settlement meeting took place, but no agreement was reached at that meeting. Although it appears that everyone present felt that the case should be settled, it also appears that there were no further settlement discussions between Harrison Interests and Bright Tunes subsequent to that date. The Bright Tunes negotiations with ABKCO, however, culminated on April 13, 1978, in a purchase by ABKCO of the HSF copyright, the United States infringement claim herein, and the worldwide rights to HSF, for $587,000, an amount more than twice the original Klein (ABKCO) offer. This purchase was made known to George Harrison by Klein himself in April or May of 1978, Harrison "was a bit amazed to find out" about the purchase. . . .

On July 17, 1978, ABKCO adopted Bright Tunes' complaint and was substituted as the sole party plaintiff in this action. In May 1979, Harrison Interests obtained leave to assert affirmative defenses and counterclaims against Klein and ABKCO for alleged breaches of fiduciary duty relating to the negotiation for and purchase of the Bright Tunes properties. . . .

The damages decision was filed on February 19, 1981. ABKCO *Music, Inc. v. Harrisongs Music, Ltd.*, 508 F. Supp. 798 (S.D.N.Y. 1981). Having determined that the damages amounted to $1,599,987, the district judge held that ABKCO's conduct over the 1975–78 period limited its recovery, substantially because of the manner in which ABKCO had become a plaintiff in this case. Particularly "troublesome" to the court was "Klein's covert intrusion into the settlement negotiation picture in late 1975 and early 1976 immediately preceding the trial on the merits." Id. at 802. He found, *inter alia*, that Klein's status as Harrison's former business manager gave special credence to ABKCO's offers to Bright Tunes and made Bright Tunes less willing to settle with Harrison Interests either before or after the liability trial. Moreover, the court found that in the course of negotiating with Bright Tunes in 1975–76, Klein "covertly furnished" Bright Tunes with certain financial information about MSL which he obtained while in Harrison's employ as business manager. The foregoing conduct, in the court's view, amounted to a breach of ABKCO's fiduciary duty to Harrison. The court held that although it was not clear that "but for" ABKCO's conduct Harrison Interests and Bright Tunes would have settled, he found that good faith negotiations had been in progress between the parties and Klein's intrusion made their success less likely, since ABKCO's offer in January 1976 was viewed by Bright Tunes as an "insider's disclosure of the value of the case." *Id.* at 803. Consequently, the district judge directed that ABKCO hold the "fruits of its acquisition" from Bright Tunes in trust for Harrison Interests, to be transferred to Harrison Interests by ABKCO upon payment by Harrison Interests of $587,000 plus interest from the date of acquisition. . . .

ABKCO . . . argues that ABKCO did not breach its fiduciary duty to Harrison because (a) no confidential information was improperly passed from ABKCO to Bright Tunes during the negotiations to purchase HSF, and (b) there was no causal relationship between ABKCO's actions and Harrison Interests' failure to obtain settlement. . . . [W]e reject appellant's arguments and affirm the decision of the district judge. . . .

There is no doubt but that the relationship between Harrison and ABKCO prior to the termination of the management agreement in 1973 was that of principal and agent, and that the relationship was fiduciary in nature. See *Meese v. Miller,* 79 A.D.2d 237, 241, 436 N.Y.S.2d 496, 499 (N.Y. App. D.V. 4th Dep't 1981). The rule applicable to our present inquiry is that an agent has a duty "not to use confidential knowledge acquired in his employment in competition with his principal." *Byrne v. Barrett,* 268 N.Y. 199, 206, 197 N.E. 217, 218 (1935). This duty "exists as well after the employment is terminated as during its continuance." *Id.; see also* Restatement (Second) of Agency § 396 (1958). On the other hand, use of information based on general business knowledge or gleaned from general business experience is not covered by the rule, and the former agent is permitted to compete with his former principal in reliance on such general publicly available information. *Byrne v. Barrett,* 268 N.Y. at 206, 197 N.E. at 218; *Restatement (Second) of Agency* § 395 comment b (1958). The principal issue before us in the instant case, then, is whether the district court committed clear error in concluding that Klein (hence, ABKCO) improperly used confidential information, gained as Harrison's former agent, in negotiating for the purchase of Bright Tunes' stock (including HSF) in 1975–76.

One aspect of this inquiry concerns the nature of three documents— schedules of MSL earnings—which Klein furnished to Bright Tunes in connection with the 1975–76 negotiations. Although the district judge did not make a specific finding as to whether each of these schedules was confidential, he determined that Bright Tunes at that time was not entitled to the information. 508 F. Supp. at 803. It appears that the first of the three schedules may have been previously turned over to Bright Tunes by Harrison. The two additional schedules which Klein gave to Bright Tunes (the detailed updating of royalty information and Klein's personal estimate of the value of MSL and future earnings) appear not to have been made available to Bright Tunes by Harrison. Moreover, it appears that at least some of the past royalty information was confidential. The evidence presented herein is not at all convincing that the information imparted to Bright Tunes by Klein was publicly available. *Cf. Franke v. Wiltschek,* 209 F.2d 493, 495 (2d Cir. 1953) (former fiduciary precluded from using confidential information in competition with former principal even if the information is readily available from third parties or by other means). Furthermore, the district judge was in a better position to assess the credibility aspects of evidence bearing on this question than we are.

Another aspect of the breach of duty issue concerns the timing and nature of Klein's entry into the negotiation picture and the manner in which he became a plaintiff in this action. In our view, the record supports the position that Bright Tunes very likely gave special credence to Klein's position as an offeror because of his status as Harrison's former business manager and prior coordinator of the defense of this lawsuit. *See, e.g.,* letter from Barash to Sheldon, dated January 19, 1976 ("Since Mr. Klein is in a position to know the true earnings of My Sweet Lord, his offer should give all of us an indication of the true value of this copyright and litigation."). To a significant extent, that favorable bargaining position necessarily was achieved because Klein, as business manager, had intimate knowledge of the financial affairs of his client. Klein himself acknowledged at trial that his offers to Bright Tunes were based, at least in part, on knowledge he had acquired as Harrison's business manager.

Under the circumstances of this case, where there was sufficient evidence to support the district judge's finding that confidential information passed hands, or, at least, was utilized in a manner inconsistent with the duty of a former fiduciary at a time when this litigation was still pending, we conclude that the district judge did not err in holding that ABKCO had breached its duty to Harrison. . . .

In this case, Klein had commenced a purchase transaction with Bright Tunes in 1971 on behalf of Harrison, which he pursued on his own account after the termination of his fiduciary relationship with Harrison. While the initial attempt to purchase Bright Tunes' catalogue was several years removed from the eventual purchase on ABKCO's own account, we are not of the view that such a fact rendered ABKCO unfettered in the later negotiations. Indeed, Klein pursued the later discussions armed with the intimate knowledge not only of Harrison's business affairs, but of the value of this lawsuit—and at a time when this action was still pending. Taking all of these circumstances together, we agree that appellant's conduct during the period 1975–78 did not meet the standard required of him as a former fiduciary.

In so concluding, we do not purport to establish a general "appearance of impropriety" rule with respect to the artist/manager relationship. That strict standard—reserved principally for the legal profession— would probably not suit the realities of the business world. The facts of this case otherwise permit the conclusion reached herein. Indeed, as Judge Owen noted in his Memorandum and Order of May 7, 1979 (permitting Harrison Interests to assert counterclaims), "The fact situation presented is novel in the extreme. Restated in simplest form, it amounts to the purchase by a business manager of a known claim against his former client where, the right to the claim having been established, all that remains to be done is to assess the monetary award." We find these facts not only novel, but unique. Indeed, the purchase, which rendered Harrison and ABKCO adversaries, occurred in the context of a lawsuit in which ABKCO had been the prior protector of Harrison's interests. Thus, although not wholly analogous to the side-switching cases involving attorneys and their former clients, this fact situation creates clear questions of impropriety. On the unique facts presented herein, we certainly cannot say that Judge Owen's findings and conclusions were clearly erroneous or not in accord with applicable law.

Appellant ABKCO also contends that even if there was a breach of duty, such breach should not limit ABKCO's recovery for copyright infringement because ABKCO's conduct did not cause the Bright Tunes/Harrison settlement negotiations to fail. See 508 F. Supp. at 803 & n. 15. Appellant urges, in essence, that a finding of breach of fiduciary duty by an agent, to be actionable, must be found to have been the proximate cause of injury to the principal. We do not accept appellant's proffered causation standard. An action for breach of fiduciary duty is a prophylactic rule intended to remove all incentive to breach—not simply to compensate for damages in the event of a breach. *See Diamond v. Oreamuno*, 24 N.Y.2d 494, 498, 248 N.E.2d 910, 912, 301 N.Y.S.2d 78, 81 (1969) ("[T]he function of [an action founded on breach of fiduciary duty] . . . is not merely to compensate the plaintiff for wrongs committed by the defendant but . . . '*to prevent* them, by removing from agents and trustees all inducement to attempt dealing for their own benefit in matters which they have undertaken for others, or to which their agency or trust relates.' ") (emphasis in original). Having found that ABKCO's conduct constituted a breach of fiduciary duty, the district judge was not required to find a "but for" relationship between ABKCO's conduct and lack of success of Harrison Interests' settlement efforts.

ABKCO argues further that the offer to sell substantially what had been gained in the purchase from Bright Tunes to Harrison for $700,000, and Harrison's rejection of that offer, see supra note 7, bars Harrison Interests from obtaining a constructive trust in this action, *per Turner v. American Metal Co.*, 268 A.D. 239, 50 N.Y.S.2d 800 (N.Y. App. D.V. 1st Dep't 1944) (where former fiduciary offers former employer what he obtained in violation of fiduciary duty at price equivalent to his cost of acquisition and former employer refuses offer, fiduciary not held liable for breach of duty), *appeal dismissed*, 295 N.Y. 822, 66 N.E.2d 591 (1946). We find this argument unpersuasive. First, in *Turner*, unlike the case at bar, there was no finding of breach of fiduciary duty. Moreover, we find somewhat disingenuous ABKCO's claim that a $700,000 offer was a "price equivalent to his cost of acquisition," which had been $587,000. In any event, it is unclear whether that which ABKCO offered Harrison Interests was equivalent to that which ABKCO had bought from Bright Tunes.

NOTE _____

In another unusual situation, the Second Circuit upheld liability imposed upon an attorney and a business manager for fraud, breach of fiduciary obligation, and civil RICO (18 U.S.C. §§ 1962 (b), (c) and (d) (1988), providing for treble damages and attorneys' fees). *Bingham v. Zolt*, 66 F.3d 553 (2d Cir. 1995.) The widow of reggae giant Bob Marley was entitled to 10% of his estate plus a life estate in an additional 45%. According to the court, the attorney, the business manager and the widow diverted millions from the estate to offshore accounts (according to them, in order to minimize estate taxes). Plaintiffs' claims for negligence, gross negligence and conversion were time-barred. However, according to the Second Circuit, the four-year RICO statute of limitations incorporates the "separate accrual rule", with each cause of action arising when the plaintiffs knew or should have known of the defendants' actions.

NOTE _____

The following is an example of a fairly typical management contract. The key issues to focus on are (i) term, (ii) commission rate, (ii) what is commissionable income, (iii) post term commissions, (iv) power of attorney provisions, and (v) key person provisions.

[Artist's Name and Address]

_____
_____
_____

As of _____, 200_

[Manager's Name and Address]

_____
_____

Dear [Manager's Name]:

In consideration of the mutual covenants and undertakings set forth in this agreement, (the "Agreement"), you (sometimes referred to as "you" or "Manager") and we/I (referred to as "us/me" or "Artist") have agreed and do hereby agree to engage you as our/my exclusive personal manager in connection with our/my activities in the recording and entertainment industries as follows:

Territory. The World.
Term. I hereby engage you as our/my exclusive worldwide personal manager for a period as follows: commencing as of the date hereof and continuing until completion of all touring activities in support of the third LP ("Third LP") embodying our/my featured performances containing substantially newly recorded, previously unreleased original musical compositions which have not been released by a record distribution company through United States Normal Retail Channels ("USNRC") on a "topline" label (the "term"). "LP," as such term is used herein, shall mean long-playing records embodying my featured performances containing

substantially newly recorded, previously unreleased original musical compositions initially released by a Major Record Company through USNRC on a "topline" label. "Major Record Company," as such term is used herein, shall mean a company regularly distributed by Sony/BMG, WEA, EMD, or Universal. In the interest of clarity, it is the intention of this Paragraph 1 that you shall be our/my worldwide exclusive personal manager for a duration embodying three LPs plus completion of three full "tour cycles" in support of those LPs. "Tour cycle," as such term is used herein, shall mean the later of the last tour date in connection with the applicable LP or commencement of actual production of the studio LP immediately subsequent to the applicable LP. Commissions payable hereunder shall include payment in connection with all forms of gross monies or other considerations payable as specified herein, including but not limited to artist royalties of any kind, "interactive" or "new technology" income of any kind, mechanical and public performance royalties, and synchronization income as well as all touring income of any kind including, without limitation, income derived from merchandising, sponsorship or endorsement activities in connection with such personal appearance tours.

Manager's Services. You shall be our/my exclusive personal manager throughout the Territory and shall confer with, counsel and advise us/me in all matters pertaining to Activities as defined herein, in our/my career in the entertainment industry including, without limitation, in connection with phonograph records, music publishing, personal appearances, motion pictures, television and the use of our/my name and likeness for commercial purposes. You agree to represent us/me in our/my professional negotiations, which may include advising and fixing the terms of other agreements that will require the use, employment and commercial exploitation of us/me in all aspects of the entertainment industry. You may also consult with our/my employers, including record labels, music video directors, and motion picture and television producers, on how to utilize our/my talents in such a manner as to best serve us/me. For the avoidance of doubt, you will not provide legal services to us/me.

Manager's Compensation:

(a) Manager shall be entitled to receive from Artist as and when received by Artist during and throughout the Term hereof and any extensions thereto, fifteen (15%) percent of Artist's Gross Income (as hereinafter defined) regardless of when earned, as a result of, or in connection with, Artist's activities in and throughout the entertainment, amusement, music, publishing, merchandising and recording industries, including any and all sums resulting from the use of Artist's artistic talents and the results and proceeds thereof ("Manager's Commission").

(b) As used in this Agreement, "Gross Income" shall mean all income or consideration of any kind paid to Artist or on Artist's behalf in connection with Artist's professional career in the entertainment industry, including, without limitation, phonograph records, publishing industries, personal appearances and commercial uses of Artist's names and likenesses. The term "Gross Income" as used herein shall include without limitation, salaries, earnings, fees, royalties, gifts, bonuses, shares of profits, shares of stock, partnership interests, percentages and the total amount paid for a television package or radio program (live or recorded), motion picture or other entertainment packages, earned (but not yet received), or received directly or indirectly by Artist or by any other person or entity on Artist's behalf. In the event that Artist receive, as all or part of Artist's compensation for activities covered hereunder, stock or the right to buy stock in any corporation, or that Artist become the packager or owner of all or part of an entertainment property in any capacity, Manager's compensation percentage shall apply to Artist's interest, and Manager shall be entitled to Manager's percentage share thereof. Should Artist be required to make any payment for such interest, Manager shall pay Manager's percentage share thereof. Notwithstanding the foregoing, Gross Income shall not include, the following:

(i) actual recording, production and other recoupable costs in connection with and promotion and exploitation of master recordings and audiovisual works as provided in a recording agreement, (e.g., musicians fees and producers fees) other than payments to Artist as a portion of those recording costs;

(ii) advances and royalties paid to third party producers, engineers, mixers, re-mixers and directors of master recordings and audio-visual works;

(iii) income derived by any entity in which Manager has a direct or indirect proprietary or income interest (but only to the extent of Manager's such interest therein);

(iv) any monies reasonably paid by or charged to Artist for an opening act, or for "sound and lights" equipment and personnel, transportation and insurance in connection with Artist's concerts and other live engagements;

(v) monies payable to Artist as "tour support" (as such term is used in the music industry) from a record company, but solely to the extent that such tour support is paid to Artist and/or on Artist's behalf to make up a deficit incurred by Artist in connection with such tour, provided that monies payable as compensation and/or salary for Artist's services shall not be deemed "tour support;"

(vi) any actual or judicial or arbitrator's award which Artist receives in the nature of actual or punitive damages, except that actual damages related to a breach of activities hereunder shall be included;

(vii) any arrangement or agreement under which s are employed or otherwise engaged by Manager or by any firm or corporation owned in whole or in part or controlled by or affiliated with Manager (including when Manager or such person, firm or corporation is acting as the package agent for an entertainment program in which Artist are so employed);

(viii) any sums paid or credited to Artist's so-called "loan out" companies as specific reimbursement for payroll taxes and guild or union pension and welfare payments;

(ix) costs incurred to collect Gross Income, including, without limitation, reasonable attorney's fees and other legal costs and auditor's costs (regardless of whether any audit recovery results).

(x) any income derived by Artist from any business investments or other non-entertainment related activities (except to the extent that Artist also perform entertainment services in connection therewith);

(c) The compensation due Manager hereunder is to be paid to the Manager from all monies or other considerations received by the Artist directly or indirectly, under contracts of employment now existing or entered into during the term of this Agreement and any extensions, renewals and substitutions thereof and for so long a time as Artist shall receive compensation under such contracts, and any extensions, renewals, substitutions or replacements. Notwithstanding anything to the contrary contained in this paragraph, Manager's Commissions with respect to product (e.g., compositions, recordings, videos, motion pictures) created by Artist *after* the term hereof ("Post-Term Product Commissions") which is otherwise commissionable hereunder shall be subject to the following commissions by Manager: Ten (10%) percent for product created during the first three (3) years after the Term; and five (5%) percent for any product created during the second three (3) years after the Term and provided that Manager shall not be entitled to receive any Post-Term Product Commissions earned after six (6) years after the Term. For purposes hereof, the year in which product is deemed created is the year in which such product is first reduced to tangible form in preparation for commercial release.

(d) Manager and Artist agree that a mutually approved accountant will be retained by Artist, at Artist's expense, to receive and disburse Artist's monies related to your transactions in the entertainment industry, which such accountant shall be irrevocably authorized by Artist to directly pay Manager his commissions and expenses pursuant to the terms hereof, provided that such accountant will promptly disburse Manager's commissions to Manager upon accountant's receipt thereof (however, in any event Manager shall have the right to be paid Manager's Commission directly from the source of such payments) via appropriate letters of direction to be executed by Artist. For so long as Artist engages an accountant or business manager to transact Artist's financial affairs, Manager will not be obligated to keep books and records related to Artist and provide Artist with accountings provided that Manager forward all monies received on behalf of Artist to such accountant or business manager. Manager shall not be obligated to provide any accountings after the expiration of the term hereof with respect to any accounting period for which Manager did not receive or disburse monies on behalf of Artist.

(e) Notwithstanding the foregoing, with regarded to publishing and BMI songwriter royalties, a fifteen (15%) percent commission will apply with regard to Gross Income from (A) Artist Versions of Artist Compositions recorded during the Term and released within one (1) year after the Term; (B) non-Artist Versions of Artist Compositions published prior to the Term to the extent a new use is obtained during the Term; and (C) non-Artist Versions of Artist Compositions unpublished prior to the Term to the extent it is published during the Term. As used herein, (i) an "Artist Composition" is that portion of a composition written in whole or in part by Artist, and (ii) an "Artist Version" of an Artist Composition is a recording embodying Artist's performance as a featured artist of an Artist Composition. For purposes of this provision, to the extent a payor of a given source of Gross Income (e.g., a performing rights society) does not distinguish between recorded versions of musical compositions and there are one or more of an Artist Composition in addition to an Artist Version, the income attributable to the Artist Version shall be determined by Manager and Artist in good faith taking into consideration all relevant factors, including, without limitation, the mechanical royalty income received with regard to each version for the period in question and whether or not the version was released as a "single." Only those contractual publishing advances pursuant to Artist's current publishing agreement with _____ dated _____ will not be commissionable (i.e., $100,000 per year maximum). In the event that you renegotiate your current publishing agreement to provide for increased advances or receive any advances in excess of the $100,000 per year, Manager shall be entitled to Manager's Commissions for such sums hereunder.

Expenses; Advances. We/I shall be solely responsible for payment of all of our/my union dues, publicity costs, promotion or exploitation expenses (with our/my prior consent), wardrobe expenses and other expenses related to our/my career, including the reasonable expenses arising from the performance by you of the services hereunder. Reasonable expenses incurred by you in rendering services under this Agreement (e.g., travel on our/my behalf, long distance telephone, postage, copying, messenger and express courier) shall be reimbursable by us/me, upon your submission of invoices for such expenses accompanied by receipts or other documents evidencing those expenses, provided that we/I will not be responsible for payment of your general office or overhead expenses. You will obtain our/my prior approval of: (i) All reimbursable travel expenses (which will be equitably prorated if travel is not solely for us/me), (ii) any single expense item in excess of $____ and (iii) aggregate monthly expenses which exceed $____. Reimbursement of expenses as aforesaid shall be due within thirty (30) days after receipt by us/me or our/my designated business manager of itemized statements setting forth the nature and amount of each such expense. During the term of this Agreement and for a period of two (2) years thereafter, you shall keep and maintain reasonable documentation of each and every expense for which you request reimbursement by us/me and all such documentation shall be provided by us/me or our/my designee for examination promptly after our/my request therefore

In the event that you advance any monies to us/me, at our/my request or with our/my consent, such advances shall be repaid out of any advances payable to us/me under a recording agreement, if not separately reimbursed by a label. In the event that there is not an advance under a recording agreement or such recording agreement advance is not sufficient to repay the monies advanced by you to us/me, we/I shall repay all such advances promptly when such funds are reasonably available to do so, but in no event shall we/I repay the entire advance later than the expiration of the term of this Agreement. Notwithstanding the forgoing, you shall have no obligation to advance us/me any monies under this Agreement.

Accounting and Audits. The compensation to which you are entitled hereunder will be calculated and paid monthly on or before the last day of each calendar month with respect to the Gross Income received by us/ me during the preceding calendar month. Each payment will be accompanied by a statement of the gross income received by us/me during the applicable calendar month and the source of such income. We/I agree to maintain a complete and accurate record of any and all monies received by us/me, which are subject to the provisions of this Agreement.

You agree to maintain a complete and accurate record of any and all monies received by you on our/my behalf, including, without limitation, any monies received as a deposit from employers of our/my talents, and will submit a monthly statement thereof to us/me in itemized detail, together with payment of those sums. Such statement will be submitted to us/me on or before the 15th day of each calendar month with respect to all monies received by you.

Upon ten (10) days' written notice, either party to this Agreement may inspect, audit and copy the books and records of the other party which directly relate to this Agreement or monies received by such party which are subject hereto. Such audit will be conducted at the expense of the party electing to audit at the location in which such books and records are maintained or at such other location as the parties may mutually agree. Any such audit shall be conducted only by a reputable certified public account or business manager familiar with the customs and practices of the entertainment industry during reasonable business hours. No party will be entitled to make more than one examination during any one (1) year period or to audit books and records with respect to any particular calendar period more than once.

It is understood that the parties shall be forever barred from maintaining or instituting an action or proceeding based upon, or in anywise relating to, any transactions which are embraced by or reflected on any statement rendered hereunder, or the accuracy of any item appearing therein, unless written objection thereto shall have been delivered by the objecting party to the other within one (1) year after the date of mailing of the statement on which such transaction or items were first reflected and unless such action or proceeding is commenced within six (6) months after delivery of such written objection. In the event, however, that it is determined as a result of an audit and/or legal action filed in connection therewith, that there is a discrepancy greater than five percent (5%) in the compensation to which one of the parties is entitled, the other party shall be responsible for the cost of the audit up to $ _____. It is understood, however, that the cost of the audit for which the other party is responsible shall be limited to the amount of the discrepancy.

Power of Attorney. Manager will have a power of attorney to enter into agreement(s) on our behalves/my behalf; such power of attorney will be limited to accepting live concert dates that we/I have approved. In addition to the foregoing, you may, subject to our/my express written approval in advance, approve and permit the use of our/my name, likeness, voice sound effect, caricature or other identifying features or characteristics in the promotion, advertising or publicity of products or services or otherwise in any so-called "merchandising" (as defined herein) endeavors.

Assignment. You shall not have the right to assign this Agreement or your duties and obligations herein, except you shall be entitled to assign this Agreement to any corporation or other entity in which you are or become a controlling stockholder or any partnership in which you are or become a partner. We/I understand that we/I may not assign any of the duties and obligations imposed upon us/me under this Agreement, provided we/I may assign our/my right to receive compensation provided we/I have provided you written notice of such an assignment.

Key person. Notwithstanding any assignment by you authorized under this Agreement, we/I will be entitled to your personal services to perform management duties under this Agreement. You shall maintain day-to-day responsibility for your duties and obligations hereunder although you shall have the right to delegate clerical or administrative services hereunder to persons solely under your direct control. In the event that you should cease for any reason to render those services on a day by day basis as our/my keyman for any period exceeding sixty (60) consecutive days, we/I may terminate this Agreement by written notice at any time thereafter during the continuation of your unavailability. Such termination will not affect our/my obligation to repay any advances previously made by you on our/my behalf. Any assignee must expressly acknowledge and agree to be bound by the provisions of this Paragraph ____.

Agency Representation. YOU HAVE ADVISED ME/US THAT YOU ARE NOT AN "EMPLOYMENT AGENT", OR "THEATRICAL AGENT" OR "ARTISTS' TALENT AGENT", BUT ACTIVE SOLELY AS A PERSONAL MANAGER; THAT YOU ARE NOT LICENSED AS A "TALENT AGENT" UNDER THE LABOR CODE OF THE STATE OF CALIFORNIA OR AS A THEATRICAL EMPLOYMENT AGENCY UNDER THE GENERAL BUSINESS LAWS OF THE STATE OF NEW YORK; THAT YOU ARE NOT LICENSED TO SEEK OR OBTAIN EMPLOYMENT OR OBTAIN ENGAGEMENTS FOR US/ME AND THAT YOU DO NOT AGREE TO DO SO, AND YOU HAVE MADE NO REPRESENTATION TO US/ME, EITHER ORAL OR WRITTEN, TO THE CONTRARY. WE/I ACKNOWLEDGE THAT YOU HAVE NEITHER OFFERED, NOR ATTEMPTED, NOR PROMISED TO OBTAIN, SEEK OR PROCURE EMPLOYMENT OR ENGAGEMENTS FOR US/ME.

Relationship of the Parties. This Agreement shall not be construed to create a partnership between us. It is specifically understood that you are acting hereunder as an independent contractor and you may appoint or engage any and all other persons, firms or corporations throughout the world in your discretion to perform any and all of the services which you have agreed to perform hereunder. Your services hereunder are not exclusive and you shall at all times be free to perform the same or similar services for others as well as engage in any and all other business activities.

Representations and Warranties: The parties hereto hereby warrant and represent as follows:
As our/my personal manager, you represent that:
You hereby agree to use your reasonable commercial endeavors to enhance and develop our/my career with respect to the Activities set forth herein; you shall always act in our/my best interests and shall provide your services to the best of your skill and ability and shall perform such

services diligently in order to enhance and develop our/my career with respect to the Activities as defined herein; you shall keep us/me regularly informed with respect to all negotiations with third parties in respect of the Activities defined herein; you shall act as a liaison with all professionals on our/my behalf with regard to the Activities defined herein when properly required and/or when reasonably requested by us/me; you shall fully consult with us/me with regard to all matters concerning the Activities defined herein and shall have due regard to our/my wishes and aspirations and always act in good faith towards us/me; and, you warrant, represent and agree that you are not under any disability, restriction or prohibition, either contractual or otherwise, with respect to your right to execute this Agreement or to fully perform its terms and conditions.

As the Artist, we/I represent that:

We/I hereby represent and warrant that we are/I am over eighteen (18) years of age;

We are/I am under no disability, restriction or prohibition with respect to our/my right to execute this Agreement and perform its terms and conditions and in particular, but without limitation, that as of the date hereof we are/I am neither bound by or under an exclusive management agreement;

We/I warrant and represent that no act or omission by us/me hereunder will violate any right or interest of any person or firm or will subject you to any liability to any person, company or entity; and,

We/I also warrant that we/I have disclosed to you each and every contract we/I have entered into that concerns our/my career(s) in the entertainment, amusement, music, recording and literary fields.

Cure of Defaults. As a condition precedent to the assertion by either party that the other party is in default in performing any obligation contained herein, the party alleging a breach shall advise the allegedly breaching party in writing specifying any such alleged default, and the allegedly breaching party shall be allowed a period of thirty (30) days after receipt of such written notice within which to cure the alleged default. The parties agree that for the purposes hereof, no alleged breach of this Agreement shall be deemed incurable with the exception of a party's criminal act or an act involving moral turpitude. It is understood, however, that termination for any crime or act of moral turpitude may not release the breaching party from that party's duty to compensate and/or reimburse the other as set forth in this Agreement.

Resolution of Disputes. Upon any dispute under or relating to the terms of this Agreement, or the breach thereof, it is agreed that the matter shall be submitted to arbitration to the American Arbitration Association, in ____ _____, _____, before a single arbitrator, and in accordance with then prevailing commercial arbitration rules of that Association. Judgment upon the award rendered by the arbitrator may be entered in any court having jurisdiction thereof. In any arbitration under this Agreement, the prevailing party shall be entitled to recover from the other party any and all costs reasonably incurred by the prevailing party in such arbitration, including without limitation, reasonable attorneys' fees.

Indemnification. The parties hereby agree to indemnify, save and hold one another, their respective agents, employees, representatives, affiliated entities, successors, heirs and designees, harmless from and against all claims, losses, damages, liabilities, costs and expenses (including, without limitation, reasonable outside legal expenses and attorneys' fees) arising out of or connected with any claim by any third party which shall be inconsistent with any agreement, warranty or representation made herein or otherwise arising out of the party's services as a result of this Agreement which has been reduced to a non-appealable settlement (with the party's consent thereto not to be unreasonably withheld) and/or judgment by a court of competent jurisdiction.

Group Provisions. The terms "Artist," "we," or "us," as used herein, refer to the musical group presently known by the name "_____," as an entertainment entity, and to each individual member of the group who is a signatory below. We warrant and represent that the undersigned constitute all of the current members of the musical group "_____" ("the Group"). We agree not to become associated with other performers in the performance of our work except for so-called "sideman," or short-term associations, unless such other performers agree to become a party to this Agreement for the balance of the Term following the date of such association. Each and all of the representations, warranties, agreements and obligations herein shall be deemed, jointly and severally, to be those of all the undersigned and the Group.

Suspension and Termination. The parties hereto shall have the following suspension and termination rights:

As our/my personal manager you shall be entitled to:

Suspension. You shall have the right, at your election, to suspend the running of the time period(s) of this Agreement and your obligations hereunder upon written notice to us/me (a) if for any reason whatsoever our/my voice shall become materially impaired; (b) if we/I shall fail, refuse, neglect, or be unable to comply with any of our/my material obligations hereunder; or, (c) if any of the representations made by us/me herein are false. Such suspension shall be for the duration of any such event or contingency, and, unless you notify us/me to the contrary in writing, the time periods for your obligations hereunder and/or the time periods during which we/I or you has the right to notify the other as to any elections hereunder shall be automatically extended by such number of days as equal the total number of days of any such suspension. During any such suspension we/I shall not render our/my services in the entertainment industry to any other person, firm or corporation, except with your prior approval therefor.

Termination. You shall have the right to terminate this Agreement in the event: (a) We/I commit a criminal act(s), an act(s) involving moral turpitude or have failed to cure a breach of this Agreement; (b) we are/ I am unable to perform our/my duties for a period of _____ or more consecutive weeks due to a medical condition or other impairment; or, (c) in the event of our/my death.

If the Agreement so terminates, we/I shall have no rights hereunder other than our/my entitlement to compensation in connection with those agreements entered into or substantially negotiated prior to the date of termination.

Notices. All notices (other than accounting statements) required or permitted under this Agreement shall be sent by personal delivery, prepaid telegram or United States registered or certified mail, return receipt requested to the address of the parties set forth herein or such other address as they shall designate by written notice. A courtesy copy of all notices given to us/me with respect to this Agreement will be sent to_____ at _____, New York, New York 10021, and a courtesy copy of all notices given to you with respect to this Agreement will be sent to _____, provided that the inadvertent failure to send such copy will not be a breach hereof or impair the effectiveness of such notice. The date of personal delivery or deposit in the mails shall be deemed the date of delivery.

Miscellaneous.

(a) Attorney's Fees: In the event of any dispute under or relating to the terms of this Agreement or the performance, breach, validity, construction, interpretation, execution or legality thereof, the prevailing party shall be entitled to recover any and all reasonable attorneys' fees and other costs incurred in the enforcement of the terms of this Agreement, or for the breach thereof.

(b) Choice of Law: This Agreement and all amendments or modifications hereof shall be governed by and interpreted in accordance with the laws of the state of Tennessee applicable to contracts executed and to be fully performed in said state. The invalidity of any clause, part or provision of this Agreement shall be restrictive in effect to said clause, part or provision, and shall not be deemed to affect the validity of the entire agreement. Any dispute arising under or concerning this Agreement shall be brought before the state or federal courts sitting in Metropolitan Nashville-Davidson County, Tennessee, and the parties hereto expressly waive any objection they have, or may have in the future have, to the jurisdiction and venue of said courts.

(c) Furtherance of Career. We/I agree at all times to devote ourselves/ myself to the furtherance of our/my career and earnings therefrom. We/I will not enter into any agreement or commitment which shall in any manner interfere with your carrying out the terms and conditions of this Agreement.

(d) Headings: No heading contained herein shall be deemed to limit in any way the contents of any paragraph or have any effect to this Agreement, whatsoever, and are inserted solely for the purpose of reference.

(e) Independent Counsel: Each of the parties hereto warrant and represent that in executing this agreement, they have relied solely upon their own judgment, belief and knowledge and the advice and recommendations of their own independently selected and retained counsel.

(f) Joint and Several Obligations. This Agreement shall be deemed between you, on the one hand, and us/me, individually, and collectively, and each of the undersigned shall be jointly and severally liable for the performance of each and all of our separate and collective obligations hereunder. All provisions hereof shall apply to each of the undersigned, individually and collectively, as if each of the undersigned had executed separate contracts with you, and regardless of the name or names under which any or all of the undersigned may perform. If this

Agreement is terminated for any reason whatsoever as to any of the undersigned, it is agreed that this Agreement shall remain in full force and effect as to each of the undersigned with whom this contract is not terminated.

(g) Merger: This Agreement embodies all the representations, terms and conditions of our/my agreement, and there is no other collateral agreement, oral or written, between us in any manner relating to the subject matter hereof. This Agreement shall not become effective until accepted and executed by you.

(h) Modification: No alteration, amendment or modification hereof shall be binding upon the parties unless confirmed by a written instrument executed by the parties hereto.

(i) No Presumption of Authorship: The parties and their counsel have participated jointly in the negotiation and drafting of this Agreement. In the event an ambiguity or question of intent or interpretation arises, this Agreement shall be construed as if drafted jointly by the parties and no presumption or burden of proof shall arise favoring or disfavoring any party by virtue of the authorship of any of the provisions of this Agreement.

(j) Non-Waiver: A waiver by either party of a breach of any provision herein shall not be deemed a waiver of any subsequent breach nor a permanent modification of such provision.

(k) Severability: Should any provision of this Agreement be void or unenforceable, such provision shall be deemed severed and this Agreement with such provision severed shall remain in full force and effect to the extent permitted by law; provided, however, that in the event such severance shall materially affect your right to receive compensation under this Agreement, you shall have the right to elect to treat your obligations under this Agreement as terminated.

(l) Successor in Interest: This Agreement shall be binding upon and inure to the benefit of parties, their respective heirs, executors, administrators, successors and assigns.

(m) Execution in Counterpart. This Contract may be executed in separate counterparts and shall become effective when such separate counterparts have been exchanged between the parties.

(n) Life Insurance: You have the right to obtain, at your own cost and expense, life insurance on the life of me/us with yourself named as sole beneficiary. We/I agree to make ourselves/myself available for all required examinations and to complete any and all documents required to effectuate such insurance policy.

ACCEPTED AND AGREED TO:_____

HOPED-FOR SUCCESS CLEAN HANDS

MANAGEMENT, LLC _____;   By: _____

An Authorized Signer

ARTIST _____

Chapter 2

TALENT CONTRACTS

2.1 INTRODUCTION

In the document-intensive business of entertainment, the acquisition of rights to talent and the process of negotiating and drafting talent agreements go to the heart of most legal and business transactions. A finished motion picture is delivered to the studio only after extensive contract negotiations and drafting for the rights to the talent and services of screenwriters, consultants, a producer, a director, cinematographer, music supervisor, actors and actresses, and scores of other individuals whose talents are required to complete a motion picture—those who are generally credited in the main or end titles of the motion picture. Transactions for rights to talent are complex and vital and are often negotiated under difficult deadlines.

In each of the industries we examine, there are scores of ever-evolving and highly detailed contracts for talent that constitute and formalize the "deal." The negotiation and drafting of these particular agreements, as well as the agreements to secure rights which are discussed in Chapter 3, below, are the focus of law practice for that segment of the bar known as "entertainment lawyers." For other industry lawyers, it is the litigation involving the enforcement of those contracts that is the focus.

Much of the complexity of these entertainment industry contracts can be traced to a number of persistent trends: *innovation*—the seemingly regular appearance of new technologies requiring ever more programming, and offering attractive new markets for old programming, *consolidation*—the continuing trend toward mergers and acquisitions on the part of existing entertainment conglomerates, *internationalization*—the increasing necessity to create programming that appeals to a worldwide audience, and *inflation*—the steady climb in the cost of programming. In addition to these factors, there are the factors of "unpredictability" and "creativity." If one looks across the spectrum of the entertainment industries, a unique phenomenon becomes apparent: The businesses are highly unpredictable with many failures and few successes. Most books, songs, records, plays, television series, and films are unsuccessful and lose money, but those few that are successful become the blockbusters that will more than offset the losses on the majority that fail. For example, the failure rate of records (measured by whether or not a particular recording fails to recoup its recording costs) has consistently been over 80 percent. Not only does the contract have to cover the phenomena of innovation, consolidation, internationalization, and inflation well into the future, it must also anticipate both the unlikely blockbuster and the more likely flop and be relevant to both scenarios (or anything in between).

Added to these complications is the reality that we are not simply dealing with an unpredictable, ever-evolving business—a business that is constantly being challenged by changes in technology. We are dealing with a creative process in which artistic vision is subjective and unpredictable. The clash between "art" and "commerce" is a constant theme both in negotiations and in litigation involving entertainment contracts, for the artistic value of any entertainment property or talent is mostly subjective. Will (and *can*) the book publishing contract address those situations where the publisher is unhappy with the book it has paid the author to write, or where the record company does not wish to release the record the artist has chosen to record, or where the director's vision for the film becomes diametrically opposed to that of the financing studio?

The form, length and number of contracts utilized in each of the various entertainment industries are quite different, reflecting the very different businesses that make up the entertainment industries. However, such contracts will contain many common provisions and address similar issues and concerns. The contract for the publication of a book may consist of a single document no greater in length than the introduction to this book, while the contracts required in the production of a major motion picture will number in the hundreds (or, in some cases, thousands) of pages. In a motion picture deal, the lengthy negotiations and eventual agreements may involve some or all of the following parties: the owner of the underlying work, any persons whose lives (or, perhaps, properties) are portrayed in the film, screenwriters, investors, a banking institution, a producer, an "errors and omissions" insurance carrier, a completion guarantor, a director, actors and actresses, stunt persons, choreographers, film composers, music publishers, record labels owning recordings in the film or releasing the soundtrack record, and a distributor.

The contracts that constitute the deal generally fall into two broad categories: Those that secure the necessary rights to produce the entertainment property and those that secure the talent. Contracts which secure the talent are often personal service contracts and include the acquisition of rights owned or controlled by the talent. A book publisher, music publisher, record company, Broadway producer, television network, or film studio, in its efforts to develop and deliver entertainment properties, will contract for both rights (in existing works) and services (in future works or employment). For instance, a book publisher may seek to secure a license agreement for the paperback rights to an existing novel from its hardcover publisher which may also be the copyright owner, while simultaneously entering into an exclusive personal service contract with the author for the writer's next three (then-unwritten) books.

Contracts for rights usually involve either copyright law (an area that we will touch upon but which is generally beyond the scope of this book) or personal rights (which are addressed in Sections 3.2 through 3.4, below).

A contract for services is more complex, subject to greater statutory restriction, and more susceptible to potential conflict and resulting litigation for a number of reasons. We are dealing with creative individuals, as opposed to pre-existing property or personal rights and future creative services that may not meet (or may exceed) expectations in industries where the future is highly unpredictable. For these reasons, a basic understanding of contract law as applied to the practice of entertainment law is essential, as is an in-depth understanding and grasp of the unique aspects of personal service contracts and the interpretation and enforcement of those contracts.

In order to deliver the finished entertainment property, the "producer" (for example, the book publisher, record company, or film studio) must first secure the talents of the many individuals required to complete the project. Due to the enormous financial commitments that most entertainment properties require today ("inflation"), and in light of the fact that the book, the record, the television pilot, sitcom, or feature film may be years in the making, many of these contracts will be long-term exclusive personal service contracts. The unpredictability element of entertainment may require the producer to structure the term of that personal service contract on the basis of options. The inflation phenomenon may give the talent the bargaining position to command payment of an extraordinary fee and profit participation, regardless of whether their services are actually utilized (a so-called pay or play clause).

Unlike other industries, the entertainment industries are, to a large degree, based upon unique, intangible, and often highly idiosyncratic talents of individual performers or artists. This characteristic makes personal service contracts, from the perspective of the producer, all the more essential and disputes relating to their enforceability all the more heated. Without the individual songwriter and the acquisition of certain rights in and to the songs he or she composes, the music publishing company cannot do business. Likewise, the motion picture company is in need of personal service contracts for many individuals in order to produce a film, including actors, actresses, director, producer, cinematographer, and composer.

The entertainment industries utilize personal service contracts in a number of different contexts. The duration of such contracts differs dramatically, depending upon the particular industry, the financial commitment of the employer, and the relative bargaining position of the parties. Traditionally, the term of a book publishing agreement with an author is based upon delivery of a satisfactory manuscript for a specific book, with an occasional option for the author's next work. In today's record business, however, the label will generally require the artist's exclusive commitment for a term that can last many years, tied to delivery of finished records—in many cases, up to eight or more albums.

Initially, the motion picture industry signed its talent to long-term personal service agreements. Commencing in the 1920s, through what was known as the "star system," actors, actresses, directors, and writers typically signed exclusively with one studio for a number of years. For example, in *De Haviland v. Warner Brothers Pictures,* note the terms and conditions under which Olivia De Haviland entered into an exclusive personal service contract with the studio for seven years (see Section 2.3.1). With the decline of movie attendance in the 1940s and thereafter, as the bargaining position of the stars increased and inflation raised the stars' salaries dramatically, the studios became less able (and also less willing) to enter into long-term personal service contracts with talent. The trend in the film industry has been toward short-duration or nonexclusive personal service contracts, and most actors, actresses, directors, and screenwriters today enter into personal service contracts on a film-by-film basis.

Nonetheless, in recent years film studios have sought and secured long-term, multi-picture contracts—often for seven- or eight-figure guaranties—with some major directors, producers, actors, and actresses. Such an exclusive agreement between producers Peter Guber and Jon Peters and Warner Bros. Pictures became the subject of litigation and a highly publicized settlement between Warner Bros. and Sony in the course of the latter's acquisition of Columbia Pictures and its effort to secure the services of Guber/Peters to run the studio. However, exclusive long-term personal service contracts still are commonplace in the television industry. They are used by both the networks and the independent television producers engaged by the networks to produce and deliver episodic television shows.

Some of the most intensive, publicized, and costly court battles in the entertainment industries involve the enforcement of exclusive long-term personal service contracts—and for good reason. In many instances, such contracts are negotiated when the relative bargaining positions between the employer and employee are unequal. These contracts, which affect the ability of talent to earn a living, address the future services of a talent whose future success (or lack thereof) cannot be anticipated at the time of execution. Finally, these contracts deal with the subjective creative process, during which the parties may disagree and an employee may unilaterally reach the conclusion that he or she can no longer work with the employer and decide to seek work elsewhere. The enforceability of a personal service contract depends upon a number of issues, including:

- Existence of a formal contract between the parties
- Whether such contract is in writing
- Whether the services are exclusive or nonexclusive
- Term of the agreement
- Applicable statutory restrictions on the term
- Provisions for options or extension of the term
- Consideration flowing to the artist
- Services to be performed by the artist
- Effect and nature of a breach of the contract by artist or company
- Availability and type of injunctive relief
- Controlling state laws and possible exclusivity of the forum hearing any disputes concerning the contract

State laws may dictate whether a formal contract exists between parties, under what terms and conditions that contract may be enforced, and for how long such contract may endure. The great majority of entertainment contracts negotiated today are entered into and performed in the states of New York and California. Because the entertainment industries are so firmly entrenched in those states, extensive regulations of the entertainment industries exist in those jurisdictions. Accordingly, a thorough understanding of the statutes of these jurisdictions is essential in order to determine the ultimate validity or invalidity of a contract. Likewise, a significant number of personal services contracts in entertainment are with minors, and the enforceability of such contracts is specifically contingent upon the applicable statutes of the jurisdiction.

We will first discuss problems involving agreements with minors, whether contracts need to be in writing and other problems encountered in making a binding agreement. We then consider the terms and conditions of the personal services contract and the remedies available under that contract.

2.2 CONTRACTS WITH MINORS

Additional considerations arise when a personal service contract involves a minor. A child artist, whether ingénue or enfant terrible, is often vital to the success of a production. Where the services of a minor must be obtained, the company seeking the minor's services will seek to secure either (or both) rights to future services (that is, a personal service contract) or rights to performance or likeness (that is, a release).

Minors have the right to disaffirm their contracts. Historically, minors are afforded this special right to protect them from naively squandering their wealth through improvident contracts with unscrupulous adults. In the entertainment industry, several child entertainers such as Shirley Temple Black and Dana Plato (teen star from television series *Diffrent Strokes*) have been left nearly bankrupt at the end of their star-studded careers as a result of contracts entered into as minors. Although some child performers have suffered great misfortune, entertainment companies can also suffer tremendous financial loss if a minor elects to disaffirm their contract. This is particularly true if the company, relying on the child performer's commitment, has already invested effort and money into developing this child's career.

To protect the interests of both minors and entertainment companies, states such as California and New York have enacted minors' entertainment contract statutes. See New York Arts and Cultural Affairs Law § 35.03; California Family Code § 6751. Under these statutes, a court is authorized to either approve or disapprove a minor's entertainment contract. If the court approves the contract, the minor loses her right to disaffirm it. Restricting a minor's right to disaffirm contracts increases the probability that an entertainment company will receive the benefits of its bargain. For further discussion on Minors' entertainment contracts, see Erika D. Munro, *Under Age, Under Contract, and Under Protected: An Overview of the Administration and Regulation of Contracts with Minors in the Entertainment Industry in New York and California,* 20 Columbia—VLA Journal of Law and the Arts 553 (1996); see also Thom Hardin, *The Regulation of Minors' Entertainment Contracts: Effective California Law or Hollywood Grandeur,* 19 Journal of Juvenile Law 376 (1998).

A minor's right to disaffirm a contract (and the California provision for approval of entertainment industry employment contracts for minors) is inapplicable to a situation where a parent or next friend has executed a valid release (under § 3344 of the California Civil Code, which recognizes the validity of parental consents to name or likeness releases), even though the subject was nude photographs of minor children published in *Hustler* magazine. See *Faloona by Frederickson v. Hustler Magazine, Inc.,* 607 F. Supp. 1341 (N.D.Tex. 1985), aff'd, 799 F.2d 1000 (5th Cir. 1986), *reh'g denied,* 802 F.2d 455 (5th Cir. 1986), *cert. denied,* 479 U.S. 1088 (1987). A New York case with virtually the same facts and holding as the *Faloona by Frederickson* decision in Texas is *Shields v. Gross,* 58 N.Y.2d 338, 448 N.E.2d 108, 461 N.Y.S.2d 254, (1983), which confirmed that under New York law a minor could not disaffirm an otherwise valid written consent from his/her parent or guardian that was specifically authorized under New York Civil Rights Law §§ 50 and 51.

A company which enters a personal services or literary property contract with a minor may also wish to contract with the minor's parents. The provisions of such an agreement may well include clauses in which the parents relinquish the custody, control, or earnings of a minor, covenant that they will not interfere with the performance of a minor's services under the contract, and, in certain circumstances, guarantee the obligation of performance by the minor. Generally, these agreements are enforceable against the minor's parents. In *Lustig v. Schoonover*, 51 N.Y.S.2d 156 (N.Y. Sup. Ct. 1944) *aff'd*, 269 A.D. 830, 56 N.Y.S.2d 415 (1945), parents who had signed a management agreement could not avoid liability even though the minor child subsequently sought to disaffirm the contract.

Companies employing minors in the entertainment industries in California are also subject to a number of administrative restrictions implemented to protect the health and safety of minors. See California Administrative Code, Title 8, Section 11750, *et seq.* In addition, the Screen Actors Guild has special provisions with respect to the employment of minors in its basic agreement. See Akiyama, "Employing Minors in the *Entertainment Industry,*" *1987 Entertainment, Publishing, and the Arts Handbook,* 465. Also see Jacobson, "Minors' Contracts in the Entertainment Industry," in *Entertainment Law* 355 (1989).

All states have general provisions that deal with minors' contracts. Although definitions of a minor vary, a majority of state statutes now provide that a minor is any person under 18 years of age. The following sections explore problems with entertainment contracts involving minors in the states of California and New York.

2.2.1 California Provisions on Minors

The age of majority in California has been 18 since 1971, under *California Civil Code § 25.* It is incumbent on the employer to make an actual determination of whether or not the employee is a minor. A minor's misrepresentation of age does not alter the consequences of dealing with the minor. See *Lee v. Hibernia Savings & Loan,* 171 P. 677 (Cal. 1918), and *Williams v. Leon T. Shettler Co.*, 276 P. 1065 (Cal. 1929).

As discussed above, the major risk in entering into a contract with a minor is that generally the contract is voidable at the option of the minor at any time, either before the minor's majority or within a reasonable time thereafter. The power to disaffirm a contract, including a personal services contract, is embodied in California Family Code § 6750.

The California Family Code controls contracts in California between a minor and a talent agency. An agreement cannot be disaffirmed if the contracting party seeking the services of the minor has complied with the court approval provisions contained in the Family Code. When the Superior Court in California approves a valid contract significant limitations are then placed on minor's ability to disaffirm (see California Family Code § 6751). The court-approval process is available with respect to contracts in which a minor is employed "to render artistic or creative services" in virtually any realm of the entertainment industry.

In California, a court-approved contract may extend to option periods. In *Warner Bros. Pictures v. Brodel,* 192 P.2d 949 (Cal. 1948), a minor attempted to disaffirm the option period in an otherwise valid contract that had previously been approved by the Superior Court. However, the Superior Court's approval of the contract was upheld, the option period was binding, and the minor's later attempt to disaffirm was denied.

The California Family Code also contains a provision to protect the earnings of child performers. See California Family Code § 6752. Enacted in 1939, this provision, known as the "Coogan Law," was created in response to the misfortune of Jackie Coogan. Jackie Coogan was an extremely successful child television star. Upon turning 18, Coogan discovered that his mother and stepfather had legally squandered all of his earnings. To limit such unseemly conduct, the Coogan law authorized courts to establish trust funds in which to deposit a minor's earnings. Although this law was a step in the right direction, it did not provide enough protection for some minors and did not change laws which authorized parents to claim their child's earnings. Thus the earliest enactment of the Coogan Law was not helpful to child stars such as Gary Coleman, whose parents also wasted his earnings legally.

In 2003, the California legislature strengthened the Coogan Law. Under the 2003 amendment, parents or guardians of minor performers must establish trust accounts for their children known as "Coogan Trust Accounts." Parents or guardians must then notify their children's employers about which financial institution the trust account has been established. Employers of child performers are required to set aside and deposit 15% of the child's gross earnings into those trust accounts. If employers do not receive the notification from the parents within a specified time, they are required to send the set-aside funds to the Actors' Fund of America. The Actors' Fund of America then has the obligation to locate performers' parents, notify them of their obligation to establish Coogan Trust Accounts, and then deposit the set-aside funds in those accounts. See California Family Code § 6752.

2.2.2 New York Provisions on Minors

Following the lead of California, in 2003 the New York legislature enacted the New York Child Performer Education and Trust Act. Modeled after California's Coogan Law, this act both allows for protections of minor performers' earnings and ensures that child performers meet educational requirements. More specifically, this act requires that 15% of the child performer's gross earnings to be placed in trust until the child reaches the age of 18. This requirement applies to all contracts with a minor who resides in or renders services in New York regardless of whether the contract is ratified by a court. Also a child performer is required to receive a work permit from the New York Department of Labor. A work permit will only be issued upon satisfaction that the child is maintaining acceptable academic performance at their school of attendance. See Section NY CLS Labor § 151. Further, employers must provide education to child performers when their schedules require them to be absent from school. See NY CLS Labor § 152.

In regards to judicial approval of contracts, until 1983, a general statute provided for minors' contracts, including judicial approval of certain types of contracts (see old New York General Obligations Law § 3–105). Under this statute, if a contract met the statutory require-ments and was duly approved by a court, the minor could not disaffirm during his minority or upon reaching his majority. In 1983, § 3–105 was repealed and replaced by *New York Arts and Cultural Affairs Law § 35.03*. The scope of the act was narrowed to focus on minors enter-ing entertainment, arts, and sports contracts. (For contracts involving employment of children as models, see N.Y. Arts and Cultural Affairs Law § 35.05.)

The case of *Prinze v. Jonas*, 345 N.E.2d 295 (N.Y.Ct.App. 1976), sug-gests a cautionary note concerning the question of whether judicial approval (or lack thereof) is the *sine qua non* of enforceability of a minor's contract under New York law. Although *Prinze* was decided under the New York General Obligations Law, cited above, the provi-sions of that law are not materially different from those of the recently enacted Arts and Cultural Affairs Law, particularly § 35.03. Thus, there is no reason to believe that future New York courts will deviate from the *Prinze* holdings.

In *Prinze*, the court recognized that a contract with a minor, even though it could not be approved by a court under the then-applicable § 3–105, could nevertheless still be found to be "reasonable and provi-dent" to the minor, and thus enforceable under N.Y. General Obliga-tions Law § 3–101. Judicial approval, therefore, was not necessarily a condition precedent to an enforceable contract with a minor.

The *Prinze* court went even further in its evaluation of the enforce-ability of an arbitration clause contained in the contract in dispute. The court held that its function was merely to review whether the arbi-tration clause was reasonable. If it was reasonable, the arbitrator, not the court, should rule on the ultimate validity of the contract itself. Thus, an arbitrator, called into the dispute only because of the contract clause, could then rely on that clause to establish jurisdiction over the dispute and resolve the validity of the contract. The arbitrator could uphold or void the contract; even in voiding, the arbitrator was still empowered to act because of the contract clause.

No New York court has faced this same conundrum under current law, but there is little reason to believe *Prinze v. Jonas* is anything other than binding precedent. Under the Arts and Cultural Affairs statutes, § 35.01 tracks the old § 3–101 as to "reasonable and provident" con-tracts in a minor's business, and § 35.03 tracks the old § 3–105 as to the grounds for judicial approval of a contract. A New York court reviewing an arbitration clause in a minor's contract would face essentially the same problems of reconciling various statutory provisions as were ana-lyzed and resolved in *Prinze*.

In New York, even if a minor has the right to disaffirm the agreement, are commissions still due and owing under the terms of a personal management agreement? As is demonstrated in the *Scott Eden Management* case that follows, the minor's ability to disaffirm may not extend to the fee for the "airplane ride" then concluded.

Scott Eden Management v. Andrew Kavovit, 563 N.Y.S.2d 1001 (Sup. Ct. N.Y. County 1990)

COPPOLA, JUSTICE

In this case of first impression, an infant actor has disaffirmed a personal services contract. He thereby seeks to avoid responsibility to his manager for commissions due in the future on income from performance contracts already obtained for him by the manager.

The salient facts are not in dispute. In 1984, when defendant Andrew M. Kavovit was twelve years of age, he and his defendant parents entered into a contract with plaintiffs ("Scott Eden") whereby Scott Eden became the exclusive personal manager to supervise and promote Andrew's career in the entertainment industry. This agreement ran from February 8, 1984 to February 8, 1986 with an extension for another three years to February 8, 1989. It provided that Scott Eden was entitled to a 15% commission on Andrew's gross compensation. "With respect to contracts entered into by [Andrew] ... during the term of this agreement ... [Scott Eden] shall be entitled to commission from the residuals or royalties of such contracts, the full term of such contracts, including all extensions or renewals thereof, notwithstanding the earlier termination of this agreement." (Paragraph "Tenth" of the Agreement.)

In 1986, Andrew signed an agency contract with the Andreadis Agency, a licensed agent selected by Scott Eden pursuant to industry requirements. This involved an additional 10% commission. Thereafter, Andrew signed several contracts for his services. The most important contract, from a financial and career point of view, secured a role for Andrew on "As the World Turns," a long-running television soap opera. Income from this employment contract appears to have commenced on December 28, 1987 and continues through December 28, 1990, with a strong possibility for renewal. One week before the contract with Scott Eden was to expire, Andrew's attorney notified Scott Eden that his "clients hereby disaffirm the contract on the grounds [sic] of infancy." Up until then, the Andreadis Agency had been forwarding Scott Eden its commissions, but by letter of February 4, 1989, Andrew's father, David Kavovit, advised Andreadis that Andrew's salary would go directly to Andrew and that he would send Andreadis its 10%. Needless to say, no further commissions were sent to Scott Eden.

The complaint seeks money damages for (1) all sums due plaintiffs for commissions relating to Andrew's personal appearances prior to February 8, 1989, the date of disaffirmance, (2) all sums due plaintiff for commissions with respect to contracts entered into by Andrew in the entertainment or promotion fields during the term of his contract with plaintiffs, "i.e., commissions from the residuals or royalties of such contracts—the full term of such contracts—including all extensions or renewals thereof," and (3) $50,000 for tortious interference with the relationship between plaintiff and the Andreadis Agency.

Issue was joined and examinations before trial were held. Defendants have now brought this motion for summary judgment upon the ground that no genuine, triable issues exist.

An infant's contract is voidable and the infant has an absolute right to disaffirm. (*General Obligations Law* Sec. 3–101; *Continental Nat. Bk. v. Strauss,* 137 N.Y. 148, 32 N.E. 1066; *Casey v. Kastel,* 237 N.Y. 305, 142 N.E. 671; *Joseph v. Schatzkin,* 259 N.Y. 241, 181 N.E. 464; and see G.O.L. Sec. 3—107 with regard to the absence of parental liability either as parties or guarantors.) This aspect of the law of contracts was well-entrenched in the common law as early as the fifteenth century (*Williston on Contracts, Third Edition Section* 223). In bringing this action, and defending the motion, plaintiffs fully recognize the principle of law involved here and in no way challenge the infant's right to disaffirm. Rather, plaintiffs rely upon a corollary to the main rule, which also evolved early in the Common Law:

After disaffirmance, the infant is not entitled to be put in a position superior to such a one as he would have occupied if he had never entered into his voidable agreement. He is not entitled to retain an advantage from a transaction which he repudiates. "The privilege of infancy is to be used as a shield and not as a sword." (Kent, vol. 2, p. 240; *Rice v. Butler,* 160 N.Y. 578), *Joseph v. Schatzkin,* 259 N.Y. 241, 244, 181 N.E. 464.

As stated differently by the same Court in an earlier case involving an infant's disaffirmance:

The theory of a rescission is that the party proceeded against shall be restored to his original position. The plaintiff cannot rescind if he retains in himself or withholds through another any fruit of the contract. *Frances v. New York and Brooklyn Elevated Railroad Co.,* 108 N.Y. 93, 97, 15 N.E. 192.

The restoration of consideration requirement found voice in CPLR 3004 which states that the infant need not tender restoration of benefits received prior to disaffirmance "but the court may make a tender of restoration a condition of its judgment, and may otherwise in its judgment so adjust the equities between the parties that unjust enrichment is avoided." (*See Williston on Contracts, Third Edition Section* 238, especially n. 9, as to the apparent historical setting of this provision.)

The restoration of consideration principle, as interpreted by the courts, has resulted in the infant being responsible for wear and tear on the goods returned by him. [Citations omitted.] In the event that the minor cannot return the benefits obtained, he is effectively precluded from disaffirming the contract in order to get back the consideration he has given. In *Vichnes v. Transcontinental & Western Air,* 173

Misc. 631, 18 N.Y.S.2d 603) the infant paid the air fare from New York to Los Angeles. On returning to New York she demanded the return of her money. Appellate Term granted summary judgment to defendant because "there is no basis for rescission here in view of the concession that the reasonable value of the transportation was the sum paid by plaintiffs" (at 631, 18 N.Y.S.2d 603).

The parties have not cited, nor has the Court found, a case dealing with the exact issue at bar, i.e. whether disaffirmance may void the contractual obligation to pay agents' commissions without any concomitant exchange being made. However, an analogy may be drawn from the case of *Mutual Milk & Cream Co. v. Prigge,* 112 App. Div. 652, 98 N.Y.S. 458. There, a minor had entered the employ of the plaintiff as a milk wagon driver and had signed a contract which included a restrictive covenant wherein the minor agreed not to solicit plaintiff's customers within three years after leaving plaintiff's employ. Several months after entering into the contract, the minor quit, pursuant to the terms of the contract, but then went to work for plaintiff's rival and solicited business from plaintiff's customers.

The Appellate Division affirmed the issuance of an injunction against the minor, who had pleaded infancy in avoidance of the contractual obligations. The court considered that the issue was not one of liability of an infant for a breach of his contract, but whether an infant should be allowed to repudiate his contract without restoring what he had received and, if restoration could not be made, without being enjoined from making use of the information he had gained from his employment by the plaintiff to the latter's damage. The Court held that the infant should be enjoined "from making use of that information, in violation of his agreement made at the time when he desired and obtained employment, and upon the faith of which he obtained the information and acquaintance." The Court further noted that "No man would engage the services of an infant if he could not impose the same condition for his own protection against the use of his formulas, trade secrets, and lists of customers that he could exact of an adult."

The rationale of the *Mutual Milk* case is applicable to this case. The work a personal manager does for and with his client is preparatory to the performance contract. Once a performance contract has been signed, the personal manager is entitled to his percentage fee, subject only to the condition subsequent that the client performs and earns his fee. This is clearly the understanding in the industry, unlike, for example, the standard in the insurance field where the initial commission is disproportionately high and the subsequent, smaller commissions are viewed as consideration for continued efforts in keeping the insurance contract current. When the client signs a performance contract, it is with the understanding that the gross amount to be paid is not solely for him. It is the expectation of all parties—the agent, the performer and, in this case, the soap opera production company, that 15% of that gross amount belongs to the personal manager. To the extent that the performer obtains that 15% for himself, he is unjustly enriched.

Here, the position adopted by defendants is no different than that advanced on behalf of the infant who had taken the airplane ride and wanted her money back or the truck driver who had milked his employer's efforts and tutelage and then refused to honor his reciprocal commitment. In each case, the infant consumed the fruits of the contract and refused to pay for that fruit, to the clear prejudice of the other party. In this case, the infant will continue to reap the benefits of his contract with plaintiff but is using his infancy as an excuse not to honor the promise made in return for that benefit.

If the argument asserted by defendants were adopted by the Court, the infant would be put in a position superior to that which he would have occupied had he never entered into the contract with plaintiff. He would be retaining an advantage from the repudiated transaction, i.e., using the privilege of infancy as a sword rather than a shield. Not only is this manifestly unfair, but it would undermine the policy underlying the rule allowing disaffirmance. If the infant may rescind the contract with the manager immediately after a lucrative performance contract is signed, yet still retain the benefits of the performance contract, no reputable manager will expend any efforts on behalf of an infant.

In this case, adjustment of the equities so as to prevent unjust enrichment, as suggested by CPLR 3004, leads to the conclusion that defendants must continue to pay to plaintiffs all commissions to which plaintiffs would be entitled under their contract, as they become due. Thus, on the first two causes of action summary judgment is denied to defendants and is granted to plaintiffs to the extent that they shall be restored to their original condition. Moreover, inasmuch as plaintiffs will no longer be involved in the day to day personal management of the infant, they will be entitled to periodic statements regarding Andrew's income and the sources thereof and they shall have the right to annual inspections of the books and records kept with regard to Andrew's income.

The third cause of action is dismissed. Plaintiffs have come forward with no proof to buttress their conclusory claim that defendants have tortiously interfered with their business relationship with the Andreadis Agency.

The Court notes that this entire situation may have arisen due to a misreading of a statute which is related to the problem at hand but irrelevant to its determination. The affidavit of David J. Kavovit makes reference to Arts and Cultural Affairs Law Sec. 35.03 as a bar to this action and that "I am advised that the agreement was void at its inception by reason of the fact that its term, including options to extend, exceeded a three year period of time" (Par. 13).

Section 35.03 (formerly G.O.L. Sec. 3–105, formerly DRL Sec. 74) provides for judicial approval of infants' contracts in order to avoid later disaffirmance. However, no such contract may be approved if it extends for a period of more than three years, whether by option or otherwise. However, the purpose of the statute was to limit the infant's right to disaffirm. If there is no judicial approval, for whatever reason, then the statute has no effect upon the infant's contract or upon his right to disaffirm (*Matter of Prinze*, 38 N.Y.2d 570, 381 N.Y.S.2d 824, 345 N.E.2d 295).

2.3 CONTRACT DURATION

2.3.1 The California Seven-Year Statute

In the 1920s and 1930s, Hollywood movie moguls developed the "star" system, which involved promotion of actors and actresses into something larger than life. At heart, it was a way to exploit the public by heightening interest in the stars and increasing the box office returns. As it developed, it was exploitation of the stars as well. The trick was to find young talent, sign them to unconscionably long contracts, and then hope that promotion and luck would make them stars in the public perception.

The usual vehicle through which a young actor or actress entered the system was a "studio" contract. In agreeing to a contract, the talent might be bound for ten years or more, at a salary that would later prove to be well below market value. At length, the California legislature tempered studio contracts by enacting a seven-year limit on the studio's ability to enforce personal service contracts. Other protections, to both employer and employee, were added.

Today, California is unique with its limitations on the duration of personal service contracts. Since so many entertainment transactions are subject to California law, the California enactments require thorough analysis. We begin with § 2855 of the California Labor Code; then we discuss important cases that have applied this legislation.

§ 2855. Enforcement of contract to render personal service;
Personal service in the production of phonorecords

(a) Except as otherwise provided in subdivision (b), a contract to render personal service . . . may not be enforced against the employee beyond seven years from the commencement of service under it. Any contract, otherwise valid, to perform or render service of a special, unique, unusual, extraordinary, or intellectual character, which gives it peculiar value and the loss of which can not be reasonably or adequately compensated in damages in an action at law, may nevertheless be enforced against the person contracting to render such service, for a term not to exceed seven years from the commencement of service under it. If the employee voluntarily continues his service under it beyond that time, the contract may be referred to as affording a presumptive measure of the compensation.

(b) Notwithstanding subdivision (a):

    (1) Any employee who is a party to a contract to render personal service in the production of phonorecords in which sounds are first

fixed, as defined in Section 101 of Title 17 of the United States Code, may not invoke the provisions of subdivision (a) without first giving written notice to the employer in accordance with Section 1020 of the Code of Civil Procedure, specifying that the employee from and after a future date certain specified in the notice will no longer render service under the contract by reason of subdivision (a).

(2) Any party to such a contract shall have the right to recover damages for a breach of the contract occurring during its term in an action commenced during or after its term, but within the applicable period prescribed by law.

(3) In the event a party to such a contract is, or could contractually be, required to render personal service in the production of a specified quantity of the phonorecords and fails to render all of the required service prior to the date specified in the notice provided in paragraph (1), the party damaged by the failure shall have the right to recover damages for each phonorecord as to which that party has failed to render service in an action which, notwithstanding paragraph (2), shall be commenced within 45 days after the date specified in the notice.

Also related to the issue of duration of employment are §§ 2924 and 2925 of the Labor Code, covering, respectively, the rights of an employer and an employee to terminate. These sections are set forth in Section 2.3.2 below.

De Haviland v. Warner Brothers Pictures, 153 P.2d 983 (Cal.Ct.App. 1944)

SHINN, J.

Defendant has appealed from a judgment declaring at an end its contract for the services of plaintiff as a motion picture actress. The ground of the decision was that the contract had run for seven years, the maximum life allowed such contracts by former Civil Code, section 1980, now section 2855 of the Labor Code. It was executed April 14, 1936, for a term of fifty-two weeks and gave the employer the right to extend the term for any or all of six successive periods of fifty-two weeks each. These options were exercised from time to time by the employer so as to cover the entire contract period. The services commenced May 5, 1936, and, except as interrupted by certain periods of suspension, were continued to August 13, 1943. The present action was commenced August 23, 1943. The contract gave the producer, defendant, the right to suspend plaintiff for any period or periods when she should fail, refuse or neglect to perform her services to the full limit of her ability and as instructed by the producer and for any additional period or periods required to complete the portrayal of a role refused by plaintiff and assigned to another artist. Plaintiff was to receive no compensation while so suspended or thereafter until she offered to resume her work. It was provided that the producer had the right to extend the term of the contract at its option, for a time equal to the periods of suspension. There were several such suspensions after December 9, 1939, and one suspension of thirty days which plaintiff agreed to and which was occasioned by her illness. In each instance defendant exercised its right to extend the term of the agreement. The several periods of suspension totaled some twenty-five weeks. The facts as to the suspensions are not in dispute; defendant's right to impose them is not questioned. Plaintiff's reason for refusing the several roles was that they were unsuited to her matured ability and that she could not faithfully and conscientiously portray them. Her good faith and motives are not in issue, but according to the contract the producer was the sole judge in such matters and she had to do as she was told. The sole question is whether the provisions for suspension, and for extension of the term of the agreement, were lawful and effective insofar as they purported to bind plaintiff beyond seven years from the date her services were commenced. If they were lawful, plaintiff still owes twenty-five weeks of service; otherwise the contract came to an end May 5, 1943. . . .

If we are to accept defendant's construction of [Sec. 2855] as amended, we must add words to the phrase used in the proviso so that it would read "for a term not beyond a period of seven years of *actual service* from the commencement of service under it." In fact, the words "of actual service" could have been used appropriately after the word "term" and also after the words "seven years" if it had been the intention to do away with the limitation of seven calendar years from the commencement of service. It is true that the exception in the first clause of contracts for exceptional services, to which the proviso relates, suggests a possible intention to take such contracts out of the general rule, but the proviso itself is the enacting clause and the controlling one. It is the clause which determines whether the general limitation was intended to be removed as to contracts for exceptional services. Defendant's contention is that there could have been only one purpose in amending the section, namely, to allow the enforcement against employees of contracts for personal services to the extent of seven years of actual service, regardless of the time over which such services might extend. With this we cannot agree. The difficulty with the argument, and which we think is insurmountable, is that the Legislature has not used the words "of service," and the failure to use those or equivalent words is far more significant as indicating the purpose of the enactment than the entire amendment as written. We cannot believe that the phrase "for a term not beyond a period of seven years" carries a hidden meaning. It cannot be questioned that the limitation of time to which section 1980 related from 1872 to 1931 was one to be measured in calendar years. It is conceded that contracts for general services are limited to seven calendar years. The substitution of years of service for calendar years would work a drastic change of state policy with relation to contracts for personal services. One would expect that such a revolutionary change, even as applied to a particular class of contracts, would be given expression in clear and unmistakable terms. . . .

We have not overlooked the earnest arguments of counsel as to whether a producer of motion pictures should or should not have the right to the exclusive services of an artist for a period of seven years of service. It is to be presumed that the Legislature considered such matters in legislating upon the subject, but the arguments do not aid us in determining what the code sections mean. While the purpose sought to be accomplished in the enactment of a statute may be considered as an aid to interpretation, the question whether the Legislature has acted at all in a given particular must find answer in the statute itself. We think the expressions of the various enactments cannot be bent to a shape that will fit defendant's argument, and that the several extensions of plaintiff's contract due to her suspensions were ineffective to bind her beyond May 5, 1943, seven years after her services commenced.

A second contention is that if defendant had not the right under the code to demand seven years of service, plaintiff has waived the right to question the validity of the extensions, which carried beyond the seven-year period. By her breaches of the contract, it is claimed, she brought into operation the provisions for extension and is now estopped to avoid them. Defendant relies upon section 3513 of the Civil Code, reading as follows: "Anyone may waive the advantage of a law intended solely for his benefit. But a law established for a public reason cannot be contravened by a private agreement." Defendant insists that the limitations of said sections 1980 and 2855 were enacted solely for the benefit of employees and not for a public reason, and may be waived. . . .

The fact that a law may be enacted in order to confer benefits upon an employee group, far from shutting out the public interest, may be strong evidence of it. It is safe to say that the great majority of men and women who work are engaged in rendering personal services under employment contracts. Without their labors the activities of the entire country would stagnate. Their welfare is the direct concern of every community. Seven years of time is fixed as the maximum time for which they may contract for their services without the right to change employers or occupations. Thereafter they may make a change if they deem it necessary or advisable. There are innumerable reasons why a change of employment may be to their advantage. Considerations relating to age or health, to the rearing and schooling of children, new economic conditions and social surroundings may call for a change. As one grows more experienced and skillful there should be a reasonable opportunity to move upward and to employ his abilities to the best advantage and for the highest obtainable compensation. Legislation which is enacted with the object of promoting the welfare of large classes of workers whose personal services constitute their means of livelihood and which is calculated to confer direct or indirect benefits upon the people as a whole must be presumed to have been enacted for a public reason and as an expression of public policy in the field to which the legislation relates. . . .

The power to restrict the right of private contract is one which does not exist independently of the power to legislate for the purpose of preserving the public comfort, health, safety, morals and welfare. The power to provide for the comfort, health, safety and general welfare of any or all employees is granted to the Legislature by article XX, section 17 1/2 of the state Constitution. Enactments exercising the power have been upheld in many instances. . . . The rights of employees as now declared by section 2855 of the Labor Code fall squarely within the prohibition of section 3513 of the Civil Code, that rights created in the public interest may not be contravened by private agreement.

Finally, it may be pointed out that the construction of the code sections contended for by defendant would render the law unworkable and would lead to an absurd result. If an employee may waive the statutory right in question by his conduct, he may waive it by agreement, but if the power to waive it exists at all, the statute accomplishes nothing. An agreement to work for more than seven years would be an effective waiver of the right to quit at the end of seven. The right given by the statute can run in favor of those only who have contracted to work for more than seven years and as these would have waived the right by contracting it away, the statute could not operate at all. It could scarcely have been the intention of the Legislature to protect employees from the consequences of their improvident contracts and still leave them free to throw away the benefits conferred upon them. The limitation of the life of personal service contracts and the employee's rights thereunder could not be waived. . . .

NOTES _____

1. An important aspect of the *De Haviland* decision is the unreported facts in the case. The original contract with the studio was for a period of less than seven years. De Haviland was a minor at the time of its execution, and accordingly, the contract was approved by the Los Angeles Superior Court as being "just, fair and conscionable and to be in the best interest of Olivia De Haviland." The extensions of the term of the contract were occasioned by De Haviland's breaches and refusals to perform. Warner Brothers, in its unsuccessful appeal, argued:

   On one occasion, Respondent [De Haviland] signed a written agreement approving the suspension dates; on another occasion Respondent herself requested and received an extension of the contract in order that she might absent herself from the studio for a period of four consecutive weeks commencing February 16, 1942. . . . Respondent alone is responsible for the term of her service extending one day beyond seven calendar years. She asked for it on February 16, 1942. She benefitted by it.

   If the statute can be waived, or if she can be estopped from hiding behind the statute, whatever its meaning may be, then in this case that statute has been waived and the estoppel exists. . . . Only a holding that L.C. 2855 is mandatory, absolute, and represents an expression of public policy and was established for a public reason, can in this case justify the granting of any relief herein to the artist.

2. In an unreported decision of the Los Angeles Superior Court filed in 1973, *Lukas aka Susan St. James v. Universal,* No. C54945, a mid-term extension was litigated under § 2855. The employment contract with Universal provided for an initial term of 26 weeks, with options for a possible total of seven years. Six months later, another employment agreement of seven-year potential was executed, with a condition that the first contract was terminated upon execution of the second. The issue raised by St. James and never resolved in that case was whether she was obligated to perform beyond the initial seven-year period under a second agreement, which she claimed was not negotiated "at arm's length."

3. In *Foxx v. Williams,* 244 Cal.App. 2d 223, 52 Cal. Rptr. 896 (2d Dist. 1966), an issue arose under § 2855. Dootone Records contended that § 2855 was inapplicable to its recording contract with comedian Red Foxx because Foxx was an independent contractor, while § 2855 applies only to an "employee." Dootone had never withheld taxes on Foxx or paid Social Security taxes or state disability assessments for him. Nor had Dootone exercised any control over the creative aspects of Foxx's material or performance. The court nonetheless found § 2855 applicable. The first two contracts between Dootone and Foxx had been denominated "contract for your personal services between Dootone Records as the employer, and you as the vocalist, and we hereby employ you for the purpose of making phonograph records." Foxx recorded in the same manner under all three of his contracts, even though the last contract did not contain the quoted language. However, Dootone selected the times and places of recording, whether to invite an audience (and, if so, whom to invite), and the equipment to be used in recording (which it operated). The court distinguished *Ketcham v. Hall Syndicate, Inc.* (see below), because Ketcham turned in completed cartoon strips, whereas Foxx's efforts were not complete until worked on by Dootone. The language of the earlier contracts, plus the consistent pattern of involvement of Dootone in the recording process, was sufficient to permit the court to find an employer-employee relationship which triggered the application of § 2855.

4. Lawyers have argued for years as to whether or not a mid-term renegotiation will serve to start the California seven-year statute running anew. One school of thought holds that only a "moment of freedom"—a release given under noncoercive circumstance—will suffice. In other words, the artist must be free to walk out of the room without signing a new contract so that the act of re-signing is perceived to be totally voluntary. Another view holds that a renegotiation involving substantial new consideration, entered into toward the end of a deal and for an independent business reason, should be sufficient to restart the seven-year period. In the case of *Melissa Manchester v. Arista Records, Inc.,* No. CV 81–2134 (C.D.Cal. Sept. 17, 1981), the court suggested (in an unpublished—and later withdrawn—opinion by Judge Robert J. Kelleher) that if the latter criteria were met, the statute could indeed be restarted. Manchester signed with Arista in 1973 while residing in New York. She later moved to California. In 1976, in order to obtain monies ($145,000) with which to fund a settlement with her manager and terminate their agreement, Manchester entered into a further contract with Arista for an additional year at Arista's option, to follow the end of the term of the original agreement. Due to late delivery of recordings by Ms. Manchester, Arista suspended the term of her agreement on several occasions so that, by the time Arista purported to exercise its one-year option under the 1976 agreement, Arista claimed that Manchester owed it three LPs, two under the original agreement and one under the additional agreement. Manchester refused to perform further, citing Labor Code § 2855. Both contracts contained forum selection and/or choice-of-law clauses selecting New York. Ms. Manchester, however, contended that to uphold these would violate the strong California public policy underlying § 2855. The court, however, was not persuaded and held that the forum selection clause of the 1973 agreement should be enforced. The 1976 contract specified New York law but did not contain a forum selection clause. The court rejected Manchester's claim that the 1976 agreement was an extension of the 1973 contract and thus invalid because of the prohibition

of waiver of employees' rights under § 2855. "This argument," Judge Kelleher said, "would effectively prevent an employee from entering into a new contract with his or her current employer until after the completion of all obligations between them. The better course is to consider the circumstances surrounding the formation of the new contract in each situation. If the new contracts was entered into at or near the time of formation of the earlier contract, and if the two contracts appear to have been entered into to avoid the application of § 2855 to a single agreement, then they should be considered a single contract for the purposes of § 2855. However, if the latter contract was entered into toward the end of the first contract, it should be treated as a separate agreement for purposes of § 2855." Each contract should be reviewed on a case by case basis, not under formalistic contract law principles but "in light of the policy consideration underlying § 2855 to protect employees." The only tie between the two contracts was that "the 1976 agreement is an option contract that Arista could exercise only if it had exercised all of its options under the 1973 contract." The second contract "was not entered into with the purpose of evading the seven-year employment limitation of § 2855."

5. In *Adams v. Irving Music, Inc.*, Case No. BC 090519, Superior Court, Los Angeles County, (unreported) Bryan Adams was granted summary judgment (effective as of 1991) in a case in which the term of Adams' songwriter agreement with Irving (which commenced in 1984) was contractually co-terminous with the term of Adams' recording agreement with Irving's then-affiliate, A&M Records, Inc. The recording agreement had been re-negotiated, and its term had been extended which, Irving claimed, also served to extend the term of the songwriter agreement until 1993.

6. There have been no reported California cases involving the seven-year statute in over a decade. Several highly publicized actions were initiated in the 1990s that would have tested the limits of the seven-year statute in light of the critical and yet-unresolved issue of midterm modification/extensions but all were settled. In *Geffen Records, Inc. v. Henley* (No. BC073696 [Superior Court, Los Angeles County]) Don Henley, who had attained enormous success both as a member of the Eagles and as a solo artist on Geffen Records sought in 1992 to invoke the statute to terminate of his 1984 solo agreement (which had been modified in 1988). In *We're Only In It For the Music v. Elektra Entertainment* (No. 9644007 Superior Court, San Francisco County), the group Metallica challenged the enforceability of their 1984 agreement under § 2855 even though the recording agreement had a New York law and forum clause. We can only speculate as the judicial outcome of these cases as both of them were dismissed as part of out-of-court settlements.

7. For additional analysis of problems arising under California's seven-year statute, see Bushkin and Meyer, "The Enforcement of Mid-Term Extensions of Employment Agreements Under California Labor Code Sec. 2855," 15 *Beverly Hills Bar Journal* 385 (1980) and "Employee Emancipation in California: The Seven Year Itch Under Labor Code Section 2855," 56 *Cal St B.J.* (1981); Blaufarb, "The Seven Year Itch: California Labor Code Section 2855," 6 *Comm/Entertainment L.J.* 653 (1984).

8. See, also, Greenberg, "Seven Years to Like: The Flight for Free Agency in the Record Business," 12 *Entertainment and Sports Lawyer* 1 (1994).

Ketcham v. Hall Syndicate, Inc., 236 N.Y.S.2d 206 (Sup. Ct. N.Y. County 1962), *aff'd*, 242 N.Y.S.2d 182 (1963)

SPECTOR, JUSTICE

On January 24, 1951 the plaintiff (the creator of the cartoon panel entitled "Dennis The Menace") and the defendant, then known as the Post-Hall Syndicate, Inc., entered into an agreement for the syndication by Hall of the cartoon panels.

The contract provided that the panels were to be delivered to Hall's office in the City of New York at least six weeks prior to the scheduled date of release.

The agreement further provided that its duration should be for the period of one year with automatic renewals from year to year without notice unless the plaintiff's share from syndication did not equal certain minimum stipulated weekly payments, in which event either party had the right to terminate it. There is no claim that the minimum returns have not been met. In fact, the evidence is quite to the contrary, and it is uncontradicted that the payments are now over five times the required minimum.

The parties performed under the contract from the date thereof until December 18, 1961 when the plaintiff wrote a letter to the defendant in which he purported to cancel and terminate the contract as of March 11, 1962. However, the plaintiff is still performing under the contract by reason of the provision in the aforesaid letter of December 18, 1961, that if the cancellation were not recognized then the plaintiff would continue to perform until such right of cancellation and termination should be established by litigation.

In answer to the plaintiff's letter, on March 8, 1962, the defendant advised the plaintiff that by reason of the payment of the minimum provided by the terms of the contract that it would deem the contract renewed for the further period of one year and that it would also deem it renewed from year to year thereafter provided the stipulated payments had been made.

The plaintiff's complaint seeks a declaratory judgment determining whether the plaintiff has the legal right to terminate the contract on the grounds (a) that it is for an indefinite term and that there is no mutuality; (b) that section 2855 of the Labor Code of the State or California provides that such a contract may not be enforced beyond seven years from the commencement of the services; and (c) that if the contract is governed by the laws of the State of California it may be cancelled and terminated since it is no longer enforceable under the aforesaid section of the Labor Code.

The questions of law are clearly defined and are (1) is the contract governed by the laws of the State of New York or the State of California; (2) if the contract is governed by the laws of California, is it terminable by reason of section 2855 of the Labor Code; and (3) is the contract, which calls for automatic renewals upon the payment of certain minimums, voidable either by reason of indefiniteness or lack of mutuality. . . .

There is no decision of the California courts which has determined whether a contract such as the one in question is governed by the above-quoted statute. Defendant contends that the contract in question established a relationship not of employer-employee but one of the status of an independent contractor and that therefore the section relied on does not apply.

Section 2750 of Article 1 of Chapter 2 of said Code defines a contract of employment as one "by which one, who is called the employer, engages another, who is called the employee, to do something for the benefit of the employer or a third person."

Edwin S. Pillsbury, Esq., plaintiff's expert on California law, testified on cross-examination that the contract in question "does not establish, in my opinion, the relationship of employer and employee in the strict sense"; and further testified that this contract would fall within the category of "an independent contractor relationship," and that Mr. Ketcham was an independent contractor by reason of the fact that there was no "right of supervision, direction and control."

Mr. Pillsbury, however, testified that section 2855 of the California Labor Code applied to independent contractors. That the second sentence of section 2855 relating to contracts to "render service of a special, unique, unusual, extraordinary, or intellectual character, which gives it peculiar value" had reference to independent contractors and that Mr. Ketcham's contract was of this type. However, he never stated the basis for his opinion, except that there was a strong public policy (in California) "to the effect that an employee should be protected by law against improvidently contracting his services away for a longer period than seven years."

Reliance is also placed by plaintiff on *De Haviland v. Warner Bros. Pictures,* 67 Cal.App. 2d 225, 153 P.2d 983. However, in that case the acting was performed by the employee at the direction of her employer at places designated by her employer. In this case, however, plaintiff's performance was delivery by him at the defendant's New York office of six daily cartoon panels per week. There was no supervision, plaintiff worked where he pleased. The provision regarding the quality of the panels is usual in certain types of sales or building contracts and does not imply supervision.

Sidney Justin, Esq. defendant's expert witness on California law, testified that he was "very intensively" acquainted with the provisions of section 2855 by reason of his employment in the legal department of Paramount Pictures Corp. because the section involved all of the employment contracts of the studio. He testified that the contract was one "to furnish materials" and similar to contracts between motion picture producers and distributors, whereas the contract in the *De Haviland* case, *supra,* was "a typical employment contract." He testified that the sole purpose of section 2855 "was to protect employees" and that there were no provisions of the Labor Code which he could find which govern independent contractors. He testified that although the word "employee" was not used in the second sentence of section 2855 (relating to unique services) it must be read into it. Since the third sentence commences: "If the employee voluntarily continues his service under it . . . ," the conclusion is inescapable that the word employee must be read into the second sentence.

Furthermore, it should be noted that the first sentence of section 2855 refers to "employee." "Employee" is defined by the same Labor Code in section 350(b) as follows:

(b) "Employee" means every person including aliens and minors, rendering actual service in any business for an employer, whether gratuitously or for wages or pay and whether such wages or pay are measured by the standard of time, piece, task, commission, or other method of calculation and whether such service is rendered on a commission, concessionaire, or other basis.

It should also be noted that the defendant is not an "employer" as defined by section 350(a) of the Labor Code as follows:

(a) "Employer" means every person engaged in any business or enterprise in this State, which has one or more persons in service under any appointment, contract of hire, or apprenticeship, express or implied, oral or written, irrespective of whether such person is the owner of the business or is operating on a concessionaire or other basis.

The above definitions add additional weight to the conclusion of the defendant's expert, whose opinion seems more compelling. The court adopts his interpretation of the statute that the sentence is only intended to include employees and would exclude independent contractors.

It is obvious that under the usual rules of statutory interpretation the provisions of section 2855 would apply only to the normal employer-employee relationship and not to situations where one of the parties was an independent contractor.

Since the second sentence was not interpreted by the California courts, I believe that we can accept our own definition of an independent contractor as laid down by our Court of Appeals in *Hexamer v. Webb*, 101 N.Y. 377, 385, 4 N.E. 755, 757:

The test to determine whether one who renders service to another does so as a contractor or not is to ascertain whether he renders the service in the course of an independent occupation, representing the will of his employer only as to the result of his work, and not as to the means by which it is accomplished. Shearm. & Redf., Neg. 76. In *Blake v. Ferris*, 5 N.Y. [48] 58, within the rule last stated, it is held that when a man is employed in doing a job or piece of work with his own means, and his own men, and employs others to help him or to execute the work for him, and under his control, he is the superior who is responsible for their conduct, no matter for whom he is doing the work. To attempt to make the primary principal or employer responsible in such cases would be an attempt to push the doctrine of *respondeat superior* beyond the reason on which it is founded. . . .

The evidence also establishes that the parties by their own conduct never considered the relationship to be that of employer-employee. There was never a withholding by the defendant for income taxes or social security; the plaintiff paid all the expenses of producing the cartoons; and the plaintiff in filing his Federal income tax return paid the "self-employment tax" which was measured by the income received from the defendant.

The contract provides that: "Should Ketcham become incapacitated or unable to deliver the material . . . or in the event of the decease of Ketcham, he or his executors shall have the privilege of employing substitute services to prepare the materials" or that the defendant "shall have the privilege of securing substitute services."

In either ebstvent Ketcham (or his estate) was still to receive the benefits of the contract (less the cost of the suitute).

Ketcham was not an employee and the contract is at best one for his services as an independent contractor. Indeed in most of its aspects it is more a contract of sale or a contract to supply a product rather than services.

There is yet another reason for holding the California Statute inapplicable. The New York Conflict of Laws rules require a finding that the contract is governed by New York Law, under the theory of "center of gravity" or the "grouping of contacts." Defendant's office is and was in New York, all of its operations (other than traveling salesmen) are conducted in New York, including the mat makers, the editorial work, financial work, photo-engravers, etc. Performance of the contract by plaintiff was to be by delivery of the panels at defendant's New York office. The contract was signed in New York by defendant and by "Kennedy Associates, Inc. by John J. Kennedy as agents for Hank Ketcham." The verified complaint sets forth that Kennedy Associates, Inc. "executed the contract as agent for the plaintiff." Plaintiff prepared the panels at various residences during the years following the execution thereof. Indeed the place where plaintiff or his substitute was to prepare the panels was of absolutely no significance. The most important contact was the place of delivery, the fixed place where all of defendant's work had to be performed. New York was the place of most significant contact when the contract was signed, was so during the intervening years and is today, and therefore New York law governs. . . .

The first, second and third affirmative defenses have been proven and therefore the California statute will not be applied.

Since we have decided that the California law is inapplicable, the remaining questions to be determined are whether the contract is indefinite and does it lack mutuality.

The issue of mutuality poses no problem. Plaintiff's argument that the contract lacks mutuality of obligation is adequately answered by a comparison of the facts in this case and those in *Wood v. Lucy, Lady Duff-Gordon*, 222 N.Y. 88, 118 N.E. 214. In this case, the defendant was expressly obligated to produce certain minimum payments to keep the contract in force, whereas in the *Wood* case, *supra*, the court merely implied an obligation on plaintiff's part to use its best efforts. There is thus certainly more basis for finding mutuality than existed in *Wood*, where the Court of Appeals found mutuality.

Whether or not the contract is indefinite presents a more difficult question and is probably the most important problem to be resolved in this case. The question, however, is not whether the contract is for an *indefinite term*, it is whether the contract, by its terms, *is indefinite as to its duration*. If it is, then judicial construction is necessary and thus plaintiff should prevail because it is well settled in New York that a contract will not be construed to require perpetual performance where another construction is available. . . . Absent a fixed or *determinable duration* or an express provision that the duration is perpetual, the contract is one terminable at will. . . .

The contract in the case at bar is not indefinite as to duration. Paragraphs 4, 5 and 6 provide specifically for termination by either party upon the happening of certain events. The contract provides that it "shall be for a period of one year . . . and shall renew itself automatically from year to year for additional periods of one year each without the giving of notice by either party to the other, except that each of the parties shall have the right to terminate this agreement at the end of any one year period hereof . . . in the event" that plaintiff's share fell below the stipulated amount and the defendant at its sole discretion, to avoid a termination of this agreement, failed to advance the difference in the minimum stipulated amount.

The plaintiff asserts that these provisions render the contract indefinite because they include no specific date for the termination of the contract. This, however, is not the kind of indefiniteness which renders the contract voidable, since specific provision is made for termination. It is this specificity which destroys the plaintiff's case. The contract is for one year and renewable from year to year, but this, from the terms of the contract itself, appears to have been the intention of the parties. The paragraphs regarding termination clearly provide for automatic renewal and just as clearly give the defendant the right to keep the contract alive in the event certain requirements for automatic renewal are met. It was the intention of the parties that the contract should run so long as the minimum receipts were realized and that during such period that neither party should be able to desert the other. The strip started as an idea and both parties were to be integral parts of its development, the plaintiff by his creative ability and the defendant by his promotion and salesmanship. The terms of the contract are clear and unambiguous and freely signed by the plaintiff and his agent.

That contracts providing for perpetual performance are not invalid is undoubtedly the law of New York, although no precise holding on this point can be found among the New York cases. . . .

For contracts which had no calendar fixed date of termination but were held as contracts for a definite term, see *Matter of Exercycle v. Maratta,* 11 A.D.2d 677, 201 N.Y.S.2d 885, *affd.* 9 N.Y.2d 329, 214 N.Y.S.2d 353; *Ehrenworth v. George F. Stuhmer & Co.,* 229 N.Y. 210, 214, 215, 128 N.E. 108, 109; *Deucht v. Storper,* City Ct., 44 N.Y.S.2d 350, 351. In *Exercycle,* the contract provided for continuation until the employee voluntarily leaves the employ of Exercycle. In *Ehrenworth,* the contract was for "as long as the plaintiff . . . remained in business." In *Deucht,* the employment was to be for so long a time as defendant "continued to employ workers, trained, developed and gathered by plaintiff." (See *Warner-Lambert Pharmaceutical Company Inc. v. John J. Reynolds, Inc.* [S.D., New York, 1959] 178 F. Supp. 655, 661.) . . .

The defendant, therefore, must prevail. Contracts which are vague as to their duration generally will not be construed to provide for perpetual performance, but where, such as the case here, the contract is not vague, no judicial construction is necessary. . . .

NOTES

1. Of course, where substantive terms *are* expressed vaguely, enforcement will be denied. The circumstances under which a court rules a contract's terms fatally indefinite are increasingly rare. A more likely result is for the court to use interpretative aids to resolve the ambiguities and save the contract. These include (1) the express language of the contract as understood in a legal context; (2) the extent to which the parties performed under the agreement and the understandings under which they performed, both stated and implied; (3) the parties' dealings in past transactions; and (4) custom and usage in the specific entertainment industry involved. The prevailing judicial view is that if the parties can reduce their understandings to writing, ambiguities will be resolved if at all possible. A deal should not be voided if its terms can be saved by interpretation. However, enforcement was denied in *Candid Productions v. International Skating Union,* 530 F. Supp. 1330 (SDNY 1982). Candid, a producer of televised sporting events (mostly skating), sought specific enforcement of a contract which (Candid claimed) gave it exclusive television rights to the World Championships. Candid had dealt with the ISU for sixteen years. Earlier contracts between the parties had provided that they would "negotiate in good faith the terms and conditions by which [Candid's] rights [would] be extended," and if the parties did not agree, ISU would "then be free to offer these rights to a third party under the same terms and conditions last offered to Candid." However, if ISU was willing to accept less favorable terms and conditions, it would give Candid the opportunity to secure the deal on those terms and conditions before ISU offered the deal to third parties. However, ISU refused to sign the contract which became the subject of the action unless the first refusal clause was deleted. In its place, the parties substituted a provision that ISU would not negotiate any further contracts for the rights for the World Championships after 1979 without first negotiating in good faith with Candid. However, ISU apparently began negotiations with CBS before commencing negotiations with Candid, and ultimately granted CBS the exclusive right to broadcast the World Championships. Candid claimed that ISU had breached its agreement to negotiate with plaintiff in good faith. In its motion for summary judgment, ISU did not contest this claim; it didn't matter, they argued: the good faith negotiation clauses upon which Candid relied were so vague and uncertain as to be unenforceable. The court agreed. Candid argued that the court should imply, "as a requirement of good faith negotiation a duty by ISU: (1) to discloses information material to Candid's ability to formulate offers; (2) to make offers and counter-offers; and (3) to continue negotiations for a sufficient minimum period of time before signing with another to permit Candid a fair opportunity to overcome in all respects the comparative attractiveness of competitive proposals. To imply such terms, however, would be to impermissively make a contract for the parties rather than to enforce any bargain the parties themselves may have reached. . . . [I]t is particularly inappropriate to imply the terms proposed by Candid for in effect Candid is asking the Court to reinsert into the contract the specific obligation that ISU expressly rejected by its demand, agreed to by the plaintiff, that the first refusal clause containing such requirement be deleted from the contract." The court also rejected Candid's alternative negative-injunction argument that the good-faith-negotiation clause contained "an express negative covenant that mandates that ISU [would] not negotiate

with others before it [had] negotiated in good faith with Candid." However, the court said, "[w]hether ISU was bound to negotiate exclusively with Candid before negotiating with anyone else, as the alleged negative covenant would require, does not relieve or assist this Court in its burden to find some standards by which to judge the parties' performance. Indeed, such negative covenant only worsens the situation for the negotiation clauses are silent as to the length of time such exclusive negotiation period is to run." The principle that "'a mere agreement to agree' is unenforceable for indefiniteness where material terms are left open for future resolution [applies] here with added force for not only one item but all terms have been left open for future negotiation. . . . To issue a decree of specific performance, as plaintiff requests, would require the Court to enter into the realm of the conjectural. An agreement to negotiate in good faith is even more vague than an agreement to agree. An agreement to negotiate in good faith is amorphous and nebulous, since it implicates so many factors that are themselves indefinite and uncertain that the intent of the parties can only be fathomed by conjecture and surmise."

2. For further discussion of obligations of good faith and fair dealings, see MacNeil, "Power of Contract and Agreed Remedies," 47 *Cornell Law Quarterly* 495 (1962); Burton, "Breach of Contract and the Common Law Duty to Perform in Good Faith," 94 *Harvard Law Review* 369 (1980); Comment, "Has the Right of First Refusal Been Thrown to the Wolves?" "*American Broadcasting Co. v. Wolf*," 1 *Cardozo Arts and Entertainment Law Review* 137 (1982).

3. In *Sellers v. American Broadcasting Co.*, 668 F.2d 1207 (11th Cir. 1982), the Court of Appeals dismissed an action in which the plaintiff attempted to enforce an "exclusive story" agreement he had made with Geraldo Rivera of ABC on contract and misappropriation grounds. The exclusive story involved information that Elvis Presley had died from an overdose of drugs, a theory which the court found neither novel, unique, nor original so as to afford the plaintiff protection under the misappropriation doctrine. Furthermore, the "contract" of the plaintiff was unenforceable as it was too vague and indefinite as to the information which Sellers was to provide regarding Elvis's death.

    The plaintiff's entire contract read as follows:

    > I, Larry L. Sellers, do hereby agree not to release this exclusive story to any reporter other than Geraldo Rivera or any network other than ABC until the network has first released said story within a reasonable period of time or thirty days. Once the story has been released, other media firms may be contracted by Larry Sellers.

    > I, Geraldo Rivera, do hereby agree to grant Larry Sellers all copy-write [sic] privileges of the exclusive Elvis Presley story and full claim for the discovery of the story by acknowledgement in any media use made of it from this day forth.

    > If the story is accepted for further investigation, all expenses incurred by Larry Sellers will be reimbursed by ABC.

    > Should the story be proven false, this contract is hereby null and void.

4. See also *De Laurentiis v. Cinematografica de Las Americas*, 215 N.Y.S.2d 60, 9 N.Y.2d 503 (1961).

2.3.2 Statutory Termination Rights in California

Circumstances change, and the initial intentions of parties to a transaction shift as well. When one party to a contract believes another party is not fulfilling the bargain, the simmering dispute begins a perceptible movement toward the courts. The pages of such publications as *Variety, The Hollywood Reporter,* and *Billboard* constantly chronicle the filing of breach of contract lawsuits. Stars walk out. Producers renege. Directors revolt.

While most suits are settled, some go the legal distance. These provide guidelines to advise others what to expect if their later disputes find a legal forum. As the following cases suggest, settling a dispute may be a good deal less painful than vindicating one's rights in court. However, if a legal fight it will be, it is best to have had competent contract drafting in the first place. That is the starting point. If that fails, then some of the limitations under which courts operate must be confronted.

This section on the circumstances of breach is a natural lead-in to the following sections that examine the remedies each side can realistically seek when the other party is in breach. Since breach and remedies for breach go hand in hand, this section examines remedies as well.

Every breach does not give rise to a right to terminate or rescind the agreement. In addition, many agreements include a "right to cure" provision that will require the party alleging a breach to notify the other party of the alleged breach, and only if the breach is not "cured" within the stated period of time will there be deemed to have been a breach of the contract. In California, the traditional "hornbook" contract law principle that a "material breach" is required in order for the non-breaching party to rescind the contract is superseded (as it applies to personal service contracts) by California Labor Code §2925. We begin our discussion with California Labor Code §2924, which permits an employer to discharge an employee, and with the decision in the Goudal case, interpreting that section.

Section 2924. *Employment for specified term; Grounds for termination by employer* An employment for a specific term may be terminated at any time by the employer in case of any willful breach of duty by the employee in the course of his employment, or in case of his habitual neglect of his duty or continued incapacity to perform it. . . .

Goudal v. Cecil B. De Mille Pictures Corp., 5 P.2d 432 (Cal.App.Ct. 1931)

Fricke, Justice Pro Tem

This is an appeal from a judgment for plaintiff in the sum of $34,531.23 in an action to recover damages for breach of a contract of employment entered into in April, 1925. Under this agreement respondent was employed by appellant as a motion picture actress for one year beginning May 19, 1925, with the option to appellant of four yearly extensions of the contract, each yearly extension to be at a specified substantial increase in compensation. Respondent entered upon her duties, and appellant twice exercised its option, extending the period of employment to May 18, 1928. On September 10, 1927, respondent was discharged by appellant. The basic question in this case is whether such termination of the employment of respondent was wrongful or whether it was justified by acts of the respondent violative of the terms of the contract. The trial court found that respondent had not violated the contract, and that her discharge was not justified.

The claim that respondent failed or refused to perform her parts as requested is based upon many incidents set forth in detail in the record. They relate to occasions when the respondent, instead of unquestioningly performing as directed by the director in charge, called attention to inconsistencies, inaccuracies, possible improvements, or lack of artistic quality in the performance called for as they appeared to her. In some instances this resulted in the suggested change being made by the director without argument; in other cases the change was made after some argument between them. In most instances where the director did not make the suggested change it appears that respondent took the question up with the president of the appellant corporation, and in a substantial number of instances he agreed with her and the changes were made. In other instances he did not agree. This presents the question, Was respondent compelled by the contract to go through her scenes as a mere puppet responding to the director's pull of the strings, regardless of whether or not he pulled the right or the wrong string, or was she called upon by the language and spirit of the contract to give an artistic interpretation of her scenes, using her intelligence, experience, artistry, and personality to the ultimate end of securing a production of dramatic merit? We believe that the latter is the correct interpretation. Suggestions and even objections as to the manner of enacting the various scenes, when made in good faith, were in the interest of the employer; in fact, it appears from the testimony that they were welcomed and encouraged in many instances, and, prior to commencing work, the president of appellant informed respondent that he did not want mannikins to work for him, that he wanted thinking people, and that, if she would explain to him why she wanted to do a thing in a particular way, he would appreciate it. By the very wording of the contract "it is agreed that the services of the artist herein provided for are of a special, unique, unusual, extraordinary and intellectual character." Even without the evidence contradicting that of appellant, the trial court was more than justified in finding that it was not true that respondent had refused or failed to perform her part of the contract.

Some of the incidents, stressed by appellant as instances of a failure of respondent to perform her contract, turn out, when reference is had to the transcript, to be dependent upon the opinion of the director as to whether respondent performed to the best of her ability; others were dependent upon the feeling of the particular director as to whether he was or was not satisfied. The declarations of several of the directors as to their dissatisfaction with the work of respondent is rather inconsistent with the testimony elsewhere of one of them that the picture "White Gold," in which respondent performed under his direction, was "the best picture I ever will make," and the testimony of the director of her last picture, that he considered it one of his best American pictures. When considering the testimony of the directors who expressed dissatisfaction with the performance of her parts by respondent, one may well wonder who was temperamental and out of step when we note in connection therewith that in the picture in which Cecil De Mille directed Miss Goudal there was no trouble whatever. There is, furthermore, a conflict in the evidence as to whether the performance given by respondent was to the best of her ability and of an artistic character. In this conflict the trial court was fully sustained in its findings against appellant.

The remaining ground urged as justifying her discharge is that respondent on certain occasions was late in arriving on the sets at the time designated by her employer. The instances cited were explained by the testimony for respondent as being due, not to any neglect or intentional absence, but to duties relating to costumes which had been voluntarily assumed by respondent with the approval of appellant, though not required by the contract, delays in appearing on the set due to the necessary consumption of time in the donning of a special wig, and, in the last picture, the only one made after the exercise of the last option by appellant to re-employ respondent for another year, delays due to the large number of costumes used, in one instance, a failure of her maid who forgot an article of clothing, and the delay of appellant in delivering to respondent the script, which determined the costumes required. . . . The case of *May v. New York Motion Picture Corporation*, 45 Cal. App. 896, 187 P. 785, so strongly relied upon by appellant, is easily distinguishable from the case at bar. The fact that the maximum salary under the contract of the plaintiff there was $125 per week as compared to the maximum salary of respondent of $5,000 per week sufficiently discloses the comparative skill of the respective artists. In that case also the plaintiff repeatedly was from one and a half to two hours late in arriving at the place of employment, on at least one occasion failed to appear after she had been notified by telephone, and on the three days preceding her discharge failed to appear for work at all, her reason for not appearing on those days being that her contract did not require her presence, a reason not sustained by the court's interpretation of the contract. The May Case involved the willful disobedience of a reasonable order incident to the employment justifying the plaintiff's discharge. There is in the case at bar no willful tardiness nor invalid excuse for absences, the instances of tardiness here being covered by the general description that those delays were occasioned by the requirements of the scenes to be enacted on those particular days, delays while respondent was actually engaged in performing her employer's business.

It may also be noted that the references to alleged breaches of the contract consist largely of incidents prior to May, 1927, when appellant, for the second time, had exercised its option to continue and extend the contract for another year, and by which time respondent had completed seven of the eight pictures in which she performed for appellant. It is rather difficult to reconcile as sincere the appellant's criticism and faultfinding as to respondent's services in the pictures made during the two years prior to May, 1927, with the fact that in that month appellant voluntarily availed itself of its option to secure the talents and services of respondent for another year. . . . The exercise of the option not only evinced a desire on the part of appellant to retain respondent's services, but expressed an approval of the manner in which she had performed her services in the past, and was an indication that a continuation of the former services was desired. Having thus placed the stamp of approval upon respondent's conduct and services as rendered prior to May, 1927, it is not reasonable that a continuance of such services and conduct was unsatisfactory, and, from appellant's viewpoint, constituted a breach of the contract warranting respondent's discharge. . . . To constitute a refusal or failure to perform the conditions of a contract of employment such as we have here, there must be, on the part of the actress, a willful act or willful misconduct (*May v. New York Motion Picture Corp.*, 45 Cal. App. 396, 187 P. 785; *Ehlers v. Langley & Michaels Co.*, 72 Cal. App. 214, 221, 237 P. 55), a condition which is absent when the actress uses her best efforts to give an artistic performance and to serve the interests of her employer. The trial court was fully warranted by the evidence in finding that respondent neither failed nor refused to perform the services required of her under the contract.

Even in the most menial forms of employment there will exist circumstances justifying the servant in questioning the order of the master. Would the discharge of a ditch digger be justified if, instead of immediately driving his pick into the ground at the point indicated, he in good faith suggested to the employer that the pipes they were to uncover lay on the other side of the highway? And when the employment is of the services of "a special, unique, unusual, extraordinary and intellectual character," as is agreed by the contract here under consideration, to be rendered "conscientiously, artistically and to the utmost of her ability," sincere efforts of the artist to secure an artistic interpretation of play, even though they may involve the suggestion of changes and the presentation of argument in favor of such changes, even though insistently presented, do not amount to willful disobedience or failure to perform services under the contract, but rather a compliance with the contract which basically calls for services in the best interests of the employer. . . .

Appellant's final point is that respondent is precluded from recovery because, after her discharge, she failed to seek other employment. The testimony of respondent is that, after her discharge, she held herself in readiness to perform her part of the contract, and did not try to secure employment elsewhere. We are referred to no evidence, and appellant's brief concedes that there is none, that respondent could, with reasonable diligence, have secured other suitable employment during the remaining period of the agreement other than, as found by the trial court, that, after the 1st day of January, following her discharge, it should have become evident to her that appellant would not accept her services and that the circumstances showed that she did not diligently seek other employment which she could have obtained. Under this finding the trial court limited the recovery to the period ending January 1, 1928, and, pursuant to a stipulation, deducted therefrom the sum of $3,000 received by respondent from other employment.

"The measure of recovery by a wrongfully discharged employee is generally and primarily . . . the agreed wage for the unexpired part of the term; and the burden is upon the employer to rebut this presumption by proof that the damages sustained were actually less." *Gregg v. McDonald,* 73 Cal. App. 748, 757, 239 P. 373, 376. "The measure of damages in such cases is the amount of the salary agreed upon for the entire period of service, less the amount which the servant has earned or with reasonable effort might have earned from other employment." *Boardman Co. v. Petch,* 186 Cal. 470, 484, 199 P. 1047, 1051; *Seymour v. Oelrichs,* 156 Cal. 782, 801, 106 P. 88, 97, 134 Am. St. Rep. 154. The case last cited calls attention to the fact that, where the action is brought before the expiration of the period of employment provided by the contract, the action is not to recover wages due, but for damages for breach of contract, and that: "The measure of damages is, therefore, prima facie, the contract price." The burden was on the defendant to show, not only that respondent remained unemployed, but also that she could by diligence have secured suitable employment elsewhere. *Rosenberger v. Pacific Coast Ry. Co.,* 111 Cal. 313, 318, 43 P. 963. Conceding that the proof would warrant the inference that respondent did not seek other employment, such proof would not establish that respondent could have secured other employment. Appellant failed to sustain the burden placed upon it by the law, and there is no proof which would warrant a reduction in the amount of damages awarded by the judgment. . . .

The judgment is affirmed.

NOTES _____

1. The company in the Goudal case could have minimized its contractual liability by including in the employment agreement a so-called pay or play clause, which would have given the company the right to discharge her by paying some liquidated sum. The following is an example of a pay or play clause from a Director's Agreement:

> PAY OR PLAY: In the event Company or Producer desires to terminate the services of Director as director of the Property, then notwithstanding that this pay or play clause is exercised prior to completion of Director's services, Director shall be entitled to retain all fixed compensation paid hereunder and Director shall be entitled to receive any unpaid balance of fixed compensation provided herein and further, should the results and proceeds of Director's services be retained and distributed as a part of at least fifty percent (50%) of the final negative, Director shall also be entitled to receive the full profit participation and contingent compensation provided herein. In the event Director has directed substantially all of the Property's principal photography, Director may not be replaced except for gross willful misconduct and shall, in any event, be entitled to all post-production creative rights and full credits.

2. See *Mason v. Lyl Productions,* 69 Cal.2d 79, 443 P.2d (1968) (producer not entitled to discharge actress from television series for failure to comply with unreasonable order).
3. See also *Loew's Inc. v. Cole,* 185 F.2d 641 (9th Cir. 1950), *cert. denied,* 340 U.S. 954 (1951), in which the court held that while MGM had the right to fire writer Lester Cole, one of the defiant "Hollywood Ten" who refused to cooperate with the House Un-American Activities Committee investigation into alleged Communist influences in the film industry, MGM did not have the right to suspend the term of Coles's agreement at the same time.

Section 2925. *Employment for specified term; grounds for termination by employee.* An employment for a specific term may be terminated by the employee at any time in case of any willful or permanent breach of the obligations of his employer to him as an employee.

Warner Bros. Pictures, Inc. v. Bumgarner, 17 Cal.Rptr. 171 (Cal.App.Ct. 1961)

Fourt, Justice

This is an action by Warner Bros. Pictures, Inc., hereinafter referred to as "Warner," for a declaration determining the status of a contract between Warner, as the employer, and James Bumgarner, also known as James Garner, hereinafter referred to as "Garner," as the employee. Garner cross-complained for damages for breach of the contract. The judgment declared the contract terminated as of March 10, 1960, and allowed Garner as damages the sum of $1,750.00. Both parties have appealed. Warner appeals " . . . from the judgment . . . and from the whole thereof." Garner appeals " . . . from that part of the judgment . . . to wit, Subdivision 3 providing that plaintiff and cross-defendant pay to defendant the sum of $1,750.00, with interest thereon at the rate of 7% per annum from March 10, 1960 up to the date of the judgment. Defendant and cross-complainant does not appeal from the rest of the judgment as set forth in Subdivisions 1, 2 and 4 thereof."
A résumé of some of the facts is as follows:

> Warner is a producer of motion pictures of different types for showing in theatres or on television. Garner is an actor who had been employed by Warner since 1955 under successive contracts, the latest of which, and the one with which we are here concerned, was made February 27, 1959, hereinafter referred to as "Garner Contract." The Garner Contract, among other things, contained a so-called [hmp1]*force majeure* clause.

> Effective mid-January, 1960, the Writers Guild of America West, Inc. declared a strike against Warner and many other producers. The writers' guild is an organization or union composed of the writers of scripts or screen plays for both theatrical and television motion pictures. The strike continued from January until June 20, 1960.

The present controversy arose when Warner, on March 2, 1960, regarded the situation as of that time as a casualty within the *force majeure* clause and notified Garner that as of March 3, 1960, his compensation would be discontinued by reason thereof.

The chronology of significant dates is as follows:

January 16, 1960—Television and feature writers struck against many feature and television producers, including Warner.

March 2, 1960—Warner elected to suspend payment of compensation to Garner alleging existence of a "casualty period" under the employment contract.

March 8, 1960—Garner objected to suspension claiming that no casualty period existed and demanded payment of salary.

March 9, 1960—Warner refused to pay salary after Garner's demand.

March 10, 1960—Garner informed Warner that Warner was in breach of contract and that he elected to treat employment contract as terminated.

June 20, 1960—Writers' guild strike ended.

When the writers' strike commenced Warner was producing ten television programs or series. A series consisted of successive episodes involving the same main characters and exhibited on television at weekly or other regular intervals. One of such series was known as "Maverick," with Garner as one of the main characters therein.

Each television episode was a motion picture filmed from a script. A script is in the form of a play with dialogue, and of the correct length to make the required episode. Scripts are written from stories, the latter being basic literary material. A script is the working tool. Scripts are the product of screen writers, and practically all of such script writers are members of the screen writers' guild. Stories are furnished to such writers by the producing company and form the basis of the required script. . . .

The preparation of motion pictures by plaintiff was not prevented, materially hampered or interrupted by reason of the writers' strike; the production of motion pictures by plaintiff was not prevented, materially hampered or interrupted by reason of the writers' strike; and the completion of motion pictures by plaintiff was not prevented, materially hampered or interrupted by reason of the writers' strike.

A large amount of statistical data was introduced to show the effect of the writers' strike on the preparation, production, and completion of theatrical and television motion pictures. The evidence shows and Warner concedes that " . . . there was at all times during the strike, both before and after March 3rd, some activity at the Studio, and some preparation, production or completion of motion pictures were at all times going on in some way and to some extent and with respect to some pictures or series." The evidence supports the finding. . . .

As already pointed out, the provisions of paragraph 15 of the contract are in the disjunctive and contain several alternatives. The first alternative relating to Warner's general activity has heretofore been discussed. Another alternative contained in paragraph 15 is that " . . . if the production of any motion picture or other production to which Artist is assigned hereunder shall be suspended, interrupted or postponed by any such cause, . . . (the continuance of any such event being hereinafter designated as the 'casualty period'), then, during the continuance of such casualty period, Producer shall not be obligated to make any weekly payments to Artist. . . . "

The trial judge in his "Memorandum Decision" made it clear that he construed the above alternative provision of paragraph 15 as not being applicable to Maverick (i.e. any Warner's production). The memorandum provides in pertinent part as follows:

The court will find that the provision "or if the production to which Artist is assigned hereunder shall be suspended, interrupted or postponed by any such cause" means the lending or assignment of the services of Artist pursuant to Paragraph 13 to a producer other than Warner Bros. and does not mean "assignment" of the Artist to one of Warner Bros. productions.

Initially it must be noted that there was no finding made concerning whether Garner was "assigned" to a production by Warner. The court did find (Finding XV) that "The production by plaintiff of the 'Maverick' series was not suspended, interrupted or postponed by reason of the writer's [sic] strike."

An examination of the record discloses that there is substantial evidence to support the trial court's determination (Finding XV) that "The production by plaintiff of the 'Maverick' series was not suspended, interrupted or postponed by reason of the writer's [sic] strike."

As of March 2, 1960, Warner had completed production on the Maverick series for 1959–1960 and had filmed one "extra" episode which was not scheduled to be telecast until September 25, 1960. In the past, Warner had not started production until May or June or later, with respect to the next air date season, and producer Trapnell testified that when he took over as Maverick producer on June 15, 1959, there was not a single completed script for the 1959–1960 season, yet Warner met its September 12 air date. Warner's executives knew that production on the Maverick series for the 1960–1961 season would ordinarily not begin until May, at the earliest, and that May production would, as the trial court found (Finding XVII), allow the maximum time necessary to meet the 1960–1961 air date commitments. The facts must be related to the manner by which Warner conducted its business.

On March 3, 1960, Warner had approximately 14 "Hermanos" writers available in its television department; at least one of the 14 had done work on a Maverick script previously. Warner had at least two stories suitable for development into Maverick scripts and, judging by both past and subsequent events, it could write a Maverick script in 15 days, or possibly rewrite an old script in as little as five days. Furthermore, the head of the television department indicated on direct examination that Warner " . . . may have had other [Maverick and Cheyenne] scripts in at this point but I don't think so."

We believe that the evidence, taken as a whole, shows that Warner was able to obtain scripts when Warner wanted them and that production of Maverick was not suspended, interrupted or postponed by reason of the writers' strike. . . .

At the conclusion of the arguments by counsel, the Reporter's Transcript discloses that the trial judge made the following statement:

The Court: Well, I am satisfied from the evidence that Warner Bros. did not have justification for laying Mr. Garner off on March 2nd. I think that is indicated by the testimony even of the plaintiff's witnesses and particularly Mr. Warner.

The trial judge in his "Memorandum Decision" stated in pertinent part as follows:

The court will find that plaintiff was not justified in stopping the payment of defendant's salary, under the provisions of paragraph 15 of the contract, for the reason that the preponderance of the evidence does not establish that a "casualty period" in fact existed; and for the further reason that the refusal to pay Garner's salary was in bad faith as evidenced, in part, by the manner in which the Bob Hope Show transaction [In which Garner was "loaned out" to the Bob Hope Show as a guest star—Eds.] was handled. Plaintiff's act in refusing to pay defendant's salary justified Garner in treating the refusal as a total breach of the contract.

When the dispute arose as to the rights of Warner Bros. to suspend Garner's salary, it could have protected itself by paying the salary and recouping the amount paid—if the suspension was justified—under the provisions of the second paragraph of numbered paragraph 17 of the contract.

A reasonable inference can be drawn from all of the evidence that Warner knew that it would not be in any trouble with respect to Maverick unless it could not start preparing another episode by May 1, 1960 (at the very earliest, since one 1960–1961 episode was already completed). Warner did in fact start preparation on two episodes in late April and by June 15 (at least three months prior to the first air date and still before the end of the writers' strike) had completed "preparation" and "production" on four "Maverick" episodes, was filming a fifth, and had four scripts in preparation.

Finally, Warner asserts as its last contention that "If Warner erroneously interpreted the contract, its action did not constitute a serious and total breach justifying a termination by Garner."

Warner's contention cannot be sustained. When Warner informed Garner that it elected not to pay Garner the stipulated weekly salary, Warner's act constituted a refusal, without cause, to pay an employee his compensation. The employee's right to *terminate* the contract where there has been a wrongful refusal to pay compensation is established by both the statutory and case law of this jurisdiction.

Labor Code section 2925 provides that "An employment for a specified term may be terminated by the employee at any time in case of any *wilful* or permanent breach of the obligations of his employer to him as an employee." (Emphasis added.) As set forth above, the trial judge in his "Memorandum Decision" stated that the "breach in this case was wilful."

In *May v. New York Motion Picture Corp.*, 45 Cal.App. 396, the court defined "wilful" in connection with what is now Labor Code section 2924, and stated at page 404 in part as follows, 187 P. 785, at page 788.

In civil cases, the word "willful," as ordinarily used in courts of law, does not necessarily imply anything blamable, or any malice or wrong toward the other party, or perverseness or moral delinquency, but merely that the thing done or omitted to be done was done or omitted intentionally. It amounts to nothing more than this: That the person knows what he is doing, intends to do what he is doing, and is a free agent. Benkert v. Benkert, 32 Cal. 467, 470; *Towle v. Matheus,* 130 Cal. 574, 577, 62 Pac. 1064; 40 Cyc. 944. . . .

Having disposed of Warner's contentions raised on its appeal from the judgment, we now turn to Garner's contentions on his limited appeal from the judgment. . . .

Garner, on April 26, 1960, filed an "Amended Cross-Complaint (Damages for breach of contract; Injunction)." As set forth above Garner was awarded the sum of $1,750 plus interest, and Garner's appeal is from that award.

The basis for the trial court's determination that Garner was entitled to judgment in the sum of $1,750 is succinctly set forth in his "Memorandum Decision" as follows:

This brings us to the question of Garner's right to recover damages.

It must be remembered that Garner was not discharged. (Emphasis added.)

As was said in Percival v. National Drama Corp., 181 Cal. 631, p. 638 [185 P. 972]: "The evidence does not show that the defendant refused to permit the plaintiff to render any services. The most that can be said of it is that defendant did not require any services of plaintiff. This fact, unless accompanied by some affirmative act indicating a discharge, is not sufficient proof thereof."

When Warner Bros. notified Garner his salary would be suspended he treated it as a breach of the contract. Warner Bros. was still anxious for him to render services under the contract.

The law is that if an employee is discharged his remedy is an action for damages. Where he has not been discharged but merely has been prevented by the employer from working, he need not treat the contract as broken but may sue on the contract and recover the agreed compensation. But in order to recover the agreed compensation he must be ready, able and willing to perform.

In this case, after declaring a breach of the contract, Garner refused to recognize it and refused to render services to or for Warner Bros.

Therefore, while Garner had the right to terminate the contract, he does not have the right to recover damages. The right he had was the option to quit his employment and sue for the salary then due, or of continuing in the employ of Warner Bros., and sue for his salary as it accrued. . . .

Garner terminated the contract about one week after the commencement of the term, and he is entitled to be paid for that period. (Emphasis added.)

In accordance with the foregoing the court will find and conclude: that the conditions that would have warranted Warner Bros. to suspend Garner's salary did not exist; that Garner was justified in terminating the contract; that Garner does not have the right to recover damages for breach of contract because he terminated the contract and was unwilling to perform further; that Garner has the right to recover one week's salary, i.e., $1,750.00, and his costs of suit. . . .

In the light of the evidence, the findings of fact based thereon and the conclusions of law which flow from the findings, it is clear that the trial court correctly determined the amount of damages to which Garner was entitled, unless this court holds as a matter of law that Warner's suspension of Garner's salary payments constituted a "wrongful discharge."

It is stated in *Percival v. National Drama Corp.*, 181 Cal. 631, 637–638, 185 P. 972, 974:

> A discharge cannot be effected by a secret, undisclosed intention on the part of the master. It must be done by some word or act communicated to the servant. "No set form of words is necessary; but any words or acts which show a clear intention on the part of the master to dispense with the servant's services, and which are equivalent to a declaration to the servant that his services will be no longer accepted, are sufficient." (26 Cyc. 987.) . . . *[T]he authorities declare that mere failure of the master to pay wages to the servant does not amount to a discharge.* (Citations omitted.) *Such failure or refusal to pay merely gives the servant the option of quitting his employment and the right to sue for the salary then due and unpaid, or of continuing in the service, with the corresponding right to require and enforce payment of the salary as it accrues.* (Emphasis added.)
>
> Even when the refusal to pay is accompanied by a refusal to permit the servant to perform the duties it has been held that no discharge was shown. . . .

The *Percival* case has been cited in later cases as authority to the effect that: (1) nonpayment of compensation in itself is not a discharge. . . . (2) no set words or language are necessary to constitute a discharge provided the circumstances show a disclosure of an unequivocal intention on the part of the employer to dispense completely with the services of the employee. . . . and (3) one of the factors entering into determining such intent would be whether the employer has gone out of business. . . .

We are not prepared to hold as a matter of law that the suspension by Warner constituted a discharge. Without belaboring the point we believe that the trial court, upon the evidence presented, was correct in its determination.

For the reasons stated, the judgment, and the whole thereof, is affirmed.

NOTES

1. For an excellent commentary on the ramifications of the Bumgarner decision, see Frackman, "Failure to Pay Wages and Termination of Entertainment Contracts in California," 52 *S. Cal. L. Rev.* 333.
2. Because Garner did not seek employment elsewhere during the duration of the litigation, injunctive relief was not sought, and it remains unresolved whether an employer may obtain an injunction against an employee who is seeking to terminate the employment agreement under Section 2925.
3. It also remains unresolved whether an employee's rights under Section 2925 would be subject to a contractual "right to cure" as, arguably, such a provision could be deemed an unenforceable waiver of a public policy Labor Code provision.
4. An employer faced with the facts of *Warner Bros. v. Bumgarner* might be best served to pay the wages of the employee "under protest."
5. The following provisions for the title "Force Majeure: Defaults and Remedies" appear in a recent record company/music production agreement:

(a) If Company's performance hereunder is delayed or becomes impossible or commercially impracticable by reason of any force majeure event, including, without limitation, any act of God, fire, earthquake, strike, civil commotion, acts of government or any order, regulation, ruling or action of any labor union or association of artists affecting Company and/or the phonograph record industry, Company, upon notice to Producer, may suspend its obligations hereunder for the duration of such delay, impossibility or impracticability, as the case may be. In the event any force majeure suspension exceeds six (6) consecutive months, Producer may terminate the term of this agreement upon ten (10) days written notice to Company; provided, that any such termination by Producer shall be effective only if the force majeure event does not affect a substantial portion of the United States recording industry, in no way involves Producer's or Artist's acts or omissions, and Company fails to terminate the suspension within ten (10) days after its receipt of Producer's notice. Company shall not withhold payment of royalties during any such suspension unless the force majeure event materially impairs Company's ability to calculate and/or pay royalties.

(b) Each of the following shall constitute an event of default hereunder:

    (i) Artist's voice and/or playing ability becomes impaired as determined by a physician reasonably designated by Company and Producer (provided that Producer shall not thwart Company's rights under this paragraph 11(b) by failing to designate a physician) or Artist ceases to seriously pursue Artist's career as an entertainer or Producer attempts to assign this agreement except as permitted hereunder or Producer and/or Artist fails, refuses or neglects to fulfill any of their respective material obligations hereunder.

    (ii) In the event Producer or Artist commences a voluntary case under any applicable bankruptcy, insolvency or other similar law now or hereafter in effect or consents to the entering of an order for relief in any involuntary case under such law or consents to the appointment of or taking possession by a receiver, liquidator, assignee, trustee or sequestrator (or similar appointees) of Producer or Artist or any substantial part of Producer's or Artist's property or Producer or Artist makes any assignment for the benefit of creditors or takes any act (whether corporate or otherwise) in furtherance of any of the foregoing.

    (iii) If a court having jurisdiction over the affairs or property of Producer or Artist enters a decree or order for relief in respect of Producer or Artist or any of Producer's or Artist's property in an involuntary case under any applicable bankruptcy, insolvency or other similar law now or hereafter in effect or appoints a receiver, liquidator, assignee, custodian, trustee or sequestrator (or similar appointee) or Producer or Artist or for any substantial part of Producer's or Artist's property or orders the winding up or liquidation of Producer's or Artist's affairs and such decree or order remains unstayed and in effect for a period of fifteen (15) consecutive days.

(c) On the occurrence of any event of default, Company, in addition to its other rights or remedies, may, by notice to Producer, elect to (i) suspend its obligations to Producer hereunder for the duration of such event (except that Company shall not suspend its obligation to pay royalties earned hereunder if Producer's failure to perform Producer's obligations is caused by reasons beyond the reasonable control of Producer), (ii) terminate the term of this agreement by written notice to Producer given at any time (whether or not during a period of suspension based on such event or based upon any other event), and thereby be relieved of all liability other than any obligations hereunder to pay royalties in respect of Masters delivered prior to termination, and/or (iii) require Artist to render Artist's exclusive recording services (and Artist's services as an individual Producer to the extent required hereunder) directly to Company in accordance with Artist's inducement letter.

(d) Producer acknowledges that its performance and the services of Artist hereunder, and the rights granted Company herein, are of a special, unique, extraordinary and intellectual character which gives them peculiar value, the
loss of which cannot be reasonably or adequately compensated in damages
in an action at law, that a breach by Producer or Artist hereunder from, or
to render performances due to Producer hereunder for, any party or person
other than Producer, including, without limitation, any successor in interest to Producer. Company shall be entitled to seek injunctive and/or other
equitable relief to prevent a breach of this agreement by Producer and/or
Artist, which relief shall be in addition to any other rights or remedies which
Company may have, whether for damages or otherwise.

2.4 CONTRACT FORMALITY AND AVAILABILITY OF INJUNCTIVE RELIEF

As stated in the reply memorandum of Warner Bros. Pictures in
the preliminary injunction phase of the Guber/Peters litigation arising out of Sony's acquisition of Columbia Pictures, "[D]reams and
expectations do not constitute an agreement." The entertainment
industries exist on ideas turned into deals. When an idea is "hot,"
immediate action is desired. Parties rush to agree, and, in the process, desire at times outraces common sense. The "deal," as it turns
out, is strictly verbal, or there are scattered memos but no single,
final, formal written agreement. The question then becomes, did
the parties actually reach agreement? Is there really a contract, with
the final writing only a memorial of the deal already concluded?
Is there a sufficient writing to satisfy the applicable statute of frauds?
If the production proceeds as envisioned, these questions are moot.
There is no problem because the idea becomes a deal that produces
a success, and everyone is happy.

But at other times, dreams die early, when the great concept does not
live up to expectations, management changes, or better opportunities
are seen elsewhere. In those circumstances, the deal sours, the parties go to war, and inevitably the questions involving contract formality
become pressing inquiries. The following three cases illustrate these
problems when one party to a transaction must argue that a contract
exists without the benefit of a signed written agreement.

2.4.1 The New York Experience

**Metro-Goldwyn-Mayer, Inc. v. Scheider, 43 A.D.2d 922, 352 N.Y.S.2d
205 (App. Div. 1st Dept. 1974), *aff'd*, 40 N.Y.2d 1069, 360 N.E.2d
930, 392 N.Y.S.2d 252 (1976)**

In September 1971, plaintiff, a producer of films, and ABC, a television broadcaster, made an agreement, pursuant to which plaintiff
was, at ABC's option to be exercised after receipt of a script, to make
a pilot film to be the precursor, if ABC exercised a second option to

that effect, of a television series to be broadcast by ABC either in the fall of 1972 or the next mid-season. By trade custom, if ABC opted for the series for fall (September) commencement of broadcast of the series, filming would be required to start no later than June; if for mid-season (January) commencement, then filming would start in November. Plaintiff then entered into an oral agreement, the basic terms of which were arrived at on or about September 30, 1971, with defendant, an actor, to play the lead in both the pilot, should ABC opt to have it made, and in the making of the series, and possible yearly series for five years, should ABC decide to proceed. As requested by defendant to relieve him of unnecessary commitments, it was further agreed that, if ABC decided not to proceed and so advised plaintiff, plaintiff's option to command defendant's services would cease. Agreed sums were to be paid defendant, depending on the extent of the work.

In February 1972, the pilot having been made, and accepted, ABC decided to proceed. Defendant was notified by plaintiff to report no later than June 5, 1972, to start filming in time for commencement of broadcast by September 15. Defendant refused. Plaintiff promptly instituted this action to enjoin defendant from working for others, and for damage for the breach. Defendant interposed a defense of Statute of Frauds, claiming the contract not to be performable within a year (section 5–701[1], General Obligations Law). Trial Term sustained the defense. We hold the agreement by its terms to have been performable within a year. ABC controlled the cutoff date and could have terminated the agreement at any option stage. Nor is it unusual for a third party to govern the possibility of performability of a contract. In any event, as the dates turned out, as chosen by ABC and ordered by plaintiff, performance for this series would have been complete before the first broadcast date, less than a year from the first agreement. And ABC retained an option to stop then or to go on from year to year thereafter. Thus, the contract was terminable at any time within a year whenever ABC chose. . . . The Statute of Frauds is not applicable and cannot serve to defeat plaintiff's claim.

NOTES _____

1. Several additional factors not evident from this decision are relevant. At the time of the initial negotiations between MGM and Scheider, Scheider was a relatively unknown actor who had had a minor part in the movie *Klute* and a supporting role in the film *The French Connection*, which was at that point in time unreleased. After filming the pilot to the TV series for MGM (entitled "Munich Project") in November of 1971, Scheider met with William Friedkin, the director who was about to shoot the film *The Exorcist*, and it may very well have been possible that Scheider wanted to star in that film at the time he refused to start filming the TV series. Also, given the release and critical acclaim received by *The French Connection*, it is safe to say that Scheider's stock (and salary) had gone up considerably since the initial negotiations.

The oral agreement reached between MGM and Scheider provided that Scheider would receive $20,000 for the pilot and, for any subsequent series, $5000 per episode in the first year, with escalations in subsequent years. The damages awarded to MGM for breach of contract were based upon the difference between the amount MGM would have paid to Scheider under the contract for the series and the $183,488 paid to the replacement actor, Robert Conrad, for the eight produced episodes of the program. The difference of $120,888 with interest, was awarded to MGM.

2. This is a New York decision. Had the case been determined under California law, the result, as to injunctive relief, would clearly have been different under California Civil Code § 3423 (see Section 2.4.2.)

3. The preceding *MGM* case can be contrasted with *Sawyer v. Sickinger,* 366 N.Y.S.2d 435 (1975), 47 A.D.2d 291 (1975), in which the plaintiff sued for injunctive relief to compel the defendant to specifically perform an oral agreement which allegedly granted to the plaintiff the exclusive option to acquire the defendant's motion picture and the related motion picture rights in a novel and to pay 1.5 percent of the producer's share of net profits from that motion picture. Such an agreement would seem to be incapable of performance within one year, and thus unenforceable under the statute of frauds. In the *Sawyer* case, correspondence of the attorney for the plaintiff distinguished ongoing negotiations with a view toward a possible contractual relationship from the actual existence of a bona fide contract. The court, referring to New York law, found that the alleged obligation to pay a percentage of profits was continuing, was not subject to termination by either party, and, accordingly, could not be performed within one year.

4. Under certain circumstances, a court may determine that a basic agreement has been entered with the understanding of the parties that certain terms will be agreed upon later. A court, faced with such an agreement, may enforce the contract and require the parties to reasonably negotiate those additional terms. Contrast the ruling in *Scheider* with that in *American Broadcasting Company, Inc. v. Wolf* (see Section 6.3).

2.4.2 Oral Agreements

Lyrick Studios v. Big Idea Productions, Inc., 420 F.3d 388 (5th Cir. 2005)

PRADO, CIRCUIT JUDGE

Appellee Lyrick Studios, Inc. ("Lyrick") contends that appellant Big Idea Productions, Inc. ("Big Idea") breached their agreement under which Big Idea provided Lyrick with an exclusive license to distribute children's cartoon programs. Lyrick sued over this breach, and the jury found in its favor. Big Idea appeals, arguing that Lyrick cannot satisfy the requirement that all transfers of copyright (such as exclusive licenses) must be in writing and signed by the transferor. Because there is no sufficient writing here, we reverse the judgment.

Phil Vischer founded Appellant Big Idea Productions, Inc., to finance and market "VeggieTales," a computer-animated Christian-themed children's cartoon he created, featuring the characters Bob the Tomato and Larry the Cucumber. Originally, Big Idea independently distributed VeggieTales to members of an organization called the Christian Bookstores Association ("CBA"). The programs were successful, and Big Idea eventually entered into a contract with a third party to distribute to the CBA. VeggieTales' sales continued to grow.

With this success, Big Idea wanted to sell its products to a larger audience. To do this, Big Idea began negotiating with Lyrick Studios, which had experience with its own successful children's programs. In February 1997, Tim Clott, Lyrick's CEO, sent Big Idea the first of three documents that are critical to this case. This document was a proposal for distribution of VeggieTales to the "general marketplace." It ended with the caveat that "for both of our protection, no contract will exist until both parties have executed a formal agreement." Big Idea's vice president of licensing and development, Bill Haljun, sent the second critical document—a fax that listed several issues still to be decided. The next day, the parties discussed the issues in a phone call and agreed to resolve them. Haljun faxed Clott a few days later, noting that "Phil is ecstatic."

Shortly afterwards, Lyrick prepared a 16-page contract. This draft agreement was never signed. In fact, several draft contracts (and suggested revisions to the drafts) were sent back and forth over the years. There were several sticking points, including DVD distribution rights, rights to stuffed animals, the possibility of a "key man" provision, and even the term of the contract. The parties agree that no formal "long-form" contract was ever signed.

Despite lacking a formal signed contract, in March 1998, Lyrick began distributing VeggieTales videocassettes. The cassettes were immediately successful; both parties made a significant profit from the relationship.

The negotiations over a written contract continued until June 1999, when the fourth and final draft was prepared by Lyrick. Like the other drafts, this one was never signed. At some point around this time, the parties' relationship became strained. . . .

In March 2001, Lyrick was acquired by HIT Entertainment, a London-based children's entertainment company, but it continued to distribute VeggieTales. In December 2001, Big Idea informed Lyrick that it was going to use a new distributor. In response, Lyrick sued Big Idea.

This lawsuit is primarily based on Lyrick's claims that Big Idea breached its exclusive license/distribution agreement by entering into an agreement with the new distributor. During discovery, Big Idea produced a document that Lyrick now contends is the third crucial document—a November 1997 internal memorandum by Bill Haljun. Haljun wrote this memo in response to a Big Idea employee's question about the 10-year term with Lyrick. In his memo, Haljun replied that "we agreed over the phone to his contract. . . . I would say that we have an agreement in force." Lyrick had not seen this internal memorandum before litigation.

The case proceeded to trial. After the close of Lyrick's evidence, Big Idea moved for judgment as a matter of law, arguing that any contract for an exclusive license of a copyrighted work, such as VeggieTales, had to be in writing. The district court denied this motion, and the case went to the jury. The jury found that there had been a contract and that Big Idea had breached it. As a result, the jury awarded Lyrick damages of $ 9,071,973 for lost profits on videocassettes and DVDs. The district court entered judgment for this amount. . . . Big Idea now appeals the district court's denial of its motion for judgment as a matter of law. We review this ruling de novo. . . .

Under § 204(a) of the Copyright Act, "[a] transfer of copyright ownership, other than by operation of law, is not valid unless an instrument of conveyance, or a note or memorandum of the transfer, is in writing and signed by the owner of the rights conveyed or such owner's duly authorized agent." A grant of an exclusive license is considered a "transfer of copyright ownership." *Section 204(a)*'s requirement, while sometimes called the copyright statute of frauds, is in fact different from a statute of frauds. Rather than serving an evidentiary function and making otherwise valid agreements unenforceable, under *§ 204(a)* "a transfer of copyright is simply 'not valid' without a writing." The writing in question "doesn't have to be the Magna Charta; a one-line pro forma statement will do." Nor does the writing have to contain any particular language. It must, however, show an agreement to transfer copyright. An after-the-fact writing can validate an agreement from the date of its inception, at least against challenges to the agreement by third parties. . . .

Here the parties dispute whether Big Idea and Lyrick have a writing that meets *§ 204(a)*'s requirement. Lyrick contends that *§ 204(a)* is satisfied with a series of documents—the letters between Haljun and Clott and the internal Haljun memorandum. Big Idea responds that the letters were just proposals and never showed a final agreement. Big Idea also argues that Haljun's internal memo is not the kind of writing that can satisfy *§ 204(a)*.

Resolving this issue requires us to examine the documents. In the first document—the February 1997 letter from Tim Clott of Lyrick to Bill Haljun of Big Idea—the opening paragraph describes the letters contents as "our proposal." The rest of the letter sets out provisions such as territory, term, rights, products, and the distribution of proceeds. The final paragraph contains some critical language: "If the above terms are acceptable to you we will begin drafting a formal agreement. (Of course, for both of our protection, no contract will exist until both parties have executed a formal agreement.)"

The second document that Lyrick relies on is Bill Haljun's faxed response. The cover sheet for this fax states, "Here is our agreement to proceed and the remaining issues and understandings which we need to resolve prior to signing a formal document." The faxed letter reads, in part, "We agree to proceed to formalize this relationship as quickly as possible with binding agreements, subject to the following clarifications and additions. Hopefully, we can resolve these issues promptly and begin the selling process . . . with the July trade show." A list of changes and proposals followed.

The final document is an internal memorandum written by Haljun in November 1997, over six months after his fax and directly responding to a concern about the proposed 10-year term. It describes the parties' negotiations and indicates that, "We agreed over the phone to his contract and thanked him very much." In recalling the discussions, Haljun indicates that Big Idea requested a minimum volume term, but Lyrick did not accept it. Continuing, the memo states that Big Idea suggested some revisions to the draft long-form contract and that Lyrick had not yet responded to those revisions. The memo concludes with language that Lyrick finds critical:

Net of all this—when we told Tim Clott we accepted his proposal and we would go forward on that basis, and they have printed catalogs, represented our products and gotten them on television, designed plush, and paid for some research, I would say that we have an agreement in force.

This memo was never sent to Lyrick. In fact, Lyrick saw it for the first time during discovery.

Lyrick contends that these three documents constitute a sufficient written agreement. This assertion raises two primary issues. First, do the first two faxes indicate that they are preliminary in nature or do they contain an actual contract? Second, can Haljun's internal memorandum constitute a "a note or memorandum of the transfer?"

The two 1997 faxes, standing alone, do not show that the parties entered into a final agreement to provide Lyrick with an exclusive license to distribute VeggieTales programs. The February fax from Lyrick indicates that it is a proposal. More importantly, it expressly states, "Of course, for both of our protection, no contract will exist until both parties have executed a formal agreement." Big Idea's fax in response also indicates a lack of finality, providing that, "We agree to proceed to formalize this relationship as quickly as possible with binding agreements." This statement indicates that the fax itself is not a binding agreement. *Section 204(a)* requires some language of finality. Finally, the continuing debate over the draft long-form contracts concerned some of the terms in the 1997 faxes (such as the term and the actual products to be distributed), which further shows that the faxes were not final contracts.

Lyrick attempts to cure these problems by turning to the internal Haljun memo. Lyrick argues that "if a writing *executed* after litigation has commenced is sufficient to satisfy *Section 204(a)*, a writing executed shortly after the agreement was reached but *communicated to* the transferee after litigation has commenced should also be sufficient. . . . " Lyrick thus tries to fit this case in the line of cases where a post-transfer writing has met § *204(a)*'s requirements. We initially note that when courts have found the post-deal writing sufficient, the party challenging the writing has been an alleged infringer who is an outsider to the deal. . . . That situation is different from the situation here, where the parties to the alleged contract disagree about whether a valid agreement actually exists. Thus, the analysis in these cases does not apply here, and the cases themselves are not relevant.

On the other hand, two Ninth Circuit cases are relevant, each for different reasons. One, *Konigsberg International, Inc. v. Rice,* addresses a post-transfer letter in the context of a dispute between the parties to the alleged contract. 16 F.3d 355 (9th Cir. 1994). The other, *Radio Television Espanola S.A. v. New World Entertainment, Ltd.,* concerns a purely internal memorandum that was not provided to the other party to the alleged transfer until litigation. 183 F.3d 922 (9th Cir. 1999).

In *Konigsberg,* two movie producers entered into an oral agreement with the author Anne Rice. Under this agreement, Rice would create a story, called a "bible," that "could form the basis for derivative works in various entertainment media." Rice would then write a novel based on the bible and the producers would have two years of movie and television rights, with an option to extend. A written contract was never signed, although Rice delivered the bible and in exchange received $ 50,000 from the producers. Rice then wrote a successful novel, *The Mummy,* based on the bible, but the producers were not able to exercise their rights. The producers claimed that Rice refused their attempts to exercise their option to extend. Therefore they sued. The district court dismissed the case because there was no writing that satisfied § *204(a)*. Rice then sent the producers' lawyer a letter stating, "As far as I am concerned, these contracts, though never signed, were honored to the letter." The producers tried to use this letter to reopen the case, arguing that this letter met § *204(a)*'s writing requirements.

The Ninth Circuit disagreed. It determined that Rice's letter was not a sufficient writing:

Rice's letter was written three and a half years after the alleged oral agreement, a year and a half after its alleged term would have expired and 6 months into a contentious lawsuit. Thus, it was not substantially contemporaneous with the oral agreement. Nor was it a product of the parties' negotiations; it came far too late to provide any reference point for the parties' license disputes. In short, Rice's letter—though ill-advised—was not the type of writing contemplated by *section 204* as sufficient to effect a transfer of the copyright to THE MUMMY.

Here, the document is more contemporaneous, entered into during the course of the parties' exchange of the long-form contracts. But *Konigsberg* shows, however, that not all documents referring to the existence of a contract, or even admitting that an agreement existed, will constitute a sufficient note or memorandum of transfer.

Radio Television Espanola is much closer to the situation here. There a television company, Television Espanola, negotiated an exclusive license with a distributor for certain programs. Afterwards, the distributor's negotiating agent drafted and signed an internal memo that listed the terms of the agreement. This memo noted that the television company was to prepare the contracts. Following this memo, the parties exchanged many letters, faxes, and memos, but never signed a contract. Trying to overcome the lack of a formal signed contract, Television Espanola pointed to several different documents it claimed satisfied *§ 204(a)*. The first was a fax in which one of the distributor's executives referred to a deal between the parties. The court concluded that this fax did not satisfy the writing requirement:

Surely, the fax references a deal, but it does not specify anything about that deal or whether that deal is for an exclusive license for the program or for other broadcast rights. A mere reference to a deal without any information about the deal itself fails to satisfy the simple requirements of *§ 204(a)*. Without more, the comment in the Garcia fax is merely a part of negotiations rather than an "instrument of conveyance" or "memorandum of the transfer."

The second document that Television Espanola relied on was also a fax. This fax, also from the distributor, discussed delivering episodes and concludes "with nothing further at this time, awaiting the contracts." The court concluded that this fax, too, failed to satisfy *§ 204(a)*. The court noted that the fax did not discuss the exclusive license and that "The statement that New World is waiting for the contracts 'undercuts the hint of finality' that the fax may otherwise contain." Finally, Television Espanola claimed that two other documents were sufficient writings. The first document was the distributor's internal deal memo, describing the deal in some detail, including the term and the total fee. The second document was a fax from Television Espanola asking the distributor to confirm the contract. Yet the court found that these documents, even when taken together with the previous ones, did not contain "language indicating finality." Rather, they discussed a pending contract and negotiations.

In rejecting Television Espanola's claim, the Ninth Circuit noted an additional reason why the internal deal memorandum was not a sufficient writing. The memo could not have satisfied *§ 204(a)* "because it was never communicated to Television Espanola." Again, not all writings will satisfy *§ 204(a)*'s requirements.

In general, this case is similar to *Radio Television Espanola*—preliminary faxes indicated that a contract would be entered into but did not provide a final contract; an internal memo, never intended to be given to the other party, described some of the terms. To be sure, there are also several differences. Haljun's internal memo indicates that he agreed over the phone and that he would say that they had an agreement in force. This is somewhat more final than the internal memorandum in *Radio Television Espanola*. These differences, however, do not change the reasoning or the result.

In the end, we conclude that the faxes themselves do not set out a final signed contract. By their own language, they are part of negotiations: Lyrick's initial fax states that "no contract will exist until both parties have executed a formal agreement." Nor do the faxes satisfy the requirements when combined with Haljun's internal memo. Like the letter in *Konigsberg* and the memo in *Radio Television Espanola*, Haljun's memo is not the kind of memorandum of transfer envisioned by *§ 204(a)*. Satisfying *§ 204(a)*'s writing requirement with a purely internal memo that was never intended to be provided to Lyrick would not further the copyright goals of predictability of ownership.

Lyrick alternatively argues that the parties acted as if they had a deal for several years, making it unfair for Big Idea to rely on a "hyper-technical" *§ 204(a)* argument. The Ninth Circuit rejected a similar argument in *Konigsberg* when it required a writing even in the face of ample evidence of an agreement, including that Rice had written the bible and had been paid for it. *Section 204(a)* requires a writing. Although Lyrick argues that enforcing this requirement would be unjust, we will not add an exception to the statute. . . .

For these reasons, we reverse the judgment of the district court. . . .

NOTES

1. Agreements that transfer ownership of copyright or grant an exclusive license in a copyright—which would include virtually all book publishing, music publishing, record, and motion picture and television acquisition agreements—must be in writing to be enforceable under copyright law. The Copyright Act of 1976, 17 U.S.C. § 204 (a) provides: "A transfer of copyright ownership, other than by operation of law, is not valid unless an instrument of conveyance, or a note or memorandum of the transfer, is in writing and signed by the owner of the rights conveyed or such owner's duly authorized agent." The Act defines a "transfer of copyright ownership" as: "an assignment, mortgage, exclusive license, or any other conveyance, alienation, or hypothecation of a copyright or any of the exclusive rights comprised in a copyright, whether or not it is limited in time or place of effect, but not including a nonexclusive license" (17 U.S.C. § 101.) Generally, a signed writing is considered valid under Section 204 if it effectuates the parties' intent to transfer ownership of copyright interest. The writing is not required to be detailed, lengthy, or even contain the words "transfer" or "copyright" as long as it evidences the mutual intent of the parties. For further discussion of the form and degree of specificity required to satisfy Section 204, see *Effects Assoc. Inc. v. Cohen*, 908 F.2d 555 (9th Cir. 1990); *Konigsberg Int'l. Inc. v. Rice*, 16 F.3d 355 (9th Cir. 1994); *Radio Television Espanola S.A. v. New World Entm't.*, 183 F.3d 922 (9th Cir. 1999).
2. The writing requirement of Section 204 does not apply to non-exclusive licenses. Therefore, non-exclusive licenses may be granted orally or implied by conduct. See *Effects Assoc. Inc. v. Cohen*, 908 F.2d 555, 558 (9th Cir. 1990) (holding that although defendant filmmaker did not obtain a written license to incorporate plaintiff's special effects footage into a film, no writing was required where plaintiff granted defendant an implied nonexclusive license); see also 3 Melville B. Nimmer & David Nimmer, *Nimmer on Copyright* § 10.03, at 49–52 (2005).
3. Much entertainment business is now transacted through email. A question has arisen as to the ability of electronic communications to effectively transfer

copyrights under Section 204. Under traditional copyright law notions, the lack of a signature places electronic communications outside the realm of effective copyright grants. However, because state rather than federal regulation traditionally governs the law of contracts, almost all states have adopted some form of the Uniform Electronic Transactions Act. California adopted this act in 1999 to give legal effect to electronic signatures. See Cal. Civ. Code § 1633.7 (2005).

§ 1633.7. Influence of electronic form on effect or enforceability of record or signature

(a) A record or signature may not be denied legal effect or enforceability solely because it is in electronic form.

(b) A contract may not be denied legal effect or enforceability solely because an electronic record was used in its formation.

(c) If a law requires a record to be in writing, an electronic record satisfies the law.

(d) If a law requires a signature, an electronic signature satisfies the law.

In 2000, Congress also enacted the Electronic Signatures in Global and National Commerce Act (E-SIGN Act). This act mandates that no signature can be denied legal effect simply because it is in electronic form. See 15 U.S.C § 7001.

4. In *Main Line Pictures, Inc v. Basinger,* 1994 WL 814244 (Cal. App. 1994) (Not Officially Published) Actress Kim Basinger, through her loan-out corporation, entered into an oral agreement with Main Line Pictures to star in the film "Boxing Helena." Basinger later reconsidered her decision to act in the film. Main Line sued Basinger and her loan-out corporation for breaching an oral contract. The jury returned a verdict of $8.9 million against Basinger indicating that although the agreements associated with the deal remained unsigned, an enforceable oral contract still existed. The appellate court reversed based on an issue unrelated to the enforceability of the oral contract. Rather, the appellate court found that the trial judge gave the jury prejudicially ambiguous jury instructions. The judge had instructed the jury to decide whether Basinger "and/or" her loan-out corporation had entered into and then breached the oral agreement. The jury could have thus found the loan-out corporation, Basinger, or both liable. Because there was no clear way to ascertain to whom the jury attributed liability, the appeals court reversed.

5. If it is established that the parties did not intend their agreement to be binding until in writing and signed, there is no enforceable oral agreement. See *Scheck v. Francis,* 26 N.Y.2d 466, 311 N.Y.S.2d 841 (1975).

6. However, a course of conduct may create a contractual obligation, even where a formal written contract is contemplated, especially if the party desiring to enforce the contract has taken action in reliance on the agreement with knowledge of the other party.

7. Singer-songwriter John Mellencamp filed an action against his music publisher seeking the return of copyrights to his songs. In one of the causes of action, Mellencamp argued there existed an oral agreement which provided that copyrights to his songs would be conveyed back to him. As evidenced in the decision of *Mellencamp v. Riva Music, Ltd.* (see Section 5.2.1), the statute of frauds barred Mellencamp's argument.

8. See also *Jillcy Film Enterprises, Inc. v. Home Box Office,* 593 F. Supp. 515 (S.D.N.Y. 1984) in which Plaintiff, Jillcy Film Enterprises, Inc., a Canadian corporation that was formed for the purpose of producing a film documentary of the making of "The Terry Fox Story" sued HBO for breach of an oral agreement (which was found to be within the statute of frauds and, therefore unenforceable) and breach of a letter agreement between Jillcy and HBO the relevant terms of which were:

    (a) HBO gave Jillcy the right to film a documentary of the filming of "The Terry Fox Story."

    (b) Within six weeks after the commencement of the film, Jillcy was to submit some rough footage of the documentary that had been filmed up to that point.

    (c) For a period of up to 90 days after the delivery of that rough footage, the parties agreed to "negotiate exclusively and in good faith with respect to the terms and provisions relating to the distribution, exhibition or other exploitation of the documentary."

    (d) Finally, the parties agreed that "in the event that you and we do not reach agreement," Jillcy would not use the documentary in the United States for the duration of the copyright in the documentary.

    Citing the *Candid* decision (see Section 2.3.1), the Court concluded "[b]ecause no definite, objective criteria or standards against which HBO's conduct can be measured were provided in the July 21, 1982 letter agreement, the provision is unenforceable on the grounds of uncertainty and vagueness and should be dismissed."

9. Entertainment transactions often move so quickly that the deal, as it evolves on cell phones and fax machines, is weeks or months ahead of the fully executed contracts that memorialize the agreement. Problems occur when the contracts do not reflect the understanding of the parties, due either to verbal modification of the agreement or ambiguities in the agreement itself. In these circumstances the parol evidence rule, an old and settled principle of law that generally provides that a party may not offer proof of a prior or contemporaneous negotiation or oral statement to contradict the clear meaning of the unambiguous terms of a written agreement, takes on significance. If the intent of a contract is clear from the language of the document, parol evidence is not admissible. If, however, the underlying contract is ambiguous, the parties may submit parol evidence concerning the facts or circumstances regarding intent of the parties. See *Meinrath v. Singer Co.* 482 F. Supp. 457 (SDNY 1979), *aff'd*, 697 F.2d 293 (2d Cir. 1982).

2.4.3 California Injunction Statutes

In reviewing the various statutory provisions of states heavily involved in the entertainment industries, most particularly California, one must consider the company's ability to enforce a personal services contract when the contract is initially entered into. Under certain statutes, an artist may have a right to terminate a contract for cause, which would obviously relieve the artist of the duty to perform under that contract. This remedy is to be distinguished from an artist's ability to cease performing and remain free from an injunction on other statutory grounds.

The collective California statutes may represent to the artist the only realistic opportunity to terminate the personal services contract prematurely and, likewise, may create an enormous number of pitfalls that the company may be subject to that ultimately may restrict or prevent enforcement of the agreement.

Two sections of the California statutes, California Civil Code § 3423 and California Code of Civil Procedure § 526 were, prior to 1994, collectively referred to as the "$6,000 per year statute." Since the extensive revisions to § 3423 enacted by the California Legislature in 1994 the two statutes are now called the "$9,000 plus" statute. The statutes basically provide that in order to provide the basis for injunctive relief, a contract must be in writing, provide for services that are unique and extraordinary, and provide for a minimum compensation (which was, until 1994, at the rate of not less than $6,000 per year).

It is obvious that, without injunctive relief, the validity, importance, and position of the exclusive personal services contract in the entertainment industry are significantly undermined. While the motion picture studio, record company, music publishing company, or television studio may still seek damages against the breaching artist, a negative injunction may be the only effective remedy in ultimately enforcing the personal services contract.

It is important to note that the $9,000 plus per year rule is not a mandatory condition placed on all employers, but, ultimately, inclusion of that clause in all entertainment service contracts would have a significant economic effect on the entertainment industry and its constituent personnel.

We consider first two important sections of the California Civil Code. Then we turn to three cases that applied the earlier $6,000 per year statute.

§ 3390. Obligations not specifically enforceable

The following obligations cannot be specifically enforced:

1. An obligation to render personal service;
2. An obligation to employ another in personal service; . . .

The amended Cal Civ Code § 3423 (1994) is as follows:

§ 3423. When injunction may not be granted

An injunction may not be granted: . . .

(e) To prevent the breach of a contract the performance of which would not be specifically enforced, other than a contract in writing for the rendition of personal services from one to another where the promised service is of a special, unique, unusual, extraordinary, or intellectual character, which gives it peculiar value, the loss of which cannot be reasonably or adequately compensated in damages in an action at law, and where the compensation for the personal services is as follows:

   (1) As to contracts entered into on or before December 31, 1993, the minimum compensation provided in the contract for the personal services shall be at the rate of six thousand dollars ($ 6,000) per annum.

   (2) As to contracts entered into on or after January 1, 1994, the criteria of subparagraph (A) or (B), as follows, are satisfied:

(A) The compensation is as follows:

(i) The minimum compensation provided in the contract shall be at the rate of nine thousand dollars ($ 9,000) per annum for the first year of the contract, twelve thousand dollars ($ 12,000) per annum for the second year of the contract, and fifteen thousand dollars ($ 15,000) per annum for the third to seventh years, inclusive, of the contract.

(ii) In addition, after the third year of the contract, there shall actually have been paid for the services through and including the contract year during which the injunctive relief is sought, over and above the minimum contractual compensation specified in clause (i), the amount of fifteen thousand dollars ($ 15,000) per annum during the fourth and fifth years of the contract, and thirty thousand dollars ($ 30,000) per annum during the sixth and seventh years of the contract. As a condition to petitioning for an injunction, amounts payable under this clause may be paid at any time prior to seeking injunctive relief.

(B) The aggregate compensation actually received for the services provided under a contract that does not meet the criteria of subparagraph (A), is at least 10 times the applicable aggregate minimum amount specified in clauses (i) and (ii) of subparagraph (A) through and including the contract year during which the injunctive relief is sought. As a condition to petitioning for an injunction, amounts payable under this subparagraph may be paid at any time prior to seeking injunctive relief.

(3) Compensation paid in any contract year in excess of the minimums specified in subparagraphs (A) and (B) of paragraph (2) shall apply to reduce the compensation otherwise required to be paid under those provisions in any subsequent contract years . . . .

In the following excerpt, Robert M. Dudnik explains the workings of §3423 as revised in 1993. Prior to January 1, 1994, an employer had to guarantee the performer compensation at the rate of $6,000 per annum. This article explains the sliding scale/optional multiple process that applies to contracts executed on or after January 1, 1994. This article is reprinted with permission from the November 1993 issue of the Entertainment Law & Finance Newsletter © 1993 NLP IP Company.

The Newly Revised California Injunction Statute

*By Robert M. Dudnik**

[A]n injunction may be issued if the compensation criteria of either subparagraph (e)(2)(A) of Section 3423 ("subparagraph (A)") or subparagraph (e)(2)(B) of Section 3423 ("subparagraph (B)") are fulfilled.

Injunctions Under Subparagraph (A)

The changes to the law mandated by subparagraph (A), when it is read with paragraph (e)(3) of Section 3423, involve: a sliding scale of guaranteed minimum compensation for each year of the contract, with the first year starting at $9,000; a requirement that specified additional compensation, over and above the guaranteed minimum, shall actually have been paid starting with the fourth year of the contract; a provision that compensation paid in any year in excess of the minimum specified for that year shall apply to reduce the compensation otherwise required to be paid in any subsequent contract years; and a provision permitting the employer to satisfy the actual payment requirement—as distinguished from the guaranteed minimum requirement—by making payment at any time prior to seeking injunctive relief.

Chart 1 illustrates the compensation requirements under a literal reading of subparagraph (A) as it is supplemented by paragraph (e)(3):

Chart 1

Contract Year	Minimum Guarantee	Amount That Must Have Actually Been Paid During The Year In Which Injunction Is Sought	Amount that Must Have Actually Been Paid From Inception Through Filing For Injunction
1	$9,000	0	0
2	$12,000	0	0
3	$15,000	0	0
4	$15,000	$30,000	$ 66,000
5	$15,000	$30,000	$ 96,000
6	$15,000	$45,000	$141,000
7	$15,000	$45,000	$186,000
		Note: $ paid in any year in excess of minimum required to be paid for that year will reduce payment requirement for later years	Note: Payable at any time prior to filing for injunction

Injunctions Under Subparagraph (B)

Subparagraph (B) permits the employer to obtain an injunction where the guaranteed minimum compensation requirement of subparagraph (A) is not satisfied; indeed, it permits an injunction even where the contract provides for no guaranteed compensation, so long as certain amounts are actually received by the performer each year. Subparagraph (B) is thus a total departure from the prior law. Chart 2 illustrates the compensation requirements under a literal reading of subparagraph (B) as supplemented by paragraph (e)(3).

Chart 2

Contract Year	Amount That Must Have Been Actually Received During The Year In Which Injunction Is Sought	Amount That Must Have Been Actually Received From Inception Through Filing For Injunction
1	$ 90,000	$ 90,000
2	$120,000	$ 210,000
3	$150,000	$ 360,000
4	$300,000	$ 660,000
5	$300,000	$ 960,000
6	$450,000	$1,410,000
7	$450,000	$1,860,000
	Note: $ paid in any year in excess of minimum required to be paid for that year will reduce payment requirement for later years	Note: Payable at any time prior to filing for injunction

Comments on the New Law

Subparagraph (A)(i)'s guaranteed minimum compensation requirement appears to provide that unless the contract guarantees the specified minimum during each year of its term, no injunction may issue (unless, of course, the requirements of subparagraph [B] are satisfied). In other words, if a five-year contract provided for no guarantee during its first year, but set forth the required guaranteed minimums for its remaining four years, it would appear that no injunction could properly issue under subparagraph (A) during any contract year, even if the actual payment requirements of subparagraph (A)(ii) were satisfied. . . .

With respect to the actual payment requirements of both subparagraph (A)(ii) and subparagraph (B), it would be surprising if royalties and other forms of contingent compensation could not be included in determining whether these requirements have been met. Not so clear, however, is the extent to which recording fund payments may be included. It would seem that the portion (if any) of a recording fund not actually utilized by the artist in recording his or her album should be included in determining the amount of compensation paid. However, determining what that portion amounts to could prove very difficult for record companies. One solution would be to contractually obligate artists with recording fund deals to submit statements under oath with respect to the amount expended in producing their albums within a specified period after delivery. Whether tour support payments may be included in determining the amount paid is an open question.

If on the first day of a contract year a performer states that he or she will no longer perform and intends to sign with a competitor, the employer may have to make a substantial payment under subparagraph (A)(ii) or subparagraph (B) to cover the full payment requirement for that particular year, since there is no provision for pro-rating. If the employer makes such a payment but fails to obtain the injunction, a question would arise as to whether it could include the payment in its claim for damages.

Another question arises from the annual payment requirements of subparagraph (e)(ii) and the "crediting" provision in paragraph (a)(3). To illustrate, assume that a performer with a contract that satisfies the guaranteed minimum requirement of subparagraph (A)(i) is actually paid $14,000 during the first contract year, $17,000 during the second, and $20,000 during the third. If this performer threatens to sign with a competitor during the fourth year, the question would arise as to what, if anything, the company must pay to satisfy the fourth year's $30,000 payment requirement of subparagraph (e)(ii), given the "crediting" provided for in paragraph (a)(3), and given the fact that the performer was paid $51,000 during the first three years, $15,000 of which was in excess of the guaranteed minimum. It could be argued that: the company need only pay an additional $15,000, since $15,000 in excess of the guaranteed minimum was paid during the first three contract years; the company need pay nothing, since the company paid $51,000 during the first three years despite the fact that the actual payment requirement during the first three years is zero; or the company must pay $30,000 on the ground that because there is no actual payment requirement during the first three years, what was actually paid is irrelevant for crediting purposes.

*Robert M. Dudnik is a partner at Mitchell Silberberg & Knupp, LLP. He served as record company counsel in the *MCA Records, Inc. v. Newton-John* case. He was assisted in preparing this article by Judith Kline.

Although the discussions of the $6,000-per-year guarantee in the following cases are no longer in effect, the decisions are still relevant to any discussion of the availability of injunctive relief under § 3423. The *Newton-John* case illustrates the hazards of terms based on fixed time periods, and the *Brockert* case illustrates that the references in § 3423 to the stature of the artist are not mere boilerplate.

MCA Records, Inc. v. Newton-John, 90 Cal.App. 3d 18, 153 Cal.Rptr. 153 (1979)

FLEMING, J.

Defendant Olivia Newton-John, a singer, appeals a preliminary injunction restraining her from recording for anyone other than plaintiff MCA Records while MCA's action is pending "or until April 1, 1982, if that date shall occur during the pendency of this action." . . . [Ms. Newton John's agreement gave her control over the recording process, and provided advances of] $250,000 for each recording received during the initial two years, and an advance of $100,000 for each recording received during the option years. The cost of producing the recordings would be borne by defendant. [The court rejected Ms. Newton-John's argument that she could not be enjoined from recording for third parties because MCA did not guarantee that she would net at least $6,000 every twelve months, because that would permit her to spend her way out of the deal. However, the court would not accept the injunctive period prescribed by the trial court.]

Defendant contends she cannot be suspended by plaintiff and at the same time enjoined from rendering personal services for others. . . . But defendant has not been suspended. She is still free to record for plaintiff, and, in the event she chooses to record, nothing in the agreement relieves plaintiff from its obligation to compensate her . . . [T]he grant of a preliminary injunction lies within the discretion of the trial court . . . and an explicit finding of irreparable harm is not required to sustain the trial court's exercise of that discretion. . . . In requesting injunctive relief plaintiff alleged that if defendant were permitted to record for a competitor, it would suffer irreparable injury, both in loss of profits and loss of goodwill. This allegation was supported by substantial evidence that defendant's services are unique. Absent any indication to the contrary, we can presume from the trial court's order granting the preliminary injunction that the court did in fact find that irreparable injury would be imminent unless the injunction were granted. . . . [However, Ms. Newton-John] contends that even if the court did not err in granting a preliminary injunction, it erred in authorizing the preliminary injunction to extend beyond the five-year term of the agreement. Plaintiff responds, in effect, that so long as defendant fails to perform her obligations under the contract, the term of the agreement, and thus of the preliminary injunction, may be extended until the seven-year statutory maximum has elapsed. (Lab. Code, § 2855.)

Because a period of five years has not yet passed since defendant began her employment on April 1, 1975, the issue of the availability to plaintiff of injunctive relief after April 1, 1980, is technically premature. Nevertheless, we consider the language in the preliminary injunction extending its possible duration to April 1, 1982, inappropriate for two reasons:

First, if defendant had performed under the contract, plaintiff would not be entitled to prevent her from recording for competitors at the end of the five-year term of the agreement. We have grave doubts that defendant's failure to perform her obligations under the contract can extend the term of the contract beyond its specified five-year maximum. . . .

Second, the injunction appealed here is merely a preliminary injunction, whose sole function is to preserve the status quo pending a final judgment in the action. . . .

Plaintiff's general duty to exercise due diligence in the prosecution of its action and to bring it to conclusion within a reasonable time (Code Civ. Proc., §§ 581a, 583) is particularly strong when, as here, the cause involves injunctive and declaratory relief (see Code Civ. Proc., §§ 527 and 1062a, which give priority to such actions). To the extent the phrase "until April 1, 1982" suggests that plaintiff, without taking further action, may prevent defendant from recording for competitors until 1982, the phrase is misleading.

The order for preliminary injunction is modified by deleting the phrase, "or until April 1, 1982, if that date shall occur during the pendency of this action," and as so modified, the order is affirmed.

NOTE

Largely as a result of this case, recording and music publishing companies changed their contract forms so that each period of the term would run for the longer of a stated time (usually twelve months) or until delivery of a specified number of recordings or compositions. In this manner, the issue of suspension (and the permissible length thereof) would no longer arise.

Although the payments required in order to secure an injunction under the amended §3423 are considerably higher than those formerly required under the earlier version of the statute, the employer must still demonstrate the requisite status. As the following case indicates, unless the talent has been the subject of an "auction" (i.e., multiple companies have been in the bidding for his/her/their services) or the artist has a proven track record, the company may encounter difficulties with the "status" branch of the statute.

Motown Record Corporation v. Brockert, 160 Cal.App. 3d 123, 207 Cal.Rptr. 574 (1984)

Johnson, Acting Presiding Judge

[The court held that Motown did not comply with the then-applicable $6000/per annum guarantee requirement of § 3423 because the contract merely reserved to Motown the option to guarantee such payments. However, the court also addressed the issue of whether or not Teena Marie was of sufficient stature to warrant application of § 3423, and held that she was not.] In 1976, [when she signed with Motown,] she was an unknown in the music business. Her experience consisted of singing with local bands at weddings, parties, and shopping centers and roles in school musicals. She had written some songs but none had been recorded or released commercially . . . Between 1979 and 1980 Teena Marie recorded four albums for Motown. All were successful. Indeed her fourth and last album, "It Must Be Magic," achieved gold record status, selling more than 400,000 copies . . . .

[On the issue of whether Teena Marie was of sufficient stature to meet the uniqueness requirements of § 3423, w]e begin our review with *Lumley v. Wagner,* [(1852) 42 Eng. Rep. 687]. Johanna Wagner was not an unknown member of a chorus line at the time her case arose. She was one of Europe's best known opera singers, niece of Richard Wagner and "cantatrice of the Court of His Majesty the King of Prussia." . . . Her contract with Lumley called for her to perform at Her Majesty's Theatre in London twice a week for three months at the rate of 100 pounds per week; a significant sum considering the wage of a unionized bricklayer in London at the same time was less than two pounds per week. (23 Encyclopedia Britannica, *supra.,* at p. 270.)

It was not uncommon for courts of that time to distinguish *Lumley v. Wagner* on the ground that there the services of an exceptional artist and a considerable sum were involved. Among the best known of these cases are *Whitwood Chem. Co. v. Hardman, supra,* 2 Ch. 416. In *Whitwood,* Lindley, L. J. stated, "I look upon *Lumley v. Wagner* rather as an anomaly to be followed in cases like it, but an anomaly which it would be very dangerous to extend." (2 Ch. at p. 428.)] *Arthur v. Oakes* (7th Cir. 1894) 63 F. 310 . . . and *Dockstader v. Reed* (1907) 121 App.Div. 846 [106 N.Y.S. 795]. In *Dockstader* the court refused to enjoin the defendant from singing for another company noting, *inter alia,* "The salary agreed to be paid defendant was quite moderate, and indicates that his part was quite ordinary, and manifestly could be easily filled." (106 N.Y.S. at p. 797.) Thus, at the time section 3423 was amended there was a discernible trend toward enforcing negative covenants against the "prima donnas" but not the "spear carriers." (See *Carter v. Ferguson* (1890) 58 Hun. 569 [12 N.Y.S. 580, 581]; and see generally, 11 *Williston on Contracts, supra,* § 1450, pp. 1042–1043; 5A Corbin on Contracts, *supra.,* § 1209, p. 417; 4 Pomeroy, *Equity Jurisprudence* (5th ed. 1941) § 1343, p. 943.)

Aside from the *Lumley* line of cases there is an even older judicial tradition which helps to explain why the California Legislature sought to limit injunctive relief to performers of star quality. A fundamental reason why courts will not order specific performance of personal services contracts is because such an order would impose on the courts a difficult job of enforcement and of passing judgment upon the quality of performance. (See 11 Williston on Contracts, *supra,* § 1423, pp. 782–783; 5A Corbin on Contracts, *supra,* § 1204, p. 400; *Poultry Producers etc. v. Barlow, supra,* 189 Cal. 278, 288–289; *Light, supra,* at p. 143.) As Corbin observes in his treatise, "An artist does not work well under compulsion, and the court might find it difficult to pass judgment upon the performance rendered." (5A Corbin, *supra*, § 1204, p. 400.)

As the court in *Lumley* candidly admitted, it had no power to compel Madame Wagner to sing at Lumley's theatre but the injunction prohibiting her from performing elsewhere might well accomplish the same result. (42 Eng. Rep. at p. 693.) Thus there is a danger an artist prohibited from performing elsewhere may feel compelled to perform under the contract and, under the stress of the situation, turn in an unsatisfactory performance. This would lead to further litigation between the parties on the adequacy of the artist's performance; the very thing the courts traditionally sought to avoid. (See, e.g., *Bethlehem Engineering Export Co. v. Christie* (2d Cir. 1939) 105 F.2d 933, 935 [125 A.L.R. 1441] (Hand, J.).) There is less likelihood of this conundrum arising if the performer is of great renown. Such a performer may well choose not to perform rather than risk her reputation by delivering a sub-par performance. . . .

It is no answer to say that by the time Motown and Jobete sought injunctive relief to enforce the exclusivity clauses Teena Marie had become a star. Motown and Jobete did not contract with a star. By their own admission they contracted with a "virtual unknown." Nothing in section 3423 prevents the companies from seeking damages from Teena Marie for breach of the exclusivity clause. . . . That section merely says for reasons of public policy the exclusivity clause of a contract can only be enforced by injunction when the contract is with a performer of requisite distinction as measured by the compensation the employer is willing to pay. . . . Moreover . . . allowing the companies, once they judge the artist to have achieved star quality, to enforce the exclusivity clause by injunction would violate the concept of fundamental fairness which is also embodied in section 3423. . . .

This is quite clear when section 3423 is read in connection with Civil Code section 3391, subdivision 2, which provides specific performance cannot be enforced against a party as to whom the contract is not "just and reasonable." Taken together those sections demand a minimum standard of fairness as a condition on equitable enforcement of an exclusivity clause in a personal services contract.

"As one grows more experienced and skillful there should be a reasonable opportunity to move upward and to employ his abilities to the best advantage and for the highest obtainable compensation." (*De Haviland v. Warner Bros. Pictures* (1944) 67 Cal.App. 2d 225 [153 P.2d 983], 235.) "[A]ny agreement that limits a person's ability to follow his vocation must be strictly construed." (*Lemat Corp. v. Barry, supra,* 275 Cal.App. 2d at pp. 678–679.) Therefore, "[a]n injunction which forbids an artist to accept new employment may be a harsh and powerful remedy. The monetary limitation in the statute is intended to serve as a counterweight in balancing the equities."

2.5 CREDIT ISSUES

Although it is estimated that he produced more than 300 films during his brief semi-legendary career, MGM's Irving Thalberg (who later was the model for Monroe Stahr in F. Scott Fitzgerald's *The Last Tycoon*) never accorded himself the customary producer billing, because in his opinion credit one awarded oneself was worthless.

This may have worked well for Thalberg, who enjoyed a unique status in 1930s Hollywood, but later generations of creative personnel have learned that billing often translates into work and money. This is why it is not unusual to see billboards upon which one actor's name is on the left above the title (known in the trade as "first position"), a second actor's name appears just to the right, but *above* the name of the first actor, while a third actor's name appears on the far right and slightly *below* the name of the first actor. Some years ago, Cary Grant and Sophia Loren resolved the first position problem by agreeing that on half the billboards, Grant's name would appear on the left, while Loren's name would appear on the left on the rest of the billboards, a very practical resolution (but one which is rarely utilized).

All matters this important produce disputes, and credit issues are no exception. The legal principles used to resolve such disputes are derived from two sources:

(1) contract law, when the affected parties have entered into agreements concerning credit, and (2) statutory and common law, when the affected parties have not entered into such agreements.

2.5.1 By Contract

Because of the importance of credit in the entertainment industry, credit often is one of the subjects specifically covered by contract. Sometimes such contracts are negotiated individually directly between the affected parties, as were the contracts in the *Gold Leaf* and *Tamarind Lithography* cases which follow. On other occasions, credit provisions appear in collective bargaining agreements such as the Writers' Guild of America agreement which is at issue in the *Ferguson* case discussed in the note following *Tamarind Lithography*.

Where contractual provisions concerning credits exist, there is no doubt they are perfectly valid and enforceable. Questions have arisen, however, concerning (1) whether a contract requiring that credit be given actually does exist; (2) what remedies are available if the credit provisions of individually negotiated contracts are breached; and (3) whether there is a right to judicial review of credit determinations made by arbitrators pursuant to collective bargaining agreements. *Cleary v. News Corp.* deals with whether a contract for credit existed at all. The *Gold Leaf* and *Tamarind* cases deal with the remedies issue. The *Ferguson* case contains an excellent description of the credit determination standards and procedures that are used by the

Writers Guild pursuant to the WGA collective bargaining agreement, and with the issue of judicial review of the credit determinations of union arbitrators.

Cleary v. News Corp., 30 F.3d 1255 (9th Cir. 1994)

WILL, SENIOR DISTRICT JUDGE (SITTING BY DESIGNATION)

Dr. James W. Cleary sued News Corporation, the [parent company of HarperCollins and Scott, Foresman and Company, the] publishers of *Robert's Rules of Order*, . . . for alleged . . . breach of contract. . . . The district court granted summary judgment in favor of the defendants. . . . For the following reasons, we affirm.

I. BACKGROUND

During the 1960s, James W. Cleary helped revise *Robert's Rules of Order* for Scott, Foresman and Company. When the 1970 edition was published, Dr. Cleary was listed on the title page as having assisted the named author, Sarah Corbin Robert, along with Henry M. Robert III and William J. Evans. The work was republished in 1980 and once again title page credit was given to Cleary, Robert III, and Evans. The most recent edition was published in 1990. The title page for this edition was virtually identical to the 1970 and 1980 versions with the most notable change being the omission of Dr. Cleary's name. Upon learning of the omission, Dr. Cleary initiated this lawsuit. . . .

Many of the facts underlying this litigation are undisputed. Currently in its ninth edition, *Robert's Rules of Order* is one of the leading sources of parliamentary law in the United States. *Robert's Rules* was first published in 1876 by General Henry Martyn Robert; he has been listed as the author of every edition of *Robert's Rules* since. After General Robert's death, members of the Robert family maintained ultimate authority over any changes. Robert's Rules Association, successor-in-interest to General Robert's rights, owns the copyright to each edition.

In 1960, Sarah Corbin Robert, General Robert's daughter-in-law, began working on what was to become the 1970 edition of *Robert's Rules*. Sarah Robert's son, Henry M. Robert III, and William J. Evans became involved in the writing and editing of the 1970 edition. In 1961, Dr. James W. Cleary was retained by Scott, Foresman to provide a critique of the previous edition of *Robert's Rules*, and in 1965, Cleary was retained as Advisory Editor to the revision.

Curtis Johnson, an employee of Scott, Foresman, testified at his deposition that prior to entering into the contract, Scott, Foresman had orally agreed to give title credit to Cleary. Johnson stated that, in light of the low royalty rate, "right from the start [name credit] was the inducement that was supposed to persuade Dr. Cleary to do the work." . . . Johnson also testified that, in fact, he did offer Cleary title credit. Most relevant to this appeal is a letter dated May 19, 1965, and addressed to

Cleary, in which Johnson discusses the proposed royalty terms at some length and concludes, "We will, of course, appropriately credit you in the new edition, as well." . . .

Subsequently, however, on September 3, 1965, Cleary entered into an agreement with Scott, Foresman concerning his role in the revision. Cleary agreed to validate the then-existing copy for the 1970 edition, to compile and complete copy for three chapters, and to write new copy for two chapters. In return, Scott, Foresman agreed to pay Cleary a royalty of three-quarters of one percent of the net receipts from sales of the 1970 edition, with Scott, Foresman reserving the right to adjust the royalty rate with respect to future editions of the book to reflect the amount of original work prepared by Cleary that remained in any subsequent edition. The contract specified that Cleary was retained on a work for hire basis and that the heirs of General Robert would retain all rights in *Robert's Rules* and in the copyright. The contract did not mention giving Cleary any title credit for the 1970 edition or any subsequent editions.

Cleary began working on the revision. According to Cleary, Sarah Robert had completed a mere outline of the work and Robert III was not producing usable material. Therefore, Cleary wrote a large amount of the new edition, which was subsequently edited by Sarah Robert and, because of her rapidly declining health, by Robert III. Cleary testified that he had contributed approximately forty percent of the final edition, Robert III had contributed forty percent, and Evans had contributed twenty percent.

In 1980, Scott, Foresman published a new edition, with minor revisions. Scott, Foresman provided Cleary with an opportunity to review the changes; none of Cleary's proposed changes were incorporated into the new edition. Cleary continued to receive title credit and three-quarters of one percent royalties for sales of the 1980 edition.

The most recent edition, referred to as the 1990 edition, was published in late 1989. It is undisputed that Cleary did not participate in the preparation of the 1990 edition. After the 1990 edition was published, Cleary learned that his name had been deleted from the title page, although he was still acknowledged in the introduction. Sarah Corbin Robert was still listed as the author, although she had died in 1972, and Robert III and Evans were listed as providing assistance. . . .

Dr. Cleary has continued to receive three-quarters of one percent royalties on sales of the 1990 edition. As part of an attempted settlement of this case, the title page of subsequent printings of the 1990 edition after the first printing listed Cleary as providing assistance just as in the 1980 version.

II. DISCUSSION

. . . Cleary claims that Scott, Foresman breached its contract when it failed to give him title credit in the 1990 edition of *Robert's Rules*. A viewing of the evidence in the light most favorable to Cleary makes it apparent that, prior to entering into the contract, Scott, Foresman had agreed to give Cleary title page credit. The contract itself, however, does not contain an attribution clause and does not mention named credit.

The parol evidence rule prohibits introduction of extrinsic evidence of a prior or contemporaneous agreement which would vary or contradict the clear and unambiguous language in a contract. . . . Notwithstanding, if "the language contained in the contract is ambiguous or silent as to essential terms then oral testimony may be properly admitted into evidence." . . . Courts will examine all the surrounding facts and circumstances of the case to determine if the contract was intended to be the complete and final expression of the parties' intent. . . .

Cleary claims that the contract was not a complete and final expression of the parties' intent because the parties intended to give Cleary title credit in the 1970 edition and subsequent reprintings. We note initially that, even if the attribution clause, though not included in the written agreement, could somehow be deemed a material term of the 1965 contract, neither the 1980 nor the 1990 editions were covered by that contract. Cleary apparently attempts to circumvent this hurdle by arguing that the contract ambiguously refers to the term "Work" by not specifying even the general contents of the work, but this argument is undermined by the clear language of the contract. The contract specifically defines the nature of the work, prescribes the number of chapters that Cleary was to produce, and provides for dates of completion. Further, the contract provides, "On any revised edition of the Work, the Publisher shall consider a further retention of the Advisory Editor's services." In using the term "Work," Scott, Foresman clearly was referring exclusively to the work-in-progress which became the 1970 edition of *Robert's Rules*.

Notwithstanding, even if we were to conclude that the terms of the 1965 contract applied to the 1980 edition and subsequent editions, we are unpersuaded by Cleary's attempts to prove that the contract was ambiguous as to a material term. Oral testimony may be introduced if the language in the contract is silent as to a material term. . . . Yet, according to Cleary's own testimony, he knew there was no provision granting him credit . . . , yet he signed the contract anyway. At his deposition, Cleary testified that at the time the contract was signed "it was not important that there be name credit, but it became in my mind more and more important as my involvement grew and grew by considerable degrees over the period of the ensuing years." . . . Even viewed in the light most favorable to Cleary, these facts indicate that he did not consider an attribution clause an essential term of the contract. Cleary was aware that the term was not in the contract and did not consider it important at the time. Therefore, oral testimony may not be used to introduce that term into the contract.

Cleary also argues that the parties implicitly intended to grant him a right to name credit. This hidden meaning is established, Cleary asserts, by the fact that in prior editions, *Robert's Rules* was published with title credit given to contributing authors. We find this argument unpersuasive. The contract does not mention name credit in any manner, and thus is not ambiguous on its face. In addition, we have already noted that under a valid work for hire arrangement, a publisher is under no obligation to provide attribution, unless such a right has been specifically reserved in the contract. *Vargas v. Esquire Inc.*, 164 F.2d 522, 526 (7th Cir. 1947). In its contract, Scott, Foresman included a work for hire clause and did not include an attribution clause. From this, it is fair to conclude that Scott, Foresman did not intend to contract to give Cleary name credit. To now introduce an attribution clause would be to introduce a term which would contradict the clear language of the contract.

Finally, Cleary argues that the defendant's subsequent acts of attributing authorship to Cleary in the 1970 and 1980 editions evince a contractual understanding that name credit would be provided. Subsequent conduct of the parties may be considered when it does not contradict the plain meaning of the contract. . . .

Because Cleary relinquished authorship as well as copyright ownership when he signed the work for hire provision, subsequent conduct and circumstances indicating an intent to provide attribution are in direct conflict with the work for hire agreement and cannot be considered. Evidence of Scott, Foresman's subsequent acts of attribution only indicates that they were complying with their previous representation that they would include his name even though they were under no contractual duty to do so. At the time of contracting, Cleary could have insisted that the agreement contain an attribution clause for the 1970 and subsequent editions; he then could have enforced that contractual right had Scott, Foresman failed to give him name credit.

Accordingly, because the plaintiff seeks to introduce extrinsic evidence which would vary the unambiguous language of the contract, we conclude that the trial court properly granted summary judgment to the defendants with respect to Cleary's breach of contract claims.

Gold Leaf Group, Ltd. v. Stigwood Group, Ltd., Sup. Ct. N.Y. County, Case No. 11768/78 (October 4, 1978)

RUBIN, J.

[After years of relentless concertizing but meager record sales, Peter Frampton was propelled to the forefront of the record world when his live album, "Frampton Comes Alive," sold some 12 million copies. On the basis of his new celebrity status, Frampton was signed to appear in the film version of *Sgt. Pepper's Lonely Hearts Club Band*. The Bee Gees, a very successful group for many years but hardly of the first rank, were also engaged to appear in the film. Obviously, Frampton was entitled to—and secured a promise of—first billing. Between the time the two artists were signed and the time the picture was to be released, two phenomena occurred: Frampton's record sales took a precipitous nose-dive, while the Bee Gees soared to the top of the heap with "Saturday Night Fever," the soundtrack that sold some 27 million copies. The producer of the film had a change of heart concerning billing. This led to injunctive proceedings, and to the following unpublished opinion of Special Term.—Ed.]

Plaintiff [Peter Frampton's loan-out corporation] moves this court for an injunction, pendente lite, restraining defendant . . . from violating the written contractual "billing" rights of Peter Frampton (Frampton). . . .

The film took approximately two years to make at a cost of over $12,000,000. A significant part of the production package is an "original motion picture soundtrack" record album. The total cost of the project, which encompasses the film and record and includes promotion, now exceeds $20,000,000.

Plaintiff seeks a temporary injunction to prevent defendants from advertising the movie and the record in a manner according . . . "the Bee Gees" the same billing credit as Frampton. While the film itself credits Frampton "top billing," the advertising as to the film and record accords "the Bee Gees" billing alongside and to the right of Frampton. Frampton claims that he has the right to have his name appear above "the Bee Gees" in connection with 1) the billing of the film, 2) the advertising of the film, 3) the art work on the cover of the record, 4) the advertising for the record and, 5) merchandising and subsidiary rights in connection with the film.

It appears that the billing provision of a contract is material in that it is not just a matter of status or prestige, but serves to protect and enhance the future marketability and commercial value of a star performer. . . . [A]n agreement was signed wherein in Paragraph 4 the credit status of Frampton is set forth as follows: "Artist shall receive the sole star billing above the title of the photoplay in a size of type one hundred per cent of the credits of any other person." In a subsequent modification, it was agreed that the Bee Gees name could be billed above the title, but below that of Frampton. . . .

The language of the agreement, even as modified by the parties, gives Frampton sole star billing in the photoplay. It is further apparent that plaintiff considered Frampton's star billing to be of prime importance and would have withheld its consent to the agreement had its artist not been so recognized.

Defendant attempts to convince the court that billing alongside but to the left of the Bee Gees is recognized as "first star billing." However, the agreement gives to Frampton "sole star billing" and plaintiff is entitled to a fulfillment of its contractual obligations. The court is aware of defendants' desire to accord its clients a greater star status as the result of their sudden surge of popularity originating from the motion picture *Saturday Night Fever*. However, in view of the contractual obligations, there is sufficient showing to enjoin defendant from billing or advertising the Bee Gees, other than on a line below Frampton, and in a size, type and prominence no greater than his in any billing or advertising concerning the [film]. . . .

The motion addressed to the record [album] presents a different problem. While it may have been the intention of the plaintiff to have paragraph 4 of the agreement apply to the soundtrack recording, the agreement is not clear and convincing in this respect. Another agreement dated January 21, 1977, between defendants' recording subsidiary, RSO Records, Inc. and Frampton's [record company], A & M Records, Inc. provides that Frampton's name be billed "in the same manner as the names of other artists are utilized in connection with said album." Furthermore, an agreement signed March 13, 1978, concerning worldwide merchandising and subsidiary rights is silent as to billing and advertising. There is, also, a question of whether plaintiff acquiesced in the design of the record album jacket. The proof required of defendants, for the purpose of this motion, is merely that they need only raise doubts of that likelihood that plaintiff will ultimately succeed in the action. It is incumbent upon plaintiff to come forth with clear and convincing evidence dispelling such doubts. As to the soundtrack recording, this the plaintiff has failed to do [so]. . . .

Accordingly, the motion for an injunction pendente lite is granted as to the motion picture and denied as to the soundtrack recording. . . .

Tamarind Lithography Workshop, Inc. v. Sanders, 143 Cal. App. 3d 571, 193 Cal.Rptr. 409 (1983)

STEPHENS, J.

The essence of this appeal concerns the question of whether an award of damages is an adequate remedy at law in lieu of specific performance for the breach of an agreement to give screen credits. Our saga traces its origin to March of 1969, at which time appellant, and cross-complainant below, Terry Sanders (hereinafter Sanders or appellant), agreed in writing to write, direct and produce a motion picture on the subject of lithography for respondent, Tamarind Lithography Workshop, Inc. (hereinafter referred to as Tamarind or respondent).

Pursuant to the terms of the agreement, the film was shot during the summer of 1969, wherein Sanders directed the film according to an outline/treatment of his authorship, and acted as production manager by personally hiring and supervising personnel comprising the film crew. Additionally, Sanders exercised both artistic control over the mixing of the sound track and overall editing of the picture.

After completion, the film, now titled "Four Stones for Kanemitsu," was screened by Tamarind at its 10th anniversary celebration on April 28, 1970. Thereafter, a dispute arose between the parties concerning their respective rights and obligations under the original 1969 agreement. Litigation ensued and in January 1973 the matter went to trial. Prior to the entry of judgment, the parties entered into a written settlement agreement, which became the premises for the instant action. Specifically, this April 30, 1973, agreement provided that Sanders would be entitled to a screen credit entitled "A Film by Terry Sanders."

Tamarind did not comply with its expressed obligation pursuant to that agreement, in that it failed to include Sanders' screen credits in the prints it distributed. As a result a situation developed wherein Tamarind and codefendant Wayne filed suit for declaratory relief, damages due to breach of contract, emotional distress, defamation and fraud. Sanders cross-complained, seeking damages for Tamarind's breach of contract, declaratory relief, specific performance of the contract to give Sanders screen credits, and defamation. Both causes were consolidated and brought to trial on May 31, 1977. A jury was impaneled for purposes of determining damage issues and decided that Tamarind had breached the agreement and awarded Sanders $25,000 in damages.

The remaining claims for declaratory and injunctive relief were tried by the court. The court made findings that Tamarind had sole ownership rights in the film, that "both June Wayne and Terry Sanders were each creative producers of the film, that Sanders shall have the right to modify the prints in his personal possession to include his credits." All other prayers for relief were denied.

It is the denial of appellant's request for specific performance upon which appellant predicates this appeal.

Since neither party is contesting the sufficiency of Sanders' $25,000 jury award for damages, the central issue thereupon becomes whether that award is necessarily preclusive of additional relief in the form of specific performance, i.e., that Sanders receive credit on all copies of the film. Alternately expressed, the issue is whether the jury's damage award adequately compensates Sanders, not only for injuries sustained as a result of the prior exhibitions of the film without Sanders' credits, but also for future injuries which may be incurred as a result of any future exhibitions of the film without his credit. Commensurate with our discussion below, we find that the damages awarded raise an issue that justifies a judgment for specific performance. Accordingly, we reverse the judgment of the lower court and direct it to award appellant the injunctive relief he now seeks.

Our first inquiry deals with the scope of the jury's $25,000 damage award. More specifically, we are concerned with whether or not this award compensates Sanders not only for past or preexisting injuries, but also for future injury (or injuries) as well.

Indeed, it is possible to categorize respondent's breach of promise to provide screen credits as a single failure to act from which all of Sanders' injuries were caused. However, it is also plausible that damages awarded Sanders were for harms already sustained at the date of trial, and did not contemplate injury as a result of future exhibitions of the film by respondent, without appropriate credit to Sanders.

Although this was a jury trial, there are findings of facts and conclusions of law necessitated by certain legal issues that were decided by the court. Finding of fact No. 12 states:

"By its verdict the jury concluded that Terry Sanders and the Terry Sanders Company are entitled to the sum of $25,000.00 in damages for all damages suffered by them arising from Tamarind's breach of the April 30th agreement." The exact wording of this finding was also used in conclusion of law No. 1. Sanders argues that use of the word "suffered" in the past tense is positive evidence that the jury assessed damages only for breach of the contract up to time of trial and did not award possible future damages that might be suffered if the film was subsequently exhibited without the appropriate credit. Tamarind, on the other hand, contends that the jury was instructed that if a breach occurred the award would be for all damages past and future arising from the breach. The jury was instructed: "For the breach of a contract, the measure of damages is the amount which will compensate the party aggrieved, for the economic loss, directly and proximately caused by the breach, or which, in the ordinary course of things, would be likely to result therefrom" and " . . . economic benefits including enhancement of one's professional reputation resulting in increased earnings as a result of screen credit, if their loss is a direct and natural consequence of the breach, may be recovered for breach of an agreement that provides for screen credit. Economic benefits lost through breach of contract may be estimated, and where the plaintiff [Tamarind], by its breach of the contract, has given rise to the difficulty of proving the amount of loss of such economic benefit, it is proper to require of the defendant [Sanders] only that he show the amount of damages with reasonable certainty and to resolve uncertainty as to the amount of economic benefit against the plaintiff [Tamarind]."

The trial court agreed with Tamarind's position and refused to grant the injunction because it was satisfied that the jury had awarded Sanders all the damages he was entitled to including past and possible future damages. The record does not satisfactorily resolve the issue. However, this fact is not fatal to this appeal because, as we shall explain, specific performance as requested by Sanders will solve the problem.

The availability of the remedy of specific performance is premised upon well established requisites. These requisites include: A showing by plaintiff of (1) the inadequacy of his legal remedy; (2) an underlying contract that is both reasonable and supported by adequate consideration; (3) the existence of a mutuality of remedies; (4) contractual terms which are sufficiently definite to enable the court to know what it is to enforce; and (5) a substantial similarity of the requested performance to that promised in the contract. . . .

It is manifest that the legal remedies available to Sanders for harm resulting from the future exhibition of the film are inadequate as a matter of law. The primary reasons are twofold: (1) that an accurate assessment of damages would be far too difficult and require much speculation, and (2) that any future exhibitions might be deemed to be a continuous breach of contract and thereby create the danger of an untold number of lawsuits.

There is no doubt that the exhibition of a film, which is favorably received by its critics and the public at large, can result in valuable advertising or publicity for the artists responsible for that film's making. Likewise, it is unquestionable that the nonappearance of an artist's name or likeness in the form of screen credit on a successful film can result in a loss of that valuable publicity. However, whether that loss of publicity is measurable dollar wise is quite another matter.

By its very nature, public acclaim is unique and very difficult, if not sometimes impossible, to quantify in monetary terms. Indeed, courts confronted with the dilemma of estimating damages in this area have been less than uniform in their disposition of same. Nevertheless, it is clear that any award of damages for the loss of publicity is contingent upon those damages being reasonably certain, specific, and unspeculative. . . .

The varied disposition of claims for breach of promise to provide screen credits encompasses two schools of thought. On the one hand, there is the view that damages can be ascertained (to within a reasonable degree of certainty) if the trier of fact is given sufficient factual data. (See *Paramount Productions, Inc. v. Smith* (9th Cir. 1937) 91 F.2d 863, *cert. den.* 302 U.S. 749 [82 L.Ed. 579, 58 S.Ct. 266].) On the other hand, there is the equally strong stance that although damages resulting from a loss of screen credits might be identifiable, they are far too imponderable and ethereal to define in terms of a monetary award. (See *Poe v. Michael Todd Co.* (SDNY 1957) 151 F.Supp. 801.) If these two views can be reconciled, it would only be by an independent examination of each case on its particular set of facts.

In *Paramount Productions, Inc. v. Smith, supra,* 91 F.2d 863, 866–867, the court was provided with evidence from which the " . . . jury might easily compute the advertising value of the screen credit." (*Id.,* at p. 867.) The particular evidence presented included the earnings the plaintiff/ writer received for his work on a previous film in which he did not contract for screen credits. This evidence was in turn easily compared with earnings that the writer had received for work in which screen credits were provided as contracted. Moreover, evidence of that artist's salary, prior to his receipt of credit for a play when compared with earnings received subsequent to his actually receiving credit, was " . . . if believed, likewise sufficient as a gauge for the measure of damages." (*Id.,* at p. 867.)

In another case dealing with a request for damages for failure to provide contracted-for screen credits, the court in *Zorich v. Petroff* (1957) 152 Cal.App. 2d 806 [313 P.2d 118] demonstrated an equal awareness of the principle. The court emphasized " . . . that there was no evidence from which the [trial] court could have placed a value upon the screen credit to be given plaintiff as an associate producer. (Civ. Code, § 3301.)" (*Id.,* at p. 811.) Incident to this fact, the court went on to surmise that because the motion picture which was at the root of the litigation was an admitted financial failure, screen credit, if given, " . . . could reasonably have been regarded as a detriment to him." (*Id.*, at p. 811.)

At the other extreme, it has been held that failure to give an artist screen credit would constitute irreparable injury. In *Poe v. Michael Todd Co., supra,* 151 F.Supp. 801, the New York district court was similarly faced with an author's claim that his contractual right to screen credit was violated. The court held: "Not only would money damages be difficult to establish, but at best they would hardly compensate for the real injury done. A writer's reputation, which would be greatly enhanced by public credit for authorship of an outstanding picture, is his stock in trade, it is clear that irreparable injury would follow the failure to give screen credit if in fact he is entitled to it." (*Id.*, at p. 803.)

Notwithstanding the seemingly inflexible observation of that court as to the compensability of a breach of promise to provide screen credits, all three cases equally demonstrate that the awarding of damages must be premised upon calculations, inferences or observations that are logical. Just how logical or reasonable those inferences are regarded serves as the determining factor. Accordingly, where the jury in the matter sub judice was fully apprised of the favorable recognition Sanders' film received from the Academy of Motion Picture Arts and Sciences, the Los Angeles International Film Festival, and public television, and further, where they were made privy to an assessment of the value of said exposure by three experts, it is reasonable for the jury to award monetary damages for that ascertainable loss of publicity. However, pecuniary compensation for Sanders' future harm is not a fully adequate remedy. (See *Rest., Contracts,* § 361, p. 648.)

We return to the remaining requisites for Sanders' entitlement to specific performance. The need for our finding the contract to be reasonable and supported by adequate consideration is obviated by the jury's determination of respondent's breach of that contract. The requisite of mutuality of remedy has been satisfied in that Sanders had fully performed his obligations pursuant to the agreement (i.e., release of all claims of copyright to the film and dismissal of his then pending action against respondents). (See Civ. Code, § 3386.) Similarly, we find the terms of the agreement sufficiently definite to permit enforcement of the respondent's performance as promised.

In the present case it should be obvious that specific performance through injunctive relief can remedy the dilemma posed by the somewhat ambiguous jury verdict. The injunction disposes of the problem of future damages, in that full compliance by Tamarind moots the issue. Of course, violation of the injunction by Tamarind would raise new problems, but the court has numerous options for dealing with the situation and should choose the one best suited to the particular violation.

In conclusion, the record shows that the appellant is entitled to relief consisting of the damages recovered, and an injunction against future injury. . . .

NOTES

1. As discussed in the *Ferguson* case below, a union member's right to credit can be decided pursuant to the union's internal procedures. *Ferguson v. Writers Guild of America, West, Inc.*, 226 Cal.App. 3d 1382, 277 Cal.Rptr. 450 (1991) involved a claim by Ferguson that his credit for "Beverly Hills Cop II" had been improperly diluted. The WGA arbitration panel awarded the following credits: "Screenplay by Larry Ferguson and Warren Skaaren; Story by Eddie Murphy & Robert D. Wachs." He asked the court to issue a peremptory writ of mandate requiring the Writers Guild to set aside its credit determination and give Ferguson sole screenplay credit and sole story credit, which was denied, the denial being affirmed by the Court of Appeal.

Writing credits are determined under the WGA's basic agreement with the Alliance of Motion Picture and Television Producers (AMPTP), the producers' trade organization as well as the WGA's credits manual. It is very common for several (even many) writers to work on the same project at different stages. When the project is completed, WGA notifies all the writers of the credits proposed by the studio. Any or all of the writers may request arbitration under the WGA credit manual. Arbitration is conducted by a panel of three WGA members, who are unknown to the applicant or to each other.

Eligible arbitrators are WGA members "with credit arbitration experience or with at least three screenplay credits of their own." Each party "can peremptorily disqualify a reasonable number of persons from the list. From the remaining potential arbitrators, the secretary selects three . . . [and] delivers to the three arbitrators all script, outline, and story material prepared or used in the creation of the screenplay. . . . [E]ach participant in the credit arbitration may examine [the materials] to assure the inclusion of everything he or she has written. Any dispute over the "authenticity, identification, sequence, authorship or completeness" of submitted literary material is resolved by a special three-member committee, which conducts for that purpose a prearbitration hearing, at which all affected writers may present testimony and other evidence."

The three arbitrators hold no hearing, and they deliberate independently of each other. Indeed, each [normally] remains unaware of the identity of the other two. . . . Each arbitrator notifies the secretary of his or her determination. The secretary then informs the parties of the decision of the majority of the arbitrators."

A dissatisfied writer may ask that the determination be put before a "policy review board" drawn from the WGA's credits committee, but the board's function is "solely to detect any substantial deviation from the policy of the Writers Guild or from the procedure set forth in the credits manual." If such deviation is found, the board can only "direct the arbitration committee to reconsider the case or to order a fresh arbitration by a new triumvirate." It cannot "reverse the decision of an arbitration committee. . . . "

The court agreed with the WGA that under the AMPTP basic agreement and the WGA credits manual, "disputes over writing credits for feature-length photoplays are nonjusticiable." The WGA membership "have agreed among themselves . . . and with the producers' association . . . that the credit-determination process can be handled both more skillfully, more expeditiously, and more economically by Writers Guild arbitration committees than by courts. The scope of judicial review in a particular case, then, is limited to a determination whether there has been a material breach of the terms of the credits manual." This limited scope of review requires the court to "examine[] only whether the parties in fact agreed to submit their controversy to arbitration, whether the procedures employed deprived the objecting party of a fair opportunity to be heard, and whether the arbitrators exceeded their powers."

With respect to Ferguson's claims of procedural irregularities, "we bear in mind that the procedures employed in the present arbitration have already been reviewed for correctness by the Writers Guild's own policy review board. The court accords considerable deference to the decision of the policy review board, because of its members' expertise in the interpretation and application of [the basic agreement] and the credits manual."

The court was also not receptive to Ferguson's claim that he was entitled to know the identity of the arbitrators. The WGA practice was "supported by important and legitimate considerations, including the necessity that arbitrators be entirely freed from both real and perceived dangers of pressure, retaliation, and litigation. . . . Ferguson apparently wishes to ask the arbitrators, inter alia, to explain and justify their conclusions regarding the various writers' contributions to the final screenplay. Even when an arbitration is conducted under more familiar rules, though, such as the commercial arbitration rules of the American Arbitration Association, the losing party is not permitted to conduct an inquisition into the arbitrators' thought processes in reaching their award. . . . "

2. The Producer's Guild of America (PGA) also has a rigorous arbitration process for determining "Produced by" credits for films and television series. The PGA created the arbitration process to ensure that the producing credit was only bestowed on those individuals who actually produced the film. Such a process became necessary because in recent years non-producers, such as financiers and distributors, have begun claiming producer credits, thereby devaluing the role of the producer. In 2006, the Academy of Motion Picture Arts and Sciences decided to solely rely on the PGA arbitration process to select which credited producers (those already with on-screen "Produced by" credits) could be eligible to win the Academy Award for Best Picture. The impetus for the Academy's decision stemmed from the 1999 Academy Awards ceremony where five so-called producers accepted Oscars for Best Picture winner, *Shakespeare in Love.*
The PGA arbitration process consists of seven steps:

First, a studio must submit to the PGA both a production for Academy Award consideration and a "Notice of Credit." The Notice of Credit is a one-page form listing names, titles, and contact information for all major creative and executive contributors to the film.
Second, upon receipt of the Notice of Credit, the PGA sends Eligibility Forms to all credited producers. The Eligibility Form is the most critical component in the process as it requires the candidate to list in detail his or her contributions to the film. The form contains several producer duties from development, pre-production, physical production, up to post-production and marketing. The candidate must indicate his or her level of responsibility for each producing task. Also, there are "free response" questions where the candidate can elaborate on both the nature of his or her involvement with the project and why he or she should be eligible to win an Academy Award.
Third, the PGA sends "Third Party Verification Forms" to all non-producer contributors on the project. These individuals must indicate which of the eligible producers they interacted with throughout the course of the film making process.
Fourth, once the PGA receives all of the documentation, a date is set for the arbitration panel to review the forms for each candidate. Each panel consists of three experienced producers selected from a list of potential panelists. Prior to panel selection, each candidate under

review has the opportunity to strike any name, in good faith, if the candidate feels that the panelist cannot remain unbiased.

Fifth, the panelists examine and debate the contributions of each producer to determine whether he or she has contributed enough to the production of the film to be considered Oscar worthy. This proceeding is completely confidential.

Sixth, the panelists weigh each producer candidate's contributions according to a scale. For motion pictures, contributions to development are weighed at 30%; pre-production at 20%; physical production at 20%; and post production and marketing together at 30%. In order to be Academy Award eligible, a producer must demonstrate responsibility for more than 50% of the functions.

Lastly, after the panel makes it decision, the producer candidates are afforded an opportunity to file an appeal with the PGA. An appeal is only warranted if the candidate can demonstrate that the panel did not have possession of material information that would have changed the outcome of the process, or that the panel acted in derelict of its duty.

The PGA arbitration process was first utilized during the selection of the eligible producers for the 2006 Academy Awards. The PGA determined that only two of the six credited producers for Best Picture nominee (and winner), *Crash*, would be eligible to receive the Academy Award. One of the ineligible producers, Bob Yari, sued the PGA and the Academy of Motion Picture Arts and Sciences claiming that the PGA arbitration process was secretive, arbitrary, and unfair. Yari also claimed that he was summarily denied right to appeal his PGA determination. At the time of this writing, this case is pending before the Los Angeles Superior Court.

3. The following is an example of a credit provision from a performer's agreement for a motion picture:

Credit

1. Subject to Paragraph 2 below, if Artist appears recognizably in the Role in the Motion Picture during its initial general theatrical release, Artist shall be entitled to receive the following cast credit:

1.1. On screen, on all positive prints of the Motion Picture, on a separate card in position among cast members, in the main titles (provided that if the credits of all other cast members appear only in the end titles, Artist's credit shall appear only in the end titles), in a size of type no smaller than that of the larger of 50% of the screen title or the credit accorded to any other cast member;

1.2. Subject to Producer's standard exclusions and exceptions as set forth in Producers Paid Advertising Exhibit attached hereto ("Excluded Advertising"), in position among cast members in the billing block, if any, of all paid advertising issued by or under the direct control of Producer, in a size of type no smaller than that of the larger of 50% of the "regular" title or the credit accorded to any other cast member in such billing block; and

1.3. In the billing block, if any, of all Excluded Advertising (or in another similar ad) issued by or under the direct control of Producer in which any cast member is accorded billing block credit, other than award, nomination or congratulatory ads in which the only individual accorded credit is the one being awarded, nominated or congratulated, ads announcing a personal appearance, radio ads and the audio portion of teasers, trailers and television ads.

2. If any other cast member is accorded credit above the screen title or the "regular" or artwork title of the Motion Picture in any particular item of paid advertising issued by or under the direct control of Producer (other than award, nomination or congratulatory ads in which the only individual accorded such credit is the one being awarded, nominated, or congratulated, ads announcing a personal appearance, radio ads and the audio portion of teasers, trailers and television ads), then Artist's credit shall also be accorded above such screen title or "regular" or artwork title in such item of paid advertising (or in another similar ad), as applicable, it being agreed that if Artist receives credit in the artwork portion of any item of paid advertising, then Producer shall not be required to accord Artist credit in the billing block of such item of paid advertising unless any other actor receives credit in both the artwork portion and billing block of such item of paid advertising.

4. The credit provision below is an example from a film agreement that specifies how the "owner," who is the screenplay writer, will be credited for her contributions to the film:

Credit: Owner shall receive credit on screen [and in paid advertising] in connection with the Picture as follows (subject to applicable guild requirements): if the Picture as initially released has the same title as the Property, in substantially the form: "Based on the _____ by _____", otherwise in substantially the form: "Based on the _____ entitled '_____' by _____". No casual or inadvertent failure by Purchaser to accord such credit, nor the failure for any reason by third parties to comply with the provisions of this paragraph, shall be deemed a breach hereof by Purchaser. [In paid advertising, the following shall apply: any reference to the size of the title shall refer to the regular as opposed to the artwork title; any reference to the "main titles" is to the credits, whether before or after the body of the Picture, where the "directed by" credit appears; the foregoing credit provisions shall apply only to the billing portion (excluding artwork and advertising copy) of advertisements issued by Purchaser or under Purchaser's direct control relating primarily to the theatrical exhibition of the Picture, and which are issued prior to the date 5 years after the initial release of the Picture, and shall not apply at any time to teasers, trailers, billboards and other outdoor advertising, radio and television advertising, group, list or special advertisements, commercial tie-ins or by-products, any advertisements of 8 column inches or less, or any advertisements which would be excepted advertisements under the Directors Guild of America Basic Agreement.

2.5.2 By Statute/Common Law

Though credits often are provided for by contract, that is not always the case. When credit disputes arise where no contract provisions exist, such disputes are resolved by referring to principles of statutory, such as the Lanham Act, or common law.

Usually, such disputes have arisen because an author, artist or performer has been denied a credit he or she wants. *Vargas v. Esquire, Smith v. Montoro* and *Lamothe v. Atlantic Recording* all are examples of such cases and are reproduced below. Vargas shows that in the absence of a contract, the general rule is that there is no statutory or common law right to claim credit; though that case was decided almost a half-century ago, the case discussed in the note that follows *Vargas* shows that it is still good law. There is, however, an exception to the general rule that arises when credits are not simply omitted but are affirmatively misrepresented. The *Smith* and *Lamothe* cases that follow both deal with credit misrepresentation.

In a surprising number of cases, credit disputes also have arisen where credit was given to someone who did not want it. The *Stephen King*, and *Ken Follett* cases below are both cases of this type.

2.5.2.1 Right to Claim Credit

Vargas v. Esquire, Inc., 164 F.2d 522 (7th Cir. 1947)

MAJOR, CIRCUIT JUDGE

This appeal is from an order, entered December 17, 1946, dismissing plaintiff's complaint and supplemental complaint for failure to state a cause of action.

Plaintiff, an artist, sued to enjoin the reproduction of certain pictures made by him and delivered to defendant, a publisher, upon the ground that the same were wrongfully used in that they were published without the signature of plaintiff and without being accredited to him. Plaintiff also sued for damages on account of such publication alleged to violate his contract and his property right in the pictures and unfairly to represent them as the work of others. Defendant moved to dismiss on the ground that the plaintiff at the time of publication had no property right in the pictures and no right to control or to direct their disposition.

The facts alleged by the complainant center about and relate largely to two contracts of which the plaintiff and defendant were parties. The complaint sets forth that in June, 1940, the parties entered into a contract, "Exhibit A," attached to and made a part of the complaint, wherein and whereby plaintiff was employed as an artist for three years, to produce art work for use by defendant in its publication and also for use in publications of a commercial nature, for a certain monthly compensation and in addition thereto a certain percent of the proceeds realized by defendant for work of a commercial nature. Under this contract plaintiff made and delivered certain pictures, one of which was reproduced each month, beginning October 1, 1940, in the magazine Esquire, published by defendant. Plaintiff also made and delivered twelve pictures each year, beginning in the fall of 1940, for a calendar published and sold the following year by defendant.

At first the pictures furnished bore plaintiff's name or signature, "Vargas," and they were reproduced and published with his name thereon. Later, by agreement of the parties, the name "Vargas" was changed to "Varga." Thereafter, the pictures made by plaintiff and published by defendant were called "Varga Girls," and the name of the plaintiff appearing thereon was "A. Varga." The name was used only in connection with pictures made by plaintiff and was thus used by the defendant until March 1, 1946. No name was on the pictures when they were furnished by plaintiff to the defendant.

The contract "Exhibit A," expired on June 30, 1943, but plaintiff continued to furnish pictures to defendant without a contract, which were published in the same manner as when the contract was in force, until May 25, 1945, when the parties entered into a second contract, "Exhibit B," attached to and made a part of the complaint.

On or about January 14, 1946, plaintiff notified the defendant that he was no longer bound by the contract, "Exhibit B," and refused to longer furnish it with pictures. Defendant at that time had twenty pictures made by plaintiff which had not as yet been published. On February 11, 1946, plaintiff caused to be instituted in the United States District Court an action by which he sought a cancellation of such contract. On May 20, 1946, the court entered its decree, allowing the relief sought by the plaintiff, finding among other things that the contract had been fraudulently obtained by defendant and ordering the same cancelled and set aside as of January 10, 1946.

It was alleged that by reason of such publication by the defendant persons seeing said magazine came to know the work of the plaintiff and that as a result plaintiff became known to millions of persons, acquired a world-wide reputation and his name, "A. Varga," likewise became known throughout the world.

The complaint alleged that on March 1, 1946, the defendant published its magazine, Esquire, which contained a two-page reproduction of a picture made by the plaintiff. At the top thereof instead of the words, "The Varga Girl," appeared the words, "The Esquire Girl." The reproduction did not bear plaintiff's signature, "A. Varga," or any other signature. The supplemental complaint made a similar allegation as to a picture produced by plaintiff appearing in Esquire for the month of May, 1946. It was also alleged in the supplemental complaint that on October 1, 1946, defendant published a certain calendar enclosed in an outside envelope on which appeared the words and figures, "The 1947 Esquire Calendar 35 Copyright Esquire Inc. 1946 Printed in U.S.A." On the envelope was a reproduction of a picture painted for defendant by plaintiff. The calendar contained in said envelope was composed of the reproduction of twelve pictures of plaintiff made and intended to be used for the Varga Esquire 1947 calendar. Each of the said pictures bore the words, "The Esquire Girl Calendar." None of such pictures carried plaintiff's name or any name, word or legend indicating them to be the work of plaintiff or any other person.

All the pictures used by the defendant both in its magazine and in connection with its 1947 calendar were furnished by plaintiff to the defendant in accordance with the terms of "Exhibit B," prior to the time that plaintiff gave notice of its cancellation. All of such pictures had been paid for by the defendant in accordance with the terms of the contract, and as to those used in defendant's magazine, plaintiff had no further monetary interest. As to those used in connection with defendant's calendar, plaintiff was entitled to a share of the proceeds derived from the sale thereof. There is no allegation, however, and no claim that defendant had refused to pay or is likely to refuse to pay to plaintiff his share of such proceeds.

It was further alleged that there was a duty upon the defendant to refrain from publishing reproductions of plaintiff's pictures without their bearing his signature and giving him due credit; that defendant, in violation of its duty in this respect, published plaintiff's work without using his name and without giving him credit therefor, and that the same constituted a misrepresentation in that it represented the pictures to be the work of another and not that of plaintiff.

"Exhibit A" (the first contract) expired long prior to the inception of the instant controversy and we think it is of little consequence insofar as it affects the issues for decision. The rights of the parties must be determined from "Exhibit B" (the second contract), which was in effect at the time that plaintiff furnished the pictures to defendant which were reproduced by it subsequent to the time that plaintiff gave notice of cancellation of such contract.

In a preamble to "Exhibit B," it is stated that Vargas for approximately three years had been preparing and furnishing to Esquire drawings for use by Esquire in connection with its publications and other printed merchandise:

"In connection with certain of these drawings, the name 'Varga,' 'Varga Girl,' and similar names have been given national publicity by Esquire and have become well known to the public. Vargas acknowledges that the success of the drawings has been due primarily to the guidance which Esquire has given him and to the publicity given to them by Esquire's publications. . . . "

The contract, after expressing the desire of the parties to enter into an agreement defining their mutual rights and obligations, contains a paragraph around which this controversy revolves and which we think is determinative of the issues involved. It provides:

"Vargas agrees for a period of ten years and six months, beginning January 1, 1944, as an independent contractor, to supply Esquire with not less than twenty-six (26) drawings during each six-months' period. . . . The drawings so furnished, and also the name 'Varga', 'Varga Girl,' 'Varga, Esq.,' and any and all other names, designs or material used in connection therewith, shall forever belong exclusively to Esquire, and Esquire shall have all rights with respect thereto, including (without limiting the generality of the foregoing) the right to use, lease, sell or otherwise dispose of the same as it shall see fit, and all radio, motion picture and reprint rights. Esquire shall also have the right to copyright any of said drawings, names, designs or material or take any other action it shall deem advisable for the purpose of protecting its rights therein."

Plaintiff's principal contention is that the publication of the reproductions of paintings produced by him, without his name appearing thereon, without credit to him and without any name appearing thereon, violated an implied agreement that the defendant would not do so. Plaintiff concedes that the contract defines defendant's rights in the pictures, but in his brief argues "that despite its broad generality, despite the fact that the defendant took all rights in the pictures, it is bound by the implied agreement not to publish them in the manner complained of."

Plaintiff cites and relies upon a number of cases in support of this alleged implied agreement. *Uproar Co. v. National Broadcasting Co.*, 1st Cir., 81 F.2d 373; *Kirke La Shelle Co. v. Armstrong Co.*, 263 N.Y. 79, 188 N.E. 163; *Manners v. Morosco*, 252 U.S. 317, 40 S.Ct. 335, 64 L.Ed 590. We have read these cases, and without attempting to discuss them in detail, we think they are inapplicable to the instant situation. In each of them an author signed a contract or license which conferred on the other party certain limited rights in a literary reproduction and reserved for the author the balance of the rights therein. The holding in each of these cases is to the effect that where certain of the rights to a literary composition were conferred and other rights retained, it would be implied that the author could not use the rights retained in such a way as to destroy or materially injure the rights conferred. Such a contractual situation is in marked contrast to that of the instant case where the plaintiff by plain and unambiguous language completely divested himself of every vestige of title and ownership of the pictures, as well as the right to their possession, control and use. The language by which the extent of the grant is to be measured, "shall forever belong exclusively to Esquire, and Esquire shall have all rights with respect thereto, including (without limiting the generality of the foregoing) the right to use, lease, sell or otherwise dispose of the same as it shall see fit," would appear to leave no room for a contention that any right, claim or interest in the pictures remained in the plaintiff after he had sold and delivered them to the defendant. Not only did plaintiff by the contract divest himself of all title, claim and interest in such drawings and designs, but also in the names "Varga," "Varga Girl," "Varga Esquire," when used in connection therewith.

Of the many cases where it has been sought to engraft an implied condition upon the terms of a written instrument, we like the rule announced in *Domeyer v. O'Connell*, 364 Ill. 467, at page 470, 4 N.E.2d 830, 832, 108 A.L.R. 476, where the language used is pertinent to the instant situation. The court stated:

"The rules concerning the construction of contracts are so well established as to require but brief attention. The object of construction is to ascertain the intention of the parties.... That intention is to be determined from the language used in the instrument and not from any surmises that the parties intended certain conditions which they failed to express. Where there is no ambiguity in the language used, from that, and that alone, may the intention of the parties be gathered.... An implied intention is one necessarily arising from language used or a situation created by such language. If such intention does not necessarily arise, it cannot be implied. On the other hand, absence of a provision from a contract is evidence of an intention to exclude such provision." As already shown, we think there is no ambiguity in the granting language of the contract, nor can there be an implied intention from the language thus employed of an intention of the parties of any reservation of rights in the grantor. The parties had been dealing with each other for a number of years, and the fact that no reservation was contained in the contract strongly indicates that it was intentionally omitted. Such a reservation will not be presumed; it must be expressed and clearly imposed. *Grant v. Kellogg Co.*, D.C., 58 F.Supp. 48, 51, *affirmed* 2d Cir., 154 F.2d 59.

Plaintiff advances another theory which needs little discussion. It is predicated upon the contention that there is a distinction between the economic rights of an author capable of assignment and what are called "moral rights" of the author, said to be those necessary for the protection of his honor and integrity. These so-called "moral rights," so we are informed, are recognized by the civil law of certain foreign countries. In support of this phase of his argument, plaintiff relies upon a work by Stephen P. Ladas entitled "The International Protection of Literary and Artistic Property" (page 575, et seq.). It appears, however, that the author's discussion relied upon by plaintiff relates to the law of foreign countries. As to the United States, Ladas in the same work states (page 802):

"The conception of 'moral rights' of authors so fully recognized and developed in the civil law countries has not yet received acceptance in the law of the United States. No such right is referred to by legislation, court decision or writers."

What plaintiff in reality seeks is a change in the law in this country to conform to that of certain other countries. We need not stop to inquire whether such a change, if desirable, is a matter for the legislative or judicial branch of the government; in any event, we are not disposed to make any new law in this respect.

Plaintiff's third and last contention is that the manner of reproduction by defendant of plaintiff's work was such as to constitute a misrepresentation and was unfair competition. The concurring opinion of Mr. Justice Holmes in *International News Service v. Associated Press*, 248 U.S. 215, 246, 247, 39 S.Ct. 68, 63 L.Ed. 211, 2 A.L.R. 293; and *Fisher v. Star Co.*, 231 N.Y. 414, 433, 132 N.E. 133, 136, 19 A.L.R. 937, are the only cases cited and relied upon as supporting this contention. We think that neither case affords any support for such theory. In both, the holding as to unfair competition rested on the premise that the defendants, without the consent or approval of the plaintiffs, had taken and used to their own advantage something in which the plaintiffs had a property right—more specifically, that the defendants had pirated or stolen plaintiff's property and used it in their business in competition with that of the plaintiffs. It is difficult to discern how there could be any pirating or unlawful taking of property in the instant case in view of the rights (heretofore discussed) which the plaintiff by contract conferred upon the defendant.

Plaintiff argues that the use of "Esquire Girl" as a title for the pictures was a representation that the author was someone other than the plaintiff. We do not agree with this contention. The title used was the name of the well-known and widely circulated magazine in which they were published, and we think the public would readily recognize the word "Esquire" referred to such magazine and not to the name of an artist.

More than that, as already shown, it was provided in the contract that both the pictures and the name "shall forever belong exclusively to Esquire, and Esquire shall have all rights with respect thereto, including . . . the right to use . . . or otherwise dispose of the same as it shall see fit." This was the basis both upon which plaintiff was paid for his pictures and upon which Esquire acquired their possession and ownership. Under these circumstances, we are of the view that there was no unfair competition by the defendant in the manner of their use.

The order appealed from is affirmed.

NOTE

In *Cleary v. News Corp.*, 30 F.3d 1255 (9th Cir. 1994), a portion of which is reproduced above, the plaintiff also alleged claims under California state law for unfair competition and infliction of emotional distress. The district court granted summary judgment in favor of the defendants on those counts as well, and the Court of Appeals affirmed. The court ruled that the Ninth Circuit "has consistently held that state common law claims of unfair competition and actions pursuant to California Business and Professions Code § 17200 are 'substantially congruent' to claims made under the Lanham Act." For reasons explained in the following paragraph, the court held the plaintiff's Lanham Act claim had been properly dismissed, and thus its state law unfair competition claims had been as well. In support of his infliction of emotional distress claims, the plaintiff asserted that Scott, Foresman had "deleted his name unilaterally and without notice to him" and that it had "failed to make a bona fide attempt to determine whether his name could be deleted at their discretion." The court, however, ruled that the "tort of intentional infliction of emotional distress requires a showing of outrageous conduct resulting in severe emotional distress. . . . Cleary has failed to produce sufficient evidence establishing either outrageous conduct, severe distress or, for that matter, any other element of this cause of action." Thus, the court ruled that summary judgment had been granted properly on this issue as well.

In addition to breach of contract and state common law claims, Cleary also brought suit under the Lanham Act, 15 U.S.C. § 1125, for alleged misattribution of his work product when his name was removed from the 1990 edition title page of *Robert's Rules*. In the context of § 43 (a) of the Lanham Act, misattribution occurs "when a product is mislabeled to mask the creator's contribution." Under the Ninth Circuit test, to constitute a violation for misattribution, the misattributed material must be "bodily appropriated" from another source rather than just merely "substantially similar." The appellate court held that the 1990 edition was not a "bodily appropriation" of the 1970 edition because the 1990 edition has been significantly revised without any participation from Cleary. Accordingly, News Corporation did not misattribute Cleary's role when his name was omitted from the title page of the 1990 edition. Therefore, the court rejected Cleary's Lanham Act claim for misattribution and affirmed the district court's grant of summary judgment in favor of News Corporation.

The two cases that follow, *Smith v. Montoro* and *Lamothe v. Atlantic Recording Corporation,* both discuss how the misattribution of credit can violate the Lanham Act.

Smith v. Montoro, 648 F.2d 602 (9th Cir. 1980)

PREGERSON, CIRCUIT JUDGE

This is an appeal from a judgment granting defendant's motion to dismiss under Fed.R.Civ.P. 12(b)(6) for failure to state a federal claim. The district court held that the complaint did not allege facts sufficient to constitute a violation of section 43(a) of the Lanham Act, 15 U.S.C. § 1125(a). Appellant argues that the district court erred since the acts alleged in the complaint are the economic equivalent of "palming off," or misuse of a trade name, thus meeting the district court's standard for stating a claim under section 43(a). For the reasons stated below, we reverse.

BACKGROUND

Paul Smith contracted to star in a film to be produced by Producioni Atlas Cinematografica ("PAC"), an Italian film company. The contract allegedly provided that Smith would receive star billing in the screen credits and advertising for the film and that PAC would so provide in any subsequent contracts with distributors of the film. PAC then licensed defendants Edward Montoro and Film Venture International, Inc., ("FVI") to distribute the film in this country under the name "Convoy Buddies." Plaintiff complains, however, that Montoro and FVI removed Smith's name and substituted the name of another actor, "Bob Spencer," in place of Smith's name in both the film credits and advertising material. Plaintiff alleges that, as a result of defendants' substitution, plaintiff has been damaged in his reputation as an actor, and has lost specific employment opportunities.

The complainant sought damages under several theories, including breach of contract, "false light publicity," violation of section 43(a) of the Lanham Act. . . .

There being no diversity of citizenship, federal subject matter jurisdiction was based solely on plaintiff's Lanham Act claim. . . .

In proceedings held on May 1, 1978, the district judge explained his "tentative view" that defendants' motion should be granted and the complaint dismissed as "not stating a valid cause of action under the Lanham Act." While noting "there are many diverging interpretations of the Lanham Act" . . . the judge stated that "[i]t is my view . . . that the Lanham Act is limited in its scope and intent to merchandising practices in the nature of, or economically equivalent to, palming off one's goods as those of a competitor, and/or misuse of trademarks and trade names." According to the district court, the acts alleged in the complaint are not the economic equivalent of palming off or misuse of a trademark or trade names. The acts are more in the nature of breaches of contract or tort which are properly the subject of state law. There is certainly in this case no intent to divert a competitor's business by misleading consumers. Plaintiff's claim is not that his name was misused, but that it wasn't used at all. Therefore, the nature of the misrepresentation alleged in this case, in my view, is not within the intended scope of the statute. . . .

Shortly after the hearing, the court issued a minute order stating that defendants' motion to dismiss was granted. Judgment was entered on May 5, 1978. . . .

DISCUSSION

A. Elements of a Claim under Section 43(a)

Section 43(a) of the Lanham Act, 15 U.S.C. § 1125(a), forbids the use of false designations of origin and false descriptions or representations in the advertising and sale of goods and services. . . . The statute provides in pertinent part as follows:

Any person who shall affix, apply, or annex, or use in connection with any goods or services a false designation of origin, or any false designation or representation and shall cause such goods or services to enter into commerce shall be liable to a civil action by any person who believes that he is or is likely to be damaged by the use of any such false designation or representation.

Appellant argues that defendants violated section 43(a) by affixing or using "a false designation or representation," i.e., another actor's name in place of appellant's, in connection with the movie's advertising and credits. Appellant claims standing under section 43(a) as a person "who believes that he is or is likely to be damaged" by the use of another actor's name in place of his. Thus, appellant's claim, although one of first impression, appears to fall within the express language of section 43(a).

The district court appears to have rejected appellant's argument on the ground that, to state a claim under section 43(a), a complaint must allege merchandising practices "in the nature of, or economically equivalent to, palming off and/or misuse of trademarks and trade names."

"Palming off" or "passing off" is the selling of a good or service of one's own creation under the name or mark of another. . . . Passing off may be either "express" or "implied." Express passing off occurs when an enterprise labels goods or services with a mark identical to that of another enterprise, or otherwise expressly misrepresents that the goods originated with another enterprise. Implied passing off occurs when an enterprise uses a competitor's advertising material, or a sample or photograph of the competitor's product, to impliedly represent that the product it is selling was produced by the competitor. . . . Such practices have consistently been held to violate both the common law of unfair competition and section 43(a) of the Lanham Act. . . .

The district court's ruling was entirely consistent with the vast majority of section 43(a) cases, however, to the extent that it indicated that a section 43(a) claim may be based on economic practices or conduct "economically equivalent" to palming off. Such practices would include "reverse passing off," which occurs when a person removes or obliterates the original trademark, without authorization, before reselling goods produced by someone else. . . . Reverse passing off is accomplished "expressly" when the wrongdoer removes the name or trademark on another party's product and sells that product under a name chosen by the wrongdoer. . . . "Implied" reverse passing off occurs when the wrongdoer simply removes or otherwise obliterates the name of the manufacturer or source and sells the product in an unbranded state. . . .

In the instant case, appellant argues that the defendants' alleged conduct constitutes reverse passing off and that appellant's complaint therefore stated a section 43(a) claim even under the district court's own standard. Appellees argue, however, that the protection afforded by the Lanham Act is limited to "sales of goods" and does not extend to claims that a motion picture shown to the public might contain false information as to origin.

The short answer to appellees' argument is that the Lanham Act explicitly condemns false designations or representations in connection with "any goods or services." The prohibitions of this section have been applied to motion picture representations. See, *e.g., Dallas Cowboys Cheerleaders, Inc. v. Pussycat Cinema Ltd.*, 467 F. Supp. 366 (SDNY), *aff'd*, 604 F.2d 200 (2d Cir. 1979). Moreover, the names of movie actors and other performers may, under certain circumstances, be registered under the Lanham Act as service marks for entertainment services. . . . Although appellant has not alleged that his name is registered as a service mark, registration of a trademark or service mark is not a prerequisite for recovery under section 43(a). See *New West Corp. v. NYM Co. of California, Inc.*, 595 F.2d 1194, 1198 (9th Cir. 1979). . . .

Appellant's allegations of "reverse passing off" are analogous to those of other complaints which have been held to state a cause of action under section 43(a). For example, in *Truck Equipment Service Co. v. Fruehauf Corp.*, 536 F.2d 1210 (8th Cir.), *cert. denied*, 429 U.S. 861 (1976), a farm equipment manufacturer used photographs of a competitor's grain trailer in its sales literature. In the photos, the competitor's labels were removed and the trailer was labeled as a product of the defendant. The court rejected the defendant-appellant's contention that the use of the photos was not a false representation prohibited by section 43(a), holding that the practice was "of the same economic nature as trademark infringement." 536 F.2d at 1216. The court also noted that "The use of another's product, misbranded to appear as that of a competitor [i.e., reverse passing off], has been repeatedly found to be 'a false designation of origin' actionable under section 43(a)." *Id.*

In *John Wright, Inc. v. Casper Corp.*, 419 F.Supp. 292 (E.D.Penn. 1976), *aff'd in relevant part sub nom. Donsco, Inc. v. Casper Corp.*, 587 F.2d 602 (3d Cir. 1978), the court stated that section 43(a) "prohibits 'reverse palming off,' i.e., conduct whereby the defendant purchases or otherwise obtains the plaintiff's goods, removes plaintiff's name and replaces it with his own." 419 F. Supp. at 325. . . .

According to appellant's complaint, defendants not only removed appellant's name from all credits and advertising, they also substituted a name of their own choosing. Appellees' alleged conduct therefore amounts to express reverse passing off. As a matter of policy, such conduct, like traditional palming off, is wrongful because it involves an attempt to misappropriate or profit from another's talents and workmanship. Moreover, in reverse palming off cases, the originator of the misidentified product is involuntarily deprived of the advertising value of its name and of the goodwill that otherwise would stem from public knowledge of the true source of the satisfactory product. . . . The ultimate purchaser (or viewer) is also deprived of knowing the true source of the product and may even be deceived into believing that it comes from a different source. . . .

In the film industry, a particular actor's performance, which may have received an award or other critical acclaim, may be the primary attraction for moviegoers. Some actors are said to have such drawing power at the box office that the appearance of their names on the theater marquee can almost guarantee financial success. Such big box office names are built, in part, through being prominently featured in popular films and by receiving appropriate recognition in film credits and advertising. Since actors' fees for pictures, and indeed, their ability to get any work at all, is often based on the drawing power their name may be expected to have at the box office, being accurately credited for films in which they have played would seem to be of critical importance in enabling actors to sell their "services," i.e., their performances. We therefore find that appellant has stated a valid claim for relief under section 43(a) of the Lanham Act. . . .

CONCLUSION

As the district court stated, a section 43(a) claim may be based on practices or conduct "economically equivalent" to palming off. We find that appellant did state such a claim by alleging that defendants engaged in conduct amounting to "express reverse palming off." Since appellant also has standing to sue under section 43(a), the district court's dismissal of the complaint for failure to state a federal claim is reversed. . . .

Lamothe v. Atlantic Recording Corporation, 847 F.2d 1403 (9th Cir. 1988)

THOMPSON, CIRCUIT JUDGE

Robert M. Lamothe and Ronald D. Jones appeal from the district court's grant of summary judgment in favor of Robinson L. Crosby and Juan Croucier, and Atlantic Recording Corp., Marshall Berle, Time Coast Music, Ratt Music, Chappell Music Co., Rightsong Music, Inc., Stephen Pearcy, Warren de Martini, Robert Blotzer, and WEA International, Inc. The district court held that summary judgment was appropriate because Lamothe and Jones failed to establish that section 43(a) of the Lanham Act, 15 U.S.C. § 1125(a), provides relief to co-authors whose names have been omitted from a record album cover and sheet music featuring the co-authored compositions. Because the court concluded that no federal cause of action existed, the court also dismissed the plaintiffs' pendent state law claims for an accounting, defamation, and misattribution of authorship.

We . . . reverse. . . .

II. FACTS

Viewing the evidence in the light most favorable to Lamothe and Jones, the nonmoving parties, the facts pertinent to this appeal are that Lamothe, Jones and Crosby are co-authors of two songs entitled "Scene of the Crime," and "I'm Insane." These works were composed while Lamothe, Jones and Crosby were members of a band called Mac Meda. After Mac Meda disbanded, Crosby joined another musical group called RATT. While Crosby was a member of RATT, he and Juan Croucier licensed the songs at issue to Time Coast Music, which in turn sub-licensed the songs to other of the defendants in this case, including Atlantic Recording. In 1984, Atlantic released an album by the group RATT entitled "Out of the Cellar," which included the recordings of the songs "Scene of the Crime" and "I'm Insane." Because of the popularity of this album, the music and lyrics for all compositions on the album were released in sheet music form by the sub-licensee Chappell Music Co. In both versions (album and sheet music), authorship of the music and lyrics of "I'm Insane" was attributed solely to Robinson Crosby and the music and lyrics of "Scene of the Crime" were attributed to Robinson Crosby and Juan Croucier. Neither Robert Lamothe nor Ronald Jones received credit for their roles in the writing of these songs.

III. ANALYSIS

. . . The principal issue on appeal is whether Lamothe and Jones have stated a claim under section 43(a) of the Lanham Act. . . .

The Lanham Act's prohibition of false designations or representations reaches either goods or services sold in interstate commerce. *Smith v. Montoro*, 648 F.2d 602, 605 (9th Cir. 1981). It has been applied to motion picture representations, *id.*, and the defendants cite no case holding that it does not similarly reach musical compositions. We also note that "[t]o recover for a violation of [section 43(a)] it is not necessary that a mark or trade-mark be registered. The dispositive question is whether the party has a reasonable interest to be protected against false advertising." *Id.* (quoting *New West Corp. v. NYM Co. of Cal.*, 595 F.2d 1194, 1198 (9th Cir. 1979)); see also *Smith*, 648 F.2d at 605 n.3 (collecting cases describing reach of section 43(a)). Finally, we recently have made clear that in cases involving false designation, the actionable "conduct must not only be unfair but must in some discernable way be competitive." *Halicki v. United Artists Communications, Inc.*, 812 F.2d 1213, 1214 (9th Cir. 1987). In the present case, the plaintiffs clearly have a legitimate interest in protecting their work from being falsely designated as the creation of another. The defendants do not dispute that the plaintiffs and Crosby are competitors in the relevant market. Having determined that the plaintiffs have an interest protected by the Lanham Act, we turn our attention to whether the defendants' conduct in this case constitutes a violation of section 43(a).

1. Prohibited Conduct Under Section 43(a)

. . . The Lanham Act applies to two different types of unfair competition in interstate commerce. The first is "palming off" or "passing off," which involves selling a good or service of one person's creation under the name or mark of another. *Smith v. Montoro*, 648 F.2d 602, 604 (9th Cir. 1981). Section 43(a) also reaches false advertising about the goods or services of the advertiser. *U-Haul Int'l, Inc. v. Jartran, Inc.*, 681 F.2d 1159, 1160 (9th Cir. 1982). Because we conclude that Lamothe and Jones, for purposes of surviving a motion for summary judgment, have produced evidence satisfying the elements of a "reverse passing off " claim, we need not decide whether the defendants' actions also constitute false advertising.

2. Passing Off

[In] [t]he leading case in this circuit discussing the "passing off" doctrine embodied in section 43(a) *Smith v. Montoro*, 648 F.2d 602 (9th Cir. 1981). . . .

[w]e concluded . . . that by deleting Smith's name from the film and advertising materials and substituting the name "Bob Spencer," the defendants had engaged in express reverse passing off.

. . . In the present case, taking the allegations of the complaint as true, the defendants engaged in express reverse palming off, by which they deprived Lamothe and Jones of recognition and profits from the release of the two songs that were their due.

The defendants' argument on appeal, reduced to its simplest form is that there can be no express reverse passing off when the designation of a product's source is partially correct. Defendants argue that the failure to attribute authorship to Lamothe and Jones is a "mere omission," which is not actionable under section 43(a). We disagree. We do not read the "falsity" requirement in origination cases so narrowly that a partially accurate designation of origin, which obscures the contribution of another to the final product, is a permissible form of competition. —Several of the cases relied on by the defendants are not applicable to this case. In those cases, removal of identifying letters or symbols from the product of another manufacturer has been said not to violate the Lanham Act. . . . In this case, however, the defendants did not simply remove all trace of the source of the product, which might itself be actionable as implied reverse passing off. . . .

Rather the defendants applied an incomplete designation of the songs' source. Thus, the implied reverse passing off cases on which the defendants seek to rely are not applicable.] . . .

In the present case, the defendants unilaterally decided to attribute authorship to less than all of the joint authors of the musical compositions. Had the defendants decided to attribute authorship to a fictitious person, to the group "RATT," or to some other person, this would be a false designation of origin. It seems to us no less "false" to attribute authorship to only one of several co-authors. . . .

The policies we identified in *Smith,* namely, ensuring that the producer of a good or service receives appropriate recognition and that the consuming public receives full information about the origin of the good, apply with equal force here. An incomplete designation of the source of the good or service is no less misleading because it is partially correct. Misbranding a product to only partially identify its source is the economic equivalent of passing off one person's product under the name or mark of another. And the Smith case makes clear that in assessing section 43(a) claims, courts are to consider whether the challenged "practices or conduct [are] 'economically equivalent' to palming off." *Smith,* 648 F.2d at 605.

3. Liability of Licensees

. . . Atlantic Recording and the other licensees or sublicensees of Crosby and Croucier argue that even if Lamothe and Jones have stated a section 43(a) claim, they cannot be held liable because they are licensees. We disagree. Some of the licensees may have been involved in affixing an incomplete designation of authorship. These licensees would be liable under section 43(a) regardless of knowledge. See 15 U.S.C. § 1125(a). The express language of section 43(a) also imposes liability upon those who "with knowledge of the falsity of such designation of origin, cause or procure the same to be transported or used in commerce." *Id.* The licensees have cited no case holding that a licensee is exempt from the prohibitions of the Lanham Act. Whether the licensees affixed the incomplete authorship or had knowledge of the false designation of origin are matters best left to the trier of fact to resolve.

IV. CONCLUSION

Because we conclude that Summary judgment was inappropriate, we reverse the decision of the district court and remand the case with instructions to reinstate Lamothe's and Jones's federal causes of action. . . .

NOTE

Relief under Section 43(a) is essentially dependent on commercial injury. In the absence of customer confusion or evidence of intentional deception, a plaintiff cannot recover damages under Section 43(a). *Bernbach v. Harmony Books,* 48 U.S.P.Q.2d

1696, 1998 WL 726009 (SDNY 1998) (Copyright Office registration erroneously listed a co-author; however, book as published listed only plaintiff, who made no showing of customer confusion or economic harm).

2.5.2.2 Right to Disclaim Credit

King v. Innovation Books, 976 F.2d 824 (2d Cir. 1992)

MINER, CIRCUIT JUDGE

[The lower court granted famed author Stephen King preliminary injunction in favor of plaintiff-appellee Stephen King, agreeing with King that defendants had] falsely designated him as the originator of the motion picture "The Lawnmower Man, . . . The injunction, which prohibits any use of King's name "on or in connection with" the movie, encompasses two forms of credit to which King objected: (i) a possessory credit, describing the movie as "Stephen King's The Lawnmower Man," and (ii) a "based upon" credit, representing that the movie is "based upon" a short story by King. For the reasons that follow, we affirm the district court's order to the extent that it prohibits use of the possessory credit, but reverse the order to the extent that it prohibits use of the "based upon" credit.

BACKGROUND

In 1970, King wrote a short story entitled "The Lawnmower Man" (the "Short Story") [which] involves Harold Parkette, a homeowner in the suburbs. Parkette begins to neglect his lawn after an incident in which the boy who usually mows his lawn mows over a cat. By the time Parkette focuses his attention again on his overgrown lawn, the boy has gone away to college. Parkette therefore hires a new man to mow his lawn. The lawnmower man turns out to be a cleft-footed, obese and vile agent of the pagan god Pan. The lawnmower man also is able to move the lawnmower psychokinetically—that is, by sheer force of mind.

After starting the lawnmower, the lawnmower man removes his clothing and crawls after the running mower on his hands and knees, eating both grass and a mole that the mower has run over. Parkette, who is watching in horror, phones the police. Using his psychokinetic powers, however, the lawnmower man directs the lawnmower after Parkette, who is chopped up by the lawnmower's blades after being chased through his house. The Short Story ends with the discovery by the police of Parkette's entrails in the birdbath behind the home. In 1978, King assigned to Great Fantastic Picture Corporation the motion picture and television rights for the Short Story. The assignment agreement, which provided that it was to be governed by the laws of England, allowed the assignee the "exclusive right to deal with the [Short Story] as [it] may think fit," including the rights

(i) to write film treatments [and] scripts and other dialogue versions of all descriptions of the [Short Story] and at all times to add to[,] take from[,] use[,] alter[,] adapt . . . and change the [Short Story] and the title[,] characters[,] plot[,] theme[,] dialogue[,] sequences and situations thereof. . . .

(ii) to make or produce films of all kinds . . . incorporating or based upon the [Short Story] or any part or parts thereof or any adaptation thereof.

In return, King received an interest in the profits of "each" film "based upon" the Short Story.

In February 1990, Great Fantastic transferred its rights under the assignment agreement to Allied [one of the defendants, another UK-based company, which] commissioned a screenplay for a feature-length film entitled "The Lawnmower Man." The screenplay was completed by August 1990, and pre-production work on the movie began in January 1991. By February 1991, Allied began to market the forthcoming movie by placing advertisements in trade magazines and journals. The picture generally was described as "Stephen King's The Lawnmower Man," and as "based upon" a short story by King. Actual filming of the movie began in May 1991. About one month later, Allied, through its United States subsidiary, licensed New Line, a domestic corporation with offices in New York and California, to distribute the movie in North America. The licensing agreement was concluded in California, and a press release announcing the distribution deal was issued from that state as well. New Line initially paid $250,000 for the distribution rights, with an additional $2.25 million to be paid thereafter.

King learned of the forthcoming movie in early October 1991, from an article in a film magazine. He then contacted Rand Holston, an agent handling King's film rights, in an attempt to gather information about the film; asked Chuck Verrill, his literary agent, to obtain a "rough cut" of the movie; and instructed Jay Kramer, his lawyer, to inform Allied that King did not like the idea of a possessory credit (a form of credit apparently portended by the article).

By letter dated October 9, 1991, Kramer advised Allied that King "did not want" a possessory credit to appear on the film. Kramer also requested a copy of the movie and the tentative movie credits King was to receive. In another letter to Allied dated October 21, 1991—written after Kramer secured a copy of the movie's screenplay—Kramer advised that "we emphatically object" to the possessory credit contained in the screenplay, and noted that he had yet to receive a copy of the tentative credits.

It appears that King learned of New Line's involvement with the film in November 1991. On King's direction, Verrill contacted New Line for a copy of the film. Verrill was informed that a copy would not be available until January 1992. Verrill contacted New Line again on February 6, 1992, but this produced no copy of the film either. Kramer and Holston shortly advised New Line, in a February 18, 1992, telephone call with New Line's President of Production Sara Risher, that King was "outraged" that the movie was being described as "Stephen King's The Lawnmower Man."

In a February 28, 1992, letter, Kramer again insisted to Risher that the possessory credit was a "complete misrepresentation," and attached copies of the October 1991 letters sent to Allied. As of this time, New Line had paid the balance of the price due to Allied for purchase of the distribution rights, had expended about $7.5 million in advertising and marketing costs, and had become committed to release the movie in theaters throughout North America.

On March 3, 1992—four days or so before release of the movie in theaters—King viewed a copy of the movie in a screening arranged by Allied and New Line. The protagonist of the two hour movie is Dr. Lawrence Angelo. Experimenting with chimpanzees, Dr. Angelo develops a technology, based on computer simulation, known as "Virtual Reality," which allows a chimp to enter a three-dimensional computer environment simulating various action scenarios. Dr. Angelo hopes to adapt the technology for human use, with the ultimate goal of accelerating and improving human intelligence.

Eventually, Dr. Angelo begins experimenting with his technology on Jobe, who mows lawns in Dr. Angelo's neighborhood and is referred to as "the lawnmower man." Jobe, a normal-looking young man, is simple and possesses a childlike mentality. Dr. Angelo is able greatly to increase Jobe's intellect with Virtual Reality technology. However, the experiment spins out of control, with Jobe becoming hostile and violent as his intelligence and mental abilities become super-human. In the build-up to the movie's climax, Jobe employs his newly acquired psychokinetic powers to chase Dr. Angelo's neighbor (a man named Harold Parkette) through his house with a running lawnmower, and to kill him. The police discover the dead man's remains in the birdbath behind his home, and, in the climax of the movie, Dr. Angelo destroys Jobe.

The film and advertising seen by King contained both possessory and "based upon" credits. On the evening of March 3, after viewing the film, King wrote to Holston:

I think The Lawnmower Man is really an extraordinary piece of work, at least visually, and the core of my story, such as it is, is in the movie. I think it is going to be very successful and I want to get out of the way. I want you to make clear to [the] trolls at New Line Pictures that I am unhappy with them, but I am shelving* any ideas of taking out ads in the trades or trying to obtain an injunction to stop New Line from advertising or exploiting the picture. I would like to talk to you late this week or early next about doing some brief interviews which will make my lack of involvement clear, but for the time being, I am just going to step back and shut up.
    *At least for the time being.

In a March 23, 1992 letter, Kramer again advised Allied of King's "long standing objection" to the possessory credit, and also took note of "the apparent failure of [Allied] to inform New Line of Mr. King's objection until the movie was about to be released." However, no objection to the "based upon" credit ever was registered until May 20, 1992.

From March through May 1992, New Line expended another $2.5 million in promotion and entered into certain hotel movie and television commitments, as well as home video arrangements.

King initiated the instant suit on May 28, 1992, seeking damages as well as injunctive relief. He claimed that the possessory and "based upon" credits violated section 43(a) of the Lanham Act, see 15 U.S.C. § 1125(a), as well as the New York common law of unfair competition and contracts, the New York General Business Law, and the New York Civil Rights Law. A motion for preliminary injunction was made on June 3, and a hearing was held on June 29.

The district court agreed with King on all of his claims and granted the injunction on July 2, concluding that the possessory credit was false on its face, that the "based upon" credit was misleading, and that the irreparable harm element of a preliminary injunction action had been satisfied. The equitable defenses of laches, estoppel and waiver interposed by Allied and New Line were rejected.

The injunction prohibited use of King's name "on or in connection with" the motion picture, and by its terms encompassed both the possessory and "based upon" credits. The injunction applied to distribution of the film by Allied abroad as well as by New Line in North America, either in theaters or on videocassette or on television. We granted appellants' application for a stay pending this expedited appeal, but conditioned the stay upon suspension of use of the possessory credit. At oral argument counsel for New Line informed us that the videocassettes of the movie now in circulation contain only the "based upon" credit.

DISCUSSION

I. Likelihood of Success on the Merits . . .

A. *The Possessory Credit*

We perceive no error in the district court's conclusion that King is likely to succeed on the merits of his objection to the possessory credit [under Section 43(a) of the Lanham Act, 15 U.S.C. § 1125(a) (1988)]. The district court was entirely entitled to conclude, from the testimony at the preliminary injunction hearing, that a possessory credit ordinarily is given to the producer, director or writer of the film; and that the credit at a minimum refers to an individual who had some involvement in, and/or gave approval to, the screenplay or movie itself. In contrast to other films for which he has been given a possessory credit, King had no involvement in, and gave no approval of, "The Lawnmower Man" screenplay or movie.

Under the circumstances, therefore, the arguments advanced by [defendants] as to why the possessory credit is not false—that the other movie credits make clear that King was not the producer, director or writer of the film, and that King has in the past received a possessory credit where he merely approved in advance of the screenplay or movie—do not alter the conclusion that King is likely to succeed on his challenge to the possessory credit. Appellants also contend that King offered no evidence of public confusion in relation to the possessory credit. As will be detailed in our discussion of irreparable harm, however, there was some such evidence offered. In any event, as the district court recognized, no evidence of public confusion is required where, as is the case with the possessory credit, the attribution is false on its face. See *PPX Enterprises, Inc. v. Audiofidelity Enterprises, Inc.*, 818 F.2d 266, 272 (2d Cir. 1987) (citations omitted).

B. The "Based Upon" Credit

As the district court recognized, a "based upon" credit by definition affords more "leeway" than a possessory credit. The district court nevertheless concluded that the "based upon" credit at issue here is misleading and likely to cause confusion to the public, reasoning in essence that the "climactic scene from the Short Story is inserted into the film in a manner wholly unrelated to the Plot of the film," and that the credit "grossly exaggerates" the relationship between the Short Story and the film. While particular findings of fact are subject to the clearly erroneous standard of review, we have said that the weighing of factors in "the ultimate determination of the likelihood of confusion is a legal issue subject to de novo appellate review." *Hasbro, Inc. v. Lanard Toys, Ltd.*, 858 F.2d 70, 75–76 (2d Cir. 1988) (citations omitted) (Lanham Act trade mark claim). We believe that in so heavily weighing the proportion of the film attributable to the Short Story in the course of finding the "based upon" credit to be misleading and confusing, the district court applied a standard without sufficient support in the testimony and applicable law.

John Breglio, an attorney of the law firm of Paul, Weiss, Rifkind, Wharton & Garrison specializing in entertainment law, testified as an expert witness for King. Breglio opined that the term "based upon," in the context of royalty obligations under King's assignment agreement, was not identical to the term "based upon" in a movie credit. After speaking of a test of "substantial similarity" between the literary work and movie, and opining that there was not substantial similarity between the Short Story and the film, Breglio went on to state that the industry standard for determining the meaning of a "based upon" movie credit is very similar to that used by copyright lawyers in examining issues of copyright infringement. Breglio further explained that this standard involved looking "at the work as a whole and how much protected material from the underlying work appears in the derivative work."

Indeed, in cases of alleged copyright infringement it has long been appropriate to examine the quantitative and qualitative degree to which the allegedly infringed work has been borrowed from, and not simply the proportion of the allegedly infringing work that is made up of the copyrighted material. See *Harper & Row v. Nation Enterprises*, 471 U.S. 539, 565–66, 85 L. Ed. 2d 588, 105 S. Ct. 2218 (1985) (citing *Sheldon v. Metro-Goldwyn Pictures Corp.*, 81 F.2d 49, 56 (2d Cir.) (L. Hand, J.), cert. denied, 298 U.S. 669, 80 L. Ed. 1392, 56 S. Ct. 835 (1936)). Accordingly, the propriety of the "based upon" credit should have been evaluated with less emphasis on the proportion of the film attributable to the Short Story, and with more emphasis on the proportion, in quantitative and qualitative terms, of the Short Story appearing in the film. Where a movie draws in material respects from a literary work, both quantitatively and qualitatively, a "based upon" credit should not be viewed as misleading absent persuasive countervailing facts and circumstances. Our concern is the possibility that under the district court's apparent approach, substantially all of a literary work could be taken for use in a film and, if unrelated ideas, themes and scenes are tacked on or around the extracted work, a "based upon" credit would be deemed misleading.

In the case before us, the apparent "core" of the ten page Short Story—a scene in which a character called "the lawnmower man" uses psychokinetic powers to chase another character through his house with a running lawnmower and thereby kill him—is used in the movie. In both the movie and the Short Story, the remains of the murdered man (who is named Harold Parkette in both works) are found in the birdbath by the police; the two police officers in both works have the same names and engage in substantially similar dialogue. As King himself described it, "the core of my story, such as it is, is in the movie." The red lawnmower seen in the movie also appears to be as described in the Short Story. A brief reference to the Pan mythology of the Short Story appears in the movie as well; dialogue between Jobe and another character includes a reference to "Pan pipes of the little people in the grass."

We recognize that several important and entertaining aspects of the Short Story were not used in the film, and that conversely the film contains a number of elements not to be found in the Short Story. However, when the resemblances between the Short Story and the motion picture at issue here are considered together, they establish to our satisfaction that the movie draws in sufficiently material respects on the Short Story in both qualitative and quantitative aspects.

Nor are there any persuasive countervailing facts or circumstances in the record to lead us away from the conclusion that the "based upon" credit is proper in this case. King himself apparently was not bothered much (if at all) by the "based upon" credit, in marked contrast to his sustained and strong objections to the possessory credit, until shortly before he initiated this suit. He has not pointed us to evidence in the record of industry or public perception of, or confusion over, the "based upon" credit beyond the thoughts offered by Breglio. Professor George Stade, Vice Chairman of the English Department at Columbia University and King's other expert witness, did opine that, despite similarities, the movie was not based upon the Short Story. However, even Professor Stade indicated at one point in his testimony that "substantial" portions of the Short Story appear in the film.

In *Gilliam v. American Broadcasting Companies, Inc.*, 538 F.2d 14 (2d Cir. 1976), we found a violation of section 43(a) by the ABC television network, which had aired, under license from the BBC, the "Monty Python's Flying Circus" programs of the British comedy group. Monty Python's agreement with the BBC gave the comedy group substantial control over any editing by the BBC. See *id.* at 17. However, ABC on its own substantially edited the programs it aired under the BBC license, so as to eliminate many thematically essential and humorous portions of the original programs. See *id.* at 24–25 & n.12. King suggests, in disputing the legitimacy of the "based upon" credit, that Allied's treatment of the Short Story is analogous to ABC's editing in Gilliam.

However, at issue in Gilliam were original Monty Python programs which were edited by ABC and then rebroadcast as Monty Python's work. We specifically noted that Monty Python was being "presented to the public as the creator of a work not [its] own, and [made] subject to criticism for work [it] has not done." *Id.* at 24 (quotation omitted). While Gilliam certainly supports the view we have taken of the possessory credit, the case is not very helpful in evaluating the accuracy of a "based upon" credit, which by definition deals with altered and derivative works.

It is undoubtedly the case that King's assignment agreement does not permit Allied to use King's name fraudulently, and we express no view as to the degree of overlap between the term "based upon" in the King assignment agreement and the term "based upon" in a theatrical credit. However, we do note that the agreement contemplates substantial alterations to the Short Story, and even obligates Allied to give King credit in the case of a film "based wholly or substantially upon" the Short Story. We think that King would have cause to complain if he were not afforded the "based upon" credit.

II. Irreparable Harm

As the district court observed, a presumption of irreparable harm arises in Lanham Act cases once the plaintiff establishes likelihood of success on a claim of literal falseness, as King has established with respect to the possessory credit. . . . Nothing in the record persuades us that the district court erred in concluding that this presumption was not rebutted.

Appellants contend that any presumption of irreparable injury was rebutted because King delayed in seeking relief. However, the greatest conceivable delay attributable to King is about eight months: from early October 1991, when he first learned of the movie, to early June 1992, when he moved for a preliminary injunction. During that time, however, King, through his agents, contacted Allied and New Line and repeatedly objected to any use of a possessory credit, and attempted to obtain the screenplay, tentative credits and film for viewing. This is not conduct that undercuts a sense of urgency or of an imminent threat, and indeed the circumstances in this case contrast with those in which we have found a delay negating the presumption of irreparable harm.

In *Citibank, N.A. v. Citytrust*, 756 F.2d 273 (2d Cir. 1985), for example, we held that an irreparable harm presumption was negated where New York's Citibank delayed bringing suit for nine months after having notice that Connecticut's Citytrust intended to open a branch in the New York area. We pointed out that Citibank made no effort to verify the opening of Citytrust's branch, made no objection concerning the branch, and had made no real objection to Citytrust's advertising in New York media markets in past years. . . . Also to be considered is that a great deal of King's alleged delay was attributable to problems in acquiring a copy of the film from appellants. See *Horgan v. Mac-Millan, Inc.*, 789 F.2d 157, 164 (2d Cir. 1986) (expressing doubt that plaintiff delayed unduly in seeking preliminary injunctive relief where only "general intentions" of alleged copyright infringer were known and plaintiff had trouble obtaining advance copy of alleged infringer's work).

The March 3 letter written by King to Rand Holston, in which King indicated that he was impressed by the movie and that he was "shelving" legal action, together with apparently similar remarks made by King to counsel at that time, could be viewed as countering an irreparable harm presumption. However, the district court did not accept this argument, and we are unable to find error in this under all the circumstances. While King refers in the letter to shelving action against New Line's advertising of the picture, King does not say in the letter that he is shelving action against Allied or action in relation to the credits appearing in the movie itself. Further, because of the references in the letter to "at least for the time being" and "at this time," King's reactions as of March 3 could be viewed as tentative in nature. Indeed, shortly after King's March 3 letter was written, Kramer again wrote to Allied to reiterate King's "long standing objection" to the movie's possessory credit.

Appellants also suggest that the presumption of irreparable harm was rebutted because King himself enjoyed the movie, continues to be a popular literary figure, and was unable to specify particular financial injury. However, we have observed that the irreparable harm in cases such as this often flows not so much from some specific reduction "in fact" to an individual's name or reputation, but rather from the wrongful attribution to the individual, in the eye of the general public, of responsibility for actions over which he or she has no control. . . .

In this connection, King testified to the obvious point that his name and artistic reputation are his major assets, and offered into evidence certain unfavorable reviews of the movie. These reviews tended to discuss the movie in possessory terms and portray the work as a kind of failure on the part of King personally—persuasive evidence of the type of damage and confusion caused by the possessory credit. One reviewer, for instance, who thought the movie uninspiring, commented sarcastically: "Coming next week to a theater near you: Stephen King's Grocery List." Another review began with the statement that "Steven [sic]

King's latest film, The Lawnmower Man, continues to reinforce the impression that he and Hollywood just don't work well together." . . .

CONCLUSION

The order of the district court granting a preliminary injunction is affirmed to the extent it prohibits use of the possessory credit, but reversed to the extent it prohibits use of a "based upon" credit.

Follett v. Arbor House Publishing Co., Inc., 497 F. Supp. 304 (SDNY 1980)

SWEET, DISTRICT JUDGE

This action presents questions arising out of the intended publication by Arbor House this fall of a book, *The Gentlemen of 16 July*, which Arbor House intends to attribute to Follett as principal author, "with Rene Louis Maurice," a pseudonym for three French authors. Follett has written *Key to Rebecca*, which will also be published by New American this fall, and seeks to restrain Arbor House from publishing *The Gentlemen of 16 July* and from using the currently proposed authorship attribution. Arbor House seeks to restrain Follett, Morrow, and New American from disparaging *The Gentlemen of 16 July* and its authorship attribution. The principal statute involved is section 43 of the Lanham Act, 15 U.S.C. § 1125, and in varying degrees counsel agree that there is no directly relevant precedent.

The issue for decision is both unique and fascinating, requiring the court to consider the practices in the publishing industry with respect to authorship attributions, the meteoric rise of Follett as a novelist, the distinction between creating and editing a literary work, and ultimately, the effect of all of this on the public. Based upon the evidence that has been presented by highly skilled counsel, at least one of whom has authored as well as litigated, an injunction must issue requiring Arbor House to indicate that *The Gentlemen of 16 July* is a work of nonfiction written by Rene Louis Maurice with Ken Follett, with attribution to be equal and in chronological order—that is, with Rene Louis Maurice first. The following constitutes the court's findings of fact and conclusions of law.

Despite the difficulty in reaching the ultimate conclusions relating to creativity and publishing integrity, the facts revealed by the testimony and the exhibits are largely undisputed.

On July 16, 1976, Albert Spaggiari and his confederates began tunnelling under the streets of Nice, France. By July 19, 1976, they had reached their goal, a bank vault, and had removed some 60 million francs of property in various forms. Subsequently, certain of the confederates were apprehended, as was Spaggiari. On March 10, 1977, by a dramatic leap from a courthouse window, Spaggiari escaped. These events were, of course, chronicled in the press at the time.

Shortly after the theft, three French journalists collaborated on a book-length account of these events. This account was published in France as "Cinq Milliards au Bout de l'Egout" under the attribution Rene Louis Maurice, the pseudonym of the three reporters. Jean Claude Simoen certified in May 1977 that he was the author of this work. Be that as it may, Clemens von Bezard, the director and principal owner of the Star Agency Establishment ("Star"), a Liechtenstein company engaged in publishing, acquiring and licensing literary rights, entered into negotiations with Simoen. As a consequence of those negotiations, Bezard testified that he acquired the right to publish the account outside France. Bezard translated the account into German and had it translated into English by Jeffrey Robinson.

In the summer of 1977, Bezard communicated with his agent in England, Burnett Rigg, to arrange for publication of the account by a British publisher. As a consequence of Rigg's efforts, William Collins Sons & Company Ltd. ("Collins") purchased the account for publication by Fontana Paperbacks, a division of Collins.

At the same time, Follett became involved, also through Rigg who acted as his agent. Follett had started his literary career by working as a reporter. By 1977 he had written ten books, including one children's novel and two thrillers, seven of which had been published under a byline other than Ken Follett. To further his knowledge of his profession, he had sought and obtained employment as an editor and had progressed to a position as deputy managing director of a publishing house.

Rigg suggested to Collins and Star that Follett be given the translation to review and, according to the final agreement between Star and Collins, to edit the work and prepare it for publication. On July 12, Follett wrote to Rigg suggesting that considerable work was required, including restructuring the story, bringing style to the writing, exploiting the drama, developing the characters and filling in gaps. On August 5, 1977, Simon King, on behalf of Collins, agreed to pay Follett 850 pounds "for refashioning the typescript" as Follett had suggested, on condition that Follett visit Nice to obtain background material. Thereafter Follett went to work to revise the manuscript which was subsequently published under the title *The Heist of the Century*.

Follett is an efficient, careful and diligent ex-reporter and editor. Fortunately for this writer, his work is carefully detailed and explicit. First, he prepared his "schema" for rewrite, a six-page document posing certain questions to which Follett sought answers. He sent this to Bezard, and it was followed up by a trip to Nice in September 1977.

In Nice, Follett was met by Bezard. They visited certain of the locations referred to in the account and were joined by Carolyn Atkinson, then a part-time employee of Bezard. The next day, Saturday, was spent without progress on the assignment, but on Sunday, Bezard, Follett and Atkinson met with Rene Cenni, one of the journalists who had written the French account. Atkinson translated and Follett meticulously recorded Cenni's answers to the questions posed in the "schema."

During this working luncheon, Follett requested by-line credit from Bezard, a request casually and quickly granted in order not to raise the issue in Cenni's presence.

On his return Follett worked daily for twelve days using the Robinson translation, a second translation of the French account, newspaper clippings, his own notes and the "schema." The work when completed contained between 42,000 and 43,000 words on 160 printed pages. It was submitted to Rigg on September 26, 1977. King's response in late November characterized the work as a "rewrite," "splendid," and "terrific."

Notwithstanding this reaction, the question of copyright and attribution was not so satisfactorily resolved. King refused Follett's requested copyright, citing Rigg, but agreed to credit Follett on the title page. Follett insisted on a copyright for his "rewrite," claimed a further financial interest in the book, and implied that legal action would be taken to enforce his position. Letters were exchanged and then on May 22, 1978, David Grossman, Follett's London agent, assured King that no copyright claim would be made by Follett, and that the attribution of "Rene Louis Maurice with Ken Follett" on the title page would be satisfactory to Follett.

The Heist of the Century was published in England in the fashion just described, namely "Rene Louis Maurice with Ken Follett" on the title page, and the pseudonym alone on the cover. It was thereafter offered to at least seven publishing houses in the United States by Zuckerman in May 1978. No publication ensued, and New American declined the book again in the fall of 1979.

Also in the fall of 1977, Follet contracted for the publication in the United States of his book *Storm Island,* which had already come out in England. It was retitled *Eye of the Needle,* and Arbor House, the publisher, embarked upon a campaign to promote the book. The book was a great success, achieving best seller status, and possessed what Donald Fine, the president and chief executive officer of Arbor House, described as "narrative drive." It was in the view of this reviewer an exciting spy story, laid in England during World War II with a challenging plot animated, as Follett explained, not only by external events but also by the characters of the protagonists. This was particularly so with respect to its dramatic denouement.

Arbor House obtained an option for Follett's next book, ultimately titled *Triple,* a tale involving espionage relating to the establishment of nuclear capacity by Israel. Follett had also conceived of a plot relating to Marshal Rommel's desert campaign and the espionage and counterespionage which was involved. Fine liked the World War II plot better than *Triple* and urged Follett to let Arbor House publish it. However, Follett decided to proceed with *Triple* partly, according to Fine, to avoid being typed as an author writing only about the World War II period. *Triple* was submitted to Arbor House in outline form late in 1978, and the manuscript was delivered early in 1979.

A dispute over editing ensued, Follett threatened litigation to bar certain changes in the manuscript, the matter was resolved, and *Triple* was published successfully, completing Follett's obligation to Arbor House.

Follett then contracted with New American for future works and received an advance against royalties of $3,000,000 for his next three books. He delivered the first of these, *Key to Rebecca*, the desert campaign book, early this year and its publication this fall was announced to the trade in the spring. *Key to Rebecca* will be a volume of 384 pages to be sold for $12.95.

In May 1980, Star, still claiming possession of the rights to *The Heist of the Century*, retained Meredith to represent its interests in the United States. On May 13, Star sent Fine the book to review for publication. Shortly after reading it, Fine determined to publish the book as *The Gentlemen of 16 July* and entered into a contract with Star which provided for a $25,000 advance royalty payment. Fine knew of New American's plans for the publication of *Key to Rebecca* in the fall.

Arbor House has prepared a jacket for *The Gentlemen of 16 July* that has the following authorship attribution.

by the author [of] TRIPLE and EYE OF THE NEEDLE
   KEN FOLLETT
   with Rene Louis Maurice

Only Follett's name is listed on the spine portion of the jacket. *The Gentlemen of 16 July* is expected to constitute 208 printed pages and to sell for $9.95.

No cases have been brought to the attention of the court relating to the question of attribution, and the testimony established contrasting practices in the publishing industry. Different attributions which frequently are used include "as told to," "by," "with," and co-authorship. One witness testified that there is no difference between "by" and "with" with respect to attribution. There are instances of publication of books under the name of one author actually written by another, without attribution, or written entirely by one author with principal attribution to another. These attributions are arrived at by negotiations with the authors and the direction of the publisher. There was testimony that if the publisher possesses all the rights, the attribution is at his discretion.

Both Arbor House and Morrow plan to promote their respective Follett books vigorously, have announced their intentions to the trade, and have invested substantial sums in the promotion and publication of their respective books. Both books are scheduled for release this fall. All parties agree that the critical and public success of each book will substantially affect sales of the other. No testimony concerning public opinion was presented, and it is difficult, if not impossible, to conceive how such evidence could be obtained as events now stand.

Much of the evidence, naturally, centered on an analysis of Follett's work which resulted in the *The Heist of the Century*, retitled for United States publication as *The Gentlemen of 16 July*, including a line-by-line comparison of Follett's product and its principal predecessor, the Robinson version. What is without challenge is that Follett added to the previous versions a prologue, an epilogue, chapter headings, about half a page of analysis of Spaggiari's psychology obtained conveniently from a next-door neighbor of Follett's who was a psychologist, and details obtained from Cenni. It is also conceded that Follett eliminated the frequent use of flashback in favor of a chronological march of events, and made alterations to Anglicize the references. In addition, the work was rewritten, and characterizations were sharpened. . . .

While there are a number of instances of re-writing of this kind, which enhance the personalities of the characters for the reader, the characterizations themselves remain essentially the same as depicted by the French authors. The incidents reported are unchanged though the sequence is altered so that each follows chronologically. There can be no doubt that to the reader of the English language, *The Heist of the Century* is a more compelling version of the historical events surrounding the Nice bank robbery than the Robinson translation. . . .

Although hired to edit according to the Star/Collins agreement, Follett did more. Fine, a concerned and capable editor who is justly proud of his ability to discern works of quality and even to improve them, drew the line between editing and authorship on a practical level. He noted that authors do not permit editors to obtain authorship credit, as a practical matter, even if the revisions are substantial. Here, Follett in fact rewrote the work. The language and presentation of the work were substantially improved and altered. Follett sought and obtained some authorship credit, though less than he felt he had earned at the time. . . .

Although the parties have attempted to frame the issues in this case in different, and in some respects contradictory fashion, the controlling question is whether the attribution to Ken Follett as the principal author of *The Gentlemen of 16 July* constitutes a false representation and false designation of origin. . . .

In *Gieseking v. Urania Records, Inc.*, 17 Misc.2d 1034, 155 N.Y.S.2d 171 (N.Y. Co. Sup. Ct. 1956), the court suggested that an author has a right under the New York Civil Rights law to ensure that any attribution to him accurately reflects his contribution to a manuscript. The court stated, "A performer has a property right in his performance that it shall not be used for a purpose not intended, and particularly in a manner which does not fairly represent his services." By analogy, it may well be that Follett is entitled to an accurate description of his role in preparing *The Gentlemen of 16 July*. Any rights which he may hold in this regard are co-extensive with his right under the Lanham Act, discussed below.

Arbor House and Meredith contend that the Lanham Act issues in this case are controlled by a determination as to whether Follett's version of *The Heist of the Century* was copyrightable under the Copyright Act, 17 U.S.C. §§ 101 *et seq.* They urge that Follett's version could have been copyrighted, since in a non-fiction work such as *The Heist of the Century,* the right to obtain a copyright derives from the form of words in which events are recounted, and not from the interpretation of the events themselves. See *Hoehling v. Universal City Studios, Inc.,* 618 F.2d 972 (2d Cir. 1980). Arbor House and Meredith point out that the form of the manuscript after Follett's editing differs substantially from that which he received as to the words used, the order of events, the development of characters and the depiction of events, so that Follett's edited version was copyrightable. . . .

However, the analysis of whether an editing or rewriting of an existing manuscript is copyrightable should not control the Lanham Act issue presented here. . . .

Although an edited version would apparently be copyrightable so long as the editor's alterations were more than "merely trivial," it could still be misleading to designate that editor as the principal author of the work. Thus the fact that Follett sought and might have been entitled to obtain a copyright interest in his edited version is not dispositive of the issue before the court.

The parties have submitted conflicting evidence as to trade practices in the publishing industry. Meredith and Arbor House contend that if an individual makes a contribution to a literary work which bears certain indicia of authorship, that person can be described as an author and the form of attribution rests within the discretion of the publisher. Follett, New American and Morrow have presented evidence that even the substantial revisions performed by Follett amount to no more than what is customarily performed by freelance editors. They contend that such alterations rarely, if ever, result in the editor's receiving authorship credit.

These industry practices are largely irrelevant to the issues in this case. Even if an attribution of authorship were consistent with industry practices, it would nevertheless be illegal under the Lanham Act if it misrepresented the contribution of the person designated as author.

The key issue, then, is whether the designation of authorship which Arbor House proposes to utilize on the cover of *The Gentlemen of 16 July* constitutes a violation of section 43(a) of the Lanham Act, 15 U.S.C. § 1125(a). . . . Section 43(a) is designed to provide a statutory cause of action for false description or advertisement of goods by any person likely to be injured by such description or advertising. . . . In order to determine whether a description or representation is false, a court should first assess the meaning of particular representations and then determine whether the claims made are false. . . . Where a description concerning goods is unambiguous, the court can grant relief based on its own findings of falsity without resort to evidence of the reaction of consumers of the goods. . . . Moreover, in order to obtain injunctive relief under the Lanham Act, a plaintiff need only establish a "likelihood of confusion or a tendency to mislead." . . .

The attribution of authorship of *The Gentlemen of 16 July* as designated on the cover and title page of the book and in Arbor House's advertisements, contains an unambiguous representation that Follett is the principal author of the book. The name Ken Follett is printed in bold typeface approximately 15 mm. high. The subtitle, "with Rene Louis Maurice," is printed in much smaller type and is only 6 mm. in height. Above Ken Follett's name, the notation "by the author of TRIPLE and EYE OF THE NEEDLE" appears in type 4 mm. high. The name Ken Follett appears on the spine of the book unaccompanied by any reference to "Rene Louis Maurice." This attribution clearly indicates that Ken Follett is the principal author of the book.

The concept of authorship is elusive and inexact. Although I do not presuppose to offer a definitive analysis of qualities which give rise to authorship, some such definition is essential to a resolution of the issue before the court. The parties have cited no cases in which the concept of authorship has been carefully dissected, and this court has discovered none.

Arbor House and Meredith contend that Follett is the principal author of *The Gentlemen of 16 July* because of his substantial contribution to the form of the book. The actual words used in the final draft were supplied in large measure by Follett. Follett altered the method of telling the story by shifting the chronology and removing flashbacks. The characters are more vividly portrayed in Follett's edited version than in the draft he received. Follett has modulated the unfolding of events carefully in order to achieve what Fine described as "narrative drive" and to enhance the dramatic effect of the plot. Follett's contribution bears certain indicia of authorship. His alterations were substantial, and the finished product bears the mark of his style and craftsmanship.

Yet, these refinements are not sufficient to render Follett the principal author of the book. Authorship connotes something more than style, form and narrative approach. It includes a special element of creativity, of the definition of scope and content. In this case, Follett received a fixed plot, a cast of characters and a set of themes and reworked these elements to make them more palatable and comprehensible to the intended audience. He neither conceived the framework or format of the book, nor played a substantial role in selecting the material to be included. Almost every significant occurrence, personality and theme can be traced directly to the materials from which Follett worked.

As a result, although Follett's revisions may have been more substantial than those which an editor would ordinarily perform in correcting, polishing and revising, it is misleading to depict him as the principal author of *The Gentlemen of 16 July*. His contributions display none of the special creative attributes which are associated with authorship. Thus, the representation that Follett is the principal author of the book is literally false. . . .

The Lanham Act . . . is designed not only to vindicate "the author's personal right to prevent the presentation of his work to the public in a distorted form," . . . but also to protect the public and the artist from misrepresentations of the artist's contribution to a finished work.

Based on the facts found and legal conclusions reached, judgment will be granted in favor of Follett, Morrow and New American. Although the court must proceed cautiously in dictating the form of presentation of *The Gentlemen of 16 July*, some accommodation is essential to assure that the public will not be misled by the attribution of authorship, yet protect Arbor House's legitimate commercial interests in publication of the work. Arbor House will be required to give equal attribution to Rene Louis Maurice and Ken Follett, in that order, and to indicate on the cover and jacket that the work is non-fiction. . . .

NOTES _____

1. In *Shostakovich v. Twentieth Century-Fox Film Corp.*, 196 Misc. 67, 80 N.Y.S.2d 575 (Sup. Ct. N.Y. County 1948), four internationally renown composers, Dmitry Shostakovich, Serge Prokofieff, Aram Khachaturian, Nicholai Miashovsky, sued Twentieth Century Fox to enjoin use of the their names and music related to the film "The Iron Curtain." The film depicted disclosures of espionage in Canada by U.S.S.R representatives. The plaintiffs sought an injunction on four grounds: 1) invasion of the right to privacy under § 51 of the Civil Rights Law, 2) publication of libelous matter, 3) deliberate infliction of injury without just cause, and 4) invasion of moral rights. The court denied the injunction on all four grounds, however focused its discussion on the libel charge.

   The gravamen of plaintiffs' charge is that by the portrayal of the espionage activities of the representatives of the U.S.S.R. in Canada and by the depicted disowning of these activities by one of these representatives a picture with an anti-Soviet theme has been published. The use of plaintiffs' music in such a picture, it is argued, indicates their "approval," "endorsement" and "participation" therein thereby casting upon them "the false imputation of being disloyal to their country." The court in the presence of and with the consent of counsel for both sides has seen the picture. There is no ground for any contention that plaintiffs have participated in its production or given their approval or endorsement thereto. It is urged that the use of plaintiffs' names and music "necessarily implies" their consent, approval or collaboration in the production and distribution of the picture because "the public at large knows that living composers receive payment for the use of their names and creations in films." The error in this reasoning is in the necessary implication. No such implication exists, necessarily or otherwise, where the work of the composer is in the public domain and may be freely published, copied or compiled by others. *Jaccard v. Macy & Co. Inc., supra; Clemens v. Belford, Clark & Co., supra.* In the absence of such implication the existence of libel is not shown and the drastic relief asked cannot be granted. . . .

2. Subsequent to the breakup of the Soviet Union, recordings featuring famed cellist Mstislav Rostropovich were licensed for U.S. distribution by a purported successor to the former government's state recording agency. The artist objected to such distribution. In *Rostropovich v. Koch International Corp.*, 34 U.S.P.Q.2d

1609, 1995 U.S.Dist.LEXIS 2785; 1995 U.S.Dist.LEXIS 10696 (SDNY 1995), the court held that Rostropovich was entitled to a jury trial on the issue of whether the size and prominence of Rostropovich's name and likeness on the covers of CDs embodying his recordings were sufficient to constitute a false endorsement under Section 43(a) of the Lanham Act.

2.6 FAVORED NATIONS CLAUSES

In the following excerpt, Michael I. Rudell and Neil J. Rosini provide an overview of Most Favored Nations clauses and explain how these clauses are used in entertainment agreements.

Michael I. Rudell and Neil J. Rosini are partners in the New York firm of Franklin, Weinrib, Rudell & Vassallo, P.C. This article is reprinted with their kind permission and was originally published in the Entertainment Law column of the *New York Law Journal,* February 24, 2006.

The Role of Most Favored Nations Clauses

By: *Michael I. Rudell and Neil J. Rosini*

MFN Clauses Defined

The "most favored nations" concept had its start not in entertainment agreements but in treaties governing international commerce. The clause would ensure that one country to a trade agreement received no worse treatment—concerning import duties, for example—than the treatment accorded another trading partner. Similarly, in entertainment agreements, an MFN clause provides that an amount, a definition, or another aspect of a contractual relationship will be computed or defined in at least as favorable a manner as the computation or definition given to one or more third parties.

Ordinarily, those third parties also are bound by agreements with the same entity and for the same project as the party receiving the benefit of the clause (e.g., a net proceeds definition for a particular movie; a royalty pool definition for a particular theatrical production). In rare cases when the recipient has great leverage, the scope of the clause might extend beyond a single project. For example, "gross receipts" might be defined on a most favored nations basis for a recipient with respect to all motion pictures produced by a film company, not just the particular motion picture to which the agreement containing the MFN clause relates.

An MFN provision may apply not to a project but rather to one or more aspects of an executive's employment agreement, such as with regard to stock option and restricted stock awards governed by an equity incentive plan. The executive may obtain the employer's promise that if anyone else gets a particular modification such as accelerated vesting upon termination, so will the executive. An executive's contract also might contain a provision that no one in a particular defined group will receive a greater number of stock options or shares of restricted stock.

The Issue of Specificity

Particularly from the perspective of the party obligated to apply the clause, the preferred MFN provisions are limited in scope and precisely written. In drafting an MFN clause, the applicable project should be named: a particular motion picture, television or live theater production, a record album or a

182 • LAW AND BUSINESS

compilation. Next, the contractual provision to be compared—an amount, a definition, or other terms—should be specified. For example, an MFN clause benefiting a recipient of contingent compensation in a motion picture might provide that for a particular film, no one else could receive a more favorable definition of contingent compensation. But because there are various levels of contingent compensation (e.g., gross receipts, adjusted gross receipts, net proceeds) involved in motion picture productions, even more specificity often would be advisable from the studio's perspective.

On the other hand, the recipient of an MFN clause may sometimes do better with a broad description because a narrowly-tailored clause may not include the full range of benefits the recipient hopes to derive. For example, a producer may compensate an individual who works in several capacities more generously in one capacity that is not implicated by an MFN clause, compared to another capacity that is. If one co-executive producer also serves as a "creative consultant," she can be compensated for both functions. A fellow co-executive producer may have a most favored nations clause that only reaches the compensation paid for executive producer services. The narrowly-written clause would not include compensation paid for similar or related functions with a different label.

For another example, in the context of contingent compensation, "adjusted gross receipts" is generally considered a more favorable participation than "net profits," but even these terms can be accorded different labels, such as "modified adjusted gross" or "net proceeds." Accordingly, the participant with a share of "adjusted gross receipts" might bargain for MFN protection respecting any form of contingent compensation no matter what the label (other than a participation in "gross receipts"). And each recipient will want to ensure that his or her entitlement is preserved even if the other party attaches a different label to the same contingent compensation.

Why Parties Use MFN Clauses

There are several reasons why one or both parties would wish to have an MFN clause. An MFN clause can eliminate significant transaction costs in both time and money through setting a specific level of compensation. (By standing firm on those terms, however, the company must be willing to lose content or services from third parties who refuse to accept that level of compensation.) MFN clauses also provide licensors and other recipients the comfort of knowing that no one else will be treated in a more favorable manner with respect to a particular term. This assurance is a security blanket for agents and other negotiating representatives who can assure their clients that a particular definition or amount is the best available for the project in question.

MFN clauses can be particularly helpful to parties with small bargaining leverage confronted by lengthy "standard terms." In the case of deal terms covering contingent compensation from motion picture exploitation, studio boilerplate is often extremely long, and if every clause were negotiated, transaction costs would be extremely high for both parties. Further, studios usually are not overly eager to negotiate such terms in a meaningful way. MFN clauses can save both sides a good deal of time and trouble while providing a measure of protection for the party contracting with the studio.

For example, it often does not make a great deal of sense for a minor participant in "net profits" from the exploitation of a property to assume the burden of negotiating a lengthy definition. This is particularly so when the benefits of such a negotiation may not be substantial. That participant is usually better advised to seek the same treatment as a participant with greater bargaining power, more at stake, and more resources to sustain the costs (principally legal fees) of a lengthy negotiation. Accordingly, a screenwriter might choose to have his or her net profits defined on the same basis as the director or author of an underlying novel.

The daunting task of negotiating a full complement of contingent compensation provisions in motion picture deals also has led to a hierarchy of side letters and riders that are commonly used in the Hollywood community. A studio may offer an actor the benefit of the best rider (the "A Rider" as opposed to the "B Rider") associated with a particular talent agency, relating to the studio's boilerplate contingent compensation provisions. The reverse effect also may come into play: for example, an actor with significant leverage may be able to negotiate uniquely beneficial terms in his deal with a studio, but the studio would then want to exclude this "superstar" tier from any MFN protection afforded to others.

MFN Clauses Appear in a Variety of Contexts

In the theater, most favored nations provisions often appear in the context of royalty pools, which provide a formula by which persons who otherwise would share in the gross weekly box office receipts of a particular production, agree instead to participate in a share of weekly operating profits (with the balance of operating profits being allocated to investors). It is usually a precondition to a royalty participant's agreement to the activation of a royalty pool that all other royalty participants be paid pursuant to the pool. However, exceptions are generally carved out for a star or the theater owner who may still be entitled to a share of gross box office receipts above a defined threshold, even when a royalty pool is in effect.

Credit is a non-monetary benefit that can be subject to MFN protection. The billing block—the text-filled box commonly seen in a film ad—is the common denominator of credits appearing in motion picture advertising, and MFN clauses typically are keyed to it. An exception from the most favored nations provision for credit to participants in the film often will be made with regard to billing in artwork afforded to a star or director. In many cases, an MFN clause also will be made subject to union requirements that are applicable to performers, directors and screenwriters.

MFN clauses are commonly used when a company assembles a product such as a compilation record album in which rights are sought from various record companies. The company assembling the compilation record may reduce the time and trouble of negotiation by assuring all licensors that they will receive the same license fee, or royalty entitlement, or both. The same concept might apply to the acquisition of rights for footage in a documentary production where, perhaps, on a per minute basis all fees will be the same.

In most instances, the clause will be self-enforcing in that the only way the recipient will know if another party has received a higher amount or better definition that triggers the clause, is for the company to disclose it. Other opportunities to learn third party deal terms do arise, however. In the event of a lawsuit, the contracts likely would be discoverable. Also, in the case of theatrical productions certain royalty participants—particularly those entitled to a share of net profits—may receive regular financial reports and have the right to inspect the books and records of the production. In addition, offering materials filed with state securities agencies may disclose compensation arrangements for major royalty participants making it relatively easy to find variations in terms.

Conclusion

Generally speaking, as with most contractual undertakings, as long as both parties are aware of differing approaches to drafting and potential outcomes, both the recipient and the offeror stand to benefit from the appropriate use of MFN treatment.

Chapter 3

ENTERTAINMENT RIGHTS: RIGHTS OF PUBLICITY, PROPERTY, AND IDEAS

3.1 INTRODUCTION

Every entertainment project begins as the exploitation of rights: rights in names, lives, intellectual properties, or ideas. It would seem at first that the only rights that need to be acquired are rights to various types of literary, artistic, dramatic, or musical property, but—especially in today's world of "docudramas" and "mockumentaries," of "reality programming" and merchandising—personal rights are involved on a regular basis. In reading the cases in the various sections which follow, it is apparent that real-life situations do not divide so neatly into separate classifications. The invasion of a celebrity's persona may require a response using not one but several legal theories. Thus, as considerations flow from one section to the next, it is important not only to study each theory in its own right, but to compare the various theories as well.

3.2 PERSONAL RIGHTS: PRIVACY

3.2.1 Introduction: Common Law

The right of privacy as a legally enforceable right is largely a twentieth-century development. As with other modern legal theories, privacy's roots are embedded in a variety of common law precedents, but its enunciation as an integrated legal theory is of recent origin. Thomas Cooley in his treatise on torts remarked on a right "to be left alone."

Then came a landmark article by Samuel Warren and Louis Brandeis, published in volume four of the *Harvard Law Review* in 1890. Titled "The Right to Privacy," the article begins its analysis with the following:

That the individual shall have full protection in person and in property is a principle as old as the common law; but it has been found necessary from time to time to define anew the exact nature and extent of such protection. Political, social, and economic changes entail the recognition of new rights, and the common law, in its eternal youth, grows to meet the demands of society. Thus, in very early times, the law gave a remedy only for physical interference with life and property, for trespasses *vi et armis*. Then the "right to life" served only to protect the subject from battery in its various forms; liberty meant freedom from actual restraint; and the right to property secured to the individual his lands and his cattle. Later, there came a recognition of man's spiritual nature, of his feelings and his intellect. Gradually the scope of these legal rights broadened; and now the right to life has come to mean the right to enjoy life—the right to be let alone; the right to liberty secures the exercise of extensive civil privileges; and the term "property" has grown to comprise every form of possession— intangible, as well as tangible.

Following this came various writings of William Prosser. In one of his later efforts, Dean Prosser enunciated the four categories included within a personal right to privacy. These are:

1. Protection against intrusion into one's private affairs;
2. Avoidance of disclosure of one's embarrassing private facts;
3. Protection against publicity placing one in a false light in the public eye; and
4. Remedies for appropriation, usually for commercial advantage, of one's name or likeness.

Most jurisdictions today have interwoven one or more of these categories into their case law. A few jurisdictions have granted statutory recognition. But in all, an uncertain process has left incomplete the protection many states afford citizens under a right of privacy.

Under Prosser's four areas of classic privacy violations, the first three protect an individual from mental harm resulting from the harsh and unwelcome glare of persona invasion. The concerns of these three differ from the theoretical underpinnings of Prosser's fourth intrusion, since the focus of the fourth is not so much on mental harm but on the proprietary interests of protecting against misappropriation of one's name or likeness for commercial gain.

Since this fourth intrusion is similar to the protections afforded by the right of publicity, courts have had difficulty distinguishing the two rights when a misappropriation of name or likeness occurs. Some courts have refused to recognize any differences at all. Courts that have recognized a common law right of publicity have chosen to distinguish the two rights on the grounds that the state's interest in enforcing them is different. Prosser stated:

The interest protected "in permitting recovery (for a privacy invasion)" is clearly that of reputation, with the same overtones of mental distress as defamation! . . . By contrast, the State's interest in permitting the proprietary interest of the individuals is closely analogous to the goals of patent and copyright law, focusing on the right of the individual to reap the reward of his endeavors and having little to do with protecting feeling. (Prosser, "Privacy," 48 *California Law Review*, p. 406)

Thus, the decision by a court to apply privacy versus publicity may depend on quite different considerations.

Since the right of privacy is a personal right, generally only persons who are injured may assert a claim. Consequently, the right is not assignable and usually does not survive the injured party's death. These limitations obviously make a publicity claim more attractive if assignment or descendibility is at issue. In addition, as a practical matter, the right of publicity is predominantly a right for celebrities whose names have commercial value; in contrast, the right of privacy is more applicable to the average individual. These characterizations are not inflexible and sedimentary, however, and celebrities for good reason at times invoke rights of privacy when unwarranted intrusions occur.

A right of privacy claim has three elements: the use of one's name or image in an (1) identifiable manner, (2) without consent, and (3) in situations in which the invasion benefits the wrongdoer. It is irrelevant how many people recognize the individual whose privacy is invaded, but recognition may be a factor in assessing damages.

A fictionalized work may give rise to a claim if the use of a name or physical characteristics makes the complainant identifiable. Whether fictionalized or not, an unauthorized depiction of an individual need not be a complete facsimile to warrant a privacy invasion. Some jurisdictions do not even require that the person be identified, but allow pictorial surroundings to constitute identification. In most jurisdictions, the complainant's actual name need not be used if a nickname or other name permits identification.

As with other personal rights, privacy rights may conflict with First Amendment rights. This raises the important question of when is there a public interest in the depictions presented? This question is discussed in Section 3.3.3.

3.2.2 The First Cases: Roberson and Pavesich

The most famous of the early privacy cases was *Roberson v. Rochester Folding Box Co.*, 171 N.Y. 538, 64 N.E. 442 (1902), in which the Court of Appeals held (in a 4–3 decision) that the unauthorized use of an individual's picture on flyers promoting the sale of flour boxes did not violate that individual's right of privacy. "The so-called right of an individual," the majority stated, "founded on the claim that he has the right to pass through this world without having his picture published, his business enterprises discussed, his successful experiments written up for the benefit of others, or his eccentricities commented on in circulars, periodicals, or newspapers, whether the comment be favorable or otherwise, does not exist in law, and is not enforceable in equity." (The absence of a common law right of privacy in New York was reiterated in *Costanza v. Seinfeld*, 181 Misc.2d 562, 693 N.Y.S.2d 897 [Sup. Ct. N.Y.Co. 1999], in which one Michael Costanza sued the creators of "Seinfeld" claiming that the character of George Costanza was based on him. Plaintiff was time-barred under §§ 50 and 51 of the New York

Civil Rights Law. However, he could not fall back on the longer limitations period applicable to common law torts.) It fell to the Georgia Supreme Court to take the first step toward protecting the right of privacy, as well as recognition (in dicta) of the right of publicity. As we will see, the positions expressed by the *Pavesich* court have taken root in subsequent statutory and case law.

Pavesich v. New England Life Insurance Co., 122 Ga. 191 (1904)

COBB, J.

[*The Atlanta Constitution* published an easily recognizable likeness of the plaintiff in an advertisement for the New England Life Insurance Company, without the participation or consent of the plaintiff (who was not insured by the company). His picture was next to that of a poorly dressed and sickly looking person. Above the picture of the plaintiff were the quotes: "Do it now. The man who did." Above the other person appeared: "Do it while you can. The man who didn't." This time the court had no trouble recognizing (or, in its view, rediscovering) the right of privacy:] "[T]he right of privacy has its foundation in the instincts of nature . . . [A]s to each individual member of society there are matters private and there are matters public so far as the individual is concerned." . . .

The right of one to exhibit himself to the public at all proper times, in all proper places, and in a proper manner is embraced within the right of personal liberty. The right to withdraw from the public gaze at such times as a person may see fit, when his presence in public is not demanded by any rule of law is also embraced within the right of personal liberty. Publicity in one instance and privacy in the other is each guaranteed. If personal liberty embraces the right of publicity, it no less embraces the correlative right of privacy; and this is no new idea in Georgia law. . . .

The right of privacy, however, like every other right that rests in the individual, may be waived by him, or by any one authorized by him, or by any one whom the law empowers to act in his behalf, provided the effect of his waiver will not be such as to bring before the public those matters of a purely private nature which express law or public policy demands shall be kept private. This waiver may be either express or implied, but the existence of the waiver carries with it the right to an invasion of privacy only to such an extent as may be legitimately necessary and proper in dealing with the matter which has brought about the waiver. It may be waived for one purpose and still asserted for another . . . Liberty includes the right to live as one will, so long as that will does not interfere with the rights of another or of the public. One may desire to live a life of seclusion; another may desire to live a life of publicity; still another may wish to live a life of privacy as to certain matters and of publicity as to others. . . .

The stumbling block [is the tension between privacy and] the liberty of speech and of the press . . . Each is a natural right, each exists, and each must be recognized and enforced with due respect for the other. . . . The right to speak and write and print has been, at different times in the world's history, seriously invaded by those who, for their own selfish purposes, desired to take away from others such privileges, and consequently these rights have been the subject of provisions in the constitutions of the United States and of this State. . . . The right of privacy [cannot] interfere with the free expression of one's sentiments and the publication of every matter in which the public may be legitimately interested. In many cases the law requires the individual to surrender some of his natural and private rights for the benefit of the public; and this is true in reference to some phases of the right of privacy as well as other legal rights. Those to whom the right to speak and write and print is guaranteed must not abuse this right; nor must one in whom the right of privacy exists abuse this right. . . .

With all due respect to Chief Judge Parker [the author of the Roberson decision] and his associates who concurred with him, we think the conclusion reached by them was the result of an unconscious yielding to the feeling of conservatism which naturally arises in the mind of a judge who faces a proposition which is novel. [While beneficial,] this conservatism should not go to the extent of refusing to recognize a right which the instincts of nature prove to exist, and which nothing in judicial decision, legal history, or writings upon the law can be called to demonstrate its non-existence as a legal right. . . .

[W]e have little difficulty in arriving at the conclusion that the present case is one in which it has been established that the right of privacy has been invaded [without constitutional exemption . . .] The defendant insurance company and its agent had no more authority to display [plaintiff's picture] in public for the purpose of advertising the business in which they were engaged [without plaintiff's consent] than they would have had to compel the plaintiff to place himself upon exhibition for this purpose . . . The plaintiff was in no sense a public character, even if a different rule in regard to the publication of one's picture should be applied to such characters. . . .

There is in the publication of one's picture for advertising purposes not the slightest semblance of an expression of an idea, a thought, or an opinion, within the meaning of the constitutional provision which guarantees to a person the right to publish his sentiments on any subject. Such conduct is not embraced within the liberty to print, but is a serious invasion of one's right of privacy, and may in many cases, according to the circumstances of the publication and the uses to which it is put, cause damages to flow which are irreparable in their nature. The knowledge that one's features and form are being used for such a purpose and displayed in such places as such advertisements are often liable to be found brings not only the person of an extremely sensitive nature, but even the individual of ordinary sensibility, to a realization that his liberty has been taken away from him, and, as long as the advertiser uses him for these purposes, he can not be otherwise than conscious of the fact that he is, for the time being, under the control of another, that he is no longer free, and that he is in reality a slave without hope of freedom, held to service by a merciless master; and if a man of true instincts, or even of ordinary sensibilities, no one can be more conscious of his complete enthrallment than he is.

So thoroughly satisfied are we that the law recognizes within proper limits, as a legal right, the right of privacy, and that the publication of one's picture without his consent by another as an advertisement, for the mere purpose of increasing the profits and gains of the advertiser, is an invasion of this right, that we venture to predict that the day will come when the American bar will marvel that a contrary view was ever entertained by judges of eminence and ability. . . .

NOTES

1. While the courts very strongly defend the right of the media to record and discuss public events, a number of recent cases have demonstrated an increasing willingness on the part of the courts to draw a tighter line around the permissible area of activity. "Reality TV" has been a staple of television in recent years. Most often, reporters go undercover to investigate allegations of wrongdoing. For example, it was permissible for an undercover reporter to tape material for a report on faulty medical tests where the taping took place in a location in which the plaintiff had "no reasonable expectation of privacy in the location or contents of the conversation." *Medical Laboratory Management Consultants v. American Broadcasting Companies*, 30 F.Supp. 2d 1182, 1998 U.S. Dist. LEXIS 20084 (D. Ariz. 1998). However, in *Sanders v. American Broadcasting Companies, Inc.*, 20 Cal.4th 907, 85 Cal.Rptr.2d 909 (1999), an investigative reporter obtained employment as a telephone answerer at a psychic hotline, where she proceeded to utilize a hidden camera to videotape her conversations with other employees which occurred inside the firm's offices. Although the court "did not hold or imply that investigative journalists necessarily commit a tort by secretly recording events and conversations in offices, stores, or other workplaces," the test is "whether a reasonable expectation of privacy is violated," and, if so, whether the invasion is "highly offensive to a reasonable person, considering, among other factors, the motive of the alleged intruder" (citing, inter alia, *Shulman v. Group W. Productions*, 18 Cal.4th 200 (1998), a case in which the producer was held liable for taping a woman accident victim after she was taken from the site of the accident and placed in a medevac helicopter.) While not deciding the ultimate issue of liability, the court held that "the cause of action is not defeated as a matter of law simply because the events or conversations upon which the defendant allegedly intruded were not completely private from all other eyes and ears." For a discussion of the effect of such cases, see Neville L. Johnson, Brian A. Rishwain and David A. Elder, "Caught in the Act, *Los Angeles Lawyer*," April 1998, p. 33.

2. A key element in the foregoing cases is the reasonable expectation of privacy. However, *People For The Ethical Treatment of Animals v. Bobby Berosini Ltd.*, 111 Nev. 615, 895 P.2d 1269 (1995) is an example of a situation in which there was no reasonable expectation of privacy: An animal rights activist (actually, a dancer in a Las Vegas show) surreptitiously videotaped the backstage activities of an animal trainer in the production, showing him shaking, punching and beating his animals. Claiming that such actions were "justified" for training, discipline, and control purposes, the trainer sued an animal rights activist who played the video on a television program, as well as the group which the activist represented. A $4.2 million verdict for the trainer for libel and invasion of privacy was reversed on appeal. The Court stated that "if [the trainer] did not think that the tape showed him doing anything wrong or disgraceful, he should not be heard to complain that the defendants defamed him merely by showing the tape." (895 P.2d at 1272.) Continuing, the court

stated that "unless the tape had been materially altered to portray something different from what [the trainer] was actually doing, then defendants have not made a statement about [him]," (*Id.* at p. 1273) and "[w]hether the beatings portrayed in the tape are justified or constitute animal abuse is a matter involving a broad spectrum of opinion, lay and expert." (*Id.* at 1274.) Such a case involves "a value judgment based on true information disclosed to or known by the public . . . [and such a statement] is not a statement of fact . . . So long as the factual basis for the opinion is readily available, the persons receiving the opinion are in a position to judge for themselves the validity of the opinion." (*Id.* at pp. 1275–77.)

3. Even famous entertainers (as well as crime victims) have reasonable expectations of privacy under some circumstances, the California Legislature has decided, enacting Sen. Bill 262 (Cal. Stats. 1998, ch. 1000), which added Civil Code § 1708.8. This statute (directed at "paparazzi," and supported by the entertainment unions) imposes liability for a "physical invasion of privacy" in a manner that is "offensive to a reasonable person" for the purpose of "captur[ing] any type of visual image, sound recording, or other physical impression of the plaintiff engaging in a personal or familial activity" (which includes intimate details of the plaintiff's life, interactions with the plaintiff's family or significant others, or other aspects of plaintiff's private affairs or concerns). Treble damages (as well as profits) are available to successful plaintiffs, in addition to injunctions and restraining orders.

3.2.3 Statutory Protection

The *Roberson* decision prompted the enactment of the first statutory protection for the right of privacy. Its scope is limited and since (as we will see) New York does not as of this writing recognize a common law right of publicity, this statute provides only limited assistance in that area. That the statute is flawed is demonstrated by the notes that follow the *Spahn* case.

New York Civil Rights Law

§50. *Right of Privacy*

A person, firm or corporation that uses for advertising purposes, or for the purposes of trade, the name, portrait or picture of any living person without having first obtained the written consent of such person, or if a minor of his or her parent or guardian, is guilty of a misdemeanor.

§51. *Action for Injunction and for Damages*

Any person whose name, portrait or picture is used within this state for advertising purposes or for the purposes of trade without the written consent first obtained as above provided may maintain an equitable action in the supreme court of this state against the person, firm or corporation so using his name, portrait or picture, to prevent and restrain the use thereof, and may also sue and recover damages for any injuries sustained by reason of such use, and if the defendant shall have knowingly used such person's name, portrait or picture in such manner as is forbidden or declared to be unlawful by the last section, the jury, in its discretion, may award exemplary damages. But nothing contained in this act shall be so construed as to prevent [the use of] the name, portrait or picture of any author, composer or artist in connection with his literary, musical or artistic productions which he has sold or disposed of with such name, portrait or picture used in connection therewith.

That the New York statute is intended (at least in part) to deal with feelings is illustrated by the following case.

Spahn v. Julian Messner, Inc., 18 N.Y.2d 324, 221 N.E.2d (1966)

KEATING, JUDGE

[Spahn won 363 major league baseball games, the most by any left-handed pitcher in history, and was elected to the Hall of Fame. Messner published a fictionalized biography of Spahn which portrayed him as a war hero. Spahn, embarrassed at being "famed," sued under the N.Y. Civil Rights Act §§ 50 and 51.]

. . . Over the years since the statute's enactment in 1903, its social desirability and remedial nature have led to its being given a liberal construction consonant with its overall purpose. [Citations omitted] But at the same time, ever mindful that the written word or picture is involved, courts have engrafted exceptions and restrictions onto the statute to avoid any conflict with the free dissemination of thoughts, ideas, newsworthy events and matters of public interest [including the "public figure" exception]. . . . But it is erroneous to confuse privacy with "personality" or to assume that privacy, though lost for a certain time or in a certain context, goes forever unprotected [citations omitted]. . . . Thus it may be appropriate to say that the plaintiff here, Warren Spahn, is a public personality, and that, insofar as his professional career is involved, he is substantially without a right to privacy. That is not to say, however, that his "personality" may be fictionalized and that, as fictionalized, it may be exploited for the defendants' commercial benefit through the medium of an unauthorized biography. The factual reporting of newsworthy persons and events is in the public interest and is protected. The fictitious is not. . . . In the present case, the findings of fact . . . establish "dramatization, imagined dialogue, manipulated chronologies, and fictionalization of events" [and] "publicizes areas of Warren Spahn's personal and private life, albeit inaccurate and distorted, and consists of a host, a preponderant percentage, of factual errors, distortions and fanciful passages" [quoting the Appellate Division opinion]. . . .

We thus conclude that the defendants' publication of a fictitious biography of the plaintiff constitutes an unauthorized exploitation of his personality for purposes of trade and that it is proscribed by section 51 of the Civil Rights Law. . . .

NOTE _____

1. The U.S. Supreme Court (387 U.S. 239 (1967)) vacated the judgment and remanded the case for reconsideration in light of *Time, Inc. v. Hill,* 385 U.S. 347, the New York Court of Appeals reaffirmed its earlier decision (21 N.Y. 2d 124 (1967)), and the U.S. Supreme Court dismissed the defendants' appeal (393 U.S. 1046 (1969)).

In *Stephano v. News Group Publications,* set forth below, the New York Court of Appeals conclusively determined that an independent common-law right of publicity did not exist in New York since the "right of publicity" is encompassed under the Civil Rights Law (§§50–51) as an aspect of the right of privacy, which is exclusively statutory in New York.

Tony Stephano, v. News Group Publications, 64 N.Y.2d 174; 474 N.E.2d 580; 485 N.Y.S.2d 220; 1984 N.Y. LEXIS 4917; 11 Media L. Rep. 1303 (1984)

Opinion of the Court (Wachtler, J)

The plaintiff, a professional model, claims that the defendant used his picture for trade or advertising purposes without his consent, and thus violated his statutory right to privacy (*Civil Rights Law, β 51*), by publishing a picture of him modeling a "bomber jacket" in a magazine article containing information regarding the approximate price of the jacket, the name of the designer, and the names of three stores where the jacket might be purchased. Plaintiff also claims that the defendant's conduct violated a common-law right of publicity. The trial court granted summary judgment to the defendant concluding that the article reported a newsworthy event of fashion news, and was not published for trade or advertising purposes. A divided Appellate Division reversed and denied summary judgment finding that factual questions were presented as to whether the defendant had used the plaintiff's picture for trade purposes and whether the article constituted an advertisement in disguise. The defendant has appealed by leave of the Appellate Division which certified a question as to the correctness of its order.

In the summer of 1981 the plaintiff agreed to model for an article on men's fall fashions. The photographic session took place on August 11, 1981. The defendant used two of the photographs taken during that session to illustrate an article entitled "Classic Mixes," which appeared under the heading "Fall Fashions" in the September 7, 1981 issue of *New York* magazine. Another photograph taken during the session was used, a week earlier, in the August 31, 1981 issue of *New York* magazine, in a column entitled "Best Bets." That column, a regular feature in the magazine, contains information about new and unusual products and services available in the metropolitan area. One of the items included in the August 31 column was a bomber jacket modeled by the plaintiff. The text above the picture states: "Yes Giorgio—From Giorgio Armani. Based on his now classic turn on the bomber jacket, this cotton-twill version with 'fun fur' collar features the same cut at a far lower price—about $225. It'll be available in the stores next week.—Henry Post Bomber Jacket/Barney's, Bergdorf Goodman, Bloomingdale's."

It is the plaintiff's contention that he agreed to model for one article only—the September 7, 1981 article on Fall Fashions—and that the defendant violated his rights by publishing his photograph in the August 31 "Best Bets" column. . . . The complaint alleges two causes of action. First the plaintiff claims that the defendant violated his civil rights by using his photograph for trade or advertising purposes without his consent. In his second cause of action the plaintiff claims that the defendant's conduct "invaded plaintiff's right of publicity." On each cause of action the plaintiff seeks $350,000 in compensatory damages and an equal amount in exemplary damages.

The defendant's answer asserts several affirmative defenses. The primary defense is that the photograph and article relating to it involve matters of legitimate public interest and concern and thus do not violate the plaintiff's rights under the *Civil Rights Law (ßß 50, 51)*, or any common-law right of publicity. The defendant also urged that the second cause of action, for invasion of the plaintiff's right of publicity, does not set forth a claim "separate and distinct" from the first cause of action.

. . . At the defendant's request, however, the parties stipulated that the note of issue would be withdrawn to afford the defendant an opportunity to move for summary judgment. In the motion for summary judgment the defendant urged that the complaint should be dismissed because the plaintiff's photograph was not published for trade or advertising purposes.

In support of the motion the defendant submitted affidavits by two of the editors involved in the publication of the "Best Bets" column of August 31, 1981. The affidavits state that the column is a regular news feature of the editorial portion of the magazine, designed to provide readers with information, sometimes including prices, concerning interesting products and services in the New York metropolitan area. They state that such information is provided solely for newsworthy purposes—"advertising concerns" play no part in deciding what to include in "Best Bets" and the magazine receives no payment for any item mentioned in the column. They further state that the item concerning the bomber jacket was included in the August 31 "Best Bets" column because the fashion editor suggested that it would be of interest to readers of *New York* magazine.

The plaintiff's affidavit in opposition to the motion stated: "While it may be that a party whose service or product is included in 'Best Bets' does not pay a direct advertising fee to be included, the benefits to the magazine are obtained in an indirect manner. Stores, designers, and retailers featured there have all advertised in *New York* magazine at other times and places, and giving them this 'breakout' feature in the 'Best Bets' column acts as barter for such advertising at another time and place." The plaintiff further stated that the designer and the stores mentioned in the August 31 column had previously advertised in *New York* magazine and observed that "the publicity benefits in the column to the designer and retail outlets mentioned are evident from a fair reading of the column."

The trial court granted summary judgment to the defendant concluding, on the basis of the exhibits submitted, that the bomber jacket item was a "newsworthy observation" and was not published for advertising or trade purposes within the contemplation of the statute. The court also held that the inclusion of information concerning the availability of the jacket at certain stores, which currently advertised in the magazine, was not sufficient to sustain the claim that the item had been published for trade or advertising purposes "without a further showing of benefit to defendant."

The Appellate Division reversed and denied the defendant's motion for summary judgment. The majority observed that the September 7 article was published for trade purposes because it was included to increase circulation. Finding that the "form and presentation" of both articles were identical the majority held that a reasonable person could conclude that the August 31 article was also used for trade purposes. "The real question", the majority stated, "is whether the public interest aspect of the August 31, 1981 article is merely incidental to its commercial purpose". The majority held that it "is also possible that this article constituted an advertisement in disguise since many of the magazine's advertisers were mentioned in the copy" *(98* AD2d 287, *291)*. One Justice concurred on the ground that a fact question was presented as to whether the plaintiff had consented to the use of his picture in both articles. . . . We now reverse.

Section 50 of the Civil Rights Law prohibits the use of "the name, portrait or picture of any living person" for advertising or trade purposes without the person's consent and declares a violation of the statute to be a misdemeanor. Section 51 of the statute provides civil remedies, including injunctive relief, compensatory damages and, if the defendant acted knowingly, exemplary damages.

The statutes have their origin in this court's 1902 decision in *Roberson v. Rochester Folding Box Co.,* 171 NY 538. In that case it was held that a young woman whose picture had been used by the defendant on flour advertisements without her consent could not recover for a violation of her right to privacy because no such right was recognized at common law. The Legislature responded the following year by amending the Civil Rights Law to establish a statutory "right to privacy" (see *Rhodes v. Sperry & Hutchinson Co.,* 193 NY 223, 227, aff'd sub nom. *Sperry & Hutchinson Co. v. Rhodes,* 220 U.S. 502). Since the adoption of the statutes, this court has repeatedly held that the right of privacy is governed entirely by statute in this State (*Arrington v. New York Times Co.,* 55 NY2d 433; *Cohen v. Hallmark Cards,* 45 NY2d 493, 497, n 2; *Gautier v. Pro-Football, Inc.,* 304 NY 354, 358).

Section 51 of the Civil Rights Law has been applied in cases, such as the *Roberson* case, where the picture of a person who has apparently never sought publicity has been used without his or her consent for trade or advertising purposes (see, e.g., *Cohen v. Herbal Concepts* 63 NY2d 379; *Flores v. Mosler Safe Co.,* 7 NY2d 276). In such cases it has been noted that the statute serves "to protect the sentiments, thoughts and feelings of an individual" (*Flores v. Mosler Safe Co., supra,* p. 280; *Cohen v. Herbal Concepts, supra*).

This history has led some courts to conclude that the statutory right to privacy is limited to the type of case which originally prompted its enactment and thus would not preclude the recognition in this State of a common-law "right of publicity" in cases where the defendant has exploited, without consent, and usually without payment, the name, picture, or portrait of an individual who has consciously sought to establish a publicity value for his personality (see, e.g., *Haelan Labs. v. Topps Chewing Gum,* 202 F2d 866, 868, cert den 346 U.S. 816; *Factors Etc. v. Pro Arts,* 579 F2d 215, cert den 440 U.S. 908; but also see *Brinkley v. Casablancas,* 80 A.D.2d 428). The statute, however, is not limited to situations where the defendant's conduct has caused distress to a person who wishes to lead a private life free of all commercial publicity.

By its terms the statute applies to any use of a person's picture or portrait for advertising or trade purposes whenever the defendant has not obtained the person's written consent to do so. It would therefore apply, and recently has been held to apply, in cases where the plaintiff generally seeks publicity, or uses his name, portrait, or picture, for commercial purposes but has not given written consent for a particular use (*Welch v. Mr. Christmas,* 57 N.Y.2d 143; cf. *Shields v. Gross,* 58 N.Y.2d 338). Thus where the written consent to use the plaintiff's name or picture for advertising or trade purposes has expired (*Welch v Mr. Christmas, supra*) or the defendant has otherwise exceeded the limitations of the consent (*Shields v. Gross, supra),* the plaintiff may seek damages or other relief under the statute, even though he might properly sue for breach of contract. The right which the statute permits the plaintiff to vindicate in such a case may, perhaps, more accurately be described as a right of publicity (*Zacchini v. Scripps-Howard Broadcasting Co.,* 433 U.S. 562). In this respect the statute parallels the common-law right of privacy which generally provides remedies for any commercialization of the individual's personality without his consent (see Prosser, Privacy, 48 Cal L Rev 383, 403; also, see, *Cohen v. Herbal Concepts, supra; Flores v. Mosler Safe Co., supra,* pp. 280–281; *Gautier v Pro-Football, Inc., supra,* p. 358). Since the "right of publicity" is encompassed under the Civil Rights Law as an aspect of the right of privacy, which, as noted, is exclusively statutory in this State, the plaintiff cannot claim an independent common-law right of publicity. . . .

The only question then is whether the defendant used the plaintiff's picture for trade or advertising purposes within the meaning of the statute when it published his picture in the "Best Bets" column without his consent.

The statute does not define trade or advertising purposes. However, the courts have consistently held, from the time of its enactment, that these terms should not be construed to apply to publications concerning newsworthy events or matters of public interest (*[citing cases]*). The exception reflects Federal and State constitutional concerns for free dissemination of news and other matters of interest to the public (*Arrington v. New York Times Co., supra,* p. 440), but essentially requires an interpretation of the statute to give effect to the legislative intent (*[citing cases]*). We have recently noted that this exception should be liberally applied (*Arrington v. New York Times Co., supra*, p. 440).

The newsworthiness exception applies not only to reports of political happenings and social trends (*Arrington v. New York Times Co., supra; Murray v. New York Mag. Co., supra*), but also to news stories and articles of consumer interest including developments in the fashion world (*Pagan v. New York Herald Tribune, supra*). Nevertheless, the plaintiff contends that the photograph in this case did not depict a newsworthy event because it is a posed picture of a professional model taken at a photographic session staged by the defendant. However, the event or matter of public interest which the defendant seeks to convey is not the model's performance, but the availability of the clothing item displayed. A fashion display is, of necessity, posed and arranged. Obviously the picture of the jacket does not lose its newsworthiness simply because the defendant chose to employ a person to model it in a controlled or contrived setting (*Pagan v. New York Herald Tribune, supra*).

The fact that the defendant may have included this item in its column solely or primarily to increase the circulation of its magazine and therefore its profits, as the Appellate Division suggested, does not mean that the defendant has used the plaintiff's picture for trade purposes within the meaning of the statute. Indeed, most publications seek to increase their circulation and also their profits. It is the content of the article and not the defendant's motive or primary motive to increase circulation which determines whether it is a newsworthy item, as opposed to a trade usage, under the Civil Rights Law (*Arrington v. New York Times Co., supra*, p. 440; *Booth v. Curtis Pub. Co., supra*). It is settled that a "'picture illustrating an article on a matter of public interest is not considered used for the purposes of trade or advertising within the prohibition of the statute ∗ ∗ ∗ unless it has no real relationship to the article ∗ ∗ ∗ or unless the article is an advertisement in disguise'" (*Murray v. New York Mag. Co.*, 27 N.Y.2d 406, 409, *supra*, quoting *Dallesandro v. Holt & Co.*, 4 A.D.2d 470, 471, app dismissed 7 N.Y.2d 735; *[citing cases]*). A contrary rule would unreasonably and unrealistically limit the exception to nonprofit or purely altruistic organizations which are not the only, or even the primary, source of information concerning newsworthy events and matters of public interest.

The plaintiff's primary contention is that his picture was used for advertising purposes within the meaning of the statute. Although the article was not presented to the public as an advertisement, and was published in a column generally devoted to newsworthy items (cf. *Gautier v. Pro-Football, Inc., supra*, pp. 358–359), the plaintiff claims that it is in fact an advertisement in disguise. In addition, although the defendant has submitted affidavits that the article was published solely as a matter of public interest, without any consideration for advertising concerns, and that the magazine received no payment for including the item in its "Best Bets" column, the plaintiff nevertheless contends that he has presented sufficient facts to require a trial on the issue.

The facts on which the plaintiff relies are entirely circumstantial. He does not claim to have personal knowledge, or direct proof, that this particular article was actually published by the defendant for advertisement purposes. The circumstances on which he bases his claim are (1) the fact that the news column contains information normally included in an advertisement identifying the designer of the jacket, the approximate price, and three places where the jacket may be purchased, and (2) the fact that some or all of those stores mentioned in the article had previously advertised products in the magazine. Those circumstances are not enough to raise a jury question as to whether the article was published for advertising purposes.

The plaintiff does not dispute the fact that the information provided in the article is of legitimate reader interest. Indeed, similar information is frequently provided in reviews or news announcements of books, movies, shows or other new products including fashions (see, e.g., *Pagan v. New York Herald Tribune, supra*). Nor does the plaintiff contend that it is uncommon for commercial publishers to print legitimate news items or reviews concerning products by persons or firms who have previously advertised in the publisher's newspaper or magazine. In short, the plaintiff has not presented any facts which would set this particular article apart from the numerous other legitimate news items concerning new products. He offers only his speculative belief that in this case the information on the jacket was included in the defendant's column for advertising purposes or perhaps, more vaguely, to promote additional advertising. That, in our view, is insufficient to defeat the defendant's motion for summary judgment. The rule exempting articles of public interest from the operation of the Civil Rights Law would, as a practical matter, lose much of its force if publishers of articles which are at least prima facie newsworthy were required to incur the expense of a trial to meet such general and insubstantial accusations of disguised advertising.

****

Accordingly, the order of the Appellate Division should be reversed, the complaint dismissed and the certified question answered in the negative.

Order reversed, with costs, complaint dismissed, and question certified answered in the negative.

NOTES

1. The statute applies only to real names, not pseudonyms. *Geisel v. Poynter Products*, 295 F. Supp. 331 (S.D.N.Y. 1968).
2. However, a "look-alike" may qualify as a "portrait or picture" of the plaintiff where the look-alike is placed in an ad in which all the other persons represented in the ad are celebrities, creating the impression that the "look-alike" is actually the real

person. *Onassis v. Christian Dior*, 122 Misc.2d 603, 472 N.Y.S.2d 254 (N.Y. Sup. Ct. N.Y. County 1984), aff'd, 110 App. Div. 2d 1095, 488 N.Y.S.2d 943 (N.Y. App. Div.1st Dep't. 1985).

3. Written consent is an absolute requirement. In *Brinkley v. Casablancas*, 80 App.Div. 2d 428, 438 N.Y.S.2d 1004 (N.Y. App. Div. 1st Dep't 1981), Christie Brinkley was able to obtain an injunction to prevent a photographer from distributing posters embodying a photograph taken at a photo session at which Ms. Brinkley posed (which was used with Ms. Brinkley's written consent in an HBO special and in ads therefor). Ms. Brinkley had selected the photo which eventually appeared on the poster and had reviewed poster proofs. Nonetheless, the issuance of the poster without her written consent was a violation of Section 51. Ms. Brinkley was held not to have waived this requirement by her participation.

4. However, once granted in an appropriate manner, consent is final. *Shields v. Gross*, 58 N.Y.2d 338, 461 N.Y.S.2d 254 (1983), involved the unsuccessful attempt on the part of actress Brooke Shields, once she had attained her majority, to prevent the future use of nude photos of her which had been taken of her when she was 10 years old pursuant to a written consent granted by her mother. The Court of Appeals held that the maternal consent was sufficient under Section 51 of the Civil Rights Act to prevent Shields from disaffirming the modeling contract under which the photos had been taken, despite the fact that the parties had failed to follow the procedure for court approval of infants' contracts under Section 3–105 of the General Obligations Law, distinguishing between a child model and a child performer, indicating as to the former that such a procedure would be impractical in view of the number of modeling engagements involved and the relatively low fees therefor. The Court of Appeals also took note of the fact that Shields did not complain that the new uses were pornographic, merely that she was embarrassed because the photographs were "not me now." Since the trial court had enjoined the future use of the photos in pornographic publications, the Court of Appeals saw no present need to discuss the question of the unenforceability of contracts violative of public policy (referring to, e.g., Penal Law §235.00 et seq.). The Court did, however, vacate the injunction which the Appellate Division had granted against the further use of the photos in advertising and trade. In a strong dissent, Jasen, J. stated that the state's strong public policy in support of the protection of children should override paternal consent with respect to its application to future uses.

5. Even in a situation in which editorial content is present and the use is not explicitly for advertising purposes, the absence of sufficient connection between the editorial content and the offending portrait or picture may give rise to a cause of action under Section 51. In *Ali v. Playgirl, Inc.*, 447 F. Supp. 723 (S.D.N.Y. 1978), defendant's magazine included a poem entitled "The Greatest," and, on the opposite page, a painting of a nude black boxer seated in his corner. In granting a preliminary injunction in favor of Ali under § 51 of the New York Civil Rights Law, Judge Gagliardi held that the painting (captioned "Mystery Man") was recognizable as a likeness of Ali, and that the identification was strengthened by the juxtaposition of the painting with the verse, the title of which used a title Ali had regularly applied to himself. There was no "informational or newsworthy dimension to defendants' unauthorized use of Ali's likeness. Instead, the picture is a dramatization, an illustration falling somewhere between representational art and cartoon, and is accompanied by a plainly fictional and allegedly libellous bit of doggerel." Ali's stature as a famous athlete would not provide a defense.

6. In some circumstances, the First Amendment may cover an advertisement which includes the name or picture of a public officer. In *New York Magazine v. Metropolitan Transit Authority*, 987 F. Supp. 254 (S.D.N.Y. 1997), the Southern District refused to permit Mayor Giuliani to direct the MTA to remove subway car cards which stated that *New York* Magazine was "possibly the only good thing in New York Rudy hasn't taken credit for." The magazine had sued claiming a violation of its civil rights under 42 U.S.C. §1983. The mayor had been the subject of articles

in the magazine, and there was a satiric aspect to the ads, so the magazine was entitled to rely on the "incidental promotion" defense described in the *Lerman* case (see 3.3.3 below).

7. On the other hand, in one case the use of a name in an advertisement was factually true but unprotected by free speech exceptions. Thus, in *Town & Country Properties, Inc. v. Riggins,* 1995 Va. LEXIS 54 (Va. 1995), involving a Virginia statute similar to New York's, the Virginia Supreme Court upheld a damage award in favor of former Washington Redskins running back John Riggins when a real estate agency used the phrase "John Riggins' Former Home" on a flyer seeking to sell the house on behalf of Riggins' ex-wife.

3.2.4 Defensive Aspects

The right of privacy must co-exist with state and federal rights of free speech. The same public official/public figure considerations that figure so strongly in the area of defamation also apply in the area of privacy, as does the concept of "newsworthiness" (even, in the *Leopold* case that follows, as to events that occurred in the past, and in some circumstances, e.g., the *Sidis* case, where the person with whom the media are concerned has assiduously sought anonymity but is still considered newsworthy). As we see in the *Rosemont* case, no public figure can exercise a monopoly with respect to his/her life story.

In *Rosemont Enterprises, Inc. v. Random House, Inc.,* 58 Misc.2d 1, 294 N.Y.S.2d 122 (N.Y. Sup. Ct. N.Y. Co. 1968), *aff'd,* 32 A.D.2d 892, 301 N.Y.S.2d 948 (N.Y. App. Dic1st Dep't. 1969), Howard Hughes sought to forestall the publication of an unauthorized biography by forming a wholly owned corporation and assigning to it the exclusive rights to his life story. In addition, the corporation bought up rights to a series of articles previously published about Hughes, to support an action for copyright infringement against Random House, whose book obviously covered some of the same events depicted in the articles. This failed, as did Hughes' claim for violation of his right of privacy under §§ 50 and 51 of the New York Civil Rights Law. In upholding the lower court's dismissal of Hughes' action, the court observed that

[a] public figure, whether he be such by choice or involuntarily, is subject to the often-searching beam of publicity and, in balance with the legitimate public interest, the law affords his privacy little protection. . . . That the New York statute gives a public figure no right to suppress truthful accounts of his life is now settled in the most unequivocal terms. . . . While plaintiff's condemnation of the literary merit and creative standards used in producing defendants' book might be of interest in a critique of the work appearing in a book review section, such arguments are wholly irrelevant in the present context. . . . The remaining ground on which plaintiff seeks to justify this suit is the assignment to it of Hughes' "right of publicity." This is a right that recognizes the pecuniary value which attaches to the names and pictures of public figures, particularly athletes and entertainers, and the right of such people to this financial benefit. . . . The publication of a biography is clearly outside the ambit of the "commercial use" contemplated by the "right of publicity" and such right can have no application to the publication of factual material which is constitutionally

protected. Just as a public figure's "right of privacy" must yield to the public interest so too must the "right of publicity" bow where such conflicts with the free dissemination of thoughts, ideas, newsworthy events, and matters of public interest.

Because of such considerations, a public figure can have no exclusive rights to his own life story, and others need no consent or permission of the subject to write a biography of a celebrity. . . .

The concept of newsworthiness is given broad application by the courts even where (as in the following case) the connection between the article and its subject is extremely attenuated. In addition, this case illustrates the degree of importance which attaches to the determination as to whether a defendant is a "publisher" or a "bookseller."

Lerman v. Flynt Distributing Co., 745 F.2d 123 (2d Cir. 1984)

CARDAMONE, J.

Defendant, a national distributor of magazines in which offensive material concerning plaintiff appeared, appeals from a judgment in plaintiff's favor. In her action plaintiff asserted causes of action for libel, violation of a statutory right of privacy, and appropriation of the common law right to publicity. In every invasion of privacy suit there is a course to be run in order for plaintiff to reach the goal or recovery. In this case, plaintiff's libel action was dismissed and her right to publicity claim fails to fit within that tort. The civil rights cause does not lie as one for advertising purposes, as that term is defined under state law; but it does state a cause of action for defendant's invasion for trade purposes of his right to privacy. Having successfully progressed that far, plaintiff would need to demonstrate a level of defendant's fault on that privacy claim sufficient to satisfy constitutional protection for freedom of the press. Here, on the final lap, plaintiff's proof falls short.

I. BACKGROUND

On February 29, 1980 the plaintiff Jackie Collins Lerman received a package at her home in London, England. An accompanying letter from a publicity agent who had formerly worked with Ms. Lerman explained that nude photographs, supposedly of plaintiff, appeared in the enclosed advance copy of *Adelina* magazine. Plaintiff discovered that the May 1980 issue of *Adelina* had misidentified her as an actress who appeared in Ms. Lerman's and her husband Oscar Lerman's movie entitled "The World is Full of Married Men." Two black and white photographs of the anonymous actress printed from the movie film appeared on pages 120–21 of the magazine. The misidentified actress appears topless in one of the pictures and in an "orgy" scene in the other. The caption identifies the photos as being

Ms. Lerman and labels her as the "starlet" who appeared in an orgy scene in the film.

The cover of the magazine proclaimed to its readers: "In the Nude from the *Playmen* archives . . . Jackie Collins." The short article accompanying the actress's photo with Ms. Lerman's name comments on the increasing willingness of "serious" actresses to appear nude in films. While Ms. Lerman authored the book and wrote the screenplay for "Married Men" and her husband directed the movie, she did not appear in the movie, clothed or otherwise, and has never appeared nude in public.

Immediately upon receipt of this package, Ms. Lerman retained a lawyer and three weeks later—on March 24, 1980—commenced an action. . . . Plaintiff sought an injunction and damages based on (a) libel (b) defendant's violation of New York's Civil Rights Law §§ 50–51 and (c) invasion of her common law right to publicity.

On March 31 the district judge issued a preliminary injunction restraining the distribution of *Adelina*. While the extent of the original defendants' compliance with that injunction is disputed, it is clear that Publishers Distributing informed all of its more than 500 nationwide wholesale customers of Ms. Lerman's lawsuit and the outstanding injunction, and requested that all unsold copies of the magazine be returned. . . .

In June 1983, . . . plaintiff proceeded to trial before a jury against Flynt Distributing. Ms. Lerman sought damages under her New York statutory privacy claim and her common law right to publicity arising from the May 1980 publication. Inasmuch as liability had already been determined in her favor by the trial court's grant of summary judgment, she also sought damages for distribution of the June 1980 and January 1981 editions of *Adelina*. After a short trial the jury returned a special verdict determining that defendant Flynt Distributing was liable for the May 1980 issue and awarding Ms. Lerman a total of $7 million in compensatory and $33 million in exemplary damages. The trial court struck $30 million from the exemplary damage award, leaving intact an award of $7 million compensatory and $3 million exemplary damages. It is from this $10 million judgment that defendant Flynt Distributing has appealed.

Since plaintiff has not cross-appealed, we need not consider whether the district court correctly dismissed plaintiff's libel claim on the ground that she failed to plead special damages. Discussion will focus primarily on two causes of action—New York's statutory action for violation of the right of privacy and the common law action for violation of the right to publicity. The parties agree that New York law governs in this diversity case.

II. GROUNDS FOR RECOVERY UNDER STATE LAW

. . . On its face the New York Privacy statute seems to provide a cause of action only for "commercial appropriation." . . .

The terms "advertising purposes" and "trade purposes" constitute the two prongs of the statute and their meaning, as construed by New York courts, is crucial to an analysis of plaintiff's claims in this case.

1. Advertising Purposes Under § 51

Where the use of plaintiff's name is solely for the purpose of soliciting purchasers for defendant's products the advertising purposes prong of the statute is violated. . . .

When the advertisement is merely incidental to a privileged use there is no violation of § 51. . . . Plaintiff cannot argue that the use of her name (accompanied by a photo of an unclad woman) in the May 1980 issue of *Adelina* was for advertising purposes. She did not show a "use for the solicitation of patronage for a particular service or product." . . . The June 1980 and January 1981 uses could be viewed as for advertising purposes since they solicited orders for back issues of *Adelina.* But, the republications in the June 1980 and January 1981 subscription solicitations were incidental to the May 1980 publication. Because the solicitations were designed simply to convey the nature and content of the past *Adelina* issues, they cannot form the advertising use prong of § 51. . . .

Trade Purposes Under §51

Next, we examine whether the uses of plaintiff's name were for "purposes of trade" under the statute. Because the media in reporting the news routinely uses names and likenesses without consent, New York courts early recognized the need to encourage the free exchange of ideas and created a broad privilege for the legitimate dissemination to the public of news and information.

. . . The trade purposes prong of the statute may not be used to prevent comment on matters in which the public has a right to be informed. . . . Where plaintiff is a public personage or an actual participant in a newsworthy event, the use of his name or likeness is not for purposes or trade within the meaning of § 51. . . . Yet, there are limits to the privilege: "While one who is a public figure or is presently newsworthy may be the proper subject of news of informative presentation, the privilege does not extend to commercialization of his personality through a form of treatment distinct from the dissemination of news or information." . . . Since "newsworthiness" and "public interest" are to be "freely defined," . . . the use of plaintiff's name in connection with the movie "The World is Full of Married Men" is a matter in which the public plainly has a legitimate interest.

Plaintiff may still be entitled to obtain the sanctions of § 51 under the trade purposes prong even where the use is in conjunction with a report on a matter of public interest, but in order to do so must meet one of two tests. First, a plaintiff may attempt to demonstrate that the use of plaintiff's name or likeness has no real relationship to the discussion, and thus is an advertisement in disguise. . . .

Alternatively, a plaintiff may claim that defendant forfeited the privilege for reporting matters on which the public has the right to be informed by proving that the defendant's use was infected with material and substantial fiction or falsity. . . . Even when so infected, for defendant to lose the newsworthy privilege plaintiff must prove that defendant acted with some degree of fault regarding the fictionalization or falsification. . . .

We cannot accept plaintiff's first argument that the photo in this case has "no real relationship" to any discussion in *Adelina*. Ms. Lerman wrote the book and screenplay that contained scenes of nudity for the film "The World is Full of Married Men." While the article in *Adelina* was vapid it did relate to the growing use of nudity in films. Insofar as the use of the name "Jackie Collins" is concerned the May 1980 use must be considered incidental to the story, and hence not objectionable as a "disguised advertisement" under § 51. . . . Further, plaintiff's status as an author and screenwriter of a film in the erotic genre makes her claim of "no connection" with these particular photographs unpersuasive. . . . Thus Ms. Lerman was not an innocent bystander without any relationship to the subject matter of the article and to the photograph.

Plaintiff's reliance on the alternative basis for defeating the newsworthy privilege rests on firmer ground, that is, the fictionalization or falsification ground. . . .

When presented with a factual error which brings an otherwise privileged newsworthy use within the trade purpose prohibition, the Supreme Court and the New York Court of Appeals have required that there be a finding of fault. . . .

We agree that plaintiff's name in all three *Adelina* issues are [sic] fictionalized or false and therefore lose the privilege that ordinarily extends to reporting matters in which the public has an interest. Further, the degree of falsity here was severe since plaintiff was not the actress pictured. Were it not for constitutional concerns this falsity would permit a properly instructed jury to find the uses here to be for trade purposes under § 51 of the New York Civil Rights law. But, precisely because of First Amendment guarantees Flynt Distributing cannot be held liable for the use of plaintiff's name unless it acted with the requisite fault, and it is on this last point that plaintiff's proof fails as we will later explain. . . .

C. Plaintiff's Claim of a Right to Publicity

In her complaint, plaintiff also included a cause of action based upon her common law right to publicity on which the district court granted her summary judgment. It is unnecessary to determine the precise outlines of that right under New York law because it is not implicated. Here, the right to publicity is essentially identical to the right to be free from commercial appropriation. . . . In light of the proof, a claim for commercial appropriation or violation of the right to publicity does not lie. . . . The right is one designed to encourage intellectual and creative works and to prevent unjust enrichment.

In a publicity case the plaintiff is not so concerned that the use occurs; he simply wants to be the one to decide when and where, and to be paid for it. . . .

Because the plaintiff must generally have developed a property interest with financial value in order to prove that he suffered damages, the right is most frequently invoked by public figures or celebrities. . . . Thus, Ms. Lerman's insistence that she is a private person insofar as these *Adelina* articles are concerned does not square with her claim that her right to publicity was appropriated. Plaintiff did not establish a prima facie cause of action for violation of her right to publicity. She has never exploited the value of her nude appearance and obviously cannot claim to have developed a property interest in the subject matter of this alleged infringement. Moreover, proof that this is not a right to publicity case is in plaintiff's demand for relief—she sought to enjoin publication and to salve her wounded feelings—neither of which are the kinds of injuries that the publicity tort is designed to remedy. There is simply no evidence that any defendant deliberately exploited plaintiff's fame and fortune. Inasmuch as the facts fail to establish a violation of plaintiff's right to publicity as a matter of law, her cause of action on that theory should have been dismissed.

D. False Light Tort Distinguishable from Right to Publicity

Despite this conclusion, we undertake a brief analysis of the false light tort because it is essential to an understanding of the application of the First Amendment to § 51. While not specifically alleged in her complaint, Ms. Lerman's action presents a classic false light claim, which is distinguishable from her right to publicity cause of action. In *Time, Inc. v. Hill,* 385 U.S. 374, 87 S.Ct. 534, 17 L.Ed.2d 456 (1967) the Supreme Court observed that New York Courts have construed the language of § 51 broadly enough to encompass false light claims. . . .

The Court stressed that where falsity is the gravamen of a § 51 claim, First Amendment guarantees permit imposition of liability only where actual malice is shown. . . .

Assuming the requisite proof of fault the facts of this case state a cause of action under [restatement] section 652E. The nude actress pictured was not Ms. Lerman. Whether or not this misidentification is defamatory to Ms. Lerman . . . we cannot conclude that such publicity is not "highly offensive to a reasonable person." . . . Hence, if a false light claim under the Restatement rubric is recognized in New York, Ms. Lerman has stated a claim under it.

In a false light case, however styled under a state statute or common law, the gravamen of the tort is falsity; not, as here, simply a factual error. Further, regardless of whether Ms. Lerman's cause of action is cast in terms of libel or false light or under the falsified trade purposes prong of § 51, the same constitutional protections apply. . . . Therefore, we must address the federal constitutional question to determine the appropriate standard of fault plaintiff should have been required to meet and to evaluate plaintiff's proof under that constitutional standard. In what follows we explain why plaintiff's proof falls short, defeating her cause against defendant.

III. CONSTITUTIONAL ISSUES

A. Public or Private Figure

To begin, the district court erroneously ruled in 1980 that the public figure question had application only to plaintiff's dismissed libel claim. . . .

No doubt defendant has shown that plaintiff successfully invited public attention to her views and has maintained continuing access to the media. Nonetheless, we agree with the district court that Ms. Lerman is not an all purpose public figure. . . .

But we believe Ms. Lerman is a limited purpose public figure required to satisfy the New York Times standard of fault. By voluntarily devoting herself to the public's interest in sexual mores, through extensive writing on this topic, reaping profits and wide notoriety for herself in the process, Ms. Lerman must be deemed to have purposefully surrendered part of what would otherwise have been her protectible privacy rights, at least those related in some way to her involvement in writing her books and screenplays. . . .

The difficult question is whether Ms. Lerman injected herself into a "public controversy" related to the offending publication. . . . The relations between the sexes and public nudity are topics of continued and general public interest and may be considered "public controversies" even though not involving political debate or criticism of public officials. A public "controversy" is any topic upon which sizeable segments of society have different, strongly held views. Certainly various groups today have vastly divergent views on the propriety of female or male nudity in films and in the print media generally. In the public controversies that daily swirl about—be they politics, pocketbook issues, or, as here, contemporary standards regarding nudity—some plunge into the arena and enter the fray. Plaintiff, as a controversial, outspoken authoress and screenwriter advocating equal nudity, was such a willing participant in this public controversy. . . .

B. Newsworthiness for First Amendment Purposes

The district court adopted plaintiff's argument that an actual malice standard of fault does not apply even if plaintiff is a public figure because the use was "completely exploitive" and outside the broad category of matters of public interest and therefore not newsworthy. This led it erroneously to conclude that the distributor could be held strictly liable for disseminating the magazine without treading on the

First Amendment. On the contrary, *Adelina* falls far short of crossing the line that would cause it to forfeit First Amendment protection. . . .

The factual error in this case would be actionable only if the distribution of *Adelina* loses First Amendment protection under a standard analogous to that which causes libelous speech to lose such protection. . . . We cannot accept a view that a publication must meet an independent standard of newsworthiness to stand under the umbrella of First Amendment protection. Even "vulgar" publications are entitled to such guarantees. . . .

The *Adelina* article unquestionably would have been within the broad definition of a newsworthy matter or a matter of public interest or concern had Ms. Lerman in fact been the "starlet" pictured. That there was a factual error does not alter the subject matter of the offending publication. . . .

C. Proof of Actual Malice

1. Actual Malice of Distributors

First Amendment guarantees have long been recognized as protecting distributors of publications. . . .

Obviously, the national distributor of hundreds of periodicals has no duty to monitor each issue of every periodical it distributes. Such a rule would be an impermissible burden on the First Amendment. At the same time a distributor as an integral part of the movement of information from the creator to the reader—the distributor here was to receive 46% of the profit from the sale of the magazine—cannot be entirely immune from liability. When a distributor acts with the requisite scienter in distributing materials defaming or invading the privacy of a private figure it must be subject to liability. . . .

The essential inquiry is whether those in charge of Flynt Distributing had serious doubts about the accuracy of the identification of Ms. Lerman in *Adelina*. . . .

Inasmuch as the district court failed to instruct the jury that it must find Flynt Distributing to have acted with actual malice, the jury's verdicts must be reversed. Nevertheless, since the record is complete with regard to Flynt Distributing's knowledge and conduct, both of which are necessary to prove a "knowing use" for punitive damages under § 51, we examine the evidence to determine whether a new trial is warranted.

2. Actual Malice in This Case

. . . The question to decide is whether the trial judge should have granted summary judgment to the defendant based on the lack of evidence of actual malice.

In the first place, plaintiff failed to offer proof sufficient even to impose a duty on defendant Flynt Distributing to inquire as to the May 1980 issue and the district court specifically found that there was no "knowing" use under § 51 by defendant of plaintiff's name in that issue. Further, there was no proof that any of defendant's employees had reason to believe that Chuckleberry (the publisher) would mis-identify Ms. Lerman as the actress pictured. . . .

Similarly, with respect to the June 1980 and January 1981 issues there is no evidence in the record showing that Flynt Distributing knew or recklessly disregarded whether these editions contained any mention of plaintiff, let alone any factual error concerning her. . . . Flynt Distributing may be held liable only if plaintiff presented clear and convincing evidence that some high level employee of the corporation acted with reckless disregard of the fact that false matter had been published by Chuckleberry. The only evidence pointing in that direction is the conceded fact that Flynt Distributing knew of plaintiff's lawsuit against Chuckleberry and Publishers Distributing for the May 1980 issue, plus a claimed failure thereafter by it to investigate. Plaintiff cites no other evidence in her brief, and careful examination of the voluminous record in this case reveals none.

Absent are any facts demonstrating that anyone in the defendant distributing company had a subjective awareness of probable falsity. Notice of the lawsuit regarding the May issue standing alone certainly is not clear and convincing evidence as to knowledge for June and January, especially given the minuscule mention of plaintiff in those issues. Moreover, mere failure to investigate, while relevant, is also not itself sufficient to show actual malice. . . .

IV. THE DAMAGE AWARDS

The jury awarded plaintiff a total of seven million dollars in compensatory damages, which the trial court refused to reduce. No doubt such an enormous verdict chills media First Amendment rights. But a verdict of this size does more than chill an individual defendant's rights, it deep-freezes that particular media defendant permanently. Putting aside First Amendment implications of "megaverdicts" frequently imposed by juries in media cases, the compensatory damages awarded shock the conscience of this Court. They are grossly excessive and obviously a product of plaintiff's counsel's appeals to the passion and prejudice of the jury. It cannot seriously be contended that Ms. Lerman's lacerated feelings are worth anything close to $7 million. No proof was offered that she sought or needed professional help because of these publications and the fact she completed a novel between March and September in 1980 refutes her contention that she was unable to work. In any event, damages under the New York statute often are only nominal since they are designed primarily to compensate for injury to feelings. . . .

Finally, we note that reputational damage to Ms. Lerman could not have been great. Only the readers of *Adelina,* a magazine of relatively modest circulation that Ms. Lerman describes as "sordid" and "obscene" would have seen the offending material. In fact, given the number of famous persons portrayed in this fashion, one wonders whether such pictures are even capable of producing genuine reputational harm. Even assuming the word would get around to those whose esteem of plaintiff would be diminished, the main source of publicity for the pictures came not from the magazine's publication, but from Ms. Lerman's lawsuit and statements to the press.

The jury also awarded a total of $33 million in punitive damages, more than plaintiff demanded in her complaint and over six times greater than plaintiff's counsel requested in this summation. This award also shocks our conscience and reinforces our conclusion that the verdicts represent appeals to passion or prejudice.

V. CONCLUSION

The availability of damages depends on plaintiff's ability to satisfy the actual malice standard of *New York Times v. Sullivan* that plaintiff as a limited purpose public figure was required to meet. Since Ms. Lerman cannot present clear and convincing evidence of defendant's requisite fault with respect to the factual error disseminated, the judgment awarding her ten million dollars in compensatory and punitive damages is reversed as a matter of law and her complaint against Flynt Distributing is dismissed.

[BONSAL, J., dissenting in part, would give the plaintiff an opportunity for further discovery and a trial on the issue of actual malice, that is whether defendant acted with knowledge of falsity or in reckless disregard of the truth.]

Even where an individual is not a prominent personality, like Howard Hughes (who had already begun to retreat from his public prominence at the time of the *Rosemont* case), a popular novelist like Jackie Collins, or a public official like Mayor Giuliani, an individual may attract public attention because of events with which he/she is involved, and this involvement may entitle the media to continue to deal with him for (in some cases, many) years.

NOTES

1. The "newsworthiness" defense is extremely broad, as illustrated by *Messenger v. Gruner + Jahr*, 208 F.3d 122 (2d Cir. 2000), in which the Second Circuit, after referring questions to the New York Court of Appeals (see *Messenger v. Gruner + Jahr printing*, 94 N.Y.2d 436 [2000]), held that there was no violation of §§ 50 and 51 where a model posed for a series of photographs to appear in *Young and Modern* (*YM*), a magazine for teenage girls, and *YM* used the photos to illustrate a "Love Crisis" column. The column began with a letter from a 14-year-old girl identified only as "Mortified," who wrote that she had gotten drunk at a party and then had sex with her 18-year-old boyfriend and two of his friends. Above the column, in bold type, was a pull-out quotation stating, "I got trashed and had sex with three guys." The photographs of plaintiff included one showing her hiding her face, with three young men gloating in the background. The captions were keyed to the columnist's advice: "Wake up and face the facts: You made a pretty big mistake;" "Don't try to hide—just ditch him and his buds;" and "Afraid you're pregnant? See a doctor."

2. Nor is a fictionalized account of a newsworthy event necessarily ineligible for First Amendment protection. *Wojtowicz v. Delacorte Press*, 43 N.Y.2d 858, 403 N.Y.S.2d 218

(2d Dept. 1978), involved the film *Dog Day Afternoon*, which was based upon a notorious Brooklyn bank robbery that originally was covered extensively in the newspapers and by a later feature in *Life* magazine. The opening scene of the movie announced the story as true and gave the date of the robbery and the fact that it had taken place in Brooklyn. However, while *Life* had mentioned the names of the wife and children of one of the robbers, the film did not use the real names of either the robbers or their relatives. The "wife," mentioned in *Life*, was a minor character in the film, and the children were mentioned only incidentally. The court rejected the wife and children's claims of invasion of privacy. The court held that no rights of privacy in New York existed apart from Civil Rights Law, §§50 and 51, and since the plaintiffs' names and likenesses were not used, no causes of action existed. (Plaintiffs' claims for defamation were reserved for further consideration.)

3. Where individuals voluntarily enter the public arena, they must expect to endure the consequences of such participation. For example, where parties voluntarily appear on talk shows and make disclosures which might constitute invasions of privacy in other contexts, they cannot sue the producers of such shows for providing the environment within which other, related disclosures occur. *Howell v. Tribune Entertainment Co.*, 106 F.3d 215, 1997 U.S.App.LEXIS 2024 (7th Cir. 1997). In this instance, the Seventh Circuit upheld the dismissal of an action brought by a 16-year-old who had appeared on the Charles Perez Show with her stepmother. When the teenager accused her stepmother of adultery and abuse, the stepmother proceeded to read a police report which described the teenager as "violent and abusive," among other things. Since the stepmother's response would have been privileged, the producer of the program could assert the same privilege. Moreover, a different rule would have a chilling effect on the media.

3.3 PERSONAL RIGHTS: PUBLICITY

The legally enforceable right of publicity is a fairly recent development. To state that the contours of the right are still being refined is clearly an understatement. For example, some jurisdictions still subsume the right of publicity under the right of privacy (this is the case in New York where, under the decision in *Stephano v. News Group* [see above], the Court of Appeals has declared that there is no common law right of publicity in New York); in others the right of publicity is wholly separate, independent and is regarded as a property right (whether at common law, pursuant to statute, or, in some cases, both).

The right of publicity is defined as the right of each individual to control and profit from the commercial value of his or her own identity. The right as recognized protects the unauthorized commercial exploitation of a celebrity's name (actual or legal), likeness, as well as other aspects of identity such as photograph, portrait, caricature, and biographical facts and records of performance. As a practical matter, celebrities are the principal parties who have value in their names and likeness.

The rationale for the right of publicity is the protection of a celebrity's proprietary interest in the development of a marketable image. Arguably, publicity rights serve social interests by guarding against unjust enrichment and promote creativity by offering financial incentive to those choosing to cultivate a unique persona.

Some jurisdictions require that for a right of publicity to be descendible the celebrity must have commercially exploited the rights during his or her lifetime, although most jurisdictions have no such prerequisite. Jurisdictions approach the right of publicity in a multitude of ways. As we see in Section 3.3.2, a number of states have adopted statutory provisions. However, state statutes do not necessarily cover all possible scenarios. In some situations, common law relief may be available for situations which are not covered by statute. This is the subject of Section 3.3.3.

One of the important issues in this area is whether rights of publicity survive the death of the celebrity concerned and, if so, whether such rights are inheritable and devisable. This is discussed in Section 3.3.4.

As is the case with the right of privacy, defenses are available when subjects are public figures, or a matter is newsworthy, and, in addition, media are permitted to utilize materials which might in other contexts violate rights of publicity where the use is designed to promote circulation. This is discussed in Section 3.3.5.

Finally, as we see in Section 3.4, Congressional enactments such as Section 43(a) of the Lanham Act, 15 U.S.C § 1125(a), unfair competition and other provisions of Federal trademark law have provided a nationwide remedy which, in many instances, is easier to achieve than relief under state right of publicity statutes and common law doctrines. Here too, however, media are accorded considerable latitude.

NOTE

See generally J. T. McCarthy, *The Rights of Publicity and Privacy* (New York: Clark Boardman & Co. 1987).

3.3.1 At Common Law

Courts have struggled with distinctions between the two rights. In 1953 a breakthrough occurred in *Haelan Laboratories, Inc. v. Topps Chewing Gum*, 202 F.2d 866 (2d Cir. 1953), *cert. denied*, 346 U.S. 816 (1953), in which the court expressly recognized a right of publicity. The court held that "in addition to and independent of the right of privacy . . . a man has a right in the publicity value of his photograph, i.e., the right to grant the exclusive privilege of publishing his picture." The court rejected the contention that the only protectible right, if any, in the publication of a celebrity's picture after it was validly assigned existed in a right of privacy. (The *Haelan* case involved the use of players' likenesses on baseball trading cards. It is noteworthy that the most recent baseball trading card case, *Cardtoons v. Major League Baseball Players*, 838 F. Supp. 1501 (N.D. Okl. 1993) reached an opposite result, because the cards involved parody characters such as "Cal Ripenwinkle" and the "Los Angeles Codgers" rather than literal depictions of the players.)

Other courts soon followed *Haelan*, including *Chaplin v. National Broadcasting Co.*, 15 F.R.D. 134 (S.D.N.Y. 1953) and continued over the next thirty years to include such notable decisions as *Martin Luther*

King, Jr. Center for Social Change, Inc. v. American Heritage Products, Inc., 296 S.E.2d 697 (Ga. 1982), which opinion was adopted and attached as Exhibit "A" by the 11th Circuit in *Martin Luther King, Jr. Center for Social Change, Inc. v. American Heritage Products, Inc.*, 694 F.2d 674 (11th Cir. 1983) discussed in this section following the *Zacchini* case below. In a right-of-publicity claim, a claimant must show the development "of a property interest with a monetary value in his or her name or face." See *Allen v. National Video, Inc.*, 610 F. Supp. 360, 367 (S.D.N.Y. 1985) (*infra*, Section 3.5.2). *See also* Nimmer, *The Right of Publicity, Law and Contemporary Problems*, vol. 19 (Chapel Hill, N.C.: School of Law, Duke University, 1954).

In the following case, the U.S. Supreme Court emphasizes the commercial nature of the right of publicity.

Zacchini v. Scripps-Howard Broadcasting Co., 433 U.S. 562 (1977)

JUSTICE WHITE DELIVERED THE OPINION OF THE COURT.

Petitioner, Hugo Zacchini, is an entertainer. He performs a "human cannonball" act in which he is shot from a cannon into a net some 200 feet away. Each performance occupies some 15 seconds. In August and September 1972, petitioner was engaged to perform his act on a regular basis at the Geauga County Fair in Burton, Ohio. He performed in a fenced area, surrounded by grandstands, at the fair grounds. Members of the public attending the fair were not charged a separate admission fee to observe his act. [Despite Zacchini's request that he not do so, a TV reporter taped Zacchini's entire act, which was then shown on the evening news, together with favorable commentary] Zacchini sued for damages for misappropriation of his "professional property." The act had been invented by his father, and had been performed only by the Zacchini family for fifty years. The Ohio appellate courts] rested petitioner's cause of action under state law on his "right to publicity value of his performance." 47 Ohio St. 2d 224, 351 N.E. 2d 454, 455 (1976). The opinion syllabus, to which we are to look for the rule of law used to decide the case, declared first that one may not use for his own benefit the name or likeness of another, whether or not the use or benefit is a commercial one, and second that respondent would be liable for the appropriation, over petitioner's objection and in the absence of license or privilege, of petitioner's right to the publicity value of his performance. *Ibid*. The court nevertheless gave judgment for respondent because, in the words of the syllabus:

A TV station has a privilege to report in its newscasts matters of legitimate public interest which would otherwise be protected by an individual's right of publicity, unless the actual intent of the TV station was to appropriate the benefit of the publicity of some nonprivileged private use, or unless the actual intent was to injure the individual. *Ibid*.

. . . [However,] we reverse the judgment of [the Ohio Supreme Court]. . . .

The Ohio Supreme Court held that respondent is constitutionally privileged to include in its newscasts matters of public interest that would otherwise be protected by the right of publicity, absent an intent to injure or to appropriate for some nonprivileged purpose. If under this standard respondent had merely reported that petitioner was performing at the fair and described or commented on his act, with or without showing his picture on television, we would have a very different case. But petitioner is not contending that his appearance at the fair and his performance could not be reported by the press as newsworthy items. His complaint is that respondent filmed his entire act and displayed that film on television for the public to see and enjoy. . . .

The Ohio Supreme Court nevertheless held that the challenged invasion was privileged, saying that the press "must be accorded broad latitude in its choice of how much it presents of each story or incident, and of the emphasis to be given to such presentation. No fixed standard which would bar the press from reporting or depicting either an entire occurrence or an entire discrete part of a public performance can be formulated which would not unduly restrict the 'breathing room' in reporting which freedom of the press requires." 47 Ohio St. 2d, at 235, 351 N.E. 2d, at 461. Under this view, respondent was thus constitutionally free to film and display petitioner's entire act.

The Ohio Supreme Court relied heavily on *Time, Inc. v. Hill,* 385 U.S. 374 (1967), but that case does not mandate a media privilege to televise a performer's entire act without his consent. Involved in *Time, Inc. v. Hill* was a claim under the New York "Right to Privacy" statute that *Life Magazine,* in the course of reviewing a new play, had connected the play with a long-past incident involving petitioner and his family and had falsely described their experience and conduct at that time. The complaint sought damages for humiliation and suffering flowing from these nondefamatory falsehoods that allegedly invaded Hill's privacy. The Court held, however, that the opening of a new play linked to an actual incident was a matter of public interest and that Hill could not recover without showing that the *Life* report was knowingly false or was published with reckless disregard for the truth—the same rigorous standard that had been applied in *New York Times* Co. v. *Sullivan,* 376 U.S. 254 (1964).

Time, Inc. v. Hill . . . involved an entirely different tort from the "right of publicity" recognized by the Ohio Supreme Court. As the opinion reveals in *Time, Inc. v. Hill,* the Court was steeped in the literature of privacy law and was aware of the developing distinctions and nuances in this branch of the law . . . *Time, Inc. v. Hill* did not involve a performer, a person with a name having commercial value, or any claim to a "right of publicity." This discrete kind of "appropriation" case was plainly identified in the literature cited by the Court and had been adjudicated in the reported cases.

The differences between these two torts are important. First, the State's interests in providing a cause of action in each instance are different. "The interest protected" in permitting recovery for placing the plaintiff in a false light "is clearly that of reputation, with the same overtones of mental distress as in defamation." Prosser, *supra,* 48 Calif. L. Rev., at 400. By contrast, the State's interest in permitting a "right of publicity" is in protecting the proprietary interest of the individual in his act in part to encourage such entertainment. As we later note, the State's interest is closely analogous to the goals of patent and copyright law, focusing on the right of the individual to reap the reward of his endeavors and having little to do with protecting feelings or reputation. Second, the two torts differ in the degree to which they intrude on dissemination of information to the public. In "false light" cases the only way to protect the interests involved is to attempt to minimize publication of the damaging matter, while in "right of publicity" cases the only question is who gets to do the publishing. An entertainer such as petitioner usually has no objection to the widespread publication of his act as long as he gets the commercial benefit of such publication. Indeed, in the present case petitioner did not seek to enjoin the broadcast of his act; he simply sought compensation for the broadcast in the form of damages. . . .

The broadcast of a film of petitioner's entire act poses a substantial threat to the economic value of that performance . . . [I]f the public can see the act free on television, it will be less willing to pay to see it at the fair. The effect of a public broadcast of the performance is similar to preventing petitioner from charging an admission fee. "The rationale for [protecting the right of publicity] is the straightforward one of preventing unjust enrichment by the theft of goodwill. No social purpose is served by having the defendant get free some aspect of the plaintiff that would have market value and for which he would normally pay." Kalven, "Privacy in Tort Law—Were Warren and Brandeis Wrong?" 31 *Law & Contemp. Prob.* 326, 331 (1966). Moreover, the broadcast of petitioner's entire performance, unlike the unauthorized use of another's name for purposes of trade or the incidental use of a name or picture by the press, goes to the heart of petitioner's ability to earn a living as an entertainer. Thus, in this case, Ohio has recognized what may be the strongest case for a "right of publicity"—involving, not the appropriation of an entertainer's reputation to enhance the attractiveness of a commercial product, but the appropriation of the very activity by which the entertainer acquired his reputation in the first place.

Of course, Ohio's decision to protect petitioner's right of publicity here rests on more than a desire to compensate the performer for the time and effort invested in his act; the protection provides an economic incentive for him to make the investment required to produce a performance of interest to the public. This same consideration underlies the patent and copyright laws long enforced by this Court. . . . The laws perhaps regard the "reward to the owner

[as] a secondary consideration," *United States v. Paramount Pictures,* 334 U.S. 131, 158 (1948), but they were "intended definitely to grant valuable, enforceable right" in order to afford greater encouragement to the production of works of benefit to the public, *Washington Publishing Co. v. Pearson,* 306 U.S. 30, 36 (1939). The Constitution does not prevent Ohio from making a similar choice here in deciding to protect the entertainer's incentive in order to encourage the production of this type of work. Cf. *Goldstein v. California,* 412 U.S. 546 (1973). . . .

There is no doubt that entertainment, as well as news, enjoys First Amendment protection. It is also true that entertainment itself can be important news. *Time, Inc. v. Hill.* But it is important to note that neither the public nor respondent will be deprived of the benefit of petitioner's performance as long as his commercial stake in his act is appropriately recognized. Petitioner does not seek to enjoin the broadcast of his performance; he simply wants to be paid for it. . . .

We conclude that although the State of Ohio may as a matter of its own law privilege the press in the circumstances of this case, the First and Fourteenth Amendments do not require it to do so. *Reversed.*

JUSTICE POWELL, WITH WHOM JUSTICE BRENNAN AND JUSTICE MARSHALL JOIN, DISSENTING

Disclaiming any attempt to do more than decide the narrow case before us, the Court reverses the decision of the Supreme Court of Ohio based on repeated incantation of a single formula: "a performer's entire act." The holding today is summed up in one sentence:

Wherever the line in particular situations is to be drawn between media reports that are protected and those that are not, we are quite sure that the First and Fourteenth Amendments do not immunize the media when they broadcast a performer's entire act without his consent.

I doubt that this formula provides a standard clear enough even for resolution of this case. In any event, I am not persuaded that the Court's opinion is appropriately sensitive to the First Amendment values at stake, and I therefore dissent.

Although the Court would draw no distinction, . . . I do not view respondent's action as comparable to unauthorized commercial broadcasts of sporting events, theatrical performances, and the like where the broadcaster keeps the profits. There is no suggestion here that respondent made any such use of the film. Instead, it simply reported on what petitioner concedes to be a newsworthy event, in a way hardly surprising for a television station—means of film coverage. The report was part of an ordinary daily news program, consuming a total of 15 seconds. It is a routine example of the press' fulfilling the informing function so vital to our system.

The Court's holding that the station's ordinary news report may give rise to substantial liability has disturbing implications, for the decision could lead to a degree of media self-censorship. Cf. *Smith v. California,* 361 U.S. 147, 150–154 (1959). Hereafter, whenever a television news editor is unsure whether certain film footage received from a camera crew might be held to portray an "entire act," he may decline coverage—even of clearly newsworthy events—or confine the broadcast to watered-down verbal reporting, perhaps with an occasional still picture. The public is then the loser. This is hardly the kind of news reportage that the First Amendment is meant to foster. . . .

In my view the First Amendment commands a different analytical starting point from the one selected by the Court. Rather than begin with a quantitative analysis of the performer's behavior—is this or is this not his entire act?—we should direct initial attention to the actions of the news media: what use did the station make of the film footage? When a film is used, as here, for a routine portion of a regular news program, I would hold that the First Amendment protects the station from a "right of publicity" or "appropriation" suit, absent a strong showing by the plaintiff that the news broadcast was a subterfuge or cover for private or commercial exploitation. . . . Since the film clip here was undeniably treated as news and since there is no claim that the use was subterfuge, respondent's actions were constitutionally privileged. I would affirm.

Martin Luther King, Jr. Center for Social Change, Inc., et al. v. American Heritage Products, Inc., et al., F.2d 674; 1983 U.S. APP. LEXIS 27928 (11ᵗʰ Circuit, 1983)

OPINION

In our previous consideration of this case, *The Martin Luther King, Jr., Center for Social Change, Inc. v. American Heritage Products, Inc.,* No. 81–7264 (11th Cir., Apr. 1, 1982), we certified the following questions to the Supreme Court of Georgia pursuant to Georgia Code Annotated ß 24–3902 permitting such procedure:

(1) Is the "right to publicity" recognized in Georgia as a right distinct from the right to privacy?
(2) If the answer to question (1) is affirmative, does the "right to publicity" survive the death of its owner? Specifically, is the right inheritable and devisable?
(3) If the answer to question (2) is also affirmative, must the owner have commercially exploited the right before it can survive his death?
(4) Assuming affirmative answers to questions (1), (2) and (3), what is the guideline to be followed in defining commercial exploitation and what are the evidentiary prerequisites to a showing of commercial exploitation?

The Supreme Court of Georgia, *The Martin Luther King, Jr., Center for Social Change, Inc. v. American Heritage Products, Inc.,* 250 Ga. 135, 296 S.E.2d 697 (1982), has answered questions (1) and (2) affirmatively and question (3) in the negative in an opinion attached hereto as Exhibit A.

Pursuant to this opinion, the opinion of the Supreme Court of Georgia, and that court's answers to the first three certified questions, we reverse the judgment of the district court and remand for further proceedings.

REVERSED and REMANDED.

Exhibit A

In the Supreme Court of Georgia

Decided: Oct. 28, 1982

38748. The MARTIN LUTHER KING, JR., CENTER FOR SOCIAL CHANGE, INC., et al. v. AMERICAN HERITAGE PRODUCTS, INC., et al. [250 Ga. 135, 296 S.E.2d 697 (1982)].

HILL, Presiding Justice.

These are certified questions regarding the "right of publicity". The certification comes from the United States Court of Appeals for the Eleventh Circuit. Code Ann. ß 24–3902, see *Miree v. United States of America, 242 Ga. 126, 131–133, 249 S.E.2d 573 (1978)*. The facts upon which the questions arise are as follows: [n1]

n1 The statement of facts is taken almost verbatim from the Court of Appeals' certification. For convenience, the parties will be identified as they appeared in the district court.

The plaintiffs are the Martin Luther King, Jr. Center for Social Change (the Center),[n2] Coretta Scott King, as administratrix of Dr. King's estate, and Motown Record Corporation, the assignee of the rights to several of Dr. King's copyrighted speeches. Defendant James F. Bolen is the sole proprietor of a business known as B & S Sales, which manufactures and sells various plastic products as funeral accessories. Defendant James E. Bolen, the son of James F. Bolen, developed the concept of marketing a plastic bust of Dr. Martin Luther King, Jr., and formed a company, B & S Enterprises, to sell the busts, which would be manufactured by B & S Sales. B & S Enterprises was later incorporated under the name of American Heritage Products, Inc.

n2 The Center is a non-profit corporation which seeks to promote the ideals of Dr. King.

Although Bolen sought the endorsement and participation of the Martin Luther King, Jr., Center for Social Change, Inc., in the marketing of the bust, the Center refused Bolen's offer. Bolen pursued the idea, nevertheless, hiring an artist to prepare a mold and an agent to handle the promotion of the product. Defendant took out two half-page advertisements in the November and December 1980 issues of *Ebony* magazine, which purported to offer the bust as "an exclusive memorial" and "an opportunity to support the Martin Luther King, Jr., Center for Social Change." The advertisement stated that "a contribution from your order goes to the King Center for Social Change." Out of the $29.95 purchase price, defendant Bolen testified he set aside 3% or $.90, as a contribution to the Center. The advertisement also offered "free" with the purchase of the bust a booklet about the life of Dr. King entitled "A Tribute to Dr. Martin Luther King, Jr."

In addition to the two advertisements in *Ebony*, defendant published a brochure or pamphlet which was inserted in 80,000 copies of newspapers across the country. The brochure reiterated what was stated in the magazine advertisements, and also contained photographs of Dr. King and excerpts from his copyrighted speeches. The brochure promised that each "memorial" (bust) is accompanied by a Certificate of Appreciation "testifying that a contribution has been made to the Martin Luther King, Jr., Center for Social Change."

Defendant James E. Bolen testified that he created a trust fund for that portion of the earnings which was to be contributed to the Center. The trust fund agreement, however, was never executed, and James E. Bolen testified that this was due to the plaintiffs' attorneys' request to cease and desist from all activities in issue. Testimony in the district court disclosed that money had been tendered to the Center, but was not accepted by its governing board. Also, the district court found that, as of the date of the preliminary injunction, the defendants had sold approximately 200 busts and had outstanding orders for 23 more.

On November 21, 1980, and December 19, 1980, the plaintiffs demanded that the Bolens cease and desist from further advertisements and sales of the bust, and on December 31, 1980, the plaintiffs filed a complaint in the United States District Court for the Northern District of Georgia. The district court held a hearing on the plaintiffs' motion for a preliminary injunction and the defendants' motion to dismiss the complaint. The motion to dismiss was denied and the motion for a preliminary injunction was granted in part and denied in part. The motion for an injunction sought (1) an end to the use of the Center's name in advertising and marketing the busts, (2) restraint of any further copyright infringement and (3) an end to the manufacture and sale of the plastic busts. The defendants agreed to discontinue the use of the Center's name in further promotion. Therefore, the court granted this part of the injunction. The district court found that the defendants had infringed the King copyrights and enjoined all further use of the copyrighted material.

In ruling on the third request for injunction, the court confronted the plaintiffs' claim that the manufacture and sale of the busts violated Dr. King's right of publicity which had passed to his heirs upon Dr. King's death. The defendants contended that no such right existed, and hence, an injunction should not issue. The district court concluded that it was not necessary to determine whether the "right of publicity" was devisable in Georgia because Dr. King did not commercially exploit this right during his lifetime. As found by the district court, the evidence of exploitation by Dr. King came from his sister's affidavit which stated that he had received "thousands of dollars in the form of honorariums from the use of his name, likeness, literary compositions, and speeches." The district court further found that "Dr. King apparently sold his copyrights in several speeches to Motown Records Corporation." *Martin Luther King, Jr., Center for Social Change, Inc. v. American Heritage Products, Inc.*, 508 F. Supp. 854 (N.D.Ga.1981).

On plaintiffs' appeal of the partial denial of the preliminary injunction, the Eleventh Circuit Court of Appeals has certified the following questions:

(1) Is the "right of publicity" recognized in Georgia as a right distinct from the right of privacy?
(2) If the answer to question (1) is affirmative, does the "right to publicity" survive the death of its owner? Specifically, is the right inheritable and devisable?
(3) If the answer to question (2) is also affirmative, must the owner have commercially exploited the right before it can survive his death?
(4) Assuming the affirmative answers to questions (1), (2) and (3), what is the guideline to be followed in defining commercial exploitation and what are the evidentiary prerequisites to a showing of commercial exploitation?

As noted by the Eleventh Circuit, this case raises questions concerning the laws of Georgia as to which there are no controlling precedents directly on point. In addition to being novel in this jurisdiction, the questions are legally alluring. Under these twin circumstances, it is necessary in the first instance to consider how the answers to the questions apply to other fact situations, and tempting in the second instance to include those considerations in writing. Hopefully having considered the various ramifications, we will resist to the extent possible the temptation to answer more than has been asked.

The right of publicity may be defined as a celebrity's right to the exclusive use of his or her name and likeness. *Price v. Hal Roach Studios, Inc.*, 400 F. Supp. 836, 843 (S.D.N.Y. 1975); *Estate of Presley v. Russen*, 513 F. Supp. 1339, 1353 (D.N.J. 1981), and cases cited. The right is most often asserted by or on behalf of professional athletes, comedians, actors and actresses, and other entertainers. This case involves none of those occupations. As is known to all, from 1955 until he was assassinated on April 4, 1968, Dr. King, a Baptist minister by profession, was the foremost leader of the civil rights movement in the United States. He was awarded the Nobel Prize for Peace in 1964. Although not a public official, Dr. King was a public figure, and we deal in this opinion with public figures who are neither public officials nor entertainers. Within this framework, we turn to the questions posed.

1. Is the "Right of Publicity" Recognized in Georgia as a Right Distinct from the Right of Privacy?

Georgia has long recognized the right of privacy. Following denial of the existence of the right of privacy in a controversial decision by the New York Court of Appeals in *Roberson v. Rochester Folding-Box Co.*, 171 N.Y. 538, 64 N.E. 442 (1902), the Georgia Supreme Court became the first such court to recognize the right of privacy in *Pavesich v. New England Life Ins. Co.*, 122 Ga. 190, 50 S.E. 68 (1905). See Prosser, Law of Torts, pp. 802–804 (1971).

In *Pavesich v. New England Life Ins. Co., supra,* the picture of an artist was used without his consent in a newspaper advertisement of the insurance company. Analyzing the right of privacy, this court held: "The publication of a picture of a person, without his consent, as a part of an advertisement, for the purpose of exploiting the publisher's business, is a violation of the right of privacy of the person whose picture is reproduced, and entitles him to recover without proof of special damage." 122 Ga. at 191(11), 50 S.E. at 68(11). If the right to privacy had not been recognized, advertisers could use photographs of private citizens to promote sales and the professional modeling business would not be what it is today.

In the course of its opinion the *Pavesich* court said several things pertinent here. It noted that the commentators on ancient law recognized the right of personal liberty, including the right to exhibit oneself before the public at proper times and places and in a proper manner. As a corollary, the court recognized that the right of personal liberty included the right of a person not to be exhibited before the public, saying: "The right to withdraw from the public gaze at such times as a person may see fit, when his presence in public is not demanded by any rule of law is also embraced within the right of personal liberty. Publicity in one instance and privacy in the other is each guaranteed. If personal liberty embraces the *right of publicity,* it no less embraces the correlative right of privacy; and this is no new idea in Georgia law." 122 Ga. at 196, 50 S.E. at 70. (Emphasis supplied.)

Recognizing the possibility of a conflict between the right of privacy and the freedoms of speech and press, this court said: "There is in the publication of one's picture for advertising purposes not the slightest semblance of an expression of an idea, a thought, or an opinion, within the meaning of the constitutional provision which guarantees to a person the right to publish his sentiments on any subject." 122 Ga. at 219, 50 S.E. at 80. The defendants in the case now before us make no claim under these freedoms and we find no violation thereof.

Observing in dicta that the right of privacy in general does not survive the death of the person whose privacy is invaded, the *Pavesich* court said: "While the right of privacy is personal, and may die with the person, we do not desire to be understood as assenting to the proposition that the relatives of the deceased can not, in a proper case, protect the memory of their kinsman, not only from defamation, but also from an invasion into the affairs of his private life after his death. This question is not now involved, but we do not wish anything said to be understood as committing us in any way to the doctrine that against the consent of relatives the private affairs of a deceased person may be published and his picture or statue exhibited." 122 Ga. at 210, 50 S.E. at 76.

Finding that Pavesich, although an artist, was not recognized as a public figure, the court said: "It is not necessary in this case to hold, nor are we prepared to do so, that the mere fact that a man has become what is called a public character, either by aspiring to public office, or by holding public office, or by exercising a profession which places him before the public, or by engaging in a business which has necessarily a public nature, gives to every one the right to print and circulate his picture." *122 Ga. at 217–218, 50 S.E. at 79–80.* Thus, although recognizing the right of privacy, the *Pavesich* court left open the question facing us involving the likeness of a public figure.[n3]

n3 Following *Pavesich, supra,* this court has continued to recognize the right of privacy. In *Bazemore v. Savannah Hospital,* 171 Ga. 257, 155 S.E. 194 (1930), the court held that the parents of a child born with his heart outside his body, who died following surgery, could maintain a suit for invasion of their privacy against the hospital, a photographer and a newspaper which respectively allowed, photographed and published a nude post mortem picture of the child.

On the other hand, in *Waters v. Fleetwood,* 212 Ga. 161, 91 S.E.2d 344 *(1956),* it was held that the mother of a 14 year old murder victim could not recover for invasion of the mother's privacy from a newspaper which published and sold separately photographs of her daughter's body taken after it was removed from a river. There the court found that publication and reproduction for sale of a photograph incident to a matter of public interest or to a public investigation could not be a violation of anyone's right of privacy. See also *Georgia Gazette Publishing Co. v. Ramsey, 248 Ga. 528,* 284 S.E.2d 386 (1981). For other Georgia cases involving the right of privacy, see *Tanner-Brice Co. v. Sims,* 174 Ga. 13(4), 161 S.E. 819 (1931); *Goodyear Tire & Rubber Co. v. Vandergriff,* 52 Ga.App. 662, 184 S.E. 452 (1935).

The "right of publicity" was first recognized in *Haelan Laboratories, Inc. v. Topps Chewing Gum, Inc.,* 202 F.2d 866 (2d Cir. 1953). There plaintiff had acquired by contract the exclusive right to use certain ball players' photographs in connection with the sales of plaintiff's chewing gum. An independent publishing company acquired similar rights from some of the same ball players. Defendant, a chewing gum manufacturer competing with plaintiff and knowing of plaintiff's contracts, acquired the contracts from the publishing company. As to these contracts the court found that the defendant had violated the ball players' "right of publicity" acquired by the plaintiff, saying (at 868): "We think that, in addition to and independent of that right of privacy (which in New York derives from statute), a man has a right in the publicity value of his photograph, i.e., the right to grant the exclusive privilege of publishing his picture, and that such a grant may validly be made 'in gross,' i.e., without an accompanying transfer of a business or of anything else. Whether it be labeled a 'property' right is immaterial; for here, as often elsewhere, the tag 'property' simply symbolizes the fact that courts enforce a claim which has pecuniary worth.

"This right might be called a 'right of publicity.' For it is common knowledge that many prominent persons (especially actors and ball-players), far from having their feelings bruised through public exposure of their likenesses, would feel sorely deprived if they no longer received money for authorizing advertisements, popularizing their countenances, displayed in newspapers, magazines, busses, trains and subways. This right of publicity would usually yield them no money unless it could be made the subject of an exclusive grant which barred any other advertiser from using their pictures."

In *Palmer v. Schonhorn Enterprises, Inc.,* 96 N.J.Super. 72, 232 A.2d 458 (1967), Arnold Palmer, Gary Player, Doug Sanders and Jack Nicklaus obtained summary judgment against the manufacturer of a golf game which used the golfers' names and short biographies without their consent. Although written as a right of privacy case, much of what was said is applicable to the right of publicity. In its opinion the court said (232 A.2d at 462): "It would therefore seem, from a review of the authorities, that although the publication of biographical data of a well-known figure does not per se constitute an invasion of privacy, the use of that same data for the purpose of capitalizing upon the name by using it in connection with a commercial project other than the dissemination of news or articles or biographies does.

"The names of plaintiffs have become internationally famous, undoubtedly by reason of talent as well as hard work in perfecting it. This is probably true in the cases of most so-called celebrities, who have attained national or international recognition in a particular field of art, science, business or other extraordinary ability. They may not all desire to capitalize upon their names in the commercial field, beyond or apart from that in which they have reached their known excellence. However, because they presently do not should not be justification for others to do so because of the void. They may desire to do it later. . . . It is unfair that one should be permitted to commercialize or exploit or capitalize upon another's name, reputation or accomplishments merely because the owner's accomplishments have been highly publicized."

In *Haelan Laboratories, supra,* the court was concerned with whether a celebrity has the right to the exclusive use of his or her name and likeness. In *Palmer, supra,* the court was concerned with whether a person using the celebrity's name for the user's commercial benefit has the right to do so without authorization. At this point it should be emphasized that we deal here with the unauthorized use of a person's name and likeness for the commercial benefit of the user, not with a city's use of a celebrity's name to denominate a street or school.

The right to publicity is not absolute. In *Hicks v. Casablanca Records,* 464 F. Supp. 426 (SDNY1978), the court held that a fictional novel and movie concerning an unexplained eleven day disappearance by Agatha Christie, author of numerous mystery novels, were permissible under the first amendment. On the other hand, in *Zacchini v. Scripps-Howard Broadcasting Co.,* 433 U.S. 562, 97 S. Ct. 2849, 53 L. Ed. 2d 965 (1977), a television station broadcast on its news program plaintiff's 15 second "human cannonball" flight filmed at a local fair. The Supreme Court held that freedom of the press does not authorize the media to broadcast a performer's entire act without his consent, just as the media could not televise a stage play, prize fight or baseball game without consent. Quoting from Kalven, "Privacy in Tort Law—Were Warren and Brandeis Wrong?", *31 Law & Contemp. Prob. 326, 332 (1966),* the Court said (433 U.S. at 576, 97 S. Ct. at 2857): "The rationale for [protecting the right of publicity] is the straight-forward one of preventing unjust enrichment by the theft of good will. No social purpose is served by having the defendant get free some aspect of the plaintiff that would have market value and for which he would normally pay."

The right of publicity was first recognized in Georgia by the Court of Appeals in *Cabaniss v. Hipsley,* 114 Ga.App. 367, 151 S.E.2d 496 (1966). There the court held that the plaintiff, an exotic dancer, could recover from the owner of the Atlanta Playboy Club for the unauthorized use of the dancer's misnamed photograph in an entertainment magazine advertising the Playboy Club. Although plaintiff had had her picture taken to promote her performances, she was not performing at the Playboy Club. The court used Dean William L. Prosser's four pronged analysis of the right of privacy, saying: " . . . Dean Prosser has analyzed the many privacy cases in an article entitled 'Privacy,' published in 48 Calif. L.Rev. 383 (1960), and in reviewing the cases he suggests that the invasion of privacy is in reality a complex of four loosely related torts; that there are four distinct kinds of invasion of four different interests of plaintiff; that there are four disparate torts under a common name. These four torts may be described briefly as: (1) intrusion upon the plaintiff's seclusion or solitude, or into his private affairs; (2) public disclosure of embarrassing private facts about the plaintiff; (3) publicity which places the plaintiff in a false light in the public eye; (4) appropriation, for the defendant's advantage, of the plaintiff's name or likeness." 114 Ga.App. at 370, 151 S.E.2d at 499–500. Finding no violation of the first three rights of privacy, the court found a violation of the fourth, saying (114 Ga.App. at 377, 151 S.E.2d 496): "Unlike intrusion, disclosure, or false light, appropriation does not require the invasion of something secret, secluded or private pertaining to plaintiff, nor does it involve falsity. It consists of the appropriation, for the defendant's benefit, use or advantage, of the plaintiff's name or likeness. . . . 'The interest protected [in the "appropriation" cases] is not so much a mental as a proprietary one, in the exclusive use of the plaintiff's name and likeness as an aspect of his identity.' Prosser, *supra,* at 406." Although Ms. Hipsley was an entertainer (i.e., a public figure), the court found she was entitled to recover from the Playboy Club (but not from the magazine which published the Club's ad) for the unauthorized use of her photograph. However the court noted a difference in the damages recoverable in traditional right of privacy cases as opposed to right of publicity cases saying (114 Ga. App. at 378, 151 S.E.2d 496): "Recognizing, as we do, the fundamental distinction between causes of action involving injury to feelings, sensibilities or reputation and those involving an appropriation of rights in the nature of property rights for commercial exploitation, it must necessarily follow that there is a fundamental distinction between the two classes of cases in the measure of damages to be applied. In the former class (which we take to include the intrusion, disclosure, and false light aspects of the privacy tort), general damages are recoverable without proof of special damages. *Pavesich v. New England Life Ins. Co., supra.* In the latter class, the measure of damages is the value of the use of the appropriated publicity."

In *McQueen v. Wilson,* 117 Ga.App. 488, 161 S.E.2d 63, reversed on other grounds, 224 Ga. 420, 162 S.E.2d 313 (1968), the Court of Appeals upheld the right of an actress, Butterfly McQueen, who appeared as "Prissie" in the movie *Gone With the Wind,* to recover for the unauthorized use of her photograph, saying: "Both before and since *Pavesich* it has been recognized that the appropriation of another's identity, picture, papers, name or signature without consent and for financial gain might be a tort for which an action would lie. . . . " 117 Ga. App. at 491, 161 S.E.2d at 65.

Thus, the courts in Georgia have recognized the rights of private citizens, *Pavesich, supra,* as well as entertainers, *Cabaniss* and *McQueen, supra,* not to have their names and photographs used for the financial gain of the user without their consent, where such use is not authorized as an exercise of freedom of the press. We know of no reason why a public figure prominent in religion and civil rights should be entitled to less protection than an exotic dancer or a movie actress. Therefore, we hold that the appropriation of another's name and likeness, whether such likeness be a photograph or sculpture, without consent and for the financial gain of the appropriator is a tort in Georgia, whether the person whose name and likeness is used is a private citizen, entertainer, or as here a public figure who is not a public official.

In *Pavesich, supra,* 122 Ga. 190, 50 S.E. 68, this right not to have another appropriate one's photograph was denominated the right of privacy; in *Cabaniss v. Hipsley, supra,* 114 Ga.App. 367, 151 S.E.2d 496, it was the right of publicity. Mr. Pavesich was not a public figure; Ms. Hipsley was. We conclude that while private citizens have the right of privacy, public figures have a similar right of publicity, and that the measure of damages to a public figure for violation of his or her right of publicity is the value of the appropriation to the user. *Cabaniss v. Hipsley, supra;* see also *Uhlaender v. Henricksen,* 316 F. Supp. 1277, 1279–1280 (Minn.1970). As thus understood the first certified question is answered in the affirmative.

2. Does the "Right of Publicity" Survive the Death of its Owner (i.e., is the Right Inheritable and Devisable)?

Although the *Pavesich* court expressly did not decide this question, the tenor of that opinion is that the right to privacy at least should be protectible after death. *Pavesich, supra,* 122 Ga. at 210, 50 S.E. at 76.

The right of publicity is assignable during the life of the celebrity, for without this characteristic, full commercial exploitation of one's name and likeness is practically impossible. *Haelan Laboratories v. Topps Chewing Gum, supra,* 202 F.2d at 868. That is, without assignability the right of publicity could hardly be called a "right." Recognizing its assignability, most commentators have urged that the right of publicity must also be inheritable. Felcher and Rubin, "The Descendibility of the Right of Publicity: Is there Commercial Life After Death?" *89 Yale L.J. 1125 (1980);* Gordon, "Right of Property in Name, Likeness, Personality and History," *55 U.L.Rev. 553 (1960);* Comment, *14* Ga.L.Rev. *831 (1980);* Note, *47* Tenn.L.Rev. *886 (1980);* Note, *33* Vand.L.Rev. *1251 (1980);* Comment, *29* Hastings L.J. *751 (1978);* Comment, *42* Brooklyn L.Rev. *527 (1976);* Comment, *22 U.C.L.A.L.Rev. 1103 (1975).*

The courts that have considered the problem are not as unanimous. In *Price v. Hal Roach Studios, Inc., supra,* 400 F. Supp. 836, the court reasoned that since the right of publicity was assignable, it survived the deaths of Stanley Laurel and Oliver Hardy. Other decisions from the Southern District of New York recognize the descendibility of the right of publicity, which has also been recognized by the Second Circuit Court of Appeals (infra).

In *Factors Etc., Inc. v. Pro Arts, Inc.,* 579 F.2d 215 (2d Cir.1978), Elvis Presley had assigned his right of publicity to Boxcar Enterprises, which assigned that right to Factors after Presley's death. Defendant Pro Arts published a poster of Presley entitled "In Memory". In affirming the grant of injunction against Pro Arts, the Second Circuit Court of Appeals said (579 F.2d at 221): "The identification of this exclusive right belonging to Boxcar as a transferable property right compels the conclusion that the right survives Presley's death. The death of Presley, who was merely the beneficiary of an income interest in Boxcar's exclusive right, should not in itself extinguish Boxcar's property right. Instead, the income interest, continually produced from Boxcar's exclusive right of commercial exploitation, should inure to Presley's estate at death like any other intangible property right. To hold that the right did not survive Presley's death, would be to grant competitors of Factors, such as Pro Arts, a windfall in the form of profits from the use of Presley's name and likeness. At the same time, the exclusive right purchased by Factors and the financial benefits accruing to the celebrity's heirs would be rendered virtually worthless."

In *Lugosi v. Universal Pictures,* 25 Cal.3d 813, 160 Cal.Rptr. 323, 603 P.2d 425 (1979), the Supreme Court of California, in a 4 to 3 decision, declared that the right of publicity expires upon the death of the celebrity and is not descendible. See *Guglielmi v. Spelling-Goldberg Productions,* 25 Cal.3d 860, 160 Cal.Rptr. 352, 603 P.2d 454 (1979), decided two days after *Lugosi, supra.* Bela Lugosi appeared as Dracula in Universal Picture's movie by that name. Universal had acquired the movie rights to the novel by Bram Stoker. Lugosi's contract with Universal gave it the right to exploit Lugosi's name and likeness in connection with the movie. The majority of the court held that Lugosi's heirs could not prevent Universal's continued exploitation of Lugosi's portrayal of Count Dracula after his death. The court did not decide whether Universal could prevent unauthorized third parties from exploitation of Lugosi's appearance as Dracula after Lugosi's death.

In *Memphis Development Foundation v. Factors Etc., Inc.*, 616 F.2d 956 (6th Cir. 1980), Factors, which had won its case against Pro Arts in New York (see above), lost against the Memphis Development Foundation under the Court of Appeals for the Sixth Circuit's interpretation of Tennessee law. There, the Foundation, a non-profit corporation, planned to erect a statue of Elvis Presley in Memphis and solicited contributions to do so. Donors of $25 or more received a small replica of the proposed statue. The Sixth Circuit reversed the grant of an injunction favoring Factors, holding that a celebrity's right of publicity was not inheritable even where that right had been exploited during the celebrity's life. [n4] The court reasoned that although recognition of the right of publicity during life serves to encourage effort and inspire creative endeavors, making the right inheritable would not. The court also was concerned with unanswered legal questions which recognizing inheritability would create. We note, however, that the court was dealing with a non-profit foundation attempting to promote Presley's adopted home place, the City of Memphis. The court was not dealing, as we do here, with a profit making endeavor.

n4 The Second Circuit has now accepted the Sixth Circuit's interpretation of Tennessee law. *Factors Etc., Inc. v. Pro Arts, Inc.*, 652 F.2d 278 (2d Cir., 1981).

In *Estate of Presley v. Russen, supra, 513 F. Supp. 1339,* the court found in favor of descendibility, quoting from Chief Justice Bird's dissent in *Lugosi v. Universal Pictures, supra, 160 Cal.Rptr. at 332, 603 P.2d at 434,* and saying: "If the right is descendible, the individual is able to transfer the benefits of his labor to his immediate successors and is assured that control over the exercise of the right can be vested in a suitable beneficiary. 'There is no reason why, upon a celebrity's death, advertisers should receive a windfall in the form of freedom to use with impunity the name or likeness of the deceased celebrity who may have worked his or her entire life to attain celebrity status. The financial benefits of that labor should go to the celebrity's heirs. . . . '" 513 F. Supp. at 1355.

For the reasons which follow we hold that the right of publicity survives the death of its owner and is inheritable and devisable. Recognition of the right of publicity rewards and thereby encourages effort and creativity. If the right of publicity dies with the celebrity, the economic value of the right of publicity during life would be diminished because the celebrity's untimely death would seriously impair, if not destroy, the value of the right of continued commercial use. Conversely, those who would profit from the fame of a celebrity after his or her death for their own benefit and without authorization have failed to establish their claim that they should be the beneficiaries of the celebrity's death. Finally, the trend since the early common law has been to recognize survivability, notwithstanding the legal problems which may thereby arise. We therefore answer question 2 in the affirmative.

3. Must the Owner of the Right of Publicity have Commercially Exploited that Right before it can Survive?

Exploitation is understood to mean commercial use by the celebrity other than the activity which made him or her famous, e.g., an inter vivos transfer of the right to the use of one's name and likeness.

The requirement that the right of publicity be exploited by the celebrity during his or her lifetime in order to render the right inheritable arises from the case involving Agatha Christie, *Hicks v. Casablanca Records, supra,* 464 F. Supp. at 429. The Hicks court cited three authorities, *Factors Etc., Inc. v. Pro Arts, Inc., supra,* 579 F.2d at 222 n. 11; *Guglielmi v. Spelling-Goldberg Prods.,* 73 Cal.App.3d 436, 140 Cal.Rptr. 775 (1977); and "see also" *Price v. Hal Roach Studios, Inc., supra,* 400 F. Supp. 836. However, footnote 11 in *Factors v. Pro Arts,* supra, shows that the issue was not decided there. The Guglielmi case, brought by an heir of Rudolpho Valentino, involved the movie "Legend of Valentino: A Romantic Fiction," and the California Court of Appeals decision in that case was affirmed on the ground of nondescendibility. *Guglielmi v. Spelling-Goldberg Productions, supra,* 603 P.2d 459. And in *Price v. Hal Roach Studios, Inc., supra,* the court said: "There cannot, therefore, be any necessity to exercise the right of publicity during one's life in order to protect it from use by others or to preserve any potential right of one's heirs." 400 F. Supp. at 846. Moreover, the Hicks court held that the fictional account of Agatha Christie's 11 day disappearance was protected by the first amendment. Thus, the finding that exploitation during life was necessary to inheritability was actually unnecessary to that decision.

Nevertheless, the Hicks dicta has been relied upon. See *Groucho Marx Productions, Inc. v. Day & Night Co.,* 523 F. Supp. 485, 490 (S.D.N.Y. 1981).[n5] However, in this case, involving the Marx brothers, it was found that, although Leo and Adolpho Marx ("Chico" and "Harpo") had not made inter vivos or specific testamentary dispositions of their rights, they had earned their livelihoods by exploiting the unique characters they created and thus had exploited their rights to publicity so as to make such rights descendible. Thus, even in the Southern District of New York where the requirement arose, exploitation beyond the "activity which made him or her famous" is not now required.

n5 On appeal of this case, the Second Circuit reversed, finding the law of California applicable, where, as noted above, the right of publicity is not inheritable. *Groucho Marx Productions, Inc. v. Day & Night Co.,* 689 F.2d 317 (2d Cir.1982).

The cases which have considered this issue, see above, involved entertainers. The net result of following them would be to say that celebrities and public figures have the right of publicity during their lifetimes (as others have the right of privacy), but only those who contract for bubble gum cards, posters and tee shirts have a descendible right of publicity upon their deaths. See *Groucho Marx Productions, Inc. v. Day & Night Co., supra,* 523 F. Supp. at 490, 491–492. That we should single out for protection after death those entertainers and athletes who exploit their personae during life, and deny protection after death to those who enjoy public acclamation but did not exploit themselves during life, puts a premium on exploitation. Having found that there are valid reasons for recognizing the right of publicity during life, we find no reason to protect after death only those who took commercial advantage of their fame.

Perhaps this case more than others brings the point into focus. A well known minister may avoid exploiting his prominence during life because to do otherwise would impair his ministry. Should his election not to take commercial advantage of his position during life ipso facto result in permitting others to exploit his name and likeness after his death? In our view, a person who avoids exploitation during life is entitled to have his image protected against exploitation after death just as much if not more than a person who exploited his image during life.[n6]

n6 Although the conclusion reached in answer to question 2 was based in part upon commercial considerations, and our answer to question 3 is based upon the absence of exploitation, the reasoning supporting the answer to question 3 also supports the answer to question 2.

Without doubt, Dr. King could have exploited his name and likeness during his lifetime. That this opportunity was not appealing to him does not mean that others have the right to use his name and likeness in ways he himself chose not to do. Nor does it strip his family and estate of the right to control, preserve and extend his status and memory and to prevent unauthorized exploitation thereof by others. Here, they seek to prevent the exploitation of his likeness in a manner they consider unflattering and unfitting. We cannot deny them this right merely because Dr. King chose not to exploit or commercialize himself during his lifetime.

Question 3 is answered in the negative, and therefore we need not answer question 4.

Certified questions 1 and 2 answered in the affirmative, question 3 answered in the negative, and question 4 not answered.

All the Justices concur, except WELTNER, J., who concurs specially.

NOTE

In the Georgia Supreme Court opinion in the *MLK* case, concurring Justice Charles Weltner stated in a separate opinion that he disagreed "most decidedly with the substantive portion of the majority opinion, for the reason that it generates more unsettling questions than it resolves." He thought that it was unnecessary for the majority to expand the "right of privacy" enumerated in Pavesich (discussed in Section 3.2.2) to add a new "right of publicity". [296 S.E.2d 697 at 706.] Justice Weltner believed that the complaint already stated a claim upon which relief could be granted under the existing "doctrine of unjust enrichment," without the need to create a new right. He suggested that in proclaiming this new "right of publicity" that "we have created an open-ended and ill-defined force which jeopardizes a right of unquestioned authenticity—free speech." Justice Weltner "vigorously dissented" to the majority's opinion concluding that the fabrication of a likeness of Dr. King for reproduction and sale was not "free speech," due to the "financial gain" inuring to the defendant. He reasoned that financial gain should not control in finding a right of publicity violation, stating that "It is rare, indeed, that any expression of sentiment beyond casual conversation is not somehow connected, directly or indirectly, to 'financial gain'." [296 S.E.2d 697 at 708.] He concluded that the doctrine of unjust enrichment would avoid what he considered to be the "quagmire" of combining considerations of "right of privacy," "right of publicity," and considerations of *inter vivos* exploitation; while retaining "our constitutional right of free speech uncluttered and uncompromised by these new impediments of indeterminate application." [supra at 709.] Since the *MLK* decision, many state statutes have addressed some of the anticipated conflicts between the right of publicity and the First Amendment by allowing limited exceptions for media reporting, newsworthy events and artistic works such as films, plays, art, and print publications.

The decision of the Georgia Supreme Court in *MLK,* adopted by the 11th Circuit, has provided one of the most expansive "right of publicity" decisions at common law in the country, and without the strictures of the usual limitations imposed by specific language reflected in other states' right of publicity statutes. The court's decision defined the right of publicity in Georgia in broad terms, with very little direction as to the limits of this right. Qualifying and limiting language on the right of publicity is usually present when a state attempts to enact a specific statute. Only at common law and based on the *MLK* decision and three prior cases (*Pavesich, Cabaniss* and the *McQueen* cases cited in *MLK*), Georgia now recognizes a separate and distinct right of publicity tort where one appropriates another's name, likeness, photograph, or sculpture, without consent, and for financial gain, whether the person is a private citizen, an entertainer, or a public figure who is not a public official. The right, once recognized, survives the death of its owner and is inheritable and devisable; and the right need not have been commercially exploited by its owner during life for such right to survive. Some of the questions left to be answered by future Georgia court decisions, or by legislative action, are the extent of the limits on the scope of such property right and the time limitation for the exclusive exploitation of this right that may be imposed upon the heirs or assignees after the owner's death.

3.3.2 Statutory Recognition

Well prior to the decisions discussed in the preceding section, the California courts had flirted with notions of the right of publicity in such well-known cases as *Lugosi v. Universal Pictures,* 603 P.2d 425 (1979), and *Guglielmi v. Spelling-Goldberg,* 603 P.2d 860 (1979). The cases created confusion as to whether in fact California law recognized a right of publicity separate from the right of privacy. The confusion has been partially resolved through legislative intervention in the enactment §3344 of the California Civil Code and its post-mortem counterpart, §990, now amended and renumbered as:

§3344.1. 3344. [Use of Name or Photograph Without Consent for Advertising]

(a) Any person who knowingly uses another's: name, voice, signature, photograph, or likeness, in any manner, on or in products, merchandise, or goods, or for purposes of advertising or selling or soliciting purchases of products, merchandise, goods or services, without such person's prior consent, or, in the case of a minor, the prior consent of his parent or legal guardian, shall be liable for any damages sustained by the person or persons injured as a result thereof. In addition, in any action brought under this section, the person who violated the section shall be liable to the injured party or parties in an amount equal to the greater of seven hundred fifty dollars ($750) *or the actual damages suffered by him or her as a result of the unauthorized use, and any profits from the unauthorized use that are attributable to the use and are not taken into account in computing the actual damages.* In establishing such profits, the injured party or parties are required to present proof only of the gross revenue attributable to such use, and the person who violated this section is required to prove his or her deductible expenses. Punitive damages may also be awarded to the injured party or parties. *The prevailing party in any action under this section shall also be entitled to attorney's fees and costs.*

(b) As used in this section, "photograph" means any photograph or photographic reproduction, still or moving, or any videotape or live television transmission, of any person, such that the person is readily identifiable.

   (1) A person shall be deemed \to be readily identifiable from a photograph when one who views the photograph with the naked eye can reasonably determine that the person depicted in the photograph is the same person who is complaining of its unauthorized use.

   (2) If the photograph includes more than one person so identifiable, then the person or persons complaining of the use shall be represented as individuals rather than solely as members of a definable group represented in the photograph. A definable group includes, but is not limited to, the following examples: a crowd at any sporting event, a crowd in any street or public building, the audience at any theatrical or stage production, a glee club, or a baseball team.

   (3) A person or persons shall be considered to not be represented as members of a definable group if they are represented in the photograph solely as a result of being present at the time the photograph was taken and have not been singled out as individuals in any manner.

(c) Where a photograph or likeness of an employee of the person using the photograph or likeness appearing in the advertisement or other publication prepared by or in behalf of the user is only incidental, and not essential, to the purpose of the publication in which it appears, there shall arise a rebuttable presumption affecting the burden of producing evidence that the failure to obtain the consent of the employee was not a knowing use of the employee's photograph or likeness.

(d) For purposes of this section, a use of a name, voice, signature, photograph, or likeness in connection with any news, public affairs, or sports broadcast or account, or any political campaign, shall not constitute a use for which consent is required under subdivision (a).

(e) The use of a name, voice, signature, photograph, or likeness in a commercial medium shall not constitute a use for which consent is required under subdivision (a) solely because the material containing such use is commercially sponsored or contains paid advertising. Rather it shall be a question of fact whether or not the use of the person's name, voice, signature, photograph, or likeness was so directly connected with the commercial sponsorship or with the paid advertising as to constitute a use for which consent is required under subdivision (a).

(f) Nothing in this section shall apply to the owners or employees of any medium used for advertising, including, but not limited to, newspapers, magazines, radio and television networks and stations, cable television systems, billboards, and transit ads, by whom any advertisement or solicitation in violation of this section is published or disseminated, unless it is established that such owners or employees had knowledge of the unauthorized use of the person's name, voice, signature, photograph, or likeness as prohibited by this section.

(g) The remedies provided for in this section are cumulative and shall be in addition to any others provided for by law.

NOTE

A "likeness" need not be literal for purposes of § 3344. *Newcombe v. Adolf Coors Co.*, 157 F.3d 686, 1998 U.S. App. LEXIS 23308 (9th Cir. 1998) involved an advertisement for Killian's Irish Red Beer which included a drawing of a baseball pitcher that Newcombe (the only man ever to win all three of the Cy Young, Most Valuable Player, and Rookie of the Year Awards) felt was sufficiently similar to a picture of himself as to constitute a "likeness." The defendants conceded that the drawing was based on an earlier picture of Newcombe. The drawing closely resembled Newcombe's characteristic stance on the pitching mound. The only major differences were a change of uniform number (from 39 to 36) and in the bill of the cap (which was a different color from the rest of the cap.) The court concluded that there was a triable issue of material fact as to the existence of a "likeness." (The court also permitted Newcombe to pursue his claim of common law misappropriation. See Sec. 3.4.2.)

3.3.2.1 Other Statutory Enactments on Right of Publicity

Currently, at least eighteen states have statutes that protect aspects of the right of publicity, including California, Florida, Illinois, Indiana, Kentucky, Massachusetts, Nebraska, Nevada, New York, Ohio, Oklahoma, Rhode Island, Tennessee, Texas, Utah, Virginia, Washington, and Wisconsin. The Indiana statute may be the most sweeping, but all four of the statutes, reproduced below (Tennessee, Kentucky, Florida and Indiana), should be studied both individually and comparatively. In an examination of the provisions of the four statutes, the only conclusion to be reached is that there is no uniform approach to the right of publicity. Of particular interest is the varied treatment of descendibility: who owns the right, and for how long.

Tenn. Code Ann. Ch. 945, §§ 47–25–1101 and 1108 (1984)

Section 1. This act shall be known and may be cited as "The Personal Rights Protection Act of 1984."

Section 2. As used in this act, unless the context otherwise requires:

(1) "Definable group" means an assemblage of individuals existing or brought together with or without interrelation, orderly form or arrangement, including but not limited to, a crowd at any sporting event, a crowd in any street or public building, the audience at any theatrical or stage production, a glee club, or a baseball team.

(2) "Individual" means human being, living or dead.

(3) "Likeness" means the use of an image of an individual for commercial purposes.

(4) "Person" means any firm, association, partnership, corporation, joint stock company, syndicate, receiver, common law trust, conservator, statutory trust or any other concern by whatever name known or however organized, formed or created, and includes not-for-profit corporations, associations, educational and religious institutions, political parties, community, civic or other organizations.

(5) "Photograph" means any photograph or photographic reproduction, still or moving, or any videotape or live television transmission, of any individual, so that the individual is readily identifiable.

Section 3.

(a) Every individual has a property right in the use of his name, photograph or likeness in any medium in any manner.

(b) The individual rights provided for in subsection (a) shall constitute property rights and shall be freely assignable and licensable, and shall not expire upon the death of the individual so protected, whether or not such rights were commercially exploited by the individual during the individual's lifetime, but shall be descendible to the executors, assigns, heirs, or devisees of the individual so protected by this act.

Section 4.

(a) The rights provided for in this act shall be deemed exclusive to the individual, subject to the assignment or licensing of such trademarks as provided in Section 3, during such individual's lifetime and to the executors, heirs, assigns or devisees for a period of ten (10) years after the death of the individual.

(b) Commercial exploitation of the property right by an executor, assignee, heir, or devisee if the individual is deceased shall maintain the right as his exclusive property until such right is terminated as provided in this subsection.

The exclusive right to commercial exploitation of the property rights is terminated by proof of the non-use of the name, likeness, or image of any individual for commercial purposes by an executor, assignee, heir or devisee to such use for a period of two (2) years subsequent to the initial ten (10) year period following the individual's death.

Section 5.

(a) Any person who knowingly uses or infringes upon the use of another individual's name, photograph, or likeness in any medium, in any manner directed to any person other than such individual, as an item of commerce for purposes of advertising products, merchandise, goods or services, or for purposes of fund raising, solicitation of donations, purchases of products, merchandise, goods or services, without such individual's prior consent, or, in the case of a minor, the prior consent of his parent or legal guardian, or in the case of a deceased individual, the consent of the executor or administrator, heirs or devisees of such deceased individual, shall be liable to a civil action.

(b) It shall be no defense to the unauthorized use defined in subsection (a) that the photograph includes more than one (1) individual so identifiable; provided that the individual or individuals complaining of the use shall be represented as individuals per se rather than solely as members of a definable group represented in the photograph.

Section 6.

(a) The chancery and circuit court having jurisdiction for any action arising pursuant to this act may grant injunctions on such terms as it may deem reasonable to prevent or restrain the unauthorized use of an individual's name, photograph or likeness.

(b) At any time while an action under this act is pending, the court may order the impounding, on such terms as it may deem reasonable, of all materials or any part thereof claimed to have been made or used in violation of the individual's rights, and such court may enjoin the use of all plates, molds, matrices, masters, tapes, film negatives, or other articles by means of which such materials may be reproduced.

(c) As part of a final judgment or decree, the court may order the destruction or other reasonable disposition of all materials found to have been made or used in violation of the individual's rights, and of all plates, molds, matrices, masters, tapes, film negatives, or other articles by means of which such materials may be reproduced.

(d) An individual is entitled to recover the actual damages suffered as a result of the knowing use or infringement of such individual's rights and any profits that are attributable to such use or infringement which are not taken into account in computing the actual damages. Profit or lack thereof by the unauthorized use or infringement of an individual's rights shall not be a criteria of determining liability.

(e) The remedies provided for in this section are cumulative and shall be in addition to any others provided for by law.

Section 7.

(a) It shall be deemed a fair use and no violation of an individual's rights shall be found, for purposes of this act, if the use of a name, photograph or likeness is in connection with any news, public affairs, or sports broadcast or account.

(b) The use of a name, photograph or likeness in a commercial medium shall not constitute a use for purposes of advertising or solicitation solely because the material containing such use is commercially sponsored or contains paid advertising. Rather it shall be a question of fact whether or not the use of the complainant individual's name, photograph or likeness was so directly connected with the commercial sponsorship or with the paid advertising as to constitute a use for purposes of advertising or solicitation.

(c) Nothing in this section shall apply to the owners or employees of any medium used for advertising, including, but not limited to, newspapers, magazines, radio and television stations, billboards, and transit ads, who have published or disseminated any advertisement or solicitation in violation of this act unless it is established that such owners or employees had knowledge of the unauthorized use of the individual's name, photograph, or likeness as prohibited by this section.

Ky. Rev. Stat., Ch. 391 (1984)
AN ACT relating to commercial rights to use the names and likenesses of public figures.
Be it enacted by the General Assembly of the Commonwealth of Kentucky:

Section 1. A New Section of KRS Chapter 391 is Created to Read as Follows:

(1) The general assembly recognizes that a person has property rights in his name and likeness which are entitled to protection from commercial exploitation. The general assembly further recognizes that although the traditional right of privacy terminates upon death of the person asserting it, the right of publicity, which is a right of protection from appropriation of some element of an individual's personality for commercial exploitation, does not terminate upon death.

(2) The name or likeness of a person who is a public figure shall not be used for commercial profit for a period of fifty (50) years from the date of his death without the written consent of the executor or administrator of his estate.

Approved April 6, 1984

Fla. Stat. Ann. Sec. 540–08 (West 1972)
Be It Enacted by the Legislature of the State of Florida:

Section 1. Sections 540.08, 540.09, and 540.10 are added to Chapter 540, Florida Statutes, to Read:

540.08 Unauthorized Publication of Name or Likeness.

(1) No person shall publish, print, display or otherwise publicly use for purposes of trade or for any commercial or advertising purpose the name, portrait, photograph or other likeness of any natural person without the express written or oral consent to such use given by:

(a) Such person; or
(b) Any other person, firm or corporation authorized in writing by such person to license the commercial use of his name or likeness; or
(c) If such person is deceased, any person, firm or corporation authorized in writing to license the commercial use of his name or likeness, or if no person, firm or corporation is so authorized, then by any one from among a class composed of his surviving spouse and surviving children.

(2) In the event the consent required in subsection (1) is not obtained, the person whose name, portrait, photograph, or other likeness is so used, or any person, firm or corporation authorized by such person in writing to license the commercial use of his name or likeness, or, if the person whose likeness is used is deceased, any person, firm or corporation having the right to give such consents, as provided hereinabove, may bring an action to enjoin such unauthorized publication, printing, display or other public use, and to recover damages for any loss or injury sustained by reason thereof, including an amount which would have been a reasonable royalty, and punitive or exemplary damages.

(3) The provisions of this section shall not apply to:

(a) The publication, printing, display or use of the name or likeness of any person in any newspaper, magazine, book, news broadcast or telecast or other news medium or publication as part of any bona fide news report or presentation having a current and legitimate public interest and where such name or likeness is not used for advertising purposes;

(b) The use of such name, portrait, photograph or other likeness in connection with the resale or other distribution of literary, musical or artistic productions or other articles of merchandise or property where such person has consented to the use of his name, portrait, photograph or likeness on or in connection with the initial sale or distribution thereof; or

(c) Any photograph of a person solely as a member of the public and where such person is not named or otherwise identified in or in connection with the use of such photograph.

(4) No action shall be brought under this section by reason of any publication, printing, display or other public use of the name or likeness of a person occurring after the expiration of forty (40) years from and after the death of such person.

(5) As used in this section, a person's "surviving spouse" is the person's surviving spouse under the law of his domicile at the time of his death, whether or not the spouse has later remarried; and a person's "children" are his immediate offspring and any children legally adopted by him. Any consent provided for in subsection (1) shall be given on behalf of a minor by the guardian of his person or by either parent.

(6) The remedies provided for in this section shall be in addition to and not in limitation of the remedies and rights of any person under the common law against the invasion of his privacy.

540.09 Unauthorized Publication of Photographs or Pictures of Areas to Which Admission is Charged.

(1) Any person who shall sell any photograph, drawing or other visual representation of any area, building or structure, the entry or admittance to which is subject to an admission charge or fee, or of any real or personal property located therein, or who shall use any such photograph, drawing or other visual representation in connection with the sale or advertising of any other product, property or service, without the express written or oral consent of the owner or operator of the area, building, structure, or other property so depicted, shall be liable to such owner or operator for any loss,

damage or injury sustained by reason thereof, including an amount which would have been a reasonable royalty, and for punitive or exemplary damages, and such unauthorized sale or use may be enjoined.

(2) The provisions of this section shall not apply to:

  (a) Photographs, drawings or other visual representations in any newspaper, magazine, book, news broadcast or telecast or other news medium or publication as part of any bona fide news report or presentation having a current and legitimate public interest and where such photographs, drawings or other visual representations are not used for advertising purposes; or

  (b) Photographs, drawings or other visual representations in which the depiction of such property is incidental to the principal subject or subjects thereof and not calculated or likely to lead the viewer to associate such property with the sale, offering for sale or advertising of any property, product or service.

(3) The remedies provided for in this section shall be in addition to and not in limitation of the remedies and rights of any person under the common law against the unauthorized sale or use for purposes of trade or advertising of photographs, drawings or other visual representations of his property.

540.10 Exemption from liability of news media.

No relief may be obtained under sections 540.08 or 540.09 Florida Statutes, against any broadcaster, publisher or distributor broadcasting, publishing or distributing paid advertising matter by radio or television or in a newspaper, magazine or similar periodical without knowledge or notice that any consent required by sections 540.08 or 540.09 Florida Statutes, in connection with such advertising matter has not been obtained, except an injunction against the presentation of such advertising matter in future broadcasts or in future issues of such newspaper, magazine or similar periodical.

Indiana Statutes, Title 32, Art. 13, Ch. 1. Rights of Publicity §32–13–1–1. Applicability

(a) This chapter applies to an act or event that occurs within Indiana, regardless of a personality's domicile, residence, or citizenship.

(b) This chapter does not affect rights and privileges recognized under any other law that apply to a news reporting or an entertainment medium.

(c) This chapter does not apply to the following:

  (1) The use of a personality's name, voice, signature, photograph, image, likeness, distinctive appearance, gestures, or mannerisms in any of the following:

    (A) Literary works, theatrical works, musical compositions, film, radio, or television programs.
    (B) Material that has political or newsworthy value.
    (C) Original works of fine art.

(D) Promotional material or an advertisement for a news reporting or an entertainment medium that:

(i) Uses all or part of a past edition of the medium's own broadcast or publication; and

(ii) Does not convey or reasonably suggest that a personality endorses the news reporting or entertainment medium.

(E) An advertisement or commercial announcement for a use described under this subdivision.

(2) The use of a personality's name to truthfully identify the personality as:

(A) The author of a written work; or

(B) A performer of a recorded performance; under circumstances in which the written work or recorded performance is otherwise rightfully reproduced, exhibited, or broadcast.

(3) The use of a personality's:

(A) Name;

(B) Voice;

(C) Signature;

(D) Photograph;

(E) Image;

(F) Likeness;

(G) Distinctive appearance;

(H) Gestures; or

(I) Mannerisms; in connection with the broadcast or reporting of an event or a topic of general or public interest.

§ 32–13–1–2. "Commercial Purpose" Defined

As used in this chapter, "commercial purpose" means the use of an aspect of a personality's right of publicity as follows:

(1) On or in connection with a product, merchandise, goods, services, or commercial activities.

(2) For advertising or soliciting purchases of products, merchandise, goods, services, or for promoting commercial activities.

(3) For the purpose of fundraising.

§ 32–13–1–3. "Name" Defined

As used in this chapter, "name" means the actual or assumed name of a living or deceased natural person that is intended to identify the person.

§ 32–13–1–4. "News Reporting or an Entertainment Medium" Defined

As used in this chapter, "news reporting or an entertainment medium" means a medium that publishes, broadcasts, or disseminates advertising in the normal course of its business, including the following:

(1) Newspapers.

(2) Magazines.

(3) Radio and television networks and stations.

(4) Cable television systems.

§ 32–13–1–5. "Person" Defined

As used in this chapter, "person" means a natural person, a partnership, a firm, a corporation, or an unincorporated association. . . .

§ 32–13–1–8. Use of Personality's Right of Publicity

A person may not use an aspect of a personality's right of publicity for a commercial purpose during the personality's lifetime or for one hundred (100) years after the date of the personality's death without having obtained previous written consent from a person specified in section 17 [IC 32–13–1–17] of this chapter.

§ 32–13–1–9. Engaging in Prohibited Conduct

A person who:

(1) Engages in conduct within Indiana that is prohibited under section 8 [IC 32–13–1–8] of this chapter;
(2) Creates or causes to be created within Indiana goods, merchandise, or other materials prohibited under section 8 of this chapter;
(3) Transports or causes to be transported into Indiana goods, merchandise, or other materials created or used in violation of section 8 of this chapter; or
(4) Knowingly causes advertising or promotional material created or used in violation of section 8 of this chapter to be published, distributed, exhibited, or disseminated within Indiana; submits to the jurisdiction of Indiana courts.

§ 32–13–1–10. Violations—Penalties

A person who violates section 8 [IC 32–13–1–8] of this chapter may be liable for any of the following:

(1) Damages in the amount of:

    (A) One thousand dollars ($1,000); or
    (B) Actual damages, including profits derived from the unauthorized use; whichever is greater.

(2) Treble or punitive damages, as the injured party may elect, if the violation under section 8 of this chapter is knowing, willful, or intentional.

§ 32–13–1–11. Establishment of Profits

In establishing the profits under section 10(1)(B) [IC 32–13–1–10(1)(B)] of this chapter:

(1) The plaintiff is required to prove the gross revenue attributable to the unauthorized use; and
(2) The defendant is required to prove properly deductible expenses.

§ 32–13–1–12. Attorney's Fees—Costs—Injunctive Relief

In addition to any damages awarded under section 10 [IC 32–13–1–10] of this chapter, the court:

(1) Shall award to the prevailing party reasonable attorney's fees, costs, and expenses relating to an action under this chapter; and

(2) May order temporary or permanent injunctive relief, except as provided by section 13 [IC 32–13–1–13] of this chapter.

§ 32–13–1–13. When Injunctive Relief not Enforceable

Injunctive relief is not enforceable against a news reporting or an entertainment medium that has:

(1) Contracted with a person for the publication or broadcast of an advertisement; and
(2) Incorporated the advertisement in tangible form into material that has been prepared for broadcast or publication.

§ 32–13–1–14. Impoundment of Items

(a) This section does not apply to a news reporting or an entertainment medium.
(b) During any period that an action under this chapter is pending, a court may order the impoundment of:

(1) Goods, merchandise, or other materials claimed to have been made or used in violation of section 8 [IC 32–13–1–8] of this chapter; and
(2) Plates, molds, matrices, masters, tapes, negatives, or other items from which goods, merchandise, or other materials described under subdivision (1) may be manufactured or reproduced.

(c) The court may order impoundment under subsection (b) upon terms that the court considers reasonable.

§ 32–13–1–15. Destruction of Items

(a) This section does not apply to a news reporting or an entertainment medium.
(b) As part of a final judgment or decree, a court may order the destruction or other reasonable disposition of items described in section 14(b) [IC 32–13–1–14(b)] of this chapter.

§ 32–13–1–16. Property Rights

The rights recognized under this chapter are property rights, freely transferable and descendible, in whole or in part, by the following:

(1) Contract.
(2) License.
(3) Gift.
(4) Trust.
(5) Testamentary document.
(6) Operation of the laws of intestate succession applicable to the state administering the estate and property of an intestate deceased personality, regardless of whether the state recognizes the property rights set forth under this chapter.

§ 32–13–1–17. Enforcement of Rights and Remedies

(a) The written consent required by section 8 [IC 32–13–1–8] of this chapter and the rights and remedies set forth in this chapter may be exercised and enforced by:

(1) A personality; or

(2) A person to whom the recognized rights have been transferred under section 16 [IC 32–13–1–16] of this chapter.

(b) If the transfer described under subsection (a) has not occurred, a person or personality to whom the rights recognized are transferred under section 18 [IC 32–13–1–18] of this chapter may exercise and enforce the rights and remedies under this chapter.

§ 32–13–1–18. Enforcement of Rights and Remedies After Death of Personality

(a) Subject to sections 16 and 17 [IC 32–13–1–16 and IC 32–13–1–17] of this chapter, after the death of an intestate personality, the rights and remedies of this chapter may be exercised and enforced by a person who possesses a total of not less than one-half ([bu412]) interest of the rights.

(b) A person described in subsection (a) shall account to any other person in whom the rights have vested to the extent that the other person's interest may appear.

§ 32–13–1–19. Termination of Rights of Deceased Personality

If:

(1) A deceased personality has not transferred the deceased person's rights under this chapter by:

(A) Contract;
(B) License;
(C) Gift;
(D) Trust; or
(E) Testamentary document; and

(2) There are no surviving persons as described in section 17 [IC 32–13–1–17] of this chapter;

The rights set forth in this chapter terminate.

§ 32–13–1–20. Rights and Remedies Supplemental

The rights and remedies provided for in this chapter are supplemental to any other rights and remedies provided by law.

NOTE _____

See S. R. Gordon and L. A. Honig, "Transfer Issues in Publicity, Privacy Rights," *Ent. L. & Finance* (May 1988).

3.3.3 Additional Recognition of the Right at Common Law

Although many states have enacted statutory rights of publicity, and although statutes such as Indiana's extend beyond name and likeness to aspects of identity, many state statutes apply only to name, likeness, and similar aspects of individual identity. In the cases that follow, none of the plaintiffs could fit themselves under an available statutory umbrella; therefore, they proceeded at common law. In *Motschenbacher,* the issue involved the plaintiff's distinctive race car (and the court nominally cast its decision in terms of privacy, although it is clear that the opinion was really based on right of publicity considerations), the *Carson* case involved a phrase associated with a talk show host, in the *Midler* and *Waits* cases, the issue was vocal style, while the *White* case involved the overall nature of the plaintiff's involvement in a game show.

Motschenbacher v. R. J. Reynolds Tobacco Co., 498 F.2d 821 (9th Cir. 1974)

KOELSCH, J.

[Motschenbacher was an internationally famous professional race car driver. His car was always red, with a distinctive white pin stripe and the number "11" on a white oval background. Defendant created and disseminated a commercial which included an altered photograph of plaintiff's car and other race cars. Plaintiff's face was not visible, and defendant had changed "11" to "71" and added a "spoiler" to plaintiff's car along with the name "Winston." The district court characterized plaintiff's action as sounding in privacy, and granted summary judgment for defendant, holding that plaintiff was unrecognizable in the commercial, and no one could infer an endorsement of defendant's product by plaintiff. The Ninth Circuit reversed.]

In California, as in the vast majority of jurisdiction, the invasion of an individual's right of privacy is an actionable tort.

California courts have observed that "[t]he gist of the cause of action . . . is not injury to the character or reputation, but a direct wrong of a personal character resulting in injury to feelings without regard to any effect which the publication may have on the property, business, pecuniary interest, or the standing of the individual in the community." . . .

It is true that the injury suffered from an appropriation of the attributes of one's identity may be "mental and subjective"—in the nature of humiliation, embarrassment and outrage . . . However, where the identity appropriated has a commercial value, the injury may be largely, or even wholly of an economic or material nature. Such is the nature of the injury alleged by plaintiff . . .

We turn now to the issue of "identifiability." Clearly, if the district court correctly determined as a matter of law that plaintiff is not identifiable in the commercial, then in no sense has plaintiff's identity been misappropriated nor his interest violated.

[A]lthough the "likeness" of the plaintiff is itself unrecognizable . . . [the lower court] wholly fails to attribute proper significance to the distinctive decoration appearing on [plaintiff's] car . . . [which] were not only peculiar to the plaintiff's cars but . . . caused some persons to think the car in question was plaintiff's and to infer that the person driving the car was the plaintiff.

Defendant's reliance on *Branson v. Fawcett Publications, Inc.*, 124 F. Supp. 429 (E.D. Ill. 1954), is misplaced. In Branson, a part-time racing driver brought suit for invasion of privacy when a photograph of his overturned racing car was printed in a magazine without his consent. In ruling that "the photograph . . . does not identify the plaintiff to the public or any member thereof" . . . the court said

[T]he automobile is pointed upward in the air and the picture shows primarily the bottom of the racer. The backdrop of the picture is not distinguishable. No likeness, face, image, form or silhouette of the plaintiff or of any person is shown. From all that appears from the picture itself, there is no one in the car. Moreover, no identifying marks or numbers on the car appear . . . Plaintiff does not even assert that the car he was driving was the same color as that which appears in the colored reproduction. . . . 124 F. Supp. at 432.

But in this case, the car under consideration clearly has a driver and displays several uniquely distinguishing features.

The judgment is reversed and the cause is remanded for further proceedings.

NOTES

1. In *Carson v. Here's Johnny Portable Toilets, Inc.*, 698 F.2d 831 (6th Cir. 1983), Carson sued for unfair competition and for violation of his rights of privacy and publicity under the laws of Michigan. Carson, longtime host of the "Tonight" show, was always introduced with the phrase "He-e-e-re's Johnny!" Carson had licensed the use of his name for men's clothing and toiletries, as well as restaurants. Defendant's "Here's Johnny" portable toilets were subtitled "The World's Foremost Commodian," and defendant's president conceded that he was aware of the identification of "Here's Johnny" with Carson and selected the phrase for that reason.

   There was no evidence that Carson created or owned the introductory phrase. There was no evidence of public confusion, i.e., that anyone thought Carson distributed or endorsed the toilets. Nevertheless, the Sixth Circuit found that defendant had violated Carson's right of publicity (although it did not believe—but did not have to decide—that his right of privacy had been violated, and rejected his claim under Section 43a of the Lanham Act, which is discussed in Section 3.5, below.) "[T]he right of publicity . . . is that a celebrity has a protected pecuniary interest in the commercial exploitation of his identity. If the celebrity's identity is commercially exploited, there has been an invasion of his right whether or not his 'name or likeness' is used. Carson's identity may be exploited even if his name, John W. Carson, or his picture is not used." The court went on to cite *Motschenbacher* and *Hirsch v. S. C. Johnson & Son, Inc.*, 90 Wis. 2d 379, 280 N.W.2d 129 (1979) (use of name "Crazylegs" on women's shaving gel violated publicity rights of famous football player known by that nickname). "It is not fatal to appellant's claim," the court concluded, "that appellee did not use his 'name.' Indeed, there would have been no violation of his right of publicity even if appellee had used his name, such as 'J. William Carson Portable Toilet' or the 'J. W. Carson Portable Toilet' [because] the appellee would not have appropriated Carson's identity as a celebrity."

The dissent would have limited the right of publicity to "an individual's name, likeness, achievements, identifying characteristics or actual performances." Judge Kennedy said that the majority holding "permits a popular entertainer or public figure, by associating himself or herself with a common phrase, to remove those words from the public domain. The phrase 'Here's Johnny' is merely associated with [Carson and] are spoken by an announcer . . . The first name is so common, in light of the millions of persons named John, Johnny or Jonathan that no doubt inhabit this world, that alone, it is meaningless or ambiguous at best in identifying Johnny Carson, the celebrity. In addition, the phrase . . . was certainly selected for its value as a double entendre. . . . The value of the phrase to appellee's product is in the risqué meaning of 'john' as a toilet or bathroom. For this reason, too, this is not a name case. . . . I do not consider it relevant that appellee intentionally chose to [utilize] a phrase that is merely associated with Johnny Carson." Judge Kennedy set forth a three-part rationale for the right of publicity: (1) vindication of the economic interests of celebrities in profiting from their fame; (2) providing financial incentives to creativity, (3) prevention of unjust enrichment and deceptive trade practices. "None of the above-mentioned policy arguments supports the extension of the right of publicity to phrases or things which are merely associated with an individual." In this case, "[t]he phrase is not part of an identity that [Carson] created. . . . Its association with him is derived, in large part, by the context in which it is said [and because appellee's use is] outside of the context in which it is associated with Johnny Carson, [it] does little to rob Johnny Carson of something which is unique to him or a product of his own efforts."

2. Although Carson had sued specifically with reference to Michigan law, the court subsequently made the injunction nationwide in scope, even though it was not clear that all other states would recognize a right of publicity under the circumstances. However, the court did say that the defendant could seek modification if it felt that use of the phrase would be legal in other jurisdictions. See *Carson v. Here's Johnny Portable Toilets, Inc.*, 810 F.2d 104 (6th Cir. 1987).

Midler v. Ford Motor Company, 849 F.2d 460 (9th Cir. 1988), *cert. denied*, 112 S.Ct. U.S. 1513 (1990)

Noonan, Circuit Judge

[In 1985, Ford and its ad agency ran a series of commercials for its cars, dubbed internally "The Yuppie Campaign," attempting to capitalize on yuppies' nostalgia for their college years. In some cases, original artists recreated their old hits. In other cases, "sound-alikes" were used. Midler, a platinum-selling Grammy winner and Academy Award nominee, expressly declined to participate. Ford then utilized one of Midler's former backup singers as a "sound-alike" who sang Midler's hit "Do You Want To Dance," closely imitating Midler's voice and style as directed by the ad agency. Neither Midler's name nor likeness were used in or in connection with the commercial.]

The district court described the defendants' conduct as that "of the average thief." They decided, "If we can't buy it, we'll take it." The court nonetheless believed there was no legal principle preventing imitation of Midler's voice and so gave summary judgment for the defendants. Midler appeals.

The First Amendment protects much of what the media do in the reproduction of likenesses or sounds. A primary value is freedom of speech and press. *Time, Inc. v. Hill,* 385 U.S. 374, 388, 87 S.Ct. 534, 542, 17 L.Ed.2d 456 (1967). The purpose of the media's use of a person's identity is central. If the purpose is "informative or cultural" the use is immune; "if it serves no such function but merely exploits the individual portrayed, immunity will not be granted." Felcher and Rubin, "Privacy, Publicity and the Portrayal of Real People by the Media," 88 Yale L.J. 1577, 1596 (1979). Moreover, federal copyright law preempts much of the area. "Mere imitation of a recorded performance would not constitute a copyright infringement even where one performer deliberately sets out to simulate another's performance as exactly as possible." Notes of Committee on the Judiciary, 17 U.S.C.A. § 114(b). It is in the context of these First Amendment and federal copyright distinctions that we address the present appeal.

Nancy Sinatra once sued Goodyear Tire and Rubber Company on the basis of an advertising campaign by Young & Rubicam featuring "These Boots Are Made For Walkin'," a song closely identified with her; the female singers of the commercial were alleged to have imitated her voice and style and to have dressed and looked like her. The basis of Nancy Sinatra's complaint was unfair competition; she claimed that the song and the arrangement had acquired "a secondary meaning" which, under California law, was protectible. This court noted that the defendants "had paid a very substantial sum to the copyright proprietor to obtain the license for the use of the song and all of its arrangements." To give Sinatra damages for their use of the song would clash with federal copyright law. Summary judgment for the defendants was affirmed. *Sinatra v. Goodyear Tire & Rubber Co.,* 435 F.2d 711, 717–718 (9th Cir. 1970), *cert. denied,* 402 U.S. 906, 91 S.Ct. 1376, 28 L.Ed.2d 646 (1971). If Midler were claiming a secondary meaning to "Do You Want To Dance" or seeking to prevent the defendants from using that song, she would fail like Sinatra. But that is not this case. Midler does not seek damages for Ford's use of "Do You Want To Dance," and thus her claim is not preempted by federal copyright law. Copyright protects "original works of authorship fixed in any tangible medium of expression." 17 U.S.C. § 102(a). A voice is not copyrightable. The sounds are not "fixed." What is put forward as protectible here is more personal than any work of authorship.

Bert Lahr once sued Adell Chemical Co. for selling Lestoil by means of a commercial in which an imitation of Lahr's voice accompanied a cartoon of a duck. Lahr alleged that his style of vocal delivery was distinctive in pitch, accent, inflection, and sounds. The First Circuit held that Lahr had stated a cause of action for unfair competition, that it could be found "that defendant's conduct saturated plaintiff's audience, curtailing his market." *Lahr v. Adell Chemical Co.,* 300 F.2d 256, 259 (1st Cir. 1962). That case is more like this one. But we do not find unfair competition here. One-minute commercials of the sort the defendants put on would not have saturated Midler's audience and curtailed her market. Midler did not do television commercials. The defendants were not in competition with her. *See Halicki v. United Artists Communications, Inc.*, 812 F.2d 1213 (9th Cir. 1987).

California Civil Code section 3344 is also of no aid to Midler [because the ad does not use her] "name, voice, signature, photograph, or likeness, in any manner." . . . The statute, however, does not preclude Midler from pursuing any cause of action she may have at common law; the statute itself implies that such common law causes of action do exist because it says its remedies are merely "cumulative." *Id.* § 3344(g).

The companion statute protecting the use of a deceased person's name, voice, signature, photograph or likeness states that the rights it recognizes are "property rights." *Id.* § 990(b) [Now §3344.1.—Eds.]. By analogy the common law rights are also property rights. Appropriation of such common law rights is a tort in California. *Motschenbacher v. R. J. Reynolds Tobacco Co.*, 498 F.2d 821 (9th Cir. 1974). . . . Midler's case is different from Motschenbacher's. He and his car were physically used by the tobacco company's ad; he made part of his living out of giving commercial endorsements. But, as Judge Koelsch expressed it in *Motschenbacher,* California will recognize an injury from "an appropriation of the attributes of one's identity." *Id.* at 824. It was irrelevant that Motschenbacher could not be identified in the ad. The ad suggested that it was he. The ad did so by emphasizing signs or symbols associated with him. In the same way the defendants here used an imitation to convey the impression that Midler was singing for them.

Why did the defendants ask Midler to sing if her voice was not of value to them? Why did they studiously acquire the services of a soundalike and instruct her to imitate Midler if Midler's voice was not of value to them? What they sought was an attribute of Midler's identity. Its value was what the market would have paid for Midler to have sung the commercial in person.

A voice is more distinctive and more personal than the automobile accouterments protected in *Motschenbacher.* A voice is as distinctive and personal as a face . . . At a philosophical level it has been observed that with the sound of a voice, "the other stands before me." D. Ihde, *Listening and Voice* 77 (1976). A fortiori, these observations hold true of singing, especially singing by a singer of renown. The singer manifests herself in the song. To impersonate her voice is to pirate her identity. See W. Keeton, D. Dobbs, R. Keeton, D. Owen, *Prosser & Keeton on Torts* 852 (5th ed. 1984).

We need not and do not go so far as to hold that every imitation of a voice to advertise merchandise is actionable. We hold only that when a distinctive voice of a professional singer is widely known and is deliberately imitated in order to sell a product, the sellers have appropriated what is not theirs and have committed a tort in California. Midler has made a showing, sufficient to defeat summary judgment, that the defendants here for their own profits in selling their product did appropriate part of her identity. *REVERSED AND REMANDED* for trial.

NOTE _____

The *Midler* case went to trial. The district court dismissed the action as against Ford Motor Co. The jury proceeded to award Ms. Midler $400,000 in damages against Ford's advertising agency, Young & Rubicam, Inc., based on the "fair market value" of Midler's voice as of May 1985, when she had been approached to do the commercial herself. Midler had sought $10,000,000 damages for the tortious imitation of her voice.

In *Waits v. Frito-Lay*, 978 F.2d 1093 (9th Cir. 1992), *cert. denied*, 506 U.S. 1080 (1993), the Court of Appeals upheld a similar claim by Tom Waits. Waits, a singer with a "raspy, gravelly singing voice (described by one fan as 'like how you'd sound if you drank a quart of bourbon, smoked a pack of cigarettes and swallowed a pack of razor blades. . . . [l]ate at night. After not sleeping for three days) sued Frito Lay over the use of a sound alike recording to advertise Doritos chips.

In November 1988, Waits sued Tracy-Locke and Frito-Lay, alleging claims of misappropriation under California law and false endorsement under the Lanham Act. The case was tried before a jury in April and May 1990. The jury found in Waits' favor, awarding him $375,000 compensatory damages, $2 million in punitive damages for voice misappropriation, and $100,000 damages for violation of the Lanham Act. The court awarded Waits attorneys' fees under the Lanham Act. The Court of Appeals affirmed the lower court decision, upholding the viability of *Midler*, stating:

"Waits' voice misappropriation claim is one for invasion of a personal property right: his right of publicity to control the use of his identity as embodied in his voice. . . . The trial's focus was on the elements of voice misappropriation, as formulated in *Midler:* whether the defendants had deliberately imitated Waits' voice rather than simply his style and whether Waits' voice was sufficiently distinctive and widely known to give him a protectible right in its use. These elements are "different in kind" from those in a copyright infringement case challenging the unauthorized use of a song or recording. Waits' voice misappropriation claim, therefore, is not preempted by federal copyright law. . . . " The Court then affirmed the compensatory damage award of $100,000 for the fair market value of Waits services $200,000 for injury to Wait's peace, happiness and feelings and $75,000 for injury to Waits' good will, professional standing and future publicity value. The Court also upheld the $2,000,000 award for punitive damages, stating : "We believe that, viewed most favorably to Waits, this evidence was adequate to support a finding of high probability that Tracy-Locke and Frito-Lay acted with malice. Despicability reflects a moral judgment, "conscious disregard" a state of mind. A rational jury could have found the defendants' conduct despicable because they knowingly impugned Waits' integrity in the public eye. A rational jury also could have found that the defendants, in spite of their awareness of Waits' legal right to control the commercial use of his voice, acted in conscious disregard of that right by broadcasting the commercial. We therefore affirm the award of punitive damages. . . ."

The Court concluded: "Waits' voice misappropriation claim and his Lanham Act claim are legally sufficient. The court did not err in instructing the jury on elements of voice misappropriation. The jury's verdict on each claim is supported by substantial evidence, as are its damage awards. Its award of damages on Waits' Lanham Act claim, however, is duplicative of damages awarded for voice misappropriation; accordingly we vacate it. Finally, the court did not abuse its discretion in awarding attorneys' fees under the Lanham Act. . . . [for malice in intentionally publishing a photo without permission.]"

Waits has been vigilant in protecting his recognizable personal property. In 2006, Waits won a Spanish court case against an advertiser for deliberately using a singer to mimic his voice. Waits brought an intellectual property case against Volkswagen-Audi and a commercial television production company, winning the right to squash sound-alike music that mimics his songs to be used in commercials. The ruling, the first in Spain that attaches likeness rights to a singer's voice, ruled that the car company and its ad agency infringed on Waits' copyrights by mimicking his sound. As of this writing, Waits is involved in a similar lawsuit against General Motors for advertisements that ran in Scandinavia for the Opal. According to news reports, GM asked for permission to use Waits' recording and was refused. GM then used a sound alike. Waits is quoted as saying "If I stole an Opel, Lancia or Audi, put my name on it and resold it, I'd go to jail. But over there they ask, you say 'no,' and they hire impersonators. They profit from the association and I lose—time, money, and credibility. What's that about?"

NOTE _____

In addition to holding that §§50 and 51 of the New York Civil Rights Law did not apply in a situation in which the use complained of was newsworthy, *Stephano v. News Group Publications, Inc.*, 64 N.Y.2d 174, 485 N.Y.S.2d 220 (1984) also held that there was no common law right of publicity in New York.

_____

White v. Samsung Electronics America, 971 F.2d 1395 (9th Cir. 1992), *cert. denied*, 508 U.S. 951 (1993)

Goodwin, J.

This case involves a promotional "fame and fortune" dispute. In running a particular advertisement without Vanna White's permission, defendants Samsung Electronics America, Inc., (Samsung) and David Deutsch Associates, Inc., (Deutsch) attempted to capitalize on White's fame to enhance their fortune. White sued, alleging infringement of various intellectual property rights, but the district court granted summary judgment in favor of the defendants. We affirm in part, reverse in part, and remand.

Plaintiff Vanna White is the hostess of Wheel of Fortune, one of the most popular game shows in television history. An estimated forty million people watch the program daily. Capitalizing on the fame which her participation in the show has bestowed on her, White markets her identity to various advertisers.

The dispute in this case arose out of a series of advertisements prepared for Samsung by Deutsch. The series ran in at least half a dozen publications with widespread, and in some cases national, circulation. Each of the advertisements in the series followed the same theme. Each depicted a current item from popular culture and a Samsung electronic product. Each was set in the twenty-first century and conveyed the message that the Samsung product would still be in use by that time. By hypothesizing outrageous future outcomes for the cultural items, the ads created humorous effects. For example, one lampooned current popular notions of an unhealthy diet by depicting a raw steak with the caption: "Revealed to be health food. 2010 A.D." Another depicted irreverent "news"-show host Morton Downey Jr. in front of an American flag with the caption: "Presidential candidate. 2008 A.D."

The advertisement which prompted the current dispute was for Samsung video-cassette recorders (VCRs). The ad depicted a robot, dressed in a wig, gown, and jewelry which Deutsch consciously selected to resemble White's hair and dress. The robot was posed next to a game board which is instantly recognizable as the Wheel of Fortune game show set, in a stance for which White is famous. The caption of the ad read: "Longest-running game show. 2012 A.D." Defendants referred to the ad as the "Vanna White" ad. Unlike the other celebrities used in the campaign, White neither consented to the ads nor was she paid.

Following the circulation of the robot ad, White sued Samsung and Deutsch in federal district court under: (1) California Civil Code § 3344; (2) the California common law right of publicity; and (3) § 43(a) of the Lanham Act, 15 U.S.C. § 1125(a). The district court granted summary judgment against White on each of her claims. White now appeals.

I. SECTION 3344

White first argues that the district court erred in rejecting her claim under section 3344. Section 3344(a) provides, in pertinent part, that "[a]ny person who knowingly uses another's name, voice, signature, photograph, or likeness, in any manner, . . . for purposes of advertising or selling, . . . without such person's prior consent . . . shall be liable for any damages sustained by the person or persons injured as a result thereof." . . .

In this case, Samsung and Deutsch used a robot with mechanical features, and not, for example, a manikin molded to White's precise features. Without deciding for all purposes when a caricature or impressionistic resemblance might become a "likeness," we agree with the district court that the robot at issue here was not White's "likeness" within the meaning of section 3344. Accordingly, we affirm the court's dismissal of White's section 3344 claim.

II. RIGHT OF PUBLICITY

White next argues that the district court erred in granting summary judgment to defendants on White's common law right of publicity claim. In *Eastwood v. Superior Court,* 149 Cal.App. 3d 409, 198 Cal. Rptr. 342 (1983), the California court of appeal stated that the common law right of publicity cause of action "may be pleaded by alleging (1) the defendant's use of the plaintiff's identity; (2) the appropriation of plaintiff's name or likeness to defendant's advantage, commercially or otherwise; (3) lack of consent; and (4) resulting injury." *Id.* at 417, 198 Cal.Rptr. 342 (citing Prosser, *Law of Torts* (4th ed. 1971) § 117, pp. 804–807). The district court dismissed White's claim for failure to satisfy *Eastwood's* second prong, reasoning that defendants had not appropriated White's "name or likeness" with their robot ad. We agree that the robot ad did not make use of White's name or likeness. However, the common law right of publicity is not so confined. . . .

The "name or likeness" formulation referred to Eastwood originated not as an element of the right of publicity cause of action, but as a description of the types of cases [in] which the cause of action had been recognized. The source of this formulation is Prosser, *Privacy,* 48 Cal.L.Rev. 383, 401–07 (1960), one of the earliest and most enduring articulations of the common law right of publicity cause of action. In looking at the case law to that point, Prosser recognized that right of publicity cases involved one of two basic factual scenarios: name appropriation, and picture or other likeness appropriation. . . .

Since Prosser's early formulation, the case law has borne out his insight that the right of publicity is not limited to the appropriation of name or likeness [citing *Motschenbacher*].

In *Midler,* this court held that, even though the defendants had not used Midler's name or likeness, Midler had stated a claim for violation of her California common law right of publicity because "the defendants . . . for their own profit in selling their product did appropriate part of her identity" by using a Midler sound-alike. . . .

In *Carson v. Here's Johnny Portable Toilets, Inc.,* 698 F.2d 831 (6th Cir. 1983), the defendant had marketed portable toilets under the brand name "Here's Johnny"—Johnny Carson's signature "Tonight Show" introduction—without Carson's permission. The district court had dismissed Carson's Michigan common law right of publicity claim because the defendants had not used Carson's "name or likeness." Id. at 835. In reversing the district court, the sixth circuit found "the district court's conception of the right of publicity . . . too narrow" and held that the right was implicated because the defendant had appropriated Carson's identity by using, *inter alia,* the phrase "Here's Johnny." Id. at 835–37.

These cases teach not only that the common law right of publicity reaches means of appropriation other than name or likeness, but that the specific means of appropriation are relevant only for determining whether the defendant has in fact appropriated the plaintiff's identity. The right of publicity does not require that appropriations of identity be accomplished through particular means to be actionable. It is noteworthy that the *Midler* and *Carson* defendants not only avoided using the plaintiff's name or likeness, but they also avoided appropriating the celebrity's voice, signature, and photograph. The photograph in *Motschenbacher* did include the plaintiff, but because the plaintiff was not visible the driver could have been an actor or dummy and the analysis in the case would have been the same. . . .

Indeed, if we treated the means of appropriation as dispositive in our analysis of the right of publicity, we would not only weaken the right but effectively eviscerate it. The right would fail to protect those plaintiffs most in need of its protection. Advertisers use celebrities to promote their products. The more popular the celebrity, the greater the number of people who recognize her, and the greater the visibility for the product. The identities of the most popular celebrities are not only the most attractive for advertisers, but also the easiest to evoke without resorting to obvious means such as name, likeness, or voice.

Consider a hypothetical advertisement which depicts a mechanical robot with male features, an African-American complexion, and a bald head. The robot is wearing black high top Air Jordan basketball sneakers, and a red basketball uniform with black trim, baggy shorts, and the number 23 (though not revealing "Bulls" or "Jordan" lettering). The ad depicts the robot dunking a basketball one-handed, stiff-armed, legs extended like open scissors, and tongue hanging out. Now envision that this ad is run on television during professional basketball games. Considered individually, the robot's physical attributes, its dress, and its stance tell us little. Taken together, they lead to the only conclusion that any sports viewer who has registered a discernible pulse in the past five years would reach: the ad is about Michael Jordan.

Viewed separately, the individual aspects of the advertisement in the present case say little. Viewed together, they leave little doubt about the celebrity the ad is meant to depict. The female-shaped robot is wearing a long gown, blond wig, and large jewelry. Vanna White dresses exactly like this at times, but so do many other women. The robot is in the process of turning a block letter on a game-board. Vanna White dresses like this while turning letters on a game-board but perhaps similarly attired Scrabble-playing women do this as well. The robot is standing on what looks to be the Wheel of Fortune game show set. Vanna White dresses like this, turns letters, and does this on the Wheel of Fortune game show. She is the only one. Indeed, defendants themselves referred to their ad as the "Vanna White" ad. We are not surprised. . . .

Because White has alleged facts showing that Samsung and Deutsch had appropriated her identity, the district court erred by rejecting, on summary judgment, White's common law right of publicity claim. . . .

IV. THE PARODY DEFENSE

In defense, defendants cite a number of cases for the proposition that their robot ad constituted protected speech. The only cases they cite which are even remotely relevant to this case are *Hustler Magazine v. Falwell*, 485 U.S. 46, 108 S.Ct. 876, 99 L.Ed.2d 41 (1988) and *L. L. Bean, Inc. v. Drake Publishers, Inc.*, 811 F.2d 26 (1st Cir. 1987). Those cases involved parodies of advertisements run for the purpose of poking fun at Jerry Falwell and L.L. Bean, respectively. This case involves a true advertisement run for the purpose of selling Samsung VCRs. The ad's spoof of Vanna White and Wheel of Fortune is subservient and only tangentially related to the ad's primary message: "buy Samsung VCRs." Defendants' parody arguments are better addressed to non-commercial parodies. The difference between a "parody" and a "knock-off" is the difference between fun and profit.

V. CONCLUSION

In remanding this case, we hold only that White has pleaded claims which can go to the jury for its decision. . . .

ALARCON, J. (DISSENTING IN PART)

I must dissent from the majority's holding on Vanna White's right to publicity claim. The district court found that, since the commercial advertisement did not show a "likeness" of Vanna White, Samsung did not improperly use the plaintiff's identity. The majority asserts that the use of a likeness is not required under California common law. According to the majority, recovery is authorized if there is an appropriation of one's "identity." I cannot find any holding of a California court that supports this conclusion. Furthermore, the record does not support the majority's finding that Vanna White's "identity" was appropriated. . . .

Notwithstanding the fact that California case law clearly limits the test of the right to publicity to name and likeness, the majority concludes that "the common law right of publicity is not so confined." Majority opinion at p. 1397. The majority relies on two factors to support its innovative extension of the California law. The first is that the *Eastwood* court's statement of the elements was permissive rather than exclusive. The second is that Dean Prosser, in describing the common law right to publicity, stated that it might be possible that the right extended beyond name or likeness. These are slender reeds to support a federal court's attempt to create new law for the state of California. . . .

The majority has focused on federal decisions in its novel extension of California Common Law. Those decisions do not provide support for the majority's decision.

In each of the federal cases relied upon by the majority, the advertisement affirmatively represented that the person depicted therein was the plaintiff. In this case, it is clear that a metal robot and not the plaintiff, Vanna White, is depicted in the commercial advertisement. The record does not show an appropriation of Vanna White's identity. . . .

The majority appears to argue that because Samsung created a robot with the physical proportions of an attractive woman, posed it gracefully, dressed it in a blond wig, an evening gown, and jewelry, and placed it on a set that resembles the Wheel of Fortune layout, it thereby appropriated Vanna White's identity. But an attractive appearance, a graceful pose, blond hair, an evening gown, and jewelry are attributes shared by many women, especially in Southern California. These common attributes are particularly evident among game show hostesses, models, actresses, singers and other women in the entertainment field. They are not unique attributes of Vanna White's identity. Accordingly, I cannot join in the majority's conclusion that, even if viewed together, these attributes identify Vanna White and, therefore, raise a triable issue as to the appropriation of her identity.

The only characteristic in the commercial advertisement that is not common to many female performers or celebrities is the imitation of the Wheel of Fortune set. This set is the only thing which might possibly lead a viewer to think of Vanna White. The Wheel of Fortune set, however, is not an attribute of Vanna White's identity. It is an identifying characteristic of a television game show, a prop with which Vanna White interacts in her role as the current hostess. To say that Vanna White may bring an action when another blond female performer or robot appears on such a set as a hostess will, I am sure, be a surprise to the owners of the show. . . .

The record shows that Samsung recognized the market value of Vanna White's identity. No doubt the advertisement would have been more effective if Vanna White had appeared in it. But the fact that Samsung recognized Vanna White's value as a celebrity does not necessarily mean that it appropriated her identity. The record shows that Samsung dressed a robot in a costume usually worn by television game-show hostesses, including Vanna White. A blond wig, and glamorous clothing are not characteristics unique to the current hostess of Wheel of Fortune. This evidence does not support the majority's determination that the advertisement was meant to depict Vanna White. The advertisement was intended to depict a robot, playing the role Vanna White currently plays on the Wheel of Fortune. I quite agree that anyone seeing the commercial advertisement would be reminded of Vanna White. Any performance by another female celebrity as a game-show hostess, however, will also remind the viewer of Vanna White because Vanna White's celebrity is so closely associated with the role. But the fact that an actor or actress became famous for playing a particular role has, until now, never been sufficient to give the performer a proprietary interest in it. I cannot agree with the majority that the California courts, which have consistently taken a narrow view of the right to publicity, would extend law to these unique facts. . . .

The majority gives Samsung's First Amendment defense short shrift because "[t]his case involves a true advertisement run for the purpose of selling Samsung VCRs." Majority opinion at p. 1401. I respectfully disagree with the majority's analysis of this issue as well.

The majority's attempt to distinguish this case from *Hustler Magazine v. Falwell*, 485 U.S. 46, 108 S.Ct. 876, 99 L.Ed.2d 41 (1988), and *L. L. Bean, Inc. v. Drake Publishers, Inc.*, 11 F.2d 26 (1st Cir. 1987), is un- persuasive. The majority notes that the parodies in those cases were made for the purpose of poking fun at the Reverend Jerry Falwell and L.L. Bean. But the majority fails to consider that the defendants in those cases were making fun of the Reverend Jerry Falwell and L.L. Bean for the purely commercial purpose of selling soft-core porno- graphic magazines. . . .

The effect of the majority's holding on expressive conduct is dif- ficult to estimate. The majority's position seems to allow any famous person or entity to bring suit based on any commercial advertisement that depicts a character or role performed by the plaintiff. Under the majority's view of the law, Gene Autry could have brought an action for damages against all other singing cowboys. Clint Eastwood would be able to sue anyone who plays a tall, soft spoken cowboy, unless, of course, Jimmy Stewart had not previously enjoined Clint Eastwood. Johnny Weismuller would have been able to sue each actor who played the role of Tarzan. Sylvester Stallone could sue actors who play blue- collar boxers. Chuck Norris could sue all karate experts who display their skills in motion pictures. Arnold Schwarzenegger could sue body builders who are compensated for appearing in public. . . .

Direct competitive advertising could also be affected. Will BMW, which advertises its automobiles as "the ultimate driving machine," be able to maintain an action against Toyota for advertising one of its cars as "the ultimate saving machine"? Can Coca Cola sue Pepsi because it depicted a bottle of Coca Cola in its televised "taste test"? Indeed, any advertisement which shows a competitor's product, or any recogniz- able brand name, would appear to be liable for damages under the majority's view of the applicable law. Under the majority's analysis, even the depiction of an obvious facsimile of a competitor's prod- uct may provide sufficient basis for the maintenance of an action for damages. . . .

The protection of intellectual property presents the courts with the necessity of balancing competing interests. On the one hand, we wish to protect and reward the work and investment of those who create intellectual property. In so doing, however, we must prevent the creation of a monopoly that would inhibit the creative expres- sions of others. We have traditionally balanced those interests by al- lowing the copying of an idea, but protecting a unique expression of it. Samsung clearly used the idea of a glamorous female game show hostess. Just as clearly, it avoided appropriating Vanna White's expression of that role. Samsung did not use a likeness of her. The performer depicted in the commercial advertisement is unmistakably a lifeless robot. Vanna White has presented no evidence that any consumer confused the robot with her identity. Indeed, no reasonable consumer could confuse the robot with Vanna White or believe that, because the robot appeared in the advertisement, Vanna White endorsed Samsung's product.

I would affirm the district court's judgment in all respects.

NOTES _____

1. In the foregoing *White* decision, the court also considered at length a Lanham Act claim by Ms. White, concluding there was a basis for finding in her favor. The court's analysis is largely duplicative of several discussions in Section 3.4 and is thus omitted at this juncture.

2. In *Wendt v. Host International,* 125 F.3d 806, 1997 U.S.App.LEXIS 25584 (9th Cir. 1997), reh. denied, 197 F.3d 1284 (9th Cir. 1999), cert. denied sub nom. *Paramount Pictures Corp. v. Wendt,* 121 S.Ct. 33, 148 L. Ed 2d 13 (2000), the court held that former "Cheers" sitcom regulars George Wendt (Norm) and John Ratzenberger (Cliff) were entitled to a jury determination of whether two seated animated robotic figures which appeared at the end of the bar in each of defendant's "Cheers" airport restaurants constituted likenesses of the plaintiffs for the purposes of Civil Code § 3344 as well as California's common law right of publicity and Section 43a of the Lanham Act (see Sec. 3.5, below).

3.3.4 Post-Mortem Availability

As we have seen in the discussion of the right of privacy, New York has no common law right of publicity and the limited right of publicity provided under §§ 50 and 51 of the Civil Rights Law does not survive death. All of the statutes set forth in the preceding section, except for §3344 of the California Civil Code, also contain provisions providing post-mortem rights. As we see below, California has a specific statute providing post-mortem rights. Where no statute exists, however, results may vary.

3.3.4.1 At Common Law

Several states recognize the descendibility of the right of publicity at common law, but have not established limits for its duration. For example, in *Martin Luther King, Jr., Center For Social Change, Inc. v. American Heritage Products, Inc.,* 250 Ga. 135, 296 S.E.2d 697 (1982) [discussed above in Section 3.3.1], the Georgia Supreme Court, responding to questions certified to it by the Eleventh Circuit in a case involving unauthorized plastic busts of Dr. King (as well as brochures and ads claiming that the busts were "an exclusive memorial" to Dr. King and "an opportunity to support the Martin Luther King, Jr., Center For Social Change," defendant's testimony being that he intended to set aside 3 percent of the $29.95 purchase price of each bust to be donated to the Center), the court looked back to the *Pavesich* case (see Sec. 3.2.2) as recognizing the right of publicity and stated that "the right of publicity survives the death of its owner and is inheritable and devisable." The court did not discuss or suggest any outside time limit.

The New Jersey common law right of publicity also survives death according to the Third Circuit. *McFarland v. Miller,* 14 F.3d 912 (3d Cir. 1994). In that case, former child star "Spanky" McFarland, who had appeared in the 1930s "Little Rascal" film comedies, sued a New Jersey restaurant called "Spanky's" which displayed pictures of McFarland in his film character. "[W]e conclude," the court stated, "that infringement of a person's right to exploit commercially his own name or the name of a character so associated with him that it identifies him in his own right is a cause of action under New Jersey law that survives the death of the person with whom the name has become identified" and passes to his personal representative.

NOTE _____

In *Zacchini* (see Sec. 3.3.1), the U.S. Supreme Court assumed that Ohio law recognized an independent right of publicity. However, in *Reeves v. United Artists Corp.,* 765 F.2d 79 (6th Cir. 1985), involving a claim by the widow of Jake LaMotta against the producers of the motion picture *Raging Bull,* a biographical account of LaMotta's life, the Sixth Circuit held that "The Ohio Supreme Court did not reach the issue of whether the right of publicity is descendible since [Zacchini] brought suit during his lifetime, but the syllabus clearly indicates the Ohio Supreme Court's recognition of that right as a part of its law concerning the invasion of privacy [and] actions for invasion of privacy in Ohio are not descendible and lapse upon death. . . ."

3.3.4.2 Under Statute

In the *Guglielmi* and *Lugosi* decisions referred to in the preceding section, the California Supreme Court made clear that if a common law right of publicity existed, it was inter vivos only. Therefore, the Legislature adopted Civil Code §990 to provide (as then-Chief Justice Rose Bird had recommended) a post-mortem right of publicity having a term of 50 years from death. As the result of the decision of the Ninth Circuit in *Astaire v. Best Film & Video Corp.,* 136 F3d 1208 (9th Cir. 1997), *cert. denied,* 525 U.S. 868, 1998 U.S. LEXIS 5584 (1998), Section 990 has been amended and renumbered as Section 3344.1. In the *Astaire* case, the widow of Fred Astaire was unsuccessful in her attempt to prevent the distributor of instructional dance videos from utilizing clips from her late husband's films, because of the statutory exemption for "film" set forth in subsection (1) of the former 990. The revised statute (SB 209) attempts to prevent future results of this type, by stating that a use that would otherwise be exempt shall not be exempt if the claimant can prove that the use is so closely connected to the sale of a product, article of merchandise, good or service as to constitute an advertising, marketing or merchandising use. The act also extends the post-mortem applicability of the provision to 70 years, and provides (in subsection (n)) that it applies to acts occurring in California regardless of the domicile of the deceased personality at the time of death.

3.3.4.2.1. Rights of Deceased Personality
California Civil Code Astaire Celebrity Image Protection Act

(a) (1) Any person who uses a deceased personality's name, voice, signature, photograph, or likeness, in any manner, on or in products, merchandise, or goods, or for purposes of advertising or selling, or soliciting purchases of, products, merchandise, goods, or services, without prior consent from the person or persons specified in subdivision (c), shall be liable for any damages sustained by the person or persons injured as a result thereof. In addition, in any action brought under this section, the person who violated the section shall be liable to the injured party or parties in an amount equal to the greater of seven hundred fifty dollars ($750) or the actual damages suffered by the injured party or parties, as a result of the unauthorized use, and any profits from the unauthorized use that are attributable to the use and are not taken into account in computing the actual damages. In establishing these profits, the injured party or parties shall be required to present proof only of the gross revenue attributable to the use and the person who violated the section is required to prove his or her deductible expenses. Punitive damages may also be awarded to the injured party or parties. The prevailing party or parties in any action under this section shall also be entitled to attorneys' fees and costs.

(2) For purposes of this subdivision, a play, book, magazine, newspaper, musical composition, audiovisual work, radio or television program, single and original work of art, work of political or newsworthy value, or an advertisement or commercial announcement for any of these works, shall not be considered a product, article of merchandise, good, or service if it is fictional or nonfictional entertainment, or a dramatic, literary, or musical work.

(3) If a work that is protected under paragraph (2) includes within it a use in connection with a product, article of merchandise, good, or service, this use shall not be exempt under this subdivision, notwithstanding the unprotected use's inclusion in a work otherwise exempt under this subdivision, if the claimant proves that this use is so directly connected with a product, article of merchandise, good, or service as to constitute an act of advertising, selling, or soliciting purchases of that product, article of merchandise, good, or service by the deceased personality without prior consent from the person or persons specified in subdivision (c).

(b) The rights recognized under this section are property rights, freely transferable, in whole or in part, by contract or by means of trust or testamentary documents, whether the transfer occurs before the death of the deceased personality, by the deceased personality or his or her transferees, or, after the death of the deceased personality, by the person or persons in whom the rights vest under this section or the transferees of that person or persons.

(c) The consent required by this section shall be exercisable by the person or persons to whom the right of consent, or portion thereof, has been transferred in accordance with subdivision (b), or if no transfer has occurred, then by the person or persons to whom the right of consent, or portion thereof, has passed in accordance with subdivision (d).

(d) Subject to subdivisions (b) and (c), after the death of any person, the rights under this section shall belong to the following person or persons and may be exercised, on behalf of and for the benefit of all of those persons, by those persons who, in the aggregate, are entitled to more than a one-half interest in the rights:

(1) The entire interest in those rights belong to the surviving spouse of the deceased personality unless there are any surviving children or grandchildren of the deceased personality, in which case one-half of the entire interest in those rights belong to the surviving spouse.

(2) The entire interest in those rights belong to the surviving children of the deceased personality and to the surviving children of any dead child of the deceased personality unless the deceased personality has a surviving spouse, in which case the ownership of a one-half interest in rights is divided among the surviving children and grandchildren.

(3) If there is no surviving spouse, and no surviving children or grandchildren, then the entire interest in those rights belong to the surviving parent or parents of the deceased personality.

(4) The rights of the deceased personality's children and grandchildren are in all cases divided among them and exercisable in the manner provided in Section 240 of the Probate Code according to the number of the deceased personality's children represented. The share of the children of a dead child of a deceased personality can be exercised only by the action of a majority of them.

(e) If any deceased personality does not transfer his or her rights under this section by contract, or by means of a trust or testamentary document, and there are no surviving persons as described in subdivision (d), then the rights set forth in subdivision (a) shall terminate.

(f) (1) A successor in interest to the rights of a deceased personality under this section or a licensee thereof may not recover damages for a use prohibited by this section that occurs before the successor in interest or licensee registers a claim of the rights under paragraph (2).

(2) Any person claiming to be a successor in interest to the rights of a deceased personality under this section or a licensee thereof may register that claim with the Secretary of State on a form prescribed by the Secretary of State and upon payment of a fee as set forth in subdivision (d) of Section 12195 of the Government Code. The form shall be verified and shall include the name and date of death of the deceased personality, the name and address of the claimant, the basis of the claim, and the rights claimed.

(3) Upon receipt and after filing of any document under this section, the Secretary of State shall post the document along with the entire registry of persons claiming to be a successor in interest to the rights of a deceased personality or a registered licensee under this section upon the World Wide Web, also known as the Internet. The Secretary of State may microfilm or reproduce by other techniques any of the filings or documents and destroy the original filing or document. The microfilm or other reproduction of any document under the provisions of this section shall be admissible in any court

of law. The microfilm or other reproduction of any document may be destroyed by the Secretary of State 70 years after the death of the personality named therein.

(4) Claims registered under this subdivision shall be public records.

(g) No action shall be brought under this section by reason of any use of a deceased personality's name, voice, signature, photograph, or likeness occurring after the expiration of 70 years after the death of the deceased personality.

(h) As used in this section, "deceased personality" means any natural person whose name, voice, signature, photograph, or likeness has commercial value at the time of his or her death, whether or not during the lifetime of that natural person the person used his or her name, voice, signature, photograph, or likeness on or in products, merchandise or goods, or for purposes of advertising or selling, or solicitation of purchase of, products, merchandise, goods, or services. A "deceased personality" shall include, without limitation, any such natural person who has died within 70 years prior to January 1, 1985.

(i) As used in this section, "photograph" means any photograph or photographic reproduction, still or moving, or any video tape or live television transmission, of any person, such that the use in connection with any news, public affairs, or sports broadcast or account, or any political campaign, shall not constitute a use for which consent is required under subdivision (a).

(k) The use of a name, voice, signature, photograph, or likeness in a commercial medium shall not constitute a use for which consent is required under subdivision (a) solely because the material containing the use is commercially sponsored or contains paid advertising. Rather, it shall be a question of fact whether or not the use of the deceased personality's name, voice, signature, photograph, or likeness was so directly connected with the commercial sponsorship or with the paid advertising as to constitute a use for which consent is required under subdivision (a).

(l) Nothing in this section shall apply to the owners or employees of any medium used for advertising, including, but not limited to, newspapers, magazines, radio and television networks and stations, cable television systems, billboards, and transit ads, by whom any advertisement or solicitation in violation of this section is published or disseminated, unless it is established that the owners or employees had knowledge of the unauthorized use of the deceased personality's name, voice, signature, photograph, or likeness as prohibited by this section.

(m) The remedies provided for in this section are cumulative and shall be in addition to any others provided for by law.

(n) This section shall apply to the adjudication of liability and the imposition of any damages or other remedies in cases in which the liability, damages, and other remedies arise from acts occurring directly in this state. For purposes of this section, acts giving rise to liability shall be limited to the use, on or in products, merchandise, goods, or services, or the advertising or selling, or soliciting purchases of, products, merchandise, goods, or services prohibited by this section.

(o) This section shall be known and may be cited as the Astaire Celebrity Image Protection Act.

NOTES

1. For a discussion of the impact of the new statute, see Joseph J. Beard, "Fresh Flowers For Forest Lawn: Amendment of the California Post-Mortem Right of Publicity Statute," *ABA Entertainment & Sports Lawyer,* Vol. 17 No. 4 (Winter 2000), p. 1.

2. The estate of Janis Joplin brought suit under the former §990 over a two-act play concerning the deceased rock singer. In *Joplin Enterprises v. Allen,* 795 F. Supp. 349 (W.D.Wash. 1992), the court held that the estate could not proceed under § 990 of the California Civil Code, because the statute by its terms covers only "merchandise, advertising, and endorsements" and specifically excludes from its coverage plays, books or musical compositions. The court also noted that California's common law right of publicity was not descendible. Thus, while the trial proceeded on other grounds, the rights of publicity claims were dismissed.

3.3.4.3 *Conflicts Problems*

As of this writing, there is no uniform rule concerning the descendibility of property rights. As we have seen, some of the state statutes (New York being the notable exception) provide for descendibility. This has been an issue in many cases where the heirs of a decedent domiciled in one state have sought to enforce publicity rights under the laws of another state. Except for statutes such as those in Indiana (and the new California Civil Code §3344.1), the outcome will generally depend upon whether the right of publicity is descendible under the law of the state in which the decedent was domiciled at the time of death.

In *Southeast Bank, N.A. v. Lawrence,* 66 N.Y.2d 910, 498 N.Y.S.2d 775 (1985), the personal representative of the estate of the late playwright Tennessee Williams, a Florida domiciliary at the time of his death, sought to enjoin defendants, the owners of a theatre located on West 48th Street in New York City, from renaming the theatre the "Tennessee Williams." In its complaint, plaintiff alleged, among other things, that the renaming of the theatre without its consent violated the decedent's descendible right of publicity.

Special Term granted plaintiff's motion for a preliminary injunction and denied defendant's cross motion to dismiss the complaint. That order was affirmed by the appellate division. The Court of Appeals reversed.

The court in its opinion said:

"The parties have assumed that the substantive law of New York is dispositive of the appeal and have addressed Florida law only tangentially. Both Special Term and the Appellate Division decided the case under what they believed to be New York law. In doing so, all have overlooked the applicable choice of law principle followed by both New York and Florida, that questions concerning personal property rights are to be determined by reference to the substantive law of the decedent's domicile. . . . For choice of law purposes, at least, rights of publicity constitute personality. . . .

Under Florida law (Fla.Stats.Ann. § 540.08), only one to whom a license has been issued during decedent's lifetime and the decedent's surviving spouse and children possess a descendible right of publicity, which is extremely limited and which Florida courts have refused to extend beyond the contours of the statute. . . . Since Tennessee Williams did not have a surviving spouse or child and did not issue a license during his lifetime, plaintiff possesses no enforceable property right. In light of this holding, we do not pass upon the question of whether a common-law descendible right of publicity exists in this State. . . ."

However, in *Prima v. Darden Restaurants, Inc.*, 78 F.Supp. 2d 337 (D.N.J. 2000), the widow of "swing"-era legend singer/songwriter Louis Prima was able to sue the Olive Garden restaurant chain in New Jersey in 1999 (for using a "sound-alike" in a commercial), although Prima had resided in Nevada from 1954 until 1976, after which, in a coma, he was in a hospital, and then a clinic, in Louisiana until his death in 1978. Defendants claimed that Louisiana law should apply, because Prima had been born there and had returned to live, work and perform there at times during his life. (This would have ended the matter, since, according to the court's interpretation, Louisiana's right of privacy subsumes the right of publicity and is not descendible.) Plaintiff, a resident of New Jersey, argued for the application of either New Jersey or Nevada law. Dismissing Prima's contacts with Louisiana as "minuscule," the court said that while Louisiana might have some interest in permitting its citizens to use Prima's persona after his death, the defendants were not citizens of Louisiana. On the other hand, New Jersey and Nevada had meaningful contacts with Prima and his widow. Since the widow was domiciled in New Jersey at the time the alleged tort occurred, and since there was no conflict between the laws of New Jersey and Nevada, the court applied New Jersey law.

3.3.5 Defensive Aspects

As we have seen in the foregoing sections, the First Amendment serves to limit the right of privacy. So, too, the First Amendment limits the right of publicity, as we see in the *New Kids on the Block* decision. However, there is a limit to the limitation, as the *Zacchini* case teaches us. The courts will not permit exploitation beyond what is reasonably necessary to convey the newsworthiness of an event.

3.3.5.1 Public Figures/Newsworthiness

New Kids on the Block v. News America Publishing, 971 F.2d 302 (9th Cir. 1992)

KOZINSKI, J.

The individual plaintiffs perform professionally as The New Kids on the Block, reputedly one of today's hottest musical acts. This case requires us to weigh their rights in that name against the rights of others to use it in identifying the New Kids as the subjects of public opinion polls.

BACKGROUND

No longer are entertainers limited to their craft in marketing themselves to the public. This is the age of the multi-media publicity blitzkrieg: Trading on their popularity, many entertainers hawk posters, T-shirts, badges, coffee mugs and the like—handsomely supplementing their incomes while boosting their public images. The New Kids are no exception; the record in this case indicates there are more than 500 products or services bearing the New Kids trademark. Among these are services taking advantage of a recent development in telecommunications: 900 area code numbers, where the caller is charged a fee, a portion of which is paid to the call recipient. Fans can call various New Kids 900 numbers to listen to the New Kids talk about themselves, to listen to other fans talk about the New Kids, or to leave messages for the New Kids and other fans.

The defendants, two newspapers of national circulation, conducted separate polls of their readers seeking an answer to a pressing question: Which one of the New Kids is the most popular? *USA Today's* announcement contained a picture of the New Kids and asked, "Who's the best on the block?" The announcement listed a 900 number for voting, noted that "any USA Today profits from this phone line will go to charity." . . .

The Star's announcement, under a picture of the New Kids, went to the heart of the matter: "Now which kid is the sexiest?" The announcement, which appeared in the middle of a page containing a story on a New Kids concert, also stated:

Which of the New Kids on the Block would you most like to move next door? STAR wants to know which cool New Kid is the hottest with our readers.

Readers were directed to a 900 number to register their votes; each call cost 95 cents per minute.

Fearing that the two newspapers were undermining their hegemony over their fans, the New Kids filed a shotgun complaint in federal court raising no fewer than ten claims: (1) common law trademark infringement; (2) Lanham Act false advertising; (3) Lanham Act false designation of origin; (4) Lanham Act unfair competition; (5) state trade name infringement; (6) state false advertising; (7) state unfair competition; (8) commercial misappropriation; (9) common-law misappropriation; and (10) intentional interference with prospective economic advantage. . . .

The district court granted summary judgment for defendants. 745 F. Supp. 1540 (C.D.Cal. 1990). . . .

I

[The Court rejected plaintiffs' trademark infringement claims, holding that the newspapers' use of the group's professional name was within the scope of the qualified privilege to make reference to trademarks for the purpose of comparison, criticism, and similar uses.] Much useful social and commercial discourse would be all but impossible if speakers were under threat of an infringement lawsuit every time they made reference to a person, company or product by using its trademark. . . . While plaintiffs' trademark certainly deserves protection against copycats and those who falsely claim that the New Kids have endorsed or sponsored them, such protection does not extend to rendering newspaper articles, conversations, polls and comparative advertising impossible. . . . Both *The Star* and *USA Today* reference the New Kids only to the extent necessary to identify them as the subject of the polls; they do not use the New Kids' distinctive logo or anything else that isn't needed to make the announcements intelligible to readers [and] nothing in the announcements suggests joint sponsorship or endorsement by the New Kids.

II

The New Kids raise three additional claims that merit brief attention.

A. The New Kids claim that *USA Today's* and *The Star's* use of their name amounted to both commercial and common law misappropriation under California law. Although there are subtle differences between these two causes of action, all that's material here is a key similarity between them: The papers have a complete defense to both claims if they used the New Kids name "in connection with any news, public affairs, or sports broadcast or account" which was true in all material respects. See Cal.Civ.Code § 3344(d). . . .

   In this case, *USA Today's* and *The Star's* use of the New Kids' name was "in connection with" news accounts: The Star ran concurrent articles on the New Kids along with its 900-number poll, while *USA Today* promised a subsequent story on the popularity of various members of the singing group. Both papers also have an established track record of polling their readers and then reporting the poll results as part of a later news story. The New Kids' misappropriation claims are barred by California Civil Code section 3344(d).

B. The New Kids' remaining claim is for intentional interference with prospective economic advantage, but they ignore the maxim that all's fair in love, war and the free market. Plaintiffs' case rests on the assumption that the polls operated to siphon off the New Kids' fans or divert their resources away from "official" New Kids products. Even were we to accept this premise, no tort claim has been made out: "So long as the plaintiff's contractual relations are merely contemplated or potential, it is considered to be in the interest of the public that any competitor should be free to divert them to himself by all fair and reasonable means. . . . In short, it is no tort to beat a business rival to prospective customers." *A-Mark Coin Co. v. General Mills, Inc.*, 148 Cal.App. 3d 312, 323, 195 Cal.Rptr. 859 (1983).

Affirmed.

3.3.5.2 Advertising and Promotion

Just as the courts have long recognized that the presence of a profit motive does not deprive a news or entertainment medium of its First Amendment rights, so have they also recognized that the survival of such a medium requires that it have the ability to promote and market itself, in order to sustain and, if possible, increase its audience. (This is mentioned in *Lerman v. Flynt Distributing Co.*, see above.) In so doing, the courts have told us, it is permissible for the medium to present brief examples of its prior offerings as part of its advertising. As the following cases illustrate, the courts take a fairly expansive view in this area. In the *Namath* case, the court is not put off by the fact that the advertising insert in question looks very much like an endorsement, while in the *Montana* case, the court permits the sale of a poster which, under normal circumstances, would most definitely engage the right of publicity. However, as we see in the *Eastwood* note, the advertising/promotion defense is not without limits.

Namath v. Sports Illustrated, 48 A.D.2d 487, 371 N.Y.S.2d 10 (1st Dept. 1975), aff'd, 39 N.Y.2d 897, 386 N.Y.S.2d 397 (1976)

CAPPAZOLI, J.

Plaintiff sought substantial compensatory and punitive damages by reason of defendants' publication and use of plaintiff's photograph without his consent. That photograph, which was originally used by defendants, without objection from plaintiff, in conjunction with a news article published by them on the 1969 Super Bowl Game, was used in advertisements promoting subscriptions to their magazine, *Sports Illustrated.*

The use of plaintiff's photograph was merely incidental advertising of defendants' magazine in which plaintiff had earlier been properly and fairly depicted and, hence, it was not violative of the Civil Rights Law (*Booth v. Curtis Publishing Co.*, 15 A.D.2d 343, 223 N.Y.S.2d 737, aff'd, 11 N.Y.2d 907, 228 N.Y.S.2d 468, 182 N.E.2d 812).

Certainly, defendants' subsequent republication of plaintiff's picture was "in motivation, sheer advertising and solicitation. This alone is not determinative of the question so long as the law accords an exempt status to incidental advertising of the news medium itself." (*Booth v. Curtis Publishing Co.*, *supra*, p. 349, 223 N.Y.S.2d p. 744.) Again, it was stated, at 15 A.D.2d p. 350, 223 N.Y.S.2d p. 744 of the cited case, as follows:

Consequently, it suffices here that so long as the reproduction was used to illustrate the quality and content of the periodical in which it originally appeared, the statute was not violated, albeit the reproduction appeared in other media for purposes of advertising the periodical.

Contrary to the dissent, we deem the cited case to be dispositive hereof. The language from the Namath advertisements, relied upon in the dissent, does not indicate plaintiff's endorsement of the magazine *Sports Illustrated*. Had that been the situation, a completely different issue would have been presented. Rather, that language merely indicates, to the readers of those advertisements, the general nature of the contents of what is likely to be included in future issues of the magazine. . . .

KUPFERMAN, J. (DISSENTING)

It is undisputed that one Joseph W. Namath is an outstanding sports figure, redoubtable on the football field. Among other things, as the star quarterback of the New York Jets, he led his team to victory on January 12, 1969 in the Super Bowl in Miami.

This feat and the story of the game and its star were heralded with illustrative photographs in the January 20, 1969, issue of *Sports Illustrated*, conceded to be an outstanding magazine published by Time Incorporated and devoted, as its name implies, to the activities for which it is famous. Of course, this was not the first nor the last time that *Sports Illustrated* featured Mr. Namath and properly so.

The legal problem involves the use of one of his action photos from the January 20, 1969, issue in subsequent advertisements in other magazines as promotional material for the sale of subscriptions to *Sports Illustrated*.

Plaintiff contends that the use was commercial in violation of his right of privacy under sections 50 and 51 of the Civil Rights Law. . . . Further, that because he was in the business of endorsing products and selling the use of his name and likeness, it interfered with this right to such sale, sometimes known as the right of publicity. *Haelan Laboratories v. Topps Chewing Gum,* 202 F.2d 866 (2nd Cir. 1953). Defendants contend there is an attempt to invade their constitutional rights under the First and Fourteenth Amendments by the maintenance of this action and that, in any event, the advertisements were meant to show "the nature, quality and content" of the magazine and not to trade on the plaintiff's name and likeness.

Initially, we are met with the determination in a similar case, *Booth v. Curtis Publishing Co.*, 15 A.D.2d 343, 223 N.Y.S.2d 737 (N.Y. App. Div.1st Dep't.) aff'd without op., 11 N.Y.2d 907, 228 N.Y.S.2d 468 182 N.E.2d 812 (1962) relied on by Baer, J., in his opinion at Special Term dismissing the complaint.

The plaintiff was Shirley Booth, the well-known actress, photographed at a resort in the West Indies, up to her neck in the water and wearing an interesting chapeau, which photo appeared in *Holiday Magazine* along with photographs of other prominent guests. This photo was then used as a substantial part of an advertisement for *Holiday*.

Mr. Justice Breitel (now Chief Judge Breitel) wrote:

Consequently, it suffices here that so long as the reproduction was used to illustrate the quality and content of the periodical in which it originally appeared, the statute was not violated, albeit the reproduction appeared in other media for purposes of advertising the periodical. [15 A.D.2d at p. 350, 223 N.Y.S.2d at p. 744]

However, the situation is one of degree. A comparison of the Booth and Namath photographs and advertising copy shows that in the Booth case, her name is in exceedingly small print, and it is the type of photograph itself which attracted attention. In the Namath advertisement, we find, in addition to the outstanding photograph, in *Cosmopolitan Magazine* (for women) the heading "The Man You Love Loves Joe Namath," and in *Life*, the heading "How to Get Close to Joe Namath."

There seems to be trading on the name of the personality involved in the defendants' advertisements. . . .

The complaint should not have been dismissed as a matter of law.

Montana v. San Jose Mercury News 34 Cal.App. 4th 790, 40 Cal.Rptr.2d 639 (Cal.Ct.App. 6th Dist. 1995)

COTTLE, P. J.

[Montana led the San Francisco 49ers to victory in the 1989 and 1990 Super Bowls. In each instance, the News ran next-day first-page stories highlighting Montana's achievements. Since the 1990 win gave the 49ers an unprecedented four Super Bowl wins in a single decade, the next Sunday News included a special "Souvenir Section" entitled "Trophy Hunters," the first page of which featured an artist's rendition of Montana. Within two weeks, the News began to sell copies of the various pages from the "Souvenir Section" in poster form. Approximately 30 percent of the posters were sold at $5 each, the balance being given away at charity events. Montana sought relief for (1) common law commercial misappropriation, and (2) violation of Civil Code §3344. The News' motion for summary judgment was granted, and the court of appeals affirmed.]

[N]o [common law] cause of action will lie for the "[p]ublication of matters in the public interest, which rests on the right of the public to know and the freedom of the press to tell it . . . "(*Dora v. Frontline Video Inc.* (1993) 15 Cal.App. 4th 536, 542, 18 Cal.Rptr.2d 790; see U.S. Const. Art. 1). Further, a matter in the public interest is not restricted to current events but may extend to the reproduction of past events (*Id. Carlisle v. Fawcett Publications, Inc.* (1962) 201 Cal.App. 2d 733, 746, 20 Cal.Rptr. 405; *Eastwood v. Superior Court* [(1983)] 149 Cal.App. 3d 409, 421, 198 Cal.Rptr. 342). . . .

[Civil Code §3344] complements rather than codifies common law misappropriation (*Lugosi v. Universal Pictures* (1979) 25 Cal.3d 813, 819, 160 Cal. Rptr. 323, 603 P.2d 425). . . . Like the common law cause of action, the statutory cause of action specifically exempts from liability the use of a name or likeness in connection with the reporting of a matter in the public interest. . . .

. . . The question [Montana] raises in this appeal is whether the relatively contemporaneous reproduction of these pages, in poster form, for resale, is [like the earlier news reports] entitled to First Amendment protection. We conclude that it is. This is because Montana's name and likeness appeared in the posters for precisely the same reason they appeared on the original newspaper front pages: because Montana was a major player in contemporaneous newsworthy sports events. Under these circumstances, Montana's claim that SJMN used his face and name solely to extract the commercial value from them fails.

Although we have been unable to locate any cases directly on point, several cases discuss First Amendment implications of the sale of posters, videotapes or movies of recognizable individuals without their consent. *Paulsen v. Personality Posters, Inc.* (1968) 59 Misc.2d 444, 299 N.Y.S.2d 501, is illustrative. There, comedian Pat Paulsen sought a preliminary injunction to bar a poster marketer from selling posters of him with the words "FOR PRESIDENT" written at the bottom. Paulsen had conducted a mock campaign for the presidency in 1968. In discussing whether Paulsen's statutorily defined right of privacy [Under §§50 and 51 of New York's Civil Rights Law—Eds.] had been abridged, the court observed "that the statute was not intended to limit activities involving the dissemination of news or information concerning matters of public interest . . . [.] [S]uch activities are privileged and do not fall within 'the purposes of trade' contemplated by Section 51 [New York's equivalent of California Civil Code section 3344], notwithstanding that they are also carried on for a profit." [Citations]. Thus, it was early held that newspapers, magazines, and newsreels are exempt from the statutory injunction when using a name or picture in connection with an item of news or one that is newsworthy and such privileged status has also been extended to other communications media including books, comic books, radio, television and motion pictures. [Citations.] Indeed, it is clear that any format of 'the written word or picture,' including posters and handbills [citation] will be similarly exempted in conjunction with the dissemination of news or public interest presentations. . . . (*Id.* 199 N.Y.S.2d at 506.)

Applying those principles to the poster of Paulsen, the court stated: "When a well-known entertainer enters the presidential ring, tongue in cheek or otherwise, it is clearly newsworthy and of public interest. A poster which portrays plaintiff in that role, and reflects the spirit in which he approaches said role, is a form of public interest presentation to which protection must be extended." (*Paulsen v. Personality Posters, Inc., supra,* 299 N.Y.S.2d at 507.)

The same could be said here. When Montana led his team to four Super Bowl championships in a single decade, it was clearly a newsworthy event. Posters portraying the 49ers' victories are, like the poster in *Paulsen,* "form[s] of public interest presentation to which protection must be extended." (299 N.Y.S.2d at 507.)

A similar conclusion was reached in *Jackson v. MPI Home Video* (N.D.Ill. 1988) 694 F. Supp. 483. In that case, the reverend Jesse Jackson sought an injunction against the unauthorized distribution of videocassettes of a copyrighted speech he gave to the 1988 Democratic convention. The court granted the injunction based on Jackson's copyright claims. At the same time, it noted that "Jackson's chances of success on [his] right to publicity claim appear less than negligible" as the "defendants claim[ed] that they were engaged in news reporting . . . "(*Id.* at 492.) The court explained that . . . [p]ublic figures possess [the right of publicity] with respect to commercial use of their names and likeness [sic]. . . . But public figures do not retain the right of publicity against the use of name and likeness in the news media." [Citation.] (*Id.* at 492.)

And in *Dora v. Frontline Video, Inc., supra,* 15 Cal.App. 4th at p. 536, 18 Cal.Rptr 790, a self-proclaimed surfing "legend" [unsuccessfully] sued the producer of a video documentary on surfing [because] the documentary contained matters of public interest and was therefore protected by the First Amendment. The court further held that the statutory exemption from liability for "public affairs" (Civ.Code, §3344, subd. (d)) applied to surfing, which "is of more than passing interest to some. It has created a life-style that influences speech, behavior, dress, and entertainment, among other things. A phenomenon of such scope has an economic impact, because it affects purchases, travel and the housing market. Surfing has also had a significant influence on the popular culture, and in that way touches many people." (*Id.* at p. 546, 18 Cal.Rptr. 790.) Again, the same public interest considerations applicable to surfing apply with equal force to professional football.

Additionally, SJMN had a right to republish its front page sports stories to show the quality of its work product. It is well established that "a person's photograph originally published in one issue of a periodical as a newsworthy subject (and therefore concededly exempt from the statutory prohibitions) may be republished subsequently in another medium as an advertisement for the periodical itself, illustrating the quality and content of the periodical, without the person's written consent." (*Booth v. Curtis Publishing Company* (1962) 15 A.D.2d 343, 223 N.Y.S.2d 737, 738–739.) In the *Booth* case, the court held that actress Shirley Booth's right of publicity was not abridged by the publication of her photograph from an earlier edition of Holiday magazine in a later edition advertising the periodical.

The same rule was applied in *Cher v. Forum Intern., Ltd.* (9th Cir. 1982) (692 F.2d 634). In that case, actress/singer Cher had been interviewed by a talk show host in connection with a planned cover story on her in *US* magazine. However, Cher and the magazine had a falling out, and plans for the story were dropped. The interviewer then sold the Cher interview to the publishers of *Star,* a tabloid, and *Forum,* a magazine. Cher sued, saying that her reputation was "degraded by the suggestion that she would give an exclusive interview to [those] publication[s]." (*Id.* at 637.) Advertisements about Cher's interview in *Forum* appeared in *Star, Penthouse, Forum,* and the *New York Daily News,* falsely stating that Cher would divulge secrets to *Forum* that she "won't tell *People* and would never tell *US.*" (*Id.* at 638.)

Applying California law, the court held that the publication of the interview in *Forum* was protected by the First Amendment. The Ninth Circuit pointed out that the California Supreme Court has acknowledged that "the right of publicity has not been held to outweigh the value of free expression. Any other conclusion would allow reports and commentaries on the thoughts and conduct of public and prominent persons to be subject to censorship under the guise of preventing the dissipation of the publicity value of a person's identity." (*Id.* at p. 638; citing *Guglielmi v. Spelling-Goldberg Productions* (1979) 25 Cal.3d 860, 873, 160 Cal.Rptr. 352, 603 P.2d 454, conc. op. of Bird, J.)

[Thus,] "[c]onstitutional protection extends to the truthful use of a public figure's name and likeness in advertising which is merely an adjunct of the protected publication and promotes only the protected publication. [Citation.] Advertising to promote a news medium, accordingly, is not actionable under an appropriation of publicity theory so long as the advertising does not falsely claim that the public figure endorses that news medium." (*Cher v. Forum Intern., Ltd.*, 692 F.2d at p. 639; see also *Namath v. Sports Illustrated* (1975) 48 A.D.2d 487, 371 N.Y.S.2d 10.)

At the hearing on the summary judgment motion in this case, SJMN submitted undisputed evidence that it sold the posters to advertise the quality and content of its newspapers. The posters were effective in this regard: they were exact reproductions of pages from the paper [without] additional information not included [therein] and they did not state or imply that Montana endorsed the newspaper. SJMN also submitted evidence showing that it set the price of the posters with the intent simply to recover its costs. Where, as here, a newspaper page covering newsworthy events is reproduced for the purposes of showing the quality and content of the newspaper, the subsequent reproduction is exempt from the statutory and common law prohibitions [and the fact that the posters were sold is without significance.] "The First Amendment is not limited to those who publish without charge . . ." (citing *Guglielmi v. Spelling-Goldberg Productions, supra,* and *Joseph Burstyn, Inc. v. Wilson* (1952) 343 U.S. 495, 501–502, 72 S.Ct. 777, 780, 96 L.Ed. 1098.)

In summary, the First Amendment protects the posters complained about here for two distinct reasons: first, because the posters themselves report newsworthy items of public interest, and second, because a newspaper has a constitutional right to promote itself by reproducing its originally protected articles or photographs. . . .

Wunderlich and Mihara, J.J, concur.

NOTE

On the other hand, the right to utilize photographs and posters for promotional purposes is not without limits, as demonstrated by *Eastwood v. Superior Court of L.A. County,* 198 Cal. Rptr.342 (Cal.Ct. App. 2d Div. 1983). There, Clint Eastwood successfully overcame a demurrer to claims brought under Civil Code §3344, his common law right of publicity, as well as his common law right of privacy (the "false light" branch) where he charged that the *National Enquirer* knowingly published a false—albeit non-defamatory—article detailing the alleged romantic involvement between Eastwood and country singing star Tanya Tucker at a time when Eastwood was living with longtime companion Sondra Locke, and included pictures of Eastwood and Tucker on the front page of the issue above the caption "Clint Eastwood in Love Triangle with Tanya Tucker." The pictures and title were also included in television ads for the issue. (Interestingly, the *Enquirer* did not contest the "false light" claim.) In overruling the demurrer on the other causes of action, the Court of Appeals observed that "California law has not imposed any requirement that the unauthorized use or publication of a person's name or picture be suggestive of an endorsement or association with the injured person," and that "to the extent [that the] use of [Eastwood's name and picture] attracted the readers' attention, the Enquirer gained a commercial advantage [and] used Eastwood's personality in the context of an alleged news account . . . to generate maximum curiosity and the necessary motivation to purchase the newspaper." This use "provided the *Enquirer* with a ready-made 'scoop'—a commercial advantage over its competitors which it would not otherwise have. Absent a constitutional or statutory proscription, we find that Eastwood can show that such use is a subterfuge or a cover-up for commercial exploitation." The court rejected the *Enquirer*'s claim that the use was covered by the "news account" exemption provided by Civil Code §3344(d). The court explained that

[a]ll fiction is false in the literal sense in that it is imagined rather than actual. However, works of fiction are constitutionally protected in the same manner as topical news stories. . . . We have no doubt that the subject of the Enquirer article . . . is a matter of public concern, which would generally preclude the imposition of liability. . . . [However, while observing that Eastwood would have to meet the standards of *New York Times v. Sullivan*,] in privacy cases the concern is with nondefamatory lies masquerading as truth, and [with respect to the statutory right of publicity,] Civil Code section 3344 does not provide exemption for a knowing or reckless falsehood. . . . [T]he First Amendment does not immunize Enquirer when the entire article is allegedly false . . . [and] the deliberate fictionalization of Eastwood's personality constitutes commercial exploiation, and becomes true when it is presented to the reader as if true with the requisite scienter. . . . "

3.4 PERSONAL RIGHTS: THE LANHAM ACT AND OTHER FEDERAL LEGISLATION

3.4.1 Introduction: A National Remedy

Celebrities may look beyond rights of privacy and publicity to assert other legal bases for their complaints about invasion of their personal rights. The legal implications of the Lanham Act, more general trademark principles, and unfair competition are discussed below. The central focus is the Federal Trademark Act, the Lanham Act, and, more specifically, Section 43a, which reads as follows:

15 U.S.C. §1125. False Designations of Origin and False Descriptions Forbidden

(a) Any person who shall affix, apply, or annex, or use in connection with any goods or services, or any container or containers for goods, a false designation of origin, or any false description or representation, including words or other symbols tending falsely to describe or represent the same, and shall cause such goods or services to enter into commerce, and any person who shall with knowledge of the falsity of such designation of origin or description or representation cause or procure the same to be transported or used in commerce or deliver the same to any carrier to be transported or used, shall be liable to a civil action by any person doing business in the locality falsely indicated as that of origin or in the region in which said locality is situated, or by any person who believes that he is or is likely to be damaged by the use of any such false description or representation.

Called by one commentator a "wild card" (Brown, "Copyright and Its Upstart Cousins: Privacy, Publicity and Unfair Competition," 33 *J. Copyright Soc. Am.* 301, 309 [1986]), the Lanham Act offers a celebrity significant protection against the unauthorized use of his or her persona.

In addition to its protection against infringement of registered trademarks, Section 43(a) of the Lanham Act provides protection against false representation likely to cause public confusion about origin and sponsorship. This section thus creates a "federal statutory tort," with "broad remedial protection" (Comment, "Whose Voice Is It Anyway? Midler v. Ford Motor Co.," 8 *Cardozo Arts & Ent. L.J.* 201, 217 [1989]).

Although one need not possess a registered trademark or servicemark in order to avail oneself of the protections of Section 43a, it is helpful to consider trademark, tradename, and service mark protections for individuals and their creative efforts. A brief description illustrates how each might be used in transforming the individual into a protected business.

Trademarks

A trademark is a sign, device, or mark by which the goods produced or dealt in by a particular individual or business are distinguished from those produced or dealt in by others. The Trademark Act defines the term "trademark" to include any word, name, symbol, or device adopted and used to identify goods and distinguish them from others.

A trademark is closely analogous to the goodwill of a business. It represents the "commercial signature" of the trademark owner placed upon the merchandise or the package in which it is sold.

The purpose of a trademark is twofold. First, a trademark's function is to designate goods as the product of a particular trader, thereby protecting the trader's goodwill as against the sale of another's products as the trader's own. Second, a trademark also assures the public that they are procuring the genuine goods they seek. It is therefore imperative that for a word, name, symbol, or device to constitute a trademark, it must point distinctly to the origin or ownership of the goods to which it is affixed. The reason for this requirement is that unless the word, name, symbol, or device clearly points out the origin or ownership of the goods, the individual or business claiming trademark protection cannot be harmed by any appropriation or imitation of them by others; nor can the public be deceived. Trademarks may be:

1. Fanciful (coined words which have been invented for the sole purpose of functioning as a trademark).
2. Arbitrary (words or symbols in common usage in the language but arbitrarily applied to goods).
3. Suggestive (words which suggest but do not primarily describe the goods or their characteristics).
4. Descriptive (marks that describe the qualities, ingredients, or characteristics of a product).

Trademark rights are protected by affixation of the mark on the goods themselves and use of the mark in interstate commerce. Trademark infringement is determined by the likelihood of confusion among the purchasing public. The similarity of the marks in sound, appearance, and meaning, and the similarities of the channels of trade and the goods are all factors in determining trademark infringement.

Tradenames

The term "tradename" is most commonly used to indicate a part or all of a business and includes individual names, surnames, and abbreviations of firm names. It is typically a name, word, or phrase used by one engaged in a business as a means of identifying products, business, or services and of establishing goodwill.

A tradename differs from a trademark in that it relates mainly to a business and its goodwill, while a trademark relates mainly to goods sold. Although the Trademark Act distinguishes between trademarks and tradenames by providing that tradenames are not entitled to registration, the protection afforded to tradenames is the same as the protection afforded to trademarks.

Service Marks

The term "service mark" under the Trademark Act includes a mark used in the sale or advertising of services to identify the services of one person and distinguish those services from the services of others. Titles, character names, and other distinctive features of radio and television programs may be registered as service marks. Moreover, entertainment services provided by individuals are among the "services" sufficient to support service mark registration. Service marks are intended to identify and afford protection to things of an intangible nature, as distinguished from the protection already provided for marks affixed to tangible goods and products. However, it is possible for a given symbol to be used in a way that it functions as both a trademark for goods and a service mark for services, and can be the object of separate registrations.

3.4.2 Use of Section 43(a) by Celebrities and Entities

Allen v. National Video, Inc., 610 F. Supp. 612 (S.D.N.Y. 1985)

MOTLEY, J.

. . . This case arises because plaintiff, to paraphrase Groucho Marx, wouldn't belong to any video club that would have him as a member. More precisely, plaintiff sues over an advertisement for defendant National Video (National) in which defendant Boroff, allegedly masquerading as plaintiff, portrays a satisfied holder of National's movie rental V.I.P. Card. Plaintiff asserts that the advertisement appropriates his face and implies his endorsement, and that it therefore violates his statutory right to privacy, his right to publicity, and the federal Lanham Act's prohibition of misleading advertising. Plaintiff, basing jurisdiction on diversity of citizenship, seeks an injunction against Boroff and defendant Smith, Boroff's agent, and damages against all defendants.

Defendants, while conceding that Boroff looks remarkably like plaintiff, deny that the advertisement appropriates plaintiff's likeness or that it poses a likelihood of consumer confusion . . .

The following facts are not in dispute. Plaintiff Woody Allen is a film director, writer, actor, and comedian. Among the films plaintiff has directed are *Annie Hall,* which won several Academy Awards, *Manhattan, Bananas, Sleeper, Broadway Danny Rose,* and, most recently, *The Purple Rose of Cairo.* In addition to being a critically successful artist, plaintiff has for more than 15 years been a major international celebrity. Although he has not often lent his name to commercial endeavors other than his own projects, plaintiff's many years in show business have made his name and his face familiar to millions of people. This familiarity, and plaintiff's reputation for artistic integrity, have significant, exploitable, commercial value.

The present action arises from an advertisement, placed by National to promote its nationally franchised video rental chain, containing a photograph of defendant Boroff taken on September 2, 1983. The photograph portrays a customer in a National video store, an individual in his forties, with a high forehead, tousled hair, and heavy black glasses. The customer's elbow is on the counter, and his face, bearing an expression at once quizzical and somewhat smug, is leaning on his hand. It is not disputed that, in general, the physical features and pose are characteristic of plaintiff.

The staging of the photograph also evokes association with plaintiff. Sitting on the counter are videotape cassettes of *Annie Hall* and *Bananas,* two of plaintiff's best known films, as well as *Casablanca* and *The Maltese Falcon.* The latter two are Humphrey Bogart films of the 1940's associated with plaintiff primarily because of his play and film *Play It Again, Sam,* in which the spirit of Bogart appears to the character played by Allen and offers him romantic advice. In addition, the title *Play It Again, Sam* is a famous, although inaccurate, quotation from *Casablanca.*

The individual in the advertisement is holding up a National Video V.I.P. Card, which apparently entitles the bearer to favorable terms on movie rentals. The woman behind the counter is smiling at the customer and appears to be gasping in exaggerated excitement at the presence of a celebrity.

The photograph was used in an advertisement which appeared in the March 1984 issue of *Video Review,* a magazine published in New York and distributed in the Southern District, and in the April 1984 issue of *Take One,* an in-house publication which National distributes to its franchisers across the country. The headline on the advertisement reads "Become a V.I.P. at National Video. We'll Make You Feel Like a Star." The copy goes on to explain that holders of the V.I.P. card receive "hassle-free movie renting" and "special savings" and concludes that "you don't need a famous face to be treated to some pretty famous service."

The same photograph and headline were also used on counter cards distributed to National's franchisees. Although the advertisement that ran in *Video Review* contained a disclaimer in small print reading "Celebrity double provided by Ron Smith's Celebrity Look-Alike's, Los Angeles, Calif.," no such disclaimer appeared in the other versions of the advertisements.

None of the defendants deny that the advertisements in question were designed, placed, and authorized by defendant National, that defendant Boroff was selected and posed as he was to capitalize on his resemblance to plaintiff and to attract the attention of movie watchers, that defendants Boroff and Smith were aware of this purpose in agreeing to supply Boroff's services, and that in fact Smith and Boroff have on other occasions offered the services of Boroff, a Los Angeles-based actor and director, as a look-alike for plaintiff. Moreover, defendants do not dispute that the photograph in question was used for commercial purposes, and that plaintiff did not give his consent to the use of the photograph.

Plaintiff maintains that these undisputed facts require the court to enter summary judgment for him on his right to privacy, right of publicity, and Lanham Act claims, he urges the court to find, as a matter of law, that defendants used his picture or portrait for commercial purposes without his permission, and that the advertisements were materially misleading and likely to result in consumer confusion as to his endorsement of National's services.

Defendants insist that other disputed facts require denial of plaintiff's motion. Although defendants concede that they sought to evoke by reference plaintiff's general persona, they strenuously deny that they intended to imply that the person in the photograph was actually plaintiff or that plaintiff endorsed National. Defendants offer their own interpretation of the advertisement to support their assertion that the photograph does not depict plaintiff. According to defendants, the idea of the advertisement is that even people who are not stars are *treated* like stars at National Video. They insist that the advertisement depicts a "Woody Allen fan," so dedicated that he has adopted his idol's appearance and mannerisms, who is able to live out his fantasy by receiving star treatment at National Video. The knowing viewer is supposed to be amused that the counter person actually believes that the customer is Woody Allen.

Defendants urge that this interpretation cannot be rejected as a matter of law, and that if defendant Boroff merely appeared as someone who looks like Woody Allen, but not as Woody Allen himself, then plaintiff's rights were not violated. Defendants further seek summary judgment against plaintiff on the basis that plaintiff has offered no actual evidence that anyone was actually deceived into thinking that the photograph was of him. . . . Plaintiff rejects defendants' explanation of the advertisement as fanciful and asserts that since all defendants knowingly participated in creating a photograph that amounts to a portrait of plaintiff to be used for advertising in a national magazine, they are all jointly and severally liable for violating plaintiff's rights. . . .

PRIVACY AND PUBLICITY CLAIMS

[Although deciding that the Lanham Act provided the appropriate remedy, the court discussed Allen's claims under §§ 50 and 51 of the

New York Civil Rights Law and held that since defendants had offered an alternative explanation for the presence of the look-alike in the ad, namely, that it was intended to portray a fan of Allen rather than Allen *himself,* unlike the situation in *Onassis,* in which the only possible explanation for the appearance of the look-alike in the ad was to suggest the real Jacqueline Kennedy Onassis, the court declined to reach this aspect of the case in deciding Allen's motion for summary judgment.]

LANHAM ACT CLAIM

Plaintiff seeks summary judgment on his claim under section 43(a) of the federal Lanham Act, 15 U.S.C. section 1125(a) (West 1982) ("the Act"), which prohibits false descriptions of products or their origins. The Act is more than a mere codification of common law trademark infringement. Its purpose is "the protection of consumers and competitors from a wide variety of misrepresentations of products and services in commerce. In enacting the section, Congress in effect created a new federal statutory tort. The section is clearly remedial and should be broadly construed." . . .

The Act has therefore been held to apply to situations that would not qualify formally as trademark infringement, but that involve unfair competitive practices resulting in actual or potential deception. . . . To make out a cause of action under the Act, plaintiff must establish three elements: (1) involvement of goods or services, (2) effect on interstate commerce, and (3) a false designation of origin or false description of the goods or services. . . .

Application of the act is limited, however, to potential deception which threatens economic interests analogous to those protected by trademark law. . . . One such interest is that of the public to be free from harmful deception. Another interest, which provides plaintiff here with standing, is that of the "trademark" holder in the value of his distinctive mark. . . .

A celebrity has a similar commercial investment in the "drawing power" of his or her name and face in endorsing products and in marketing a career. The celebrity's investment depends upon the goodwill of the public, and infringement of the celebrity's rights also implicates the public's interest in being free from deception when it relies on a public figure's endorsement in an advertisement. The underlying purposes of the Lanham Act therefore appear to be implicated in cases of misrepresentations regarding the endorsement of goods and services.

The Act's prohibitions, in fact, have been held to apply to misleading statements that a product or service has been endorsed by a public figure. See *Geisel v. Poynter Products, Inc.* 283 F. Supp. 261 (S.D.N.Y. 1968) [see Section 4.10, *infra.*]

In *Cher v. Forum International, Ltd.,* 213 USPQ 96 (C.D. Cal 1982), plaintiff, a popular singer and actress, brought a similar Lanham Act claim. Plaintiff sued when an interview she had granted to *US* magazine was sold to *Forum* magazine, a publication of Penthouse International. *Forum* published the interview and advertised it widely, falsely implying that plaintiff read and endorsed *Forum* and had granted the magazine an exclusive interview. *Id.* at 99–100. The court held that the Act "extends to misrepresentations in advertising as well as labeling of products and services in commerce," *id.* at 102, and noted that no finding of an actual trademark is required under the Act. *Id.* "The Lanham Act proscribes any false designation or representation in connection with any goods or services in interstate commerce," a standard which plaintiff Cher had met. *Id.*

Geisel and *Cher* suggest that the unauthorized use of a person's name or photograph in a manner that creates the false impression that the party has endorsed a product or service in interstate commerce violates the Lanham Act. Application of this standard to the case at bar, however, is complicated by defendants' use of a look-alike for plaintiff, rather than plaintiff's actual photograph, as in *Cher,* or pseudonym, as in *Geisel.* Unlike the state law privacy claim discussed in the foregoing section, the plaintiff's Lanham Act theory does not require the court to find that defendant Boroff's photograph is, as a matter of law, plaintiff's "portrait or picture." The court must nevertheless decide whether defendant's advertisement creates the likelihood of consumer confusion over whether plaintiff endorsed or was otherwise involved with National Video's goods and services. . . .

This inquiry requires the court to consider whether the look-alike employed is sufficiently *similar* to plaintiff to create such a likelihood—an inquiry much like that made in cases involving similar, but not identical, trademarks. The court therefore finds it helpful, in applying the likelihood of confusion standard to the facts of this case, to refer to traditional trademark analysis.

Reference to this analysis is justified since the likelihood of confusion standard is applied to a wide variety of trademark and trademark-related causes of action. The standard is "the heart of a successful claim" under both the Lanham Act and common law trademark infringement. . . . Other cases have held that the standard is applied in state law unfair competition cases as well as in trademark cases. . . .

In *Standard and Poor's,* the Second Circuit suggested six factors for a court to consider in deciding the issue of likelihood of confusion: (1) the strength of plaintiff's marks and name; (2) the similarity of plaintiff's and defendant's marks; (3) the proximity of plaintiff's and defendant's products; (4) evidence of actual confusion as to source or sponsorship; (5) sophistication of the defendant's audience; and (6) defendant's good or bad faith, 683 F.2d at 708, 216 USPQ at 843. . . .

The first factor outlined in *Standard and Poor's,* the strength of plaintiff's mark, concerns the extent to which plaintiff has developed a favorable association for his mark in the public's mind. . . . There is no dispute that plaintiff's name and likeness are well-known to the public, and that he has built up a considerable investment in his unique, positive public image. Plaintiff's "mark," to analogize from trademark law, is a strong one.

The similarity of the "marks"—i.e., the similarity of plaintiff to defendant Boroff—is the question posed by the second *Standard and Poor's* factor, and has already been addressed above. While the court was unable to hold that defendant Boroff's photograph was as a matter of law plaintiff's portrait or picture, the resemblance between the two is strong and not disputed.

Under the third factor, proximity of the products, the court notes that while plaintiff does not own a video rental chain, he is involved in producing and distributing his own motion pictures, and he is strongly identified with movies in the public mind. The audience at which National Video's advertisement was aimed—movie watchers—is therefore the same audience to which plaintiff's own commercial efforts are directed. There is no requirement under the Act that plaintiff and defendant actually be in competition. . . .

The court has declined to rely on plaintiff's proffered consumer survey, and plaintiff has submitted no other evidence of actual confusion. Under the fourth *Standard and Poor's* factor, such evidence, although highly probative of likelihood of confusion, is not required. . . .

The sophistication of the relevant consuming public is measured under the fifth factor. The average reader of *Video Review* or customer of National Video is likely to be comparatively sophisticated about movies, such that a good number of them arguably would realize that plaintiff did not actually appear in the photograph. This is relevant to the question of whether the advertisement contained plaintiff's "portrait or picture." However, given the close resemblance between defendant Boroff's photograph and plaintiff, there is no reason to believe that the audience's relative sophistication eliminates all likelihood of confusion; at a cursory glance, many consumers, even sophisticated ones, are likely to be confused.

The final factor is the good or bad faith of defendants. While plaintiff has not established that defendants acted intentionally to fool people into thinking that plaintiff actually appeared in the advertisement, defendants admit that they designed the advertisement intentionally to evoke an association with plaintiff. They must therefore at least have been aware of the risk of consumer confusion, which militates against a finding that their motives were completely innocent. Defendants may not have intended to imply that plaintiff actually endorsed their product, but they happily risked creating that impression in an attempt to gain commercial advantage through reference to plaintiff's public image. The failure of defendant National to include any disclaimer on all but one of the uses of the photograph also supports a finding of, at best, dubious motives.

A review of all these factors leads the court to the inescapable conclusion that defendant's use of Boroff's photograph in their advertisement creates a likelihood of consumer confusion over plaintiff's endorsement or involvement. In reaching this conclusion, the court notes several distinctions between plaintiff's Lanham Act and privacy claims which make this case more appropriate for resolution under the Lanham Act.

First and most important, the likelihood of confusion standard applied herein is broader than the strict "portrait or picture" standard under the Civil Rights Law. Evocation of plaintiff's general persona is not enough to make out a violation of section 51, but it may create a likelihood of confusion under the Lanham Act. . . .

Second, the likelihood of confusion standard is easier to satisfy on the facts of this case. Enough people may realize that the figure in the photograph is defendant Boroff to negate the conclusion that it amounts to a "portrait or picture" of plaintiff as a matter of law. All that is necessary to recover under the Act, however, is that a *likelihood* of confusion exist. While defendants, as noted above, have urged an interpretation of the advertisement which might defeat a finding of "portrait or picture," the court finds that no such explanation can remove the likelihood of confusion on the part of "any appreciable number of ordinarily prudent" consumers. . . .

Third, although the question of identifiability under the Civil Rights Law is generally one of fact for the jury, the likelihood of confusion standard may be applied by the court. While confusing similarity is technically a question of fact, it has sometimes been regarded as "one for the court to decide through its own analysis, comparison, and judgment." . . . It has therefore been held to be appropriate for summary adjudication. . . .

In seeking to forestall summary judgment, defendants Smith and Boroff maintain that the disclaimer which they insisted be included in the advertisement would have avoided consumer confusion. The court disagrees. Even with regard to the one version of the advertisement in which the requisite disclaimer was included, there exists a likelihood of consumer confusion. The disclaimer, in tiny print at the bottom of the page, is unlikely to be noticed by most readers as they are leafing through the magazine. Moreover, the disclaimer says only that a celebrity double is being used, which does not in and of itself necessarily dispel the impression that plaintiff is somehow involved with National's products or services. To be effective a disclaimer would have to be bolder and make clear that plaintiff in no way endorses National, its products, or its services. . . .

Smith and Boroff also argue that they lacked sufficient control over the design of the advertisement and its placement to be jointly and severally liable to plaintiff along with National. This contention, too, is without merit. There is no dispute that defendants all knowingly agreed to include Boroff in the advertisement as a look-alike for plaintiff and that the pose and props in the photograph were intended in create an association with plaintiff. Defendants Smith and Boroff will not now be heard to plead ignorance when they intentionally created at least the risk of confusion.

The court concludes, on the undisputed facts before it, that a likelihood of consumer confusion exists in this case as a matter of law. Plaintiff's motion for summary judgment on his Lanham Act claim therefore is granted against all defendants. The motion of defendants Smith and Boroff for summary judgment is denied.

Having established a likelihood of consumer confusion, plaintiff is entitled to injunctive relief under the Act. . . .

Defendants have argued that any injunction against them must be limited in geographical scope to New York State. While such a limitation might be required for an injunction under the New York Civil Rights Law, given the differences in privacy law among different jurisdictions, an injunction under the Lanham Act need not be so limited. Plaintiff enjoys a nationwide reputation and defendants advertised a nationally franchised business through a national magazine. The harm sought to be prevented is clearly not limited to the New York area, and the injunction must therefore be national in scope.

Plaintiff seeks an injunction preventing defendants from presenting defendant Boroff as plaintiff in advertising. Defendant Boroff argues that any such injunction would interfere impermissibly with his ability to earn a living and his First Amendment rights.

As defendants correctly point out, the scope of injunctions against misleading commercial speech should be limited to that necessary to avoid consumer confusion. For this reason, disclaimers are favored over outright bans. . . . The court has already found, however, that the disclaimer appended to one of the advertisements before the court was inadequate as a matter of law to dispel a likelihood of consumer confusion. Nevertheless, the court hesitates sweepingly to enjoin defendant Boroff from ever appearing as a look-alike for plaintiff, since that could interfere with his ability to make money and express himself in settings where there is no likelihood of consumer confusion.

What plaintiff legitimately seeks to prevent is not simply defendant Boroff dressing up as plaintiff, but defendant *passing himself off* as plaintiff or an authorized surrogate. Therefore, defendant must be enjoined from appearing in advertising that creates the likelihood that a reasonable person might believe that he was really plaintiff or that plaintiff had approved of his appearance. . . . Defendant may satisfy the injunction by ceasing his work as a Woody Allen look-alike, but he may also satisfy it by simply refusing to collaborate with those advertisers, such as National Video in this case, who recklessly skirt the edge of misrepresentation. Defendant may sell his services as a look-alike in any setting where the overall context makes it completely clear that he *is* a look-alike and that plaintiff has nothing to do with the project—whether that is accomplished through a bold and unequivocal disclaimer, the staging of the photograph, or the accompanying advertising copy. This injunction applies as well to defendant Smith in his role as agent for Boroff. . . .

Difficult questions of law and fact are presented by plaintiff's claim that the photograph of defendant Boroff used in defendant National Video's advertisements constitutes a "portrait or picture" of Woody Allen, entitling him to relief under New York's privacy statute. The court concludes that this case is more properly regarded as one for unfair competition under the Lanham Act, and that plaintiff may gain full relief on this theory. There is no question that the advertisement in question creates at least a likelihood of consumer confusion as to whether plaintiff endorses National Video. Plaintiff therefore is entitled to summary judgment on his Lanham Act claim and an injunction against such potentially confusing use of defendant's photograph. . . .

NOTES

1. See also *Allen v. Men's World Outlet, Inc.*, 679 F. Supp. 360 (S.D.N.Y. 1988). Allen was granted an injunction against the use of an Allen look-alike in the advertising of a discount clothing retailer.

2. The issue of false implication of endorsement through the use of "look-alikes" was one of the claims raised in *Tin Pan Apple, Inc. v. Miller Brewing Co., Inc.*, 737 F. Supp. 826 (S.D.N.Y. 1990), in which the rap group The Fat Boys (who were all under legal drinking age and whose material included strong anti-drug, anti-alcohol, stay-in-school messages) sued, *inter alia*, for false designation and unfair competition under Lanham Act § 43a, unfair business practices, false advertising and unfair competition under the New York General Business Law §§ 349 et seq., and violation of plaintiffs' privacy rights under §§ 50 and 51 of the New York Civil Rights Law, as well as trade libel and disparagement. Miller had run a national TV beer ad featuring three Fat Boys look-alikes (one of whom was comic Joe Piscopo) performing in the Fat Boys style. The Fat Boys had been approached to appear in the ad, but had refused. Plaintiffs claimed that the ad falsely represented that the Fat Boys approved of and solicited orders for alcoholic beverages, which would be contrary to their image and message, and that the ad had injured their business (including in their claims the purported loss of tour sponsorship from Coca-Cola, Inc.). Among the defenses raised in defendants' motion to dismiss was that of parody (a protected form of artistic expression which the Second Circuit had recognized in *Cliffs Notes, Inc. v. Bantam Doubleday Dell Publishing, Inc.*, 886 F.2d 490 (2d Cir. 1989), but the court rejected the claim that the ad was a permissible parody and held that plaintiffs could proceed with their Lanham Act claims as well as their claims under §§ 349 and 350 of the New York General Business Law. However, the court agreed with the defendants that "sound-alikes" did not fall afoul of the Civil Rights Law, and also agreed that the plaintiffs had failed to state claims for defamation and trade disparagement.

3. Elements of identity such as those in the Allen case also figured strongly in *Estate of Elvis Presley v. Russen*, 513 F. Supp. 1339 (D.N.J. 1981). There, preliminary injunctive relief was granted against the promoter of "THE BIG EL SHOW," a re-creation of a live Presley concert utilizing the services of an impersonator, which was advertised as "Reflections on a Legend . . . A Tribute to Elvis Presley." During his lifetime, Presley had toured under the title "Elvis In Concert," and he had utilized a unique "Elvis pose" (jumpsuit, mike in hand, apparently singing) as well as the symbols "TCB" and a lightning bolt, as well as the name "TCB" for his accompanying band. After Presley's death, his estate and the estate's licensees continued to use these indicia of identity. Although the promoter had the right to stage his show, he could not utilize the unique Presley indicia, which would tend to lead customers to believe that the show was authorized by the Estate, a false designation of origin.

4. Similarly, *NFL v. Wichita Falls Sportswear, Inc.*, 532 F. Supp. 651 (W.D.Wash. 1982) discusses extensively the Lanham Act implications of the unauthorized use of NFL team colors, jersey designs, etc.

5. The Federal Trademark Dilution Act of 1995 (104 HR 1295) may have an impact in matters of the kind discussed above. Under the Act, an injunction is available to prevent "dilution of the distinctive quality" of a "famous mark by commercial use in commerce." As is typically the case in this area, there are exemptions for fair use, non-commercial use, and all forms of news reporting and commentary. Dilution is defined as "the lessening of the capacity of a famous mark to identify and distinguish goods and services, regardless of the presence or absence of (1) competition

between the owner of the famous mark and other parties, or (2) the likelihood of confusion, mistake or deception." Whether or not the mark is registered is only one of seven specific tests prescribed in the statute for determining whether a mark is "distinctive and famous," the other being the degree of inherent or acquired distinctiveness of the mark, the duration and extent of use, the duration and extent of advertising and publicity, the geographical extent of use, the channels of trade in which the mark is used, and the degree of recognition accorded the mark.

6. In addition, the "trade dress" doctrine may be helpful in an appropriate case. *Two Pesos Inc. v. Taco Cabana Inc.*, 505 U.S. 763 (1992) provided protection under Section 43a for the distinctive manner in which a product is presented. This case involved two competing chains of Mexican-style restaurants. Although the plaintiff had not established secondary meaning, the inherent distinctiveness of its trade dress was sufficient. According to Mr. Justice White, "Denying protection for inherently distinctive nonfunctional trade dress until after secondary meaning has been established would allow a competitor, which has not adopted a distinctive trade dress of its own, to appropriate the originator's dress in other markets and to deter the originator from expanding into and competing in these areas. As noted above, petitioner concedes that protecting an inherently distinctive trade dress from its inception may be critical to new entrants to the market and that withholding protection until secondary meaning has been established would be contrary to the goals of the Lanham Act." See Lisa I. Fried, "Trade Dress Suits Knock Knockoffs Off Store Shelf," *National Law Journal*, 9/18/95, P. B.1.

7. Where the likelihood of confusion exists, even the use of one's own name can be enjoined. This happened in a state action not involving the Federal Trademark Act. The proprietor of a radio and television sales and repair business in upstate New York (Edward J. Sullivan) had conducted business under the name "Ed Sullivan's Radio & TV." After a New York gossip columnist by the name "Ed Sullivan" became a nationally famed television variety show host, Edward J. Sullivan and others attempted to incorporate "Ed Sullivan's Radio & TV, Inc." Even though Edward J. Sullivan had conducted a radio (then radio and television) sales and repair business for some time, and there was no direct competition between the two Eds, the variety show host had endorsed brands of television sets. There was no indication in the businessman's corporate name that his activities were limited to sales and repair of equipment. And the fields of activity of the two Ed Sullivans were sufficiently similar that consumers might be confused into believing that there was some relationship between them. The Appellate Division observed that "[a]lthough, in fact, but one isolated store in Buffalo is involved at the present time, nevertheless the state of facts may so change as to encompass a situation wherein there may be a series or a chain of similar stores throughout the country, in which case indeed, unless [the television star Ed Sullivan] had taken this present, prompt action, he might at a later date encounter great difficulty in obtaining an injunction because of his own laches." Also, at this stage the corporate enterprise would suffer minimal inconvenience in dropping the diminutive prefix, a situation which might not hold true at some future time. *Sullivan v. Ed Sullivan Radio & T.V.*, 1 App.Div.2d 609, 152 N.Y.S.2d 227 (1st Dept. 1956).

3.4.3 Defensive Matters

The same balancing of interests which we saw in operation in the areas of defamation, privacy, and publicity is also encountered in cases involving Section 43a and other areas of trademarks and service marks. As we see in the following cases, artistic considerations are often invoked to justify name uses that in other contexts would probably be impermissible. In addition, as we see in the decision in *Pump, Inc. v. Collins*, there are some instances in which the junior of two marks will prevail.

Rogers v. Grimaldi, 875 F.2d 994 (2d Cir. 1989)

JON O. NEWMAN, CIRCUIT JUDGE

Appellant Ginger Rogers and the late Fred Astaire are among the most famous duos in show business history. Through their incomparable performances in Hollywood musicals, Ginger Rogers and Fred Astaire established themselves as paragons of style, elegance, and grace. A testament to their international recognition, and a key circumstance in this case, is the fact that Rogers and Astaire are among that small elite of the entertainment world whose identities are readily called to mind by just their first names, particularly the pairing "Ginger and Fred." This appeal presents a conflict between Rogers' right to protect her celebrated name and the right of others to express themselves freely in their own artistic work. Specifically, we must decide whether Rogers can prevent the use of the title "Ginger and Fred" for a fictional movie that only obliquely relates to Rogers and Astaire.

Rogers appeals from an order of the District Court for the Southern District of New York (Robert W. Sweet, Judge) dismissing on summary judgment her claims that defendants-appellees Alberto Grimaldi, MGM/UA Entertainment Co., and PEA Produzioni Europe Associate, S.R.L., producers and distributors of the motion picture "Ginger and Fred," violated the Lanham Act, 15 U.S.C. § 1125(a) (1982), and infringed her common law rights of publicity and privacy. Rogers v. Grimaldi, 695 F. Supp. 112 (SDNY1988). Although we disagree with some of the reasoning of the District Court, we affirm.

BACKGROUND

Appellant Rogers has been an international celebrity for more than fifty years. In 1940, she won an Academy Award for her performance in the motion picture "Kitty Foyle." Her principal fame was established in a series of motion pictures in which she co-starred with Fred Astaire in the 1930s and 1940s, including "Top Hat" and "The Barkleys of Broadway."

There can be no dispute that Rogers' name has enormous drawing power in the entertainment world. Rogers has also used her name once for a commercial enterprise other than her show business career. In the mid-1970s, she licensed J. C. Penney, Inc. to produce a line of GINGER ROGERS lingerie. Rogers is also writing her autobiography, which she hopes to publish and possibly sell for adaptation as a movie.

In March 1986, appellees produced and distributed in the United States and Europe a film entitled "Ginger and Fred," created and directed by famed Italian film-maker Federico Fellini. The film tells the story of two fictional Italian cabaret performers, Pippo and Amelia, who, in their heyday, imitated Rogers and Astaire and became known in Italy as "Ginger and Fred." The film focuses on a televised reunion of Pippo and Amelia, many years after their retirement. Appellees describe the film as the bittersweet story of these two fictional dancers and as a satire of contemporary television variety shows.

The film received mixed reviews and played only briefly in its first run in the United States. Shortly after distribution of the film began, Rogers brought this suit, seeking permanent injunctive relief and money damages. Her complaint alleged that the defendants (1) violated section 43(a) of the Lanham Act, 15 U.S.C. § 1125(a) (1982), by creating the false impression that the film was about her or that she sponsored, endorsed, or was otherwise involved in the film, (2) violated her common law right of publicity, and (3) defamed her and violated her right to privacy by depicting her in a false light.

After two years of discovery, the defendants moved for summary judgment. In opposition to the motion, Rogers submitted a market research survey purporting to establish that the title "Ginger and Fred" misled potential movie viewers as to Rogers' connection with the film. Rogers also provided anecdotal evidence of confusion, including the fact that when MGM/UA publicists first heard the film's title (and before they saw the movie), they began gathering old photographs of Rogers and Astaire for possible use in an advertising campaign.

The District Court granted summary judgment to the defendants. Judge Sweet found that defendants' use of Rogers' first name in the title and screenplay of the film was an exercise of artistic expression rather than commercial speech. 695 F. Supp. at 120. He then held that "[b]ecause the speech at issue here is not primarily intended to serve a commercial purpose, the prohibitions of the Lanham Act do not apply, and the Film is entitled to the full scope of protection under the First Amendment." *Id.* at 120–21. The District Judge also held that First Amendment concerns barred Rogers' state law right of publicity claim. *Id.* at 124. He also rejected Rogers' "false light" claim without elaboration.

DISCUSSION

I. Lanham Act. . . .

The District Court ruled that because of First Amendment concerns, the Lanham Act cannot apply to the title of a motion picture where the title is "within the realm of artistic expression," 695 F. Supp. at 120, and is not "primarily intended to serve a commercial purpose," *id.* at 121. Use of the title "Ginger and Fred" did not violate the Act, the Court concluded, because of the undisputed artistic relevance of the title to the content of the film. *Id.* at 120. In effect, the District Court's ruling would create a nearly absolute privilege for movie titles, insulating them from Lanham Act claims as long as the film itself is an artistic work, and the title is relevant to the film's content. We think that approach unduly narrows the scope of the Act.

Movies, plays, books, and songs are all indisputably works of artistic expression and deserve protection. Nonetheless, they are also sold in the commercial marketplace like other more utilitarian products, making the danger of consumer deception a legitimate concern that warrants some government regulation. . . .

Poetic license is not without limits. The purchaser of a book, like the purchaser of a can of peas, has a right not to be misled as to the source of the product. Thus, it is well established that where the title of a movie or a book has acquired secondary meaning—that is, where the title is sufficiently well known that consumers associate it with a particular author's work—the holder of the rights to that title may prevent the use of the same or confusingly similar titles by other authors. . . . Indeed, it would be ironic if, in the name of the First Amendment, courts did not recognize the right of authors to protect titles of their creative work against infringement by other authors. . . .

Though First Amendment concerns do not insulate titles of artistic works from all Lanham Act claims, such concerns must nonetheless inform our consideration of the scope of the Act as applied to claims involving such titles. Titles, like the artistic works they identify, are of a hybrid nature, combining artistic expression and commercial promotion. The title of a movie may be both an integral element of the filmmaker's expression as well as a significant means of marketing the film to the public. The artistic and commercial elements of titles are inextricably intertwined. Film-makers and authors frequently rely on word-play, ambiguity, irony, and allusion in titling their works. Furthermore, their interest in freedom of artistic expression is shared by their audience. The subtleties of a title can enrich a reader's or a viewer's understanding of a work. Consumers of artistic works thus have a dual interest. They have an interest in not being misled and they also have an interest in enjoying the results of the author's freedom of expression. For all these reasons, the expressive element of titles requires more protection than the labeling of ordinary commercial products.

Because overextension of Lanham Act restrictions in the area of titles might intrude on First Amendment values, we must construe the Act narrowly to avoid such a conflict. . . .

Rogers contends that First Amendment concerns are implicated only where a title is so intimately related to the subject matter of a work that the author has no alternative means of expressing what the work is about. This "no alternative avenues of communication" standard derives from *Lloyd Corp. v. Tanner,* 407 U.S. 551, 566, 67, 92, S.Ct. 2219, 2227–28, 33 L.Ed.2d (1972), and has been applied by several courts in the trademark context. . . .

In the context of titles, this "no alternative" standard provides insufficient leeway for literary expression. In *Lloyd,* the issue was whether the First Amendment provided war protesters with the right to distribute leaflets on a shopping center owner's property. The Supreme Court held that it did not. But a restriction on the *location* of a speech is different from a restriction on the *words* the speaker may use. . . . As the Supreme Court has noted, albeit in a different context, "[W]e cannot indulge the facile assumption that one can forbid particular words without running a substantial risk of suppressing ideas in the process." *Cohen v. California,* 403 U.S. 15, 26, 91 S.Ct. 1780, 1788, 29 L.Ed.2d 284 (1971). (This Circuit employed the "no alternative avenues of communication" standard in *Dallas Cowboys Cheerleaders, Inc. v. Pussycat Cinema, Ltd.,* 604 F.2d 200, 206 (2d Cir. 1979). As we stated in *Silverman,* however, that case involved a pornographic movie with blatantly false advertising. 870 F.2d at 48 n. 5. Advertisements for the movie were explicitly misleading, stating that the principal actress in the movie was a former Dallas Cowboys' cheerleader. We do not read *Dallas Cowboys Cheerleaders* as generally precluding all consideration of First Amendment concerns whenever an allegedly infringing author has "alternative avenues of communication." [Note in original].)

Thus, the "no alternative avenues" test does not sufficiently accommodate the public's interest in free expression, while the District Court's rule—that the Lanham Act is inapplicable to all titles that can be considered artistic expression—does not sufficiently protect the public against flagrant deception. We believe that in general the Act should be construed to apply to artistic works only where the public interest in avoiding consumer confusion outweighs the public interest in free expression. In the context of allegedly misleading titles using a celebrity's name, that balance will normally not support application of the Act unless the title has no artistic relevance to the underlying work whatsoever, or, if it has some artistic relevance, unless the title explicitly misleads as to the source or the content of the work. (This limiting construction would not apply to misleading titles that are confusingly similar to other titles. The public interest in sparing consumers this type of confusion outweighs the slight public interest in permitting authors to use such titles. [Note in original].)

The reasons for striking the balance in this manner require some explanation. A misleading title with no artistic relevance cannot be sufficiently justified by a free expression interest. For example, if a filmmaker placed the title "Ginger and Fred" on a film to which it had no artistic relevance at all, the arguably misleading suggestions as to source or content implicitly conveyed by the title could be found to violate the Lanham Act as to such a film.

Even where a title surpassed the appropriately low threshold of minimal artistic relevance but was explicitly misleading as to source or content, a violation could be found. To illustrate, some titles—such as "Nimmer on Copyright" and "Jane Fonda's Workout Book"—explicitly state the author of the work or at least the name of the person the publisher is entitled to associate with the preparation of the work. Other titles contain words explicitly signifying endorsement, such as the phrase in a subtitle "an authorized biography." If such explicit references were used in a title and were false as applied to the underlying work, the consumer's interest in avoiding deception would warrant application of the Lanham Act, even if the title had some relevance to the work.

Many titles, however, include a well-known name without any overt indication of authorship or endorsement—for example, the hit song

"Bette Davis Eyes," and the recent film "Come Back to the Five and Dime, Jimmy Dean, Jimmy Dean." To some people, these titles might implicitly suggest that the named celebrity had endorsed the work or had a role in producing it. Even if that suggestion is false, the title is artistically relevant to the work. In these circumstances, the slight risk that such use of a celebrity's name might implicitly suggest endorsement or sponsorship to some people is outweighed by the danger of restricting artistic expression, and the Lanham Act is not applicable. . . .

Similarly, titles with at least minimal artistic relevance to the work may include explicit statements about the content of the work that are seriously misleading. For example, if the characters in the film in this case had published their memoirs under the title "The True Life Story of Ginger and Fred," and if the film-maker had then used that fictitious book title as the title of the film, the Lanham Act could be applicable to such an explicitly misleading description of content. But many titles with a celebrity's name make no explicit statement that the work is about that person in any direct sense; the relevance of the title may be oblique and may become clear only after viewing or reading the work. As to such titles, the consumer interest in avoiding deception is too slight to warrant application of the Lanham Act. Though consumers frequently look to the title of a work to determine what it is about, they do not regard titles of artistic works in the same way as the names of ordinary commercial products. Since consumers expect an ordinary product to be what the name says it is, we apply the Lanham Act with some rigor to prohibit names that misdescribe such goods. . . . But most consumers are well aware that they cannot judge a book solely by its title any more than by its cover. We therefore need not interpret the Act to require that authors select titles that unambiguously describe what the work is about nor to preclude them from using titles that are only suggestive of some topics that the work is not about. Where a title with at least some artistic relevance to the work is not explicitly misleading as to the content of the work, it is not false advertising under the Lanham Act.

This construction of the Lanham Act accommodates consumer and artistic interests. It insulates from restriction titles with at least minimal artistic relevance that are ambiguous or only implicitly misleading but leaves vulnerable to claims of deception titles that are explicitly misleading as to source or content, or that have no artistic relevance at all.

With this approach in mind, we now consider Rogers' Lanham Act claim to determine whether appellees are entitled to summary judgment. . . .

Rogers essentially claims that the title "Ginger and Fred" is false advertising. Relying on her survey data, anecdotal evidence, and the title itself, she claims there is a likelihood of confusion that (1) Rogers produced, endorsed, sponsored, or approved the film, and/or (2) the film is about Rogers and Astaire, and that these contentions present triable issues of fact. In assessing the sufficiency of these claims, we accept Judge Sweet's conclusion, which is not subject to dispute, that the title "Ginger and Fred" surpasses the minimum threshold of artistic relevance to the film's content. The central characters in the film are nicknamed "Ginger" and "Fred," and these names are not arbitrarily chosen just to exploit the publicity value of their real life counterparts but instead have genuine relevance to the film's story. We consider separately the claims of confusion as to sponsorship and content.

The title "Ginger and Fred" contains no explicit indication that Rogers endorsed the film or had a role in producing it. The survey evidence, even if its validity is assumed, indicates at most that some members of the public would draw the incorrect inference that Rogers had some involvement with the film. But that risk of misunderstanding, not engendered by any overt claim in the title, is so outweighed by the interests in artistic expression as to preclude application of the Lanham Act. We therefore hold that the sponsorship and endorsement aspects of Rogers' Lanham Act claim raise no "genuine" issue that requires submission to a jury. (The survey sampled 201 people who said they were likely to go to a movie in the next six months. Half of those surveyed were shown a card with the title "Ginger and Fred" on it; the other half were shown an actual advertisement for the movie. Of these 201, 38 percent responded "yes" to the question: "Do you think that the actress, Ginger Rogers, had anything to do with this film, or not?" Of these respondents, a third answered yes to the question: "Do you think Ginger Rogers was involved in any way with making this film or not?" In other words, about 14 percent of the total 201 surveyed found that the title suggested that Rogers was involved in making the film.)

(Appellees contend that the survey used "leading" questions, making the survey results invalid. Without resolving this issue, we will assume for the purposes of this appeal that the survey was valid. [Note in original].)

Rogers' claim that the title misleads consumers into thinking that the film is *about* her and Astaire also fails. Indeed, this case well illustrates the need for caution in applying the Lanham Act to titles alleged to mislead as to content. As both the survey and the evidence of the actual confusion among the movie's publicists show, there is no doubt a risk that some people looking at the title "Ginger and Fred" might think the film was about Rogers and Astaire in a direct, biographical sense. For those gaining that impression, the title is misleading. At the same time, the title is entirely truthful as to its content in referring to the film's fictional protagonists who are known to their Italian audience as "Ginger and Fred." Moreover, the title has an ironic meaning that is relevant to the film's content. As Fellini explains in an affidavit, Rogers and Astaire are to him "a glamorous and care-free symbol of what American cinema represented during the harsh times which Italy experienced in the 1930s and 1940s." In the film, he contrasts this elegance and class to the gaudiness and banality of contemporary television, which he satirizes. In this sense, the title is not misleading; on the contrary, it is an integral element of the film and the film-maker's artistic expressions.

This mixture of meanings, with the possibly misleading meaning not the result of explicit misstatement, precludes a Lanham Act claim for false description of content in this case. To the extent that there is a risk that the title will mislead some consumers as to what the work is about, that risk is outweighed by the danger that suppressing an artistically relevant though ambiguous title will unduly restrict expression.

For these reasons, we hold that appellees are entitled to summary judgment on Rogers' claim that the title gives the false impression that the film is about Rogers & Astaire. . . .

B. False-Light Defamation

Rogers claims that the film portrays her in a false light by depicting the dance pair in the film in a tawdry and "seedy" manner. . . . We need not dwell long on this claim, nor need we decide which state's law governs it. The film is manifestly not about Rogers. It is about a pair of fictional characters who are like Rogers and Astaire only in their imagination and in the sentimental eyes of their fictional audience. We know of no state law that provides relief for false-light defamation against a work that clearly does not portray the plaintiff at all.

CONCLUSION

In sum, we hold that section 43(a) of the Lanham Act does not bar a minimally relevant use of a celebrity's name in the title of an artistic work where the title does not explicitly denote authorship, sponsorship, or endorsement by the celebrity or explicitly mislead as to content. . . . Under these standards, summary judgment was properly entered on the undisputed facts of this case, rejecting the Lanham Act . . . as well as the claim for false-light defamation.

We therefore affirm the judgment of the District Court.

GRIESA, DISTRICT JUDGE, CONCURRING IN THE RESULT:

I concur with the result reached in the majority opinion, but have substantial disagreement with the opinion otherwise.

At the outset, a brief word about the development of the issues is in order.

The original claim of Rogers, as stated in the complaint, did not have any separate allegation about the title of the film as such. The complaint was directed against "the Film." The first cause of action, claiming violation of Rogers' right of publicity, was directed against the production and distribution of the Film. The second alleged that the Film depicted Rogers in a false light. The third cause of action, under the Lanham Act, was directed against the Film and its advertising. In her submissions on the summary judgment motion, Rogers focused mainly on the alleged wrongdoing of defendants in entitling the Film and in promoting and advertising the Film.

Judge Sweet's opinion treated the issue as relating to "the Film's title and screenplay." He discussed promotion and advertising, but not as a significant separate claim. His holding was that the Film (including the title and the screenplay) is entitled to First Amendment protection and does not violate the Lanham Act or state law rules.

On appeal, the only issues raised by Rogers relate to the title and to the advertising and promotion. No claim is made regarding the screenplay. The only issue dealt with in the majority opinion is that relating to the title. I have no objection to this feature of the majority opinion. My objection is to how the issue is handled.

LANHAM ACT

According to the majority, Judge Sweet's Lanham Act ruling creates a broad immunity which would prevent a remedy in instances of "flagrant deception." To deal with this problem, the majority attempts to set out more precise standards by which lawful titles are to be differentiated from unlawful ones. It is said that the Lanham Act

... should be construed to apply to artistic works only where the public interest in avoiding consumer confusion outweighs the public interest in free expression.

To implement this vague and fluid test, the majority goes on to articulate two specific rules. *First,* titles which are artistically relevant to an underlying work but are "explicitly misleading" violate the Lanham Act. *Second,* titles which are artistically relevant but "ambiguous or only implicitly misleading" do not violate the Lanham Act.

I do not believe that anything in Judge Sweet's opinion, sensibly read, would interfere with the protection of the public against "flagrant deception." But whatever may be the problem with Judge Sweet's opinion, the cure offered by the majority is far worse than the ailment.

Judge Sweet's reasoning can be briefly summarized as follows. Since the two main characters of the Film, Pippo and Amelia, are depicted as having made their living by imitating Ginger Rogers and Fred Astaire, there is, in a unique but entirely lawful manner, a reference to Ginger Rogers in the Film. The name "Ginger" is relevant to both the Film's screenplay and its title. The screenplay and title are within the realm of artistic expression, and are thus entitled to an appropriately broad measure of protection under the First Amendment, a level of protection greater than would be accorded if this were commercial speech. The possibility that alternate avenues of expression might have been used does not create a valid Lanham Act claim. The judge noted that there is nothing in the record to suggest an intention to use Ginger Rogers' name to deceive the public into coming to the movie under the mistaken belief that it was about the true Rogers and Astaire. 695 F.Supp. 113, 120–21.

The essential points of Judge Sweet's rationale are echoed in the majority opinion, which states that the title "is an integral element of the film and the film-maker's artistic expression," and that "the expressive element of titles requires more protection than the labeling of ordinary commercial products." However, the majority opinion expresses the concern that the district court's ruling would create "a nearly absolute privilege for movie titles," because of what are thought to be broad statements about the First Amendment protection accorded to artistic speech as distinct from commercial speech.

In my view, this concern is unfounded. Judge Sweet's discussion of First Amendment protection for artistic expression was his basis for deciding *this case*. He did not purport to write a treatise or attempt to say how various other cases with different facts should be treated. This is not to say that the ruling would not, justifiably, have some general precedential effect. It is undoubtedly true that most titles which are artistically relevant to the underlying work would be protected under the First Amendment from Lanham Act claims. However, Judge Sweet did not purport to write the law covering all possible situations.

The problem of an overly expansive ruling really lies with the majority opinion and its unfortunate attempt to establish a rule based on the asserted difference between explicitly misleading titles and those which are ambiguous or only implicitly misleading.

All the judges involved here agree that the title "Ginger and Fred" does not violate the Lanham Act. Although the title may mean different things to different people, the artistic relationship between the title and the Film protects both from the strictures of the statute.

However, this unique case would seem to be an inappropriate vehicle for fashioning a general rule of the kind announced by the majority. The unusual circumstances here do not provide a valid illustration of the general proposition (which I regard as dubious indeed) that there is a legal boundary between implicitly misleading titles and explicitly misleading ones. The majority opinion does not use the facts of this case to define the asserted distinction, but seeks to give substance to the announced rule through the use of certain hypothetical examples.

The majority attempts to give illustrations of titles which would be artistically relevant but explicitly misleading. It is said that if the titles "Nimmer on Copyright" and "Jane Fonda's Work-out Book" were used in a manner which was "false as applied to the underlying work" there would be liability under the Lanham Act. But these examples really go nowhere. It is not specified what the underlying works would be where such titles would be false but "artistically relevant." The simple fact is that if either of these titles was used in connection with some bogus work, it would be a simple case of the copying of a legally protected title. . . . Thus the illustrations have nothing whatever to do with the kind of problem under discussion here.

The majority opinion states that, in the present case, the title would have been explicitly misleading if it had been "The True Life Story of Ginger and Fred." Of course, this awkward assemblage could hardly be expected to come under the consideration of a director such as Fellini. If, by some strange circumstance, it had been used, and if the majority opinion's legal doctrine were applied to it, lawyers might debate extensively about whether it was indeed misleading, and if so, whether it fell into the explicit or the implicit category. But the fact is that the example does not pose a realistic legal problem.

Coming to the other branch of the rule created by the majority, the opinion attempts to give illustrations of titles which would be artistically relevant and implicitly misleading—*i.e.*, which "impliedly suggest

that the named celebrity had endorsed the work or had a role in producing it." The examples given are the song "Bette Davis Eyes" and the
film "Come Back to the Five and Dime, Jimmy Dean, Jimmy Dean." But
these examples in no way illustrate the majority's proposition. No one
can seriously think that these titles imply or suggest that Bette Davis or
James Dean endorsed or had a role in producing the song or the film.

In my view, the rule of the majority opinion, involving the two purported categories, is not well founded. It should be left to future courts,
dealing with real cases, to determine if there are to be exceptions to
the First Amendment protection which would seem to be generally afforded to artistically relevant titles. To say the least, the hypotheticals in
the majority opinion are a poor basis for arriving at serious legal propositions. When and if an actual case arises, it may not fit within either
of the categories posited by the majority. Also, it is most likely that the
distinction between explicitly and implicitly misleading titles will prove
to be unsound and unworkable. . . .

NOTES _____

1. This decision was followed in *Rosa Parks v. LaFace Records,* 76 F. Supp. 2d 775 (E.D.
   Mich. 1999) (Hackett, J.). A group recording artist named Outkast released an
   album which included a song entitled "Rosa Parks." Ms. Parks, of course, is justly
   revered as the woman who dramatized and energized the civil rights movement by
   refusing to move to the rear of a public bus in Birmingham, Alabama, in 1963. While
   Outkast's song was entitled "Rosa Parks," and included the line "Ah, ha, hush that
   fuss. Everybody move to the back of the bus," the song was not about Ms. Parks. The
   album and the song were released to great acclaim, and the song received a Grammy
   nomination. Ms. Parks objected to the use of her name in association with music
   that contained, according to Ms. Parks, "profanity, racial slurs, and derogatory language directed at women." Nevertheless, District Judge Barbara K. Hackett granted
   defendants' motion for summary judgment, according First Amendment protection
   because "the song at issue makes unmistakable reference to [Ms. Parks'] symbolic
   act a total of ten times" and the use of Ms. Parks' name and the quoted phrase is
   "metaphoric and symbolic." The Sixth Circuit did not quite agree as to freedom of
   expression prevailing over privacy rights by reversing the trial court's grant of summary judgment. *Rosa Parks v. LaFace Records, et al,* 329 F.3rd 437 (6th Cir. 2003). The
   District Court had found, in regard to the artistic relationship between the song's
   title and its contents, that ". . . the relationship is so obvious that the matter is not
   open to debate." The Appellate Court decided that the relationship "is certainly not
   obvious" and that based upon a 'translation' of the rap lyrics: "We believe that reasonable people could find that the use of Rosa Parks' name as the title to this song
   was not justified as being metaphorical or symbolic of anything for which Rosa Parks
   is famous." "There is a genuine issue of material fact whether the use of Rosa Parks'
   name as a title . . . is artistically related to the content of the song . . . or whether the
   use of the name Rosa parks is nothing more than a misleading advertisement for the
   sale of the song." 329 F.3rd at 446, 447, 450. [Note: It appears from this decision that
   the 6th Circuit was more concerned about protecting the claims of a civil rights legend
   over the first amendment defense by a rap/hip hop group. Upon the reversal of Rosa
   Parks' Lanham Act and Right of Publicity claims and remand to the trial court (her
   defamation claim dismissal was affirmed), the case was later settled].
2. A service mark infringement action was brought by the operator of a karate instruction school, who asserted he had been known as the "Karate Kid" for years.
   He objected to the use of the appellation in the title to the movie, *Karate Kid,*
   and its two sequels. He also alleged violation of his right of publicity under the

New York Civil Rights statute. In *DeClemente v. Columbia Pictures Industries,* 860 F. Supp. 30 (E.D.N.Y. 1994), the court held that the use of the name in the title of the movie did not infringe plaintiff's registered service mark. The court also dismissed the plaintiff's right of publicity claim, noting that New York does not recognize a common law right and the New York statute does not protect nicknames.

Trademark registration does not automatically foreclose others from using a trade name, nor does prior use always equate with "seniority." As we see in the following cases, the realities of the marketplace have a great deal of relevance. Although the court in *Pump, Inc. v. Collins Management* performs an analysis similar to that undertaken by the court in *Allen v. National Video,* the outcome is opposite to that in the *Allen* case.

Pump, Inc. v. Collins Management, 746 F. Supp. 1159 (D. Mass. 1990)

YOUNG, J.

[The Court granted defendants' motion to dismiss in a service mark infringement case. Pump, Inc., had registered a mark for a musical group consisting of the word "Pump" resting on what appeared to be a barbell. "Pump" stood for "Promoting Unlimited Mind Power," and the device appeared on all promotional materials associated with the band.] . . . The alleged purpose of the band Pump is to promote physical self-improvement as an alternative to drugs, thereby providing a positive role model for today's youth. . . . The four original members of the band were all bodybuilders.

The band Pump has played several concerts . . . at high schools in Massachusetts, Rhode Island and Connecticut. . . .

The band has released two singles promoting an anti-drug message, "Cracked" and "White Line Fever." "Cracked" received radio airplay on radio station WHJY in Providence, Rhode Island in May of 1987.

The band Pump also recorded a version and made a video of Elvis Costello's song "Pump It Up." It filmed videos for "Cracked" and "White Line Fever" in March 1987. The filming of Pump's videos was the subject of a front-page article in the March 21, 1987 edition of the North Attleboro *Sun Chronicle,* as well as a piece on the local Channel 6 evening news. Pump, Inc., sent its three videos, along with footage of interviews with the band, to cable television networks, including [MTV] and Colony Interconnect and the local North Attleboro station Visioncable. The videos were subsequently aired on Visioncable and . . . Colony Interconnect.

Through its then-manager . . . the band Pump mailed letters to over 200 corporations seeking corporation sponsors. No corporation agreed to sponsor the band, although several sent acknowledgment letters. Pump, Inc., did, however, receive letters of recognition supporting its anti-drug stance from former First Lady Nancy Reagan, Arnold Schwarzenegger, Kathleen Sullivan of CBS, and former Boston Celtics player M.L. Carr.

The band Pump was inactive from mid-1988 until shortly after the initiation of this lawsuit. [The current manager] was in California during August and September, 1989, attempting without success to promote the band. On December 19, 1989, Pump performed live at Alhambras in Westport, Massachusetts and was paid $1,000.

Pump, Inc. has never turned a profit [despite $70,000 in promotional expenditures, $20,000 in the year preceding the action. The band has been re-formed] with five new musicians, none of whom are bodybuilders . . . [and] is currently seeking a record contract [which it does not presently have], and, to this end, it has retained the services of an attorney. . . .

Aerosmith is a world-famous rock band that has sold millions of albums worldwide since the early 1970s. . . . Aerosmith's songs and videos have been repeatedly played and shown throughout the country. Its concerts routinely sell out large arenas at home and abroad. . . .

On September 12, 1989, Aerosmith released to considerable publicity its latest album, entitled "Pump." The album has already sold over 1,800,000 copies in the United States and 600,000 copies abroad, earning it "platinum" honors in the record industry. Its first two single cuts, "Love In An Elevator" and "Janie's Got A Gun," have become hits.

The cover of the Aerosmith "Pump" album portrays one pickup truck driving up on top of another pickup truck from behind. Written on the door of the truck on top, in prominent white capital letters, is the word "Pump." The registered Aerosmith logo is also featured prominently on the cover. A recent readers' poll in *Rolling Stone* magazine named the "Pump" cover as one of America's "Best Album Covers" during 1989. . . .

As is customary practice in the music industry, Aerosmith has promoted its current tour as "the Pump tour." . . .

There has been recent publicity that Aerosmith's members have given up drugs and have been placing more attention on physical fitness. On an MTV special . . . [a] band member . . . responded to a reporter's question "Why is the album entitled Pump?" with the comment, "Now that we're off drugs we're all pumped up." . . .

The band Pump and Aerosmith both appeal to predominantly teenage audiences aged 15–24 but even though the members of Aerosmith live near Norton, Massachusetts, where Pump, Inc. is domiciled, there is no evidence that Aerosmith was aware of the band Pump's existence before the institution of this lawsuit. . . .

[The leader of the band Pump] first learned of the existence of the Aerosmith "Pump" album in mid-September when four acquaintances of his—including the vocalist who had earlier sung background vocals for the band Pump on the song "Pumped"—informed him of the new release and asked him if he was associated with Aerosmith [which he denied.] None of the four mistakenly thought that the album was a release of the band Pump; all were aware that the recording was an Aerosmith album. No non-acquaintance has expressed any confusion. . . .

In the "normal" infringement case, a large, well-established senior user seeks to prevent a lesser-known junior user from trading off her business goodwill. . . .

Here, it borders on ridiculous to argue, as counsel for Pump, Inc. did at oral argument, that Aerosmith adopted the name "Pump" in the hope that purchasers would mistake its album for one of the band Pump. A world-famous group such as Aerosmith, enjoying a strong base of loyal teenage support, would have absolutely no reason for stealing the name of an unknown band to sell its records. Indeed, such action would be irrational. The Aersomith name sells well enough on its own.

Rather, Pump's best argument is reverse confusion—that in the future, anyone who hears of the band Pump, or buys a Pump record will think that the band is sponsored by or affiliated with Aerosmith. In more general terms, this is the case of a little-known senior user being infringed by a more powerful junior user. Given Aerosmith's notoriety, its actions in releasing and promoting the album "Pump" have effectively robbed Pump, Inc. of the ability to use its service mark and have rendered the plaintiff's mark devoid of independent value. Aerosmith has preempted the market with regard to the term "pump." Any time the plaintiff seeks to promote itself by reference to "Pump," consumers will think of Aerosmith first.

In support of its allegations of reverse confusion, Pump, Inc. refers the Court to *Big O Tire Dealers, Inc. v. Goodyear Tire & Rubber Co.*, 408 F. Supp. 1219 (D. Colo. 1976), *aff'd,* 561 F.2d 1365 (10th Cir. 1977). . . . In that case, the plaintiff alleged that Goodyear infringed on its tradmark "BIG FOOT" for automobile tires by promoting and marketing a custom polysteel radial tire under the name, "BIGFOOT." Goodyear apparently came up with the name "BIGFOOT" innocently enough, but was informed of the plaintiff's "BIG FOOT" tire a month before it instituted a massive nationwide multi-media advertising campaign. When negotiations between the parties failed, Goodyear went ahead with its planned promotion efforts spending millions of dollars and literally flooding the market. Actual instances of confusion between "BIG FOOT" and "BIGFOOT" tires resulted, with some consumers even believing, mistakenly, that Big O was trading off Goodyear's goodwill—not vice versa. The district court ruled in favor of the smaller and weaker Big O. . . .

[W]hether the confusion alleged by the plaintiff is forward or reverse[, however], likelihood of confusion must still be established. . . .

The First Circuit has identified eight factors that must be weighed in assessing likelihood of confusion: (1) the similarity of the service marks; (2) the similarity of the goods; (3) the relationship between the parties' channels of trade; (4) the relationship between the parties' advertising; (5) the classes of prospective purchasers; (6) evidence of actual confusion; (7) the defendant's intent in adopting its mark; and (8) the strength of the plaintiff's mark. . . .

1. SIMILARITY OF THE MARKS

Pump, Inc.'s entire case is premised on the similarity between the name of plaintiff's band and the title of the latest Aerosmith Album. Indeed, both use the word "Pump" prominently, spelled in an identical manner. But the designs differ greatly. . . .

While "phonetically identical," the two marks are used in different contexts and with different visual displays. . . .

The presence of the Aerosmith logo in conjunction with the "Pump" name would therefore seem to render any similarity between the marks inconsequential. The Court, however, is mindful of its duty to consider the evidence in a light most favorable to Pump, Inc. So doing, the Court cannot for purposes of this review state that the two marks are dissimilar. . . . This similarity, though, is tenuous, based solely on the use of the same word. Alone, it does not mandate a finding of likelihood of confusion.

2. SIMILARITY OF THE GOODS

The parties offer the same services ("goods") to the public—musical entertainment. Aerosmith, however, points out that while they use the term "Pump" as the title of an album, the plaintiff uses it as the name of a band. True, this is the primary use of the mark by Pump, Inc., but this is not its sole use. Pump, Inc. also uses its service mark on T-shirts and cassettes that it has sold at its high-school concerts [as well as on its singles and videos.] In short, Pump, Inc. uses its mark "Pump" in the same manner as Aerosmith uses its registered mark "Aerosmith"—to promote and identify the band and its recordings. Aerosmith's argument to the contrary ignores the fact that both parties use the term "Pump" to promote a wide array of goods and services associated with musical entertainment. . . .

3. CHANNELS OF TRADE, ADVERTISING AND PROSPECTIVE PURCHASERS

Aerosmith argues vehemently that the parties do not have the same channels. . . .

They assert that Pump, Inc. is a gimmick group of singing bodybuilders that have an audience limited to persons interested in bodybuilding, whereas Aerosmith is an internationally known and popular band with widespread audience appeal.

These factors, however, cut in favor of Pump, Inc. as well. The differences between the parties are of degree, not of kind. The Court is already familiar with Aerosmith's music and has listened carefully to the tape supplied by Pump, Inc. Accordingly, even a tone deaf middle-aged judge whose musical tastes incline toward folk melodies can here rule confidently that both the band Pump and Aerosmith are rock groups playing roughly similar kinds of music. Aerosmith, moreover, depends on music store sales, radio and video royalties, and live concert proceeds for its profits. Pump, Inc. seeks precisely this—which is why it has attempted to obtain a recording contract. Both bands either advertise, or intend to advertise through posters, T-shirts, jewelry and media exposure. Finally, both have a nearly identical class of prospective purchasers: young persons who enjoy rock music. . . .

Viewing the evidence favorably to Pump, Inc., it satisfies this standard. A contrary ruling would, in effect, insulate better known, more successful parties from challenge whenever they attempt to steal names or ideas from unknown parties with limited market strength. Consequently, these factors favor Pump, Inc.

4. EVIDENCE OF ACTUAL CONFUSION . . .

Pump, Inc. has presented four affidavits as proof of actual confusion. . . . The four allegedly confused persons give, interestingly, nearly identical accounts. [Two] saw displays of the Aerosomith "Pump" album in record stores; [two] heard of the album on the radio. Each alleges that he or she was confused as to the association of the band Pump with the "Pump" album and enquired . . . as to any affiliation [and was informed] that there was no connection whatsoever.

Several considerations weigh against a finding of actual confusion in this case. First, each of the four admitted that he or she was aware that the "Pump" album was an Aerosmith album. . . .

Second, the mere inquiries [to the Pump, Inc. leader] as to any affiliation between Aerosmith and the band Pump, while relevant, is insufficient evidence of actual confusion. . . .

Third, each of the four persons is a friend or acquaintance of [the leader. One,] for example, sang background vocals in recording the song "Pumped." . . .

There is not a shred of evidence in the record that anyone unaffiliated with [the leader] or Pump, Inc. was confused by the appearance of the Aerosmith album—either that Aerosmith's album was in fact the band Pump's or that Pump, Inc. was now working with Aerosmith to promote an anti-drug message. There is simply no evidence that anyone ever bought the Aerosmith album thinking it came from the band Pump.

This factor favors Aerosmith.

5. AEROSMITH'S INTENT IN ADOPTING THE MARK

Pump, Inc. has presented no evidence that Aerosmith intentionally appropriated the plaintiff's mark "Pump." Nor has it presented evidence that any of the defendants were even aware of the band Pump's existence before the filing of this lawsuit. The closest that Pump, Inc. comes in this regard is a rather cryptic allegation that the individual members of Aerosmith live "within a seven mile radius of Norton, Massachusetts," where Pump, Inc. has its headquarters.

Even if true, this inference upon inference does not demonstrate bad faith.

6. STRENGTH OF THE PLAINTIFF'S MARK

'Strong' marks are accorded broader protection against infringement than are 'weak' marks.

The First Circuit has looked to the following factors in determining the strength of a plaintiff's mark: (1) the length of time it has been used and the plaintiff's renown in its field; (2) the strength of the mark in the field; and (3) the plaintiff's actions in promoting its mark.

Judged against these factors, the mark of Pump, Inc. is extremely weak. Giving Pump, Inc. every benefit of the doubt, the mark has only been in use since early 1987, and the band's failure to get a record contract indicates that neither it nor the mark is well-known in the music industry. Certainly Pump, Inc. has pointed to no evidence to the contrary. Until December 19, 1989, the band's only concerts—totalling at most twenty—were at local high schools as part of anti-drug rallies. Moreover, [the leader's] efforts to promote Pump, Inc., admittedly substantial from a personal point of view, apparently ended sometime in 1988, and were only rekindled in recent months. The band itself was inactive from 1988 until after the institution of this lawsuit.

Again, this factor favors Aerosmith.

7. SUMMARY

Weighing each of the eight factors examined above, the Court concludes that Pump, Inc. has failed to demonstrate any likelihood of confusion, much less a substantial one. While there is some surface similarity between the marks themselves, and while the parties offer similar services and utilize similar means of reaching similar audiences, the Court is swayed by the following factors: the dissimilar manner in which the word "Pump" is used by the parties; the weak evidence of actual confusion; the weakness of the mark of Pump, Inc.; and Aerosmith's lack of bad faith. Consequently, summary judgment in favor of Aerosmith is appropriate on the claim of service mark infringement. . . .

NOTES _____

1. In *Sullivan v. CBS Corporation et al*, 385 F.3d 772; 2004 U.S. App. LEXIS 20062; 72 U.S.P.Q.2D (BNA) 1586; 32 Media L. Rep. 2516 (7th Circuit, 2004), we see another case of and inflated sense of proprietariness. The owner of the trademark in the band name "Survivor" brought an action alleging trademark infringement, federal and common law trademark dilution, unfair competition and deceptive trade practices against CBS and others to prevent them from using the mark "Survivor" from their popular television show "Survivor" on CDs and merchandise. The Court of Appeals affirmed the lower court's decision that plaintiff could not demonstrate any likelihood of confusion as to the origin of the CDs or merchandise related to the TV show, nor could he show any likelihood of dilution of his service mark. The Court stated "This case turns, in our view, on Sullivan's failure to submit enough evidence on the likelihood of confusion point to survive summary judgment. Sullivan had to submit evidence that, if believed by a trier of fact, would show that consumers are likely to be confused as to the source of the CDs and merchandise at issue. In assessing the likelihood of confusion, courts have identified seven relevant factors that help in deciding the ultimate question: (1) the similarity of the marks; (2) the similarity of the products; (3) the area and manner of concurrent use; (4) the degree of care likely to be used by consumers; (5) the strength of the plaintiff's mark; (6) whether any actual confusion exists; and (7) the defendant's intent to palm off its goods as those of the plaintiff. *Promatek Indus., Ltd. v. Equitrac Corp.,*

300 F.3d 808, 812 (7th Cir. 2002). The district court found that similarity of the marks, similarity of the products, degree of care, strength of mark, actual confusion, and intent all favored CBS. Area and manner of concurrent use favored Sullivan. . . .”

"Sullivan claims that his mark is famous enough to make consumers think the Series' merchandise is likely to come from his band. But he offered no evidence to back up this guess. He might have offered specifics on how well-known the name "Survivor" still is today as the identifier of a rock band, but he did not. Survivor has not released a new album in the United States since 1993. Sullivan offered nothing about how much money he spends promoting the Band, or on advertising for the Band, nor did he provide any evidence of how much money the Band has earned. Sullivan presented newspaper articles mentioning the Band, but these stories were not about the Band; they either announced the Band's upcoming performance, or identified Survivor as the band that recorded a particular song. There is simply no evidence that "Survivor" the Band enjoys fame and recognition as the originator of any products other than rock albums and concert t-shirts. . . . On both of the CDs issued by CBS, not only is the "Survivor" mark on display in its entirety, but each CD announces its affiliation with the CBS television show. The first CD, which contains music composed for the show, states that it is "The Official Soundtrack to the Hit CBS TV Series." The second CD announces that it is "Music Inspired by the Hit CBS TV Series." CBS has, in short, taken substantial steps to make the association between its CDs and its television show readily apparent from the face of the CD. It is important to note that Sullivan makes no claim that his trade-mark precludes CBS from calling its show "Survivor." He wants only to force it to stop using that name on the associated musical CDs and merchandise. Not only is the mark different in the ways we have described, but CBS has taken extra steps to assure that their products are readily differentiated. . . . Both Sullivan and CBS market similar merchandise, but Survivor the Band sells t-shirts only at their concerts, whereas CBS sells Survivor the Series t-shirts, hats, and other merchandise through various outlets. As with the CDs, Survivor the Series' merchandise prominently displays the entire "Survivor" mark. Taking these facts as a whole, we conclude that no rational factfinder could conclude that any consumer would be confused as to the source of the merchandise. Series' merchandise is not sold through the same outlets as the Band's merchandise, nor is it advertised in the same manner or in similar outlets. . . .”

"Sullivan finally takes issue with the district court's finding that no evidence of actual confusion exists. Sullivan asks us to disregard the results of a CBS survey demonstrating no actual confusion. That survey, he claims, improperly focused on confusion about music, not trade identities; it was limited to only one CD; and it failed to include any questions about other merchandise. This court has upheld similar surveys, however. See *Henri's, 717 F.2d at 356–57*. Sullivan had ample opportunity to conduct his own survey, but he chose not to. . . .”

"Sullivan was not required to conduct his own survey, but he presented no other evidence of actual confusion or likelihood of confusion other than the evidence we have already discussed, with one exception. That exception is a presentation showing the results of searches conducted on two automated search engines. The search engines retrieved web sites related to both the Band and the Series. This does not mean, however, that the search engine was "confused" as to the source of the sites. It is responding to a query that asks for all records listing "Survivor" as the author. But those results just take us back to the same point about confusion: would a consumer, looking at the different web-sites, think that CBS and the Band were somehow from the same source? No evidence of such confusion exists, and the websites contain the same additional information from CBS that distinguishes its "Survivor" from all others. Because there is no triable issue of fact on likelihood of confusion, we conclude that CBS's "Survivor" mark does not infringe Sullivan's "Survivor" mark.

2. In addition, the scope of coverage of a trademark will not be unreasonably extended. In *Pirone v. Macmillan, Inc.*, 894 F.2d 579 (2d Cir. 1990), defendant Macmillan published The 1988 Macmillan Baseball Engagement Calendar, using "Macmillan"

(in addition to using it as part of the title) on the back cover, the title page, and the copyright page. The book consisted of weekly calendars on each right-hand page, with pictures on each left-hand page. Among the pictures of such stars as Lou Gehrig and Mickey Mantle were two pictures of Babe Ruth and a picture of a baseball autographed by Babe Ruth. Ruth, of course, had had commercial endorsements during his lifetime, and after his death, his daughters registered "Babe Ruth" as a trademark for "paper articles, namely, playing cards, writing paper, and envelopes." Babe Ruth League, Inc., was licensed to use the trademark for its amateur baseball league, and Curtis Management Group, Inc., was authorized to license the mark to third parties on a royalty basis. The Second Circuit affirmed the trial court's grant of summary judgment with respect to the Ruth daughters' federal and common law trademark infringement and unfair competition claims, and the lower court's dismissal of their claims for infringement of the common law right of privacy, for violation of §§ 50 and 51 of the New York Civil Rights Law, and unfair competition.

On the trademark claims, the court observed that

[t]he owner of the mark acquires only the right to prevent his goods from being confused with those of others and to prevent his own trade from being diverted to competitors through their use of misleading marks. . . . [Rejecting the daughters' claim that their registration of two specific pictures of Babe Ruth extended their rights to every photograph ever taken of him, the court stated that] an individual's likeness is not a consistently represented fixed image—different photographs of the same person may be markedly dissimilar. Thus, a photograph of a human being, unlike a portrait of a fanciful cartoon character, is not inherently "distinctive" in the trademark sense of tending to indicate origin. . . . Whatever rights [the daughters] may have in the mark "Babe Ruth," Macmillan's use of Ruth's name and photographs can infringe those rights only if that use was a "trademark use," that is, one indicating source or origin [which was not the case here]. . . . Here, the calendar uses the name and image of Babe Ruth . . . to identify a great baseball player enshrined in the history of the game. Such use is not a trademark use and not an infringement.

"[The daughters'] unfair competition claim is broader, since Section 43(a) [of the Lanham Act] is violated by the use of any "symbol" as a "false designation of origin" or as any "representation," whether or not a registered trademark is involved. 15 U.S.C. § 1125(a). While these pictures of Ruth are in a sense symbols, they in no way indicate origin or represent sponsorship. . . . The pictures of Ruth no more indicate origin than does the back cover's picture of Jackie Robinson stealing home plate. Both covers are merely descriptive of the calendar's subject matter. In neither case would any consumer reasonably believe that Ruth or Robinson sponsored the calendar. . . . The source of the calendar is clearly indicated by the numerous references to Macmillan. . . . [Here, there was no possibility of confusion, hence no possibility of infringement. As to the privacy claims, the court observed that §§ 50 and 51 applied only to living persons, and that the New York courts had held that the Civil Rights Law preempted any common law publicity claims.]

3.5 ACQUISITION OF RIGHTS: IDEAS AND OTHER PROPERTY

3.5.1 Ideas

Every entertainment project ever made began with a creative idea. Everyone agrees that this is so. But the value of ideas, by themselves, is debated in the entertainment industry. Some think them very valuable, and entire books have been written telling people just how to go about selling their ideas. See, e.g., Robert Kosberg with Mim Eichler, *How to Sell Your Idea to Hollywood* (Harper Perennial, 1991); Carlos de Abreu & Howard Jay Smith, *How to Sell Your Story-Book-Screenplay Idea*

(Custos Morum Publishers, 1995). The contrary view is that "the idea" is one of Hollywood's "most overrated" commodities. According to this view, "[a]n idea is just an idea. If it's good, all that remains is the work" (Richard Walter, *Screenwriting: The Art, Craft and Business of Film and Television Writing*, 152–53 [Plume, 1988]).

The law too is ambivalent about ideas. It provides some protection to those who submit ideas to others (against the unauthorized use of those ideas), and it also provides some protection for those who receive idea submissions (against unwarranted claims by those who submitted them). Part of the law's ambivalence is explained by nothing more than its efforts to balance competing interests. The competing interests in question were noted long ago by Lord Mansfield: "We must take care to guard against two extremes equally prejudicial: The one that men of ability, who have employed their time for the service of the community, may not be deprived of their just merits and the reward of their ingenuity and labor; the other, that the world may not be deprived of improvements, nor the progress of the arts be retarded" (*Sayre v. Moore*, 1 East 361, 101 Eng.Rep. 140, quoted in *Stanley v. CBS*, 35 Cal.2d 653, 221 P.2d 73 [1950] [Stanley, J., dissenting]).

The law's ambivalence about ideas also is explained by its history. At one time, the law provided no protection whatsoever against unauthorized *dramatizations* of copyright-protected *literary works* (like novels)— let alone against the unauthorized use of mere ideas. When copyright law was amended in 1891 to create a right to dramatize copyright-protected literary works, Congress made it clear that it was only protecting "expression," not "ideas." See Lionel S. Sobel, "The Law of Ideas, Revisited," 1 *UCLA Entertainment Law Review* 9, 14–15 (1994).

Of course, the distinction between expression and ideas is not marked by a bright or distinct line. The two opinions in Section 3.5.1 of this chapter—*Nichols v. Universal Pictures, Zambito v. Paramount, and Universal v. Film Ventures*—all deal with that distinction and demonstrate how difficult it is to apply in actual cases. They also illustrate just how much similarity of detail must exist for copyright infringement to be proved.

In the 1950s, courts were confronted with several cases in which ideas had been used without authorization (or at least without compensation) under circumstances that seemed unfair, even though no copyrights had been infringed. Thus some courts—especially those in California—embarked on a search for legal doctrines other than copyright that would provide protection for ideas. The first two cases in Section 3.5.2 of this chapter—*Desny v. Wilder* and *Mann v. Columbia Pictures*—show that this search led courts to conclude that ideas could be protected by contract and confidential relationship law, under certain circumstances. The first two major cases in Section 3.5.2.1—*Blaustein v. Burton* and *Murray v. NBC*—deal with a related issue: whether the idea for which protection is sought must be novel in order to be protected by contract or whether non-novel ideas will be protected too.

3.5.1.1 Copyright Law: Idea versus Expression

Copyright law is the place where legal protection for literary and dramatic works is found, so it is logical that this is the first place that plaintiffs look for protection when their ideas are used without authorization, especially if those ideas were embedded in a copyright-protected book, play or movie. Copyright law, however, does not protect ideas and never has. See, e.g., Copyright Act § 102(b), 17 U.S.C. § 102(b) ("In no case does copyright protection for an original work of authorship extend to any idea.")

Thus, when relying on copyright law, it is necessary for a plaintiff to show that copyright-protected "expression" was used by the defendant. The first two cases below, *Nichols v. Universal Pictures* and *Zambito v. Paramount*, are representative of dozens of cases in which courts ruled that copyright-protected expression had not been used. Contrast the facts of these two cases with those of the third case in this section, *Universal v. Film Ventures*, where the court found that copyright-protected expression had been used. Taken together, these cases should give you a good sense of how much detail must be copied in order to prove copyright infringement.

Nichols v. Universal Pictures Corp., 45 F.2d 119 (2d Cir. 1930), *cert. denied*, 282 U.S. 902 (1931)

L. HAND, CIRCUIT JUDGE

The plaintiff is the author of a play, "Abie's Irish Rose," which it may be assumed was properly copyrighted. . . . The defendant produced publicly a motion picture play, "The Cohens and The Kellys," which the plaintiff alleges was taken from it. As we think the defendant's play too unlike the plaintiff's to be an infringement, we may assume, arguendo, that in some details the defendant used the plaintiff's play, as will subsequently appear, though we do not so decide. It therefore becomes necessary to give an outline of the two plays.

"Abie's Irish Rose" presents a Jewish family living in prosperous circumstances in New York. The father, a widower, is in business as a merchant, in which his son and only child helps him. The boy has philandered with young women, who to his father's great disgust have always been Gentiles, for he is obsessed with a passion that his daughter-in-law shall be an orthodox Jewess. When the play opens the son, who has been courting a young Irish Catholic girl, has already married her secretly before a Protestant minister, and is concerned to soften the blow for his father, by securing a favorable impression of his bride, while concealing her faith and race. To accomplish this he introduces her to his father at his home as a Jewess, and lets it appear that he is interested in her, though he conceals the marriage. The girl somewhat reluctantly falls in with the plan; the father takes the bait, becomes infatuated with the girl, concludes that they must marry, and assumes that of course they will, if he so decides. He calls in a rabbi, and prepares for the wedding according to the Jewish rite.

Meanwhile the girl's father, also a widower, who lives in California, and is as intense in his own religious antagonism as the Jew, has been called to New York, supposing that his daughter is to marry an Irishman and a Catholic. Accompanied by a priest, he arrives at the house at the moment when the marriage is being celebrated, but too late to prevent it, and the two fathers, each infuriated by the proposed union of his child to a heretic, fall into unseemly and grotesque antics. The priest and the rabbi become friendly, exchange trite sentiments about religion, and agree that the match is good. Apparently out of abundant caution, the priest celebrates the marriage for a third time, while the girl's father is inveigled away. The second act closes with each father, still outraged, seeking to find some way by which the union, thus trebly insured, may be dissolved.

The last act takes place about a year later, the young couple having meanwhile been abjured by each father, and left to their own resources. They have had twins, a boy and a girl, but their fathers know no more than that a child has been born. At Christmas each, led by his craving to see his grandchild, goes separately to the young folks' home, where they encounter each other, each laden with gifts, one for a boy, the other for a girl. After some slapstick comedy, depending upon the insistence of each that he is right about the sex of the grandchild, they become reconciled when they learn the truth, and that each child is to bear the given name of a grandparent. The curtain falls as the fathers are exchanging amenities, and the Jew giving evidence of an abatement in the strictness of his orthodoxy.

"The Cohens and The Kellys" presents two families, Jewish and Irish, living side by side in the poorer quarters of New York in a state of perpetual enmity. The wives in both cases are still living, and share in the mutual animosity, as do two small sons, and even the respective dogs. The Jews have a daughter, the Irish a son; the Jewish father is in the clothing business; the Irishman is a policeman. The children are in love with each other, and secretly marry, apparently after the play opens. The Jew, being in great financial straits, learns from a lawyer that he has fallen heir to a large fortune from a great-aunt, and moves into a great house, fitted luxuriously. Here he and his family live in vulgar ostentation, and here the Irish boy seeks out his Jewish bride, and is chased away by the angry father. The Jew then abuses the Irishman over the telephone, and both become hysterically excited. The extremity of his feelings makes the Jew sick, so that he must go to Florida for a rest, just before which the daughter discloses her marriage to her mother.

On his return the Jew finds that his daughter has borne a child; at first he suspects the lawyer, but eventually learns the truth and is overcome with anger at such a low alliance. Meanwhile, the Irish family who have been forbidden to see the grandchild, go to the Jew's house, and after a violent scene between the two fathers in which the Jew disowns his daughter, who decides to go back with her husband, the Irishman takes her back with her baby to his own poor lodgings. The lawyer, who had hoped to marry the Jew's daughter, seeing his plan foiled, tells the Jew that his fortune really belongs to the Irishman, who was also related to the dead woman, but offers to conceal his knowledge, if the Jew will share the loot. This the Jew repudiates, and, leaving the astonished lawyer, walks through the rain to his enemy's house to surrender the property. He arrives in great dejection, tells the truth, and abjectly turns to leave. A reconciliation ensues, the Irishman agreeing to share with him equally. The Jew shows some interest in his grandchild, though this is at most a minor motive in the reconciliation, and the curtain falls while the two are in their cups, the Jew insisting that in the firm name for the business, which they are to carry on jointly, his name shall stand first.

It is of course essential to any protection of literary property, whether at common-law or under the statute, that the right cannot be limited literally to the text, else a plagiarist would escape by immaterial variations. That has never been the law, but, as soon as literal appropriation ceases to be the test, the whole matter is necessarily at large, so that, as was recently well said by a distinguished judge, the decisions cannot help much in a new case. . . . [W]hen the plagiarist does not take out a block in situ, but an abstract of the whole, decision is more troublesome. Upon any work, and especially upon a play, a great number of patterns of increasing generality will fit equally well, as more and more of the incident is left out. The last may perhaps be no more than the most general statement of what the play is about, and at times might consist only of its title; but there is a point in this series of abstractions where they are no longer protected, since otherwise the playwright could prevent the use of his "ideas," to which, apart from their expression, his property is never extended. Nobody has ever been able to fix that boundary, and nobody ever can. In some cases the question has been treated as though it were analogous to lifting a portion out of the copyrighted work; but the analogy is not a good one, because, though the skeleton is a part of the body, it pervades and supports the whole. In such cases we are rather concerned with the line between expression and what is expressed. As respects plays, the controversy chiefly centers upon the characters and sequence of incident, these being the substance.

We did not in *Dymow v. Bolton,* 11 F.2d 690, hold that a plagiarist was never liable for stealing a plot; that would have been flatly against our rulings in *Dam v. Kirk La Shelle* Co., 175 F. 902, 41 L.R.A. (N.S.) 1002, 20 Ann. Cas. 1173, and *Stodart v. Mutual Film* Co., 249 F. 513, affirming my decision in (D.C.) 249 F. 507; neither of which we meant to overrule. We found the plot of the second play was too different to infringe, because the most detailed pattern, common to both, eliminated so much from each that its content went into the public domain; and for this reason we said, "this mere subsection of a plot was not susceptible of copyright." But we do not doubt that two plays may correspond in plot closely enough for infringement. How far that correspondence must go is another matter. Nor need we hold that the same may not be true as to the characters, quite independently of the "plot" proper, though, as far as we know, such a case has never arisen. If *Twelfth Night* were copyrighted, it is quite possible that a second comer might so closely imitate Sir Toby Belch or Malvolio as to infringe, but it would not be enough that for one of his characters he cast a riotous knight who kept wassail to the discomfort of the household, or a vain and foppish steward who became amorous of his mistress. These would be no more than Shakespeare's "ideas" in the play, as little capable of monopoly as Einstein's Doctrine of Relativity, or Darwin's theory of the Origin of Species. It follows that the less developed the characters, the less they can be copyrighted; that is the penalty an author must bear for marking them too indistinctly.

In the two plays at bar we think both as to incident and character, the defendant took no more—assuming that it took anything at all—than the law allowed. The stories are quite different. One is of a religious zealot who insists upon his child's marrying no one outside his faith; opposed by another who is in this respect just like him, and is his foil. Their difference in race is merely an obbligato to the main theme, religion. They sink their differences through grandparental pride and affection. In the other, zealotry is wholly absent; religion does not even appear. It is true that the parents are hostile to each other in part because they differ in race; but the marriage of their son to a Jew does not apparently offend the Irish family at all, and it exacerbates the existing animosity of the Jew, principally because he has become rich, when he learns it. They are reconciled through the honesty of the Jew and the generosity of the Irishman; the grandchild has nothing whatever to do with it. The only matter common to the two is a quarrel between a Jewish and an Irish father, the marriage of their children, the birth of grandchildren and a reconciliation.

If the defendant took so much from the plaintiff, it may well have been because her amazing success seemed to prove that this was a subject of enduring popularity. Even so, granting that the plaintiff's play was wholly original, and assuming that novelty is not essential to a copyright, there is no monopoly in such a background. Though the plaintiff discovered the vein, she could not keep it to herself; so defined, the theme was too generalized an abstraction from what she wrote. It was only a part of her "ideas."

Nor does she fare better as to her characters. It is indeed scarcely credible that she should not have been aware of those stock figures, the low comedy Jew and Irishman. The defendant has not taken from her more than their prototypes have contained for many decades. If so, obviously so to generalize her copyright, would allow her to cover what was not original with her. But we need not hold this as matter of fact, much as we might be justified. Even though we take it that she devised her figures out of her brain de novo, still the defendant was within its rights.

There are but four characters common to both plays, the lovers and the fathers. The lovers are so faintly indicated as to be no more than stage properties. They are loving and fertile; that is really all that can be said of them, and anyone else is quite within his rights if he puts loving and fertile lovers in a play of his own, wherever he gets the cue. The plaintiff's Jew is quite unlike the defendant's. His obsession is his religion, on which depends such racial animosity as he has. He is affectionate, warm and patriarchal. None of these fit the defendant's Jew, who shows affection for his daughter only once, and who has none but the most superficial interest in his grandchild. He is tricky, ostentatious and vulgar, only by misfortune redeemed into honesty. Both are grotesque, extravagant and quarrelsome; both are fond of display; but these common qualities make up only a small part of their simple pictures, no more than any one might lift if he chose. The Irish fathers are even more unlike; the plaintiff's a mere symbol for religious fanaticism and patriarchal pride, scarcely a character at all. Neither quality appears in the defendant's, for while he goes to get his grandchild, it is rather out of a truculent determination not to be forbidden, than from pride in his progeny. For the rest he is only a grotesque hobbledehoy, used for low comedy of the most conventional sort, which any one might borrow, if he chanced not to know the exemplar.

The defendant argues that the case is controlled by my decision in *Fisher v. Dillingham* (D.C.) 298 F. 145. Neither my brothers nor I wish to throw doubt upon the doctrine of that case, but it is not applicable here. We assume that the plaintiff's play is altogether original, even to an extent that in fact it is hard to believe. We assume further that, so far as it has been anticipated by earlier plays of which she knew nothing, that fact is immaterial. Still, as we have already said, her copyright did not cover everything that might be drawn from her play; its content went to some extent into the public domain. We have to decide how much, and while we are as aware as any one that the line, wherever it is drawn, will seem arbitrary, that is no excuse for not drawing it; it is a question such as courts must answer in nearly all cases. Whatever may be the difficulties a priori, we have no question on which side of the line this case falls. A comedy based upon conflicts between Irish and Jews, into which the marriage of their children enters, is no more susceptible of copyright than the outline of Romeo and Juliet. . . .

Zambito v. Paramount Pictures, 613 F. Supp. 1107 (E.D.N.Y.), *aff'd*, 788 F.2d 2 (2d Cir. 1985)

DISTRICT JUDGE MCLAUGHLIN

This is an action for copyright infringement. . . . Plaintiff Zambito, an archaeologist-screenwriter, asserts that defendants' movie, "Raiders of the Lost Ark" ("Raiders"), infringes copyrightable material contained in his screenplay, "Black Rainbow" ("Rainbow"). Both sides have moved for summary judgment on the issue of substantial similarity. For the reasons set forth below, defendants' motion for summary judgment is granted and plaintiff's motion is denied.

FACTS

For the purpose of this motion only, defendant concedes the validity of plaintiff's copyright and defendants' access to the plaintiff's copyrighted work. Thus, the only task facing the Court is to determine whether the two works are sufficiently similar to raise a genuine issue of copyright infringement; if such an issue exists a trial is, of course, required.

"RAINBOW"

Plaintiff's screenplay, "Black Rainbow," is the story of archaeologist Zeke Banarro's ("Zeke") expedition to the Andes of Peru in search of pre-Columbian gold artifacts. In the preamble to "Rainbow," Zeke is introduced as "a legitimate archaeologist who became a renegade treasure hunter or huaquero."

In the opening scene, Zeke is informed by his former lover, Michael Colby, a female museum curator, that Zeke has been replaced as head of an expedition to Peru. Undaunted, Zeke finances his own "bootleg" expedition with the help of a cocaine dealer who fronts Zeke the money in exchange for Zeke's promise to smuggle cocaine from Peru.

Upon arrival in Peru, Zeke and his sidekick, Justo, a Peruvian Indian native, pause to taste the pleasures of cocaine and prostitutes. After assembling an entourage of Indian natives and taking as a partner, Alvarado, who supplied horses and pack animals, the party then proceeds on the expedition.

Along the way, Tumba, Alvarado's servant/mistress, gives birth to a son. Shortly thereafter, Alvarado offers Tumba's services as a prostitute in return for the other Indians' share of the treasure. Zeke seeks to prevent this exploitation by pacifying the natives with cocaine. Ironically, Tumba, who is understandably grateful for this act of humanity, rewards Zeke with sexual favors.

Later, an old Indian mystic tells Zeke that he can locate the cave with the great anaconda snakes, and hopefully the treasure, by observing the reflection of the sun off the side of the cliffs. Upon locating the cave, the party rappels down the side of the cliff, fights off the anacondas with Molotov cocktails, and uncovers the treasure in a burial site inside the cave.

As they are about to begin their trek back from the cliff top, the expedition is confronted by the script's principal antagonist, Von Stroessner, and his band of thieves. As it turns out, Von Stroessner was hired by Michael Colby and the museum to follow Zeke and liberate him of his new-found treasure. A fight ensues, in which Zeke and Von Stroessner are wounded and several Indians are killed. Zeke ultimately shoots Von Stroessner in cold blood.

The expedition party continues the journey back, only to be confronted by the Peruvian National Guard. In the ensuing gunfire, Justo is mortally wounded, the remaining Indians are killed, and Zeke and Alvarado are forced to flee through the dense jungle carrying what little gold they can carry. Zeke ultimately shoots Alvarado in a quarrel over the remaining treasure, and the story ends with Zeke hiking back to civilization.

"RAIDERS"

"Raiders of the Lost Ark," by now familiar to movie-goers everywhere, is the swashbuckling adventure story of archaeologist Indiana Jones ("Indy"). After a brief introductory expedition to South America in 1936, which is foiled by Indy's arch-rival, Belloq, a French mercenary archaeologist, Indy returns home only to find that his services are required by the United States Army. It seems that army intelligence has revealed that Hitler is digging outside of Cairo for the lost Ark of the Covenant. Hitler, we are told, seeks to take advantage of the Ark's vast supernatural powers. Indy's mission, should he choose to accept it, is to beat Hitler's to the Ark.

Indy flies to Nepal where he locates Marion Ravenwood, his former lover and the daughter of his mentor. Marion has the headpiece to the Staff of Ra, which is the key to locating the Ark. When attached to a staff and placed in a miniature map room in the ancient city outside Cairo, the headpiece will direct the sun's rays to the location of the Well of Souls, in which the Ark is hidden. After Indy saves Marion from several ruthless Nazis, who are also after the headpiece, the pair heads for Cairo.

There, Indy discovers that Hitler has hired his old rival, Belloq, to direct the excavation. Belloq takes great interest in Marion, who has since been abducted by the Nazis.

Meanwhile, Indy and Sallah, an Egyptian friend, manage to sneak into the excavation and descend into the map room, where they discover the location of the Well of Souls. As they are about to descend into the Well, they discover that its floor is covered with tiny asps. Indy fends off the snakes by dousing them with fuel oil and setting them afire.

Indy and Sallah place the Ark in a crate and hoist it to their helpers waiting above. Once Sallah has ascended, the Nazis, who have observed

Indy's discovery, thrust Marion into the well with Indy and seal it up. The two manage to escape through the wall, however, to a neighboring catacomb.

After blowing up a Nazi airplane, Indy realizes that the Ark is now aboard a truck headed for Cairo. In a famous "chase" scene, Indy, riding a white steed, catches up with the Nazi caravan, gains control of the truck, fends off the Nazis, and escapes into the maze of the streets of Cairo.

Indy and Marion depart Cairo with the Ark aboard a ship, only to be overtaken by a Nazi U-boat. Indy, who managed to elude capture, follows the Nazis to an unidentified Mediterranean Island only to be taken captive once again. With Indy and Marion tied up nearby, Belloq and the Nazis open the Ark in a ritualistic ceremony. The grotesque spirits released therefrom converge upon the Nazis in a bizarre swoop of destruction. Only Indy and Marion, who in Old Testament fashion have kept their eyes closed throughout, are spared.

Back in Washington, D.C., as the film closes, we see the crated Ark being transported to an army warehouse where, among thousands of other identical crates, it will lie forever forgotten.

DISCUSSION

Although the question whether two works are substantially similar usually presents a factual issue that does not lend itself to summary judgment, the Second Circuit has recognized the appropriateness of summary judgment in copyright actions, "permitting courts to put 'a swift end to meritless litigation' and to avoid lengthy and costly trials." Clearly, summary judgment is appropriate where, after reviewing the comparing works, the Court concludes either that any similarity between the works concerns only non-copyrightable elements or that no reasonable jury, properly instructed, could find the works substantially similar.

The test for substantial similarity has been succinctly described as "whether an average lay observer would recognize the alleged copy as having been appropriated from the copyrighted work." In assessing whether a properly instructed jury may find two works substantially similar, it is helpful to review a few basic principles delineating the scope of copyright protection.

It is, of course, well-settled that a copyright protects only an author's original expression of an idea, not the idea itself. . . . In addition, a copyright affords no protection to so-called "scenes a faire," i.e., characters, settings or events which necessarily follow from a certain theme or plot situation.

Plaintiff concedes, as he must, that a basic idea of an archaeologist searching for artifacts is unprotectible. He argues, however, that actionable similarities lie in the characters, devices and action employed in expressing that idea. Defendant, of course, argues that any similarities existing between the two works are, in fact, unprotectible scenes a faire. I agree.

It is unnecessary to discuss every alleged similarity in the two works; a brief discussion of the salient portions of plaintiff's argument is illustrative.

First, it is noted that the mood and "feel" of the two works are completely different. "Rainbow" is, for the most part, a somber, vulgar script replete with overt sexual scenes, cocaine smuggling and cold-blooded killing. "Raiders," on the other hand, is a tongue-in-cheek, action-packed, Jack Armstrong, all-American adventure story.

Nor is there substantial similarity in the settings of the two works. "Rainbow" is set almost entirely in a Peruvian jungle. Although "Raiders" begins with a very brief expedition to a booby-trapped cave in a South-American jungle, most of the story is set in and around Cairo. Thus, any similarity of locale is simply too insignificant to warrant protection.

Plaintiff fares no better in his claim of character infringement. As the Second Circuit has stated, "[s]tirring one's memory of a copyrighted character is not the same as appearing to be substantially similar to that character, and only the latter is infringement." A review of plaintiff's claims of character infringement indicates that no jury could reasonably find the characters substantially similar.

Plaintiff argues, initially, that actionable similarity lies between the two protagonists, Zeke Banarro and Indiana Jones. Any similarity ends, however, with the fact that both are male and both are archaeologists. Zeke is basically a serious, self-interested, individual who betrays both the museum for which he works and his illegitimate "backer," strikes out on his own, and ends up shooting his adversaries in cold-blood. Indy, on the other hand, is a larger-than-life adventurer who, in matinee-idol fashion, remains loyal to truth, justice and the American way.

Nor does actionable similarity exist regarding the principal antagonists, Belloq in "Raiders" and Von Stroessner in "Rainbow." Belloq is an articulate, cultured French archaeologist who is Indy's established rival. Although not a Nazi himself, Belloq has been hired by Hitler to find the lost Ark.

Von Stroessner, whose full name is Juan Jos de Maria Lopez y Von Stroessner, is described as a mestizo thief who preys upon archaeologists. Plaintiff claims that the name Von Stroessner was chosen to depict the character as a post-war Nazi. Nothing in the script, however, indicates that Von Stroessner is, in fact, a Nazi. Indeed, it is ultimately revealed that Von Stroessner was hired, not by the Nazis, but by the museum where Zeke formerly was employed.

Plaintiff's assertion that he intended the Von Stroessner character to depict a Nazi does not present an actionable claim. The law of copyright protects the author's actual expression of an idea, and not the idea as it existed in the author's imagination. Clearly, "no character infringement claim can succeed unless plaintiff's original conception sufficiently developed the character, and defendants have copied this development and not merely the broader outlines."

In any event, even if the distorted inference that Von Stroessner is a Nazi could be drawn, no actionable similarity would lie. It is significant that "Raiders" is set in the late-1930's, the Nazi era. "Rainbow," on the other hand, obviously takes place in a contemporary setting, as is evidence from various references to the World Trade Center, the King Tut exhibit at the Metropolitan Museum of Art, Laurence Rockefeller, and the cocaine trade. Thus, any similarity caused by a remote reference to Nazism is, to say the least, superficial.

Finally, and incredibly, plaintiff asserts a similarity between Marion Ravenwood of "Raiders" and a combination of Tumba, the pregnant Indian mistress, and Michael Colby, the ambitious museum curator, of "Rainbow." The only similarities between these characters, however, are that they are female and that they share the common experience of a sexual encounter with the respective protagonists.

Upon close inspection, plaintiff's remaining claims of actionable similarity fall within the category of unprotectible scenes a faire. That treasure might be hidden in a cave inhabited by snakes, that fire might be used to repel the snakes, that birds might frighten an intruder in the jungle, and that a weary traveler might seek solace in a tavern, all are indispensable elements to the treatment of "Raiders" theme, and are, as a matter of law, simply too general to be protectible.

Moreover, these scenes were given dissimilar treatment in the respective works. For instance, in "Rainbow," the party's access to the cave was hindered by giant anaconda snakes that ultimately were frightened away by Molotov cocktails. In "Raiders," the floor of the Well of Souls was covered by hundreds of tiny asps and a cobra, that were fended off by burning them with fuel oil.

Likewise, an examination of plaintiff's claim that both scripts utilize sunlight to locate the treasure reveals a similarity too general to afford protection. In "Rainbow," the treasure-filled cave is located by observing the reflection of the sun off a crystallized rock formation on the side of a cliff. In "Raiders," however, the location of the Well of Souls is determined in a map room by observing the reflection of the sun through the headpiece of the Staff of Ra.

Finally, plaintiff's claim of dialogue infringement involves generalized insignificant pieces of dialogue which also necessarily flow from a common theme.

In short, having thoroughly reviewed all the plaintiff's claims (and having thoroughly enjoyed both scripts), I am led ineluctably to the conclusion that a "comparison of the two works reveals that their similarity exists only at a level of abstractions too basic to permit any inference that defendants wrongfully appropriated any 'expression' of plaintiff's ideas."

Accordingly, defendants' motion for summary judgment is granted and plaintiff's motion is denied. . . . The complaint is hereby dismissed.

Universal City Studios, Inc. v. Film Ventures International, Inc. 543 F. Supp. 1134 (C.D.Cal. 1982)

UNITED STATES DISTRICT JUDGE KENYON

. . . Findings of Fact

1. This is a civil action . . . for copyright infringement. . . . This preliminary injunction proceeding involves Plaintiffs' claim that Defendants have infringed the copyrights in the motion pictures "Jaws" and "Jaws 2." . . .

6. Prior to January, 1974, Peter Benchley ("Benchley") created and wrote a book entitled "Jaws," which is a fictional story about a great white shark that terrorizes the inhabitants of a coastal town on the Atlantic seaboard. Benchley has secured the exclusive rights and privileges in and to the copyright of the book "Jaws" and has received from the Register of Copyrights a Certificate of Registration identified as No. A-497539. Benchley subsequently assigned to Universal and The Zanuck/Brown Company all motion picture and allied rights in the book "Jaws."

7. Universal is the owner of the copyright in a motion picture entitled "Jaws." Prior to June 20, 1975, Universal produced the motion picture "Jaws" based on the book "Jaws" written by Benchley. Universal has received from the Register of Copyrights a Certificate of Registration identified as No. LP-4455.

8. Since approximately June 20, 1975, Universal has exhibited the motion picture "Jaws" throughout the United States and the world to millions of members of the public. Defendants have had access to Benchley's book "Jaws" and Universal's motion picture "Jaws."

9. [In 1980] Defendants . . . produced . . . a motion picture about a great white shark that terrorizes the inhabitants of a coastal town on the Atlantic seaboard. . . .

   That motion picture has been distributed in the United States using the title "Great White" and will be referred to hereinafter as "Great White." Defendants had no permission or consent from Universal or Benchley to produce or distribute "Great White." . . .

12. The expression . . . in "Great White" and the motion picture "Jaws" is substantially similar. . . . For example, and without limitation, the basic story points, the major characters, the sequence of incident, and the development and interplay of the major characters and story points of "Great White" are substantially similar to these elements in "Jaws."

13. Substantial similarity of the basic story points is found in the following comparisons:

    a. The local politician, a gubernatorial candidate in "Great White" and the mayor in "Jaws," both of whom play down the news of the shark in the interest of local tourism.

    b. In "Great White" the action revolves primarily around a salty, English-accented skipper and a local shark expert who go out in a boat to hunt the shark; in "Jaws" the action similarly revolves primarily around a salty English-accented skipper, a shark expert, and the local police chief who go out in a boat to hunt the shark.

    c. In the finale of "Great White" the skipper is eaten by the shark, and then the shark expert kills the shark by detonating dynamite which the shark has swallowed. In the finale of "Jaws" the skipper is eaten by the shark, and then the police chief kills the shark by exploding a canister of compressed air which the shark has swallowed.

14. Furthermore, all the major characters in "Great White" have substantially similar counterparts in "Jaws":

   a. The shark in both films becomes a principal character in its own right. The two sharks are maniacal and demonic, attacking people and boats for reasons beyond satisfying hunger. In addition, when hunted, both sharks attack the hunters rather than flee. The presence of the sharks in the waters of the coastal resorts in each film is unusual.

   b. The salty skippers, both of whom have heavy English-type accents and are experienced shark hunters, are substantially similar. The skipper in the two works accompanies the expedition in search of the shark and is killed in the finale.

   c. The politicians in both films are also substantially similar; they are concerned about the effect that the news would have on tourism. Specifically, in "Great White" the gubernatorial candidate is concerned about the windsurfing regatta and his political campaign; in "Jaws" the mayor is concerned about the Fourth of July weekend. Moreover, in "Great White," after the shark expert's child is injured by the shark, the politician apologizes to the father in the hospital and as an act of contrition personally hunts for the shark. In "Jaws" after the police chief's child has gone into a state of shock because of the shark, the politician apologizes to the father in the hospital and as an act of contrition signs a contract hiring the salty skipper to hunt the shark.

   d. Finally, the local shark expert in "Great White," Peter Benton (James Franciscus) is a combination of two characters in "Jaws": the shark expert (Richard Dreyfuss) and the local police chief (Roy Scheider). As the shark expert in "Jaws," Richard Dreyfuss tries to warn the town of the dangers of the shark; in "Great White," the shark expert does the same thing. In "Jaws," the local police chief has a blond wife and a child injured by the shark; in "Great White," James Franciscus has a blond wife and a child injured by the shark.

15. There is also substantial similarity between the development and interplay of the major characters and story points. The following non-inclusive list of comparisons of major incidents and the sequence of action indicates substantial similarity in the expression of the ideas of the two works at issue:

   a. The opening scene in both films depicts teenagers playing on the beach. In "Great White" there are many underwater shots of a windsurf, repeated musical bass tones to indicate the approach of the shark and to build tension, and the windsurf becomes the first victim of the shark. In "Jaws" there are many underwater shots of a swimmer, repeated bass tones to indicate the approach of the shark and to build tension, and the swimmer becomes the first victim.

   b. In "Great White" the action then shifts to the shark expert and his wife at home. After their daughter returns home, the expert goes out to search for the missing windsurf and finds part of the surfboard. He examines the surfboard and determines that a shark is responsible. In "Jaws" the police chief and his wife are at home. After their son returns home, the police chief receives a phone call which informs him that the swimmer is missing. The police chief finds part of the swimmer's body (which was initially discovered by his assistant) and concludes that a shark is responsible.

c. In "Great White" there is a boat scene in which, to the accompaniment of bass tones, the shark approaches the boat, bumps it, and causes a girl to fall into the water. The girl is rescued before the shark attacks. In "Jaws" there is a similar boat scene in which, again to the sound of bass tones, the shark approaches the boat, bumps it, and causes a boy to fall into the water. The boy is also rescued before the shark attacks.

d. In "Great White" the empty boat of a local fisherman is found floating in the water. After examining the arm of the fisherman discovered in the hull, the expert tries to warn the politician about the dangers of the shark. In "Jaws" the police chief and the scientist find the empty boat of a local fisherman floating in the water. After examining the body of the dead fisherman and a shark's tooth found in the hull, the two men try to warn the politician about the dangers of the shark.

e. The scare technique of a false alarm is present in both films. In "Great White" a broken surfboard, which looks like the fin of a shark, floats through the water. In "Jaws" a bathing cap, which looks like the head of a shark, floats through the water.

f. Both politicians agree to take security measures. In "Great White" several boats with armed spotters are placed around the bay and underwater netting is installed. The gubernatorial candidate refuses to cancel the windsurfing regatta. In "Jaws" several boats with armed spotters are placed around the harbor. The Fourth of July festivities are not cancelled by the mayor.

g. In both works, the shark attacks a dinghy. The dinghy is capsized, and the shark's consumption of the occupant is shown.

h. In "Great White" a local newsman and his cameraman, in order to obtain publicity, decide to lower raw meat off the pier as shark bait. The shark grabs the bait, breaking off part of the pier. People fall off the pier; some manage to reach shore as the shark attacks. In "Jaws" two bounty-hunters, seeking the monetary award, decide to lower raw meat off the pier as shark bait. The shark grabs the bait and breaks off part of the pier. One of the men falls off the pier and into the water, but manages to swim back to shore before the shark attacks.

i. The apologies and acts of contrition by the politicians in both films, which have already been described, also indicate substantial similarity in the major incidents and sequence of events in the two works.

j. The final scene in both movies involving the swallowing of the skipper and the explosion of the shark (described more fully above) is also evidence of similarity of the expression of the idea through major incidents and sequence of events. . . .

CONCLUSIONS OF LAW

. . . 11. Plaintiffs contend that there is sufficient similarity of expression to mandate a finding of infringement because there is substantial similarity between the basic story points, the major characters, the sequence of incident, and the development and interplay of the major characters and story points of their copyrighted works, "Jaws" and "Jaws 2," and "Great White." On the other hand, Defendants argue that neither the basic idea nor the scenes a faire present in Plaintiffs' motion pictures is protected and that upon elimination of these elements from "Jaws" and "Jaws 2," "virtually no similarity remains" with respect to "Great White." In essence, most, if not all, of that which Plaintiffs present as evidence of substantial similarity of expression in support of their contention of copying, Defendants characterize as unprotected elements which do not constitute expression of ideas and are not even subject to review for infringement.

12. The Court rejects Defendants' overly expansive view of that which falls within the unprotected sphere of general ideas and scenes a faire and, instead, adopts Plaintiffs' characterization of that which constitutes the expression of ideas. . . . The similarity in the basic story lines, the major characters, the sequence of events, and the interplay and development of the characters and the plot is substantial. These similarities are set forth more fully in Findings of Fact Numbers 12–15. And while the two films are not identical, "[d]uplication or near identity is not necessary to establish infringement." To put it simply, Defendants have captured the "total concept and feel" of Plaintiffs' motion picture, "Jaws."

3.5.1.2 Idea Submissions

The *Nichols, Zambito,* and *Universal/Film Ventures* cases (in Section 3.5.1 above) are widely accepted as having been correctly decided. If after reading those cases, you thought that Ms. Nichols and Mr. Zambito *should* have received more protection than they did, then you understand why courts began to apply contract and confidential relationship law in idea submission cases.

Idea submission cases involve two types of legal issues. The first concerns the circumstances that must exist in order for a contract or confidential relationship to exist between the person who submits an idea and the person to whom it is submitted. The second concerns the characteristics an idea must have in order for it to be protected (assuming a contract or confidential relationship is found).

3.5.1.2.1 Implied Contract

The leading case concerning the circumstances which will permit a finding that an implied-in-fact contract does exist between an idea-submitter and the recipient of the idea is *Desny v. Wilder*. Read it carefully. While it held that Mr. Desny was entitled to go forward with a trial of his claim against Billy Wilder and Paramount Pictures, it also established fairly rigorous conditions that had to be satisfied for him to prevail. Those conditions have been incorporated into jury instructions used in subsequent idea-submission cases, like *Mann v. Columbia Pictures.* Moreover, those conditions for recovery are not always satisfied, as they weren't in the *Mann* case. In many garden-variety idea-submission cases the *Desny* requirements simply cannot be satisfied. Moreover, California is a minority of one in the idea submission area. As we see in *Murray v. NBC,* in Section 3.5.2.2, other states require that the idea be at a minimum novel; moreover, there must be a confidential relationship between the submitter and the recipient. *Blaustein v. Burton* and *Faris v. Enberg,* along with the *Murray* case, illustrate the elements that are required in order to establish a confidential relationship.

Desny v. Wilder, 46 Cal.2d 715, 299 P.2d 257 (1956)

SCHAUER, JUSTICE

Plaintiff appeals from a summary judgment rendered against him in this action to recover the reasonable value of a literary composition, or of an idea for a photoplay, a synopsis of which composition, embodying the idea, he asserts he submitted to defendants for sale, and which synopsis and idea, plaintiff alleges, were accepted and used by defendants in producing a photoplay. . . .

[I]t appears from the present record that defendant Wilder at the times here involved was employed by defendant Paramount Pictures Corporation (sometimes hereinafter referred to as Paramount) either as a writer, producer or director, or a combination of the three. In November 1949, plaintiff telephoned Wilder's office. Wilder's secretary, who was also employed by Paramount, answered, and plaintiff stated that he wished to see Wilder. At the secretary's insistence that plaintiff explain his purpose, plaintiff "told her about this fantastic unusual story. . . . I described to her the story in a few words. . . . I told her that it was the life story of Floyd Collins who was trapped and made sensational news for two weeks . . . and I told her the plot. . . . I described to her the entrapment and the death, in ten minutes, probably. She seemed very much interested and she liked it. . . . The main emphasis was the central idea, which was the entrapment, this boy who was trapped in a cave eighty-some feet deep. I also told her the picture had never been made with a cave background before." Plaintiff sought to send Wilder a copy of the story but when the secretary learned of its length of some 65 pages she stated that Wilder would not read it, that he wanted stories in synopsis form, that the story would first be sent to the script department, and "in case they think it is fantastic and wonderful, they will abbreviate it and condense it in about three or four pages, and the producers and directors get to see it." Plaintiff protested that he preferred to do the abbreviating of the story himself, and the secretary suggested that he do so. Two days later plaintiff, after preparing a three or four page outline of the story, telephoned Wilder's office a second time and told the secretary the synopsis was ready. The secretary requested plaintiff to read the synopsis to her over the telephone so that she could take it down in shorthand, and plaintiff did so. During the conversation the secretary told plaintiff that the story seemed interesting and that she liked it. "She said that she would talk it over with Billy Wilder and she would let me know." Plaintiff on his part told the secretary that defendants could use the story only if they paid him "the reasonable value of it. . . . I made it clear to her that I wrote the story and that I wanted to sell it. . . . I naturally mentioned again that this story was my story which has taken me so much effort and research and time, and therefore if anybody used it they will have to pay for it. . . . She said that if Billy Wilder of Paramount uses the story, 'naturally we will pay you for it.' " Plaintiff did not remember whether in his first telephone conversation with the secretary anything was said concerning his purpose of selling the story to defendants. He did not at any time speak with defendant Wilder. It seems clear, however, that one of the authorized functions of the secretary was to receive and deliver messages to Wilder and hence, as is developed infra, that on this record her knowledge would be his knowledge. Plaintiff's only subsequent contact with the secretary was a telephone call to her in July 1950, to protest the alleged use of his composition and idea in a photoplay produced and exhibited by defendants. The photoplay, as hereinafter shown in some detail, closely parallels both plaintiff's synopsis and the historical material concerning the life and death of Floyd Collins. It also includes a fictional incident which appears in plaintiff's synopsis and which he claims is his creation, presumably in the sense of being both original and novel in its combination with the facts from the public commons or public domain.

. . . In his opening brief plaintiff states "It is conceded *for purposes of argument* [italics added] that the synopsis submitted by plaintiff to defendants was not sufficiently unique or original to be the basis for recovery under the law of plagiarism or infringement. It is conceded that the plaintiff first obtained the central idea or theme of his story, which involves the entrapment of a man in an underground cave and the national interest promoted by the attempt to rescue him, from the Floyd Collins incident which occurred in the 1920's.

"It is appellant's [plaintiff's] contention, however, that in spite of this, the lower court committed reversible error in granting a summary judgment in this case for the reason that the summary judgment had the effect of denying the plaintiff the right to prove that his idea or synopsis was the subject of a contract wherein the defendants promised to pay him for it if they used it. It is clear that 'ideas,' as such, may still be the subject of a contract in California and may be protected, as such, even though not protectible under the laws of plagiarism."

Plaintiff also asserts that he "is not suing defendants for plagiarizing his idea but is suing defendants because they agreed to pay him the reasonable value of the use of his idea and story synopsis if they used his idea" and that "defendants so used plaintiff's idea and synopsis but refused to pay him as they agreed." But the complaint, as already shown, alleges that "Plaintiff conceived, originated and completed [and offered for sale to and defendants accepted submission of and thereafter used] a certain untitled literary and dramatic composition (hereinafter called 'Plaintiff's Property') based upon the life of Floyd Collins."

If plaintiff is seeking to recover for a mere abstract, unprotectible idea, he must meet certain rules; if he seeks recovery for a literary composition in which he conceivably had a property right, the rules are quite different, as will subsequently be shown. . . .

Defendants concede, as they must, that "the act of disclosing an unprotectible idea, if that act is in fact the bargained-for exchange for a promise, may be consideration to support the promise." They then add, "But once the idea is disclosed without the protection of a contract, the law says that anyone is free to use it. Therefore, subsequent use of the idea cannot constitute consideration so as to support a promise to pay for such use." And as to the effect of the evidence defendants argue that plaintiff "disclosed his material before . . . [defendants] did or could do anything to indicate their willingness or unwillingness to pay for the disclosure. The act of using the idea, from which appellant attempts to imply a promise to pay, came long after the disclosure. . . . Accordingly, even if a promise to pay could be found . . . it came after the disclosure had been made and is therefore unenforceable." The conclusion of law asserted in the last sentence, insofar as it might be applicable to an express (whether proved by direct or by circumstantial evidence) promise to pay for the service (the conveyance of the idea) previously rendered from which a profit has been derived, for reasons which hereinafter appear, is not tenable. . . .

From what has been indicated above it appears necessary for us in the proper disposition of this case, having in mind the problems which apparently will confront the trial court at a trial on the merits and the duty imposed on us by section 53 of the Code of Civil Procedure, to consider not only (1) the rules for recovery pertaining to the conveyance of ideas, as such, but also (2) the question whether the synopsis of plaintiff's untitled composition could on any view of the evidence be deemed entitled to the status of a literary property, and (3) the rules defining rights of recovery, so far as pertinent on this record, if plaintiff has a literary property in his composition.

The Law Pertaining to Ideas. Generally speaking, ideas are as free as the air and as speech and the senses, and as potent or weak, interesting or drab, as the experiences, philosophies, vocabularies, and other variables of speaker and listener may combine to produce, to portray, or to comprehend. But there can be circumstances when neither air nor ideas may be acquired without cost. The diver who goes deep in the sea, even as the pilot who ascends high in the troposphere, knows full well that for life itself he, or someone on his behalf, must arrange for air (or its respiration-essential element, oxygen) to be specially provided at the time and place of need. The theatrical producer likewise may be dependent for his business life on the procurement of ideas from other persons as well as the dressing up and portrayal of his self-conceptions; he may not find his own sufficient for survival. As counsel for the Writers

Guild aptly say, ideas "are not freely usable by the entertainment media until the latter are made aware of them." The producer may think up the idea himself, dress it and portray it; or he may purchase either the conveyance of the idea alone or a manuscript embodying the idea in the author's concept of a literary vehicle giving it form, adaptation and expression. It cannot be doubted that some ideas are of value to a producer.

An idea is usually not regarded as property, because all sentient beings may conceive and evolve ideas throughout the gamut of their powers of cerebration and because our concept of property implies something which may be owned and possessed to the exclusion of all other persons. . . .

The principles above stated do not, however, lead to the conclusion that ideas cannot be a subject of contract. As Mr. Justice Traynor stated in his dissenting opinion in *Stanley v. Columbia Broadcasting System* (1950), . . . 35 Cal.2d 653, 674, 221 P.2d 73: "The policy that precludes protection of an abstract idea by copyright does not prevent its protection by contract. Even though an idea is not property subject to exclusive ownership, its disclosure may be of substantial benefit to the person to whom it is disclosed. That disclosure may therefore be consideration for a promise to pay. . . . Even though the idea disclosed may be 'widely known and generally understood' [citation], it may be protected by an express contract providing that it will be paid for regardless of its lack of novelty." . . .

In other words the recovery may be based on contract either express or implied. The person who can and does convey a valuable idea to a producer who commercially solicits the service or who voluntarily accepts it knowing that it is tendered for a price should likewise be entitled to recover. In so holding we do not fail to recognize that freelance writers are not necessarily members of a learned profession and as such bound to the exalted standards to which doctors and lawyers are dedicated. So too we are not oblivious of the hazards with which producers of the class represented here by defendants and their related amici are confronted through the unsolicited submission of numerous scripts on public domain materials in which public materials the producers through their own initiative may well find nuclei for legitimately developing the "stupendous and colossal." The law, however, is dedicated to the proposition that for every wrong there is a remedy (Civ. Code, § 3523) and for the sake of protecting one party it must not close the forum to the other. It will hear both and seek to judge the cause by standards fair to both. To that end the law of implied contracts assumes particular importance in literary idea and property controversies.

The Law Pertaining to Contracts, Express, Implied-in-Fact and Implied by Law, and Quasi Contractual Obligations, as Related to Ideas and Literary Property. . . . We agree that whether a contract be properly identified as express or as implied-in-fact or inferred from circumstances; or whether the bargain meets the subjective test of a meeting of minds or is held to reside in the objective evidence of words and acts with or without a meeting of minds; or whether the obligation be recognized as implied by law from acts having consensual aspects (and therefore often termed implied-in-fact); or whether the obligation be imposed by law because of acts and intents which, although tortious rather than consensual, should in justice give rise to an obligation resembling that created by contract and, hence, should be termed quasi-contractual, is important here to the extent that we recognize the situations and discriminate appropriately in the governing rules. . . .

If it were not for precedent we should hesitate to speak of an implied-in-fact contract. In truth, contracts are either made in fact or the obligation is implied in law. If made in fact, contracts may be established by direct evidence or they may be inferred from circumstantial evidence. The only difference is in the method of proof. In either case they would appear to be express contracts. Otherwise, it would seem that they, or the presumed contractual obligation, must be implied at law. A so-called "implied-in-fact" contract, however, as the term is used by some writers, may be found although there has been no meeting of the minds. Even an express contract may be found where there has been no meeting of minds. The classic example of this situation is set up by the parol evidence rule. The law accepts the objective evidence of the written contract as constituting the contract and, subject, of course, to certain exceptions, precludes oral evidence to show that the minds of the parties did not meet in the writing. Professor Williston recognizes in effect, if not specifically, that the law implies (or construes) contractual obligations in many cases where there is no true contract in the historically conventional sense and that such implied obligations are of the nature of, and governed by the rules applicable to, contracts termed implied-in-fact by many writers. In a paper published in 14 *Illinois Law Review* 85, 90, Mr. Williston says: "The parties may be bound by the terms of an offer even though the offered expressly indicated dissent, provided his action could only lawfully mean assent. A buyer who goes into a shop and asks and is given [told] the price of an article, cannot take it and say 'I decline to pay the price you ask, but will take it at its fair value.' He will be liable, if the seller elects to hold him so liable, not simply as a converter for the fair value of the property, but as a buyer for the stated price." . . .

Whether the resulting "contract" . . . is classified as express (as may be fictionized by the law's objective test) or as implied-in-fact (as also may be fictionized by the law) or whether in the same or slightly differing circumstances an obligation shall be "implied" and denominated "quasi contractual" because it is strong-armed by the law from non-consensual acts and intents, is probably important in California—and for the purposes of resolving the problems now before us—principally as an aid to understanding the significance of rulings and discussions in authorities from other jurisdictions. Here, our terminology and the situations for application of the pertinent rules are simplified by codification.

Our Civil Code declares that (§ 1619) "A contract is either express or implied"; (§ 1620) "An express contract is one, the terms of which are stated in words" and (§ 1621) "An implied contract is one, the existence and terms of which are manifested by conduct." The same code further provides that (§ 1584) "[T]he acceptance of the consideration offered with a proposal, is an acceptance of the proposal"; (§ 1589) "A voluntary acceptance of the benefit of a transaction is equivalent to a consent to all the obligations arising from it, so far as the facts are known, or ought to be known, to the persons accepting"; (§ 1605) "Any benefit conferred . . . upon the promisor, by any other person, to which the promisor is not lawfully entitled . . . is a good consideration for a promise"; and (§ 1606) "[A] moral obligation originating in some benefit conferred upon the promisor . . . is also a good consideration for a promise, to an extent corresponding with the extent of the obligation, but no further or otherwise." . . .

From what has been shown respecting the law of ideas and of contracts we conclude that conveyance of an idea can constitute valuable consideration and can be bargained for before it is disclosed to the proposed purchaser, but once it is conveyed, i.e., disclosed to him and he has grasped it, it is henceforth his own and he may work with it and use it as he sees fit. In the field of entertainment the producer may properly and validly agree that he will pay for the service of conveying to him ideas which are valuable and which he can put to profitable use. Furthermore, where an idea has been conveyed with the expectation by the purveyor that compensation will be paid if the idea is used, there is no reason why the producer who has been the beneficiary of the conveyance of such an idea, and who finds it valuable and is profiting by it, may not then for the first time, although he is not at that time under any legal obligation so to do, promise to pay a reasonable compensation for that idea—that is, for the past service of furnishing it to him—and thus create a valid obligation. . . . But, assuming legality of consideration, the idea purveyor cannot prevail in an action to recover compensation for an abstract idea unless (a) before or after disclosure he has obtained an express promise to pay, or (b) the circumstances preceding and attending disclosure, together with the conduct of the offered acting with knowledge of the circumstances, show a promise of the type usually referred to as "implied" or "implied-in-fact." . . .

Such inferred or implied promise, if it is to be found at all, must be based on circumstances which were known to the producer at and preceding the time of disclosure of the idea to him and he must voluntarily accept the disclosure, knowing the conditions on which it is tendered. Section 1584 of the Civil Code ("[T]he acceptance of the consideration offered with a proposal, is an acceptance of the proposal") can have no application unless the offered has an opportunity to reject the consideration—the proffered conveyance of the idea—before it is conveyed. Unless the offered has opportunity to reject he cannot be said to accept. . . . The idea man who blurts out his idea without having first made his bargain has no one but himself to blame for the loss of his bargaining power. The law will not in any event, from demands stated subsequent to the unconditioned disclosure of an abstract idea, imply a promise to pay for the idea, for its use, or for its previous disclosure. The law will not imply a promise to pay for an idea from the mere facts that the idea has been conveyed, is valuable, and has been used for profit; this is true even though the conveyance has been made with the hope or expectation that some obligation will ensue. So, if the plaintiff here is claiming only for the conveyance of the idea of making a dramatic production out of the life of Floyd Collins he must fail unless in conformity with the above stated rules he can establish a contract to pay.

From plaintiff's testimony, as epitomized above, it does not appear that a contract to pay for conveyance of the abstract photoplay idea had been made, or that the basis for inferring such a contract from subsequent related acts of the defendants had been established, at the time plaintiff disclosed his basic idea to the secretary. Defendants, consequently, were at that time and from then on free to use the abstract idea if they saw fit to engage in the necessary research and develop it to the point of a usable script. Whether defendants did that, or whether they actually accepted and used plaintiff's synopsis, is another question. And whether by accepting plaintiff's synopsis and using it, if they did accept and use it, they may be found to have implicitly—by the rules discussed—agreed to pay for whatever value the synopsis possessed as a composition embodying, adapting and implementing the idea, is also a question which, upon the present summary judgment record, is pertinent for consideration in reaching our ultimate conclusion. That is, if the evidence suggests that defendants accepted plaintiff's synopsis, did they not necessarily accept it upon the terms on which he had offered it? Certainly the mere fact that the idea had been disclosed under the circumstances shown here would not preclude the finding of an implied (inferred in fact) contract to pay for the synopsis embodying, implementing and adapting the idea for photoplay production. . . .

The basic distinction between the rights in and to literary productions as they may exist at common law and as they are granted by statutory copyright is that the common law protects only a property right while the copyright statute grants a limited monopolistic privilege. (34 Am.Jur. 401, § 2.) Plaintiff here has no statutory copyright. His claim as to the synopsis, therefore, necessarily must rest in a common law property right or in contract. He has chosen to rest it in contract. If plaintiff has a literary composition it may be the subject of a property right and its use by defendants, if established, could entitle him to remedies, notwithstanding the concessions he has made, which would be unavailable if he had only an idea to be appropriated or to be the subject of contract.

Literary property which is protectible may be created out of unprotectible material such as historical events. It has been said (and does not appear to have been successfully challenged) that "There are only thirty-six fundamental dramatic situations, various facets of which form the basis of all human drama." (Georges Polti, "The Thirty-Six Dramatic Situations"; see also, Henry Albert Phillips, "The Universal Plot Catalog"; Eric Heath, "Story Plotting Simplified.") It is manifest that authors must work with and from ideas or themes which basically are in the public domain. History both in broadly significant and in very personal aspects has furnished a wealth of material for photoplays. The Crusades, The French Revolution, The War Between the States, the lives, or events from the lives, of rulers, ministers, doctors, lawyers, politicians, and military men, among others, all have contributed. Events from the life of the late General William Mitchell are even now the basic theme of a current showing. Events from the life of Floyd Collins were avowedly the basic theme of plaintiff's story. Certainly, it must be recognized that a literary composition does not depend upon novelty of plot or theme for the status of "property," if it is entitled to that status at all. The terms "originality" and "novelty" have often been confused, or used without differentiation, or with meanings which vary with different authorities. We therefore suggest the sense in which we use them. A literary composition may be original, at least in a subjective sense, without being novel. To be original it must be a creation or construction of the author, not a mere copy of another's work. The author, of course, must almost inevitably work from old materials, from known themes or plots or historical events, because, except as knowledge unfolds and history takes place, there is nothing new with which to work. But "Creation, in its technical sense, is not essential to vest one with ownership of rights in intellectual property. Thus, a compiler who merely gathers and arranges, in some concrete form, materials which are open and accessible to all who have the mind to work with like diligence is as much the owner of the result of his labors as if his work were a creation rather than a construction." . . .

Writing—portraying characters and events and emotions with words, no less than with brush and oils—may be an art which expresses personality. Accordingly, the language of Mr. Justice Holmes, speaking for the Supreme Court in a copyright case relating to circus posters is apropos: "Others are free to copy the original. They are not free to copy the copy. . . . The copy is the personal reaction of an individual upon nature. Personality always contains something unique. It expresses singularity even in handwriting, and a very modest grade of art has in it something irreducible, which is one man's alone. That something he may copyright unless there is a restriction in the words of the act." (*Bleistein v. Donaldson Lithographing Co.* (1903), 188 U.S. 239, 249–250, 23 S.Ct. 298, 47 L.Ed. 460.) As indicated, the theme of a writer must almost inevitably be neither novel nor original. The finished work probably will not be novel because it deals only with the public domain or public commons facts. But the completed composition may well be the original product of the researcher who compiles or constructs it. He gives it genesis, and genesis in this sense requires only origin of the composition, not of the theme. The composition will be the property of the author. Whether it possesses substantial value, and to what extent, if any, it may be entitled to copyright protectibility, may be quite another matter.

The time of the author; his resourcefulness in, opportunity for and extent of, research; his penetration in perception and interpretation of source materials; the acumen of his axiological appraisals of the dramatic; and his skill and style of composition, including the art of so portraying accurate narration of events long passed as to arouse vivid emotions of the present, are all elements which may contribute to the value of his product. Some of those elements in varying quanta and proportions must exist in any literary composition; thereby the composition reflects the personality of the author. And any literary composition, conceivably, may possess value in someone's estimation and be the subject of contract, or, conversely, it may be considered totally devoid of artistic, historic, scientific or any practical value. Obviously the defendants here used someone's script in preparing and producing their photoplay. That script must have had value to them. As will be hereinafter shown, it closely resembles plaintiff's synopsis. Ergo, plaintiff's synopsis appears to be a valuable literary composition. Defendants had an unassailable right to have their own employees conduct the research into the Floyd Collins tragedy—an historical event in the public domain—and prepare a story based on those facts and to translate it into a script for the play. But equally unassailable (assuming the verity of the facts which plaintiff asserts) is plaintiff's position that defendants had no right—except by purchase on the terms he offered—to acquire and use the synopsis prepared by him. . . . We are satisfied that, for the purposes of this appeal, plaintiff's dictation to defendant Wilder's secretary of the synopsis of his composition, embodying the core of his idea and his concept of a desirable entertainment media adaptation of it, is equivalent to submission of the synopsis in typed form.

Under the principles of law which have been stated it appears that for plaintiff to prevail on this appeal the record must indicate either that the evidence favors plaintiff, or that there is a triable issue of fact, in respect to the following questions: Did plaintiff prepare a literary composition on the Floyd Collins tragedy? Did he submit the composition to the defendants for sale? Did the defendants, knowing that it was offered to them for sale, accept and use that composition or any part thereof? If so, what was the reasonable value of the composition?

It is not essential to recovery that plaintiff's story or synopsis possess the elements of copyright protectibility if the fact of consensual contract be found. . . .

The Law Applied to the Facts. Here, as conceded by defendants for purposes of their summary judgment motion, plaintiff, in accordance with his testimony, submitted his synopsis to them through defendant Wilder's secretary and such submission included a declaration by both plaintiff and the secretary that defendants were to pay for his story if they used it. The mere fact that at the time of plaintiff's first telephone call to Wilder's office he described the central idea of the story to the secretary in response to her insistence that he explain the purpose of his call would not as a matter of law deprive plaintiff of the right to payment for the story as discussed by him and the secretary when he again spoke with her two days later and at her request read his synopsis to her, for her to take down in shorthand for defendants' consideration; the two conversations appear to have been parts of a single transaction and must be construed as such. The affidavits submitted on behalf of defendants by Wilder and by an officer of Paramount to the effect that neither Wilder nor Wilder's secretary had authority to negotiate contracts for the purchase of scripts do not compel the conclusion as a matter of law that an implied (inferred) contract binding defendants to pay for plaintiff's story was not created if (as is hereinafter shown) the record discloses any substantial evidence indicating that defendants did accept and make use of plaintiff's composition. . . .

With respect to whether defendants used plaintiff's composition, it may be first noted that defendants presented no affidavits in any way denying such use, but merely exhibited their photoplay to the court for purposes of comparison between plaintiff's synopsis and defendants' production. Defendants also produced extracts from a magazine and newspaper to which plaintiff had already freely testified in his deposition that he had referred in preparing his story. A script of the photoplay was, however, attached to plaintiff's complaint as an exhibit, and plaintiff has provided an outline comparing his synopsis with defendants' scenario. Defendants in their brief have likewise outlined the story of their photoplay.

In defendants' motion picture script the trapped man expresses a fear of the curse of dead Indians, as did Collins in the fictional portion of plaintiff's synopsis. Other similarities between plaintiff's story and the scenario of defendants' picture are these:

DEFENDANTS' SCENARIO

Cave where Mimosa trapped was on property owned by him and father. Mimosa operated Indian Curio Shop. Mimosa cave open to tourist trade. Mimosa's difficulty in extricating himself from cave was due to large flat slab wedged against wall of his cell, which slanted across him, pinning him down.

Mimosa's father calls sheriff.

Tatu is first reporter to arrive; tells Mimosa not to worry, as "they'll get you out."

Tatu suggests setting up a drill on top of the mountain and going straight down; this is done.

Local miners object that drilling is unnecessary.

Tatu comments that the news story is "Big. As big as they come, I think. Maybe bigger than Floyd Collins," and refers to fact that reporter on Collins story received a Pulitzer Prize.

Carnival trucks are described, and persons operating concessions are shown; excursion train is referred to; rescue equipment assembled and public address system used.

Mimosa's father protests.

Doctor diagnoses pneumonia.

Tatu is only reporter who saw Mimosa.

Other reporters are suspicious of the "whole set-up and criticized and complained about Tatu's control of the situation"; one threatened to "take this all the way to Santa Fe. To the Governor."

Mimosa dies.

PLAINTIFF'S STORY

Cave where Collins trapped was underneath father's farm.

Collins sold Indian relics to tourists.

Crystal Cave open to tourist trade.

Rock wedge fell across Collins' left ankle and pinioned both legs, holding him prisoner.

Collins' father spread alarm.

Miller is first reported to reach Collins, and tells him, "The world is coming, old man."

Lt. Bourdon says, "There is only one way to save Collins without maiming him, and that is to sink a shaft to him."

Opposition develops between the natives and the rescue crew.

Collins story carried on front page of Louisville newspaper every day; Miller was later awarded Pulitzer Prize.

Cave City took on appearance of Klondike gold rush town; special reporters came; special trains stopped to unload travelers and equipment; occasion regarded as picnic by many.

Collins' father resented the behavior.

Doc Haslet fears pneumonia.

Miller is only reporter who saw Collins.

Some reporters make accusations expressing strong suspicions with respect to lack of good faith in rescue of Collins; governor summons Board of Military Inquiry; two reporters considered whole thing a giant publicity scheme and hoax. Collins dies.

For the purposes of appellate review of this summary judgment proceeding it is apparent from the comparisons above tabulated, and from the outlines which are set out in the margin, that a factual issue, rather than one of law, is presented as to whether defendants used plaintiff's synopsis or developed their production independently thereof.... Particularly does this appear true in view of the fact that plaintiff submitted his synopsis to defendants in November 1949, and that as early as July 1950, the latter were producing their photoplay which, despite their assertion that it "does not purport to be a biography of the life of Floyd Collins.... Its characters, plot and development are wholly imaginative," obviously does bear a remarkable similarity to plaintiff's story both in respect to the historical data and the fictional material originated by plaintiff.

It has been suggested that this court view the photoplay (which defendants in their brief offer to make available) in order to determine whether a triable issue of fact exists. The scope of the implications in that suggestion is persuasive to us that the issues here are not for summary disposition. In the light of the conclusions we have reached on the evidence already discussed it appears that viewing the photoplay would relate merely to the weight of the evidence. . . . We therefore find it unnecessary to view the film.

At the trial the trier of fact should proceed with nicety of discrimination in applying the evidence to resolve the issues. Inasmuch as plaintiff's story is taken from the public domain, and as both his story and that of defendants are in principal substance historically accurate, it must be borne in mind that the mere facts that plaintiff submitted and offered to sell to defendants a synopsis containing public domain material and that thereafter defendants used the same public domain material, will not support an inference that defendants promised to pay for either the synopsis or for the idea of using the public domain material. The plaintiff can have no property right in the public domain facts concerning Floyd Collins or in the abstract idea of making a photoplay dramatizing those facts. On the other hand, the fact that plaintiff used the public domain material in constructing his story and synopsis would afford no justification whatsoever for defendants to appropriate plaintiff's composition and use it or any part of it in the production of a photoplay—and this, of course, includes the writing of a scenario for it—without compensating plaintiff for the value of his story. And the further fact, if it be a fact, that the basic idea for the photoplay had been conveyed to defendants before they saw plaintiff's synopsis, would not preclude the finding of an implied (inferred-in-fact) contract to pay for the manuscript, including its implemented idea, if they used such manuscript. . . .

NOTES

1. Following the ruling in *Desny,* motion picture and television production companies sought to protect themselves from idea submission claims by declining unsolicited scripts or treatments from unknown individuals, and in limiting access to the receipt of submissions from established industry professionals like agents, managers and entertainment attorneys. It also became an industry-wide practice to require the signing of a broad program material submission release, or film script release, in conjunction with any submission. An example of a typical program material submission release form for television is provided below. As expected after *Desny,* the language in this program submission release form is very broad in its protection of the television production company from any future liability, in the event they subsequently produce a similar program. It appears from the language in Paragraphs 4 and 5 of the release that, absent distinctly novel or original content, only a clear case of copyright infringement would prevail to defeat this release if it was later alleged that the submitted material was "substantially copied" by the production company in a subsequent program.

PROGRAM MATERIAL RELEASE FORM

_____, 20____

Title and/or Theme of Material

Submitted Hereunder:

_____*Program:*

_____

Big Time Pictures Television

A Division of Interplanetary Entertainment, Inc.

1234 Whatever Street

Burbank, CA 91505

Gentlemen:

I am today submitting to you certain program material, the title and/or theme of which is indicated above (which material is hereinafter referred to as the "program material") upon the following express understanding and conditions.

1. I acknowledge that I have requested permission to disclose to you and to carry on certain discussions and negotiations with you in connection with such program material.

2. I agree that I am voluntarily disclosing such program material to you at my request. I understand that you shall have no obligation to me in any respect whatsoever with regard to such material until each of us has executed a written agreement which, by its terms and provisions, will the only contract between us.

3. I agree that any discussions we may have with respect to such program material shall not constitute any agreement expressed or implied as to the purchase or use of any such program material which I am hereby disclosing to you either orally or in writing..

4. If such material submitted hereunder is not new or novel, or was not originated by me, or has not been reduced to concrete form, or if because other persons including your employees have heretofore submitted or hereafter submit similar or identical program material which you have the right to use, then I agree that you shall not be liable to me for your use of such program material and you shall not be obligated in any respect whatsoever to compensate me for such use by you.

5. I further agree that if you hereafter produce or distribute a television program or programs based upon the same general idea, theme or situation and/or having the same setting or background and/or taking place in the same geographical area or period of history as the said program material, then, unless you have substantially copied the expression and development of such idea, theme or situation, including the characters and story line thereof, as herewith or hereafter submitted to you by me in writing, you shall have no obligation or liability to me of any kind or character by reason of the production or distribution of such program(s), nor shall you be obligated to compensate me in connection therewith.

I acknowledge that but for my agreement to the above terms and conditions, you would not accede to my request to receive and consider the said program material which I am submitting to you herewith.

Very truly yours,

_____

Writer

2. Unlike the situation in the *Desny* case, the idea-submitter in *Mann v. Columbia Pictures, Inc.*, 128 Cal.3d 628, 180 Cal.Rptr. 522 (1982) did not condition submission of her work on appropriate payment. Ms. Mann (apparently, an amateur) wrote *Women Plus,* "a brief description of six characters in a beauty salon setting, together with a short narration of a number of scenes" which she registered with the Writers' Guild of America (registration not being limited to WGA members.) Ms. Mann had a friend who in turn had a friend (Caplan) who was described to Ms. Mann as "an important man at Columbia [Pictures]" who would have Ms. Mann's work "reviewed by a Columbia reader" as a favor to Ms. Mann. Although Mann never stated it, she expected to be paid if her work was used. In fact, Caplan was a "production manager" (i.e., production cost calculator) for an independent company which had a relationship with Columbia. He had no involvement with creative matters or with compensation to creative personnel. Caplan turned Ms. Mann's work over to a fellow employee of the production company. There was no record of a rejection letter with respect to *Women Plus,* nor was Ms. Mann's material found in Columbia's records. Some four years after Ms. Mann's submission, Columbia released *Shampoo.* Ms. Mann recognized several similarities between *Shampoo* and *Women Plus,* and sued for breach of an implied-in-fact contract. A jury verdict for Ms. Mann was set aside by the trial judge, who granted judgment n.o.v. to the defendants. The Court of Appeal affirmed. The court characterized Ms. Mann's work as "no more than a collection of ideas which was never developed in the form of a script or a story . . . Mann's abstract ideas are not literary property. [citing *Desny v. Wilder*]. The material allegedly used by defendants must also constitute protectible property if Mann is to recover in quasi-contract. (*Weitzenkorn v. Lesser* [1953] 40 Cal.2d 778, 795.) "Therefore, the proof necessary to recover upon the theory of a contract implied in law is the same as that required by the tort action for plagiarism." (*Ibid.*) The lower court correctly determined that "there is no substantial similarity" between *Shampoo* and plaintiff's outline as to form and manner of expression, the portion which may be protectible property. [Therefore, Ms. Mann] cannot recover upon a quasi-contractual theory for the alleged use of her ideas. (*Ibid.*; 1 Witkin, Summary of Cal. Law [8th ed. 1973] Contracts, § 4, pp. 31–32.) . . . [Since the trial court properly rendered judgment for defendants on plagiarism,] the trial court's dismissal of the count for quasi-contract is necessarily affirmed [because of the absence of evidence that Ms. Mann's work had reached Warren Beatty and Robert Towne, the creators of *Shampoo.* There was, on the other hand, ample evidence of independent prior creation of the *Shampoo* screenplay by them.] . . .

   "For this court to find that Mann and Columbia entered an implied-in-fact contract, plaintiff must demonstrate that she clearly conditioned her offer of *Women Plus* upon an obligation to pay for it, or its ideas, if used by Columbia; and Columbia, knowing the condition before it knew the ideas, voluntarily accepted their disclosure (necessarily on the specified basis) and found them valuable and used them. [Citing *Desny*] . . . [Moreover, if] the two defendants did not use her ideas in the 'shooting script,' the fact that the motion picture may strongly resemble *Women Plus* does not afford plaintiff a cause of action against Columbia for breach of an implied contract. . . . "

3. The abstract (and clichéd) nature of the plaintiffs' idea was a decisive factor in *Robinson v. Viacom International,* 1995 WL 417076, 1995 CCH Copyright Law Decisions ¶ 27,480 (SDNY 1995), which discussed the idea/expression dichotomy discussed at the beginning of this chapter, and which illustrates the majority rule requiring novelty as a condition to an implied contract. Summary judgment was granted to Viacom in a case in which plaintiffs claimed they were entitled to compensation for misappropriation of an idea for a sitcom. The premise was that a 1980s family was haunted by "America's favorite sitcom family" of the 1950s. The earlier family was visible only to the 1980s family. The plaintiffs claimed misappropriation of (1) plot, (2), characters, (3) total concept and feel (i.e., mood), (4) setting, (5) format, and (6) pace. However, the court stated, "[J]uxtaposition of the two families constitutes an idea, not an expression, and plaintiffs may not be granted a monopoly in this idea, *even if the plaintiffs' formulation is novel.*" (Emphasis added.) Plaintiffs' plot ideas were not sufficiently developed to merit protection, especially in light of their derivative nature (most actually constituting clichés gleaned from a long line of family-based sitcoms—not unlike the situation in the *Murray* case (below). There was no character development, and "the broad theme of a 1950's sitcom family interacting with a contemporary family is an unprotectible idea." The court similarly minimized the significance of the setting (middle class suburb), format (comedy with prologue), pace (up tempo), and other elements. In addition to rejecting plaintiffs' claim of a contract implied in fact, the court granted summary judgment to the defendants on plaintiffs' deceptive business practices claim (involving New York General Business Law §§ 349–350) and their Lanham Act claim. Plaintiffs' attempt to revive their claim in state court was also unavailing, the First Department affirming dismissal of plaintiffs' action because they had failed to rebut defendants' prima facie showing that plaintiffs' idea was not novel. *Robinson v. Viacom International,* 242 A.D.2d 481, 663 N.Y.S.2d 817 (1997).

4. In *Nadel v. Play-by-Play Toys,* 200 F.3d. 368, 2000 WL 310 268 (2d Cir. 2000), the Southern District had granted summary judgment to the defendant, holding that New York law required that the idea must be totally novel, not simply that the idea be novel as to the defendant. However, the Second Circuit interpreted several earlier decisions by the New York courts as permitting recovery if an idea were novel as to the defendant, even if not totally original with the plaintiff. Moreover, plaintiff contended that pursuant to industry custom and usage, ideas were assumed to be disclosed on a confidential basis, with compensation to the idea-submitter if an idea was used. Because of the issues concerning "particular" and "general" novelty, and because of plaintiff's claims that a contract existed (either express, or implied in fact), the Second Circuit reversed and remanded. In an idea-submission case, the court said, general novelty is required, whereas in a misappropriation/breach of contract case, novelty to the defendant is sufficient.

3.5.1.2.2 Confidential Relationships

As indicated above, there is a conflict among the states concerning idea submission claims. The majority rule is the New York rule applied in the *Murray* case which held that an idea must be novel to be protected. The minority rule is the California rule applied in *Blaustein* which held that non-novel ideas may be protected by contract too, if a confidential relationship exists between the plaintiff and the defendant. When you read these cases, consider which rule makes more sense to you and do so from two perspectives. First, consider which rule would make more sense if you (or your client) were an aspiring screenwriter. Then consider which rule would make more sense if you (or your client) were a movie or television production company that is bombarded with thousands of ideas every year (many of which are unsolicited and unwanted).

Blaustein v. Burton, 9 Cal.App.3d 161, 88 Cal.Rptr. 319 (1970)

FRAMPTON, ASSOCIATE JUSTICE PRO TEM

Appellant, in his deposition, testified that he had been in the motion picture business since 1935. After serving as a reader, a story editor, the head of a story department, and an editorial supervisor, he became a producer of motion picture films in 1949. The films he has produced include *Broken Arrow; Mr. 880; Half Angel; Just One More Chance; Take Care of My Little Girl; The Day the Earth Stood Still; The Outcasts of Poker Flat; Don't Bother to Knock; Desiree; The Racers; Storm Center; Cowboy; Bell, Book and Candle; The Wreck of the Mary Deare; Two Loves; The Four Horsemen of the Apocalypse; and Khartoum.* The functions of a producer of a motion picture are to (1) generate the enthusiasm of the various creative elements as well as to bring them together; (2) search out viable locations which would be proper for the artistic side of the production and would be proper from the logistic physical production side; (3) create a budget that would be acceptable from the physical point of view as well as satisfactory from the point of view of implementing the requirements of the script; (4) make arrangements with foreign government where the photography would take place; (5) supervise the execution of the script, the implementation of it onto film; (6) supervise the editing of all the production work down through the dubbing process and the release printing process, at least through the answer print process with Technicolor in this case; (7) the obligation of consulting with the United Artists people on advertising and publicity; (8) arrange casting; (9) engage the interests of the kind of star or stars that they (the United Artists' people) would find sufficiently attractive to justify an investment, and (10) develop the interest of a proper director.

During 1964, appellant conceived an idea consisting of a number of constituent elements including the following: (a) the idea of producing a motion picture based upon William Shakespeare's play *The Taming of the Shrew;* (b) the idea of casting respondents Richard Burton and Elizabeth Taylor Burton as the stars of this motion picture; (c) the idea of using as the director of the motion picture Franco Zeffirelli, a stage director, who at that time had never directed a motion picture and who was relatively unknown in the United States; (d) the idea of eliminating from the film version of the play the so-called "frame" (i.e., the play within a play device which Shakespeare employed), and beginning the film with the main body of the story; (e) the idea of including in the film version the two key scenes (i.e., the wedding scene and the wedding night scene) which in Shakespeare's play occur offstage and are merely described by a character on stage; (f) the idea of filming the picture in Italy, in the actual Italian settings described by Shakespeare.

On April 6, 1964, appellant met with Hugh French, an established motion picture agent who was then, and was at the time of the taking of the deposition (March 20, 1968), the agent for respondent Richard Burton. Prior to such meeting, appellant knew that Mr. French was Mr. Burton's agent and Mr. French knew that appellant was a motion picture producer, as appellant and Mr. French had been involved in business dealings together in the past. At such meeting, appellant first asked Mr. French "if he could tell me anything about the availability of Mr. and Mrs. Burton." Mr. French replied: "Well, they have many commitments; but, as you know, they are always interested in good ideas or good scripts or good projects." Appellant then replied: "Well, I have a thought about a picture for the Burtons, but it makes no sense to discuss it unless you would be interested in it or unless you tell me that they would be available to consider a production beyond their current commitments." Mr. French responded: "No, indeed, I would like to hear what you have in mind." Appellant then said that he thought there would be something uniquely attractive at that time to do a film based on Shakespeare's "Taming of the Shrew" with respondents as the stars of the picture. Mr. French's reaction was "instantaneous and affirmative." Appellant then asked Mr. French if the idea had ever been previously discussed, and Mr. French replied no, that to his knowledge it had not been. Mr. French further stated that he would discuss appellant's idea with Mr. Burton, and would try to arrange a meeting in New York between appellant and the Burtons.

Thereafter, at Mr. French's suggestion and with tickets arranged for by Mr. French, appellant attended the opening of Mr. Burton's stage production of *Hamlet* in New York City on April 9, 1964. At that time, Mr. French introduced appellant to Mr. Burton as "the man who had been talking about *Taming of the Shrew*." Because of Mr. Burton's preoccupation with his stage production, it was not possible at that time for appellant to have a private meeting with the Burtons, so appellant proceeded on to London, where he was engaged in production work on another motion picture.

Upon arriving in London, appellant decided to explore the possibility of using the services of Franco Zeffirelli as the director of *The Taming of the Shrew* motion picture. Accordingly, on May 11, 1964, appellant met with John Van Essen, Mr. Zeffirelli's agent, in London. Appellant related his idea to Mr. Van Essen, and his disclosure thereof to Mr. French. To appellant's inquiry as to the possible availability of Mr. Zeffirelli, Mr. Van Essen replied "that he thought it was just a splendid idea, that he was absolutely certain that his client would agree with his reaction, but that he would telephone him in France and discuss it with him as quickly as he could reach him. . . . " Thereafter, appellant, together with Mr. Van Essen, met with Mr. Zeffirelli in Paris on May 22, 1964. Appellant there related his idea in some detail to Mr. Zeffirelli, and Mr. Zeffirelli's response was: "I can't tell you how much I would like to do it, but why would the Burtons accept me?" Appellant replied " . . . that is my job, to generate their enthusiasm for you . . . [and] I think there is a very good chance of my persuading them to accept you."

On May 25, 1964, appellant, while still in London, telephoned to Mr. French in Los Angeles, suggested the idea of Mr. Zeffirelli acting as director of the proposed motion picture, told of the meeting with Zeffirelli, and suggested that this information be communicated to Mr. and Mrs. Burton. . . .

Upon his return to Los Angeles, appellant met with Martin Gang on June 25, 1964. Mr. Gang at that time was appellant's lawyer. Mr. Gang's firm was also the attorneys for respondents Richard Burton and Elizabeth Taylor Burton. Aaron Frosch, a New York lawyer, acted as general counsel for Mr. and Mrs. Burton. At the meeting between appellant and Mr. Gang, appellant disclosed his above described idea, and related his dealings up to that point with Mr. French. Appellant told Mr. Gang that "Mr. French has so far been unable to arrange a meeting" with Mr. and Mrs. Burton. Mr. Gang offered to attempt to arrange such a meeting. Mr. Gang thereupon phoned Aaron Frosch and informed him of appellant's desire to meet with Mr. and Mrs. Burton and of the reasons for such a meeting. Mr. Frosch stated that he believed that he could arrange such a meeting, suggesting that appellant phone him upon appellant's arrival in New York.

Upon his arrival in New York, appellant phoned Mr. Frosch's secretary on June 29, 1964, and was told to contact Richard Hanley, appointments secretary for Mr. and Mrs. Burton. Appellant did phone Mr. Hanley, who recognized him and stated "It looks fine. Richard and Elizabeth know you are here and we will get it set up as quickly as we can." On the afternoon of June 30, 1964, Mr. Hanley phoned appellant and said: "Can you come up to see them?" Appellant proceeded to Mr. and Mrs. Burton's hotel suite, was introduced to Mr. Burton by Mr. Hanley, and then met for a period alone with Mr. Burton. Later, Mrs. Burton joined them. At the beginning of the conversation between appellant and Mr. Burton regarding *The Taming of the Shrew*, Mr. Burton commented upon what a good idea it was for Mrs. Burton and him to make such a motion picture, adding, "I don't know how come we hadn't thought of it."

After Mrs. Burton joined them, appellant explained in full his ideas regarding the proposed project. This included the use of Mr. Zeffirelli as the director. Mr. Burton said of Zeffirelli "I think he is a marvelous idea. The idea of who directs this picture is naturally very important, and I just think you have made a very good choice. And you have met with him?," to which appellant replied in the affirmative. They then discussed the cost of the film, and of appellant's prior discussion with Mr. Zeffirelli relative to the cost area. Mr. Burton stated "Well, certainly with you as an experienced producer, you can contribute that part of it to him."

There then was a discussion of possible conflicting commitments, and Mr. Burton stated with reference to another project, "Well, look, we are not actually committed to that, and I do believe that could be pushed back anyway. This idea is such a good one and this picture is so important that we do it that I think we should plan on doing it. And we can try to juggle our other productions to fit this." Toward the end of the meeting, Mr. Burton stated, "Well, let's plan to go ahead now. Elizabeth and I would like to do this. We think Zeffirelli is a good idea. We will accept him. You tell me you have worked out a potential deal with him." Appellant had discussed Mr. Zeffirelli's connection with the proposal with Mr. Van Essen. Mr. Burton instructed appellant to work out appropriate arrangements with Aaron Frosch. The meeting ended with a mutual expression of looking forward to working together.

After the above meeting, and before appellant left the United States, he called Martin Gang in California from New York City. In this telephone conversation, he told Mr. Gang "Look, you do whatever you think is right about structuring a deal with Aaron Frosch, and you know I am not going to be difficult about my end of this because this is a very important picture to me and I don't want you to feel that we have got to fight with anybody, whatever might come up, about any fees and my participation and so forth. It's a picture I want very badly to do, and please keep me in touch." Mr. Gang replied, "Congratulations. I will get onto it right away and keep you informed."

Upon appellant's return to London, where he was working on another motion picture, he met with Mr. Van Essen and proceeded further with the negotiation of a deal for the services of Mr. Zeffirelli as director. Appellant reported progress made in these negotiations in a letter dated July 7, 1964, which he sent to Martin Gang.

On August 11, 1964, appellant received a phone call in London from Mickey Rudin, who was then a partner in Mr. Gang's law firm. Mr. Rudin worked in close contact with Mr. Frosch in connection with *The Taming of the Shrew.* Mr. Rudin represented Mr. and Mrs. Burton in connection with *The Taming of the Shrew,* and as far as Mr. Gang knows, has continued to do so even after Mr. Rudin disassociated from the Gang firm. In the phone call of August 11, 1964, appellant asked Mr. Rudin what percentage share of the gross receipts from the motion picture *The Taming of the Shrew* appellant would receive if he were paid no guaranteed fee; what percentage share he would receive if he were paid a guaranteed fee of $50,000, and what percentage share he would receive if he were paid a guaranteed fee of $100,000. Mr. Rudin replied that he would think about it and let appellant know.

About November 27, 1964, appellant "felt that there was nothing to do but wait until the Burtons are in a position to and have an inclination to make a commitment."

On December 30, 1964, appellant met with Mr. Gang and Mr. Rudin in Mr. Gang's office in Los Angeles. At this meeting appellant learned that his position in the project was in jeopardy. At this time both Mr. Rudin and Mr. Gang advised appellant that he had no legal rights in the project, and appellant "simply accepted that."

In March 1965, a meeting was held in Dublin, Ireland, where Mr. Burton was filming another motion picture, attended by Mickey Rudin, among others. The meeting concerned *The Taming of the Shrew* project, including appellant's participation in connection therewith. Following this meeting, Mr. Rudin stopped off in London, en route back to Los Angeles, and on March 18, 1965, phoned appellant. In that phone conversation, Mr. Rudin stated to appellant that "[he] might not be the producer if the picture is ever made." Mr. Rudin further stated, "under any conditions, however, there would be a reward for your contribution to the project." On March 20, 1965, appellant addressed a letter to Messrs. Rudin and Gang in which he said in part: "There's no point rehashing the various elements involved; nor is there any point attempting to 'try the case,' particularly with my own attorney. I realize I must simply accept whatever Aaron Frosch and you agree is proper 'reward' for my contribution. But it's important to me, Mickey, that you understand I can never consider any such payment to be a satisfactory substitute for the function that has been denied me on a project I initiated." In conversations with Mr. Van Essen (face to face) and with Mr. Zeffirelli (via telephone) on March 25, 1965, appellant was advised that the suggestion that appellant not be the producer of the film had come from "the other side" and from "the Burton lawyer." Appellant understood this reference to be directed toward Mr. Aaron Frosch and so advised both Mr. Zeffirelli and Messrs. Gang and Rudin.

Upon Mr. Rudin's return to Los Angeles, he reported events at the Dublin meeting to his then partner, Martin Gang. Mr. Gang wrote to appellant on April 27, 1965, stating that Mr. Rudin had reported to him that "there is no question in anybody's mind that this was your idea, of *Taming of the Shrew* and bringing Zeffirelli in was your idea, and this is so recognized by all the principals, including Mr. Burton and Mr. Zeffirelli."

In December 1965, appellant heard rumors of a "deal" being made for the production of *The Taming of the Shrew* involving the respondents and was informed by Mr. Gang that discussions to this effect were then taking place with Columbia Pictures Corporation. In a letter to Mr. Gang dated January 3, 1965, but, in fact, written and sent on January 3, 1966, appellant suggested the possibility of informing Columbia of his participation in the project, noting that "Burton has acknowledged the obligation involved," and stating, "I should imagine Columbia wouldn't hesitate to acknowledge Burton's (and Zeffirelli's) obligation to me as an obligation of the production—provided it's discussed at the proper time, which is during the negotiations of the entire deal." Mr. Gang's response to this suggestion was to advise appellant against contacting Columbia since by doing so "he might upset the possibility of any deal being made because Columbia wouldn't want to get involved in litigation, and that if he wanted to get any rewards out of it for any reason, without giving any legal opinions, that it would be best not to upset that apple cart." Appellant did not communicate with Columbia.

Thereafter, a motion picture based upon William Shakespeare's play *The Taming of the Shrew* was produced and exhibited commencing in or about March 1967. The motion picture stars respondents Richard Burton and Elizabeth Taylor Burton, and is directed by Franco Zeffirelli. The motion picture was financed and distributed by Columbia Pictures Corporation, although at the time of taking Mr. Gang's deposition (March 26, 1968), the formal contract between Columbia and the respondents remained to be completed. Mr. Rudin has represented Mr. and Mrs. Burton in the negotiations with Columbia. The motion picture as completed utilizes the following ideas disclosed by appellant to respondents: (1) It is based upon the Shakespearean play *The Taming of the Shrew;* (2) it stars Elizabeth Taylor Burton and Richard Burton in the roles of Katherine and Petruchio, respectively; (3) the director is Franco Zeffirelli; (4) it eliminates the "frame," i.e., the play within a play device found in the original Shakespearean play, and begins with the main body of the story; and (5) it includes an enactment of the two key scenes previously referred to by appellant which in Shakespeare's play occur off-stage.

In addition, the film was photographed in Italy, although not in the actual locales in Italy described by Shakespeare.

Respondents have paid no monies to appellant, nor have they accorded him any screen or advertising credit.

Respondents, while not challenging the foregoing statement of facts, except to say that they do not acquiesce in the claimed "characterizations" and "conclusions" contained therein, urge that critical facts have been omitted therefrom. These critical facts, according to respondents, as revealed by the record, are as follows: In connection with appellant's meeting on April 6, 1964, with Hugh French, motion picture agent for respondent Richard Burton, appellant, was, according to his own testimony, familiar with the function of an agent for an established star in the motion picture industry. Appellant was aware of the role usually played by an agent for an established star, which was to screen projects submitted to the star, in turn submitting them to the star for a determination of interest. If there is interest, the agent usually pursues it further on the star's behalf.

Appellant was aware that an agent for a major star cannot commit the star without the star's approval. This is the practice in very close to 100 percent of the cases and in that sense differs from other agencies. The "few cases" in which the star permits his agent to make commitments on his behalf "are very rare."

Appellant testified in his deposition that there is nothing unique about doing Shakespeare on the screen. It has been done many times. It has been done by leading stars of the caliber of Laurence Olivier. Respondent Richard Burton has himself previously appeared in a motion picture made of Shakespeare's *Hamlet.* Shakespearean productions in motion picture form have been made in the United States, with leading stars, and also in England, the Soviet Union and other countries of the World.

Appellant testified that there is nothing unique about the idea of making a motion picture entitled *The Taming of the Shrew,* based on Shakespeare's play of that title. Such has been done in the United States before the making of the film here in issue, and the earlier film featured in its leading roles (Petruchio and Katherine) stars who were then married to each other and who were perhaps the leading idols of the screen at the time, Mary Pickford and Douglas Fairbanks. The Pickford-Fairbanks film *The Taming of the Shrew* was done in the 1930's. The declaration of Norman B. Rudman filed in support of the motion disclosed that the earlier version of the film also (1) eliminated the "frame" (the play within a play device utilized by Shakespeare), and (2) depicted on screen the wedding night scenes which in the Shakespearean original occurs off-stage and are merely described by narration.

Appellant testified in his deposition that there was nothing unique or unusual about doing *The Taming of the Shrew* with two of the leading actors of the time, in the sense that it had been done once before, but "there was something unusual about the particular notion of doing it under other circumstances." There is nothing unique about a stage director of good repute coming directly from the stage to motion pictures and directing a major motion picture. Such has been done often in the past by such directors as Rouben Mamoulian, Josh Logan, Danny Mann, Orson Welles, Elia Kazan, and by Mike Nichols, who directed the film *Who's Afraid of Virginia Woolf,* which starred the respondents in its leading roles, as his first film production.

Appellant testified further in his deposition that there is nothing unique about a non-American director directing English speaking actors in a film. Zeffirelli speaks quite good English, was distinguished for his directorial work in the field of opera and had done many stage productions in different languages in Italy, France and England. Zeffirelli was well known and distinguished as a director of at least one Shakespearean production, *Romeo and Juliet,* prior to his direction of the respondents in *The Taming of the Shrew.*

Appellant testified further, by way of deposition, that he asked Mr. French to communicate with the Burtons to ascertain whether or not they would be interested in doing *The Taming of the Shrew.* Appellant was interested in this from a business point of view so that he might have an interest in the film as a producer. One of appellant's objects was to negotiate a co-production or joint venture agreement with respondents under which he would be engaged as producer of the film under specific terms and conditions, and respondents would be committed to star in the film, their services to begin on a given start date. Appellant's company and respondents or their company would be co-venturers and co-owners of the film. The negotiations did not result in a co-production or joint venture agreement.

Appellant testified further, by way of deposition, that his interest in the possibility of using the services of Franco Zeffirelli as director of the motion picture was based upon Zeffirelli's potential in contributing to the commercial success of the picture to such extent that appellant could point out its commercial potential to a possible distributor whose prime interest would be commercialism. The key elements of the picture, so far as appellant was concerned, besides the play itself, were Mr. and Mrs. Burton to play the leads. In appellant's letter of July 11, 1964, addressed to Mr. Martin Gang, his attorney, he stated that if Mr. Zeffirelli were not available as director of the film, respondent Burton might himself direct the film; the only requirement was that there be a top-flight director.

In appellant's first meeting with John Van Essen, Zeffirelli's agent, which occurred in London on May 11, 1964, he told Van Essen that interest in the project had been expressed by the Burtons' agent, and by the Burtons through their agent, but that nothing had been done beyond that and that appellant had not yet met with the Burtons personally to discuss the subject. Appellant urged Mr. Van Essen to discuss the matter with Zeffirelli, but did not enjoin the former from discussing it with others as such an injunction is implicit in any discussion with an agent. Before meeting the Burtons, appellant had possibly discussed the matter of the picture informally with one David Chasman of United Artists.

When Mr. Gang, at appellant's request, telephoned Aaron Frosch on June 25, 1964, to assist appellant in obtaining an audience with the Burtons, Mr. Frosch had already known about the proposal of the Burtons doing a film *The Taming of the Shrew* because of appellant's approach to Mr. Zeffirelli, who was also a client of Mr. Frosch's office.

Appellant, since the meeting with respondents of June 30, 1964, has not seen them personally nor had any conversations with them. He has no written contract in connection with the proposed project signed by respondents, or either of them, or any agent of the respondents wherein he was promised the position of producer of the film *The Taming of the Shrew. . . .*

The rights of an idea discloser to recover damages from an idea recipient under an express or implied contract to pay for the idea in event the idea recipient uses such idea after disclosure is discussed in *Desny v. Wilder,* 46 Cal.2d 715, 731–739 [299 P. 2d 257]. . . .

It is held that " . . . if a producer obligates himself to pay for the disclosure of an idea, whether it is for protectible or unprotectible material, in return for a disclosure thereof he should be compelled to hold to his promise. There is nothing unreasonable in the assumption that a producer would obligate himself to pay for the disclosure of an idea which he would otherwise be legally free to use, but which in fact, he would be unable to use but for the disclosure.

"The producer and the writer should be free to make any contract they desire to make with reference to the buying of the ideas of the writer; the fact that the producer may later determine, with a little thinking, that he could have had the same ideas and could thereby have saved considerable money for himself, is no defense against the claim of the writer. This is so even though the material to be purchased is abstract and unprotected material." (*Chandler v. Roach,* 156 Calliope.2d 435, 441–442 [319 P. 2d 776].)

An idea which can be the subject matter of a contract need not be novel or concrete. (*Donahue v. Ziv Television Programs, Inc.,* 245 Cal.2d 593, 600 [54 Cal.Rptr. 130]; *Minniear v. Tors,* 266 Cal.2d 495, 502 [72 Cal.Rptr. 287].) . . .

We are of the opinion that appellant's idea of the filming of Shakespeare's play *The Taming of the Shrew* is one which may be protected by contract.

Express or implied contracts both are based upon the intention of the parties and are distinguishable only in the manifestation of assent. . . .

The making of an agreement may be inferred by proof of conduct as well as by proof of the use of words. . . . Whether or not the appellant and respondents here, by their oral declarations and conduct, as shown by the depositions and affidavits, entered into a contract whereby respondents agreed to compensate appellant in the event respondents used appellant's idea, is a question of fact which may not be properly resolved in a summary judgment proceeding, but must be resolved upon a trial of the issue. . . .

Statute of Frauds. Respondents urge that the agreement is barred by the statute of frauds, section 1624 subdivision 1 of the Civil Code.

The application of section 1624 subdivision 1 of the Civil Code to the transaction here under consideration rests upon a triable issue of fact. The trier of fact might conclude that from the negotiations and conduct of the parties and their agents there was an implied contract. That is, the respondents may be found to have made an implied promise of payment, conditioned upon subsequent use, in return for appellant's act of disclosing his idea—not in return for his promise to disclose such idea. This being a unilateral contract (a promise for an act—see Rest., Contracts, §§ 12 and 55), it does not fall within the section of the statute of frauds dealing with contracts not to be performed within one year. (Rest., Contracts, § 198, com. a.) If the trial court should find that appellant disclosed his idea to respondents on the condition that respondents would not use the idea unless they compensated appellant for such use, and respondents accepted the disclosure on that condition, then the compensation would, at respondents' option, take one of two forms: they would engage appellant as producer of the film or pay him the monetary equivalent. Since it appears from the record that appellant has made his disclosure and respondents have elected not to engage him as producer of the film, all that remains to be done is payment by respondents. Where a contract has been fully performed by one party and nothing remains to be done except the payment of money by the other party, the statute of frauds is inapplicable. . . . Furthermore, to fall under the bar of subdivision 1 of section 1624 of the Civil Code, the contract must, by its terms, be impossible of performance within a

year. If it is unlikely that it will be so performed, or the period of performance is indefinite, the statute does not apply. . . .
The judgment is reversed.

NOTE

In the preceding case, it appears that the plaintiff's producer status and his preexisting relationships in the industry were such that his very involvement in a proposed project was assumed to be with a view toward a joint venture or an equivalent relationship. In *Faris v. Enberg*, 97 Cal.3d 309, 158 Cal. Rptr. 704 (Cal. 1979), on the other hand, the developer of an idea for a television sports quiz show appears to have been a novice, without an established industry status. Faris called television station KTLA and left a message with a secretary that he had created a sports television show that would interest Dick Enberg (an up and coming sportscaster). He left his name and number. When Enberg called back, Faris told Enberg that he intended to produce the show and that he wanted to speak with Enberg "about participating in the show as the master of ceremonies." Enberg was interested, and the two met the next day at KTLA. Faris described the show and gave Enberg a copy of the format. Faris told Enberg that the show was his "creation" and "literary property." Faris discussed the possibility of Enberg's serving as master of ceremonies, "or, if he desired, actually participating with me in the production of the show . . . as a part owner thereof. . . . [I]f you will come with me and do the show, you can have a piece of the show. You can own it. You won't have to work for a salary for somebody else." Enberg told Faris he was going to talk the next week with some KTLA producers about a sports show. He asked Faris to leave a copy of the format for further review. Faris did not expressly authorize Enberg to discuss the format with anyone or to give it to anyone else. He stated that had Enberg told Faris that Enberg planned to disclose the format to, or discuss it with, anyone else, or that he had a commitment to another sports quiz show, Faris would not have disclosed his idea or left a copy of the format with Enberg. Thereafter, a quiz show called "Sports Challenge" appeared on television with Enberg as master of ceremonies. "There is absolutely no evidence," the court stated, "that plaintiff expected, or indicated his expectation of receiving compensation for the service of revealing the format to Enberg [and eventually selling it]. To the contrary, the sole evidence is that plaintiff voluntarily submitted it to Enberg for the sole purpose of enabling Enberg to make a determination of his willingness to enter into a future business relationship with plaintiff . . . [Faris] appears at all times to have intended to produce [the show] himself, and sought out Enberg, as a master of ceremonies. He obviously hoped to make his idea more marketable by hiring a gifted sports announcer as his master of ceremonies [and] sought to entice [Enberg] by promises of a 'piece' of the enterprise for his involvement. . . . There is no reason to think that Enberg, or anyone else with whom Enberg spoke, would have believed that Faris' submission was an offer to sell something, which if used would oblige the user to pay . . . Based on the clear holding of *Desny* an obligation to pay could not be inferred from the mere fact of submission on a theory that everyone knows that the idea man expects to be paid. Nor could it be inferred from the comment by Faris that the format was his 'creation' and 'literary property.' In *Desny* the court held that the mere submission of an idea by a writer could not create the obligation. So, necessarily, the converse must also be the case: that knowledge on the part of the recipient that the submitter is a writer possessing his or her unprotected literary creation could not create an obligation to pay. Plaintiff's statements that he would not have revealed the format or idea to Enberg had he known that Enberg was going to show it to anyone else were not germane since he never told this to Enberg. . . . Plaintiff attempted to impose a contract on the facts of this case by asserting that Enberg solicited the submission, returned plaintiff's phone call and asked to keep a copy of the format. We do not agree. Faris solicited Enberg's involvement. It would be entirely inconsistent with *Desny* to hold that an implied-in-fact contract could be created because a telephone call was returned or because a request was made for an opportunity to read the work that was unconditionally submitted. . . . " Nor was there a breach of fiduciary obligation. While "copyright protectability of a literary work is not a necessary element of proof in a cause of action for breach of confidence . . . [i]n order to prevent the unwarranted creation or extension of a monopoly and restraint on progress in art, a confidential relationship will not be created from the mere submission of an idea to another. There must exist evidence of the communication of the confidentiality of the submission or evidence from which a confidential relationship can be inferred. Among the factors from which such an inference can be drawn are: proof of the existence of an implied-in-fact contract (*Davies v. Krasna*, 245 Cal.2d 535 [54 Cal.Rptr. 37]); proof that the material submitted was protected by reason of sufficient novelty and elaboration (*Fink v. Goodson-Todman Enterprises, Ltd.*, 9 Cal.3d 996 [88 Cal.Rptr. 649]); or proof of a particular relationship such as partners, joint adventurers, principal and agent or buyer and seller under certain circumstances. (*Blaustein v. Burton*, 9 Cal.3d 161, 187 [88 Cal.Rptr.319]; *Thompson v. California Brewing Co.*, 150 Cal.2d 469, 475 [310 P.2d 436].) . . . We do not believe that the unsolicited submission of an idea to a potential employee or potential business partner, even if that person then passes the disclosed information to a competitor, presents a triable issue of fact for confidentiality. Here, no rational receiver of the communications from Faris could be bound to an understanding that a secret was being imparted. One could not infer from anything Enberg did or said that he was given the chance to reject disclosure in advance or that he voluntarily received the disclosure with an understanding that it was not to be given to others. To allow the disclosure which took place in this case to result in a confidential relationship, without something more, would greatly expand the creation of monopolies and bear the concomitant danger to the free communication of ideas. Our conclusion that evidence of knowledge of confidence or from which a confidential relationship can be implied is a minimum prerequisite to the protection of freedom in the arts. In the instant case, there was no direct evidence that either party believed that the disclosure was being made in confidence . . . [nor were there] other special facts [present] from which the relationship can be inferred: there was no implied-in-fact contract; the material was not protectible; and they were not yet partners or joint adventurers, and there was no buyer/seller or principal/agent relationship. Plaintiff might argue that he and Enberg were joint adventurers, but such was only Faris' unfulfilled hope. There was no evidence of more than a conversation which might have developed into a relationship later on. . . . "

Murray v. National Broadcasting Company, Inc., 844 F.2d 988 (2d Cir.), *cert. denied*, 488 U.S. 955 (1988)

ALTIMARI, CIRCUIT JUDGE

It was almost a generation ago that a young comedian named Bill Cosby became the first black entertainer to star in a dramatic network television series. That program, I Spy, earned Cosby national recognition as an actor, including three Emmy Awards (1966, 1967 and 1968) for best performance in a dramatic series, and critical acclaim for the portrayal of a character without regard to the actor's race. Although keenly aware of the significance of his achievement in breaking the color line on network television, Cosby set his sights then on "accomplish[ing] something more significant for the Negro on TV." In an interview in 1965, he envisioned a different approach to the situation comedy genre made popular by The Dick Van Dyke Show.

The *Daily News* described Cosby's "dream" series as not unlike other situation comedies. There'll be the usual humorous exchanges between husband and wife. . . . Warmth and domestic cheerfulness will pervade the entire program.

Everything on the screen will be familiar to TV viewers. But this series will be radically different. Everyone in it will be a Negro.

. . . "I'm interested in proving there's no difference between people," [explained Cosby]. "My series would take place in a middle-income Negro neighborhood. People who really don't know Negroes would find on this show that they're just like everyone else."

Nearly twenty years later, on September 20, 1984, Cosby's dream for a "color-blind" family series materialized with the premier of The Cosby Show—a situation comedy about a family known as the Huxtables. Bill Cosby stars in the leading role as Heathcliff ("Cliff") Huxtable together with his TV wife Clair and their five children.

Plaintiff-appellant Hwesu Murray, an employee of defendant-appellee ("NBC"), claims in the instant case that in 1980, four years prior to the premier of The Cosby Show on NBC's television network, he proposed to NBC a "new" idea for a half-hour situation comedy starring Bill Cosby. In a written proposal submitted to NBC, Murray described his series called Father's Day as "wholesome . . . entertainment" which will focus upon the family life of a Black American family. . . . The leading character will be the father, . . . a devoted family man and a compassionate, proud, authority figure. . . .

. . . The program may well resemble Father Knows Best and The Dick Van Dyke Show. It will be radically different from The Jeffersons, Good Times, Different Strokes, and That's My Mama. The father will not be a buffoon, a supermasculine menial, or a phantom. The program will show how a Black father can respond with love . . . , and will present . . . a closely-knit family. . . .

On this appeal from an order . . . granting defendants-appellees' motion for summary judgment, we are asked to determine whether, under New York law, plaintiff has a legally protectible interest in his idea which he maintains was used by NBC in developing The Cosby Show. Because we agree with the district court's conclusion that, under New York law, lack of novelty in an idea precludes plaintiff from maintaining a cause of action to prevent its unauthorized use, we affirm the district court's order granting summary judgment and dismissing the complaint.

BACKGROUND

Plaintiff Hwesu S. Murray has been employed in the television industry for the past ten years. Murray holds a Bachelor of Arts degree in English and graduate degrees in broadcast journalism and law. In 1979, defendant-appellee NBC hired Murray as a Unit Manager and financial analyst in its sports division. A year later, plaintiff contacted an NBC official outside of NBC Sports about some "extracurricular" ideas he had for future television programs, and the official apparently instructed him to submit his proposals in writing. Soon thereafter, in June 1980, plaintiff submitted five written proposals, one of which was entitled "Father's Day." Murray allegedly informed NBC that if it were interested in any of the proposals, he expected to be named executive producer and to receive appropriate credit and compensation as the creator of the eventual program. Plaintiff also allegedly told NBC that his ideas were being submitted in confidence.

Murray's proposal for "Father's Day" is the subject matter of this action. The NBC official who originally had requested it encouraged Murray to "flesh out" his proposal and submit it to Josh Kane, then an NBC vice-president and a top official with NBC Entertainment, the division of NBC responsible for network television programming. Plaintiff thereupon submitted to Kane an expanded proposal for Father's Day. In a two-page memorandum dated November 1, 1980, Murray first suggested that Bill Cosby play the part of the father. At that time, plaintiff also made several other casting suggestions, including roles for a working spouse and five children, and again indicated that the proposed series would "combine humor with serious situations in a manner similar to that of the old Dick Van Dyke Show" but "with a Black perspective." Murray's expanded proposal concluded with the observation that, "[l]ike Roots, the show will attempt to depict life in a [closely-knit] Black family, with the addition of a contemporary, urban setting."

NBC apparently decided not to pursue Murray's proposal. On November 21, 1980, Kane returned the Father's Day submission to plaintiff and informed him that "we are not interested in pursuing [its] development at this time."

Four years later, in the fall of 1984, The Cosby Show premiered on NBC. The Cosby Show is a half-hour weekly situation comedy series about everyday life in an upper middle-class black family in New York City. The father, played by Bill Cosby, is a physician, and the mother is a lawyer. In its first season, The Cosby Show soared to the top of the Nielsen ratings and has become one of the most popular programs in television history. The show is highly regarded by critics and is also a huge commercial success.

Less than a month after viewing the premiere, plaintiff wrote to NBC to advise it that The Cosby Show had been derived from his idea for Father's Day. In January 1985, NBC responded through its Law Department, stating its position that " 'Father's Day' played absolutely no role in the development of 'The Cosby Show' . . . [since m]uch of the substance and style of 'The Cosby Show' is an outgrowth of the humor and style developed by Bill Cosby throughout his career." NBC further maintained that The Cosby Show was developed and produced by The Carsey-Werner Company ("Carsey-Werner"), an independent production company and the executive producers of the series.

In his complaint, plaintiff claimed that The Cosby Show's portrayal of a strong black family in a nonstereotypical manner is the essence of Father's Day, and "[i]t is that portrayal of Black middle-class life that originated with plaintiff." Murray also alleged that Josh Kane showed plaintiff's Father's Day proposal to his superiors at NBC, including defendant-appellee Brandon Tartikoff, President of NBC Entertainment. Tartikoff, together with Cosby and Carsey-Werner, have been credited with the creation and development of The Cosby Show. Plaintiff maintains that NBC and Tartikoff deliberately deceived plaintiff into believing that NBC had no interest in "Father's Day" and then proceeded to develop and eventually produce plaintiff's idea as The Cosby Show.

Plaintiff's complaint stated a number of causes of action arising out of defendants' alleged appropriation of his idea. Among those relevant to this appeal are . . . various state law claims, including . . . breach of implied contract. . . . Plaintiff sought, inter alia, damages and declaratory and injunctive relief as the "sole owner of all rights in and to the idea, proposal and property [known as] 'Father's Day.' "

In a decision dated July 15, 1987, 671 F.Supp. 236 (SDNY), the district court considered whether plaintiff's idea was "property" that could be subject to legal protection. Since the parties agreed that New York law applied to plaintiff's claims, the district court proceeded to analyze defendants' motion for summary judgment in light of the New York Court of Appeals decision in *Downey v. General Foods Corp.*, 31 N.Y.2d 56, 334 N.Y.S.2d 874, 286 N.E.2d 257 (1972). In *Downey*, the New York court established the general proposition that "[l]ack of novelty in an idea is fatal to any cause of action for its unlawful use." The district court, therefore, determined that the "sole issue" before it was the novelty of plaintiff's Father's Day proposal, and accordingly assumed, for purposes of defendants' motion, that defendants in fact used plaintiff's idea in the development of The Cosby Show.

In focusing on the novelty of plaintiff's proposal, the district court determined that Murray's idea was not subject to legal protection from unauthorized use because Father's Day merely combined two ideas which had been circulating in the industry for a number of years—namely, the family situation comedy, which was a standard formula, and the casting of black actors in nonstereotypical roles. The district court found that, to the extent Father's Day, in Murray's words, "may well resemble 'Father Knows Best' and 'The Dick Van Dyke Show,'" it could not be considered novel. In addition, the portrayal of a black family in nonstereotypical roles, according to the court, precluded a finding of novelty because 1) the television networks already had cast some black actors, including Bill Cosby himself, e.g., I Spy (1965–68), The Bill Cosby Show (1969–71), and Fat Albert and the Cosby Kids (1972–79), in such roles, and 2) the idea of combining the family situation comedy theme with an all-black cast already had been suggested publicly by Bill Cosby some twenty years before the creation of The Cosby Show. The district court also determined that Murray's casting of Bill Cosby in the lead role in Father's Day was no mere coincidence. Rather, it was "further evidence that Cosby is connected—even in plaintiff's mind—with the concept that plaintiff seeks to monopolize."

In view of the foregoing, the district court granted defendants' motion for summary judgment and dismissed the various claims presented in the complaint, concluding that the lack of novelty in plaintiff's proposal was fatal to any cause of action for unauthorized use of that idea.

DISCUSSION

. . . As the district court recognized, the dispositive issue in this case is whether plaintiff's idea is entitled to legal protection. Plaintiff points to "unique"—"even revolutionary"—aspects of his Father's Day proposal that he claims demonstrate "genuine novelty and invention," which preclude the entry of summary judgment against him. Specifically, plaintiff contends that his idea suggesting the nonstereotypical portrayal of black Americans on television is legally protectible because it represents a real breakthrough. As he stated in his affidavit in opposition to defendants' motion,

[w]hen I created "Father's Day," I had in mind . . . a show that . . . would portray a Black family as it had never been shown before on television. . . . I also . . . desire[d] to produce a show with strong and positive role models for the Black community, and to make a statement regarding the love and integrity of the Black family to the world. I think every Black person in this country knows there has been a need for this, and that never before on television had there been a portrayal of a Black family as I created it for "Father's Day."

Murray claims that the novelty of his idea subsequently was confirmed by the media and the viewing public which instantly recognized the "unique" and "revolutionary" portrayal of a black family on The Cosby Show.

We certainly do not dispute the fact that the portrayal of a non-stereotypical black family on television was indeed a breakthrough. Nevertheless, that breakthrough represents the achievement of what many black Americans, including Bill Cosby and plaintiff himself, have recognized for many years—namely, the need for a more positive, fair and realistic portrayal of blacks on television. While NBC's decision to broadcast The Cosby Show unquestionably was innovative in the sense that an intact, nonstereotypical black family had never been portrayed on television before, the mere fact that such a decision had not been made before does not necessarily mean that the idea for the program is itself novel.

Consequently, we do not agree with appellant's contention that the non-stereotypical portrayal of a black middle-class family in a situation comedy is novel because

[t]o argue otherwise would be the equivalent of arguing that since there had always been baseball, and blacks in baseball, there was nothing new about Jackie Robinson playing in the major leagues—or that since there had always been schools in Little Rock, Arkansas, and blacks in schools, there was nothing new about integrating schools in Little Rock.

As appellees persuasively point out in response to this analogy, Murray has "confuse[d] the 'idea' with its execution. . . . Indeed, the idea of integration . . . had been discussed for decades prior to the actual events taking place." Similarly, we believe, as a matter of law, that plaintiff's idea embodied in his Father's Day proposal was not novel because it merely represented an "adaptation of existing knowledge" and of "known ingredients" and therefore lacked "genuine novelty and invention."

We recognize of course that even novel and original ideas to a greater or lesser extent combine elements that are themselves not novel. Originality does not exist in a vacuum. Nevertheless, where, as here, an idea consists in essence of nothing more than a variation on a basic theme—in this case, the family situation comedy—novelty cannot be found to exist. The addition to this basic theme of the portrayal of blacks in nonstereo-typical roles does not alter our conclusion, especially in view of the fact that Bill Cosby previously had expressed a desire to do a situation comedy about a black family and that, as the district court found, Cosby's entire career has been a reflection of the positive portrayal of blacks and the black family on television.

Appellant would have us believe that by interpreting New York law as we do, we are in effect condoning the theft of ideas. On the contrary, ideas that reflect "genuine novelty and invention" are fully protected against unauthorized use. But those ideas that are not novel "are in the public domain and may freely be used by anyone with impunity." Since such non-novel ideas are not protectible as property, they cannot be stolen.

In assessing whether an idea is in the public domain, the central issue is the uniqueness of the creation. Murray insists that there is at least a question of fact as to the novelty of Father's Day because The Cosby Show is indisputably unique. In support of this contention, plaintiff points to the fact that NBC contracted with Carsey-Werner for the right of NBC to broadcast The Cosby Show. The contract apparently was executed by the parties before there had been any written development of the proposed series. The "program idea" for The Cosby Show, however, was described in the contract as "unique, intellectual property." According to plaintiff, the inescapable conclusion is that the idea—whether it be Father's Day or The Cosby Show—could not possibly have been in the public domain if NBC expressly contracted to purchase it from Carsey-Werner.

We disagree. The Carsey-Werner contract contemplates a fully-produced television series. The contract refers to, inter alia, the program format, titles, set designs, theme music, stories, scripts, and art work as well as to the "program idea." Taken together, these elements no doubt would be considered original and therefore protectible as property. On the other hand, we think it equally apparent that the mere idea for a situation comedy about a nonstereotypical black family—whether that idea is in the hands of Murray, Carsey-Werner, NBC, or anyone else—is not novel and thus may be used with impunity.

Finally, as an alternative attack on the propriety of the district court's order granting summary judgment, plaintiff posits that even if his idea was not novel as a matter of law, summary judgment still was inappropriate because his proposal was solicited by defendants and submitted to them in confidence. In this regard, Murray relies on *Cole v. Phillips H. Lord, Inc.*, 262 A.D. 116, 28 N.Y.S.2d 404 (1st Dep't 1941). Murray contends that Cole stands for the proposition that when an idea is protected by an agreement or a confidential relationship, a cause of action arises for unauthorized use of that idea irrespective of the novelty of the subject matter of the contract. Plaintiff's reliance on Cole is misplaced in light of subsequent cases, particularly the New York Court of Appeals decision in *Downey v. General Foods Corp.*, 31 N.Y.2d 56, 334 N.Y.S.2d 874, 286 N.E.2d 257 (1972). See also *Ferber v. Sterndent Corp.*, 51 N.Y.2d 782, 433 N.Y.S.2d 85, 86, 412 N.E.2d 1311 (1980) ("[a]bsent a showing of novelty, plaintiff's action to recover damages for illegal use of 'confidentially disclosed ideas' must fail as a matter of law"); *Educational Sales Programs*, 317 N.Y.S.2d at 844 ("[o]ne cannot be forever barred from using a worthwhile but unoriginal idea merely because it was once asked to be treated in confidence").

Consequently, we find that New York law requires that an idea be original or novel in order for it to be protected as property. Since, as has already been shown, plaintiff's proposal for Father's Day was lacking in novelty and originality, we conclude that the district court correctly granted defendants' motion for summary judgment. . . .

CONCLUSION

Our review of New York intellectual property law leads us to the inescapable conclusion that the district court did not err in deciding that there was no material issue of fact as to the novelty of plaintiff's proposal. In our judgment, the basic premise underlying the concept of novelty under New York law is that special protection is afforded only to truly innovative ideas while allowing the free use of ideas that are "merely clever or useful adaptation[s] of existing knowledge." In this case, the record indicates that plaintiff's idea for a situation comedy featuring the nonstereotypical portrayal of a black family simply was not uniquely plaintiff's creation. Accordingly, we affirm the district court's order granting summary judgment and dismissing the complaint.

Affirmed.

PRATT, CIRCUIT JUDGE (DISSENTING)

Today this court holds that the idea underlying what may well be the most successful situation comedy in television history was, in 1980, so unoriginal and so entrenched in the public domain that, as a matter of law, it did not constitute intellectual property protected under New York law. Because I am convinced that the novelty issue in this case presents a factual question subject to further discovery and ultimate scrutiny by a trier of fact, I respectfully dissent.

At least for purposes of this appeal, it is given that Murray presented NBC with an idea for a television series; that, after showing interest in Murray's initial idea, NBC then asked him to submit a more detailed proposal; and that NBC then actually used his proposal in developing The Cosby Show, but at the same time refused to provide any compensation to Murray. The only question on appeal is whether there is evidence to indicate that Murray's idea possessed the novelty and originality required under New York law. . . .

I agree with the majority that there is some evidence that Murray's idea was not novel. But clearly, there is also evidence indicating novelty. Initially, there is the admission by NBC, in its agreement with Carsey-Warner, that the television series is "unique, intellectual property." Although NBC argues, and the majority agrees, that this clause refers to a "fully-produced television series," and not Murray's program idea, such analysis ignored two important facts.

First, the "unique, intellectual property" language is found in the remedies section of the development agreement. This section gives NBC the right to prevent the loss of its "unique, intellectual property" should Carsey-Werner fail to perform. However, if Carsey-Werner does not perform—that is, if it subsequently refuses to develop the television series—the only "unique, intellectual property" to be protected is the program's underlying idea. In other words, from the outset NBC wanted to make certain that if its relationship with Carsey-Werner faltered, the novel idea it had given Carsey-Werner would be protected from disclosure. And because, for purposes of this appeal, we must assume that NBC got its idea from Murray, the Carsey-Werner development agreement, at a minimum, constitutes admissible evidence that Murray's idea was unique, thus making the novelty determination a question of fact.

That the "unique, intellectual property" mentioned in the agreement refers to Murray's basic idea underlying the series rather than a fully-produced series, also finds support in the second fact the majority ignores. The definition section of the development agreement specifically defines this "property," not, as the majority contends, as "titles, set designs, theme music, stories, scripts, and art work"—indeed, these are separately defined in the agreement as the "elements" to be developed by Carsey-Werner—but rather, the development agreement defines the actual "property" exclusively to be the "story, literary property, program idea, and/or program format which form(s) the basis" for the television series. This provision provides additional evidence that it was Murray's underlying idea, not the developed elements of the series as a whole, which NBC desired to protect as unique and novel property.

Nor is the agreement the only piece of evidence indicating an issue of fact as to novelty. In 1985, NBC admitted that Murray had "rights" in his idea, but determined it had no interest in acquiring those rights. At trial, both Cosby and Tartikoff stated that they believed The Cosby Show to be novel and unique. NBC admitted that the reason it formally returned rejected submissions, as it did in Murray's case, was that the "material belong[ed] to the submitter." In short, there is substantial evidence, both within and independent of the Carsey-Werner development agreement, which directly conflicts with the majority's holding that, as a matter of law, Murray's idea was not novel.

The fact that the basic idea had been expressed by Cosby some fifteen years before Murray submitted his proposal to NBC does not erase these factual issues. To say, as a matter of law, that an idea is not novel because it already exists in general form, would be to deny governmental protection to any idea previously mentioned anywhere, at anytime, by anyone. I do not believe New York law defines "novelty" so strictly, especially in the area of mass communications, an area long recognized by state courts as "a specialized field having customs and usages of its own" where "a property right exists" in "a combination of ideas evolved into a programs." Indeed, in a market the very existence of which depends on the generation and development of ideas, it may be impossible to formulate a concept that has not previously been expressed by someone, somewhere.

Novelty, by its very definition, is highly subjective. As fashion, advertising, and television and radio production can attest, what is novel today may not have been novel 15 years ago, and what is commonplace today may well be novel 15 years hence. In this instance, where Cosby expressed the concept almost a decade and a half before Murray submitted his proposal, where it was Murray's idea that NBC actually used, where there is no evidence indicating NBC knew anything of the program idea until Murray submitted it, and where substantial conflicting evidence exists as to the "novelty" of the idea under New York law, there seems to be at least a triable issue.

The majority's decision prematurely denies Murray a fair opportunity to establish his right to participate in the enormous wealth generated by The Cosby Show. Accordingly, I would reverse the district court judgment and remand the case for further consideration.

NOTE _____

As we have seen in the *Nadel* decision (see 3.5.1.2.1, note 3, above), novelty to the defendant can be the basis for a claim in this area. However, as underscored by the unreported decision of the Second Circuit in *Khreativity Inc. v. Mattel, Inc.*, 2000 WL 1843223 (2d Cir. 2000), liability will not lie where "the idea was simply an insignificant variation on ideas already known to" the defendant.

3.5.2 Negotiated Acquisitions

The preceding sections of this chapter have covered the many legal principles that must be considered in deciding *whether* certain rights must be acquired, or instead may be used without permission. While this is a very important part of the lawyer's job—and is the part that requires lawyers to make greatest use of "the law"—it is not the only thing that lawyers do. When legal analysis leads to the conclusion that rights should be acquired, the "transactional" phase of entertainment law begins. In this phase, the terms or "deal points" of the acquisition are negotiated, and if an agreement on the deal points is reached, the agreement is reduced to a writing (or should be).

Most of the time, the parties to entertainment industry agreements have a common understanding of what their agreements permit and require; and most of the time, they govern themselves accordingly. Voluntary compliance with agreements is never newsworthy, and by definition does not result in litigation.

On occasion, however, disagreements do arise. Sometimes, the parties disagree about the meaning of certain provisions of their contract. Other times, one party argues that it did not agree to convey more than may be conveyed as a matter of law, and therefore the other party did not actually acquire it. Examples of both types of cases follow.

3.5.2.1 The Scope of Acquired Rights: By Contract

When, as is often the case, rights are acquired by written agreement, the scope of the rights acquired is fixed by the language of that agreement. Should disputes arise, they are simply disputes concerning the meaning of that agreement consistent with the intent of the parties; and such disputes are resolved in entertainment industry cases using the same techniques of contract interpretation that are used in cases arising in all other industries.

The cases in this subsection of the book are a representative sampling (chosen from among dozens that are available) of decisions that interpret rights acquisition agreements. Certain general principles are applied by judges in interpreting agreements (e.g., give effect to the plain meaning of the agreement's words, and give effect to the parties' intentions). Nonetheless, contract interpretation cases are fact-specific; they turn, in other words, on the specific language of the agreements at issue and on the circumstances that existed when they were negotiated. Therefore, the following cases are not included because they contain a "rule of law." Instead, they are included because they illustrate why, as a factual matter, disputes arose.

Such disputes typically arise with the advent of new technologies. When the home video industry was born, the question that arose was whether grants of "television rights" included the right to release videocassettes. *Cohen v. Paramount Pictures Corp.*, 845 F.2d 851 (9th Cir. 1988), caused major shock waves to rumble through Hollywood when the court determined that a grant of rights "to record [a song] in any manner, medium, form or language" and to exhibit the film in which the song had been recorded "by means of television" was not broad enough to permit the studio to manufacture and distribute videocassettes. Subsequently, two other circuit court decisions addressed the same issue. In *Rey v. Lafferty,* the First Circuit reached the same conclusion as had the Ninth Circuit in Cohen; but in *Bloom v. Hearst Entertainment,*

Inc. (noted below) the Fifth Circuit reached the opposite conclusion, based on similar contract language.

While reading all of these cases, think about whether other language could have been used in drafting the agreements to make the intentions of the parties clearer than these agreements did.

Landon v. Twentieth Century-Fox Film Corp., 384 F. Supp. 450 (S.D.N.Y. 1974)

LASKER, J.

In 1944 Margaret Landon entered into an agreement with Twentieth Century-Fox Film Corporation (Fox) to sell, among other things, "motion picture rights" to her book entitled *Anna and the King of Siam.* In 1972 Fox produced 13 films which were broadcast on the CBS Television network as a weekly serial entitled "Anna and the King."

This suit presents the question whether the 1944 agreement between Landon and Fox authorized Fox to produce and exhibit the 1972 series through defendant CBS. In addition to her assertion that the series infringed her copyright in the literary property *Anna and the King of Siam,* Landon raises the novel claim that the 1944 agreement constituted a tying arrangement in violation of Section 1 of the Sherman Act, 15 U.S.C. § 1, on the grounds that Fox allegedly acquired the original copyright "on condition that" it also acquire the copyright renewal rights. She also argues that the assignment of the renewal copyright is unenforceable for lack of consideration. Landon's final claim is that production and exhibition of the television series constituted tortious misconduct on the part of defendants, that is, defamation, invasion of her right of privacy, misappropriation of literary property and wrongful attribution to Landon of credit for the series, which she claims to have "mutilated" her literary property. . . .

The heart of Landon's contention that the series infringed her copyright is that the granting language of the 1944 agreement gave Fox the right to produce only motion pictures of feature length intended for first exhibition in movie theaters, and not those intended for first exhibition on television. The grant clauses of the agreement provide, in relevant part:

FIRST: The Owner does hereby grant, convey and assign unto the Purchaser, its successors and assigns forever:

(a) The sole and exclusive motion picture rights and motion picture copyright throughout the world in and to said literary property. . . .

(b) The sole and exclusive right to make, produce, adapt, sell, lease, rent, exhibit, perform and generally deal in and with the copyright motion picture versions of said literary property, with or without sound accompaniment and with or without the interpolation of musical numbers therein, and for such purposes to adapt one or more versions of said literary property, to add to and subtract from the literary property, change the sequence thereof, change the title of said literary property, use said title, or any of its components, in connection with works or motion pictures wholly or partially independent of said literary property, change the characters in said literary property, change the descriptions of the said characters, and use all thereof in new versions, adaptations and sequels in any and all languages, and to register and obtain copyright therein, throughout the world. . . .

(c) The sole and exclusive right to broadcast by means of the method generally known and described as television, or any process analogous thereto, any of the motion picture versions of said literary property produced pursuant hereto. The Owner specifically reserves to herself the right to broadcast the literary property by television direct from living actors; provided, however, that the Owner agrees that, for a period from the date hereof until eight (8) years after the date of general release of the first motion picture produced by the Purchaser based upon the literary property, or until ten (10) years after the date hereof, whichever period first expires, she will not exercise or grant the right to broadcast the literary property, or any part thereof, by television, or by any other device now known or hereafter to be devised by which the literary property may be reproduced visually and audibly for an audience not present at a performance thereof and with living actors speaking the roles thereof. The Owner grants to the Purchaser the exclusive option to license, lease and/or purchase said reserve rights to broadcast the literary property by television from living actors, or otherwise, at the same price and upon such bona fide terms as may be offered to the Owner by any responsible prospective buyer and which shall be acceptable to the Owner.

(d) The right to broadcast by means of radio processes, portions of said literary property, or the motion picture version or versions thereof, in conjunction with or exploitation of or as an advertising medium or tie-up with the production, exhibition and/or distribution of any motion picture based on said literary property, provided that, in exercising said radio broadcasting rights, Purchaser shall not broadcast serially an entire photoplay produced hereunder. Except as herein stated, the Owner agrees that she will not permit the said literary property or any part thereof to be broadcast by any method or means until two years after the general distribution date of the first motion picture made by the Purchaser based upon the said literary property, or four years after the date hereof, whichever period first expires. This restriction on broadcasting, however, shall not in any way affect or restrict the rights on television herein granted.

(e) The right to publish, copyright or cause to be published and copyrighted in any and all languages, in any and all countries of the world, in any form or media (including, but not limited to, press books, press notices, trade journals, periodicals, newspapers, heralds, fan magazines and/or small separate booklets) synopses revised and/or abridged versions of said literary property, not exceeding 7,500 words each, adapted from the said literary property or from any motion picture and/or television version thereof, with or without sound accompaniment, produced, performed, released or exhibited pursuant hereto.

It is evident that the grant clauses are broadly drafted and do not contain or suggest the purported distinction between motion pictures made for first exhibition on television and those made for theater presentation. Clause (c) expressly grants to Fox the sole right to "make" and "generally deal in" an apparently unlimited number of "motion picture versions" of the property. It confers the right to use and modify the plot, characters and title in "new versions, adaptations, and sequels," again without apparent limit on the number of such versions. Clause (f) cedes the "exclusive" right to broadcast on television "any of the motion picture versions" of the property produced pursuant to the agreement.

The broad construction of the phrase "motion picture versions" to include the 1972 series is confirmed by related provisions of the agreement. These indicate that when the parties sought to reserve to Landon certain rights, they did so carefully and specifically. Such reservations are themselves strong evidence that if Landon had intended to reserve the right to make and exhibit filmed television versions of the property, she and her noted and experienced literary agents, the William Morris Agency, knew how to do so. For example, Clause (g) gives Fox the right to broadcast by radio portions of the property for advertising or promotional purposes, but by express language states that Fox "shall not broadcast serially an entire photoplay. . . . " Significantly the provision states that "[t]his restriction on broadcasting . . . shall not in any way affect or restrict the rights on television herein granted." Clause (f), the television clause, specifically reserves to Landon the right to "broadcast the literary property by television direct from living actors," but contains a covenant providing that she shall not exercise even that limited right for a period of years. In view of this covenant obviously drafted to protect Fox from Landon's competition with Fox's own films, it is far-fetched to believe that the parties so carefully restricted Landon's right to exhibit live television performances only to leave her completely free to show an unlimited number of filmed television versions of the property. . . .

We conclude that the only reasonable construction of the 1944 agreement is that Fox was granted the right to make an unlimited number of motion picture versions of the property, without limitation as to length, or place of first exhibition. This conclusion is consistent with the law in this Circuit as to the interpretation of copyright grants. *Bartsch v. Metro-Goldwyn-Mayer, Inc.*, 391 F.2d 150 (2d Cir.), *cert. denied*, 393 U.S. 826, 89 S.Ct. 86, 21 L.Ed.2d 96 (1968) is precisely in point. There the copyright owners of a musical play assigned to Bartsch in 1930 the "motion picture rights" in the play together with the right to "copyright, vend, license and exhibit" motion picture photoplays throughout the world. There was no television clause in the assignment. Later in 1930, Bartsch assigned his rights to Warner Brothers, which in turn transferred its rights to MGM. MGM produced and distributed a feature-length motion picture based on the musical play in 1935. In 1958 MGM licensed the picture for exhibition on television and Bartsch's widow, to whom his copyright interest had devolved, sued to enjoin the broadcast. The issue was comparable to ours: whether, under the terms of original grant by the copyright authors to Bartsch in 1930 (and then from Bartsch to Warner), the right to "copyright, vend, license and exhibit . . . motion picture photoplays" included the right to license a broadcaster to exhibit the picture on television without a further express grant by the copyright owner (Bartsch). In deciding that the grant did include such a right, Judge Friendly emphasized that Bartsch's assignment to Warner was "well designed to give [Warner] the broadest rights" with respect to the right to produce motion pictures, and noted that " '[e]xhibit' means to 'display' or to 'show' *by any method,* and nothing in the rest of the grant sufficiently reveals a contrary intention." 391 F.2d at 154 (emphasis added). The court stated the rule which controls the present case:

As between an approach that "a license of rights in a given medium (e.g., 'motion picture rights') includes only such uses as fall within the unambiguous core meaning of the term (e.g., exhibition of motion picture film in motion picture theaters) and exclude any uses which lie within the ambiguous penumbra (e.g., exhibition of motion picture film on television)" and another whereby "the licensee may properly pursue any uses which may reasonably be said to fall within the medium as described in the license," [Professor Nimmer] prefers the latter. So do we. . . . If the words are broad enough to cover the new use, it seems fair that the burden of framing and negotiating an exception should fall on the grantor; if Bartsch or his assignors had desired to limit "exhibition" of the motion picture to the conventional method where light is carried from a projector to a screen directly beheld by the viewer they could have said so. 391 F.2d at 155.

There was no question in *Bartsch* that the parties were aware of the possibilities of television even in 1930. In the present case, involving a 1944 agreement, there is, of course, no question on that score either: the Landon contract is sprinkled with references to television and one does not have to roam far into the penumbral meanings of "motion picture versions" to conclude that the term was intended by the parties to embrace rather than exclude the right to produce a television series. Indeed, Clause (h) of the agreement, (to which, curiously, the parties pay only passing attention) expressly refers to "any motion picture and/or television version . . . produced, performed, released or *exhibited pursuant hereto.*" (emphasis supplied) *Goodis v. United Artists Television, Inc.,* 425 F.2d 397 (2d Cir. 1970) also supports our conclusion that the 1944 agreement authorized the 1972 television series. . . .

Significantly, the right to make "sequels," critically absent in *Goodis,* is explicitly expressed in the language before us. Clause (c) of the agreement recites the usual "additions" and "alterations" provisions in regard to adapting the property to the film medium and then grants the "sole and exclusive right" to use the property in "new versions, adaptations and sequels . . . and to register and obtain copyright therein, throughout the world." Such broad language, particularly when read in combination with the grant in Clause (f) of the "sole and exclusive right" to broadcast on television "any of the motion picture versions" which the contract gives Fox the "sole and exclusive" right to make (Clause (c)), leads inescapably to the conclusion that Fox is entitled to summary judgment on the infringement claim.

We have carefully considered Landon's argument that, at the least, the presence of genuine issues as to material facts precludes the grant of summary judgment to Fox. Apart from the fact that such an assertion is undercut by her own motion for similar relief, the argument is without merit. Landon contends first that Fox's contracting practices as reflected in a number of other agreements drafted during the 1940's demonstrate that Fox often and explicitly contracted for the right to produce "television versions," and that its failure to do so here is probative of its intent as to the 1944 agreement. The contention is effectively rebutted by the undisputed facts that (1) Fox maintained both East coast and West coast legal departments, each with its own drafting style, and (2) Landon's contract was drafted in the office which, as a matter of consistent practice, did not use the magic words "television versions" to acquire the rights in issue here, relying instead on general language to achieve the same result. In any event, contracts made between Fox and other copyright owners have little probative value as to what Fox and Landon intended in their particular agreement. . . .

Landon also contends that "motion picture versions" is a term of art whose meaning can be established only by extrinsic "technical evidence." It is, of course, a familiar principle that where the terms of a contract are ambiguous, such evidence may be introduced, not to vary the meaning of a contract but to establish the intent of the parties. But in the context here, the terms of the contract are not ambiguous and do not raise a triable issue of fact. . . .

Plaintiff also argues that it was not her intention to grant to Fox the right to make television versions of the property. She takes the position that her intentions in 1944 present an issue of disputed fact requiring a trial on the merits. The argument is wide of the mark for two reasons. First, it is axiomatic that evidence of plaintiff's intent is admissible only insofar as it was expressed to Fox. Her affidavit is silent on the question whether she ever expressed to Fox in 1944 the construction of the agreement she presses on the present motions, and it is undisputed that she had very little, if any direct contact with Fox at all. Albert B. Taylor, an executive with William Morris Agency (plaintiff's literary agents) with some familiarity with the negotiation of the 1944 agreement, does not state that he, or any other employee of the Agency communicated Landon's understanding of the agreement to Fox. More to the point, the opposing affidavit of Helen Strauss, who was personally responsible for plaintiff's account and for negotiation on Landon's behalf of the Fox agreement, states that in 1944 Strauss understood the agreement to convey to Fox all film rights, including television rights, while reserving to Landon "dramatic rights," including the right to televise a "live" dramatic rendition of the property.

In sum, there is no genuine issue as to any material fact and defendants are entitled to summary judgment as to the infringement claim. . . .

The second count of the complaint alleges as an unlawful tying arrangement Fox's requirement that it acquire the renewal copyright as a condition to its purchase of the original copyright. As plaintiff concedes, there is no reported case recognizing such a cause of action. Assuming, without deciding, that such an arrangement may violate the anti-trust laws, the particular claim asserted here is fatally deficient. As the Second Circuit has recently stated, the exercise of actual coercion by the defendant (as distinguished from the mere presence of market power) is a necessary element of an unlawful tying arrangement. See *Capital Temporaries, Inc. of Hartford v. The Olsten Corporation*, 506 F.2d 658 (2d Cir. 1974). . . . As we read *Capital Temporaries*, to state a valid claim plaintiff would have to allege that (1) she wished to sell only the original copyright at the time she signed the 1944 agreement, (2) expressed that fact to Fox, and (3) that sale of the renewal copyrights was forced upon her by virtue of the superior economic strength or market dominance of Fox. However, neither the complaint nor any supporting affidavit suggest the presence of these elements. Indeed, the contrary appears: Landon testified at her deposition (at p. 266) in connection with the question of copyright renewals that she did not have any discussion "at all" on that subject at the time the agreement was negotiated. Neither her own affidavit on the present motion nor those of her literary agents refer to any such discussions or any proposed modification of the draft agreement in connection with renewals.

As to Fox's market dominance, the record indicates that Landon's agents offered the literary property to various theater companies and film companies but that Fox was the "only film company to make an offer, despite efforts on my part to secure offers from other film companies." (Opposing Affidavit of Helen Strauss, at Paragraph 5.) Although Fox, as the only interested buyer may have been in a position to drive a hard bargain with Landon, the exercise of such power is not the kind of conduct proscribed by the antitrust laws, and indeed there is no evidence that Fox exercised it all. Indeed the Strauss affidavit (Paragraph 5) states that *Anna and the King of Siam* was, as a factual work rather than a novel, not an easily saleable property but that Fox paid "a good purchase price" for it.

Moreover, even if plaintiff's claim of an unlawful tying arrangement were otherwise sufficient, it would be barred by the four-year Statute of Limitations in 15 U.S.C. § 16(b). . . .

In the present case, however, the alleged violation arises from a single act—the 1944 agreement—by a single defendant. As a general rule, claims based on anti-competitive agreements to which the plaintiff is a party accrue at the time of their execution. . . .

Landon's final claim charges that certain episodes in the 1972 television series "fail to retain and give appropriate expression to the theme, thought and main action of plaintiff's work," resulting in damage to her privacy and reputation and the literary property itself. (Complaint, Paragraph 24.) As fleshed out by the material in support of her motion, the basis of this allegation is that her book was a serious literary work concerned with the struggle for human rights, whereas the television series was light in tone, and punctuated with bursts of dubbed laughter from the audience.

It is undisputed that the television credits stated that the scripts were "based on" plaintiff's literary property, with screenwriting credit given to the actual authors of the series in the same titles as Landon's name appears.

For several reasons, the claim is insufficient as a matter of law. Even without permission from an author or the existence of a written agreement with him, any person may truthfully state that a work is "based on" or "suggested by" the work of that author. I Nimmer, Copyright, § 110.41 at p. 447; *Geisel v. Poynter Products, Inc.*, 295 F. Supp. 331, 353 (S.D.N.Y. 1968). Although plaintiff would have a valid claim against defendants if they had falsely attributed the authorship of the series to her, see *Granz v. Harris,* 198 F.2d 585, 589 (2d Cir. 1952), her claim must fail where, as here, she contracted to (1) *require* Fox to give her appropriate credit "for her contribution to the literary material upon which such motion pictures shall have been based" (1944 Agreement, Article X); and (2) grant Fox the right to:

reproduce . . . spoken words taken from and/or *based on* the text or theme, of said literary property . . . in . . . motion pictures, using for that purpose all *or a part of the theme,* text and/or dialogue contained in said literary property. . . . [and] adapt one or more versions of said literary property, to add to and subtract from the literary property, change the sequence thereof, change the title . . . in connection with works or motion pictures *wholly or partially independent of said* literary property . . . *change the characters . . .* change the *descriptions of the said characters,* and use all thereof in new versions, adaptations and sequels. . . . (Agreement, Article I, paragraphs (b), (c)). (Emphasis added.)

These provisions clearly grant Fox the right to alter the literary property substantially and to attribute to plaintiff credit appropriate to her contribution. Accordingly, we find that Fox did not violate the agreement or engage in tortious conduct when it truthfully stated that the series was "based on" the property. . . .

NOTE ⎯⎯⎯⎯⎯⎯⎯⎯⎯⎯⎯⎯⎯⎯⎯⎯⎯⎯⎯⎯⎯⎯⎯⎯⎯⎯⎯⎯⎯⎯

In *Goodis v. United Artists Television, Inc.,* 425 F.2d 397 (2d Cir. 1970), Warner Bros acquired exclusive motion picture rights to the novel *Dark Passage,* under a contract on Warner's' standard form which contained additional specially negotiated clauses to cover radio and television broadcast rights. After producing a film of the book, which was shown in theatres and on television, Warner Brothers assigned its contract rights to UA, which produced a television film series based on the book, entitled "The Fugitive."

The issue was whether an episodic series designed solely for television was included under the grant of rights to "broadcast and transmit *any photoplay produced hereunder* by the process of television . . . "

The contract permitted "such changes, *variations, modifications, alterations, adaptations, arrangements, additions in* and/or eliminations and omissions from *said Writings and/or the characters, plot,* dialogue, *scenes, incidents, situations, action,* language and theme thereof" as the producer might elect. (This language was very similar to that in the *Landon* case.) Goodis specifically retained only "[t]he right to broadcast said Writings by television from the performances given by living actors." Judge Waterman (with whom Judge Kaufman agreed) overturned the summary judgment which the district judge had granted to UA, and remanded the case for trial, stating that "the right to make 'additions in . . . said writings' and in the characters and plot of *Dark Passage* does not necessarily go so far as to show that there is no genuine issue as to whether the characters of *Dark Passage* may be depicted in photoplay adventures which bear little relationship to the 'said writings' of *Dark Passage.*

Viewed in the context of the entire contract, the 'additions' and 'alterations' clauses . . . could be read in a more restrictive manner to permit only those alterations necessary to adapt a written story to the medium of film. Similarly, use of the word 'unlimited' with respect to the rights to alter and supplement could have been intended only to prevent Goodis from protesting that his story had been distorted or mutilated." In addition, Judge Waterman wanted a full trial because "our disposition of this appeal may affect the interpretation of other contracts which convey some of the divisible rights in a given story but do not explicitly mention among the conveyed rights the right to make subsequent stories employing the same character, i.e., 'sequels' [and because] a proper decision as to what the parties intended in this case may largely depend upon the general custom and expectations of authors and of members of the publishing, broadcasting, and film vocations [and] we have before us no evidence as to these customs and expectations. Many authors have used characters they created in one novel in a whole series of subsequent works; surely it would be rash of us to hold on summary judgment that the sale of rights in one of an author's works ends, without specific mention that it ends, the author's exclusive ownership of the valuable characters he created in that one work, when he may well desire to create sequels of his own using these same characters. . . . " Judge Lumbard, however, found it "difficult to imagine a broader transfer of rights than that which these parties drafted."

Rey v. Lafferty, 990 F.2d 1379 (1st Cir.), *cert. denied,* 510 U.S. 828 (1993)

CYR, CIRCUIT JUDGE

Margret Rey . . . owns the copyright to the "Curious George" children's books. . . .

Lafferty Harwood & Partners ["Lafferty"] . . . appeals the district court order awarding Rey damages . . . [on account of Lafferty's licensing of] certain . . . "Curious George" products . . . [including videos].

I. BACKGROUND

"Curious George" is an imaginary monkey whose antics are chronicled in seven books, written by Margret and H. A. Rey, which have entertained readers since the 1940s. A mischievous personality consistently lands Curious George in amusing scrapes and predicaments. The more recent "monkey business"—leading to the present litigation—began in 1977 when Margret Rey granted Milktrain Productions an option to produce and televise 104 animated "Curious George" film episodes. The option agreement was contingent on Milktrain's obtaining financing for the film project. . . .

Milktrain approached [Lafferty], a Canadian investment firm, to obtain financing for the project. [Lafferty] agreed to fund the venture by selling shares in the project to investors (hereinafter: the "Milktrain Agreement"); [Lafferty] and its investors were to divide a 50% share of Milktrain's profits on the films and on any future ancillary products.

With the financing commitment in place, Rey granted Milktrain and [Lafferty] a limited license "to produce (within a two-year period from the date of exercise) one hundred and four (104) four minute film episodes based on the ["Curious George"] character solely for broadcast on television" (hereinafter: the "Rey License"). Rey was to receive a fee for assisting with the editing and production of the episodes, and an additional royalty amounting to 10% of the revenues from any film telecasts. . . .

The film project soon encountered delays and financial setbacks. By early 1979, though only 32 of the 104 episodes had been completed, the original investment funds had been virtually exhausted. In order to rescue the project and complete the films to Rey's satisfaction, [Lafferty] offered to arrange additional financing. In consideration, [Lafferty] insisted that the Milktrain Agreement be revised to permit [Lafferty] to assume control of the film production process and to receive higher royalties on the completed episodes. Milktrain assented to these revisions, and the revised Milktrain Agreement . . . was signed on November 5, 1979. . . .

On November 5, 1979, concurrently with the execution of the Revised Milktrain Agreement, a revised version of the Rey License (hereinafter: the ["Revised License"]) was executed . . . superseding the original Rey License. The [Revised License] recited that the original Rey License had granted Milktrain and [Lafferty] the right to produce and distribute animated "Curious George" films "for television viewing." . . .

As agreed, [Lafferty] undertook to arrange further financing to complete the film project. . . .

Production of the 104 TV episodes was completed in 1982. . . .

Beginning in 1983, the "Curious George" TV episodes were licensed [by Lafferty] to Sony Corporation, which transferred the images from the television film negatives to videotape. [Lafferty] takes the position that the Sony video license was entered pursuant to the [Revised License]. . . .

On February 8, 1991, Rey filed suit against . . . [Lafferty], in connection with [Lafferty]'s continuing, allegedly unauthorized production of the . . . Sony videos. Rey's complaint alleged violations of federal copyright, trademark and unfair-competition statutes, breach of contract, and violations of Mass. Gen. L. ch. 93A ("chapter 93A"); it sought to enjoin further violations and to recover unpaid royalties on the . . . videos. . . .

After a four-day bench trial, the district court found for Rey on her claims for breach of contract. . . .

II. DISCUSSION

. . . [Lafferty]'s claim to the Sony video royalties is . . . complicated: . . . might they [the videos] . . . have been covered by the grant of rights in the [Revised License], which licensed [Lafferty] to produce the 104 episodes "for television viewing"? The district court thought not: the parties' "reference to television viewing . . . in a licensing agreement . . . does not include [video technology] . . . which probably was not in existence at the time that the rights were given."

a. "New Uses" and Copyright Law

For purposes of the present appeal, we accept the uncontested district court finding that the relevant video technology "was not in existence at the time that the rights" were granted under the [Revised License] in January 1979. Consequently, it must be inferred that the parties did not specifically contemplate television "viewing" of the "Curious George" films in videocassette form at the time the [Revised License] was signed. Such absence of specific intent typifies cases which address "new uses" of licensed materials, i.e., novel technological developments which generate unforeseen applications for a previously licensed work. See Melville B. Nimmer and David Nimmer, 3 Nimmer on Copyright § 10.10[B] at 10–85 (1992) ("Nimmer") ("the . . . fact that we are most often dealing with a later developed technological process (even if it were known in some form at the time of execution) suggests that the parties' ambiguous phraseology masks an absence of intent rather than a hidden intent which the court simply must 'find' ").

Normally, in such situations, the courts have sought at the outset to identify any indicia of a mutual general intent to apportion rights to "new uses," insofar as such general intent can be discerned from the language of the license, the surrounding circumstances, and trade usage. See, e.g., *Murphy v. Warner Bros. Pictures, Inc.*, 112 F.2d 746, 748 (9th Cir. 1940) (grant of "complete and entire" motion picture rights to licensed work held to encompass later-developed sound motion picture technology); *Filmvideo Releasing Corp. v. Hastings*, 446 F. Supp. 725 (SDNY 1978) (author's explicit retention of "all" television rights to licensed work, in grant of motion picture rights predating technological advances permitting movies to be shown on television, included retention of right to show motion picture on television). Where no reliable indicia of general intent are discernible, however, courts have resorted to one of several interpretive methods to resolve the issue on policy grounds.

Under the "preferred" method, see 3 Nimmer at 10–85, recently cited with approval in *SAPC, Inc. v. Lotus Development Corp.*, 921 F.2d 360, 363 (1st Cir. 1990), the court will conclude, absent contrary indicia of the parties' intent, that "the licensee may properly pursue any uses which may reasonably be said to fall within the medium as described in the license." 3 Nimmer at 10–86. Under this interpretive method, the courts will presume that at least the possibility of nonspecific "new uses" was foreseeable by the contracting parties at the time the licensing agreement was drafted; accordingly, the burden and risk of drafting licenses whose language anticipates the possibility of any particular "new use" are apportioned equally between licensor and licensee. See, e.g., *Bartsch v. Metro-Goldwyn-Mayer, Inc.*, 391 F.2d 150, 155 (2d Cir.), cert. denied, 393 U.S. 826, 21 L. Ed. 2d 96, 89 S. Ct. 86 (1968) ("if the words [of the license] are broad enough to cover the new use, . . . the burden of framing and negotiating an exception should fall on the grantor" of the licensed rights).

An alternative interpretive method is to assume that a license of rights in a given medium (e.g., 'motion picture rights') includes only such uses as fall within the unambiguous core meaning of the term . . . and excludes any uses which lie within the ambiguous penumbra (e.g., exhibition of motion picture film on television). Thus any rights not expressly (in this case meaning unambiguously) granted are reserved. See 3 Nimmer at 10–85; see also *Bourne Co. v. Walt Disney Co.*, 1992 Copyr. L. Rep. (CCH) P 26,934 (S.D.N.Y. 1992) ("if the disputed use was not invented when the parties signed their agreement, that use is not permitted under the contract"). This method is intended to prevent licensees from "'reaping the entire windfall' associated with the new medium," *Cohen v. Paramount Pictures Corp.*, 845 F.2d 851, 854 (9th Cir. 1988) (quoting Neil S. Nagano, Comment, Past Software Licenses and the New Video Software Medium, 29 U.C.L.A. L. Rev. 1160, 1184 (1982)), and is particularly appropriate in situations which involve overreaching or exploitation of unequal bargaining power by a licensee in negotiating the contract. See, e.g., *Bartsch*, 391 F.2d at 154 & n.2 (citing *Ettore v. Philco Television Broadcasting Corp.*, 229 F.2d 481 (3d Cir. 1955) (suggesting narrow construction where licensor was not "an experienced businessman" and had no "reason to know of the . . . potential" for new uses at the time he signed the relevant agreement)). It may also be appropriate where a particular "new use" was completely unforeseeable and therefore could not possibly have formed part of the bargain between the parties at the time of the original grant. *Cohen*, 845 F.2d at 854; *Kirke La Shelle Co. v. Paul Armstrong Co.*, 263 N.Y. 79, 188 N.E. 163 (1933). Obviously, this method may be less appropriate in arm's-length transactions between sophisticated parties involving foreseeable technological developments; in such situations, narrow construction of license grants may afford an unjustifiable windfall to the licensor, who would retain blanket rights to analogous "new uses" of copyright material notwithstanding the breadth of the bargained-for grant. See generally 3 Nimmer at 10–85 ("it is surely more arbitrary and unjust to put the onus on the licensee by holding that he should have obtained a further clarification of a meaning which was already present than it is to hold that the licensor should have negated a meaning which the licensee might then or thereafter rely upon"). [The problem becomes particularly acute when the analogous technology develops so rapidly as to supplant the originally contemplated application of the licensed work, rendering the parties' original bargain obsolete. Thus, for example, broad grants of "motion picture rights," made before technological advances permitted the combination of moving images with sound, later were held, typically, to encompass the rights to sound motion picture technology; a narrower holding would have left the original license virtually worthless, despite its broad language, and would have provided the licensor with an undeserved windfall. See, e.g., *Murphy*, 112 F.2d at 748; *L.C. Page & Co. v. Fox Film Corp.*, 83 F.2d 196 (2d Cir. 1936).]

b. Video Technology as "New Use."

These fine-tuned interpretive methods have led to divergent results in cases considering the extension of television rights to new video forms. Thus, for example, in *Rooney v. Columbia Pictures Industries Inc.*, 538 F. Supp. 211 (SDNY), aff'd, 714 F.2d 117 (2d Cir. 1982), cert. denied, 460 U.S. 1084, 76 L. Ed. 2d 346, 103 S. Ct. 1774 (1983), the court determined that a series of contracts granting motion picture distributors a general license to exhibit plaintiffs' films "by any present or future methods or means" and "by any means now known or unknown" fairly encompassed the right to distribute the films by means of later-developed video technology.

The contracts in question gave defendants extremely broad rights in the distribution and exhibition of pre-1960 films, plainly intending that such rights would be without limitation unless otherwise specified and further indicating that future technological advances in methods of reproduction, transmission and exhibition would inure to the benefit of defendants.

Similarly, in *Platinum Record Co. v. Lucasfilm, Ltd.*, 566 F.Supp. 226, 227 (D. N.J. 1983), the court held that videocassette rights were encompassed by a broad synchronization license to "exhibit, distribute, exploit, market, and perform [a motion picture containing licensed musical composition] . . . perpetually throughout the world by any means or methods now or hereafter known." Again, the court rested its holding on the "extremely broad and completely unambiguous" contractual grant of general rights to applications of future technologies, which was held to "preclude any need in the Agreement for an exhaustive list of specific potential uses of the film." Id.

By contrast, in *Cohen*, 845 F.2d 851 at 853–54, the Ninth Circuit concluded that a 1969 contract granting rights to "the exhibition of [a] motion picture [containing a licensed work] . . . by means of television," but containing a broad restriction reserving to the licensor "all rights and uses in and to said musical composition, except those herein granted," did not encompass the right to revenues derived from sales of the film in videocassette form. After deciding that "the general tenor of the [contract] section [in which the granting clause was found] contemplated some sort of broadcasting or centralized distribution, not distribution by sale or rental of individual copies to the general public," see id. at 853, the court stressed that the playing of videocassettes, with their greater viewer control and decentralized access on an individual basis, did not constitute "exhibition" in the sense contemplated by the contract.

Though videocassettes may be exhibited by using a television monitor, it does not follow that, for copyright purposes, playing videocassettes constitutes "exhibition by television." . . . Television requires an intermediary network, station, or cable to send the television signals into consumers' homes. The menu of entertainment appearing on television is controlled entirely by the intermediary and, thus, the consumer's selection is limited to what is available on various channels. Moreover, equipped merely with a conventional television set, a consumer has no means of capturing any part of the television display; when the program is over it vanishes, and the consumer is powerless to replay it. Because they originate outside the home, television signals are ephemeral and beyond the viewer's grasp. Videocassettes, of course, allow viewing of a markedly different nature. . . . By their very essence, . . . videocassettes liberate viewers from the constraints otherwise inherent in television, and eliminate the involvement of an intermediary, such as a network. Television and videocassette display thus have very little in common besides the fact that a conventional monitor or a television set may be used both to receive television signals and to exhibit a videocassette. It is in light of this fact that Paramount argues that VCRs are equivalent to "exhibition by means of television." Yet, even that assertion is flawed. Playing a videocassette on a VCR does not require a standard television set capable of receiving television signals by cable or by broadcast; it is only necessary to have a monitor capable of displaying the material on the magnetized tape.

Id. at 853–54.

Most recently, in *Tele-Pac, Inc. v. Grainger,* 168 A.D.2d 11, 570 N.Y.S.2d 521, appeal dismissed, 79 N.Y.2d 822, 580 N.Y.S.2d 201, 588 N.E.2d 99 (1991), the court held (one judge dissenting) that a license to distribute certain motion pictures "for broadcasting by television or any other similar device now known or hereafter to be made known" did not encompass the videocassette film rights. "Transmission of sound and images from a point outside the home for reception by the general public . . . is implicit in the concept of 'broadcasting by television.' Conversely, while one may speak of 'playing,' 'showing,' 'displaying,' or even perhaps 'exhibiting' a videotape, we are unaware of any usage of the term 'broadcasting' in that context." Id. at 523.

c. Video Rights and the [Revised License]

Although the question is extremely close, under the interpretive methodology outlined above we conclude that the [Revised License]'s grant of rights to the 104 film episodes "for television viewing" did not encompass the right to distribute the "Curious George" films in videocassette form.

First, unlike the contracts in *Rooney and Lucasfilm,* the [Revised License] contained no general grant of rights in technologies yet to be developed, and no explicit reference to "future methods" of exhibition. Compare *Lucasfilm,* 566 F.Supp. at 227; *Rooney,* 538 F.Supp. at 228. Rather, the [Revised License] appears to contemplate a comparatively limited and particular grant of rights, encompassing only the 104 film episodes and leaving future uses of "Curious George" to later negotiation in the ancillary products agreement. Although the [Revised License] conversely contains no "specific limiting language," compare *Cohen,* 845 F.2d at 853, we believe such limitation is reasonably inferable from the situation of the parties and the "general tenor of the section" in which the "television viewing" rights were granted.

Second, as properly noted in *Cohen,* "television viewing" and "videocassette viewing" are not coextensive terms. Even though videocassettes may be, and often are, viewed by means of VCRs on home television screens, see, e.g., *Sony Corp. of America v. Universal City Studios, Inc.,* 464 U.S. 417, 429, 78 L. Ed. 2d 574, 104 S. Ct. 774 (1984) (noting prevalent use of videocassette recorders for "time-shifting" of commercial television programming); *Rooney,* 538 F. Supp. at 228 ("whether the exhibition apparatus is a home videocassette player or a television station's broadcast transmitter, the films are 'exhibited' as images on home television screens"), still, as the Ninth Circuit pointed out, a "standard television set capable of receiving television signals" is not strictly required for videocassette viewing. *Cohen,* 845 F.2d at 854. "It is only necessary to have a monitor capable of displaying the material on the magnetized tape." Id. Indeed, a number of non-television monitors recently marketed in the United States permit videocassette viewing on computer screens, flat-panel displays, and the like. Thus, we find insufficient reliable indicia of a contrary mutual intent on the part of Rey and [Lafferty] to warrant disturbing the district court's implicit determination that the language of the [Revised License] is not "broad enough to cover the new use." *Bartsch,* 391 F.2d at 155.

Finally, any lingering concerns about the correctness of the district court's interpretation are dispelled by the evidence that the [Revised License] (including its "television viewing" clause) was drafted and proposed by [Lafferty], a professional investment firm accustomed to licensing agreements. Rey, an elderly woman, does not appear to have participated in its drafting, and, indeed, does not appear to have been represented by counsel during the larger part of the transaction. Under these circumstances, . . . ambiguities in the drafting instrument are traditionally construed against the licensor and the drafter. See also Nimmer at 10–71 ("ambiguities [in licensing agreements] will generally be resolved against the party preparing the instrument of transfer"); *U.S. Naval Institute v. Charter Communications, Inc.,* 875 F.2d 1044, 1051 (2d Cir. 1989) (interpreting ambiguous copyright assignment against sophisticated drafting party); see generally, e.g., *Merrimack Valley Nat'l Bank v. Baird,* 372 Mass. 721, 724, 363 N.E.2d 688, 690 (1977) ("as a general rule, a writing is construed against the author of the doubtful language . . . if the circumstances surrounding its use and the ordinary meaning of the words do not indicate the intended meaning of the language").

Accordingly, as the Sony videocassette sales were not encompassed by the [Revised License] . . . , and we affirm the award . . . to Rey. . . .

NOTES

1. As discussed by the court in the *Rey* decision, *Cohen v. Paramount Pictures Corp.,* 845 F.2d 851 (9th Cir. 1988), held that the 1968 grant to the studio of the right to include plaintiff's song in the soundtrack of the film "Medium Cool" and to exhibit the film "by means of television" was held to exclude distribution on home video cassettes, where the basic technology existed at the time of the grant and the contract reserved "all rights and uses except those . . . herein granted." A contrary result was reached in *Bloom v. Hearst Entertainment, Inc.,* 33 F.3d 518 (5th Cir. 1994), in which a grant of rights which included "worldwide motion picture and television rights" was held to be ambiguous, despite a contractual reservation of all rights not expressly granted. "At its most basic level," the court asked, "what is a video, if not a motion picture displayed on a television set? This observation is also supported by the precise definitions of the relevant terms. Webster's Ninth New Collegiate Dictionary defines video as follows: "a recording of a *motion picture or television program* for playing through a *television set*" (emphasis provided). It is not unreasonable to conclude that video rights lie at the intersection of motion picture and television rights, and hence, a grant of motion picture and television rights could include video rights as well."

    Despite the presence of a general "reservation of all rights not granted" clause, "in light of the specific recitals of rights reserved immediately following it, this general reservation clause is of little benefit . . . [H]aving chosen not to specifically reserve the video rights in their reservation clause, the appellants cannot prosper by this boilerplate, catch-all clause. . . . "

2. In *Bourne v. Walt Disney Co.,* 68 F.3d 621 (2d Cir. 1995), cert. denied 517 US. 1240 (1996), the Second Circuit held that when Disney conveyed music publishing rights in certain film music to Bourne's predecessor in interest reserving a license to use such compositions "in synchronism with any and all of the motion pictures which may be made by [Disney]," such reservation was sufficiently broad to permit Disney to manufacture and distribute videocassettes embodying "Pinocchio" but not to permit use of the licensed compositions in television commercials promoting the sale thereof.

    The Second Circuit distinguished *Cohen* and *Rey,* as well as *Tele-Pac, Inc. v. Grainger,* 570 N.Y. 2d 521 (1st Dept. 1991), stating that the latter cases did not present the precise issue of whether the term *motion pictures* would permit videocassette synchronization. Citing the Senate Report on what became the 1976 Copyright Act ("the physical form in which the motion picture is fixed—film, tape, disc, and so forth, is irrelevant . . . " S.Rep. No. 72, 92d Cong. 1st Sess. 5 [1971]), the court agreed with the decision in Bloom, and found that the language was broad enough to encompass home video, and in response to Bourne's argument that videocassette technology was unknown during the 1930s when the deal was made, the court cited evidence produced by Disney indicating that home viewing of motion pictures was already in contemplation at that time.

3. See, also, *Boosey & Hawkes Music Publishers, Ltd. v. Walt Disney Co.,* 145 F.3d 481 (2d Cir. 1998), in which a 1939 grant of rights "to record in any manner, medium or form . . . in [a] motion picture" was sufficient to cover home video, where the court found (at p. 486) that Disney had provided unrefuted evidence that a "nascent market for home viewing of feature films existed by 1939."

4. *Kelly v. William Morrow,* 186 Cal.3d 1625, 231 Cal.Rptr. 497 (1986) involved a claim that Joseph Wambaugh's *Lines and Shadows,* an account of the activities of San Diego police officers assigned to the Border Alien Robbery Force (BARF), a unit formed to control criminal activities in the Mexican border area, exceeded the scope of the written waiver executed by Kelly, a member of BARF. Following publication of the book, Kelly (who had been paid $5,000 for the waiver) sued for invasion of privacy, libel, slander, breach of contract, fraud, and negligent infliction of emotional distress, claiming the book contained false statements and inaccuracies, portrayed him as frivolous, flippant, and irresponsible toward his job as a police officer, and related fictitious events. While reversing the trial court's dismissal of the other claims in the action, the court of appeal sustained the lower court's dismissal of Kelly's breach of contract action. The waiver included "the exclusive and irrevocable right and license to use, simulate and portray [Kelly's] likeness, activities, experiences and career and to use [his] name in and in connection with the production, exhibition, advertising and other exploitation of a motion picture, photoplay or photoplays and book, or other printed material [and] the right to depict and/or portray [Kelly] to such extent and in such manner, either factually or fictionally as [defendants in their] discretion and pursuant to any contract with [Kelly] may determine and the right to distribute, exhibit or otherwise exploit any such photoplay by any method and in any manner, including theatrically and nontheatrically and by means of television or otherwise." The court found viable causes of action for defamation, libel and slander. "Fairly construed," the court stated, "[E]xtracts [from the book submitted by Kelly] depict Kelly as lecherous, heavy-drinking, promiscuous, unfaithful and untruthful to his wife, loud, raucous, blasphemous, profane, acting as a pimp for his fellow officers, and vacuous. Kelly labels marital discord episodes written vividly and profusely as false as well as happenings on the border during BARF forays. Kelly denies the attribution to him of remarks concerning BARF squad members as being psychotic, alcoholic, dangerous, and violent." In addition, "Kelly alleges a number of statements in the book are false. The breach of contract and fraud causes of action plead the waiver granted Wambaugh the right to depict Kelly factually or fictionally but not both. Kelly claims the book is half factual and half fictional [,] the waiver does not constitute a consent to the mix of fact and fiction in the book, [and] the waiver requires the defendants to elect a factual or a fictional account of his BARF adventures because the word 'or requires a choice between the two and prohibits their commingling into a factual-fictional account." Applying normal rules of construction, the court said, "or" would typically be seen as disjunctive, i.e., "either one or the other."

"The waiver is replete with suggestions Kelly's depiction is not limited to either a factual or fictional portrayal . . . 'Depict' means to form a likeness by drawing or painting, or in other ways as tapestries or carvings and to portray in words (*Webster's Third New Internat. Dict., op. cit. supra,* at p. 605). 'Portray' is to represent by drawing or painting, to make a picture or image, and to describe in words: present a verbal picture of (a novelist who [portrays] life the way most of us see it—Bernice Matlowsky) . . . to play the role of: represent dramatically. . . . "

A book about Kelly's life and BARF experiences in wholly factual terms would be a combination of autobiographical data typically found in a 'Who's Who' of Podunk and a police report on a BARF incident. While occasionally interesting, such factual stuff does not find its way to the bestseller lists and we surmise the subject is not paid $5,000 for the right to use his name. The use in the waiver of the words 'simulate,' 'depict,' 'portray' and our own reading of historical documentaries and novels compel the conclusion Kelly consented to publication of a mixed bag of fact and fiction. The demurrer to the breach of contract cause of action was correctly sustained." On the issues of defamation, privacy and emotional distress, however, "[w]e cannot say as a matter of law the rights given in the waiver include a license to defame, slander and libel Kelly. The waiver is not clear or certain. The waiver is ambiguous. The waiver does not suggest Kelly was aware he waived his rights to privacy. . . . We conclude the extent of the privileges conferred by the waiver must be determined in the light of the circumstances in which it was executed. Kelly's entitlement to a prepublication review under the terms of the waiver must likewise be considered. Whether Kelly sold his birthright to privacy for a mess of pottage when he signed the waiver can only be determined by a trier of fact."

3.5.2.2 The Scope of Acquired Rights: Legally Imposed Limitations

Sometimes the meaning of a contract is clear, but one party contends that greater rights were transferred by the contract than the law itself permits, and therefore the other party did not effectively acquire all of the rights it thought it had. While generally American law permits people to make their own deals—to sell or license, in other words, whatever they may own—there are certain provisions of copyright law which do have the effect of preventing copyright owners from conveying everything that others might be willing and even anxious to acquire. Three such provisions of copyright law are the compulsory mechanical license provision of the Copyright Act of 1976, the termination of transfer provisions of the Copyright Act of 1976, and the renewal provision of the Copyright Act of 1909.

The "compulsory mechanical license" provision of the Copyright Act (17 U.S.C. §115) has the effect of preventing songwriters and music publishers from granting *exclusive* licenses to recording artists or record companies, at any price. Moreover, if an agreement between a music publisher and a record company were to purport to grant the record company exclusive recording or *mechanical* rights to a song, the "compulsory mechanical license" would make the exclusivity clause of that agreement completely unenforceable. The compulsory mechanical license provision of the Copyright Act, as it currently reads, is set out below and is followed by an excerpt from a case which explains its history and its impact on the size of the mechanical fees that are paid for music recording licenses. It is important to note that Section 115 of the Copyright Act now covers "digital phonorecord deliveries" (digital "downloads") as well as traditional hard copies.

The "termination of transfers" provisions of the Copyright Act of 1976 [17 U.S.C. §203 and §304(c)] have the effect of permitting authors (or their lawful heirs) to terminate assignments and licenses, after a period of time, even if they had expressly agreed by contract not to do so. These provisions are set forth below.

The renewal provisions of the Copyright Act of 1909 have the effect of invalidating agreements which purport to transfer rights to be exercised during the copyright renewal term, under certain circumstances. Two significant cases illustrating this effect are reproduced below.

Copyright Act of 1976, 17 U.S.C. §115(a)(1)

In the case of nondramatic musical works, the exclusive rights . . . to make and to distribute phonorecords of such works, are subject to compulsory licensing under the conditions specified by this section.

(a) Availability and Scope of Compulsory License.—

(1) When phonorecords of a nondramatic musical work have been distributed to the public in the United States under the authority of the copyright owner, any other person, including those who make phonorecords or digital phonorecord deliveries may, by complying with the provisions of this section, obtain a compulsory license to make and distribute phonorecords of the work . . . if his or her primary purpose in making phonorecords is to distribute them to the public for private use, including by means of a digital phonorecord delivery. . . .

Recording Industry Ass'n of America v. Copyright Royalty Tribunal, 662 F.2d 1 (D.C. Cir. 1981)

CIRCUIT JUDGE MIKVA

These consolidated cases present various challenges to a rulemaking proceeding of the Copyright Royalty Tribunal ("Tribunal"), in which the Tribunal increased the royalty payable under the compulsory license for making and distributing phonorecords of copyrighted musical works. . . .

The royalty determinations challenged in this proceeding concern the compulsory license for phonorecords under the Copyright Act. Once the creator of a nondramatic musical work has allowed phonorecords of that work to be produced and distributed, the statute requires him to grant a license upon request to any other person who proposes to make and distribute phonorecords of the work, at a royalty rate set by law. This compulsory licensing scheme is one of several established by the Copyright Act, and determination of the appropriate royalty rates is one of the principal functions Congress . . . [originally] assigned to the Copyright Royalty Tribunal [and which now are assigned to Copyright Arbitration Royalty Panels].

The phonorecord compulsory licensing system dates back to 1909, when Congress first extended a composer's copyright protection to include the right to control manufacture of "parts of instruments serving to reproduce mechanically the musical work." Industry representatives expressed a fear that this protection ran the risk of "establishing a great music monopoly" because the Aeolian Company, a manufacturer of player-piano rolls, was acquiring exclusive contract rights from composers and publishers. The music industry has undergone major transformations in the intervening years, but record producers have continued to argue that a danger of monopolization and discriminatory practices exists, and Congress has concluded that a compulsory licensing system is still warranted.

Although the availability of the compulsory license under the 1909 Act has been very important to the structure of the recording industry, the statutory procedures for invoking the license have rarely been used. The usual effect of the system is to make the statutory royalty rate a ceiling on the price copyright owners can charge for use of their songs under negotiated contracts: if the owner demands a higher price in voluntary negotiations, the manufacturer can turn to the statutory scheme, but if the owner is willing to accept less than the statutory rate, he is free to do so.

Copyright Act of 1976, 17 U.S.C. §203

Termination of transfers and licenses granted by the author

(a) Conditions for Termination.—In the case of any work other than a work made for hire, the exclusive or nonexclusive grant of a transfer or license of copyright or of any right under a copyright, executed by the author on or after January 1, 1978, otherwise than by will, is subject to termination [by the author, or certain of the author's heirs] under the following conditions:

. . . .

(3) Termination of the grant may be effected at any time during a period of five years beginning at the end of thirty-five years from the date of execution of the grant; or, if the grant covers the right of publication of the work, the period begins at the end of thirty-five years from the date of publication of the work under the grant or at the end of forty years from the date of execution of the grant, whichever term ends earlier.

(4) The termination shall be effected by serving an advance notice in writing. . . .

(5) Termination of the grant may be effected notwithstanding any agreement to the contrary, including an agreement to make a will or to make any future grant.

(b) Effect of Termination.—Upon the effective date of termination, all rights under this title that were covered by the terminated grants revert to the author, authors, and other persons owning termination interests . . . , but with the following limitations:

(1) A derivative work prepared under authority of the grant before its termination may continue to be utilized under the terms of the grant after its termination, but this privilege does not extend to the preparation after the termination of other derivative works based upon the copyrighted work covered by the terminated grant. . . .

(4) A further grant, or agreement to make a further grant, of any right covered by a terminated grant is valid only if it is made after the effective date of the termination. As an exception, however, an agreement for such a further grant may be made between the [author, or the

author's heirs] . . . and the original grantee or such grantee's successor in title, after the notice of termination has been served. . . .

Copyright Act of 1976, 17 U.S.C. §304(c)

Termination of Transfers and Licenses Covering Extended Renewal Term.— In the case of any copyright subsisting in either its first or renewal term on January 1, 1978, other than a copyright in a work made for hire, the exclusive or nonexclusive grant of a transfer or license of the renewal copyright or any right under it, executed before January 1, 1978 . . . , otherwise than by will, is subject to termination [by the author, or certain of the author's heirs] . . . under the following conditions:

(3) Termination of the grant may be effected at any time during a period of five years beginning at the end of fifty-six years from the date copyright was originally secured, or beginning on January 1, 1978, whichever is later. . . .

(5) Termination of the grant may be effected notwithstanding any agreement to the contrary, including an agreement to make a will or to make any future grant.

(6) . . . In all cases the reversion of rights is subject to the following limitations:

(A) A derivative work prepared under authority of the grant before its termination may continue to be utilized under the terms of the grant after its termination, but this privilege does not extend to the preparation after the termination of other derivative works based upon the copyrighted work covered by the terminated grant. . . .

(D) A further grant, or agreement to make a further grant, of any right covered by a terminated grant is valid only if it is made after the effective date of the termination. As an exception, however, an agreement for such a further grant may be made between the author or [the author's heirs] and the original grantee or such grantee's successor in title, after the notice of termination has been served. . . .

NOTE

The Sonny Bono Copyright Term Extension Act of 1998, P.L. 105–298, 112 Stat. 2827 (105th Cong. 2d. Sess.) extended the term of copyright by an additional 20 years for any copyright subsisting in its renewal term on the effective date of the Sonny Bono Copyright Term Extension Act of 1998, and added a new Section 304(d) which permits recapture of the additional twenty years where the author or owner of the termination right has not previously exercised such termination right.

Miller Music Corp. v. Charles N. Daniels, Inc., 362 U.S. 373 (1960)

MR. JUSTICE DOUGLAS DELIVERED THE OPINION OF THE COURT.

Petitioner, a music publisher, sued respondent, another music publisher, for infringement of petitioner's rights through one Ben Black, as coauthor, in the renewal copyright of the song "Moonlight and Roses." Respondent's motion for summary judgment was granted, and the Court of Appeals affirmed by a divided vote. The case is here on a petition for a writ of certiorari which we granted.

The facts are stipulated. Ben Black and Charles Daniels composed the song and assigned it to Villa Moret, Inc., which secured the original copyright. Prior to the expiration of the 28-year term, Black assigned to petitioner his renewal rights in this song in consideration of certain royalties and the sum of $1,000. Black had no wife or child; and his next of kin were three brothers. Each of them executed a like assignment of his renewal expectancy and delivered it to petitioner. These assignments were recorded in the copyright office. Before the expiration of the original copyright, Black died, leaving no widow or child. His will contained no specific bequest concerning the renewal copyright. His residuary estate was left to his nephews and nieces. One of the brothers qualified as executor of the will and renewed the copyright for a further term of 28 years. The probate court decreed distribution of the renewal copyright to the residuary legatees. Respondent then obtained assignments from them.

The question for decision is whether by statute the renewal rights accrue to the executor in spite of a prior assignment by his testator. Section 24 of the Copyright Act of 1909, after stating that "the proprietor of such copyright shall be entitled to a renewal and extension of the copyright in such work for the further term of twenty-eight years," goes on to provide:

That ... the author of such work, if still living, or the widow, widower, or children of the author, if the author be not living, or if such author, widow, widower, or children be not living, then the author's executors, or in the absence of a will, his next of kin shall be entitled to a renewal and extension of the copyright in such work for a further term of twenty-eight years when application for such renewal and extension shall have been made to the copyright office and duly registered therein within one year prior to the expiration of the original term of copyright.

An assignment by an author of his renewal rights made before the original copyright expires is valid against the world, if the author is alive at the commencement of the renewal period. *Fisher Co. v. Witmark & Sons* so holds. It is also clear, all questions of assignment apart, that the renewal rights go by statute to an executor, absent a widow or child. *Fox Film Corp. v. Knowles.*

Petitioner argues that the executor's right under the statute can be defeated through a prior assignment by the testator. If the widow, widower, and children were the claimants, concededly no prior assignment could bar them. For they are among those to whom §24 has granted the renewal right, irrespective of whether the author in his lifetime has or has not made any assignment of it. Petitioner also concedes—and we see no rational escape from that conclusion—that where the author dies intestate prior to the renewal period leaving no widow, widower, or children, the next of kin obtain the renewal copyright free of any claim founded upon an assignment made by the author in his lifetime. These results follow not because the author's assignment is invalid but because he had only an expectancy to assign; and his death, prior to the renewal period, terminates his interest in the renewal which by §24 vests in the named classes. The right to obtain a renewal copyright and the renewal copyright itself exist only by reason of the Act and are derived solely and directly from it.

We fail to see the difference in this statutory scheme between widows, widowers, children, or next of kin on the one hand and executors on the other. The hierarchy of people granted renewal rights by §24 are first, the author if living; second, the widow, widower, or children, if he or she is not living; third, his or her executors if the author and the widow, widower, or children are not living; fourth, in absence of a will, the next of kin. True, these are disparate interests. Yet Congress saw fit to treat them alike. It seems clear to us, for example, that by the force of §24, if Black had died intestate, his next of kin would take as against the assignee of the renewal right. Congress in its wisdom expressed a preference for that group against the world, if the author, the widow, the widower, or children are not living. By §24 his executors are placed in the same preferred position, unless we refashion §24 to suit other policy considerations. Of course an executor usually takes in a representative capacity. He "represents the person of his testator" as *Fox Film Corp. v. Knowles* states. And that normally means that when the testator has made contracts, the executor takes cum onere. Yet it is also true, as pointed out in *Fox Film Corp. v. Knowles* that "it is no novelty" for the executor "to be given rights that the testator could not have exercised while he lived." It is clear that under this Act the executor's right to renew is independent of the author's rights at the time of his death. What Congress has done by §24 is to create contingent renewal rights. Congress has provided that, when the author dies before the renewal period arrives, special rules in derogation of the usual rules of succession are to apply for the benefit of three classes of people—(1) widows, widowers, and children; (2) executors; and (3) next of kin. We think we would redesign §24 if we held that executors, named as one of the preferred classes, do not acquire the renewal rights, where there has been a prior assignment, though widows, widowers, and children or next of kin would acquire them. Certainly *Fox Film Corp. v. Knowles* states that what one of the three could have done, either of the others may do. Mr. Justice Holmes speaking for the Court said:

No one doubts that if Carleton had died leaving a widow she could have applied as the executor did, and executors are mentioned alongside of the widow with no suggestion in the statute that when executors are the proper persons, if anyone, to make the claim, they cannot make it whenever a widow might have made it. The next of kin come after the executors. Surely they again have the same rights that the widow would have had.

The legislative history supports that view:

Instead of confining the right of renewal to the author, if still living, or to the widow or children of the author, if he be dead, we provide that the author of such work, if still living, may apply for the renewal, or the widow, widower, or children of the author, if the author be not living, or if such author, widow, widower, or children be not living, then the author's executors, or, in the absence of a will, his next of kin. It was not the intention to permit the administrator to apply for the renewal, but to permit the author who had no wife or children to bequeath by will the right to apply for the renewal.

The category of persons entitled to renewal rights therefore cannot be cut down and reduced as petitioner would have us do. Section 24 reflects, it seems to us, a consistent policy to treat renewal rights as expectancies until the renewal period arrives. When that time arrives, the renewal rights pass to one of the four classes listed in §24 according to the then-existing circumstances. Until that time arrives, assignees of renewal rights take the risk that the rights acquired may never vest in their assignors. A purchaser of such an interest is deprived of nothing. Like all purchasers of contingent interests, he takes subject to the possibility that the contingency may not occur. For example, an assignment from an author and his wife will be ineffective, if on his death another woman is the widow. Examples could be multiplied. We have said enough, however, to indicate that there is symmetry and logic in the design of §24. Whether it works at times an injustice is a matter for the Congress, not for us.

Affirmed.

MR. JUSTICE HARLAN, with whom MR. JUSTICE FRANKFURTER, MR. JUSTICE WHITTAKER, and MR. JUSTICE STEWART join, dissenting. . . .

Stewart v. Abend, 495 U.S. 207, 110 S.Ct. 1750 (1990)

JUSTICE O'CONNOR[NM DELIVERED THE OPINION OF THE COURT].

The author of a pre-existing work may assign to another the right to use it in a derivative work. In this case the author of a pre-existing work agreed to assign the rights in his renewal copyright term to the owner of a derivative work, but died before the commencement of the renewal period. The question presented is whether the owner of the derivative work infringed the rights of the successor owner of the pre-existing work by continued distribution and publication of the derivative work during the renewal term of the pre-existing work.

I

Cornell Woolrich authored the story "It Had to Be Murder," which was first published in February 1942 in Dime Detective Magazine. The magazine's publisher, Popular Publications, Inc., obtained the rights to magazine publication of the story and Woolrich retained all other rights.

Popular Publications obtained a blanket copyright for the issue of Dime Detective Magazine in which "It Had to Be Murder" was published.

The Copyright Act of 1909 provided authors a 28-year initial term of copyright protection plus a 28-year renewal term. In 1945, Woolrich agreed to assign the rights to make motion picture versions of six of his stories, including "It Had to Be Murder," to B. G. De Sylva Productions for $9,250. He also agreed to renew the copyrights in the stories at the appropriate time and to assign the same motion picture rights to De Sylva Productions for the 28-year renewal term. In 1953, actor Jimmy Stewart and director Alfred Hitchcock formed a production company, Patron, Inc., which obtained the motion picture rights in "It Had to Be Murder" from De Sylva's successors in interest for $10,000.

In 1954, Patron, Inc., along with Paramount Pictures, produced and distributed, "Rear Window," the motion picture version of Woolrich's story "It Had to Be Murder." Woolrich died in 1968 before he could obtain the rights in the renewal term for petitioners as promised and without a surviving spouse or child. He left his property to a trust administered by his executor, Chase Manhattan Bank, for the benefit of Columbia University. On December 29, 1969, Chase Manhattan Bank renewed the copyright in the "It Had to Be Murder" story pursuant to 17 U.S.C. §24. Chase Manhattan assigned the renewal rights to respondent Abend for $650 plus 10% of all proceeds from exploitation of the story.

"Rear Window" was broadcast on the ABC television network in 1971. Respondent then notified petitioners Hitchcock (now represented by co-trustees of his will), Stewart, and MCA Inc., the owners of the "Rear Window" motion picture and renewal rights in the motion picture, that he owned the renewal rights in the copyright and that their distribution of the motion picture without permission infringed his copyright in the story. Hitchcock, Stewart, and MCA nonetheless entered into a second license with ABC to rebroadcast the motion picture. In 1974, respondent filed suit against these same petitioners, and others, in the United States District Court for the Southern District of New York, alleging copyright infringement. Respondent dismissed his complaint in return for $25,000.

Three years later, the United States Court of Appeals for the Second Circuit decided *Rohauer v. Killiam Shows, Inc.*, 551 F.2d 484, cert. denied, 431 U.S. 949 (1977), in which it held that the owner of the copyright in a derivative work may continue to use the existing derivative work according to the original grant from the author of the pre-existing work even if the grant of rights in the pre-existing work lapsed. [The Copyright Act of 1976 codified the definition of a "derivative work" as "a work based upon one or more preexisting works, such as a translation, musical arrangement, dramatization, fictionalization, motion picture version . . . or any other form in which a work may be recast, transformed, or adapted."] Several years later, apparently in reliance on Rohauer, petitioners re-released the motion picture in a variety of media, including new 35 and 16 millimeter prints for theatrical exhibition in the United States, videocassettes, and videodiscs. They also publicly exhibited the motion picture in theaters, over cable television, and through videodisc and videocassette rentals and sales.

Respondent then brought the instant suit in the United States District Court for the Central District of California against Hitchcock, Stewart, MCA, and Universal Film Exchanges, a subsidiary of MCA and the distributor of the motion picture. Respondent's complaint alleges that the re-release of the motion picture infringes his copyright in the story because petitioners' right to use the story during the renewal term lapsed when Woolrich died before he could register for the renewal term and transfer his renewal rights to them. Respondent also contends that petitioners have interfered with his rights in the renewal term of the story in other ways. He alleges that he sought to contract with Home Box Office (HBO) to produce a play and television version of the story, but that petitioners wrote to him and HBO stating that neither he nor HBO could use either the title, "Rear Window" or "It Had to Be Murder." Respondent also alleges that petitioners further interfered with the renewal copyright in the story by attempting to sell the right to make a television sequel and that the re-release of the original motion picture itself interfered with his ability to produce other derivative works.

Petitioners filed motions for summary judgment, one based on the decision in *Rohauer* and the other based on alleged defects in the story's copyright. Respondent moved for summary judgment on the ground that petitioners' use of the motion picture constituted copyright infringement. Petitioners responded with a third motion for summary judgment based on a "fair use" defense. The District Court granted petitioners' motions for summary judgment based on *Rohauer* and the fair use defense, and denied respondent's motion for summary judgment, as well as petitioners' motion for summary judgment alleging defects in the story's copyright. Respondent appealed to the United States Court of Appeals for the Ninth Circuit and petitioners cross-appealed.

The Court of Appeals reversed, holding that respondent's copyright in the renewal term of the story was not defective. The issue before the court, therefore, was whether petitioners were entitled to distribute and exhibit the motion picture without respondent's permission despite respondent's valid copyright in the pre-existing story. Relying on the renewal provision of the 1909 Act, respondent argued before the Court of Appeals that because he obtained from Chase Manhattan Bank, the statutory successor, the renewal right free and clear of any purported assignments of any interest in the renewal copyright, petitioners' distribution and publication of "Rear Window" without authorization infringed his renewal copyright. Petitioners responded that they had the right to continue to exploit "Rear Window" during the 28-year renewal period, because Woolrich had agreed to assign to petitioners' predecessors in interest the motion picture rights in the story for the renewal period.

Petitioners also relied, as did the District Court, on the decision in *Rohauer v. Killiam Shows, Inc.* In *Rohauer,* the Court of Appeals for the

Second Circuit held that statutory successors to the renewal copyright in a pre-existing work under § 24 could not "depriv[e] the proprietor of the derivative copyright of a right . . . to use so much of the underlying copyrighted work as already has been embodied in the copyrighted derivative work, as a matter of copyright law." The Court of Appeals in the instant case rejected this reasoning, concluding that even if the pre-existing work had been incorporated into a derivative work, use of the pre-existing work was infringing unless the owner of the derivative work held a valid grant of rights in the renewal term.

The court relied on *Miller Music Corp. v. Charles N. Daniels* in which we held that assignment of renewal rights by an author before the time for renewal arrives cannot defeat the right of the author's statutory successor to the renewal rights if the author dies before the right to renewal accrues. . . . The Court of Appeals reasoned that "[i]f *Miller Music* makes assignment of the full renewal rights in the underlying copyright unenforceable when the author dies before effecting renewal of the copyright, then a fortiori, an assignment of part of the rights in the underlying work, the right to produce a movie version, must also be unenforceable if the author dies before effecting renewal of the underlying copyright." Finding further support in the legislative history of the 1909 Act and rejecting the *Rohauer* court's reliance on the equities and the termination provisions of the 1976 Act, 17 U.S.C. §§ 203(b)(1), 304(c)(6)(A), the Court of Appeals concluded that petitioners received from Woolrich only an expectancy in the renewal rights that never matured; upon Woolrich's death, Woolrich's statutory successor, Chase Manhattan Bank, became "entitled to a renewal and extension of the copyright," which Chase Manhattan secured "within one year prior to the expiration of the original term of copyright." Chase Manhattan then assigned the existing rights in the copyright to respondent.

The Court of Appeals also addressed at length the proper remedy, an issue not relevant to the issue on which we granted certiorari. We granted certiorari to resolve the conflict between the decision in *Rohauer* and the decision below. Petitioners do not challenge the Court of Appeals' determination that respondent's copyright in the renewal term is valid and we express no opinion regarding the Court of Appeals' decision on this point.

II

Petitioners would have us read into the Copyright Act a limitation on the statutorily created rights of the owner of an underlying work. They argue in essence that the rights of the owner of the copyright in the derivative use of the pre-existing work are extinguished once it is incorporated into the derivative work, assuming the author of the pre-existing work has agreed to assign his renewal rights. Because we find no support for such a curtailment of rights in either the 1909 Act, the 1976 Act, or the legislative history of either, we affirm the judgment of the Court of Appeals.

Petitioners and Amicus Register of Copyrights assert, as the Court of Appeals assumed, that § 24 of the 1909 Act, and the case law interpreting that provision, directly control the disposition of this case. Respondent counters that the provisions of the 1976 Act control, but that the 1976 Act reenacted § 24 in § 304 and, therefore, the language and judicial interpretation of § 24 are relevant to our consideration of this case. Under either theory, we must look to the language of and case law interpreting § 24.

The right of renewal found in § 24 provides authors a second opportunity to obtain remuneration for their works. . . .

Since the earliest copyright statute in this country, the copyright term of ownership has been split between an original term and a renewal term. Originally, the renewal was intended merely to serve as an extension of the original term; at the end of the original term, the renewal could be effected and claimed by the author, if living, or by the author's executors, administrators or assigns. Congress altered the provision so that the author could assign his contingent interest in the renewal term, but could not, through his assignment, divest the rights of his widow or children in the renewal term. The 1831 renewal provisions created "an entirely new policy, completely dissevering the title, breaking up the continuance . . . and vesting an absolutely new title eo nomine in the persons designated." In this way, Congress attempted to give the author a second chance to control and benefit from his work. Congress also intended to secure to the author's family the opportunity to exploit the work if the author died before he could register for the renewal term. "The evident purpose of [the renewal provision] is to provide for the family of the author after his death. Since the author cannot assign his family's renewal rights, [it] takes the form of a compulsory bequest of the copyright to the designated persons."

In its debates leading up to the Copyright Act of 1909, Congress elaborated upon the policy underlying a system comprised of an original term and a completely separate renewal term. "It not infrequently happens that the author sells his copyright outright to a publisher for a comparatively small sum." The renewal term permits the author, originally in a poor bargaining position, to renegotiate the terms of the grant once the value of the work has been tested. "[U]nlike real property and other forms of personal property, [a copyright] is by its very nature incapable of accurate monetary evaluation prior to its exploitation." "If the work proves to be a great success and lives beyond the term of twenty-eight years, . . . it should be the exclusive right of the author to take the renewal term, and the law should be framed . . . so that [the author] could not be deprived of that right." With these purposes in mind, Congress enacted the renewal provision of the Copyright Act of 1909, 17 U.S.C. § 24. With respect to works in their original or renewal term as of January 1, 1978, Congress retained the two-term system of copyright protection in the 1976 Act.

Applying these principles in *Miller Music Corp. v. Charles N. Daniels, Inc.*, this Court held that when an author dies before the renewal period arrives, his executor is entitled to the renewal rights, even though the author previously assigned his renewal rights to another party. . . . The legislative history of the 1909 Act echoes this view: "The right of renewal is contingent. It does not vest until the end [of the original term]. If [the author] is alive at the time of renewal, then the original contract may pass it, but his widow or children or other persons entitled would not be bound by the contract." Thus, the renewal provisions were intended to give the author a second chance to obtain fair remuneration for his creative efforts and to provide the author's family a "new estate" if the author died before the renewal period arrived.

An author holds a bundle of exclusive rights in the copyrighted work, among them the right to copy and the right to incorporate the work into derivative works. By assigning the renewal copyright in the work without limitation, as in *Miller Music,* the author assigns all of these rights. After *Miller Music,* if the author dies before the commencement of the renewal period, the assignee holds nothing. If the assignee of all of the renewal rights holds nothing upon the death of the assignor before arrival of the renewal period, then a *fortiori*, the assignee of a portion of the renewal rights, e. g., the right to produce a derivative work, must also hold nothing. Therefore, if the author dies before the renewal period, then the assignee may continue to use the original work only if the author's successor transfers the renewal rights to the assignee. This is the rule adopted by the Court of Appeals below and advocated by the Register of Copyrights. Application of this rule to this case should end the inquiry. Woolrich died before the commencement of the renewal period in the story, and, therefore, petitioners hold only an unfulfilled expectancy. Petitioners have been "deprived of nothing. Like all purchasers of contingent interests, [they took] subject to the possibility that the contingency may not occur."

The reason that our inquiry does not end here, and that we granted certiorari, is that the Court of Appeals for the Second Circuit reached a contrary result in *Rohauer v. Killiam Shows, Inc.* Petitioners' theory is drawn largely from *Rohauer.* The Court of Appeals in *Rohauer* attempted to craft a "proper reconciliation" between the owner of the pre-existing work, who held the right to the work pursuant to *Miller Music,* and the owner of the derivative work, who had a great deal to lose if the work could not be published or distributed. Addressing a case factually similar to this case, the court concluded that even if the death of the author caused the renewal rights in the pre-existing work to revert to the statutory successor, the owner of the derivative work could continue to exploit that work. The court reasoned that the 1976 Act and the relevant precedents did not preclude such a result and that it was necessitated by a balancing of the equities:

[T]he equities lie preponderantly in favor of the proprietor of the derivative copyright. In contrast to the situation where an assignee or licensee has done nothing more than print, publicize and distribute a copyrighted story or novel, a person who with the consent of the author has created an opera or a motion picture film will often have made contributions literary, musical and economic, as great as or greater than the original author. . . . [T]he purchaser of derivative rights has no truly effective way to protect himself against the eventuality of the author's death before the renewal period since there is no way of telling who will be the surviving widow, children or next of kin or the executor until that date arrives.

The Court of Appeals for the Second Circuit thereby shifted the focus from the right to use the pre-existing work in a derivative work to a right inhering in the created derivative work itself. By rendering the renewal right to use the original work irrelevant, the court created an exception to our ruling in *Miller Music* and, as petitioners concede, created an "intrusion" on the statutorily created rights of the owner of the pre-existing work in the renewal term.

Though petitioners do not, indeed could not, argue that its language expressly supports the theory they draw from *Rohauer,* they implicitly rely on §7 of the [1909] Act, . . . which states that "dramatizations . . . of copyrighted works when produced with the consent of the proprietor of the copyright in such works . . . shall be regarded as new works subject to copyright under the provisions of this title." Petitioners maintain that the creation of the "new," i.e., derivative, work extinguishes any right the owner of rights in the pre-existing work might have had to sue for infringement that occurs during the renewal term.

We think, as stated in *Nimmer on Copyright,* that "[t]his conclusion is neither warranted by any express provision of the Copyright Act, nor by the rationale as to the scope of protection achieved in a derivative work. It is moreover contrary to the axiomatic copyright principle that a person may exploit only such copyrighted literary material as he either owns or is licensed to use." The aspects of a derivative work added by the derivative author are that author's property, but the element drawn from the pre-existing work remains on grant from the owner of the pre-existing work. So long as the pre-existing work remains out of the public domain, its use is infringing if one who employs the work does not have a valid license or assignment for use of the pre-existing work. It is irrelevant whether the pre-existing work is inseparably intertwined with the derivative work. Indeed, the plain language of § 7 supports the view that the full force of the copyright in the pre-existing work is preserved despite incorporation into the derivative work. This well-settled rule also was made explicit in the 1976 Act:

The copyright in a compilation or derivative work extends only to the material contributed by the author of such work, as distinguished from the preexisting material employed in the work, and does not imply any exclusive right in the preexisting material. The copyright in such work is independent of, and does not affect or enlarge the scope, duration, ownership, or subsistence of, any copyright protection in the pre-existing material.

Properly conceding there is no explicit support for their theory in the 1909 Act, its legislative history, or the case law, petitioners contend, as did the court in *Rohauer,* that the termination provisions of the 1976

Act, while not controlling, support their theory of the case. For works existing in their original or renewal terms as of January 1, 1978, the 1976 Act added 19 years to the 1909 Act's provision of 28 years of initial copyright protection and 28 years of renewal protection. See 17 U.S.C. §§ 304(a) and (b). For those works, the author has the power to terminate the grant of rights at the end of the renewal term and, therefore, to gain the benefit of that additional 19 years of protection. See 17 U.S.C. §304(c). In effect, the 1976 Act provides a third opportunity for the author to benefit from a work in its original or renewal term as of January 1, 1978. Congress, however, created one exception to the author's right to terminate: The author may not, at the end of the renewal term, terminate the right to use a derivative work for which the owner of the derivative work has held valid rights in the original and renewal terms. See § 304(c)(6)(A). The author, however, may terminate the right to create new derivative works. For example, if the petitioners held a valid copyright in the story throughout the original and renewal terms, and the renewal term in "Rear Window" were about to expire, petitioners could continue to distribute the motion picture even if respondent terminated the grant of rights, but could not create a new motion picture version of the story. Both the court in *Rohauer* and petitioners infer from this exception to the right to terminate an intent by Congress to prevent authors of pre-existing works from blocking distribution of derivative works. In other words, because Congress decided not to permit authors to exercise a third opportunity to benefit from a work incorporated into a derivative work, the Act expresses a general policy of undermining the author's second opportunity. We disagree.

The process of compromise between competing special interests leading to the enactment of the 1976 Act undermines any such attempt to draw an overarching policy out of § 304(c)(6)(A), which only prevents termination with respect to works in their original or renewal copyright terms as of January 1, 1978, and only at the end of the renewal period. More specifically, § 304(c)

was part of a compromise package involving the controversial and intertwined issues of initial ownership, duration of copyright, and reversion of rights. The Register, convinced that the opposition . . . would scuttle the proposed legislation, drafted a number of alternative proposals. . . . Finally, the Copyright Office succeeded in urging negotiations among representatives of authors, composers, book and music publishers, and motion picture studios that produced a compromise on the substance and language of several provisions. . . .

. . . "Because the controversy surrounding the provisions disappeared once the parties reached a compromise, however, Congress gave the provisions little or no detailed consideration. . . . Thus, there is no evidence whatsoever of what members of Congress believed the language to mean." Litman, Copyright, Compromise, and Legislative History, 72 Cornell L. Rev. 857, 865–868 (1987).

In fact, if the 1976 Act's termination provisions provide any guidance at all in this case, they tilt against petitioners' theory. The plain language of the termination provision itself indicates that Congress assumed that the owner of the pre-existing work possessed the right to sue for infringement even after incorporation of the pre-existing work in the derivative work:

> A derivative work prepared under authority of the grant before its termination may continue to be utilized under the terms of the grant after its termination, but this privilege does not extend to the preparation after the termination of other derivative works based upon the copyrighted work covered by the terminated grant. 17 U.S.C. §304(c)(6)(A)

Congress would not have stated explicitly in § 304(c)(6)(A) that, at the end of the renewal term, the owner of the rights in the pre-existing work may not terminate use rights in existing derivative works unless Congress had assumed that the owner continued to hold the right to sue for infringement even after incorporation of the pre-existing work into the derivative work.

Accordingly, we conclude that neither the 1909 Act nor the 1976 Act provides support for the theory set forth in *Rohauer*. And even if the theory found some support in the statute or the legislative history, the approach set forth in *Rohauer* is problematic. Petitioners characterize the result in *Rohauer* as a bright-line "rule." The Court of Appeals in *Rohauer*, however, expressly implemented policy considerations as a means of reconciling what it viewed as the competing interests in that case. While the result in *Rohauer* might make some sense in some contexts, it makes no sense in others. In the case of a condensed book, for example, the contribution by the derivative author may be little, while the contribution by the original author is great. Yet, under the *Rohauer* "rule," publication of the condensed book would not infringe the pre-existing work even though the derivative author has no license or valid grant of rights in the pre-existing work. Thus, even if the *Rohauer* "rule" made sense in terms of policy in that case, it makes little sense when it is applied across the derivative works spectrum. Indeed, in the view of the commentators, *Rohauer* did not announce a "rule," but rather an "interest-balancing approach."

Finally, petitioners urge us to consider the policies underlying the Copyright Act. They argue that the rule announced by the Court of Appeals will undermine one of the policies of the Act—the dissemination of creative works—by leading to many fewer works reaching the public. Amicus Columbia Pictures asserts that "[s]ome owners of underlying work renewal copyrights may refuse to negotiate, preferring instead to retire their copyrighted works, and all derivative works based thereon, from public use. Others may make demands—like respondent's demand for 50% of petitioners' future gross proceeds in excess of advertising expenses . . .—which are so exorbitant that a negotiated economic accommodation will be impossible." These arguments are better addressed by Congress than the courts.

In any event, the complaint that the respondent's monetary request in this case is so high as to preclude agreement fails to acknowledge that an initially high asking price does not preclude bargaining. Presumably, respondent is asking for a share in the proceeds because he wants to profit from the distribution of the work, not because he seeks suppression of it.

Moreover, although dissemination of creative works is a goal of the Copyright Act, the Copyright Act creates a balance between the artist's right to control the work during the term of the copyright protection and the public's need for access to creative works. The copyright term is limited so that the public will not be permanently deprived of the fruits of an artist's labors. But nothing in the copyright statutes would prevent an author from hoarding all of his works during the term of the copyright. In fact, this Court has held that a copyright owner has the capacity arbitrarily to refuse to license one who seeks to exploit the work.

The limited monopoly granted to the artist is intended to provide the necessary bargaining capital to garner a fair price for the value of the works passing into public use. When an author produces a work which later commands a higher price in the market than the original bargain provided, the copyright statute is designed to provide the author the power to negotiate for the realized value of the work. That is how the separate renewal term was intended to operate. At heart, petitioners' true complaint is that they will have to pay more for the use of works they have employed in creating their own works. But such a result was contemplated by Congress and is consistent with the goals of the Copyright Act. . . .

. . . In this case, the grant of rights in the pre-existing work lapsed and, therefore, the derivative work owner's rights to use those portions of the pre-existing work incorporated into the derivative work expired. Thus, continued use would be infringing; whether the derivative work may continue to be published is a matter of remedy, an issue which is not before us. To say otherwise is to say that the derivative work nullifies the "force" of the copyright in the "matter employed." Whether or not we believe that this is good policy, this is the system Congress has provided, as evidenced by the language of the 1909 Act and the cases decided under the 1909 Act. Although the dissent's theory may have been a plausible option for a legislature to have chosen, Congress did not so provide.

III

. . . For the foregoing reasons, the judgment of the Court of Appeals is affirmed and the case is remanded for further proceedings consistent with this opinion.

It is so ordered.

JUSTICE WHITE (CONCURRING IN THE JUDGMENT)

Although I am not convinced, as the Court seems to be, that the decision in *Miller Music Corp. v. Charles N. Daniels, Inc.* was required by the Copyright Act, neither am I convinced that it was an impermissible construction of the statute. And because *Miller Music,* in my view, requires the result reached by the Court in this case, I concur in the judgment of affirmance.

JUSTICE STEVENS WITH WHOM THE CHIEF JUSTICE AND JUSTICE SCALIA JOIN (DISSENTING)

. . . The statutory background supports the conclusion that Congress intended the original author to be able to sell the right to make a derivative work that could be distributed for the full term of the derivative work's copyright protection. . . .

The legislative history confirms that the copyright in derivative works not only gives the second creative product the monopoly privileges of excluding others from the unconsented use of the new work, but also allows the creator to publish his or her own work product. The authority to produce the derivative work, which includes creative contributions by both the original author and the second artist, is dependent upon the consent of the proprietor of the underlying copyright. But once that consent has been obtained, and a derivative work has been created and copyrighted in accord with that consent, "a right of property spr[ings] into existence," that Congress intended to protect. Publication of the derivative work does not "affect the force or validity" of the underlying copyright except to the extent that it gives effect to the consent of the original proprietor. That owner—and in this case, the owner of a renewal of the original copyright—retains full dominion and control over all other means of exploiting that work of art, including the right to authorize other derivative works. The original copyright may have relatively little value because the creative contribution of the second artist is far more significant than the original contribution, but that just means that the rewards for creativity are being fairly allocated between the two artists whose combined efforts produced the derivative work. . . .

The critical flaw in the Court's analysis is its implicit endorsement of the Court of Appeals reasoning that:

If *Miller Music* makes assignment of the full renewal rights in the underlying copyright unenforceable when the author dies before effecting renewal of the copyright, then a fortiori, an assignment of part of the rights in the underlying work, the right to produce a movie version, must also be unenforceable if the author dies before effecting renewal of the underlying copyright.

That reasoning would be valid if the sole basis for the protection of the derivative work were the contractual assignment of copyright, but Woolrich did not just assign the rights to produce a movie version the way an author would assign the publisher rights to copy and vend his work. Rather, he expressed his consent to production of a derivative work under §7. The possession of a copyright on a properly created derivative work gives the proprietor rights superior to those of a mere licensee. . . .

I respectfully dissent.

NOTES _____

1. For a detailed analysis of the consequences of the decision in *Stewart v. Abend* see Lionel S. Sobel, "View from the 'Rear Window': A Practical Look at the Consequences

of the Supreme Court's decision in *Stewart vs. Abend*" in the 12 *Entertainment Law Reporter* (June 1990).

2. In *Mills Music, Inc. v. Snyder,* 469 U.S. 153, 105 S.Ct. 638 (1985) the U.S. Supreme Court in a 5–4 ruling, which was disappointing to authors, upheld the continuing right of music publishers to receive mechanical royalty income from sound recordings that were licensed prior to a proper termination under 17 U.S.C. §304(c). The decision addressed the extent of the application of the termination of transfers right granted to authors under the Copyright Act of 1976 in Sections 203 and 304(c). The case involved the popular song "Whose Sorry Now" and the attempted termination under 17 U.S.C. §304(c) by the heirs of the author (Snyder) of a 1940 assignment of the copyright and exclusive publishing rights granted to Mills Music by the author of the renewal term of the copyright.

The publishing contract assigning the renewal copyright from Snyder to Mills Music authorized the publisher to issue licenses and collect royalties, in return for payment of 50% of the royalties collected to Snyder. During the renewal period Mills Music directly or through the Harry Fox Agency issued over 400 mechanical licenses to record companies to record and release records containing the song. The primary question answered by the Court was: after lawful termination of the publisher's rights under the initial grant, who is entitled to collect and receive the mechanical royalties earned post termination from licenses issued pre-termination? Under 17 U.S.C. §304(c)(6)(A), a derivative work (i.e. the recording of a song, or a movie based upon a book) prepared under authority of the grant before its termination may continue to be utilized by the licensee *under the terms of the grant* after termination of the grant.

Justice Stevens, in writing for the majority, held that the right of Snyder's heirs to terminate the rights of Mills Music to collect royalties during the post-termination period, which were generated from pre-termination licenses, was an exception to the right of termination in §304(c)(6)(A). The Court reasoned that under the statute a derivative work is allowed to continue to be utilized "under the terms of the grant" issued by Mills Music. Under the terms of that grant the record labels were required to continue to pay mechanical royalties to Mills Music (who then would have an obligation to pay 50% of these royalties to the author's heirs). Notwithstanding the intent of Congress to give authors a fresh start after the termination in recapturing their copyrights, a publisher's pre-termination license of a derivative work consisting of recordings of the song could not be terminated by author's heirs, and the author's share in the royalties therefore would not be improved. Under this ruling the majority decision implies that the termination right only applies to the ability to grant *future* licenses, primarily because any pre-termination licenses of derivative works would still be collected and paid to Mills Music under the terms of the old licenses.

In a strong dissent by Justice White, joined by Brennan, Marshall and Blackmon, it was stated that the majority's reading of the derivative works exception to termination by the author was clearly unsupported by the legislative history. Section §304(c)(6)(A) was designed to protect the owners of derivative works, such as record labels and film producers, from having to renegotiate rights in underlying works such as novels and plays on which the films were based. Justice White declared that the decision by the majority was not consistent with congressional intent, particularly in view of the preference for authors' interests, which the termination provisions express. The dissenters also noted that the majority opinion does not explain how a terminated publisher is allowed to continue to collect royalty income from licensees of derivative rights after termination and then distribute 50% of that income to the author according to a terminated grant, i.e. the publishing contract. This appears in opposition to the language of §304(c)(5): "Termination of the grant may be effected notwithstanding any agreement to the contrary, including an agreement to make a will or to make any future grant." The derivative works clause was a compromise between the concerns of providing increased compensation to authors and promoting public access to existing derivative works. The dissent argued that there is no reason why, upon termination of the grant to Mills Music, the heirs of Snyder could not be substituted as the licensor receiving future royalties from the existing owners of the derivative works "under the terms of the grant" from Mills Music.

In view of the majority ruling, it will require further action by Congress to amend the statutory language in order to correct this interpretation. So far such an amendment appears unlikely in the near future given the time that has passed since the decision in *Mills Music* and the anticipated resistance from music publishers and organizations like the National Music Publishers Association ("NMPA").

Chapter 4

CONTRACT PERFORMANCE AND EXPLOITATION OBLIGATIONS

4.1 DELIVERY STANDARDS

In each of the entertainment industries, the applicable agreements will specify standards for acceptable performance on the part of the artist, the performer, the writer, or whoever else is furnishing services and/or materials to the company.

In the recording industry, for example, the agreement will customarily provide that master recordings must be "technically and commercially satisfactory for the manufacture and sale of phonograph records," a phrase which means, first, that the recordings must comply with the audio standards established by the major U.S. record companies (an essentially objective standard), and, second, that the company must believe that the public will buy records manufactured from the masters, a far more subjective standard. In the literary publishing industry, a typical book contract requires that the manuscript be "satisfactory in form and content" to the publisher.

In the film and television industries, the company usually insists upon approvals over all key personnel (e.g., the line producer, director, screenwriter, principal cast members, director of photography, composer) as well as the budget and the script, approvals which are exercised at important points throughout the production and delivery process. The company will frequently require changes in content and/or personnel. Therefore, it is highly unusual to encounter a relationship such as that which director Woody Allen enjoyed with Orion Pictures for many years which Orion put up the funds for Allen's pictures but reportedly had no input along the way and, when a picture was delivered, Orion had but two choices: to release the picture as delivered, or sell it back to Allen.

As a general rule, the degree of subjectivity with which delivery standards are infused increases in more or less direct proportion to the relative level of investment. The greater the investment (relative to industry norms), the more subjective the company will be.

4.1.1 Delivery Clauses

4.1.1.1 Book Publishing

In the area of book publishing, satisfactory manuscript clauses have been the subject of substantial litigation. The following are examples of such clauses and what happens if the book is considered an unsatisfactory manuscript.

Author agrees to deliver to Publisher on or before _____ (date) in duplicate, and in final revised form and content satisfactory to Publisher, an English-language manuscript of approximately _____ (number) words. Unless postponed by mutual agreement, failure to make timely delivery of the manuscript on or before the date shall be deemed just cause for Publisher, at its option, to terminate this Agreement by giving written notice, whereupon Author agrees to repay forthwith all monies which may have been advanced hereunder and shall further pay other damages as Publisher may sustain by reason of such breach. The foregoing does not exclude any other remedies at law or equity that the publisher may have. It is understood and agreed that no duty shall devolve upon Publisher under this Agreement until such time as the manuscript has been completed to the satisfaction of Publisher. It is understood that in the ordinary course of preparing the manuscript for the printer Publisher is authorized to exercise editorial privilege and to make the manuscript conform to its house style in spelling, punctuation and usage.

If, in the opinion of Publisher, the manuscript is unacceptable or unsatisfactory to Publisher, Publisher may reject it by written notice within sixty (90) days of delivery, in which event any sums previously advanced under this agreement shall be repaid by Author, this Agreement shall be deemed terminated, and there shall be no further obligation upon Publisher to publish the Work or to make any further payment hereunder.

4.1.1.2 Music Publishing

Delivery requirements in music publishing agreements usually include the "delivery commitment" of a certain number of new compositions to the publisher. Compare the delivery requirements of the following two provisions:

Your **"Delivery Commitment"** for each Contract Year shall consist of fifteen (15) 100% newly-written compositions (or the equivalent in compositions only partly written by you), together with notice to us of the completion of delivery of the requisite number of compositions (with titles, names of co-writers and percentages subject to this Agreement, as well as the name(s) of any co-writer(s) and/or co-publisher(s) and the respective share(s) of each such third party).

Your "delivery commitment" for each Contract Year shall consist of: fifteen (15) 100% newly written compositions or the equivalent in compositions only partly written by Writer are embodied on four or more LP length recordings that are initially released commercially in the U.S. during such Contract Year (in CD and cassette formats) by a "**Major Record Company**"(*i.e.,* Sony-BMG, WEA, EMD, Universal, or another company then regularly distributed by one of such companies and distributing such record) and upon which mechanical royalties are actually payable in the U.S. at rates not less than 75% of current U.S. statutory rate set under the Copyright Law together with notice of the completion of delivery of the requisite number of compositions (with titles and percentages subject to this Agreement) and confirmation of release (record label information accompanied by a commercial copy of each record).

4.1.1.3 Recorded Music

Look at following delivery commitment from this major label recording agreement. If you were a recording artist or a recording artist's representative how might you modify this clause to allow for more artistic control?

Delivery Obligations:

1. During each Contract Period you will Deliver to Label commercially satisfactory Masters. Masters that you Deliver in fulfillment of your Recording Commitment (other than the first Album during the initial Contract Period shall be deemed satisfactory, provided such Masters are technically satisfactory and feature first class performances of the same quality, style, and caliber as Artist's prior successful Recordings. Such Masters will embody the featured vocal performances of Artist of contemporary selections, not recorded "live" or "in concert" (other then with Label's prior consent), and that have not been previously recorded by Artist, whether hereunder or otherwise. (Any Masters delivered hereunder that were partially or completely recorded prior to the term of this agreement will be deemed to have been recorded during the initial Contract Period.) Neither Multiple Record Albums nor Joint Recordings may be recorded as part of your Recording Commitment hereunder without Label's written consent. Without limiting the foregoing, Label has the right to reject any Master that Label reasonably believes is either offensive to reasonable standards of public taste or in violation of the rights of others.

2. During each Contract Period, you will cause the Artist to perform for the recording of Masters and you will deliver to Label those Masters (the "Recording Commitment") necessary to satisfy the following schedule:

Contract Period	Recording Commitment
initial Contract Period	one (1) Album
first Option Period	one (1) Album
second Option Period	one (1) Album
third Option Period	one (1) Album
fourth Option Period	one (1) Album

3. Each Album in fulfillment of your Recoding Commitment will be Delivered to Label within five (5) months after the commencement date of the Contract Period concerned.

4. You will not deviate from the Delivery schedule specified in paragraph 3 without Label's written consent; timely Delivery as provided therein is a material obligation hereunder. You agree not to commence the recording of any Record hereunder until five (5) months after the date of Delivery to Label of the immediately preceding Record in fulfillment of your Recording Commitment hereunder. Each Record will consist entirely of Masters made in the course of that recording project.

5. (a) (1) You agree to Deliver to Label each Master hereunder in the form of a Digital Master. You will concurrently deliver all multitrack tapes recorded in connection with the recording project, including, without limitation, all twenty four (24) track master tapes. Without limiting any of Label's rights or remedies hereunder, not less than two (2) weeks prior to Label's of pre-mastering (e.g., equalization and the making of reference dubs or the equivalent thereof in the applicable configurations) for a particular set of Master Recordings hereunder (including remixes of Master Recordings, regardless of whether such remixes will be commercially released), you shall deliver to Label for the applicable set of Master Recordings the lyrics to the Compositions embodied on such Masters, which lyrics shall be typed an in an easily readable form.

(2) Upon Label's request, you agree to Deliver a 96Khz/24 bit 2 channel stereo version and a 5.1 channel surround sound version of each recording embodied on a Master hereunder for use on DVD Audio discs, provided that any such costs will not be deducted from the Recording Fund of the Album concerned, but will be additional Recording Costs to be paid by Label pursuant to a mutually approved budget, and provided further that such additional costs shall be recoupable solely from sales of configurations embodying such surround sound version.

(b) You shall comply with Label's policies with respect to samples, and you and Artist hereby warrant and represent that all information supplied by you or the Artist to Label in that regard is and shall be complete and correct. As of the date hereof, Label's policies with respect to all samples embodied in any Master Recording (including remixes of Master Recordings, regardless of whether such remixes will be commercially released) are as follows:

(1) Prior to Label's authorization of pre-mastering (e.g., equalization and the making of reference dubs or the equivalent thereof in the applicable configurations) for a particular set of Master Recordings hereunder, you shall deliver the following to Label for the applicable set of Master Recordings:

(i) A detailed list of any and all samples embodied in each Master Recording:

(ii) A written clearance or license for the perpetual, nonrestrictive use of each such sample interpolated in each Master Recordings in any and all media from the copyright holder(s) of the Master Recordings and the Composition sampled.

(iii) Any and all necessary information pertaining to credit copy required by the copyright holder(s) of each sample interpolated in each Master Recording.

(2) No Master Recording will be scheduled for release and no Master Recording shall be deemed to be delivered to Label hereunder (and no Advances due on Delivery, if any, will be paid) until such written sample clearances (including credit copy, if any) have been obtained and approved by Label.

(3) If any such sample clearance provides for an advance, a flat-fee "roll-over" payment and/or royalty payment for Net Sales of the applicable Master Recording and your record royalty account hereunder is in an unrecouped position at that the time such royalties are due, then, notwithstanding anything to the contrary contained herein, you shall be solely responsible for making, and shall make such payment(s) to the applicable Person promptly upon receipt from Label of such Person's accounting statement thereof. If Label makes any such payment(s), such payment(s) will constitute an Advance and will be recoupable from all monies becoming payable by Label to you or the Artist under this agreement.

(c) Provided you have complied with your other material obligations hereunder and Label is in receipt of all items described in paragraph _____ below, the date of Delivery of a Record in fulfillment of your Recording Commitment will be the date of receipt of such Digital by Label's Vice President of Pre-production at the address specified on page ___ hereof; concurrently therewith, you will send a written notice that you have so delivered to Label's Senior Vice President of Business and Legal Affairs.

6. Label's election to make payment to you which was to have been made upon Delivery of Masters or to release a Record derived from such Masters will not be deemed to be its acknowledgment that such "Delivery" was properly made, and Label will not be deemed to have waived either its rights to require such complete and proper performance thereafter or its remedies for your failure to perform in accordance therewith. Your isolated failure to deliver an ancillary item required for Delivery hereunder (e.g., a mechanical license) will not delay payment of the Advance otherwise due upon Delivery, provided Label reasonably believes that it will not be harmed in any way by virtue of such delay and that actual delivery will eventually be made. If Label chooses to release any Album in fulfillment of your Recording Commitment hereunder prior to the Delivery of such Album, Label will pay an Advance due upon the Delivery of such Album promptly after the United States release of the Album.

4.1.1.4 Film

Film delivery has two components: physical and legal delivery. Physical delivery refers to delivery of the technical elements such as the original negative, trailers, photo stills, audio materials, and the soundtrack. Legal delivery refers to documents such as the chain of title, underlying agreements, Errors and Omission insurance, cast and crew agreements, MPAA ratings, clearances of any photos or product placements, and any music licenses.

The clause below is an example of a film delivery provision.

Production

Provided only that Producer is able to obtain production financing for the Picture, then Producer shall cause the Picture to be produced subject to Distributor's approval rights and delivered to Distributor as follows:

A. *Technical Requirements.*

(i) The Picture shall be filmed in color on Eastman Kodak color film stock in 35mm with an aspect ratio of 1.85:1, and have a running time of not less than ninety-five (95) minutes and not more than one hundred fifteen (115) minutes (excluding the end titles) and shall not be filmed with the use of a hard matte;

(ii) The Picture shall follow the final shooting script approved by Distributor as of the commencement of principal photography of the Picture (*i.e.*, Producer shall not make any changes therein which would materially alter the storyline, including plot and character elements necessary to the storyline as contained in the approved shooting script without the prior written approval of a Business Affairs executive of Distributor, excepting only minor changes required by the exigencies of production);

(iii) The Picture shall qualify for an MPAA rating not more restrictive than "PG" unless otherwise agreed to in writing by Distributor;

(iv) Distributor shall be furnished with "cover shots" and alternate scenes and dialogue (which Distributor shall designate prior to commencement of principal photography) and can be incorporated into the Picture to render it suitable for exhibition on United States network prime-time television and a television version (the "Television Version") of the Picture which shall have a running time of not less than ninety-three (93) minutes and fourteen (14) seconds; and which shall be in accordance with applicable network "Standards and Practices" regulations of which Distributor informs Producer and similar family cable requirements regarding the content of motion pictures of which Distributor informs Producer. Such cover shots and alternate scenes and dialogue shall be such that the same can be integrated into such prime-time network version and family cable versions of the Picture without materially changing or impairing the continuity of the storyline of the Picture; and

(v) The Picture's main and end title credits shall conform to Distributor's standard policies and practices, and in no event shall the end title credits have a running time in excess of three (3) minutes.

B. *Insurance.* Producer shall obtain all normal and customary insurance coverage for the Picture (including cast insurance for principal personnel, liability insurance and Errors and Omissions Insurance), and shall provide satisfactory evidence thereof to Distributor Prior to commencement of principal photography of the Picture.

C. *Delivery Date.* Producer shall deliver the Picture not later than 16 weeks after the scheduled completion of principal photography of the Picture, but in no event later than _____, 199_ (200_), and in this regard, time is of the essence.

D. *Cutting Rights.* Distributor shall have the right, in connection with the marketing, distribution and exploitation of the Picture to cut, edit or alter the Picture or any part thereof as is required to comply with censorship requirements, exhibition requirements, rating and length requirements, compliance with law, and release exigencies. In addition, after Delivery (as hereafter defined) of the Picture to Distributor, Distributor shall have all other rights to cut and edit the Picture for all other forms of media and exploitation, including without limitation television exhibition (*e.g.,* to meet broadcast time requirements), airline and/or ship exhibition requirements and other non-theatrical exhibition requirements as Distributor may see fit in its sole discretion. The Chairman of _____ shall be the individual who has the right of "final cut" of the Picture.

4.2 THE COMPANY'S OBLIGATIONS

4.2.1 The Fiduciary Duty Claim

Claims are made on a regular basis that companies are fiduciaries for authors, performers, songwriters and other talent. A "fiduciary" is "a person holding the character of a trustee, or a character analogous to that of a trustee, in respect to the trust and confidence involved in it and the scrupulous good faith and candor which it requires [,a] person having [the] duty, created by his undertaking, to act primarily for another's benefit in matters connected with such undertaking" (*Black's Law Dictionary 625* [6th ed. 1990]). In addition to being required to perform to a higher standard than that applied to normal business dealings (good faith and fair dealing), a fiduciary may be exposed to a statute of limitations which is considerably longer than that applicable to normal business relationships.

As the following cases indicate, the company is not normally considered a fiduciary. Where rights are conveyed outright by an artist to a company subject to a duty on the part of the company to pay royalties, the relationship that is created is essentially that of debtor and creditor. However, as we see in the *Contemporary Mission* case and the *Van Valkenburgh* discussion in Section 4.2.2, below, the acceptance of special duties and/or certain types of particularly disloyal behavior may render the company liable for far more extensive damages than would otherwise be the case. See also *Art Buchwald v. Paramount Pictures Corp.* in Section 5.5.

Rodgers v. Roulette Records, Inc., 677 F. Supp. 731 (S.D.N.Y. 1988)

Kram, District Judge

[Rodgers sued defendants for failure to account and to pay royalties, on a number of theories, including, among others, breach of contract and breach of fiduciary duty. Defendants moved for summary judgment, claiming that the applicable statute of limitations had run, and that they were entitled to judgment as a matter of law on the other claims, including the claim of breach of fiduciary duty. The court granted defendants' motion on seven of eight claims, including the claim for breach of fiduciary duty.]

FACTUAL BACKGROUND

... The Contract [i.e., the applicable recording agreement, which was signed on April 23, 1957] provided that "Jimmy" Rodgers would record at least eight record sides for defendant, the compositions to be chosen by defendant. Plaintiff was restricted from making recordings for anyone else during the term of the agreement and for five years thereafter. Defendant was to pay plaintiff royalties in the amount of three percent (3%) of the "retail list price of double-faced records sold in the U.S. and paid for" ... [with royalties at half rate on foreign sales]. ...

Defendant would charge against plaintiff's account the entire cost of the recording sessions and any advances made by defendant to plaintiff. Statements were to be issued twice a year, on September 1st and March 1st. The Contract provided that all recordings belonged solely to defendant company and gave defendant the right to assign, lend, lease or sell to any person, firm or company, matrices, stampers or master recordings from which records ... may be manufactured or sold and shall have the right to grant permission to any such person, firm or company ... to manufacture and sell records therefrom.

Plaintiff claims that either the Contract or industry custom requires defendants to pay royalties for sales made by licensees ... whereas defendant Levy [Morris Levy, president of Roulette—Ed.] asserts that Roulette had no contractual obligation to charge license fees. ... Roulette Records' comptroller, Howard Fisher, acknowledges, however, that royalties were to be computed by applying the royalty rate to record sales or to license fees. ...

Plaintiff claims that he has made approximately 100 recordings for plaintiff, but has received insufficient or no royalties since the early sixties because defendants underreported domestic sales, failed to report foreign sales, failed to report sales by licensees, and ascribed too low a royalty rate to many of the songs. ...

Plaintiff also alleges that defendants failed to provide accounting statements as required under the Contract. ... [He] claims not to have received any accounting statements until 1981, yet it is apparent that plaintiff's agents received at least some accounting reports since the time the Contract was signed. ...

Plaintiff claims that these accounting statements misrepresented the royalties and sales of plaintiff's songs.

Between 1957 and 1960, defendant Roulette Records advanced money to plaintiff and charged his account with costs for recording, totalling approximately $26,000. Over the next twenty-five years, defendants credited plaintiff's account with royalties in an amount approximating

$20,000. . . . After commencement of the lawsuit, defendant Roulette Records acknowledged that it owed plaintiff an additional $14,000 for royalties due for the early 1980's. Plaintiff alleges that this amount is but a small fraction of the actual amount due from 1960 through the present. . . .

DISCUSSION

[The Court proceeded to decide, *inter alia,* (1) that the account between plaintiff and defendant was not "an open, mutual account," so that the six-year statute of limitations would apply to each accounting in turn, instead of commencing to run on the entire history of the account only from the last accounting, (2) that plaintiff's claim of conversion was barred by the three-year statute of limitations applicable to such actions and, in addition, that plaintiff had failed to prove title to specific, identifiable monies, as opposed to a general claim for payment out of monies title to which belonged to defendants, and (3) that defendant was also entitled to summary judgment on plaintiff's fraud claim, applying New York's two-year fraud statute of limitations and holding that it applied to each successive statement, since plaintiff had (as the statute required) "knowledge of facts sufficient to suggest to a person of ordinary intelligence the probability that he has been defrauded".]

. . . Since plaintiff claims that the misrepresentation upon which the fraud claim was based was each of the allegedly false royalty statements, the alleged fraudulent dispossession of royalties occurred with the issuance of each allegedly false royalty statement. The critical question is thus when plaintiff discovered or reasonably should have discovered the fraud.

Plaintiff claims not to have discovered the fraud until shortly before he filed his lawsuit in 1984. . . . Plaintiff asserts that the royalty statements appeared accurate mathematically . . . and that nothing in the royalty statements indicated that defendants were defrauding plaintiff . . . [Plaintiff stated that] "I did not have any expectation that monies would be forthcoming as I was not aware of any exploitation by Roulette or its licensees, if any, of my songs recorded for Roulette." . . . At the same time, however, plaintiff alleges in his complaint that his "songs sold millions of copies at around the time of their release and have continued to sell through and including the present time." . . . Moreover, plaintiff recorded over 100 songs for defendants, representing "a healthy portion of their better-selling records," [according to plaintiff]. . . . It is inconceivable that plaintiff or his agents did not notice that his songs were being released on records between 1960 and 1984.

. . . Plaintiff's agents should have known that royalties were understated given plaintiff's apparent popularity. At the very least plaintiff or his agents should have investigated the status of his royalties given the apparent discrepancy between the sale of millions of [copies of] his songs and the veritable trickle of royalties flowing back to plaintiff. Such an investigation would necessarily have to have gone beyond mere reliance on defendants' royalty statements. Reliance on statements suspected of being false cannot be the due diligence required of plaintiff.

Additionally, plaintiff is not entitled to recover under his fraud claims as a matter of law [because of the absence of] a false representation upon which plaintiff detrimentally relied. . . . Plaintiff alleges that, at the time of contracting, defendant promised to pay royalties and provide accountings while secretly never intending to do so. While this allegation would state a claim for fraud under New York law, see *Bower v. Weisman,* 650 F. Supp. 1415, 1422 (S.D.N.Y. 1980) (citing *Sabo v. Delman,* 3 N.Y.2d 155, 162, 164 N.Y.S.2d 714, 718, 143 N.E.2d 906, 909 (1957)) (Note: The Court notes the existence of contrary authority in New York courts. See, e.g., *CB Western Financial v. Computer Consoles,* 122 A.D.2d 10, 504 N.Y.S.2d 179, 182 (N.Y. App. Div. 2d Dep't. 1986) (a "cause of action for fraud in inducing a contract cannot be based solely upon a failure to perform contractual promises of future acts.")) See *Deerfield Communications Corp. Chesebrough-Ponds, Inc.,* 68 N.Y.2d 954, 510 N.Y.S.2d 88, 89, 502 N.E.2d 1003, 1004 (1986) (plaintiff did not produce evidence which suggested that defendant misrepresented an existing fact which induced the contract) plaintiff has not produced evidence, beyond defendants' failure to perform, to suggest that defendants never intended to perform their contractual obligations. *Soper v. Simmons Int'l, Ltd.,* 632 F. Supp. 244, 249 (S.D.N.Y. 1986) (proof of undisclosed intention not to perform contract must be based on sufficient evidence in addition to mere nonperformance) (cases cited therein). As such, defendants are entitled to summary judgment on the fraudulent inducement claim.

Finally, plaintiff's fraud claim fails for the simple reason that the fraud they [sic] allege is nothing more than the breach of contract. . . . [T]he alleged fraudulent misrepresentations were the allegedly false royalty statements. Any wrongdoing by defendants stems from a breach of their contractual obligations. For these reasons, defendants' motions [for summary judgment on the fraud claims] are granted. . . .

Defendants move for summary judgment on plaintiff's action for an accounting. In order to establish a right to an accounting, which is an action in equity, plaintiff must demonstrate the existence of a fiduciary relationship between himself and defendant, or the existence of a joint venture or other special circumstances warranting equitable relief. *Grossman v. Laurence Handprints-N.J., Inc.,* 90 A.D.2d 95, 455 N.Y.S.2d 852, 858 (2d Dept. 1982); see *Sanshoe Trading Corp. v. Mitsubishi Int'l Corp.,* 122 Misc.2d 585, 470 N.Y.S.2d 991, 1993 (N.Y. Sup. Ct. 1984), *aff'd,* 104 A.D.2d 337, 479 N.Y.S.2d 149 (N.Y. App. Div. 1st Dep't. 1984). Plaintiff claims that a fiduciary relationship exists because defendants collected money on behalf of plaintiff in the form of royalties or license fees. This claim fails for a few reasons.

No fiduciary relationship exists in this case between Rodgers and defendants; instead, the parties enjoy a contractual relationship. In

Sanshoe, the court held that a fiduciary relationship did not exist between a sales agent and the company for whom the agent made sales, even though the company collected money which it had an obligation to pass on to plaintiff. 470 N.Y.S.2d at 993. . . . See also *Van Valkenburgh, Nooger & Neville, Inc. v. Hayden Publishing Company,* 33 A.D.2d 766, 306 N.Y.S.2d 599 (N.Y. App. Div. 1st Dep't. 1969) (no fiduciary relationship where purely commercial relationship exists), *aff'd* 30 N.Y.2d 34, 330 N.Y.S.2d 329, 281 N.E.2d 142 (1972), *cert. denied* 409 U.S. 875, 93 S.Ct. 125, 34 L.Ed.2d 128 (1972).

Similarly in this case, the fact that Roulette or Levy collected royalties or fees which it [sic] had an obligation to pass on to plaintiff did not make them plaintiff's fiduciaries. In addition, never having received [anything specifically earmarked as] plaintiff's property . . . defendants could not have been acting as their fiduciary. Since defendants were not fiduciaries to plaintiff, an accounting is not available. . . .

Plaintiff claims that defendants breached a fiduciary duty by negotiating for unconscionably low royalty fees with defendants' licensees. Defendants are entitled to summary judgment for a number of reasons.

First, as stated above, there was no fiduciary relationship to be breached. Second, plaintiff could not identify any royalty or license fee that was unconscionably low. Third, plaintiff alleged, but did not establish, that defendants had a duty to negotiate royalty or license fees with third parties. Defendants claim that no such obligation existed. The record nowhere indicates an obligation for defendants to negotiate on plaintiff's behalf. Indeed, the nature of the alleged duty was simply that defendants had a duty to ensure that plaintiff received the ultimate yield due from the licensing arrangements. . . . At best, plaintiff had a contractual or implied contractual right to receive royalties for recordings which Roulette decided to license to third parties. Defendants' motions for summary judgment on this claim are thus granted.

Mellencamp v. Riva Music Ltd., 698 F. Supp. 1154 (S.D.N.Y. 1988)

CONBOY, DISTRICT JUDGE

Plaintiff John J. Mellencamp, professionally known as John Cougar Mellencamp, is a songwriter, performer, and recording artist who has enjoyed enormous success in recent years. Defendants (collectively "the Riva companies") are affiliated corporations owned and/or controlled by William A. Gaff. On May 12, 1977, Mellencamp entered into a written publishing agreement with defendant G. H. Music, Ltd. Pursuant to the 1977 agreement, Mellencamp assigned to G. H. Music the worldwide copyrights in and to the compositions to be authored by him during the term of the agreement. The 1977 agreement was modified by a written agreement, dated February 28, 1979, and by letter agreement, dated February 21, 1980. On June 15, 1981, John Cougar, Inc. entered into a written publishing agreement with defendant Riva Music, Ltd. whereby

John Cougar, Inc. assigned Mellencamp's songwriting and composing services and copyrights to Riva. On June 1, 1983, Mellencamp entered into a third publishing agreement with defendant Riva Music, Inc. Finally, by written agreement dated July 26, 1985, among Riva Music, Inc., Riva Music, Ltd., G. H. Music, Ltd, Mellencamp, and John Cougar Inc., each of the prior publishing agreements was amended in certain respects. In exchange for the assignment of the copyrights, Mellencamp received a percentage of the royalties earned from the exploitation of his music.

By virtue of the publishing agreements, according to the complaint, the Riva companies became fiduciaries for Mellencamp's interests. In his first and second claims, Mellencamp alleges that defendants breached their fiduciary duties by failing to actively promote his songs and to use their best efforts to obtain all the monies rightfully due him from third parties. In his third claim, Mellencamp contends that the Riva companies breached the various publishing agreements controlling their relationship by consistently underreporting royalties due him and by failing to timely render royalty statements and payments. In his fourth and final claim, Mellencamp contends that he entered into a binding agreement with the Riva companies pursuant to which the defendants agreed to release him from all obligations under the publishing contracts and to return all the rights to and in his musical compositions in exchange for $3 million dollars. . . . [Since the Court granted summary judgment to the defendants with respect to Mellencamp's fourth claim on the basis of straight contract and copyright analysis, the Court's discussion of the fourth claim is omitted—Eds.]

Defendants now move pursuant to Rule 12(b) (6) to dismiss the complaint on the ground that it fails to state any valid claim for relief. Specifically, defendants contend (1) that the first two claims fail as a matter of law because no fiduciary duties are owed by a publisher to an author under a publishing agreement [and] (2) that the third claim fails to specify which of the publishing agreements were breached, who the parties to the agreements were, and which provisions of the agreements were breached, and also fails to include a necessary party. . . .

ANALYSIS

I. Fiduciary Duties

Under New York law, the existence of fiduciary obligations in a particular relationship cannot be determined by recourse to fixed formulas or precedents:

Broadly stated, a fiduciary relationship is one founded upon trust or confidence reposed by one person in the integrity and fidelity of another. It is said that the relationship exists in all cases in which influence has been reposed and betrayed. The rule embraces both technical fiduciary relations and those informal relations which exist whenever one man trusts in, and relies upon, another (see *Mobil Oil Corp v. Rubenfeld,* 72 Misc.2d 392, 399–400, 339 N.Y.S.2d 623, *aff'd.* 77 Misc.2d 962, 357 N.Y.S.2d 589, revs. on other grounds 48 A.D.2d

428, 370 N.Y.S.2d 943). Such a relationship might be found to exist, in appropriate circumstances between close friends (see *Cody v. Gallow,* 28 Misc.2d 373, 214 N.Y. S.2d 127) or even where confidence is based upon prior business dealings (see *Levine v. Chussid,* 31 Misc.2d 412, 221 N.Y.S.2d 311).

> *Penato v. George,* 52 A.D.2d 939, 942, 383 N.Y.S.2d 900, 904–05
> (2d Dep't 1976).

Notwithstanding this broad rule, defendants, relying on *Van Valkenburgh, Nooger & Neville, Inc. v. Hayden Publishing Co.,* 30 N.Y.2d 34, 330 N.Y.S.2d 329, 281 N.E.2d 142 (1972), *cert. denied,* 409 U.S. 875, 93 S.Ct. 125, 34 L.Ed.2d 128 (1972), argue that the relationship between an author and a publisher can never be a fiduciary relationship. *Van Valkenburgh* does not support this proposition.

There, a publisher and an author entered into a written agreement which provided, *inter alia,* that the publisher was obligated to use its best efforts to promote the author's books. *Id.,* 30 N.Y.2d at 43, 330 N.Y.S.2d at 331, 281 N.E.2d at 144. The agreement also provided that the author would receive a 15% royalty on all books sold. *Id.* The trial court found that the publisher did not use its best efforts to promote the books, the publisher occupied a fiduciary relationship to the author, and the publisher failed to act in good faith in that relationship. *Id.* at 44, 330 N.Y.S.2d at 332, 281 N.E.2d at 144. On appeal, the Appellate Division determined that no fiduciary relationship existed between the parties. *Id.* Instead, the court concluded, the relationship between the parties was one of ordinary contract. *Id.* The court also concluded that the publisher did not breach its duty of good faith but found that the publisher did breach its contractual obligation to use its best efforts to promote the author's books. *Id.* The New York Court of Appeals affirmed, concluding that "it *could* be found, as a matter of law, *on the record,* that there was no fiduciary relationship." *Id.* at 46, 330 N.Y.S.2d at 334, 281 N.E.2d at 145 (emphasis added). See also *Lane v. Mercury Record Corp.,* 21 A.D.2d 602, 252 N.Y.S.2d 1011 (1st Dep't 1964) (a royalty or percentage arrangement would not in and of itself establish a fiduciary relationship), *aff'd,* 18 N.Y.2d 889, 276 N.Y.S.2d 626, 223 N.E.2d 35 (1966). The Court did not hold that fiduciary obligations could never arise in a relationship based at least in part on publishing agreements.

(1) The complaint as drafted, however, goes further than this, suggesting that fiduciary obligations attach to the publisher-author relationship as a matter of law and, consequently, that the Riva companies' alleged failure to meet their express or implied contract obligations amounts to a breach of trust. In addition, there is language in several older state cases, as well as in federal cases interpreting New York state law, that arguably supports the view that a publisher-author contract creates a "technical fiduciary relation." If these cases can be so interpreted, they are directly at odds with the greater weight of authority which teaches that the conventional publisher-author arrangement is not a per se fiduciary relationship. Commenting on the ambiguities in the caselaw, Judge Haight observed that "[t]he legal responsibilities

attendant upon this status . . . are far from clear." *Warfield v. Jerry Vogel Music Co., Inc.*, 1978 Copyright L. Rep. (CCH) para. 25,005, at 15,033 (SDNY Mar. 21, 1978). These cases warrant discussion.

(2) Under New York law, every contract includes an implied covenant of good faith and fair dealing which precludes a party from engaging in conduct that will deprive the other contracting party of his benefits under their agreement. *Filner v. Shapiro*, 633 F.2d 139, 143 (2d Cir.1980). A contract is also deemed to include any promise which a reasonable person in the position of the promisee would be justified in believing was included. *Rowe v. Great Atlantic & Pacific Tea Co., Inc.*, 46 N.Y.2d 62, 69, 412 N.Y.S.2d 827, 831, 385 N.E.2d 566, 570 (1978). When the essence of a contract is the assignment or grant of an exclusive license in exchange for a share of the assignee's profits in exploiting the license, these principles imply an obligation on the part of the assignee to make reasonable efforts to exploit the license. *Havel v. Kelsey-Hayes*, 83 A.D.2d 380, 382, 445 N.Y.S.2d 333, 335 (4th Dep't 1981). See also *Zilg v. Prentice-Hall, Inc.*, 717 F.2d 671 (2d Cir.1983) (promise of publisher to publish book which it has obtained exclusive rights to implies good faith effort to promote the book). The critical point here is that a publisher's obligation to promote an author's work is one founded in contract rather than on trust principles.

While it is true that several of the cases cited by plaintiff discuss certain "trust elements that are part of the relationship between a writer and a publisher," *Nolan v. Sam Fox Publishing Company, Inc.*, 499 F.2d 1394, 1400 (2d Cir.1974), it is apparent that the courts were in fact discussing a publisher's implied-in-law contract obligations or were relying on trust principles in situations where the publisher tolerated or participated in tortious conduct against the author. For example, in *Schisgall v. Fairchild Publications*, 207 Misc. 224, 137 N.Y.S.2d 312 (Sup. Ct. N.Y. County 1955), the plaintiff-author alleged that his publisher refused to fill existing orders for his book, withdrew his book from sale, and refused to transfer the rights to the book back to the author, all for "the single purpose to abort or destroy . . . the defendant's interests." *Id.* at 232, 137 N.Y.S.2d at 319. In determining whether the alleged conduct created tort liability in addition to liability in contract, the court observed that "the intentional infliction of injury without just cause is prima facie tortious." *Id.* at 230, 137 N.Y.S.2d at 317.

As a preliminary matter, however, the court had to determine whether the plaintiff could be deemed to have suffered any injury in the absence of express contractual obligations or rights governing the complained of conduct. In response to defendant's assertion that the plaintiff retained no protectible interest in his literary product because he assigned all his rights to the defendant, the court stated:

[A]s I read the contract, even though there be an absolute assignment, there was such an assignment on the basis of the business to be done—such a transfer of rights and property to the defendant as did not denude the plaintiffs of a certain right and interest, and that arrangement resulted in that kind of relationship that *fair dealing* was required between the parties. It is not the express contractual reservation of rights per se on which plaintiffs rely, but upon the defendant's breach of the special relationship thus created—plus the defendant's intentional purpose to destroy. It is not necessary to use the magic words of "fiduciary relationship," or to hold that a "relationship of trust and confidence" was created by the contract, or to find that defendant became a "trustee" of the copyright for the benefit of the plaintiffs (as well as of the defendant). As Chief Judge Cardozo put it in *Wood v. Lucy, Lady Duff-Gordon,* 222 N.Y. 88, 91, 118 N.E. 214: "The law has outgrown its primitive stage of formalism when the precise word was the sovereign talisman, and every slip was fatal. It takes a broader view today. *A promise may be lacking and yet the whole writing may be 'instinct with an obligation,' imperfectly expressed.*" Similarly, the special relationship here may not be specifically expressed, and yet the whole factual situation may be instinct with a duty which should be imposed by law upon the publisher.

The law implies a promise on the defendant's part to endeavor to make the book and copyright productive, since that is the very purpose of the assignment of literary rights and the correlative obligation to pay royalties, *In re Waterson, Berlin & Snyder Co. v. Irving Trust Co.,* 48 F.2d 704 [2nd Cir. 1981]. Id. at 230–31, 137 N.Y.S.2d at 317–18 (emphasis added).

Despite the reference to "fiduciary relationship" and "relationship of trust," it is clear, in context, that the court was talking about a publisher's implied-in-law contract obligation to use its best efforts to promote an author's work, where the publisher has exclusive rights in the work. The single case cited in the court's discussion of the "special relationship" between author and publisher, *Wood v. Lucy, Lady Duff-Gordon,* 222 N.Y. 88, 91, 118 N.E. 214 (1917) (Cardozo, C.J.), is the seminal authority on an exclusive licensee's implied promise to use reasonable efforts to generate profits from the license. The court's reliance on contract principles is confirmed later in the opinion:

If the defendant acted merely as a contracting party (at legal liberty perhaps to breach its agreement on payment of damages), that is one thing. But if the defendant went further, and acted with intent to inflict injury beyond that contemplated as a result of the mere breach of contract, I would hold that the contract does not grant the defaulter immunity from tort liability. *Even though the act would not be actionable in tort if the defendant "elected" to breach its contract in furtherance of its legitimate business interests,* it is tortious (as well as a breach of contract) if there be no self-interest involved, but rather the sole purpose be that of injury to another. Id., 207 Misc.2d at 232, 137 N.Y.S.2d at 319 (emphasis added).

The holding of Schisgall is that a publisher who breaches his implied contract obligation to exploit an author's work with no motive other than to injure the author, is liable for prima facie tort. See *Nifty Foods Corp. v. Great Atlantic & Pacific Tea Co.,* 614 F.2d 832, 838 n. 7 (2d Cir. 1980) ("*Schisgall*... involved the deliberate and unjustified destruction of a property right entrusted under a contract").

Relying on the two paragraphs from 207 Misc.2d at pages 230–31, 137 N.Y.S.2d at 317–18 of *Schisgall* quoted above, the court in *Manning v. Miller Music Corp.*, 174 F. Supp. 192, 195–96 (S.D.N.Y. 1959), characterized the relationship between publisher and author as one involving fiduciary obligations. But as in *Schisgall,* the court did not hold that the publisher's breach of contract obligations gave rise to liability as a fiduciary, nor was such liability even at issue. The question in *Manning* was whether the plaintiffs, composers of a song who assigned their copyrights to a publisher, had standing to maintain a suit for infringement against a third party. *Id.* at 194. The court concluded that the "peculiar relationship between the author and his publisher," *id.* at 195, gives the authors standing to bring suit against a third party infringer when the publisher fails to do so. "It is this fiduciary relationship imposing equitable obligations upon the publisher beyond those ordinarily imposed by law upon those dealing fully at arms' length, which gives the plaintiffs standing to sue here." *Id.* at 196. Analogizing the situation to a stockholder's derivative action, *id.* at 196, the court reasoned that plaintiffs could maintain the infringement action as long as the publisher was joined as a nominal defendant. *Id.* Notably, the court concluded that it would be inappropriate to force plaintiffs to institute "a separate action in *contract* against the publisher" to achieve the same end. *Id.* at 197 (emphasis added). See also *Cortner v. Israel,* 732 F.2d 267, 271 (2d Cir.1984) (when a composer assigns a copyright title to a publisher in exchange for the payment of royalties, an equitable trust relationship is established between the two parties which gives the composer standing to sue for infringement of the copyright). In a similar vein, the court in *Nelson v. Mills,* 278 A.D. 311, 104 N.Y.S.2d 605 (1951), *aff'd,* 304 N.Y. 966, 110 N.E.2d 892 (1953), held that a publisher's actual promotion of a song which infringed the author's was a "breach of contract or trust." *Id.* at 312, 104 N.Y.S.2d at 606. But the court also asserted, echoing Schisgall, that "the defendant was not obligated to promote the sale of plaintiff's song." *Id.* at 312, 104 N.Y.S.2d at 607.

(3) To the extent the cases discussed above intended to posit a per se rule that a publisher with exclusive rights in a work is a fiduciary for the author's interests, they must be rejected as inconsistent with *Van Valkenburgh.* The better view, and the one consistent with *Van Valkenburgh,* is that the "trust elements" in a publisher-author relationship come into play when the publisher tolerates infringing conduct, *Manning, Cortner,* or participates in it, *Nelson v. Mills.* Ordinarily, however, the express and implied obligations assumed by a publisher in an exclusive licensing contract are not, as a matter of law, fiduciary duties. See *Sobol v. E. P. Dutton, Inc.,* 112 F.R.D. 99, 104 (S.D.N.Y. 1986) (Weinfeld, J.); *Ekern v. Sew/Fit Company, Inc.,* 622 F. Supp. 367, 373 (N.D.Ill. 1985) (citing *Van Valkenburgh*). Cf. *Beneficial Commercial Corp. v. Murray Glick Datsun,* 601 F. Supp. 770, 772 (S.D.N.Y. 1985) (absent assumption of control or responsibility and corresponding repose of trust, arm's length business transaction does not give rise to fiduciary

relationship). Accordingly, since plaintiff's first two claims are predicated solely upon the professional relationship between the parties and do not plead any specific conduct or circumstances upon which trust elements are implicated, they are dismissed. In the unlikely event that plaintiff can repair his pleadings in this regard, he is given leave to re-plead within twenty days of the date of this order. . . .

NOTES

1. In *Waverly Productions, Inc. v. RKO General, Inc.*, 217 Cal.App. 2d 721, 22 Cal.Rptr. 73 (Cal. Ct. App. 2d Dist. 1963), the court held that (except with respect to the duty to account for film rentals received) a film distributor was not a fiduciary with respect to the production company licensor.
2. Under Illinois law, "[a] fiduciary duty must be established by more than just a showing of a contractual relationship plus a subservient party's reliance on the trust placed in the other party." The determination is based on "(1) the degree of business experience between the parties, and (2) the extent to which the allegedly subservient party entrusts the handling of his business and financial affairs to the other party." In a case involving an oral license from the widow of rock legend Frank Zappa to a video distributor, the court found that the widow had business experience and that the licensee lacked "overwhelming business influence over [Mrs.] Zappa in their relationship." *Glovarama, Inc. v. Maljack Productions. Inc.*, 1998 WL 102742 (N.D. Ill. 1998).

Wolf v. Superior Court, 1130 Cal. Rptr. 2d 860 (Ct. App. 2003)

PERLUSS, P.

Petitioners Gary K. Wolf and his company Cry Wolf!, Inc. (hereinafter referred to collectively as Wolf), seek a writ of mandate to compel the trial court to vacate its order sustaining, without leave to amend, the demurrer of real party in interest, Walt Disney Pictures and Television (Disney), to Wolf's cause of action for breach of fiduciary duty. At issue is whether one contracting party's right to contingent compensation in the form of a percentage of future revenues in the control of the other contracting party creates a fiduciary relationship in an otherwise arm's length business transaction. Because a contingent entitlement to future compensation within the exclusive control of one party does not make that party a fiduciary in the absence of other indicia of a confidential relationship, we deny the request for a writ of mandate.

FACTUAL AND PROCEDURAL BACKGROUND

The operative second amended complaint alleges that Gary Wolf is the author of the novel entitled Who Censored Roger Rabbit? (1981). In or about August 1983, Wolf entered into a written agreement with Disney (the 1983 Agreement) in which Wolf assigned to Disney the rights to the novel and the Roger Rabbit characters. In exchange for acquiring the rights, Disney agreed to pay Wolf a stated, fixed compensation upon execution of the agreement; a percentage of the "net profits," as defined by the parties, from a motion picture based on the novel; and additional, contingent compensation in the amount of 5 percent of any future gross receipts Disney earned from merchandising or other exploitation of the Roger Rabbit characters. The 1983 Agreement provided that Disney was not "under any obligation to exercise any of the rights" granted to it and could assign or license any and all rights granted under the 1983 Agreement as Disney "s[aw] fit."

Disney then developed and coproduced, along with Steven Spielberg's Amblin Entertainment, a motion picture entitled Who Framed Roger Rabbit (1988) based upon Wolf's novel and its characters. After a dispute arose between Wolf and Disney regarding certain terms contained in the 1983 Agreement, the parties entered into a 1989 agreement that confirmed Wolf's entitlement to the contingent compensation set forth in the 1983 Agreement. In addition, the 1989 agreement granted Wolf certain audit rights.

According to the complaint, each time Wolf attempted to exercise its audit rights, Disney failed to provide access to pertinent records. In addition, Disney allegedly underreported revenues it received in connection with the Roger Rabbit characters and failed to disclose the nature of its third party agreements concerning the characters and the compensation received. Wolf alleges such conduct not only constitutes a breach of contract but also amounts to a breach of fiduciary duty. Wolf claims that Disney is a fiduciary because Disney enjoyed "exclusive control over the books, records and information concerning the exploitation [of the Roger Rabbit characters] and the revenue and Gross Receipts Royalties derived therefrom." . . .

CONTENTIONS

Wolf contends its contingent entitlement to future compensation in the form of a percentage of revenues from Disney's exploitation of the Roger Rabbit characters, together with Disney's exclusive control over the information pertaining to such revenues, necessarily creates a fiduciary relationship. . . .

DISCUSSION

1. The Trial Court Did Not Err in Sustaining Without Leave to Amend the Demurrer to the Breach of Fiduciary Duty Cause of Action

A fiduciary relationship is " 'any relation existing between parties to a transaction wherein one of the parties is in duty bound to act with the utmost good faith for the benefit of the other party. Such a relation ordinarily arises where a confidence is reposed by one person in the integrity of another, and in such a relation the party in whom the confidence is reposed, if he voluntarily accepts or assumes to accept the confidence, can take no advantage from his acts relating to the interest of the other party without the latter's knowledge or consent. . . . ' " (*Herbert v. Lankershim,*

(1937) 9 Cal.2d 409, 483 [71 P.2d 220]; see also *Rickel v. Schwinn Bicycle Co.,* (1983) 144 Cal. App. 3d 648, 654 [192 Cal. Rptr. 732] [" 'A "fiduciary relation" in law is ordinarily synonymous with a "confidential relation." It is . . . founded upon the trust or confidence reposed by one person in the integrity and fidelity of another, and likewise precludes the idea of profit or advantage resulting from the dealings of the parties and the person in whom the confidence is reposed.' "])

Traditional examples of fiduciary relationships in the commercial context include trustee/beneficiary, directors and majority shareholders of a corporation, business partners, joint adventurers, and agent/principal.

Inherent in each of these relationships is the duty of undivided loyalty the fiduciary owes to its beneficiary, imposing on the fiduciary obligations far more stringent than those required of ordinary contractors. As Justice Cardozo observed, "Many forms of conduct permissible in a workaday world for those acting at arm's length, are forbidden to those bound by fiduciary ties. A trustee is held to something stricter than the morals of the market place. Not honesty alone, but the punctilio of an honor the most sensitive is then the standard of behavior." (*Meinhard v. Salmon,* (N.Y. 1928) 249 N.Y. 458 [164 N.E. 545, 546].)

Wolf concedes the complaint is devoid of allegations showing an agency, trust, joint venture, partnership or other "traditionally recognized" fiduciary relationship and further admits that the complaint cannot be amended to state facts alleging such a relationship. Nonetheless, he argues that the absence of a "traditionally recognized" fiduciary relationship is not dispositive on the question whether a fiduciary duty exists. Because Wolf's contractual right to contingent compensation necessarily required Wolf to repose "trust and confidence" in Disney to account for the revenues received, and because such revenues and their sources are in the exclusive knowledge and control of Disney, Wolf claims the relationship is "confidential" in nature and necessarily imposes a fiduciary duty upon Disney, at least with respect to accounting to Wolf for the gross revenues received.

a. A Contingent Entitlement to Future Compensation Does Not, Alone, Give Rise to a Fiduciary Relationship.

Contrary to Wolf's contention, the contractual right to contingent compensation in the control of another has never, by itself, been sufficient to create a fiduciary relationship where one would not otherwise exist. (See, e.g., *Downey v. Humphreys,* (1951) 102 Cal. App. 2d 323, 332 [227 P.2d 484] [the obligation to pay money is a debt; "A debt is not a trust" and does not create a fiduciary relationship, "whether [debtor's] liability is certain or contingent"]; *Wiltsee v. California Emp. Com. (1945)* 69 Cal. App. 2d 120, 125, 128 [158 P.2d 612] [employment contract entitling employee to 25 percent of future profits neither created a joint venture nor gave rise to a fiduciary relationship]. Equally without merit is Wolf's contention that a fiduciary relationship exists because he necessarily reposed "trust and confidence" in Disney to perform its contractual obligation—that is, to account for and pay Wolf the contingent compensation agreed upon in the contract. Every contract requires one party to repose an element of trust and confidence in the other to perform. For this reason, every contract contains an implied covenant of good faith and fair dealing, obligating the contracting parties to refrain from " 'doing anything which will have the effect of destroying or injuring the right of the other party to receive the fruits of the contract . . . .' "

b. The Profit-sharing Aspect of an Agreement Alone Does Not Give Rise to a Fiduciary Relationship.

Wolf cites a number of cases for the proposition that profit or revenue-sharing agreements are inherently fiduciary in nature. None of them, however, supports its claim. For example, in *Nelson, supra,* 29 Cal.2d 745, the court addressed whether an agreement to share the profits of the operation of the business, though without an equity interest in the business, gave rise to a fiduciary obligation in the absence of a partnership. Distinguishing an agreement to share profits that "is merely to provide a measure of compensation for services or the use of money" from one that "extends beyond and bestows ownership and interest in the profits themselves" (*id. at p. 750*), the court held that it was the plaintiff's "effort, skill, management and tact" that was "pertinent in determining the nature of the relationship of the parties and in defining the correlative rights and duties flowing from a contract which gave to the plaintiff a share in the net profits from operation." (*Id. at p. 752.*) In rejecting the defendant's claim that the plaintiff was not entitled to profits because no partnership had been formed, and finding instead an obligation to share and to account for profits, the court held that it was "unnecessary to place a precise legal designation on the relationship" because the respective obligations imposed on the parties in the contract showed at least a joint venture giving rise to a fiduciary obligation. (*Id. at p. 750.*)

Stevens v. Marco, (1956) 147 Cal. App. 2d 357 [305 P.2d 669] (Stevens), also cited by Wolf, is similarly unavailing. In *Stevens,* the plaintiff agreed to assign his invention to the defendant, who in turn, agreed to secure patent protection and to give the plaintiff a percentage of the net revenues from the product's sales. (*Id. at p. 363*). . . . Reversing a nonsuit and explaining that the plaintiff had stated facts potentially establishing a fiduciary relationship thereby shifting the burden of proof, the court observed, "Where an inventor entrusts his secret idea or device to another under an arrangement whereby the other party agrees to develop, patent and commercially exploit the idea in return for royalties to be paid the inventor, there arises a confidential or fiduciary relationship. [Citations]. . . . At a minimum, the court explained, there were sufficient facts for a jury to find that "the parties were allied in an enterprise *similar* to that of joint venturers for mutual gain. The royalty agreements between the parties [were] not . . . merely 'a contract of assignment and sale[,' but] plainly indicated that [defendant] was to exploit and develop the use of the patents for their *joint profit* and that any subsequent improvements made by either would accrue to their *mutual benefit*." (Id. at 374, italics added.)

In contrast to the facts in *Nelson* and *Stevens,* there are no allegations in the instant complaint of the formation of a joint venture or a relationship "akin" to a joint enterprise. To the contrary, the agreement created a debtor/creditor relationship, expressly providing that in exchange for compensation, both certain and contingent, Disney, as the new owner of the rights, could exploit those rights or not exploit them as it saw fit. Disney was under no obligation to maximize profits from the enterprise or obtain Wolf's approval for its contracts. Instead, in authorizing Disney to use those rights as it saw fit, the contract plainly allowed an opportunity for nonmutual profit that is absent in fiduciary relationships.

Trying to fit its complaint within the principles articulated in *Nelson* and *Stevens,* Wolf argues that a fiduciary duty exists because Disney's exploitation of the characters, if profitable, would inure to the parties' joint benefit. Yet even distribution agreements, negotiated at arm's length, do not create a fiduciary relationship between the product's owner and the distributor even though both parties stand to benefit from the distributor's sales of the product. (*Recorded Picture Company [Production] Ltd. v. Nelson Entertainment, Inc.* 53 Cal.App.4th 350, 370 [61 Cal. Rptr. 2d 742] (1997); *Waverly Productions, Inc. v. RKO General, Inc.* 217 Cal. App. 2d 721, 732–734 [32 Cal. Rptr. 73](1963) (Waverly).) If those agreements, where no ownership rights over property are transferred, do not create a fiduciary relationship, neither do contracts, such as the one between Wolf and Disney, involving the sale of all rights to the new owner to exploit as it sees fit.

c. Wolf's Contractual Right to an Accounting Does Not Create a Fiduciary Relationship.

Relying on *Waverly,* Wolf alternatively argues that fiduciary duties exist with respect to Disney's obligation to provide an accounting even though the relationship itself is not otherwise fiduciary in character. In *Waverly,* a distribution company (RKO) entered into an agreement with a producer to distribute two of the producer's motion pictures. The distributor then entered into sublicensing agreements with foreign distributors. The producer sued RKO, claiming RKO breached its fiduciary duty by subcontracting the distribution duties to foreign distributors who made little or no effort to distribute the films. Rejecting the producer's claim that the distributor was a fiduciary, the court held, "The [distribution] contract is an elaborate one which undertakes to define the respective rights and duties of the parties. . . . A mere contract or a debt does not constitute a trust or create a fiduciary relationship." (*Waverly, supra,* 217 Cal. App. 2d at pp. 731–732.) Noting that the trial court had correctly held that although not a fiduciary, RKO did have an obligation to account to the producer for rentals received from its sublicensees *Id. at 731*, the court also stated its holding in the following language: "We think it clear that RKO was not a fiduciary with respect to the performance of the terms of this contract (except as to accounting for rentals received) and that arguments predicated on the assumption that it was are directed to a false issue." *Id. at 734.*

Seizing on the court's parenthetical reference to RKO's obligation to provide an accounting, Wolf argues that *Waverly* acknowledged the existence of a fiduciary relationship between the distributor and the producer with respect to the accounting that applies equally to issues surrounding Disney's contractual obligation to account to Wolf, even if their contract does not otherwise create a fiduciary relationship. Wolf misapprehends the import of the *Waverly* court's recognition of the producer's right to an accounting of proceeds received from subdistributors. Either a relationship is fiduciary in character or it is not. Whether the parties are fiduciaries is governed by the nature of the relationship, not by the remedy sought. *Waverly* recognized simply that RKO had a duty to account, not that RKO was a fiduciary with respect to its accounting obligation.

The duty to provide an accounting of profits under the profit-sharing agreement in *Waverly* is appropriately premised on the principle, also expressed in *Nelson*, that a party to a profit-sharing agreement may have a right to an accounting, even absent a fiduciary relationship, when such a right is inherent in the nature of the contract itself. As the court in *Nelson* observed, the right to obtain equitable relief in the form of an accounting is not confined to partnerships but can exist in contractual relationships requiring payment by one party to another of profits received. That right can be derived not from a fiduciary duty, but simply from the implied covenant of good faith and fair dealing inherent in every contract, because without an accounting, there may be no way " 'by which such [a] party [entitled to a share in profits] could determine whether there were any profits . . . .' " (*Nelson, supra,* 29 Cal.2d at *p. 751* quoting *Kirke La Shelle Co. v. Paul Armstrong Co., supra,* 263 N.Y. 79.) Here, the parties do not dispute that the contract itself calls for an accounting. That contractual right, however, does not itself convert an arm's length transaction into a fiduciary relationship.

d. The Need to Shift the Burden of Proof in Profit-sharing Cases Does Not Create a Fiduciary Relationship.

Wolf's final argument for finding a fiduciary relationship based on Disney's contingent obligation to pay future compensation rests on the practical assessment that, without such a finding and the corresponding shift in the burden of proof that such a relationship affords, Wolf will be unable to prove any breach by Disney because all information regarding the proper calculation of contingent compensation is within Disney's exclusive control. Wolf asserts that this total dependence on financial information from Disney demonstrates that it has reposed trust and confidence in the integrity and fidelity of Disney, thereby establishing a fiduciary relationship.

We agree with Wolf that, in contingent compensation and other profit-sharing cases where essential financial records are in the exclusive control of the defendant who would benefit from any incompleteness, public policy is best served by shifting the burden of proof to the defendant, thereby imposing the risk of any incompleteness in the records on the party obligated to maintain them. Ordinarily, "a party has the burden of proof as to each fact the existence or nonexistence of which is essential to the claim for relief or defense that he is asserting," but this rule applies only "[e]xcept as otherwise provided by law." (*Evid. Code, § 500.*) On occasion courts have held that, " 'Where the evidence necessary to establish a fact essential to a claim lies peculiarly within the knowledge and competence of one of the parties, that party has the burden of going forward with the evidence on the issue although it is not the party asserting the claim.' " [Citation omitted.]

"In determining whether the normal allocation of the burden of proof should be altered, the courts consider a number of factors: the knowledge of the parties concerning the particular fact, the availability of the evidence to the parties, the most desirable result in terms of public policy in the absence of proof of the particular fact, and the probability of the existence or nonexistence of the fact. In determining the incidence of the burden of proof, 'the truth is that there is not and cannot be any one general solvent for all cases. It is merely a question of policy and fairness based on experience in the different situations.'" [Citations omitted.]

In cases where the financial records essential to proving the contingent compensation owed are in the exclusive control of the defendant, fundamental fairness, the "lodestar" for analysis under *Evidence Code section 500* (*Adams v. Murakami* 54 Cal.3d 105, 119 [284 Cal. Rptr. 318, 813 P.2d 1348] (1991)), requires shifting the burden of proof to the defendant. In such cases, the essential facts as to the contingency and the amount owed lie in the exclusive knowledge and control of the defendant, placing the defendant in a far better position to prove satisfaction of its payment obligation. (See, e.g., *Thomas v. Lusk* 27 Cal.App.4th 1709, 1717 [34 Cal. Rptr. 2d 265] ["the burden of proving an element of a case is more appropriately borne by the party with greater access to information"].) Imposing the burden of proof on a defendant to prove it has fulfilled its payment obligations to plaintiff in these types of contract cases, moreover, is consistent with the long-standing rule that a debtor defending a lawsuit to recover money under a promissory note bears the burden of proving that its payment obligation has been satisfied.

Although we therefore agree that the burden of proving a plaintiff has been paid contingent compensation in accord with the parties' agreement is properly placed on a defendant in exclusive control of essential financial records (thereby imposing on the defendant the risk of any incompleteness in such records), this determination regarding evidentiary burdens does not alter the contractual nature of the parties' relationship. Considerations of fairness and practicality, while relevant to an analysis under *Evidence Code section 500,* cannot serve to create a fiduciary relationship where one does not otherwise exist.

DISPOSITION

The petition for writ of mandate is denied. . . .

JOHNSON, J., DISSENTING.

. . . I write separately, however, to register my disagreement with the majority opinion affirming the trial court's order sustaining a demurrer to Wolf's breach of fiduciary duty cause of action. This ruling is based on a finding Disney owed no fiduciary duty, *as a matter of law,* to accurately and honestly account to Wolf for his 5 percent share of the gross receipts attributable to the company's exploitation of Wolf's intellectual product.

The majority opinion implies there can be no fiduciary duty to keep honest and accurate books . . . unless the relationship between the two parties is a fiduciary relationship for all purposes. The majority argues the relationship defined in this contract falls short of being a joint venture, largely because Disney lacks a contractual duty to exploit any of Wolf's figures or other intellectual property, and thus does not qualify as a fiduciary relationship. . . .

I differ with the majority opinion on both counts.

First, in my view, evidence may develop establishing Disney and Wolf were involved in a joint venture—at least, a contingent joint venture and one which Disney elected to activate—despite any language in the contract to the contrary. . . . This arrangement had some key attributes of a joint venture, at least once Disney elected to make the movie starring "Roger Rabbit," and then to exploit the characters in other ways. Later in the proceeding, evidence may emerge demonstrating that once Disney decided to make the movie and exploit the characters Wolf created, the two of them embarked on a joint venture. If so, Disney would owe a fiduciary duty to its co-adventurer even though the terms of the written contract did not define a joint venture and despite the fact Disney had managed to insert contract language asserting this was only to be a debtor-creditor relationship.

Second, . . . Disney does not necessarily escape a fiduciary duty to honestly and accurately account to the author of the intellectual property for the receipts earned from the intellectual property on which that author's compensation is based. Under the terms of this contract, Disney undertook the accounting responsibility for the author as well as itself—a responsibility arguably carrying with it a fiduciary duty to accurately and honestly report the true receipts and profits. Accountants, like lawyers, owe a fiduciary duty to their clients. . . .

Disney may not be an accounting firm, but it employs the accountants and bookkeepers who perform the accounting function Disney contracted to carry out. In a very real sense, Disney *is* Wolf's accountant with respect to the complete and accurate and honest maintenance of the books as to any transactions involving exploitation of Wolf's characters. That itself may create a fiduciary relationship. (Or, alternatively Disney is simultaneously occupying the roles of both accountant and client. In that case, in its role as accountant it is duty bound not to supply negligently or intentionally false information to Wolf, who obviously is a third person known to be relying on that information in its dealings with Disney in the latter's role as client.)

In either event, contrary to a bank-depositor relationship or many other relationships where one business entity maintains records for another, in this instance Wolf necessarily depended entirely on Disney's accounting department and the other Disney employees providing raw information to that department. He was not able to "reconcile" his checkbook based on his own records, or the equivalent. Nor was Wolf in a position to verify the accuracy and completeness of the raw data—the true gross receipts from exploitation of his characters—purportedly recorded in the reports he received. Even if the contract by its terms is ambiguous on this issue, evidence may well develop during the course of these proceedings demonstrating Disney's promise to perform this function created a fiduciary relationship—in this instance, a fiduciary relationship limited to the accounting aspect of the total relationship between Disney and Wolf. . . .

4.2.2 The Obligation to Exploit

Having thus determined that the company does not normally occupy the role of a fiduciary toward the talent, we turn next to the determination of the scope of the company's duty to exploit the results of the talent's contribution. The normal rule in such situations is set forth in the *Wood* and *Zilg* cases; however, as we see in the notes on the *Contemporary Missions* and *Van Vallenburgh* cases which follow, the addition of specific exploitation commitments may give rise to potentially serious consequences in the event that the company fails to carry them out, and the company's ability to exploit subsequently acquired competing properties may be limited by its contractual undertakings in an earlier agreement.

Wood v. Lucy, Lady Duff-Gordon., 222 N.Y. 88, 118 N.E. 214 (1917),
rearg. denied **222 N.Y. 643 (1918)**

CARDOZO, J.

[In a 5–2 decision, the Court of Appeals upheld the complaint against a demurrer.] The defendant styles herself as a "creator of fashions." Her favor helps a sale. Manufacturers of dresses, millinery, and like articles are glad to pay for a certificate of her approval. The things which she designs, fabrics, parasols, and what not, have a new value in the public mind when issued in her name. She employed the plaintiff [pursuant to a written, signed agreement] to help her to turn this vogue into money. He was to have the exclusive right, subject always to her approval, to place her indorsements on the designs of others. He was also to have the exclusive right to place her own designs on sale, or to license others to market them. In return she was to have one-half of 'all profits and revenues' derived from any contracts he might make. . . . The plaintiff says that he kept the contract on his part, and that the defendant broke it. She placed her indorsement on fabrics, dresses, and millinery without his knowledge, and withheld the profits. He sues her for the damages, and the case comes here on demurrer.

. . . The defendant insists . . . that [the agreement] lacks the elements of a contract because the plaintiff does not bind himself to anything. It is true that he does not promise in so many words that he will use reasonable efforts to place the defendant's indorsements and market her designs. We think, however, that such a promise is fairly to be implied. . . . A promise may be lacking, and yet the whole writing may be "instinct with an obligation," imperfectly expressed (Scott, J., in *McCall Co. Wright*, 133 App. Div. 62, 117 N.Y. Supp. 775; *Moran v. Standard Oil Co.*, 211 N.Y. 187, 198, 105 N. E. 217). If that is so, there is a contract.

The implication of a promise here finds support in many circumstances. The defendant gave an exclusive privilege. She was to have no right for at least a year to place her own indorsements or market her own designs except through the agency of the plaintiff. The acceptance of the exclusive agency was an assumption of its duties. [Citations omitted.] We are not to suppose that one party was to be placed at the mercy of the other. [Citations omitted.] Many other terms of the agreement point the same way. We are told at the outset by way of recital that: "The said Otis F. Wood possesses a business organization adapted to the placing of such indorsements as the said Lucy, Lady Duff-Gordon, has approved."

The implication is that the plaintiff's business organization will be used for the purpose for which it is adapted. But the terms of the defendant's compensation are even more significant. Her sole compensation for the grant of an exclusive agency is to be one-half of all the profits resulting from the plaintiff's efforts. Unless he gave his efforts, she could never get anything. Without an implied promise, the transaction cannot have such business "efficacy, as both parties must have intended that at all events it should have." Bowen, L. J., in the Moorcock, 14 P. D. 64, 68. But the contract does not stop there. The plaintiff goes on to promise that he will account monthly for all moneys received by him and that he will take out all such patents and copyrights and trade-marks as may in his judgment be necessary to protect the rights and articles affected by the agreement. It is true, of course, as the Appellate Division has said, that if he was under no duty to try to market designs or to place certificates of indorsement, his promise to account for profits or take out copyrights would be value-less. But in determining the intention of the parties the promise has a value. It helps to enforce the conclusion that the plaintiff had some duties. His promise to pay the defendant one-half of the profits and revenues resulting from the exclusive agency and to render accounts monthly was a promise to use reasonable efforts to bring profits and revenues into existence. For this conclusion the authorities are ample. [Citations omitted.]

Zilg v. Prentice-Hall, Inc., 717 F.2d 671 (2d Cir. 1983), *cert denied*, 466 U.S. 938 (1984)

WINTER, CIRCUIT JUDGE

. . . Gerard Colby Zilg is the author of *DuPont: Behind the Nylon Curtain,* an historical account of the role of the DuPont family in American social, political and economic affairs. Early in 1972, after one partially successful and several unsuccessful efforts to find a publisher for his proposed book Zilg's agent introduced him to Bram Cavin, a senior editor in P-H's Trade Book Division. Cavin expressed interest in the book, and he and Zilg submitted a formal proposal to John Kirk, P-H's Editor-in-Chief at that time. Kirk approved the proposal, which described the future book

as a thoroughly documented study of the major role the DuPont family has played in the development of modern America and its corporate and social institutions. After skimming lightly over the family's origins in France and its development of its gunpowder business up to and through the Civil War, the book will concentrate on the period after that conflict right down to the present day. The story—essentially one of money and power—is going to be told in human terms and in the lives of the members of the family and their actions. The family will be looked upon as a unit in its relations to the outside world. But it will also be shown to be, as many families frequently are, one torn by feuds and struggles over the money and the power. . . .

Zilg submitted the first half of his completed manuscript to Cavin in November 1972, and the remainder a year later. Cavin authorized acceptance of the work on behalf of P-H apparently without the participation of Peter Grenquist, who had become president of P-H's Trade Book Division sometime after execution of the contract but before submission of the manuscript. P-H's legal division scrutinized the manuscript for libelous content and concluded that, if a libel action were brought, P-H "would ultimately prevail" because the subject matter of the work was constitutionally privileged and the plaintiffs would have to prove actual malice. The division's opinion noted, however, that litigation against the DuPonts would be very costly.

A decision was made to accept the manuscript, which was distributed to selected wholesalers, reviewers and booksellers. Copies were also sent to the editorial director of the Book of the Month Club ("BOMC").

Although BOMC decided not to offer the book as a selection of its main club, a subsidiary, the Fortune Book Club, which appealed to a readership composed largely of business executives, did choose it as a selection.

A committee of various P-H department representatives, including the book's editor, met on March 28, 1974 to discuss production plans. The sales estimates of committee members varied from 12 to 15 thousand copies for the first year although by May two members were predicting sales of only 10 thousand. Estimates of from 15 to 20 thousand sales over a five year period were also made. Cavin, an ardent supporter of the book, made estimates of 20 to 25 thousand in the first year and 25 to 35 thousand over five years. The committee decided on a first printing of 15,000 copies at a retail price of $12.95 per copy. At a later meeting, the committee decided to devote roughly $15,000 to advertising.

Although the literary or scholarly merits of the book are not our concern, its nature, tone and marketability among various audiences are key facts in this litigation, for they bear upon the book's prospects for commercial success and illuminate the negative reactions which later set in at P-H. The book is a harshly critical portrait of the DuPont family and their role in American social, political and economic history. Indeed, it is a harshly critical portrait of that history itself. The reactions of readers and reviewers in the record indicate that the book is polarizing, the difference in viewpoint depending in no small measure upon the politics of the beholder. A significant number of readers regard the book as a strident caricature, drawing every conceivable inference against the DuPont family and firms with which members of the family were or are associated. One judge at BOMC, for example, described it as "300,000 words of pure spite." On the other hand, the book has a loyal band of admirers. It received a favorable review in many newspapers, including the *New York Times* Book Review section. Its comprehensiveness and the extensive research on which it was based were frequently noted. The book also has some appeal to another audience, namely readers with a taste for gossip about the rich and powerful, particularly readers in Delaware. Indeed, it was once first in nonfiction sales in that state.

In the American market, the book's appeal is somewhat limited by the fact that it is not a work critical of business on grounds that reform of capitalism is necessary to save it, a viewpoint with mainstream appeal. Rather, it represents a Marxist view of history. Also weighing against its overall marketability were its size (586 pages of text, 2 inches thick, three and one-half pounds), complexity (almost 200 family members with the surname DuPont and 170 years of American history) and price ($12.95 in 1974 dollars).

Prior to June 1974, Grenquist appears not to have been aware of the nature and tone of the book, of the intensity of negative feeling that it might arouse in some readers or of evidence of serious inaccuracies. He may have been reassured partly by Cavin's enthusiasm and partly by the book's selection by the Fortune Book Club. That selection itself remains something of a mystery since the Club's inside reader concluded it was "a bad book, politically crude and cheaply journalistic." However, instead of accepting his recommendation that it "be fed back to the author page by page," BOMC contracted with P-H to have it adopted by the Fortune Book Club.

In June 1974, a chain of events was set in motion which apprised Grenquist of the negative aspects of Zilg's work. A member of the DuPont family obtained an advance copy of the manuscript from a bookseller and, predictably outraged, turned it over to the Public Affairs Department of the DuPont Company. Members of that department sought to locate individuals in P-H's management whom they knew personally in order to speak privately about the book, but to no avail. They advised the family member to do nothing before the book was published.

In July, the DuPont Company learned that the book had been accepted as a Fortune Book Club selection and decided to act before publication anyway. Harold Brown of DuPont ("DuPont-Brown") telephoned Vilma Bergane, a manager of Fortune Book Club, having received her name from the managing editor of *Fortune Magazine*. He told her the book had been read by several persons, some of whom were attorneys, and that the book was "scurrilous" and "actionable." Bergane passed on a version of DuPont-Brown's remarks to F. Harry Brown, Editor-in-Chief of BOMC ("BOMC-Brown"). DuPont-Brown then told BOMC-Brown that DuPont family attorneys found the book abusive and that he was to try to locate someone at P-H with whom to discuss the book. He also told BOMC-Brown that the DuPont Company did not intend to throw its weight around. BOMC-Brown referred DuPont-Brown to Peter Grenquist at P-H.

Some days later, apparently in an effort to quash rumors or inaccurate messages to the contrary, DuPont-Brown telephoned Grenquist to assure him that DuPont was not attempting to block publication of the book, initiate litigation, or even approach P-H in any kind of adversarial posture. One such rumor, allegedly passed on to Cavin by an editor at BOMC who does not remember the conversation, was that DuPont had gone to *Fortune Magazine* and threatened to pull all its advertising. *Fortune,* owned by Time, Inc., had no connection with the Fortune Book Club at this time.

Meanwhile, BOMC-Brown decided to look into the matter personally. Over the July 27–28 weekend, he "spent a horrible two days reading" the book and decided it was an unsuitable selection for the Fortune Book Club. He later stated that he felt no pressure from the DuPont Company in reaching this decision. In view of the nature of the book and the Club's audience of business executives, his decision seems an inevitable result of his reading the book. BOMC immediately notified P-H of its decision not to distribute the book. The reason given was BOMC's belief that the book was malicious and had an objectionable tone.

P-H's own detailed examination of the manuscript may also have induced or heightened skepticism on Grenquist's part. A toning down was found to be necessary even after the book was in page proof. Mistakes of fact, such as a statement that Irving S. Shapiro (DuPont's Chief Executive Officer) had served as an Assistant District Attorney in Queens County, New York, were discovered. More serious matters also came to light. The original manuscript attacked Judge Harold R. Medina for matters irrelevant to the DuPonts and in a fashion which the district court characterized as libelous. Zilg admitted at trial that there was no factual foundation for this attack. Some eyebrows may well have been raised when this passage was discovered and deleted, since it was not only unfounded but also irrelevant.

P-H continued to correct and tone down the book, hoping to reverse BOMC's decision not to offer it through the Fortune Book Club. A certain defensiveness also began to creep into P-H's attitude toward the book. On August 2, Grenquist circulated a memorandum which noted that questions had arisen regarding both the tone of the book and Zilg's approach and recommended that the adjective "polemical" henceforth be used because "[t]he book is a polemical argument and no pretense is made that it is anything else." More importantly, he also cut the first printing from 15,000 copies to 10,000, stating that 5,000 copies were no longer needed for BOMC. The proposed advertising budget was also slashed from $15,000 to $5,500.

Judge Brieant held that the DuPont Company had a constitutionally protected interest in bringing the "scurrilous" nature of the book and its unsuitability as a Fortune Book Club selection to the attention of senior officials at BOMC and P-H. He expressly found that the Company did not engage in coercive tactics but limited its actions to the expression of its good faith opinion.

As to P-H Judge Brieant found that the publishing contract required the publisher to "exercise its discretion in good faith in planning its promotion of the Book, and in revising its plans." This obligation required that Prentice-Hall use "its best efforts . . . to promote the book fully and fairly." He held that P-H breached this obligation because it had no "sound" or "valid" business reason for reducing the first printing by 5,000 volumes and the advertising budget by $9,500, which allowed the book to go briefly out of stock (although wholesalers had ample copies) just as it gained sales momentum. He expressly found that since BOMC did its own printing of club selections, the first printing cut could not be attributed to the cancellation of the BOMC order. He also found that the book would have sold 25,000 copies had P-H not taken these actions.

Having concluded that P-H had no sound or valid business reason for reducing the first printing and advertising budget, Judge Brieant held that P-H "privished" Zilg's book on the basis of the testimony of plaintiff's expert, William Decker. Decker testified that publishers often mount a wholly inadequate merchandising effort after concluding that a book does not meet prior expectations in either quality or marketability. Such "privishing is intended to fulfill the technical requirements of the contract to publish but to avoid adding to one's losses by throwing good money after bad . . . "

We agree with Judge Brieant that DuPont did not tortiously interfere with Zilg's beneficial commercial relationships. We disagree, however, with his conclusion that P-H breached its contract with Zilg and reverse that judgment.

I. TORTIOUS INTERFERENCE BY DUPONT

[Finding that New York would follow the Restatement (Second) of Torts (1977), the Court held that although DuPont's actions were a cause in fact of BOMC's decision to drop the book, a reading of §§ 766 and 767 led to the conclusion that DuPont had limited itself to a "good faith expression of views" without threats of litigation or economic coercion.]

. . . Such communications seem to me socially beneficial because they promote the free flow of ideas. . . . Authors have no exclusive right to the ear of those who disseminate their works, for intelligent decisions by publishers and others distributing books are enhanced by the free flow of information. . . .

2. P-H's Breach of Contract

. . . Judge Brieant [erred when he] read the contract in question to oblige P-H "to use its best efforts . . . to promote the Book fully . . . " and found that the decision to cut the first printing and original advertising budget resulted in a loss of sales momentum when the book was briefly out of stock. These actions by P-H he held, breached its agreement with Zilg because they lacked a sound or valid business reason.

Putting aside for the moment P-H's motive in slashing the first printing and advertising budget, we note that Zilg neither bargained for nor acquired an explicit "best efforts" or "promote fully" promise, much less an agreement to make certain specific promotional efforts. . . .

While P-H obligated itself to "publish" the book once it had accepted it, the contract expressly leaves to P-H's discretion printing and advertising decisions. Working as we must in the context of a surprising absence of case law on the meaning of this not uncommon agreement, we believe that the contract in question establishes a relationship between the publisher and author which implies an obligation upon the former to make certain efforts in publishing a book it has accepted notwithstanding the clause which leaves the number of volumes to be printed and the advertising budget to the publisher's discretion. This obligation is derived both from the common expectations of parties to such agreements and from the relationship of those parties as structured by the contract. . . .

Zilg, like most authors, sought to take advantage of a division of labor in which firms specialize in publishing works written by authors who are not employees of the firm. Under contracts such as the one before us, publishing firms print, advertise and distribute books at their own expense. In return for performing these tasks, and for bearing the risk of a book's failure to sell, the author gives the publisher exclusive rights to the book with certain reservations not important here. Such contracts provide for royalties on sales to the author, often on an escalating basis, i.e., higher royalties at higher levels of sales.

While publishers and authors have generally similar goals, differences in perspective and resulting perceptions are inevitable. An author usually has a bigger stake in the success or failure of a book than a publisher who may regard it as one among many publications, some of which may lose money. The author, whose eggs are in one basket, thus has a calculus of risk quite different from the publisher so far as costly promotional expenditures are concerned. The publisher, of course, views the author's willingness to take large risks as a function of the fact that it is the publisher's money at peril. Moreover, the publisher will inevitably regard his or her judgment as to marketing conditions as greatly superior to that of a particular author.

One means of reconciling these differing viewpoints is "up-front" money—$ 6,500 in Zilg's case—which provides a token of the publisher's seriousness about the book. Were such sums not bargained for, acquisition of publishing rights would be virtually costless and firms would acquire those rights without regard to whether or not they had truly decided to publish the work.

However, up-front money alone cannot fully reconcile the conflicting interests of the parties. Uncertainty surrounds the publication of most books and publishers must be cautious about the size of up-front payments since they increase the already considerable economic risks they take by printing and promoting books at their own expense. Negotiating such matters as the number of volumes to be printed and the level of advertising efforts might be possible but such bargaining in the case of each author and each book would be enormously costly. There is never a guarantee of ultimate agreement, and if a set of negotiations fails over these issues, the bargaining must begin again with another publisher. Moreover, publishers must also be wary of undertaking obligations to print a certain number of volumes or to spend fixed sums on promotion. They will strongly prefer to have flexibility in reacting to actual marketing conditions according to their own experience. . . .

Once P-H had accepted the book, it obtained the exclusive right to publish it. Were the clause empowering the publisher to determine promotional expenses read literally, the contract would allow a publisher to refuse to print or distribute any copies of a book while having exclusive rights to it. In effect, authors would be guaranteed nothing but whatever up-front money had been negotiated, and the promise to publish would be meaningless. We think the promise to publish must be given some content and that it implies a good faith effort to promote the book including a first printing and advertising budget adequate to give the book a reasonable chance of achieving market success in light of the subject matter and likely audience. . . .

However, the clause empowering the publisher to decide in its discretion upon the number of volumes printed and the level of promotional expenditures must also be given some content. If a trier of fact is free to determine whether such decisions are sound or valid, the publisher's ability to rely upon its own experience and judgment in marketing books will be seriously hampered. We believe that once the obligation to undertake reasonable initial promotional activities has been fulfilled, the contractual language dictates that a business decision by the publisher to limit the size of a printing or advertising budget is not subject to second guessing by a trier of fact as to whether it is sound or valid. . . .

Given the line we draw, a breach of contract might be proven by Zilg in two ways. First, he might demonstrate that the initial printing and promotional efforts were so inadequate as not to give the book a reasonable chance to catch on with the reading public. Second, he might show that even greater printing and promotional efforts were not undertaken for reasons other than a good faith business judgment. Because he has shown neither, we reverse the judgment in his favor.

As to P-H's initial obligation, Zilg has not shown that P-H's efforts on behalf of his book did not give it a reasonable chance to catch on with the reading public. It printed or reprinted 13,000 volumes (3,000 over the volume of sales at which the highest royalty was triggered), authorized an advertising budget of $5,500 (1974 purchasing power), distributed over 600 copies to reviewers, purchased ads in papers such as *the New York Times* and *Wall Street Journal,* and made reasonable efforts to sell the paperback rights. The documentary record shows that Grenquist took a continued interest in marketing the book, made suggestions as to promoting it effectively and ordered that "rave reviews" be sent to BOMC as late as January, 1975.

The fact that initial decisions as to promotional efforts were trimmed is of no relevance absent evidence that the actual efforts made were so inadequate that the book did not have a reasonable chance to catch on with the reading public. The record is barren of such evidence. . . .

So long as the initial promotional efforts are adequate under the test we outline above, a publisher's printing and advertising decisions do not breach a contract such as that before us unless the plaintiff proves that the motivation underlying those decisions was not a good faith business judgment. Zilg failed to produce such evidence. His case was based on the theory that economic coercion by the DuPont Company caused P-H to reduce its promotional efforts. Judge Bricant found against him on this issue and, for reasons stated above, we affirm this determination. . . .

. . . [T]he contract between P-H and Zilg left the decisions in question to the business judgment of the publisher, the author's protection being in the publisher's experience, judgment and quest for profits. P-H's promotional efforts were, in Decker's words, "adequate," notwithstanding the reduction of the first printing and the initial advertising budget. Indeed, those reductions, coming on the heels of BOMC's decision not to distribute the book, appear to be a rational reaction to that news. Decker himself testified that the Fortune Book Club selection was an important barometer of marketability since it was an independent judgment that the book had an audience. Zilg's contract with P-H did not compel the publisher to ignore the implications of BOMC's change of heart.

Affirmed in part, reversed in part. . . .

PIERCE, CIRCUIT JUDGE (CONCURRING). . . .

NOTES

1. The "reasonable efforts" standard, of course, will not apply where the company accepts express obligations of a higher order (a major reason why companies strenuously resist the inclusion of specific promotional and marketing commitments.) Thus, in *Contemporary Mission, Inc, v. Famous Music Corporation,* 557 F.2d 918 (2d Cir. 1977), Famous, a record distributor, promised Contemporary, a production company that it would "select and appoint, within the first year of the agreement, at least one person to personally oversee the nationwide promotion of the sale of records, to maintain contact with Contemporary and to submit weekly reports to Contemporary; [that it would] spend, within the first year of the agreement, no less than $50,000 on the promotion of records; and [that it would] release, within the first two years of the agreement, at least four separate single records" delivered by the production company. The agreement also contained a non-assignability clause. Famous proceeded to sell its record division to ABC Records, Inc. ABC then informed Contemporary that ABC "was not going to have any relationship with Contemporary." The Second Circuit rejected Famous' argument that it had complied with its contractual obligations by appointing the product manager and spending the $50,000. These obligations, the court said, were but two of many created by the [subject] agreement. Under the doctrine of *Wood v. Lucy, Lady Duff-Gordon,* Famous had an obligation to use its reasonable efforts to promote [Contemporary's records] on a nationwide basis. That obligation could not be satisfied merely by technical compliance with the spending and appointment requirements of . . . the agreement. Even assuming that Famous complied fully with those requirements, there was evidence from which the jury could find that Famous failed to adequately promote *Virgin* [Contemporary's record]. The question is a close one, particularly in light of [Famous' CEO's] obvious commitment to the success of *Virgin* and in light of the efforts that were in fact exerted and the lack of any serious dispute between the parties prior to the sale to ABC. However, there was evidence that Famous prematurely terminated the promotion of the first single record, "Got To Know," shortly after its release, and that Famous limited its promotion of the second record, "Kyrie," to a single city, rather than promoting it nationwide. Moreover, there was evidence that, prior to the sale to ABC, Famous underwent a budget reduction and cut back its promotional staff. From this, the jury could infer that the promotional effort was reduced to a level that was less than adequate. On the whole, therefore, we are not persuaded that the jury's verdict should be disturbed. Because the record continued to sell, despite ABC's refusal to support it, and because the single rose from #80 to #61 on the Billboard "Hot Soul Singles" chart, "it cannot be gain-said that if someone had continued to promote it, and if it had not been withdrawn from the market, it would have sold more records than it actually did."

2. The following clause is an example of a foreign exploitation obligation provision from a major label recording agreement.

Foreign Release Commitment

Provided neither you nor Artist is in material breach of this agreement, Company agrees to commercially release each such Album timely Delivered under this agreement in the United Kingdom, Canada, Germany and Australia within one hundred twenty (120) days after Company's initial release of the applicable Album in the United States (the "Foreign Release Deadline Period"). If Company fails to so release any such Album, then, as your sole remedy, you shall have the right, within thirty (30) days following the expiration of the Foreign Release Deadline Period to notify Company in writing of such failure and of your desire that Company correct such failure in the applicable territory. If Company does not commercially release such Album in the territory specified in your notice within sixty (60) days after Company receives such notice from you (the "Foreign Release Cure Period"), then, upon your written request, Company will enter into an agreement with a licensee selected by you, approved by Company and actually engaged in the business of manufacturing and distributing Records in the territory in which Company fails to release such Album (the "License Territory"), upon terms and conditions approved by Company, regarding the grant by Company to such licensee of a license for the manufacture and distribution in the License Territory of Records derived from such Album, provided that such license is entered into within sixty (60) days following the expiration of the Foreign Release Cure Period. Fifty percent (50%) of Net Receipts derived from such licenses will be credited to your royalty account under this agreement and the balance shall be retained by Company for its own account. It is specifically understood and agreed that, if Company shall fail to fulfill any such release commitment, Company shall have no liability whatsoever to you, and your only remedy shall be as set forth in this paragraph.

And circumstances may arise which obviate a company's obligations to exploit particular material, as evidenced by the following case.

Third Story Music, Inc. v. Waits, 41 Cal.App. 4th 798, 48 Cal.Rptr. 2d 747 (Cal. Ct. App. 2d Dist. 1995), *rev. denied (Mar. 21, 1996)*

EPSTEIN, ACTING PJ

This case involves a dispute between a [music publisher/production company and a singer/songwriter.] The issue is whether a promise to market music, or to refrain from doing so, at the election of the promisor, is subject to the implied covenant of good faith and fair dealing, where substantial consideration has been paid by the promisor. We conclude that the implied covenant does not apply.

FACTUAL AND PROCEDURAL SUMMARY

[Waits was an exclusive songwriter/recording artist signed to TSM, which licensed distribution rights in Wait's recordings to Asylum Records (now Elektra/Asylum), pursuant to contractual provisions which gave the distributor the worldwide right "to manufacture, sell, distribute and advertise" (copies of Waits' recordings) or, "at [its] election, [to] refrain from any or all of the foregoing." TSM received advances against future royalties from record sales. These advances began at $8,800 per annum and progressed to the point where TSM received $50,000 plus an additional $100,000, and later $150,000 per LP. The parties operated on the basis of an interrelated series of agreements beginning in 1972 until 1993, at which time a third party distributor approached E/A's sister company Warner Special Products, which licensed "aftermarket" projects and other re-releases, for a license to compile and issue an LP of previously-unreleased recordings made by Waits during the term of the TSM/EA agreements. Warner refused to grant the license without Waits' approval. Waits refused. TSM then sued the Warner entities for damages, claiming that Warner had no right to insist upon Waits' approval and that Warner had therefore breached the implied covenant of good faith and fair dealing. Warner's demurrer was sustained because of the clause permitting the distributor to refrain from exploiting the recordings. TSM appealed, contending that such discretionary power must be exercised in good faith, and that Warner's insistence upon Waits' approval of the proposed license was not in good faith.]

DISCUSSION

I

When an agreement expressly gives to one party absolute discretion over whether or not to perform, when should the implied covenant of good faith and fair dealing be applied to limit its discretion? Both sides rely on different language in the recent Supreme Court decision in *Carma Developers (Cal.) Inc. v. Marathon Development California Inc.* 2 Cal.4th 342, 6 Cal.Rptr. 467, 826 P.2d 710 (1992) to answer that question. In *Carma,* the parties had entered into a lease agreement which stated that if the tenant procured a potential sublessee and asked the landlord for consent to sublease, the landlord had the right to terminate the lease, enter into negotiations with the prospective sublessee, and appropriate for itself all profits from the new arrangement. In the passage relied upon by TSM, the court recognized that "[t]he covenant of good faith finds particular application in situations where one party is invested with a discretionary power affecting the rights of another." 2 Cal. 4th at 372, 6 Cal.Rptr.2d 467, 826 P.2d 710. The court expressed the view that "[s]uch power must be exercised in good faith." *Id.*

At the same time, the Carma court upheld the right of the landlord to freely exercise its discretion to terminate the lease in order to claim for itself—and deprive the tenant of—all profit from the expected sublease. In this regard, the court stated: "We are aware of no reported case in which a court has held the covenant of good faith may be read to prohibit a party from doing that which is expressly permitted by an agreement. On the contrary, as a general matter, implied terms should never be read to vary express terms." [Internal citations omitted] "The general rule [regarding the covenant of good faith] is plainly subject to the exception that the parties may, by express provisions of the contract, grant the right to engage in the very acts and conduct which would otherwise have been forbidden by an implied covenant of good faith and fair dealing. . . .

This is in accord with the general principle that, in interpreting a contract 'an implication . . . should not be made when the contrary is indicated in clear and express words.' 3 Corbin, *Contracts*, 564, p. 298 (1960). . . . [I]f the defendants were given the right to do what they did by the express provisions of the contract there can be no breach." 2 Cal.4th at p. 374, 6 Cal.Rptr.2d 467, 826 P.2d 710, quoting VTR, *Incorporated v. Goodyear Tire & Rubber Company* (S.D.N.Y. 1969) 303 F. Supp. 773, 777–778.

. . . In situations such as the present one, where a discretionary power is expressly given by the contractual language, the quoted passages from Carma set up an apparent inconsistency between the principle that the covenant of good faith should be applied to restrict exercise of a discretionary power and the principle that an implied covenant must never vary the express terms of the parties' agreement. We attempt to reconcile the two.

II

We first emphasize a long-established rule concerning implied covenants. To be imposed "(1) the implication must arise from the language used or it must be indispensable to effectuate the intention of the parties; (2) it must appear from the language used that it was so clearly within the contemplation of the parties that they deemed it unnecessary to express it; (3) implied covenants can only be justified on the grounds of legal necessity; (4) a promise can be implied only where it can be rightfully assumed that it would have been made if attention had been called to it; (5) there can be no implied covenant where the subject is completely covered by the contract." *Lippman v. Sears, Roebuck & Co.* 44 Cal.2d 136, 142, 280 P.2d 775 (1955); *City of Glendale v. Superior Court* 18 Cal.App. 4th 1768, 23 Cal.Rptr.2d 305 (1993).

- [The court proceeded to review some of the cases cited in *Carma*:
- *Perdue v. Crocker National Bank* 38 Cal.3d 913, 216 Cal.Rptr. 345, 702 P.2d 503 (1985), where, although the bank was given discretion to set NSF check charges, the court held that an open term (such as price) had to be filled in good faith, and the court proceeded to impose an objective standard. Use of the implied covenant was "indispensable" and "justified by legal necessity."
- *Cal. Lettuce Growers v. Union Sugar Co.* 45 Cal.2d 474, 289 P.2d 785 (1955). Again, although the contract permitted the buyer to set the price of sugar beets, which would have rendered the contract illusory, the court held that the implied covenant obligated the buyer to use good faith, and proceed to establish an objective price to preserve the enforceability of the agreement.
- A number of cases require reasonable efforts to generate profits where exclusive promotional or licensing rights are granted solely in return for

royalties based on exploitation: *Zilg v. Prentice-Hall, Inc.* (2d Cir. 1983) 717 F.2d 671, 79–681; *Wood v. Lucy, Lady Duff-Gordon* 222 N.Y. 88, 118 N.E. 214 (1917).]

In each of these cases, the courts were forced to resolve contradictory expressions of intent from the parties: the intent to give one party total discretion over its performance and the intent to have a mutually binding agreement. In that situation, imposing the duty of good faith creates a binding contract where, despite the clear intent of the parties, one would not exist. Faced with that choice, courts prefer to imply a covenant at odds with the express language of the contract rather than literally enforce a discretionary language clause and thereby render the agreement unenforceable. . . .

[The court proceeded to discuss *April Enterprises, Inc. v. KTTV* 147 Cal.App. 3d 805, 195 Cal.Rptr. 421(1983), cited by TSM. The contract gave the station the right to erase tapes after they were broadcast. However, the contract also gave the producer the right to sell the old shows in syndication. Judgment dismissing the complaint was reversed: the covenant might be applied in order to reconcile the conflicting contract provisions.]

The court in *April Enterprises* used the implied covenant to interpret an ambiguous discretionary power. As we have seen, the implied covenant of good faith is also applied to contradict an express contractual grant of discretion when necessary to protect an agreement which otherwise would be rendered illusory and unenforceable. Does a different result ensue where the contract is unambiguous, otherwise supported by consideration, and the implied covenant is not needed to effectuate the parties' expressed desire for a binding agreement? We believe it does, and the cases cited by the court in *Carma* illustrate this point.

[*Balfour, Guthrie & Co. v. Gourmet Farms* 108 Cal.App. 3d 181, 166 Cal. Rptr. 422 (1980). Grain producer agreed that broker could set price of grain to be purchased from producer based on market rate when price was set. Broker paid an advance. Broker had discretion to set prices after a missed margin call, which would occur if the value of the grain dropped a certain percentage below the amount of the advance. This occurred, and the court upheld the right of the broker to set the price in a falling market.]

[*Brandt v. Lockheed Missiles & Space Co.* 154 Cal.App. 3d 1124, 201 Cal. Rptr. 746 (1984). Employment contract provided that if the company considered the employee's invention worthwhile, and secured a patent on it, the company would pay the employee $600, and could, but was not obligated to, grant him an additional "Special Invention Award" and that the decision of Lockheed's committee would be "final and conclusive." Having faithfully followed the contractual procedure, the court stated that it could not reasonably be said that in doing so Lockheed had violated the implied covenant of good faith and fair dealing.]

[*Gerdlund v. Electronic Dispensers International* 190 Cal.App. 3d 263, 235 Cal.Rptr. 279 (1987). Company terminated sales representative under clause permitting termination on 30 days' notice "at any time and for any reason." Holding that the 30-day notice provision constituted sufficient consideration, the appellate court reversed the lower court's application of the implied covenant of good faith and fair dealing, saying that "[a] provision for termination by one or either party after notice for a fixed period is enforceable and does not render the contract illusory."]

In each of these cases, as in *Carma,* one of the parties was expressly given a discretionary power but regardless of how such power was exercised, the agreement would have been supported by adequate consideration. There was no tension between the parties' express agreement and their intention to be bound, and no necessity to impose an implied covenant to create mutuality. The conclusion to be drawn is that courts are not at liberty to imply a covenant directly at odds with a contract's express grant except in those relatively rare instances when reading the provision literally would, contrary to the parties' clear intention, result in an unenforceable, illusory agreements. In all other situations where the contract is unambiguous, the express language is to govern. . . .

The illusory promise [of exploitation] was not . . . the only consideration given by the [distributor,] . . . which promised to pay TSM a guaranteed minimum amount no matter what efforts were undertaken. It follows that, whether or not an implied covenant is read into the agreement, the agreement would be supported by consideration and would be binding. [The guaranteed payments involved do not appear to be large in relation to what might be earned from the [recorded performances] of a successful recording artist. But unless the consideration given was so one-sided as to create an issue of unconscionability, the courts are not in a position to decide whether legal consideration agreed to by the parties is or is not fair. The [payments in this case] amounted to more than the peppercorn of consideration the law requires. [Note in original.]

As we see it, [Elektra/Asylum] bargained for and obtained all rights to Waits' [recordings] . . . and paid legally adequate consideration. That it chose not to grant a license in a particular instance cannot be the basis for complaint on the part of TSM as long as [Elektra/Asylum] made the agreed minimum payments and paid royalties when it did exploit the work . . . TSM was free to accept or reject the bargain offered and cannot look to the courts to amend the terms that prove unsatisfactory. . . .

HASTINGS AND ROBERT KLEIN, JJ, CONCUR.

4.3 LIMITS ON EXPLOITATION

4.3.1 Creative Control

Actors and actresses frequently seek approval of the director and the script. No one wants to be caught in a flop, and producers and studios are well aware of the box office history of the previous films of the performers they cast. In addition, television shows such as "Entertainment Tonight" broadcast box office numbers, and they appear on a regular basis in the Los Angeles Times and other print publications, and financial and other information once of interest only to industry insiders has grown increasingly fascinating to the general public as well.

The following case and arbitration summaries illustrate the consequences that may flow from a grant of creative control. In *Parker v. Twentieth Century-Fox Film Corporation,* script and director approvals were among the weapons Shirley MacLaine employed successfully to ward off an assignment to what she considered an inferior (and potentially career-limiting) assignment. In the *Cimino* and *Beatty* arbitrations, we see that the power of "final cut" in the hands of a director is truly enormous, but that it must nonetheless be exercised in good faith, in the absence of special circumstances.

Parker v. Twentieth Century-Fox Film Corporation, 3 Cal.3d 176, 474 P.2d 689 (1970)

BURKE, J

Defendant Twentieth Century-Fox Film Corporation appeals from a summary judgment granting to plaintiff the recovery of agreed compensation under a written contract for her services as an actress in a motion picture. As will appear, we have concluded that the trial court correctly ruled in plaintiff's favor and that the judgment should be affirmed.

Plaintiff [Shirley MacLaine] was to play the female lead in defendant's contemplated production of a motion picture entitled *Bloomer Girl* [under a contract which] provided [for] a minimum "guaranteed compensation" of $53,571.42 per week for 14 weeks commencing May 23, 1966, for a total of $750,000. Prior to May 1966 defendant decided not to produce the picture and by a letter dated April 4, 1966, it notified plaintiff of that decision and that it would not "comply with our obligations to you under" the written contract.

By the same letter and with the professed purpose "to avoid any damage to you," defendant instead offered to employ plaintiff as the leading actress in another film tentatively entitled *Big Country. Big Man* (hereinafter, *Big Country*). The compensation offered was identical, as were 31 of the 34 numbered provisions or articles of the original contract. Unlike *Bloomer Girl,* however, which was to have been a musical production, *Big Country* was a dramatic "western type" movie. *Bloomer Girl* was to have been filmed in California; *Big Country* was to be produced in Australia. Also, certain terms in the proffered contract varied from those of the original. Plaintiff was given one week within which to accept; she did not and the offer lapsed. Plaintiff then commenced this action seeking recovery of the agreed guaranteed compensation.

The complaint sets forth two causes of action. The first is for money due under the contract; the second, based upon the same allegations as the first, is for damages resulting from defendant's breach of contract. . . .

The general rule is that the measure of recovery by a wrongfully discharged employee is the amount of salary agreed upon for the period of service, less the amount which the employer affirmatively proves the employee has earned or with reasonable effort might have earned from other employment. . . . However, before projected earnings from other employment opportunities not sought or accepted by the discharged employee can be applied in mitigation, the employer must show that the other employment was comparable, or substantially similar, to that of which the employee has been deprived; the employee's rejection of or failure to seek other available employment of a different or inferior kind may not be resorted to in order to mitigate damages. . . .

In the present case defendant has raised no issue *of reasonableness of efforts* by plaintiff to obtain other employment; the sole issue is whether plaintiff's refusal of defendant's substitute offer *of Big Country* may be used in mitigation. Nor, if the *Big Country* offer was of employment different or inferior when compared with the original *Bloomer Girl* employment, is there an issue as to whether or not plaintiff acted reasonably in refusing the substitute offer. Despite defendant's arguments to the contrary, no case cited or which our research has discovered holds or suggests that reasonableness is an element of a wrongfully discharged employee's option to reject, or fail to seek, different or inferior employment lest the possible earnings therefrom be charged against him in mitigation of damages.

Applying the foregoing rules to the record in the present case, with all intendments in favor of the party opposing the summary judgment motion—here, defendant—it is clear that the trial court correctly ruled that plaintiff's failure to accept defendant's tendered substitute employment could not be applied in mitigation of damages because the offer of the *Big Country* lead was of employment both different and inferior, and that no factual dispute was presented on that issue. The mere circumstance that *Bloomer Girl* was to be a musical review calling upon plaintiff's talents as a dancer as well as an actress, and was to be produced in the City of Los Angeles, whereas *Big Country* was a straight dramatic role in a "Western Type" story taking place in an opal mine in Australia, demonstrates the difference in kind between the two employments; the female lead as a dramatic actress in a western style motion picture can by no stretch of imagination be considered the equivalent of or substantially similar to the lead in a song-and-dance production.

Additionally, the substitute *Big Country* offer proposed to eliminate or impair the director and screenplay approvals accorded to plaintiff under the original *Bloomer Girl* contract . . . and thus constituted an offer of inferior employment. No expertise or judicial notice is required in order to hold that the deprivation or infringement of an employee's rights held under an original employment contract converts the available "other employment" relied upon by the employer to mitigate damages, into inferior employment which the employee need not seek or accept. . . .

SULLIVAN, ACTING CIRCUIT JUDGE (DISSENTING)

The basic question in this case is whether or not plaintiff acted reasonably in rejecting defendant's offer of alternate employment. The answer depends upon whether that offer (starring in *Big Country, Big Man*) was an offer of work that was substantially similar to her former employment (starring in *Bloomer Girl*) or of work that was of a different or inferior kind. To my mind this is a factual issue which the trial court should not have determined on a motion for summary judgment. The majority have not only repeated this error but have compounded it by applying the rules governing mitigation of damages in the employer-employee context in a misleading fashion. Accordingly, I respectfully dissent. . . .

Although the majority appear to hold that there was a difference "in kind" between the employment offered plaintiff in *Bloomer Girl* and that offered in *Big Country* . . . , an examination of the opinion makes crystal clear that the majority merely point out differences between the two *films* (an obvious circumstance) and then apodictically assert that these constitute a difference in the *kind of employment*. The entire rationale of the majority boils down to this: that the "*mere circumstances*" that *Bloomer Girl* was to be a musical review while *Big Country* was a straight drama "demonstrates the difference in kind" since a female lead in a western is not "the equivalent of or substantially similar to" a lead in a musical. This is merely attempting to prove the proposition by repeating it. It shows that the vehicles for the display of the star's talents are different but it does not prove that her employment as a star in such vehicles is of necessity different in kind and either inferior or superior. . . .

It seems to me that *this inquiry* involves, in the instant case at least, factual determinations which are improper on a motion for summary judgment. Resolving whether or not one job is substantially similar to another or whether, on the other hand, it is of a different or inferior kind, will often (as here) require a critical appraisal of the similarities and differences between them in light of the importance of these differences to the employee. This necessitates a weighing of the evidence. . . .

The majority do not confront the trial court's misuse of judicial notice. They avoid this issue through the expedient of declaring that neither judicial notice nor expert opinion (such as that contained in the declarations in opposition to the motion) is necessary to reach the trial court's conclusion. *Something*, however, clearly is needed to support this conclusion. Nevertheless, the majority make no effort to justify the judgment through an examination of the plaintiff's declarations. Ignoring the obvious insufficiency of these declarations, the majority announce that "the deprivation or infringement of an employee's rights held under an original employment contract" changes the alternate employment offered or available into employment of an inferior kind. . . .

NOTE _____

Although the court in *Parker* stressed creative control issues, the decision in *David Lynch v. CIBY 2000,* Case No. CV 97–9022 (C.D. Ca.) granting summary judgment for plaintiff in a "pay or play" case relied on *Payne v. Pathe Studios, Inc.,* 6 Cal.App. 2d 136 (1935) cited with approval in *de la Palaise v. Gaumont-British Picture Corp., Ltd.,* 39 Cal.App. 2d 461 (1940) for the proposition that "[T]he duty to mitigate does not apply when an employee seeks minimum [guaranteed] compensation." The court also rejected defendant's argument that the "pay or play" clause was a liquidated damages provision and unenforceable as a penalty under Cal. Civil Code § 1671(b).

4.3.1.1 The Cimino and Beatty Arbitrations

However, the directors have had perhaps the most heated battles with studios over who will have "final cut"—the right to determine what will ultimately be shown to the public. It is generally conceded that film is a "director's medium" (although Ralph Rosenblum, a leading editor and author of *When the Shooting Stops . . . The Cutting Begins: A Film Editor's Story,* regards editing as "a major center of film creation").

Two arbitrations conducted under the aegis of the Directors Guild of America illustrate the power of final cut—those between *Michael Cimino/ SweetwaterFilms, Ltd and Gladden Entertainment Corp. re: "The Sicilian" (DGA Case No. 2183,* decided by Arbitrator Murray L. Schwartz on July 23, 1987), and between *Warren Beatty/JRS Productions, Inc. and Paramount Pictures Corp. re: "Reds" (DGA Case No. 1738,* decided by Arbitrator Edward Mosk on April 15, 1985). (The authors gratefully acknowledge the assistance of Elliot Williams, General Counsel of the DGA, in making the opinions available for our analysis.)

In *Cimino,* the director had the right of final cut, after good faith consultation with Gladden, so long as he delivered a film of not less than 105 minutes nor more than 125 minutes in length by a contractually specified date. The initial version (the "rough cut") ran 155 minutes, and producer David Begelman became concerned that Cimino would be unable to meet the target running time and delivery date. The parties met and agreed to an extension of the delivery date, in return for which Cimino agreed that Begelman might "cut the film behind him" if the film as delivered exceeded 125 minutes.

Cimino proceeded to deliver a 125-minute version, which Begelman rejected as "a bad joke," lacking full and complete continuity (a contention which Cimino's attorney rejected). At a subsequent meeting between Begelman and Cimino, Begelman suggested a number of cuts which would reduce the running time by about 20 minutes. Cimino thereupon delivered two further, alternative versions, one at 121:30, the other at 143 minutes. At this point, Begelman notified Cimino that neither version was satisfactory and that Cimino's services were no longer required.

Cimino's position in the arbitration was simple: He had, in fact, timely delivered a proposed final cut meeting the stipulated time requirements, after good faith consultation with Gladden. Gladden, on the other hand, took the position that Cimino's proposed final cut was unusable, since he had achieved the requisite length by deleting every scene (a total of 14) showing physical violence. While Cimino's position was that this approach permitted him to focus upon interrelationships between characters against the unchanging background of Sicily, Gladden took the position that the film was intended not as a character study but rather a depiction of the struggle of the legendary bandit Turi Giuliano against the Mafia, the state, the police, and the church. In addition, Gladden claimed that the cuts rendered the film incomprehensible, a position with which a large number of witnesses agreed, including Mario Puzo, author of the underlying novel, and Steve Shagan and Gore Vidal, who worked on versions of the screenplay. The only witnesses siding with Cimino were his editor and, perhaps, his attorney.

Arbitrator Murray L. Schwartz observed, at the outset, that:

A director's final cut is an uncommon, if not rare, event [and] is solely a matter of private contract between the director and producer . . . [A]bsent qualifying language in the personal services agreement, a director with final cut has ultimate decision-making authority over creative and artistic decisions about the final version of the picture. . . . It gives the producer the benefit of the name and reputation of the director in the financing, distribution, and exhibition of the film..

Arbitrator Schwartz pointed out that Cimino had spent some 6 to 12 months editing the longer version, that he had merely designated the 14 scenes to be cut, and that he had never viewed the 125-minute version as a whole. After being told by Begelman that the shorter version was "a failure," Cimino did not argue with Begelman or attempt to discuss the shorter version with him any further (which the arbitrator felt was Cimino's obligation), nor did Cimino proceed to screen it or do anything else with it during the ensuing six weeks between the initial submission of the short version and the May 1 outside delivery date.

"In short," said the arbitrator,

. . . the only attention Cimino paid to the short version was during the several days in March when he was attempting to satisfy "the letter of the agreement." This inattention is a far cry from the attention, care and review that, according to the testimony, directors normally accord to the versions they submit as their final cuts.

Moreover, the arbitrator pointed out that although Cimino was entitled to a copy of the shorter version, he never requested one and submitted a copy of the longer version—not his purported final cut—to the distributor for use in publicity trailers (even though the longer version contained the deleted scenes).

As additional justification for its position, Gladden pointed out that Cimino's purported final cut was not "in accordance with the screenplay." Although the Gladden/Cimino agreement contained no such requirement, it did contain a clause permitting Gladden to take over the picture "upon the occurrence [sic] of any event which permits such takeover under the completion bond guarantor for the Picture," and the completion bond *did* require that the picture be produced "in accordance with the Approved Screenplay," in default of which the completion bond guarantor had the right to take over the picture. However, the arbitrator rejected Gladden's attempt to incorporate such a major point by implication, observing that such language had been dropped from an earlier draft of the Gladden/Cimino agreement and that even under the completion bond agreement, takeover was basically justified only by a budget overrun or by a delay in production.

Indeed, in light of seriously conflicting testimony as to the extent to which the obligation of a director to shoot the approved screenplay would supersede the director's right of final cut, Arbitrator Schwartz stated that he:

would be loathe [sic] to interfere on this basis alone with Cimino's creative authority under the right of final cut. [On the other hand,] this factor cannot be considered in isolation. According to the evidence, in practically every case in which directors with final cut had made what were considered to be significant cuts or changes, there had been extensive consultation with the producer before those changes were made final. As such, in the circumstances of this case, mere substantial consistency with the screenplay—if it existed—cannot of itself control.

The arbitrator stated that under the circumstances, it appeared that "in effect, [Cimino's] first cut, made as a 'proposal,' became his final cut, despite his awareness that [Begelman] had rejected it absolutely [and] that behavior scarcely amounts to consultation, let alone 'good faith consultation,' as required by the contract."

Observing that "it is—and should be—a rare case in which an arbitrator will be asked to deny a director his final cut [and that] a director's claim of final cut is not vulnerable to every claim of procedural irregularity or creative misjudgment," but requires the producer to bear "a heavy burden of establishing even a prima facie case that further inquiry is warranted," the arbitrator proceeded to find that this *was* such a rare case, that Cimino did not treat the short version he submitted as a realistic attempt at a final cut, that Cimino had failed to engage in good faith consultation, and that Cimino could not prevent Gladden from proceeding to re-edit the picture.

The *Beatty* arbitration, by contrast, involved the attempt by Paramount to permit the ABC television network to make cuts in *Reds* in order to accommodate commercials, although the agreement between Beatty and Paramount permitted cuts only to accommodate network "standards and practices" (that is, censorship). Beatty had final cut under the original agreement under which he undertook to produce and direct the film. The conditions imposed upon him (apart from the obligation to comply with censorship requirements) were to timely deliver a film of 95–140 minutes in length, with a rating no worse than "R." In the event, Paramount accepted and released a film of 195 minutes in length. Beatty received the Academy Award for Best Director. In 1982, despite what Arbitrator Mosk characterized as Beatty's "grave concern about any release of REDS [*sic*] on network television, fearing that changes in the picture would be required which would be objectionable to [him]," Paramount entered into a license agreement with ABC, which granted ABC the right "to edit the film and elements thereof for purposes of time segment requirements." However, in 1984, in order to secure Beatty's cooperation in Paramount's efforts to acquire an extension for a proposed Paramount production of *Dick Tracy* (which was ultimately produced under the aegis of the Walt Disney Company, to moderate but not overwhelming success), Barry Diller, then chairman of Paramount, verbally agreed that Paramount would repurchase the network exhibition rights from ABC if the version which ABC proposed to televise proved unacceptable to Beatty. Beatty did not object to the proposed deletion of 1 minute 12 seconds for purposes of "standards and practices," but he did object in a timely manner to ABC's proposal to delete 6 minutes 25 seconds in order to accommodate commercials.

Arbitrator Mosk observed that:

Since the evidence is uncontradicted that Paramount gave Beatty almost unrestricted "final cut" on Dick Tracy, it is fair to conclude that the assertedly inflexible company policy regarding the right of abridgment for television could also be modified for Beatty in the case of Reds and was so modified.... [Indeed, under the contractual language,] the senior Paramount executives have an obligation to seek to prevent an abridgment of the picture even for otherwise permitted censorship cuts.... ABC could not acquire from Paramount any greater rights than Paramount had acquired from Beatty.

The arbitrator refused to consider the merits of the cuts which ABC proposed to make, stating that "it would not matter even if the arbitrator believed that the ABC editing had improved the picture as against the theatrical version.... Who is right on this creative issue is not for the arbitrator to determine."

With respect to Paramount's assertion that the implied covenant of good faith and fair dealing required that Beatty cooperate in the attempt to achieve a solution to ABC's time problems, the arbitrator observed that the operative agreement "did not set any objective standards on Beatty's ultimate decision with regard to the ABC cuts," and that Beatty's exercise of his contractual rights "cannot amount to conduct which violates the implied covenant of good faith and fair dealing."

NOTES

1. In *Preminger v. Columbia Pictures Corp.* 267 N.Y.S.2d 594 (N.Y. Sup. Ct. N.Y. County 1966), it was permissible for a television syndicator to allow its sublicensees to make minor cuts in order to insert commercials and to comply with time period constraints. Although director Preminger had a "final cut" clause, the court held that it applied only to the theatrical version, that this was a general clause, and that the clause granting television rights (which made no provision for "final cut") was a more specific grant and therefore took precedence over Preminger's theatrical "final cut" clause. The court cited *Autry v. Republic Productions,* 213

F.2d 667, 669 (9th Cir. 1954) for the proposition that a grant of television rights implied a privilege to cut and edit. The court noted that Preminger was well aware of the custom and practice of cutting for commercials, and had made provision for approval of such cuts in earlier agreements with respect to other films. Since the cuts were within normal parameters, Preminger was not entitled to prevent them.

2. For a further discussion of this issue, see Dana Harris, "Who Gets Final Cut?," *The Hollywood Reporter,* February 2–8, 1999, p. 18.

4.3.2 Mutilation

Even in the absence of contractual provisions reserving artistic control to the creators of an entertainment project, creators may have other avenues available through which to seek relief, as is illustrated in the *Gilliam, Chesler,* and *Bobbs-Merrill* decisions that follow.

Gilliam v. American Broadcasting Companies, 538 F.2d 14 (2d Cir. 1976)

[The Monty Python comedy group was extremely popular in England on the basis of its BBC television series. In 1973, BBC licensed Time-Life Films to distribute the series in the United States. ABC, which had previously attempted unsuccessfully to obtain from the group the right to broadcast excerpts from the Python shows, secured a license from Time-Life to broadcast two 90-minute specials, each consisting of three 30-minute Python programs not previously aired in the United States.

Although BBC had assured the group that the programs would be shown in their entirety, in fact each segment was edited by Time-Life to allow for the insertion of commercials (BBC did not show commercials). As aired, the first special included only 66 of the original 90 minutes, having been edited further by ABC to remove material ABC considered offensive or obscene. Although the BBC/Time-Life license permitted editing "for insertion of commercials, applicable censorship or governmental . . . rules and regulations," the underlying Python-BBC agreement contained no such broad grant. The BBC could only make "minor alterations" and "such other alterations as in its opinion are necessary in order to avoid involving the BBC in legal action or bringing the BBC into disrepute." Changes of the latter type could only be made by BBC through a procedure requiring an approach to the group, and only after the group unreasonably refused to do so.

Dismayed at the first program the group tried to negotiate with ABC over editing of the second special. When these negotiations failed, Monty Python sought a preliminary injunction against the showing of the special. U.S. District Court Judge Lasker denied the motion. . . .

The Second Circuit reversed]

LUMBARD, J.

. . . ABC presented the appellants with their first opportunity for broadcast to a nationwide network audience in this country. If ABC adversely misrepresented the quality of Monty Python's work, it is likely that many members of the audience, many of whom, by defendant's admission, were previously unfamiliar with appellants, would not become loyal followers of Monty Python productions. The subsequent injury to appellants' theatrical reputation would imperil their ability to attract the large audience necessary to the success of their venture. Such an injury to professional reputation cannot be measured in monetary terms or recompensed by other relief. . . .

In concluding that there is a likelihood of infringement here, we rely especially on the fact that the editing was substantial, i.e., approximately 27 percent of the original program was omitted, and the editing contravened contractual provisions that limited the right to edit Monty Python material. . . . Judge Lasker denied the preliminary injunction in part because he was unsure of the ownership of the copyright in the recorded program. Appellants first contend that the question of ownership is irrelevant because the recorded program was merely a derivative work taken from the script in which they hold the uncontested copyright. Thus, even if BBC owned the copyright in the recorded program its use of the work would be limited by the license granted to BBC by Monty Python for the use of the underlying script. We agree. . . .

Since the copyright in the underlying script survives intact despite the incorporation of that work into a derivative work, one who uses the script, even with the permission of the proprietor of the derivative work, may infringe the underlying copyright. . . .

One who obtains permission to use a copyrighted script in the production of a derivative work . . . may not exceed the specific purpose for which the permission was granted. . . .

The rationale for finding infringement when a licensee exceeds time or media restrictions on his license—the need to allow the proprietor of the underlying copyright to control the method in which his work is presented to the public—applies equally to the situation in which a licensee makes an unauthorized use of the underlying work by publishing it in a truncated version. Whether intended to allow greater economic exploitation of the work, as in the media and time cases, or to ensure that the copyright proprietor retains a veto power over revisions desired for the derivative work, the ability of the copyright holder to control his work remains paramount in our copyright law. We find, therefore, that unauthorized editing of the underlying work, if proven, would constitute an infringement of the copyright in that work similar to any other use of a work that exceeded the license granted by the proprietor of the copyright.

If the broadcast of an edited version of the Monty Python program infringed the group's copyright in the script, ABC may obtain no solace from the fact that editing was permitted in the agreements between BBC and Time-Life or Time-Life and ABC. BBC was not entitled to make unilateral changes in the script and was not specifically empowered to alter the recordings once made; Monty Python, moreover, had reserved to itself any rights not granted to BBC. Since a grantor may not convey greater rights than it owns, BBC's permission to allow Time-Life, and hence ABC, to edit appears to have been a nullity. . . .

Although a holder of a derivative copyright may obtain rights in the underlying work through ratification, the conduct necessary to that conclusion has yet to be demonstrated in this case. It is undisputed that appellants did not have actual notice of the cuts in the October 3 broadcast until late November. Even if they are chargeable with the knowledge of their British representative, it is not clear that she had prior notice of the cuts or ratified the omissions, nor did Judge Lasker make any finding on the question. While [Monty Python's representative], on September 5, did question how ABC was to broadcast the entire program if it was going to interpose 24 minutes of commercials, she received assurances from BBC that the programs would not be "segmented." . . .

On the present record, it cannot be said that there was any ratification of BBC's grant of editing rights. ABC, of course, is entitled to attempt to prove otherwise during the trial on the merits.

Aside from the question of who owns the relevant copyrights, ABC asserts that the contracts between appellants and BBC permit editing of the programs for commercial television in the United States. ABC argues that the scriptwriters' agreement allows appellants the right to participate in revisions of the script only *prior* to the recording of the programs, and thus infers that BBC had unrestricted authority to revise after that point. This argument, however, proves too much. A reading of the contract seems to indicate that Monty Python obtained control over editing the script only to ensure control over the program recorded from that script. Since the scriptwriters' agreement explicitly retains for the group all rights not granted by the contract, omission of any terms concerning alterations in the program after recording must be read as reserving to appellants exclusive authority for such revisions. . . .

Finally, ABC contends that appellants must have expected that deletions would be made in the recordings to conform them for use on commercial television in the United States. ABC argues that licensing in the United States implicitly grants a license to insert commercials in a program and to remove offensive or obscene material prior to broadcast. According to the network, appellants should have anticipated that most of the excised material contained scatological references inappropriate for American television and that these scenes would be replaced with commercials, which presumably are more palatable to the American public.

The proof adduced up to this point, however, provides no basis for finding any implied consent to edit. Prior to the ABC broadcast, Monty Python programs had been broadcast on a regular basis by both commercial and public television stations in this country without interruption or deletion. Indeed, there is no evidence of any prior broadcast of edited Monty Python material in the United States. These facts, combined with the persistent requests for assurances by the group and its representatives that the programs would be shown intact belie the argument that the group knew or should have known that deletions and commercial interruptions were inevitable.

Several of the deletions made for ABC, such as elimination of the words "hell" and "damn," seem inexplicable given today's standard television fare. If, however, ABC honestly determined that the programs were obscene in substantial part, it could have decided not to broadcast the specials at all, or it could have attempted to reconcile its differences with appellants. The network could not, however, free from a claim of infringement, broadcast in substantially altered form a program incorporating the script over which the group had retained control.

It also seems likely that appellants will succeed on the theory that, regardless of the right ABC had to broadcast an edited program, the cuts made constituted an actionable mutilation of Monty Python's work. This cause of action, which seeks redress for deformation of an artist's work, finds its roots in the continental concept of droit morale, or moral right, which may generally be summarized as including the right of the artist to have his work attributed to him in the form in which he created it. . . .

American copyright law, as presently written, does not recognize moral rights or provide a cause of action for their violation, since the law seeks to vindicate the economic, rather than the personal, rights of authors. Nevertheless, the economic incentive for artistic and intellectual creation that serves as the foundation for American copyright law . . . cannot be reconciled with the inability of artists to obtain relief for mutilation or misrepresentation of their work to the public on which the artists are financially dependent. Thus courts have long granted relief for misrepresentation of an artist's work by relying on theories outside the statutory law of copyright, such as contract law, *Granz v. Harris,* 198 F. 2d 5, 85 (2d Cir. 1952) (substantial cutting of original work constitutes misrepresentation), or the tort of unfair competition, *Prouty v. National Broadcasting Co.,* 26 F. Supp. 265, (Mass. 1939). See Strauss, "The Moral Right of the Author," 128–38, in *Studies on Copyright* (1963). Although such decisions are clothed in terms of proprietary right in one's creation, they also properly vindicate the author's personal right to prevent the presentation of his work to the public in a distorted form.

Here, the appellants claim that the editing done for ABC mutilated the original work and that consequently the broadcast of those programs as the creation of Monty Python violated the Lanham Act Sec. 43(a), 15 U.S.C. Sec. 1125(a). This statute, the federal counterpart to state unfair competition laws, has been invoked to prevent misrepresentations that may injure plaintiff's business or personal reputation, even where no registered trademark is concerned. . . . It is sufficient to violate the Act that a representation of a product, although technically true, creates a false impression of the product's origin.

We find that the truncated version at times omitted the climax of the skits to which appellants' rare brand of humor was leading and at other times deleted essential elements in the schematic development of a story line. We therefore agree with Judge Lasker's conclusion that the edited version broadcast by ABC impaired the integrity of appellants' work and represented to the public as the product of appellants what was actually a mere caricature of their talents. We believe that a valid cause of action for such distortion exists and that therefore a preliminary injunction may issue to prevent repetition of the broadcast prior to final determination of the issues.

GURFEIN, J. (CONCURRING)

I concur with my brother Lumbard's scholarly opinion, but I wish to comment on the application of Section 43(a) of the Lanham Act, 15 U.S.C. Sec. 1125(a).

I believe that this is the first case in which a federal appellate court has held that there may be a violation of Section 43(a) of the Lanham Act with respect to a common-law copyright. The Lanham Act is a trademark statute, not a copyright statute. Nevertheless, we must recognize that the language of Section 43(a) is broad. It speaks of the affixation or use of false designations of origin or false descriptions or representations, but proscribes such use "in connection with any goods or services." It is easy enough to incorporate trade names as well as trademarks into Section 43(a) and the statute specifically applies to common law trademarks, as well as registered trademarks. Lanham Act Sec. 45, 15 U.S.C. Sec. 1127.

In the present case, we are holding that the deletion of portions of the recorded tape constitutes a breach of contract, as well as an infringement of a common-law copyright of the original work. There is literally no need to discuss whether plaintiffs also have claim for relief under the Lanham Act or for unfair competition under New York law. . . .

The Copyright Act provides no recognition of the so-called *droit moral* or moral right of authors.

Nor are such rights recognized in the field of copyright law in the United States. . . . An obligation to mention the name of the author carries the implied duty, however, as a matter of contract, not to make such changes in the work as would render the credit line a false attribution of authorship.

So far as the Lanham Act is concerned, it is not a substitute for *droit moral* which authors in Europe enjoy. If the licensee may, by contract, distort the recorded word, the Lanham Act does not come into play. If the licensee has no such right by contract, there will be a violation in breach of contract. The Lanham Act can hardly apply literally when the credit line correctly states the work to be that of the plaintiff which, indeed it is, so far as it goes. The vice complained of is that the truncated version is not what the plaintiffs wrote. But the Lanham Act does not deal with artistic integrity. It *only* goes to misdescription of origin and the like. . . . The misdescription of origin can be dealt with, as Judge Lasker did below, by devising an appropriate legend to indicate that the plaintiffs had not approved the editing of the ABC version. With such a legend, there is no conceivable violation of the Lanham Act.

NOTE

In *Seroff v. Simon and Schuster. Inc.*, 162 N.Y.S.2d 770 (N.Y. Sup. Ct N.Y. County 1957), the author of the biography *Rachmaninoff* brought a libel suit against his publisher for damage to his reputation resulting from a mistranslated French version of the book. Although the court recognized what has been called the "moral right" of an author or artist to protection from deformation or alteration of his or her work it also found that these rights can be transferred or surrendered through contract.

The parties entered into a standard publishing contract in which the author granted additional rights of translation and foreign publication. With respect to these translation rights, the relationship between author and publisher became one of joint venture because the proceeds of the sale were to be shared equally between author and publisher. The only duty assumed by the publisher was to take reasonable care in the sale of the foreign translation rights, and this duty was discharged when Simon & Schuster sold the French rights to a publisher of fine repute. The French firm acted as an independent contractor, and the author could not hold Simon & Schuster responsible for its mistranslation.

Gilliam involved a complete absence of authority to perform the cuts to which the creators objected. However, as we see in the following cases, relief may be available to the creator in varying degrees despite the presence of very broad grants of rights to alter or adapt the creator's work.

NOTE

It is also important to bear in mind the scope of the doctrine of *droit morale*, i.e., moral rights, discussed in Gilliam, above, which is recognized in many countries of the world. There are two principal moral rights: (1) paternity, i.e., the right to be acknowledged as the creator of the work and (2) integrity, i.e., the right to have the work represented as the author created it. Thus, in *Turner Entertainment Co. v. Huston*, Court of Appeal of Versailles [France], 12/19/94, it was held that the moral rights of director/writer John Huston and his co-writer Ben Maddow would be violated by the broadcast of a colorized version of "The Asphalt Jungle," which Huston had deliberately shot in black-and-white at a time when films were frequently shot in color. "Huston's renown," the court stated, "is based on the interplay of black and white, creating an atmosphere . . . [which] would be jeopardized by colorization." The court also noted that "John HUSTON had opposed the colorization of his works during his life."

4.3.3 Censorship and Regulation of Content and Attendance

The issue of censorship is ever present. Private and public groups regularly attempt to regulate the content of what is to be available to the entertainment-consuming public and/or the availability of the material itself. Private efforts include the television boycott activities of Rev. Donald Wildmon and his American Family Association, the mid-1980s record-labeling pressure by the Parents' Music Resource Center (led by Mrs. "Tipper" Gore), and similar organized pressure groups. Public efforts include obscenity prosecutions (such as the one which followed after the *Navarro* case, below), as well as legislative efforts such as the Washington statute which was held unconstitutional in the *Soundgarden* case (see Note).

Government may be on firmer ground when it comes to regulating access to venues, when acting in *loco parentis* under the police power. The Memphis and San Antonio ordinances which are noted below do not attempt to regulate the content of what is presented in live concert and stage productions; however, they limit the ability of minors to attend such presentations. As we see in the notes discussing the *City of Renton* and *Stanglin* cases, the Supreme Court will allow a considerable latitude to localities in limiting access by the very young to places and performances considered to be potentially harmful. However, government cannot condition access to public facilities upon approval of content, as we see in the *Cinevision* case.

Skyywalker Records, Inc. v. Navarro, 739 F. Supp. 578 (S.D.Fla. 1990).

GONZALES, J.

This is a case between two ancient enemies: Anything Goes and Enough Already.

Justice Oliver Wendell Holmes, Jr., observed in *Schenck v. United States*, 249 U.S. 47 (1919), that the First Amendment is not absolute and that it does not permit one to yell "Fire" in a crowded theater. Today, this court decides whether the First Amendment absolutely permits one to yell another "F" word anywhere in the community when combined with graphic sexual descriptions.

Two distinct and narrow issues are presented: whether the recording *As Nasty As They Wanna Be (Nasty)* is legally obscene; and second, whether the actions of the defendant Nicholas Navarro (Navarro), as Sheriff of Broward County, Florida, posed an unconstitutional prior restraint upon the plaintiffs' right to free speech. . . .

THE PLAINTIFFS

The plaintiff Skyywalker Records, Inc. (Skyywalker) is a Florida corporation headquartered in Miami, Florida. The [individual] plaintiffs . . . constitute the group known as "2 Live Crew" whose recording . . . is the subject of this lawsuit. . . .

The plaintiffs have brought this action under section 1983, Title 42 of the United States Code, which provides a federal statutory remedy for unlawful deprivations of federal rights including those liberties guaranteed under the United States Constitution. The plaintiffs also seek a declaration of their legal rights, under the Federal Declaratory

Judgment Act, 28 U.S.C. 2201(a), and injunctive relief under section 2202(b) thereof. This court has previously denied the plaintiffs' motion for a preliminary injunction by *ore tenus* entered April 19, 1990. There is no prayer for money damages.

Because this is a civil action, the party with the burden of proof must prevail by a preponderance of the evidence. On the issue of obscenity, the defendant Navarro has the burden of proof. As to the prior restraint claim, however, the plaintiffs have the burden to prove, beyond a preponderance of the evidence, that the defendant's actions were unconstitutional.

It must be emphasized at the outset that this decision does not criminalize the plaintiffs' conduct, nor does it charge anyone with a crime. That is a matter for the police and the criminal courts to determine. Whether the plaintiffs are guilty of a crime can only be decided if criminal charges are brought, a trial by jury conducted, and all other due process requirements have been met. Whether *As Nasty As They Wanna Be* is criminally obscene is left for the determination of another court on another day. . . .

In deciding whether a specific work is or is not obscene, the court must apply the controlling test enunciated in *Miller v. California,* 413 U.S. 15 [1 Media L. Rptr. 1441] (1973). To be obscene, there must be proof of all three of the following factors: (1) the average person, applying contemporary community standards [the Court defined Palm Beach, Dade and Broward Counties as the relevant community] would find that the work, taken as a whole, appeals to the prurient interest, (2) measured by contemporary community standards, the work depicts or describes, in a patently offensive way, sexual conduct specifically defined by the applicable state law, and (3) the work, taken as a whole, lacks serious literary, artistic, political, or scientific value. Id; *also see Memoirs,* 383 U.S. at 419 (to be obscene, all three elements must be met and each element must be "independently" evaluated); *Penthouse International, Ltd v. McAuliffe,* 610 F.2d 1354, 1363 [5 Media L. Rptr. 2531] (5th Cir. 1980) (same); *United States v. Various Articles of Obscene Merchandise,* 709 F.2d 132, 135 (2nd Cir. 1983) (same). . . .

THE FIRST MILLER TEST: PRURIENT INTEREST

This court finds, as a matter of fact, that the recording . . . appeals to the prurient interest. The Supreme Court has defined prurient as "material having a tendency to excite lustful thoughts." *Roth,* 354 U.S. at 487 n.20. Appeals only to "normal healthy sexual desires" are not adequate to meet the test. *Brockett v. Spokane Arcades, Inc.,* 472 U.S. 491, 498 (1985). The material must exhibit a "shameful or morbid interest in nudity, sex, or excretion." *Id.* (readopting definition in *Roth,* 354 U.S. at 487 n.20).

Nasty appeals to the prurient interest for several reasons. First, its lyrics and the titles of its songs are replete with references to female and male genitalia, human sexual excretion, oral-anal contact, fellatio, group sex, specific sexual positions, sado-masochism, the turgid state of the male sexual organ, masturbation, cunnilingus, sexual intercourse, and the sounds of moaning. Florida's Legislature has provided a valuable source of evidence in the form of its obscenity statutes for determining what is sexual conduct. The initial provision is section 847.001(11), Florida Statutes, which defines "sexual conduct" to include "actual or simulated sexual intercourse, deviate sexual intercourse, . . . masturbation, . . . sadomasochistic abuse; [or] actual lewd exhibition of the genitals." Section 847.001(2), Florida Statutes, defines deviate sexual intercourse as sexual conduct between unmarried persons involving contact between the penis and the anus, the mouth and the penis, or the mouth and the vulva. Section 847.001(8) defines sadomasochistic abuse as satisfaction from sadistic violence derived by inflicting harm upon another. These definitions cover most, if not all, of the sexual acts depicted in *As Nasty As They Wanna Be.*

Furthermore, the frequency and graphic description of the sexual lyrics evinces a clear intention to lure hearers into this activity. The depictions of ultimate sexual acts are so vivid that they are hard to distinguish from seeing the same conduct described in the words of a book or in pictures in periodicals or films.

It is also noteworthy that the material here is music. It is true that it would be difficult, albeit not impossible, to find that mere sound without lyrics is obscene. Music is sufficiently subjective that reasonable persons could disagree as to its meaning. But, the focus of the *Nasty* recording is its lyrics. Based on the evidence at trial, music of the "rap" genre focuses upon verbal messages accentuated by a strong beat. 2 Live Crew itself testified that the *Nasty* recording was made to be listened and danced to. The evident goal of this particular recording is to reproduce the sexual act through musical lyrics. It is an appeal directed to "dirty" thoughts and the loins, not to the intellect and the mind.

The court has also given some, but not great, weight to the plaintiffs' commercial motive. Of course, the fact that the plaintiffs made a profit from the public distribution of the Nasty recording is not relevant in determining obscenity. See *Ginzburg v. United States,* 383 U.S. 463, 474 [1 Media L. Rptr. 1409] (1966). However, the court can consider the manner in which the material was distributed and promoted to determine if the "leer of the sensualist" permeates the work. *Id.* at 465–66, 468, 475–76. In Ginzburg, the court found that publishers of certain magazines and books had directed their advertising in such a way as to commercially exploit erotica solely for the sake of their prurient appeal. Id. at 466. For example, the advertisements sent to potential customers "stressed the sexual candor of the respective publications, and openly boasted that the publishers would take full advantage of what they regarded [as] an unrestricted license allowed by law in the expression of sex and sexual matters." *Id.* at 469. The court went on to note that, "the deliberate representation of petitioners' publications as erotically arousing, for example, stimulated the reader to accept them as prurient; he looks for titillation not for saving intellectual content." *Id. at 470.*

Consideration of the creator's intent to appeal to the prurient interest is still a valid consideration today, even after *Miller v. California.* See *Splawn v. California,* 431 U.S. 595 [2 Media L. Rptr. 188 1] (1977); *Pinkas,* 436 U.S. 293 [3 Media L. Rptr. 2329] (1978).

The record at trial indicates that the plaintiffs' commercial exploitation of this work was done in a manner calculated to make a salacious appeal. The title of the recording . . . in addition to the names of many of the songs and the illustration on the recordings' insert certainly fit within the confines of the Ginzburg case for materials "look[ing] for titillation."

One of the more interesting points suggested by the evidence at trial, but not dwelt on by the defendant, was that 2 Live Crew made two apparently identical albums with the only difference being the sexually explicit lyrics. The plaintiffs' own expert, John Leland, testified that the *Nasty* recording, without the salacious lyrics, would not have been expected to sell more than 500,000 copies nationwide. To date, the *Nasty* version has sold 1.7 million copies. The identical recording sans sexual lyrics (*Clean*) has sold only 250,000 copies. The difference between the actual sales of the two recordings can reasonably be found to have been motivated by the "leer of the sensualist." The plaintiffs cannot claim they needed the vulgar lyrics to promote their message since the plaintiffs' own experts testified that music from neither the "rap" or "hip-hop" genre does not require the use of such language.

Finally, the plaintiffs rely upon testimony, both lay and expert, that the Nasty recording did not actually physically excite anyone who heard it and indeed, caused boredom after repeated play. However, based on the graphic deluge of sexual lyrics about nudity and sexual conduct, this court has no difficulty in finding that [*Nasty*] appeals to a shameful and morbid interest in sex.

THE SECOND MILLER TEST: PATENTLY OFFENSIVE

The court also finds that the second element of the Miller test is satisfied in that the *Nasty* recording is patently offensive. This is a question of fact, which must be measured by contemporary community standards. See *Miller,* 413 U.S. at 30.

It is quite true that not all speech with sex as its topic is obscene. See *Roth,* 354 U.S. at 487. [*Nasty*] is another matter.

The recording depicts sexual conduct in graphic detail. The specificity of the descriptions makes the audio message analogous to a camera with a zoom lens, focusing on the sights and sounds of various ultimate sex acts. Furthermore, the frequency of the sexual lyrics must also be considered. With the exception of part B on Side 1, the entire *Nasty* recording is replete with explicit sexual lyrics. This is not a case of subtle references or innuendo, nor is it just "one particular scurrilous epithet" as in *Cohen v. California,* 403 U.S. 15, 22 (1971).

. . . States may outlaw certain portrayals of sexual conduct and nudity if they constitute "hardcore pornography." See *Jenkins v. Georgia*, 417 U.S. 153 [1 Media L. Rptr. 1504] (1974). In *Jenkins*, the Supreme Court reversed a conviction for distribution of the film "Carnal Knowledge" which contained scenes of a woman with a bare midriff and several lovemaking sessions. Id at 161. This depiction was held by the court to not be within the hardcore category. As noted by the court,

While the subject matter of the picture is, in a broader sense, sex, and there are scenes in which sexual conduct including "ultimate sexual acts" is to be understood to be taking place, the camera does not focus on the bodies of the actors at such times. There is no exhibition whatever of the actors' genitals, lewd or otherwise, during these scenes. There are occasional scenes of nudity, but nudity alone is not enough to make material legally obscene under the Miller standards. Id at 161.

In *Miller*, the Supreme Court gave two examples of the type of conduct subject to state regulation: "(a) Patently offensive representations or descriptions of ultimate sexual acts, normal or perverted, actual or simulated. (b) Patently offensive representation or descriptions of masturbation, excretory functions, and lewd exhibition of the genitals." 413 U.S. at 25. The conduct described in the *Nasty* recording is certainly within the scope of the Florida statutes. The state law, of course, is not dispositive on the question of whether this particular community would be patently offended, but it is entitled to significant weight. *Smith*, 431 U.S. at 307–08.

While the above facts are sufficient to support a finding that this material is patently offensive, there are additional considerations that support such a finding. First, the *Nasty* lyrics contain what are commonly known as "dirty words" and depictions of female abuse and violence. It is likely that these offensive descriptions would not of themselves be sufficient to find the recording obscene. [Citations omitted.] When these terms are used with explicit sexual descriptions, however, they may be considered on the issue of patent offensiveness. Secondly, the material here is music which can certainly be more intrusive to the unwilling listener than other forms of communication. Unlike a video tape, a book, or a periodical, music must be played to be experienced. A person can sit in public and look at an obscene magazine without unduly intruding upon another's privacy; but, even according to the plaintiffs' testimony, music is made to be played and listened to. A person laying on a public beach, sitting in a public park, walking down the street or sitting in his automobile waiting for the light to change is, in a sense, a captive audience. While the law does require citizens to avert their ears when speech is merely offensive, they do not have an obligation to buy and use ear plugs in public if the state legislature has chosen to protect them from obscenity.

Finally, in determining whether the Nasty recording is patently offensive, it is again proper to consider the plaintiffs' commercial exploitation of sex to promote sales. As noted by the Supreme Court in *Ginzburg v. United States*, 383 U.S. 463, 470 Media L. Rptr. 1409 (1966), representations of a publication as erotically arousing "would tend to force public confrontation with the potentially offensive aspects of the work; the brazenness of such an appeal heightens the offensiveness of the publications to those who are offended by such material." Such is the case here, as already discussed. Again, while this factor has not been given great weight, it is entitled to consideration.

THE THIRD MILLER TEST: SOCIAL VALUE

The final factor under *Miller* is whether the Nasty recording, taken as a whole, lacks serious literary, artistic, political, or scientific value. This factor is not measured by community standards. The proper inquiry is whether a reasonable person would find serious social value in the material at issue. See *Pope v. Illinois, U.S.*, 107 S.Ct. 1918, 1921 Media L. Rptr. 1001 (1987). The plaintiffs correctly note that the value of a work can pass muster under *Miller* if it has serious merit, measured objectively, even if a majority of the community would not agree.

As a preliminary matter, it is again important to note what this case is not about. Neither the "Rap" or "Hip-Hop" musical genres are on trial. The narrow issue before this court is whether the [Nasty] recording . . . is legally obscene.

This is also not a case about whether the group 2 Live Crew or any of its other music is obscene. The third element of the *Miller* test focuses upon the social value of the particular work, not its creators. The fact that individuals of whom we approve hold objectionable ideas or that people of whom we do not approve hold worthy ideas does not affect judicial review of the value of the ideas themselves.

The Philistines are not always wrong, nor are the guardians of the First Amendment always right. This court must examine the *Nasty* recording for its content; the inquiry is objective, not *ad hominem*.

Finally, this court's role is not to serve as a censor or an art and music critic. If the *Nasty* recording has serious literary, artistic, political, or scientific value, it is irrelevant that the work is not stylish, tasteful, or even popular.

The plaintiffs themselves testified that neither their music nor their lyrics were created to convey a political message.

The only witness testifying at trial that there was political content in the *Nasty* recording was Carlton Long, who was qualified as an expert on the culture of black Americans. This witness first stated that the recording was political because the 2 Live Crew, as a group of black Americans, used this medium to express themselves. While it is doubtless true that *Nasty* is a product of the group's background, including their heritage as black Americans, this fact does not convert whatever they say, or sing, into political speech. Professor Long also testified that the following passages from the recording contained political content: a four-sentence phrase in the song "Dirty Nursery Rhymes" about Abraham Lincoln, the word "man" in the Georgie Porgie portion of the same song, and the use of the device of "boasting" to stress one's manhood. Even giving these isolated lyrics the meaning attributed by the expert, they are not sufficient in number or significance to give the *Nasty* recording, as a whole, any serious political value.

In terms of science, Professor Long also suggested that there is cultural content in 2 Live Crew's recording which rises to the level of serious sociological value. According to this witness, white Americans "hear" the *Nasty* recording in a different way than black Americans because of their different frames of references. Long identifies three cultural devices evident in the work here: "call and response," "doing the dozens" and "boasting." The court finds none of these arguments persuasive.

The only examples of "call and response" in the *Nasty* recording are portions where males and females yell, in repetitive verse, "Tastes Great-Less Filling" and, in another song, assail campus Greek-letter groups. The phrases alone have no significant artistic merit nor are they examples of black American culture. In the case of "Tastes Great—Less Filling," this is merely a phrase lifted from a beer commercial.

The device of "doing the dozens" is a word game composed of a series of insults escalating in their satirical content. The "boasting" device is a way for persons to overstate their virtues such as sexual prowess.

While this court does not doubt that both "boasting" and "doing the dozens" are found in the culture of black Americans, these devices are also found in other cultures. "Doing the dozens" is commonly seen in adolescents, especially boys, of all races. "Boasting" seems to be part of the universal human condition.

Professor Long also cited to several different examples of literary devices such as rhyme and allusion which appear in *Nasty,* and points to the song title "Dick Almighty" as an example of the literary device of personification. This, of course, is nonsense regardless of the expert's credentials. "A quotation from Voltaire in the fly leaf of a book," noted the Supreme Court in *Miller,* "will not constitutionally redeem an otherwise obscene publication." 413 U.S. at 25 n.7 (quoting *Kois v. Wisconsin,* 408 U.S. 229, 231 (1972)).

Prior to *Miller,* the government had to demonstrate that a work was utterly without redeeming social value to be judged obscene. See *Memoirs,* 383 U.S. at 419. The present test is less stringent, only requiring proof of an absence of serious social worth. This leads to the plaintiffs' strongest argument: that the *Nasty* recording has serious artistic value. This category of social worth is broad enough to include the value contributed by the political, literary, and cultural aspects of the particular work.

The plaintiffs stress that the *Nasty* recording has value as comedy and satire. Certainly, people can and do laugh at obscenity. The plaintiffs point to the audience reaction at trial when the subject recording was played in open court. The audience giggled initially, but the court observed that after the initial titillation, it fell silent.

In a society where obscenity is forbidden, it is human nature to want to taste forbidden fruit. It is quite another thing to say that this aspect of humanity forms the basis for finding that *Nasty* has serious artistic value. Furthermore, laughter can express much more than enjoyment and entertainment. It is also a means of hiding embarrassment, concealing shame, and releasing tension. The fact that laughter was only heard at the time that the first song of the tape was played is probative on what the audience's outbursts really meant. It cannot be reasonably argued that the violence, perversion, abuse of women, graphic depictions of all forms of sexual conduct, and microscopic descriptions of human genitalia contained on this recording are comedic art.

The *Nasty* recording is not comedy, but is first and foremost, music. Initially, it would appear very difficult to find a musical work obscene. As noted by the American Civil Liberties Union, the meaning of music is subjective and subject only to the limits of the listener's imagination.

Music nevertheless is not exempt from a state's obscenity statutes. Musical works are obscene if they meet the *Miller* test. Certainly it would be possible to compose an obscene oratorio or opera and it has probably been done.

The plaintiffs claim that this case is novel since it seeks to determine whether music can be obscene. The particular work here, although belonging to the general category of music, however, is to be distinguished from a purely instrumental work, or other more common recordings with a fairly equal emphasis on music and lyrics. The focus of the *Nasty* recording is predominately on the lyrics. Expert testimony at trial indicates that a central characteristic of "rap" music is its emphasis on the *verbal* message. Rhythm is stressed over melody, not for its own sake, but to accentuate the words of the song. The pounding beat and the presence of near continuous lyrics support this conclusion. 2 Live Crew's music is explicitly clear as to its message. Although music and lyrics must be considered jointly, it does not significantly alter the message of the *Nasty* recording to reduce it to a written transcription. The Supreme Court's decision in *Kaplan v. California,* 413 U.S. 115 (1973), is applicable here. The court held that an expression by words alone, albeit in a written form, can be legally obscene even if there are no accompanying pictorial depictions. Id at 118–119. The case at bar is an extension of the law to the extent that words, as lyrics in music, can be obscene.

The key to judging the *Nasty* recording is to consider it as a whole. 2 Live Crew has "borrowed" components called "riffs" from other artists. Taking the work in its entirety, the several riffs do not lift *Nasty* to the level of a serious artistic work. Once the riffs are removed, all that remains is the rhythm and the explicit sexual lyrics which are utterly without any redeeming social value.

Obscenity is not a required element for socially valuable "rap" or "hip-hop" music. 2 Live Crew itself proved this point by the creation of its *Clean* recording. . . .

One of the plaintiffs' expert witnesses testified at trial that material is art if it causes a reaction in the audience perceiving it. If that reaction is an appeal to the prurient interest in a patently offensive way, and if the material lacks serious literary, artistic, political or scientific, the law does not call that art—it calls it obscenity and when so proven beyond a reasonable doubt is a crime in Florida.

Obscenity? Yes!

The [*Nasty*] recording . . . taken as a whole, is legally obscene.

The court so finds by a preponderance of the evidence although the standard of proof presents no real issue.

The court also finds [*Nasty*] to be legally obscene under the *Miller* test by clear and convincing evidence, which standard the plaintiffs maintain is the correct burden of proof . . .

NOTES _____

1. The Eleventh Circuit subsequently reversed, holding that the trial judge had impermissibly proceeded on the basis of his own subjective assessment of community standards rather than on the basis of objective evidence. *Skyywalker Records. Inc. v. Navarro*, 968 F.2d 134 (11th Cir.), *cert. denied*, 506 U.S. 1022 (1992).

2. Following the decision of the district court in the *Navarro* case, a Florida jury subsequently found Skyywalker Records, Inc., and 2 Live Crew not guilty of criminal obscenity charges that were brought against them with respect to the Nasty record. However, a Miami record store owner was found guilty of violating the obscenity statute in selling the *Nasty* record and fined $1,000.00.

3. In the next election after these proceedings, Sheriff Nick Navarro was defeated for re-election.

4. Washington's "Erotic Sound Recordings" statute (House Bill 2554, Laws of 1992, ch. 5, codified as RCW 9.68.050, .060, .070 and .090, also known as the "Erotic Music Statute") was declared unconstitutional on its face in *Soundgarden v. Eikenberry*, 123 Wash.2d 750, 871 P.2d 1050, 1994 Wash. LEXIS 255 (1994) and its enforcement was permanently enjoined.

5. Municipalities have adopted ordinances aimed at preventing minors from attending concerts or other presentations deemed harmful to them by the authorities. For example, see *City of San Antonio. Texas. Ordinance 61,850* (Effective November 14, 1985), which provides that "[n]o person having control over a City-owned facility [a definition which includes anyone who may produce, direct, participate or perform] shall intentionally, knowingly, or recklessly allow or permit a child under the age of fourteen (14) years to enter or to remain within a leased area in a City-owned facility within one hour before or at any time during a performance is scheduled, if such person (1) knows, or (2) has knowledge of sufficient facts and circumstances from which a reasonable person would know that the performance is or will be a performance obscene as to a child, unless such child is admitted with a parent or legal guardian."

6. In *City of Renton v. Playtime Theatre, Inc.*, 475 U.S. 41 (1986), the Supreme Court upheld (by a 7 to 2 vote, with Justices Brennan and Marshall dissenting) an ordinance prohibiting adult motion picture theaters from locating within 1,000 feet of any residential zone, church, park, or school. Playtime had claimed that the ordinance violated Playtime's rights under the First and Fourteenth Amendments. The Court stated that the ordinance was content-neutral and dealt only with the time, place, and manner of performance, serving a substantial government interest in preserving the quality of urban life (citing *Young v. American Mini Theatres, Inc.*, 427 U.S. 50 [1976]). Although the city of Renton had not itself undertaken studies of the impact that such theatres would have on Renton itself, the Court stated that Renton was entitled to refer to the experience of other neighboring cities, as long as that experience was reasonably believed to be relevant to Renton's own situation. Additionally, Renton did not attempt to bar all

entertainment of the type offered by Playtime, having left more than 5 percent of the entire area of the city open to such uses.

7. In *City of Dallas v. Stanglin*. 490 U.S. 19, 109 S.Ct. 1591(1989), the Supreme Court upheld a local ordinance establishing a category of "Class E" dance halls, admission to which was restricted to persons between 14 and 18 years of age. Since such a dance hall might experience attendance of as many as 1,000 teenagers on a given night, such experiences did not engage the "associational" values of the First Amendment sufficiently to override the city's interest in protecting its teenagers from corrupting influences. (The decision was 7–0, with Justices Stevens and Blackmun concurring.)

In the preceding cases and ordinances, the public authority was acting in loco parentis. Although reference is made to content in the ordinances involved, the standards employed have been upheld repeatedly when expressed with sufficient particularity, especially when applied for the protection of minors. However, courts are suspicious of any attempt to regulate content where adults are concerned. This is illustrated clearly in the following case.

Cinevision v. City of Burbank, 745 F.2d 560 (9th Cir. 1984), *cert. denied*, 471 U.S. 1054 (1985)

[The City authorized Cinevision to promote summer concerts at City-owned Starlight Bowl for a five-year period. The contract required Cinevision to submit, in advance, "a description of the nature and content of each show or performance and the names of the participants," and reserved to the City "the right to disapprove and cancel any show or performance which has the potential of creating a public nuisance or which would violate any State law or City ordinance." In 1977, Richman, an opponent of the concerts, was elected to the City Council. Despite his opposition, the concerts continued through 1977 and 1978. In 1979, however, objecting to "hard rock" music and the potential attraction of narcotics users to the community, the Council rejected 6 out of 8 proposed concerts. Cinevision sued the City and Councilman Richman under 42 U.S.C. § 1983, claiming a violation of its civil rights. The jury awarded Cinevision $20,000 damages against the City and Richman jointly, and an additional $5,000 against Richman for his "willful, wanton, malicious or oppressive conduct." The district court also awarded Cinevision $119,288 attorneys' fees.]

REINHARDT, CIRCUIT JUDGE

. . . Other circuits and district courts presented with the issue have held, and we agree, that music is a form of expression that is protected by the first amendment. Therefore, "[i]f the[City Council] passed an ordinance forbidding the playing of rock and roll music . . . they would be infringing a First Amendment right. . . .

even if the music had no political message—even if it had no words— and the defendants would have to produce a strong justification for thus repressing a form of speech." *Reed v. Village of Shorewood*, 104 F.2d 943, 950 (7th Cir. 1983). . . .

The City suggests that because Cinevision does not seek to "express" its views, it has no first amendment right to promote concerts for profit. However, even though concert promoters generally promote concerts for profit, they still enjoy the protections of the first amendment. See, e.g., *Joseph Burstyn, Inc. Wilson,* 343 U.S. 495, 501–02. . . . In fact, promoters of theatrical productions and concerts have previously succeeded in challenging a municipality's denial of access to governmentally owned property. See *Southeastern Promotions Ltd. Conrad,* 420 U.S. 546 (1975). . . . Thus, under the first amendment, there clearly are rights to promote protected expression for profit—including musical expression. As a promoter of protected musical expression, Cinevision enjoys first amendment rights. . . .

. . . To have access to live musical expression, the public must necessarily rely on concert promoters to make arrangements for musicians to perform. The role of the promoter in ensuring access to the public is at least as critical as the role of the bookseller or theater owner: in fact, it would seem to be far easier for an individual to obtain printed material or a film on his or her own than to arrange personally for live entertainment by a nationally known musical group. Thus, a concert promoter, like a bookseller or theater owner, is a type of "clearing-house" for expression. Moreover, as a practical matter, a promoter, like Cinevision, is in a far better position than concert-goers or individual performers to vindicate first amendment rights, and ensure public access to live musical entertainment.

The City's argument that Cinevision enjoyed no first amendment right to promote the six rejected concerts is based in large part on the fact that an executive officer of Cinevision did not know specifically what songs each performer would sing; therefore, the City argues, Cinevision, by promoting the concerts was not engaging in "expression" protected by the first amendment. As we have noted, however, theater owners and booksellers, even if they are not "expressing" themselves, further a first amendment interest in making protected materials available to the public. Moreover, it would be anomalous to require a promoter to know exactly what songs an entertainer will sing before any first amendment rights attach—just as it would be to require a bookseller to read all of the books he plans to sell or a theater-owner to view all of the movies he intends to show. In fact, not even the City Council members knew the songs that each proposed performer would sing. Rather than objecting to any particular songs, various Council members objected to certain types of music, labeling all music of which they disapproved as "hard rock."

We recognize, as the Council members obviously did, that the musical expression of some performers reflects a particular political view and that some performers may, apart from their music, represent a particular ideology or way of life. However unsophisticated or ill-informed the members of the City Council may have been regarding current forms of popular music, it is difficult to believe that they would not have been aware of the differences between Jackson Browne and Donnie and Marie

Osmond, or the differences between Pete Seeger and Pat Boone, or Joan Baez and Merle Haggard. It is hardly necessary to know what specific songs these artists will sing in order to know that their very appearances carry differing political or social messages. In any event, constitutional safeguards are not applicable only to musical expression that implicates some sort of ideological content. Rather, all-political and non-political-musical expression, like other forms of entertainment, is a matter of first amendment concern. Consequently, promoters of musical expression of all types enjoy the protections of the first amendment. . . .

Governmental regulation of a place determined to be a public forum is limited by the constraints of the first amendment. . . . As the City correctly points out, public ownership of the Bowl does not compel the conclusion that it is a public forum. [By allowing concerts] by a variety of performers, the City transformed publicly owned property into a public forum for expressive activity, even if the expressive activity is promoted by a single entity. Moreover, assuming that, as the City claims, the Starlight Bowl is "remote, fenced, seldom used, and locked when not in use," that does not affect its status as a public forum. . . .

. . . Although the City was not required to open the Starlight Bowl and is not required to leave it open indefinitely, it cannot, absent a compelling governmental interest, open the forum to some and close it to others solely in order to suppress the content of protected expression. . . . Here, although the prohibitions against the concerts are content-related, there are neither compelling state interests that justify the City's denial of access to the Starlight Bowl, nor narrowly drawn standards designed to prevent arbitrary decision-making. . . . The contract in this case provides an overbroad standard for the City Council's disapproval of the proposed concerts . . . [and] does not adequately limit the discretion of the City Council in approving or disapproving the proposals. Thus, it fails to meet the requirements of the first amendment. Objections to the proposed concert centered on the content of the music—it was "hard rock" music that the City Council wanted to exclude from the Starlight Bowl. . . . Given the evidence before us, we must reject the City of Burbank's suggestion that "hard rock" concerts are a per se public nuisance justifying their exclusion from the Starlight Bowl because of their content. In addition, a general fear that state or local narcotics or other laws will be broken by people attending the concerts cannot justify a content-based restriction on expression. Normally, law enforcement officers can deal adequately and effectively with unlawful activity of that nature at the time it occurs. That is a proper exercise of the police power; censorship is not. Even if the performers planned to advocate unlawful, subversive activities, which the City has not alleged here, that expression could only be suppressed if it were directed at producing, and were likely to produce, imminent lawless action. Moreover, there is reason to question the extent to which any good faith concern over problems relating to law enforcement (irrelevant as those concerns may be for purposes of the first amendment) played a serious part in the Council's determinations. The facts surrounding the

Todd Rundgren concert illustrate this point. Even though the members of the Police Commission who made a recommendation concerning the proposed concert suggested that the City Council approve the concert, the City Council disapproved it. The pre-concert investigation report prepared by the Police Department expressly stated that there had been "no problems" at any of Rundgren's concerts in other cities. In fact, in 1976, Todd Rundgren performed in the Starlight Bowl and, according to the Chief of Police, there were no security or traffic congestion problems; "[t]he crowd, for the most part, was orderly, and there were no citizen complaints." Similarly, although there was no evidence whatsoever that there had been any problems at his previous concerts, the City Council rejected a proposed Jackson Browne concert. We recognize, of course, that a municipality may have legitimate concerns about the collateral effects of concerts in an amphitheater like the Starlight Bowl: a municipality has a significant interest in controlling the noise level of a concert, crowd overflow, and traffic congestion. For that reason, content-neutral, time, place and manner regulations that are narrowly drafted to further such significant governmental interests do not violate the first amendment. For example, a City may under some circumstances regulate the decibel level of concerts or place time restrictions on concerts when music is performed above a certain volume. However, there are no time, place, or manner regulations involved here. . . .

Despite our holding that the City violated Cinevision's first amendment rights, we do not mean to suggest that a municipality that wishes to dedicate a facility to the promotion of drama or opera is powerless to do so, or that a governmental entity can never regulate access to a forum on the basis of the type of entertainment to be presented. The dedication of a museum to the exhibition of contemporary art, a theater to the production of Shakespeare's works or the performance of plays intended for children, or an auditorium to ballet or other forms of dance, may in some instances encourage diversity of entertainment and promote, rather than abridge, first amendment values. A court must, however, scrutinize closely a government's dedication of a forum to a particular type of expression and fully consider a number of factors before deciding the constitutionality of such an action [and] review with particular care any claim that the governmental body is actually attempting to suppress controversial, political, or other forms of expression, rather than attempting to promote certain limited forms of entertainment. Any willful or purposeful effort by a municipality to suppress protected expression clearly conflicts with the first amendment. . . .

Once it is clearly established that the purpose of the conduct is not to suppress protected expression, the reviewing court should consider the category of expression that a municipality has dedicated the use of a public forum to, how that category is defined, and what standards will be used to determine whether particular performances or works fall within that category. The exclusive use of an auditorium or theater for a form of expression that is well defined, historically recognized, readily identifiable, and susceptible to objective classification is likely to be found permissible (e.g., opera, ballet, Shakespeare, 19th Century French dramatists). However, the more subjective the standard used, the more likely that the category will not meet the requirements of the first amendment; for, when guided only by subjective, amorphous standards, government officials retain the unbridled discretion over expression that is condemned by the first amendment.

The way in which a public forum dedicated to a certain form of expression is operated may also be significant in determining the constitutionality of the limitation. When decisions about what forms of expression will be permitted or which individuals will be allowed to express themselves in a public forum are made by a body like the City Council, those decisions must be scrutinized most carefully—if only because such a body is at all times, by its very nature, the object of political pressures. . . . To the extent the decision-maker is removed from the heat of the political process, or is free to make an independent judgment, the constitutional problem is less acute. For example, the selection of exhibits by a professionally trained museum curator is far less likely to result in first amendment questions than the veto of proposed museum exhibits by a group of local elected officials. Similarly, a decision by a professional concert promoter, or even a civil service employee with particular training or expertise in the field of entertainment or facilities management, will have a better chance of surviving first amendment scrutiny than a similar decision made by a mayor or other elected officials. Another relevant factor in determining whether a public forum may be devoted exclusively to one form of expression is whether other forums are available for the presentation of that form of expression. The fact that there are few, if any, alternative forums for a particular form of expression would tend to support the constitutionality of the municipality's action; restricting the use of the forum would under those circumstances provide the public with access to expression that it would not otherwise have.

Finally, the nature of the previous use of a forum may also be a relevant consideration. Specifically, if a facility was previously open to various forms of expression but access is then limited so that certain forms may no longer be performed or exhibited, the argument that the municipality intends to suppress, rather than to promote, expression may under some circumstances be stronger. . . .

The City Council also considered arbitrary and unlawful factors in disapproving the proposed concerts. Discussion at the City Council meeting indicated that Todd Rundgren and Patti Smith were rejected—at least in part—because members of the Council thought that their performances would attract homosexual crowds. Councilman Richman explicitly stated that Rundgren and Smith attracted homosexual crowds and "that's not what we want." The only "evidence" supporting that assertion was a Burbank police report indicating that a police department in another city where Rundgren and Smith had performed apparently stated that a large number of homosexuals had attended the concerts. Other arbitrary factors were considered by the Council in rejecting some of the proposed concerts. For example, Richman in the past had indicated opposition to performers who attracted "black audiences." The vice-mayor objected to Patti Smith's proposed concert because she often said "off-the-wall things." Finally, the discussion at the City Council meeting strongly suggests that the proposed Jackson Browne concert was rejected solely because of Browne's views, and the views of the crowd he would attract, on nuclear power. . . .

Moreover, there were no consistent content-neutral standards used to evaluate the proposed entertainers; rather, the City Council rejected groups with both favorable and unfavorable police reports. The only standard consistently applied is that performers who played what the members of the Burbank City Council thought to be "hard rock" music or who were perceived by the officials to be unorthodox in the least were disapproved. . . .

The qualified immunity of officials acting in an executive capacity protects them from section 1983 claims concerning good faith actions taken within the scope of their authority. Councilman Richman does not challenge the jury's finding that he acted in bad faith. Thus, for purposes of resolving the immunity question, we need only decide whether Councilman Richman was acting in a legislative or an executive capacity in voting on Cinevision's proposed concerts issue, . . . "[i.e., w]hether actions . . . are, in law and fact, an exercise of legislative power depends not on their form but upon 'whether they contain matter which is properly to be regarded as legislative in its character and effect.'" *INS v. Chadha*, 462 U.S. 919, 103 S.Ct. 2764, 77 L.Ed.2d 317 (1983). . . .

Here, after considering the character and effects of the City Council's act, we conclude that, as the district court recognized, the City Council was simply monitoring and administering the contract by voting on the various proposed concerts. Administration of a municipal contract—a contract between a private party and a municipality—would generally seem to be an executive function. . . . Administration of a contract does not involve the formulation of policy "as a defined and binding rule of conduct." Rather, it is more the type of ad hoc decision making engaged in by an executive.

We hold that in voting to disapprove all of Cinevision's proposed concerts for the 1979 season, Councilman Richman acted in his executive, rather than legislative capacity. He therefore enjoyed only a qualified immunity. Because the jury found that he acted in bad faith, we affirm the award of damages against Councilman Richman. . . .

We conclude that the district court did not abuse its discretion in awarding attorneys' fees. We therefore affirm the District Court's fee award. . . .

SNEED, CIRCUIT JUDGE CONCURRED.

4.3.4 Private Actions Against Creators and Distributors

As we have seen in the preceding section, the ability of government to interfere with the flow of entertainment (whether prior to or after release) is extremely limited. However, the issue of interference does not end with an examination of the role of government, because even a successful entertainment defendant will incur substantial costs and therefore private actions can have the same chilling effect upon expression as censorship by public authorities. A number of actions have involved claims that audience members have been inspired to commit crimes after seeing specific films or television programming. In a number of cases, for example, *Davidson v. Time Warner, Inc.* 25 Med.L. Rptr. 1705 (S.D. Tex. 1997), plaintiffs have claimed that crimes were inspired by record lyrics. In a slightly different scenario, the heirs of a murder victim were allowed to proceed with their action against the publisher of a manual for contract killers and a book on how to construct silencers. *Rice v. Paladin Enterprises. Inc.*, 128 F.3d 233 (4h Cir.) *cert denied* sub nom *Paladin Enterprises, Inc. v. Rice*, 523 U.S. 1074 (1998). In this case, the publisher stipulated that it had the intent that purchasers of the books make use of them, a factor not present in the two decisions that follow. In *Byers v. Edmondson*, the inclusion of an assertion that the creators and distributors of "Natural Born Killers" either intended that audience members copy the behavior depicted in the film or knew or should have known that imitative behavior would result was sufficient to overcome a motion to dismiss.

Byers v. Edmondson, 712 So.2d 681 (La.App. 1 Cir.), *writ denied* **726 So. 2d 29 (1998),** *cert denied* **sub nom.** *Time Warner Entertainment Co., L.P. v. Byers,* **526 U.S. 1005 (1999)**

CARTER. JUDGE.

This is an appeal from a trial court judgment dismissing a negligence and intentional tort claim on a peremptory exception raising the objection of no cause of action.

FACTS

[Byers died as the result of wounds she received during a convenience store holdup. Plaintiffs claimed that defendants Edmondson and Darrus had gone] upon a crime spree culminating in the shooting and permanent injury to Patsy Ann Byers as a result of seeing and becoming inspired by the movie "Natural Born Killers" [produced and directed by Oliver Stone and distributed by Warner Bros. Inc.] . . . a film which they knew or should have known would cause and inspire people such as . . . Edmondson and . . . Darrus, to commit crimes such as the shooting of Patsy Ann Byers, and for producing and distributing a film which glorified the type of violence [Edmondson and Darrus] committed against Patsy Ann Byers by treating individuals who commit such violence as celebrities and heroes. . . . "[According to plaintiffs, defendants should be held liable for producing and distributing a movie and video]" which they knew, intended, were substantially certain or should have known would cause or incite "such crime sprees . . . for negligently and/or recklessly failing to take steps to minimize violent content of the video or to minimize glorification of senselessly violent acts and those who perpetrate such conduct [and] for negligently and/or recklessly failing to warn viewers of the potential deleterious effects upon teenage viewers caused by repeated viewing of the film and video."

[The defendants moved to dismiss for, *inter alia,* failure to state a cause of action, asserting] that they owed no duty to plaintiffs to ensure that none of the viewers of the movie would decide to imitate actions depicted in the fictional film [or] that they owed a duty to prevent harm inflicted by others absent a "special relationship" obligating the defendant to protect the plaintiff from such harm. They further asserted that imposition of such a duty would violate the First Amendment to the United States Constitution and Article 1, Section 7 of the Louisiana Constitution. [In their moving papers, the defendants pointed out that a similar action had been dismissed by a Georgia court some two years earlier.]

[The trial court granted defendants' motion,] finding that the "law simply does not recognize a cause of action such as that presented in Byers' petition." Byers appealed the judgment of the trial court, assigning as error the trial court's finding that Byers' cause of action was proscribed by Louisiana law and United States and Louisiana constitutional guarantees of free speech.

[SUFFICIENCY OF THE COMPLAINT]

When a [complaint] states a cause of action as to any ground or portion of the demand, [a motion to dismiss must be denied.] Any doubts are resolved in favor of the sufficiency of the [complaint]. *Treasure Chest Casino, L.L.C. v. Parish of Jefferson,* 691 So.2d at 755.

In resolving the issue of whether Byers has a cause of action against the Warner defendants for the shooting, we must determine if the Warner defendants owed a duty to Byers to prevent her from being shot by two people who viewed "Natural Born Killers" and went on a crime spree shortly thereafter. If we find that such a duty exists under Louisiana law, we must further decide whether the imposition of such a duty violates the guarantee of free speech contained in the First Amendment to the United States Constitution and in Article l, Section 7 of the Louisiana Constitution.

DUTY

Byers alleges that the Warner defendants are liable to Byers under Louisiana tort law in that they were negligent and committed an intentional tort. However, before we can find that a cause of action has been set forth based on a negligence or intentional tort theory of recovery under the facts of this case, we must first determine whether a duty was owed by the Warner defendants to Byers. A duty represents a legally enforceable obligation to conform to a particular standard of conduct. *Penton v. Clarkson,* 93–0657, p. 6 (La. App. lst Cir. 3/11/94), 633 So.2d 918, 922. Louisiana courts have traditionally applied a duty-risk analysis to determine whether a plaintiff has stated a cause of action in tort against a particular defendant. See *Meany v. Meany,* 94–0251, p. 6 (La.7/5/94), 639 So.2d 229, 233. This approach is most helpful in cases where the only issue is whether the defendant stands in any relationship to the plaintiff as to create any legally recognized obligation of conduct for the plaintiffs benefit. *Pitre v. Opelousas General Hospital,* 530 So.2d 1151, 1155 Oia.1988). The existence of duty is a question of law for the court to decide from the facts surrounding the occurrence in question. *Harris v. Pizza Hut of Louisiana, Inc.,* 455 So.2d 1364, 1371 (La. 1984). When no duty exists, a court will dismiss a petition as a matter of law for failure to state a cause of action. See *Pitre v. Opelousas General Hospital,* 530 So.2d at 1158.

The factual allegations which must be accepted as true are that Edmondson and Darrus viewed "Natural Born Killers" and began a crime spree shortly thereafter; Byers was shot while Edmondson and Darrus were on this crime spree; the Warner defendants produced, directed and marketed "Natural Born Killers" for the movie theatres and for video; the Warner defendants did not warn viewers of the film or video of the potential deleterious effects that repeated viewing of the film could have on teenage viewers; the Warner defendants were negligent through the production of a film which they knew, should have known or intended would cite people such as Edmondson and Darrus to commit violent acts such as the one committed against Byers; the film glorified the type of violence committed by Edmondson and Darrus against Byers through its treatment of individuals in the film who committed such acts as celebrities and heroes; and the Warner defendants failed to take steps to minimize the violent content of the film or the glorification of senselessly violent acts in the film. Thus, Byers essentially contends that the Warner defendants owed her a duty to not produce this film in the form in which it was released and/or to protect her from viewers who would imitate the violent acts or crimes committed by the film's two main characters and cause her harm.

We recognize that in Louisiana, a defendant does not owe a duty to protect a person from the criminal acts of third parties absent a special relationship which obligates the defendant to protect the plaintiff from such harm. [Citation omitted.] We further note that in the present case, Byers has not, nor can she allege the existence of such a special relationship.

However, we agree with Byers that based on the allegations of the petition which we must accept as true for purposes of a [motion to dismiss for failure to state a] cause of action, the Warner defendants

627. Motion pictures are a significant medium for the communication of ideas and are protected by the first amendment just like other forms of expression. *Joseph Burstyn, Inc. v. Wilson,* 343 U.S. 495, 501–02, 72 S.Ct 777, 780, 96 L.Ed. 1098 (1952).

However, the freedom of speech guaranteed by the First Amendment is not absolute. There are certain limited classes of speech which may be prevented or punished by the state consistent with the principles of the First Amendment: (1) obscene speech; (2) libel, slander, misrepresentation, obscenity, perjury, false advertising, solicitation of crime, complicity by encouragement, conspiracy, and the like; (3) speech or writing used as an integral part of conduct in violation of a valid criminal statute; and (4) speech which is directed to inciting or producing imminent lawless action, and which is likely to incite or produce such action. *McCollum v. CBS, Inc.,* 249 Cal.Rptr. at 192–93.

Byers argues that "Natural Born Killers" falls within the incitement to imminent lawless activity exception to the First Amendment. The constitutional guarantee of free speech does not permit a state to forbid or proscribe advocacy of the use of force or of law violation except where such advocacy is directed to inciting or producing imminent lawless action and is likely to incite or produce such action. *Brandenburg v. Ohio,* 395 U.S. 444, 447, 89 S.Ct. 1827, 1829, 23 L.Ed.2d 430 (1969). Thus, to justify a claim that speech should be restrained or punished because it is (or was) an incitement to lawless action, the court must be satisfied that the speech (1) was directed or intended toward the goal of producing imminent lawless conduct and (2) was likely to produce such imminent conduct. Speech directed to action at some indefinite time in the future will not satisfy this test. Moreover, speech does not lose its First Amendment protection merely because it has "a tendency to lead to violence." See *Hess v. Indiana,* 414 U.S. 105, 108–09, 94 S.Ct. 326, 328–29, 38 L.Ed.2d 303 (1973).

Byers' [allegation] that the Warner defendants intended to incite viewers of the film to begin, shortly after viewing the film crime sprees such as the one that led to the shooting of Patsy Byers [must be accepted] as true for purposes of the [motion to dismiss, and] would fall into the unprotected category of speech directed to inciting or producing imminent lawless action and which is likely to incite or produce such action.

We note that in *Rice v. Paladin Enterprises, Incorporated,* 128 F.3d 233 (4th Cir.1997), the United States Fourth Circuit Court of Appeal held that the publisher of a book which contained step-by-step instructions on how to be a hit man could be civilly liable for the deaths of victims killed by a third person who followed the instructions in the book to murder the victims. The issue before the court was whether the book was protected under the First Amendment. The court found that the particular book was not protected speech. The United States Supreme Court denied writs. *Paladin Enterprises, Incorporated v. Rice,* 118 S.Ct. 1515, 140 L.Ed.2d 668 (1998).

In *Rice*, it was stipulated by Paladin that it not only knew that the book's instructions might be used by murderers, but, it actually intended to provide assistance to murderers and would be murderers.

The U.S. Fourth Circuit further stated:

In other words, the First Amendment might well circumscribe the power of the state to create and enforce a cause of action that would permit the imposition of civil liability, such as aiding and abetting civil liability, for speech that would constitute pure abstract advocacy, at least if that speech were not "directed to inciting or producing imminent lawless action, and . . . likely to incite or produce such action." Brandenburg, 395 U.S. at 447, 89 S.Ct. at 1829. The instances in which such advocacy might give rise to civil liability under state statute would seem rare, but they are not inconceivable. Cf Schenck v. United States, 249 U.S. 47, 39 S.Ct. 247, 63 L.Ed. 470 (1919) (criminal conspiracy prosecution predicated upon subversive advocacy). . . .

After carefully and repeatedly reading Hit Man in its entirety, we are of the view that the book so overtly promotes murder in concrete, non-abstract terms that we regard as disturbingly disingenuous both Paladin's cavalier suggestion that the book is essentially a comic book whose "fantastical" promotion of murder no one could take seriously, and amici's reckless characterization of the book as "almost avuncular," see Br. of Amici at 8–9. The unique text of Hit Man alone, boldly proselytizing and glamorizing the crime of murder and the "profession" of murder as it dispassionately instructs on its commission, is more than sufficient to create a triable issue of fact as to Paladin's intent in publishing and selling the manual.

Paladin, joined by a spate of media amici, including many of the major networks, newspapers, and publishers, contends that any decision recognizing even a potential cause of action against Paladin will have far-reaching chilling effects on the rights of free speech and press. . . . That the national media organizations would feel obliged to vigorously defend Paladin's assertion of a constitutional right to intentionally and knowingly assist murderers with technical information which Paladin admits it intended and knew would be used immediately in the commission of murder and other crimes against society is, to say the least, breathtaking. But be that as it may, it should be apparent from the foregoing that the indisputably important First Amendment values that Paladin and amici argue would be imperiled by a decision recognizing potential liability under the peculiar facts of this case will not even arguably be adversely affected by allowing plaintiffs' action against Paladin to proceed. In fact, neither the extensive briefing by the parties and the numerous amici in this case, nor the exhaustive research which the court itself has undertaken, has revealed even a single case that we regard as factually analogous to this case.

Paladin and amici insist that recognizing the existence of a cause of action against Paladin predicated on aiding and abetting will subject broadcasters and publishers to liability whenever someone imitates or "copies" conduct that is either described or depicted in their broadcasts, publications, or movies. This is simply not true. In the "copycat" context, it will presumably never be the case that the broadcaster or publisher actually intends, through its description or depiction, to assist another or others in the commission of violent crime; rather, the information for the dissemination of which liability is sought to be imposed will actually have been misused vis-a-vis the use intended, not, as here, used precisely as intended. It would be difficult to overstate the significance of this difference insofar as the potential liability to which the media might be exposed by our decision herein is concerned.

And, perhaps most importantly, there will almost never be evidence proffered from which a jury even could reasonably conclude that the producer or publisher possessed the actual intent to assist criminal activity. In only the rarest case, as here where the publisher has stipulated in almost taunting defiance that it intended to assist murderers and other criminals, will there be evidence extraneous to the speech itself which would support a finding of the requisite intent; surely few will, as Paladin has, "stand up and proclaim to the world that because they are publishers they have a unique constitutional right to aid and abet murder." Appellant's Reply Br. at 20.

Moreover, in contrast to the case before us, in virtually every "copycat" case, there will be lacking in the speech itself any basis for a permissible inference that the "speaker" intended to assist and facilitate the criminal conduct described or depicted. Of course, with few, if any, exceptions, the speech which gives rise to the copycat crime will not directly and affirmatively promote the criminal conduct, even if, in some circumstances, it incidentally glamorizes and thereby indirectly promotes such conduct. 128 F.3d at 249, 254, 265.

In holding that plaintiffs' allegations of intent state a cause of action, we do not address the issue of whether the Warner defendants may later invoke the protection of the First Amendment guarantee of free speech to bar Byers' claim after discovery has taken place. It is only by accepting the allegations in Byers' petition as true that we conclude that the film falls into the incitement to *imminent* lawless activity exception to the First Amendment. We agree with *Rice v. Paladin* . . . that the mere foreseeability or knowledge that the publication might be misused for a criminal purpose is not sufficient for liability. Proof of intent necessary for liability in cases such as the instant one will be remote and even rare, but at this stage of the proceeding we find that Byers' cause of action is not barred by the First Amendment. Since we have determined that the allegations of plaintiffs' petition bring the case at this stage into the incitement to imminent lawless activity exception, we need not address Byers' claim that the film constitutes obscene speech.

CONCLUSION

For these reasons, the judgment of the trial court is reversed and the matter is remanded to the trial court for further proceedings consistent with the views expressed herein. Costs of this appeal are assessed to the Warner defendants.

REVERSED AND REMANDED.

NOTES

1. On March 12, 2001, the judge to whom the case was remanded dismissed the complaint, citing First Amendment concerns and the absence of intent on the part of Warner Bros. and Stone to incite unlawful activity. The plaintiffs indicated that they would appeal.
2. For a critical analysis of this case, see Stephen F. Rohde, "Killer Defense," *Los Angeles Lawyer*, vol. 23 no. 2 (April 2000), p. 28.

Chapter 5

REMEDIES

5.1 SELF-HELP

There are tried and true remedies available in our legal system for those who feel, rightly or wrongly, aggrieved. Among them are damages for breach of contract, statutory damages, injunctive relief, rescission and reversion, bankruptcy protection and arbitration awards. We start out with one of the more unusual and innovative remedies, self-help. More often found in situations such as tree limbs extending over a neighbor's driveway, landlord—tenant disputes or the "repo man" for a bank, self-help can be applied in unexpected venues and circumstances.

In every one of the entertainment industries, there is a constant battle for attention. Record companies vie for the privilege of setting up special displays right next to the check-out counters of record stores. Book publishers want their books displayed at eye level. Movie distributors want their preview shown first.

Unfortunately, for a variety of reasons, many works receive less attention than their creators believe they should. Frustration sets in. Perhaps a recording artist is on tour and finds the local record stores out of stock when he arrives in a city where he is to play. Or a novelist arrives for a book signing and there are not enough copies of her book to provide one for each prospective buyer. Or a television network might want to broadcast NFL games instead of late season baseball games. It's a tough world out there.

The distributor of a creative product is generally only required to make a reasonable effort to exploit the creator's work, and courts are loath to place themselves in the position of marketing and distribution specialists. It can be very frustrating for the creator.

As we see in the case that follows, one enterprising author used self-help to correct what he saw as an undersupply of his work by resorting to portions of the Uniform Commercial Code. The results, however, were less than satisfactory.

Dodd, Mead & Company, Inc. v. Lilienthal, 514 F. Supp. 105 (S.D.N.Y. 1981)

DUFFY, DISTRICT JUDGE

[Defendant author entered into an exclusive publishing agreement with plaintiff publisher to sell his book *The Zionist Connection* in the U.S. and Canada. From 1978 through 1979, the publisher printed 14,500 copies and spent more than $66,000 in manufacturing and marketing. Defendant became dissatisfied with the publisher's efforts when he learned that the publisher was not planning on printing any more copies, and the book could not be found in some bookstores. In late 1979, defendant and his company printed their own copies of *The Zionist Connection,* substituting their own names as publisher and deleting plaintiff's name. In this action, the publisher sought a permanent injunction to prevent defendant from selling defendant's version of the book and damages.]

Defendants make three principal arguments in opposition to plaintiff's summary judgment motion and in support of their cross-motion for summary judgment.

First, defendants argue that according to the terms of the contract between the parties, plaintiff retained the right to buy books at a substantial discount from the publisher and to re-sell them without restriction. When the plaintiff allegedly breached this term of the contract by refusing to print further copies of the book, they were entitled, defendants assert, to "cover" by printing up their own copies. Second, defendants argue that Dodd Mead abandoned the copyright and therefore cannot enforce it. Finally, defendants assert that Lilienthal's first amendment right to disseminate his work to the public precludes Dodd Mead's claim for copyright infringement. For the reasons that follow, these arguments are unavailing. . . . .

Lilienthal argues that Dodd Mead failed to adequately promote the book and to adequately distribute copies to bookstores around the country. Starting in the spring of 1979, Lilienthal began receiving letters from the public indicating that his book was not available in bookstores. Then, Lilienthal learned from his previous publisher that Dodd Mead did not intend to re-print the book.

When Lilienthal requested an explanation by Dodd Mead, Dodd Mead stated in a letter dated September 18, 1979 that they did not intend to print more than the 12,500 copies of the book already printed until Lilienthal paid a $42,359.77 debt owed to Dodd Mead. Lilienthal then replied by letter to Dodd Mead stating that he had paid approximately this amount into an escrow account pending his accountant's analysis of the debt.

In October, 1979, Dodd Mead printed an additional 2,000 copies of the book. Lilienthal claims to have had no knowledge of this printing, at least until after October 23, 1979, when Lilienthal signed a contract with another printer to print approximately 2,000 copies of the book.

It is Lilienthal's contention that when Dodd Mead failed to publish the book at his request, he had the right to "cover" by substituting books printed at his own expense under the New York Uniform Commercial Code 2–712.

N.Y.U.C.C. Law 2–711 provides in part:

> (1) Where the seller fails to make delivery or repudiates or the buyer rightfully rejects or justifiably revokes acceptance then with respect to any goods involved, . . . the buyer may cancel and . . . (a) "cover." . . .

N.Y.U.C.C. Law 2–712 provides:

> (1) After a breach within the preceding section the buyer may "cover" by making in good faith and without unreasonable delay any reasonable purchase of or contract to purchase goods in substitution for those due from the seller.
>
> (2) The buyer may recover from the seller as damages the difference between the cost of cover and the contract price together with any incidental or consequential damages as hereinafter defined (Section 2–715) but less expenses saved in consequence of the seller's breach.
>
> (3) Failure of the buyer to effect cover within this section does not bar him from any other remedy.

Lilienthal, however, has failed to demonstrate any breach of the contract by Dodd Mead which triggered a right to cover. There is no indication that Dodd Mead failed to meet specific orders for books made by Lilienthal in accordance with the October 4 letter. Lilienthal's major grievance is that Dodd Mead was not printing enough books to keep up with the public's demand. If proven, this may or may not have constituted a breach of contract. Such a determination, however, will have to be made in the state court action. In any case, Dodd Mead's alleged failure to meet the public demand did not permit Lilienthal to publish his own copies in contravention of the contract between the parties. Lilienthal's obvious remedy under these circumstances was to follow the terms of the contract which at paragraph 17 provided:

If at any time during the continuance of this Agreement the work shall be out of print for six months in all editions, including reprints, whether under the imprint of the Publishers or another imprint, and if, after written notification from the Author, the Publishers shall fail to place the work in print within six months from the date of receipt of such notification, then this Agreement will terminate and all of the rights granted to the Publishers here under shall revert to the Author. The Author shall have the right for thirty days after such termination to purchase from the Publishers all copies or sheets (if any) remaining at the cost of manufacture and the plates and engravings of illustrations (if in existence) at one-half their cost to the Publishers, including composition, all f.o.b. point of shipment.

Unfortunately, the record before me does not show that Lilienthal pursued this avenue. He cannot be permitted now to sue for damages on the contract and, at the same time, to breach the contract egregiously by printing his own copies. Defendants' argument that Dodd Mead abandoned its exclusive right under the copyright is also without merit. In order for the holder of a copyright to abandon his rights thereunder, he must perform some overt act which manifests an intent to surrender rights in the copyrighted material. [Citations omitted.] Here, Dodd Mead never abandoned the copyright in Lilienthal's work. Between December, 1978 and October, 1979, Dodd Mead printed 14,500 copies and spent more than $66,500 on its manufacturing and marketing. There is absolutely no evidence to suggest Dodd Mead intended to give up its exclusive rights in the book. . . . .

Plaintiff's motion for summary judgment is therefore granted, and defendants' cross-motion for summary judgment is denied. The defendants are hereby permanently enjoined from publishing, selling, marketing or otherwise disposing of any copies of the book entitled *The Zionist Connection*. The case is referred to Magistrate Bernikow for an inquest to determine damages. SO ORDERED.

To demonstrate that not just disgruntled authors try the self-help remedy, the following case offers a corporate slant to self-help.

ESPN, Inc. v. Office of The Commissioner of Baseball, 76 F. Supp. 2nd 383 (S. D. N. Y., 1999)

SHIRA A. SCHEINDLIN, U.S.D.J

[ESPN, all-sports channel, entered into an agreement with Major League Baseball in 1996 to telecast the regular season major league baseball games on Wednesday and Sunday nights. As part of the agreement, ESPN agreed that it would not make any commitment that would conflict with the telecasting of the baseball games, provided that ESPN would have the ability to preempt up to ten games a season with Baseball's prior written approval, "which shall not be unreasonably withheld or delayed." In 1998, ESPN entered into an agreement with the National Football League to telecast regular season football games on Sunday nights.

When ESPN asked Baseball to permit it to preempt baseball games to be broadcast on three Sunday nights in September 1998 and 1999 for three NFL games, Baseball refused. ESPN broadcast the NFL games anyway. Baseball terminated the agreement, alleging that ESPN was in breach. ESPN commenced an action alleging Baseball had breached the agreement by, among other things, unreasonably withholding its approval of ESPN's preemption requests in 1998 and 1999. As part its decision on omnibus evidentiary motions by the parties, the Court ruled with respect to ESPN's motion to preclude Baseball from proving that ESPN could not engage in self-help as follows:]

It is ESPN's position in this litigation that Baseball's disapproval of its preemption requests in 1998 and 1999 was "unreasonable." Moreover, ESPN intends to argue that if Baseball unreasonably withheld approval of ESPN's preemption requests, ESPN was legally entitled to engage in "self-help" by treating Baseball's refusal as a "nullity" and broadcasting football games rather than baseball games on the six relevant Sunday nights. In contrast, Baseball contends that ESPN had no right to self-help regardless of the reasonableness of Baseball's decision to withhold its approval for preemption. . . .

By its motion, ESPN seeks to preclude Baseball from introducing testimony or argument to the effect that, even if Baseball unreasonably withheld its approval of ESPN's preemption requests, ESPN had no right to engage in self-help. Although ESPN has cast its motion in terms of presentation of evidence and argument to the jury, ESPN raises a purely legal issue that must be resolved by this Court as a matter of law. Accurately phrased, ESPN seeks a ruling that if Baseball unreasonably withheld its approval of ESPN's preemption requests, ESPN had the right to telecast NFL games instead of baseball games and therefore did not breach the 1996 Agreement. However, if Baseball is correct and ESPN had no right to preempt the baseball games in the absence of written permission from Baseball, then, as a matter of law, ESPN breached the 1996 Agreement when it preempted baseball games in 1998 and 1999 without Baseball's approval.

C. RIGHT TO "SELF-HELP"

1. Landlord-Tenant Law Inapplicable

ESPN's theory of "self-help" is based entirely on three landlord-tenant cases which it cites for the proposition that

where a written contract provides that a proposed action by one party requires approval by the other party, but that such approval "shall not be unreasonably withheld", if the approving party unreasonably withholds approval . . . . the party who sought the approval may engage in "self-help"—it may proceed as if its request had been granted.

BB MIL at 3 (citing Lexann Realty Co. v. Deitchman, 83 A.D.2d 540, 441 N.Y.S.2d 472 (1st Dep't 1981); Kruger v. Page Management Co., 105 Misc. 2d 14, 432 N.Y.S.2d 295 (Sup. Ct. N.Y. Co. 1980); Cedarhurst Park Apts., Inc. v. Milgrim, 55 Misc. 2d 118, 284 N.Y.S.2d 330 (D. Ct. Nassau Co. 1967)). However, none of these cases nor the proposition they stand for is applicable to the instant dispute which involves a commercial contract rather than a residential lease.

Each of the cases relied upon by ESPN concern a tenant's ability to sublet his or her apartment. Each involved a standard residential lease which provided that the tenant could only sublet his or her apartment with the prior written approval of the landlord and that such approval could not be "unreasonably withheld." All three tenants sought permission to sublet, and all three landlords refused their requests. The court in each case, after determining that the landlord's refusal was unreasonable, went on to find that "where consent is unreasonably withheld . . . the landlord is deemed to have granted] consent." Lexann Realty, 441 N.Y.S.2d at 473.

See also *Kruger*, 432 N.Y.S.2d at 302 ("Where a landlord has agreed not to withhold consent unreasonably and violates such an agreement, the Courts have held that the tenant may ignore the restrictive covenant and sublet the premises."); *Cedarhurst Park*, 284 N.Y.S.2d at 331 (finding that where landlord unreasonably withheld consent, the "actions of the tenant . . . in subletting the apartment to subtenants . . . was legal and permitted under the case law on this subject in [New York]"). However, the courts based their decisions regarding a tenant's ability to sublet despite a landlord's unreasonable refusal not on principles of contract law but on principles of real property law which disfavors "provisions or covenants in a lease restricting assignment or subletting." See *Kruger*, 432 N.Y.S.2d at *300*. As the court in Kruger explained, restrictions on a tenant's ability to assign or sublet are restraints which courts do not favor. They have been construed with the utmost jealousy and very easy modes have always been countenanced for defeating them. The reason is such are restraints on the free alienation of land and tend to prevent full utilization of the land, which is contrary to the best interests of society.

Id. (internal quotations and citations omitted). Moreover, Lexann and Kruger were decided pursuant to section 226-b of the Real Property Law of New York which specifically addresses a tenant's right to sublet and a landlord's ability to restrict that right. n[13]

n13 Cedarhurst was decided in 1967, eight years before the 1975 enactment of section 226-b.

In light of the unique public policy considerations underlying landlord-tenant law, the holdings of Lexann, Kruger and Cedarhurst are irrelevant here and provide no basis for ESPN's contention that it had a legal right to ignore Baseball's disapproval of its request for preemption and to "proceed as if its request had been granted." As Baseball argues persuasively in its opposition brief, "this special caselaw disfavoring restrictions on real property has no bearing on commercial cases." See BB Op. at 4.

2. Commercial Contract Law

In its unsuccessful attempt to craft a "self-help" remedy from landlord-tenant caselaw, ESPN has confused and twisted basic precepts governing commercial contracts. As set forth in the discussion of election of remedies, see supra Part II.A., it is black-letter law that when one party to a contract materially breaches, the nonbreaching party has two options: it can terminate the agreement and sue for total breach, or it can continue the contract and sue for partial breach. See *ARP Films, Inc. v. Marvel Entertainment Group, Inc.*, 952 F.2d 643 (2d Cir. 1991); *Estate of John Lennon v. Leggoons, Inc.*, 1997 U.S. Dist. LEXIS 8829, 95 Civ. 8872, 1997 WL 346733, *1 (S.D.N.Y. 1997); *Inter-Power of New York, Inc. v. Niagara Mohawk Power Corp.*, 259 A.D.2d 932, 686 N.Y.S.2d 911, 913 (N.Y. App. Div. 3d Dep't. 1999); Farnsworth, Contracts ß 8.19 (3d ed. 1999). "There is, however, no third option allowing the party claiming a breach to invoke 'self-help' and only perform those obligations it wishes to perform." BB Op. at 2. n[14] n14 Indeed, the term "self-help" is commonly used among commentators to refer to a party's right to suspend its performance in response to a material breach and, if the breaching party fails to cure within a specified time, to terminate the contract. See Farnsworth, Contracts ß 8.15 (3d ed. 1999). Thus, "self-help" in the context of commercial contracts is merely another way of describing the first option set forth above—a party can terminate the agreement and sue for total breach.

Applying this well-settled principle to the instant case, if ESPN believed that Baseball had materially breached the contract by withholding its approval of ESPN's preemption requests, then it had two—and only two—courses of action. First, it could have terminated the contract and commenced litigation against Baseball for total contract damages. This option would have allowed ESPN to show NFL games in place of baseball games because ESPN would no longer be obligated to produce baseball game telecasts on Sunday nights or any other night. Second, ESPN could have continued to perform while suing Baseball for partial breach. Under this option, ESPN could not have substituted NFL games for baseball games because it would still be bound by its contractual promise to broadcast baseball games on Sunday nights absent Baseball's prior written approval to preempt those games. [n15]

n15 In addition, because Baseball denied ESPN's preemption requests in February 1998 and February 1999—more than six months before the September 1998 and September 1999 games—ESPN had ample opportunity to seek injunctive relief from the courts, well before it was required to broadcast the September baseball games.

ESPN chose neither of these options. It clearly did not terminate the 1996 Agreement, and, in fact, it does not seek to do so now. Nor did ESPN continue to perform under the agreement. Although ESPN "continued to pay Baseball the entire rights fee called for by the contract and continued to telecast all other baseball games and other programming called for by the 1996 Agreement," see ESPN Reply at 4, it did not broadcast baseball games "on each Sunday night of the regular season period" as it was obligated to do under the contract. That ESPN performed its other obligations merely goes to the materiality of ESPN's Sunday night breach; it does not excuse ESPN's nonperformance of a contractual obligation. Again, a party is only excused from performance when it terminates a contract in response to a material breach.

In Estate of John Lennon v. Leggoons, Inc., the defendant also resorted to its own form of self-help in response to plaintiff's alleged breach of the contract. See *Leggoons,* 1997 WL 346733, at *1. Leggoons involved a licensing agreement pursuant to which Bag One granted defendant Leggoons the exclusive right "to use the signature of John Lennon [**40] and artwork created by John Lennon" in exchange for guaranteed royalty payments by Leggoons. See id. Bag One commenced litigation when Leggoons stopped making its contractually required royalty payments. See id. Leggoons asserted a counterclaim alleging that Bag One had violated the contract's exclusivity provision by licensing the use of the John Lennon name to another company. See id. Leggoons claimed that it was "entitled to stop making [royalty] payments because of Bag One's prior breach of the Agreement." Id.

Despite Leggoons's "self-help" justification, the court granted Bag One's motion for summary judgment on its contract claim. The court first stated the general principle set forth above: "It is well-settled that the non-breaching part has a choice when faced with a breach by the other party; it can stop performance and sue for total breach or affirm the contract by continuing to perform while suing in partial breach." Id. The court then found that

> a party that elects to continue to receive benefits under a contract (in this case, the right to sell Lennon merchandise) cannot unilaterally suspend its performance (in this case, payment of guaranteed royalty) as a means of self-help to remedy a breach by the other party. Leggoons did not terminate the agreement when it learned of Ones' breach, but rather continued to conduct business pursuant to the license. Accordingly, Leggoons affirmed the license and is liable to Bag One for . . . unpaid guaranteed royalties.

Id.

Other courts faced with claims of "self-help" have reached similar conclusions. See, e.g., *ARP Films,* 952 F.2d at 649 (rejecting plaintiff's contention that its decision to withhold royalty payments and reports was proper "self-help measure designed to force [defendant] to repent from its repudiation, and did not amount to a material breach" because plaintiff could not affirm contract while "refusing to perform its end of the bargain"); *V.S. Int'l, S.A. v. Boyden World Corp.,* 862 F. Supp. 1188, 1197 *(S.D.N.Y. 1994)* (despite defendant's breach and "in view of plaintiffs' affirmance, [plaintiffs'] refusal to perform their end of the bargain by making requisite licensing payments was impermissible" as plaintiffs could not "engage in self-help, by withholding their payment of licensing fees which they were contractually obligated to remit to defendant"); *Richard Subaru, Inc. v. Subaru of New England,* 8 F. Supp. 2d 164, 169 (D. Conn. 1998) (plaintiff's "self-help solution [of relocating car dealership without permission of dealer] . . . was a clear breach of the terms and conditions of exclusivity as well as location of dealership facility"; moreover, "it is beyond dispute that [plaintiff] knew of his obligations . . . and he took a roll of the legal dice with his [decision to relocate]").

ESPN argues that Leggoons and the other cases cited above are inapplicable because those cases

> involve a factually different context in which, in response to an alleged breach, the non-breaching party continued to accept the benefits of the contract but failed to continue to make payments due under the contract to the breaching party. In such instances, the failure to make payments was held to be a breach of the contract in itself.

ESPN Reply at 4. ESPN's attempt to distinguish these cases is unavailing. Although ESPN "made payments due under the contract," see id., it failed to fulfill another contractual obligation, namely its explicit duty to produce Baseball game telecasts "on each Sunday night of the regular season period" absent the prior written approval of Baseball, see 1996 Agreement, Ex. O to Kheel Aff., at 4. ESPN has essentially drawn a false distinction between the obligation to make money payments and the obligation to render other contractual performances, such as telecasting baseball games. To use ESPN's own words as set forth above, "in response to [Baseball's] alleged breach, [ESPN] continued to accept [the exclusive right to broadcast baseball games] but failed to [show baseball games on Sunday nights during the regular season as it was obligated to do] under the contract." ESPN Reply at 4. Moreover, the failure to show baseball games on Sunday nights, like the failure to make payments, is "a breach of the contract in itself." Id. It is undisputed that ESPN preempted Baseball games on six Sunday nights without the prior written approval of Baseball, and the failure to broadcast Sunday night baseball games absent Baseball's approval is a breach of ESPN's obligation to telecast baseball games on Sunday nights.

ESPN's failure to show baseball games on six Sunday nights over a period of two baseball seasons may be immaterial in light of its fulfillment of other contractual obligations such as payment and Wednesday night broadcasts. However, ESPN's failure cannot be excused as a form of self-help. Indeed, the phrase "self-help" merely masks the fact that in response to Baseball's alleged breach, ESPN elected the one course of action that was impermissible. It continued the contract but failed to fully perform its obligations under the contract. ESPN performed only those obligations that it chose to perform, and such selective performance is a remedy that contract law does not countenance.

3. Terms of 1996 Agreement

Finally, as a matter of contract interpretation, ESPN's theory of "self-help" violates the plain language of the 1996 Agreement in that it allows ESPN to unilaterally determine when preemption is appropriate.

As set forth above, ESPN is obligated to broadcast baseball games on Sunday nights unless it obtains Baseball's permission to preempt those games. The terms of the preemption provision are as follows:

With the prior written approval of Baseball, which shall not be unreasonably withheld or delayed, ESPN may . . . preempt any [Baseball game telecast] hereunder, up to a maximum of ten [Baseball game telecasts] per year, for an event of significant viewer interest.

1996 Agreement, Ex. O to Kheel Aff., at 48–49. Although the preemption provision (as well as the rest of the contract) is silent as to who determines whether Baseball is "unreasonably" withholding its approval, [16] it clearly does not contemplate that the final arbiter of reasonableness will be ESPN. That is, the contract does not permit ESPN to preempt the ten baseball games of its choice. Instead, Baseball has a contractual right to approve or disapprove ESPN's desired substitutions. Although Baseball's decision to withhold approval must be reasonable, ESPN cannot be the judge of whether Baseball is acting reasonably because Baseball's approval right would be rendered meaningless; ESPN could simply preempt the ten games of its choice and determine that any objections Baseball expressed were "unreasonable."

n16 That the parties failed to provide for any method of dispute resolution in the foreseeable event they disagreed as to whether Baseball's disapproval was reasonable is surprising to say the least. It is unfortunate, as evidenced by this litigation, that the contract did not set forth a procedure for empanelling arbitrators who could resolve any preemption dispute expeditiously and fairly. Indeed, the parties could have explicitly named an arbitrator or a panel of arbitrators in the contract rendering dispute resolution that much more efficient and expedient.

The point of this analysis is that to credit ESPN's self-help theory would effectively appoint ESPN the final arbiter of reasonableness and render superfluous the terms of the preemption provision. If ESPN had a legal right to "self-help" in that it could preempt games whenever it believed that Baseball's disapproval was unreasonable, then Baseball would effectively have no right to disapprove. Under ESPN's theory of self-help, the preemption provision would read as follows: "ESPN may . . . preempt any [Baseball game telecast] hereunder, up to a maximum of ten [Baseball game telecasts] per year, for an event of significant viewer interest whenever ESPN thinks such preemption is reasonable." This does not, however, comport with the plain language of the contract. [n17]

n17 Although to some extent this reading can be seen as appointing Baseball the final arbiter of its own reasonableness, that is not the case. Because the parties failed to provide for any method of dispute resolution, the final arbiter with respect to the preemption provision is the court. As an academic matter, the issue then becomes which party bears the burden of commencing litigation.

In the instant case that burden properly falls on ESPN for two reasons. First, it is ESPN who seeks to alter the status quo by requesting an exemption from its duty to perform a contractual obligation. Second, the provision contemplates that Baseball will perform, or fail to perform, first in time by either granting or withholding its approval of ESPN's requests for preemptions. Accordingly, and in compliance with contract principles, if ESPN believes Baseball is in breach it must either terminate and sue for total breach or continue the contract and sue for partial breach. If the parties had wanted to allocate the burden differently, they could have drafted a different preemption provision. For example, Baseball would bear the burden of commencing litigation under the following construction: "ESPN may . . . preempt any [Baseball game telecast] hereunder, up to a maximum of ten [Baseball game telecasts] per year, for an event of significant viewer interest, provided that ESPN is not unreasonable with respect to which baseball games it chooses to preempt."

* * *

For all the foregoing reasons, ESPN had no right to engage in its version of "self-help" regardless of whether Baseball unreasonably withheld its approval of ESPN's preemption requests. Accordingly, ESPN breached the 1996 Agreement as a matter of law when it preempted baseball games in September 1998 and September 1999 without Baseball's prior written approval. Whether ESPN's breaches are material is a matter of fact for the jury to determine.

5.2 RESCISSION/REVERSION

One of the causes of action encountered frequently in complaints filed in entertainment industry litigation is a count seeking rescission. Often, the plaintiff holds a sincere belief that there are legitimate grounds to undo the agreement; in other cases, the approach is based upon changed circumstances under which the plaintiff, if successful, would be able to make a more advantageous deal elsewhere. As the *Nolan* case indicates, rescission, carrying with it a reversion of the rights originally transferred, will rarely be granted unless there is a total failure of consideration. Moreover, as the *Peterson* case demonstrates, limits may be placed upon the scope of the remedy even where rescission is granted. Finally, as *Shepherd v. Maximus Entertainment Group, Inc.* establishes, the remedies of rescission and reversion are alive and well.

Nolan v. Williamson Music Inc., 300 F. Supp. 1311 (S.D.N.Y. 1969), *aff'd*, 499 F.2d 1394 (1974)

[Nolan, a member of the famed singing group The Sons of the Pioneers (which, during its early years, included a young singer who went on to fame as cowboy star Roy Rogers), wrote an extremely popular country/western song, "Tumbling Tumbleweeds," which he sold to Sam Fox Publishing Company in return for Fox's promise to pay stated composer royalties. In most instances, these were a percentage of royalties received by the "Publisher" (defined in the contract as Fox, "its successors and assigns forever").

After publishing the song for 12 years, Fox conveyed it to Williamson, which, in turn, agreed to pay Fox between 50% and 66 2/3% of Williamson's receipts, and paid Fox an advance of $17,500. As between Fox and Williamson, Fox continued to have the duty to account to and to pay Nolan his share of royalties (essentially, 33 1/3% of "Publisher's" receipts).

In 1960, when he became entitled to renew the copyright on "Tumbling Tumbleweeds," Nolan (as required pursuant to his original contract with Fox) assigned the renewal to Fox, which, in turn, executed a further assignment to Williamson.

While Fox never notified Nolan of the assignments to Williamson, Williamson had taken out an ad in *Variety* at the time of the original assignment, announcing that it had acquired "the sensational Western song, 'Tumbling Tumbleweeds' by Bob Nolan." In addition, Williamson had registered the assignment in the Copyright Office. Further, Gray, who was Nolan's business manager for some 19 years, learned of the assignment in the course of representation of a different client.

Throughout the period following the assignment to Williamson, Fox essentially paid Nolan 33 1/3% of what Williamson paid Fox, not 33 1/3% of what Williamson collected. In addition, Fox failed to pay Nolan 74% of the royalties due Nolan for a six-year period (including a total failure to pay him any foreign royalties for that period).

Nolan sued seeking to rescind the contract and recover his copyright, by reason of fraud. In addition, Nolan sought royalties and damages for copyright infringement.]

EDELSTEIN, DISTRICT JUDGE

The basic claim which plaintiff has urged in this suit is that he had the legal right to, and, in fact, did rescind his agreements with Fox by the May 29, 1963 notice. Plaintiff argues that rescission is justified in this case because over the years Fox has allegedly committed the following breaches: (1) non-payment of all royalties earned by foreign sources (this is conceded by Fox); (2) non-payment of the royalties due from domestic performing income; (3) non-payment of all of the royalties due on octavo editions of the song, electrical transcriptions, synchronizations, and on lyric uses of the song; (4) assignment of the copyright and its renewal term to Williamson; (5) payment of royalties by Fox based only on Fox's receipts from Williamson; [etc.]. . . .

The court finds that it was not a breach of contract for Sam Fox to assign the copyright to Williamson. The 1934 transfer from plaintiff to Sam Fox of "all rights of every kind, nature and description" which plaintiff had in the copyright was clearly absolute on its face. Furthermore, the agreement specifically provided that the conveyance was to "Publisher, its successors and assigns." Whether a contract is assignable or not is, of course, a matter of contractual intent, and one must look to the language used by the parties to discern that intent. Clearly the language just quoted contemplated that the agreement was to be assignable. Williston on Contracts sec. 423 (3rd ed. 1962).

The plaintiff . . . seems to be saying, however, that this contract involved such personal elements of trust and confidence that it was not assignable without the consent of the parties despite the clear language to the contrary. This argument, though, is not premised upon any reliable evidence adduced at the trial which would demonstrate that Nolan entered into his agreement with Fox because of any personal trust and confidence which he placed in Fox. Further, rescission of copyright exploitation agreements much like the one in issue in the case at bar was also sought in the case of *In re Waterson, Berlin & Snyder Co.* when the original assignee of the copyrights at issue there attempted to assign them to other publishers. The District Court, 36 F.2d 94 (S.D.N.Y. 1929), granted rescission in that case on the ground that the agreements were not assignable because of the degree of personal trust involved in them. The Court of Appeals, however, reversed that decision and held that the copyrights could be assigned further. *In re Waterson, Berlin & Snyder Co.*, 48 F.zd704 (2d Cir. 1931).

Plaintiff's assertions of fraud are based in part upon the allegation that Fox concealed from plaintiff its relationship with Williamson by never giving plaintiff actual notice of the assignment. The evidence, however, does not support a finding of fraud in this regard. . . . [T]he court has already held that the contract was assignable without Fox's first having to obtain the plaintiff's consent. Further, far from demonstrating an intent to conceal the assignment, the evidence shows that the defendants openly announced the fact of their arrangement in ... *Variety* [and] the assignment was registered in the Copyright Office and the Fox-Williamson relationship was noted on the copies of sheet music which were distributed.

In this regard it is also important to note that ... [Gray] had, at the least, notice that Williamson was publishing the song, and since Gray was plaintiff's authorized business agent in general and specifically acted as such with regard to "Tumbling Tumbleweeds," this notice is imputable to plaintiff. See, e.g., *Farr v. Newman,* 14 N.Y.2d 183, 250 N.Y.S.2d 272, 199 N.E.2d 369, 4 A.L.R.3d 215 (1964).

The other part of plaintiff's claim of fraud is predicated upon the failure of Fox to render clearer and more detailed accountings to plaintiff and to pay him all of the royalties which were due him. Again, however, the reliable evidence fails to demonstrate fraud. Essentially what plaintiff is really complaining of here is mere breaches of contract by Fox; fraud consists of something more than the mere breach of a contract. . . . [R]escission can be permitted only when the complaining party has suffered breaches of so material and substantial a nature that they affect the very essence of the contract and serve to defeat the object of the parties.

Cases which have considered the problem of rescission in situations analogous to the one presented by the case at bar have granted rescission only after finding the equivalent of a total failure in the performance of the contract. In *Raftery v. World Film Corp.* [180 App. Div. 475, 167 N.Y.S. 1027 (1st Dept. 1917)], the plaintiff temporarily turned over to the defendant prints from which movies were to be made and then distributed. The contract provided that the defendant was to render weekly accounts of the earnings on the movies and to pay the plaintiff fifty percent thereof. The prints were to be returned at the expiration of the contract term. The court found that the defendant never paid plaintiff the full amount due, deliberately maintained a set of fictitious records, deliberately rendered false accountings, refused to permit inspection of the records as was required by the contract, and failed to return the prints to the plaintiff. Based on all of these factors rescission was granted. . . . [A]nd finally in *DeMille Co. v. Casey,* 115 Misc. 646, 189 N.Y.S. 275 (N.Y. Sup.Ct. 1921), a contract permitting the defendant to produce motion pictures based on plaintiff's plays was rescinded when royalty payments ceased and the defendant, because of various sublicensing agreements over which he had lost effective control, was no longer in a position to comply with the contract and to protect the plaintiff's future interest. . . .

Although defendant has been guilty of diverse breaches, these breaches involve a failure to comply fully with the contractual provisions for payment of royalties in various categories, and as to these breaches, it is clear to the court that plaintiff may be rendered whole by an award of monetary damages. Moreover, there seems little danger that Nolan will be deprived of his royalties in the future. This is not a case where the defendant has repudiated his obligation to pay royalties, nor is this a case in which plaintiff's song has not been exploited fully in the past or threatened with not being fully exploited in the future. . . .

It is the judgment of this court that plaintiff's agreements with Fox are not rescinded. Plaintiff is entitled to the payment of royalties due him under his 1934 and 1960 agreements with Fox and the court directs an accounting limited to the period commencing six years prior to the commencement of this action, except that this six-year limitation does not apply to the money due plaintiff for royalties derived from foreign mechanical income [which, Fox conceded, had never been paid at all, and as to which Fox waived the application of the statute of limitations]. . . .

[After findings by a Special Master, the Court found for Nolan in the amount of $94,148, including interest and costs. Both sides appealed.]

Nolan v. Sam Fox Publishing Company, Inc., 499 F.2d 1394 (2d Cir. 1974)

WATERMAN, CIRCUIT JUDGE

. . . [The *Variety* ad] is, of course, patently inconsistent with the theory that Fox and Williamson were intent on concealing their relationship. Moreover, Williamson's name was displayed on all the sheet music copies of the song published by it. Nolan argues, however, that nowhere in the *Variety* announcement or on the sheet music was Williamson identified as the "publisher." This omission, in and of itself, surely would not demonstrate fraud. In addition, it is significant that the assignment from Fox to Williamson was recorded at the Copyright Office. Inasmuch as that assignment was recorded, we need not even reach the question of whether Nolan can be charged with knowledge of the assignment because of the recording, for it suffices to say here that this recordation further illustrates that Williamson and Fox had no intention whatever of concealing their relationship from Nolan or from anyone else. . . . [In addition, it] is unimportant what Gray actually did or did not tell Nolan about the knowledge Gray obtained. Whatever knowledge Gray had is imputed to Nolan. . . .

Although the existence of fraud is a sufficient ground for permitting rescission it is not a necessary one. Rescission has also been allowed, despite the absence of any showing of fraud, in cases in which a publisher has made none of the royalty payments. The rationale of these decisions is, of course, that an essential objective of a contract between a composer and publisher is the payment of royalties, and a complete failure to pay means this objective has not been achieved. Here, however, Fox did pay 26% of the royalties due to Nolan for the applicable six-year period, and this partial payment of royalties due distinguishes this case from cases where there was total failure to pay the required royalties. . . .

Peterson v. Highland Music, Inc., 140 F.3d 1313 (9th Cir. 1998)

FLETCHER, CIRCUIT JUDGE

This case involves an attempt by the Kingsmen, a musical group, to secure a rescission of the contract by which they assigned to others the rights to their popular recording of the hit song, "Louie, Louie." The group made the recording over thirty years ago. They then sold the [recording, the "]Masters["][4] . . . in return for nine per cent of any profits or licensing fees that the recording might generate. [However, t]he Kingsmen have never received a single penny of the considerable royalties that "Louie, Louie" has produced over the past thirty years.

In 1993, the Kingsmen brought suit in federal district court in California for rescission of the contract, basing their claim entirely on actions (or inactions) by the defendants that fell within the four-year statutory limitations period. After a full trial, the district court ruled in plaintiffs' favor and granted the rescission, restoring possession of the Masters to the Kingsmen. . . . The judge [in a subsequent action then] ruled, on summary judgment, that the rescission enforced in the original action was effective as of the date when the Kingsmen formally declared their intention to rescind—the date of the filing of the complaint—and that defendants must [return the Masters and] pay to the Kingsmen any royalties or profits that accrued thereafter, whether from licenses entered into after the date of rescission or from licenses that preexisted that date. The district court also issued an order in aid of enforcement of its first judgment, commanding defendants to turn over the Masters to plaintiffs forthwith. . . . Defendants . . . contend that the district court erred in holding that the statute of limitations does not bar remedy of rescission in this case. In California, the statute of limitations for an action seeking rescission of a contract is four years. See Cal.Code Civ. Proc. 337. Specifically, the statute provides that an aggrieved party must commence such an action within four years "from the date upon which the facts that entitled the aggrieved party to rescind occurred." *Id.* Both parties agree that the period of limitations has long since run with respect to the first occasions on which defendants breached their agreement. Both parties also agree that defendants have breached their agreement repeatedly over the course of the past thirty years, and did so, repeatedly, within four years of the time that plaintiffs commenced this action. Defendants' claim is that, even in the face of multiple and continuing breaches of the agreement, the California statute should be read to bar any action that is not commenced within four years of the first occasion on which an aggrieved party could have requested rescission. Defendants cite no authority for this proposition, and we reject it.

In analyzing requests for rescission where there have been multiple breaches under an installment contract, California courts have held that each breach starts the clock afresh for statute of limitations purposes. In *Conway v. Bughouse, Inc.*, 105 Cal.App. 3d 194, 164 Cal.Rptr. 585 (1980), for example, a California appeals court looked to the manner in which money would be paid under a pension contract in determining how a party's failure to make any given payment should affect the tolling of the statute of limitations.

[T]he total amount of money to be paid to [the pensioner] is not a fixed sum which is to be paid out over a period of time. To the contrary, the total amount owed is unascertainable until the date of [the pensioner's] death because each payment is separate and contingent upon [the survival of the pensioner and his adherence to the terms of the contract]. As each payment is separable from the others and is not a part of a total payment, the agreement should logically be considered an installment contract for purposes of determination of the application of the statute of limitations. *Id. at 199–200, 164 Cal.Rptr. 585.*

The same holds true in the present case: There is no fixed amount to be paid out over time under the Kingsmen's contract, but rather a continuing obligation to pay a portion of the profits and royalties on "Louie, Louie" as the recording gets used over time.

The district court in this case made it clear that, in determining whether rescission was warranted and appropriate, it was relying upon breaches that had occurred within the limitations period. To find for defendant under these circumstances would be to hold that California law forever bars a party from seeking a remedy of rescission after it has once passed up the opportunity to do so, regardless of the nature of any future breaches of the other party's obligations. We have found no authority that would support such a reading of California law. We therefore affirm the district court's conclusion that the statute of limitations does not bar rescission of the contract in this case . . .

[T]he district court found that the rescission of the Kingsmen's contract was effective as of the date of the filing of the Kingsmen's complaint. We agree. Under California law, "a party to a contract [can] rescind it and . . . such rescission [can] be accomplished by the rescinding party by giving notice of the rescission and offering to restore everything of value which [the rescinding party has] received." *Runyan v. Pacific Air Indus.*, 2 Cal.3d 304, 311, 85 Cal.Rptr. 138, 466 P.2d 682 (1970); see also *Id.* at 311–13, 85 Cal.Rptr. 138, 466 P.2d 682. When a party gives notice of rescission, it has effected the rescission, and any subsequent judicial proceedings are for the purpose of confirming and enforcing that rescission. See *Id.* at 311–12, 85 Cal. Rptr. 138, 466 P.2d 682. Thus, when the Kingsmen filed suit in 1993, they rescinded the contract and became owners of the Masters. The lawsuit that followed confirmed that their rescission was a proper one and resulted in an order enforcing that rescission. The district court correctly ruled that, as the owners of the Masters, the Kingsmen are entitled to all income derived from the exploitation of the recordings following September 29, 1993, the date of the notice of rescission.

NOTE

For a discussion of the Peterson case and related considerations, see Jeanette M. Bazis, "Remedies and Roadblocks in the Recovery of Unpaid Music Royalties," *ABA Entertainment & Sports Lawyer,* vol. 17, no. 4 (Winter 2000), p. 18.

Thom Shepherd v. Maximus Entertainment Group, Inc., 2005 Tenn. App. LEXIS 557 (2005)

OPINION BY: WILLIAM C. KOCH, JR.

OPINION: This appeal involves a dispute between a country music songwriter and a music publishing company arising out of an "exclusive co-publishing agreement" relating to the song "Riding with Private Malone" and other works. Because of the parties' dispute, ASCAP declined to release royalties for "Riding with Private Malone" to either the songwriter or the publisher. The songwriter filed suit in the Chancery Court for Davidson County seeking a determination that the publishing company had breached the agreement and that he was entitled to receive the royalties held by ASCAP because all the rights to "Riding with Private Malone" had reverted to him. Both parties filed motions for summary judgment. The trial court concluded that the songwriter was not entitled to the withheld royalties. After the trial court denied his motion to amend his complaint to seek money damages, the songwriter appealed. We have concluded that the trial court erred by holding that the songwriter was not entitled to the withheld royalties and that the trial court properly denied the songwriter's motion to amend his complaint.

I

Thom Shepherd wrote the country music song "Riding with Private Malone." On December 1, 2001, after the song achieved a measure of commercial success, Mr. Shepherd entered into a music publishing contract with Maximus Entertainment Group, Inc. ("Maximus"). The "Exclusive Co-Publishing Agreement" drafted by Maximus covered three sets of compositions: the song "Riding with Private Malone," several other songs Mr. Shepherd had previously written, and all songs Mr. Shepherd would write and compose during the three-year term of the agreement. The agreement specified that all of the songs would be "co-published" by Mr. Shepherd and Maximus.

In the agreement, Mr. Shepherd assigned Maximus 12.5% of his copyright interest in the song "Riding with Private Malone" and 50% of his copyright interest in the other songs he had previously written, as well as the songs he would write or compose during the term of the agreement. Maximus's interest in the song "Riding with Private Malone" would last for five years, but Maximus's interest in the other songs covered by the agreement would continue for the full term of the copyrights to the songs, including any renewals, extensions, or revivals of the copyrights.

In return, Maximus agreed to make several types of payments to Mr. Shepherd. First, Maximus agreed that Mr. Shepherd would receive 87.5% of the total royalties from "Riding with Private Malone" and 75% of the total royalties from all of the other songs covered by the agreement. Second, Maximus agreed to pay Mr. Shepherd advances against royalty income in the amount of $40,000 during the first year of the agreement, $45,000 during the second year of the agreement, and $50,000 during the third year of the agreement. The yearly advances were to be paid in monthly installments due on the first day of each month. Third, Maximus agreed to pay Mr. Shepherd an initial non-recoupable bonus of $20,000.00 for "Riding with Private Malone" and an additional one-time advance of $2,666.66 for the other songs Mr. Shepherd had previously written.

The agreement also contained several provisions regarding the reversion of Maximus's interest in the songs to Mr. Shepherd. All of Maximus's rights in the song "Riding with Private Malone" would automatically revert to Mr. Shepherd at the end of five years. Maximus's rights in any of the songs Mr. Shepherd wrote during the term of the agreement would also automatically revert to Mr. Shepherd at the end of five years if the songs had not been commercially exploited during that time. Maximus's interest in the songs other than "Riding with Private Malone" written before December 1, 2001 that were covered by the agreement would revert to Mr. Shepherd at the end of the agreement only if Mr. Shepherd repaid Maximus the initial $2,666.66 advance he was to receive for those songs. Finally, Maximus's interest in all of the songs, including "Riding with Private Malone," would automatically and immediately revert to Mr. Shepherd if (1) one of the principals of Maximus left the company during the term of the agreement, (2) Maximus declared or was forced to declare bankruptcy, or (3) Maximus defaulted in making any of the payments required by the agreement. The agreement provided that Maximus would have five days to cure after receiving written notice of any default from Mr. Shepherd.

Maximus paid Mr. Shepherd the first monthly advance and the $20,000 non-recoupable bonus for "Riding with Private Malone" but failed to make any of the other payments required by the agreement. On May 15, 2002, Mr. Shepherd's attorney sent Maximus a letter stating that Maximus was in breach of the agreement for failure to pay the required monthly advances, that Maximus had five days to cure the default, and that if Maximus did not cure the default within that time, the agreement would automatically terminate, and Maximus's interest in all the songs covered by the agreement would automatically revert to Mr. Shepherd. Mr. Shepherd's attorney received no response to this letter. Accordingly, on June 3, 2002, Mr. Shepherd's attorney wrote Maximus a second letter stating that due to Maximus's default under the agreement as outlined in his first letter and Maximus's failure to cure its default, the agreement had been terminated, and all of the rights Mr. Shepherd had previously granted to Maximus had reverted to Mr. Shepherd.

Maximus refused to recognize the reversion of its interest in "Riding with Private Malone." As a result, the American Society of Composers,

Authors and Publishers ("ASCAP"), which collects and distributes royalties from the public performance of songs, refused to release over $ 25,000 in royalties representing Maximus's 12.5% interest in "Riding with Private Malone" without a judicial determination of who was entitled to the funds. Accordingly, on September 12, 2002, Mr. Shepherd filed suit against Maximus in the Davidson County Chancery Court seeking a declaration that Maximus's rights in all of the songs governed by the agreement had reverted to him. . . . . On December 2, 2002, Maximus, this time represented by counsel, filed its "Amended Answer."

In its "Amended Answer," Maximus admitted that it had not paid Mr. Shepherd all of the monthly advances required by the parties' agreement. In light of this admission, Mr. Shepherd filed a motion for partial summary judgment. Mr. Shepherd argued that Maximus had admitted its default and that the undisputed facts showed that Maximus had received written notice of the default and had failed to cure the default within the requisite time. Therefore, Mr. Shepherd claimed he was entitled, as a matter of law, to a judgment that Maximus had breached the agreement, that the agreement had been terminated, and that all rights in the compositions covered by the agreement, including rights to royalties, had reverted to him.

Maximus responded by filing its own motion for summary judgment. Maximus again admitted that it failed to pay Mr. Shepherd all of the monthly advances required by the agreement, acknowledged that it received the written notice of default and notice of termination from Mr. Shepherd's attorney, and stated that all of its rights in all compositions other than "Riding with Private Malone" had reverted to Mr. Shepherd. However, Maximus argued that because it had paid Mr. Shepherd an initial $20,000 non-recoupable bonus for "Riding with Private Malone," its 12.5% interest in that song would still continue for five years in spite of the fact that it breached the agreement by failing to make the monthly advance payments, and in spite of the fact that the agreement had thereby been terminated.

In a memorandum opinion filed March 20, 2003, the trial court concluded that Maximus's rights relating to the song "Riding with Private Malone" were separate from its rights with respect to the other songs covered by the agreement and that its default on its obligations with respect to the other songs did not affect its rights with respect to "Riding with Private Malone." Accordingly, the court denied Mr. Shepherd's motion for partial summary judgment and granted Maximus's motion for summary judgment. The trial court entered an order reflecting its conclusions on March 31, 2003. Mr. Shepherd then filed a motion for an interlocutory appeal and a motion for permission to amend his complaint to add a claim for money damages against Maximus. Given that the March 31, 2003 order was a final order, the trial court denied Mr. Shepherd's motion for an interlocutory appeal. The trial court also denied Mr. Shepherd's motion to amend the complaint. Mr. Shepherd filed a timely notice of appeal.

II

The Agreement's Reversion Provisions

Mr. Shepherd argues that the trial court erred by denying his motion for partial summary judgment and granting Maximus's motion for summary judgment because the trial court misinterpreted the reversion provisions of the agreement. This issue is particularly amenable to disposition by summary judgment because questions involving the meaning of a written contract are questions of law rather than questions of fact. We have determined that the trial court misinterpreted the reversion provisions in the parties' "Exclusive Co-Publishing Agreement."

* * * * * * * * * * * * * *

B

The operative facts in this case are essentially undisputed. Maximus admits that it failed to make the payments required by the agreement, that it failed to cure its breach within the required time after receiving written notice from Mr. Shepherd's attorney, and that the agreement was therefore terminated. Maximus's only defense to Mr. Shepherd's claim is that the song "Riding with Private Malone" was an exception to the reversion provisions. Thus, this case can be determined solely by reference to the terms of the parties' written agreement. Where, as here, the terms of an agreement are "plain and unambiguous" on a particular point, the interpretation of the agreement is a question of law. *Bratton v. Bratton*, 136 S.W.3d 595, 601 (Tenn. 2004); *Standard Fire Ins. Co. v. Chester-O'Donley & Assocs.*, 972 S.W.2d 1, 5–6 (Tenn. Ct. App. 1998). Because the parties' rights can be determined by the resolution of legal questions alone, the trial court correctly concluded that this case was an appropriate one for resolution by summary judgment. The primary question on appeal, then, is whether the trial court erred in its interpretation of the reversion provisions of the parties' agreement. This is a question of law that we review de novo. *Security Fire Prot. Co. v. Huddleston*, 138 S.W.3d 829, 834 (Tenn. Ct. App. 2003); *Gen. Const. Contractors Ass'n v. Greater St. Thomas Baptist Church*, 107 S.W.3d 513, 520 (Tenn. Ct. App. 2002).

The reversion provisions at issue are contained in paragraphs three and nine of the agreement. Paragraph three, titled "Compensation," contains a miscellaneous provision that reads as follows:

In the event that Publisher fails to timely pay Songwriter the Monthly Advance pursuant to paragraph 3(b) hereof on the first business day of each month of the Term hereof, in such case of failure to pay the Monthly Advance, this Agreement shall automatically terminate and all rights in the Compositions shall automatically revert to Songwriter and Songwriter shall have no further obligation to Publisher under this Agreement. Publisher shall have five (5) days to cure Publisher's failure to timely pay the Monthly Advance due hereunder.

Paragraph nine, under the heading "Copyright/Reversion," provides:

With the exception of "Riding With Private Malone" the rights herein granted hereunder shall be for the full term of copyright of the Compositions, including any renewals, extensions and revivals of copyright in any and all languages throughout the universe. In the event of Publisher's default in payment per the provisions otherwise set forth herein, all copyrights in the Compositions delivered hereunder during the Term shall automatically and immediately revert to Songwriter, effective immediately thereupon. Publisher shall acknowledge such reversion, in writing, within five (5) business days of Songwriter's written notice to Publisher of such breach and resulting reversion of copyrights.

The meaning of the reversion provisions quoted above is plain and unambiguous, particularly in light of the definitions contained in the agreement. The agreement states that references to the "Publisher" mean Maximus, and that references to the "Songwriter" mean Mr. Shepherd. The agreement defines the term "Compositions" to mean "all original musical compositions" and states that the songs set forth on Exhibit A to the agreement - *i.e.*, "Riding with Private Malone"—are "further defined as Compositions delivered hereunder." Using these definitions, the first sentence of the portion of paragraph three quoted above can be restated as follows:

In the event that [Maximus] fails to timely pay [Mr. Shepherd] the Monthly Advance . . ., this Agreement shall automatically terminate and all rights in [all original musical compositions] shall automatically revert to [Mr. Shepherd].

The second sentence of paragraph nine can similarly be restated as follows:

In the event of [Maximus's] default in payment per the provisions otherwise set forth herein, all copyrights in [all original musical compositions] delivered hereunder during the Term shall automatically and immediately revert to Songwriter.

The plain and unambiguous meaning of these provisions is that Maximus's interests in all of the songs governed by the agreement—including "Riding with Private Malone"—would automatically and immediately revert to Mr. Shepherd if Maximus failed to make any of the payments required under the agreement.

In spite of the plain language of the agreement quoted above, Maximus contends that the song "Riding with Private Malone" was intended to be an "exception" to these reversion provisions. Maximus offers two main arguments in support of this contention. First, Maximus argues that because the agreement contains *other* provisions that explicitly distinguish between "Riding with Private Malone" and the other songs covered by the agreement, we should interpret these reversion provisions as making the same distinction. However, the "interpretation" suggested by Maximus is not really an interpretation at all. Instead, Maximus, dissatisfied with the consequences resulting from the plain terms of an agreement that it drafted, is asking this court to rewrite these reversion provisions to insert an exception for the song "Riding with Private Malone." This we cannot do. The courts must interpret contracts as they are written. *Bob Pearsall*

Motors, Inc. v. Regal Chrysler-Plymouth, Inc., 521 S.W.2d 578, 580 (Tenn. 1975); *Bradson Mercantile, Inc. v. Crabtree*, 1 S.W.3d 648, 652 (Tenn. Ct. App. 1999). Courts do not concern themselves with the wisdom or folly of a contract, *Chapman Drug Co. v. Chapman*, 207 Tenn. 502, 516, 341 S.W.2d 392, 398 (1960); *Brooks v. Networks of Chattanooga, Inc.*, 946 S.W.2d 321, 324 (Tenn. Ct. App. 1996), and we will not relieve parties from contractual obligations simply because these obligations later prove to be burdensome or unwise. *Atkins v. Kirkpatrick*, 823 S.W.2d 547, 553 (Tenn. Ct. App. 1991); *Ballard v. N. Am. Life & Cas. Co.*, 667 S.W.2d 79, 82 (Tenn. Ct. App. 1983); *Carrington v. W. A. Soefker & Son, Inc.*, 624 S.W.2d 894, 897 (Tenn. Ct. App. 1981).

Second, Maximus argues that its admitted breach of the contract does not require it to surrender its five-year, 12.5% interest in the song "Riding with Private Malone" because the initial $ 20,000 non-recoupable bonus payment it made to Mr. Shepherd was intended to be the sole consideration for this interest. However, there is nothing in the agreement to suggest that the parties viewed the additional $ 20,000 bonus for "Riding with Private Malone" to be the sole consideration for Maximus's five-year, 12.5% interest in the song. Moreover, this argument runs directly counter to the express language of the reversion provisions in the agreement. Paragraph three states that in the event Maximus fails to pay the required monthly advances, "this Agreement shall automatically terminate and all rights in the Compositions shall automatically revert" to Mr. Shepherd. Paragraph nine goes even further, stating that if Maximus defaults on making *any* of the payments required in the agreement, "all copyrights in the Compositions delivered hereunder during the Term shall automatically and immediately revert" to Mr. Shepherd. Thus, while the initial $ 20,000 bonus payment Mr. Shepherd received for "Riding with Private Malone" was separate from the other consideration contemplated by the agreement, it was not severable from that other consideration.

* * * * * * * * * * * *

V

The trial court erred in interpreting the reversion provisions of the agreement. Under these provisions, Maximus's default in making any of the payments required by the agreement triggered automatic termination of the agreement and reversion to Mr. Shepherd of Maximus's interest in all of the songs covered by the agreement, including "Riding with Private Malone." Accordingly, the trial court erred in denying Mr. Shepherd's motion for partial summary judgment and in granting Maximus's motion for summary judgment. . . . . . For these reasons, we reverse the summary judgment for Maximus and remand the case with directions to enter a summary judgment for Mr. Shepherd regarding the disputed rights to "Riding with Private Malone" and for any further proceedings that may be required. We tax the costs of this appeal to Maximus Entertainment Group, Inc. for which execution, if necessary, may issue.

5.3 INJUNCTION

The entertainment industries run on a fuel consisting in equal parts of great enthusiasm and high expectations. At least, this is usually the case at the outset of a deal. However, creative and business interests often diverge, tempers rise, and all at once the parties are at logger-heads. Litigation begins. The company will want to secure an injunction to prevent the artist from leaving the production. One side or the other will seek an injunction. In many cases, the grant or denial of the injunction will for practical purposes often end the litigation, with the artist often returning to work in the former instance or a settlement favorable to the artist following thereafter in the latter instance.

The standards for a preliminary injunction are discussed in the second part of the Introduction. Special problems in securing injunctions in California are considered in Section 2.4.

A "negative injunction" to prevent a party from working elsewhere has particular appeal in the entertainment industries. While the normal legal response to contract breach in other situations is damages for the loss incurred, how does one accurately measure the loss of a star attraction or unique talent? The lost profits from a proposed, but unrealized, venture may be too speculative to be proved to a court's satisfaction. While money damages are an effective remedy in some situations, the employers of talent have often turned to another weapon in order to effectively deal with a defecting performer by indirectly forcing their return to the fold. That weapon is the negative injunction.

The enforcement of the personal services contract through a negative injunction dates to the landmark English case decided in 1852, *Lumley v. Wagner,* 1 De G.M.&G 604, 42 Eng.Rep. 687 (1852). A young opera singer, Johanna Wagner, was under contract to Her Majesty's Theatre of London. When she attempted to breach that contract and join a rival troupe, Her Majesty's Theatre sued both her and her new employer. As to Ms. Wagner, the court pointed to the provision in her contract where she was to render her exclusive services to Her Majesty's Theatre for a number of months. The Chancellor granted a negative injunction preventing Wagner from performing for the rival company with the stated reasoning that, while a court could not specifically enforce the contract, an injunction preventing her performing elsewhere might cause the defendant to return and perform her prior contractual obligations. While the Chancellor's reasoning was unavailing in Wagner's case, in that she did not return to Her Majesty's Theatre, the grounds for a negative injunction were established.

Other nineteenth-century English cases expanded on *Lumley v. Wagner.* In *Webster v. Dillon,* 30 L.T.R.(n.s.) 71 (1857), the court held that it was not necessary to include a specific clause in a contract specifying that injunctive relief was permissible. It was sufficient that the contract terms made it clear the services were to be exclusive, and that it could be determined, from the nature of the services, that they were unique and difficult to obtain from a substitute.

A second case, *Grimston v. Cunningham*, (1894) 1 Q.B. 125, involved an English actor who was in a road company touring the United States. Dissatisfied with the roles assigned to him, he abandoned the tour and returned to England, only to face a day in court when he signed with another company. He was enjoined from performing in England during the time his contract with the road company in the United States was still running. This rather extensive restriction meant it was not necessary for an employer to show competitive harm in order to obtain a negative injunction; the loss of a performer's unique services was enough. Even so, under concepts that an injunction cannot be unduly harsh or burdensome, the absence of competitive harm may cause a court to deny an injunction. Yet another English case that dealt with competitive harm, or the lack thereof, was *Marco Prod., Ltd. v. Pagola*, (1945) K.B.111.

Early entertainment cases in the United States involving the negative injunction looked to the English precedents for support. Both *Daly v. Smith*, 38 N.Y. Sup. Ct. 158 (1874) and *Mapleson v. Del Puente*, 13 Abb. N.Cas. 144 (N.Y. 1883) noted the availability of the injunction when conditions paralleled those examined in the English cases just cited. Thus, the negative injunction was effectively transferred to U.S. jurisdictions and has been a principal deterrent to contract "jumping" ever since.

A court will not issue a negative injunction if it feels it will be unduly harsh or burdensome. The court is influenced by: 1) the length of time the injunction is to run, 2) the extent of geographical area in which the defendant is to be prohibited from seeking alternative work, 3) the types of work prohibited by the requested injunction, and 4) the likelihood that the injunction will produce positive results.

The time left under the original contract is important, although courts have issued injunctions that effectively prohibit important types of alternative employment for three or more years. In *Warner Bros. Pictures, Inc. v. Nelson* (1937) 1 K.B. 209, actress Bette Davis was enjoined from making films or appearing on stage in England for the remainder of her contract or three years, whichever was shorter. The court did refuse plaintiff's request that, during this time, the actress be barred from all entertainment work. Even so, the length of time preventing her pursuit of her chief career was formidable.

The Davis case involved another issue of the harshness of a negative injunction. When it appeared that Davis would not make further films for Warner Brothers, she was suspended from the company payroll and was still not being paid under her studio contract when suit was brought against her. The court indicated it would not order an injunction unless the company indicated a firm willingness to lift the suspension. In other words, one cannot both suspend a performer without pay and also restrain the performer from working elsewhere.

In recent years, U.S. courts have become increasingly reluctant to grant injunctions which have the effect of putting performers completely out of work. In earlier cases, *Harry Rodgers Theatrical Enterprises v. Comstock*,

232 N.Y.S.1 (1928) (competing producer wished to sign highly paid vaudeville performer already under long-term contract; when negotiations for release failed, performer signed with competing producer anyway, and negative injunction issued, perhaps impelled to some degree by performer's testimony that he didn't remember signing the contract) and *King Records, Inc. v. Brown,* 252 N.Y.S.2d 988 (1964) (exclusive recording artist prevented from recording for larger company during contract term under agreement entered into via company established by artist and manager). However, in the absence of such circumstances (*Machen v. Johansson* below) and even in a case involving conduct the court found totally reprehensible (*ABC v. Wolf,* below) courts in recent years have demonstrated an increasing reluctance to grant injunctions against entertainment figures.

The uniqueness of the performer's talents (or the lack thereof, as demonstrated in *Motown Records Corp. v. Brockert,* in Sec. 2.4.2) is a central issue when the company seeks to obtain a negative injunction against the performer. Uniqueness is largely an element of proving irreparable harm, but it bears on the issue of inadequacy of legal damages as well. Uniqueness to the extent that the performer is impossible to replace is not required. A showing of great difficulty and inconvenience in finding a substitute performer of similar talents is generally sufficient. Can the company feel secure if it includes in its talent agreements clauses reciting that the performer concedes that his/her talents are "special, unique, extraordinary, etc."? No. The courts will scrutinize such clauses just as they do the rest of the agreement. In fact, in *Wilhelmina Models, Inc. v. Abdulmajid,* 413 N.Y.S.2d 21 (1st Dept. 1979), the court stated that the fact that such a clause appeared in every agreement entered into by a model agency was an indication that the subject of the agreement was *not* unique.

Machen v. Johansson, 174 F. Supp. 522 (S.D.N.Y. 1959)

KAUFMAN, DISTRICT JUDGE

In this action tried to me without a jury the plaintiff seeks to enjoin the defendant from engaging in a boxing match with Floyd Patterson, the heavyweight champion of the world, scheduled to be held in New York City on June 25, 1959, approximately two weeks from today. He asks that this injunction continue until the defendant shall have engaged in a return boxing match with the plaintiff.

Plaintiff's claim for an injunction is grounded upon the contention that the defendant had agreed to a rematch with the plaintiff and had also agreed not to engage in any fights in the United States and specifically not to fight Floyd Patterson anywhere in the world before the rematch with the plaintiff had been held.

Defendant has refused to honor the alleged agreement for a rematch and to recognize the document of September 13th on several grounds: (1) He contends that [defendant] Ahlquist [the promoter of the bout] was never his agent, actual or apparent, and was never given authority to sign this agreement in his behalf, and that Flaherty [Machen's manager] had been specifically informed that defendant would not agree to a rematch; (2) that the agreement was obtained by coercion and duress [Machen's manager informed Ahlquist the night before the match that Machen would not fight unless Ahlquist first agreed in writing to a return match if Machen lost, a threat which could have been economically catastrophic for Ahlquist—Eds.]; (3) that the agreement for a rematch is void and unenforceable for lack of consideration and is further invalid because its terms are indefinite and uncertain. Other grounds are urged, such as the inability of the International Boxing Club, named in the document of September 13th as the promoter of the rematch, to perform because of its dissolution pursuant to a decree of Judge Ryan in an anti-trust suit brought against it. *United States v. International Boxing Club*, D.C., 150 F. Supp. 397; 171 F. Supp. 841; 358 U.S. 242, 79 S. Ct. 245, 3 L.Ed.2d 270.

As I have already stated, plaintiff seeks drastic relief by his prayer for an injunction restraining the defendant from engaging in the boxing match with Floyd Patterson now scheduled for June 25th and for a continuance of this injunction until Johansson shall have engaged with the plaintiff in a rematch. I am convinced that the applicable law prevents me, in the light of the facts in this case, from granting the equitable relief sought by the plaintiff. Furthermore, even if such relief could be granted, I would deny the injunction in the exercise of my discretion. I, therefore, find it unnecessary to determine whether Ahlquist had actual or apparent authority to enter into the September writing on behalf of Johansson or to agree to any provisions for a rematch in his behalf. Likewise it becomes unnecessary to decide whether the document of September 13th was extracted by duress or coercion or whether it was based on adequate consideration.

By reason of this disposition it follows also that any alleged violation of Judge Ryan's decree or assertion of a conspiracy to violate the Sherman Act, 15 U.S.C.A. 1–7, 15 note, need not be dealt with. In short, I make no findings or conclusions concerning the validity of the writing of September 13, 1958, or the enforceability of any part of that writing except the negative covenant contained in paragraph 5 thereof.

Meaning of the Negative Covenant

Even were I to assume that the writing of September 13, 1958, constitutes a valid agreement between Machen and Johansson for a return fight in the event of Machen's defeat in the September 14, 1958, fight, I would be compelled to hold that Machen is not entitled to the injunction he seeks.

It is black letter law that although a contract may be valid it may not necessarily provide the basis for equitable relief. This is not to say that the aggrieved party is left without any remedy. The usual form of redress in cases of breach of contract is money damages. Only in the most unusual case will a court of equity act upon the person of the defendant to restrain him from doing some act which the plaintiff claims may cause him irreparable injury. This is particularly true where, as in this case, the plaintiff seeks to restrain the defendant from freely practicing his trade. His right to this relief must be clear, reasonable and well defined.

In order to determine what rights and obligations may flow from the writing of September 13, 1958, I must first determine what the parties intended to achieve by that writing. My task in this case is to examine the words employed by the parties against the background of all of the circumstances under which the contract was drawn. It is only by interpreting the words of others that we may give meaning to their expressions. In the words of Professor Corbin:

> In reading each other's words, men certainly see through a glass darkly; . . . the best that a judge can do is to put himself so far as possible in the position of that person or persons [whose meaning and intention are in issue], knowing their history and experience . . . and then to determine what his own meaning and intention would have been. Corbin, Contracts 13, 23 (1951).

So viewing the contract, it is clear on its face that the parties intended to ensure Machen an opportunity to fight Johansson in a return match in the event that Machen lost to Johansson in Sweden. The return bout was to be held in Chicago under the auspices of the International Boxing Club specifically during the last week of January or the first two weeks of February, 1959. No provision was made in the agreement for a postponement or for any alternative time within which the fight was to be held. It, therefore, appears that it was the intent of the parties that Johansson was to have performed the affirmative aspect of the contract by the end of the second week of February 1959 and that if he failed to do so he would have breached his obligation. As I have already stated, there was included in the writing of September 13, 1958, a negative covenant providing that Johansson "will not box anyone in the United States and will not box Floyd Patterson under any conditions any place in the world until the above agreements have been fulfilled." If plaintiff is entitled to the injunction he seeks, that right flows from this negative covenant. However, while the covenant clearly exhibits an intention to place some restrictions on Johansson's activities as a fighter, it provides me with no clue as to the period of time during which those restrictions were intended to run. The only temporal limitation to be found in the negative covenant is contained in the words "until the above agreements have been fulfilled." The "above agreements" must have reference to the provision relating to the return fight. Thus, the contract is subject to two possible interpretations:

(1) that the negative covenant would run until the time when the return match was scheduled to be held, i.e., no later than February 14, 1959;

(2) that it would run until such time as the return fight was actually held, or until a tender of performance by Johansson was refused by Machen, even if that time ran indefinitely beyond the dates specified in the agreement.

I am compelled to conclude that the parties never intended that the negative covenant run beyond February 14, 1959, the last date for performance of the return bout provision. It may be conjectured that Flaherty was fearful that Johansson, should he defeat Machen and thereby gain a reputation which would be readily saleable in the United States, [and] would not be able to resist the temptation to exploit that reputation in the months between the original Machen-Johansson fight and the return. Had Johansson engaged in an interim bout and lost, it would have seriously impaired his reputation and thus have detracted from the value of the return bout agreement. This is the eventuality against which Flaherty sought to protect his fighter.

However, plaintiff would have me adopt a different interpretation of the covenant. He now urges that, in contracting to fight Johansson, Machen gave to Johansson "the opportunity to make an important improvement in his competitive position in the boxing world." The instant covenant, plaintiff argues, was intended to prevent Johansson from utilizing his advanced position in competition with Machen until Machen shall have an opportunity to engage him in a return fight. However, a consideration and evaluation of all of the evidence in the case leads me to the conclusion that the interpretation advanced by plaintiff is the less probable of the two possible alternatives.

Under plaintiff's theory, the negative covenant could run on without restriction for an indefinite length of time. This might conceivably be for the remainder of Johansson's life should he never agree to a return match with Machen. Plaintiff concedes that the possible advancement in Johansson's position as a fighter was one of the primary inducements on Johansson's part in entering into the contract for the September 14, 1958, fight with Machen. It is difficult to believe that Ahlquist, if he was acting in Johansson's behalf, or Johansson himself, would ever agree to a contract term which might forever bar Johansson from the beneficial enjoyment of that advanced position.

I find that plaintiff has failed to establish that at the time the parties entered into the alleged agreement of September 13, 1958, they intended the negative covenant to run beyond February 14, 1959, the last date upon which the return fight was to be held.

THE INJUNCTIVE RELIEF SOUGHT

However, even were I to conclude that the parties intended to restrict Johansson's right to fight indefinitely and until such time as he would agree to engage Machen in a return fight, I would not enforce such a covenant by injunction.

Plaintiff urges upon me that the instant covenant is similar to that category of restrictive covenants ancillary to contracts of employment, where the employee, having gained a professional advantage through the employment, may properly be restrained from using that advantage in such a way as to do serious injury to his employer after the employment has terminated. Plaintiff argues that, by engaging Johansson in the initial fight, he advanced Johansson's professional standing, and that it was, therefore, reasonable for him to restrain Johansson from using that advanced standing to harm Machen.

Defendant, on the other hand, answers that restrictive covenants based upon a promise to refrain from competition are not valid unless they are ancillary either to a contract for the transfer of good will or other property, or to an existing employment or contract of employment. Restatement of Contracts, 515. Defendant asserts that he was never an employee of Machen's nor was he ever engaged in a transfer of good will.

I need not pass upon the correctness of this proposition of law. I find that the instant covenant even as interpreted by plaintiff is not enforceable by injunction for two reasons:

(1) It is not reasonable in its terms;
(2) The granting of an injunction would inflict serious injury on the defendant, while not providing the plaintiff with the protection he seeks.

(a) Reasonableness of the terms of the covenant

Injunctive relief is an extraordinary remedy to be granted sparingly. *Worthington Pump & Machinery Corp. v. Douds,* 97 F. Supp. 656, 661 (S.D.N.Y. 1951). Where restrictive covenants have been enforced they have usually been sharply defined as to time and area. *See* 9 A.L.R. 1468 et seq. and cases cited therein. While it is true that there are cases in which restrictive covenants, running for the life of the one restrained, have been enforced, in such cases the restriction extended to a very limited area only. *See Fitch v. Dewes,* 2 A.C. 158 (Eng. 1921). The instant covenant is extremely broad geographically. It prevents Johansson from fighting anyone in the United States and from fighting Floyd Patterson anywhere in the world. If such a restriction is imposed upon Johansson for an indefinite period of time it would be tantamount to denying him the right to advance himself within his trade or to fight in the United States which, it was testified to, offers the most fertile field for fights. I find that this would constitute an unreasonable restraint.

(b) The ineffectiveness of the remedy sought

Finally there is no way that an injunction could be framed to secure for plaintiff the results he seeks without at the same time placing Johansson under an intolerable restriction. "Equity not infrequently withholds relief which it is accustomed to give where it would be burdensome to the defendant and of little advantage to the plaintiff." *Di Giovanni v. Camden Fire Ins. Ass'n,* 1935, 296 U.S. 64, 71–72, 56 S.Ct. 1, 5, 80 L.Ed. 47.

A restriction running for only a limited period would be ineffective. Let us explore this further. Were I to restrain Johansson from fighting Patterson or fighting anyone in the United States for, let us say, one year, he might well return to Sweden, engage in several contests in Europe during the year, and then, upon the expiration of the injunction, again contract to meet Patterson. This would neither safeguard Machen's reputation nor secure for him a return match.

Nor would a longer term injunction be satisfactory. Were I to restrain Johansson from fighting for two or three years the damage to him would be very great. He would be unable to advance his position by fighting in the United States during a period that might well represent a relatively large portion of his effective ring career. Yet the benefit to plaintiff from such a restriction would be small. Machen would undoubtedly engage in bouts with other fighters during the period when Johansson was under the restriction. Indeed, he has already engaged in one such fight since his defeat by Johansson on September 14, 1958. Each time Machen fought, the outcome would have an impact, for good or ill, upon his standing as a fighter. These subsequent fights, and not any activity upon Johansson's part, would form the basis of the sports world's evaluation of Machen's abilities. Thus, while it may be argued that at this moment Johansson in effect carries Machen's reputation into the ring with him, this is a situation which will be of but short duration.

In summary, I find that plaintiff has failed on a number of grounds to demonstrate his right to the extraordinary relief he seeks:

(1) There is nothing to indicate that the parties intended that the negative covenant was to run beyond February 14, 1959 and in fact it is apparent that the parties intended the restriction to run only until that date.

(2) If the covenant was intended to run indefinitely beyond February 13, 1959, it is unenforceable because it would place an unreasonable restriction upon defendant.

(3) No injunction could be framed which would provide plaintiff with the results he asks without placing defendant under an intolerable and unreasonable burden.

Any one of these grounds would be sufficient in itself to deny plaintiff the relief sought. . . .

American Broadcasting Cos., Inc. v. Wolf, 52 n.y.2d 398, 438 n.y.s.2d 482 (1981)

COOKE, CHIEF JUDGE

This case provides an interesting insight into the fierce competition in the television industry for popular performers and favorable ratings. It requires legal resolution of a rather novel employment imbroglio.

The issue is whether plaintiff American Broadcasting Companies, Incorporated (ABC), is entitled to equitable relief against defendant Warner Wolf, a New York City sportscaster, because of Wolf's breach of a good faith negotiation provision of a now expired broadcasting contract with ABC. In the present circumstances, it is concluded that the equitable relief sought by plaintiff—which would have the effect of forcing Wolf off the air—may not be granted.

I

Warner Wolf, a sportscaster who has developed a rather colorful and unique on-the-air personality, had been employed by ABC since 1976. In February 1978, ABC and Wolf entered into an employment agreement which, following exercise of the renewal option, was to terminate on March 5, 1980. The contract contained a clause, known as a good-faith negotiation and first-refusal provision, that is at the crux of this litigation: "You agree, if we so elect, during the last ninety (90) days prior to the expiration of the extended term of this agreement, to enter into good faith negotiations with us for the extension of this agreement on mutually agreeable terms. You further agree that for the first forty-five (45) days of this renegotiation period, you will not negotiate for your services with any other person or company other than WABC-TV or ABC. In the event we are unable to reach an agreement for an extension by the expiration of the extended term hereof, you agree that you will not accept, in any market for a period of three (3) months following expiration of the extended term of this agreement, any offer of employment as a sportscaster, sports news reporter, commentator, program host, or analyst in broadcasting (including television, cable television, pay television and radio) without first giving us, in writing, an opportunity to employ you on substantially similar terms, and you agree to enter into an agreement with us on such terms." Under this provision, Wolf was bound to negotiate in good faith with ABC for the 90-day period from December 6, 1979, through March 4, 1980. For the first 45 days, December 6 through January 19, the negotiation with ABC was to be exclusive. Following expiration of the 90-day negotiating period and the contract on March 5, 1980, Wolf was required, before *accepting* any other offer, to afford ABC a right of first refusal; he could comply with this provision either by refraining from accepting another offer or by first tendering the offer to ABC. The first-refusal period expired on June 3, 1980, and on June 4 Wolf was free to accept any job opportunity, without obligation to ABC.

Wolf first met with ABC executives in September 1979 to discuss the terms of a renewal contract. Counterproposals were exchanged, and the parties agreed to finalize the matter by October 15. Meanwhile, unbeknownst to ABC, Wolf met with representatives of CBS in early October. Wolf related his employment requirements and also discussed the first refusal-good faith negotiation clause of his ABC contract. Wolf furnished CBS a copy of that portion of the ABC agreement. On October 12, ABC officials and Wolf met, but were unable to reach agreement on a renewal contract. A few days later, on October 16, Wolf again discussed employment possibilities with CBS.

Not until January 2, 1980, did ABC again contact Wolf. At that time, ABC expressed its willingness to meet substantially all of his demands. Wolf rejected the offer, however, citing ABC's delay in communicating with him and his desire to explore his options in light of the impending expiration of the 45-day exclusive negotiation period.

On February 1, 1980, after termination of that exclusive period, Wolf and CBS orally agreed on the terms of Wolf's employment as sports-caster for WCBS-TV, a CBS-owned affiliate in New York. During the next two days, CBS informed Wolf that it had prepared two agreements and divided his annual compensation between the two: one covered his services as an on-the-air sportscaster, and the other was an off-the-air production agreement for sports specials Wolf was to produce. The production agreement contained an exclusivity clause which barred Wolf from performing "services of any nature for" or permitting the use of his "name, likeness, voice or endorsement by, any person, firm, or corporation" during the term of the agreement, unless CBS con-sented. The contract had an effective date of March 6, 1980.

Wolf signed the CBS production agreement on February 4, 1980. At the same time, CBS agreed in writing, in consideration of $100 received from Wolf, to hold open an offer of employment to Wolf as sportscaster until June 4, 1980, the date on which Wolf became free from ABC's right of first refusal. The next day, February 5, Wolf submitted a letter of resignation to ABC.

Representatives of ABC met with Wolf on February 6 and made vari-ous offers and promises that Wolf rejected. Wolf informed ABC that they had delayed negotiations with him and downgraded his worth. He stated he had no future with the company. He told the officials he had made a "gentlemen's agreement" and would leave ABC on March 5. Later in February, Wolf and ABC agreed that Wolf would continue to ap-pear on the air during a portion of the first-refusal period, from March 6 until May 28. (The agreement also provided that on or after June 4, 1980, Wolf was free to "accept an offer of employment with anyone of [his] choosing and immediately begin performing on-air services." The par-ties agreed that their rights and obligations under the original employ-ment contract were in no way affected by the extension of employment. [Note in original])

ABC commenced this action on May 6, 1980, by which time Wolf's move to CBS had become public knowledge. The complaint alleged that Wolf, induced by CBS, breached both the good-faith negotiation and first-refusal provisions of his contract with ABC. ABC sought spe-cific enforcement of its right of first refusal and an injunction against Wolf's employment as a sportscaster with CBS.

After a trial, Supreme Court found no breach of the contract, and went on to note that, in any event, equitable relief would be inappro-priate. A divided Appellate Division, while concluding that Wolf had breached both the good-faith negotiation and first-refusal provisions, nonetheless affirmed on the ground that equitable intervention was unwarranted. There should be an affirmance.

II

Initially, we agree with the Appellate Division that defendant Wolf breached his obligation to negotiate in good faith with ABC from

December, 1979 through March 1980. When Wolf signed the production agreement with CBS on February 4, 1980, he obligated himself not to render services "of any nature" to any person, firm or corporation on and after March 6, 1980. Quite simply, then, beginning on February 4, Wolf was unable to extend his contract with ABC; his contract with CBS precluded him from legally serving ABC in any capacity after March 5. Given Wolf's existing obligation to CBS, any negotiations he engaged in with ABC, without the consent of CBS, after February 4 were meaningless and could not have been in good faith.

At the same time, there is no basis in the record for the Appellate Division's conclusion that Wolf violated the first-refusal provision by entering into an oral sportscasting contract with CBS on February 4. The first-refusal provision required Wolf, for a period of 90 days after termination of the ABC agreement, either to refrain from accepting an offer of employment or to first submit the offer to ABC for its consideration. By its own terms, the right of first refusal did not apply to offers accepted by Wolf prior to the March 5 termination of the ABC employment contract. It is apparent, therefore, that Wolf could not have breached the right of first refusal by accepting an offer during the term of his employment with ABC. (In any event, the carefully tailored written agreement between Wolf and CBS consisted only of an option prior to June 4, 1979. Acceptance of CBS's offer of employment as a sportscaster did not occur until after the expiration of the first-refusal period on June 4, 1979. [Note in original]) Rather, his conduct violates only the good-faith negotiation clause of the contract. The question is whether this breach entitled ABC to injunctive relief that would bar Wolf from continued employment at CBS. To resolve this issue, it is necessary to trace the principles of specific performance applicable to personal service contracts.

III

A

Courts of equity historically have refused to order an individual to perform a contract for personal services (e.g., 4 Pomeroy, Equity Jurisprudence [5th ed.], 1343, at pp. 943–944; 5A Corbin, *Contracts*, 1204; see *Haight v. Badgeley*, 15 Barb. 499; Willard, *Equity Jurisprudence*, at pp. 276–279). Originally this rule evolved because of the inherent difficulties courts would encounter in supervising the performance of uniquely personal efforts (e.g., 4 Pomeroy, *Equity Jurisprudence*, 1343; 5A Corbin, *Contracts*, 1204; see, also, *De Rivafinoli v. Corsetti*, 4 Paige Ch. 264, 270). During the Civil War era, there emerged a more compelling reason for not directing the performance of personal services: the Thirteenth Amendment's prohibition of involuntary servitude. It has been strongly suggested that judicial compulsion of services would violate the express command of that amendment (*Arthur v. Oakes*, 63 F. 310, 317; Stevens, Involuntary Servitude by Injunction, 6 Corn.L.Q. 235; Calamari & Perillo, *The Law of Contracts*

[2d ed.], 16–5). For practical, policy and constitutional reasons, therefore, courts continue to decline to affirmatively enforce employment contracts.

Over the years, however, in certain narrowly tailored situations, the law fashioned other remedies for failure to perform an employment agreement. Thus, where an employee refuses to render services to an employer in violation of an existing contract, and the services are unique or extraordinary, an injunction may issue to prevent the employee from furnishing those services to another person for the duration of the contract (see, e.g., *Shubert Theatrical Co. v. Gallagher,* 206 App. Div. 514, 201 N.Y.S. 577). Such "negative enforcement" was initially available only when the employee had expressly stipulated not to compete with the employer for the term of the engagement (see, e.g., *Lumley v. Wagner,*1 De G.M.&G. 604, 42 Eng. Rep. 687; *Shubert Theatrical Co. v. Rath,* 271 F. 827, 830–833; 4 Pomeroy, *Equity Jurisprudence* [5th ed.], 1343, at p. 944). Later cases permitted injunctive relief where the circumstances justified implication of a negative covenant (see, e.g., *Montague v. Flockton,* L. R. 16 Eq. 189 [1873], 4 Pomeroy, *Equity Jurisprudence* [5th ed.], 1343; 5A Corbin, *Contracts,* 1205). In these situations, an injunction is warranted because the employee either expressly or by clear implication agreed not to work elsewhere for the period of his contract. And, since the services must be unique before negative enforcement will be granted, irreparable harm will befall the employer should the employee bepermitted to labor for a competitor (see 5A Corbin, *Contracts,* 1206, at p. 412).

B

After a personal service contract terminates, the availability of equitable relief against the former employee diminishes appreciably. Since the period of service has expired, it is impossible to decree affirmative or negative specific performance. Only if the employee has expressly agreed not to compete with the employer following the term of the contract, or is threatening to disclose trade secrets or commit another tortious act, is injunctive relief generally available at the behest of the employer (see, e.g., *Reed, Roberts Assoc. v. Strauman,* 40 N.Y.2d 303, 386 N.Y.S.2d 677, 353 N.E.2d 590; *Purchasing Assoc. v. Weitz,* 13 N.Y.2d 267, 246 N.Y.S.2d 600, 196 N.E.2d 245; *Town & Country House & Home Serv. v. Newbery,* 3 N.Y.2d 554, 170 N.Y.S.2d 328, 147 N.E.2d 724). Even where there is an express anticompetitive covenant, however, it will be rigorously examined and specifically enforced only if it satisfies certain established requirements (see, e.g., *Reed, Roberts Assoc. v. Strauman, supra,* 40 N.Y.2d at 307–308, 386 N.Y.S.2d 677, 353 N.E.2d 590; *Purchasing Assoc. v. Weitz, supra,* at 272–273; see, generally, Calamari & Perillo, *The Law of Contracts* [2d ed.], 16–19, at 601–602). Indeed, a court normally will not decree specific enforcement of an employee's anticompetitive covenant unless necessary to protect the trade secrets, customer lists or good will of the employer's business, or perhaps when the employer is exposed to special harm because of the unique nature of the employee's services (see, e.g., *Reed, Roberts Assoc. v. Strauman, supra,* 40 N.Y.2d at p. 308, 386 N.Y.S.2d 677, 353 N.E.2d 590; *Purchasing Assoc. v. Weitz, supra,* 13 N.Y.2d at pp. 272–273, 246 N.Y.S.2d 600, 196 N.E.2d 245; *Lepel High Frequency Labs. v. Capita,* 278 N.Y. 661, 16 N.E.2d 392, *aff'g.* 253 App. Div. 799, 2 N.Y.S.2d 628; 6A Corbin, *Contracts,* 1394). And, an otherwise valid covenant will not be enforced if it is unreasonable in time, space, or scope or would operate in a harsh or oppressive manner (e.g., *Reed, Roberts Assoc. v. Strauman,* 40 N.Y.2d, at p. 307, 386 N.Y.S.2d 677, 353 N.E.2d 590 *supra; Clark Paper & Mfg. Co. v. Stenacher,* 236 N.Y. 312, 140 N.E. 708; 6A Corbin, *Contracts,* 1394). There is, in short, general judicial disfavor of anticompetitive covenants contained in employment contracts (e.g., *Reed, Roberts Assoc. v. Strauman, supra,* 40 N.Y.2d at 307, 386 N.Y.S.2d 677, 353 N.E.2d 590).

Underlying the strict approach to enforcement of these covenants is the notion that, once the term of an employment agreement has expired, the general public policy favoring robust and uninhibited competition should not give way merely because a particular employer wishes to insulate himself from competition (e.g., *Clark Paper & Mfg. Co. v. Stenacher,* 236 N.Y. 312, 319–320, 140 N.E. 708, *supra;* 6A Corbin, *Contracts,* 1394, at 100). Important, too, are the "powerful considerations of public policy which militate against sanctioning the loss of a man's livelihood" (*Purchasing Assoc. v. Weitz,* 13 N.Y.2d at 272, 246 N.Y.S.2d 600, 196 N.E.2d 245, *supra*). At the same time, the employer is entitled to protection from unfair or illegal conduct that causes economic injury. The rules governing enforcement of anticompetitive covenants and the availability of equitable relief after termination of employment are designed to foster these interests of the employer without impairing the employee's ability to earn a living or the general competitive mold of society.

C

Specific enforcement of personal service contracts thus turns initially upon whether the term of employment has expired. If the employee refuses to perform during the period of employment, was furnishing unique services, has expressly or by clear implication agreed not to compete for the duration of the contract, and the employer is exposed to irreparable injury, it may be appropriate to restrain the employee from competing until the agreement expires. Once the employment contract has terminated, by contrast, equitable relief is potentially available only to prevent injury from unfair competition or similar tortious behavior or to enforce an express and valid anticompetitive covenant. In the absence of such circumstances, the general policy of unfettered competition should prevail.

IV

Applying these principles, it is apparent that ABC's request for injunctive relief must fail. There is no existing employment agreement between the parties; the original contract terminated in March 1980. Thus, the negative enforcement that might be appropriate during the term of employment is unwarranted here. Nor is there an express anticompetitive covenant that defendant Wolf is violating, or any claim of special injury from tortious conduct such as exploitation of trade secrets. In short, ABC seeks to premise equitable relief after termination of the employment upon a simple, albeit serious, breach of a general contract negotiation clause. (Even if Wolf had breached the first-refusal provision, it does not necessarily follow that injunctive relief would be available. Outside the personal service area, the usual equitable remedy for breach of a first-refusal clause is to order the breaching party to perform the contract with the person possessing the first-refusal right (e.g., 5A Corbin, *Contracts,* 1197, at pp. 377–378). When personal services are involved, this would result in an affirmative injunction ordering the employee to perform services for plaintiff. Such relief, as discussed, cannot be granted.[Note in original]) To grant an injunction in that situation would be to unduly interfere with an individual's livelihood and to inhibit free competition where there is no corresponding injury to the employer other than the loss of a competitive edge. Indeed, if relief were granted here, any breach of an employment contract provision relating to renewal negotiations logically would serve as the basis for an open-ended restraint upon the employee's ability to earn a living should he ultimately choose not to extend his employment. Our public policy, which favors the free exchange of goods and services through established market mechanisms, dictates otherwise.

Equally unavailing is ABC's request that the court create a non-competitive covenant by implication. Although in a proper case an implied-in-fact covenant not to compete for the term of employment may be found to exist, anticompetitive covenants covering the post-employment period will not be implied. Indeed, even an express covenant will be scrutinized and enforced only in accordance with established principles.

This is not to say that ABC has not been damaged in some fashion or that Wolf should escape responsibility for the breach of his good-faith negotiation obligation. Rather, we merely conclude that ABC is not entitled to equitable relief. Because of the unique circumstances presented, however, this decision is without prejudice to ABC's right to pursue relief in the form of monetary damages, if it be so advised.

Accordingly, the order of the Appellate Division should be affirmed.

FUCHSBERG, JUDGE (DISSENTING)

I agree with all the members of this court, as had all the Justices at the Appellate Division, that the defendant Wolf breached his undisputed obligation to negotiate in good faith for renewal of his contract with ABC. Where we part company is in the majority's unwillingness to mold an equitable decree, even one more limited than the harsh one the plaintiff proposed, to right the wrong.

Central to the disposition of this case is the first-refusal provision. . . .

One need not be in the broadcasting business to understand that the restriction ABC bargained for, and Wolf granted, when they entered into the original employment contract was not inconsequential. The earnings of broadcasting companies are directly related to the "ratings" they receive. This, in turn, is at least in part dependent on the popularity of personalities like Wolf. It therefore was to ABC's advantage, once Wolf came into its employ, especially since he was new to the New York market, that it enhance his popularity by featuring, advertising and otherwise promoting him. This meant that the loyalty of at least part of the station's listening audience would become identified with Wolf, thus enhancing his potential value to competitors, as witness the fact that, in place of the $250,000 he was receiving during his last year with ABC, he was able to command $400,000 to $450,000 per annum in his CBS "deal." A reasonable opportunity during which ABC could cope with such an assault on its good will had to be behind the clause in question.

Moreover, it is undisputed that, when in late February Wolf executed the contract for an extension of employment during the 90-day hiatus for which the parties had bargained, ABC had every right to expect that Wolf had not already committed himself to an exclusivity provision in a producer's contract with CBS in violation of the good-faith negotiation clause (see majority opn. at 397–398, at p. 483 of 438 N.Y.S.2d, at 364 of 420 N.E.2d). Surely, had ABC been aware of this gross breach, had it not been duped into giving an uninformed consent, it would not have agreed to serve as a self-destructive vehicle for the further enhancement of Wolf's potential for taking his ABC-earned following with him.

In the face of these considerations, the majority rationalizes its position of powerlessness to grant equitable relief by choosing to interpret the contract as though there were no restrictive covenant, express or implied. However, as demonstrated, there is, in fact, an express three-month negative covenant which, because of Wolf's misconduct, ABC was effectively denied the opportunity to exercise. Enforcement of this covenant, by enjoining Wolf from broadcasting for a three-month period, would depart from no entrenched legal precedent. Rather, it would accord with equity's boasted flexibility (see 11 Williston, *Contracts* [3d ed.], 1450, at pp. 1043–1044; 6A Corbin, *Contracts,* 1394, at 100; see, generally, 20 N.Y. Jur. [rev.], Equity, 79, 83, 84).

That said, a few words are in order regarding the majority's insistence that Wolf did not breach the first-refusal clause. It is remarkable that, to this end, it has to ignore its own crediting of the Appellate Division's express finding that, as far back as February 1, 1980, fully a month before the ABC contract was to terminate, "Wolf and CBS orally agreed on the terms of Wolf's employment as sportscaster for WCBS-TV" (majority opn., at p. 399, at p. 484 of 438 N.Y.S.2d, at 365 of 420 N.E.2d; see *American Broadcasting Cos. v. Wolf,* 76 A.D.2d 162, 166, 170–171, 430 N.Y.S.2d 275). It follows that the overt written CBS-Wolf option contract, which permitted Wolf to formally accept the CBS sportscasting offer at the end of the first-refusal period, was nothing but a charade.

Further, on this score, the majority's premise that Wolf could not have breached the first-refusal clause when he accepted the producer's agreement, exclusivity provision and all, *during* the term of his ABC contract, does not withstand analysis. So precious a reading of the arrangement with ABC frustrates the very purpose for which it had to have been made. Such a classical exaltation of form over substance is hardly to be countenanced by equity (see *Washer v. Seager*, 272 App.Div. 297, 71 N.Y.S.2d 46, *aff'd* 297 N.Y. 918, 79 N.E.2d 745).

For all these reasons, in my view, literal as well as proverbial justice should have brought a modification of the order of the Appellate Division to include a 90-day injunction—no more and no less than the relatively short and certainly not unreasonable transitional period for which ABC and Wolf struck their bargain. . . .

NOTES

1. On the other hand, in *Zink Communication v. Elliott*, 1990 WL 176382 (SDNY), *aff'd* without opinion, 923 F.2d 846 (2d Cir. 1990), the defendant's breach of a contract with the plaintiff to host a television game show which was being developed by the plaintiff for the Fox network and subsequent contract with a competing production company to host another game show ("To Tell the Truth") resulted in the issuance of a permanent injunction barring the defendant from appearing on the "To Tell the Truth" or any other game show. After determining that the plaintiff had properly exercised its option to employ Zink on an exclusive basis to host its game show, "Get the Picture," the court distinguished *Wolf* on the basis that it involved a contract for employment which had expired, while in the case at hand the contract for employment had not expired. The decision then applied the four elements (articulated in *Wolf*) required for the issuance of an injunction: failure to perform during period of employment, an exclusive underlying agreement, unique services, and irreparable harm to the plaintiff. The most difficult issues were whether Gordon Elliott's attributes as a game show host were sufficient to meet the "uniqueness" requirement and whether irreparable harm was shown. While actual harm was not established, the court, relying on equitable principle of fair dealing and policy considerations in the face of a defendant who breached a contract "with impunity," found a sufficient showing of harm with respect to the respective game shows.

2. In *KGB Inc. v Giannoulas*, 164 Cal.Rptr., 571, 104 Cal.App. 3d 844 (1980), the California Court of Appeals vacated an injunction against the former employee of a radio station which prevented him from wearing a chicken suit, a costume he had worn while appearing as the station's mascot. The court expressed a number of concerns regarding the injunction, including the fact that there was no showing of irreparable harm. In addition, the court addressed the fact that the employer was seeking an injunction after the term of the contract:

   In California under section 16600 [of the Business & Professions Code], even reasonableness may not save an injunction like that here. There is authority in California for enjoining employee performance, after breach of an entertainment contract, *during the term of the contract*, under Civil Code section 3423, permitting injunctions for breach of special service contracts. (See *MCA Records, Inc. v. Newton-John*, 90 Cal.App. 3d 18, 23, 153 Cal.Rptr. 153., which is discussed in Sec. 2.4, above) The court in *Newton-John*, however, expressed grave doubts whether such an injunction would be legal beyond the term of the employment contract. (*Id.* at p. 24, 153 Cal.Rptr. 153.) Those doubts are shared by the court in *Lemat Corp. v. Barry*, 275 Cal.App. 2d 671, 679, 80 Cal.Rptr. 240; see also dictum in *Loew's*

Inc. v. Cole (9th Cir. 1950) 185 F.2d 641, 657. Here the written contract of employment expired on September 15, 1979, if it was not sooner terminated, as alleged, in late May 1979.

3. As the preceding note indicates, courts tend to be hostile toward attempts of employers to prevent former employees from earning a living. This tendency is further illustrated by *Earthweb, Inc. v. Schlack,* 71 F. Supp. 2d 299 (SDNY 1999), in which the court found a one-year post-employment non-competition clause excessive where a "dot com" employee moved from one Internet-based company to another. (It should be noted that in an officially unreported opinion, which appears at 205 F.3d 1322, 2000 WL 232057 (2d Cir. 2000), the Second Circuit remanded the case to the district court for clarification concerning his grounds for denial of preliminary injunction.) The court rejected the former employer's contention that the employee would inevitably disclose the former employer's trade secrets. In *Nigra v. Young Broadcasting of Albany, Inc.,* No. 3338–98, Supreme Court, Albany County, the court ruled that an on-air personality who had performed for station WTEN for ten years, and who had strong and long-standing family ties in the Albany, New York, area, was not sufficiently unique to be barred from working for another station in the same area (at a salary considerably higher than that offered by WTEN) and should not be required to move to another area to obtain employment. However, in *Midwest Television, Inc. v. Oloffson,* 298 Ill. App. 3d 548, 699 N.E.2d 230 (Ill. App. ct. 1998), the court held that the station had demonstrated sufficient "permanence" in its relationship with its audience, and sufficient uniqueness in the on-air personality, to enforce a one-year, 100-mile non-competition radius.

4. If an injunction cannot be obtained against the performer to prevent the performer from working for a third party, can the company instead obtain an injunction against the third party to prevent the performer from working for the third party? At least in California, the answer seems to be *no.* See *Beverly Glen Music, Inc. v. Warner Communications Inc.,* 178 Cal. App. 3d 1142, 224 Cal.Rptr. 260 (Cal.Ct. App. 1986), in which the court observed that to grant an injunction preventing a second record company from utilizing the artist's services would be the functional equivalent of an injunction against the artist (which was unavailable under the California injunction statutes).

5. As to the duration of an injunction, it is generally held that the injunction will endure for the duration of the term of the contract including all unexercised option periods. See *Warner Bros Pictures v. Brodel,* 31 Cal.2d 766, 192 P.2d 949 (1948). However, English courts generally will not issue an injunction for the entire contract period, as held in *Warner Bros. Pictures v. Nelson,* 1 K.B. 209 (1937).

6. Of course, not all negative covenants seek to bar a performer totally from performing for third parties. Recording agreements typically provide that the artist will not re-record material recorded for the record label for a certain period of time, generally a number of years succeeding both the date of the recording of the material and the date of termination of the recording agreement (the clause is customarily referred to as the "rerecording restriction"). Usually, the negative covenant runs for five (5) years from the date of release of the artist's recording of the album or composition for the first label or until two (2) years after the date of termination or expiration of the term of the recording agreement with the first label, whichever is later. The purpose of this clause is to prevent an artist who has been dropped or whose contract has expired from immediately recording the same songs again for a new record label—thereby causing direct competition with recordings of the identical songs previously released on records owned by the first record company. The rationale for a minimum of a five year restrictive period is that it is thought that this period of time is sufficient for the first record label to adequately exploit its sales of such recordings, while allowing enough time to pass where the artist will probably no longer be interested in recording and releasing this old material. This period of time is generally not a problem for most artists unless the first

record label did not release or adequately market the prior recordings, or if the artist desires to immediately record and release with the new label a "live" concert recording which would normally contain many of the artist's prior "hits."

5.4 DAMAGES

The traditional remedy for breaches of entertainment industry contracts is money damages. Sometimes money damages are compensatory, sometimes they are coupled with other relief, sometimes they are punitive, sometimes they are constrained by statute, sometimes they are symbolic and nominal, sometimes they seem inadequate and sometimes the parties just don't get any damages at all.

Compensatory damages must have a reasonable foundation upon which an award may be calculated, which, in turn, requires some sort of "track record" or basis in custom and practice in the industry.

In *Freund v. Washington Square Press, Inc.*, 34 N.Y.2d 379, 357 N.Y.S.2d 857 (1974), plaintiff writer entered into an agreement with defendant publisher, granting defendant the exclusive right to publish plaintiff's book on modern drama. The agreement provided for an advance to plaintiff and royalties based on sales. Defendant had an 18 month period in which to publish a hard bound version of the book. If defendant did not publish within 18 months, the agreement terminated and the rights to the book reverted to plaintiff; plaintiff would also keep whatever monies he had received to date (i.e., the advance). Defendant did not publish the hard bound version within the 18 month period. At trial, the court found that defendant had breached the agreement and set the matter down for hearing on damages. Plaintiff sought to recover for:

"...(1) delay of his academic promotion; (2) loss of royalties which would have been earned; and (3) the cost of publication if plaintiff had made his own arrangements to publish. The trial court found that plaintiff had been promoted despite defendant's failure to publish, and that there was no evidence that the breach had caused any delay. Recovery of lost royalties was denied without discussion. The court found, however, that the cost of hardcover publication to plaintiff was the natural and probable consequence of the breach and, based upon expert testimony, awarded $10,000 to cover this cost. It denied recovery of the expenses of paperbound publication on the ground that plaintiff's proof was conjectural.

The Appellate Division (3 to 1) affirmed, finding that the cost of publication was the proper measure of damages...... It is axiomatic that, except where punitive damages are allowable, the law awards damages for breach of contract to compensate for injury caused by the breach-injury which was foreseeable, i.e., reasonably within the contemplation of the parties, at the time the contract was entered into....

In other words, so far as possible, the law attempts to secure to the injured party the benefit of his bargain, subject to the limitations that the injury—whether it be losses suffered or gains prevented—was foreseeable, and that the amount of damages claimed be measurable with a reasonable degree of certainty and, of course, adequately proven . . . But it is equally fundamental that the injured party should not recover more from the breach than he would have gained had the contract been fully performed. . . .

Measurement of damages in this case according to the cost of publication to the plaintiff would confer greater advantage than performance of the contract would have entailed to plaintiff and would place him in a far better position than he would have occupied had the defendant fully performed. Such measurement bears no relation to compensation for plaintiff's actual loss or anticipated profit. Far beyond compensating plaintiff for the interests he had in defendant's performance of the contract—whether restitution, reliance or expectation (see Fuller & Perdue, "Reliance Interest in Contract Damages," 46 Yale L.J. 52, 53–56)—an award of the cost of publication would enrich plaintiff at defendant's expense. . . .

As for plaintiff's expectation interest in the contract, it was basically two-fold—the "advance" and the royalties. (To be sure, plaintiff may have expected to enjoy whatever notoriety, prestige or other benefits that might have attended publication, but even if these expectations were compensable, plaintiff did not attempt at trial to place a monetary value on them.) There is no dispute that plaintiff's expectancy in the "advance" was fulfilled—he has received his $2,000. His expectancy interest in the royalties—the profit he stood to gain from the sale of the published book—while theoretically compensable, was speculative. Although this work is not plaintiff's first, at trial he provided no stable foundation for a reasonable estimate of royalties he would have earned had defendant not breached its promise to publish. In these circumstances, his claim for royalties fails for uncertainty. . . .

Since the damages which would have compensated plaintiff for anticipated royalties were not proved with required certainty, we agree with the dissent in the Appellate Division that nominal damages alone are recoverable. . . . Though these are damages in name only and not at all compensatory, they are nevertheless awarded as a formal vindication of plaintiff's legal right to compensation which has not been given a sufficiently certain monetary valuation. . . .

. . . In this case, unlike the typical construction contract, the value to *plaintiff* of the promised performance—publication—was a percentage of sales of books published and not the books themselves. Had the plaintiff contracted for the printing, binding and delivery of a number of hardbound copies of his manuscript, to be sold or disposed of as he wished, then perhaps the construction analogy, and measurement of damages by the cost of replacement or completion, would have some application.

Here, however, the specific value to plaintiff of the promised publication was the royalties he stood to receive from defendant's sales of the published book. . . . In this case, the consequence to plaintiff of defendant's failure to publish is that he is prevented from realizing the gains promised by the contract—the royalties. But, as we have stated, the amount of royalties plaintiff would have realized was not ascertained with adequate certainty and, as a consequence, plaintiff may recover nominal damages only.

Accordingly, the order of the Appellate Division should be modified to the extent reducing the damage award of $10,000 for the cost of publication to six cents, but with costs and disbursements to the plaintiff."

And then there are times when plaintiffs don't always get what they want, but if they try sometimes, they get what they need to quote the Rolling Stones. In *Barrera and Burgos v. Brooklyn Music, Ltd. et al*, 346

F. Supp. 2d 400; 2004 U.S. Dist LEXIS 12450 (S.D.N.Y. 2004), plaintiffs fared a bit better, but only a bit. Plaintiffs were visual artists. They developed an abstract photograph of a green silo in Vermont. They left the photo with a designer for review only. They did not authorize any use of the photo. Approximately one year later, they found the photo on the cover of a CD produced by defendant Brooklyn Music, Ltd. ("BML"). The plaintiffs then registered their copyright in the photo. Plaintiffs commenced an action for copyright infringement. Upon BML's default, the matter was set down for an assessment of damages. Plaintiffs submitted an expert witness affidavit from Gary Elsner, an expert in licensing stock photographs, in support of their damage claims. Plaintiffs claimed actual damages of $72,000 as a reasonable license fee for the photo and $1,440,000 in profits consisting of the licensing payments made to BML by K-tel International, Inc. for the rights to exploit BML's entire catalog which included the CD with plaintiffs' photo on the cover. BML did not submit any evidence in opposition to plaintiffs' claimed damages. In assessing the damages, the magistrate recommended the following:

Actual Damages

The Copyright Act states, in pertinent part: "an infringer of copyright is liable for either (1) the copyright owner's actual damages and any additional profits of the infringer, as provided by *[17 U.S.C. β 504(b)]*; or (2) statutory damages, as provided by subsection [*17 U.S.C. β 504(c)*]." *17 U.S.C. β 504(a)* ("*β 504(a)*"). Actual damages are primarily measured by "the extent to which the market value of the copyrighted work at the time of the infringement has been injured or destroyed by the infringement." See *Fitzgerald Publ'g Co., Inc. v. Baylor Publ'g Co., Inc.*, 807 F.2d 1110, 1118 (2d Cir. 1986). In appropriate circumstances, actual damages may be taken to be a reasonable license fee—that is, the fair market value of a license authorizing defendants' use of the copyrighted work. See *On Davis v. The Gap, Inc.*, 246 F.3d 152, 164–68 (2d Cir. 2001).

Typically, the plaintiffs sell prints of their work through art galleries and do not sell or license their work for commercial purposes. Since they were unfamiliar with the market for such licensed work, the plaintiffs retained Elsner, to assess the fair market value of a license to use the Photograph as the defendants did.

Elsner has extensive work experience in the stock photograph industry, [n1] extending over a period of more than thirty-five years. As a senior executive for several stock photography agencies and as the president of his own consulting company, Elsner has handled more than three hundred copyright infringement claims for both individual photographers and stock photography agencies. By virtue of his knowledge and experience in the field, the Court finds Elsner has sufficient knowledge, skill and experience in the stock photograph industry to qualify him to provide an opinion about a reasonable license fee for the defendants' use of the Photograph.

n1 "Stock photograph" refers to a photograph that is already in existence, as opposed to a newly created photographic work that a photographer is commissioned by a client to produce. See *Baker v. Urban Outfitters. Inc.*, 254 F. Supp. 2d 346, 353 (S.D.N.Y. 2003).

* * * * *

The calculation of a reasonable license fee for use of a photograph may be based on such factors as the type of use, size of use, and circulation. See *Baker,* 254 F. Supp. 2d at 353–354. In his analysis, Elsner also considers the type of media in which the Photograph is reproduced, the size of the image of the Photograph in relation to the materials in which it is used, the geographic scope of the market in which the infringing use was made, and whether the use of the photograph contains a "credit line" that completely and accurately identifies the author(s) of the photograph.

Based on these considerations and on his review of the documents, photographs, and websites relevant to this action, Elsner assesses that a reasonable license fee, assuming the use of a complete and accurate credit line, would include: 1)$2,500 for the use of the Photograph on the front and back covers of the CD, assuming worldwide distribution of not more than 100,000 CDs; 2)$3,500 for the use of the Photograph in advertisements of the CD, including those in print and on the Internet; 3)$1,000 for the use of the Photograph on the CD divider; and 4)$2,000 for the four uses within the booklet that accompanied the CD. Accordingly, Elsner computes a license fee of $9,000 ("base license fee"). Elsner states that this figure should be augmented to account for the fact that the defendants' uses of the Photograph credit Barrera only partially—with the statement "Photography by Javier"—and do not credit Burgos at all. According to Elsner, it is customary in the music industry to triple the license fee for a photograph if credit is not properly given to the photographer(s). Augmented on this basis, the license fee would be $27,000 ("augmented license fee").

The factors used by Elsner to compute the base license fee are ones that reliably could be expected to determine the value of a license for use of a stock photograph. Moreover, the inclusion of a credit line would likely have significant value to a photographer, in view of the additional notoriety and business opportunities such credit might bring. Conversely, it is reasonable to conclude that a photographer would charge a significantly higher fee to a licensee who wishes to omit a credit line from its usage of a photograph. Elsner's application of all these factors was informed by his review of pertinent materials in this action. Accordingly, the Court finds that Elsner computed the base and augmented license fees through the application of reliable principles and methods, and with sufficient bases in fact.

Elsner opines that license fee should be augmented further—by $45,000, five times the base license fee—to account for the fact that the defendants' use of the Photograph was unauthorized. He states that it is the custom and practice in the photography industry for photographers and stock photography agencies to charge such an additional fee when they discover an unauthorized use of photographs whose copyrights they hold. Elsner further explains:

> Most agencies will accept payment of a fee multiplied by either three or four times the customary license fee if the matter is immediately settled when brought to the attention of the infringing party. On occasion, a multiplier of not less than ten times the customary license fee or an amount equal to the limits of the statutory damages provided under copyright law is demanded when litigation has to be commenced in order to resolve the issues of the infringement.
> Elsner Declaration, P 11.

Since the plaintiffs have applied for actual damages, pursuant to *§ 504(a) & (b),* this additional $45,000 may only be awarded if it represents compensation for an injury caused by the defendants' infringing activities. The additional $45,000, which allegedly reflects the fact that defendants' use of the Photograph was unauthorized, cannot logically represent part of the fair market value of a license *authorizing* such use. Neither Elsner's declaration nor any of the other materials before the Court identify any other injury cognizable under *ß ß 504(a) & (b)* for which the additional $45,000 would provide compensation. The portion of Elsner's declaration quoted above suggests that a photographer or stock photography agency might demand such an additional fee in order to avoid the need to resort to litigation to resolve an infringement dispute. However, the injuries compensable through actual damages, as contemplated by *ß ß 504(a) & (b)*, do not encompass the need to engage in litigation. Other sections of the Copyright Act govern the recovery of litigation expenses for copyright infringement actions. See *17 U.S.C. ß ß 412, 505* (providing for recovery of litigation costs and a reasonable attorney's fee when certain copyright registration requirements are met). It would be inappropriate to circumvent the scheme put in place by those other provisions of the Copyright Act by awarding such compensation under the rubric of actual damages. The plaintiffs' application for damages includes a separate request for the award of litigation costs, and that request is addressed below. Accordingly, the Court finds that there is no basis in the record before the Court for the additional $45,000 in actual damages suggested by the Elsner Declaration.

In light of the foregoing, the Court finds that the plaintiffs have established actual damages of $27,000, the reasonable license fee for the defendants' use of the Photograph.

Profits from the Defendants' Infringement

In addition to actual damages, a copyright owner electing to seek damages under *ß 504(b)* is entitled to recover "any profits of the infringer that are attributable to the infringement and are not taken into account in computing the actual damages." *17 U.S.C. ß 504(b)*. The statute provides further: "in establishing the infringer's profits, the copyright owner is required to present proof only of the infringer's gross revenue, and the infringer is required to prove his or her deductible expenses and the elements of profit attributable to factors other than the copyrighted work." *Id.* However, for the purposes of *ß 504(b)*, "gross revenues" includes only "gross revenues reasonably related to the infringement, not unrelated revenues." *On Davis*, 246 F.3d at 160; *see also* Fournier v. Erickson, 242 F. Supp. 2d 318, 327 (S.D.N.Y. 2003) (holding that in a copyright action alleging that advertisements for one of defendant's software product lines made infringing use of plaintiff's work, plaintiff may offer evidence of defendant's gross revenues stemming from sales of that software product line, but not from sales of defendant's other products and services).

The plaintiffs contend that the monthly payments provided for in the 1998 Agreement are gross revenues of BML attributable to the defendants' infringement. However, under circumstances that are unclear from the record before the Court, the 1998 Agreement was terminated by the parties prior to the end of the two-year period during which contractual monthly payments were to be made. This leaves considerable doubt about what portion of the contractual monthly payments were actually made to BML. Moreover, the plaintiffs have not established that monthly payments made pursuant to the 1998 Agreement were gross revenues reasonably related to the infringement, as required by On Davis, while the amount of the payments is partly a function of the amount of royalties due to BML from K-tel for sales of BML albums licensed to K-tel, the 1998 Agreement suggests that the CD was just one of many music albums that K-tel licensed from BML since at least 1997. Moreover, the 1998 Agreement expressly states that K-tel would continue to license and distribute additional recordings owned by BML. More significantly, the principal object of the 1998 Agreement was to grant K-tel certain rights entitling it to purchase a controlling interest in BML. The contention that the funding that K-tel was to provide to BML in exchange for such rights represents gross revenues reasonably related to the sale of the CD is not plausible.

For the foregoing reasons, the Court finds that any payments made to BML by K-tel pursuant to the 1998 Agreement are not gross revenue within the meaning of β 504(b). Accordingly, the plaintiffs' application for an award of profits attributable to the defendants' infringement of the Photograph should be denied."

The magistrate denied plaintiffs' request for an award of attorney's fees and costs, stating:

"In this action, the defendants' infringement began no later than 1998, prior to the effective date of the plaintiffs' registration of their copyright in the Photograph, April 1, 1999. Thus, if the Photograph was unpublished at the time the infringement commenced, the plaintiffs are ineligible for recovery of their attorney's fee. If, on the other hand, the Photograph was published prior to the time the infringement commenced, such publication would necessarily have occurred more than three months prior to the effective date of the copyright registration. In this case, too, the plaintiffs cannot recover their attorney's fee."

Similarly, the magistrate denied plaintiffs' application for court costs, but recommended the entry of a permanent injunction against BML's use of the photo. In *Barrera and Burgos v. Brooklyn Music, Ltd.*, et al, 346 F. Supp. 2d 400; 2004 U.S. Dist LEXIS 18883 (S.D.N.Y. 2004), the Court accepted the magistrate's recommendation in part and rejected it in part, awarding plaintiffs actual damages of $27,000, no profits, no attorney's fees, a permanent injunction and court costs of $130.

NOTES _____

1. One way in which experienced creators (or, at least, creators with some negotiating power) avoid the necessity of providing a foundation for an award of damages is to include a liquidated damages clause. One such example is the so-called pay or play clause, in which the failure to utilize the services of a performer gives rise to an entitlement to a specified (or easily calculated) sum of money. In *Parker v. Twentieth Century-Fox Film Corporation*, 3 Cal.3d 176, 474 P.2d 689 (1970), actress Shirley MacLaine recovered a minimum "guaranteed compensation" of $53,571.42 per week for 14 weeks commencing May 23, 1966, for a total of $750,000, when the film she was to appear in (a musical, in which she was to be the sole lead performer) was canceled and she was offered instead the female lead in a western to be shot in Australia, a part which she declined. Because of the creative control provisions of her contract (which could not be honored due to time constraints) and the court's determination that the alternative casting was not reasonably equivalent to the part MacLaine would have played in the picture which the studio had canceled, the court held that she was entitled to invoke the pay or play clause.
2. The company can also benefit by including a pay or play clause, since, in a normal case, such a clause will protect the company against consequential damages.

However, companies sometimes attempt to avoid the obligation of paying even the pay or play amount.

3. Contract disputes which would normally give rise to contractual damages only can sometimes evolve into situations in which punitive damages are available. While film agreements almost never extend beyond a single project, the pattern in television is quite the opposite. Most talent agreements contemplate a relationship that may last several years. Quite often, actors are more or less unknown when they are engaged to perform in a series. Weekly fees will be prescribed at the outset, as will restrictions on outside activities. All at once, an actor or actress may find himself or herself a major national celebrity, and fees which once seemed astronomical may now appear minor league; similarly, restrictions on outside activities which once seemed almost academic may now prohibit the performer from taking up lucrative and/or career-enhancing projects.

Then, too, people change: they and their interests can undergo considerable transformation over time. The grueling weekly grind of series television may result in boredom, personal friction between members of the cast and/or the production staff, and other distractions. Additionally, producers may feel the need to revisit old arrangements as the fortunes of a series wax and wane.

The case of Valerie Harper illustrates the sort of problems that occur in the area of talent agreements. The *Harper* case is discussed in detail in two articles in 12 Los Angeles Lawyer (April 1989): "Valerie Harper v. Lorimar: Entertainment Industry Customs on Trial," by Barry Langberg (the attorney who successfully represented Ms. Harper) (at p. 19) and "Valerie's Version: Vindicated, Not Vengeful," by Robert M. Snider (at p. 20).

Harper commenced her work in the sitcom "Valerie" under a short-form agreement (customarily known as a "deal memo") that called for the eventual preparation of a more formal agreement containing "customary provisions" to be negotiated in good faith. Apparently, according to testimony summarized in the Langberg article, the production company never really expected to prepare a long-form agreement, a fairly common practice in the entertainment industry. (Indeed, an old industry joke used to be that you would know your series was being cancelled when you received the first draft of your long-form agreement.)

Apparently, Harper developed an idea for a sitcom, in which she would star, which received some favorable response at NBC and which was ultimately developed by Lorimar into the "Valerie" series. Because of her involvement with the creative genesis of the project, Harper was to have some measure of creative input and not merely perform as an actress, although this was not mentioned in the deal memo, which Langberg describes (at p. 20) as "standard" and which provided for a profit participation.

Over a two-year period, during which the series' ratings gradually improved, relations between Harper and Lorimar deteriorated, according to Langberg, "when the executive producers increasingly excluded Harper from the creative process." After the second season, there were negotiations concerning creative as well as monetary issues, and demand was made for the formal agreement called for by the deal memo. No formal agreement was forthcoming. Claiming that Lorimar was in breach, Harper failed to appear for the commencement of shooting for the third season, following which Lorimar brought suit seeking injunctive relief. After one episode had been filmed without her, Harper returned to work on the basis of a letter from Lorimar confirming settlement terms.

The parties' testimony differed on what occurred next. Harper claimed that she was again excluded from the creative process, while Lorimar contended that she interfered with production and was a disruptive influence. According to Langberg (at p. 21), post-trial juror interviews indicated that the jurors found that Harper was acting in good faith in an attempt to assist in achieving quality results. In any case, Harper's performance in the second episode turned out to be her last.

Lorimar amended its breach of contract action to drop its request for injunctive relief, while Harper counter-claimed for breach of contract, breach of the implied covenant of good faith and fair dealing, and certain other counts. After a jury trial, Harper and her husband, Tony Caciotti, were awarded $1.85 million in damages and a one-eighth share of (according to Snider, at p. 20) 1987 and 1988 profits of $10 to $15 million.

The case, *Lorimar Productions, Inc. v. A.V. Productions, Inc.*, L.A. Sup. Ct. Case No. WEC 115546, illustrates, according to Langberg (at p. 22) "the typical conflict between the apparently customary procedures in the entertainment industry on the one hand and the formalities of the law on the other hand." Langberg observes that legal rules "often conflict with the assumptions that one or both of the parties have made during the course of their dealings" and that "failure to execute an agreement, or leaving terms to future negotiations, opens the door to results in the courtroom that are unpredictable" (*Id.*). He further warns against "nebulous and unspecific promises, both verbally in addition to the contract and in the contract itself," such as "promises of 'creative input' or 'good faith approvals' not spelled out in specific detail" (*Id.*, p. 23).

Sometimes, the Court seems to want to award damages, but is constrained by the facts and the law from doing so.

Ronnie Greenfield et al v. Philles Records, Inc. et al 98 N.Y.2d 562; 780 N.E.2d 166; 750 N.Y.S.2d 565; 2002 N.Y. LEXIS 3146 (2002)

OPINION:

GRAFFEO, J.

In this contract dispute between a singing group and their record producer, we must determine whether the artists' transfer of full ownership rights to the master recordings of musical performances carried with it the unconditional right of the producer to redistribute those performances in any technological format. In the absence of an explicit contractual reservation of rights by the artists, we conclude that it did.

In the early 1960s, Veronica Bennett (now known as Ronnie Greenfield), her sister Estelle Bennett and their cousin Nedra Talley, formed a singing group known as "The Ronettes." They met defendant Phil Spector, a music producer and composer, in 1963 and signed a five-year "personal services" music recording contract (the Ronettes agreement) with Spector's production company, defendant Philles Records, Inc. The plaintiffs agreed to perform exclusively for Philles Records and in exchange, Philles Records acquired an ownership right to the recordings of the Ronettes' musical performances. [n1] The agreement also set forth a royalty schedule to compensate plaintiffs for their services. After signing with Philles Records, plaintiffs received a single collective cash advance of approximately $15,000.

n1 Defendants acknowledge that the agreement did not restrict the ability of the Ronettes to earn income from concert performances and appearances on television or in movies, or to sell the reproduction rights to those performances.

The Ronettes recorded several dozen songs for Philles Records, including "Be My Baby," which sold over a million copies and topped the music charts. Despite their popularity, the group disbanded in 1967 and Philles Records eventually went out of business. Other than their initial advance, plaintiffs received no royalty payments from Philles Records.

Beyond their professional relationship, however, was the story of the personal relationship between Spector and plaintiff Ronnie Greenfield. They married in 1968 but separated after a few years. Greenfield initiated a divorce proceeding against Spector in California and a settlement was reached in 1974. As part of that agreement, Spector and Greenfield executed mutual general releases that purported to resolve all past and future claims and obligations that existed between them, as well as between Greenfield and Spector's companies.

Defendants subsequently began to capitalize on a resurgence of public interest in 1960s music by making use of new recording technologies and licensing master recordings of the Ronettes' vocal performances for use in movie and television productions, a process known in entertainment industry parlance as "synchronization." The most notable example was defendants' licensing of "Be My Baby" in 1987 for use in the motion picture "Dirty Dancing." Defendants also licensed master recordings to third parties for production and distribution in the United States (referred to as domestic redistribution), and sold compilation albums containing performances by the Ronettes. While defendants earned considerable compensation from such licensing and sales, no royalties were paid to any of the plaintiffs.

As a result, plaintiffs commenced this breach of contract action in 1987, alleging that the 1963 agreement did not provide Philles Records with the right to license the master recordings for synchronization and domestic redistribution, and demanded royalties from the sales of compilation albums. Although defendants initially denied the existence of a contract, in 1992 they stipulated that an unexecuted copy of the contract would determine the parties' rights. Defendants thereafter argued that the agreement granted them absolute ownership rights to the master recordings and permitted the use of the recordings in any format, subject only to royalty rights. Following extensive pretrial proceedings (160 AD2d 458; 243 AD2d 353; 248 AD2d 212, 670 N.Y.S.2d 73), Supreme Court ruled in plaintiffs' favor and awarded approximately $ 3 million in damages and interest.

The Appellate Division affirmed, concluding that defendants' actions were not authorized by the agreement with plaintiffs because the contract did not specifically transfer the right to issue synchronization and third-party domestic distribution licenses. Permitting plaintiffs to assert a claim for unjust enrichment, the Court found that plaintiffs were entitled to the music recording industry's standard 50% royalty rate for income derived from synchronization and third-party licensing. We granted leave to appeal.

We are asked on this appeal to determine whether defendants, as the owners of the master recordings of plaintiffs' vocal performances, acquired the contractual right to issue licenses to third parties to use the recordings in connection with television, movies and domestic audio distribution. [n2] The agreement between the parties consists of a two-page document which apparently was widely used in the 1960s by music producers signing new artists. Plaintiffs executed the contract without the benefit of counsel.

The parties' immediate objective was to record and market the Ronettes' vocal performances and "make therefrom phonograph records and/or tape recordings and other similar devices (excluding transcriptions)." [n3] The ownership rights provision of the contract provides:

n2 Whether defendants were allowed to use the Ronettes' performances on compilation albums and the amount of compensation that Supreme Court awarded for that use have not been raised on appeal.

n3 "Transcriptions" were large discs used for reproducing musical performances for radio broadcasts.

'All recordings made hereunder and all records and reproductions made therefrom together with the performances embodied therein, shall be entirely [Philles'] property, free of any claims whatsoever by you or any person deriving any rights of interest from you. Without limitation of the foregoing, [Philles] shall have the right to make phonograph records, tape recordings or other reproductions of the performances embodied in such recordings by any method now or hereafter known, and to sell and deal in the same under any trade mark or trade names or labels designated by us, or we may at our election refrain therefrom.'

Plaintiffs concede that the contract unambiguously gives defendants unconditional ownership rights to the master recordings, but contend that the agreement does not bestow the right to exploit those recordings in new markets or mediums since the document is silent on those topics. Defendants counter that the absence of specific references to synchronization and domestic licensing is irrelevant. They argue that where a contract grants full ownership rights to a musical performance or composition, the only restrictions upon the owner's right to use that property are those explicitly enumerated by the grantor/artist.

Despite the technological innovations that continue to revolutionize the recording industry, long-settled common-law contract rules still govern the interpretation of agreements between artists and their record producers. [n4] The fundamental, neutral precept of contract interpretation is that agreements are construed in accord with the parties' intent (*see Slatt v Slatt*, 64 N.Y.2d 966, 967, 488 N.Y.S.2d 645, 477 N.E.2d 1099, *rearg. denied* 65 N.Y.2d 785, 482 N.E.2d 568, 492 N.Y.S.2d 1026 [1985]). "The best evidence of what parties to a written agreement intend is what they say in their writing" (*Slamow v Del Col*, 79 N.Y.2d 1016, 1018, 584 N.Y.S.2d 424, 594 N.E.2d 918 [1992]). Thus, a written agreement that is complete, clear and unambiguous on its face must be enforced according to the plain meaning of its terms (*see e.g. R/S Assocs. v New York Job Dev. Auth.*, 98 N.Y.2d 29, 32, 744 N.Y.S.2d 358, 771 N.E.2d 240, *rearg. denied* 98 NY2d 693 [2002]; *W.W.W. Assocs. v Giancontieri*, 77 N.Y.2d 157, 162, 565 N.Y.S.2d 440, 566 N.E.2d 639 [1990]).

n4 The dynamics of recording contracts were altered with the extension of federal statutory copyright protections to sound recordings in 1971. All the master recordings involved in this dispute predate that copyright statute.

Extrinsic evidence of the parties' intent may be considered only if the agreement is ambiguous, which is an issue of law for the courts to decide (*see W.W.W. Assocs. v Giancontieri*, 77 NY2d at 162). A contract is unambiguous if the language it uses has "a definite and precise meaning, unattended by danger of misconception in the purport of the [agreement] itself, and concerning which there is no reasonable basis for a difference of opinion" (*Breed v Insurance Co. of N. Am.*, 46 N.Y.2d 351, 355, 413 N.Y.S.2d 352, 385 N.E.2d 1280 [1978], *rearg. denied* 46 N.Y.2d 940 [1979]). Thus, if the agreement on its face is reasonably susceptible of only one meaning, a court is not free to alter the contract to reflect its personal notions of fairness and equity (*see e.g. Teichman v Community Hosp. of W. Suffolk*, 87 N.Y.2d 514, 520, 640 N.Y.S.2d 472, 663 N.E.2d 628 [1996]; *First Natl. Stores v Yellowstone Shopping Ctr.*, 21 N.Y.2d 630, 638, 290 N.Y.S.2d 721, 237 N.E.2d 868, *rearg. denied 22 NY2d 827* [1968]).

The pivotal issue in this case is whether defendants are prohibited from using the master recordings for synchronization, and whatever future formats evolve from new technologies, in the absence of explicit contract language authorizing such uses. Stated another way, does the contract's silence on synchronization and domestic licensing create an ambiguity which opens the door to the admissibility of extrinsic evidence to determine the intent of the parties? We conclude that it does not and, because there is no ambiguity in the terms of the Ronettes agreement, defendants are entitled to exercise complete ownership rights, subject to payment of applicable royalties due plaintiffs.

New York has well-established precedent on the issue of whether a grantor retains any rights to artistic property once it is unconditionally transferred. In *Pushman v New York Graphic Soc.* (287 N.Y. 302, 39 N.E.2d 249 [1942]), for example, this Court considered whether the common law permitted an artist who unconditionally sold a painting to enjoin the owner from making reproductions of the artwork. Citing numerous authorities for the proposition that the unconditional sale of a work of art transfers all property rights to the buyer, we held that the defendants could reproduce the painting because "an artist must, if he wishes to retain or protect the reproduction right, make some reservation of that right when he sells the painting" (id. at 308). A broad grant of ownership rights, coupled with the absence of a reservation clause, was similarly dispositive in *Burnett v Warner Bros. Pictures* (67 N.Y.2d 912, 501 N.Y.S.2d 815, 492 N.E.2d 1231 [1986], *aff g* 113 A.D.2d 710, 493 N.Y.S.2d 326). In that case, the plaintiffs had assigned all of their rights in a play that was later adapted into a movie, "Casablanca," and subsequently led to the defendant's spinoff television series. We affirmed the Appellate Division's conclusion that if "the plaintiff intended to retain certain rights, specific clauses to that effect should have been included in the agreement" because the parties' contract assigned "all imaginable rights" to *Warner Brothers* (113 A.D.2d at 712–713).

In analogous contexts, other courts have recognized that broad contractual provisions, similar to those in the Ronettes agreement, convey virtually unfettered reproduction rights to license holders in the absence of specific exceptions to the contrary. In *Boosey & Hawkes Music Publs. Ltd. v Walt Disney Co.* (145 F.3d 481 [2d Cir 1998]), the plaintiff granted distribution rights in foreign countries to Igor Stravinsky's musical composition "The Rite of Spring," including the "right, license, privilege and authority to record [the composition] in any manner, medium or form" (*id.* at 484) for use in the motion picture "Fantasia" to the Walt Disney Company. After Disney reproduced the song in videocassette and laser disc versions for foreign distribution, the plaintiff sought breach of contract damages on the basis that the agreement did not explicitly provide for distribution in new technological mediums.

The United States Court of Appeals for the Second Circuit reiterated its precedent that "'licensee[s] may properly pursue any uses which may reasonably be said to fall within the medium as described in the license'" (*id. at 486*, quoting *Bartsch v Metro-Goldwyn-Mayer,* 391 F.2d 150, 155 [2d Cir], *cert denied* 393 US 826 [1968]). As applied to the facts of *Boosey,* the Second Circuit concluded that the broad language employed in the contract granted Disney the authority to use the musical composition in the videocassette version of the movie in the absence of any contractual indication otherwise. [n5] Thus, the language of the contract was the controlling factor in interpreting the agreement:

n5 *See also Batiste v Island Records,* 179 F.3d 217, 223 (5th Cir 1999) (grant of unconditional rights to a musical composition included the licensing of a record containing a digital sample of the song), *cert denied* 528 US 1076 (2000); *Maljack Prods. v GoodTimes Home Video Corp.,* 81 F.3d 881, 885 (9th Cir 1996) (unconditional grant of motion picture music rights included right to synchronize music in videocassette format); *Ingram v Bowers,* 57 F.2d 65, 65 (2d Cir 1932) (artist failed to reserve any property interest in recordings of his musical performances); *Chambers v Time Warner,* 123 F. Supp. 2d 198, 200–201 (S.D.N.Y. 2000) (agreements permitted the conversion of master recordings to digital format), *vacated on other grounds* 282 F3d 147 (2d Cir 2002).

"If the contract is more reasonably read to convey one meaning, the party benefitted by that reading should be able to rely on it; the party seeking exception or deviation from the meaning reasonably conveyed by the words of the contract should bear the burden of negotiating for language that would express the limitation or deviation." (145 F3d at 487).

We agree with these prevalent rules of contract construction—the unconditional transfer of ownership rights to a work of art includes the right to use the work in any manner (*see generally Pushman,* 287 N.Y. at 308) unless those rights are specifically limited by the terms of the contract (*see Burnett,* 67 NY2d 912, 492 N.E.2d 1231, 501 N.Y.S.2d 815; *Boosey & Hawkes Music Publs.,* 145 F.3d at 486–487; *see generally, Hellman v Samuel Goldwyn Prods.,* 26 N.Y.2d 175, 309 N.Y.S.2d 180, 257 N.E.2d 634 [1970]). However, if a contract grants less than full ownership or specifies only certain rights to use the property, then other, unenumerated rights may be retained by the grantor (*see e.g., Warner Bros. Pictures v Columbia Broadcasting Sys.,* 216 F.2d 945, 948 [9th Cir 1954], *cert denied* 348 US 971 [1955]; *see generally Cohen v Paramount Pictures Corp.,* 845 F.2d 851 [9th Cir 1988]).

In this case, plaintiffs concede that defendants own the master recordings. Notably, the agreement explicitly refers to defendants' "right to make phonograph records, tape recordings or *other reproductions* of the performances embodied in such recordings by *any method now or hereafter known,* and to sell and deal in the same" (emphasis added). Plaintiffs contend that the breadth of the ownership provision is limited by the agreement's introductory paragraph, which states that defendants' purpose for purchasing plaintiffs' performances was to make "phonograph records and/or tape recordings and other similar devices." However, when read in conjunction with the ownership provision, a reasonable meaning emerges—the phrase "other similar devices" refers to defendants' right to reproduce the performances by any current or future technological methods. We also reject plaintiffs' assertion that the royalty schedule restricts the scope of defendants' ownership rights. That section of the agreement provides compensation rights to plaintiffs; it does not inhibit defendants' ability to use the master recordings. We therefore hold that the Ronettes agreement, "read as a whole to determine its purpose and intent" (*W.W.W. Assocs. v Giancontieri*, 77 N.Y.2d at 162), is susceptible to only one reasonable interpretation—defendants are authorized to license the performances for use in visual media, such as movies and television commercials or broadcasts, and for domestic release by third parties in audio formats.

Plaintiffs' reliance upon *B.J. Thomas v Gusto Records* (939 F.2d 395 [6th Cir], *cert denied* 502 US 984 [1991]) is misplaced. In *Thomas*, the United States Court of Appeals for the Sixth Circuit purportedly applied New York law and held that the parties' agreements were ambiguous regarding the artists' right to royalties from domestic licensing because the contracts were silent on the issue. The dispute in *Thomas*—whether the contract's compensation clause entitled the plaintiffs to royalties from the issuance of domestic licenses—is not the same as the question posed in this case, which concerns the scope of owners' rights to use their property. Furthermore, *Thomas'* suggestion that the failure of a contract to address certain categories of royalties allows a court to look beyond the four corners of the document to discern the parties' true intent conflicts with our established precedent that silence does not equate to contractual ambiguity (*see e.g. Reiss v Financial Performance Corp.*, 97 N.Y.2d 195, 199, 738 N.Y.S.2d 658, 764 N.E.2d 958 [2001]; *Trustees of Freeholders & Commonalty of Town of Southampton v Jessup*, 173 N.Y. 84, 90, 65 N.E. 949 [1903] ["an ambiguity never arises out of what was not written at all, but only out of what was written so blindly and imperfectly that its meaning is doubtful"]).

It follows that *Caldwell v ABKCO Music & Records* (269 A.D.2d 206, 703 N.Y.S.2d 97 [2000]), which cites *Thomas* for the proposition that "rights not specifically granted by an artist in an agreement are reserved to the artist and the owner of such property, absent the clearest language, is not free to do with it whatever the owner wishes" (269 A.D.2d at 207), is not to be followed. Nor does *Warner Bros. Pictures v Columbia Broadcasting Sys.* (216 F.2d 945) lead us to a different conclusion since the agreement in that case did not purport to confer full ownership rights—it was restricted to only certain aspects of the "Maltese Falcon" story.

We realize that our conclusion here effectively prevents plaintiffs from sharing in the profits that defendants have received from synchronization licensing. *However sympathetic plaintiffs' plight (Emphasis added)*, we cannot resolve the case on that ground under the guise of contract construction. Our guiding principle must be to neutrally apply the rules of contract interpretation because only in this way can we ensure stability in the law and provide guidance to parties weighing the risks and advantages of entering a binding agreement.

Defendants acknowledge that the royalty schedule for domestic sales encompasses the sale of records, compact discs and other audio reproductions by entities holding domestic third-party distribution licenses from Philles Records. In light of that concession, we remit this case to Supreme Court to recalculate plaintiffs' damages for royalties due on all such sales. Damages should be determined pursuant to the applicable schedule incorporated in the agreement rather than based on industry standards.

* * * * *

Accordingly, the order of the Appellate Division should be modified, without costs, and the case remitted to Supreme Court for further proceedings in accordance with this opinion and, as so modified, affirmed."

The damages continue to be litigated in this case. In 2005, the Appellate Division rejected plaintiffs' claim that they should be permitted to establish damages for royalties on sales of home-use audio-visual products (*Greenfield et al v. Philles Records, Inc.* et al, 16 A.D. 3d 228; 790 N.Y.S. 2d 604; 2005 N.Y. App. Div. LEXIS 2697) (1st Dept. 2005) and denied defendants' attempt to deduct foreign VAT taxes or use the prices and packaging deductions in third party agreements for the calculation of monies due plaintiffs (*Greenfield et al v. Philles Records, Inc.* et al, 2005 NY Slip Op 8613; 23 A.D. 3d 214; 803 N.Y.S. 2d 548; 2005 N.Y. App. Div. LEXIS 12382 (1st Dept. 2005)).

And then there are times when parties end up with nothing, even though they have a valid contract.

PolyGram Records, Inc. et al v. Legacy Entertainment Group, Inc., 2006 Tenn. App. LEXIS 41 (Court of Appeals of Tennessee at Nashville 2006)

OPINION: CLEMENT, J.

Three competing parties claim rights to commercially exploit performances of legendary performer Hank Williams that were recorded and broadcast by WSM Radio in the 1950s. Polygram Records, Inc., claims exclusive phonograph exploitation rights, relying on a contract Williams entered into with its predecessor in interest, MGM Records. Legacy Entertainment Group, LLC., claims rights of exploitation to the recordings under a chain of title. Williams' heirs, Hank Williams, Jr., and Jett Williams, contend neither Legacy nor Polygram have contractual rights to exploit Williams' performances embodied in the WSM recordings, and further contend the rights passed to his heirs. The trial court summarily dismissed the claims of Polygram and Legacy, finding neither own rights to exploit the recorded performances, and the rights belong to Williams' heirs. Legacy and Polygram appeal. We affirm the trial court.

OPINION

From 1947 through January of 1953, Hank Williams was under contract with MGM Records, Inc. [n1] during which term Williams assigned unto MGM his "exclusive personal services . . . for the purpose of making phonograph records . . ." During the same period, specifically 1951 and 1952, Hank Williams and his band, The Drifting Cowboys, frequently performed live and by pre-recordings on a WSM radio program known as Mother's Best Flour. The pre-recordings were preserved on acetate records [n2] for broadcast on days Williams and the Drifting Cowboys were on tour or otherwise unavailable. WSM only used the acetate recordings to facilitate daily broadcasts of the Mother's Best Flour program; it never exploited the acetate recordings to produce phonograph records.

n1 Williams entered into three separate recording contracts with MGM Records. He signed the first one, which was for a one year term, on March 6, 1947, and it took effect April 1, 1947. The second and third contracts were for two year terms each and had identical language as the first. The second and third contracts spanned from 1949–1952.

n2 Radio acetate transcriptions were defined in one of the parties' briefs as "large discs used for reproducing musical performances on radio stations." *See Greenfield v. Philles Records, 98 N.Y.2d 562, 780 N.E.2d 166, 750 N.Y.S.2d 565 (N.Y. 2002).*

In 1997, Legacy Entertainment Group acquired the 1951 and 1952 acetate recordings for the purpose of producing and selling compact disc formats of Williams' performances from the Mother's Best Flour program. Legacy acquired the acetate recordings from Hillous Butrum, who had acquired the recordings from Les Leverett, a former employee of WSM. Leverett, who worked as a photographer for WSM, found the recordings in or near a trash bin at WSM in the 1960s when the radio station was moving its offices. Though it is not fully evident from the record, apparently WSM was discarding a lot of its possessions during the move, the acetate recordings of the Mother's Best Flour program being some of many discards. Leverett dug through the trash bin, [n3] retrieved some of the acetate recordings and took them home for his personal collection. After letting them collect dust for several years, Leverett sold to Butrum whatever interest, if any, he had in the recordings.

n3 There is some discrepancy over whether the Mother's Best Flour recordings had actually made it into the trash bin before Leveret acquired them, but all parties agree that WSM had at least expressed its intention to dispose of them.

As Legacy was preparing to commercially exploit the Mother's Best Flour performances of Hank Williams by producing and selling them on compact discs, the technological progeny of phonograph records, Polygram learned of Legacy's intentions and informed

Legacy that Polygram owned the exclusive exploitation rights of Williams' performances for phonograph records and compact discs. After discussions between Polygram and Legacy failed, Polygram filed this action against Legacy, claiming it had the exclusive rights to exploit the recordings. Hank Williams, Jr. and Jett Williams, as Hank Williams' heirs, joined Polygram as co-plaintiffs against Legacy, claiming they succeeded to Hank Williams' rights in the recordings, and in addition thereto, the rights of publicity in his name and likeness.

In April of 2000, the trial court summarily dismissed Polygram's claims finding it had no property interest in the recordings. Subsequently, in 2003, Legacy and the heirs filed cross motions for summary judgment. The trial court ruled in favor of the heirs and dismissed Legacy's claims. Polygram and Legacy appeal those rulings.

* * * *

ANALYSIS

The parties present a total of eleven issues, the essence of most of which are substantially similar. We have, therefore, recast those issues we have identified as dispositive in order to facilitate a more cohesive assessment of the matters at issue on appeal.

Legacy's Claims

Legacy claims it owns the right to commercially exploit several recordings of performances by Hank Williams from the WSM radio program, Mother's Best Flour. This claim is based on a chain of title that is comprised of many links. Unfortunately for Legacy, some critical links are missing, the absence of which is fatal to its claim.

The chain of title Legacy relies on comprises a long and windy road during which there was a brief stop in a trash can at a radio station. If a song were written about this matter favorable to Legacy's claim, it might be entitled, "I Found a Gold Mine in the Radio Station Trash." Indeed, although Legacy may have acquired certain tangible rights to WSM's acetate tapes, and the performances by Hank Williams from the 40s and 50s embodied therein are golden, the gold attendant to Hank Williams' performances may not be mined by Legacy. Accordingly, an appropriate title attributable to Legacy's claim would be, "Your Bucket Has a Hole in It."

Legacy's chain of title begins with the relationship between Hank Williams and radio station WSM, which broadcast the Mother's Best Flour and made acetate recordings to facilitate the broadcasts in Hank Williams' absence, when he was on the road. The evidence in the record is undisputed that the recordings were solely for the purpose of broadcasting Hank Williams' performance on the Mother's Best Flour show in his absence and that WSM never used the recordings for any other purpose, nor did anyone else. Evidence of the fact WSM had no further use of the acetate recordings or the performances embodied therein, the acetate recordings were discarded in the 1960s by WSM during its move from downtown Nashville.

It was while the acetate recordings were awaiting their intended disposition by the janitorial staff that Les Leverett, an employee of WSM [n4] noticed them. Leverett requested permission to keep the recordings for himself. Receiving a favorable reply, though no contractual rights of any kind or character from WSM, Leverett removed the recordings from the trash and took them home, where they collected dust for several years. On July 12, 1982, Hillous Butrum, a former band member of the Drifting Cowboys, entered into a contract with Leverett whereby he acquired the acetates and "All right, title and interest Leverett has in and to said taped radio shows,. . . . " The agreement between Butrum and Leverett provided that Butrum would endeavor to exploit the recordings and then pay Leverett 40% of all monies earned. [n5]

n4 Leverett was not an executive or officer of WSM; he was employed as a photographer for WSM.

n5 Butrum explained in his deposition the economic deal with Legacy was conditioned upon Legacy getting the requisite consent from the Williams estate to exploit Williams' performances. We have not considered this evidence for purposes of our opinion because the Chancellor granted Legacy's motion to have all of Butrum's deposition excluded because Butrum died before his deposition was completed. Nevertheless, we add this footnote so that others will not mistakenly believe Butrum intended to exploit Williams' performances without the consent of the Williams estate.

Butrum, however, did not intend to exploit Williams' performances as originally recorded. He planned to enhance the acetate recordings by removing "skips" and hissing noises present in the originals and by adding additional background music. After Butrum dubbed the additional music and voice overs, he filed for and obtained copyrights for the re-mixed recordings. Thereafter, Butrum sold the acetate recordings along with the re-mixed masters and copyrights therein to Legacy pursuant to a written contract dated September 12, 1997.

The evidence in the record established for purposes of summary judgment that Legacy acquired physical possession, if not some fashion of ownership of the tangible components of the acetate recordings. [n6] Moreover, the evidence established for purposes of summary judgment that Legacy acquired whatever legal rights and interests, if any, Butrum and Leverett had in the recordings. However, the record is devoid of any evidence showing that Butrum or Leverett owned any right, title or interest in the intangible property rights to the performances of Hank Williams preserved by the acetates.

n6 With this statement, we are not declaring that Legacy has a right to the physical acetates, but only that they may have acquired such a right. We will not give a ruling regarding the lawful owner of the physical acetates because that issue is not before us.

Possession of a tangible embodiment of a work or performance such as the recordings at issue conveys no rights or ownership interests to the intangible rights embodied therein, especially the right to commercially exploit the performances embodied therein. The Supreme Court of the United States has clearly drawn this distinction between tangible rights and intangible rights. In a case wherein the rights to a book were at issue, the Court explained:

Even the transfer of the manuscripts of a book will not, at common law, carry with it a right to print and publish the work, without the express consent of the author, as the property of the manuscript, and the right to multiply the copies, are two separate and distinct interests.

Stephens v. Cady, 55 U.S. 528, 530–531, 1852 WL 6761, 14 L. Ed. 528 (1852)
[citations omitted.]

Accordingly, we must examine Legacy's claim realizing the rights it acquired to the physically tangible acetate recordings are distinct from the rights it acquired, if any, to exploit the performances recorded therein.

Legacy claims to have acquired intangible rights to the performances when it acquired the recordings from Butrum. It also contends it acquired copyrights to the performances embodied in the recordings; however, the record does not establish that it acquired any copyrights in the recordings or performances therein except for those owned by Butrum. As for Butrum's copyright interests, the record provides little information other than the copyright registration numbers associated with Butrum's copyrights. Even though the record is incomplete, it is evident Butrum's copyrights only pertain to the enhancements by Butrum, which afforded Butrum, and thus Legacy, no copyright ownership interest in the original performances by Hank Williams. As Butrum dubbed background music onto the original recordings and made other improvements thereto, whatever copyrights Butrum may have would be limited to his "derivative work," exclusive of the original performances. "The copyright in a derivative work extends only to the material contributed by the author of such work, as distinguished from the preexisting material employed in the work, and does not imply any exclusive right in the preexisting material." *Murray Hill Publications, Inc. v. ABC Communications, Inc.*, 264 F.3d 622, 630 (6th Cir. 2001) (quoting *17 U.S.C. β 103(b)*). Accordingly, the copyright Legacy acquired from Butrum was most limited; it only pertained to Butrum's contributions, and thus did not constitute a copyright interest to the original performances of Hank Williams.

Legacy may have acquired certain tangible rights in the WSM tapes Leverett retrieved from the trash at WSM. Moreover, it may have acquired the copyrights of Butrum, limited as they are. Nevertheless, there is no evidence to support Legacy's claim that it acquired any rights to the performances of Hank Williams embodied in the recordings.

Moreover, there is no evidence to support Legacy's claim that it acquired rights to exploit the name and likeness of Hank Williams in association with the WSM recordings. This novel claim is based on the absence of proof that Williams retained such rights in his contract with WSM for the 1951 and 1952 performances. We find this claim is also without merit.

Tennessee recognizes the property right in the use of one's name, photograph or likeness. This property right is identified as the "right of publicity." In commenting on the nature of the right of publicity, this court has stated,

the recognition of individual property rights is deeply embedded in our jurisprudence. These rights are recognized in *Article I, Section 8 of the Tennessee Constitution* and have been called "absolute" by the Tennessee Supreme Court. . . . In its broadest sense, property includes all rights that have value. It embodies all the interests a person has in land and chattels that are capable of being possessed and controlled to the exclusion of others. Chattels include intangible personal property such as choses in action or other enforceable rights of possession. . . . Tennessee's common law thus embodies an expansive view of property. Unquestionably, a celebrity's right of publicity has value. It can be possessed and used. It can be assigned, and it can be the subject of a contract. Thus, there is ample basis for this Court to conclude that it is a species of intangible personal property.

State ex rel Elvis Presley v. Crowell, 733 S.W.2d 89, 96–97 (Tenn. Ct. App. 1987)
(citations omitted).

The right of publicity was adopted by the General Assembly of Tennessee as a result of the foregoing controversy.

(a) Every individual has a property right in the use of that person's name, photograph, or likeness in any medium in any manner.
(b) The individual rights provided for in subsection (a) constitute property rights and are freely assignable and licensable, and do not expire upon the death of the individual so protected, whether or not such rights were commercially exploited by the individual during the individual's lifetime, but shall be descendible to the executors, assigns, heirs, or devisees of the individual so protected by this part.

Tenn. Code Ann. β 47–25–1103.

We are unwilling to infer, indeed to jump to the illogical conclusion that Hank Williams assigned these rights without limitation based on the mere fact his heirs cannot establish that the 1951 informal agreement with WSM provided to the contrary. [n7] Moreover, we concur with the trial court's finding that these rights belong to the heirs of Hank Williams. *See Presley, 733 S.W.2d at 96–97* (holding that a celebrity's right of publicity is survivable at death and passes to the celebrity's heirs).

n7 *See Gracey v. Maddin,* 769 S.W.2d 497 (Tenn. Ct. App. 1989) wherein this court declined to infer, in the absence of an agreement from the individual or his estate, the assignment of the right to the use of his name as an asset of the partnership, after retirement or death, without proof of the individual's consent.

We therefore affirm the dismissal of the claims of Legacy Entertainment Group, LLC.

Polygram's Claim

Polygram claims it has the exclusive rights to exploit as phonograph records (including compact discs) [n8] the 1951 and 1952 recordings of Hank Williams embodied in the acetate recordings of Mother's Best Flour. Polygram's claim hinges on the 1947 contract between MGM

Records and Hank Williams, to which Polygram is the successor in interest to MGM's rights. The trial court found no genuine issue of material fact that would allow Polygram to have an interest in the Mother's Best Flour recordings. We agree with the trial court.

n8 This is based on the provision in the agreement that MGM "shall have the right to make records or other reproductions of the performances embodied in such recordings by any method now or hereafter known, . . . "

Because Polygram's claim hinges entirely on the contract between MGM Records and Hank Williams, an examination of the rights and responsibilities of the parties to the contract is necessary. "The purpose of interpreting a written contract is to ascertain and to give effect to the contracting parties' intentions." *Marshall v. Jackson & Jones Oils, Inc.*, 20 S.W.3d 678, 681 (Tenn. Ct. App. 1999) (citing *Bob Pearsall Motors, Inc. v. Regal Chrysler-Plymouth, Inc.*, 521 S.W.2d 578, 580 (Tenn. 1975) (other citations omitted). To discern the intentions of MGM and Williams, we must consider the four corners of the contract, the circumstances in which the contract was made, and the parties' actions in carrying out the contract, *see Marshall*, 20 S.W.3d at 681, and give the words of the contract their usual and ordinary meaning." *Gredig v. Tennessee Farmers Mutual Ins. Co.*, 891 S.W.2d 909, 912 *(Tenn. Ct. App. 1994)* (citing *St. Paul Surplus Lines Ins. Co. v. Bishops Gate Ins. Co.*, 725 S.W.2d 948, 951 *(Tenn. Ct. App. 1986))* (other citations omitted).

The contract between Williams and MGM was in the form of a letter from MGM to Williams employing Williams' "exclusive personal services . . . for the purpose of making phonograph records, as [MGM] may require." The contract also provided, "during the period of this contract [Williams] will not perform for the purpose of making phonograph records for any person other than [MGM]. . . . "

Polygram claims its predecessor in interest, MGM, had an "exclusive services" contract with Williams that included the period when the Mother's Best Flour performances were recorded. We agree with this claim but only to the extent the exclusivity pertains to recordings made for the purpose of making phonograph records. We have considered the language of the contract on which Polygram wants us to focus our attention. That portion reads, "All recordings and all records and reproductions made therefrom, together with the performances embodied therein, shall be entirely our property, free of any claims whatsoever by you or any person deriving any right or interest from you." We, however, may not restrict our reading to this one excerpt because we must look to the four corners of the contract to appreciate the intentions of the parties. *See Marshall, 20 S.W.3d at 681.* In considering the entire contract, we find it significant that the first page of the contract places its focus on "*recordings made for the purpose of making phonograph records.*" (Emphasis added).

Although the contract provided that Williams could not perform for anyone else "for the purpose of making phonograph records," nothing in the contract affords MGM or Polygram the present right to exploit recordings of performances by Hank Williams that were for purposes other than producing phonograph records, such as a pre-recorded radio broadcast. [n9] Moreover, there is no evidence in the record to establish that the Mother's Best Flour performances were recorded for the purpose of making phonograph records. Accordingly, the trial court correctly found the performances by Hank Williams embodied in the Mother's Best Flour acetate recordings did not fall within the purview of the contract between MGM and Hank Williams. [n10] We therefore affirm the summary dismissal of Polygram's claims.

n9 Whether Polygram had the legal right to preclude others from exploiting the 1951 and 1952 performances as phonograph records or compact discs is a different issue. We recognize that another provision of the MGM agreement precluded Williams from performing any musical compositions recorded under the MGM agreement "for the purpose of making phonograph records, within five years after our recording is made. . . . " The five year exclusivity period has long since expired; thus the provision is inapplicable to the matters at issue, and we decline to volunteer an advisory opinion.

n10 Polygram contends the trial court misunderstood the nature of the rights Polygram was asserting. The trial court held that Polygram's "claims depend upon its having a property interest in those recordings. . . . " This, however, is not a misunderstanding because Polygram would need at the very least an intangible property interest in the recordings to have a claim. The trial court's failure to use the word intangible does not mean it misunderstood the nature of Polygram's asserted rights. Polygram's claim could only be sustained if it had a property interest in the recordings, intangible or otherwise, and the contract between MGM and Williams does not afford Polygram that interest.

Rights Possessed By The Heirs Of Hank Williams

In addition to summarily dismissing the claims of Legacy and Polygram, the trial court granted summary judgment in favor of the heirs of Hank Williams, concluding there was no genuine dispute of material fact as to the heirs' ownership of the rights to control the use of and/or exploit Hank Williams' performances in the acetate recordings of the Mother's Best Flour radio broadcasts. The trial court's dismissal of all claims of Legacy and Polygram based upon the conclusions that neither has any right or interest in the recordings at issue, and our affirmance thereof, renders the issue moot because neither Legacy or Polygram have standing to challenge the rights of the heirs of Hank Williams.

IN CONCLUSION

The judgment of the trial court is affirmed in all respects, and costs of appeal are assessed against Polygram Records, Inc. and Legacy Entertainment Group, LLC.

This is the first page of the contract (see page 521) at issue:

The first paragraph reads: "This contract for the personal services of musicians is made between Loew's Incorporated (M. G. M. Records Division) as the employer and you and the musicians who make up the orchestra represented by you as leader."

The second paragraph reads: "We hereby employ the exclusive personal services of you and such musicians individually, and the musicians will perform together for us under your leadership for the purpose of making phonograph records, as we may require."

The last paragraph reads: "During the period of this contract you will not perform for the purpose of making phonograph records for any person

MGM RECORDS

A DIVISION OF LOEW'S INCORPORATED

701 SEVENTH AVENUE
NEW YORK 19, NEW YORK
PHONE: CIRCLE 7-7900

March 6, 1947

Mr. [illegible] Williams
c/o [illegible]
[illegible]
Nashville 3, Tenn.

Dear Mr. Williams:

This contract for the personal services of musicians is made between Loew's Incorporated (M. G. M. Records, Division) as the employer and you and the musicians who make up the orchestra represented by you as leader.

We hereby employ the exclusive personal services of you and such musicians individually, and the musicians shall perform together for us under your leadership for the purpose of making phonograph records, as we may require.

Recordings will be made at recording sessions in studios designated by us at mutually agreeable times. A minimum of 8 record sides shall be recorded during the period of this contract, and additional recordings shall be made at our election. The musical compositions to be recorded shall be mutually agreed upon between you and us, and each recording shall be subject to our approval as satisfactory, for manufacture and sale. As to each recording session a separate Form B contract shall be entered into. No recording shall be made by dubbing.

We will pay you in respect of recordings made hereunder, [redacted] on both sides thereof, and [redacted] records sold embodying performances hereunder on only one side thereof; [redacted] Royalties for records sold outside of the United States [redacted] are to be payable only when [redacted] are received by us in the United States. [redacted]

For the services of the musicians hereunder, we will make a non-returnable payment to the musicians within fourteen days after the services are rendered, [redacted]; and such payments shall be charged against your royalties when earned. We will render an accounting to you within forty-five days after February 28th and after August 31st of each year during which records made hereunder are sold.

During the period of this contract you will not perform for the purpose of making phonograph records for any person other than us, and after the expiration of this contract you will not perform any musical compositions recorded hereunder for any other person for the purpose of making phonograph records, within five years after our recording is made; and you acknowledge that your services are unique

other than us, and after the expiration of this contract you will not perform any musical compositions recorded hereunder for any other person
for the purpose of making phonograph records within five years after our
recording is made; and you acknowledge that your services are unique
and extraordinary."

At least one of the parties plans to appeal.

One caveat to remember: the Williams contract is ancient by recording industry standards and contains none of the all-encompassing grant
of rights language that contemporary recording contracts have (i.e. "to
manufacture, sell, lease, license, distribute and advertise and otherwise
fully exploit the Masters in any and all media and by any method now
or hereafter known in any field or manner of use involving sound alone
or sight and sound together both directly to consumers and indirectly
through distributors, dealers, resellers, agents and other third parties") or broad language regarding exclusivity (i.e., "Company hereby
engages Artist's exclusive services as a recording artist in connection
with the production of master recordings ("Masters") embodying the
original performances of Artist and Artist hereby accepts such engagement and agrees to exclusively render such services to Company during
the Term hereof and all extensions and renewals").

5.5 BANKRUPTCY

5.5.1 The Availability of Bankruptcy Protection

In re Watkins, 210 B.R. 394 (N.D. Ga. 1997)

Creditors moved to dismiss recording artists' Chapter 11 cases as bad
faith filings. The Bankruptcy Court, Stacey Cotton, Chief Judge, held
that Chapter 11 cases filed by successful recording artists p/k/a "TLC",
when negotiations with their former manager and related production
and publishing companies and record company broke down, were
not filed solely in attempt to reject their existing management, publishing, production and recording agreements, and therefore did not
have to be dismissed as "bad faith" filings. Motions of LaFace Records,
Pebbitone, Inc. and Perri Reid denied.

ORDER

Before the court are movant LaFace Records' ("LaFace") Motion
to Dismiss or Abstain, and movant Pebbitone, Inc. and Perri Reid
d/b/a Pebbitone Music's (collectively, "Pebbitone") Motion to
Dismiss. LaFace and Pebbitone contend that Tionne Watkins
("Watkins"), Lisa Lopes ("Lopes"), and Rozonda Thomas ("Thomas")
p/k/a "TLC" (collectively, "Debtors" or "TLC") did not file their
respective Chapter 11 petitions in good faith. Upon review of the
authorities and evidence presented, the court found and concluded
the following.

FACTS

Debtors Watkins and Lopes signed a Production Agreement with Pebbitone dated February 28, 1991. At or about the same time, they entered into an Exclusive Songwriter's Agreement and a Co-Publishing Agreement (collectively, "Songwriting Agreement") with Pebbitone Music. The Production and Songwriting Agreements were amended on April 2, 1991, to reflect the addition of Debtor Thomas. Debtors and Movant Perri Reid also entered into a Management Agreement with the members of TLC. [Note: The production and publishing companies were owned by personal manager Perri Reid, who was the wife of L.A. Reid, president of LaFace Records]. On May 10, 1991, Movants Pebbitone Inc. and LaFace entered into a Recording Agreement granting LaFace exclusive rights to distribute Debtors' recordings and use the name "TLC" in the sale, promotion or exploitation of such recordings. Thereafter, "TLC" signed an undated Inducement Letter with LaFace guarantying performance and delivery of up to seven (7) albums should Pebbitone fail to deliver them under certain circumstances. Pursuant to those agreements, Debtors began recording and performing under the group name "TLC" and have enjoyed tremendous success as one of the largest selling female groups in the music business.

In the ensuing years, tension and disagreements developed between Debtors and Pebbitone. Debtors terminated their management relationship with Perri Reid and employed Hiram Hicks as their personal manager in 1993. Debtors also employed entertainment counsel, Stephen Barnes ("Barnes"), to renegotiate the contract or a buy-out of the Pebbitone Production Agreement. Apparently those efforts continued until they reached an impasse in May 1995. At that time, Pebbitone granted LaFace the right to negotiate directly with Debtors, subject to its approval. LaFace commenced negotiations with Debtors, through counsel, but made little progress. In June 1995, Debtors' counsel advised LaFace for the first time that Debtors were contemplating the filing of bankruptcy petitions. Counsel also indicated that Debtors would seek to reject their contracts with Movants. At the request of LaFace, the case filings were delayed for a short period; however, on July 3, 1995, Debtors filed their respective Chapter 11 cases.

During the period immediately preceding the filing, several conversations occurred between Barnes and representatives of LaFace and Pebbitone. On June 28 and June 30, letters were exchanged between Clifford Lovette ("Lovette") of LaFace, Pebbitone's attorney, Kenneth Kraus ("Kraus"), and Barnes. These letters reflect a growing tension between the parties that appears to have arisen, in part, from the disclosure of Debtors' contemplated bankruptcy filings. Prior to and during negotiations, Debtors were experiencing financial problems. They found it necessary to obtain loans from LaFace in March 1995 as follows: Watkins-$88,815.41; Lopes-$147,291.45; and Thomas-$113,815.40. These loans were evidenced by demand promissory notes. If not paid on demand, the notes are payable directly from Debtors' royalties. The LaFace loan proceeds generally were used to catch up on delinquent bills and arrearage payments. For example: The undisputed testimony of Debtors and their accountant, Bruce Kolbrenner ("Kolbrenner"), establishes that each Debtor was behind on car payments, house payments, credit cards payments, automobile insurance payments, or other similar liabilities. Each testified that their financial problems had begun as early as 1994. They were continually confronted with difficulties in meeting monthly payments and were constantly behind in paying their debts. On several accounts, Debtors were delinquent in excess of three months. Prior to July 1995, Debtors received six Pebbitone royalty statements for the period commencing in 1991 and ending December 31, 1994. The December 31, 1994 statement was the latest received prior to commencement of Debtors' cases. It reflects a negative balance of $576,828.98. This statement was amended post-petition to increase the negative balance to $827,695.12.

While LaFace conveyed to Debtors' counsel a willingness to make further funding advances to assist Debtors with regard to their financial problems, however, no amount was specified or provided. Nevertheless, each Debtor concluded that she needed to file a Chapter 11 case and create the potential for modification and rejection of their music industry contracts.

DISCUSSION

The issue before the court is whether Debtors' petitions were filed in good faith. This issue has been considered on several occasions by the Eleventh Circuit. *See, In re Dixie Broadcasting, Inc.,* 871 F.2d 1023 (11th Cir.1989), *cert. denied, Dixie Broadcasting, Inc. v. Radio WBHP, Inc.,* 493 U.S. 853, 110 S.Ct. 154, 107 L.Ed.2d 112 (1989); *In re Waldron,* 785 F.2d 936 (11th Cir.1986), *cert. dismissed sub nom., Waldron v. Shell Oil Co.,* 478 U.S. 1028, 106 S.Ct. 3343, 92 L.Ed.2d 763 (1986); *and In re Albany Partners, Ltd.,* 749 F.2d 670 (11th Cir.1984). In *Albany Partners,* the Eleventh Circuit instructs that: Although "good faith" is required for confirmation of a reorganization plan, *11 U.S.C. § 1129(a)(3), Chapter 11* does not expressly condition the right to file or maintain a proceeding on the "good faith" of the debtor when the proceeding is initiated. However, *§1112(b)* of the Code permits a bankruptcy court to convert or dismiss a case for "cause". The provision lists nine examples of cause, but the list is not exhaustive. The pertinent legislative history states, "The court will be able to consider other factors as they arise, and use its equitable powers to reach an appropriate result in individual cases." H.R.Rep. No. 595, 95 Cong., 1st Sess. 406 (1977), U.S.Code Cong. & Admin. News 1978, pp. 5787, 6362. Accordingly, the determination of cause under *§1112(b)* is "subject to judicial discretion under the circumstances of each case." *In the Matter of Nancant,* 8 B.R. 1005, 1006 (Bankr. D.Mass.1981).The equitable nature of this determination supports the construction that a debtor's lack of "good faith" may constitute cause for dismissal of a petition.

In *Waldron,* it posited: "The Bankruptcy laws are intended as a shield, not as a sword." *In re Penn Central Transportation Co.,* 458 F.Supp. 1346, 1356 (E.D.Pa.1978). Congress could not have intended that the debt free financially secure [debtors] be permitted to engage the bankruptcy machinery solely to avoid an enforceable contract. *785 F.2d at 940.* Other courts have held that the court should not permit rejection or avoidance of contracts simply because a better offer has become available. *See, Matter of Northwest Place Ltd.,* 73 B.R. 978 (Bankr. N.D.Ga.1987) (Kahn, J.), *aff'd., In re Northwest Place Ltd.,* 108 B.R. 809 (N.D.Ga.1988); *In re Southern California Sound Systems, Inc.,* 69 B.R. 893 (Bankr.S.D.Cal.1987); *In re Carrere,* 64 B.R. 156 (Bankr.C.D.Cal.1986).

Further, in *In re Dixie Broadcasting, Inc.,* the Eleventh Circuit held that "[a]lthough there is no precise test for determining bad faith, courts have recognized factors which show 'an intent to abuse the judicial process and the purposes of the reorganization provisions.'" *871 F.2d at 1027* (citations omitted). In considering the question of bad faith, courts have noted a number of factors that may be indicia of bad faith. *See, e.g., In re Dixie Broadcasting, Inc.,* 871 F.2d at 1027; *In re Phoenix Piccadilly, Ltd.,* 849 F.2d 1393, 1394 (11th Cir.1988); *In re Natural Land Corp.,* 825 F.2d 296, 298 (11th Cir.1987); *In re Davidoff,* 185 B.R. 631, 635–636 (Bankr.S.D.Fla.1995); *Matter of Northwest Place Ltd.,* 73 B.R. at 981. The court will only consider those factors that have been raised or that the court deems applicable in these cases.

Movants argue that Debtors' petitions were not filed in good faith. They assert that Debtors are not financially distressed and experienced no serious creditor pressure prior to their case filings; that Debtors misled the court by failing to schedule certain assets, by scheduling inaccurate values, and by overstating their liabilities; that Debtors failed to adjust their extravagant lifestyles post-petition and continued to make payments to insiders; that Debtors engaged in certain post-petition actions which indicate bad faith; and that the true impetus behind Debtors' case filings is their desire to reject Movants' contracts.

1. *Whether Debtors Were Financially Distressed*

Movants assert that creditors holding the greater dollar amount of each Debtor's indebtedness had made no demands for payment. It is undisputed that Debtors' largest obligations are held by LaFace, Pebbitone or industry professionals, [i.e . . . .managers, publishers, and record and production companies . . .]. None of these creditors were pressuring Debtors for payment. However, the negative royalty balance due Pebbitone is payable only from royalties. LaFace's indebtedness is evidenced by demand notes which, if not paid when due, are also recoverable from Debtors' royalties. All such royalties flow directly through the hands of Movants, LaFace and Pebbitone. Thus, there was no need for Movants to pressure Debtors. They controlled the source and payment of Debtors' royalties. Similarly, the professionals, advisors and managers were so intricately involved or related to the music industry and the management of Debtors' business and financial affairs that they too had no real need to press for payment.

The undisputed testimony of Debtors and their accountant establishes that each Debtor was experiencing difficulty in making automobile payments, house payments, credit card payments, automobile insurance payments, or other similar liabilities. Each Debtor scheduled one or more automobile finance or lease creditors, a real property mortgage creditor and utilities, credit card and telephone creditors. Ms. Lopes and Ms. Watkins also scheduled medical obligations. These creditors comprise the majority in number, but a minority in total amount of indebtedness. Beginning as early as 1994, Debtors were consistently behind or experiencing financial difficulty in meeting their monthly obligations. On some of their accounts, Debtors experienced delinquencies of three or more months. In fact, when loans were obtained from LaFace, the proceeds were used to catch up delinquent bills and arrearage payments.

Ms. Watkins used the LaFace loan proceeds to purchase an automobile and to pre-pay her rent for one year because she was concerned about a place to live and the uncertainty of having sufficient funds to pay her monthly rental payments. She also had one suit pending. Ms. Thomas was being pressed by credit card companies demanding payment. She also faced uncertainty regarding her ability to pay bills from month-to-month. Her schedules reflect that at least one of her accounts was in the hands of a collection agency. When asked how Debtors came to the decision to file for relief, she stated that "[we pulled] out our pockets with nothing in them. That is exactly how we decided. None of us could pay our bills." Ms. Lopes testified that her delinquent payment history resulted in additional creditor pressure as future payments became due. She expressed great concern over her inability to pay her bills. She appeared convinced that relief in this court was necessary because she didn't have money in the past and "had financial trouble for about . . . two years." Further, she was facing foreclosure on the Diamond Circle property, and she had been sued by two other creditors. Thus, each Debtor credibly testified that she was receiving regular and consistent pressure from creditors.

It was, therefore, the non-industry and non-professional creditors who were pressing Debtors for payment. By their very nature, these obligations represented debts which most affected each Debtor's daily life. The fact that Movants and industry professionals had no need to press for payment does not negate the existence of pressure from other creditors. The court finds that each Debtor was, in fact, experiencing *bona fide* financial distress and creditor pressure that warranted Chapter 11 relief.

2. *Debtors' Solvency*

There is no insolvency requirement for a Title 11 case. As stated in a leading bankruptcy treatise: It is worth noting that a chapter 7 "debtor" need not be insolvent to be eligible for chapter 7 relief. Nor does the standard established for those persons who "may be" a debtor under chapter 7 contain any specific or implied requirement that such persons be heavily burdened by debts. Under this subdivision any person not within the excluded class who owes debts in any amount, no matter how small, may file a petition for liquidation. [L. King, *2 Collier on Bankruptcy* §109.02 at 109–11 (15th ed.1996)]. With a few non-relevant exceptions, a person eligible for relief under Chapter 7 is eligible for relief under Chapter 11 of the Bankruptcy Code. *11 U.S.C. §109(d)*.

Further, creditors filing an involuntary petition need only show that a debtor is not paying such person's debts as they become due. *11 U.S.C. §303(h)(1)*. In the court's view, Congress has not imposed a greater burden upon a voluntary debtor than an involuntary debtor. Although a debtor's assets may exceed liabilities, the debtor's income or cash flow may be insufficient to pay those debts as they become due. Such debtor is, nevertheless, financially distressed because of the inability to pay. The court finds that each of these Debtors was unable to pay her debts as they matured. Further, based upon their known financial circumstances, Debtors believed themselves to be insolvent. *Section 303(h)(1)* provides . . . [T]he court shall order relief . . . only if (1) the debtor is generally not paying such debtor's debts as such debts become due . . . ; The evidence indicates that two debtors, Ms. Thomas and Ms. Watkins, may have become solvent post-petition. This results from the post-petition accrual of royalties sufficient to satisfy Pebbitone's negative royalty balance and a surplus of $1,800,000 or $600,000 due each Debtor. As for Ms. Lopes, the issue is somewhat more doubtful due to the $1,300,000 damage claim of Lloyds of London. While this claim is disputed, the court cannot simply ignore its existence since it may be resolved adversely to Ms. Lopes. *In re Chi-Feng Huang*, 23 B.R. 798 (9th Cir.BAP 1982).

In determining whether to file *Chapter 11* cases, Debtors were reasonably entitled to rely upon the latest financial information available to them at the time. That information indicated a negative royalty balance in excess of $576,000. The possible post-petition solvency of Debtors Thomas and Watkins does not establish, however, that they were able to pay their debts when due at the time their cases were filed. In fact, the evidence shows that each of these Debtors was unable to do so. Therefore, Debtors are not precluded from invoking the protection provided by the Bankruptcy Code.

Movants also contend that the court should consider Debtors' ancillary income prospects in determining Debtors' solvency. First, this so-called "ancillary income" is prospective only. It is speculative at best. Further, Movants' expert, Lance Grode ("Grode"), acknowledged that he had not based his opinions on the historical experience of these Debtors. In the final analysis, the market place is the best determinant of Debtors, ability to earn income. In fact, Debtors have not earned ancillary income approximating Grode's projections. Even if they can, that does not change each Debtor's financial condition at the time her case was filed. It would support their prospects for reorganization.

Finally, Grode's testimony is of doubtful probative value as he acknowledged that some of the amounts stated were not his, but were provided by other persons who were not before the court.

3. Whether Debtors Disguised Their Financial Condition

Movants point to the failure to schedule certain assets and values. They contend that Ms. Lopes failed to schedule Left-Eye Productions, Left-Eye Management and Left-Eye Music, and that all three Debtors failed to schedule the group name "TLC," PYT Inc., the "MTV" contract and the "Waiting to Exhale" soundtrack contract. Without a doubt, a full and fair disclosure requires scheduling these assets. The question, however, is whether the omissions were willful and intended to mislead creditors and the court.

In paragraph 16(a) of Ms. Lopes "Statement of Financial Affairs," she listed both Left Eye Productions and Left Eye Management, Inc. She testified that she did not list the Left-Eye entities in Schedule "B"-Personal Property-because they had no significant value in her judgment. In fact the Left-Eye entities share office space with The Howard Agency, which provides the office furnishings, a copier, fax machine and computer equipment for use by Left-Eye. Testimony elicited not one example of a successful artist being managed or produced by Left-Eye. The court, therefore, is satisfied that the Left-Eye entities were disclosed, although not listed in Schedule "B". The court finds Ms. Lopes' testimony to be credible and is satisfied that her failure to list the Left-Eye entities in Schedule "B" was not an effort to disguise her financial condition, but was based on her belief that they had no significant value.

Debtors credibly testified that PYT, Inc. is their new touring company which has not yet engaged in business and has no value. This appears to be based largely on the fact that their last tour lost about $300,000. They further testified that Suki-Suki was their old touring company. It is no longer in business having lost a substantial amount of money on their last tour. Tiz Biz is their publishing company which was scheduled with an "unknown" value. There is no evidence to establish that it was incorrectly scheduled. Although certain post-petition deposits were made into the Tiz Biz account, each Debtor denied knowledge of them. No evidence was presented to refute Debtors' asserted values on July 3, 1995. Acknowledging that it should have value, they testified credibly that they don't know what it should be. Based upon this unrefuted testimony, the court is satisfied that these omissions were the result of Debtors' good faith belief that they had no value. The evidence does not establish that the omissions were for the purpose of misleading the court and creditors. Further, there is adequate means within the Bankruptcy Code to deal with willful omissions and misstatements. The harsh sanction of dismissal is not warranted.

With regard to the "MTV" contract, it appears that each Debtor was paid $10,000 pre-petition in return for executing a letter extension of a contingent option or exclusivity agreement for possible future personal services. The May 4, 1994 agreement referred to in the letter extension is not in evidence. The evidence does not establish any value for this agreement beyond the $10,000 pre-petition payment to each Debtor. Presumably, terms, conditions and benefits would have been negotiated at such time as MTV "obtained a pilot order." While it should have been scheduled, at least as an executory personal service option, it does not appear to be a material omission. As for the "Waiting to Exhale" contract, it bears a post-petition date on its face and was apparently negotiated by or through LaFace. Since it was executed post-petition, there is no requirement that it be scheduled, even if based upon pre-petition negotiations. The court finds and concludes that Debtors' failures to schedule the "MTV" and "Waiting to Exhale" contracts are not material omissions made in bad faith to disguise their financial condition or to mislead the court and creditors.

Next, it is undisputed that the name "TLC" is owned by Pebbitone. Debtors testified that they did not list the name "TLC" for that reason. The court finds this testimony to be credible. The owner of the name (Pebbitone) and licensee (LaFace) are scheduled. Further, the existence and use of the name "TLC" by Debtors is openly and popularly known. Both Movants are inextricably involved with the group name. Common sense suggests that Debtors' group popularity as "TLC" and the scheduling of the Pebbitone and LaFace executory contracts was sufficient disclosure to enable creditors to ascertain the existence and use of the group name. The omission simply does not appear to be an attempt to disguise Debtors' financial conditions.

Finally, Movants contend that Debtors overstated their liabilities. First, Debtors acknowledged that they each scheduled the Internal Revenue Service ("IRS") as priority unsecured claims as follows: Lopes-$59,057, Thomas-$52,667 and Watkins-$47,227. These amounts were scheduled as "estimated" taxes. Debtors' accountant testified that these figures were incorrectly calculated because he included the loan proceeds from LaFace as income on Debtors' tax returns. There is no evidence to support a finding that Debtors knew or should have known of such errors when their cases were filed.

Movants also assert that Pebbitone's negative royalty balance is not an indebtedness and that each Debtor is responsible for only one-third of the total. Debtors each scheduled unrecouped royalties of $566,434.48. All agree that Pebbitone's December 31, 1994 statement actually reflects $576,828.98. Further, it was amended post-petition to increase the amount to approximately $827,000. Paragraph 21 of the Production Agreement states "[a]ll of the terms, conditions, warranties, representations, *and obligations* applicable to the Artist contained in this contract *shall apply jointly and severally to each individual member of the Artist*" (emphasis added). Each Debtor properly scheduled the entire claim amount because of their joint and several liability for the repayment from their royalties. The Supreme Court in *Johnson v. Home State Bank (In re Johnson)*, 501 U.S. 78, 85, 111 S.Ct. 2150, 2155, 115 L.Ed.2d 66 (1991) held that " §102(2) establishes, as a '[r]ul[e]' of construction' that the phrase 'claim against the debtor includes claim against property of the debtor.'" It concluded, . . . insofar as Congress did not expressly limit §102(2) to nonrecourse loans but rather chose general language broad enough to encompass such obligations, we understand Congress' intent to be that §102(2) extend to all interests having the relevant attributes of nonrecourse obligations regardless of how these interests come into existence. *Id. at* 86–87, 111 S.Ct. at 2155–56. *See also, Matter of Hutcherson*, 186 B.R. 546 (Bankr.N.D.Ga.1995) (Drake, J.).

When Debtors' cases commenced, Pebbitone's latest statement showed, and Debtors believed themselves to have, an approximate $576,000 negative royalty balance. This balance is payable only from Debtors' future royalties. Thus, Pebbitone held a claim against each Debtor's property or right to property. The court concludes, therefore, that each Debtor properly listed the Pebbitone claim. Debtors did not omit assets and values or overstate liabilities in an attempt to disguise their financial conditions.

4. *No Lifestyle Adjustments By Debtors*

Movants contend Debtors have made no adjustment in their lavish lifestyles. The cases cited by Movants are Chapter 7 cases under *11 U.S.C. §707* involving substantial abuse. This provision applies only to Chapter 7 cases involving primarily consumer debt. *11 U.S.C. §103(b)*. Therefore, the cases cited under *§707* are neither applicable nor persuasive with regard to the *Chapter 11* good faith issue.

In every *Chapter 11* case there is a presumption of some degree of financial mismanagement. Undoubtedly each Debtor leads a lavish lifestyle compared to most people. They acknowledge no real post-petition lifestyle adjustment. However, that result is due at least in part to the availability of post-petition, non-estate personal services earnings or because Movants have consented to Debtors use of funds. If the funds are property of the estate, Movants have consented to their use. If they are not property of the estate, Movants have not cited, and the court has not found, any authority that restricts Debtors' use of their non-estate or exempt property.

There is no evidence that estate funds have been misapplied. In fact, it appears Debtors have primarily used funds which they contend are from post-petition personal services. Neither the creditors nor the U.S. Trustee have contested the use of cash collateral or the fact that Debtors have generated and used proceeds from post-petition personal services. The court concludes that the failure of Debtors to alter their lifestyles post-petition does not establish bad faith in the filing of their cases.

5. *Payment To Insiders*

Payments to or for family members have been disclosed throughout Debtors' monthly reports. It is unclear whether the payments were made from post-petition personal service earnings or from cash collateral whose use was consented to by Movants. The care or support of family members is a serious matter which is not, *per se,* improper or undesirable. Supporting one's family or family members is a normal and desirable societal goal. The proper inquiry is whether the payments are a misuse of estate funds and harmful to the estate and creditors. While questioning their propriety, Movants have presented no evidence to show that the insider payments were improper or detrimental to these estates. In fact, the court finds these post-petition actions to be of little or no relevance with regard to Debtors' prior determination to file these cases. The court finds that the post-petition payments to insiders do not support a finding that these cases were filed in bad faith and that they should be dismissed. If estate funds are being misapplied or improperly disbursed, there are adequate means available to deal with it without resorting to the drastic sanction of dismissal.

6. *Failure To Seek Advances From LaFace*

Movants further contend that the failure of Debtors to seek advances from LaFace constitutes bad faith. Debtors testified that they did not want to resort to further advances because they would merely get deeper in debt. Their response is credible. Common sense tells us that debtors cannot borrow themselves out of debt.

7. *Pre-petition Statements Regarding Case Filing and Intent To Reject Contracts*

Movants contend that the sole purpose of these case filings is to reject their contracts for a better deal. They point to Barnes' statement to LaFace that Debtors would be filing bankruptcy petitions and would reject Movants' contracts. There was no showing that the statement was made under circumstances that suggest bad faith. The fact that a statement is made in the course of negotiations does not automatically make it a declaration in bad faith. While the parties had been negotiating in an effort to resolve their differences, these cases were not filed until they reached an impasse. Even then Debtors delayed filing for a short period at the request of LaFace. Having considered the demeanor of the witnesses and the circumstances surrounding the statement, the court is satisfied that this was merely a statement of intention by Debtors' counsel.

8. *Debtors' Post-petition Conduct*

Movants also point to certain post-petition conduct as an indication of bad faith. First, they point to the failure of Ms. Watkins and Ms. Thomas to attend the first scheduled §341 meeting. In fact, all three Debtors attended a rescheduled §341 meeting. While the court does not condone the failure to attend a regularly scheduled §341 meeting, the failure to do so does not establish that the petitions were filed in bad faith. Dismissal for failure to appear, particularly when they subsequently appeared, is too drastic a sanction for the offense. Next, Movants point to the attempt by Ms. Watkins to purchase a home for which she made a deposit of $80,000 and requested court authorization to borrow in excess of $200,000 to complete the purchase. When Movant objected to that request, the motion was withdrawn. This is clearly unusual. However, Ms. Watkins' monthly financial report indicates that LaFace provided the funds to make the $80,000 deposit. A simple objection would have prevented such use. Further, it has been asserted that these funds were earnings from post-petition personal services and were not property of the estate. If true, Ms. Watkins was free to use those funds in her discretion. The evidence does not establish this to be an improper disbursement. Movants have not shown Ms. Watkins' actions to be in bad faith and the sanction of dismissal is not warranted. This is particularly true since one of the Movants actively consented to the transaction.

9. *Were Petitions Filed Merely to Reject Unprofitable Contracts*

Finally, Movants contend that Debtors' cases were filed solely to reject certain contracts between the parties. This court agrees that where the *sole* objective of a solvent debtor is to reject a contract in favor of a better one, the petition is in bad faith as it serves no useful reorganization purpose. *In re Waldron*, 785 F.2d at 940–941. However, the evidence does not support Movants' position. While Debtors did move to reject Movants' contracts shortly after filing, this fact alone does not establish bad faith. The real question is whether Debtors were experiencing *bona fide* financial problems that warranted bankruptcy relief. For the reasons set forth herein, the court finds and concludes that they were.

10. *Likelihood of Reorganization*

It appears likely that Debtors can propose reorganization plans within a reasonable time. The evidence establishes that Debtors have earned post-petition royalties under their present contacts sufficient to pay the $827,000 negative royalty balance to Pebbitone plus $600,000 net to each Debtor. Lovette testified that LaFace had offered to renegotiate the contracts with Debtors with an estimated gross value to Debtors of $16,000,000. Further, Debtors' income prospects may increase substantially if they reject Movants' contracts. For these reasons, the court concludes there is a reasonable likelihood that Debtors can propose reorganization plans within a reasonable time. Accordingly, the motions to dismiss will be denied.

For the reasons set forth herein, the court also concludes that abstention is not appropriate in this case as resolution of the issues is in the best interest of Debtors and their creditors. Accordingly, it is: ORDERED that Movants' LaFace and Pebbitone's Motions to Dismiss are denied, and it is FURTHER ORDERED that Movant LaFace's Motion to Abstain is also denied.

The clerk is directed to serve a copy of this order upon Debtors, Debtors' counsel, counsel for Pebbitone, Inc. and Perri Reed, counsel for LaFace Records, and the United States Trustee.

IT IS SO ORDERED.

NOTES _____

1. *In the Matter of Taylor,* 913 F.2d 102 (3d Cir. 1990), a member of the group known as "Kool and the Gang" filed a Chapter 11 bankruptcy petition and sought to reject his exclusive music publishing agreement. His publisher objected (citing, among other grounds, that the petition was not filed in "good faith") and asked the court to dismiss the action. In the first reported appellate decision on the issue, the court held that executory contracts for personal services may be rejected.

2. After some years and many revisions, Congress passed a new bankruptcy act, supported by the banking and credit card industry, titled the Bankruptcy Abuse Prevention and Consumer Protection Act of 2005 ("BAPCPA"). Record companies have long been displeased with bankruptcy act provisions that have permitted recording artists to get out of their contracts while leaving large unrecouped advances. The usual reason for rejection of recording contracts by artists in bankruptcy is to be able to sign contracts with another record label, so that royalties from the sale of their new recordings will not be recouped from, or "cross-collateralized" with, outstanding advances from their old recordings. Artists like James Taylor in *Matter of Taylor,* 913 F.2d 102 (3d Cir. 1990), Willie Nile in *In the Matter of Noonan,* 17 B.R. 793 (SDNY 1982) [Chapter 11 debtor allowed to convert to Chapter 7 for the purpose of rejecting recording contract] and the members of music group TLC in *In re Watkins* have all accomplished this, as have many others, primarily by first showing that the debtor was experiencing "real financial hardship". However, as the *Carrere* case below shows, unless an artist can prove real financial hardship, bankruptcy trustees and the courts are less inclined to allow executory contract rejection. Earlier draft bills, which did not make it through Congress, included provisions amending 11 U.S.C. § 365 in order to make it more difficult for recording artists to use bankruptcy as a tool for getting out of their contracts with record companies. The new Act does not contain any additional provisions which would alter the rights available to artists under §365 and their right to reject executory contracts upon a showing of real financial hardship at the time of filing of the petition.

3. In the case *In re Levon Helm,* 335 B.R. 528 (Bankr. S.D.N.Y 2006), the debtor, who is a famous musician, former member of The Band and actor, attempted in his Chapter 11 bankruptcy to reject an exclusive royalty collection services agreement with Royalty Recovery, Inc. ("RRI"). Under the Agreement entered in 2004, RRI was to be paid 40%-50% of all royalties collected from third parties from the exploitation of Helm's recordings and songwriting interests. The engagement of RRI was exclusive, irrevocable, in perpetuity and for the territory of the Universe [as the court noted ". . . in the event that Debtor's work is being used at the space station and beyond . . ."]. RRI opposed rejection of its contract primarily contending: 1) that the Agreement was not an executory contract subject to rejection under §365 alleging that the Agreement had been fully performed by the parties; and 2) under the sound business judgment test, the Debtor had not established that rejection of the Agreement would increase the benefit to the Debtor's estate and creditors.

If a contract has been fully performed except for payment due from the debtor, it is not an executory contract and may not be rejected. The Court thought that RRI's characterization of the Agreement as "fully performed" ignored reality and the plain language of the contract. Since no royalties had yet been collected by RRI; and past, present, and future royalties were still to be identified, earned and collected; much of the services of RRI (and Debtor) were still to be performed. The Court noted that RRI had failed to cite "a single case that indicates that a contract perpetual in term, exclusive in nature and universal in territory, is no longer executory." Therefore, the Court found that the Agreement was clearly an executory contract and subject to rejection by the debtor-in-possession.

In order to meet the business judgment test, the debtor must "establish that rejection will benefit the estate. Once the debtor meets its burden, the non-debtor party bears the burden of proving that the debtor's decision derives from bad faith, whim or caprice." Helm stated that, in his considered business judgment, the matters delegated to RRI under the Agreement were matters within the ordinary competence of an attorney familiar with entertainment law, which could be administered and collected at a far lower cost than a 40%–50% commission. Since a reasonable business person could arrive at this same conclusion, the burden then shifted to RRI to prove otherwise, or to show that Debtor's decision was made in bad faith, or from whim or caprice. RRI failed to offer evidence to the contrary. The Court found, in rejecting the Agreement, the Debtor's "royalties can be collected for less, and that this consequent savings in collection commissions would provide an economic benefit to the estate." Debtor's Motion to Reject is granted.

In re Carrere, 64 B.R. 156 (U.S.D.C. C.D. Ca. 1986)

MUND, BANKRUPTCY JUDGE

STATEMENT OF FACTS

[Carrere had been a member of the cast of the ABC soap opera "General Hospital" for three years, her contract guaranteeing her an average of 1.4 performances per week, at a salary of $600–700 for each 60-minute program in which she appeared. She made a guest appearance on the "A Team," under an agreement under which, if she became a regular cast member, she would earn considerably more than she would on "General Hospital." Carrere filed a voluntary petition under Chapter 11, and attempted to reject the executory ABC contract.]

In her declaration in support of the motion to reject, Carrere makes it clear that her primary motivation . . . was to reject the contract with ABC so as to enter into the more lucrative contract with A Team. In fact, she claims she did not enter into the contract with A Team until she had obtained advice that the bankruptcy would allow her to reject the contract with ABC. In her schedules she claims unsecured debt only. Her stated liabilities are $76,575 and her assets are $13,191. The amount of debts is disputed by ABC.

ABC vigorously opposed the rejection of its contract and has sought extensive discovery concerning Carrere's liabilities and motivations in filing this bankruptcy. ABC also brought a motion to dismiss the Chapter 11 proceeding on the grounds that it was filed in bad faith.

ANALYSIS

The key issue to be determined by this Court is whether a debtor, who is a performer under a personal services contract, is entitled to reject the contract by virtue of the provisions of 11 U.S.C. sec. 365. . . .

A Personal Services Contract is Not Property of the Estate in Chapters 7 or 11

The concept of sec. 365 is that the trustee, in administering the estate, may assume (and even assign) contracts which are advantageous to the estate and may reject contracts which are not lucrative or beneficial to the estate. 2 Collier on Bankruptcy (15th ed.) para. 365.01. It is not the trustee's duty to benefit the debtor's future finances, but he is to maintain the property of the estate for the benefit of the creditors.

The threshold issue to be determined is whether the ABC contract is "property of the estate." If it is not, the trustee has no standing to assume or reject it. [Note: The practical issue raised here is whether Carrere may deprive ABC of a cause of action for a negative injunction if she seeks further employment under the A Team Contract.] . . .

11 U.S.C. sec. 541(a)(6) states that property of the estate does not include "earnings from services performed by an individual debtor after the commencement of the case." . . . [P]ost-petition earnings from personal services contracts are thus excluded from the Chapter 7 or Chapter 11 estate. Does this exclude the contract itself? . . . The language of sec. 541(a)(6) . . . is an enactment of case law which specified that where an executory contract between the debtor and another is based upon the personal service or skill of the debtor, the Trustee does not take title to the debtor's rights in the contract. *Ford, Bacon & Davis, Inc. v. M.A. Holahan,* 311 F.2d 901 (5th Cir. 1962). . . .

Under the Code, it has been held that a contract for personal services is excluded from the estate pursuant to both sec. 541(a)(6) and sec. 365(c). *In re Bofill,* 25 B.R. 550 (Bankr. S.D.N.Y. 1982) [and *Matter of Noonan,* supra]. . . .

Since the trustee has no interest in the contract, he has no standing to act at all under sec. 365. Therefore, he cannot assume or reject the contract.

The Rights of a Debtor-in-Possession Are No Greater Than Those of a Trustee

. . . Upon the filing of a Chapter 11, Ms. Carrere created a new entity called a debtor-in-possession. . . . She is granted the rights and duties of a trustee (11 U.S.C. sec. 323). Therefore, while the debtor (Tia Carrere) may have duties under the ABC contract and may wish to reject those duties, the debtor-in-possession (who represents the estate of Tia Carrere) has no rights or duties whatsoever in the contract and therefore is a stranger to it. . . .

. . . The contract never comes under the jurisdiction of the Bankruptcy Court. The Court has no interest, the estate has no interest, and even if the debtor-in-possession were allowed by consent of all parties to assume the contract under 11 U.S.C. sec. 365, the assumption would not create an asset of the estate, for the proceeds would never be an asset of the estate, nor would the contract be assignable. Therefore, no rights of assumption are vested in the debtor-in-possession.

The only one who has rights or duties under the contract is the debtor herself. But the statutory scheme of sec. 365(d)(1) does not allow the debtor to reject an executory contract. It only allows the trustee to do so.

Therefore, this Court finds that sec. 365 . . . does not apply to a personal services contract in a bankruptcy case under Chapter 7 or 11, whether or not a trustee has been appointed.

It Would Be Inequitable to Allow the Contract to Be Rejected

Beyond the legal arguments described above, the Court is concerned about the good faith issue of allowing a debtor to file for the primary purpose of rejecting a personal services contract. A personal services contract is unique and money damages will often not make the employer whole. . . .

The Bankruptcy Court is a court of equity, as well as a court of law. It would be inequitable to allow a greedy debtor to seek the equitable protection of this Court when her major motivation is to cut off the equitable remedies [e.g., negative injunction] of her employer.

For that reason, this Court finds that there is not "cause" to reject this contract, if the major motivation of the debtor in filing the case was to be able to perform under the more lucrative A Team contract. It is clear that for Carrere this is the major motivation, even if it is not the sole motivation. Therefore, rejection is denied for lack of cause.

Rejection Would Not Relieve the Debtor of a Possible Negative Injunction.

There is yet another issue that arises and impacts on the ultimate outcome of such cases: if rejection were permitted, what would be its effect on the creditor's right to seek a negative injunction against the debtor?

Rejection of an executory contract constitutes a breach, which is deemed to have occurred immediately before the date of the filing of the petition (11 U.S.C. sec. 365(g)(1)). The claim for monetary damages thus becomes a claim in the estate (11 U.S.C. sec. 502(g)).

But a rejection under the Bankruptcy Code only affects the monetary rights of the creditor. It does not disturb equitable, non-monetary rights that the creditor may have against the debtor because of the breach of contract.

. . . California law has given ABC an equitable remedy: to seek a negative injunction against Carrere and thereby prevent her from performing elsewhere. Rejection of the ABC contract would not interfere with

ABC's rights to seek that equitable remedy. Rejection would merely categorize any claim for monetary damages as pre-petition debt. Therefore, whether this Court were to allow rejection or not, Carrere cannot use the Bankruptcy Code to protect her from whatever non-monetary remedies are enforceable under state law.

On both the legal and equitable grounds set forth above, Carrere's Motion to Reject the contract is denied.

NOTES

1. In a significant unreported decision in 1988, the United States Bankruptcy Court for the Central District of California, in a bankruptcy petition involving the members of the recording group "Concrete Blonde," held that where the primary purpose of the bankruptcy filing was to reject an executory personal service contract (in that case, a recording agreement with IRS Records), the contract was not dischargeable in bankruptcy. In that case all three members of the group simultaneously filed voluntary petitions under Chapter 7 after delivering one record to the record company. The bankruptcy schedules did not evidence other significant debts or a distressed financial condition. In addition, 18 days after the filing of the bankruptcy petitions, the group performed a "showcase" concert at the Roxy in West Hollywood, California to attract the attention of other record companies. This evidence was sufficient to convince Bankruptcy Judge Mund that the subject personal service contracts could not be assumed by the Trustee or rejected by the Trustee or the Debtor and, accordingly, the Bankruptcy Code did not affect the future enforceability of those recording agreements. Subsequent to the decision Concrete Blonde and IRS settled their differences, and Concrete Blonde went on to release very successful records. See United States Bankruptcy Court for the Central District of California, Action No. LA 87–18212.

2. Many entertainment agreements attempt to modify the effect of the Bankruptcy Code on the agreement by a specific contractual provision. Common in book publishing agreements, these clauses attempt to force a reversion of rights to the author in the event of a voluntary or involuntary filing of bankruptcy by the publisher. These clauses are known as *ipso facto* provisions. Although they were enforceable under the former Bankruptcy Act, Section 541(c) of the Bankruptcy Code now invalidates these provisions in agreements that attempt to circumvent the Bankruptcy Code by a restriction of transfer or termination of interest that is conditional upon a bankruptcy action.

3. For a detailed discussion of the effect of bankruptcy on entertainment industry contracts, see Leslie A. Cohen and David L. Neale, "Bankruptcy and Contractual Relations in the Entertainment Industry—An Overview," in *1990 Entertainment, Publishing and the Arts Handbook 375* (1990). Also see Jennifer A. Brewer, "Bankruptcy & Entertainment Law: The Controversial Rejection of Recording Contracts," 11 Am. Bankr. Inst. L. Rev. 581 (2003) and Risa C. Letowsky, "Broke or Exploited: The Real Reason Behind Artist Bankruptcies," 20 *Cardozo Arts & Ent. L.J.* 625 (2002).

5.5.2 The Consequences of Bankruptcy

The question of whether or not bankruptcy protection is available in a given instance is only the first part of the analysis. What happens *afterward?* What happens to rights granted by the debtor prior to the bankruptcy, and who gets the revenues derived from the exploitation of those rights?

Section 365(g) of the Bankruptcy Code provides that the rejection of an executory contract constitutes a breach on the part of the debtor, but this may be small consolation where (as is usually the case) a debtor's assets don't begin to cover outstanding indebtedness.

However, Section 365(n) of the Bankruptcy Code provides some relief: licensees of intellectual property rights may elect [under Section 365(n)(1)] to retain the rights previously licensed to them. Section 101(56) contains a broad definition of intellectual property, including "copyrights" (which, under Section 102 of 17 U.S. Code include "literary works; musical works, including any accompanying words; dramatic works, including any accompanying music; pantomimes and choreographic works; . . . motion pictures and other audiovisual works; [and] sound recordings.") Thus, licensees in every area with which this book is concerned can elect to continue to exploit the rights licensed to them when their licensors go bankrupt, subject, of course, to the obligation to continue to pay royalties. Moreover, while the licensee retains the right to recoup advances if it elects to retain the licensed rights, any rights of set-off are waived. The licensee will still have the right to assert a claim of breach of contract, but the licensee may not assert a claim that it is entitled to priority over other creditors.

Who gets the post-bankruptcy royalties? The issue is addressed in the following cases.

Waldschmidt v. CBS, Inc., 14 B.R. 309 (U.S.D.C. M.D. Tenn. 1981)

WISEMAN, DISTRICT JUDGE

This action involves a dispute between the bankruptcy trustee for the estate of musician George Jones and the defendant CBS, Inc., concerning who is entitled to the royalties from the sale of certain records made by Mr. Jones pursuant to his recording contract with CBS. Because the recordings were made by Mr. Jones prior to the date of his voluntary bankruptcy petition, the trustee argues that any royalties derived from their sale are the property of Mr. Jones' estate and therefore should pass to the trustee. CBS, on the other hand, argues that because the royalties actually stem from services rendered under a personal services contract—the recording contract between Mr. Jones and CBS—they are not the property of Mr. Jones' estate and do not pass to the trustee. CBS's argument is important because it also alleges that under the contract it is entitled to recoup from these royalties certain advances it made to Mr. Jones prior to his bankruptcy. CBS's fear is that if the royalties are deemed the property of the estate, its right of recoupment would dissipate and it would be forced to proceed as an ordinary creditor of Mr. Jones to recover the money it advanced to him. The advances far exceed the royalties collected to date, and if treated like any other creditor, CBS would be unable to recover the full amount of the advances.

Each party in this action has moved for summary judgment pursuant to Rule 56, F.R.C.P. Because no genuine issue regarding any material fact exists, this cause is ripe for summary judgment. Having reviewed the pertinent facts and law, this Court now makes the following determinations: (1) that the royalties are the property of Mr. Jones' estate; (2) that although the royalties are the property of the estate, CBS is entitled to recoup the full amount of the advances from these royalties; and (3) that the trustee is entitled to an accounting of the royalties and of the amounts recouped by CBS. . . .

The threshold issue in this case is whether the royalties constitute "property" within the meaning of section 70(a)(5) of the old Bankruptcy Act. That section provides in relevant part:

(a) The trustee of the estate of a bankrupt . . . shall . . . be vested by operation of law with the title of the bankrupt as of the date of the filing of the petition initiating a proceeding under this title, except insofar as it is to property which is held to be exempt, to all of the following kinds of property wherever located. . . . (5) property, including rights of action, which prior to the filing of the petition he could by any means have transferred. . . .

CBS bases its argument that the royalties are not property within the scope of section 70(a)(5) on two grounds. First, CBS argues that because the recording contract between Mr. Jones and CBS was one for personal services, both the contract itself and any rights growing out of it—such as the right to royalties—were nontransferable and nonseverable as of the date of the bankruptcy petition, December 13, 1978. Second, CBS argues that even if Mr. Jones had transferable rights in the royalties in December 1978, royalty rights are not the type of property intended to be covered by section 70(a)(5). The trustee counters CBS's contentions by arguing that Mr. Jones had unquestionable rights in any royalties collected by CBS from sales of his records, that these rights were clearly alienable by Mr. Jones, and that "property" as meant by section 70(a)(5) includes the rights to the royalties here in dispute.

In regard to the first point of contention, this Court finds that nothing in the nature of the recording contract itself prevents the rights to the royalties from passing to the trustee. As CBS argues, it is generally true that a contract for personal services is "nonassignable." What this rule means, however, is simply that the performance of the particular personalized service itself is nondelegable, not that the right to payment for any such service may not be assigned once performance has occurred. *See* Corbin, Corbin on Contracts 805 (1952). . . .

. . . CBS argues that Mr. Jones was still obligated under the contract to certain promotional activities, as well as live performances, before he was entitled to receive the royalties.

While it is true that Mr. Jones did have certain obligations outstanding under the overall contract with CBS, this Court cannot agree that Mr. Jones' right to the royalties was expressly conditioned on such additional activity. Mr. Jones completed performance of the basic contractual duties upon which the receipt of royalties was conditioned by making the master recordings from which the records were ultimately pressed. Mr. Jones did have other obligations under the contract, but these obligations did not affect his right to royalties from the record sales. If anything, Mr. Jones' further obligations seemed designed to boost record sales, and it is only in that respect that they affected the royalties. This Court rejects CBS's argument, then, and accepts the contention of the trustee that any contingency that did exist in Mr. Jones' contract regarding the royalties would at most affect the marketability of Mr. Jones' interest, but not its assignability. See *In re Malloy,* 2 B.R. 674 (Bankr. M. D. Fla. 1980).

Having concluded that the personal services nature of the recording contract does not preclude passage to the trustee of Mr. Jones' rights to the royalties, this Court must now decide whether these rights are in fact the sort of "property" intended to pass to the trustee under section 70(a)(5). Although the definition of property under section 70(a)(5) has been considered by the courts on numerous occasions, no case appears to have addressed this particular question directly. Despite the absence of a specific precedent, the voluminous case law that has evolved under section 70(a)(5) does provide guidelines for this Court's inquiry. Taking the existing interpretations into consideration, this Court concludes, in this case of apparent first impression, that the royalty rights here are property under section 70(a)(5) of the Bankruptcy Act.

It is well established that the term "property" as employed in section 70(a)(5) is to be given a broad interpretation. . . . The simple fact that Mr. Jones could not actually collect the royalties until some time after the date of his bankruptcy petition, then, does not prevent his rights to those royalties—which effectively accrued before his bankruptcy—from being considered property under section 70(a)(5). . . .

While "property" under section 70(a)(5) is thus broadly defined, its scope is not unlimited. As the Supreme Court noted in *Segal,* "[L]imitations on the term do grow out of other purposes of the Act; one purpose . . . is to leave the bankrupt free after the date of his petition to accumulate new wealth in the future." 382 U.S. at 379, 86 S. Ct. at 514, 15 L.Ed.2d at 432. Elaborating on this restriction, the Court in *Lines v. Frederick,* 400 U.S. 18, 19, 91 S.Ct. 113, 114, 27 L. Ed. 2d 124, 127 (1970), stated,

The most important consideration limiting the breadth of the definition of "property" lies in the basic purpose of the Bankruptcy Act to give the debtor a "new opportunity in life and a clear field for future effort, unhampered by the pressure and discouragement of preexisting debt. The various provisions of the bankruptcy act were adopted in the light of that view and are to be construed when reasonably possible in harmony with it so as to effectuate the general purpose and policy of the act."

(citing *Local Loan Co. v. Hunt,* 292 U.S. 234, 244–45, 54 S. Ct. 695, 699, 78 L.Ed. 1230, 1235 (1984)). The test for determining whether the inclusion of certain items in the estate is consistent with the purpose and policy of the Bankruptcy Act is whether the bankrupt's claim to the asset is "sufficiently rooted in the pre-bankruptcy past and so little entangled with the bankrupt's ability to make an unencumbered fresh start that it should be regarded as 'property' under 70a(5)." *Segal v. Rochelle,* 882 U.S. 375, 380, 86 S. Ct. 511, 515, 15 L. Ed2d 428, 432 (1966). This Court believes that Mr. Jones' interest in the royalties meets this test and should be considered the property of his estate under section 70(a)(5). . . .

In characterizing assets for the purposes of section 70(a)(5), the courts have developed no clear mode of classification. Indeed, the Supreme Court itself has stated that "property" as meant by section 70(a)(5) "has never been given a precise or universal definition." Moreover, "it is impossible to give any categorical definition to the word . . . , nor can we attach to it in certain relations the limitations which would be attached to it in others." *Kokoszka v. Belford,* 417 U.S. 642, 645, 94 S.Ct. 2431, 2433, 41 L.Ed.2d 374, 378–79 (1974). Rather than erecting hard and fast categories, then, the courts have taken a case-by-case approach and analyzed each asset on an individualized basis. Essentially, the courts have applied a balancing test to each specific situation, employing the *Segal* formula and weighing the degree of relation between the asset and the "pre-bankruptcy past" against the potential effect that placing the asset in the estate would have on the bankrupt's ability to make an "unencumbered fresh start" after bankruptcy.

Applying this balancing test to the facts of this case, this Court finds that Mr. Jones' rights to the royalty payments are indeed sufficiently rooted in the pre-bankruptcy past to warrant inclusion of the royalties within Mr. Jones' estate. The recordings involved here, from which the royalties derive, were completed prior to the filing of the bankruptcy petition. Moreover, while Mr. Jones did have certain outstanding obligations under his contract with CBS, his right to payment was not so conditioned on his performance of these additional duties that the royalties should not be deemed property under section 70(a)(5). Moreover, including the royalties within the estate would not unduly handicap Mr. Jones' efforts to make an unencumbered fresh start because the royalties are in fact derived from recordings made prior to Mr. Jones' bankruptcy. As this Court is aware from other proceedings involving Mr. Jones, he has already devised a plan to repay his creditors and is presently once again engaged in recording and public appearances. . . .

Although the royalty payments owed to Mr. Jones were not due *in toto* on any one specific date, the arrangement between Mr. Jones and CBS did require a regularized system of accounting and payment to Mr. Jones at six-month intervals. Moreover, nothing in the fact of Mr. Jones' bankruptcy has (or had) any effect at all upon CBS's obligation to pay the royalties. That obligation matured upon the completion of the recordings by Mr. Jones, and nothing has since occurred to alter it. While the example of wages is not a perfect analogy—for there is no perfect analogy to this case—the reasoning of the Sixth Circuit in this respect is persuasive. Coupled with this Court's previous conclusion that any impediment to Mr. Jones' ability to start anew is far outweighed by the pre-bankruptcy nature of the royalties' roots, *Aveni* provides ample basis for including the royalties within the estate.

This Court thus rules that the royalties owed by CBS, Inc., to George Jones because of recordings made by Mr. Jones prior to the date of his bankruptcy petition are property within the scope of section 70(a)(5) of the Bankruptcy Act and pass to the trustee for the benefit of the estate. The argument of CBS is accordingly rejected. . . .

Although this Court has ruled that the royalties are the property of the estate under section 70(a)(5), this Court also holds that CBS is entitled to recoup the full amount of its advances to Mr. Jones from these royalties.

The trustee attempts to argue that CBS must proceed with its claim under the restrictive setoff provisions of section 68 of the Bankruptcy Act, instead of possessing a general right of recoupment. The trustee apparently seeks to argue not only that recoupment is covered by section 68 but also that the set-off and recoupment processes are equivalent. The trustee is sorely mistaken on both points.

In the first place, no authority exists to support the trustee's assertion that recoupment is within the ambit of section 68. Indeed, there is ample authority to the contrary. . . .

Additionally, the recoupment process is different from the requirements for set-off. While set-off under section 68 is limited to instances involving mutuality of obligation, recoupment is subject to no such limitation. . . . The only real requirement regarding recoupment is that a sum can be reduced only by matters or claims arising out of the same transaction as the original sum. . . . Despite the trustee's contention, the advances and royalties involved in this case unquestionably arise from the same transaction. Both grow out of the recording contract between Mr. Jones and CBS. In fact, no dispute over the royalties would exist but for the express provision in the contract calling for advances and their recoupment from royalties. Additionally, no question exists regarding the enforceability of such a contract provision against the bankruptcy trustee. . . . In view of these considerations, CBS is clearly entitled to recoup its advances from the royalties at issue in this case. . . .

As a final point, this Court rules that the trustee is entitled to an accounting of all royalties received by CBS from the sale of recordings made by George Jones prior to the date of his bankruptcy. The trustee is also entitled to an accounting of all advances to date recouped by CBS from these royalties. Because this Court has held that the royalties are the property of the estate, but subject to CBS's right of recoupment, the trustee must have all information regarding the royalties and advances. The trustee now stands in the place of the bankrupt with regard to these royalties. Should CBS recoup its advances and there be undepleted royalties, these would pass to the trustee for the benefit of the estate. The trustee must know if that event is a possibility, and if so, at what point in time it might occur. An accounting is thus necessary so that the trustee may be fully informed. Accordingly, this Court hereby orders CBS, Inc., to provide the trustee with an accounting of the royalties received and any advances recouped therefrom.

NOTES

1. In *In re Prize Frize, Inc.*, 32 F.3d 426 (9th Cir. 1994), the Ninth Circuit held that license fees (the contract provided for both fixed payments and percentage royalties) paid for the use of technology, patents and proprietary rights are "royalties" within the meaning of Section 365(n)(2)(b), so that if the licensee elected to retain the licensed rights, the payments would have to continue and the licensee would have to forgo any potential right of set-off.

2. What happens when the bankrupt is the licensee? Personal services contracts are not assignable without the consent of the party to whom the services are to be rendered. Thus, in *Catapult Entertainment, Inc. v. Perlman (In re Catapult Entertainment, Inc.)*, 165 F.3d 747 (9th Cir.), *cert denied*, 120 S.Ct. 369, 68 USLW 3263 (1999), a licensee debtor could not assume a license after entering bankruptcy reorganization. Since many corporations are organized in Delaware, and since a corporation may file for bankruptcy either in the state in which its place of business is located or in its state of incorporation, many bankruptcies are filed in Delaware. *In re Access Beyond Technologies*, 237 B.R. 32 (Bankr. D. Del. 1999) has reached the same conclusion as *Catapult*. However, the First Circuit has taken the opposite view. *Institut Pasteur v. Cambridge Biotech Corp.*, 104 F.3d 489 (1st Cir.), *cert denied*, 521 U.S. 1120 (1997). See Evan M. Jones, "Catapult to Oblivion: Recent Court Decisions Threaten Ability of Bankruptcy Debtors to Retain or Sell Intellectual Property Licenses," *Ent. L. Rptr* vol. 21, no. 5, p. 4 (1999).

5.5.3 Protective Registration

In some deals, transactions are set up in the form of security interests. Until a few years ago, entertainment attorneys routinely filed UCC-1's in the debtor's home jurisdiction as they would in ordinary transactions. However, as the following case indicates, this proved to be insufficient. Where copyright interests are involved, the security interest must be filed in the Copyright Office. However, as the *Sherman* note (p. 551) indicates, advances are not loans, and need not be evidenced by a security document.

In re Peregrine Entertainment, Ltd. 116 B.R. 174, 16 U.S.P.Q. 2d 1017 (U.S.D.C., C.D.Ca 1990)

KOZINSKI, DISTRICT JUDGE

This appeal from a decision of the bankruptcy court raises an issue never before confronted by a federal court in a published opinion: Is a security interest in a copyright perfected by an appropriate filing with the United States Copyright Office or by a UCC-1 financing statement filed with the relevant secretary of state?

National Peregrine, Inc. (NPI) is a Chapter 11 debtor in possession whose principal assets are a library of copyrights, distribution rights, and licenses to approximately 145 films, and accounts receivable arising from the licensing of these films to various programmers. NPI claims to have an outright assignment of some of the copyrights; as for the others, NPI claims it has an exclusive license to distribute in a certain territory, or for a certain period of time.

In June 1985, Capitol Federal Savings and Loan Association of Denver (Cap Fed) extended to American National Enterprises, Inc., NPI's predecessor by merger, a six million dollar line of credit secured by what is now NPI's film library. Both the security agreement and the UCC-1 financing statements filed by Cap Fed describe the collateral as "[a] inventory consisting of films and all accounts, contract rights, chattel paper, general intangibles, instruments, equipment, and documents related to such inventory, now owned or hereafter acquired by the Debtor." Although Cap Fed filed its UCC-1 financing statements in California, Colorado, and Utah, it did not record its security interest in the United States Copyright Office.

NPI filed a voluntary petition for bankruptcy on January 30, 1989. On April 6, 1989, NPI filed an amended complaint against Cap Fed, contending that the bank's security interest in the copyrights to the films in NPI's library and in the accounts receivable generated by their distribution were unperfected because Cap Fed failed to record its security interest with the Copyright Office. NPI claimed that, as a debtor in possession, it had a judicial lien on all assets in the bankruptcy estate, including the copyrights and receivables. Armed with this lien, it sought to avoid, recover, and preserve Cap Fed's supposedly unperfected security interest for the benefit of the estate.

The parties filed cross-motions for partial summary judgment on the question of whether Cap Fed had a valid security interest in the NPI film library. The bankruptcy court held for Cap Fed. . . .

The Copyright Act provides that "[a]ny transfer of copyright ownership or other document pertaining to a copyright" may be recorded in the United States Copyright Office, 17 U.S.C. 205(a). . . .

It is clear from the preceding that an agreement granting a creditor a security interest in a copyright may be recorded in the Copyright Office. See G. Gilmore, *Security Interests in Personal Property* 17.3, at 545 (1965). Likewise, because a copyright entitles the holder to receive all income derived from the display of the creative work (see 17 U.S.C. 106), an agreement creating a security interest in the receivables generated by a copyright may also be recorded in the Copyright Office, Thus, Cap Fed's security interest could have been recorded in the Copyright Office; the parties seem to agree on this much. The question is, does the UCC provide a parallel method of perfecting a security interest in a copyright? One can answer this question by reference to either federal or state law; both inquiries lead to the same conclusion.

Even in the absence of express language, federal regulation will preempt state law if it is so pervasive as to indicate that "Congress left no room for supplementary state regulation," or if "the federal interest is so dominant that the federal system will be assumed to preclude enforcement of state laws on the same subject." *Hillsborough County v. Automated*

Medical Laboratories, Inc., 471 U.S. 707, 713 (1985) (internal quotations omitted). Here, the comprehensive scope of the federal Copyright Act's recording provisions, along with the unique federal interests they implicate, support the view that federal law preempts state methods of perfecting security interests in copyrights and related accounts receivable.

The federal copyright laws ensure "predictability and certainty of copyright ownership," "promote national uniformity" and "avoid the practical difficulties of determining and enforcing an author's rights under the differing laws and in the separate courts of the various States." *Community for Creative Non-Violence v. Reid*, 109 S. Ct. 2155, 2177 (1989); H.R. Rep. No. 1476, 94th Cong., 2d Sess. 129 (1976). As discussed above, section 205(a) of the Copyright Act establishes a uniform method for recording security interests in copyrights. A secured creditor need only file in the Copyright Office in order to give "all persons constructive notice of the facts stated in the recorded document" (17 U.S.C. 205[c]). Likewise, an interested third party need only search the indices maintained by the Copyright Office to determine whether a particular copyright is encumbered. See *Northern Songs, Ltd. v. Distinguished Productions, Inc.*, 581 F. Supp. 638, 640– 41 (SDNY 1984); Circular 12, at 8035–4. . . .

A recording system works by virtue of the fact that interested parties have a specific place to look in order to discover with certainty whether a particular interest has been transferred or encumbered. To the extent there are competing recordation schemes, this lessens the utility of each; when records are scattered in several filing units, potential creditors must conduct several searches before they can be sure that the property is not encumbered. See *Danning v. Pacific Propeller, Inc.* (*In re Holiday Airlines Corp.*), 620 F.2d 731 (9th Cir. 1980), *cert. denied*, 449 U.S. 900 (1980); *Red Carpet Homes of Johnstown, Inc. v. Gerling* (*In re Knapp*), 575 F.2d 341, 343 (2d Cir. 1978); UCC 9401, Official Comment para. 1. It is for that reason that parallel recordation schemes for the same types of property are scarce as hen's teeth; the court is aware of no others, and the parties have cited none. No useful purposes would be served—indeed, much confusion would result—if creditors were permitted to perfect security interests by filing with either the Copyright Office or state offices. See G. Gilmore, *Security Interests in Personal Property* 17.3, at 545 (1965); see also *Nimmer on Copyright*, 10.05[A] at 10–44 (1989) ("a persuasive argument . . . can be made to the effect that by reasons of Sections 201(d)(1), 204(a), 205(c), and 205(d) of the current Act . . . Congress has preempted the field with respect to the form and recordation requirements applicable to copyright mortgages").

If state methods of perfection were valid, a third party (such as a potential purchaser of the copyright) who wanted to learn of any encumbrances thereon would have to check not merely the indices of the U.S. Copyright Office but also the indices of any relevant secretary of state. Because copyrights are incorporeal—they have no fixed situs— a number of state authorities could be relevant. Thus, interested third parties could never be entirely sure that all relevant jurisdictions have been searched. This possibility, together with the expense and delay of conducting searches in a variety of jurisdictions, could hinder the purchase and sale of copyrights, frustrating Congress's policy that copyrights be readily transferable in commerce.

Moreover, as discussed at greater length below, the Copyright Act establishes its own scheme for determining priority between conflicting transferees, one that differs in certain respects from that of Article Nine. Under Article Nine, priority between holders of conflicting security interests in intangibles is generally determined by who perfected his interest first (UCC 9312[5].) By contrast, section 205(d) of the Copyright Act provides: "As between two conflicting transfers, the one executed first prevails if it is recorded in the manner required to give constructive notice under subsection (c), within one month after its execution in the United States or within two months after its execution outside the United States, or at any time before recordation in such manner of the later transfer . . . " (17 U.S.C. 205[d]). Thus, unlike Article Nine, the Copyright Act permits the effect of recording with the Copyright Office to relate back as far as two months. . . .

Because the Copyright Act and Article Nine create different priority schemes, there will be occasions when different results will be reached, depending on which scheme was employed. The availability of filing under the UCC would thus undermine the priority scheme established by Congress with respect to copyrights. This type of direct interference with the operation of federal law weighs heavily in favor of preemption. See generally *Bonito Boats, Inc. v. Thunder Craft Boats, Inc.*, 109 S.Ct. 971 (1989).

The bankruptcy court below nevertheless concluded that security interests in copyrights could be perfected by filing either with the copyright office or with the secretary of state under the UCC, making a tongue-in-cheek analogy to the use of a belt and suspenders to hold up a pair of pants. According to the bankruptcy court, because either device is equally useful, one should be free to choose which one to wear. With all due respect, this court finds the analogy inapt. There is no legitimate reason why pants should be held up in only one particular manner: Individuals and public modesty are equally served by either device, or even by a safety pin or a piece of rope; all that really matters is that the job gets done. Registration schemes are different in that the way notice is given is precisely what matters. To the extent interested parties are confused as to which system is being employed, this increases the level of uncertainty and multiplies the risk of error, exposing creditors to the possibility that they might get caught with their pants down.

A recordation scheme best serves its purpose where interested parties can obtain notice of all encumbrances by referring to a single, precisely defined recordation system. The availability of parallel state recordation systems that could put parties on constructive notice as to encumbrances on copyrights would surely interfere with the effectiveness of the federal recordation scheme. Given the virtual absence of dual re-cordation schemes in our legal system, Congress cannot be presumed to have contemplated such a result. The court therefore concludes that any state recordation system pertaining to interests in copyrights would be preempted by the Copyright Act.

The court therefore concludes that the Copyright Act provides for national registration and "specifies a place of filing different from that specified in [Article Nine] for filing of the security interest" (UCC 9302[3][a]). Recording in the U.S. Copyright Office, rather than fil-ing a financing statement under Article Nine, is the proper method for perfecting a security interest in a copyright.

EFFECT OF FAILING TO RECORD WITH THE COPYRIGHT OFFICE

Having concluded that Cap Fed should have, but did not, record its security interest with the Copyright Office, the court must next deter-mine whether NPI as a debtor in possession can subordinate Cap Fed's interest and recover it for the benefit of the bankruptcy estate. As a debtor in possession, NPI has nearly all of the powers of a bankruptcy trustee (see 11 U.S.C. 1107[a]), including the authority to set aside preferential or fraudulent transfers, as well as transfers otherwise void-able under applicable state or federal law. See 11 U.S.C. 544, 547, 548.

Particularly relevant is the "strong arm clause" of 11 U.S.C. 544(a)(1), which, in respect to personal property in the bankruptcy estate, gives the debtor in possession every right and power state law confers upon one who has acquired a lien by legal or equitable proceedings. If, under the applicable law, a judicial lien creditor would prevail over an adverse claim-ant, the debtor in possession prevails; if not, not. *Wind Power Systems, Inc. v. Cannon Financial Group, Inc. (In re Wind Power Systems, Inc.)*, 841 F.2d 288, 293 (9th Cir. 1988); *Angeles Real Estate Co. v. Kerxton (In re Construction General Inc.)*, 737 F.2d 416, 418 (4th Cir. 1984). A lien creditor gener-ally takes priority over unperfected security interests in estate property because, under Article Nine, "an unperfected security interest is subordi-nate to the rights of . . . [a] person who becomes a lien creditor before the security interest is perfected" (UCC 9301[1][b]). But, as discussed previ-ously, the UCC does not apply to the extent a federal statute "governs the rights of parties to and third parties affected by transactions in particular types of property" (UCC 9104). Section 205(d) of the Copyright Act is such a statute, establishing a priority scheme between conflicting trans-fers of interests in a copyright.

As between two conflicting transfers, the one executed first prevails if it is recorded, in the manner required to give constructive notice under subsection (c), within one month after its execution in the United States or within two months after its execution outside the United States, or at any time before recordation in such manner of the later transfer. Otherwise, the later transfer prevails if recorded first in such manner, and if taken in good faith, for valuable consideration or on the basis of a binding promise to pay royalties, and without notice of the earlier transfer (17 U.S.C. 205[d]). For the reasons discussed above, the federal priority scheme preempts the state priority scheme.

Section 205(d) does not expressly address the rights of lien creditors, speaking only in terms of competing transfers of copyright interests. To determine whether NPI, as a hypothetical lien creditor, may avoid Cap Fed's unperfected security interest, the court must therefore consider whether a judicial lien is a transfer as that term is used in the Copyright Act.

As noted above, the Copyright Act recognizes transfers of copyright ownership "in whole or in part by any means of conveyance or by operation of law" (17 U.S.C. 201[d][1]). Transfer is defined broadly to include any "assignment, mortgage, exclusive license, or any other conveyance, alienation, or hypothecation of a copyright . . . whether or not it is limited in time or place of effect" (17 U.S.C. 101). A judicial lien creditor is a creditor who has obtained a lien "by judgment, levy, sequestration, or other legal or equitable process or proceeding" (11 U.S. C. 101[32]). Such a creditor typically has the power to seize and sell property held by the debtor at the time of the creation of the lien in order to satisfy the judgment or, in the case of general intangibles such as copyrights, to collect the revenues generated by the intangible as they come due. See, e.g., Cal. Civ. P. Code 701.510, 701.520, 701.640. Thus, while the creation of a lien on a copyright may not give a creditor an immediate right to control the copyright, it amounts to a sufficient transfer of rights to come within the broad definition of transfer under the Copyright Act. See *Phoenix Bond & Indemnity Co. v. Shamblin* (*In re Shamblin*), 890 F.2d 123, 127 n.7 (9th Cir. 1989) (under the Bankruptcy Code, "[t]his court has consistently treated the creation of liens on the debtor's property as a transfer").

Cap Fed contends that, in order to prevail under 17 U.S.C. 205(d), NPI must have the status of a bona fide purchaser, rather than that of a judicial lien creditor. See *Pistole v. Mellor* (*In re Mellor*), 734 F.2d 1396, 1401 (9th Cir. 1984) (judicial lien creditor does not have the same rights as a bona fide purchaser); cf. 11 U.S.C. 544(a)(3) (for real estate in the bankruptcy estate, debtor in possession has the rights of a bona fide purchaser). Cap Fed, in essence, is arguing that the term transfers. For the reasons expressed above, the court rejects this argument. The Copyright Act's definition of transfer is very broad and specifically includes transfers by operation of law (17 U.S.C. 201 [d][1]). The term is broad enough to encompass not merely purchasers, but lien creditors as well. NPI therefore is entitled to priority if it meets the statutory good faith, notice, consideration, and recording requirements of section 205(a). As the hypothetical lien creditor, NPI is deemed to have taken in good faith and without notice. See 11 U.S.C. 544(a). The only remaining issues are whether NPI could have recorded its interest in the Copyright Office and whether it obtained its lien for valuable consideration.

In order to obtain a lien on a particular piece of property, a creditor who has received a money judgment in the form of a writ of execution must prepare a notice of levy that specifically identifies the property to be encumbered and the consequences of that action. See Cal. Civ. P. Code 699.540. If such a notice identifies a federal copy-right or the receivables generated by such a copy-right, it and the underlying writ of execution, constitute "document[s] pertaining to a copyright" and therefore, are capable of recordation in the Copyright Office. See 17 U.S.C. 205(a); Compendium of Copyright Office Practices II paras. 1602–1603 (identifying which documents the Copyright Office will accept for filing). Because these documents could be recorded in the Copyright Office, NPI as debtor in possession will be deemed to have done so.

Finally, contrary to Cap Fed's assertion, a trustee or debtor in possession is deemed to have given valuable consideration for its judicial lien. Section 544(a)(1) provides: "The trustee [or debtor in possession] shall have, as of the commencement of the case . . . the rights and powers of, or may avoid any transfer of property of the debtor or any obligation incurred by the debtor that is voidable by . . . a creditor that extends credit to the debtor at the time of the commencement of the case, and that obtains, at such time and with respect to such credit, a judicial lien on all property on which a creditor on a simple contract could have obtained such a judicial lien . . . " (11 U.S.C. 544[a][1]). The act of extending credit, of course, constitutes the giving of valuable consideration. See *First Maryland Leasecorp v. M/V Golden Egret,* 764 F.2d 749, 753 (11th Cir. 1985); *United States v. Cahall Bros.,* 674 F. 2d 578, 581 (6th Cir. 1982). In addition, the trustee's lien—like that of any other judgment creditor—is deemed to be in exchange for the claim that formed the basis of the underlying judgment, a claim that is extinguished by the entry of the judgment.

Because NPI meets all of the requirements for subsequent transferees to prevail under 17 U.S.C. 205(d)—a transferee who took in good faith, for valuable consideration and without notice of the earlier transfer—Cap Fed's unperfected security interest in NPI's copyrights and the receivables they generated is trumped by NPI's hypothetical judicial lien. NPI may therefore avoid Cap Fed's interest and preserve it for the benefit of the bankruptcy estate.

CONCLUSION

The judgment of the bankruptcy court is reversed. The case is ordered remanded for a determination of which movies in NPI's library are the subject of valid copyrights. The court shall then determine the status of Cap Fed's security interest in the movies and the debtor's other property. To the extent that interest is unperfected, the court shall permit NPI to exercise its avoidance powers under the Bankruptcy Code. It is so ordered.

NOTES _____

    1. In an age of inflated entertainment costs, outside financing of projects has become both more commonplace and large-scale. Inherent and vital to financing is

the ability to provide security for the loans, and among the most obvious and ultimately valuable assets one can secure in an entertainment project is a copyright covering the work being financed, generally accomplished through floating liens on future copyrights. Prior to the district court's decision in *Peregrine*, there was widespread belief that a properly filed UCC financing statement would provide a security interest in a copyright. It remains unresolved how one would perfect a security interest in an unregistered or future copyright. *In re Avalon Software, Inc.*, 209 B.R. 517 (Bankr. D. Ariz. 1997) holds that a security interest in a copyrightable work is not perfected unless both the work and the UCC-1 are filed with the Copyright Office. This includes copyrightable modifications to the original program. However, stating that "the Peregrine court's analysis only works if the copyright was registered," *In re World Auxiliary Power Co.*, 244 B.R. 149 (Bankr. N.D. Cal. 1999) concludes that where no copyright registration has been filed, a security interest is perfected when the UCC-1 is filed with the California Secretary of State. For safety's sake, lenders must require that they be notified when a work subject to an "after acquired interest" clause has been created so that a further copyright registration and security interests can be filed. Moreover, it should be noted that because of the traditionally slow processing time of the U.S. Copyright Office, coupled with the fact that filings are made under title and not by debtor, searches for prior security interests are both difficult and uncertain.

2. There are three distinct categories of collateral that could be secured by the borrower in a film financing transaction: (1) the contract rights and accounts receivable related to the motion picture, which would include amounts payable for pre-sales and amounts paid via distribution or syndication agreements; (2) the actual physical film (the negatives, prints, and soundtrack that make up the motion picture); and (3) the copyright in the film. Each of the three distinct classes of collateral is secured in a different way. The contract rights and accounts receivable, as well as the physical film, are generally secured by the borrower through provisions of the UCC as adopted and modified by the applicable state. As seen in the *Peregrine* case, perfection of a security interest in the copyright is not covered by UCC Article 9 but, rather, the 1976 Copyright Act. A lender who seeks to obtain security interest in the copyright to the motion picture it is financing will generally require the borrower to execute a mortgage of copyright, which would be filed with the Copyright Office and released upon full repayment of the loan. See Peter A. Levitan, "A Primer of Selected Copyright Concerns in Motion Picture Practice," 1990 *Entertainment Publishing and the Arts Handbook*, at 3.

3. In *Septembertide Publishing B.V. v. Stein and Day, Inc.*, 884 F.2d 675 (2d Cir. 1989), the issue was whether a commercial printer (which had a security agreement with the publisher) or an author (who did *not* have a security agreement) was entitled to two-thirds of an advance due from the licensee of the paperback rights to a novel written by the author, when the publisher went bankrupt. Holding that the author was an intended third-party beneficiary of the agreement between the publisher and the printing house, the Court found (on this basis as well as on custom and usage in the industry) that the author was therefore entitled to two-thirds of the advance payable by the licensee of the paperback edition, the share prescribed in the agreement between the author and the now-bankrupt publisher.

4. In *In re Sherman*, 627 F.2d 594 (2d Cir. 1980), an insurance company was permitted to recoup a bankrupt agent's advance commissions from commissions actually earned subsequent to filing of the petition. These were advances, not loans. No "security interest" was involved, and therefore the company was not required to perfect its interest under UCC.

5. An assignment of the right to receive royalties from a copyrighted work does not constitute a "transfer of copyright ownership" within the meaning of 107 of the Copyright Act of 1976; such assignments are not "other documents pertaining to

copyright" (17 U.S. C. 205). Therefore, such an assignment need not be recorded in the Copyright Office, and a subsequent IRS lien will not take precedence over the rights of the assignee. *BMI v. Hirsch,* 104 F.3d 1163 ((9th Cir. 1997).

5.6 ARBITRATION

It may be a good idea to consider the desirability of attempting to negotiate arbitration clauses when representing entry-level recording artists, songwriters and other creative personnel. However, there is no clear answer; as with so many other contemporary issues, it depends.

While it would probably be impossible to develop an empirical method of proving it, the level of bitterness reflected in the cases in this chapter should be sufficient to convince even the most casual observer that litigation involving creative talents is extremely hazardous to ongoing business relationships and frequently impacts creativity negatively. Companies do not relish the negative implications which attend publicity surrounding litigation with persons under contract to them. Because of the enormous costs in time, money, and psychological damage that litigation customarily entails, transactional attorneys frequently seek to include arbitration clauses in their agreements. The standard American Arbitration Association arbitration clause is:

"Any controversy or claim arising out of or relating to this contract, or the breach thereof, shall be settled by arbitration administered by the American Arbitration Association in accordance with its Commercial [or other] Arbitration Rules [including the Optional Rules for Emergency Measures of Protection], and judgment on the award rendered by the arbitrator(s) may be entered in any court having jurisdiction thereof."

The arbitration clause may be expanded to include arbitration in specific contexts (international, construction, employment, patents, domain names) and to take into consideration timing, private statutes of limitation, number and method of selection of arbitrators, arbitrator qualifications, locales, governing law, available remedies, etc. Sample arbitration clauses are available on-line at the American Arbitration Association website, http://www.adr.org/sp.asp?id = 22020.

Parties to any existing dispute may commence an arbitration under the Rules of the American Arbitration Association by filing at any regional office of the Association three copies of a written submission to arbitrate under these rules, signed by the parties. It must contain a statement of the matter in dispute, the amount involved (if any), the remedies sought, and the hearing local requested, together with the appropriate filing fee as provided in the schedule of administrative fees. Parties may agree to submit and conduct their dispute on-line exclusively via the Internet. The AAA Supplementary Procedures provide for all party submissions to be made online, and for the arbitrator, upon review of such submissions, to render an award and to communicate it to the parties via the Internet.

State statutes (e.g., Article 75 of the New York Civil Practice Law & Rules, Title 9 (1280 et seq.) of the California Code of Civil Procedure) and a federal statute (Federal Arbitration Act, 9 U.S.C.A. 1 et seq.) provide detailed legislative schemes which may be utilized if parties decide to forgo resort to the American Arbitration Association. Some states require arbitration (mandatory arbitration) for cases involving lesser amounts (under $50,000). There are commercial operations such as the Judicial Arbitration & Mediation Service (JAMS)(www.jamsadr.com), the Center for Dispute Settlement (www.cdsusa.org), Resolute Systems, Inc. (www.resolutesystems.com), and National Arbitration and Mediation (NAM) (www.namadr.com) which provide experts, retired judges and experienced attorneys as arbitrators.

Arbitration is strongly favored as a matter of public policy, *Cohen v. Wedbush, Noble, Cooke, Inc.*, 841 F.2d 282 (9th Cir. 1989), and any doubts concerning the scope of an arbitration clause are to be resolved in favor of arbitration. *French v. Merrill, Lynch, Pierce, Fenner & Smith Co.* 784 F.2d 902 (9th Cir. 1989). In *Graham v. Scissor-Tail, Inc.*, 28 Cal.3d 807, 623 P.2d 165 (1981), promoter Bill Graham was required to arbitrate a dispute under a standard American Federation of Musicians date agreement; however, he did not have to accept an arbitrator selected solely by the union, which the court found unconscionable. (In *Taylor v. Nelson*, 615 F. Supp. 533 (W.D.Va. 1985), *rev'd on other grounds*, 788 F.2d 220 (1986) the same form arbitration clause was held unenforceable against the promoter. The AF of M has since abandoned its former policy in favor of a more impartial format.) While ideally arbitration provides a quick, easy, inexpensive and definitive alternative to conventional litigation, it is well to remember that "[a]rbitrators do not have to follow the law or the rules of evidence." W. F. Rylersdaam, Alternative Dispute Resolution, *Cal. Bar J.* March 2000, p. 10. Moreover, experience with three-member panels indicates that because of the difficulty of meshing the schedules of the three members, the schedules of the attorneys, clients, and non-party witnesses as well as the frequently disjointed nature of such proceedings, such arbitrations often take longer than conventional litigation and are very expensive and produce awards that are not models of clarity. Bear in mind that an arbitration proceeding concludes with the entry of an award, and resort must then be made to the appropriate judicial forum for the confirmation, vacatur, or modification of the award. The initiation of an arbitration proceeding may also result in court practice in the form of a motion to compel or stay arbitration, adding yet another layer of cost, time and resources to the procedure.

An arbitrator has very broad powers during the course of the hearings except that with respect to pre-hearing discovery, pursuant to Rule R-21 of the Commercial Arbitration Rules of the American Arbitration Association, the Arbitrator may direct (i) the production of documents and other information, (ii) the identification of any witnesses to be called, and (iii) a schedule for further hearings to resolve the dispute. The parties are required to exchange copies of all exhibits intended to be used in the hearing at least five (5) days prior to the hearing. Under

Section 43 of the same Rules, the arbitrator may grant "any remedy or relief . . . deem[ed] just and equitable and within the scope of the agreement of the parties," including, but not limited to, specific performance of contracts. A judgment entered upon an arbitration award will not be set aside by motion or on appeal, except upon jurisdictional grounds or by reason of the corruption of the arbitrator(s), or unless the award is totally irrational. American Arbitration Association awards do not set forth reasons for the decision. This, plus the lack of a transcript (which is commonplace), prevents meaningful court review, because while "an award will be vacated if it is in 'manifest disregard of the law' . . . [t]his standard requires [that t]he error must have been obvious and capable of being readily and instantly perceived by the average person qualified to serve as an arbitrator." *Ripa v. Cathy Parker Management, Inc.*, 1998 WL 241621 (SDNY 1998).

The most extensive use of arbitration as a procedure to determine disputes in the entertainment industries is through collective bargaining agreements entered into between unions acting on behalf of creative personnel and the companies which utilize their services, e.g., actors (represented by the Screen Actors Guild), screenwriters (Writers Guild of America), directors (Directors Guild of America, which also represents production managers and technical coordinators in motion pictures), vocalists (American Federation of Television and Radio Artists). Actors Equity Association acts on behalf of performers, stage managers, and assistant stage managers for live theatrical productions. Both sides to these agreements recognize the need for expeditious resolution of disputes, with binding effect, available on short notice, so that films, television, Broadway productions and other entertainment presentations may move forward without delay.

In the following case, the District Court's decision illustrates the unassailability of the arbitration award.

Robert Lewis Rosen Associates, Ltd. V. William Webb, 2005 U.S. Dist. LEXIS 10413 (SDNY 2005)

HON. HAROLD BAER, JR., DISTRICT JUDGE:

Plaintiff Robert Lewis Rosen Associates, Ltd. ("RLR") seeks an Order from this Court allowing the entry of a money judgment, pursuant to this Court's previous Opinion and Order dated November 24, 2003, and subsequent Judgment dated November 26, 2003. The motion is Granted.

I. BACKGROUND

RLR is a New York corporation that manages individuals' entertainment careers. William Webb ("Webb") used RLR's services as a personal manager, representative and advisor for his career as a television sports director until the relationship soured and RLR initiated arbitration before the American Arbitration Association. On July

31, 2003, an Award was rendered in RLR's favor and on November 24, 2003, this Court issued an Opinion and Order ("Opinion") that confirmed the Award in its entirety. The Arbitration Award provided, inter alia, that:

1. Respondent William Webb shall pay Claimant RLR the sum of Three Hundred Fifty-Five Thousand Eighty-Four Dollars and Thirty-Two Cents ($355,084.32), which reflects amounts due Claimant as of May 31, 2003. This sum includes manager's fees due, the costs of this arbitration including fees of the American Arbitration Association and the Arbitrator's compensation, attorneys' fees and other related costs. Payments shall be rendered forthwith but in no event later than thirty days after Webb's receipt of this Award.
2. Additional payments due Claimant RLR pursuant to the 2000 Fox Renewal, the 2001 MSG Renewal and the 2005 and 2006 Fox Renewal shall be made within thirty days after William Webb's receipt of these payments.
3. Interest at the rate of six per cent (6%) per annum shall accrue after payments are due in accordance with Paragraphs (1) and (2) above. *Robert Lewis Rosen Assocs. v. Webb, 2003 U.S. Dist. LEXIS 21317 at *9–10 (SDNY Nov. 24, 2003).*

On November 26, 2003, this Court entered a separate Judgment that provided as per the Court's Opinion, "petitioner's motion to confirm the arbitration award is granted, the award of $ 355,084.32 with interest of 6% per annum is confirmed [and] respondent's motion to vacate the award or in the alternative, for a stay is denied." Nov. 26, 2003 Judgment, Dckt. # 23. The Judgment was silent with regard to "Additional payments" that may become due in the future, e.g., the 2000 Fox Renewal, the 2001 MSG Renewal and the 2005 and 2006 Fox Renewal. Each of which represents an unmatured renewal and each of which was included in the Arbitration Award and were reflected in this Court's Opinion that confirmed that Award. *Robert Lewis Rosen, 2003 U.S. Dist. LEXIS 21317, 2003 WL 22801698 at *9.* The first Judgment did not set out the renewals since it was unknown as to whether those renewals would ever mature. The question then is whether a new judgment must be fashioned and is it too late.

On February 4, 2005, RLR petitioned this Court to enter an additional judgment against William Webb with respect to these "Additional payments" which became due pursuant to the award within 30 days of payment following the networks' decision to renew Webb's contracts. Webb argues that because these payments were not spelled out in the November 26, 2003, Judgment, the money is now uncollectible. After oral argument and consideration of all the materials provided to the Court, I conclude that the Court having confirmed the Arbitration Award in its entirety, the "Additional payments" in the Arbitration Award were included and are now due and owing and RLR is entitled to such relief as was provided in the Award. [n1]

n1 According to the Clerk of the Court, it is not uncommon for courts to clarify Judgments that confirm arbitration awards where there is no way at the time of entry for the prevailing party to execute on such a judgment, and that's what this Order does.

II. DISCUSSION

Webb argues that the November 26, 2003 Judgment represents the final and complete award due to RLR and as such RLR cannot now collect commissions on the renewals. Because the Judgment does not explicitly provide for the "Additional payments," Webb argues RLR should have amended the Judgment pursuant to *Rule 59(e)* and the time to do so has long since passed. Creative perhaps but unavailing. This relief is not an increase in the Judgment because it was already awarded when the Court confirmed the entire Arbitration Award in its Opinion in November 2003. As such, *Rule 59(e)* plays no role in my decision on this issue. So a new judgment is not necessary and the renewals having only now become due, this application is not too late.

This is a somewhat novel issue because the rationale underlying *Rule 59(e)* has not been applied to confirmation of arbitration awards and subsequent judgments to clarify those awards.

When an arbitration award is confirmed, unless the court specifies otherwise, it includes the entire award. *Barbier v. Shearson Lehman Hutton, Inc.,* 752 F. Supp. 151, 158 (SDNY 1990), aff'd in part, rev'd in part, 948 F.2d 117 (2d Cir. 1991) (citing *Florasynth, Inc. v. Pickholz,* 750 F.2d 171, 176 (2d Cir. 1984)) (confirmation of an arbitration award is "a summary proceeding that merely makes what is already a final arbitration award a judgment of the court."). A judgment that confirms an arbitration award "should reflect what would have happened had the parties immediately complied with the awards instead of going to court." *Americas Ins. Co. v. Seagull Compania Naviera, S.A.,* 774 F.2d 64, 67 (2d Cir. 1985) citing *Marion Mfg. Co. v. Long,* 588 F.2d 538, 541 (6th Cir. 1978). If an arbitration award is upheld in a reviewing court, the rights of the parties are determined from the date of the award and not the date of the court's judgment confirming the award. *Marion Mfg.,* 588 F.2d at 541. Any other result would defeat the purpose of arbitration which is to finally decide the issues between the arbitrating parties without judicial intervention. As such, when this Court confirmed the Arbitration Award, it confirmed the entire Award, which necessarily includes the future contract renewal payments.

Section 13 of the FAA provides that a judgment confirming an award, once entered, has the same force and effect as a judgment in a standard civil action and is "subject to all provisions of law" relating to judgments. *9 U.S.C. β 13.* Webb argues that because the Judgment provided a specific sum and did not include language about the additional payments due to contract renewal, it was not intended to be part of the final Judgment and cannot later be changed. The relevant part of the November 2003 Judgment states that "petitioner's motion to confirm the arbitration award is granted, the award of $ 355,084.32 with interest of 6% per annum is confirmed [and] respondent's motion to vacate the award or in the alternative, for a stay is denied." Notwithstanding the fact that the previous clause reiterates the Court's intention to confirm the Award, Webb has chosen to read ambiguity into the Judgment and contends that no additional payments can ever be due because no further monies are detailed. But because Arbitration Awards are confirmed in their entirety or specifically changed or vacated, and in this case the Court expressly denied Defendant's motion to vacate, any arguments about ambiguity or the effects of final judgment are unavailing.

III. CONCLUSION

For the above stated reasons RLR is entitled to judgment against William Webb in the additional sum of one hundred and six thousand, four hundred forty one dollars and seventy two cents ($106,441.72) in satisfaction of the monies owed per the Arbitration Award as a result of the 2000 Fox Renewal, the 2001 MSG Renewal and the 2005 and 2006 Fox Renewal, plus interest at the rate of six percent 6% per annum beginning 30 days from the date Webb received the payments.

In addition, within 30 days from the date hereof, RLR is Ordered to provide William Web with an accounting of all monies received to date in connection with the Arbitration Award to determine if there were any overpayment, and such overpayment, if any, will be offset against the money due. The Clerk of the Court is instructed to close this motion and any other motions and remove this case from my docket.

IT IS SO ORDERED

Chapter 6

LITERARY PUBLISHING

6.1 INTRODUCTION

Headlines of the Wall Street Journal ("WSJ") characterize changes in the literary publishing business: "Harper Collins Plans to Control its Digital Books" (Harper Collins plans to produce digital copies of its books and then make them available to search services offered by such companies as Google, Inc., Yahoo, Inc., Microsoft Corp. and Amazon. com while maintaining physical possession of the digital files) (WSJ, Dec. 12, 2005); "Google will Return to Scanning Copyrighted Library Books," (Google plans to resume scanning copyrighted library books into its search engine, despite the efforts of some publishers and authors to block it from doing so without the copyright holders' permission) (WSJ, Nov. 1, 2005); "Google This: Amazon Plans to Settle Portions of Books Online" (Amazon plans to introduce two new programs next year to allow consumers to buy online access to entire books, giving publishers and authors another way to generate revenue from their content) (WSJ, Nov. 4, 2005).

With the advent of the internet, the business of literary publishing took on a new dimension. Digital books, books online, and the googling of copyrighted library books all created a new arena for authors and their publishers. Significant copyright issues arose, and as of the writing of this Chapter, significant issues remain unsettled.

Long before films, radio, television, and other technologies, the printed word was a medium of entertainment. A tremendous proportion of the raw material of the other media is derived from print sources. In addition, the recent history of the literary publishing industry bears many similarities to the recent histories of the other industries we survey in the remainder of this book.

Writers such as Erle Stanley Gardner, Louis L'Amour, Agatha Christie, Georges Simenon, P. G. Wodehouse, Catharine Cookson and Barbara

Cartland have written hundreds of books, with aggregate sales in the hundreds of millions. The novels of such mass-market-oriented authors as John Grisham (who received a reported $6 million for the movie rights to his first novel, *A Time To Kill*), Stephen King, Scott Turow, Patricia Cornwall, James Patterson, James Clavell, and Danielle Steel, as well as the works of more "serious" writers such as Hemingway, Fitzgerald, and Faulkner, have become the stuff of movie and television fare.

Whereas early American writers such as James Fenimore Cooper and Washington Irving had to pay to publish their works, by the nineteenth century book publishing had emerged as an American business. The roles of writer and publisher diverged, and patterns emerged which have spread to the other industries, molded and adapted in each industry to suit its own needs and customs. Ironically, with the advent of the Internet and the ease of self-publishing, those roles may merge again in the future. Our initial focus, therefore, is on trends which have developed in literary publishing.

6.2 THE BUSINESS OF LITERARY PUBLISHING

Publishing houses began as family businesses. Ownership passed from generation to generation, and an intimate relationship between the company ownership and its group of authors was the norm. While many small general interest and specialty publishers survive, many of the larger publishing houses have been absorbed by multinational conglomerates, with potential negative consequences for authors in two respects: first, because these enterprises are publicly held and must answer to stockholders and public markets generally, there is a greater hesitancy to gamble on moderate sellers or unknowns; and second, again because of the need to generate steady, sizeable profits, there is less one-on-one involvement between publishing house editors and authors than prevailed in the past.

Book publishing is big business. Only television commands more total revenue than print publishing, an ascendancy gained only as recently as the early 1980s. Let us examine some of the "players."

Expansion and consolidation characterize the publishing side of the business as well as the retail side. As of 2002, the five large New York publishers had US sales of $4.102 billion and worldwide sales of $5.68 billion. The leading publishers by annual sales were:

Random House	$2.1 billion worldwide
Penguin Group	$1.3 billion worldwide
HarperCollins	$1.1 billion worldwide
Simon & Schuster	$690 million (estimated)
AOL/Time Warner	$415 million

(http://parapub.com/statistics/)

Bertlesmann AG, the world's third largest entertainment conglomerate (after AOL Time Warner Inc. and The Walt Disney Company), acquired Random House, which gives Bertelsmann (which also owns Bantam Doubleday Dell) the largest single share of the U.S. literary publishing market. Random House imprints include Random House, Alfred A. Knopf, Ballantine, Crown, Fawcett, Fodor's and Modern Library. Pearson Plc, a UK conglomerate (owner of the Financial Times, paperback giant Penguin, the educational publisher Addison Wesley Longman, as well as 50% owner of The Economist) acquired Simon & Schuster (except for its consumer publishing business) from Viacom Inc. Even with its reduced scope, Simon & Schuster remains the second largest American trade publisher. Time Warner Inc. publishes such magazines as *Time, Life, Fortune, Sports Illustrated,* and *Money,* and owns leading paperback house Warner Books, direct mail operations Time-Life Books and Record and Book-of-the-Month Club, and such traditional publishers as Little, Brown & Co.

Each of these conglomerates operates in many different areas of the entertainment industries, and it is therefore no accident that the conglomerates are also involved in literary publishing. For example, in addition to the publishing interests described above, Bertelsmann owns worldwide record operations through its BMG and Ariola Records groups. Australia-based News Corp. (whose chairman, Rupert Murdoch, became a U.S. citizen in order to qualify to own television stations) controls major newspapers on three continents, as well as 20th Century Fox, Fox Broadcasting, and HarperCollins (formerly Harper & Row and U.K. publisher Collins). Holtzbrinck, a German Publishing house, owns U.S. publishers Henry Holt & Co. and Farrar Straus Giroux. The importance of literary publishing to the conglomerates varies considerably. Bertelsmann derived 37.8% of its $14 billion annual worldwide revenues in 1998 from this source, while AOL Time Warner, Inc. derived only 5.4% of its annual revenues and Disney only 0.7% from literary publishing.

Part of the reason that entertainment conglomerates are attracted to literary publishing is the cross-marketing potential of tie-ins between books and radio, television, and films, as illustrated by such phenomena as Oprah Winfrey's book club; talk show host Rush Limbaugh's leading of the best-seller lists in 1992 and 1993; by sales of such volumes as a cookbook by Oprah Winfrey's cook (a 400,000-copy first printing); the Bubba Gump Shrimp Co. Cookbook (a 700,000-copy first printing, the largest ever for a hardcover cookbook), which followed the phenomenal box-office success of "Forrest Gump"; and the trade paperback edition of "Schindler's List," which passed the 1,000,000 sales mark in 1994 after the success of the Steven Spielberg film (Daisy Maryles, "Embraced by the List," *Publishers Weekly,* January 2, 1995, p. 50).

The increasing internationalization of the entertainment industries, which is discussed throughout this book, evidenced in the literary publishing industry by the ownership described above, is further underscored by the presence in recent years in top U.S. positions of such figures as Alberto Vitale, an Italian, chief executive of Random House, Inc.; Sonny Mehta, an Indian, head of Alfred A. Knopf; and Tina Brown, an Englishwoman, editor of the *New Yorker* (and subsequently the new magazine, *Talk*).

However, internationalization does not stop with ownership by foreign conglomerates or the appointment of foreign nationals to lead U.S. publishing houses. Foreign revenues have become increasingly important to American publishers: some 60% to 70% of U.S. publishers' revenues from sources other than U.S. hard copy sales comes from foreign subpublishing Jennifer Nix, "A Broad Book Biz," *Daily Variety*, June 23, 1998, p. 24.

There are six large publishers, 3–400 medium-sized publishers, and 86,000 small/self-publishers, according to the Para Publishing Web site (http://parapub.com/statistics).

Expansion, concentration, and cross-ownership in publishing have had their counterpart in book retailing as well. The small mom and pop bookshop faces increasing competition from large chains. It is estimated that Barnes & Noble (which includes B. Dalton/Pickwick), Borders-Waldenbooks (a subsidiary of mass-market retailer K Mart, with over 1,000 stores), and Crown Books now account for approximately 50 percent of U.S. retail book sales. Because of the steady growth of Barnes & Noble and Borders-Waldenbooks, third-largest chain Crown Books was forced to seek Chapter 11 protection. Meanwhile, the dominance of the big chains has in turn, provoked an anti-trust suit from the American Booksellers Association, a trade organization of some 4,500 independent bookshops (down from 5100 in 1991) (*ABA* v. *Barnes & Noble and Borders et al*, U.S. District Court, District of Northern California). From 1992 to 1998, the chain store share of the book market increased from 22% to 26%, while the independent share declined from 33% to 19% (*Los Angeles Times*, April 27, 1998, p. D2).

Online hard-copy distribution also poses a threat to traditional bookstores. Amazon.com, losing money but growing, offers access to millions of titles. Barnes & Noble (bn.com) is waging a battle with Amazon.com for pre-eminence in on-line publishing and Borders Group is a distant third.

Online publishing, downloading of books directly to the consumer and e-books are still very new, but many see this as a revolution in literary publishing. Some question whether paper books will be a thing of the past as soon as 2009, the year Microsoft has predicted that the majority of books will be available in e-book form. In 2000, Microsoft entered into agreements with Barnesandnoble.com, Random House, and Simon & Schuster to make popular titles available free of charge on Pocket PCs employing Microsoft's Reader software, and Time Warner's Ipublish.com was announced as the first dedicated Web-publishing venture by a U.S. book publisher.

As a possible precursor of things to come, Stephen King's novella "Riding The Bullet" generated enormous excitement in its first two days of literary life as an e-book. Simon & Schuster reported 400,000 orders in the first 24 hours after the work became available on retail websites, although customers experienced delays and inability to download due to software problems. Orders ultimately exceeded 500,000 copies. Sales of digital reading devices were expected to exceed 500,000 copies by the end of 2000. King generated more controversy in the publishing world by posting sequential serial chapters of "The Plant" on-line on a "pay as you go" subscription basis. When King interrupted the installments (or put "The Plant" on hiatus and "furled its leaves" as he called it) in December 2000, *his* net profit (direct to him) was $463,832.27.

These trends have ominous implications for traditional literary publishers: Authors whose names have "marquee" value may decide that their works can be marketed without the assistance of old-line publishers, and they may elect to forego advances in favor of potentially greater "back-end" earnings. For those who are less famous and for traditional publishers, there will be additional pressure to spend marketing dollars in order to attract attention in an increasingly hits-driven business.

6.3 THE SCOPE OF LITERARY PUBLISHING CONTRACTS

The basic literary work may be only the beginning of the process by which a "story" is created and sold through numerous media. Serializations may occur before and after publication, and "books on tape" have grown increasingly important. A book may be turned into a movie, the movie may become a play or a musical, and the movie may provide the push for a paperback tied to the film (with the title of the book sometimes being changed to the title of the movie). The book which has become a movie may then be transformed into a television series (for example, *M*A*S*H*), the movie into a television series, the book into a sequel, the sequel into a movie, and on and on. The first contract between the publisher and author is crucial in determining who has control over the process. Several other contracts are likely to be entered into before the creative work reaches its ultimate saturation of all available markets. In addition to the contract between the publisher and author, there are likely to be contracts for paperback, foreign, and merchandise licensing and for motion picture, television, and video/audiocassette options. There is usually also a contract between the author and a literary agent. This contract is discussed in Section 6.3.6. The publisher/author contract is the tablesetter that may greatly determine—or, indeed, foreclose—what can or cannot be included in later agreements. This contract is discussed in detail in Section 6.4. However, in light of the fact that sales of hardback copies are usually the "tail" of an increasingly diffuse "dog," it is important to note three important areas which can be of enormous importance to an author.

6.3.1 Paperback Licensing

On the assumption that the prospective book has possibilities for both hardcover and paperback markets, the hardback publisher generally obtains paperback exploitation rights in the original publisher-author contract. In the usual scenario, the publisher-author contract allows the original publisher to sublicense the paperback edition to another company. In very rare cases, the hardcover publisher will obtain the paperback rights but there will be restrictions in the contract limiting the range of companies to whom the paperback rights can be licensed. For the most established writers, it is not unusual to arrange at the outset for the paperback publishing rights to be handled by a different publisher than the publisher of the hardcover edition.

6.3.2 Foreign Licensing

While the publisher's first draft agreement will almost always include foreign publication rights (at far lower royalty rates than those which apply to domestic sales), authors frequently dispose of foreign publication rights separately from rights for the U.S. and Canada. A foreign license may involve translating the work into another language. One question to be resolved is the extent to which the original publisher (or the author) has an opportunity to review the quality and faithfulness of the translation. Unless the work is a "literary" work, it is very rare for the author to secure approval over translations. The precise limits of the territory within which the foreign translation may be distributed must be included. In this connection, it should be remembered that country-by-country licenses are ineffective in the European Union, since the EC Treaty forbids territorial restrictions within the 17 countries now belonging to the Union. The precise purposes for which the license is granted must be defined. The foreign licensee will often be required to put up advances and/or guarantees "in front." This is of major importance, since audits are expensive and a U.S. licensee may not wish to undertake these costs if they can be avoided. Prompt repatriation of royalties is an issue in this area; in order to control inflation, foreign countries sometimes impose so-called blocked currency restrictions, which prevent or delay local licensees from remitting dollars to the U.S. In such cases, the value of royalties affected by such restrictions may diminish and even disappear before the blockage is lifted.

6.3.3 Merchandise Licensing

Literary works at times attain such popularity that items in clothing, toys, posters, and other merchandise may have substantial commercial possibilities. *Geisel v. Poynter Products,* Inc., 295 F. Supp. 331 (S.D.N.Y 1968), emphasizes what happens when the ownership of a creative product is not properly protected. The facts of the case also illustrate the marketing possibilities for characters in a literary work, sometimes several years after the original work featuring the characters first appears. The merchandise licensing agreement must define precisely for what purposes the license is granted in terms of what product can be produced, what degree of quality control exists, and how long the license runs. Restrictions on territorial areas and types of marketing should also be negotiated.

6.3.4 Motion Picture/Television Licensing

Here, too, the literary publisher will seek to include the rights in its basic agreement with the author. However, quite a few films have been based upon novels acquired prior to their publication. Potentially "hot" properties are often circulated in pre-publication galley proofs or even in manuscript form. If an author can retain film/television rights, he/she can potentially realize far more income than would be the case if the deal went through the literary publisher. On the other hand, the imprimatur of a major publisher may induce a higher level of interest among film and television producers than might otherwise be the case.

Typically, the prospective producer's first step is to obtain an option on the work, pending a decision as to whether the work is translatable to film and whether the appropriate financing and talent can be obtained. In the normal case, an option agreement will provide for an initial option period of one year, with one or two potential renewal periods before the potential licensee must ultimately exercise the option or let it drop. The option agreement will typically provide for a set fee for the option(s) with a further payment when the option is exercised, which may be limited to a fixed dollar amount or may include a fee plus a percentage of the proceeds (usually, net profits). Sometimes the option payments are advances against the ultimate purchase price; in other situations, they are not. The dollars will vary greatly depending upon the stature of the book (sometimes, the stature of the author) and whether the film is made originally for theatrical release or is made strictly for television.

The option agreement should define not only the length and cost of the option but also the terms of the ultimate agreement in the event the option is exercised. The option contract, as well as the license which will come into existence if the option is exercised, must define the creative control retained by publisher or author, the time limits on the license as well as an outside date by which the film must be made or the rights relinquished, the precise scope of the license (e.g., does the producer get prequel, sequel and spin-off rights, which would permit the producer to make a series of films, or does the license cover only one picture?), and, of course, the royalty or fee arrangements.

Frequently, the ability of the prospective licensee to exercise its options will be conditioned on the occurrence of one or more specific events, e.g., the preparation of a first draft of the script, the signing of a name director or actor, etc.

6.3.5 Other Media Licensing

Literary publishing agreements have for many years included catch-all "new technologies" clauses. Until a few years ago, little attention was paid to these. However, as technologies evolve, such clauses receive greater attention. Some print publishers find it advantageous to put their works directly into other media forms, such as audio books or videocassettes. The basic publisher-author agreement should cover this possibility (see Section 6.4); the publisher may then find itself licensing the rights for an audio book or videocassette to another company if the publisher itself does not have such capacity. The original publisher will be concerned over the timing of the release of the audio book version, so that the "buzz" attending the printed version of the book will have the fullest possible impact on sales of the audio book version. The publisher will also be concerned about the quality of the audio book version and the conformity between the advertising and marketing materials utilized in connection with the printed audio book versions.

6.3.6 Author-Literary Agent

Authors who write for the mass market usually require a literary agent to represent them. The agent in this role assumes somewhat different responsibilities than agents or managers in other entertainment fields, but there are also similarities. The general legal requirements of agents, including those of a fiduciary relationship to the client, are discussed at length in Chapter 1 (see Section 1.3). The agreement between the author and the literary agent should specify how long the contract is to run, the different types of income on which the agent's fees will be based, and, in rare cases, representations by the agent as to what can be done for the author and the ability of the agent to act on the author's behalf. In general, the agent promises good-faith efforts to market the author. The reality is that a young author's big opportunity may lie in obtaining the services of a reputable and well-established literary agent.

The following provides an example of an agreement between an author and a literary agent, again subject to negotiation between the parties:

Literary Agency Agreement

AGREEMENT made this Xth day of MONTH 20xx between XXXXX (hereinafter called "Author"), whose address is XXXXXX, and YYYYYYY (hereinafter called "Agent), whose principal address is YYYYYYYY.

1. Author appoints YYYYYY as sole and exclusive agent to represent her interests with regard to a book-length writing project tentatively entitled **XXXXXX** by ZZZZZZZZZZZ (hereinafter called Work), and its Derivatives (hereinafter defined as any and all works and ancillary products based on the Work), throughout the world, under the following terms and conditions.

   a. Agent will negotiate the Author's writing contract for the Work with the publisher, proprietor, or other entity as applicable. Agent agrees to provide Author in a timely fashion with copies of all drafts and redrafts of proposed contract between Author and ZZZZZZZZZZ.

   b. Agent agrees to make no agreements on Author's behalf without Author's prior written approval, and no agreement shall bind Author without Author's consent and signature.

   c. No power of attorney of any kind or nature is given to the Agent by the Author.

2. In the event that the Agent is unable to negotiate an agreement with a publisher, producer or other entity that is satisfactory to the Author, the Author may terminate this Agreement any time after six (6) months from the date of this Agreement provided that the Author notify the Agent in writing thirty (30) days prior to termination.

3. Agent agrees to monitor publisher, producer, or other entity for compliance with contract terms.

4. Agent may, on Author's behalf and with Author's prior written approval, do the following: approve and permit any and all publicity and advertising, approve and permit the use of Author's name, bibliography, photograph, likeness, voice, literary, and artistic materials for purposes of advertising and publicity and in the promotion and advertising of any and all products and services related to the Work.

5. Agent and Author will be responsible for paying the following expenses as indicated:

   a. The Agent shall pay for phone, postage, and light photocopying as it relates to Agent's efforts on Author's behalf.

   b. The Author agrees, however, to reimburse Agent for any expenses that it may incur on Author's behalf related to large amounts of photocopying, travel, or any single expenditure exceeding $50. Agent must secure Author's verbal approval before incurring such expenses. The Agent will not travel on the Author's behalf without prior written approval of the Author. Should the Agent incur the expenses herein described, Agent will provide author with monthly expense reports.

6. Author agrees to do all the reasonable things necessary and desirable to promote her writing career. Author will not enter into any agreement or commitment that shall in any manner interfere with Author's carrying out the terms and conditions of this or any agreement entered into as part of our relationship. Author agrees not to employ, during the term of the Agreement, any other person or entity to act for her in the capacity in which she has engaged Agent by this Agreement. The Agent is willing to forgo the commission provided for in paragraph seven (7) in the event that the Work goes out of print. Likewise, the Agent is willing to forgo said commission on subsidiary rights contracts should the original subsidiary rights contracts lapse.

7. In consideration for Agent's services, Agent is irrevocably entitled to the following commissions: On all monies, whether royalties or fees, earned by Author for the Work or Derivatives published or produced during the term of this Agreement or arising out of any agreement entered into during the term of this Agreement related either to the Work or Derivatives, a commission equal to fifteen percent (15%). Agent will receive said commissions for the life of the Work and/or Derivatives contracted for during the term of this Agreement even in the event that the Work or the Derivatives are published or produced subsequent to the termination of this Agreement as well as contracts or licenses renewed or entered into after the termination of this Agreement.

8. All payments shall be paid directly to Agent from publisher, producer, or other entity.

9. This instrument sets forth the entire agreement between Agent and Author with respect to the subject matter hereof and no modification, amendment, waiver, termination or discharge of any provision hereof shall be binding upon the parties unless communicated by a written instrument executed by both Agent and Author.

10. This Agreement shall not be construed as creating a partnership between Agent and Author. It is specifically understood that Agent is acting as an independent contractor.

11. Author represents and warrants that she has been advised of her right to seek legal counsel of her own choosing in connection with the negotiation and execution of this Agreement.

12. Author represents and warrants that she is wholly free to enter into this Agreement and to grant the rights herein granted to Agent, and that she is not a party to any agreements, and that she does not have any obligations, which conflict with any of the above provisions.

13. This Agreement, or any part of Agent's rights hereunder, may be assigned to any person, Agent, or corporation which acquires all or substantially all of Agent's assets or which is owned or controlled by Agent. The Author is free to assign this contract to any entity that furnishes the Author's services.

14. This Agreement shall be construed in accordance with the laws of the State of XXXXXXXXXX.

In witness whereof, the Author and the Agent have duly executed this Agreement to be effective as of the date first above written.

Author's Signature: Witness to Author's Signature:

_____   _____
XXXXXXXXXX

Agent's Signature: Witness to Agent's Signature

_____   _____

6.4 PUBLISHER–AUTHOR AGREEMENT IN DETAIL

Because of the vast variety of books published for today's markets, no single form could ever be appropriate for all publisher-author agreements. A law school casebook, for example, has little potential for later adaptation to the silver screen. A grant of rights to the publisher as to motion picture rights, therefore, is not an item likely to consume a great deal of negotiating time. When the prospective book is a novel by a well-known author, however, the ability to license the work for motion pictures and television may be a central issue. Thus, the following comments may or may not apply to any particular publisher-author agreement. The points discussed are those that must be considered when approaching such agreements, with an initial decision to be made as to their applicability.

6.4.1 Rights Granted and Assigned

The rights granted by the author to the publisher run the gamut and must be carefully negotiated. The publisher is likely to ask for exclusive, worldwide, perpetual rights in a work, including the right to issue (or sublicense others to issue) higher-quality (and higher-priced) trade paperback editions; book clubs; reprint licensing; mass-market paperback reprints; selections for anthologies, textbooks, abridgements, and condensations; periodical and broadcast selections; digests; transcriptions; special editions for the handicapped, the theatre, motion pictures, and television; radio; educational pictures, merchandising; foreign language; export; and "all others." The author will want to limit such grants and, at a minimum, retain royalty rights in all such possible uses of the work. An author should not assume that the publisher is entitled to every one of these rights; to the contrary, the author (depending, in each instance, upon relative bargaining strength) should consider each item separately negotiable.

Audio book and online distribution rights are of increasing importance, and should not be regarded as incidental to the main purpose of the agreement.

6.4.2 Delivery of Satisfactory Manuscript

The manuscript provisions define who has ultimate creative control over the work, the delivery date for the manuscript (and the consequences for late delivery), the rights and duties of the publisher to edit and comment, and what will constitute delivery. Typically, the agreement requires that the manuscript be "satisfactory in form and content" to the publisher. Such clauses have been the basis for substantial litigation discussed in Section 6.4.3, indicating that where such a clause appears (and provided the publisher has provided good faith editorial guidance) the good faith decision of the publisher is determinative. The Authors Guild, on the other hand, prefers its own model "Satisfactory Manuscript Clause" (which, unless the author has extreme clout, will not be accepted by any publisher):

(a) Author shall deliver a manuscript which, in style and content, is professionally competent and fit for publication. A manuscript shall be deemed professionally competent and fit for publication if it substantially follows Author's prior works and or Author's style at the time the contract between Author and Publisher is signed.

(b) Publisher shall be deemed to have agreed that the manuscript complies with the conditions of (a) above unless, within 60 days of the manuscript's receipt, Publisher sends the author a written statement of the respects in which Publisher maintains the manuscript is not, in style and content, professionally competent and fit for publication. Author may, within 60 days after receipt of that statement, submit changes in the manuscript.

(c) If the manuscript (with any changes by the author) is not, in style and content, professionally competent and fit for publication, and Publisher has given the statement required by (b) above, Publisher may terminate this contract by written notice to Author given within 60 days after receipt of the changes pursuant to (b) above, or if no changes are submitted, within 90 days after Publisher sent the statement pursuant to (b) above.

(d) If the contract is terminated pursuant to (c) above:

> (i) Author shall be entitled to retain _____ percent of the total advance and shall receive any portion of that amount not yet paid, and
>
> (ii) if Author has received more than _____ percent of the total advance, Author shall re-pay to Publisher any portion that exceeds percent of the total advance7, but only from those proceeds, if any, received by Author under a subsequent contract for publication of the work by another publisher.

NOTES

Satisfactory Manuscript Clauses

Standard publishing contracts usually contain a clause requiring that "the author shall deliver . . . the complete and final manuscript of the Work, in content and form satisfactory to the Publisher . . . " Perle & Williams, *The Publishing Law Handbook,* sec. 2.06 (1988). Under these clauses publishers can reject a manuscript and require the author to return the advance by concluding in its subjective view that a manuscript is not satisfactory. As with any contract there is a requirement of good faith, but this still gives publishers wide latitude for rejecting a manuscript, including, *inter alia,* potential liability for publication, the publisher's own financial circumstances, likelihood of commercial success or excessive length.

This issue rose to prominence again recently when Joan Collins prevailed in a contract dispute with Random House which allowed her to keep a $1.3 million advance and collect $1.2 million due under her publishing contract for a novel Random House characterized as "trash." "*Collins Keeps Random House Advance,*" *Pub. Weekly,* Feb. 19, 1995, at 13. This victory was due to the highly unusual clause only requiring the author to deliver a "complete" manuscript, rather than a more stringent and common "satisfactory manuscript" clause. The case is unlikely to set any significant precedent since the clause at issue is so rare. While some authors are able to negotiate "comparable performance" clauses, requiring the manuscript be of similar quality to the author's previous books, most agreements have some variation on the standard "satisfactory manuscript" clause.

Duty to Provide Editorial Assistance

1. In *Gregory v. Simon & Schuster, Inc.,* 23 Med. L. Rptr. 1626, 1994 WL 381481 (S.D.N.Y. 1994), aff'd, 60 F.3d 812 (2d Cir. 1995) (no opinion), a former ballet dancer entered a publishing agreement to deliver her autobiography. The contract gave the Publisher the right to terminate the contract if the final revised complete manuscript was not "reasonably satisfactory" to the Publisher. The Publisher terminated the contract after reviewing three versions of the manuscript and the author brought suit to recover the balance of the advance. The court interpreted the clause to incur an obligation to act "rationally and not arbitrarily" with the decision resting on the publisher's own judgment and not to impose an "objective reasonable person standard." However, the contract included a nonstandard "reasonable editorial assistance" clause which the Publisher conceded raised a triable issue, which precluded the court from granting the Publisher's motion for summary judgment.

2. In *Gates v. Billboard Pub., Inc.,* 81 A.D.2d 776, 439 N.Y.S.2d 17 (1st Dep't. 1981), the court affirmed a denial of a publisher's motion for summary judgment where the publisher refused to publish a book in the form submitted by plaintiff. The court concluded that whether the circumstances justified rejection and whether

"the publisher made a good faith exercise of its right of editing and whether such refusal excused further performance by the plaintiff" were triable issues. The court suggested the First Amendment would be a bar to specific performance compelling publication.

3. In *Academy of Chicago v. Cheever,* 144 Ill.2d 24, 578 N.E.2d 981, 18 Med. L. Rptr. 2327 (1991), a publisher and John Cheever's widow sought declaratory judgment concerning a contract governing publication of the deceased author's uncollected works. The primary dispute concerned the length and content of the proposed book. The Supreme Court of Illinois found the contract void and unenforceable because numerous essential terms were missing from the agreement, including the fact that it did not specify criteria by which the Publisher would determine whether the manuscript was satisfactory as to form and content.

Acceptable Grounds for Rejection of Manuscript

1. In *Demaris v. G.P. Putnam,* 379 F. Supp. 294 (C.D. Cal. 1973), the publisher had a reputable attorney review an author submitted manuscript. Based on the attorney's legal opinion that publication of the manuscript would put the Publisher in danger of being sued for invasion of privacy and common law copyright, the author was not entitled to receive additional advance payment because of his failure to submit a manuscript "satisfactory to the publishers." *See also Random House v. Damore,* Index No. 14406/86 (N.Y. Sup. Ct. N.Y. Co. 1987) (Publisher not required to render editorial assistance to the author where the manuscript may have raised legal problems, was twice the length contracted for and the author issued an ultimatum that the publisher accept or reject the manuscript as is). But cf *Random House v. Curry,* 747 F. Supp. 191 (S.D.N.Y. 1990) (questions of fact precluding summary judgment were raised by the authors' assertion that the editor rejected the manuscript because the author refused to retain a quote that the author could not verify and refused to delete a negative treatment of the editor's friend); *Holt, Rinehart & Winston v. Wolman,* 47 A.D.2d 874, 368 N.Y.S.2d 813 (1st Dep't 1975) (triable issue raised as to whether the use of plagiarized material breached a warranty of originality, whether the material constituted fair use, and whether proper consents were obtained).

2. In *William Morrow & Co. v. Astrachan,* 15 Med. L. Rptr. 2424 (N.Y. Civ. Ct. N.Y. Co. 1988), a publisher sought the return of an advance from an author when a manuscript, which took eight years to deliver, was longer than originally agreed upon in the publishing contract. The publisher offered editorial assistance, which the author refused. Furthermore, the author issued an ultimatum that publisher accept the longer manuscript. The author subsequently sold the manuscript to another publisher. The court granted the first publisher's motion for summary judgment, finding the publisher acted in good faith. The court ordered the author to return the advance.

3. In *Little Brown & Co. v. Klein,* 22 Med. L. Rptr. 1085, 1993 WL 643380 (N.Y. Sup. Ct. N.Y. Co. 1993), the author submitted a proposal for a book on the day to day activities of President Bush and his family. In his proposal, he stated that he had the agreement of the White House to spend a day with the President and have "access to key players for a week." The author also stated that the book would be submitted in time for the release to coincide with the 1992 Republican and Democratic conventions. Thereafter, the White House withdrew their consent giving the author access and suggested that after the election such access might be possible. On the publisher's motion for summary judgment for return of the advance, the court found that the "cooperation of the Bushes and the timing of the delivery of a satisfactory manuscript formed the essence of the Contract" and that the entire advance must be returned.

4. In *Goodyear Publishing v. Mundell,* 74 A.D. 2d 556, 427 N.Y.S.2d 242 (1st Dep't. 1980), the statute of limitations did not bar a publisher's suit for breach of contract launched within six years of nonsubmission of an acceptable manuscript by the date provided. The court found that alleged supervening oral agreements would not alter the parties' duties and responsibilities when the contract contained a clause stating "this agreement may not be changed by oral modification." *See also G.P. Putnam's Sons v. Owens,* 51 A.D. 2d 527, 378 N.Y.S.2d 637 (1st Dep't. 1976) (publisher's cause of action accrued when author failed to submit manuscript by time limit in contract, not when publisher later exercised its right to terminate).

6.4.3 Delivery Standards

In each of the entertainment industries, the applicable agreements will specify standards for acceptable performance on the part of the artist, the performer, the author, or whoever else is furnishing services and/or materials to the company.

Interestingly enough, almost all the reported cases involving delivery standards have arisen in the book publishing industry. As the following cases demonstrate, this is not a completely subjective standard, although economic considerations may be taken into account, and the company must be wary lest it be held to have waived the benefit of a delivery standards clause.

Random House, Inc. v. Gold, 464 F. Supp. 1306 *aff'd. mem,* 607 F.2d 998 (S.D.N.Y. 2d Cir. 1979)

POLLACK, DISTRICT JUDGE

This is an action to recover sums paid to the defendant as advances under a contract for the publication of up to four books to be written by defendant. Defendant has counter-claimed, alleging a breach of the contract in bad faith. . . .

In 1970, Random House and Gold entered into an agreement . . . which called for the publication of four literary works to be written by Gold with an option to cancel the fourth book. The contract was drawn on a printed form customarily used for arrangements pertaining to a single book. The form was adapted by Random House to cover the proposed books involved herein.

Prior to the execution of the 1970 agreement, Random House had published several other works by Gold, including two books published pursuant to a 1965 contract. The latter two books were quite successful, and Gold received advances and royalties from them in excess of $100,000.

The 1970 agreement provided for the payment of advances of $150,000, payable to Gold in ten equal annual installments. The advances were against and on account of all moneys accruing to Gold under the agreement. The contract required Gold to submit manuscripts for the works "in content and form satisfactory to the publisher" and in accordance with a delivery schedule set forth therein.

The 1970 contract also provided that Gold had the right to terminate the agreement with respect to a fourth work if he had earned $150,000 or more from the publication of works #1, 2 and 3. . . .

Gold wrote and delivered the first two works and Random House accepted and published them. In January 1973, Random House paid Gold the fourth installment of the agreed advances, making a total of $60,000 thereon to that date. As of December 1973, Gold's royalties on the two published works totaled $9,304.71.

On July, 30, 1973, James Brown, Gold's literary agent, delivered the manuscript of the third work, a novel entitled *Swiftie the Magician.* James Silberman, the editor-in-chief at Random House, read the manuscript and also asked another fiction editor, Joe Fox, to read it. Silberman also asked his staff to check on the financial results of the Gold contract. His secretary reported to him that Random House had paid a total of $60,000 and that the two published books had earned a total of $11,579.35, as of March 31, 1973.

Fox reported to Silberman on August 23, 1973. He admitted he was not a fan of Gold's work, and criticized the manuscript as shallow and badly designed. In considering whether Random House should agree to publish the book, Fox asked whether Random House was behind financially on the contract with Gold.

On September 11, 1973, Silberman sent some of Fox's comments to Gold, with a covering letter stating that he was "uneasy" about the manuscript. Gold went to work on a revision of the manuscript.

On December 20, 1973, just ten days before another installment of the agreed advances would have fallen due and after being assured by Random House's attorneys that in their opinion Gold would have to repay about $50,000 if the contract were terminated, Silberman wrote to Brown, stating that the manuscript was unsatisfactory in form and content and that Random House was terminating the agreement pursuant to Paragraph 2 thereof. Silberman testified that he decided to reject the book after reading a second, revised manuscript. He did not give the second manuscript to Fox or to anyone else to read. He could not remember exactly why he thought that the work was not a good book, and he did not keep a written memorandum of his criticisms, but said that they were the same as those in the Fox memo. Silberman admitted that he was conscious of the financial circumstances of the Gold contract at the time he decided to reject the book.

On January 2, 1974, Silberman and Brown spoke over the telephone about the third work by Gold. Silberman offered to renegotiate the terms of the Gold contract, and told Brown that the manuscript for the third work would be acceptable to Random House on different terms.

After the rejection by Random House, Brown offered the Gold manuscript for *Swiftie the Magician* to McGraw-Hill, which accepted the work for publication and paid Gold an advance of $10,000. . . .

Random House now seeks to recover from Gold the amount of all the advances paid to Gold in excess of the royalties accrued with respect to the two published works, or approximately $50,000. It contends that the sum represents an "unearned" advance which Gold agreed to repay in the event the contract was terminated.

Gold denies that he is obligated to repay all the advances he had received, viz., the $60,000 (less accrued royalties) and maintains that he is entitled to the $90,000 balance of the agreed advances because Random House breached the agreement in bad faith. Gold argues that he is at least entitled to an additional $15,000 for that part of the agreed advances attributable to the two works accepted and published by Random House. . . .

Gold contends that Random House acted in bad faith when it rejected the *Swiftie* manuscript because it gave undue and improper weight to financial considerations in the making of that decision and to escaping from the remaining financial obligations if it rejected the third work. Gold points to the plaintiff's offer to accept and publish the third work on different terms. Gold has offered no authority, however, for the proposition that a publisher's financial circumstances and the likelihood of a book's commercial success must be excluded from the range of factors that may be weighed in the decision to accept or reject a manuscript offered for publication, and this Court declines to endorse such a view. The requirement that a manuscript be satisfactory to the publisher gives it the right to reject a work if it acts in good faith; the publisher is not bound to incur the significant costs of publication if it declines to accept the risk of financial loss. There has been no other suggestion that Random House's view of the manuscript as unsatisfactory from its viewpoint was not held honestly and in good faith, and Gold's claim of a breach of contract in bad faith has not been established by a preponderance of the credible evidence. . . .

Random House seeks to recover the entire amount of the advances paid to Gold, less the sum of royalties accrued on the published works. Random House's claim for repayment, however, lacks any support in the express language of the agreement of the parties.

Paragraph "2" of the contract states that, "*as to any undelivered works*," (emphasis added):

. . . the Author agrees to repay forthwith all unearned amounts which may have been advanced hereunder, and Publisher will not be liable for any further advance installments.

Similarly, with respect to repayment of moneys advanced on published works, paragraph "9" of the contract states in harmony with the foregoing quotation from paragraph "2" that:

Any such advance shall not be repayable, provided that the Author has delivered the manuscript in conformity with Paragraph 2 and is not otherwise in default under this agreement.

The quoted sentence from paragraph "9" refers to "*the* manuscript" rather than to *all four* manuscripts, and in the face of the express limitation on recovery of advances to "any undelivered works," the manuscript referred to in the proviso of paragraph "9" must be interpreted to distinguish delivered from undelivered works. This is cogent evidence that paragraphs "9" and "2" must be interpreted as applying independently to each of the four contemplated manuscripts. Thus, since Gold delivered the first two manuscripts in conformity with paragraph "2," advances attributable to those manuscripts are not repayable.

The evidence as a whole makes clear that, in effect, the parties made four separable arrangements in the adapted printed form, one for each work.

The notion of the plaintiff that the contract which it drew (adapted) is to be read as providing for a forfeiture by the defendant of all the advances it had received over a four year period because the plaintiff decided not to publish the third work, does violence to the contract, common sense and industry practice. Plaintiff's vice-president and editor-in-chief, Mr. Silberman testified that where separate works have been contracted for, an allocation is to be made of advances to each of the several works involved and that such an arrangement is common in the publishing industry. Moreover, when used in such a contract "all moneys earned" applies to each of the several works separately. . . .

The defendant Gold received $60,000 advanced against the possibility of four works. He failed to deliver the third manuscript in satisfactory form and the contract was terminated as to the third and fourth works. As to those "undelivered works," Gold must repay the portion of his advance attributable to them, or $30,000, which was not earned by the timely delivery of a satisfactory manuscript. Gold's promise to repay advances did not extend to delivered, accepted and published works, however, and Gold may retain the $30,000 attributable to the two published books. . . .

Random House contends that it was not obligated to continue to pay any part of the advances due in the years 1974 through 1979. This contention, however, is also without support in the terms of the contract.

The *only* circumstance in which Random House was permitted to suspend all advance payments, notwithstanding its acceptance and publication of one or more of the four works was the disability of the author. Paragraph "9" states in part:

If the Author becomes physically or mentally incapacitated prior to delivery of *all the Works,* Publisher may discontinue payments of installments and will have no further obligation to make such payments for the duration of the disability. (Emphasis added.)

In this provision of paragraph "9," the rights and obligations of the publisher are clearly expressed: it may suspend all advance payments even where, for example, a disability delays delivery of a fourth manuscript after three works have been delivered and published. In contrast, there is no similar provision in the contract allowing Random House to suspend *all* payments when the contract is terminated *in part* as to undelivered works.

Paragraph "2," on which Random House relies, grants the publisher only partial relief from the continuing obligation to make advance payments. It provides:

If the Author fails to deliver any manuscript . . . , as to any undelivered works, . . . Publisher will not be liable for any further advance installments.

Conversely, as to delivered and published works, Random House remains liable for further advance installments after a partial termination of the contract.

Therefore, with respect to the six advances due for the years 1974 through 1979, Random House is not liable for those attributable to the two "undelivered works," but Random House is liable for the portion of those installments attributable to the delivered and published books, or $45,000. . . .

Accordingly, the further findings and conclusions of this Court are as follows:

(1) Random House rejected the manuscript for *Swiftie the Magician,* the 3rd work, as unsatisfactory in form and content in good faith, and was privileged to terminate the 1970 agreement as to the third and fourth works, the undelivered works.
(2) Random House is entitled to recover from Gold the advances paid as to the undelivered works, or $30,000.
(3) Random House is *not* entitled to recover from Gold the advances paid as to the two published books.
(4) Gold is *not* entitled to recover from Random House the unpaid advances attributable to the undelivered works.
(5) Gold is entitled to recover from Random House the unpaid advances attributable to the two published books, or $45,000.
(6) Therefore, Gold is entitled to recover from Random House the net amount of $15,000, plus interest and costs, and the Clerk is directed to enter judgment accordingly. . . .

Harcourt Brace Jovanovich, Inc. v. Goldwater, 532 F. Supp. 619 (S.D.N.Y. 1982)

GRIESA, JUDGE

. . . In early 1977 a proposal was submitted to Harcourt Brace Jovanovich, which I will refer to hereafter as HBJ, for the publication of the memoirs of Barry Goldwater.

The proposal was to have Stephen Shadegg act as the actual writer, working closely with Goldwater who was to provide the material and work and comment on the substance of what was presented.

Shadegg had previously had a long relationship with a literary agent by the name of Oscar Collier and he relied on Collier to market this proposal. Oscar Collier was associated as a literary agent with his daughter, Lisa Collier.

The Collier firm submitted the proposal to certain publishers, including HBJ, in early 1977. An editor at HBJ by the name of Carol Hill received the proposal. She talked about it to her editor-in-chief, Daniel Okrent. There was a meeting involving Hill, Okrent and the Colliers. The HBJ people were very enthusiastic and quickly agreed to publish the Goldwater memoirs on the basis of the proposal which had been submitted.

There is testimony demonstrating that although the HBJ people were enthusiastic about having the Goldwater memoirs, they had reservations about the writer Shadegg. There is a dispute as to whether they communicated these reservations to the Colliers. Whether they did or did not communicate the reservations is unimportant. But it is important to note that the HBJ people did have reservations and would have preferred another writer.

However, it is also to be noted that the Colliers furnished the HBJ people with four books previously written by Shadegg, a writer of long experience, who had engaged in journalistic writing as well as having written books, political biographies and so forth. The HBJ people were fully on notice as to exactly the degree of talent possessed by Shadegg.

There was a meeting in Washington, D.C., the main purpose of which was to meet Senator Goldwater. The contract was then signed January 26, 1977. It names Stephen Shadegg and Barry Goldwater as the authors and HBJ as the publisher.

The contract contains . . . certain paragraphs referring to the concept of the manuscript being "satisfactory to the publisher in form and content," particularly paragraph 2 which states as follows: "The author will deliver to the publisher on or before October 1, 1978, one copy of the manuscript of the work as finally revised by the author and satisfactory to the publisher in form and content."

The agreement provided for an advance totaling $200,000, a remarkably high advance. $65,000 was to be paid at the time of contract signing. Another $75,000 was due on delivery and acceptance of the completed manuscript. The balance of $60,000 was due on publication.

There was an exchange of letters in February 1977 between Hill and Goldwater in which Hill in effect offered to do a vigorous job of editing and Goldwater made it clear that he welcomed such editing. He stated in his letter of February 15, 1977 that Hill should not hesitate to criticize or make suggestions, even though he might be a little bullheaded here and there.

The project began between Shadegg and Goldwater. One of the things which was a feature of these memoirs was that Goldwater had over the years collected what he called the Alpha File. It consisted of memos and notes of conversations he had with other political and governmental leaders in the United States and he had dictated these notes and memos and prepared them at the time of various meetings and events.

These items had been collected in the Alpha File and one of the ideas of the memoirs was to publish materials of substance, anecdotes and so forth, from the Alpha File, to the extent they did not involve purely personal information or the normal kind of information which sometimes is held back until the death of certain living people in order not to hurt them.

In any event, materials from the Alpha File were turned over to Shadegg and other materials were given to Shadegg. Goldwater commenced consulting with Shadegg and Shadegg set to work writing.

This process continued over the period of time involved in the lawsuit. Shadegg would write a section and submit it to Goldwater; Goldwater would comment, offer criticisms, provide additional material, and so forth.

On June 22, 1977, Shadegg wrote a letter to Hill enclosing a draft of seven chapters, approximately 30,000 words. At the same time Shadegg sent Oscar Collier the same draft material. The letter to Hill concluded with the following paragraph:

"We would be most interested in having your comments and your suggestions. One of the problems we face is how much to put in and how much to leave out. The available material is almost overwhelming. Your objective viewpoint will be extremely helpful."

Hill did not communicate with either Shadegg or Goldwater in response to the receipt of this draft material. This caused understandable puzzlement on the part of Shadegg and Goldwater. They were eager to have her reaction and they did not have it.

Goldwater has made it clear in his testimony in the case that he expects and needs editorial work on the part of a publisher. He has published a number of books and feels the need of editorial work. He expected it here and he was particularly puzzled that none was forthcoming.

Goldwater relied on Shadegg for the principal communications with either the publisher or the agent and, pursuant to this, Shadegg made inquiries of Oscar Collier as to what was going on. Shadegg has testified that he placed one telephone call to Hill at about this time which was not returned. He candidly admitted at trial that he did not act more persistently in going to Hill directly because he was angry and hurt at the lack of what he considered a normal response.

In any event, in September of 1977, there was a discussion between Hill and Oscar Collier. Hill gave a general unfavorable comment about the seven-chapter draft, criticizing the tone, the lack of drama and what she considered flat writing. . . .

Even Hill's comments to Collier did not involve normal, detailed editorial work. They did not convey specific comments as to what should be cut or what should be added or what was unclear or any of the other things that one would expect in editorial work.

Consequently, in connection with the first seven chapters, it is clear that Hill did not perform any editorial work, either directly with the authors or indirectly through Collier.

The evidence indicates strongly that Hill was considering, and to some degree pursuing, the idea of replacing Shadegg with another writer.

In late September 1977, an item appeared in the *Washington Post* indicating that Goldwater was looking for a ghost writer. Goldwater and Shadegg heard about this. They inquired and were told by Hill that there was nothing to it. Hill wrote them a letter of reassurance which indicated that she was in fact enthusiastic about the book and expected that it would be an important one.

Thus, in her only direct contact with the authors at this juncture, Hill was not only withholding her negative views of the draft, she was indicating support and enthusiasm.

Behind the scenes, there were certain maneuvers going on about the possibility of getting a new writer. Apparently there was talk at HBJ on this subject, and the desire for a possible new writer was known. This resulted in some communications with a literary agent about a possible writer by the name of Clay Blair. Hill went so far as to write the agent to try to see if Clay Blair would be available. Hill did not expressly mention the Goldwater project. She spoke in veiled terms, at least to the outsiders. But the point is that a new writer for the Goldwater book was definitely on her mind. . . .

As I have already described, Oscar Collier had received from Hill some general negative comments, which he conveyed to Shadegg and which were in turn conveyed to Goldwater.

There is a letter dated November 14, 1977 to Hill from Lisa Collier indicating that comments had been passed on and that work was going forward.

The intention of Shadegg and Goldwater and their agents was to keep going ahead with the writing in the hopes that whatever problems there were would work out with the further production of manuscript. Obviously, the authors had an obligation under the contract to write and they continued to fulfill that obligation.

In the absence of any editorial work forthcoming from Hill, Shadegg solicited comments from Oscar Collier, who made detailed suggestions on draft material. These comments were not the substitute of editorial work from the publisher. They tended to deal with rather trivial points about precise phrasing and so forth. But at least Shadegg was soliciting what assistance he could from the agent.

On July 13, 1978, 24 chapters were sent to Hill. These were sent by Goldwater. The idea had been adopted that if Goldwater himself submitted the material there might be a better chance of getting some editorial work from Hill. Also it was hoped that the production of a substantial part of the book would encourage some progress with the publisher.

The Goldwater letter of July 13, 1978 concludes with the following:

If you have any suggestions or would like to make some we could arrange to meet in Arizona at your convenience, in Washington or even New York. Let me know your honest opinion of what has been done so far and let me have any suggestions as soon as possible that might be incorporated in further writing.

The letter was not responded to. Hill made no attempt to communicate with Shadegg or Goldwater in order to offer the kind of opinions, suggestions, or comments which had been solicited in the Goldwater letter.

Hill has testified that she felt that the materials submitted in the 24-chapter package were poor and she was very concerned about whether the book could be successfully marketed. She asked two other editors at HBJ to read the materials. The other two editors were also negative about the contents of the 24-chapter package.

However, as I have said, there was no attempt to communicate with the authors and go over the matter in detail and see what, if anything, could be done to remedy the perceived difficulties.

Hill's communications again were with the agents, particularly with Oscar Collier. She conveyed her negative impression of the 24 chapters in a general way and, at this time, expressly suggested that another writer be brought in. This suggestion was rejected by Oscar Collier.

At this time Hill indicated to Oscar Collier that HBJ would probably not publish the book and would probably reject the manuscript.

Oscar Collier and Hill discussed seeking another publisher. It was indicated to Collier that he was free to do this and Collier, in order to cover the contingency he was faced with, and in order to ensure publication of the book, commenced inquiries about the possibility of another publisher.

However, Shadegg and Goldwater kept on working on the book to finish it and the intention still was to submit the final manuscript to HBJ pursuant to the existing contract.

It should be noted that on August 31, 1978, Hill sent a memo to the head of the firm, Mr. Jovanovich, which stated, among other things, "that the original idea was to have Taylor Branch rewrite the manuscript when it was delivered." Taylor Branch was a writer who had been favored by the HBJ people for this project if they could have chosen the writer.

The memo has significance, in indicating that there was an intention to refrain from doing editorial work with Shadegg in the hopes that another writer could come in and do the job.

On September 29, 1978, the full manuscript was submitted to HBJ. It contained revisions of materials earlier submitted and certain additional chapters. The full manuscript was submitted with a letter from Oscar Collier which attempted to explain what Collier felt were the merits of the manuscript.

There was further review by Hill and certain of her colleagues at HBJ, and submission to a freelance manuscript reader. All took a very negative view of the manuscript. However, one suggestion by an associate editor was that the manuscript be reworked and that the authors be bargained down to a lower advance.

On August 31, 1978, HBJ wrote Oscar Collier returning the manuscript, stating that it was unacceptable, and demanding the return of the $65,000 advance.

Prior to this time neither Hill nor any other editor at HBJ had communicated directly with Shadegg or Goldwater regarding the manuscript material. No one at that firm attempted to do so. There was never any detailed comment about what should be added, what should be deleted, what was unclear, or about any other specific matters in the manuscript. There was no such comment made either directly to Shadegg or Goldwater, or indirectly through the agent, Collier.

Following the rejection of the manuscript by HBJ, there were discussions by Collier with a few other publishers. The result was that the book was bought by William Morrow & Company who agreed to pay an advance of $80,000. The same manuscript which had been rejected by HBJ was the one submitted to Morrow.

An experienced editor at Morrow by the name of Howard Cady has testified that he found the manuscript fascinating. He saw problems with it but felt that it could yield a best-selling book.

Prior to entering into any agreement with Shadegg and Goldwater, Cady went to see Shadegg in Phoenix, Arizona, where Shadegg lived to see whether he could work with Shadegg. This was in January 1979.

Cady found Shadegg thoroughly professional and cooperative. Cady had certain comments that were discussed with Shadegg at that time, and the two developed an immediate working relationship.

Over the next few weeks, after Morrow had bought the rights to the book, Cady sent off to Shadegg in Phoenix communications with detailed comments about items to cut, questions to be answered and so forth. In other words, Cady was engaging in the normal editorial activity. . . .

The book was ready for galley proofs in a relatively short time. It was published in the fall of 1979 by Morrow under the title "With No Apologies" and it became a best-seller.

Cady has testified that the process he went through with Shadegg was a normal editorial process. There were substantial cuts of superfluous material, which he has testified is not unusual in work on a manuscript of a book being prepared under contract. The cuts were made leaving what Cady felt was valuable narrative and commentary material.

As far as additions to the manuscript which had been submitted to Cady, he said that there was less than 1 percent of the material in the present book which was added pursuant to his requests and questions. Again Cady said this involved normal editorial effort.

We come to the conclusions of law to be drawn. It is true that under the contract which was in force here between HBJ and the authors, the publisher has a very considerable discretion as to whether to refuse a manuscript on the ground that it is unsatisfactory to the publisher in form and content.

It cannot be, however, that the publisher has absolutely unfettered license to act or not to act in any way it wishes and to accept or reject a book for any reason whatever. If this were the case, the publisher could simply make a contract and arbitrarily change its mind and that would be an illusory contract. It is no small thing for an author to enter into a contract with a publisher and be locked in with that publisher and prevented from marketing the book elsewhere.

It is clear, both as a matter of law and from the testimony in this case, that there is an implied obligation in a contract of this kind for the publisher to engage in appropriate editorial work with the author of a book. Both plaintiff's and defendants' witnesses testified to this effect, based on the custom of the trade.

It is clear that an author who is commissioned to do a work under a contract such as this generally needs editing to produce a successful book. There has been testimony by Goldwater, as I have mentioned, to the effect that he feels the need of editing work and expected it here. The letters from both Shadegg and Goldwater to the publisher indicated their desire for editorial work on the part of the publisher.

In a general way, it is clear that the editorial work which is required must consist of some reasonable degree of communication with the authors, an interchange with the authors about the specifics of what the publisher desires; about what specific faults are found; what items should be omitted or eliminated; what items should be added; what organizational defects exist, and so forth. If faults are found in the writing style, it seems elementary that there should be discussion and illustrations of what those defects of style are. All of this is necessary in order to allow the author the reasonable opportunity to perform to the satisfaction of the publisher.

If this editorial work is not done by the publisher, the result is that the author is misled and, in fact, is virtually prevented from performing under the contract.

There is no occasion in this decision to determine the full extent or the full definition of the editorial work which is required of a publisher under the contract. Here there was no editorial work. I emphasize, no editorial work. There was nothing approaching any sensible editorial activity on the part of the publisher. There were no comments of a detailed nature designed to give the authors an opportunity to remedy defects, even though such comments were specifically invited and requested. . . .

As far as any qualms about having Shadegg as writer, it should be emphasized that the contract was with Shadegg as well as with Goldwater. The contract was not with Goldwater alone. And, as I have already indicated, the publisher entered into this contract with a full opportunity to determine the exact abilities and talents of Shadegg.

In a given situation it could be that after a contract is entered into of the kind we have here, and after draft material is submitted, the material is so hopeless that editorial work might be fruitless. It is difficult to imagine such a situation occurring but I suppose it is conceivable. But this was far from the case here.

I note that the publisher claims that there were no revelations of fact, no "revelatory material" as the term has been used. It is difficult to even comprehend that claim. The book as it was published is full of facts. It is full of conversations with illustrious personages. It is full of comments and judgments in detail about presidents and other public figures, presidential administrations and so forth. It is simply not true that the book had no factual material in it of a valuable nature.

It is quite clear that the bulk of the manuscript which was submitted to HBJ must have contained valuable and interesting factual material. This is not the case of a manuscript of no merit which ended up unpublished or was published in a book of clearly low-grade quality.

A distinguished editor, Howard Cady, found the manuscript fascinating. He edited the manuscript in the normal way and produced a successful book.

Consequently, I conclude that HBJ breached its contract with Shadegg and Goldwater by wilfully failing to engage in any rudimentary editorial work or effort. Consequently, HBJ cannot rely on the concept that the manuscript was unsatisfactory in form and content and can be rejected. HBJ had no right under its contract to reject that manuscript.

I have examined the legal authorities cited by the parties. No case directly in point has been referred to. I would note particularly that the case most heavily relied upon by HBJ, *Random House, Inc. V. Gold,* 464 F. Supp. 1306 (SDNY), aff'd mem., 607 F.2d 998 (2d Cir. 1979), holds that the type of contract involved in the present case requires the publisher to act in good faith, and notes the obvious point that, allowing unfettered license to publishers to reject a manuscript submitted under contract would permit "overreaching by publishers attempting to extricate themselves from bad deals." 464 F. Supp. at 1308 n.1. In the present case, for the reasons already stated, it must be concluded that HBJ did not act in good faith.

This concludes my findings on the issues I have set out to deal with.

Nance v. Random House, Inc., 212 F. Supp. 2d 268, 274 (S.D.N.Y. 2002)

STEIN, U.S. DISTRICT JUDGE:

John J. Nance, a successful author of action novels, brings this breach of contract action against Bantam Doubleday Dell Publishing Group ("Doubleday") and St. Martin's Press, Inc. Jurisdiction exists in this Court because the controversy is between citizens of different states. See 28 U.S.C. § 1332. Nance alleges that defendants rejected his manuscript for a work of fiction in bad faith and fraudulently induced him to write an additional draft of the work that they never intended to publish. The publishers have moved for summary judgment dismissing the complaint and granting them summary judgment on their counterclaim for the return of the advances they paid to Nance prior to terminating his contract. Since the parties' contract required that Nance's manuscript be satisfactory to the publishers and Nance has failed to come forward with any issues of material fact that would establish that the publishers rejected the manuscript in bad faith, both of defendants' motions are granted.

I. BACKGROUND

Nance is a commercial air pilot and author of eight novels, all of which are aviation-based thrillers. Prior to entering into the contract at issue in this action, Doubleday published the hardcover edition, and St. Martin's published the paperback edition, of Nance's novels *Pandora's Clock*—a *New York Times* bestseller—and *Medusa's Child.* In February 1997, Nance signed a contract (the "Contract") with Doubleday and St. Martin's for the publication of three additional novels over a three-year period. (Compl. P 9; Coyne Aff. P 3, Ex. 1.) The Contract stated that Nance would receive $ 1 million per book, with payments to be made first, upon signing the Contract; second, upon the completion of specified outlines and manuscripts "complete and satisfactory to [the] Publisher;" and third, upon publication of each novel. (Coyne Aff., Ex. 1, cl. 3, 7.) With respect to the editorial process, the Contract provided that the parties would agree on a schedule for revising submitted work, but that "should Publisher conclude that the Work or any portion thereof as first submitted cannot be revised to its satisfaction within a timely period or should Publisher find the revised Work or any portion thereof unacceptable for any reason, Publisher may reject it." (Id., cl. 3(b).)

The first novel foreseen in the three-book Contract, *The Last Hostage,* was published in the spring of 1998. (Compl. P 13.) Nance's literary agent Olga Wieser submitted an outline for the second work, entitled *Blackout,* on January 6, 1998. (Coyne Aff. P 12, Ex. 2; Nance Dep. (I) at 77–78.) As described in the outline, Blackout's plot involved a commercial air flight whose pilot is blinded by a mysterious laser and forced to land the plane with the help of his terrified passengers. Shawn Coyne, a Senior Editor at Doubleday who had worked with Nance on *The Last Hostage,* sent Wieser comments the following day. (Coyne Aff. P 12, Ex. 3; Nance Dep. (I) at 79–80.) Nance sent a revised outline to Coyne and Matthew Shear, then Vice President and Publisher for St. Martin's, and subsequently met with Shear and Joseph Veltre, then an Assistant Editor at St. Martin's, to discuss the outline. (Coyne Aff. PP 13, 15, Ex. 4; Shear Dep. at 173; Veltre Dep. at 12–13; Nance Dep. (I) at 98.) In February, Nance submitted another revised outline, which the publishers accepted the following month and sent Nance an advance payment of $150,000 pursuant to the Contract. (Coyne Aff. P 16, Ex. 7; Nance Dep. (I) at 101–02, 228.)

Nance then drafted a manuscript based on the approved outline and sent Coyne the first 17 chapters of *Blackout* in April. (Coyne Aff. P 17, Ex. 9; Nance Dep. (I) at 119–120.) Coyne responded in writing that the manuscript was "coming along nicely" and shared some of his concerns with the submission, such as the need to increase suspense by with holding certain plot details until later in the work. (Coyne Aff., Ex. 10.) Nance submitted the rest of the draft of *Blackout* in July. (Coyne

Aff. P 18; Compl. P 23.) Coyne subsequently wrote Nance that while the manuscript had "a lot of great things going," some areas of the plot needed to be made more suspenseful or credible and that he intended to share the draft with the editors at St. Martin's before sending a more formal response. (Coyne Aff. P 18, Ex. 11.)

The resulting comments were largely unfavorable. In an eight-page, single-spaced letter dated September 2, 1998, Coyne, Shear, and Veltre described specific problems with the plot, characterization and pacing of the manuscript. (Coyne Aff. PP 20–24, Ex. 13; Nance Dep. (I) at 155–56.) Most fundamentally, the editors felt that the submitted draft of *Blackout* lacked the elements that had made *Pandora's Clock* a bestseller—the combination of a "high concept plot," i.e., a single theme unifying the book, with a "very personal story." (Coyne Aff., Ex. 13 at 1–2.) While *Pandora's Clock* kept readers "glued to the page" with its story of a deadly virus transported on a plane, Nance's two subsequent novels—*Medusa's Child* and *The Last Hostage*—lacked the same narrative drive and thus sold fewer copies. The draft of *Blackout,* they believed, became bogged down in "the inner workings of the various strata of the American political, intelligence, and justice systems." (Id. at 2.) The editors invited Nance to provide them with a plan for revisions once he had identified "the missing big idea" that would appeal to his readers and "get [sales] back to the *Pandora* level." (Id. at 2, 8.)

The following week, Nance submitted a revised outline with a new "high concept"—a nuclear bomb hidden at the base of the Hoover Dam, the instructions for disarming which are contained on a computer diskette passed to an unwitting passenger on a flight from Hong Kong to Los Angeles. (Coyne Aff. PP 25–27, Ex. 14.) The device of a pilot blinded by lasers was retained, but it was reduced to a subsidiary element to the main nuclear bomb story. The editors were unimpressed by Nance's changes and instead sent him their own suggested outline for *Blackout.* (Coyne Aff. P 28, Ex. 15.) The letter also cautioned, "our acceptance of the [first *Blackout*] outline did not imply that we would accept the first draft of *Blackout,* which we have decided not to do. And, should you choose to follow our suggested revised outline . . . we'll still have to evaluate this next draft and determine its acceptability." In early November, Nance submitted another revised outline based on the editors' suggestions. (Coyne Aff. P 29, Ex. 16.) Shortly thereafter, Coyne informed Wieser that Nance should draft a manuscript based on the revised outline. (Coyne Aff. P 29.)

Nance submitted part of the second draft of *Blackout* on December 1, 1998, noting in his cover letter that he "absolutely must know immediately if there is anything in the evolving copy that does not fully meet the expectations of the approved outline." (Coyne Aff. P 30, Ex. 17; Nance Dep. (I) at 230–31.) Coyne responded that the editors would be unable to evaluate the work until they had received the entire manuscript. (Coyne Aff. P 31, Ex.18, Nance Dep. (I) at 233.) By early January 1999, Nance had submitted the entire second draft of *Blackout.* (Coyne Aff. P 32, Exs. 19–21; Nance Dep. (I) at 238–243.)

Unfortunately for Nance, the second *Blackout* manuscript fared no better in the judgment of the editors than the first. William Thomas, the Editor-in-Chief of Doubleday, formally terminated the Contract in a letter of February 8, 1999, writing that "after two rewrites the manuscript is editorially unacceptable and there is no likelihood that a further revision will solve the editorial problems," including the work's lack of suspense, "wooden" dialogue, "cartoon-like" characters, and "awkward" prose. (Coyne Aff. P 38, Ex. 22.)

Shortly thereafter, Nance sold the second *Blackout* manuscript to publisher Penguin Putnam, Inc. for an advance of $550,000. (Nance Aff. P 71.) Putnam published the hardcover edition of the novel in February 2000. Defendants then sought to recover the advances they had paid to Nance for *Blackout* and the unwritten third novel. Although the parties attempted to resolve their differences, and Nance voluntarily repaid $15,000 to defendants, settlement discussions ultimately broke down and Nance filed this action. (Kovner Aff. P 9; Ex. 5, Nance Dep. (II) at 46–47, 52–53.)

II. DISCUSSION

. . . The Contract provided that Nance's manuscripts had to be "complete and satisfactory to [the] Publisher," and further stated that the publishers could reject a manuscript if they found it "unacceptable for any reason." (Coyne Aff., Ex. 1, cl. 7, 3(b).) Courts have interpreted such clauses to grant publishers wide discretion to terminate publishing contracts, "provided that the termination is made in good faith, and that the failure of the author to submit a satisfactory manuscript was not caused by the publisher's bad faith." Doubleday & Co. v. Curtis, 763 F.2d 495, 501 (2d Cir. 1985). See also Random House, Inc. v. Gold, 464 F. Supp. 1306, 1308 (SDNY), aff'd, 607 F.2d 998 (2d Cir. 1979); Random House, Inc. v. Curry, 747 F. Supp. 191, 193 (SDNY 1990); Harcourt Brace Jovanovich, Inc. v. Goldwater, 532 F. Supp. 619, 624 (SDNY 1982). "Dishonesty" or "willful neglect" are evidence of bad faith. See Curtis, 763 F.2d at 501. In sum, the requirement that a work be "complete and satisfactory to [the] Publisher" gives the publisher the right to reject the work as long as it acts in good faith.

Nance contends that the publishers rejected *Blackout* not on its own merits but in response to the low sales figures for Nance's two previous books, *Medusa's Child* and *The Last Hostage*. Even assuming that the rejection of a manuscript based on poor sales of prior works constitutes bad faith—which is not clear, see Gold, 464 F. Supp. at 1308 (declining to hold that rejecting a book for financial reasons was bad faith)—Nance has failed to come forward, after extensive discovery in this action, with any evidence that defendants rejected his draft due to disappointing sales of his most recent novels. While the editors' letter of September 2, 1998 does refer to the relative sales performances of Nance's last three books, these remarks are made within the context of a detailed and lengthy editorial analysis of the shortcomings in the plot, characters and pacing of the submitted draft. To draw the inference from the September 2 letter that the publishers had already decided to reject *Blackout* because Nance's two prior novels had not sold enough copies is sheer conjecture and insufficient to withstand a summary judgment motion. Cf. Curry, 747 F. Supp. at 193.

Nor does anything else in the record support an inference of bad faith. Coyne's favorable comments about early versions of the outline and manuscript were coupled with detailed criticisms of the plot and characterization. Nowhere did Coyne represent that there were no problems with the manuscript or that publication was guaranteed, and the fact that he praised certain aspects of early drafts and outlines does not indicate an attempt to deceive or mislead Nance. See Curtis, 763 F.2d at 501, n. 4. Similarly, Nance's contention that the editors exhibited bad faith by rejecting a manuscript when they had previously approved its outline also fails, since the Contract clearly states that "acceptance of the outline for a Work and payment of the portion of the advance due as a result thereof shall not, in any way, limit or restrict the Publisher's right to determine, following delivery of the complete manuscript of the Work, whether the complete manuscript is satisfactory." (Coyne Aff., Ex. 1, cl. 3(b).)

It is indisputable that the editors at Doubleday and St. Martin's spent considerable time and effort working with Nance on the *Blackout* manuscript. Indeed, the final version of *Blackout* that Nance eventually sold to Putnam was based on an outline written by the editors that differed significantly from Nance's original proposal. The case therefore differs from Goldwater, 532 F. Supp. at 624, and Dell Publ'g Co. v. Whedon, 577 F. Supp. 1459, 1462 (SDNY 1984), in which the publishers rejected works without giving the authors any editorial suggestions or opportunities for revision. Finally, Putnam's subsequent publication of *Blackout* is not evidence of defendants' bad faith, since it is well-established that evaluations of editorial acceptability are based on the subjective judgment of the publisher. See, e.g., Gold, 464 F. Supp. at 1308–09. What in good faith may be acceptable to one publisher may be, in equally good faith, not acceptable to a different publisher.

Because Nance has not raised any triable issue of fact that defendants rejected his manuscript in bad faith, the publishers' motion for summary judgment on Nance's claim for breach of contract is granted.

C. Fraud

Nance alleges that defendants fraudulently induced him to make extensive revisions on the *Blackout* manuscript, when in fact they had no good faith intention of considering the manuscript at all due to the sales record of his previous books. (See Compl. PP 52–57.) Since, as noted above, Nance has come forward with no evidence that the publisher rejected the manuscript in bad faith, this claim must also fail.

Nance's fraud claim also fails as a matter of law because it is qualitatively equivalent to his breach of contract claim. Pursuant to New York law, "a contract action cannot be converted to one for fraud merely by alleging that the contracting party did not intend to meet its contractual obligations." *International Cabletel, Inc. v. Le Groupe Videotron Ltee, 978 F. Supp. 483, 486 (SDNY 1997) (quoting Rocanova v. Equitable Life Assurance Soc'y, 83 N.Y.2d 603, 614, 612 N.Y.S.2d 339, 634 N.E.2d 940 (1994)). See also Bridgestone/Firestone, Inc. v. Recovery Credit Servs., Inc., 98 F.3d 13, 19–20 (2d Cir. 1996).* The essence of Nance's fraud claim is that the defendants never intended to consider his manuscript in good faith. The claim is based on the same facts as the breach of contract claim and therefore fails as a matter of law. See *Papa's-June Music, Inc. v. McLean, 921 F. Supp. 1154, 1162 (SDNY 1996).* Accordingly, defendants' motion for summary judgment dismissing Nance's fraud claim is granted.

D. Defendants' Counterclaim

Since the publishers did not breach the Contract, they are entitled to summary judgment on their counterclaim for return of advances paid pursuant to the Contract. See *Maysek & Moran, Inc. v. S.G. Warburg & Co., 284 A.D.2d 203, 204, 726 N.Y.S.2d 546 (1st Dep't 2001)* (noting that "on a motion for summary judgment, the construction of an unambiguous contract is a question of law for the court to pass on"). Clause 3(b)(ii) of the Contract provides:

If the manuscript for Work # 2 is rejected, the Author shall retain fifty percent (50%) of monies previously advanced for Work # 2 and all other monies paid to the Author for Work # 2 shall be returned to Publisher, and Publisher shall not be obligated make any further payments hereunder for that Work. *Thereafter, the Author may grant the rights to Work # 2 to another publisher, subject to the Author's obligation to repay Publisher the retained sum out of first and all monies received from such other publisher for Work # 2.* Further, in the event of rejection of Work # 2, Publisher may, at its option, terminate this Agreement for Work # 3 as well, and the Author shall repay Publisher all sums theretofore advanced for Work # 3. (emphasis added.)

It is uncontested that, of the total amount Nance received from defendants, $250,000 represents advances for *Blackout* and $100,000 represents an advance for Work # 3. (Compl. P 48; Kovner Aff. P 7.) Since Nance received an advance of $550,000 from Putnam for *Blackout,* he is obligated to repay the $250,000 advance defendants paid for *Blackout* as well as the $100,000 advance for Work # 3, less the $15,000 he has already returned.

CONCLUSION

Because Nance has not identified any evidence from which a trier of fact could conclude that the publishers rejected his *Blackout* manuscript in bad faith, defendants' motion for summary judgment dismissing the complaint is granted. Because the publishers were entitled to terminate the Contract on the basis of a manuscript that they found unsatisfactory, summary judgment is granted to defendants on their counterclaim for the return of $335,000 in advances paid to Nance.

Doubleday & Company, Inc. v. Curtis, 763 F.2d 495 (2d Cir.1985), *cert. denied,* 474 U.S. 912 (1985)

KAUFMAN, CIRCUIT JUDGE

Mindful of the limited function of the judiciary in the private contractual realm, and aware of the dangers arising from judicial interference with the editorial process, we are today required to interpret an agreement entered into by an author and his publisher.

This dispute arose when, pursuant to the terms of a standard publishing agreement, Doubleday & Co. rejected as unsatisfactory a manuscript submitted by Tony Curtis. Each party then sued for breach of contract; Doubleday brought an action for recovery of the advance it remitted Curtis, and Curtis counterclaimed for anticipated earnings.

After a nonjury trial, the district court dismissed both actions. Judge Sweet rejected Curtis's claim, finding that Doubleday's unfavorable evaluation of the manuscript had been made in good faith and, assuming the publisher had a duty under the contract to provide editorial assistance to Curtis, this obligation had been fulfilled. Doubleday's complaint was dismissed on the basis that the company had waived its right to demand return of its advance. For the reasons set forth below, we affirm the dismissal of Curtis's counterclaims, but reverse the dismissal of Doubleday's claim. . . .

In the early 1970s, Tony Curtis, a respected dramatic and comedic actor, sought to enrich his career by becoming a novelist. He prepared a manuscript—later titled *Kid Andrew Cody and Julie Sparrow* ("Kid Cody")—and enlisted the aid of Irving Paul ("Swifty") Lazar, a well-known literary agent. Doubleday & Co., the venerable New York publishing house, foresaw within Curtis the potential for great commercial success and entered into a two-book contract with him in the winter of 1976.

As part of their arrangement, Doubleday promised to pay Curtis royalties on hardcover sales, and a share of the proceeds from the sale of subsidiary rights (e.g., paperback rights), provided Curtis could deliver—within a specified period of time—final manuscripts, "satisfactory to Publisher in content and form." The agreement was a standard industry form, and did not elaborate on the meaning of the penultimate condition—"satisfactory to Publisher in content and form."

Amid much fanfare, *Kid Cody* was accepted for publication. The final draft was generally acknowledged to have been a joint effort of Curtis and Larry Jordan, a Doubleday editor. Through a series of face-to-face meetings in New York, the experienced Jordan was able to assist the novice Curtis in the successful completion of his first novel.

Inspired by Curtis's literary debut and somewhat intrigued by an eight-page outline for his next novel, Doubleday agreed to renegotiate the contract governing publication of the second book. On September 7, 1977, the parties executed the document that spawned this litigation. Curtis was to receive one hundred thousand dollars as an advance to be charged against future royalties. One-half of the advance was paid upon the signing of the contract, with the balance due on "acceptance of complete satisfactory manuscript." In addition, Curtis was to receive fifty percent of any proceeds Doubleday might earn from the sale of reprint rights. Doubleday's performance was again contingent upon Curtis's ability to produce a "satisfactory" manuscript by a date no later than October 1, 1978. This deadline, as well as the conditions relating to acceptable "form" and "content," were expressly stated to be "of the essence of the Agreement." The document further stated that failure to comply with the satisfaction clause granted the publisher the right to terminate the contract, and require Curtis to return any sums advanced. As with the *Kid Cody* contract, this agreement did not speak to the methods and standards by which the publisher would determine whether a manuscript was "satisfactory." Indeed the contract omitted any reference to the plot, subject, title, length or tone of the proposed novel.

If Doubleday's arrangement with Curtis appeared to favor the publishing house, the company's subsequent reprint agreement with New American Library ("NAL") epitomized the firm's bargaining acumen. NAL promised to pay Doubleday $200,000 merely for the right to publish Curtis's second novel in paperback, in the event it was accepted for publication by Doubleday. NAL's position was thus wholly dependent upon Doubleday's opinion of the manuscript. Indeed, no matter how inferior or unsaleable the novel might prove to be, if Doubleday published the work before December 31, 1980, NAL was bound by the terms of the contract and Doubleday was ensured a handsome profit.

The great expectations that surrounded the project never materialized. It was not until April 1980 that Curtis delivered even a partial first draft of his would-be second novel, *Starstruck*, a rags-to-riches story of a lascivious Hollywood starlet. Doubleday appeared unperturbed, however, and blithely ignored the October 1978 deadline. Equally generous was NAL, which willingly extended its own deadline one year to December 31, 1981.

Those portions of *Starstruck* that Curtis had forwarded to Doubleday were routed from one editor's desk to another, finally coming to rest in August 1980 with Adrian Zackheim, then a stranger to Curtis. Zackheim's review of the first half of *Starstruck* was slow but painstakingly thorough. After four months of intermittent reading—totaling perhaps fifty hours—he sent Curtis a seven-page letter. In it, Zackheim criticized the numerous inconsistencies and inherent contradictions that pervaded the manuscript and exhorted Curtis to tighten the plot. Yet, sprinkled among this criticism was praise for the author's story-telling ability. To this end, Zackheim emphasized he was generally "charmed" with the "wonderful possibilities" of *Starstruck* and was not expecting substantial changes in "the basic outlines of the novel."

The following months, however, did not prove conducive to *Starstruck*'s completion. The few telephonic and face-to-face conversations between Curtis and Zackheim contrasted dramatically with the considerable contact Curtis had maintained with Larry Jordan. To a large extent, the dearth of communication was a product of circumstance rather than neglect. Curtis was preoccupied with complex divorce proceedings, and his visits to New York became more and more infrequent. Zackheim, for his part, was willing to review changes and additions piecemeal, but Curtis eschewed this alternative.

The spring of 1981 elapsed without any significant progress being made on the manuscript. As a result, Doubleday executives became increasingly anxious that they would be unable to accept *Starstruck* for publication before the December 31, 1981 deadline with NAL. The prevailing sentiment at Doubleday was that it would prove fruitless to appeal to NAL for a further extension.

In early August, Curtis finally forwarded to Zackheim what he represented to be a completed draft of the book. Zackheim was appalled at the product, and reluctantly concluded that *Starstruck* was unpublishable. Not only had Curtis ignored suggestions involving the story's first half, but he had composed such an unexpectedly poor conclusion that *Starstruck* was transformed from a potential success into an almost certain debacle.

Without apprising Curtis of his impressions, Zackheim asked his supervisor at Doubleday, Elizabeth Drew, to read the revised manuscript. Drew's response, in the form of an intrafirm memorandum, clearly demonstrates the dilemma then confronting Doubleday. She acknowledged that rejecting *Starstruck* would require forfeiture of the lucrative reprint arrangement with NAL, but nonetheless recommended that Doubleday abandon the book. In her opinion, *Starstruck* was "junk, pure and simple," and could not be "edited into shape or even rewritten into shape." To accept the manuscript for publication solely because of the NAL contract was, in Drew's words, "not a way to sleep nights, at least not if one's concerned with ethics."

As a final means of salvaging the book and the NAL deal, Zackheim approached Lazar and suggested that Curtis submit the manuscript to a "novel doctor" in an attempt to put the shine back on the fallen *Starstruck*. When Lazar demurred, Doubleday finally admitted defeat. It cancelled the reprint deal with NAL, formally terminated the September 1977 agreement with Curtis and demanded repayment of the original $50,000 advance. When Curtis refused, Doubleday commenced this litigation. . . .

Characterizing the litigation as a "dispute about creativity and the respective responsibilities of an author and his publisher," the district court dismissed Doubleday's complaint and Curtis's litany of counterclaims. 599 F.Supp. 779 (SDNY 1984). In considering whether to infer a duty to edit from a clause requiring delivery of a manuscript "satisfactory to the publisher," the court acknowledged that New York's appellate courts had yet to resolve this issue. Without deciding the issue, Judge Sweet concluded that, "[e]ven if a duty to provide editorial services is accepted as required under New York law, here, Doubleday performed it." *Id.* at 784.

Turning to the question of bad faith, the trial judge deemed the testimony of Doubleday's witnesses credible, and held that the decision to reject Curtis's manuscript had been animated by a genuine belief that *Starstruck* was unpublishable. Curtis's remaining counterclaims were summarily dismissed as contrary to the relevant provisions of the 1976 and 1977 contracts.

Finally, the court dismissed Doubleday's claim seeking recovery of the $50,000 advance. Judge Sweet held that Doubleday had waived the "time of the essence" clause by accepting Curtis's manuscript nearly eighteen months after the original deadline had passed. Moreover, the court found that because Doubleday had led Curtis to believe that *Starstruck* would eventually be published, it had also waived its right to a return of the advance even if it found the manuscript unsatisfactory. . . .

We note at the outset that Curtis has never defended his August 1981 manuscript as a work of publishable quality. Rather, Curtis maintains that but for Doubleday's inability and unwillingness to provide adequate editorial assistance, *Starstruck* would have met the "satisfactory to publisher" condition. Curtis concedes that his proposed interpretation is not supported by a literal reading of the 1977 agreement. On its face, the document is completely silent regarding any obligation on Doubleday's part to ensure that Curtis's rough drafts are transformed, through the company's affirmative efforts, into a polished novel.

Our task, then, is to delineate the extent to which New York law requires us to infer such an obligation from the agreement. Because New York's appellate courts have not yet addressed this question, we must attempt to divine the likely response of our state brethren.

The 1977 agreement expressly granted Doubleday the right to terminate the contract if it deemed Curtis's manuscript to be unsatisfactory. In similar circumstances—where the satisfactory performance of one party is to be judged by another party—New York courts have required the party terminating the contract to act in good faith. . . .

This principle—that a contract containing a "satisfaction clause" may be terminated only as a result of honest dissatisfaction—would seem especially appropriate in construing publishing agreements. To shield from scrutiny the already chimerical process of evaluating literary value would render the "satisfaction" clause an illusory promise, and place authors at the unbridled mercy of their editors.

A corollary of this duty to appraise a writing honestly is an obligation on the part of the publisher not to mislead an author deliberately regarding the work required for a given project. A willful failure to respond to a request for editorial comments on a preliminary draft may, in many instances, work no less a hardship than would an unjustifiable rejection of a final manuscript. A publisher's duty to exercise good faith in its dealings toward an author exists at all stages of the creative process.

Although we hold that publishers must perform honestly, we decline to extend that requirement to include a duty to perform skillfully. The possibility that a publisher or an editor—either through inferior editing or inadvertence—may prejudice an author's efforts is a risk attendant to the selection of a publishing house by a writer, and is properly borne by that party. To imply a duty to perform adequate editorial services in the absence of express contractual language would, in our view, represent an unwarranted intrusion into the editorial process. Moreover, we are hesitant to require triers of fact to explore the manifold intricacies of an editorial relationship. Such inquiries are appropriate only where contracts specifically allocate certain creative responsibilities to the publisher.

Accordingly, we hold that a publisher may, in its discretion, terminate a standard publishing contract, provided that the termination is made in good faith, and that the failure of an author to submit a satisfactory manuscript was not caused by the publisher's bad faith. . . .

Evaluating the Doubleday-Curtis relationship in light of these principles, we are convinced that *Starstruck's* failure was not attributable to any dishonesty, willful neglect or any other manifestations of bad faith on the part of Doubleday. The factual landscape illustrates the complete frustration experienced by Doubleday's editors, who were forced to harmonize an inferior manuscript, a lucrative reprint agreement and a recalcitrant author. Zackheim sincerely endeavored to assist Curtis in the completion of his manuscript. Although Zackheim's suggested revisions may have been offered somewhat belatedly, the evidence indicates that he extended numerous offers to discuss the novel with Curtis, as well as to review portions of the second draft. Indeed, it was Curtis who refused these renderings of assistance. That Zackheim's editing was perhaps inadequate is beside the point, as is any comparison with Larry Jordan. Curtis neither alleged, nor does the record support a finding that Doubleday deliberately or even recklessly assigned *Starstruck* to an editor unfit or unsuited for the project.

Admittedly, the selection of an editor is a matter of paramount importance to a writer, but we note once again that the power to control this decision—like all aspects of the publication process—could have been reserved to Curtis in his contract.

Turning our attention to the actual termination of the contract, we believe the district court's finding that Doubleday rejected *Starstruck* in good faith is amply supported by the record before us. Zackheim and Drew were in complete agreement that no amount of in-house editing could save the project. Moreover, the suggestion that Curtis consult a "novel doctor"—though perhaps somewhat humiliating—appears to have been made sincerely, rather than as a strategem for avoiding the responsibilities attendant to a difficult editing job.

Curtis argues with some force that Doubleday terminated his contract in November 1981 primarily because of the impending NAL deadline. Although we agree the two events were not unconnected, we choose to characterize the relationship between them quite differently. Were it not for the extremely lucrative arrangement with NAL, it is likely that Doubleday would have abandoned *Starstruck* without hesitation, and perhaps at a much earlier date. Only the prospect of a commercially profitable reprint deal prevented Zackheim from rejecting the August 1981 manuscript immediately. Doubleday's decision to sacrifice financial reward for "ethics," as Zackheim's superior Drew framed the choice, can hardly be said to constitute an act of bad faith.

In light of all the circumstances, we agree with the district court's finding that Doubleday exercised good faith in its dealings with Curtis, and thus affirm the dismissal of Curtis's counterclaim. . . .

In dismissing Doubleday's complaint, which sought recovery of the $50,000 advance paid to Curtis, the district court found that Doubleday had waived its right to demand return of the advance. Because the issue was not properly before the court, we conclude dismissal on that basis was improper.

Among the cardinal principles of our Anglo-American system of justice is the notion that the legal parameters of a given dispute are framed by the positions advanced by the adversaries, and may not be expanded *sua sponte* by the trial judge. The dismissal of Doubleday's claim based on an issue never pleaded by Curtis—or even implicitly raised at trial—is inconsistent with the due process concerns of adequate notice and an opportunity to be heard. Moreover, such a result runs counter to the spirit of fairness embodied in the Federal Rules of Civil Procedure. . . .

Chodos v. West Publishing Company, 292 F.3d 992, 1003 (9th Cir. 2002)

REINHARDT, CIRCUIT JUDGE

This case presents the question whether a publisher retains the right to reject an author's manuscript written pursuant to a standard industry agreement, even though the manuscript is of the quality contemplated by both parties. In this case, attorney Rafael Chodos entered into a standard Author Agreement with the Bancroft-Whitney Publishing Company under which he agreed to write a treatise on the intriguing subject of the law of fiduciary duty. The agreement is widely used in the publishing industry for traditional literary works as well as for specialized volumes. Bancroft-Whitney thought that the treatise would be successful commercially and that it would result in substantial profits for both the author and the publisher. After Chodos had spent a number of years fulfilling his part of the bargain and had submitted a completed manuscript, Bancroft-Whitney's successor, the West Publishing Company, came to a contrary conclusion. It declined to publish the treatise, citing solely sales and marketing reasons. Like a good lawyer, Chodos responded by suing for damages, first for breach of contract, and then, after amending his complaint to drop that claim, in quantum meruit. The district court held that under the terms of the contract West's decision not to publish was within its discretion, and granted summary judgment in West's favor. Chodos appeals, and we reverse.

I. BACKGROUND

The facts that are relevant to liability are undisputed. Those that are relevant to the amount of the recovery are set forth for narrative purposes only and do not constitute findings. Should the district court be requested to determine that amount on remand, such determination shall be based solely on the facts as they are developed in that court.

Rafael Chodos is a California attorney whose specialty is the law of fiduciary duty. His practice consists primarily of matters involving fiduciary issues such as partnership disputes, corporate dissolutions, and joint ventures. Prior to being admitted to the bar in 1977, Chodos worked as a software engineer. Beginning in approximately 1989, Chodos began developing the idea of writing a treatise on the law of fiduciary duty that included a traditional print component as well as an electronic component that incorporated search engines, linking capabilities, and electronic indexing. Chodos sought to draw on both his legal and technological expertise, and was motivated in part by the fact that there was, and continues to be, no systematic scholarly treatment of the law of fiduciary duty.

In early 1995, Chodos sent a detailed proposal, which included a tentative table of contents, to the Bancroft-Whitney Corporation. Bancroft was at the time a leading publisher of legal texts. William Farber, an Associate Publisher, promptly responded to Chodos's proposal, and informed him that the Bancroft editorial staff was enthusiastic about both the subject matter and the technological features of the proposed project. In July, 1995, Bancroft and Chodos entered into an Author Agreement, which both parties agree is a standard form contract used to govern the composition of a literary work for hire.

The Author Agreement provided for no payments to Chodos prior to publication, and a 15% share of the gross revenues from sales of the work. Farber informed Chodos that a typical successful title published by Bancroft grossed $1 million over a five-year period, although Chodos's work, of course, might be more or less successful than the average. Chodos sought publication of the work not only for the direct financial rewards, but also for the enhanced professional reputation he might receive from the publication of a treatise, which in turn might result in additional referrals to his practice and increased fees for him.

From July, 1995 through June, 1998, Chodos's principal professional activity was the writing of the treatise. He significantly limited the time spent on his law practice, and devoted several hours each morning as well as most weekends to the book project. Chodos estimates that he spent at least 3600 hours over the course of three years on writing the treatise and developing the accompanying electronic materials. He did so with the guidance of Bancroft staff. For example, in late 1995 or early 1996, Farber instructed Chodos that because

Bancroft viewed the book as a practice aid and not as an academic work, he should delete an introductory chapter that was primarily historical and disperse the historical material throughout the text, in footnote form. As Chodos completed each of the chapters, he submitted them to Bancroft on a CD-ROM; the seventh and final chapter was sent to the publisher in February, 1998. When finished, the book consisted of 1247 pages.

In mid-1996, Bancroft-Whitney was purchased by the West Publishing Group, and the two entities merged at the end of the year. The Bancroft editors, now employed by West, continued to work with Chodos in preparing the work for publication, although West did establish a management position that ultimately had a direct bearing on Chodos's career as a treatise-writer, that of Director of Product Development and Management for the Western Market Center. Between February and June, 1998, after the entire treatise had been submitted, Chodos reviewed the manuscript to ensure that the formatting was consistent and that no substantive gaps existed. In the summer of 1998 the West editors provided him with detailed notes and suggestions, to which he diligently responded. In November, 1998, West again sent Chodos a lengthy letter including substantive editorial suggestions related to the organization of the book. In early December, 1998, West sent Chodos yet another letter, this time apologizing for delays in publication, and assuring him that publication would take place in the first quarter of 1999. Burt Levy, who replaced Farber as Chodos's editor, informed Chodos that copy editors were preparing the manuscript for release in the early part of that year.

After receiving no communication from Levy in January, 1999, Chodos contacted West to check on the status of his treatise. On February 4, 1999, Chodos received a response from Nell Petri, a member of the marketing department. Petri informed Chodos that West had decided not to publish the book because it did not "fit within [West's] current product mix" and because of concerns about its "market potential." West admits, however, that the manuscript was of "high quality" and that its decision was not due to any literary shortcomings in Chodos's work.

The decision not to publish the treatise on fiduciary duty was made by Carole Gamble, who joined West as Director of Product Development and Management for the Western Market Center at about the same time that Chodos completed the manuscript. In late 1998, West developed new internal criteria to guide publication decisions. Applying these criteria, Gamble decided not to go forward with the publication of the treatise. She did not in fact read what Chodos had written, but instead reviewed a detailed outline of the treatise and the original proposal for it. Gamble did not prepare a business analysis prior to making her decision. After Chodos informed West that in his view the publisher had breached its contract, West did prepare an economic projection that concluded that the publication of Chodos's work would be an unprofitable venture. Thus, this legal action was born.

Proceedings Below

Chodos filed an action against West for breach of contract in Los Angeles Superior Court in March, 1999, shortly after the publisher's decision not to publish his work, and West removed the case to federal court on the basis of diversity jurisdiction. Chodos immediately moved for summary judgment, which was denied. Shortly thereafter, he amended his complaint to seek restitution on a quantum meruit basis and dropped the breach of contract claim. West moved to dismiss the amended complaint for failure to state a claim, and the motion was denied. At the conclusion of discovery, West moved for summary judgment, and Chodos sought to amend the complaint again, in order to add a claim for fraud. The district court granted West's motion and entered judgment in its favor; it simultaneously denied Chodos leave to amend his complaint.

II. DISCUSSION

Chodos makes two alternative arguments: first, that the standard Author Agreement is an illusory contract, and second, that if a valid contract does exist, West breached it. Under either theory of liability, Chodos contends that he is entitled to recover in quantum meruit.

A. The Author Agreement Is Not Illusory

In support of his first argument, Chodos correctly notes that in order for a contract to be enforceable under California law, it must impose binding obligations on each party. *Bleecher v. Conte,* 29 Cal. 3d 345, 350, 213 Cal. Rptr. 852, 698 P.2d 1154 (1981). The California Supreme Court has held that "if one of the promises leaves a party free to perform or to withdraw from the agreement at his own unrestricted pleasure, the promise is deemed illusory and it provides no consideration." *Mattei v. Hopper,* 51 Cal. 2d 119, 122, 330 P.2d 625 (1958). Chodos contends that because the contract required him to produce a work of publishable quality, but allowed West, in its discretion, to decide unilaterally whether or not to publish his work, the contract violates the doctrine of mutuality of obligation and is therefore illusory.

California law, like the law in most states, provides that a covenant of good faith and fair dealing is an implied term in every contract. *Carma Developers (Cal.) v. Marathon Dev. Cal.,* 2 Cal. 4th 342, 372–73, 826 P.2d 710, 6 Cal. Rptr. 2d 467 (1992); *see Russell v. Princeton Laboratories, Inc.,* 50 N.J. 30, 231 A.2d 800, 805 (N.J. 1967) (noting that a "majority of the courts" read a good-faith obligation into contracts providing one party with discretion); *Boston Road Shopping Center v. Teachers Annuity Ins. Ass'n of America,* 13 A.D.2d 106, 213 N.Y.S.2d 522, *aff'd.* 11 N.Y.2d 831, 182 N.E.2d 116, 227 N.Y.S.2d 444 (N.Y. 1962). Thus, a court will not find a contract to be illusory if the implied covenant of good faith and fair dealing can be read to impose an obligation on each party. *See, e.g., Third Story Music v. Waits,* 41 Cal. App. 4th 798, 805–06, 48 Cal. Rptr. 2d 747 (1995) ("The implied covenant of good faith is also applied to contradict an express contractual grant of discretion when necessary to protect an agreement which otherwise would be rendered illusory and unenforceable."). The covenant of good faith "finds particular application in situations where one party is invested with a discretionary power affecting the rights of another." *Carma, 2 Cal. 4th at 372.*

It is correct that the agreement at issue imposes numerous obligations on the author but gives the publisher "the right in its discretion to terminate" the publishing relationship after receiving the manuscript and determining that it is unacceptable. However, we conclude that the contract is not illusory because West's duty to exercise its discretion is limited by its duty of good faith and fair dealing. *See, e.g., Asmus v. Pacific Bell,* 23 Cal. 4th 1, 15–16, 999 P.2d 71, 96 Cal. Rptr. 2d 179 (2000); *Third Story Music Inc,* 41 Cal. App. 4th at 803–04; see also *Wood v. Lucy, Lady Duff-Gordon,* 222 N.Y. 88, 91, 118 N.E. 214 (1917) ("We are not to suppose that one party was to be placed at the mercy of the other."). More specifically, because the standard Author Agreement obligates the publisher to make a judgment as to the quality or literary merit of the author's work—to determine whether the work is "acceptable" or "unacceptable"—it must make that judgment in good faith, and cannot reject a manuscript for other, unrelated reasons. *See* Third Story Music, 41 Cal. App. 4th at 804. Thus, Chodos's first argument fails.

B. West Breached the Agreement

Chodos's alternative argument—that a contract exists and it was breached—is more persuasive. West contends that the Author Agreement allowed it to decline to publish the manuscript after Chodos completed writing it for *any* good-faith reason, regardless of whether the reason was related to the quality or literary merit of Chodos's manuscript. However, West's right to terminate the agreement is a limited one defined in two related provisions of the agreement. The first, the "acceptance clause," establishes that West may decline to publish Chodos's manuscript if it finds the work to be "unacceptable" in form and content. The acceptance clause, paragraph eight of the agreement, provides that:

After timely receipt of the Work or any portion of the Work prepared by Author, Publisher shall review it as to both form and content, and notify Author whether it is acceptable or unacceptable in form and content under the terms of this Agreement. In the event that Publisher determines that the Work or any portion of the Work is unacceptable, Publisher shall notify Author of Publisher's determination and Publisher may exercise its rights under paragraph 4.

The second relevant provision (referred to in the acceptance clause as West's "rights under paragraph 4") allows West to terminate the publishing agreement if the author does not cure a failure in performance after being given an opportunity to do so. This provision, numbered paragraph four of the contract and entitled "Author's Failure to Perform," states:

If Publisher determines that the Work or any portion of it is not acceptable to publisher as provided in paragraph 8 [the acceptance clause] . . . after thirty (30) days following written notice to author if Author has not cured such failure in performance Publisher has the right in its discretion to terminate this Agreement.

The district court agreed with West that in determining whether a manuscript is satisfactory in form and content under the acceptance clause of the standard Author Agreement, the publisher may in good faith consider solely the likelihood of a book's commercial success and other similar economic factors. We unequivocally reject the view that the relevant provisions of the Author Agreement may be so construed in the absence of additional language or conditions.

The expansive reading of the acceptance clause suggested by West is inconsistent with the language of the two contract clauses. Under the agreement, the publisher may deem a manuscript unacceptable only if it is deficient in "form and content." Thus, had Chodos submitted a badly written, poorly researched, disorganized or substantially incomplete work to West, the publisher would have been well within its rights to find that submission unacceptable under the acceptance clause—as it would were it to reject any work that it believed in good faith lacked literary merit. A publisher bargains for a product of a certain quality and is entitled to reject a work that in its good faith judgment falls short of the bargained-for standard. Nothing in the contract, however, suggests that the ordinary meaning of the words "form and content" was not intended, and nowhere in the contract does it state that the publisher may terminate the agreement if it changes its management structure or its marketing strategy, or if it revises its business or economic forecasts, all matters unrelated to "form and content."

To the contrary, the fact that the contract required West to afford Chodos an opportunity to cure any deficient performance supports our straightforward reading of the acceptance clause as a provision that relates solely to the quality or literary merit of a submitted work. As noted above, if West determined that Chodos's submission was unacceptable, he was to be given a period of time to cure his failure in performance. The inclusion of this provision indicates that a deficiency in "form and content" is one that the author has some power to cure. Chodos has no power to "cure" West's view that the marketplace for books on fiduciary duty had changed; nor could he "cure" a change in West's overall marketing strategy and product mix; nor, indeed, could he be expected to do much about a general downturn in economic conditions. The text and structure of the contract thus demonstrate that West's stated reasons for terminating the agreement were not among those contemplated by the parties.

The uncontroverted evidence in this case is that Chodos worked diligently in cooperation with West—indeed, with West's encouragement—to produce a work that met the highest professional standard, and that he was successful in that venture. His performance was induced by an agreement that permitted rejection of the completed manuscript only for deficiencies in "form and content." Chodos thus labored to complete a work of high quality with the expectation that, if he did so, it would be published. He devoted thousands of hours of labor to the venture, and passed up substantial professional opportunities, only for West to decide that due to the vagaries of its internal reorganizations and changes in its business strategies or in the national economy or the market for legal treatises, his work, albeit admittedly of high quality, was for naught. It would be inequitable, if not unconscionable, for an author to be forced to bear this considerable burden solely because of his publisher's change in management, its poor planning, or its inadequate financial analyses at the time it entered into the contract, or even because of an unexpected change in the market-place. Moreover, to allow a publisher to escape its contractual obligations for these reasons would be directly contrary to both the language and the spirit of the standard Author Agreement.

West urges us to affirm the district court's ruling because, in its view, it is well-accepted that, regardless of the contract's failure to mention economic circumstances or market demands, publishers have broad discretion under the acceptance clause of the standard Author Agreement to reject manuscripts for any good faith commercial reason. For this proposition, the district court cited two cases from the Second Circuit involving that same clause. Although at least one of the cases contains dicta that would support the district court's decision, both are distinguishable factually and legally. Moreover, to the extent that either case suggests that a publisher bound by the standard Author Agreement may terminate the contract for *any* reason so long as it acts in good faith, we respectfully reject that view.

In *Doubleday & Co. v. Curtis*, 763 F.2d 495, 496 (2d Cir. 1985), a publisher rejected a manuscript by the well-known actor but neophyte author, Tony Curtis, on the basis of its poor literary quality. There, as here, the publishing agreement allowed the publisher to reject a submission if it was not satisfactory as to "form and content". *Id.* However, in *Doubleday*, in direct contrast to the circumstances here, it was agreed that the manuscript was *unsatisfactory* in form and content. *Id.* at 500. In *Doubleday*, Curtis's claim was that the publisher had a good-faith obligation under the contract to re-write his admittedly unsatisfactory manuscript and to transform it into one of publishable quality. *Id.* The Second Circuit held that a publisher's good faith obligation does not stretch that far; thus, the Second Circuit's essential holding in *Doubleday* has no bearing on the present case.

It is true that the Second Circuit appears to have stated its holding in *Doubleday* more broadly than the case before the court warranted. The court said:

We hold that a publisher may, in its discretion, terminate a standard publishing contract, provided that the termination is made in good faith, and that the failure of an author to submit a satisfactory manuscript was not caused by the publisher's bad faith.

Id. at 501. Still, read in context, the holding does not make it clear whether the court meant that a publisher may reject a manuscript for reasons wholly unrelated to its literary worth or that it may do so only if it determines in good faith that the submitted work is unsatisfactory on its literary merits. If the former is the Second Circuit's view of the law, we respectfully disagree.

The district court also relied on *Random House, Inc. v. Gold,* 464 F. Supp. 1306 (SDNY 1979). That case is more apposite than *Doubleday* in that the district court there held that a publisher may consider economic circumstances when evaluating a manuscript's "form and content" under the standard publishing agreement. *Id. at 1308–09.* Although we disagree with that holding for the reasons set forth above, and are certainly not bound by it, we note that even in *Random House* the court did not go so far as to state that economic considerations may be the *sole* reason for a publisher to decline to publish a manuscript that is in every other respect acceptable. In *Random House,* as in *Doubleday,* the submitted manuscript was not of publishable quality. In contrast to Chodos's work, the editor at Random House considered the manuscript at issue to be "shallow and badly designed." *Id. at 1308.*

In sum, we reject the district court's determination that West acted within the discretion afforded it by the Author Agreement when it decided not to publish Chodos's manuscript. Because West concedes that the manuscript was of high quality and that it declined to publish it solely for commercial reasons rather than because of any defect in its form and content, we hold as a matter of law that West breached its agreement with Chodos.

C. Chodos May Pursue A Quantum Meruit Claim

The district court ruled that if West breached the contract, Chodos could proceed in quantum meruit, but only if the damages were not determinable under the contract. It also stated that a question of material fact existed as to whether contract damages were determinable. It then granted West summary judgment on the quantum meruit claim because it held that there was no breach of contract. As we have already determined above, the district court erred in finding that no breach occurred. Accordingly, we must consider the remaining issues relevant to Chodos's quantum meruit claim.

Under California law, a party who has been injured by a breach of contract may generally elect what remedy to seek. In a leading case on election of remedies, the California Supreme Court stated:

It is well settled in this state that one who has been injured by a breach of contract has an election to pursue any of three remedies, to wit: He may treat the contract as rescinded and may recover upon a quantum meruit so far as he has performed; or he may keep the contract alive, for the benefit of both parties, being at all times ready and able to perform; or, third, he may treat the repudiation as putting an end to the contract for all purposes of performance, and sue for the profits he would have realized if he had not been prevented from performing.

Alder v. Drudis, 30 Cal. 2d 372, 381–82, 182 P.2d 195 (1947) *(internal quotation marks omitted).*

In employment contracts and contracts for personal services, like the one before us, the first option, an action in quantum meruit, is generally limited to cases in which the breach occurs after partial performance and the party seeking a recovery does not thereafter complete performance. "Where [a party's] performance is not prevented, the injured party may elect instead to affirm the contract and complete performance. If such is his election, his exclusive remedy is an action for damages." *B.C. Richter Contracting Co. v. Continental Casualty Co.,* 230 Cal. App. 2d 491, 500, 41 Cal. Rptr. 98 (1964) *(citing House v. Piercy,* 181 Cal. 247, 251, 183 P. 807 (1919)). Thus, if a plaintiff has fully performed a contract, damages for breach is often the only available remedy. *Oliver v. Campbell,* 43 Cal. 2d 298, 306, 273 P.2d 15 (1954).

The California Supreme Court has, however, recognized an exception to the general rule. In *Oliver,* the court stated:

> The remedy of restitution in money is not available to one who has fully performed his part of a contract, if the only part of the agreed exchange for such performance that has not been rendered by the defendant is a sum of money constituting a liquidated debt; *but full performance does not make restitution unavailable if any part of the consideration due from the defendant in return is something other than a liquidated debt.*
>
> *Id. at 306 (adopting Restatement of Contracts § 350) (emphasis added).*

Assuming that Chodos fully performed his end of the bargain by delivering a completed manuscript to West, then whether Chodos can recover on a quantum meruit claim turns on whether the 15% of the gross revenues provided for in the agreement constitutes a "liquidated debt." According to Black's Law Dictionary, "[a] debt is liquidated when it is certain what is due and how much is due. That which has been made certain as to amount due by agreement of parties or by operation of law." *Black's Law Dictionary* 931 (6th ed. 1990). The term "liquidated debt" is similar to the term "liquidated damages," which the California courts have defined as "an amount of compensation to be paid in the event of a breach of contract, the sum of which is fixed and certain by agreement. . . ." *Kelly v. McDonald,* 98 Cal. App. 121, 125, 276 P. 404 (1929) (citation omitted), *overruled in part on other grounds, McCarthy v. Tally,* 46 Cal. 2d 577, 297 P.2d 981 (1956).

Chodos's entitlement to 15% of the revenues from his book on fiduciary duty is not a liquidated debt under California law, as it was not a certain or readily ascertainable figure. The mere existence of a fixed percentage royalty in a contract does not render that royalty a "liquidated debt," if the revenues to which that percentage figure is to be applied cannot be calculated with reasonable certainty. Here, it is impossible to determine even now what those revenues would have been had West not frustrated the completion of the contract. Had West honored its contractual obligations and published the treatise, the revenues would have depended on any number of circumstances, including how West chose to market the book, and how it was received by readers and critics. Accordingly, under *Oliver,* Chodos is entitled to sue for restitution for the time and effort he reasonably invested in writing the manuscript. *See also O'Hare v. Peacock Dairies,* 26 Cal. App. 2d 345, 79 P.2d 433, 442–43 (Cal. 1938) (holding future profits to be unascertainable where plaintiffs are owed a future revenue stream from a dairy that had ceased operation). We express no opinion as to how restitution should be calculated in this case, nor do we intimate any suggestion as to the appropriate amount of such recovery.

III. CONCLUSION

Because West breached its contract with Chodos by rejecting his manuscript for a reason not permitted by the contract between the parties and because Chodos is entitled to recover for the breach in quantum meruit, we REVERSE the district court's grant of summary judgment in West's favor, and REMAND the case to the district court with instructions to enter summary judgment as to liability in Chodos's favor, and for further proceedings consistent with this opinion. *See Bachelder v. America West Airlines,* 259 F.3d 1112, 1132 (9th Cir. 2001) (reversing a district court's grant of summary judgment for the defendant and directing that judgment be entered for the plaintiff where both sides had moved for summary judgment below). We AFFIRM the district court's denial of Chodos's motion to amend his complaint.

NOTES ──────────────────────────────────

1. In *Dell Publishing Co. v. Whedon,* 577 F. Supp. 1459 (SDNY 1984), the publisher reviewed the author's outline for the book before contracting with the author; an advance was paid on the basis of the outline. Under these circumstances, the court held there was an implied duty for the publisher in good faith to offer suggestions to the author as to what needed to be revised to make the manuscript satisfactory. Editorial assistance had to be offered, and a manuscript could not be rejected without this degree of assistance. The publisher's failure to comply with these procedures prevented the publisher from recovering the advances made to the author.

2. In *William Morrow & Co. v. Davis,* 583 F. Supp. 578 (SDNY 1984), a three-sided dispute erupted between the publisher (William Morrow & Co.), a celebrity (Bette Davis) who was to have her autobiography written, and an author (Mickey Herskowitz) who was to assist the celebrity in the writing. The court denied the publisher's motion for summary judgment, holding that triable issues of fact existed as to what is meant by contract language that requires the authors to deliver a manuscript satisfactory to plaintiff publisher in form and content.

   The court held that each of the three principals in the case had set forth reasonable interpretations as to what was satisfactory in the context of the dealings among the three. Only a trial on the matter could determine what would constitute a satisfactory manuscript. These circumstances, the court held, raised an implied duty for the publisher in good faith to offer suggestions to the author as to what needed to be revised to make the manuscript satisfactory. Editorial assistance had to be offered, and a manuscript could not be rejected without this degree of assistance. The publisher's failure to comply with these procedures prevented the publisher from recovering the advances made to the author.

3. In *Polygram Records, Inc. v. Buddy Buie Productions, Inc.*, 520 F. Supp. 248 (SDNY 1981), a record company was held to have accepted an album on the date when it was physically delivered to the company by a recording artist, rather than a later date. Although the company's artists & repertoire representative testified that he had not in fact accepted the album, the company had proceeded to pay the balance of the advance applicable to the album (which was so noted on the check stub), which balance was due only upon delivery and acceptance of the album. Because "delivery" occurred on a date earlier than that asserted by the company, the company's attempt to exercise its option for a subsequent album was held to be untimely. Record companies have since adopted rather strict and specific rules governing "delivery," typically providing that the making of payments by the company does not constitute a waiver of the rules and that delivery is deemed to occur on the last day of the month during which all rules have been satisfied.

6.4.4 Non-Compete Clause

The publisher's form agreement often contains provisions which require the author to agree not to publish a future book that is based on the material of the book under contr ally sweeping and are potentially applicable to a wide range of works that the author might want to undertake. One can sympathize with a publisher's not wanting an author to come out immediately or in close proximity to the publisher's release with a competing work that will undercut the sales of the book in question. However, the publisher is rarely willing to provide reciprocal guarantees; indeed, the publisher may have several competing books in the same field. This suggests that the author should grant no more than a very limited, specific noncompetition provision.

The Authors Guild has made these comments about noncompete clauses:

These clauses can cause an author considerable harm. A publisher might claim that the characters in a novel or children's story could not be used in sequels; that the author of a textbook could not write other works on the same subject; or that one cookbook or other specialized work is all that an author could write, without the publisher's release from the non-compete clause. We do not think these claims are valid. These clauses, absolute restrictive covenants, are probably unenforceable; and they may violate the antitrust laws.

Non-compete clauses should be deleted. If the publisher refuses, the clause should be tightened. There should be a reasonably short time period, after which it expires. The types of books to which it applies should be stated specifically. Authors of textbooks should be particularly careful that they limit the effect of the clause, so that the contract for one book on a subject does not prevent them from writing other texts on the subject for other age groups, or for different types of classes or schools.

6.4.5 Publication

Several provisions in the publisher-author contract spell out the publisher's publication rights and duties. The publisher will normally secure the exclusive right to publish. An approximate timetable for publication of hard-cover and paperback editions may be established. The author will seek—and the publisher will resist—a specific recitation of duties on the part of the publisher to advertise and market the book. The publisher has an implied duty to promote a work, but this duty is limited to a reasonable "first push," and no case has yet extended this implied duty any further. Therefore, the author will want to attempt to obtain specific commitments, such as an advertising budget and promotion and marketing schedule. The publisher will just as resolutely resist either a general commitment to use its best efforts or a detailed list of specific undertakings.

Typically, the publisher will agree that if the book is not published within a specified time frame (frequently, 18 months following acceptance of the manuscript) the author has the right to recapture it. In such cases, the contract will customarily provide that if the author then places the book with a third-pa rty publisher, the author will be required to repay advances made by the original publisher. In addition, if the book is published but thereafter goes out of print (i.e., is deleted from the publisher's catalog or "list"), the author has the right to demand that the book be put back into print or that the publishing rights be returned to the author.

NOTE _____

Even famous authors have complaints about their publisher's efforts to sell and exploit a book. In 1996, Joe McGinnis, best-selling author of *Blind Faith,* returned a $1,000,000 advance from Crown Publishing for a book about the O. J. Simpson trial to instead devote his efforts to writing *The Miracle of Castel di Sangro,* a book about a soccer team from a small town in Italy. Upon publication of *Miracle,* McGinnis criticized his publisher, Little, Brown & Company, for everything from a mediocre book cover to a cancelled tour to legal problems regarding the final chapter of the book. Despite the fact that Little, Brown took out full page ads in *The New York Times* and other newspapers, the book failed to create much interest or sales. Small publishers, on the other hand, face a dilemma when an author achieves a certain amount of success. It is a common practice for writers to jump to large publishing houses at the first sign of success, primarily for the increased marketing support and advances available.

6.4.6 Copyright

While many publishers readily agree that the copyright is to be retained by the author (a very different practice from those prevailing in the recording, film and television industries, and to a far lesser degree in the music publishing industry) some publishers will insist that the copyright be assigned by the author. In any event, the ownership of the copyright is a question that is distinct from the granting of rights under Section 6.4.1 below. The contract should be precise both as to copyright ownership and the rights to license that flow from ownership.

6.4.7 Royalties and Other Payments

These very important provisions in the publisher-author contract require close scrutiny. Beyond the issue of the percentage actually named for the royalty, of equal and perhaps even greater importance is the definition of what that percentage is based on.

(a) A hardback book contract will often prescribe a royalty of 10 percent of the suggested retail list price for the first 10,000 copies, 12.5 percent on the next 5,000, and 15 percent on all copies in excess of 15,000.

(b) On trade paperbacks, a new author or an author without a track record of substantial sales can usually anticipate a royalty in the area of 6 percent on up to 10,000 or 20,000 copies, increasing to 7.5 percent thereafter.

(c) On mass market editions, 8 percent on the suggested retail price of the first 150,000 copies and ten percent of the retail price thereafter.

(d) On audio work editions, 8 percent of net sales revenues.

(e) On electronic versions, 25 percent of net electronic sales receipts (all monies actually received by the Publisher from sales of the Electronic Versions, less any applicable taxes, handling or processing fees paid by the publisher, customer refunds resulting from bonafide offering, billing or other errors in the transmission of the Work and commissions or fees payable to third parties incurred in connection with effecting the transaction or transmission of the Electronic Version to the customer).

As further evidence of the impact of the Internet, Random House has announced its e-book royalty policy—it will split its electronic book sales revenue evenly with its writers (David Kirkpatrick, "Publisher to Split E-Book Revenue," *The New York Times,* Nov. 7, 2000, Sec. C, p. 2).

Advances are often included in publisher-author agreements. The advances may be paid on the signing of the contract, or it may be paid in stages, as parts of the manuscript are submitted. Advances vary greatly according to the likely commercial success of the book and are generally non-refundable but recoupable out of sales.

Expenses incurred by the author in preparing or later helping market the book should be reimbursed by the publisher, but this is not a given and must be dealt with in the original publisher-author agreement.

Virtually every publisher will have its own standard provisions governing when and how accountings and payments are to be made, as well as the time allowed for the author to audit the publisher's books and records (and, if unsatisfied, bring suit). Such provisions are generally not very negotiable, since the publisher will want the greatest possible uniformity in this area. If the publisher does not include a provision allowing audits the author must insist upon it since there is no automatic right of audit. Most publishers will balk at including a provision for interest on late payments of royalties and/or on underpayments disclosed as the result of audit, but again, it will be a matter of relative bargaining strength.

6.4.8 Warranties and Indemnities

The provisions for warranties and indemnities attempt to shift the burden to the author if suit is brought by a third party claiming copyright violations, libel, invasions of privacy, or other actionable claims against the author's work. These provisions are typically quite broad and extend not only to breach but also to *alleged* breach. The publisher may include a right to withhold royalties pending disposition of the matter. Obviously, this could tie up the author's income for years and subject the author to substantial liability. Before acceding to these types of provisions, an author should attempt to narrow the coverage. For example, the Authors Guild suggests that an author be held responsible only for situations in which he or she knew of the violation. In any event, substantial time should be spent scrutinizing the warranties and indemnities provisions to calculate the variety of situations that might be called into play.

NOTE _____

The importance of warranties and indemnities have taken on an interesting guise in *Lacoff v. Buena Vista Publishing,* 705 N.Y.S. 2d 183 (N.Y. Supp. 2000) and *Keimer v. Buena Vista Books,* 75 Cal. App. 4th 1220 (1999), rev. denied 2000. The courts in *Lacoff* and *Keimer* have taken opposing views regarding whether the cover of the book "The Beardstown Ladies' Common-Sense Investment Guide" is commercial speech and subject to state advertising laws or noncommercial speech protected by the First Amendment. The cover of the best-selling book *The Beardstown Ladies' Common-Sense Investment Guide* boasted a "23.4% annual return" on investments in the stock market. In truth, the annual rate of return for the Beardstown Ladies' investments was 9.1 percent. In *Lacoff,* the New York State Supreme Court held that while the book cover was part commercial and part noncommercial, it was protected by the First Amendment and not subject to state false advertising laws. In *Keimer,* the California First District Court of Appeal held that the statement on the book cover was commercial speech and subject to the state's deceptive practices laws. The conflict in these two decisions remains to be resolved, but book publishers and other media are clearly concerned about the chilling effect of the California ruling.

6.4.9 Future Revisions

Most books have only a limited commercial life, although certain types of books (texts, cookbooks, etc.) have continued vitality if revised and updated. The author will of course try to insist that any revisions, updates, abridgments, be done by the author, while the publisher will reason that such a provision gives the author a virtual veto over any such project and, in any case, that if the author has gone on to other projects the author may not be willing to devote the time and attention that is required. The rights and duties of the author to participate in the revisions should be carefully negotiated, including provisions for when the author is unable or unwilling to participate. If the author fails to perform requested revisions within a specified time period, the publisher will want the right to look elsewhere.

6.4.10 Option for Next Book

Some publisher-author contracts attempt to bind an author to a future contract by giving the publisher an option on the next work. As we see in the case of *Pinnacle Books, Inc. v. Harlequin Enterprises, Ltd.,* (in Section 6.6) if a publisher does not draw such a clause very carefully, it may be construed as simply an unenforceable "agreement to agree." The Authors Guild deplores the next-book option clause and urges authors to watch for and then refuse such a clause. In general, there is little reason to bind an author to a one-way option. At most, a publisher might be given a "right of first negotiation" (i.e., a provision for a period during which the author is prohibited from negotiating with third parties so that the author and the original publisher can negotiate a possible deal for a follow-up book) or a so-called right of first refusal (i.e., the right to match any third-party offer). Where a right of first refusal applies and the author is able to elicit one or more third party offers, this sets some objective market value on the author's present worth but still gives the original publisher the first opportunity to publish the new work. While a right of first negotiation will not have a "chilling" effect on the ability of the author to secure a deal with a third-party publisher, the author needs to understand that the existence of a right of first refusal or other matching right can, under some circumstances, have a "chilling" effect on the market value of the author's next book, since some publishers are wary of bidding in such circumstances.

6.4.11 Other Provisions

Numerous other provisions are included in typical publisher-author contracts. Typically, the contract is not assignable by the author but may be assigned by the publisher. The author may want restrictions placed on the publisher's ability to assign (for example, the author may want to insist that the assignment be made only to a publisher of equivalent or greater financial responsibility than the original publisher). In the event of an alleged breach by the publisher, the author will be required to notify the publisher and the publisher will have an opportunity to cure, usually in a period of 30 or 60 days. The publisher's right to publicize the book by using the author's name and likeness is also standard, but at times the language is overly broad and should be narrowed so that other publicity rights of the author are not impaired.

When there is more than one author, care must be exercised in defining the authors' joint and several liabilities, not only to the publisher but also to each other. Finally, there are often provisions as to proofreading duties, responsibility for an index, payment to others for use of copyrighted materials, governing law, ability to modify the agreement, an integration clause, notice procedures, number of copies of the work provided to the author, bankruptcy of the publisher, and procedures for adjudication of disputes. All should be carefully examined.

NOTE _____

For a treatise on this area, see Mark A. Fischer, E. Gabriel Perle and John Taylor Williams, *Perle & Williams on Publishing Law, Third Edition* (New York: Aspen Law & Business 1999) (regularly supplemented).

What follows is a Literary Publishing Agreement between an author and a publisher that contains many of the provisions heretofore described. It is important to recognize that this Agreement is subject to negotiation.

Literary Publishing Agreement

AGREEMENT made this __th day of _____, between _____("the AUTHOR') and _____ ("the PUBLISHER') with reference to a work tentatively titled

(insert name of work)

(hereinafter "the WORK").

WHEREBY, in consideration of the promises set forth in this Agreement, the AUTHOR and the PUBLISHER agree that:

1. Grant of Rights

The AUTHOR grants to the PUBLISHER the exclusive rights to publish, reproduce, and distribute the WORK, in formats described in Paragraph 4, in all languages, and to exercise and grant to third parties the rights to the WORK described in Paragraph 6. throughout the world ("the TERRITORY") for the full term of copyright available to the WORK in the TERRITORY.

2. Manuscript Delivery

(a) The AUTHOR shall deliver to the PUBLISHER on or before 1 October 2002 a rough draft of the WORK approximately 208 book pages in length, the WORK to be complete and satisfactory to the PUBLISHER in content and form (complete and satisfactory shall include requirements 2(d)[l] and [2] below). A satisfactory manuscript will also include a one(1)-page summary of the WORK suitable to serve as the basis of marketing and promotional copy.

(b) [1] In determining whether the manuscript is satisfactory and acceptable in content, the PUBLISHER'S editorial staff and outside reviewers may consider accuracy and adequacy of treatment of subject matter, completeness of bibliographic information and conformity to the description of the WORK and targeted readership included in the AUTHOR'S proposal or other communication between the AUTHOR and the PUBLISHER. The parties agree that, if the manuscript (1) conforms to the description of the Work and targeted readership, and (2) is of a quality comparable to other works published by the PUBLISHER, it shall be considered satisfactory and acceptable.

[2] The manuscript will be considered satisfactory and acceptable in form if it is delivered on computer disk(s) compatible with the PUBLISHER'S conversion software (most recent versions of MicrosoftWord, MicrosoftWorks, ClarisWorks, AmiProfessional, WordPerfect, or as a last resort in ASCII format) along with one double-spaced, hard copy and if it generally conforms to the guidelines of the latest edition of _____.

(c) The PUBLISHER shall use its best efforts to advise the AUTHOR within sixty (60) days of its receipt of a complete manuscript for the WORK whether or not the complete manuscript is acceptable to the PUBLISHER. If the PUBLISHER does not judge an initially submitted manuscript to be satisfactory, the PUBLISHER will provide specific counsel to the AUTHOR of the changes that are needed. The AUTHOR shall have ninety (90) days in which to submit a revised manuscript, it being agreed that, if AUTHOR makes the changes requested by the PUBLISHER, the manuscript shall be accepted. If the AUTHOR does not receive such notice of acceptance or request for changes from the PUBLISHER within such sixty (60)-day period, the AUTHOR may at any time thereafter give written notice by registered mail to the Vice President and Publisher of Zondervan Publishing House (with a copy to the AUTHOR'S editor) demanding notice of acceptance or a request for changes, such notice from the AUTHOR to specify that failure to respond within fifteen (15) days from the receipt of such notice shall be deemed acceptance. If the AUTHOR receives no response from the PUBLISHER within fifteen (15) days from the PUBLISHER'S receipt of such demand, the manuscript shall be deemed accepted by the PUBLISHER. However, acceptance of the manuscript as satisfactory does not relieve the AUTHOR of the responsibility to correct problems that may be discovered by the PUBLISHER in the course of the PUBLISHER'S editing process.

(d) The AUTHOR shall at the AUTHOR'S expense obtain and deliver to the PUBLISHER with the complete manuscript:

[1] written permissions for world rights, all editions, required by the PUBLISHER for any quotations from other sources included in the WORK by the AUTHOR, and

[2] all illustrations, maps, charts, and photographs mutually agreed to by the PUBLISHER and the AUTHOR for the WORK together with written permission for world rights, all editions, for their use as part of the WORK. If the AUTHOR fails to do so, the PUBLISHER may obtain such items and charge the costs incurred, including both permission fees and the PUBLISHER'S clerical costs, to the AUTHOR'S royalty account.

(e) If the PUBLISHER and the AUTHOR mutually agree to publish an index as part of the WORK, the PUBLISHER will have one prepared and charge the costs incurred to the AUTHOR'S royalty account. If the AUTHOR makes a timely delivery of a satisfactory index in order to meet the PUBLISHER'S production schedule, the PUBLISHER shall use such index.

(f) The parties agree that, for the AUTHOR to fulfill her obligations under this Paragraph 2, she requires active editorial assistance from the PUBLISHER. The PUBLISHER therefore agrees that, commencing upon execution of this Agreement through the PUBLISHER'S acceptance or rejection of the manuscript in accordance herewith, if the AUTHOR so requests, the PUBLISHER shall ensure that AUTHOR'S editor (i) is reasonably available to consult with the AUTHOR, and (ii) provides the AUTHOR with consistent and meaningful editorial assistance and creative guidance.

(g) Except to the extent of books in progress previously disclosed to the PUBLISHER, including the book tentatively entitled *I'm Pregnant, Now What?*, the WORK shall be the AUTHOR'S next book, whether written by the AUTHOR alone or written by the AUTHOR in collaboration with others, and the AUTHOR will not undertake to write another book, either by the AUTHOR alone or in collaboration with others, before delivery to the PUBLISHER of the complete and final manuscript of the WORK in accordance with Paragraph 2 and the delivery by the AUTHOR to the PUBLISHER of other materials in accordance with Paragraphs 2(d)[1] and 2.(d)[2].

3. Editing and Proofs

(a) The WORK as edited by the PUBLISHER shall be submitted to the AUTHOR for review in manuscript for computer-generated copy.

(b) The AUTHOR shall read, revise and correct, and return to the PUBLISHER all edited copy submitted by the PUBLISHER to the AUTHOR for the AUTHOR'S review and approval, not to be unreasonably denied or delayed. If the AUTHOR does not return such copy within twenty (20) working days after receipt unless mutually agreed otherwise by AUTHOR and PUBLISHER, the PUBLISHER may publish the WORK in the form in which it was submitted to the AUTHOR for review.

(c) The title, cover, and jacket of each edition of the WORK will be mutually acceptable to the AUTHOR and the PUBLISHER, such approval not to be unreasonably denied or delayed.

4. Publication

(a) The PUBLISHER shall publish a hard cover edition of the WORK in such style and manner as the PUBLISHER deems appropriate (subject to AUTHOR'S rights hereunder) within twelve (12) months from the date of the PUBLISHER'S acceptance of the manuscript for the WORK, provided the AUTHOR has complied with Paragraphs 2(a), (d) and 3 and has responded in a satisfactory way to any requests made under Paragraph 9(e). Except as otherwise provided herein, all details of publication, including manufacture, format and design, distribution, pricing, advertising and promotion, and distribution of free copies, shall be determined by the PUBLISHER.

(b) The PUBLISHER shall give the AUTHOR seventy-five (75) copies of the PUBLISHER'S first edition of the WORK free-of-charge. The AUTHOR reserves the non-exclusive right to sell copies of the WORK in connection with appearances and lectures given by the AUTHOR or by means of direct marketing solely to consumers via the AUTHOR'S own web site or whose names appear on customer lists proprietary to the AUTHOR, but not to rental lists, subject to the following:

[1] Commencing on publication of the WORK hereunder, all copies of the WORK sold by the AUTHOR in connection with the AUTHOR'S exercise of rights reserved by the AUTHOR under this Paragraph 4(b) shall be purchased by the AUTHOR from the PUBLISHER in accordance with Subparagraph 4(b).

[2] The AUTHOR may purchase copies of the WORK from the PUBLISHER for purposes of exercising rights reserved by the AUTHOR under this Paragraph 4(b) in accordance with the following:

(i) If when an order for copies of the WORK is received from the AUTHOR and sufficient inventory of the WORK is available in the PUBLISHER'S warehouse the discount off the suggested retail price at the time an order from the AUTHOR is received shall be: sixty percent (60%) for one through five hundred (1–500) copies;

and sixty-five percent (65%) for over five hundred copies of the WORK, purchased in case lot quantities only;

(ii) If the AUTHOR chooses to buy copies of the WORK off of any of PUBLISHER'S press runs in quantities greater than one thousand (1,000) copies, the applicable discount will be seventy-five percent (75%) off the suggested retail price for that printing;

[3] Copies ordered by the AUTHOR shall be shipped within thirty (30) days if at the time an order is received the PUBLISHER has sufficient inventory to fill the order;

[4] Payment shall be made for copies purchased pursuant to this Paragraph 4(b) within thirty (30) days of the AUTHOR'S receipt of the PUBLISHER'S invoice for copies shipped;

[5] Shipment of copies of the WORK purchased off PUBLISHER'S print runs here under shall be FOB the printer. Copies of the WORK purchased from PUBLISHER'S inventory hereunder shall be FOB the PUBLISHER'S warehouse; there shall be a separate charge for any special packaging requested by the AUTHOR;

[6] Copies purchased pursuant to this Paragraph 4(b) shall be non returnable;

[7] No royalties shall be payable by the PUBLISHER to the AUTHOR on copies of the WORK purchased by the AUTHOR pursuant to this Paragraph4(b).

[8] If the AUTHOR determines to distribute any copies purchased hereunder in any manner other than in connection with the AUTHOR'S exercise of rights reserved by the AUTHOR under this Paragraph4(b),the AUTHOR shall inform the PUBLISHER and the purchase price for such copies shall be adjusted, if necessary, so that the AUTHOR pays for such copies in a manner consistent with the PUBLISHER'S discount schedules.

5. Royalties

(a) The PUBLISHER shall pay the AUTHOR royalties on sales, less returns, of copies of the PUBLISHER'S English language editions of the WORK as follows:

[1] except as other wise provided below, twenty percent (20%) of the net amount received (net amount received being the PUBLISHER'S suggested retail price less the discounted amount; but not less bad debt) by the PUBLISHER on sales of the first twenty thousand (20,000) copies; twenty-two percent(22%) of the net amount received by the PUBLISHER on sales of the next twenty thousand (20,000) copies; and twenty-four percent (24%) of the net amount received by the PUBLISHER thereafter on sales of all hardcover editions and trade paperback editions sold by the PUBLISHER in the United States and Canada through normal book trade channels;

[2] except as otherwise provided below, fourteen percent (14%) of the net amount received on sales of all mass market paperback editions sold by the PUBLISHER in the United States and Canada through normal book trade channels;

[3] eight percent (8%)of the net amount received on any audio recording of all or parts of the WORK or of adaptations of the WORK if read by a freelance narrator or ten percent (10%) of the net amount received if read by the AUTHOR and sold by the PUBLISHER in the TERRITORY, through normal book trade channels and on sale of copies for export;

[4] twelve percent (12%) of the net amount received on all copies of hardcover, trade paperback, and mass market paperback editions and sets of sheets sold for export;

[5] six percent (6%) of the net amount received on all copies of any of the PUBLISHER'S editions of the WORK or on audio recordings sold directly by the PUBLISHER to the consumer in response to direct promotion to the consumer, such as mail order campaigns, telephone sales, and electronic bulletin boards, sponsored by the PUBLISHER;

[6] no royalties on any copies of any of the PUBLISHER'S editions of the WORK or on audio recordings given to the AUTHOR, salesmen's samples, damaged copies, returned copies, copies given away for publicizing the WORK to promote sales, given to non-commercial educational or missionary organizations, or sold at or below manufacturing cost. (When copies of the WORK are put on sale at remainder prices, the PUBLISHER shall use its best efforts to offer copies of the WORK to the AUTHOR at the remainder price.)

(b) [1] If the PUBLISHER publishes its own Spanish language edition of the WORK, the PUBLISHER shall pay the AUTHOR royalties on sales, less returns often percent (10%) of the net amount received on sales of all hardcover, trade paper back, and mass market editions.

[2] If the PUBLISHER publishes its own Portuguese language edition of the WORK, the PUBLISHER shall pay the AUTHOR royalties on sales, less returns of five percent (5%)of the PUBLISHER'S retail list price on sales of all hard cover, trade paper back, and mass market editions.

Advance

(c) The PUBLISHER will advance to the AUTHOR the sum of _____ Dollars against all royalties and payments due the AUTHOR for said WORK payable as follows:

[1] _____ upon full execution of this Agreement, and

[2] _____ within thirty (30) days of acceptance of a manuscript satisfactory in content and form for the WORK.

[3] If the manuscript is not delivered by the agreed date (or any extensions there of agreed to by the PUBLISHER)or satisfactory in content and form, all monies advanced to the AUTHOR for that book of the WORK will be returned to the PUBLISHER (by each of AUTHOR and the AGENT as provided below), provided that the PUBLISHER has given the AUTHOR written notice of its intent to exercise such termination right of that book of the WORK unless a satisfactory manuscript is delivered to the PUBLISHER within twenty (20) business days after receipt of such notice.

Author's Agent

(d) The AUTHOR has irrevocably appointed _____ ("the AGENT") as the AUTHOR'S literary agent for this Agreement and the AGENT shall be entitled to compensation as described in (e) below. However, the PUBLISHER shall send all notices and requests both to the AGENT and directly to the AUTHOR.

Divided Payment

(e) The AUTHOR agrees that all amounts due to the AUTHOR under this Agreement ,including all advances, royalties, and payments shall be divided and paid eighty-five percent (85%) to the AUTHOR and fifteen percent 15%) to the AGENT. Should the AUTHOR waive or assign the AUTHOR'S royalty or a portion thereof *for* any reason, the percent due the AGENT will still be paid. However, if the AUTHOR is required to repay any such amounts, AUTHOR shall repay her percentage of such amount and AGENT shall repay its percentage of such amount (it being agreed that AUTHOR shall have no liability to PUBLISHER *for* any failure of AGENT to make a required repayment). The PUBLISHER shall prepare quarterly reports *for* both the AUTHOR and the AGENT, accounting *for* all sales of the WORK and indicating total copies in print. The terms of this Paragraph 5(f) may not be amended or deleted without the prior written consent of the AGENT. The AGENT'S Tax Identification Number is:

6. Subsidiary Rights

(a) The subsidiary rights to the WORK granted to the PUBLISHER, and the allocation of proceeds received by the PUBLISHER *from* the grants of such rights to third parties, are:

	AUTHOR'S Percentage	PUBLISHER'S Percentage
[1] periodical or newspaper publication prior to book publication, subject to the AUTHOR'S approval;	60	40
[2] periodical or newspaper publication following book publication, including syndication rights, subject to the' AUTHOR'S approval as to placement and such rights to revert to the AUTHOR if not exercised within twelve (12) months of publication;	60	40
[3] permissions, including publication of portions of the WORK in anthologies, subject) of the AUTHOR'S approval;	60	40

[4]	condensations and abridgments, subject to the AUTHOR'S approval;	60	40
[5]	book club publication, such rights to revert to the AUTHOR if not exercised within twelve (12) months of publication;	60	40
[6]	publication of editions *for* premium or special use or *for* direct sale to consumers;	60	40
[7]	foreign-language publication (including the right to sublicense the other rights granted in this Agreement to foreign language publishers);	60	40
[8]	English-language publication outside the United States and Canada (including the right to sublicense the other rights granted in this Agreement to English language publishers);	60	40
[9]	paperback reprint editions;	60	40
[10]	hardcover reprint editions;	60	40
[11]	audio recordings of all or parts of the WORK or of adaptations of the WORK; however, if PUBLISHER has not released an audio version within twelve (12) months of publication of print edition, audio rights will revert to the AUTHOR upon request;	60	40
[12]	the right to record and transmit and display the WORK in 'its entirety by any means, electronic or otherwise in the form in which the WORK is published by the PUBLISHER, including the right to include the WORK in information storage and retrieval systems and databases;	60	40
[13]	non-exclusive public reading rights, including the right to authorize the reading of parts of the WORK on radio		

or television (it being understood that PUBLISHER may grant such rights for publicity purposes without charge and without payment to the AUTHOR);	60	40
[14] Braille, large-type, and other editions for the handicapped (the PUBLISHER may grant such rights to recognized non-profit organizations for the handicapped without charge and without payment to the AUTHOR)	60	40

(b) The PUBLISHER will exercise these rights (and will make reasonable efforts to cause its licensees to exercise these rights) in a manner consistent with the reputation and persona of the AUTHOR, and copies of all sublicenses will be sent to the AUTHOR. Further, the PUBLISHER only issues sublicense to publishers that it has come to trust as reputable and compatible with the AUTHOR'S reputation and persona.

(c) If the PUBLISHER itself desires to exercise any of the rights described above (as opposed to licensing such rights to third parties),other than those rights for which royalty rates are already provided in Paragraph 5. Hereof, the AUTHOR and the PUBLISHER shall negotiate in good faith the royalties payable thereon.

7. Accounting

(a) Following first publication of the WORK by the PUBLISHER, an accounting of all of the AUTHOR'S earnings under the term of this Agreement, accompanied by payments of amounts due on such accounting, shall be rendered no later than May 31, August 31, November 30, and February 28 of each year for the three-month period ending the preceding March 31, June 30, September 30, and December 31, respectively.

(b) The PUBLISHER may retain a reasonable reserve against returns on any accounting statement, provided the amount of the reserve held is clearly indicated and provided the subsequent statement clearly indicates how such reserve has been applied. Any reserve held shall be related to sales and returns of the WORK during the accounting period for which the reserve is held and the PUBLISHER'S reasonable expectation of sales and returns at the time the accounting statement for such period is prepared. On request, the PUBLISHER shall provide a written explanation of any reserve.

(c) If the AUTHOR receives an overpayment of royalties, after the advance has been earned back, because of copies reported sold but subsequently returned, the PUBLISHER may deduct the amount of the overpayment from further sums due the AUTHOR under this Agreement. If any such overpayment is not recouped in six accounting periods, the AUTHOR, upon request, shall pay the PUBLISHER the unrecouped balance (subject to the AGENT'S obligations under Paragraph 5(e).

(d) Any sums owed by the AUTHOR to the PUBLISHER under Paragraph 4(b), 7(c),and/or Paragraph 14 may be deducted from any amounts due the AUTHOR by the PUBLISHER under any other agreement between them.

8. *Right to Audit*

(a) Upon written request from the AUTHOR, the PUBLISHER shall provide the following information: the number of copies of each edition of the WORK printed by the PUBLISHER; the date of each printing; the cumulative number of copies sold, returned, distributed free-of-charge, remaindered, destroyed or lost; copies of any licenses made by the PUBLISHER; and any other information the AUTHOR may reasonably request on the basis that it is required in order to ascertain the accuracy of accountings rendered.

(b) The AUTHOR may upon written notice examine the PUBLISHER'S records relating to the WORK during normal business hours under such conditions as the PUBLISHER may reasonably prescribe. If an error is discovered as a result of any such examination, the party in whose favor the error was made shall promptly pay the other the amount of the error. Any such examination shall be at the AUTHOR'S expense unless errors of accounting in the PUBLISHER'S favor amounting to five percent (5%) or more of the total sum paid to the AUTHOR under this Agreement are found, in which event the PUBLISHER shall contribute to the cost of the examination up to the amount of the error determined as a result of the examination and will also pay to the AUTHOR the amount of such shortfall as may be discovered.

9. *Warranties*

(a) The AUTHOR warrants to the PUBLISHER that:

[1] the AUTHOR is the sole author of the WORK and sole owner of the rights granted in this Agreement, has not assigned, pledged or otherwise encumbered them and has the right to enter this Agreement;

[2] the WORK is an original work, has never before been published in whole or in part in any form in the TERRITORY, is not in the public domain in any country in the TERRITORY and does not infringe any copyright or any other proprietary or personal right; and

[3] the WORK contains no material that is libelous, in violation of any right of privacy or publicity, or harmful so as to subject the PUBLISHER to liability to any third party or otherwise contrary to law.

(b) In the event the AUTHOR enters into a contract with a writer who will assist the AUTHOR in the completion of the WORK, the AUTHOR shall provide to the PUBLISHER a copy of the work-for hire agreement between the AUTHOR and such writer which provides for the writer's services if so requested by the PUBLISHER. The Author shall be an additional insured under the terms of the Publisher's insurance for litigations based on claims for libel, privacy and related torts and copyright infringement.

(c) The AUTHOR shall indemnify the PUBLISHER from any loss, damage, expense (including reasonable attorneys' fees), recovery or judgment arising from any breach or alleged breach of any of the AUTHOR'S warranties, subject to the limitations stated below.

[1] Each party shall promptly inform the other of any claim made against either which, if sustained, would constitute a breach of any warranty made by the AUTHOR to the PUBLISHER in this Agreement. The PUBLISHER shall defend any such claim made against the PUBLISHER with counsel of the PUBLISHER'S selection. The AUTHOR shall fully cooperate with the PUBLISHER in such defense and may join in such defense with counsel of the AUTHOR'S selection at the AUTHOR'S expense.

[2] If the PUBLISHER wishes to settle on its own behalf any claim made against the PUBLISHER, the PUBLISHER shall consult with the AUTHOR and give serious consideration to any objections the AUTHOR may have, and the AUTHOR and the PUBLISHER shall attempt in good faith to agree in writing on the percentage of any such settlement costs which each shall bear. Failing such agreement, the PUBLISHER may on its own behalf settle any such claim made against the PUBLISHER on terms the PUBLISHER deems advisable. In such event, the PUBLISHER may recover from the AUTHOR amounts paid in settlement if settlement costs are incurred because of a breach of a warranty made by the AUTHOR to the PUBLISHER in this Agreement. Alternatively, the AUTHOR may, at the AUTHOR'S discretion, provide security reasonably acceptable to the PUBLISHER for the further costs of defending the claim, in which event the PUBLISHER shall not settle without the AUTHOR'S written consent.

[3] If any such claim is successfully defended, the AUTHOR'S indemnity shall be limited to fifty percent (50%) of the costs (including reasonable attorneys' fees) incurred by the PUBLISHER in the defense of the claim.

[4] If any such claim is made, the PUBLISHER may withhold a portion of payments due the AUTHOR under this Agreement to cover the AUTHOR'S obligations stated above. (Amounts withheld shall be reasonably related to the PUBLISHER'S reasonable assessment of the damages claimed and of the anticipated defense costs.) The PUBLISHER shall deposit monies so withheld in an interest-bearing account pending disposition of the claim; monies withheld and the interest thereon will be first applied to satisfy the AUTHOR'S obligation to indemnify the PUBLISHER, and the balance remaining shall be promptly remitted to the AUTHOR after the disposition of the claim or after the claim has in the PUBLISHER'S opinion been abandoned. If monies are withheld under this provision because a claim is made, but such claim does not result in litigation within one year from the date on which the claim is first asserted, the Publisher shall release monies being withheld unless at such time the Publisher is either actively conducting settlement discussions relating to the claim or actively defending the claim by correspondence.

(d) The AUTHOR shall be responsible for any claims made against any third party to which the PUBLISHER grants subsidiary rights to the WORK to the same extent as the AUTHOR is responsible to the

PUBLISHER under the indemnification provisions of this Agreement. The warranties and indemnities made by the AUTHOR in this Agreement shall survive the termination of this Agreement.

(e) Prior to the first publication of the WORK, the PUBLISHER shall have the WORK read by the PUBLISHER'S counsel at the PUBLISHER'S expense. If the AUTHOR makes changes in the WORK as are recommended by the PUBLISHER'S counsel, the AUTHOR'S indemnity for a judgment shall be limited to fifty percent (50%) to the extent that such judgment arises from a matter within the scope of the review by the PUBLISHER'S counsel and as to which the AUTHOR made full disclosure to the PUBLISHER. If the AUTHOR will not make changes recommended by the PUBLISHER'S counsel, the PUBLISHER shall not be required to publish the WORK and shall have the right to recover from the AUTHOR any advances made to the AUTHOR under this Agreement. When such advances are fully repaid, this Agreement shall terminate.

10. Reserved Rights

(a) The AUTHOR reserves all rights to the WORK not granted to the PUBLISHER in this Agreement including, without limitation, motion picture, television, video, radio and live stage rights and all electronic rights other than those specified in Section 6.(a)[12]. In exercising such rights, the AUTHOR shall reserve for the PUBLISHER'S benefit the rights granted to the PUBLISHER in this Agreement and in addition, shall comply with the following: In connection with the AUTHOR'S disposition of reserved motion picture, television, video, radio dramatic adaptation, or live-stage dramatic adaptation rights, the AUTHOR shall not make any grant of publication rights without the PUBLISHER'S written consent and shall in no event make any grant of novelization, photonovel, comic book, or similar rights. The PUBLISHER will consent to the publication of synopses of motion picture, video, and television dramatic adaptations of the WORK, provided no such synopsis exceeds 10,000 words in length, no such synopsis is offered for sale (except as it may appear in motion picture-television fan magazines or souvenir programs) and each such synopsis is published with an appropriate copyright notice.

(b) All rights to the WORK that are granted to the PUBLISHER and any inquiry concerning those rights to the WORK received by the AUTHOR shall be referred by the AUTHOR to the PUBLISHER for response.

11. Non-Competition

For a period of five (5) years following first publication of the WORK, the AUTHOR shall not without the PUBLISHER'S prior consent publish or permit to be published any book: by the AUTHOR or by the AUTHOR in collaboration with others that is likely to conflict with sales of the WORK because it is of the same genre as, and materially and significantly overlaps in content with, the WORK.

12. Copyright

(a) The PUBLISHER shall print a copyright notice in conformity with the United States Copyright Act and the Universal Copyright Convention in the name of AUTHOR in each copy of the WORK printed by the PUBLISHER and require its licensees to do the same. The PUBLISHER shall register the copyright on the WORK with the United States Copyright office promptly after first publication and may record this Agreement with the United States Copyright Office.

(b) Any textual or illustrative material prepared for the WORK by the PUBLISHER at its expense may be copyrighted separately as the PUBLISHER deems appropriate.

(c) All references to copyright in this Agreement shall reflect any amendment made subsequent to the date of this Agreement in the copyright laws of the United States, in any international copyright convention or in the copyright laws of any other country within the TERRITORY. Both parties shall execute such documents as may be necessary to effectuate copyright to the WORK in accordance with this Agreement.

(d) In the event of any infringement of the copyright to the WORK, the PUBLISHER may employ such remedies as it deems advisable and may name the AUTHOR a co-plaintiff in any litigation the PUBLISHER may commence. The PUBLISHER shall bear the entire expense of any such litigation. Any recovery shall be applied first to reimburse the PUBLISHER for its expenses; the balance shall be divided between the AUTHOR and the PUBLISHER as follows: that portion which is based on actual damages shall be divided in proportion to the losses from such infringement suffered by each, and that portion which is based upon the infringers' profits, statutory damages, or punitive damages shall be divided equally.

13. Author's Rights of Termination

(a) If the PUBLISHER does not publish the WORK within the time specified in Paragraph 4(a) for reasons other than first serial or book club use, delays of the AUTHOR in returning the copyedited manuscript or proofs, the AUTHOR'S failure to comply with requests made by the PUBLISHER'S counselor delays caused by circumstances beyond the PUBLISHER'S control and if the PUBLISHER at any time thereafter receives written notice from the AUTHOR demanding publication, the PUBLISHER shall within ninety (90) days of the PUBLISHER'S receipt of such written demand either publish the WORK or revert to the AUTHOR in writing all rights to the WORK granted to the PUBLISHER in this Agreement, subject to any outstanding licenses, which shall be assigned to the AUTHOR, and the AUTHOR shall retain any advance payments made under this Agreement for the WORK prior to such reversion as liquidated damages for the PUBLISHER'S failure to publish the WORK.

(b) [1] If the WORK is out-of-print and the PUBLISHER receives from the AUTHOR a written request for a reversion of rights for the WORK, the PUBLISHER shall within six (6) months of the PUBLISHER'S receipt of such request do one of the following: (i) announce that it will reissue an edition of the WORK under one of its imprints within one (1) year from the date of the request; or (ii) enter a license providing for the publication in the United States of an edition of the WORK within eighteen (18) months from the date of the license; or (iii) revert in writing to the AUTHOR the rights granted to the PUBLISHER in this Agreement for the WORK, provided the AUTHOR is not indebted to the PUBLISHER for any sum owing to it under this Agreement. (If the PUBLISHER does announce that it will reissue an edition of the WORK but has not reissued an edition one (1) year after the PUBLISHER'S receipt of a request for reversion, the rights for the WORK shall on such date automatically revert to the AUTHOR). Before the PUBLISHER sells copies of the WORK at remainder prices to third parties, such copies will be offered to the AUTHOR at PUBLISHER'S cost. Printer-ready-files will also be available at processing cost to the AUTHOR.

[2] Any reversion shall be subject to grants of rights made to third parties prior to the date of the reversion and the right of the AUTHOR and the PUBLISHER to participate in the proceeds from such grants.

[3] The WORK shall be considered out-of-print if (i) no English language edition is available for sale through ordinary channels of the book trade in the United States from the order fulfillment department of the PUBLISHER or a licensee of the PUBLISHER and no license is in effect which provides for the distribution of an edition of the WORK through ordinary channels of the book trade in the United States within eighteen (18) months from the date of the AUTHOR'S request for a reversion, or (ii) during any calendar year, the AUTHOR does not earn at least two hundred dollars ($200) in royalties.

14. Publisher's Rights of Termination

If the AUTHOR does not deliver the complete manuscript for the WORK within three (3) months of the delivery date in Paragraph 2(a) or, if requested to do so, does not deliver a revised, complete manuscript for the WORK within the times specified in Paragraph 2(a)or, if the manuscript delivered to the PUBLISHER is unsatisfactory for the WORK, the PUBLISHER shall not be required to publish the WORK and shall have the right exercisable at the PUBLISHER'S discretion at any time thereafter to Recover from the AUTHOR and the AGENT (in accordance with Paragraph 5(e) above) any advances made for the WORK under this Agreement. When the AUTHOR repays her advances, the Agreement shall terminate.

15. Force Majeure

The failure of the PUBLISHER to publish or reissue the WORK shall not be a breach of this Agreement or give rise to any right of termination or reversion if such failure is caused by restrictions of governmental agencies, labor disputes, inability to obtain materials necessary for manufacture of the WORK or any other reason beyond the PUBLISHER'S control; in the event of delay from any such cause, the publication or reissue shall be postponed for a period of time reasonably related to such cause.

16. Marketing Plan

The PUBLISHER agrees to prepare a promotion and marketing plan for the WORK so as to give the WORK an opportunity to become and remain a viable product in the marketplace. The marketing plan will be prepared in consultation with the AUTHOR and will be delivered to the AUTHOR three (3) months prior to publication of the WORK.

17–25. General Provisions

17. No advertisements, other than for other works by the AUTHOR published by the PUBLISHER, shall be included in any edition of the WORK published by the PUBLISHER or under license from the PUBLISHER without the AUTHOR'S written consent. At the AUTHOR'S request, the PUBLISHER shall include in each edition of the WORK published by the PUBLISHER, and use reasonable efforts to cause licensees to include in each edition of the WORK that they publish reference to the AUTHOR'S websites, including www.ruthgrahanncintyre.com and www.forpregnancyhelp.com.

18. The PUBLISHER may use the AUTHOR'S name, likeness, and biographical data, subject to AUTHOR'S approval of each such use, on any editions of the WORK published by the PUBLISHER and in any advertising, publicity, or promotion for the WORK and may extend these rights in connection with grants of the subsidiary rights made by the PUBLISHER, subject to AUTHOR'S approval of each use, except that such approval will not be required of international sub licensees of known reputation to the PUBLISHER.

19. (a) If the PUBLISHER is required by law to withhold and pay to any U.S. or foreign government taxing authority any portion of amounts due the AUTHOR under this Agreement, such payments shall be deducted from the amounts due the AUTHOR hereunder.

    (b) If any foreign taxes, bank charges or agents' commissions are imposed on any payments due the PUBLISHER from the exercise of any right granted in this Agreement, the appropriate allocation of proceeds between the PUBLISHER and the AUTHOR from the exercise of such right shall be made on amounts received after such charges have been paid.

20. In the event of the bankruptcy, insolvency, or liquidation of the PUBLISHER, this Agreement shall terminate and all rights granted to the PUBLISHER shall revert to the AUTHOR automatically and without the necessity of any demand or notification.

21. This Agreement shall be binding upon and inure to the benefit of the heirs, executors, or administrators and assigns of the AUTHOR and the successors and assigns of the PUBLISHER and may not be assigned by either without the written consent of the other, with the following exceptions. The AUTHOR may assign the AUTHOR'S right to receive payment under this Agreement upon written notice to the PUBLISHER. The PUBLISHER may upon written notice to the AUTHOR assign this Agreement to any company that acquires or succeeds to all or a substantial portion of the assets of the PUBLISHER.

22. If under any provision of this Agreement, the PUBLISHER is required to obtain the AUTHOR'S approval, such approval shall not be unreasonably withheld or delayed. If the PUBLISHER fails to receive a response from the AUTHOR within such time as the PUBLISHER may

reasonably designate to accommodate its schedule for publication, promotion, or the exercise of rights when any approval is requested (but no less than five (5) business days), the approval requested shall be deemed granted.

23. This Agreement contains the entire understanding of the AUTHOR and the PUBLISHER with reference to the WORK; there are no warranties other than those expressly stated in this Agreement. No waiver or modification of any provision of this Agreement shall be valid unless in writing and signed by both parties. No waiver of any breach shall be deemed a waiver of any subsequent breach. If any provision of this Agreement is held to be invalid or unenforceable, the remaining provisions shall not be affected.

24. Regardless of its place of physical execution or performance, the provisions of this Agreement shall in all respects be construed according to, and the laws of the State of _____ hereto shall in all respects govern the rights and liabilities of the parties.

25. The caption headings of this Agreement are inserted for convenience only and are without substantive effect.

IN WITNESS **WHEREOF,** the parties have signed this Agreement to be effective as of the date first stated above.

AUTHOR:
PUBLISHER:

6.5 THE IMPACT OF CUSTOM AND USAGE

Authors are often so anxious to publish that they pay little attention to the small print of contract provisions. Despite a heightened consciousness of the pitfalls of indiscriminate contract signing, and in some cases due to a serious imbalance in bargaining power, many authors still sign whatever is thrust before them. Later, whether it be next month, next year, or several years later, many authors live to regret their hasty actions.

The time of contracting, of course, is the time to plan for the future. As *Geisel v. Poynter Products*, demonstrates, one must anticipate any number of future contingencies, even those that occur 20 or 30 years down the road, and it is also crucial to familiarize oneself with the customs and usages of a particular industry before entering into contractual relationships within that industry.

Stein and Day Incorporated v. Morgan below illustrates the limits of custom and usage which will not override the express provisions of a literary publishing agreement. In the more recent decision in *Tasini v. The New York Times,* below, the digital age presents the question of whether the transfer of a work to an electronic database constitutes a revision under the Copyright Act in the absence of an express grant of digital rights.

In *Geisel v. Poynter Products, Inc.*, 295 F. Supp. 331 (S.D.N.Y. 1968) plaintiff (better known as "Dr. Seuss") entered into an oral agreement in 1932 with defendant Liberty Publishing Corporation, publishers of Liberty Magazine, for the preparation and sale to Liberty of a series of one-page "cartoon essays" to be published in a series of weekly issues of Liberty. Several decades later, the extent of the rights transferred to Liberty became one of the issues in plaintiff's action in which he sought to prevent the manufacture, sale and distribution of three-dimensional figures based on the cartoons published by Liberty. Since the evidence about the terms of the oral contract was inconclusive regarding the extent of the rights transferred to Liberty, the Court looked to custom and usage in the magazine publishing industry in 1932. The court stated:

This evidence demonstrates that plaintiff agreed to prepare cartoons for publication in *Liberty Magazine;* that the cartoons were published; that plaintiff received $300 a page; that the only copyright upon this material was in the name of Liberty Publishing Company; and that plaintiff did not *expressly* reserve any rights in the cartoons.

There is evidence, and the Court so finds, that, with certain exceptions which do not apply in this case, the custom and usage in 1932 in the magazine trade were that an agreement for the sale of a work between authors or their agents and magazines was oral and not a formal written contract. . . . The agreement was usually reached after *only* monetary terms were discussed. . . . This contrasts with the custom in the book publishing field in which similar contracts were written. . . .

In this case, there was no *express* agreement that *Liberty Magazine* would hold the copyright in trust for plaintiff or that plaintiff reserved any rights in the cartoons. However, much evidence was offered by both sides with respect to the issue whether there was any settled and established custom and usage in the magazine publishing trade in 1932 by which any terms or conditions were implied in fact or understood to be part of a contract between an author or his agent and a weekly magazine; and if so, what were those implied-in-fact terms.

Evidence was also offered with respect to the issue whether there was any settled and established custom and usage concerning what the magazine was impliedly agreeing to in fact with respect to the extent of the magazine's use of the purchased material; and concerning the alleged practice of a magazine to hold its copyright in trust for the author and to reassign its copyright upon the request of the author. . . .

The court continued:

Plaintiff offered the testimony of three witnesses with respect to the above mentioned customs and usages in 1932 in the magazine publishing trade: Bennett Cerf, Leland Hayward and plaintiff himself.

Mr. Cerf has been a *book* publisher since 1925 and has himself written books as well as articles for periodicals. . . . Plaintiff's books are published by the firm of which Cerf is chairman of the board . . . ; and, in fact, plaintiff is the president of a division of that firm. . . . Mr. Cerf is an eminent personality in the field of book publishing. However, his testimony with respect to customs and usages in the *magazine* trade is found by the Court to be tenuous and unpersuasive. He repeatedly admitted his unfamiliarity with magazine customs . . . and with contracts between magazines and authors or their agents. . . . Furthermore, some of his testimony presents internal inconsistencies and self-contradictions. . . .

On the basis of the great weight of the credible evidence, the Court finds that during the relevant period it was the custom and usage in the magazine trade for the magazine to obtain a copyright upon the entire contents of the magazine. . . .

However, the author or artist could also obtain a separate copyright upon his particular work . . .

Virtually all the testimony was in agreement on the proposition, which the Court finds established, that there was a settled custom and usage in the magazine publishing trade in the early 1930s by which a term or condition defining the scope of rights was implied in fact or understood to be part of the agreement between the author or his agent and the magazine. . . .

After reviewing the evidence of custom and usage from both plaintiff and defendant, the court held that "the custom and usage in 1932 in the magazine trade implied in fact in the *Geisel-Liberty Magazine* agreement a provision whereby all rights or complete rights were assigned to *Liberty Magazine*," that the terms 'all rights' or 'complete rights' [had] a nontechnical and literal meaning" and that Geisel had sought "to impart to these words a connotation that is diametrically opposite to their plain, colloquial sense."

The court approved the manufacture, distribution and sale of three-dimensional figures fairly representing Geisel's characters and indicating their origin, so long as Poynter neither stated nor implied that Geisel had endorsed the products.

NOTES _____

1. In a later case, the court declared the widow of an artist rather than *Playboy* magazine to be the owner of works created by the artist for the magazine between 1974 and 1984. Despite the presence of check endorsements reciting that they constituted "payment in full for all right, title and interest in and to [the artwork items]," the works could not be considered to have been created as "works for hire" because, inter alia, the checks were endorsed only after the works had been created, which did not meet the requirements of the "work for hire" provisions of Section 101 of the Copyright Act of 1976 and testimony indicated that under magazine industry custom and usage, a publisher in such a situation acquired one-time rights only. *Playboy Enterprises, Inc. v. Dumas*, 831 F. Supp. 295 (SDNY 1993).

2. In *Warner Bros. Pictures, Inc. v. Columbia Broadcasting System, Inc.*, 216 F.2d 945 (9th Cir.), *cert. denied*, 348 U.S. 971 (1954), custom and usage helped to defeat Warner Bros.' claim that by purchasing film rights to Dashiell Hammett's *The Maltese Falcon*, Warner Bros. had thereby acquired exclusive rights to Hammett's fictional detective, Sam Spade. Hammett and CBS claimed the right to use Sam Spade in new adventures.

   The Court concluded that the omission of a reference to characters in the grant of rights defeated Warner Bros.' claim, stating (at 949):

   > The conclusion that these rights are [excluded] is strongly buttressed by the fact that historically and presently detective fiction writers have and do carry the leading characters with their names and individualisms from one story into succeeding stories. This was the practice of Edgar Allen Poe, Sir Arthur Conan Doyle, and others; and in the last two decades of S. S. Van Dine, Earle [sic] Stanley Gardner, and others. . . . If the intention of the contracting

parties had been to avoid this practice which was a very valuable one to the author, it is hardly reasonable that it would be left to a general clause following specific grants . . .

Stein and Day, Incorporated v. Morgan, 5 Med.L.Rptr. 1831 (Sup. Ct. N.Y. County 1979)

STECHER, J.

This is an action tried without a jury. After [trial] I make the following findings:

On Sept. 6, 1972, the parties entered into a written agreement pursuant to which the defendant Morgan would write, and the plaintiff Stein and Day Incorporated would publish, two books: one was to be entitled *Anchor Woman* and the other *NBC, A Biography of the Corporation*. By its terms [Para. 8] the author agreed to deliver to the Publisher on or before [see Cl. 19(B)] a copy of the manuscript complete and satisfactory to the Publisher, and ready for press. . . . If the Author fails to deliver the manuscript in a form acceptable to the Publisher within the specified time, unless extended in writing by the Publisher, the Publisher may decline to publish the Work and recover any and all amounts that may have been advanced to the Author, and terminate this agreement subject to the Publisher's right to recover any and all amounts that may have been advanced to the Author.

19(B). Delivery Date—*Anchor Woman*, Sept. 15, 1973.
NBC, A Biography of the Corporation, Sept. 15, 1971.

An advance of $35,000 was given to Mr. Morgan in four quarterly installments beginning Dec. 15, 1972 conditioned upon the scheduled delivery of portions of *Anchor Woman*.

Anchor Woman was timely delivered, published and has earned royalties for the defendant of $20,424.51. None of the royalties have been paid to the defendant but have been applied, in accordance with the terms of the contract, against the advance.

The *NBC* book was never delivered. At some time in 1974, Morgan, who had been with NBC in a variety of capacities for some twenty years and had by this time left NBC's employ, discussed with Mr. Stein, president of the plaintiff, his reluctance to write the *NBC* book. In his words, he was in a "no win" situation—he didn't wish to write a critical book for it would be rejected as "sour grapes" and he did not wish to write a laudatory book. Morgan and Stein agreed that, in lieu of the NBC book, the defendant would deliver a novel entitled *First Lady*. Sometime in June or July 1975, Stein received about 130 pages of *First Lady*. This portion of the draft and Stein's criticism were delivered to Morgan's agent, Mrs. Pryor, under cover of Stein's letter of July 13, 1975 and, thereafter, by letter dated July 23, 1975. Morgan wrote to Stein agreeing in substance with the criticism.

Between July and October what purported to be a complete *First Lady* novel was delivered to the plaintiff. By letter of Oct. 15, 1975, Stein sent to Morgan's agent a criticism of the novel written by one of Stein's senior editors whose conclusion it was that the draft was not worth editing. Stein requested that the book be rewritten. A week later, Mrs. Pryor requested the return of the manuscript concluding that there was no point to resubmission.

Upon the return of the manuscript, Mrs. Pryor attempted to sell it to at least four other well known publishers and each of them rejected the manuscript. She had and has no plans for submitting it anew to any publishers.

The plaintiff pursuant to the provisions of the agreement set forth above seeks to recoup that portion of the advance which was not covered by the royalties earned by *Anchor Woman*. No portion of the advance was allocated to either book, it being the intention of the parties that the entire advance be covered by both books and that the royalties from both books, together, be charged against the entire $35,000 advance. No claim is made by the plaintiff concerning the timeliness of delivery of the manuscript; the claim involves solely the question of acceptability to the publisher.

The defendant contends presumably that objectively the manuscript was "acceptable" and argues with greater emphasis that the custom of the publishing industry bars a refund of any portion of the advance.

There can be no doubt that the publisher was motivated in refusing this manuscript by "an honest dissatisfaction" with *First Lady* [see *Baker v. Chock Full o' Nuts Corp.*, 30 A.D. 2d, 329, 332] and that the rejection was made in good faith.

The defendant offered testimony that the custom of the publishing industry with respect to an unsatisfactory manuscript required that all sums advanced to the time of submission of the manuscript be retained by the author; that no further installments of the advance need be paid; that if the manuscript is thereafter sold to another publisher, it is the author's obligation, from the new consideration, to reimburse the first publisher to the extent of the advance; and that in the absence of sale to a new publisher, the publisher making the advance absorbs the loss represented by the advance. The testimony as to custom was uncontradicted.

A custom of an industry cannot overcome the express language of a written agreement. If custom and language are consistent both shall be enforced; but where, as here, they are in conflict, the express language shall prevail [UCC 1–205 subd 4]. The parties expressly agreed that if the manuscript was not acceptable to the publisher, the publisher was entitled to recoup his advance. In this case, it was the intention of the parties that the advance be recouped less those sums of money attributable to royalties earned. It would thus appear that the plaintiff was entitled to judgment for the amount of the advance which exceeded royalties. In accordance with the stipulation of the parties, however, there shall be deducted from the amount to which the plaintiff is entitled a reserve held by the publisher against another book as set forth in Exhibit (I) for identification dated June 30, 1978 in the sum of $1,194.82.

Accordingly, the plaintiff is entitled to judgment in the net amount of $13,380.67 with interest from Oct. 14, 1977, the date of the plaintiff's demand for reimbursement and judgment may be entered accordingly.

The issue of custom and usage has followed us to the Internet, as we see in the following case, but the result (as well as the reasoning) is considerably different from that in *Geisel*.

Tasini v. The New York Times Company, Inc., 206 F.3d 161 (2d Cir. 1999), cert. granted sub nom. New York Times Company, Inc. v. Tasini, 121 S.Ct. 425 (2000)

WINTER, J.

Six freelance writers appeal from a grant of summary judgment dismissing their complaint. The complaint alleged that appellees had infringed appellants' various copyrights by putting individual articles previously published in periodicals on electronic databases available to the public. [The lower court] held that appellees' use of the articles was protected by the "privilege" afforded to publishers of "collective works" under Section 201(c) of the Copyright Act of 1976 ("Act" or "1976 Act"), 17 U.S.C. 201(c). We reverse and remand with instructions to enter judgment for appellants.

BACKGROUND

Appellants [were not employed by defendants and did not write works-for-hire. They were the holders of the copyrights in their articles]. [Defendants] (collectively, "Publishers") are periodical publishers who regularly create "collective works," *see* 17 U.S.C. 101, that contain articles by freelance authors as well as works created for-hire or by employees . . . [T]he Publishers' general practice was to negotiate due-dates, word counts, subject matter and price; no express transfer of rights under the Author's copyright was sought . . .

The gist of the Authors' claim is that the copyright each owns in his or her individual articles was infringed when the Publishers provided them to the [other defendants'] electronic databases. [The Publishers] argue that the Publishers own the copyright in the "collective works" that they produce and are afforded the privilege, under Section 201(c) of the Act, of "reproducing and distributing" the individual works in "any revision of that collective work." 17 U.S.C. 201(c). The crux of the dispute is, therefore, whether one or more of the pertinent electronic databases may be considered a "revision" of the individual periodical issues from which the articles were taken.

DISCUSSION

. . . These works were published with the Authors' consent . . . [However,] Section 201(c) does not permit the Publishers to license individually copyrighted works for inclusion in the electronic databases. . . .

Section 201 of the Act provides, *inter alia,* that as to contributions to collective works, the "[c]opyright in each separate contribution . . . is distinct from copyright in the collective work as a whole, and vests initially in the author of the contribution." 17 U.S.C. 201(c). Correspondingly, Section 103, which governs copyright in compilations and derivative works, provides in pertinent part that:

The copyright in a compilation or derivative work extends only to the material contributed by the author of such work, as distinguished from the preexisting material employed in the work, and does not imply any exclusive right in the preexisting material.

17 U.S.C. 103(b). Section 101 states that "[t]he term 'compilation' includes collective works." 17 U.S.C. 101. It further defines "collective work" as "a work, such as a periodical issue, anthology, or encyclopedia, in which a number of contributions, constituting separate and independent works in themselves, are assembled into a collective whole." *Id.*

Publishers of collective works are not permitted to include individually copyrighted articles without receiving a license or other express transfer of rights from the author. However, Section 201(c) creates a presumptive privilege to authors of collective works. Section 201(c) creates a presumption that when the author of an article gives the publisher the author's permission to include the article in a collective work, as here, the author also gives a non-assignable, non-exclusive privilege to use the article as identified in the statute. It provides in pertinent part that:

In the absence of an express transfer of the copyright or of any rights under it, the owner of copyright in the collective work is presumed to have acquired only the privilege of reproducing and distributing the contribution as part of that particular collective work, any revision of that collective work, and any later collective work in the same series. 17 U.S.C. 201(c).

Under this statutory framework, the author of an individual contribution to a collective work owns the copyright to that contribution, absent an express agreement setting other terms. *See id.* The rights of the author of a collective work are limited to "the material contributed by the [collective work] author" and do not include "any exclusive right in the preexisting material." 17 U.S.C. 103(b). Moreover, the presumptive privilege granted to a collective-work author to use individually copyrighted contributions is limited to the reproduction and distribution of the individual contribution as part of: (i) "that particular [*i.e.,* the original] collective work"; (ii) "any revision of that collective work"; or (iii) "any later collective work in the same series." 17 U.S.C. 201(c). Because it is undisputed that the electronic databases are neither the original collective work—the particular edition of the periodical—in which the Authors' articles were published nor a later collective work in the same series, appellees rely entirely on the argument that each database constitutes a "revision" of the particular collective work in which each Author's individual contribution first appeared. We reject that argument.

We begin, as we must, with the language of the statute. *See Lewis v. United States,* 445 U.S. 55, 60 (1980). The parameters of Section 201(c) are set forth in the three clauses just noted. Under ordinary principles of statutory construction, the second clause must be read in the context of the first and third clauses. [Citations omitted.] The first clause sets the floor, so to speak, of the presumptive privilege: the collective-work author is permitted to reproduce and distribute individual contributions as part of "that particular collective work." In this context, "that particular collective work" means a specific edition or issue of a periodical. *See* 17 U.S.C. 201(c). The second clause expands on this, to permit the reproduction and distribution of the individual contribution as part of a "revision" of "that collective work," *i.e.,* a revision of a particular edition of a specific periodical. Finally, the third clause sets the outer limit or ceiling on what the Publisher may do; it permits the reproduction and distribution of the individual contribution as part of a "later collective work in the same series," such as a new edition of a dictionary or encyclopedia.

The most natural reading of the "revision" of "that collective work" clause is that Section 201(c) protects only later editions of a particular issue of a periodical, such as the final edition of a newspaper. Because later editions are not identical to earlier editions, use of the individual contributions in the later editions might not be protected under the preceding clause. Given the context provided by the surrounding clauses, this interpretation makes perfect sense. It protects the use of an individual contribution in a collective work that is somewhat altered from the original in which the copyrighted article was first published, but that is not in any ordinary sense of language a "later" work in the "same series."

In this regard, we note that the statutory definition of "collective work" lists as examples "a periodical issue, anthology, or encyclopedia." 17 U.S.C. 101. The use of these particular kinds of collective works as examples supports our reading of the revision clause. Issues of periodicals, as noted, are often updated by revised editions, while anthologies and encyclopedias are altered every so often through the release of a new version, a "later collective work in the same series." Perhaps because the "same series" clause might be construed broadly, the House Report on the Act noted that the "revision" clause in Section 201(c) was not intended to permit the inclusion of previously published freelance contributions "in a new anthology or an entirely different magazine or other collective work," *i.e.,* in later collective works not in the same series. H.R. Rep. No. 94–1476, at 122–23 (1976), *reprinted in* 1976 U.S.C.A.A.N. 5659, 5738.

Moreover, Publishers' contention that the electronic databases are revised, digital copies of collective works cannot be squared with basic canons of statutory construction. First, if the contents of an electronic database are merely a "revision" of a particular "collective work,"*e.g.,* the August 16, 1999 edition of The New York Times, then the third clause of Section 201(c)—permitting the reproduction and distribution of an individually copyrighted work as part of "a later collective work in the same series"—would be superfluous. [Citations omitted.] An electronic database can contain hundreds or thousands of editions of hundreds or thousands of periodicals, including newspapers, magazines, anthologies, and encyclopedias. To view the contents of databases as revisions would eliminate any need for a privilege for "a later collective work in the same series."

Second, the permitted uses set forth in Section 201(c) are an exception to the general rule that copyright vests initially in the author of the individual contribution. Reading "revision of that collective work" as broadly as appellees suggest would cause the exception to swallow the rule. [Citation omitted.] Under Publishers' theory of Section 201(c), the question of whether an electronic database infringes upon an individual author's article would essentially turn upon whether the rest of the articles from the particular edition in which the individual article was published could also be retrieved individually. However, Section 201(c) would not permit a Publisher to sell a hard copy of an Author's article directly to the public even if the Publisher also offered for individual sale all of the other articles from the particular edition. We see nothing in the revision provision that would allow the Publishers to achieve the same goal indirectly through NEXIS.

Appellees' reading is also in considerable tension with the overall statutory framework. Section 201(c) was a key innovation of the Copyright Act of 1976. Because the Copyright Act of 1909 contemplated a single copyright, authors risked losing their rights by allowing an article to be used in a collective work. *See* 3 Melville Nimmer & David Nimmer, Nimmer on Copyright 10.01[A] (1996 ed.) (discussing doctrine of indivisibility). To address this concern, the 1976 Act expressly permitted the transfer of less than the entire copyright, *see* 17 U.S.C. 201(d), in effect replacing the notion of a single "copyright" with that of "exclusive rights" under a copyright. *Id.* 106, 103(b) [Statutory provisions omitted] . . . Were the permissible uses under Section 201(c) as broad and as transferable as appellees contend, it is not clear that the rights retained by the Authors could be considered "exclusive" in any meaningful sense.

[The NEXIS database can hardly be deemed a "revision" of each edition of every periodical that it contains.]

Moreover, NEXIS does almost nothing to preserve the copyrightable aspects of the Publishers' collective works, "as distinguished from the preexisting material employed in the work." 17 U.S.C. 103(b). The aspects of a collective work that make it "an original work of authorship" are the selection, coordination, and arrangement of the preexisting materials. [Citations omitted.] However, as described above, in placing an edition of a periodical such as the August 16, 1999 New York Times, in NEXIS, some of the paper's content, and perhaps most of its arrangement are lost. Even if a NEXIS user so desired, he or she would have a hard time recapturing much of "the material contributed by the author of such [collective] work." 17 U.S.C. 103(b). In this context, it is significant that neither the Publishers nor NEXIS evince any intent to compel, or even to permit, an end user to retrieve an individual work only in connection with other works from the edition in which it ran. Quite the contrary, The New York Times actually *forbids* NEXIS from producing "facsimile reproductions" of particular editions . . .

What the end user can easily access, of course, are the preexisting materials that belong to the individual author under Sections 201(c) and 103(b) . . .

We emphasize that the only issue we address is whether, in the absence of a transfer of copyright or any rights thereunder, collective-work authors may re-license individual works in which they own no rights. Because there has by definition been no express transfer of rights in such cases, our decision turns entirely on the default allocation and presumption of rights provided by the Act. Publishers and authors are free to contract around the statutory framework . . .

CONCLUSION

We therefore reverse and remand with instructions to enter judgment for appellants.

NOTE _____

The lower court rejected defendant *Newsday*'s contention that a legend on the checks it used to pay for freelance pieces made those checks, once endorsed, express transfers of copyright pursuant to Section 204(a) of the Copyright Act, *Tasini v. New York Times Co.*, 972 F. Supp. 804, 810–811 (SDNY 1997), a conclusion with which the Second Circuit agreed, noting that The New York Times had since revised its form to include rights of the type involved in the *Tasini* decision.

6.6 THE "NEXT BOOK" OPTION

Pinnacle Books, Inc. v. Harlequin Enterprises, Ltd., 519 F. Supp. 118 (S.D.N.Y.), aff'd, 661 F.2d 910 (2d Cir. 1981)

DUFFY, J.

This is an action for a permanent injunction and damages resulting from the allegedly unlawful interference of defendant Harlequin Enterprises Limited ["Harlequin"] with the contractual relationship between plaintiff Pinnacle Books, Inc. ["Pinnacle"] and its most successful author, Don Pendleton ["Pendleton"]. Pinnacle claims that Harlequin induced Pendleton to breach his contract with Pinnacle and to enter into an agreement with Harlequin pursuant to which it will publish new books in or relating to a series of paperback men's action/adventure books entitled "The Executioner" [sometimes referred to herein as the "Series"]. Pinnacle now moves for summary judgment . . .

Pinnacle is a publisher of mass-market and trade paperback books. The company has offices in New York City and Los Angeles. It has been publishing "The Executioner" series since the inception of the series in 1969.

Pinnacle has published thirty-eight different titles in "The Executioner" series and sold approximately twenty million copies. Pendleton, the author of the Series, is the copyright owner of the Series.

In 1976, Pinnacle and Pendleton entered into an agreement whereby Pinnacle agreed to publish books 29 through 38 . . . [which included the following option clause]:

VII. The Author grants the Publisher the option to renew this contract for the books in THE EXECUTIONER series following the ten books covered hereby on terms to be agreed, and, if, after extending their best efforts, the parties are unable to reach an agreement thereon, then Author shall be free to offer rights in such other books in THE EXECUTIONER series to any other publisher, provided the publication thereof does not occur until the expiration of 3 months following the first publication of the tenth book hereunder.

The manuscript for the last book under the 1976 Agreement was delivered to Pinnacle on December 14, 1979. By that time, Andrew Ettinger, the Editorial Director of Pinnacle, had begun negotiations with Pendleton for an extension of the 1976 Agreement. These discussions between Ettinger and Pendleton occurred as early as September 8, 1978 and continued until November 1979, at which time Ettinger left Pinnacle and joined Harlequin. According to Ettinger, he was unable to consummate a renewal of the 1976 Agreement before he left Pinnacle because an outstanding dispute between Pendleton and Pinnacle regarding foreign royalty rights had not been resolved. By late 1979, however, an acceptable resolution of the dispute had been reached and Pendleton was ready and willing to discuss an extension of the 1976 Agreement.

Negotiations between Pinnacle and Pendleton continued until about February 10, 1980. According to Pinnacle, the discussions had been congenial and the conditions established by Pendleton had either been satisfied in full or could have been met if the parties had proceeded with the negotiations in good faith and using their best efforts.

Meanwhile, Harlequin, a Canadian publisher and distributor of paperback books throughout the world, also had developed an interest in Pendleton. Having achieved spectacular success in the romance novel market, Harlequin was exploring the feasibility of entering the action/adventure line of book publishing. Ettinger, who was now affiliated with Harlequin, began meeting with Pendleton in early January 1980 to discuss the possibility of Harlequin becoming Pendleton's publisher. On about February 10, 1980, Pendleton advised Pinnacle that, at Harlequin's invitation, he was planning to visit its Toronto headquarters where he expected Harlequin to discuss the possibility of licensing to it rights in "The Executioner" series. Pendleton also indicated that he wished to halt discussions on the Pinnacle offer until he heard from Harlequin. At the conclusion of his discussion with Harlequin, Pendleton signed a preliminary agreement to license the Series and its characters to Harlequin. On May 15, 1980, Pendleton signed the formal agreement with Harlequin pursuant to which twelve books in "The

Executioner" series and four to six spin-offs from that Series would be published annually by Harlequin.

Pinnacle instituted this action in September 1980 against Harlequin seeking injunctive and compensatory relief. Pinnacle alleges that Harlequin, although fully aware of Pendleton's contractual obligations to Pinnacle and that Pinnacle was still negotiating with Pendleton, induced Pendleton to break off negotiations with Pinnacle just as final agreement on new contract terms was near. Pinnacle now moves for summary judgment. Harlequin argues against the motion for summary judgment on the grounds that the option clause on which Pinnacle bases its case is unenforceable. . . .

To succeed in an action for interference with contractual relations, the plaintiff must establish first and foremost the existence of a valid contract. . . .

In the instant case, Pinnacle accuses Harlequin of interfering with the option clause in the 1976 Agreement. As noted above, that clause provides that, after Pendleton has fulfilled his obligation to deliver books 29 through 38 of "The Executioner" Series, the parties would use their "best efforts" to negotiate a new contract "on terms to be agreed" for delivery of an unspecified number of new Executioner books. Clause VII of the 1976 Agreement. Harlequin contends that this clause is unenforceable because either (i) it is nothing more than an unenforceable "agreement to agree"; or (ii) the material terms of the "best efforts" clause are too vague.

Harlequin's first contention that the "best efforts" clause is an unenforceable "agreement to agree" is inappropriate in this case. Clause VII of the 1976 Agreement does not require that any agreement actually be achieved but only that the parties work to reach an agreement actively and in good faith. . . .

Harlequin is correct, however, in arguing that the "best efforts" clause is unenforceable because its terms are too vague. "Best efforts" or similar clauses, like any other contractual agreement, must set forth in definite and certain terms every material element of the contemplated bargain. It is hornbook law that courts cannot and will not supply the material terms of a contract.

Essential to the enforcement of a "best efforts" clause is a clear set of guidelines against which the parties' "best efforts" may be measured. . . . The performance required of the parties by a "best efforts" clause may be expressly provided by the contract itself or implied from the circumstances of the case. . . .

In the case at bar, there simply are no objective criteria against which either Pinnacle or Pendleton's efforts can be measured.

Pinnacle's argument that the parties' obligations under the "best efforts" clause are clear from the circumstances of the case is without merit. While it is possible to infer from the circumstances the standard of performance required by a "best efforts" clause where the parties have agreed to work toward a specific goal, . . . it is not so here where the parties have agreed only to negotiate. The performance required by a contract to negotiate with best efforts, unlike the performance required by a distribution contract or a patent assignment, simply cannot be ascertained from the circumstances. Unless the parties delineate in the contract objective standards by which their efforts are to be measured, the very nature of contract negotiations renders it impossible to determine whether the parties have used their "best" efforts to reach a new agreement. Certainly, no party to a negotiation, no matter what the circumstances, is required to make a particular offer nor to accept particular terms. What each party offers or demands in the course of any negotiation is a matter left strictly to the business judgment of that party. Thus, absent express standards, a court cannot decide that one party's offer does not constitute its best efforts; nor can it say that the other party's refusal to accept certain terms does not constitute its best efforts.

In the instant case, therefore, where the parties agreed only to negotiate and failed to state the standards by which their negotiation efforts were to be measured, it is impossible to determine whether Pinnacle or Pendleton used their "best efforts" to negotiate a new agreement. For instance, there simply is no objective standard by which the court can determine whether Pinnacle's offer constituted its best efforts; nor can it decide whether Pendleton's participation in negotiations with Pinnacle for over a year were his best efforts. In short, the option clause is unenforceable due to the indefiniteness of its terms. Accordingly, Pinnacle's motion for summary judgment is denied [as is plaintiff's motion for temporary injunction pending appeal.]

NOTE _____

In *Thompson v. Liquichimica of America, Inc.*, 481 F. Supp. 365 (SDNY 1979), a "best efforts" clause was distinguished from an agreement to agree and was held enforceable. The court found it to constitute a "closed proposition discrete and actionable." The Pinnacle court disagreed with the reasoning in *Thompson*. In addition, *Pinnacle* distinguished the *Thompson* situation, asserting the terms of the agreement in *Thompson* were more specific and provided sufficient criteria against which the parties' efforts could be measured. See 519 F. Supp. at 122. Even so, despite the Pinnacle court's attempted distinguishing of *Thompson*, the two cases stand in contrast with each other.

Chapter 7

MUSIC PUBLISHING

7.1 AN OVERVIEW OF THE MUSIC PUBLISHING INDUSTRY

As the Internet, new technologies and digital uses expand and reinvent the ways in which we use, listen to and purchase music; the music publishing industry will continue to undergo dramatic change. Without question, music publishing will continue to change and adapt as new technologies and new music alter the business that was once comprised of piano copies and performance rights, and was later transformed, first by phonorecords, radio and television and then CDs, MTV, DVDs, the Internet and a multitude of digital opportunities. The "players" may change, and the economic models upon which they base their businesses are already changing. Therefore, the customs and usages which have prevailed in the past will evolve or, in some cases, disappear altogether as new models emerge with the new technologies. Nevertheless, if past experience is any guide, music deals in the Internet age and digital era will probably continue to be made with an eye toward how business has been done in the past. Therefore, it makes sense to review the business as we see it now.

The song—its creation, discovery, protection, licensing, exploitation, and resultant income—has been and remains the focus of the music publishing industry. The functions of the music publisher include working on a creative level with songwriters in the composing of new songs, protecting and enforcing their copyrights, seeking potential licensees for songs, entering into licensing arrangements for such uses, and collecting and disbursing the resulting income.

Just as the songs have changed, technology has changed the way in which music publishers do business: It has enlarged potential sources of income and made the industry much more complex. Virtually all of the technological innovations affecting the entertainment industries in recent decades, including cable television, videocassettes, CD-ROMs, interactive media, ring tones, Itunes, satellite transmission, online delivery of music, pay-per-view, compact discs, and other digital sound formats (for example, new "digital juke boxes," which permit tracking of—and payment for—actual usages, are beginning to replace older, conventional jukeboxes the music license fee for which was some $50 per box per year), have resulted in the expansion of the music publishing business through new outlets and greater usage of music. In a report first published in 2004, NMPA indicated that in the year 2001 worldwide music publishing revenues exceeded $6.63 billion (*NMPA International Survey of Music Publishing Revenues, Twelfth Edition*).

Technological advances have also presented, and will continue to present, legal and business challenges to the publishing industry. As musicians and producers found a new way of recording through digital "sampling" of pre-existing recordings, publishers and record labels were faced with the immediate question of when such sampling constitutes a copy of a pre-existing composition requiring a license or poses the possibility of a claim for infringement and such issues as appropriate fees, claims of copyright ownership, and damages for infringement. As a practical matter, in most situations where a significant sample of a musical composition is used, the publisher and producer/artist/label are able to work out a mutually satisfactory license arrangement. In the case of *Grand Upright Music, Ltd. v. Warner Bros. Records, Inc.* (see Section 7.8), we see the potential problems that can result from releasing a record with "uncleared samples." Furthermore, in the cases that follow courts have different interpretations of whether a sample license is required.

Ring tones, master tones, and ring backs for cell phones (which we will refer to here collectively as ring tones) became another new source of revenue for music publishers that also raised legal and business issues that will continue to be debated and negotiated. Who has the right to license the musical composition for a ring tone, under what license terms and for what fee? As to the party that had the right to grant such licenses for this new profit source, disputes and conflicts emerge as the artist, the songwriters, the publisher, the record company and the performing rights societies have all claimed rights to license and collect for ring tone licenses. The ring tone (and/or master tone or ring back) license has been developed. Most ring tone licenses are on a limited territory basis (e.g., U.S. and Canada) as the conflicts between the various claimants of the ring tone license right may preclude the grant of a worldwide license until rights are further established. One reason for the keen interest today in ring tones is the profit potential as ring tones use a small portion of a song in a format that commands a substantially higher retail price that a download of the entire recording (in many cases now as much as $2.99 for a ring tone versus $.99 for the entire song). Current ring tone royalties in the United States are often the greater of 10 cents to 12 cents for each download of a song to a phone for a ring tone or 10–12% of the retail price (or net sales) from the ring tone license.

Subscription music services are another new music delivery system that challenges music publishing's traditional notions of mechanical royalties, performance income and synchronization licenses (the three primary (and previously distinct) sources of income for publishers and songwriters). Recognizing that the new subscription model posed great opportunity and risk to music rights holders while challenging the traditional license and income models, the music publishers (through the National Music Publishers' Association (NMPA)) and the labels (through the Recording Industry Association of America (RIAA)) entered into an agreement in 2001 on the licensing of new subscription services on the Internet. Under the agreement, the labels and on-line services had access to all songs licensed by the Harry Fox Agency who would issues licenses for subscription services offering on-demand streaming and limited downloads (sometime called "tethered downloads" that can only be played a limited number of times or for a limited period). The license provided that the labels paid the publishers a $1M advance towards "to be determined" royalties for the first year and $750,000 advances for the two years following. By 2005, the negotiations broke down, as the on-line subscription services, labels and publishers were unable to agree on rates for such services and uses. The most recent position of the publishers is that in consideration for the use of the songs on the subscription services, publishers and writers should be entitled a royalty based on the greater of 12% of gross, a certain per-play penny rate or 25% of gross paid for all content, rates which the services and labels have not agreed to pay.

Webcasting is yet another new technology that both poses new challenges and provides opportunities for music publishing. This generally refers to the streaming of audio on the Internet. It is sometimes called "Internet radio." For an interesting summary webcasting license and rights issues see the RIAA site at http://www.riaa.com/issues/licensing/webcasting_faq.asp#whatis. These new models and all the other online and digital uses of music challenge the music publishing (and record) industry, as issues of copyright owner compensation, a satisfactory monitoring system for programming, and the allocation of license fees for transglobal broadcast of copyrighted material through multiple territories, have yet to be resolved. While the information superhighway poses enormous potential opportunities for music publishers it also creates risks and problems, causing creators such as lyricist Hal David ("Promises, Promises") to state that songwriters feel like "road kill on the information highway." Efforts to ease the impact of new technologies upon the music and recording industries have not been uniformly successful. For example, the Audio Home Recording Act of 1992, which imposed a basic 2 to 3 percent surcharge on the manufacturers and distributors of digital audio recorders and digital recording "blanks," allocated one-third of all such digital royalty income to music publishing rights (split equally between songwriters and publishers) but did not specify how the income would be allocated among individuals.

Coinciding with the rapid growth of digital downloads, which is seen by many to be the bright future for music sales, there has been an increase in disputes in many major territories outside of the United States between record companies and music publishers as to the prevailing rate for the use of the song in a digital download. Like the disputes over subscription rates, this fight over digital rates in a growth segment of an otherwise stagnated sales market promises to be widespread, difficult, and not concluded in the foreseeable future.

One primary reason that music publishing and new technologies have so challenged one another is the fragmented and specialized nature of music publishing rights that are held by thousands of parties with, in many cases, very different interests. The Harry Fox Agency, the U.S. organization that represents music publishers for mechanical (and other) licensing, represents over 28,000 music publishers. An LP of material may be owned by scores of parties, some of whom want to see new technology uses and others who may not and, in many cases rights to these songs are controlled by different parties in different territories.

Prior to the explosive growth of the record business beginning in the 1950s, marked by the advent of the LP, stereo, and rock and roll, the role of the music publisher was quite different from what it has been since that time. In the early years of this century, music publishers made most of their money from the sale of printed music. They hired "song pluggers" (such as the young Irving Berlin and George Gershwin) to play their numbers on pianos set up in music stores to encourage the purchase of printed music. The song pluggers also auditioned numbers for theatrical, vaudeville, and cabaret performers in the hope of achieving exposure for the catalogs of their employers.

With the organization of the American Society of Composers, Authors, and Publishers (ASCAP), a second major source of income—from so-called small performing rights—emerged. Fees were collected from live performances and later from radio (and still later from TV) by ASCAP and by its competitor, Broadcast Music, Inc. (BMI), which arrived on the scene in the 1940s. SESAC, the third performing rights society in the United States, began an aggressive campaign in recent years to attract writers and publishers in the Latin and pop market fields (signing Bob Dylan and Neil Diamond in 1995).

The record business grew slowly. As was the case with vaudeville and cabaret performers, early recording artists rarely wrote their own material and were receptive to the offerings of the song pluggers, a situation that continued to prevail until the emergence of the self-contained rock-and-roll and "folk performers," who tended to write their own material. Artists such as Bing Crosby, Frank Sinatra, and Doris Day rarely, if ever, wrote their own material nor, for the most part, did the great big-band names such as Tommy Dorsey, Harry James, Benny Goodman, and Artie Shaw.

As the primary revenue sources for music publishers shifted from printed music and live performances to "mechanical royalties" from phonograph records and fees from radio and then TV airplay, so too did the role of the music publisher. The song plugger was gradually replaced by the "professional manager," who bears some relationship to the A&R (artists and repertoire) person in the record business. "Professional managers" attempt to convince recording artists and producers to record their companies' catalogs, but they are perhaps more oriented toward talent scouting—that is, finding young writers or, preferably, writer/performers with recording potential whom the publisher can develop and in whom the publisher can invest. As the post-Beatles popular music trend has clearly moved in the direction of the artist/songwriter, the publisher has followed that trend in pursuing the songwriter who can record and perform his or her own songs.

This is not to say that song plugging or the nonartist songwriter are no longer parts of the business. Country music still relies heavily on both "staff writers" of publishing companies and outside material for many of its artists. Many of the hits in that genre are the direct result of the publisher's plugging the right song to the right artist. In addition, pop music has developed a roster of "superstar" songwriters, such as Diane Warren as well as many songwriter-producers such as Dr. Dre, the Neptunes, Timbaland, and David Foster, who have the gift of creating songs that contemporary hit radio wants to play. Because radio airplay has become increasingly difficult to obtain and because such airplay is generally a prerequisite to a "hit" record, publishers of writers who are perceived as writing hit songs see great demand for those songs that the producer, label, or manager think will ignite or jump start a recording career. (Of course, given the ease of entry to the Internet, the growth of "streaming audio," and the availability of exposure through such outlets as i-Tunes and Rhapsody the significance of conventional radio airplay can be expected to diminish considerably.). Moreover, the proliferation of unauthorized musical websites with global reach has served to emphasize the importance of collective enforcement, both by individual publishing companies and by trade organizations.

The structure of the music publishing industry is similar to that of the recording industry in certain respects and different in others. The similarity stems from the consolidation that has occurred in recent years in virtually all of the entertainment industries. As the business became much more international in scope and as deal inflation dramatically drove up the cost of signing the next potential superstar songwriter or buying a catalog of songs, the concentration of a larger proportion of the music publishing industry in a few conglomerates was inevitable. As a result, more songs were bought and sold in the 1980s than in all of the preceding decades of the twentieth century combined, and the catalog purchase agreement became as familiar to the industry as the songwriter agreement.

In 2006, the five largest music publishing companies controlled nearly two thirds of market share and revenues of the music publishing market. The two largest of these, EMI Music Publishing and Warner/Chappell (the latter owned by Warner Music Group), each administer catalogs of well over a million songs, including a large proportion of the "standards," i.e., those songs which demonstrated sustained staying power ("staying power" that was extended by the Sonny Bono Copyright Extension Act that extended the term of copyright in the U.S. to life plus seventy years). Each of these companies was itself the result of numerous purchases and/or mergers, largely in the 1980s. Warner Chappell Music resulted from a 1987 merger between Warner Bros. Music and Chappell Music Group, which had itself been sold in 1984 by PolyGram Records. EMI Music bought SBK in 1989 for an estimated $337 million for approximately 250,000 songs, which consisted largely of the catalog of CBS Songs that SBK had acquired in 1986 for an estimated $125 million.

The remaining three global music publishing companies are Universal Music Publishing (a subsidiary of Vivendi Universal (which includes Universal Records and France's Vivendi the owner of major pay television outlet Canal Plus), which itself acquired former major PolyGram and Rondor Music (the former publishing arm of A&M Records, Sony-ATV Music (formerly CBS Music, which bought Nashville-based Tree International in 1988 for about $40M and bought Acuff-Rose Music in 2002 for about $157M), and BMG Music Publishing. In fact, it is hard to find an American record company that does not have its own affiliated music publishing company, and those that do not often are new companies that will include a "first refusal" clause for publishing in their artist recording agreements.

Where the structure of the music publishing business differs from that of the record industry is in the existence of a wide range of independent music publishers. This situation came about largely due to the difference between the record and music publishing businesses in the "hard copy" world. Labels relied on a distribution system dominated by six (at this point four, due to mergers,) companies to sell their product, while a publisher with a hit song could do business with a telephone and a fax machine. Because publishers were not as reliant on a distribution system for their business, many more of them were able to survive and prosper as independents. Significant remaining independent publishers that are affiliated with labels include Chrysalis Music, while there are significant independent music publishers who operate otherwise, such as Peer Music, Bug Music, and Windswept Pacific. In addition, almost every motion picture studio or production company has its own publishing company, which generally will own and control almost all of the newly composed music included in its motion pictures and television programming.

The industry also includes a number of private publishing companies owned by songwriters (among those who have or have had their own companies: Paul McCartney, Bob Dylan, Dr. Dre, Bruce Springsteen, and Paul Simon.). Many new artist-songwriters, following this example and wanting to have full control over their songs for all uses, have retained ownership (and in many cases all control) of all of their songs, administering songs themselves or though their representatives (in many cases paralegals within their lawyers' offices). In such cases, the writers(s) will enter into subpublishing agreements for collection and licensing outside the U.S. and Canada. This trend has created new markets and opportunity for publishing administrators (such as Randall Wixen, who administers the works of Neil Young, the Doors and Jackson Browne) and has allowed new companies such as Kobalt to emerge and compete with the majors and independents with new models of administration deals, collection and accounting.

7.2 SOURCES OF REVENUE

How do the music publishing revenues which have exceeded $6.63 billion in one year break down? These revenues were derived from the following sources:

- Fees from so-called small performing rights—payment for the playing of music on radio and television, in concert halls, arenas, bars, and other locales, and via "streaming" over the Internet.
- "Mechanical royalties" paid for the use of musical compositions on phonograph records in all of the various formats, including tape and CD (and, of course, via download). The phrase "mechanical royalties" comes from the fact that the earliest music publishing royalties were derived from player-piano's perforated-paper music rolls.
- Royalties from printed editions of songs. Although print was the principal source of income before the explosion of records, television, film, and radio, its proportionate share of the publishing pie is now quite small. The print field includes educational materials, including teaching materials for learning various instruments, single piano or vocal sheets of top songs, and "personality" folios of particular artist or "mixed" folios (for example, "Hits of the Sixties"). There are three significant print publishers in the United States: Hal Leonard, Alfred Publications, and Cherry Lane Music.
- Fees from the "synchronization" of music in television and film soundtracks, which may involve the license to use the music on commercial television, pay television, home video devices, or some combination thereof or in radio or television commercials.
- Royalties from ring tones, subscriptions services, "streaming" uses of music, webcasting, and other online and digital uses of music

There are other types of income—so-called grand rights uses—either on the living stage or by way of a television or film dramatization of a song (for example, "The Ballad of Billy Joe") or the use of its title (for example, "Blue Velvet" or "Sea of Love"). There is also the use of lyrics or titles on materials such as greeting cards, balloons, lyric magazines, and T-shirts.

According to the last NMPA study, the leading source of publishing income (in 2001) is now "performance based revenue" (including income from live performance and the public performance of recorded music), which was nearly $3.18 billion and is now followed by "distribution based income," (i.e., "mechanical" royalties, which includes "synchronization" revenues, of $2.42 billion). Traditional mechanical income has been declining since 2000 (when record sales began their decline) and music publisher and songwriters increasingly look to synchronization licenses and new technology and digital opportunities (e.g., ring tones, digital downloads and subscription services to offset such trends). Print revenues (which includes the music rental market) accounts for about 12% of the yearly world publishing market with sales of $804 million.

The United States accounted for about 29.3% of the total worldwide revenue, followed by Germany with 12.2%, Japan with 11.5% and the U.K. with 10.1%

For many years music publishing revenues have essentially been divided equally between the writer and publisher, a practice followed throughout most of the world. Thus, in theory, 50 cents of every dollar collected by the publisher will be paid to the songwriter and 50 cents will be retained by the publisher in most deals. The two great exceptions to this split are "small performing rights" fees and co-publishing situations.

7.2.1 Small Performance Fees

Small performance fees are monies paid for the public performance of music in non-dramatic situations (e.g., concerts, radio broadcasts, Internet streaming), collected by performing rights "societies" (such as ASCAP, BMI, and SESAC in the United States; GEMA in Germany; SACEM in France; JASRAC in Japan; and Performing Rights Society (PRS) in the United Kingdom). The U.S. societies, after deducting their own administration fees), pay half of their income directly to the songwriter and half directly to the publisher. Generally speaking, the songwriter's half is inviolate.

7.2.2 Co-publishing Agreements

Songwriters who are artists recording their material or songwriters with a track record of releases and who want a publishing deal with an advance, can usually negotiate the retention of a portion of the copyrights in their songs through what is known as a "co-publishing" agreement. Once a variation agreement that was an exception to the standard songwriter agreement (which would vest the entire copyright with the publisher), the co-publishing deal became in the 1970s and into the new millennium the new standard agreement between major music publishers and writers (though many artists in this era and today would not give up any portion of the copyrights to their songs for any price).

In its simplest and most common form, a co-publishing agreement provides for the co-ownership of specified songs by two or more parties, usually—but not necessarily—on a 50/50 percentage basis. There is a designated administrator of the songs and a split of the net income after payment of writer royalties. A co-publishing agreement may be described in terms of a 75/25 percentage overall split. This generalization refers to the fact that in a simple 50/50 percentage co-publishing agreement, the writer will generally receive 50 cents of every dollar as author of the song(s) and half of the net income (or another 25 cents) for a total of 75 percent of most sources of income.

7.3 PRINCIPAL TYPES OF AGREEMENTS

The number and variety of types of agreements utilized by publishers have increased substantially as the business has expanded and writers' needs for publishers' services have become increasingly diverse, but the single-song publishing agreement and exclusive songwriter agreement (ESWA) are still alive and well. The ESWA is common in situations where the writer is very reliant upon the publisher's song plugger efforts to make the song happen. Likewise many writers who record their own material and seek to retain full ownership of their copyrights merely need a company to administer and collect; they will enter into administration agreements. Others will negotiate foreign subpublishing agreements in certain territories.

We have already mentioned the co-publishing agreement, which is discussed in more detail in Section 7.4. Following are some of the most common publishing agreements. It should be kept in mind that as patterns of exploitation evolve (e.g., increased incidence of downloads by individual song rather than albums, increased utilization of subscription radio rather than record purchases), the nature and economics of the various types of agreements discussed below will inevitably evolve to meet the new realities.

7.3.1 Songwriter Agreement

Whether for a single song, a number of specified songs, all songs written during an exclusive term, or some songs written during a specified term (for example, songs written and recorded by the writer as a recording artist), a songwriter agreement stipulates that the writer receive royalties of 50 percent of the income (with or without an advance against royalties). The songwriter transfers 100 percent of the copyright and administration rights to the publisher. Again, subject to the songwriter's (or his/her heirs') right to recapture the U.S. copyrights in the songs 35 years after the grant, the assignment of copyright is usually perpetual and worldwide. Where the songwriter is not also a recording/performing artist, advances will typically be smaller than those which are paid to writer/performers, since exploitation possibilities will usually be less frequent. Few truly established songwriters will sign an ESWA; they will insist upon retaining all or part of their copyrights. This is especially true where a songwriter is a frequent collaborator with (and/or producer of) the recording.

7.3.2 Administration Agreement

Under an administration agreement, the songwriter retains 100 percent of the copyright, the publisher undertakes the same functions as under the co-publishing or participation agreement, and the publisher receives an "administration fee" (usually 15 to 20 percent of gross income, depending on the songwriter's bargaining strength and the amount of advances the administrating publisher is called on to make). In contrast to the co-publishing/participation type of agreement, the administrator's rights usually expire after a stated period—perhaps three years, or three years following the delivery of the final songs under the agreement, or until advances have been recouped or reimbursed. In the latter case, an outside termination date of a year or two following the term will be specified.

7.3.3 Collection Agreement

As in an administration agreement, the publisher acquires no ownership rights under a collection agreement, merely rights for a term of years (typically, three years). Under this type of agreement, however, the publisher generally does not undertake any affirmative obligation to exploit the songs, but merely agrees to handle the paperwork of registration, licensing, and collection. The collection fee under such an agreement will generally range from 5 to 15 percent of gross receipts, settling most often at around 10 percent. These percentages may vary if advances are involved.

7.3.4 Foreign Subpublishing Agreement

Since well over half of music publishing income derives from records and TV and radio performances, and since territories such as the United Kingdom, Germany, Japan, France, Italy, the Netherlands, Scandinavia, Australia, and New Zealand yield hundreds of millions of dollars of publishing income, U.S. publishers enter into deals with subpublishers in these and other territories which are quite similar to U.S. administration agreements. These agreements will typically include provisions imposing additional artistic and economic controls on the subpublisher. For example, a typical subpublishing agreement may provide that the subpublisher will not license a so-called "local cover recording" (a recording of a song produced and recorded in the local territory by an artist other than the artist who originally recorded that song) unless the translated or adapted lyrics have been approved by the original publisher. There may be a prohibition against licensing songs for films and/or TV. Clauses may provide that timely payment of advances and royalties is "of the essence." These agreements tend to be for short terms—three years is typical. In all important territories, the majors have their own subsidiary or affiliated subpublishers.

7.3.5 Catalog Purchase Agreement

The owner of a musical composition or catalog of compositions may decide to sell the copyright(s) in a transaction (if it involves multiple copyrights) known as a catalog purchase. The transaction can include 25% of one song or rights in a million compositions. If an entire company is being sold the transaction might be either a stock or asset acquisition (with tax impact being a major issue in the decision). Any purchase of the copyright (and so-called "publisher's share of income" in respect of the copyright(s)) usually involves due diligence by the purchasers to establish and verify chain of title and the terms of existing licenses and subject agreements (that might impact valuation of the song) coupled with a financial review of historic earnings to establish an average of the publisher's share of income over a period of years (usually three to five) which is known as the "net publisher's share (NPS)." The purchase price of the catalog is then, in most cases based upon a multiple of the NPS. The range of multiples has been between five times NPS and twenty times NPS. NPS might be defined in the agreement as follow:

"Net Publisher's Share" ("NPS"). The annual gross receipts, including receipts from non-affiliated foreign third-party subpublishers, which are attributable to the Compositions less all third-party expenses actually paid or incurred by Seller attributable to those receipts. No advances paid to Seller are included in NPS except to the extent recouped by the payor thereof.

Selling an on going publishing company with existing writer agreements and royalty obligations makes for a more complex transaction and, in any purchase, the warranties and indemnities will be a focus of buyer and seller alike.

7.4 NEGOTIATION OF A CO-PUBLISHING AGREEMENT

As in most other areas of entertainment law practice, there is no standard co-publishing agreement or approved form. As a practical matter, every major music publisher has a basic form, or series of forms to meet different needs, that create the basis of the publishing agreement negotiation. Some of these agreements are as few as five pages in length, others thirty or more.

Generally, as is the case in record deals, the artist wants a long commitment, few company options, large advances and royalties, and significant creative control. The company wants to minimize its commitment in an uncertain business, more options if there is success, lower advances and royalties, and control over most administration rights. Somewhere between these two positions will lie the negotiated agreement. As the co-publishing agreement is the one commonly negotiated today, following is a brief summary of some of the points that are addressed and negotiated. All such agreements have several basic deal points that go to the heart of the negotiation and the contract: (1) What rights are granted and for how long? (2) Which songs? (3) Who controls? (4) How much?

In most cases, the first draft of the deal submitted by the publishing company will provide that the publisher retains its rights to the songs covered by the agreement for the life of copyright (subject, of course, to the statutory right of termination available to the songwriter with respect to the U.S. copyright after 35 years.) However, in recent years, songwriter/ co-publishers have with increasing frequency sought (and now commonly secure) the right to the reversion of their songs at earlier dates (usually from 5 to 15 years after the end of the term of the agreement sometimes conditioned upon repayment to the publisher of any unrecouped advances or advances plus, typically, a premium of 10% or 15% of the amount repaid and occasionally subject to an outside limit on the retention period, (e.g., no longer than 15 years post-term). As is the case with the songwriter agreement, the publisher will undertake to administer the songs—that is, establish song files, register the copyrights, issue licenses, collect funds, take enforcement action against copyright infringements (and, likewise, defend infringement claims brought against the song), and account to and pay the songwriter.

The term of such a deal will usually run for an initial period lasting until the later of twelve months or delivery of one (or, less commonly, two) albums which contain a specified minimum number of songs which are subject to the deal (typically 80% of the songs) or, where the writer is not also a recording artist, delivery of a specified number of songs (typically, 8 to 12, although, where the publisher insists that a song must be recorded and commercially released in order to count against the writer's delivery commitment, the number may drop to 4 or 5 depending on the size of the advance), with two or three options in the company's favor to renew for like periods. Such agreements commonly provide for advances, either on a periodic basis (e.g., monthly, quarterly) or upon the occurrence of stated events (e.g., release of an album, completion of delivery commitment, attainment of specified "chart" positions). Advances are entirely dependent upon negotiating power; thus, an unknown but promising band might receive $10 thousand or $15 thousand to sign, another $20 thousand to $40 thousand upon securing a recording agreement with a major company, another $30 thousand to $40 thousand upon the initial commercial release of the first album under the deal, and, perhaps, "sales kickers" of $25 thousand to $50 thousand when the album reaches U.S. SoundScan sales of 250,000 units, 500,000 units, and so on. Optional album advances are typically 66 2/3% of the earnings of the preceding album during the first 12 months following release, with minimum and maximum numbers which will escalate from those applicable to the first album. For example, if the first album advances to the point of release amounted to $75,000, the optional minimum/maximum figures might be $100,000–$200,000, $150,000–$300,000, and $200,000–$400,000. In some agreements, if the writer's account is unrecouped at the date of release of the next LP (or contract year, in the case of a non-artist writer) the advance otherwise due is often reduced by the amount of the unrecouped balance (in most cases to a "sub-floor" of a lowered advance.

Typically, a deal of this type will be exclusive, although it is not uncommon in publishing deals that tie into affiliated company recording agreements to see deals that cover only compositions written *and recorded* by the writer (or extend only to the "controlled compositions"). A publisher may seek to acquire every unpublished song the songwriter ever wrote, everything written during the term, and/or everything recorded or released within six months thereafter. The songwriter may seek to limit the scope by specifying that only certain prior compositions are to be included and that only songs recorded during the term are subject to the agreement, or that there will be a reversion back to the writer of songs unrecorded during the term. Many attorneys will argue that pre-existing songs (referred to in the vernacular as "back catalog") should count against the writer's delivery commitment; a frequent compromise is to count those songs which are first recorded and released during the term of the agreement, up to a limit of perhaps two or three such songs in any one contract period. In some instances, additional advances may be paid for songs written by the writer but recorded only by third parties, but in such cases, advances are usually keyed to chart or sales success.

Territory is open to negotiation. However, if the publisher is paying a significant advance, it will almost always insist upon world-wide rights. A prior subpublishing deal may, however, restrict the territory to, for example, "The Universe excluding Papua New Guinea." In the new world of the Internet, of course, split rights deals present hitherto-undreamed-of complications, since the situs of an Internet transaction has yet to be determined. For example, if a German computer user downloads a recording from a U.S. site, will the German publisher collect the mechanical royalty or will it be collected by the U.S. publisher?

Administration rights are almost always exclusive to the publisher in these types of deals. However, the contract may impose restrictions regarding the exercise of certain rights, requiring the prior approval of or consultation with the writer. Many of these are creative issues that will have varying degrees of importance to different writers. For example, some writers love to have their songs in motion pictures and/or commercials, while others are hostile to the concept. Certain writers want prior approval on changes in lyrics, change of title, use of the title in a motion picture, or use in certain types of commercials (e.g., alcohol, tobacco, firearms, personal hygiene products.) A songwriter might wish to control or have rights with respect to the "first use" mechanical license (which is a condition precedent to the ability of third parties to release "cover recordings."). Writers will generally prohibit commercial use of "demo" recordings without their consent, and they will want approval over name and likeness usages. Generally publishers are willing to grant some restrictions on usage, provided they do not impede their ability to make reasonable use of the songs and recoup their advances. Restrictions and controls in publishing agreements are further discussed in Section 7.6.

Income from the United States in a co-publishing agreement generally follows the 75/25 percentage split, with the songwriter receiving 50 percent of mechanical income and synchronization licenses and the 50 percent songwriters' share of performance income which is paid directly by the performing rights society. Income from print sales is generally subject to a different royalty split. After payment of writer royalties, there are certain other items taken "off the top" which may be negotiable. Some publishers will ask for an administration fee (5 to 10 percent, or more). In almost all cases the costs of copyright registration, lead sheets, collection of income, and making approved demonstration records ("demos") will be deductible. After a net income figure is ascertained, including foreign income as discussed in Section 7.5, this amount is split between the publisher and the songwriter's "publishing designee," most commonly on the agreed 50/50 basis.

7.4.1 Example of Co-publishing Agreement (Year-to-Year Term)

Dear _____:

The following, when signed by you and by us, will constitute the terms and conditions of the exclusive co-publishing agreement between you and us (the "Agreement"):

1. *Term:*

1.1. The Term of this Agreement shall consist of an initial period of two (2) **"Contract Years"** (as defined below) commencing as of the above date. In addition, we shall have two options each to renew such Term for a period of one (1) Contract Year in each instance.

1.2. The options are exercisable by notice (all references to **"notice"** in this Agreement are to notice in the manner prescribed in paragraph 9 below) within thirty (30) days following the completion of delivery of your **"Delivery Commitment"** (as defined below) for the applicable Contract Year, **provided** that we shall in no event be required to exercise an option prior to the end of the eleventh month of the then-current Contract Year.

1.3. Contract Year/Delivery Commitment:

1.3.1. A **"Contract Year"** shall continue for the later of twelve (12) months or, until thirty (30) days following completion of your **"Delivery Commitment"** for such Contract Year.

1.3.2. Your **"Delivery Commitment"** for each Contract Year shall consist of twelve (12) newly-written 100% compositions (or the equivalent in compositions only partly written by you) together with notice to us of the completion of delivery of the requisite number of compositions (with song titles, names of co-writers and percentages subject to this Agreement, as well as the name(s) of any co-writer(s) and/or co-publisher(s) and the respective ownership share(s) of each such third party).

2. *Territory:* The World.

3. *Scope of Agreement:*

3.1. Subject Compositions:

    3.1.1. Subject to those requirements and/or restrictions set forth in paragraphs 3.2. and 3.3., below, your music publishing designee and we will each own an undivided 50% share of your interest in all songs currently owned or controlled by you, which are not subject to an existing third party agreement set forth on Schedule "A", including, without limitation, all songs included on the attached Schedule "A" (**"Existing Compositions"**) and all songs written or co-written by you during the Term subject to the provisions of paragraph 3.1.2., below, in the case of co-written compositions (collectively referred to below as **"Subject Compositions"** or **"SCs"**), and we will have exclusive administration of the SCs throughout the Territory during the "Administration Period" (as defined below). A composition first recorded and/or released during the Term or within sixty (60) days following the expiration of the Term shall be deemed to have been written and composed during the Term unless you can conclusively prove that such composition was written after the Term.

    3.1.2. In the case of co-written compositions, such co-ownership and administration shall only extend to your fractional interest which shall be calculated by multiplying 100% by a fraction, the numerator of which is the number one and the denominator of which is the total number of contributing writers, unless we have received notice within sixty (60) days following the initial U.S. release of the specific composition indicating either (a) different ownership shares (accompanied by a fully executed writer acknowledgment of such shares utilizing the form on the attached Schedule "C") or (b) a dispute among the contributing writers and/or their respective publishers concerning the ownership shares of the applicable co-written composition(s).

3.2. Administrative Requirements and Restrictions:

Although it is intended that we and our foreign subsidiaries, affiliates and licensees have the fullest possible rights to administer and exploit SCs, to utilize your name and approved likeness (subject to paragraph 3.2.5. below) in connection therewith and to execute PA forms (and other routine copyright documents, copies of which we shall provide to you upon our receipt of notice from you requesting same) in your name and on your behalf as your attorney-in-fact (which appointment is coupled with an interest and is therefore irrevocable), neither we nor our foreign subsidiaries or subpublishers shall do any of the following (nor shall we authorize any affiliate or licensee to do any of the following) without your prior written consent in each instance (which consent, unless expressly provided otherwise, shall not be unreasonably withheld by you):

    3.2.1. (A) Change or authorize any change in the English-language title and/or lyric of any SC, alter the harmonic structure of any SC, or alter the melody of any SC (except insubstantial changes necessary to accommodate the syllabic requirements of foreign languages) or register any local translation of an SC with a performing rights society unless a recording embodying such translation has been released;

(B) Except to the extent that the rules and regulations of local mechanical and/or performing rights societies prescribe the share of royalties to be allocated to local adapters/translators/arrangers (which share shall be deducted "off the top" in determining "Gross Receipts", as defined in paragraph 4.2.3., below), all fees and/or royalties to any such persons shall be borne by us;

3.2.2. Issue a mechanical license for the use of any SC in a "topline" LP at less than the prevailing statutory or society rate, except in connection with those types of uses for which reduced-rate licenses are customarily granted in the country in question (**provided,** that our inadvertent, non-repetitive failure to obtain your prior written consent to such license at less than the full rate shall not be deemed to be a breach of this Agreement) and **provided,** further, that we will issue mechanical licenses as required by the terms of your current "controlled compositions" and related clauses (as annexed hereto as Schedule "B"), as well as with the corresponding clauses of any future agreement in respect of your recording and/or producing services, so long as such clauses comply with the provisions of paragraph 7.2.1.1., below.

3.2.3. Authorize the use of the title or lyric of any SC or any portion thereof as the title of a play, film or TV program, or authorize the dramatization of any SC or exploit any so-called "grand rights";

3.2.4. Authorize the inclusion of any SC in: (1) a videogame or film or television program, except as may be required pursuant to any blanket or similar license under foreign performing rights or mechanical rights society regulations now or hereafter in effect, (2) any commercial, political advertisement, or public service announcement (consent may be withheld in your sole discretion) or (3) any merchandising "tie-in";

3.2.5. Utilize any name, photograph or likeness of, or biographical material concerning, you (**provided,** that any such material [as well as any album cover artwork] utilized by a record company with your written consent, or under circumstances deemed to constitute consent pursuant to the applicable agreement with such company, shall be deemed approved for use hereunder, free of charge as between you and us but subject to any necessary third-party clearance). Notwithstanding the foregoing, our use of your name in connection with our administration and/or exploitation of SCs, or in connection with advertising and publicity for our publishing companies, to designate our writers and catalog, or (with your consent) in respect of a profile of you on our so-called "web site" (such advertising, publicity and web site use being at no cost to you) all of which shall not require your consent or prior approval.

3.2.6. Commercially exploit any demo recording (such consent may be withheld in your sole discretion).

3.3. Reassignment of Administration Rights:

3.3.1. You shall be entitled to a reassignment administration rights of your 50% copyright interest in all SCs (so that the SCs would then be co-administered by you and us upon our receipt of notice requesting such reassignment as of the end of the accounting period during which occurs the *later of* (1) the five year anniversary of the end of the Term *or* (2) the recoupment of all advances hereunder Subject to such co-administration rights in such SCs, the **"Administration Period"** with respect to such SC shall be life of copyright.

4. *Collection and Division of Income:*

4.1. We will be entitled to collect (and shall employ best efforts consistent with our reasonable business judgment to collect) all writer/publisher income (except the writer's share of public performances collected by societies and any other amount normally paid directly to songwriters by a disbursing agent) generated by each SC (including pre-Term earnings on Existing Compositions not subject to collection by third parties under presently-existing agreements listed on Schedule "A").

4.2. Royalties/Gross Receipts/Net Income Share:

4.2.1. We shall pay you 75% of mechanicals (and 70% in respect of synchronization and other income except the publisher's share of public performance income which we will split 50% to you and /50 to us) of the **"Net Income"** (as defined below) from SCs.

4.2.3. As used herein, **"Gross Receipts"** shall be deemed to be the following:

(A) Amounts received by us in the United States (or credited to our account in reduction of an advance previously received by us in the United States) in respect of the use or exploitation of SCs by any means, including but not limited to, from licensees and performing and mechanical rights societies and received by way of damages and/or settlements in connection with lawsuits and other proceedings brought with respect to SCs (it being understood and agreed that our share of amounts collected by our foreign music publishing subpublishers (which shall be calculated by them "at the source", *i.e.,* as received by them from performing and mechanical rights societies and other licensees, and shall not be reduced by intermediate distribution between various units of our music publishing group) shall be deemed to be 90% of such amounts (other than the publisher's share of public performance income and mechanical income from "local cover recordings," as defined below), 80% of the publisher's share of public performance income, and 80% of mechanical income from "local cover recordings" (i.e., recordings of SCs not performed and/or produced by you in whole or in part, which are initially recorded and commercially released outside of the United States). Consistent with the foregoing, and not in limitation thereof, no administration fee shall be charged and/or deducted hereunder.

4.2.4. **"Net Income"** is hereby defined as Gross Receipts less

(A) Actual copyright registration fees, the actual and reasonable costs of preparing lead sheets and other direct out-of-pocket administration expenses (excluding general overhead);

    (B) Actual and reasonable out-of-pocket audit, litigation and collection expenses (prorated in the event that such expenses are incurred in an action involving other compositions we control); and

    (C) "Demo costs" (approved by both parties in writing) to the extent not recouped from your songwriter's royalties with respect to SCs.

5. *Advances*:

We shall make the following nonrefundable payments (subject to any withholding which may be required by the rules and regulations of any taxing authority having jurisdiction), which shall be fully recoupable from your share of Net Income hereunder:

5.1. In respect of the first Contract Year:

    5.1.1. $55,000. payable in 12 equal monthly installments commencing January 1, 2006.

5.2. In respect of the second Contract Year:

    5.2.1. $50,000. payable in 12 equal monthly installments commencing on the first day of the second Contract Year.

5.3. In the event that we exercise our first renewal option, an amount (payable in equal installments on the first day of each calendar quarter) equal to 66% of your combined writer/publisher royalties and Net Income share hereunder (as reported on your royalty statements for the first four quarters of the immediately preceding Contract Year), but not less than $50,000, nor more than $80,000.

5.4. In the event that we exercise our second renewal option, an amount (payable in equal installments on the first day of each calendar quarter) equal to 66% of your combined writer/publisher royalties and Net Income share hereunder (as reported on your royalty statements for the first four quarters of the immediately preceding Contract Year), but not less than $60,000. nor more than $90,000.

5.5. In the event that you request an advance (**"Extra-contractual Advance"**) at a time when such advance is not due hereunder, such Extra-contractual Advance shall constitute a pre-payment (in whole or in part, as applicable) of the next advance(s) becoming due and payable hereunder.

6. *Accounting and Payment*:

6.1. We will account to you (and make payment where appropriate) within 60 days following the end of each semi-annual calendar period. However, if the amount due for a specific statement is less than $50., payment (but not the statement) may be deferred until the aggregate amount due to you exceeds $50. The exchange rates used by third parties in accounting to us shall be used by us in accountings hereunder.

6.2. We will only be required to account and pay with respect to amounts actually received by us in the United States (or credited to our account in reduction of an advance previously received by us in the United States); *provided,* that amounts collected by our foreign music publishing subsidiaries shall (subject to the "blocked currency" provisions set forth below) be deemed to have been reported by them to us no later than the end of the semi-annual accounting period next following the semi-annual period during which such amounts are actually collected by or credited to our account by such subsidiaries.

6.3. Audit and Suit:

6.3.1. You (or a certified public accountant or attorney on your behalf) shall have the right to audit our books and records as to each statement for a period of three (3) years after such statement is received (or deemed received as provided below). Legal action with respect to a specific accounting statement or the accounting period to which such statement relates shall be barred if not commenced in a court of competent jurisdiction within four (4) years after such statement is received (or deemed received as provided below).

6.3.2. For the purposes of calculating such time periods, you shall be deemed to have received a statement when due unless we receive notice of nonreceipt from you (in the manner prescribed in paragraph 9, below) within ninety (90) days thereafter. However, your failure to give such notice shall not affect your right to receive such statement (and, if applicable, your royalty and/or Net Income payment) after such ninety-day period.

6.4. In "blocked currency" situations, we shall not be required to pay you until the blockage shall have been removed, but if requested to do so, we shall deposit blocked currency royalties in the local currency in a depository of our choice and give you reasonably prompt notice of the particulars concerning such deposit.

6.5. All payments hereunder shall be subject to all applicable taxation statutes, regulations and treaties.

7. *Warranties and Representations:*

7.1. By your signature below, and in each instance in which SCs are delivered to us (**"delivery"** to include a CD and/or cassette copy together with complete writer and publisher splits and society affiliations and satisfactory written clearance of any and all so-called "samples" embodied in any SC), you warrant and represent (1) that you have the right to do so, (2) that such SC does not infringe any third party's rights or violate any applicable criminal statute, including but not limited to such third party's copyright, trademark, servicemark, or right of privacy or publicity, (3) that the SC is not defamatory and (4) that, you and your music publishing designee are and will remain affiliated with ASCAP, BMI or another recognized performing rights society (and in the event of your failure to so affiliate and for the purpose of preventing loss of income due to such failure, we shall be entitled to claim 100% of the publisher's share with the performing rights society and account to you for income derived therefrom per paragraph 4.2.2. until such time as you formally affiliate and notify us of such affiliation). In each instance in which we provide you with a document which is necessary to vest our rights and/or interests in the SCs as provided herein, you shall execute and return such document to us within ten (10) business days following your receipt of same. In the event that you fail to do so, in addition to any other rights and/or remedies available to us hereunder, we shall be entitled to execute such document (copies of which we shall provide to you upon our receipt of notice from you requesting same) in your names and on your behalf as your attorney-in-fact (which appointment is coupled with an interest and is therefore irrevocable).

7.2. Additional Warranties and Representations:

7.2.1. Except as set forth in the annexed Schedule "B," neither you nor your music publishing designee, nor anyone acting on your and/or your music publishing designee's behalf or deriving rights from or through you or your music publishing designee (A) has received or will receive an advance, loan or other payment from a performing rights society recoupable from any monies other than the so-called "writer's share" of public performance income, record company or other third party which is or may be recoupable from (or otherwise subject to offset against) monies which would otherwise be collectible by us hereunder, (B) is presently subject to any so-called "controlled compositions" clause under a recording agreement or (C) is presently subject to any provision of a recording agreement which would allow a record company to charge any amount against mechanical royalties.

7.2.1.1. Notwithstanding the foregoing, we shall comply with the licensing requirements of the "controlled compositions" clause of any recording or producing agreement into which you (or an entity furnishing your services) may enter subsequent to the date of this Agreement, and your and/or such entity's acceptance of such clause shall not constitute a breach of this Agreement, provided:

(A) for "top-line" LPs the applicable mechanical rate in the United States is not less than 3/4ths of the statutory compulsory mechanical license rate in effect on the date of initial recording of the first record embodying a specific SC, and the rate in Canada is 3/4ths of the full rate in effect on the date of delivery of masters to your record company in the U.S.;

(B) the per-record maximums are not less than 10 times such rate in the case of full-length records (LPs, cassettes, CDs) (with your reasonable efforts to secure in such recording agreement payment on 50% of LP-length "free goods"), 3 times such rate in the case of 12" singles, and 2 times such rate in the case of 7" singles or cassette singles; and

(C) no advances or other charges under the recording agreement are recoupable from, or capable of being offset against, mechanical royalties in respect of SCs (with the exception of budget overruns, and union late-payment penalties).

7.2.1.2. If (and to the extent that) one or more of the standards set forth above is not met, and/or in the event of any recoupment and/or offset pursuant to subsection 7.2.1.1.(C), above, we shall nonetheless calculate our share of income as though such standards had been met and no such recoupment or offset had occurred.

7.2.2. Notwithstanding the foregoing, in the event that any record company to whom you (or an entity furnishing your services) are or may hereafter be under contract charges any advance(s) or other amount(s) against mechanical royalties earned by the SCs from recordings made under such recording agreement or reduces the amount of mechanical royalties otherwise due to you because the mechanical royalties payable with respect to "outside material" embodied in your recordings causes aggregate mechanical royalties to exceed the per-record maximum rate(s) prescribed in the controlled compositions clause of your recording agreement or fails to pay mechanical royalties in respect of all records for which record royalties are payable, then, in addition to any other rights and remedies available to us, we shall be entitled to (A) send a letter of direction in your name advising your record company of the terms of this paragraph 7 and instructing such record company (upon recoupment from record and/or video royalties of any portion(s) of the advance(s) or other amount(s) so charged) to re-credit us directly to the same extent (not to exceed the total amount originally recouped from or charged against mechanical royalties) and (B) reimburse ourselves from any and all monies (including your writer royalties and/or Net Income share) earned or due hereunder, for any amount charged against mechanical royalties, except to the extent later recovered through the re-crediting process.

7.2.3. In the event of a breach of this paragraph 7.2., we shall (in addition to any other remedies available to us) be entitled to reimburse ourselves from monies otherwise becoming due to you or your music publishing designee hereunder to the extent that monies are not collectible by us by reason thereof.

8. *Indemnities; Cure of Breaches; Waiver:*

8.1. Indemnity:

8.1.1. Each party will indemnify the other against any loss or damage (including court costs and reasonable outside attorneys' fees) due to a breach of this Agreement by that party which results in a final judgment against the other party or which is settled with the other party's prior written consent (not to be unreasonably withheld). In addition, your indemnity shall extend to the "deductible" under our errors-and-omissions policy without regard to judgment or settlement.

8.1.2. Each party shall give the other prompt notice of any third party claim which such party receives in respect of any SC and each party shall make a good faith effort to consult with the other prior to responding to such claim. Notwithstanding the foregoing, we shall not incur more than $5,000 in respect of any specific claim without your prior consent.

8.1.3. Each party is entitled to be notified of any action against the other brought with respect to any SC, and to participate in the defense thereof. However, if you wish to participate in the defense by counsel other than our errors and omissions counsel, such participation shall be at your sole cost and expense. Furthermore, in respect of any action alleging that any SC infringes a third party's rights or violates any applicable criminal statute, including but not limited to such third party's copyright, trademark, servicemark, or right of privacy or publicity, we shall at all times have the right to tender the defense thereof to you (i.e., require you to assume the obligation of defense).

8.1.4. If a claim is made against us and/or with respect to any SC, we may withhold a reasonable amount (i.e., an amount reasonably related to the scope of the claim and potential liability including anticipated reasonable outside attorneys' fees and litigation costs) from monies due or to become due to you, but if requested to do so by notice in the manner prescribed in paragraph 9, below, we will notify you of the amount on legal hold and we will refund it (together with interest on the amount released at the regular savings and loan passbook interest rate prevailing in Los Angeles from time to time during the period of withholding) if (and to the extent that) suit is not brought with respect to that sum within one (1) year thereafter, and provided that you have fully responded in writing to any written inquiry we have made in respect of such claim, and we won't withhold if you provide us with a satisfactory commercial surety bond.

8.2. Cure of Breaches: Neither party will be deemed in breach unless the other party gives notice and the notified party fails to cure within thirty (30) days (15 days in the case of payment of monies) after receiving notice; *provided,* that if the alleged breach is of such a nature that it cannot be completely cured within 30 days, the notified party will not be deemed to be in breach if the notified party commences the curing of the alleged breach within such 30-day period and proceeds to complete the curing thereof with due diligence within a reasonable time thereafter. However, either party shall have the right to seek injunctive relief to prevent a threatened breach of this Agreement by the other party. All payments required to be made by us hereunder shall be subject to any rights and/or remedies which may otherwise be available to us in the event of a breach of this Agreement on your part not cured in the manner prescribed above.

8.3. Waiver: The waiver of the applicability of any provision of this Agreement or of any default hereunder in a specific instance shall not affect the waiving party's rights thereafter to enforce such provision or to exercise any right or remedy in the event of any other default, whether or not similar.

9. *Notices/Statements/Consents:*

9.1. Except as expressly provided otherwise herein, any notices shall be sent by certified mail (return receipt requested), registered mail, Federal Express or Airborne Express to you and to us at the following addresses, or to such other addresses as the parties may designate from time to time by notice in like manner:

To You:
To Us:

9.2. Statements (and payments, if applicable) shall be sent by ordinary mail to your address in paragraph 9.1., above.

9.3. Approval/Consent:

9.3.1. Where the consent or approval of a party is required, it shall not be unreasonably withheld (unless expressly provided otherwise herein) and shall be deemed given unless the party whose consent or approval has been requested delivers notice of nonconsent or disapproval to the other party within fifteen (15) days after receipt of notice requesting such consent or disapproval.

9.3.2. Notwithstanding the foregoing, with respect to the use of any SC pursuant to paragraph 3.2. above, consent or approval shall be deemed to have been given unless we are notified of disapproval by fax or email from you or your manager or attorney within seven (7) business days (three (3) business days in respect of uses pursuant to 3.2.4.(2)) following your receipt of faxed notice requesting such consent or approval (such notices to be given to the parties at their respective fax numbers or email addresses set forth in paragraph 9.1., above).

10. *Law and Forum:*

10.1. This Agreement has been entered into in, and is to be interpreted in accordance with the laws of, the State of Tennessee. All actions or proceedings seeking the interpretation and/or enforcement of this Agreement shall be brought only in the State or Federal Courts located in Davidson County, all parties hereby submitting themselves to the jurisdiction of such courts for such purpose.

10.2. Service of Process:

10.2.1. Service of process in any action between the parties may be made by registered or certified mail addressed to the parties' then-current addresses for notice as prescribed in paragraph 9, above.

10.2.2. Service shall become effective thirty (30) days following the date of receipt by the party served (unless delivery is refused, in which event service shall become effective thirty (30) days following the date of such refusal).

Very truly yours,

By:_____

AGREED AND ACCEPTED:

7.5 COMPUTATION OF FOREIGN INCOME ("RECEIPTS" VERSUS "AT THE SOURCE")

In publishing parlance, a deal can be either a "receipts" deal or a "source" deal. Under a receipts deal, the division of income between publisher and writer (or publisher and co-publisher/participant) is based on what is collected by the original publisher from subpublishers and other licensees, not necessarily on all the income generated by specific uses.

Most music publishing income, whether generated within or outside of the United States, is initially handled by mechanical and performing rights collecting societies. We have already mentioned performing rights societies. There are *mechanical* rights licensing societies as well. In the United States, the Harry Fox Agency, Inc. (not really a society but rather a subsidiary of the National Music Publishers Association), represents more than 21,000 publishers for this purpose, while

STEMRA (the Netherlands), SDRM (France), NCB (Scandinavia), and other national societies perform the same function elsewhere around the world. Foreign income is processed and paid over to local subpublishers, who deduct their administration fees and remit the balance to the originating publisher in the United States. Under a *receipts* deal, the U.S. publisher would in turn deduct its publisher/administration/collection percentage (whichever is applicable) and pay over the remainder to the songwriter (or co-publisher or participant). Under a *source* deal, by contrast, the fee of the foreign subpublisher is absorbed by the originating U.S. publisher out of the U.S. publisher's percentage of income.

Clearly, the income resulting to the songwriter/co-publisher/participant can be reduced considerably under a receipts deal. Indeed, in the hands of an unscrupulous publisher, application of the receipts concept can have an effect that is little short of catastrophic. For example, under a receipts deal providing for the publisher to keep 25 percent of its receipts and pay over 75 percent to the writer/co-publisher, if the original publisher subpublishes to a foreign affiliate under an agreement allowing that foreign affiliate to keep 25 percent of gross receipts, and that foreign affiliate in turn subpublishes to affiliates in other foreign countries under agreements allowing *them* to retain 25 percent of gross receipts, the following is the result:

$1.00	collected by ultimate subpublisher.
$0.75	remitted to intermediate subpublisher.
$0.5625	remitted to original publisher.
$0.4218	paid to songwriter/co-publisher/participant.

If the client's bargaining strength is such that the publisher is able to insist on a receipts deal (which is the case in most songwriter and co-publishing agreements today), the agreement should, at least, specify the maximum percentage that may be retained by the publisher's foreign subpublishers for the purpose of calculating the ultimate division of income (e.g., "all royalties shall be based on "receipts" (U.S. share of foreign gross being 90% generally and 80% of publisher performances and local cover mechanicals").

7.6 MUSIC PUBLISHER OBLIGATION

7.6.1 The Obligation to Exploit

As with many different types of agreements in the entertainment industry, music publishing contracts usually contain clauses embodying variations on the theme that earnings from compositions are inherently speculative, that the publisher does not guarantee any particular level of success, and, incidentally, that the publisher is not really obligated to do *anything* except the customary housekeeping details (registration of copyright, setting up of song files, and so on), and accounting and payment for royalties if compositions are exploited. In this regard, the contract in the *Schroeder* case in Section 6.6.1, is fairly typical of U.S.

contracts as well as English contracts in lacking specific affirmative obligations on the part of the publisher. Under what circumstances and to what result can an author allege that the publisher is a fiduciary with special duties to the writer and, having failed to fulfill its duties, has lost its right to enforce the agreement?

Subsequent to the *Schroeder* decision, many English publishers adopted the custom of providing in their agreements that songs not exploited by two years following the end of the term would revert to the songwriter, especially in cases where advances and other commitments were less than robust. Such provisions are not uncommon in American agreements but are not routinely agreed to by publishers.

7.6.2 The Obligation to Account and Pay

The payment to writers, monitored by proper accounting procedures, is a primary responsibility of any music publisher. As the *Nolan* case in Section 6.2 illustrates, a publisher may not, absent express contractual provisions so permitting, sell its rights in a manner that diminishes the writer's contractual expectancy. By the same token, the writer is more than a mere creditor; as the *Waterson* case illustrates, a purchaser of a bankrupt catalog must continue to account to and pay the writers, who have an equitable lien on the copyrights. However, in reading the *Waterson* case, it is important to keep in mind that it was decided during an era when sheet music and song plugging were the primary exploitation vehicles. As *Zilg v. Prentice-Hall, Inc.* and *Third Story Music v. Waits* (both in Sec. 4.2.2) indicate, the obligation to exploit is not open-ended, and the level of effort will be reduced by the presence of substantial advances. In the *Evans* case that follows we see that a publisher's duty to account may not extend to share the foreign tax credits it receives.

In re Waterson, Berlin & Snyder Co., 48 F.2d 704 (2d Cir. 1931)

HAND, CIRCUIT JUDGE

The bankrupt was a music publisher. Prior to bankruptcy it had purchased from the petitioner Fain, and others, musical compositions, including words and music, under agreements all of which were identical except as to royalty rates and advance royalties. There were agreements made with twenty-two such composers.

The provisions of the royalty contracts important for consideration are illustrated by the following taken from the contract with one of the composers:

For the Consideration of the sum of One dollar, in hand paid to Jimmie Monaco, party of the first part, by Waterson, Berlin & Snyder Co., party of the second part, the receipt whereof is hereby acknowledged, the said party of the first part does hereby sell, set over and transfer unto the said party of the second part, its successors and assigns, a certain song or musical composition, including the words and music thereof, bearing the title "You Went Away Too Far and Stayed Away Too Long" or any other title, name or style the said party of the second part may at any time give to said composition, together with the right to take out a copyright for or upon the same, and each and every part thereof, including the words and music, to the full extent in all respects as the party of the first part could or might be able to do if these presents had not been executed.

And The Said Party of the second part hereby covenants and agrees in the event of the publication by it of the said song or musical composition, to pay to the party of the first part 1 cents upon each and every ordinary printed pianoforte copy sold and paid for of the said song or musical composition hereafter sold by the party of the second part in the United States, except as hereinafter mentioned or specified, such payment to be made only upon a full and complete compliance with all and singular the terms and conditions herein contained on the part of the party of the first part. And it is hereby expressly agreed that out of the first royalties to which the party of the first part may be entitled by or under the terms of this agreement the sum of $500.00 dollars, paid as advance Royalty, shall be deducted. . . .

And The Party of the first part hereby covenants and represents to Waterson, Berlin & Snyder Co., for the purpose of inducing it to accept an assignment of said song and musical composition, and to enter into and execute this agreement and make the payment above mentioned, that he has not heretofore sold, mortgaged, hypothecated, or otherwise disposed of or incumbered any right, title or interest in or to said song or musical composition or any part thereof, and has not made or entered into an agreement with any person, firm or corporation in any wise affecting the said song, words or musical composition, and that he is the author and composer and absolute owner thereof, and has the full right, power and authority to make this assignment and agreement.

We agree to pay 33/13% jointly of all revenue received from Mechanical reproduction less any expense incurred.

Settlement On This Agreement shall be made semi-annually within thirty (30) days after the first days of January and July, respectively, during the whole term in existence of the copyright of said song and musical composition, according to such correct and proper statements of account as may be available on such days. Any such payment when made and accepted shall operate as a release to the said party of the second part, his successors or assigns, from any further claim or liability for any royalty up to the date thereof.

[After the publishing company went bankrupt, the trustee proposed to sell its compositions, free from royalty claims, whereupon the writers filed a petition] alleging that in entering into their contracts they had relied on the reputation and organization of Waterson, Berlin & Snyder Company as leading musical publishers to popularize their publications and to increase sales of the songs, that the bankruptcy of the publishers had disabled them from further performance of the contracts to publish, and that, if the receiver was permitted to sell the compositions and copyrights free from royalty claims, purchasers would publish them without obligation to pay further royalties to the composers, who would thus be deprived of all revenue from their productions. The petitioners prayed for an order directing the receiver or trustee in bankruptcy to reassign the copyrights to them, or, in the alternative, not to sell without provision for the payment of future royalties to the composers, and for other and further relief.

The District Judge, though finding that each agreement involves "a transfer, absolute on its face, in exchange for a covenant by the publisher for the payment of certain agreed royalties," held that the "royalty contracts . . . involve such personal elements of trust and confidence that they are not assignable without the consent of the parties," and that they may "be rescinded by the composers when the publisher, as here, is unable or definitely refuses to fulfill his obligations thereunder." He therefore granted the petition and ordered that the royalty contracts be rescinded and that the trustee in bankruptcy should reassign each copyright to the composer upon the return to the bankrupt estate of any unearned advance royalties paid thereon to such composer.

The trustee has taken this appeal, which raises the questions (1) whether the trustee has a right to sell the copyrights at all; (2) whether, if he has a right to sell them at all, he may sell them free and clear of royalties.

. . . We find difficulty in taking the view adopted by the District Judge . . . because it disregards the unqualified grant to the publisher, and because it appears to give no weight to the labor, skill, and capital which a publisher expends in putting a song on the market. The expense of maintaining an organization, of building up a business and making it available to the composers of songs, as well as the more direct cost of making plates, advertising, and distributing the songs so as to give them popularity, largely go for nought if a rescission of the contracts be ordered on the sole condition that the composers return unearned advance royalties. Such a disposition seems specially inequitable where in the case of some, if not many, of the songs there are no unearned advances whatever. . . .

In the case at bar there was an agreement to pay "33/13% . . . of all revenue received from Mechanical reproductions less any expenses incurred," as well as to pay one cent upon each copy of the songs sold. Such a provision involved an implied covenant to work the copyright so far as was reasonable under all the circumstances. Under the doctrine of the Werderman Case [an earlier precedent], any purchaser of the copyrights who took with notice of such a covenant would take them subject to it, and, we believe, also subject to payment of royalties, without which the obligation to work the copyright would be futile. . . .

Courts in the United States have enforced rights resembling an equitable servitude binding on a third party who has acquired personal property from one who is under a contract to use it for a particular purpose or in a particular way. . . .

In both [the U.K. and the U.S.], where there has been a conveyance upon an agreement to pay the grantor sums of money based upon the earnings of property transferred, the courts have implied a covenant to render the subject-matter of the contract productive—if the property was a mine, a covenant to mine, quarry, or drill; if it consisted of a patent or copyright, a covenant to work the patent or copyright. . . .

The difference between the English and American decisions lies in the fact that our courts have allowed rescission where there has been a failure on the part of the grantee or assignee to act in accordance with his obligation to render the property conveyed productive, while the English courts have refused to allow it except for fraud. . . .

To allow rescission, the default must be such that it "destroys the essential objects of the contract," *Rosenwasser v. Blyn Shoes, Inc.*, 246 N.Y. at page 346, 159 N. E. 84, 85, or it "must be so fundamental and pervasive as to result in substantial frustration." *Buffalo Builders' Supply Co. v. Reeb*, 247 N. Y. at page 175, 159 N. E. 899, 901.

In our opinion a rescission could only be decreed in the case at bar if there had been a gross failure to work the copyrights, which has nowhere been indicated. Moreover, such a drastic remedy as rescission has often been withheld, and an equitable lien upon the subject-matter involved has been substituted even where rescission might have been allowed. This is illustrated in various cases where conveyances of land have been made in consideration of maintenance and support. Rescission has sometimes been granted because of a fundamental breach of the contract on the part of the grantee. . . . But in other cases the relief afforded has been through the imposition of an equitable lien upon the property conveyed, enforceable at the suit of the grantor. . . .

In the case at bar, within a month after August 1, 1929, which was the date when royalty payments became due under the contract, and only about three weeks after the adjudication, the receiver called for bids and attempted to sell the copyrights. Any default in working the copyrights had not been long enough in itself to justify a rescission and the proposed sale cannot be said to have been an act that would "result in substantial frustration" of the composer's rights upon the record before us. We can see no justification for decreeing rescission unless the transfer of title to the bankrupt, "its successors and assigns," though absolute in form, be held as naught.

It may be that the songs, or some of them, are worth much more than when they were copyrighted, and it is not unlikely that a large part of their value is due to the labor and expense laid out upon them by the bankrupt as entrepreneur. The trustee in bankruptcy ought to be able to retain for the creditors these contributions to the copyrighted songs, as well as any fortuitous increment, if the right of the composers to receive royalties from working the copyrights can be reasonably safeguarded.

Whether or not the copyrights may have become burdened with equities in favor of the composers, their title is in the bankrupt estate. The assignments were absolute, and Waterson, Berlin & Snyder Company would have had no right to take out the copyrights had it not been the "proprietor" within the meaning of the Copyright Act. . . .

In our opinion there is a middle course between the extreme doctrine of [earlier English cases] and the [later] cases which have allowed rescission for failure to work a patent, which we should take in the circumstances here. In view of the absolute terms of the transfer, the presence of the word "assigns" in the instrument of conveyance, and the statutory requirement that one who takes out a copyright must be the "proprietor," we see no reason to imply a covenant that Waterson, Berlin & Snyder Company must itself publish the songs. The composers cannot object if the trustee sells the copyrights. . . .

But it is a different matter to say that the sale of the copyrights should be free from all equities on behalf of the composers. In ordinary circumstances, and between the original parties, it may be that the only remedy of the composers would be an action at law for breach of the promise to pay royalties. Even between the original parties, rescission would be granted at the suit of the composers, if the publisher failed to work the copyrights in good faith, so that they might so far as possible yield royalties and thus afford the measure of compensation agreed upon. But, even where the publisher failed to work the copyrights, it could not be said that there would be actually no remedy at law, for the courts allow actions at law because of failure to observe such implied covenants. . . .

The damages for the breach of such a covenant, however, would necessarily be determined by estimates that at best could be no more than speculative substitutes for the definite royalties prescribed by the contracts. Accordingly a court of equity would decree a rescission where the breach was so fundamental as to amount to frustration, because the remedy at law would be inadequate. . . . A restrictive covenant affecting the use is imposed in such cases, and rescission is granted for failure to observe it.

It is true that the royalties on the songs are definitely provided to be paid only "in the event of the publication" by Waterson, Berlin & Snyder Company, but, where the words of assignment of the musical compositions are absolute, it is unreasonable to suppose that there may be no exploitation of the songs, except by Waterson, Berlin & Snyder Company. It seems to us equally unreasonable to suppose that the trustee may sell them free from all rights of the composers and thus deprive the latter of the only means of fixing the royalties which they have been promised. In our opinion, while the copyrights may be sold by the trustee, they should be sold subject to the right of the composers to have them worked in their behalf and to be paid royalties according to the terms of the contracts. . . .

We can discover no justification for decreeing a rescission . . . because the facts here do not warrant a remedy so extreme and so disastrous to the bankrupt estate. If the purchaser at the trustee's sale should fail to work any copyright that he purchased, when it was reasonably practicable to do so, rescission doubtless might be granted at the instance of the composer in some future suit. If the trustee shall be unable within a reasonable time to obtain a purchaser who will take title subject to the terms mentioned, the District Court should direct a reassignment of any copyright thus affected upon repayment of any unearned advance royalties upon such copyright. Rescission ought to be allowed only where there is manifestly no purpose to render the copyright productive to the composer. . . .

If a right to rescind the contract may be granted because of a fundamental breach of the implied obligation to work the copyrights, surely a lien may be imposed for royalties accruing through the use of the copyright by a sub vendee, for in no other way can the right of a composer to receive royalties be preserved in a case where the publisher has parted with title. . . .

The order of the District Court is reversed, and the proceeding is remanded, with directions to enter an order in accordance with the views expressed in this opinion.

NOTES

1. In *Harris v. Emus,* 734 F.2d 1329 (9th Cir. 1984), the foregoing case was distinguished, the court holding that a mere license would not be transferable in bankruptcy.

2. Publishers and virtually all other companies in entertainment who account to third parties for royalties seek by contract to shorten the otherwise available statute of limitations on accounting matters. Rather than be subject to various state statutes of limitation which would force the publisher to both keep all accounting records and be exposed to liability for six years or more, many agreements will limit to one to three years the period of time within which the royalty participant may object to an accounting, audit the books and records of a publisher, or initiate an action against the publisher. The provisions are common and have been upheld. See *Elliott-McGowan Productions v. Republic Productions,* 145 F. Supp. 48 (SDNY 1956).

3. Such a clause may provide: "You or a Certified Public Accountant on your behalf shall have the right to audit our books and records as to each statement for a period of two (2) years after such statement is received or deemed received as provided below. Legal action with respect to a specific accounting statement or the accounting period to which such statement relates shall be barred if not commenced in a court of competent jurisdiction within three (3) years after such statement is received, or deemed received as provided herein."

4. In *Weatherly v. Universal Music Publishing Group,* 125 Cal. App. 4th 913 (Ct. App. 2004), the California Court of Appeal allowed a songwriter to bring suit against his publisher ten years after the contractual statute of limitations had expired. Plaintiff Weatherly sued his publisher in 2002 based on misleading royalty statements from 1990. Upon conducting and audit in 2001, Weatherly learned that he had been receiving 25% less royalties than he had expected. Weatherly mistakenly believed that his royalty statements from 1990 indicated that he was being paid royalties based on 100% of all foreign income received when he was actually only being paid on 75% of such income. Universal Music Publishing argued that Weatherly's ten-year long delay in conducting an audit amounted to a lack of diligence that barred Weatherly from taking advantage of the delayed discovery doctrine. The court chose not to honor the contractual statute of limitations and, thus allowed Weatherly to use the delayed discovery doctrine because "a defendant cannot hinder the plaintiff's discovery through misrepresentations and then fault the plaintiff for failing to investigate." The *Weatherly* court thus held that "the right to conduct an audit is not dispositive of diligence where there is evidence that the plaintiff was "hindered" from discovering the breach by the defendant's misrepresentations."

5. In *Newsome v. Brown,* 75 U.S.P.Q.2d (BNA) 1903 (SDNY 2005), songwriter Betty Newsome sued world renowned performer, James Brown, and his music publisher in 2001 alleging copyright infringement of the 1966 hit song, "It's a Man's Man's Man's World." Newsome argued that the defendants acted improperly when they filed an original copyright notice solely in the name of James Brown in 1966 and later an amended copyright notice in 1994 listing Brown and Newsome as co-authors. The New York Southern District Court determined that

the essence of Newsome's claim was *not* copyright infringement, but rather *ownership* because Newsome claimed that she was the sole owner and creator of the song. The court examined whether Newsome's ownership claim was barred by the three year statute of limitations contained in the 1976 Copyright Act. In granting summary judgment for the defendants, the court found that Newsome "knew or had reason to know" of the injury about 35 years prior to the filing of the current complaint. The court determined this because Newsome had previously sued James Brown in 1966 for not crediting her as a writer on "It's a Man's Man's Man's World." That lawsuit resulted in a settlement agreement in 1967 that credited Newsome and Brown as co-authors. The court also noted that, as a result of that settlement agreement, Newsome had received $250,000 in royalties. Therefore, the court held that Newsome's ownership claim was outside the statute of limitations window by over three decades and thus barred. As an alternative claim to relief, the defendants also argued that Newsome's claims were barred by the doctrine of laches. The court agreed and found that Newsome had unreasonably delayed in filing suit, thus prejudicing the defendants' ability to put on a defense.

Evans v. Famous Music Corporation, 754 N.Y.S.2d 259 (N.Y. App. Div 2003)

Order, Supreme Court, New York County (Richard Lowe, III, J.), entered August 14, 2002, which, insofar as appealed from as limited by the briefs, denied defendant's motion for summary judgment dismissing the breach of contract cause of action and granted plaintiffs' cross motion for partial summary judgment as to liability on their breach of contract claim, unanimously reversed, on the law, without costs, plaintiffs' cross motion for partial summary judgment denied and summary judgment dismissing the breach of contract cause of action granted.

Plaintiffs Ray Evans, Ginny Mancini, John L. Mercer, Amanda Mercer Neder, The Johnny Mercer Foundation, Margaret Whiting and Barbara Whiting Smith are composers, songwriters and musicians, or their heirs, assigns and successors in interest. Defendant Famous Music Corporation (Famous), a wholly owned subsidiary of Viacom, Inc., is a music publishing company which has entered into various contracts with plaintiffs and/or their predecessors in interest, inter alia, for the payment of royalties.

At issue are six contracts each containing a standard provision that the artist is to receive an amount equal to 50% of "all net sums actually received" by Famous, less all expenses and charges and less all deductions for taxes. Pursuant to these contracts, Famous licensed the use of the plaintiffs' compositions in various forms throughout the world through its subpublishers. In exchange for a fee, these foreign subpublishers administer Famous's catalog of songs and collect royalties for uses in their respective countries. After deducting their fees and the taxes imposed by the foreign jurisdictions, the foreign subpublishers remit to Famous the balance, generally on a semi-annual basis. It is undisputed that Famous had paid the plaintiffs 50% of the amount it had received from its foreign subpublishers. However, plaintiffs contend, inter alia, that Famous regularly received a foreign tax credit for such payments on its

United States income tax and that Famous breached its contractual obligation to reimburse them for their proportional share of monies recouped from credits Famous received against the payment of foreign taxes.

Plaintiffs commenced the instant action, alleging breach of contract, unjust enrichment and "money had and received" by Famous. Famous interposed an answer asserting affirmative defenses based on a failure to state a cause of action, statute of limitations and the doctrine of laches, estoppel and waiver. Subsequently, Famous moved for summary judgment and plaintiffs cross-moved for partial summary judgment on their breach of contract claim.

In granting partial summary judgment to plaintiffs, the motion court found, inter alia, that the subject contracts clearly and unambiguously required Famous to share with plaintiffs the benefit of any foreign tax credit that may have been received by virtue of the payment of foreign taxes on the royalty income generated by plaintiffs' compositions. In particular, the motion court found that the contractual term "all net sums actually received" encompassed all monies and other value received by Famous, including the benefit of all credits for foreign tax payments. The motion court further determined that it was the intention of the parties that the artist would receive half the net profit realized by Famous after the deduction of amounts disbursed to cover the taxes Famous was to pay on the gross receipts. Since Famous deducted the foreign tax payments from the gross receipts when calculating the "net sums" upon which plaintiffs' royalty payments are based, the motion court concluded that plaintiffs were underpaid and that such underpayment constituted a breach of the contracts' payment clauses. We reverse.

It is well settled that a court may not, under the guise of interpretation, fashion a new contract for the parties by adding or excising terms and conditions if to do so would contradict the clearly expressed language of the contract. In the instant matter, the motion court's findings contradict the clearly expressed language of the subject contracts inasmuch as the benefit of any foreign tax credit was not contemplated by the parties. Although it is argued that the contractual language entitles plaintiffs to half the value of any benefit of a foreign tax credit, the specific language of these contracts specifically identifies and delineates all of the royalties in which plaintiffs are entitled to share. Under fundamental principles of contract interpretation, the failure to identify the foreign tax credit benefit indicates that such benefit was not envisioned by the parties to be an intended term in any of the subject contracts.

1. For additional readings and resources, the following books should be consulted:

   (1) Randy Poe, *Music Publishing: A Songwriters Guide* 2d ed. (Cincinnati: Writer's Digest Books, 1997). A well-organized and insightful overview of the music publishing business that addresses such topics as sources of publishing income, how music publishing companies work, and how to start a publishing company.

(2) Donald Farber, ed., *Entertainment Industry Contracts Negotiating and Drafting Guide* (New York: Matthew Bender, 1986, update 2005). A four-volume set of entertainment industry agreements with detailed commentary of each paragraph in the margins. Songwriters and music publishers covered in Chapter 168 by Evan Medow.

(3) Jeffrey Brabec and Todd Brabec, *Music, Money and Success: The Insiders Guide to Making Money in the Music Business,* 5th ed. (New York: Schirmer Trade Books, 2006).

(4) Mark Halloran, ed., *The Musician's Business and Legal Guide* 3d ed. (Englewood Cliffs, N.J.: Prentice-Hall, 2001).

(5) Al Kohn and Bob Kohn, *Kohn on Music Licensing,* 3d Ed. (Englewood Cliffs, NJ: Aspen Law & Business 2002). Like the Passman book listed below, indispensable to any practitioner in this area. (Comes with disk.)

(6) Donald S. Passman, *All You Need To Know About The Music Business,* Revised 5th ed. (New York: Simon & Schuster, 2003).

(7) Simon Garfield, *Money for Nothing: Greed and Exploitation in the Music Industry* (London: Faber and Faber, 1986). A fascinating, if somewhat one-sided series of stories involving the legal and business side of the music industry in the United Kingdom.

(8) Sidney Shemel and M. William Krasilovsky, *This Business of Music,* 9th ed. (New York: Billboard Publications, Inc., 2003). A classic survey of the music business done in a practical way. Part Two (Chapters 15–32) is devoted to music publishing.

(9) Howard Siegel, ed., *Entertainment Law* 2d ed. (Albany: New York State Bar Association, 1996). A collection of articles by experts in the various areas of entertainment law. Music publishing is covered in Chapter 2 by Michael J. Perlstein.

(10) Jeffrey L. Graubart, "Self-Publishing and the Songwriter/Music Publisher," 8 *Ent. Law Rptr.* 3 (September 1986), and Donald E. Biederman, "Self-Publishing, Etc.: A Rejoinder," 8 *Ent. Law Rptr.* 6 (October 1986). Concerning the advantages and disadvantages of functioning as one's own music publisher instead of dealing with an outside publisher.

7.7 PERFORMING RIGHTS

The following passages from Jeffrey Brabec and Todd Brabec's *Music, Money, and Success: The Insider's Guide To Making Money In the Music Business* (Fifth Edition) are an excellent discussion of performing rights.

The performing rights area—the world of ASCAP, BMI, SESAC and foreign country societies—represents for most songwriters, film and TV composers and music publishers their greatest source of continuing royalty income. Throughout the world, writers and publishers receive each year more than $4 billion in royalties from this right of copyright, yet very few understand what the right is, where these royalties come from, which organizations negotiate and collect them, how do these organizations compute royalties, how do the services offered by these organizations compare with one another, and how do you leave one organization to join another. Considering that performance royalties continue well beyond the lives of many writers (life of the author plus 70 years in many cases), knowledge of this area is a necessity for anyone involved in any aspect of music.

The Performing Right

Despite its name, the performing right has nothing to do with artists or performers. It is a right of copyright that is set forth in the U.S. Copyright Law, as well as the laws of most countries, and that applies to the payment of license fees by music users when those users perform the copyrighted musical compositions of writers and publishers. This right recognizes that a writer's creation is a property right and its use requires permission as well as compensation. Performances can be songs heard on the radio or on a jukebox; underscore in a television series; or music performed live or on tape at a Las Vegas show, an amusement park, a sporting event, a major concert venue, a local rock and roll, country or jazz club, or a symphonic concert hall. Performances can be music channels on an airplane, music at a convention, or music on hold on a telephone. Music users (those that pay the license fees) include the major television networks, U.S. local television and radio stations, pay cable services (HBO, Showtime), basic cable (USA Network, MTV, VH1, A&E, the Nashville Network), concert halls, Web sites, the hotel industry, colleges and universities, nightclubs, bars and grills, and many others. In short, in most situations where music is played (with the exception of the home), a user is paying a license fee, an organization is collecting those fees, and writers and publishers are being paid royalties for the performances of their copyrighted works.

In the United States, this right's primary recognition came as part of the 1909 Copyright Act, with further definition under the 1976 Copyright Revision Act. The right covers the non-dramatic performance of copyrighted musical works. It does not involve dramatic rights, also known as grand rights, where performances of a composition are licensed directly by the copyright owner. Dramatic, or grand rights, include works being performed in musicals (the live theatre), operas, ballets, and so on. Compositions, though considered dramatic in the context of their original theatre or opera setting, are generally under the non-dramatic right when performed individually on radio or television. In the United States, three organizations negotiate license fee agreements with the users of music and distribute those fees back to the writers and publishers whose music and lyrics are being performed. The organizations are the American Society of Composers, Authors, and Publishers (ASCAP), Broadcast Music, Inc. (BMI), and SESAC.

Types of License Agreements

The most common type of license agreement signed by users with ASCAP and BMI is the "blanket license." This license allows a user (a radio or television station, for instance) to perform any works in the ASCAP or BMI repertory during the term of the license for a specific negotiated fee. This unlimited access to repertory includes all of the past works of writer and publisher members or affiliates as well as the works written by such members or affiliates during the entire term of the license agreement with ASCAP or the writer and publisher affiliation agreement with BMI. The license also covers the works of writers who are members of foreign societies (PRS, SOCAN, APRA, etc.). The blanket license allows a user to perform the copyrighted works of writers and publishers without worrying about infringement litigation (performing copyrighted works without permission), the administrative record keeping of what is being performed, or the identity of the correct parties to be paid and what the payment is to be. Blanket licenses are negotiated agreements in which the license fee paid by the user can be, among others, a flat dollar fee, a per subscriber or gross revenue fee, a fee based on net receipts from sponsors, or based on such other objective factors as the number of full-time students for universities, the seating capacity and the types of equipment used in nightclubs, and live entertainment expenditures for hotels. License agreements have a maximum term of five years.

A per program license is where a station pays a license fee only for each program using ASCAP or BMI music that is not otherwise licensed directly or at the source. The fee is dependent on the advertising revenues the program has generated for the station. They also pay an incidental music fee for music uses not contained in specific programs and ambient uses in local news programs. The core provisions of this license were set by the court decision in the U.S. v ASCAP application of Buffalo Broadcasting (S.D. N.Y. 1993).

Two other forms of license involve the writer and publisher (the copyright owner) making an agreement directly with a user or directly with a program producer (a film or television producer, who then grants the license to a user). These latter two forms of license are permitted under the ASCAP and BMI agreements with writers and publishers, as those agreements are nonexclusive and enable a writer to license his or her works directly even though he or she is a member of ASCAP or an affiliate of BMI. . . .

Components of ASCAP and BMI Income

The primary job of ASCAP and BMI is to negotiate license fee agreements with the users of music for the non-dramatic performance of copyrighted works and to pay those fees back to writers and publishers based on the performances of their compositions. Knowledge of the sources making up each organization's total income is important, as it relates directly to the royalties paid for music and lyrics in any area. . . .

Domestic

In the domestic area (U.S. users of music), the largest single source of revenue comes from television, with radio in second place and general (concert halls, nightclubs, hotels, etc.) and background music operations third. The remainder of each organization's total income comes from the symphonic and concert field, new media uses and interest on investments. Using ASCAP as a guide, since it does publish financial figures, the society's 2004 total receipts figure of $698 million included $217 million from television, $182 million from radio stations, $88 million from the general licensing area and $4.8 million from the symphonic and concert area. To illustrate comparative growth, the 1972 ASCAP year of $69 million in receipts showed $33 million from television, $18 million from radio, $8 million from the general licensing area and $314,000 from the symphonic field.

Foreign

In recent years, the greatest area of income growth for both ASCAP and BMI has been the royalties received from foreign performing right organizations. The reasons for this growth have primarily been due to the ever-increasing popularity of the U.S. repertory overseas as well as the substantial increase in the number of radio and television stations in foreign countries. For certain years, exchange rate fluctuations can affect the amount of incoming foreign money. Every major country of the world has a performing rights society that collects for ASCAP and BMI writers and publishers when their works are performed in the foreign territory. These societies forward those monies to ASCAP and BMI, which in turn distribute them to their members or affiliates. Through agreements with these foreign societies, ASCAP and BMI also collect for foreign writers and publishers whose works are performed in the U.S. and forward those monies to the particular society of which the foreign writer or publisher is a member.

In 2004 ASCAP received approximately $206 million from foreign societies for foreign performances of its writers' and publishers' works. BMI's 2004 foreign receipts figure is estimated at $186 million. By contrast, in 1987 ASCAP's foreign collections totaled $50 million, with BMI's at approximately $30 million. Considering that most major music publishers collect performance money directly from foreign societies through local subpublishers, most of the foreign money received and distributed by ASCAP and BMI is writer money. The top countries sending performance money to the U.S. are the United Kingdom (PRS), Germany (GEMA), Japan (JASRAC), Italy (SIAE), France (SACEM), Canada (SOCAN), Netherlands (BUMA), Australia/New Zealand (APRA), Spain (SGAE), and Switzerland (SUISA).

Interim Fees

Of increasing importance to the amount of royalties being paid to writers and publishers are the situations where users and the performing right organizations are not able to reach final agreements on what license fees should be for a particular period of time. The result of not being able to negotiate a final agreement has been that many users (the television networks, the local television industry, the pay and basic cable industry, etc.) as well as ASCAP and BMI have litigated the matter or gone to a rate court in order for third parties (judges or magistrates) to set what the fees should be in a given area. In many of these cases, the user continues to pay at the old agreement rate or pay an "interim" court-set rate pending the final outcome of the trial or hearing and all of its appeals. In interim fee cases, many years or decades can elapse before final license fees for an area are determined and paid.

Methods of Payment

ASCAP

Live Performances

ASCAP conducts a census survey (100% pickup) of all songs performed in the top 200 grossing U.S. concert tours as well as all songs at ten major venues (Madison Square Garden, Radio City Music Hall, Hollywood Bowl, etc.). Song use information is gathered from set lists and generally is split 95% to the headliners and 5% to the opening act. The split between one headliner and two opening acts would be 90/10 and a co-headliner split would be 50/50. Tours are ranked according to revenue (the #1 tour, the 18th tour, etc.) and payments reflect the economic value of each tour. Live tour payments commenced in 1993. The Symphony Concert, Recital, and Educational Survey covers licensed symphony orchestras and serious concert artists on a census basis as well as all works performed in licensed educational institutions that pay the guest artist or ensemble $1,500 or more. Other educational institution's concerts are surveyed on a sample basis. The fees from other live performances not covered by these surveys are distributed as a surrogate on the basis of all performances on television and all feature performances on radio. ASCAP writers as well as foreign society writers who have performances primarily in venues not surveyed or whose catalogs have prestige value for which they would not otherwise be compensated can apply for financial awards under the ASCAPLU$ Awards system.

Per Program Distributions

In the local television area, stations either have blanket or per program licenses with ASCAP. A station with a per-program license pays a license fee only for each program using ASCAP music in an amount dependent on that program's revenues.

Under the blanket license, local stations pay license fees without regard to the specific musical content or revenues of any particular program. Since specific license fees can be allocated to specific television programs under the per program license, ASCAP distributes the fees from each specific program to the writers and publishers with music contained in that program.

The Internet

ASCAP Internet licenses are based upon, among other things, revenue and traffic, and they cover individual sites and aggregators as well as other new business models. Internet distributions to writers and publishers commenced in 1997.

BMI

Local Television

For local television programming, BMI employs a combination of a census survey (100% pickup) of certain types of programs and a sample survey of other types of programs. Any network series that goes to syndication, any series that is made for first-run local television syndication, and any feature film or television movie of the week are covered by a census survey of performances. For all original programs produced only for a particular local television station, BMI employs a sample survey of performances whereby a performance on a local station is multiplied by a statistical multiplier based on the ratio of stations logged to stations licensed. Currently, the rates on blanket stations are weighted to reflect the license fees paid by a station or group of stations.

Live Performance Payments/Internet

Royalty payments are calculated for each BMI licensed work used in the opening and headliner's acts for all dates on the 200 top grossing tours. Tour payments began in 1996 and are based on set lists.

BMI uses radio and television performances as a proxy for the distribution of much of its other live performance money. Certain licensed concerts in the symphonic world are also paid on a census basis. Internet distributions began in 1998.

For further reading and the complete text see Jeffrey Brabec and Todd Brabec *Music, Money, and Success: The Insider's Guide To Making Money In the Music Business* (5th ed.) (New York: Schirmer Trade Books, 2006).

7.7.1 Blanket Licensing

Blanket licensing is the predominant mode under which radio and television stations obtain the right to utilize music. In return for an annual fee ranging from a few hundred dollars to a percentage of the user's revenues, the user obtains the right to use the licensor's entire catalog as and when it pleases. The blanket license has been the subject of considerable litigation, the following case being perhaps the most widely known recent example.

Buffalo Broadcasting Co. v. ASCAP, 744 F.2d 917 (2d Cir. 1984), *cert. denied*, 469 U.S. 1211 (1985)

NEWMAN, CIRCUIT JUDGE

[The Southern District enjoined ASCAP's and BMI's blanket licensing of music in programming "syndicated" to local television stations as an unreasonable restraint of trade in violation of Section 1 of the Sherman Antitrust Act. A "blanket" license permits the licensee to perform publicly any musical composition in the repertory of the licensor. Finding the evidence insufficient as a matter of law, the Second Circuit reversed.]

The [plaintiff class] includes approximately 450 owners who, because of multiple holdings, own approximately 750 local television stations. . . . Since 1949 most [of these] stations have been represented in negotiations with ASCAP and BMI by the All-Industry Television Station Music License Committee ("the All-Industry Committee") . . .

The subject matter of this litigation is music transmitted by television stations to their viewer-listeners. Television music is classified as either theme, background, or feature. Theme music is played at the start or conclusion of a program and serves to enhance the identification of the program. Background music accompanies portions of the program to heighten interest, underscore the mood, change the pace, or otherwise contribute to the overall effect of the program. Feature music is a principal focus of audience attention, such as a popular song sung on a variety show.

More particularly, we are concerned with the licensing of non-dramatic performing rights to copyrighted music [pursuant to] 17 U.S.C. 106(4) (1982). Also pertinent to this litigation is the so-called synchronization right, or "synch" right, that is, the right to reproduce the music onto the soundtrack of a film or a videotape in synchronization with the action. The "synch" right is a form of the reproduction right also created by statute as one of the exclusive rights enjoyed by the copyright owner. *Id.* 106(1). The Act specifically accords the copyright owner the right to authorize others to use the various rights recognized by the Act, including the performing right and the reproduction right, *id.* 106, and to convey these rights separately, *id.* 201(d)(2). The Act recognizes that conveyance of the various rights protected by copyright may be accomplished by either an exclusive or a non-exclusive license. 101.

Music performed by local television stations is selected in one of three ways. It may be selected by the station itself, or by the producer of a program that is sold to the station, or by a performer spontaneously. The stations select music for the relatively small portion of the program day devoted to locally produced programs. The vast majority of music aired by television stations is selected by the producers of programs supplied to the stations. In some instances these producers are the major television networks, but this litigation is not concerned with performing rights to music on programs supplied to the local stations by the major networks because the networks have blanket licenses from ASCAP and BMI and convey performing rights to local stations when they supply network programs. Apart from network-produced programs, the producers of programs for local stations are "syndicators" supplying the stations with "syndicated" programs. Most syndicated programs are feature length movies or one-hour or half-hour films or videotapes produced especially for television viewing by motion picture studios, their television production affiliates, or independent television program producers. However, the definition of "syndicated program" that was stipulated to by the parties also includes live, non-network television programs offered for sale or license to local stations. These syndicated programs are the central focus of this litigation. The third category of selected music, songs chosen spontaneously by a performer, accounts for a very small percentage of the music aired by the stations. These spontaneous selections of music can occur on programs produced either locally or by the networks or by syndicators.

Syndicators wishing to include music in their programs may either select pre-existing music (sometimes called "outside" music) or hire a composer to compose original music (sometimes called "inside" music). Most music on syndicated programs, up to 90% by plaintiffs' estimate, is inside music commissioned through the use of composer-for-hire agreements between the producer and either the composer alone or the composer and a corporation entitled to contract for a loan of the composer's services. Composer-for-hire agreements are normally standard form contracts. The salary paid to the composer, sometimes called "up front money," varies considerably from a few hundred dollars to several thousand dollars. The producer for whom a "work made for hire" was composed is considered by the Act to be the author and, unless the producer and composer have otherwise agreed, owns "all of the rights comprised in the copyright." . . . However, composer-for-hire agreements for syndicated television programs typically provide that the producer assigns to the composer and to a music publishing company the performing right to the music composed pursuant to the agreement.

When the producer wishes to use outside music in a film or videotape program, it must obtain from the copyright proprietor the "synch" right in order to record the music on the soundtrack of the film or tape. "Synch" rights vary in price, usually within a range of $150 to $500. When the producer wishes to use inside music, as is normally the case, it need not obtain the "synch" right because it already owns this right by virtue of the "work made for hire" provision of the Act.

Whether the producer decides to use outside or inside music, it need not acquire the television performing right since neither the making of the program nor the selling of the program to a television station is a "performance" of the music that would require a performing right. The producer is therefore free either to sell the program without the performing right and leave it to the station to obtain that right, or to obtain the performing right from the copyright proprietor, usually the composer and a publishing company, and convey that music performing right to the station along with the performing rights to all other copyrighted components of the program. If the producer obtains the music performing right from the copyright proprietor and conveys it to the station, the transaction is known as "source licensing" or "clearance at the source." If the station obtains the music performing right directly from the copyright proprietor, the transaction is known as "direct licensing."

The typical arrangement whereby local television stations acquire music performing rights in syndicated and all other programs is [via] a blanket license permitting television performance of all of the music in the [societies'] repertories . . . for a fee normally set as a percentage of the station's revenue. That fee, after deduction of administrative expenses, is distributed to the copyright proprietors on a basis that roughly reflects the extent of use of the music and the size of the audience for which the station "performed" the music. The royalty distribution is normally divided equally between the composer and the music publishing company.

In addition to offering stations a blanket license, ASCAP and BMI also offer a modified form of the blanket license known as a "program" or "per program" license. The program license conveys to the station the music performing rights to all of the music in the ASCAP or BMI repertory for use on the particular program for which the license is issued. The fee for a program license is a percent of the revenue derived by the station from the particular program, *i.e.*, the advertising dollars paid to sponsor the program.

The blanket license contains a "carve-out" provision exempting from the base on which the license fee is computed the revenue derived by the station from any program presented by motion picture or transcription for which music performing rights have been licensed at the source by the licensor, i.e., ASCAP or BMI. The program license contains a more generous version of this provision, extending the exemption to music performing rights licensed at the source *either* by ASCAP/BMI *or* by the composer and publisher. Thus, for film and videotaped syndicated programs, a station can either obtain a blanket license for all of its music performing rights and reduce its fee for those programs licensed at the source by ASCAP/BMI, or obtain program licenses for each of its programs that use copyrighted music and avoid the fee for those programs licensed at the source by either ASCAP/BMI or by the composers and publishers. . . .

[The Court then proceeded to review the decades-long history of litigation between the broadcasters and other users of music and the societies, which had resulted in decisions and consent decrees limiting the rights which could be obtained by the societies.] [O]perators of movie theaters . . . .successfully challenged the blanket license they were obliged to take from ASCAP in order to exhibit films with music from the ASCAP repertory. *Alden-Rochelle, Inc. v. ASCAP*, 80 F. Supp. 888 (SDNY 1948). *See also M. Witmark & Sons v. Jensen*, 80 F. Supp. 843

(D. Minn. 1948), *appeal dismissed,* 177 F.2d 515 (8th Cir. 1949). [In 1950, the ASCAP consent decree was modified so that it] prohibits ASCAP from acquiring exclusive music performing rights, limiting it solely to non-exclusive rights. ASCAP is also prohibited from limiting, restricting, or interfering with the right of any member to issue to any user a non-exclusive license for music performing rights [and must] offer to any television or radio broadcaster a program license. ASCAP is also required "to use its best efforts to avoid any discrimination among the respective fees fixed for the various types of licenses which would deprive the licensees or prospective licensees of a genuine choice from among such various types of licenses." Finally, in the event license applicants believe they are being overcharged, the decree permits any applicant for a blanket or program license to apply to the District Court for the determination of a "reasonable" fee, and in such a proceeding, "the burden of proof shall be on ASCAP to establish the reasonableness of the fee requested by it."

[After local television stations challenged ASCAP's blanket rate in 1951, the parties agreed in 1954] to set the per program license rate at 9% of the revenue of programs using ASCAP music and to reduce the blanket license rate to 2.05% of total station revenue, less certain deductions. . . .

In 1961 local television stations requested from ASCAP a modified blanket license that excluded syndicated programs. When ASCAP refused, the stations sued in the consent decree court to require ASCAP to issue such a license. The District Court declined to require such a license, *United States v. ASCAP (Application of Shenandoah Valley Broadcasting, Inc.),* 208 F. Supp. 896 (SDNY 1962), aff'd, 331 F.2d 117 (2d Cir.), *cert. denied,* 377 U.S. 997, 84 S.Ct. 1917, 12 L.Ed.2d 1048 (1964). In affirming, this Court observed that if the blanket license was serving to restrain trade unreasonably in violation of the antitrust laws, the stations' remedy was to urge the Department of Justice to seek modification of the consent decree or to initiate a private suit. 331 F.2d at 124.

Rather than press an antitrust challenge, the stations initiated another round of fee determination pursuant to the consent decree. That litigation, known as the *Shenandoah* proceeding, was settled upon the parties' agreement that the form of blanket and program licenses then in use "may be entered into lawfully by each party to this proceeding" and that the rate for the blanket license was reduced to 2% of 1964–65 revenue plus 1% of incremental revenue above that base. *United States v. ASCAP (Application of Shenandoah Valley Broadcasting, Inc.),* Civ. No. 13–95 (SDNY July 28, 1969) (final order). The All-Industry Committee reported to the stations that this rate reduction would save them approximately $53 million through 1977, an estimate that was exceeded because of the rapid growth of station revenue.

Thereafter, while the local television stations took blanket licenses from ASCAP and BMI, the legality of the license was challenged by a network licensee, CBS. [The Second Circuit ultimately ruled] that the blanket license had not been proven to be a restraint of trade. *CBS, Inc. v. ASCAP,* 620 F.2d 930 (2d Cir. 1980), *cert. denied,* 450 U.S. 970, 101 S.Ct. 1491, 67 L.Ed.2d 621 (1981) . . .

. . . [In the instant case, the District Court injunction] bars ASCAP and BMI from offering either blanket or program licenses and also prohibits them from conveying performing rights with respect to such programs on any basis at all. . . .

Is There a Restraint?

We think the initial and, as it turns out, dispositive issue on the merits is whether the blanket licensing of performing rights to the local television stations has been proven to be a restraint of trade. . . .

[T]rade is restrained, sometimes unreasonably, when rights to use individual copyrights or patents may be obtained only by payment for a pool of such rights, but that the opportunity to acquire a pool of rights does not restrain trade if an alternative opportunity to acquire individual rights is realistically available [and] a plaintiff will not be held to have an alternative "available" simply because some imaginable possibility exists . . . ."An antitrust plaintiff is not obliged to pursue any imaginable alternative, regardless of cost or efficiency, before it can complain that a practice has restrained competition." . . .

. . . [In] *NCAA v. Board of Regents of the University of Oklahoma,*—U.S.—, 104 S.Ct. 2948, 82 L.Ed.2d 70 (1984) . . . the Court was . . . concerned, as we are here, with an agreement whereby a pool of rights was conveyed. In determining that the agreement constituted a restraint, the Court stated, "[S]ince as a *practical* matter all member institutions need NCAA approval, members have no *real* choice but to adhere to the NCAA's television controls." *Id.* at 2963 (emphasis added) (footnote omitted). Thus, the restraining effect of the challenged agreement arose not by virtue of its terms alone, but because as a "practical" matter no "real" alternative existed whereby individual negotiations could occur between member schools and television broadcasters. NCAA thus reinforces our view that the first issue is whether the local television stations have proven that they lack, as a "practical" matter, a "real" alternative to the blanket license for obtaining music performing rights.

In reaching the conclusion that plaintiffs had proven the lack of realistically available alternatives to the blanket license, Judge Gagliardi gave separate consideration to three possibilities: the program license, direct licensing, and source licensing. We consider each in turn.

[1] *Program License.* Judge Gagliardi based his conclusion that a program license is not realistically available to the plaintiffs essentially on two circumstances: the cost of a program license and the reporting requirements that such a license imposes on a licensee. "The court therefore concludes that the per program license is too costly and burdensome to be a realistic alternative to the blanket license." 546 F. Supp. at 289 (footnote omitted). Without rejecting any subsidiary factual finding

concerning the availability of a program license, we reject the legal conclusion that it is not a realistic alternative to the blanket license.

The only fact found in support of the conclusion that the program license is "too costly" is that the rates for such licenses are seven times higher than the rates for blanket licenses. The program license rate is 9%; the blanket license rate is between 1% and 2%. This difference in rates does not support the District Court's conclusion for several reasons. First, the rates are charged against different bases. The blanket license rate is applied to a station's total revenue; the program license rate is applied only to revenue from a particular program. Since the base for the blanket license fee includes revenue from network programs, for which the networks have already acquired performing rights by virtue of their blanket licenses, as well as some local programs that use no music, it is inevitable that the rate for a local station's blanket license will be less than the rate for a program license taken solely to permit use of music on a particular program.

Second, the degree of difference between the two rates is largely attributable to the stations themselves. In negotiating a revision of license rates in [an earlier litigation], the All-Industry Committee elected not to press for reduction of the program license rate and instead concentrated on securing a reduction of the blanket license rate, believing, as it informed the broadcasters it represented, that "the critical matter at this time was to get the best possible blanket license." Having preferred to win a lower price for only the blanket license, the stations are in no position to point to the widened differential between rates to show that program licenses are not realistically available.

Third, the only valid test of whether the program license is "too costly" to be a realistic alternative is whether the price for such a license, in an objective sense, is higher than the value of the rights obtained. . . . Within reasonable price ranges, the program license is not an unrealistic alternative to the blanket license simply because the rate for the latter is less. The differential in rates may reflect the inherent difference in the bundle of rights being conveyed. Even if the blanket license is objectively the "better buy" for most users, the program license would be a realistic alternative so long as it was fairly priced for those who might find it preferable for reasons other than price. . . .

Thus, while the relative cheapness of the blanket rate does not necessarily mean that it is not a restraint, the absence of evidence that the program license has been artificially priced higher than is reasonable for value received bars any conclusion that the program license is "too costly" to be a realistic alternative. . . .

In addition to cost, Judge Gagliardi considered the program license not realistically available because of the burdens of required record-keeping that accompany its use. This conclusion is similarly flawed by the lack of evidence that the record-keeping requirements have been unnecessarily imposed. . . .

The lack of evidence that the program license is not realistically available has a two-fold significance in determining whether the blanket license has been shown to be a restraint. First, the program license itself remains as an alternative to the blanket license for the local stations to acquire performing rights to the music on all of their syndicated programs. That consequence is not necessarily determinative since the program license is in reality a limited form of the blanket license and, like the blanket license, is subject to the objection that its use by stations would continue the present practice whereby no price competition occurs among individual songs with respect to licensing of performing rights. However, the availability of the program license has a second and more significant consequence: The program license provides local stations with a fallback position in the event that they forgo the blanket license and then encounter difficulty in obtaining performing rights to music on some syndicated programs either by direct licensing or by source licensing. Whether those alternatives were proven to be unavailable as realistic alternatives is our next inquiry.

[2] *Direct Licensing.* The District Court concluded that direct licensing is not a realistic alternative to the blanket license without any evidence that any local station ever offered any composer a sum of money in exchange for the performing rights to his music. That evidentiary gap exists despite the 21-year interval between entry of the [consent decree] and the trial of this case, during which the local stations had ample opportunity to determine whether performing rights could be directly licensed.

The District Court declined to attach any significance to the absence of purchase offers from stations directly to copyright proprietors for two related reasons. Judge Gagliardi concluded, first, that direct licensing could not occur without the intervention of some agency to broker the numerous transactions that would be involved and, second, that the television stations lack the market power to induce anyone to come forward and perform that brokering function. 546 F. Supp. at 290. We have no quarrel with the first proposition. Some intermediary would seem essential to negotiate performing rights licenses between thousands of copyright proprietors and hundreds of local stations, in the same manner that the Harry Fox Agency for years has brokered licenses for "synch" rights between copyright proprietors and program producers.

However, we see no evidentiary support for the District Court's second proposition—that no one would undertake the brokering function for direct licensing of performing rights. Judge Gagliardi was led to this conclusion, not on the basis of any evidence of an expressed reluctance on anyone's part to broker direct licensing, but because of his view of the difference between the market power of [a national network] and that of the local television stations. . . .

[However,] plaintiffs in this case do not discharge their burden of proving that local stations cannot realistically obtain direct licenses by showing that they have less market power than [a national network.] The issue is whether the local stations have been shown to lack power sufficient to give them a realistic opportunity to secure direct licenses. To conclude that they do not simply because no one of them is as powerful as CBS disregards the functioning of a market. Sellers are induced to sell by a perception of aggregate demand, existing or capable of stimulation. . . . The plaintiffs have not presented evidence to show that a brokering mechanism would not handle direct licensing transactions if the stations offered to pay royalties directly to copyright proprietors. . . .

[3] *Source Licensing.* As Judge Gagliardi noted, the "current availability and comparative efficiency of source licensing have been the focus of this lawsuit." The availability of source licensing is significant to the inquiry as to whether the blanket license is a restraint because so much of the stations' programming consists of syndicated programs for which the producer could, if so inclined, convey music performing rights. Most of these syndicated programs use composer-for-hire music. As to such music, the producer starts out with the rights of the copyright, including the performing right, by operation of law, 17 U.S.C. 201(b), unless the hiring agreement otherwise provides. Thus it becomes important to determine whether the stations can obtain from the producer the music performing right, along with all of the other rights in a syndicated program that are conveyed to the stations when the program is licensed. As to "inside" music, source licensing would mean that the producer would either retain the performing right and convey it to the stations, instead of following the current practice of assigning it to the composer and a publishing company, or reacquire the performing right from the composer and publisher for conveyance to the stations. As to "outside" music, source licensing would mean that the producer would have to acquire from the copyright proprietor the performing right, in addition to the "synch" right now acquired.

Plaintiffs sought to prove that source licensing was not a realistic alternative by presenting two types of evidence: "offers" from stations and analysis of the market. Prior to bringing this lawsuit, the stations had not sought to obtain performing rights via source licensing [but] plaintiffs began in mid-1980, a year and one-half after the suit was filed, to create a paper record designed to show the unavailability of source licensing.

Various techniques were used. Initially, some stations simply inserted into the standard form of licensing agreement for syndicated programs a new clause specifying that the producer has obtained music performing rights and that the station need not do so. No offer of additional compensation for the purchase of the additional rights was made. Not surprisingly most producers declined to agree to the proposed clause. . . .

Another approach, evidenced by King Broadcasting Co.'s letter to MCA, attached a music performing rights rider to the standard syndication licensing agreement and added, "If [*sic*] an additional fee is in order, we would certainly consider favorably any such reasonable fee." . . . Metromedia, Inc., owner of several stations, went further and asked Twentieth Century-Fox Television ("Fox"), "Since you are the 'seller,' what is the price you would affix to the altered product [the syndication license including music performing right]?" In reply Fox made the entirely valid point that since syndication licensing without music performing rights had been the industry practice for years, it was Metromedia's "responsibility to advise us in what manner you would like" to change the current arrangements. Notably absent from all of the correspondence tendered by the plaintiffs is the customary indicator of a buyer's seriousness in attempting to make a purchase—an offer of a sum of money.

Judge Gagliardi properly declined to give any probative weight to the plaintiff's transparent effort to assemble in the midst of litigation evidence that they had seriously tried to obtain source licensing. . . . Nevertheless the District Court concluded that source licensing was not a realistic alternative because the syndicators "have no impetus to depart from their standard practices and request and pay for television performing rights merely in order to pass them along to local stations." This conclusion does not follow from some of the Court's factual findings and rests on a view of the syndication market that is contradicted by other findings.

The District Court viewed the syndication market as one in which the balance of power rests with the syndicators and the stations have no power to "compel" a reluctant syndicator to change to source licensing. Yet the Court found that there are eight major syndicators, and that they distribute only 52% of all syndicated programs, *id.* at 281, hardly typical of a non-competitive market. Moreover, the Court characterized production of syndicated programs as a "risky business.". . . a finding fully supported by the evidence. It may be that the syndicator of a highly successful program has the upper hand in negotiating for the syndication of that program and would not engage in source licensing for music in that program simply to please any one station, but it does not follow that the market for the wide range of syndicated programs would be unresponsive to aggregate demand from stations willing to pay a reasonable price for source licensing of music performing rights. . . .

Defendants vigorously assert that whatever reluctance producers may have to undertake source licensing reflects their view of the efficiency of the blanket license. They contend that the blanket license may not properly be found to be a restraint simply because producers of syndicated programs regard it as efficient. We need not determine whether defendants have correctly analyzed the motivation of those syndicators who have expressed reluctance to undertake source licensing. Our task, in determining whether plaintiffs have presented evidence sufficient to support a conclusion that the blanket license is a restraint of trade, is not to psychoanalyze the sellers but to search the record for evidence that the blanket license is functioning to restrain willing buyers and sellers from negotiating for the licensing of performing rights to individual compositions at reasonable prices. Plaintiffs have simply failed to produce such evidence.

Instead they suggest that source licensing is not a realistic alternative because the agreements producers have made with composers and publishers are a "contractual labyrinth," and because the composers have precluded price competition among songs by "splitting" performing rights from "synch" But plaintiffs have made no legal challenge to the "composer-for-hire" contracts by which "inside" music is customarily obtained for syndicated programs, with provisions for producers to assign performing rights to composers and publishers. And composers have not "split" performing rights from "synch" rights; they have separately licensed distinct rights that were created by Congress. Moreover, the composers' grant of a performing rights license to ASCAP/BMI is on a non-exclusive basis. That circumstance significantly distinguishes this case from *Alden-Rochelle,* where ASCAP's acquisition of exclusive licenses for performing rights was held to restrain unlawfully the ability of motion picture exhibitors to obtain music performing rights directly from ASCAP's members.

[4] *The Claimed Lack of Necessity.* Plaintiffs earnestly advance the argument that the blanket license, as applied to syndicated programming, should be declared unlawful for the basic reason that it is unnecessary. In their view, the blanket license is suspect because, where it is used, no price competition occurs among songs when those who need performing rights decide which songs to perform. The resulting absence of price competition, plaintiffs urge, is justifiable only in some contexts such as night clubs, live and locally produced programming of television stations, and radio stations, which make more spontaneous choices of music than do television stations.

There are two fundamental flaws in this argument. First, it has not been shown on this record that the blanket license, even as applied to syndicated television programs, is not necessary. If all the plaintiffs mean is that a judicial ban on blanket licensing for syndicated television programs would not halt performance of copyrighted music on such programs and that some arrangement for the purchase of performing rights would replace the blanket license, we can readily agree. Most likely source licensing would become prevalent, just as it did in the context of motion pictures in the aftermath of *Alden-Rochelle.* But a licensing system may be "necessary" in the practical sense that it is far superior to other alternatives in efficiency and thereby achieves substantial saving of resources to the likely benefit of ultimate consumers, who usually end up paying whenever efficient practices are replaced with inefficient ones.

Moreover, the evidence does not establish that barring the blanket license as to syndicated programs would add any significant price competition among songs that the blanket license allegedly prevents. When syndicators today decide what music to select for their programs, they do so in the vast majority of instances, by deciding which composer to hire to compose new music for their programs. As to that "inside" music, which plaintiffs estimate accounts for 90% of music on syndicated programs, there is ample price competition: Prices paid as "up front" money in order to hire composers vary significantly. Even when syndicators consider use of pre-existing music (for which copyright protection has not expired), there is some price competition affecting the choice of that "outside" music because prices for "synch" rights vary. . . .

The second flaw in the argument is more fundamental. Even if the evidence showed that most of the efficiencies of the blanket license could be achieved under source licensing, it would not follow that the blanket license thereby becomes unlawful. The blanket license is not even amenable to scrutiny under section 1 unless it is a restraint of trade. The fact that it may be in some sense "unnecessary" does not make it a restraint. This is simply a recognition of the basic proposition that the antitrust laws do not permit courts to ban all practices that some economists consider undesirable. Since the blanket license restrains no one from bargaining over the purchase and sale of music performance rights, it is not a restraint unless it were proven that there are no realistically available alternatives . . . It is . . . irrelevant whether, as plaintiffs contend, the blanket license is not as useful or "necessary" in the context of syndicated programming on local television stations as it is in other contexts. Not having been proven to be a restraint, it cannot be a violation of section 1.

. . . Without doubting that the context in which the blanket license is challenged can have a significant bearing on the outcome, we hold that the local television stations have not presented evidence in this case permitting a conclusion that the blanket license is a restraint of trade in violation of section 1.

The judgment of the District Court is therefore reversed.

NOTES

1. The controversies concerning public performance licensing continue unabated in many forums. In recent years, a number of cases regarding various aspects of performance licensing have shifted the focus from the networks and independent television stations to the cable programmers and operators. The big issues in those cases were: Who is liable for a performance fee, and what is a reasonable fee for a license? Also, new digital technology and the Internet have raised a multitude of additional problems.

2. In 1993, Magistrate Judge Dolinger filed a 226-page Opinion and Order under the *Buffalo Broadcasting* decision setting the final blanket and per-program license fees through 1995 for local stations and O&Os ("owned and operated companies"). The per-program rate has since been reduced from 9 times to approximately 1.5 times the pro-rated blanket rate.

3. The full-length opinion in *Buffalo Broadcasting* makes repeated references to the lengthy litigation brought by CBS against ASCAP and BMI, whose actions haves frequently been challenged over the years, including antitrust inquiries initiated by the United States government, resulting in different consent decrees. See *United States v. ASCAP,* 1940–43 Trade Cas. (CCH) 56,104 (SDNY 1941); *United States v. BMI,* 1940–43 Trade Cas. (CCH) 56,098 (SDNY 1941); *United States v. ASCAP,* 1950–51 Trade Cas. (CCH) 62,595 (SDNY 1950); and *United States v. BMI,* 1966 Trade Cas. (CCH) 71,941 (SDNY 1966).

4. The court in its *Buffalo Broadcasting* decision discussed at several points a nondramatic performing right. In a footnote, the court explained this right as follows: A non-dramatic performing right is the right to perform a musical composition

other than in a dramatic performance, which the ASCAP blanket license defines as "a performance of a musical composition on a television program in which there is a definite plot depicted by action and where the performance of the musical composition is woven into and carries forward the plot and its accompanying action." See 3 *Nimmer on Copyright* 10.10[E] (1984).

5. The court in *Buffalo Broadcasting* noted limitations on the per-program license as follows:

The program license is not an alternative means of obtaining performing rights to individual compositions since it permits the licensee to use all compositions in the repertory of the licensor for an individual program. Its use would not afford a station a choice among competitive prices of performing rights for individual compositions. Nevertheless, to whatever extent it is available, it is an alternative means of obtaining performing rights needed to broadcast one program. Moreover, the program license, if available, may facilitate the stations' efforts to pursue direct licensing and source licensing, as we discuss later in the text. In any event, the parties joined issue as to whether it is a realistically available alternative, the District Court ruled on the issue, and we review that ruling.

7.7.2 Split Licensing

In a business such as cable TV, in which programming passes through more than one conduit, the performing rights societies have tried repeatedly to collect license fees at each stage. Just as regularly, they have been turned down. For example, Turner Broadcasting System was successful in arguing that ASCAP's refusal to issue a "through-to-the-viewer" license to WTBS was in violation of the 1950 Consent Decree. See *United States v. American Society of Composers, Authors and Publishers/Application of Turner Broadcasting System, Inc.* 782 F. Supp 778 (S.D.N.Y 1991), aff'd, 956 F.2d 21 (2d Cir.), *cert. denied,* 112 S.Ct. 1950 (1992). A similar result was reached in the following case.

U.S. v. ASCAP, In re Fox Broadcasting Co., 870 F. Supp. 1211 (SDNY 1995).

CONNER, D. J.

[The then-fledgling Fox Network distributed programming via satellite to 8 stations owned and operated by Fox ("O&O's," in industry parlance) and 134 affiliates, who, in turn, transmitted it to their audiences.]

[When] Fox commenced operations . . . ASCAP treated Fox's programs in the same way that it handled syndicated programming—by licensing the programming at the local station level pursuant to the interim fee arrangement in place at that time for the local stations. In late 1991, ASCAP [demanded] that Fox [obtain] a license for the transmission of its programs to the Fox [Network] stations . . .

[T]herefore, Fox filed this application, seeking a determination of whether ASCAP could require it to obtain a license from the transmission of its programs to its affiliates and O&Os . . .

We hold that ASCAP is not entitled to collect a fee from Fox for the transmission of Fox's programs to its affiliates, and that, even if it were, the reasonable retrospective fee would be $0. The music performances in Fox's programming were included in the license fees set for the local stations through the end of 1995, and ASCAP may not be paid two license fees for one broadcast of a musical performance to the viewing audience. Prospectively, Fox may indeed be a "network" that ASCAP should license on a through-to-the-viewer basis. If ASCAP wishes to license Fox as it does ABC, NBC and CBS, however, it must exclude revenue from Fox programs from the total revenues used to calculate the license fees collected from the local stations in order to reflect the fact that the Fox programs will no longer be licensed at the local level. . . .

It has long been recognized that ASCAP may not "split" rights in order to collect more than one license fee for any one use of the music in its repertory. This prohibition is apparent in several provisions of the Consent Decree and in the case law applying the Decree.

In 1948, the Court first indicated that collecting fees at more than one level for particular music use was forbidden. In *Alden-Rochelle, Inc. v. American Society of Composers, Authors and Publishers,* 80 F. Supp. 888, *as amended,* 80 F. Supp. 900 (S.D.N.Y 1948), the Court held that ASCAP's practices in licensing music use in motion pictures violated the anti-trust laws. . . .

Although ASCAP has collected its license fees for the broadcast of Fox's programs from the local stations from Fox's inception in 1986, and will continue to do so through December 31, 1995, ASCAP, Fox and Fox's local stations are, of course, free to restructure the terms of their relationship for license terms beginning in January 1996. Indeed, we believe that ASCAP is correct in its argument that Fox should be licensed on a through-to-the-viewer basis as ABC, NBC and CBS are. In practical terms, Fox does present itself to the public as a fourth network, and its revenues are substantial. Every week, it distributes a substantial amount of programming, clearly identified to the viewing public as Fox programming, to approximately 142 local television stations. . . .

7.8 SAMPLING

Many records embody digital samples of other recordings that require licenses from both the owner of the sound recording that is be utilized and the owner of the musical composition. When a license for use of the song being sampled is not secured before the release, the results can be disastrous as is seen in the *Grand Upright* case, the classic expression in the area:

Grand Upright Music, Ltd. v. Warner Bros. Records, Inc., 780 F. Supp. 182 (U.S.D.C., SDNY 1991).

KEVIN THOMAS DUFFY, DISTRICT JUDGE

"Thou shalt not steal" [footnote omitted] has been an admonition followed since the dawn of civilization. Unfortunately, in the modern world of business this admonition is not always followed. Indeed, the defendants in this action for copyright infringement would have this court believe that stealing is rampant in the music business and, for that reason, their conduct here should be excused. The conduct of the defendants herein, however, violates not only the Seventh Commandment, but also the copyright laws of this country.

This proceeding was instituted by Order To Show Cause to obtain a preliminary injunction against the defendants for the improper and unlicensed use of a composition "Alone Again (Naturally)" written and performed on records by Raymond "Gilbert" O'Sullivan. Defendants admit "that the Biz Markie album 'I Need A Haircut' embodies the rap recording 'Alone Again' which uses three words from 'Alone Again (Naturally)' composed by Gilbert O'Sullivan and a portion of the music taken from the O'Sullivan recording." . . .

Each defendant who testified knew that it is necessary to obtain a license—sometimes called a "clearance"—from the holder of a valid copyright before using the copyrighted work in another piece. Warner Bros. Records, Inc. had a department set up specifically to obtain such clearances. WEA International, Inc. knew it had to obtain "consents, permissions or clearances." . . . Cold Chillin' Records, Inc. knew that such clearances were necessary.

Clearly, the attorneys representing Biz Markie and acting on his behalf also knew of this obligation. Biz Markie's attorneys sent copies of an August 16 letter, addressed to counsel for Cold Chillin' Records, Inc., to the other defendants. That letter contains the following:

In light of the fact that Cold Chillin' knew that other sample clearance requests were pending at that time, it follows that Cold Chillin' should have known that similar denials of permission by rights holders of other samples used on the album and single might be forthcoming, for which similar action would have been appropriate. Nevertheless, instead of continuing to communicate with our client and us and otherwise cooperating to ensure that all rights were secured prior to release of the album and single, as it did in the situation involving the Eagles samples, Cold Chillin' unilaterally elected to release the album and single, perhaps with the thought that it would look to Biz for resolution of any problems relating to sampling rights, or the failure to secure such rights, that may arise in the future.

Consequently, if any legal action arises in connection with the samples in question, such action will not arise due to the fact that Biz used the samples in his recorded compositions, but rather, due to the fact that Cold Chillin' released such material prior to the appropriate consents being secured in connection with such samples.

From all of the evidence produced in the hearing, it is clear that the defendants knew that they were violating the plaintiff's rights as well as the rights of others. Their only aim was to sell thousands upon thousands of records. [Footnote omitted.] This callous disregard for the law and for the rights of others requires not only the preliminary injunction sought by the plaintiff but also sterner measures.

The argument suggested by the defendants that they should be excused because others in the "rap music" business are also engaged in illegal activity is totally specious. The mere statement of the argument is its own refutation.

The application for the preliminary injunction is granted. . . . This matter is respectfully referred to the United States Attorney for the Southern District of New York for consideration of prosecution of these defendants under 17 U.S.C. 506(a) and 18 U.S.C. 2319.

The resolution of any issue left open in this civil matter should have no bearing on the potential criminal liability in the unique circumstances presented here.

Newton v. Diamond, 349 F.3d 591 (9th Cir. 2003)

SCHROEDER, CHIEF JUDGE

This appeal raises the difficult and important issue of whether the incorporation of a short segment of a musical recording into a new musical recording, i.e., the practice of "sampling," requires a license to use both the performance and the composition of the original recording. The particular sample in this case consists of a six-second, three-note segment of a performance of one of his own compositions by plaintiff, and accomplished jazz flutist, James W. Newton. The defendants, the performers who did the sampling, are the members of the musical group Beastie Boys. They obtained a license to sample the sound recording of Newton's copyrighted performance, but they did not obtain a license to use Newton's underlying composition, which is also copyrighted.

The district court granted summary judgment to the defendants. In a scholarly opinion, it held that no license to the underlying composition was required because, as a matter of law, the notes in question—C—D flat—C, over a held C note—lacked sufficient originality to merit copyright protection. The district court also held that even if the sampled segment of the composition were original, Beastie Boys' use was de minimis and therefore not actionable. We affirm on the ground that the use was de minimis.

Background and Procedural History

The plaintiff and appellant in this case, James W. Newton, is an accomplished avant-garde jazz flutist and composer. In 1978, he composed the song "Choir," a piece for flute and voice intended to incorporate elements of African-American gospel music, Japanese ceremonial court music, traditional African music, and classical music, among others. According to Newton, the song was inspired by his earliest memory of music, watching four women singing in a church in rural Arkansas. In 1981, Newton performed and recorded "Choir" and licensed all rights in the sound recording to ECM Records for $5000. The license covered only the sound recording, and it is undisputed that Newton retained all rights to the composition of "Choir." Sound recordings and their underlying compositions are separate works with their own distinct copyrights. 17 U.S.C. § 102(a)(2), (7).

The defendants and appellees include the members of the rap and hip-hop group Beastie Boys, and their business associates. In 1992, Beastie Boys obtained a license from ECM Records to use portions of the sound recording of "Choir" in various renditions of their song "Pass the Mic" in exchange for a one-time fee of $ 1000. Beastie Boys did not obtain a license from Newton to use the underlying composition.

The portion of the composition at issue consists of three notes, C—D flat—C, sung over a background C note played on the flute. When played on the sound recording licensed by Beastie Boys, the segment lasts for approximately six seconds. The score to "Choir" also indicates that the entire song should be played in a "largo/senza-misura" tempo, meaning "slowly/without-measure." Apart from an instruction that the performer sing into the flute and finger simultaneously, the score is not further orchestrated.

The dispute between Newton and Beastie Boys centers around the copyright implications of the practice of sampling, a practice now common to many types of popular music. Sampling entails the incorporation of short segments of prior sound recordings into new recordings. The practice originated in Jamaica in the 1960s, when disc jockeys (DJs) used portable sound systems to mix segments of prior recordings into new mixes, which they would overlay with chanted or 'scatted' vocals. Sampling migrated to the United States and developed throughout the 1970s, using the analog technologies of the time. The digital sampling involved here developed in the early 1980s with the advent of digital synthesizers having MIDI (Musical Instrument Digital Interface) keyboard controls. These digital instruments allowed artists digitally to manipulate and combine sampled sounds, expanding the range of possibilities for the use of pre-recorded music. Whereas analog devices limited artists to "scratching" vinyl records and "cutting" back and forth between different sound recordings, digital technology allowed artists to slow down, speed up, combine, and otherwise alter the samples.

Pursuant to their license from ECM Records, Beastie Boys digitally sampled the opening six seconds of Newton's sound recording of "Choir." Beastie Boys repeated or "looped" this six-second sample as a background element throughout "Pass the Mic," so that it appears over forty times in various renditions of the song. In addition to the version of "Pass the Mic" released on their 1992 album, "Check Your Head," Beastie Boys included the "Choir" sample in two remixes, "Dub the Mic" and "Pass the Mic (Pt. 2, Skills to Pay the Bills)." It is unclear whether the sample was altered or manipulated, though Beastie Boys' sound engineer stated that alterations of tone, pitch, and rhythm are commonplace, and Newton maintains that the pitch was lowered slightly.

Newton filed the instant action in federal court on May 9, 2000, alleging violations of his copyright in the underlying composition. . . . The district court . . . granted summary judgment in favor of Beastie Boys on the copyright claims on May 21, 2002. The district court held that the three-note segment of the "Choir" composition could not be copyrighted because, as a matter of law, it lacked the requisite originality. The court also concluded that even if the segment were copyrightable, Beastie Boys' use of the work was de minimis and therefore not actionable. Newton appealed.

Whether Defendants' Use was De Minimis

We may affirm the grant of summary judgment on any basis supported by the record and need not reach each ground relied upon by the district court. Assuming that the sampled segment of the composition was sufficiently original to merit copyright protection, we nevertheless affirm on the ground that Beastie Boys' use was de minimis and therefore not actionable.

For an unauthorized use of a copyrighted work to be actionable, there must be substantial similarity between the plaintiff's and the defendants' works. This means that even where the fact of copying is conceded, no legal consequences will follow from that fact unless the copying is substantial. The principle that trivial copying does not constitute actionable infringement has long been a part of copyright law. Indeed, as Judge Learned Hand observed over 80 years ago: "Even where there is some copying, that fact is not conclusive of infringement. Some copying is permitted. In addition to copying, it must be shown that this has been done to an unfair extent." This principle reflects the legal maxim, *de minimis non curat lex* (often rendered as, "the law does not concern itself with trifles").

The leading case on de minimis infringement in our circuit is *Fisher v. Dees, 794 F.2d 432 (9th Cir. 1986),* where we observed that a use is de minimis only if the average audience would not recognize the appropriation. This observation reflects the relationship between the de minimis maxim and the general test for substantial similarity, which also looks to the response of the average audience, or ordinary observer, to determine whether a use is infringing. To say that a use is de minimis because no audience would recognize the appropriation is thus to say that the works are not substantially similar.

On the facts of *Fisher,* this court rejected the de minimis defense because the copying was substantial: the defendant had appropriated the main theme and lyrics of the plaintiff's song, both of which were easily recognizable in the defendant's parody. Specifically, the defendant copied six of the thirty-eight bars to the 1950s standard, "When Sunny Gets Blue," to make the parody, "When Sonny Sniffs Glue," and paralleled the original lyrics with only minor variations. However, despite the works' substantial similarities, we held that the use was nevertheless non-infringing because, as a parody, it was "fair use" under

17 U.S.C. § 107. We explained that the defendant's successful fair use defense precluded a finding that the use was insubstantial or unrecognizable because "the parodist must appropriate a substantial enough portion of [the original] to evoke recognition."

This case involves not only use of a composition, as was the case in *Fisher*, but also use of a sound recording of a performance of that composition. Because the defendants licensed the sound recording, our inquiry is confined to whether the unauthorized use of the composition itself was substantial enough to sustain an infringement claim. Therefore, we may consider only Beastie Boys' appropriation of the song's compositional elements and must remove from consideration all the elements unique to Newton's performance. Stated another way, we must "filter out" the licensed elements of the sound recording to get down to the unlicensed elements of the composition, as the composition is the sole basis for Newton's infringement claim.

In filtering out the unique performance elements from consideration, and separating them from those found in the composition, we find substantial assistance in the testimony of Newton's own experts. His experts reveal the extent to which the sound recording of "Choir" is the product of Newton's highly developed performance techniques, rather than the result of a generic rendition of the composition. As a general matter, according to Newton's expert Dr. Christopher Dobrian, "the contribution of the performer is often so great that s/he in fact provides as much musical content as the composer." This is particularly true with works like "Choir," given the nature of jazz performance and the minimal scoring of the composition. Indeed, as Newton's expert Dr. Oliver Wilson explained:

The copyrighted score of "Choir," as is the custom in scores written in the jazz tradition, does not contain indications for all of the musical subtleties that it is assumed the performer-composer of the work will make in the work's performance. The function of the score is more mnemonic in intention than prescriptive.

And it is clear that Newton goes beyond the score in his performance. For example, Dr. Dobrian declared that "Mr. Newton blows and sings in such a way as to emphasize the upper partials of the flute's complex harmonic tone, [although] such a modification of tone color is not explicitly requested in the score." More generally, Dr. Wilson explained Newton's performance technique as follows:

The Newton technique produces a musical event in which the component sounds resulting from the simultaneous singing of one or more pitches and the interaction of this pitch or pitches with the various components of the multiphonic array of pitches produced on the flute create a relatively dense cluster of pitches and ambient sounds that sometimes change over time.

Whatever copyright interest Newton obtained in this "dense cluster of pitches and ambient sounds," he licensed that interest to ECM

Records over twenty years ago, and ECM Records in turn licensed that interest to Beastie Boys. Thus, regardless of whether the average audience might recognize "the Newton technique" at work in the sampled sound recording, those performance elements are beyond consideration in Newton's claim for infringement of his copyright in the underlying composition. Having licensed away his interest in the recording of his performance, Newton's only claim is for a violation of his rights in the three-note sequence transcribed in the composition.

Once we have isolated the basis of Newton's infringement action—the "Choir" composition, devoid of the unique performance elements found only in the sound recording—we turn to the nub of our inquiry: whether Beastie Boys' unauthorized use of the composition, as opposed to their authorized use of the sound recording, was substantial enough to sustain an infringement action. In answering that question, we must distinguish between the degree and the substantiality of the works' similarity. The practice of music sampling will often present cases where the degree of similarity is high. Indeed, unless the sample has been altered or digitally manipulated, it will be identical to the original. Yet as Nimmer explains, "[if] the similarity is only as to nonessential matters, then a finding of no substantial similarity should result." 4 Nimmer § 13.03[A][2], at 13–48. This reflects the principle that the substantiality requirement applies throughout the law of copyright, including cases of music sampling, even where there is a high degree of similarity.

The high degree but limited scope of similarity between the works here place Newton's claim for infringement into the class of cases that allege what Nimmer refers to as "fragmented literal similarity." 4 Nimmer § 13.03[A][2], at 13–45. Fragmented literal similarity exists where the defendant copies a portion of the plaintiff's work exactly or nearly exactly, without appropriating the work's overall essence or structure. Because the degree of similarity is high in such cases, the dispositive question is whether the similarity goes to trivial or substantial elements. The substantiality of the similarity is measured by considering the qualitative and quantitative significance of the copied portion in relation to the plaintiff's work as a whole. This focus on the sample's relation to the plaintiff's work as a whole embodies the fundamental question in any infringement action, as expressed more than 150 years ago by Justice Story: whether "so much is taken that the value of the original is sensibly diminished, or the labors of the original author are substantially to an injurious extent appropriated by another." *Folsom v. Marsh, 9 F. Cas. 342, 348, F. Cas. No. 4901 (C.C. Mass. 1841)* (No. 4901). Courts also focus on the relationship to the plaintiff's work because a contrary rule that measured the significance of the copied segment in the defendant's work would allow an unscrupulous defendant to copy large or qualitatively significant portions of another's work and escape liability by burying them beneath non-infringing material in the defendant's own work, even where the average audience might recognize the appropriation.

Thus, as the district court properly concluded, the fact that Beastie Boys "looped" the sample throughout "Pass the Mic" is irrelevant in weighing the sample's qualitative and quantitative significance.

When viewed in relation to Newton's composition as a whole, the sampled portion is neither quantitatively nor qualitatively significant. Quantitatively, the three-note sequence appears only once in Newton's composition. It is difficult to measure the precise relationship between this segment and the composition as a whole, because the score calls for between 180 and 270 seconds of improvisation. When played, however, the segment lasts six seconds and is roughly two percent of the four-and-a-half-minute "Choir" sound recording licensed by Beastie Boys. Qualitatively, this section of the composition is no more significant than any other section. Indeed, with the exception of two notes, the entirety of the scored portions of "Choir" consist of notes separated by whole- and half-steps from their neighbors; the remainder of the composition calls for sections of improvisation that range between 90 and 180 seconds in length. Although the sampled section may be representative of the scored portions of the composition, Newton has failed to offer any evidence as to this section's particular significance in the composition as a whole. Instead, his experts emphasize the significance of Newton's performance, the unique elements of which Beastie Boys properly licensed.

Yet Newton maintains that the testimony of his experts creates a genuine issue of material fact on the substantiality of the copying. To the extent the expert testimony is relevant, it is not helpful to Newton. On the key question of whether the sample is quantitatively or qualitatively significant in relation to the composition as a whole, his experts are either silent or fail to distinguish between the sound recording, which was licensed, and the composition, which was not. Moreover, their testimony on the composition does not contain anything from which a reasonable jury could infer the segment's significance in relation to the composition as a whole: rather, Dr. Dobrian described the three-note sequence at issue as "a simple 'neighboring tone' figure." The district court cited two pieces by Gyorgy Ligeti and Jacob Druckman employing similar figures. This evidence is consistent with the opinion of Beastie Boys' expert, Dr. Lawrence Ferrara, who stated that the sampled excerpt from the "Choir" composition "is merely a common, trite, and generic three-note sequence, which lacks any distinct melodic, harmonic, rhythmic or structural elements." Dr. Ferrara also described the sequence as "a common building block tool" used over and over again by major composers in the 20th century, particularly the '60s and '70s, just prior to James Newton's usage."

Having failed to demonstrate any quantitative or qualitative significance of the sample in the "Choir" composition as a whole, Newton is in a weak position to argue that the similarities between the works are substantial, or that an average audience would recognize the appropriation. In this respect, the minimal scoring of the "Choir" composition bears emphasis, as does the relative simplicity of the relevant portion of the composition. On the undisputed facts of this case, we conclude that an average audience would not discern Newton's hand as a composer, apart from his talent as a performer, from Beastie Boys' use of the sample. The works are not substantially similar: Beastie Boys' use of the "Choir" composition was de minimis. There is no genuine issue of material fact, and the grant of summary judgment was appropriate.

Conclusion

Because Beastie Boys' use of the sound recording was authorized, the sole basis of Newton's infringement action is his remaining copyright interest in the "Choir" composition. We hold today that Beastie Boys' use of a brief segment of that composition, consisting of three notes separated by a half-step over a background C note, is not sufficient to sustain a claim for copyright infringement. We affirm the district court's grant of summary judgment on the ground that Beastie Boys' use of the composition was de minimis and therefore not actionable.
AFFIRMED

GRABER, CIRCUIT JUDGE, DISSENTING:

I respectfully dissent. The majority has laid out correctly the legal principles that apply in this case, and I agree with the majority's assumption that the sampled portion of "Choir" qualifies as "original" and therefore is copyrightable. However, on the record before us, a jury reasonably could find that Beastie Boys' use of the sampled material was not de minimis. Therefore, summary judgment is inappropriate.

As the majority observes, a use is de minimis only if an average audience would not recognize the appropriation. The majority is correct that James Newton's considerable skill adds many recognizable features to the performance sampled by Beastie Boys. Even after those features are "filtered out," however, the composition, standing alone, is distinctive enough for a jury reasonably to conclude that an average audience would recognize the appropriation of the sampled segment and that Beastie Boys' use was therefore not de minimis.

Newton has presented evidence that the compositional elements of "Choir" are so compositionally distinct that a reasonable listener would recognize the sampled segment even if it were performed by the featured flautist of a middle school orchestra. It is useful to begin by observing that the majority's repeated references to the sampled segment of "Choir" as a "3-note sequence" are overly simplified. The sampled segment is actually a three-note sequence sung above a fingered held C note, for a total of four separate tones. Even passages with relatively few notes may be qualitatively significant. The opening melody of Beethoven's Fifth Symphony is relatively simple and features only four notes, but it certainly is compositionally distinctive and recognizable.

The majority is simply mistaken in its assertion that Newton's experts did not present evidence of the qualitative value of the compositional elements of the sampled material sufficient to survive summary judgment. The majority is similarly mistaken when it says that Newton's experts failed to distinguish between the sound recording and the composition. To the contrary, Newton presented considerable expert evidence that the composition *alone* is distinctive and recognizable.

First, Newton offered a letter from Professor Olly Wilson of the University of California at Berkeley. Professor Wilson acknowledges that much of the distinctiveness of the sampled material is due to Newton's performance and that the copyrighted score does not fully convey the quality of the piece as performed. Nevertheless, Professor Wilson concludes that the score:

> . . . clearly indicates that the performer will simultaneously sing and finger specific pitches, gives a sense of the rhythm of the piece, and also provides the general structure of this section of the piece. Hence, in my opinion, the digital sample of the performance . . . is clearly a realization of the musical score filed with the copyright office.

Second, Newton presented a letter from Professor Christopher Dobrian of the University of California, Irvine. The majority deals with Professor Dobrian's evidence by stating: "Dr. Dobrian described the three-note sequence at issue as 'a simple, "neighboring tone" figure.'" As the passage quoted below demonstrates, the majority fundamentally misreads Professor Dobrian's statement by taking it out of context; in the process the majority reverses his intended meaning. Professor Dobrian actually concludes:

> Applying traditional analysis to this brief excerpt from Newton's "Choir"—i.e., focusing solely on the notated pitches—a theorist could conclude (erroneously, in my opinion) that the excerpt contains an insignificant amount of information because it contains a simple "neighboring-tone" figure: C to D-flat and back to C. . . . If, on the other hand, one considers the special playing technique *described in the score* (holding one fingered note constant while singing the other pitches) and the resultant complex, expressive effect that results, it is clear that the "unique expression" of this excerpt is not solely in the pitch choices, but is actually in those particular pitches performed in that particular way on that instrument. These components in this particular combination are not found anywhere else in the notated music literature, and they are *unique and distinctive* in their sonic/musical result. (Emphasis added.)

It is important to note that Professor Dobrian is *not* talking about Newton's performance of the sampled portion. Rather, he is speaking of the distinctiveness *of the underlying composition*. The "playing technique" is not a matter of personal performance, but is a built-in feature of the score itself. In essence, Dobrian is stating that *any* flautist's performance of the sampled segment would be distinctive and recognizable, because the score itself is distinctive and recognizable.

The majority, then, misreads the record when it states that Newton failed to offer evidence that the sampled material is qualitatively significant. In fact, Newton presented evidence, as described above, to show that an average and reasonable listener would recognize Beastie Boys' appropriation of the *composition* of the sampled material.

Because Newton has presented evidence establishing that reasonable ears differ over the qualitative significance of the composition of the sampled material, summary judgment is inappropriate in this case. Newton should be allowed to present his claims of infringement to a jury. I therefore dissent from the majority's conclusion to the contrary.

Bridgeport Music v. Dimension Films, 401 F.3d 647 (6th Cir. 2004)

Guy, jr., Circuit Judge

Plaintiffs, Bridgeport Music, Inc., Westbound Records, Inc., Southfield Music, Inc., and Nine Records, Inc., appeal from several of the district court's findings with respect to the copyright infringement claims asserted against No Limit Films. This action arises out of the use of a sample from the composition and sound recording "Get Off Your Ass and Jam" ("Get Off") in the rap song "100 Miles and Runnin'" ("100 Miles"), which was included in the sound track of the movie *I Got the Hook Up* (*Hook Up*). Specifically, Westbound appeals from the district court's decision to grant summary judgment to defendant on the grounds that the alleged infringement was *de minimis* and therefore not actionable. Bridgeport, while not appealing from the summary judgment order, challenges instead the denial of its motion to amend the complaint to assert new claims of infringement based on a different song included in the sound track of *Hook Up*. Finally, Bridgeport, Southfield, and Nine Records appeal from the decision to award attorney fees and costs totaling $41,813.30 to No Limit Films under *17 U.S.C. § 505*. For the reasons that follow, we reverse the district court's grant of summary judgment to No Limit on Westbound's claim of infringement of its sound recording copyright, but affirm the decision of the district court as to the award of attorney fees and the denial of Bridgeport's motion to amend.

I

The claims at issue in this appeal were originally asserted in an action filed on May 4, 2001, by the related entities Bridgeport Music, Southfield Music, Westbound Records, and Nine Records, alleging nearly 500 counts against approximately 800 defendants for copyright infringement and various state law claims relating to the use of samples without permission in new rap recordings. In August 2001, the district court severed that original complaint into 476 separate actions, this being one of them, based on the allegedly infringing work and ordered that amended complaints be filed.

The claims in this case were brought by all four plaintiffs: Bridgeport and Southfield, which are in the business of music publishing and exploiting musical composition copyrights, and Westbound

Records and Nine Records, which are in the business of recording and distributing sound recordings. It was conceded at the time of summary judgment, however, that neither Southfield Music nor Nine Records had any ownership interest in the copyrights at issue in this case. As a result, the district court ordered that they be jointly and severally liable for 10% of the attorney fees and costs awarded to No Limit Films.

Bridgeport and Westbound claim to own the musical composition and sound recording copyrights in "Get Off Your Ass and Jam" by George Clinton, Jr. and the Funkadelics. We assume, as did the district court, that plaintiffs would be able to establish ownership in the copyrights they claim. There seems to be no dispute either that "Get Off" was digitally sampled or that the recording "100 Miles" was included on the sound track of *I Got the Hook Up*. Defendant No Limit Films, in conjunction with Priority Records, released the movie to theaters on May 27, 1998. The movie was apparently also released on VHS, DVD, and cable television. Fatal to Bridgeport's claims of infringement was the Release and Agreement it entered into with two of the original owners of the composition "100 Miles," Ruthless Attack Muzick (RAM) and Dollarz N Sense Music (DNSM), in December 1998, granting a sample use license to RAM, DNSM, and their licensees. Finding that No Limit Films had previously been granted an oral synchronization license to use the composition "100 Miles" in the sound track of *Hook Up*, the district court concluded Bridgeport's claims against No Limit Films were barred by the unambiguous terms of the Release and Agreement. Although Bridgeport does not appeal from this determination, it is relevant to the district court's later decision to award attorney fees to No Limit Films.

Westbound's claims are for infringement of the sound recording "Get Off." Because defendant does not deny it, we assume that the sound track of *Hook Up* used portions of "100 Miles" that included the allegedly infringing sample from "Get Off." The recording "Get Off" opens with a three-note combination solo guitar "riff" that lasts four seconds. According to one of plaintiffs' experts, Randy Kling, the recording "100 Miles" contains a sample from that guitar solo. Specifically, a two-second sample from the guitar solo was copied, the pitch was lowered, and the copied piece was "looped" and extended to 16 beats. Kling states that this sample appears in the sound recording "100 Miles" in five places; specifically, at 0:49, 1:52, 2:29, 3:20 and 3:46. By the district court's estimation, each looped segment lasted approximately 7 seconds. As for the segment copied from "Get Off," the district court described it as follows:

The portion of the song at issue here is an arpeggiated chord—that is, three notes that, if struck together, comprise a chord but instead are played one at a time in very quick succession—that is repeated several times at the opening of "Get Off." The arpeggiated chord is played on an unaccompanied electric guitar. The rapidity of the notes and the way they are played produce a high-pitched, whirling sound that captures the listener's attention and creates anticipation of what is to follow.

No Limit Films moved for summary judgment, arguing (1) that the sample was not protected by copyright law because it was not "original"; and (2) that the sample was legally insubstantial and therefore does not amount to actionable copying under copyright law.

Mindful of the limited number of notes and chords available to composers, the district court explained that the question turned not on the originality of the chord but, rather, on "the use of and the aural effect produced by the way the notes and the chord are played, especially here where copying of the sound recording is at issue." The district court found, after carefully listening to the recording of "Get Off," "that a jury could reasonably conclude that the way the arpeggiated chord is used and memorialized in the 'Get Off' sound recording is original and creative and therefore entitled to copyright protection." No Limit Films does not appeal from this determination.

Turning then to the question of *de minimis* copying in the context of digital sampling, the district court concluded that, whether the sampling is examined under a qualitative/quantitative *de minimis* analysis or under the so-called "fragmented literal similarity" test, the sampling in this case did not "rise to the level of a legally cognizable appropriation." Westbound argues that the district court erred both in its articulation of the applicable standards and its determination that there was no genuine issue of fact precluding summary judgment on this issue.

On October 11, 2002, the district court granted summary judgment to No Limit Films on the claims of Bridgeport and Westbound; dismissed with prejudice the claims of Southfield and Nine Records; denied as moot the motion of Bridgeport and Westbound for partial summary judgment on the issue of copyright ownership; and entered final judgment accordingly. Bridgeport and Westbound appealed. The facts relevant to the earlier denial of Bridgeport's motion to amend the complaint will be discussed below. No Limit Films filed a post-judgment motion for attorney fees and costs, which the district court granted for the reasons set forth in its memorandum opinion and order of April 24, 2003. Bridgeport, Southfield Music, and Nine Records appealed from that award.

II

In granting summary judgment to defendant, the district court looked to general *de minimis* principles and emphasized the paucity of case law on the issue of whether digital sampling amounts to copyright infringement. Drawing on both the quantitative/qualitative and "fragmented literal similarity" approaches, the district court found the *de minimis* analysis was a derivation of the substantial similarity element when a defendant claims that the literal copying of a small and insignificant portion of the copyrighted work should be allowed. After listening to the copied segment, the sample, and both songs, the district court found that no reasonable juror, even one familiar with the works of George Clinton, would recognize the source of the sample without having been told of its source. This finding, coupled with findings concerning the quantitatively small amount of copying involved and the lack of qualitative similarity between the works, led the district court to conclude that Westbound could not prevail on its claims for copyright infringement of the sound recording.

Westbound does not challenge the district court's characterization of either the segment copied from "Get Off" or the sample that appears in "100 Miles." Nor does Westbound argue that there is some genuine dispute as to any material fact concerning the nature of the protected material in the two works. The heart of Westbound's arguments is the claim that no substantial similarity or *de minimis* inquiry should be undertaken at all when the defendant has not disputed that it digitally sampled a copyrighted sound recording. We agree and accordingly must reverse the grant of summary judgment.

A. Digital Sampling of Copyrighted Sound Recordings

At the outset it is important to make clear the precise nature of our decision. Our conclusions are as follows:

1. The analysis that is appropriate for determining infringement of a musical composition copyright, is not the analysis that is to be applied to determine infringement of a sound recording. We address this issue only as it pertains to sound recording copyrights.
2. Since the district court decision essentially tracked the analysis that is made if a musical composition copyright were at issue, we depart from that analysis.

"In most copyright actions, the issue is whether the infringing work is substantially similar to the original work. . . . The scope of inquiry is much narrower when the work in question is a sound recording. The only issue is whether the actual sound recording has been used without authorization. Substantial similarity is not an issue. . . . " Bradley C. Rosen, Esq., 22 CAUSES OF ACTION § 12 (2d ed. 2003).

3. We would agree with the district court's analysis on the question of originality if the composition copyright had been at issue. Having concluded that the statute requires a different analysis for sound recording copyrights, however, we also find that the requirement of originality is met by the fixation of sounds in the master recording. Only an actual physical copy of a master recording will be exactly the same as the copyrighted sound recording. We assume that Westbound will be able to establish it has a copyright in the sound recording and that a digital sample from the copyrighted sound recording was used in this case.
4. This case involves "digital sampling" which is a term of art well understood by the parties to this litigation and the music industry in general. Accordingly, we adopt the definition commonly accepted within the industry.
5. Because of the court's limited technological knowledge in this specialized field, our opinion is limited to an instance of digital sampling of a sound recording protected by a valid copyright. If by analogy it is possible to extend our analysis to other forms of sampling, we leave it to others to do so.
6. Advances in technology coupled with the advent of the popularity of hip hop or rap music have made instances of digital sampling extremely common and have spawned a plethora of copyright disputes and litigation.

7. The music industry, as well as the courts, are best served if something approximating a bright-line test can be established. Not necessarily a "one size fits all" test, but one that, at least, adds clarity to what constitutes actionable infringement with regard to the digital sampling of copyrighted sound recordings.

B. Analysis

We do not set forth the arguments made by Westbound since our analysis differs somewhat from that offered by the plaintiff. Our analysis begins and largely ends with the applicable statute. *Section 114(a) of Title 17 of the United States Code* provides:

The exclusive rights of the owner of copyright in a sound recording are limited to the rights specified by clauses (1), (2), (3) and (6) of section 106, and do not include any right of performance under section 106(4).

Section 106 provides:

Subject to sections 107 through 122, the owner of copyright under this title has the exclusive rights to do and to authorize any of the following:

    (1) to reproduce the copyrighted work in copies or phonorecords;

    (2) to prepare derivative works based upon the copyrighted work;

    (3) to distribute copies or phonorecords of the copyrighted work to the public by sale or other transfer of ownership, or by rental, lease, or lending;

    (4) in the case of literary, musical, dramatic, and choreographic works, pantomimes, and motion pictures and other audiovisual works to perform the copyrighted work publicly;

    (5) in the case of literary, musical, dramatic, and choreographic works, pantomimes, and pictorial, graphic, or sculptural works, including the individual images of a motion picture or other audiovisual work, to display the copyrighted work publicly; and

    (6) in the case of sound recordings, to perform the copyrighted work publicly by means of a digital audio transmission.

Section 114(b) states:

(b) The exclusive right of the owner of copyright in a sound recording under clause (1) of section 106 is limited to the right to duplicate the sound recording in the form of phonorecords or copies that directly or indirectly recapture the actual sounds fixed in the recording. The exclusive right of the owner of copyright in a sound recording under clause (2) of section 106 is limited to the right to prepare a derivative work in which the actual sounds fixed in the sound recording are rearranged, remixed, or otherwise altered in sequence or quality. The exclusive rights of the owner of copyright in a sound recording under clauses (1) and (2) of section 106 do not extend to the making or duplication of another sound recording that consists entirely of an independent fixation of other sounds, even though such sounds imitate or simulate those in the copyrighted sound recording. The exclusive rights of the owner of copyright in a sound recording under clauses (1), (2), and (3) of section 106 do not apply to sound recordings included in educational television and radio programs (as defined in section 397 of title 47) distributed or transmitted by or through public broadcasting entities (as defined by section 118(g)): *Provided,* That copies or phonorecords of said programs are not commercially distributed by or through public broadcasting entities to the general public.

Before discussing what we believe to be the import of the above quoted provisions of the statute, a little history is necessary. The copyright laws attempt to strike a balance between protecting original works and stifling further creativity. The provisions, for example, for compulsory licensing make it possible for "creators" to enjoy the fruits of their creations, but not to fence them off from the world at large. *17 U.S.C. § 115*. Although musical compositions have always enjoyed copyright protection, it was not until 1971 that sound recordings were subject to a separate copyright. If one were to analogize to a book, it is not the book, *i.e.,* the paper and binding, that is copyrightable, but its contents. There are probably any number of reasons why the decision was made by Congress to treat a sound recording differently from a book even though both are the medium in which an original work is fixed rather than the creation itself. None the least of them certainly were advances in technology which made the "pirating" of sound recordings an easy task. The balance that was struck was to give sound recording copyright holders the exclusive right "to duplicate the sound recording in the form of phonorecords or copies that directly or indirectly recapture the actual sounds fixed in the recording." *17 U.S.C. § 114(b)*. This means that the world at large is free to imitate or simulate the creative work fixed in the recording so long as an actual copy of the sound recording itself is not made. That leads us directly to the issue in this case. If you cannot pirate the whole sound recording, can you "lift" or "sample" something less than the whole. Our answer to that question is in the negative.

Section 114(b) provides that "the exclusive right of the owner of copyright in a sound recording under clause (2) of section 106 is limited to the right to prepare a derivative work in which the actual sounds fixed in the sound recording are rearranged, remixed, or otherwise altered in sequence or quality." In other words, a sound recording owner has the exclusive right to "sample" his own recording. We find much to recommend this interpretation.

To begin with, there is ease of enforcement. Get a license or do not sample. We do not see this as stifling creativity in any significant way. It must be remembered that if an artist wants to incorporate a "riff" from another work in his or her recording, he is free to duplicate the sound of that "riff" in the studio. Second, the market will control the license price and keep it within bounds. The sound recording copyright holder cannot exact a license fee greater than what it would cost the person seeking the license to just duplicate the sample in the course of making the new recording. Third, sampling is never accidental. It is not like the case of a composer who has a melody in his head, perhaps not even realizing that the reason he hears this melody is that it is the work of another which he had heard before. When you sample a sound recording you know you are taking another's work product.

This analysis admittedly raises the question of why one should, without infringing, be able to take three notes from a musical composition, for example, but not three notes by way of sampling from a sound recording. Why is there no *de minimis* taking or why should substantial similarity not enter the equation. Our first answer to this question is what we have earlier indicated. We think this result is dictated by the applicable statute. Second, even when a small part of a sound recording is sampled, the part taken is something of value. No further proof of that is necessary than the fact that the producer of the record or the artist on the record intentionally sampled because it would (1) save costs, or (2) add something to the new recording, or (3) both. For the sound recording copyright holder, it is not the "song" but the sounds that are fixed in the medium of his choice. When those sounds are sampled they are taken directly from that fixed medium. It is a physical taking rather than an intellectual one.

This case also illustrates the kind of mental, musicological, and technological gymnastics that would have to be employed if one were to adopt a *de minimis* or substantial similarity analysis. The district judge did an excellent job of navigating these troubled waters, but not without dint of great effort. When one considers that he has 800 other cases all involving different samples from different songs, the value of a principled bright-line rule becomes apparent. We would want to emphasize, however, that considerations of judicial economy are not what drives this opinion. If any consideration of economy is involved it is that of the music industry. As this case and other companion cases make clear, it would appear to be cheaper to license than to litigate.

Since our holding arguably sets forth a new rule, several other observations are in order. First, although we followed no existing judicial precedent, we did not pull this interpretation out of thin air. Several law review and text writers, some of whom have been referenced in this opinion, have suggested that this is the proper interpretation of the copyright statute as it pertains to sound recordings. Since digital sampling has become so commonplace and rap music has become such a significant part of the record industry, it is not surprising that there are probably a hundred articles dealing with sampling and its ramifications. It is also not surprising that the viewpoint expressed in a number of these articles appears driven by whose ox is being gored. As is so often the case, where one stands depends on where one sits. For example, the sound recording copyright holders favor this interpretation as do the studio musicians and their labor organization. On the other hand, many of the hip hop artists may view this rule as stifling creativity. The record companies and performing artists are not all of one mind, however, since in many instances, today's sampler is tomorrow's samplee. The incidence of "live and let live" has been relatively high, which explains why so many instances of sampling go unprotested and why so many sampling controversies have been settled.

Second, to pursue further the subject of stifling creativity, many artists and record companies have sought licenses as a matter of course. Since there is no record of those instances of sampling that either go unnoticed or are ignored, one cannot come up with precise figures, but it is clear that a significant number of persons and companies have elected to go the licensing route. Also there is a large body of pre-1971 sound recordings that is not protected and is up for grabs as far as sampling is concerned. Additionally, just as many artists and companies choose to sample and take their chances, it is likely that will continue to be the case.

Third, the record industry, including the recording artists, has the ability and know-how to work out guidelines, including a fixed schedule of license fees, if they so choose.

Fourth, we realize we are announcing a new rule and because it is new, it should not play any role in the assessment of concepts such as "willful" or "intentional" in cases that are currently before the courts or had their genesis before this decision was announced.

Finally, and unfortunately, there is no Rosetta stone for the interpretation of the copyright statute. We have taken a "literal reading" approach. The legislative history is of little help because digital sampling wasn't being done in 1971. If this is not what Congress intended or is not what they would intend now, it is easy enough for the record industry, as they have done in the past, to go back to Congress for a clarification or change in the law. This is the best place for the change to be made, rather than in the courts, because as this case demonstrates, the court is never aware of much more than the tip of the iceberg. To properly sort out this type of problem with its complex technical and business overtones, one needs the type of investigative resources as well as the ability to hold hearings that is possessed by Congress.

These conclusions require us to reverse the entry of summary judgment on Westbound's claims against No Limit Films.

NOTES

Today, in most "sampling" situations the original music publisher of the underlying work that is being sampled settles its claim for copyright infringement by settling with the new song's publisher for a split of the copyright. Such a sample settlement agreement usually follows a quote process (which now almost always occurs before release) whereby the underlying publisher quotes (in most all cases) a percentage of the copyright (which can be 10% or 100% but is usually in the 25% to 50% range) for which the publisher will settle its claim and participate in the ownership, administration and income of a portion of the new song. The following are excerpts from such a sample settlement agreement to show the basic premise and structure of the settlement:

WHEREAS, "Composers" as designated on the annexed Schedule A wrote the musical composition designated as "New Composition" on the annexed Schedule A.

WHEREAS, the New Composition incorporates portions of the pre-existing musical composition designated as "Original Composition" on Schedule A, written by "Original Composer(s)" (as designated on Schedule A) and as part of this settlement the Original Composer(s) shall be deemed co-writers of the New Composition under the provisions set forth in paragraph 1.2., below;

WHEREAS, the New Composition is embodied on the LP Album described on the annexed Schedule A (the "Recording");

WHEREAS, Co-Publisher I and Co-Publisher II individually and collectively warrant and represent that their respective writer(s) have heretofore entered into an agreement with them pursuant to which Co-Publisher I and Co-Publisher II have exclusive administration in and to such writer(s)' right, title and interest in and to the New Composition, and

WHEREAS, Publisher warrants and represents that Original Composer(s) have heretofore entered into an agreement with Publisher pursuant to which Publisher has exclusive administration in and to Original Composer(s)' right, title and interest in and to the Original Composition and the New Composition.

NOW, THEREFORE, for and in consideration of the mutual covenants herein set forth, the parties hereby agree as follows:

1. Ownership of Copyright:

    1.1. The parties hereto shall jointly own the New Composition in the shares set forth on Schedule A, including all of the worldwide right, title and interest, the copyright, the right to copyright, and any and all renewal rights therein and thereto, for the full term of copyright and all extension and renewal terms in each and every country of the world. Nothing contained herein shall be deemed to grant to Co-Publisher I, Co-Publisher II or Composers any right, title or interest in or to the Original Composition. For the purposes of this paragraph 1.1., the term Composers shall exclude Original Composers.

    1.2. It is understood and agreed that all songwriter credits in respect of the New Composition shall be as set forth on Schedule A, however, an inadvertent failure to accord such credit shall not be deemed a breach of this agreement, provided such failure is prospectively cured.

2. Copyright Registration:

    2.1. The New Composition shall be registered for copyright in the names of each party hereto (to reflect each party's Respective Ownership Interest as set forth in Schedule A) in the Copyright Office of the United States of America. If the New Composition has heretofore been registered for copyright in the name of Co-Publisher I and Co-Publisher II, Co-Publisher I and Co-Publisher II shall simultaneously herewith execute and submit an assignment of the appropriate interest therein, in favor of Publisher (in the form annexed hereto as Exhibit "A") as may be necessary to conform record title in the copyright (i.e., title as shown in the records of the Copyright Office of the United States of America) with each party's Respective Ownership Interest.

    2.2. In the event that Co-Publisher I and Co-Publisher II fail to execute and deliver such assignment to Publisher within ten (10) business days following receipt of written notice (all references to "**notice**" in this Agreement are to notice in the manner prescribed in ¶11 below) from Publisher requesting same, Publisher shall have the right to do so in the name of Co-Publisher I and Co-Publisher II, as Co-Publisher I and Co-Publisher II's attorney-in-fact, such appointment being coupled with an interest and therefore irrevocable and will send a copy of such assignment to Co-Publisher I and Co-Publisher II.

3. Administration Rights:

    3.1. Except for print rights with respect to the entire Composition, which shall be non-exclusive to each party, each party shall each have the separate right in the United States and Canada to administer and exploit the New Composition, to print, publish, use and license the use of the New Composition, and to execute any and all licenses and agreements whatsoever affecting or respecting its respective share of the New Composition, including but not limited to licenses for mechanical reproduction, print uses, public performance and synchronization uses and subpublication, provided that (a) no such licenses or agreements shall be exclusive, (b) no mechanical license shall be issued by any party at less than the then current statutory rate (with reduced rates to be permitted, however, in any such licenses, for those types of sales or distributions for which music publishers customarily grant such reduced rates to non-affiliated record companies); provided, however, Co-Publisher I and Co-Publisher II hereby acknowledge and agree that Publisher's Respective Share of the New Composition shall under no circumstances be subject to or affected by any so-called "controlled composition" clause contained in any recording agreement for the services of Artist (as designated on Schedule A), (c) synchronization licenses, licenses for commercials and other such licenses, shall only be issued jointly by the parties (and approval may be withheld by any party in its sole discretion), (d) all licenses and agreements shall provide for all proceeds to be paid directly to each party in accordance with each party's Respective Share, as set forth in Schedule A, and (e) a true copy of each license or agreement issued by one party affecting any other party shall be promptly furnished to each other party. The administration rights outside of the United States and Canada are covered by ¶13.3. below.

3.2. Notwithstanding anything to the contrary herein, Artist (as defined on Schedule "A") shall have the right to create promotional synchronization videos (commonly known as "music videos") for MTV/VH1, embodying the Composition, without any additional consideration payable therefor, provided that such videos are not embodied in theatrical motion pictures, commercials, CD-Roms, CD Plus or DVD Discs and provided, that compensation is not received for the sale or licensing of such music videos, and provided that at such time said videos are exploited for payment, the appropriate license shall be filed and negotiated in good faith. Further notwithstanding anything to the contrary herein, Co-Publisher I and Co-Publisher II shall have the right to re-mix or re-edit the New Composition, provided that the interests of Publisher and Original Composer(s) in such versions shall not be diminished.

Chapter 8

SOUND RECORDINGS

8.1 DEVELOPMENT OF THE INDUSTRY

Thomas Edison, the inventor of the first recording and recorded music playing devices, could not have predicted the complexity of the record business as it developed. The content of early records featuring limited genres has expanded to seemingly limitless selections. The media have also evolved from the piano roll to digital distributions over the Internet. Not since the inception of the audio recording industry has there been such a shift in the technological and economic base of the business as exists right now. It is almost ironic that while there has been a steady deterioration of the physical goods based economy, both new music and technology have created amazing new opportunities for digitally recording, distributing and promoting music globally. The old order is dying while the new digitally based industry is growing at a seemingly simultaneous and symmetrical rate.

At the turn of the century, the record industry, dominated by two companies, the Victor Talking Machine Company (later to become RCA) and the Columbia Graphophone Company, found an enormous market for recordings of spoken words and classical and vaudeville show tunes. Although the growth of the record industry was tempered by the advent of radio in the 1920s and television in the late 1940s, by 1950 U.S. record sales were approximately $189 million. However, the arrival of the long-playing record, "hi-fi" and rock 'n roll caused a revolution. By the early 1960s, records had become a vast, mass-market phenomenon, which grew even larger with successive technological improvements: eight-track cartridges, audiocassettes, and eventually the repurchase of older favorite albums as well as new releases on CD. In 1980, record sales, which had enjoyed exponential growth from the 1950s through 1978, suddenly suffered an unprecedented decline in sales and profits. This result was partially attributable to competition for entertainment dollars from new media: video games, videocassettes, and cable television. That recession lasted approximately six years. Beginning in 1984, the record business enjoyed increased sales and profits, largely from sales of its superstar artists, such as Michael Jackson, R.E.M., U2 and Madonna together with the development of digital compact disc technology.

When rock first rolled in the mid-1950s, the record industry experienced the growth and a proliferation of small independent record labels that were able to record and market both rhythm and blues and rock and roll music. Such successful independent labels included Sam Phillips' Sun Records, Chess Records (Muddy Waters, Howlin' Wolf, and Chuck Berry), and Atlantic Records. Two other developments contributed to the strong development of the record business in the 50s: In 1955, Columbia Record Club emerged and major record labels began alternate distribution of their records through mail order. In 1957, the first stereo record was released. The modern-day record business may be said to have been launched in 1962 with the coming of the Beatles to America. For the next 15 years the industry experienced a great growth period. But, by 1999, the legitimate global record business was subject to massive pirate inroads, including illegal downloads, burning and bootlegging which amounted to approximately $38 billion per year.

Between 1962 and 2004 there was significant consolidation in the record business to the extent that today four multinational (major label) companies, each part of larger conglomerates, control and account for more than 90 percent of physical product sales of recorded music world wide. Those companies are: 1) America based Warner Music Group (consisting of Warner Bros. Records, Elektra Records, Atlantic Records, and affiliated labels); 2) British company EMI (consisting of Capitol EMI Records and Virgin Records); 3) Sony/BMG Music which formed from the merger of Japan based Sony Music, Inc. (including Sony and Epic Records, which was once part of the CBS empire purchased by Sony in 1989); and BMG Entertainment (Bertelsmann Music Group, including U.S. based Arista Records and J Records), part of the German-owned conglomerate Bertelsmann; and 4) Universal Music Group, a division of Universal Studios, Inc., which was acquired in 2000 by French conglomerate Vivendi which includes Universal, PolyGram (acquired from the Dutch conglomerate Philips) along with the Mercury, Island, A&M Geffen Records and Interscope Records. Of the approximately 60,331 albums released world wide in 2005, approximately 11,070 (18.4%) were released by the major labels.

While record companies are responsible for recording and promoting records, distribution companies are responsible for physically distributing records to the various retail outlets. While each major label is affiliated with a major distribution company owned by the same parent company, it is not axiomatic that a major label will be distributed by a co-owned distributor. The distributors act as a separate business and may distribute other major label titles. Into the 1970s, the record industry relied in large measure on a series of independent record distributors that acted as intermediaries between the record manufacturers and retailers. In the 1980s the independent distribution system began to break down as more and more independent labels such as Arista, Motown, and A&M left independent distribution in favor of distribution by one of the major distributors.

Consolidation in the record distribution business has been accompanied by a simultaneous movement among the majors to create or affiliate with independent record companies that find and develop new talent to feed the worldwide distribution networks that the major labels have established. In some cases, these affiliated labels begin as start-ups that nurture and develop young artists to a certain level beyond which they need the marketing and promotional expertise of the majors. In others cases, they were founded by established veterans with industry financing. Examples of successful independents include Priority, Matador, LaFace, Interscope, Maverick, Tommy Boy, Radioactive, Mammoth, and American. Many of these labels have been on the cutting edge of new music, and the desire to capitalize on this reputation has enticed the majors to purchase or to create strategic joint label and distribution alliances with these independents. Despite increasing consolidation within the industry, the nature of the record business continues to allow the independent record label to not only survive but to occasionally flourish. Of the approximately 60,331 albums released world wide in 2005, approximately 49,261 (81.6%) were released by independent labels.

Another significant development in the record business includes the development and growth of the music video as a promotion tool for the sale of records through MTV, VH-1, and other music lifestyle outlets. In addition, extended-length DVD concert and music documentary DVDs have established new sources of revenue and deals for the record companies, TV broadcasters, and artists through retail sales, pay and cable television licensing. The content of music lyrics became a significant legal issue beginning in the 1980s and continues on a number of fronts. The major labels in the record industry, pressed with the threat of potential legislation in several jurisdictions to require mandatory "stickering" of records with controversial lyric content, agreed upon a voluntary warning sticker policy. Lyric liability suits were brought in civil actions, largely by families of suicide victims who claimed that such deaths were incited or caused by lyrics to certain songs. Simultaneously, in criminal courts both recording and performing artists were accused of obscenity.

Digital technology has created as many challenges for the modern music business as it has opportunities. With the onset of digital "sampling" in the 1980s to illegal Internet downloads, home copying, first via blank cassettes, now via CD "rippers" and "burners" and "file sharing" over peer to peer exchange technologies, all of which cost the U.S. record industry billions of dollars each year. Legislation and legal action has been slow to respond as law and policy continue to chase technology. Until 1995, Section 107 of the Copyright Act did not include a performance right in sound recordings. That year, the Digital Performance in Sound Recordings Act was passed which provided an exclusive right with respect to interactive and subscription services which would give the listener the ability to select or to predict what would be broadcast. The Digital Millennium Copyright Act of 1998 provided for a compulsory license for other digital broadcast services of a non-interactive, non-predictable nature.

8.2 CONTRACTS IN THE RECORD INDUSTRY

8.2.1 Some Background Statistics

The break-even point for a record company's investment on sales is high and reflects the high-risk nature of the business. Although the cost of manufacturing a CD is low, the costs of recording, advertising, promotion, marketing and distribution remain very high. The investment in many recordings yields rare success. Of the approximately 11,070 new releases by the major labels in 2005, the average total sale was approximately 18,455 albums per title. Of the approximately 49,260 new releases by the independent labels in 2005, the average total sale was approximately 787 albums per title. While there is no manufacturing cost on the Internet, legal download sales are still a small part (though growing) of the income generated from recordings. An artist's career can be enhanced with the excitement of signing a record deal, but this is only an opportunity and the probability is that the artist will never release a second album with that record company. Physical albums sold at retail have steadily declined over the past years while digital download sales have increased. In 2004 and 2005 respectively, *Billboard* reported that 681,437,000 and 618,951,000 albums were sold world wide which represents a 9.2% decrease. However, *Billboard* also reported legal digital download singles (track) sales in 2004 and 2005 respectively at 142,594,000 and 352,655,000, which represents a 147.3% increase. These trends continued through the first months of 2006. Cassette tape, CD single and vinyl records sales are negligible.

8.2.2 Quick Economics

The remainder of this chapter is intended to make the reader aware of the basic economics and music industry customs that influence the structure and negotiation of recording contracts. There are thousands, perhaps millions, of artists who seek to enter into a recording agreement with a third-party company with hopes that, with a record company's investment of money and personnel, the artist will achieve the notoriety and translated sales of recorded products to provide the artist with a short term livelihood, long term career, and financial security. The job of identifying artists is primarily undertaken by artist and repertoire (A&R) representatives. These individuals research to find new talent using the Internet, local and regional community contacts, and their own resources to discover talent. Only officers of the record company have the authority to sign artists to what is usually an exclusive recording agreement.

Record companies provide funding, creative guidance, and administration services for the production of recordings. The label has consent or approval rights over the recording budget and elements, including the selection of the studio, producer, mixing and mastering engineers. The cost of a major label album for a new contemporary music artist ranges from $100,000 to $500,000. From this amount (recording "fund") the recording must be produced and any remaining balance will be "advanced" to the artist. The entire recording fund is typically subject to recoupment by the label. This means that the label will be entitled to repay itself the recording costs from any amount that is owed to the artist by the label as royalties.

In addition to the recording fund, a label will "advance" the costs of certain promotions, including independent (third party) radio promotion, financial support for a tour to the extent the income from the tour does not cover the tour costs ("deficit tour funding"), production of a promotional video (that also may be available for sale), and other items that are set forth in the recording agreement. The money advances for these promotions are, to some negotiated extent, recoupable as well. The result is that there is usually about $300,000 to $1,000,000 advanced to an artist's recoupable account. In the calculation of royalties, a general rule of thumb is that each royalty percentage point is worth about 10 cents. If the artist received a 15% royalty, this will translate to about $1.50 per album sold. Sales of singles, licensing of songs for use in compilations, movies, TV and other media as well as download sales would generate additional revenue from which the label would be entitled to recoup advanced money in some negotiated proportion as well. But assuming the label advances $500,000, the artist will not be paid royalties under the recording contract until the album has sold at least about 300,000 copies. The record company would have collected all income from the sale of the albums from the music distributor, less the distributor's fee of about 30% to 40% of the retail price, which is applied to the label's general operating costs. So, usually at about 250,000 copies (or less if the advance was under $500,000) sold, a label will break even, depending on the actual amount advanced.

Any royalties payable to other creative contributors, like producers and high-end mixing engineers, are paid from the artist's "all-in" royalty rate. That means that the $1.50 must be shared with others thus reducing the artist's payment. All advances to the artist are only repayable through recoupment. If an insufficient number of albums are sold to achieve recoupment of advances, the artist does not have to pay the deficiency to the label. This is the risk the label takes. However, if the artist does not sell or license a promising number of recordings, the label has the right not to exercise its option to make further recordings with the artist and the recording contract may therefore be terminated by the label. As noted earlier, very few of the new artists' signings break even; perhaps one in twenty. Thus, the business, at the major label level, has always been a business built on hit singles and albums. This reality remains true today.

A strange reality is that if the recordings and artist is unusually successful (platinum plus album sales: 1,000,000 albums and more), and the artist becomes an asset rather than a liability to the company, the negotiation leverage changes and a company will re-negotiate many financial terms of the recording agreement, including royalties, recording funds, and personal artist advances, among other terms.

Artist revenues are generally generated from four separate activities: (1) recording (record deal and related licensing the use of the recordings to third parties), (2) publishing (separate income generated from song writing and related licensing the use of the compositions to third parties), (3) touring, and (4) merchandise sales. While it is not a subject of this chapter, it is worth noting that most artists "signed" to an exclusive recording agreement with a major label or major independent record company usually will have the opportunity to enter separate third-party agreements with a publisher, booking agency (tour) and merchandising company. It is worth noting that record companies do not usually participate in these other revenue streams. However, there are growing instances where record companies, both majors and independents, seek, to some extent, to participate in these revenues. These requests or requirements are justified by the current decline in CD sales, resulting in enhanced record label risks, for which more collateral is sought. Sometimes, greater artist royalties or money advances are traded by the artist for more label participations in revenue streams. Another justification is that the record deal is usually the deal that enhances (or makes possible) artist revenues in the three remaining areas.

8.2.3 Artist Recording Agreement

The most common agreement is the exclusive recording agreement between the recording artist and the record company for the recording and distribution of records. The increasing sophistication of the business in recent years and the increasing potential income from the sale of recordings has caused the agreement to become significantly more complex. In the 1920s singer Bessie Smith signed a recording contract that was less than one page. Today, a first draft of an artist recording agreement with a major label will be in excess of 70 single-spaced pages. Independent label agreements address the same basic terms but usually with more brevity: about 15 to 40 pages. Many negotiations, arbitrations, and litigations arise from the various deal points in most every recording agreement. What an artist will get and what the label will give depend on two basic issues: (1) What leverage does the artist have (multiple offers from other labels, a proven successful career, and a great artist)?; and (2) What does the artist ask for during the negotiation? The initial offer from a label is not drafted in the artist's favor. If the artist's representative does not ask for certain accommodations, the label will not offer it. Only through experience is a negotiator fully educated about what to negotiate, why, and how. The following is a fairly typical exclusive recording agreement (with commentary), that contains common deal points based on underlying concepts present in every competently drafted agreement:

8.2.3.1 Parties and Exclusivity

[Artist(s)]_____individually and p/k/a [professionally known as (name(s))_____]

or

[Artist, Inc. f/s/o (for services of) [Artist(s)name(s) _____]

We hereby engage your exclusive services for the making of *Masters and Records* and you hereby accept such engagement and agree to *exclusively* render such services to us in the Territory during the Term of this Agreement. You are sometimes called "Artist" herein; all references in this agreement to "you," "your," "Artist," and their possessive forms and the like shall be understood to refer to you alone. We may be referred to as "Company" "we" "us," "our" or the possessive forms thereof.

Comment:

(1) Artists may enter the agreement individually or through entities called "loan out" companies. The establishing and contracting through such companies protects the individual from certain liabilities. The company is authorized to furnish the services of the artist. To assure this is the case, the record company will require the artist to sign an "inducement letter" which assures the label that the artist will remain responsible for performing the personal services required under the recording agreement. "Masters" refer to the recordings from which replications can be made. "Records" is still acknowledged as an acceptable general term for audio (and audio-visual) recorded products. Terms such as "LP" (long playing records), "CD" "Album" or others may be used to identify the same thing.

(2) Recording agreements are almost always "exclusive" in that the artists agree to render exclusive recording services during the term of the agreement for the label. Exceptions, which may be reflected in the agreement, include recording work as a "sideman" on another artist's recording session and performances on soundtrack records. An additional exclusive provision is what is known as the "re-recording restriction," which restricts an artist from making another recording of a song that artist has recorded for the company, usually for a period of the longer of two years following the end of the term or five years following the release of the original recording. The point is to prevent the artist from re-recording and re-releasing a recording that could compete with the label's version.

(3) The record company often signs an agreement with several individuals doing business as a group. This factor creates unique problems due to the reality that many groups disband, fire members, and hire new members. In addition, individuals within the group may pursue simultaneous solo careers. Accordingly, the recording contract will contain "leaving member" clauses, which will usually give the label options to renew the agreement if members leave the group.

8.2.3.2 Term

An initial period commencing on the date of this Agreement and continuing until six months following the "Delivery" (as defined below) of the number of Masters required to be Delivered during said period ("Initial Period"), plus three separate, consecutive options to extend the term for further periods ("Option Periods"), upon the same terms and conditions applicable to the Initial Period, except as otherwise hereinafter set forth (the "Term"). Each Option Period, if we exercise our option therefor, shall commence upon the expiration of the immediately preceding period and shall continue until five months following the Delivery of the Masters required to be Delivered during such *Option Period*. Such options shall be exercised, if at all, by notice to you at any time prior to the date the Term would otherwise expire. Notwithstanding the foregoing, if, as of the date when the then-current period would otherwise have expired, we have not exercised our option to extend the Term for a further period, then: (a) you shall immediately send a notice to us specifically referencing this paragraph and stating that our option has not yet been exercised; (b) we shall be entitled to exercise our option at any time before receiving said notice or within 5 business days thereafter; and (c) the current period shall be deemed to have continued until we exercise our option or until the end of such 5 business day period (whichever shall occur first). Notwithstanding the foregoing (a) in no event shall the Term hereof be longer than 21 months following the date of Delivery of the Masters required to be Delivered during the Initial Period and (b) to the extent that the Term is extended for all three Option Periods hereunder, in no event shall the Term expire prior to 21 months following the date of Delivery of the Masters required to be Delivered during the Initial Period.

Comment:

Note that the term is not for a certain period of years. Usually the term is defined as an Initial Period within which one or more record albums must be delivered. The artist would want the number of albums to be delivered during the initial period to be "firm" which means the label must record and release the albums or pay the artist a negotiated amount if not released. Such a provision is called "pay or play." The company then has options to require the artist to record and deliver more albums. Absent any provision to the contrary, the company generally has the authority to terminate the agreement at any time and not release any album. It may elect to do so if the company feels, for whatever reasons, that it cannot achieve financial or artistic success with the recording or artist.

8.2.3.3 Delivery

The terms "Delivery," "Deliver," and "Delivered" as used in this Agreement shall mean the actual receipt by us of a completed, fully-edited, mixed, and equalized two-track stereo tape, in the format customarily used by us for the manufacture of Records at the time of Delivery (currently 2.0 DDP file set masters in Yellowbook CD-ROM, 8mm Exabyte or DVD-R for audio-only Records) for each format (e.g., compact disc) of each Master comprising the applicable Masters required to be Delivered during the applicable period, which tapes shall in all respects be in the proper form for the production of the parts necessary for the manufacture or creation of Records, together with: (1) one complete copy of the final multi-channel for all applicable Masters prior to mixdown in DVD-R format; (2) the Producer's Package; (3) all required consents, approvals, licenses and permissions in respect of each such Master and Artwork; and (4) using our then-standard form therefor, a complete and accurate summary regarding all Samples embodied in each Master, and all consents, licenses and documentation in connection with such Samples. Your Delivery obligation shall include all union session reports and the delivery of a track-by-track list identifying the performers on and timings of (and titles, writers and publishers of each Composition embodied on) each Master (including any "hidden" Recordings on any Record) and shall describe such perform-ers' performances.

Comment:

Although what establishes delivery depends on compliance with a number of technical requirements, delivery not only is required for payment of any balance of initial money due the artist and producer who make the record-ing, it starts the time running on many other important matters including the length of ther term. There are many incentives built in this provision to assure that the record company gets what it needs before the benefits start flowing to the artists.

8.2.3.4 Technically and Commercially Satisfactory

Each Master shall be subject to our approval as *technically and commercially satisfactory*, and shall not be deemed Delivered unless and until such approval is given. Without limiting the preceding sentence, no Master shall be deemed Delivered if, in our rea-sonable, good faith opinion, such Master or material embodied in such Master would constitute an invasion of any Person's rights (including copyright infringement, libel or slander) or would violate our standards of decency or any applicable rules, reg-ulations, statutes or laws. Upon our request, you shall cause Artist to re-record any Composition until a technically and commercially satisfactory Master shall have been obtained. Only Masters Delivered in full compliance with the provisions of this agree-ment shall be applied in fulfillment of the Recording Commitment and no payments shall be required to be made to you in connection with any Masters which are not in full compliance. Each Master shall be delivered to us at [our office] or such other place as we may notify you.

Comment:

The label wants to have the final approval as to whether the recordings are technically satisfactory in that they sound competitive with other commercially viable recordings. The label also will seek the same authority to determine whether the recorded content is also commercially viable as a financial and ar-tistic matter. Generally the artist will want such approvals to be mutual at most.

8.2.3.5 Territory

The term "**Territory**" as used in this Agreement shall mean the universe.

Comment:

When entering a contract with a major label with world wide distribution capacity, "the universe" or "the world" is reasonable territory as the artist usu-ally wants to be distributed as broadly as possible. An independent label may not have such a reach without affiliating with other labels around the world. Therefore, the artist may request the right to license the masters to third party labels in territories where the independent label has no reach or is unable to secure affiliations within a certain period of time.

8.2.3.6 Delivery Commitment for Albums

For the Initial Period, you shall record and Deliver a sufficient number of Mas-ters, but no less than ten (14), sufficient to constitute one complete long play album ("Album") of customary length to be Delivered within six (6) months following the commencement of the Initial Period. For each Option Period, you shall record and Deliver an Album within six (6) months following the commencement of the applicable Option Period. In the event that you fail to timely fulfill any of your recording and Delivery commitments in accordance with all of the terms and conditions of this Agreement, we shall have the right, upon written notice to you at any time prior to the Delivery of the applicable minimum recording commitment, to terminate this Agreement without further obligation to you as to unrecorded or undelivered Masters.

8.2.3.7 Video

We may, but are under no obligation to, produce one or more audio–visual devices ("Videos") in connection with the Masters. We shall mutually agree on the budget and director for the Video. Video production costs shall be advanced by us and shall be recoupable against monies otherwise due you hereunder. Notwithstanding the foregoing, in the event we determine to produce a Video in connection with the first Album hereunder, the budget for such Video shall not exceed One Hundred Thousand ($100,000) Dollars without our prior written mutual consent. You agree to make yourself available on reasonable notice to participate in the planning, preparation of storyboards, pre- and post- production activities, filming and selection and performance of the musical selections to be included in any such Videos. In the event a Video is commercially exploited (i.e., not used solely for promotional use), we shall credit to your account a royalty of ten (10%) [a negotiated point] for sales of Videos through normal U.S. retail channels and not returned, subject to a reasonable reserve. Artist waives any entitlement to mechanical royalties in connection with the controlled compositions as embodied on a Video.

Comment:

Videos are important promotional tools for replay on TV, over the Internet, and for use as a part of the artist's press kit. The costs to produce a video vary but for pop music videos, the amount can equal the cost of producing an album. The cost is considered a "recording cost" that is recoupable against the artist's royalties. Sometimes the label will agree to recoup up to 50% of the video production costs from the sale of records and 100% from the sale of Videos. Because they are rarely sold, this is a generally accepted term. Generally, decisions to produce a video, the budget amount, the director selection and the master/song selection, is either the label's decision upon consulting the artist or is a mutual decision between artist and label. Technically, the publishing (composition) license is usually waived provided the video is being use for promotion purposes. In the event the video is sold in some fashion (like as an inclusion in a pop video compilation or DVD) some arrangement for payment is usually made.

8.2.3.8 Creative

With respect to each Master required to be Delivered hereunder, the studio, producer, material and times of recording shall be mutually selected by us. Each such composition selection shall be subject to our approval and you shall consult with us in advance of recording any composition. Each Master shall consist of newly recorded studio performances. Each Master shall be subject to our approval as commercially satisfactory.

Comment:

The "creative controls" are a very important issue to artists. If the label has the final say as to what the artist can record, where and how it is recorded and produced, and whether it is commercially and technically satisfactory, the artist may (rightly) feel that the art and the business decisions are out of the artist's control. The extent to which an artist preserves creative control depends on the relative negotiation strengths (leverage) of the parties, including the artistic authority of the artist. An established songwriter/performer with proven success will have more leverage than an unproven teen artist that does not write his or her own music.

8.2.3.9 Grant of Rights

a. You hereby grant us the right to manufacture, sell, lease, license, distribute and advertise and otherwise fully exploit the Masters in any and all media and by any method now or hereafter known in any field or manner of use involving sound alone or sight and sound together both directly to consumers and indirectly through distributors, dealers, resellers, agents and other third parties. All Masters recorded during the Term shall be deemed *works made for hire* for us by Artist and by all other persons rendering services in connection with the Masters. The Masters (*excluding the copyrights in the underlying musical compositions*) from the inception of recording, and all recordings and other reproductions made from the Masters together with the performances embodied thereon and all copyrights therein in the Territory and all renewals and extensions thereof shall be entirely our property, free of any claims by Artist or any other person, firm or corporation. We shall have the right to register the copyright in the Masters in Company's name. If for any reason, the Masters are determined not to be "works made for hire," then this Agreement shall constitute a transfer by you to us of all of your right, title and interest in and to the Masters.

b. We shall have the exclusive and worldwide right to manufacture, sell, distribute and advertise recordings embodying the Masters under any trademarks, trade names or labels and to lease, license, convey or otherwise use or dispose of the Masters by any method now or hereafter known, to include the Masters on records with masters by third parties, and to perform publicly recordings and other reproductions embodying the Masters or in its discretion, to refrain from doing any of the foregoing. "*Recordings*" and "*Records*" as used herein shall mean all forms, means and methods of recording and reproduction by which sound may be recorded now or hereafter known, manufactured or sold for primarily home use, juke box use, Internet or computer transmission, or use on or in any means of transportation, including without limitation, magnetic recording tape, film, electronic video recordings and any other medium or device for the production of artistic performances whether embodying sound alone or sound synchronized with visual images.

c. You grant to us the right to use and publish and to permit others to use and publish your name (given or professional) and *approved* photographs, portraits, likenesses and biographical material concerning you and the name(s) (given or professional) and photographs, portraits, likenesses and biographical material concerning any person whose performance is embodied on the Masters for publicity, sale, *merchandising*, advertising and trade purposes in connection with the Masters. You warrant and represent that you have the right to use your given or any professional name you may use from time to time and that such use does not and will not infringe on the rights of any third party. You hereby authorize us to conduct a trademark search of your professional names now being used and any other professional name you may use from time to time. All costs incurred in connection with any such *trademark search* shall be recoupable from monies otherwise due to you hereunder. If any such search indicates that a professional name you may use from time to time should not be so used, we and you shall *mutually agree upon a substitute name.* You will not, during the Term, alter the name under which you perform professionally without our prior written consent. Notwithstanding the foregoing, we are not obligated to conduct any trademark search hereunder and are entitled to rely on your warranty and representation herein.

d. In the event we release Records embodying Masters hereunder in physical format, you shall have the right to sell such Records directly to consumers *at live music venues* where you are performing during the License Term and you shall have the right to purchase all such Records from us at a price to equal our usual outside wholesale price for full album-length Records and at our customary artist price for other configurations; provided, that you shall not have the right to buy more than 2,000 units of any particular Record in respect of any one-year period during the License Term. Such purchases by you shall be *royalty bearing.*

e. The selection, preparation and cost of artwork (the "Artwork") shall be mutually selected by you and us [or Company may want final approvals]. Company shall own all right, title and interest in and to the copyright and trademarks associated with the Artwork.

Comment:

(1) Record labels normally insist on perpetual, worldwide ownership of recordings created under the agreement. However, an artist with significant bargaining leverage may be able to restrict the territory to one or more countries, allowing that artist to enter into foreign record agreements without the consent or participation of the original record company, although, with respect to Internet sales, there may be problems identifying the source of particular sales and enforcing collection proceedings. Also, if the artist has unusual leverage, a reversion of copyright (transfer back to the artist) may be negotiated at some future time. The length of time would depend on what might be a reasonable time within which the label could recoup its investment and make a profit from the catalog. An artist's lawyer would want to make certain that the publishing income from "controlled compositions" (those compositions written by artist) are not "cross collateralized." That is, the income from compositions (including mechanical royalties, which are royalties, form the sale of physical products like CDs) are not to be applied against the artist's recoupable account. This is a major deal point. If the publishing is not cross-collateralized, the entire amount of royalties and other licensing fees generated from songwriting is paid directly to the songwriter.

(2) The ownership and total control of the sound recording copyright, as embodied in the Masters, is the central asset of the record company. This is the main point of the business: to own a catalog of master recordings that it can exploit in all media and through all mediums usually "now known or hereafter devised." Such exploitations include those undertaken directly by the record company, those accomplished through third-party licenses and those through the outright sale (assignment) of masters.

(3) The artist usually wants the right to approve all (or some) of the personal elements used for promotion. Traditionally, merchandising rights have not been generally granted to record companies but, lately, have been requested and even required by some labels. The justification is that but for the notoriety built by company promotion, merchandise

sales would not be so significant. Also, the steady decline in CD sales, coupled with continuing major costs of promotion, justifies label participation in other artist revenue streams. With so many artists now promoting recordings over web sites and otherwise, it is difficult to find an unused band name. If the artist is not using a personal given name or a name secured by trademark registration, it may be necessary, to avoid trademark problems, for the label to conduct a name search and, if necessary, participate in the selection of an alternative name that the label feels will complement the artist's image, music and promotion.

(4) Sales by the artist of CDs at live performances are a major source of income for the developing artist. Sometimes the CDs are provided at wholesale and vended by artist just like any other retailer. In this event, the label may require the artist to register "stage sales" with SoundScan (a service to validate retail sales which count toward placing a recording on the trade charts). Royalties (and recoupments) apply to such sales. Other labels will provide CDs at manufacturing and handling costs (about $3/CD) and allow the artist to keep whatever it can collect. Still other labels may provide a number of CDs at no cost in lieu of money "tour support" (which would be a recoupable advance to help underwrite the hard costs incurred on a tour that is primarily to promote the recording).

(5) The status of any existing recordings previously distributed or otherwise sold by the artist can be a major issue. What if the artist has self-released one or more albums (not uncommon). The label may wish to purchase this catalog and thereby own the sound recording copyright, license it from the artist should any of the masters be needed, allow the artist to continue to sell the recordings with some restrictions (local or stage sales only, CD sales over the artist site only, no sales for a period of years while the label promotes the new recordings, etc.), or prevent the artist form selling such recordings at all during the term.

8.2.3.10 Web Site

We shall have the exclusive right throughout the Territory during the License Term, free from any claims whatsoever by you, Artist or any other person: (i) to establish and maintain a site (the "Company-Artist Site," which term shall include the content of such site) on the Internet having the address (i.e., Uniform Resource Locator, or "URL") "[Artist].com" or any similar designation based on or containing Artist's professional name as we shall mutually approve (the "Artist URL"); (ii) to couple the Artist URL with any such other appropriate suffixes (e.g., top-level domains such as .com, .net, .co .uk, etc.), which we determine in our sole discretion is necessary or desirable and to register the Artist URL and any such suffixes in our name in any and all territories with the appropriate entities and to secure any and all renewals and extensions thereof on your behalf, it being understood that you hereby appoint us as your attorney-in-fact for such purposes; (iii) to refer to the Company-Artist Site as the "official" site relating to you; and (iv) to include the Artist URL on Records embodying any Master hereunder and in advertising and marketing materials therefor. *We shall be the sole and exclusive owner of the Company-Artist Site* and the operation and content thereof shall be controlled by us. Within 6 months following the expiration or earlier termination of the Term, to the extent so requested by you in writing, we shall, to the extent of our rights, *assign to you all our rights in and to the Artist URL* on an "as is" basis.

To the extent that you or Artist maintain a site utilizing the Artist's professional name or featuring the Artist's name, image(s) and or likenesses (the "Artist Maintained Site") we shall have the right to link to the *Artist Maintained Site* from the Company-Artist Site and you or Artist shall create a prominent link from the Artist Maintained Site to the Company-Artist Site.

Comment:

The label will generally own and control an official site for at least the term of the agreement (until the artist is no longer required to deliver recordings to the label). An artist that already owns a developed web site (as most do) may be allowed to maintain that site provided there is a link to the "official" site. Also, the label may allow the artist to sell CDs, downloads and merchandise over the artist site on terms similar to stage sales.

8.2.3.11 Release and Commercial Availability Commitment

You acknowledge that the sale of Records is speculative and agree that our judgment with regard to any matter affecting the sale, distribution and exploitation of such Records shall be binding and conclusive upon you. Except as expressly set forth to the contrary in this paragraph, nothing contained in this Agreement shall obligate us to sell, license, or distribute Records manufactured from Masters hereunder. Provided you are in material breach of this Agreement, and if we are in receipt of Delivered Masters, together with all materials therefor, we agree to commercially release Records *in physical form* embodying each such Master in the United States within 60 days following your Delivery of the applicable Master(s) and our receipt of the applicable Performance Video in connection therewith and, following such release, shall continue to make each such Master commercially available in Records in *non-physical form* in the United States during the License Term.

Comment:

From the artist's perspective, an essential element of the contract is the label's commitment to record and to release the record. While the agreement will almost always provide for the recording of a minimum number of masters (or "side" if the master is a single master) during each contract period, the company will be reluctant to guarantee the release of records. While a company will often agree to release a record within four to six months following delivery of the masters for the "commitment" record, a company may refuse to release an album by an unproven artist between October 1 of a given year and January 15 of the following year for fear that the album will be buried by the typical fourth quarter (holiday season) avalanche of product from established artists. Typically, the artist's sole remedy in the event that the company fails to complete the release is to terminate the term of the agreement. In some cases, the company will additionally agree to sell the unreleased album back to the artist in return for repayment of the recording costs of the album. In the Internet era, of course, the delivery commitment may change from "albums" to "sides," and the occurrence of release commitments will undoubtedly increase to reflect the ubiquity of the Web.

8.2.3.12 Recording Fund and Advances

a. During the Initial Period, Company shall advance a recording fund ("*Fund*") for the production of the required Masters in an amount of $250,000 of which an initial "*Personal Advance*" of $50,000 shall be paid to you upon signing this Agreement ("First Album").

b. The Fund for additional Masters during the Option Periods, if any, shall be an amount equal to sixty-seven (67%) percent of the amount of the royalties, after the retention of reserves, not to exceed twenty (20%) percent for purposes of computing the Fund only, less Recording costs attributable to the immediately preceding Album, as such term is defined below, earned by you hereunder from net sales through normal retail channels in the United States ("*USNRC Net Sales*"), of the immediately preceding Album delivered hereunder during the twelve-month period immediately following the initial commercial release in the United States of such preceding Album. "Net sales" means 85 percent of the gross sales to wholesale and retail customers, less returns, credits and reserves against anticipated returns and credits. Notwithstanding the forgoing, the Fund for each Album delivered for each Option Period shall have the minimum and maximum amounts as follows:

Second Album:	*Min:* $200,000	*Max:* $250,000	*Personal Advance:* $50,000
Third Album:	$300,000	$400,000	$75,000
Fourth Album:	$400,000	$500,000	$100,000

c. The Fund shall include all costs incurred in connection with the production and Recording of the applicable Masters, including but not limited to, recording studio costs, arranging fees, producer advances and fees, musician advances and fees, union payments, "sample" clearances, equipment, tape and tape editing, mixing and engineering fees and costs, album cover artwork and additional packaging costs for packaging other than standard industry record packaging (collectively referred to herein as "*Recording Costs*"). All such Recording Costs approved by Company shall be advanced by Company and shall be recoupable from monies otherwise due you hereunder. We shall have final approval [or mutual approval] of all compositions to be recorded hereunder, as well as the studio, recording sessions, producer, engineer, musicians and other artists, if any, involved with the production and recording of such compositions. The Fund and Recording Costs, as well as all other monies advanced to Artist or on Artist's behalf pursuant to this Agreement shall constitute advances ("*Advances*") hereunder and shall be recoupable by Company from any monies otherwise due Artist hereunder.

d. You will timely submit to Company all bills, invoices, receipts, vouchers and similar substantiation of Recording Costs incurred in connection with the Masters. Any expenditures in excess of the agreed upon Fund are subject to Company's prior written approval and if not approved in writing by Company, such expenditures shall be your sole responsibility.

e. Any *Fund balance* remaining after payment of all Recording Costs and your compliance with all Delivery requirements shall be payable to you as you may request, in writing, as a recoupable Advance.

Comments:

(1) Recording funds are the most common way to budget albums. From the fund, a certain amount may be earmarked up-front to go to the artist. For new artists, this amount is intended to provide enough income to pay the artist's costs of living and general overhead for a period of at least the time it takes to record an album and (unless the artist is a multiple-member band) there may be some left to underwrite the artist's cost of living while touring the album for about a year after its release. It the album and act is not experiencing success at that point, the company will probably not exercise an option for another album. In other words, the advance to the artist is opportunity money, not retirement money.

(2) The fund for the ensuing albums usually is determined by the sales of the previous album with stated minimums and maximums. The 67% formula is generally accepted. The minimum is important. As noted earlier, if the album and artist are unusually successful, a company will re-negotiate many financial terms of the recording agreement, including the funds and the personal artist advances, among other terms. The numbers suggested would be typical for a new "baby act." If there was signing competition for such act or if it was a re-signing of an established act whose contract has expired, the amounts would be greater. This relative value also applies to royalties (discussed below) and all other material terms.

(3) The recording costs are all recoupable and represent the hard costs of making an album. The cost of promoting an artist is usually not charged as a recording cost or as a recoupable cost. Such costs include all in-house generated marketing and promotion programs. However, if independent (third-party) radio promoters are engaged to "work" radio, that amount may be a recoupable advance of 50% to 100% of such amount. Unused amounts from the fund are advanced to the artist. Usually, this creates an incentive for the artist to not overspend on recording costs.

8.2.3.13 Per Record Costs

You shall be solely responsible for and shall pay all monies becoming payable to you, Artist, producers, engineers, and all other parties rendering services or otherwise in respect of sales or other exploitations of Records derived from Masters hereunder, provided that we shall pay mechanical royalties becoming payable to the copyright proprietors of musical compositions embodied thereon.

Comment:

Technically, the artist is usually responsible for engaging the services of the producer, who in turn is technically charged with engaging and overseeing the procedure and costs of studios, recording engineers, mixing engineers and mastering engineers and related staff. The producer submits an invoice for services of these technical parties to the label administrator, who then pays these individuals upon receiving from them the required documentation that assigns any copyright interests or right to claims therein to the label. Those who may be entitled to receive a royalty (producers and some top-level mixers) may request and receive a "letter of direction" which enables them to be paid their royalty directly from the label and not through the artist.

8.2.3.14 Royalties

We shall credit to your royalty account "Royalties" as described herein. Royalties shall be computed by applying the applicable royalty rate specified herein to the applicable Royalty Base Price in respect of Net Sales of the Record concerned. The "Basic U.S. Rate" of 14% shall be the royalty rate on 90% of USNRC Net Sales of Records (U.S. retail sales) consisting entirely of Masters made hereunder in physical form for the First Album. For subsequent albums the Basic U.S. Rate shall be:

Second Album:	15%
Third Album:	16%
Fourth Album:	17%

In determining USNRC Net Sales of Records, Company shall be entitled to deduct a container or packaging charge of 25% for Records including but not limited to singles, compact discs and "new media" records. No deduction shall apply to electronic transmission and "streaming audio" configurations. No royalties shall be due for Records given away as so-called "free goods" or promotional items, whether in conjunction with special sales plans, record clubs, or other promotional programs, provided, however, such free goods shall not exceed 15% of the total number of Records manufactured.

(a) Additional Royalty: In the event any Record which solely embodies Masters required to be recorded and Delivered hereunder shall have USNRC Net Sales to equal or in excess of 500,000 but less than 1,000,000 royalty-bearing copies, we shall pay you an additional royalty to escalate to .5%. In the event any such Record shall have further USNRC Net Sales to equal or in excess of 1,000,000 royalty-bearing copies, we shall pay you a further additional royalty to escalate to 1%, but only with respect to those USNRC Net Sales to equal or in excess of 1,000,000 royalty-bearing copies of that particular Record.

(b) Basic Foreign Rate: The royalty rate (the "Foreign Rate") for Net Sales of Records sold for distribution outside the United States by Company or its Principal Licensees shall be computed at the applicable percentage of the royalty rate that would otherwise apply to Net Sales in the United States of the Record concerned as follows:

   (1) 90% Canada
   (2) 80% U.K., Japan, Australia, Germany, France
   (3) 75% Spain, Italy Luxembourg, Belgium, Sweden, Finland, Norway Denmark
   (4) 66 2/3% Rest of the world

(c) Digital Distributions: 100% of the otherwise applicable U.S. rate for Records for digital downloads or ring tones; 75% for all other Digital media.

(d) Flat-fee or Royalty Licensing: The royalty rate for any Masters hereunder licensed by us or our Principal Licensees (other than for On-Demand Usages) shall be 50% of Net Receipts.

(e) Proration: As to any Record not consisting entirely of Masters Delivered under this Agreement, the royalty rate otherwise payable to you with respect to sales of any such Record shall be prorated by multiplying such royalty rate by a fraction, the numerator of which is the number of Masters Delivered under this Agreement embodied on such Record and the denominator of which is the total number of Masters embodied thereon.

(f) No Royalty Payable: No royalties (including mechanical royalties) shall be payable in respect of: (i) Records given away or sold at below stated wholesale prices for promotional purposes; (ii) Records sold as scrap, salvage, overstock or "cut-outs"; (iii) "sampler" Records given away or sold below $5.00; and (iv) Records sold below cost. No royalties shall be payable on any sales by our licensees until payment or credit therefor against advances previously taken has been received by us in the United States.

Comment:

(1) The artist's royalty typically begins at the rate of at least 14% of the suggested retail price (or 28% if the royalty is calculated based on the wholesale price). The artist royalty is generally "all-in," *i.e.*, the royalty rate includes the artist's royalty as well as the producer's royalty and perhaps a top-notch mixer royalty. As discussed in numeric detail below, Net Sales to which a royalty is applied is usually reached by language in the record contract providing for reductions that have the effect of reducing that

amount. While packaging costs were at one time quite substantial, they are no longer. Nevertheless, the packaging deduction persists and is now considered a general overhead cost accommodation for the label. A balance has been met with some labels not charging any such costs on digital distributions (even though there clearly are no such packaging costs). The royalty rate may be applied to 90% of USNRC Net Sales of Records. This further 10% deduction is a remnant of the days when about 10% of records were expected to be returned as literally broken goods damaged in shipment the replacement of which was an additional cost to the label. To eliminate this deduction is a major deal point which the label may just off-set by requiring a lower royalty rate or a higher escalation level or a smaller escalation percentage. It is a game of pennies. The company will be mindful that it can give here and there as long as the penny rate remains within an acceptable range. The artist's lawyer must try to push the penny rate to the maximum a company will allow or build in benefits for the artist that may pay-out in the back-end in the event the label is allowed to recoup its up-front money sooner. Advances and royalties for superstar artists do not conform to any pattern or range; they are determined strictly by negotiations, but major artists can command tens of millions of dollars in advances and their royalties can range 20% and up. They may fashion joint venture deals, in which the label recoups its out-of-pocket costs off the top and then divides the balance equally with the artist.

(2) "Top-line" (full retail sales) royalty rates are lowered when applied to foreign countries, singles, military outlet, and record club sales. The justification is that the costs of distributing and promoting abroad require added costs and perhaps third-party label assistance. Sales to record clubs, military outlets, and single sales all require volume discounts. Escalations in royalties are paid as a reward for sales at a high level. By the time an album has sold gold (500,000 units) or platinum (1,000,000 units), the record company has usually recouped the recording costs and usually more through the artist's relatively small royalty amount. Therefore, the company has already been making money. The escalator is a sharing of what amounts to usually be some sort of profit with the artist. In virtually all modern contracts, record royalties escalate both when a particular album achieves specified sales thresholds. Typically, the rate rises by a half a percentage point at net paid sales of 500,000 copies through normal U.S. retail channels, and another half a percentage point at 1,000,000 such units.

(3) One of the major issues now concerns royalties on downloads and audio streaming or other digital distributions. A major label's form may provide for no reduced royalty or may provide for a reduced royalty (for example, 75% of the otherwise applicable base rate); a 15% to 25% distribution fee, and a 50/50 split on the balance; or a combination of factors, all of which will tend to yield a lower royalty to the artist. The traditional record industry has only just embraced the Internet, and the companies face high costs to establish, maintain and promote their delivery systems, and at least a period of uncertain sales (not to mention piracy.) In addition to selling albums, companies will contract with various digital distribution "aggregators" to sell single downloads, ring tones based on the master record-

ings ("ring tones or master ring tones). Subscription models are also under consideration.

(4) When the masters are licensed to third parties for synchronizations with visual images such as TV and motion pictures. The proceeds are usually split 50/50 after deductions for delineated costs of such licensing. This revenue is 100% subject to recoupment. Masters may also be used (licensed) by the company for audio exploitations by other companies such as compilations or other "couplings". The royalty is generally pro-rated in such events. The revenue is entirely subject to recoupment.

8.2.3.15 Deficit Tour Advance

We may, in our sole discretion, provide you, upon your request, with deficit tour advances in an amount also subject to our sole discretion, which shall be fully recoupable against royalties due you by us herein.

Comment:

In many cases the label will offer, and the artist should request as an additional advance, "deficit tour support." This is an advance of money to the artist while it is on the road promoting an album that represents the difference between the amount of money the artist is making from performance fees and merchandising income, on one hand, and the reasonable hard costs of touring, on the other hand. Should there be a deficiency (deficit), the label will pay the difference as a recoupable advance so the artist does not lose money. This is a common scenario for new acts who may tour with a major act as an opening act. Such performances do not pay well and are undertaken primarily for exposure to the audience.

8.2.3.16 Statements, Reserves, and Audit Rights

a. Statements: Statements as to royalties earned under this Agreement for sales of Records embodying Masters shall be sent by us to you within 60 days after the end of each quarter-annual [or semi-annual] calendar period. Concurrently with the rendition of each statement, we shall pay you all royalties shown to be due by such statement, after deducting all Recording Costs paid by us, all other permitted charges and all advances made to you hereunder prior to the rendition of the statement.

b. Reserves: We shall be entitled to maintain a single account with respect to all Recordings subject to this Agreement. We may maintain reasonable **reserves** for physical Records but not to exceed 25% of Records distributed. Such reserves must be fully **liquidated** within one year from the period in which such reserve was initially made.

c. Audit Right: You shall be deemed to have consented to all accountings rendered by us under this Agreement and said accountings shall be binding upon you and shall not be subject to any objection by you for any reason unless specific objection, in writing, stating the basis thereof, is given to us within 2 years after the date rendered, and after such written objection, unless suit is instituted within 1 year after the date upon which we notify you that we deny the validity of the objection. You shall have the right at your sole cost and expense to appoint a Certified Public Accountant to examine our books as same pertain to the Recordings subject hereto, provided that any such examination shall be for a reasonable duration, shall take place at our offices during normal business hours on reasonable written notice and shall not occur more than once in any calendar year. If we agree that there has been an under-crediting of royalties to you exceeding ten percent (10%) of the total royalties reported as credited by us to your account hereunder for the period covered by such examination or if an under-crediting of royalties exceeding such amount is established by a court of competent jurisdiction, we shall reimburse you in the amount of all reasonable fees paid by you to the auditors concerned in connection with such audit, up to a maximum amount of $25,000 per audit. We shall pay interest to you on the payable portion (i.e., the portion in excess of any then-unrecouped Advances) of any agreed upon or so-established under-crediting of royalties hereunder at the prime rate as quoted in the "Money Rate" section of The Wall Street Journal or any other similarly-reputable published source, calculated on the basis of a 365-day year. Up to one (1) time per each [week] of the License Term, solely as an accommodation to you, following your written request, we shall provide you with up to date information relating to the sales of Masters embodying Masters hereunder; provided, that our failure to so provide you with such information shall not be deemed to be a breach of this Agreement.

Comment:

Receipt of statements and payments is customarily sixty days after each semi-annual period (periods ending June and December). Reserves are allowed to recognize that there are records sold that are then returned. The label does not get paid from the distributor until a certain amount of time has passed after sale, so this waiting period is passed on to the artist. The reserve amount can vary from 20% to 30%. It must be liquidated (paid) eventually. A year from sale is usually long enough. This is a fairly artist-friendly audit right in that it provides for payment of audit costs in the event there is a proven 10% discrepancy. This is unusual to secure for an artist. For a gold or platinum selling album, it would be perhaps malpractice not to recommend an audit because discrepancies are expected and companies open their books without much, if any, objection. A "look-back" period of two years is common; three years is possible.

8.2.3.17 Controlled Compositions

(a) All musical compositions or material recorded that are written or composed in whole or in part by you, Artist or any producer of the Masters, or that are owned or controlled, directly or indirectly, in whole or in part, by you, Artist or any producer of the Masters (herein called "Controlled Compositions") shall be and are hereby licensed to us for the United States, at a royalty per selection equal to 75% of the minimum statutory per selection rate (without regard to playing time) effective on the earlier of: (i) the date a particular Master is Delivered hereunder; or (ii) the date such Master is required to be Delivered hereunder (the "Effective Date") (the "U.S. Per Selection Rate"); and for Canada, at a royalty per selection equal to 75% of the statutory per selection rate (without regard to playing time) effective on the Effective Date, or, if there is no statutory rate in Canada on such date, 75% of the per selection rate (without regard to playing time) then generally utilized by major record companies in Canada (the "Canadian Per Selection Rate). With respect of all Controlled Compositions, we are hereby granted the irrevocable gratis right throughout the Territory to reprint the lyrics on the jackets, sleeves and other packaging of Records derived from Masters hereunder and on any related web-sites which sell or promote the respective Master whether in physical or non-physical form, and in advertising and promotional materials related thereto.

(b) Notwithstanding the foregoing, the maximum aggregate mechanical royalty rate that we shall be required to pay in respect of any Record, regardless of the total number of compositions contained therein, shall not exceed 11 times the U.S. Per Selection Rate or the Canadian Per Selection Rate, respectively. It is specifically understood that in the event that any Record contains other compositions in addition to the Controlled Compositions and the aggregate mechanical royalty rate for said Record shall exceed the applicable rate provided in this paragraph, the aggregate rate for the Controlled Compositions contained thereon shall be reduced by the aforesaid excess over said applicable rate. Additionally, we shall have the right with respect to any Record, the aggregate mechanical royalty rate for which exceeds the applicable rate provided in this paragraph to deduct such excess payable thereon from any and all monies payable to you pursuant to this Agreement. All mechanical royalties payable hereunder shall be paid on 100% of Publishing Net Sales. We may maintain reasonable reserves with respect to payment of mechanical royalties. If any Record contains compositions that are not Controlled Compositions, you shall use your reasonable efforts to obtain for our benefit mechanical licenses covering such compositions in a form no less favorable to us than those contained in the then current standard form Harry Fox Agency license; however, if such license contains terms less favorable to us than those contained in this Agreement which are applicable to Controlled Compositions, then we shall have the right to reduce mechanical royalties payable with respect to Controlled Compositions or to otherwise charge your account under this Agreement for any such excess or differential.

Comment:

(1) A sound recording involves two different properties and copyrights: the recording itself (the sound recording) and the song which is performed on the recording (the musical composition). Record companies must pay a royalty for each use. An "artist royalty" is paid for the performance on the sound recording and a "mechanical (publishing license) royalty" is paid to the writer(s) of a composition. The performer and writer may or may not be the same person. If they are, the money is much better for the successful writer performer. If the song was written by the artist, the "controlled composition" will provide that such song is deemed licensed to the record company at the contractually-specified rate. If, however, the song is owned or controlled by a third party, a separate license, called a "mechanical license" (because the first such licenses were issued when sound was reproduced by needles scratching—mechanically—on wax discs) must be obtained. A short agreement between the record label and music publisher grants the label a license to use the musical composition in CD format or via electronic distribution on payment of an agreed-upon royalty. Most publishers use the so-called "Harry Fox" form and most controlled compositions require the artist to secure licenses for third-party compositions on terms no less favorable than those provided in the Harry Fox form, this being the form utilized by The Harry Fox Agency, Inc. (a subsidiary of the National Music Publishers' Association, which acts as mechanical licensing agent for more than 20,000 publishers, liaises with foreign mechanical rights collection societies, and maintains a Far East office in Singapore). A compulsory mechanical license

may be obtained pursuant to Section 115 of the Copyright Act of 1976, 17 U.S.C. 115, but only (1) if an authorized recording of the song has already been commercially released and (2) if the license is obtained no later than 30 days after records are manufactured, and before records are distributed. In addition, Section 115 imposes strict and onerous reporting and payment requirements. A negotiated license is clearly preferable. Although record companies are frequently late in securing mechanical licenses (often due to lack of information from their artists and producers), this can be very costly.

(2) The recording agreement will also attempt to limit the amount of mechanical royalties to be paid by the record label in the U.S. and Canada through what is known as a "controlled compositions" clause. This clause reduces the mechanical royalties required to be paid by the record label to the music publisher for compositions appearing on the artist's album, and "controlled" (generally those written) by the artist, to a rate less than the statutory rate (previously set by the now disbanded Copyright Royalty Tribunal) under copyright law. Typically, the rate will be 75% of the minimum U.S. statutory rate and 75% of the corresponding Canadian industry rate, as of one of three dates: (A) the date of commencement of recording (favored by the record companies), (B) the date of initial release of the subject record (obtainable by artists with strong bargaining positions), (C) the date of sale (obtainable only by the very strongest artists.) In addition, the company will insist upon limiting the amount of mechanical royalties it will pay with respect to a specific record, typically, 10 to 12 times (11 being most common) the 75% rate. Further, the company will refuse to pay mechanicals on "free goods" (although, where the artist has decent bargaining power, the company may agree to pay mechanicals on 50% of Album-length "free goods," but never on singles.) This "cap" applies to the album as a whole, so that if an artist selects compositions owned or controlled by third parties, and the record company is required to pay higher rates for the use of these compositions, the mechanicals applicable to controlled compositions will be reduced thereby. If the use of such outside songs causes the mechanicals on a particular record to exceed the contractual cap, the excess will typically be chargeable against the artist's record royalties. In the event the artist is in a competitive position, a 100% statutory rate on up to 11 compositions is possible to negotiate.

(3) By allowing the record company to pay 75% of the statutory rate as opposed to 100% thereof, the artist is essentially granting the company a 25% share in the artist's mechanical royalty. Again, in the game of pennies, this amounts to quite a bit. The label benefit is also enhanced by the cap of the compositions to which the royalty applies. For example, if the full statutory rate (as of January 2006) is 9.1 cents per composition, there are 12 songs on the album, and the recording artist wrote all songs, the artist would receive $1.092 per album sold. If the artist is paid 75% of the full rate on a cap of 10 songs, the amount is $.68 per album sold. If 100,000 albums were sold, the writer would receive $109,200 vs. $68,000. Consider the difference at gold and platinum! Furthermore, mechanical roy-

alties are paid from the first sale and a vigilant artist's lawyer will make sure such royalties are not subject to any recoupment (not cross collateralized).

8.2.3.18 Warranties, Representations, and Indemnity

You and Artist warrant and represent:

(a) that neither you nor Artist are under any disability, restriction or prohibition, whether contractual or otherwise, with respect to your or Artist's right to execute this Agreement and perform its terms and conditions;

(b) that we shall not be required to make any payments of any nature for, or in connection with, the rendition of your or Artist's services or the acquisition, exercise or exploitation of rights by us pursuant to this Agreement, except as specifically provided hereinabove;

(c) that no materials hereunder, or any use thereof, will violate any law or infringe upon or violate the rights of any third party; and

(d) that Artist shall not perform any selection recorded hereunder for record purposes for anyone other than us for use in the Territory for a period of 5 years after the initial date of release of the respective Record containing such selection.

(e) You agree to and do hereby indemnify, save and hold us harmless from any and all loss and damage (including court costs and reasonable attorneys' fees) arising out of, connected with or as a result of any inconsistency with, failure of, or breach or threatened breach by you or Artist of any warranty, representation, agreement, undertaking or covenant contained in this Agreement including, without limitation, any claim by any third-party in connection with the foregoing. We shall give you notice of any third-party claim to which the foregoing indemnity applies and you shall have the right to participate in the defense of any such claim through counsel of your own choice and at your expense. Pending the determination of any such claim, we may withhold payment of all monies under this Agreement in any amount reasonably consistent with such claim, provided that if litigation has not been commenced within 1 year of such claim first being made, we will pay such withheld monies to you; however, such payment to you shall not limit our right to withhold sums at a later date if litigation based on such claim is thereafter commenced. We shall accrue interest on such withheld monies at the then prevailing average interest rate applicable to passbook savings accounts in savings accounts in commercial banks within the State of _____.

Comment:

Subparagraph (d) contains the "re-recording restriction" which restricts an artist from making another recording of a song that artist has recorded for the company, usually for a period of the longer of two years following the end of the term or five years following the release of the original recording. The point is to prevent the artist from re-recording and re-releasing a recording that could compete with the label's version.

8.2.3.19 Injunctive Relief

You expressly acknowledge that Artist's services hereunder are of a special, unique and intellectual character, which gives them peculiar value, and that in the event of a breach by you or Artist of any term, condition or covenant hereof during the Term or the License Term, as applicable, we will be caused immediate irreparable injury. You and Artist expressly agree that we shall be entitled to injunctive and other equitable relief, as permitted by law, to prevent a breach of this Agreement, or any portion thereof, by you or Artist, which relief shall be in addition to any other rights or remedies, for damages or otherwise, available to us.

8.2.3.20 Notices

All notices to you shall be in writing and shall be sent postage prepaid by registered or certified mail, return receipt requested, addressed to you at your address first above. All notices to us shall be in writing and shall be sent postage prepaid by registered or certified mail, return receipt requested, addressed to our address first above written with a simultaneous copy sent in the same manner to [Artist's lawyer].

8.2.3.21 Logos, Artwork, Merchandise, etc.

All logos, designs or other merchandising or promotional artwork created by us for use in connection with Artist's name and/or the sale of Artist's Recordings shall belong entirely to us and may not be used by any person or entity other than us, unless you pay to us 50% of all amounts incurred by us in the creation or acquisition of such materials and unless you pay any monies due to third parties in connection with such use.

Comment:

The payment obligation is often traded away in the event the label acquires any merchandise rights from the artist. Basically, the label does not want the artist to take the art developed and paid for by the label (as an advance) and generate income by way of merchandising in which the label does not participate. If the label should offer a merchandise deal, it should advance all costs of the merchandise, allow final approvals on design, limit its rights to distribute in areas where it has a capacity to sell, possess non-exclusive rights (as much as possible) and agree to split at least 50/50 with artist all revenues after deducting the label's advanced costs off the top. Furthermore, like publishing income, the merchandise income should not be cross-collateralized against other recoupable costs (recording costs, promotion costs, etc.).

8.2.3.22 Miscellaneous

This Agreement sets forth the entire agreement between the parties with respect to the subject matter hereof. No modification, amendment, waiver, termination or discharge of this Agreement shall be binding unless confirmed by a written instrument signed by an officer of ours. No modification or amendment of this Agreement shall be binding upon you unless confirmed by a written instrument signed by you. A waiver of any term or condition of this Agreement in any instance shall not be deemed or construed as a waiver of such term or condition for the future, or of any subsequent breach thereof. All of our rights and remedies in this Agreement shall be cumulative and none of them shall be in limitation of any other remedy or right available to us. Should any provision of this Agreement be adjudicated by a court of competent jurisdiction as void, invalid or inoperative, such decision shall not affect any other provision hereof, and the remainder of this Agreement shall be effective as though such void, invalid or inoperative provision had not been contained herein. No breach of this Agreement by us shall be deemed material unless within 30 days after you learn of such breach, you serve written notice thereof on us specifying the nature thereof and we fail to cure such breach, if any, within 30 days after receipt of such notice. No breach of this Agreement by you shall be deemed material unless within 30 days after we learn of such breach, we serve written notice thereof on you specifying the nature thereof and you fail to cure such breach, if any, within 30 days after your receipt of such notice. The foregoing sentence shall not be applicable to any breach, alleged breach or threatened breach of the exclusivity provisions of this Agreement, or to the provisions of paragraph 13(d) of this Agreement, or to any breach, alleged breach or threatened breach or otherwise for which a cure period is already provided for in this Agreement. We shall have the right without your consent to assign this Agreement in whole or in part to any subsidiary, parent company, affiliate, or to any third party acquiring a substantial portion of our assets or stock. This Agreement shall be deemed to have been made in the State of _____ and its validity, construction, performance and breach shall be governed by the laws of the State of _____ applicable to agreements made and to be wholly performed therein. You agree to submit to the jurisdiction of the Federal or State courts located in _____ in any action which may arise out of this Agreement and said courts shall have exclusive jurisdiction over all disputes between us and you pertaining to this Agreement and all matters related thereto.

8.2.3.23 Love and Affection

Every Company staffer agrees to treat you with love and affection. You in turn agree to treat us with a modicum of respect. Although impolite disregard of this paragraph is not to be considered a formal breach of the entire Agreement, bad karma resulting therefrom lays on the soul of the perpetrator.

If the foregoing is in accordance with your agreement with us, please so indicate by signing in the appropriate place below.

Very truly yours,
COMPANY
By: [Company Officer]
The Artist p/k/a _____
By: _____

Comment:

Record companies frequently deal with groups rather than individual artists. The company wants to have all members of a group under contract, but the company must cope with the reality that membership in a band undergoes frequent change. The contract must deal with the possibility that one or more members of the group may depart and that others will take their places. Not only must the contract keep continuity with the group as presently constituted, but it must also attempt to determine whether departing members are still committed to some kind of contract with the label.

8.3 ROYALTY CALCULATIONS

The calculation of record royalties is complicated. The framework for the following illustration is provided by Lionel S. Sobel, who is a former Professor of Loyola Law School, Los Angeles, editor and publisher of *Entertainment Law Reporter,* and a co-author of the Third Edition of this book. Prices, products and rates have changed since the article was first published, but the basic calculations and analysis remains valid.

Recording Artist Royalty Calculations: Why Gold Records Don't Always Yield Fortunes

Every industry has a benchmark for success. In the record business, that benchmark is the "Gold Record." Awarded by the Recording Industry Association of America to albums that sell 500,000 copies, Gold

Records mean fame and fortune for their artists. Or do they? The answer, like the answer to so many questions in the entertainment business, is yes and no. Yes, a Gold Record means fame. But does it always mean fortune? The answer to this question, at least insofar as recording artists are concerned, may be "no." And the explanation for this apparent anomaly has nothing to do with creative, unethical, or fraudulent accounting practices on the part of record companies. The explanation is found in the royalty provisions of recording contracts, many of which are customary in the industry. What follows is an explanation for how a recording artist may be entitled to no royalties at all, even though his or her album ships gold.

The following explanation requires some introductory caveats. First, the hypothetical on which this explanation is based is just that—a hypothetical. Like all good law school problems, the facts of the "hypo" are intended to be realistic. But they are not the facts of any actual case, and (admittedly) they have been selected to illustrate certain points clearly (and even dramatically). Second, the hypo includes—among its assumed facts—several contract provisions, all of which have a critical bearing on the outcome of royalty calculations. These provisions are believed to mirror provisions which appear in the contracts used by several actual record companies. But the provisions used in the hypo are only "samples." There is no industry-wide "standard" contract, and the provisions described below do not appear in all record company contracts. Further, even contracts that do contain the provisions on which this article is based are printed on paper; they are not carved in stone. In other words, everything is negotiable. The outcome of negotiations over these provisions, or any others, depends on how badly the artist wants the deal as compared to how badly the record company wants it. As always, relative "clout" (as well as negotiator skill) will determine the exact language of any record contract's actual royalty provisions.

Finally, as it is the dominant product, the analysis is limited to CDs. Before 1986, vinyl records and cassette tapes (in addition to the then new CD) were viable products, in both album and single configurations. Today, royalties and fees generated through the sale and licensing of master recordings through various digital distributions are still contemplated under the recording contract language. In concert with technology, these physical and non-physical product sales are diversifying and growing quickly. Exploitations and payments of royalties and fees through digital downloads, film and TV licenses, master ringtones, digital juke boxes, on-line subscription services, video game licenses, and more are assigned a value for which payments are calculated and paid under essentially the same formula framework as applies to CDs.

The Hypothetical

Ann Artiste signed her first-ever record contract with XYZ Records in the spring of 2006. The contract gave her a $150,000 "recording fund" from which her recording costs, including an advance to the album producer, were to be paid. Artiste completed recording her first album by the fall of 2006, and copies of it began shipping in January 2007. XYZ Records was delighted with the album, and Artiste was thrilled when the album shipped "gold." However, when she received her first royalty statement, for the period from January through June 2007, her thrill turned to bitterness, because the statement showed that she was not entitled to any royalties whatsoever—that in fact the album was still seriously "in the hole" to the tune of negative $36,579.

The statement indicated that 500,000 CDs were shipped. The statement also showed that 6,000 of the albums were given away free to radio stations, critics, movie producers and others for promotion. The balance was shipped to record stores and distributors. Two CDs were designated as "free goods" for every ten that were billed. The recording costs for the album had come to $110,000, (a relatively modest cost) and her producer received a $30,000 advance against his royalties. This meant that $10,000 was left in the recording fund when the album was completed. The Artiste received that $10,000 as an advance against her royalties.

XYZ's suggested retail price is $15.98 for CD's. Artiste's contract with XYZ provides that she is to receive an "all-in" royalty of 14% of the album's suggested retail price. However, because this is an all-in rate, the album producer's royalty is paid out of Artiste's 14%. (Each percentage is often referred to as a "point"). In this hypothetical, the producer's royalty is 3% (3 points) of suggested retail, thus reducing Artiste's royalty to an effective rate of 11%. Royalty rates often escalate when sales exceed 500,000 units, but such escalations did not come into play on Artiste's first statement because only 500,000 units had been shipped.

Artiste's contract further provides that royalties are not payable at all for records given away for promotional purposes to disc jockeys, radio and television stations, motion picture companies, distributors, sub-distributors, dealers, consumers, employees, publishers, reviewers, critics or others. Moreover, the contract provides that royalties will be paid only on 90% of those records actually sold. The contract authorizes a number of specific "recoupable" costs before royalties are paid including recording costs and money advances made by XYZ to Artiste. XYZ also is authorized to deduct a "packaging charge" of 25% of the suggested retail price of CD's.

The contract further provides that the combined mechanical license rates payable by XYZ to music publishers for all compositions embodied in an album shall not exceed 75% of the then-current statutory mechanical license fee multiplied by 10 (the "cap") for each album sold at XYZ's invoiced price. Artiste agrees to indemnify and hold XYZ harmless from mechanical license fees in excess of the amounts specified. If XYZ is required to pay such excess, the payments shall be a direct debt from Artiste to XYZ which XYZ may also recoup from royalties otherwise payable to Artiste. If videos are produced, XYZ would pay the cost of producing those videos, but the amount paid would be treated as a recoupable advance against Artiste's royalties. One video of a song on the album was produced at a cost of $75,000. Finally, the contract provides that in computing the number of records sold, XYZ shall have the right to deduct returns and credits of any nature and to withhold reasonable reserves therefore from payments otherwise due Artiste. Such reserves withheld by XYZ, are limited to 25% of payments otherwise due Artiste in connection with such records. The statement showed that XYZ withheld $125,000 in reserves.

Royalty Calculations Based on Hypothetical Contract

Albums on which Artiste was entitled to receive royalties:

500,000	CD's shipped
−6,000	CD's given free to D.J.'s
494,000	shipped, 2 free with every 10
×10/12	to determine number actually "sold"
=411,666	
=90%	to calculate number on which royalties are payable (a significant reduction based on the old vinyl "breakage" custom)
=370,500	CDs on which royalties payable

Gross royalties:

$15.98	suggested retail price
−4.00	packaging deduction of 25%
=$11.98	on which royalties are payable
×14%	royalty rate for CD's
=$1.677	royalty per CD sold
370,500	CD's sold
×$1.677	royalty per CD
$621,328	gross CD royalties

Deductions

Next, XYZ calculated the deductions it was permitted to take from the total gross royalties Artiste's album had earned. The easiest deductions to determine were $110,000 in recording costs for producing the album, $30,000 advance to the album producer, $10,000 fund balance ($150,000 recording fund) that Artiste received as an advance against her royalties, and $75,000 cost of producing the video. These amounts were deductible in full.

XYZ also was entitled to deduct "excess" mechanical license fees. (The terms "mechanical royalties" and "mechanical licenses" are synonymous.) The relevant contract clause provided that XYZ would have to pay no more than 75% of the then-current statutory mechanical license fee multiplied by 10 for each album sold at XYZ's invoiced price. Any excess could be deducted from Artiste's royalties. The CD contained 12 songs.

Since all of these songs were written by someone *other* than Artiste, XYZ in fact had to pay mechanical license fees for all 12 songs on the CD. Moreover, section 115 of the Copyright Act requires mechanical license fees to be paid "for every phonorecord made and distributed in accordance with the license," which includes records that are given away free. Since January 1, 2006, the statutory mechanical license fee has been 9.1 cents per song, per record. This means that XYZ had to pay mechanical license fees at this rate for all 500,000 copies of the album that were shipped—not merely for those that were "sold." The third-party songwriters (who are not bound by the recording agreement between XYZ and Artiste) were paid the full 9.1 cents per song on all 12 songs and not the 75% rate with the 10 song cap to which Artiste was subject. The total amount of these fees came to $546,000 calculated as follows:

Mechanical License Fees

Total mechanical license fees paid by XYZ to third-party songwriters on all 12 songs:

$.091	license fee per song
×12	songs per CD (cap)
=$1.092	mechanical license fee per CD
×500,000	CDs shipped
$546,000.00	total CD mechanical license fees

The clause in Artiste's agreement specifies that XYZ will be solely responsible for the mechanical license fees up to 75% of the statutory rate on CDs and Artiste is responsible for the excess. As a result, XYZ had to pay 100% of the statutory rate:

Mechanical license fees that XYZ was responsible for under the agreement with Artiste:

$.091
×75%
×10 songs cap
=$0.6825
×500,000 CDs shipped
=$341,250

The difference between XYZ's responsibility for mechanical license fees under the agreement and the total mechanical license fees is the "excess mechanical fees." Artiste is responsible for excess mechanical fees.

$546,000.00	total mechanical license fees
−$341,250	XYZ's responsibility for mechanical license fees
=$204,750	excess mechanicals paid by XYZ—which amount is also was deductible from Artiste's gross royalties

Producer's Royalties

Since Artiste's royalty rate was an "all-in rate," XYZ was entitled to deduct the producer's royalties as well. In this hypothetical, the royalty provisions of the producer's contract are identical to those in Artiste's contract, except that his rates are net (i.e., not "all-in") and are 3% for CD's. The producer's royalties are calculated like this:

$15.98	suggested retail price
−$4.00	packaging deduction of 25%
$11.98	on which royalties are payable
$11.98	on which royalties are payable
×3%	royalty rate for CDs
$.3594	royalty per CD sold
×370,500	CD's sold
=$133,157	gross producer royalties

Since the producer previously received a $30,000 advance against his royalties, an additional $103,157 was payable to him on account of album sales.

Reserves Against Returns

Finally, XYZ withheld and deducted $125,000 in reserves against possible returns, (25% of shipped CDs).

XYZ therefore totaled its deductions as follows:

$110,000	recording costs
$30,000	advance to producer
$10,000	advance to Artiste
$75,000	video production costs
$204,750	excess mechanicals
$103,157	royalties payable to producer
$125,000	reserve against possible returns
=$657,907	total deductions

Royalties Payable

Accordingly, no royalties were payable to Artiste, at that time, because her "gold album" was still substantially "unrecouped":

$621,328	total gross royalties
−$657,907	total deductions
=(−$36,579)	

Of course, Artiste has not really done as badly as it appears at first. She did receive $10,000 in royalties in advance. And the $125,000 reserve for returns is only that—a reserve. Her recording contract provides that the reserve must be "liquidated" by XYZ within two accounting periods following the period for which the reserve was withheld. Since the contract also provides XYZ will render accountings twice a year, XYZ will have to credit Artiste's account with that $125,000 in one year, if there are no returns; and that by itself would result in an additional royalty check to her. Finally, the advances paid by XYZ are its investment risk which is secured by its ability to recoup advances from Artiste's royalties (collateral). Therefore, Artiste is not required to pay back any deficiency from her own funds as would be the case if it were a loan.

Effects of Contract Modifications

This is not meant to suggest that "gold records" never produce substantial royalties. In fact, even in this hypothetical, Artiste's royalties would have been dramatically more significant had small changes been negotiated in just four provisions of her contract with XYZ.

Negotiable Modifications

First, historically, record companies paid royalties on 90% (rather than 100%) of records sold, because records used to be brittle and broke in shipment. Since record stores did not pay for broken records, record companies did not want to pay royalties for them either. A 10% breakage factor became customary between record companies on the one hand and stores and recording artists on the other. Today, however, records do not break in shipment, and some record companies do pay royalties on 100% of all records "sold." Assume that XYZ had been asked, and had agreed, to pay Artiste on 100% of her albums sold (rather than on 90%).

Second, with respect to free goods, record companies customarily shipped 3 free singles and 2 free albums with every 10 singles and albums sold to record stores. On the other hand, some record companies have reduced or even eliminated the number of free goods they ship. Assume that XYZ had been asked, and had agreed, to reduce the number of free albums it ships from the customary "2 on 10" to "15 on 100."

Third, the deductibility of video production expenses often is a subject of negotiation. From the record company's point of view, those expenses are equivalent to recording costs, which are fully deductible by record companies in calculating artist royalties, and thus ought to be fully deductible as well. From the recording artist's point of view, video production expenses are equivalent to advertising and promotional expenses which are not deducted by record companies in calculating artist royalties. Assume that in this hypothetical, the issue of video production expenses had been raised in negotiation, and assume those negotiations had resulted in a compromise that permitted XYZ to deduct 50% (rather than 100%) of Artiste's video production expenses.

Fourth, assume that the "excess mechanicals" provision of Artiste's contract had been modified in three small ways. Assume that XYZ had been asked, and had agreed, to pay mechanicals on all albums "distributed" (rather than only on albums "sold"). Assume that XYZ had been asked, and had agreed, that the 75% rate limitation would apply only to "controlled compositions" (i.e., those written or otherwise owned by Artiste herself). Finally, assume that XYZ had been asked, and had agreed, to pay the mechanicals on all 12 songs.

New Royalty Calculations

Artiste's Gross Royalties

500,000	CDs shipped
−6,000	CD's given free to D.J.'s
494,000	shipped, 15 free with every 100 sold
×100/115	to determine number actual "sold"
=429,566	sold and on which royalties payable
$15.98	suggested retail price of CD's
−$4.00	packaging deduction of 25%

$11.98	on which CD royalties are payable
×14	% royalty rate for CD's
$1.677	royalty per CD sold
×429,566	CD's sold
=$720,382	gross CD royalties

Producer's Royalties

429,566	CD's sold
×$0.3594	royalty per CD
=$154,386	total gross royalties

Since the producer received a $30,000 advance against his royalties, an additional $124,386 was payable to him on account of album sales.

Deductions

$110,000	recording costs
$30,000	advance to producer
$10,000	advance to Artiste
$37,500	video production costs
$0	excess mechanicals
$124,386	royalties payable to producer
$125,000	reserve against possible returns
=$436,886	total deductions

Royalties Payable to Artiste

$720,382	gross royalties
−$436,886	deductions
=$283,496	royalties payable

Thus, by virtue of small changes in four contract provisions, Artiste's royalties, in this hypothetical, leap from negative $36,579 to $283,496! The value of understanding the value and the effect of negotiable deal points becomes very clear.

Mechanical Royalties Revisited

Observe how much more benefit there is for the recording artist that also writes songs—especially those that are the main or sole writer. Mechanical royalties (as all music writing/publishing income) is a separate compensable activity. To benefit the writer, mechanical (and other publishing) income should never be "cross-collateralized" (subject to application against recoupable amounts by the label). In this way, mechanical royalties, whether at a 75% rare or 100% rate, are payable to the writer from the first sale ("record one"). This means that those who record and don't write may not see any royalties (other than advances) while the writer will make substantial income from that source. This reality often raises participation issues within bands. In any event, to be paid up to $.091 per song, or any part thereof, on any record as a mechanical, in addition to royalties and fees to writers on or master use licenses, digital distributions, and other income that flows from the recording contract (not to mention even more publishing income from sources outside the recording contract) is very substantial especially upon achieving "gold."

Even More

For a more detailed discussion and analysis of the negotiation of recording agreements and related music publishing issues review the following books are recommended:

Don Passman, *All You Need to Know About the Music Business,* 5th ed. (Free Press, Simon & Schuster, 2003).

Jeffrey Brabec and Todd Brabec, *Music, Money and Success,* 5th ed. (Schirmer Trade Books, 2006).

Chapter 9

FILM

9.1 THE CHANGING SCENE IN THE MOTION PICTURE INDUSTRY

The changing scene in the motion picture industry can best be gleaned from headlines in the Wall Street Journal ("WSJ"): "Movies May Hit DVD, Cable Simultaneously" (reporting that cable companies and movie studios are considering strategies to release movies through video-on-demand cable services the same day they come out on DVD) (WSJ, Jan. 4, 2006); "Universal to Supply Films in Digital Form" (Universal Studios agreed to distribute its films to as many as 4,000 screens running new digital equipment in the United States) (WSJ, Oct. 31, 2005); "Paramount Nears Sale of DreamWorks Library" (Viacom agreed to sell the film library of recently acquired DreamWorks studio in a deal that values the library at $900 million) (WSJ, Mar. 17, 2006); "Movie Debut: Films for Sale by Download" (Broadband Internet users will be able to legally purchase and keep an electronic copy of the movie Brokeback Mountain by using their computers) (WSJ, Apr. 3, 2006); and "Coming Attraction: Downloadable Movies from Amazon" (an article that discusses negotiations between Amazon.com, Inc. and major movie studios to movie content available for Internet rental and purchase) (WSJ, Mar. 10, 2006).

Although the cost of producing a major studio movie increased by nearly 600 percent between 1980 and 1998, the cost of producing a film at one of the major studios in 1998 decreased 1.3 percent—to $52.7 million—and a 2000 report indicated a further decline in production costs in 1999 of $1.2 million per film, to $51.5 million. However, based on recent Motion Picture Association ("MPAA") statistics, this downward trend has been reversed. In 2004, the average cost to make and market a MPAA film was $98 million, which reflects $63.6 million in negative costs and $34.4 million in print and advertising costs.

Despite the large cost of producing and marketing films and the great risk involved, the film industry is still a profitable venture. In 2004, the total domestic box office amounted to some $9.54 billion, a 25% increase over five years ago. The top five films of 2004 pulled in more than $200 million each, and "Shrek II," "Spider Man II," and "The Passion of the Christ" each surpassed the $300 million mark. This growth is consistent with the worldwide trend. In 2004, the worldwide box office was $25.24 billion, representing a 24% increase over 2003's box office of $20.34 billion.

In 2004, the average ticket price for the United States was $6.21, a 3% increase over the 2003 average. However, despite the rising ticket costs, in 2004 the number of moviegoers reached its highest point in five years. Although Academy Award best film nominees like "Brokeback Mountain," "Crash," "Munich," "Capote" and "Good Night, and Good Luck" generate artistic interest, these five films combined only added up to $185 million in 2005. Instead, audiences still seem to prefer "big, spangly movies full of wonder or . . . stories with a minimum of ideology and a maximum of happy endings" (WSJ, Feb. 3, 2006). For example, "Star Wars: Episode III: Revenge of the Sith" made roughly $370 million in 2005, and "Harry Potter and the Goblet of Fire," which opened in November, 2005, has to date earned about $285 million.

As reported in the WSJ, Dec. 29, 2005, Hollywood did not fare badly in terms of the box office for 2005. Although U.S. theatres took in eight percent less money in the first nine months of 2005 than they did in the same period in 2004, the movies of the major Hollywood studios—Fox, Sony, Warner Bros., Disney, Paramount and Universal—taken together, were up, not down. From January 1 to September 30, 2005, the movies of the six majors took in $4.7 billion compared to $4.5 billion in the same period in 2004. They did so by increasing their slice of the total box-office pie from 68% in 2004 to 75% in 2005.

Despite the profitability of the film industry, studios are more determined than ever to cut production costs across the board. The reason for this is that the rate of return on their investments from theatrical distribution is low—an estimated 5 percent—and most of their profits come from home video and television distribution. The object now is to make cheaper, better films. Costs are being cut in three distinct ways:

1. Although proven box office superstars like George Clooney, Reese Witherspoon, Tom Cruise, Tom Hanks, Julia Roberts, and Jim Carrey command eight-figure guarantees (often cast as advances against shares of gross receipts, whereas most "above the line" talent—principal actors, producers, writers, directors—share only in the net—the definition of *net* being a major bone of contention discussed below), many actors, even relatively major ones command far less than the fees they formerly received. Furthermore, many stars like Nick Nolte and Tim Allen have in recent years voluntarily accepted significantly less than their regular rates to land desirable roles.
2. The studios have demonstrated a greater readiness to drop or to cancel productions with potential runaway budgets.

3. Some of the perks are being eliminated for all but the A-list stars. For example, studios have begun to cut back or eliminate production house-keeping deals, under which star talents are provided with office space (sometimes buildings) on the lot, together with staff and development/production funds.

In the United States, the film industry is dominated by six major film studios that engage in the financing, production, and distribution of films, and some are involved with exhibition as well. Most of the majors are subsidiaries of multinational conglomerates: Universal (owned by NBC/GE); Sony Pictures (a unit of Japan's giant electronics multinational); Twentieth Century Fox (a subsidiary of Australian-based News Corporation); Warner Brothers, Inc. (a unit of AOL Time Warner Inc.); Paramount Pictures (a subsidiary of Viacom, Inc., which owns Showtime, The Movie Channel, and CBS Inc.); and The Walt Disney Corporation (which releases under a variety of names and also controls ABC, ESPN, and, of course, its signature theme parks around the world).

At this point most of the more famous production companies are owned (or at least financed in whole or in part) by major studios. Miramax (which won more Academy Awards during the 1990s than any of the major studios for such films as *The English Patient* and *Shakespeare in Love*) is owned and financed by Disney. Castle Rock (of which Rob Reiner, director of *When Harry Met Sally* and *A Few Good Men,* is a principal) and New Line Cinema were acquired by Turner Entertainment which, in turn, was acquired by Time Warner, Inc. (and later merged into AOL.). Other top producers such as Jerry Bruckheimer (whose production company has an agreement with Disney) and Arnon Milchan's Regency Enterprises (formerly allied with Warner Brothers, now at Twentieth Century Fox) have agreements with major studios for financing and/or distribution.

It is very difficult for an independent film company to survive over the long term without an agreement with a major studio. The reason for this is that independents are not diversified conglomerates, so one or two flops can exert a tremendous impact on a company that survives on a hit-by-hit basis. Also, the major studios enjoy a regular revenue stream from exploitation of their substantial movie libraries in home video and on cable and satellite. In fact, Ted Turner was able to create the basis for a cable network (TNT) merely by purchasing MGM's film library. The independents do not have such vast libraries, so their revenue streams are precarious. Thus, in recent years, most key independent companies have been acquired by major studios (Focus Features, Miramax, New Line) so that the whole notion of an "independent" company is questionable. However, every so often, a film will be produced for next to nothing, and achieve huge numbers. Artisan's *Blair Witch Project* ($1 million production cost, $175 million domestic box office) is an example of this phenomenon. Studios and other distributors and exhibitors flock in growing numbers to events such as the

Sundance Film Festival and the American Film Market hoping to find similar gems. While "small" films have shown up very well in the Academy Awards and other awards arenas in recent years, the vast majority of the country's screens are effectively controlled by the majors, and it's very difficult for a true independent to reach a broad market.

Overall, the film industry is a complex organization involving all aspects of law in some way, shape, or form. However, the key to understanding the law is to understand the industry itself. This chapter attempts to provide an overview of the film industry.

NOTE

An extremely lively literature has developed around the film business. Some representative examples:

(a) Nestor Almendros, *A Man with a Camera* (New York: Farrar Straus Giroux, 1984). Observations on the art of cinematography by an Academy Award winner.

(b) Steven Bach, *Final Cut* (New York: Wm. Morrow & Co., 1985). The amazing story of the making of *Heaven's Gate,* which destroyed United Artists as a viable studio.

(c) Peter Bart, *The Gross: The Hits, The Flops—The Summer that Ate Hollywood* (New York: St. Martin's Press, 1999). An intense look at the summer season of 1998, and the filmmaking machinations behind it.

(d) Stan Berkowitz and David Lees, *The Movie Business: A Primer* (New York: Vintage Books [Random House] 1981). An overview of the filmmaking process, less technical and more anecdotal than Squire, *The Movie Business Book.*

(e) Bernie Brillstein (with David Rensin), *Where Did I Go Right?* (New York: Little Brown & Co., 1999).

(f) Roger Corman (with Jim Jerome), *How I Made a Hundred Movies in Hollywood and Never Lost a Dime* (New York: Random House, 1990). A memoir by the "King of the B Movies." Truly a legend in his own time, Corman launched or assisted the careers of talents as diverse as Jack Nicholson, Dennis Hopper, Jonathan Demme, Ron Howard, and James Cameron.

(g) Bill Daniels, David Leedy, and Steven D. Sills, *Movie Money: Understanding Hollywood's (Creative) Accounting Practices* (Los Angeles: Silman-James Press, 1998).

(h) William Goldman, *Adventures in the Screen Trade* (New York: Warner Books, 1984). A funny, caustic inside look at the business from one of the great screenwriters (*Marathon Man, Butch Cassidy & The Sundance Kid, All the President's Men*). A classic in the field. The "sequel," *Which Lie Did I Tell?,* was published by Pantheon Books (New York, 2000).

(i) Mark Litwak, *Dealmaking in the Film & Television Industry* (Los Angeles: Silman James, 1994).

(j) Sidney Lumet, *Making Movies* (New York: Alfred A. Knopf, 1995). A director's-eye view of the process, by the maker of more than forty films.

(k) David McClintick, *Indecent Exposure* (New York: Wm. Morrow & Co., 1982). The battle for control of Columbia Pictures. Although not specifically relevant to today's facts, it illustrates a recurrent Hollywood theme.

(l) Schuyler M. Moore, *The Biz: The Basic Business, Legal and Financial Aspects of the Film Industry* (Los Angeles: Silman-James, 2000). An excellent (and often hilarious) primer on how the industry works (or *fails* to work).

(m) Pierce O'Donnell and Dennis McDougal, *Fatal Subtraction: How Hollywood Really Does Its Business* (New York: Doubleday, 1992). The story of the epic battle between Art Buchwald and Paramount, told by Buchwald's attorney, with an introduction by Buchwald.

9.2 PRODUCING FILMS

9.2.1 The Evolution of the Studio Model

From the early 1920s until a few years after World War II, the major studios controlled virtually every aspect of film financing, production, and distribution (including the lion's share of exhibition). Actors and directors generally worked exclusively for specific studios under long-term contracts and exercised little or no control over the films to which they were assigned or the roles they played. After World War II, however, came the twin terrors of television and antitrust litigation. The studios were forced to divest themselves of their theatre holdings and to deal with a new, independent attitude on the part of major stars such as Kirk Douglas (producer of *Spartacus*) and Jimmy Stewart (producer of *Rear Window*). The old star system came apart rather quickly. Since that time, actors and directors have almost always worked on a film-by-film basis. While the studios still serve as the primary (but by no means only) source of financing, they no longer possess the power to assign talent to productions in which they do not wish to participate. Nor do they necessarily control every aspect of production. Top actors will often have the right of approval over scripts, directors, and other creative elements.

However, negotiation on a film-by-film basis is not the sole business model. Some actors, directors, writers, and producers have secured long-term contracts with major studios. Mel Gibson, Eddie Murphy, Jerry Bruckheimer, and James Cameron's Lightstorm Entertainment have, or have had, multiple-picture deals with major studios.

Studios generally have few problems finding the funds to finance movies. Their biggest problem is deciding which movies to finance. Although many of them have reduced the level of their support for the development process, hundreds of projects—few of which will ever reach theatres—are "in development" at each studio at any given time. A studio will put up a small fund for preliminary steps such as acquiring rights to pre-existing works, commissioning scripts, and making initial payments to producers. For the production phase, most studios have arrangements with banks. Major studios are low-risk for bank loans because of their track records and because they have "slates" of cross-collateralized pictures providing multi-million dollar assets to serve as collateral. Furthermore, although a film may be a failure at the box office, most studio films make back their investments over the long-term with the ancillary markets much as home videos, DVDs, broadcast and cable television.

Nevertheless, American studios, confronted with the huge production budgets attached to some recent films, have turned more and more to co-financing arrangements (e.g., Twentieth Century Fox and Paramount on *Titanic*, Dreamworks SKG and Paramount on *Saving Private Ryan*) under which (typically) the studios will contribute production monies in agreed shares; one studio will acquire rights for the U.S. and Canada, the other for the rest of the world; and revenues will be apportioned in accordance with a prearranged formula, another strategy followed by studios as well as independents is so-called off-balance-sheet financing, in which interests in slates of films are syndicated to outside investors. For example, Castle Rock Entertainment made a six-year, eight-picture deal with Chase Manhattan Bank in August 1998 under which Chase would provide $200 million to finance two-thirds of the production costs of eight films, the distributing studio would take a 15 percent fee off the top, and Chase would recoup its investment from the remainder. (See Carl Diorio, "Major Moolah" *The Hollywood Reporter,* January 29, 1999, p. 14.)

9.2.2 Producing Films: The Studio Model

9.2.2.1 Acquisition of Underlying Rights

Every project in the entertainment industry begins with a creative expression of an idea. Typically, the prospective producer of a film begins by acquiring the rights to an existing play, book, screenplay, or treatment for a screenplay (literary option/purchase agreement). Sometimes (as illustrated in Robert Altman's bitterly satirical *The Player*) the project begins with just an idea—a "pitch." The purchase of rights is usually made in the form of an option agreement calling for an initial period of one year with one or more potential extensions of one year each. If the owner of the underlying material has a number of eager suitors, the option payments (as well as the ultimate payment upon exercise of option) can be quite substantial, and the exercise of the option may be subject to conditions precedent. Conditions can include the requirement of obtaining a funding commitment from a studio or a firm commitment from a leading actor or director, or, perhaps, the creation of a final script. In most cases, the option payments are small and no conditions attach. Usually, an agreement for the purchase of rights of an idea calls for payments in a range between five figures and millions. Factors that determine the value include the past record of the writer, the marketability of the idea, and whether a major actor or director is interested in the project.

From the standpoint of the producer, it is important to get the broadest possible grant of rights, including the right to distribute the film in all formats presently known and that may be invented in the future. A major studio will not accept anything less than complete rights to all markets including, but not limited to, domestic and international theatrical release, the home video market, broadcast and cable television (including pay-per-view), and Internet distribution. Home video, once considered an ancillary market, now accounts for four times as much studio revenue as theatrical distribution, at least in the United States.

In addition to all rights in the basic work, the producer also will want to acquire all rights in the characters embodied in the property, in order to do remakes, sequels (and even "prequels" such as the "first" episode of *Star Wars*), spin-offs featuring characters from the original work in new stories, and to exploit all of these derivative works in all present or future formats.

Many deals involve adaptations of pre-existing materials. An existing work (e.g., a John Grisham bestseller) is somewhat "pre-sold"; there is already a "buzz." But many projects are based on original material. However, where original material is involved, a studio will generally be more hesitant to enter the development process and, where material is offered by a writer, will normally accept only something at or close to a shooting script. On the other hand, proven writers can sometimes get deals on the basis of an outline or a treatment. (In his classic *Adventures in the Screen Trade*, veteran writer William Goldman tells how he would put together a dozen outlines and send them around to see if he could generate any interest; if not, he'd junk the twelve and write twelve more, until he found something saleable.) Joe Eszterhas, author of the screenplay for *Jagged Edge* and other films, once sold an unfinished script for $3,000,000. This script went through revisions, as is the case with most films, but the studio eventually returned to the original script and the film was released to considerable success as *Basic Instinct*. Eszterhas wasn't finished pushing the envelope: he went on to make a $4,000,000 deal with Paramount Pictures on the basis of a "pitch." Eszterhas was to receive $1,000,000 for signing, a further $500,000 on completion of a second draft, $1,900,000 when the film was greenlighted, and another $500,000 if the film surpassed a certain box office threshold.

The literary option/purchase agreement used to acquire the underlying rights contains, among other terms, the following: (A) The length of the initial option period and any extensions; (B) The price of the option periods and any extensions, and whether those payments are applicable against the purchase price; (C) "Set up bonuses," if any; (D) The purchase price for the rights, and if based on a percentage of the budget, "floors" and "ceilings;" (E) If there are additional writing services to be rendered (in the case of an optioned screenplay, for instance), what writing steps will be commissioned and for what fees (see Screenwriter Agreement contained in another part of this chapter); (F) The rights granted, the rights reserved, and reversion of the rights; (G) With respect to the rights reserved, holdbacks, rights of first negotiation, and matching rights; (H) Credit.

During the option period, the producer may develop the project (e.g., by commissioning a script in the case of a book option, by attaching cast, etc.) with the protection of knowing that the rights to the material cannot be optioned or sold to others. If the project goes into production, the producer will exercise the option or the option will be deemed automatically exercised, and the rights will transfer to the producer. If the project does not go into production, the option will expire and the author is free to dispose of these rights elsewhere.

The Memorandum Agreement and Standard Terms and Conditions which follows are representative of the basic terms and conditions contained in an option to acquire rights in an underlying property (screenplay/fiction).

If music is to be a part of the film, then the studio is required to enter into a Master Use License with the record company which owns the underlying rights to the recording and a Film Synchronization and Performance License with the music publisher who owns the underlying rights to the musical composition embodied on the recording. Representative examples of the three agreements follow; all of which are subject to negotiations between the contracting parties.

1 *Memorandum Agreement*

Basic Terms and Conditions—Option—Screenplay (Fiction)

A. Producer.
B. Seller.

B1. *Conditions Precedent.* All of Producer's obligations hereunder are conditioned upon its approval of the so-called "chain of title" for this project, including valid copyright and title reports and registrations.

C. *Work.* The original screenplay written by Seller entitled " " and all versions, revisions and elements thereof and notes, working papers, treatments and other material in connection therewith, including the respective themes, plots, characters, settings, titles and stories contained therein.

D. *Motion Picture.* The first motion picture, if any, produced hereunder by Producer based solely on the Work.

E. Grant Period.

E.1. The Option (as defined in Paragraph 1.1 of the Standard Terms and Conditions attached hereto) granted hereunder is granted for a period (the "Grant Period") commencing on the date hereof and ending on the date six (6) months after the date of execution hereof. Simultaneously with the execution hereof, Seller shall execute and deliver to Producer a Short-Form Option in the form attached hereto as Exhibit E.1, and Producer shall have the irrevocable right to file such short-form option as Producer deems necessary.

E.2. Producer shall have the right, but not the obligation, before the expiration of the Grant Period, to exercise the Option by making the payment to Seller described in Paragraph G.1 below, and if such payment is made, the Option shall automatically be deemed exercised. Upon exercise of the Option, Producer shall automatically and irrevocably acquire all the rights set forth in Paragraph 1 of the Standard Terms and Conditions, including the right to date and file the assignment in the form attached hereto as Exhibit E.2 (the "Assignment"), which Assignment Seller is executing and delivering to Producer contemporaneously herewith, it being agreed that such

Assignment shall be deemed to be null and void if the Option expires hereunder.

F. *Compensation.* In full and complete consideration to Seller for entering into and for fully performing all of the terms and conditions hereof, and for all rights granted hereunder, Producer shall pay to Seller upon the complete execution hereof an amount equal to US$.

G. *Contingent Payments.* If the following events occur, and provided Seller has not materially breached any of Seller's representations, warranties or obligations, Seller shall be entitled to receive the following contingent payments:

G.1. If Producer elects to exercise the Option pursuant to Paragraph E.2 above, an amount equal to US$;

G.2. If Producer produces a feature-length prequel, sequel or remake motion picture based upon the Motion Picture intended for initial theatrical release in the U.S., and Seller is accorded sole "separated rights" in the Work, provided Seller is not engaged to render services in connection with such prequel, sequel or remake, an amount equal to % of the amounts paid pursuant to Paragraph G.1 above, payable within ten (10) days after the commencement of principal photography of such prequel, sequel or remake, it being agreed that if Seller is accorded shared "separated rights" in the Work, the amount payable pursuant to this paragraph shall be reduced by fifty percent (50%);

G.3. If Producer produces a live-action episodic television series based upon the Motion Picture (the "Series") for initial broadcast in the U.S. on a free television network (*i.e.,* ABC, CBS, NBC or Fox) during prime time, and Seller is accorded sole "separated rights" in the Work, provided Seller is not engaged to render services in connection with such Series, a first-run royalty in an amount equal to the following for each episode of such Series so produced and broadcast, depending upon the length of such episode, payable within thirty (30) days after such broadcast, provided that (i) if such Series is not live-action or is produced for initial broadcast in the U.S. on other than a free television network during prime time, the amounts payable pursuant to this paragraph shall be reduced by fifty percent (50%), provided that such amounts shall only be reduced by twenty-five percent (25%) if such Series is produced for initial broadcast in the U.S. on HBO during prime time and (ii) if Seller is accorded shared "separated rights" in the Work, the amounts payable pursuant to this paragraph shall be reduced by fifty percent (50%);

G.3.1. For each episode that is thirty (30) minutes or less in length, US$;

G.3.2. For each episode that is more than thirty (30) minutes and up to sixty (60) minutes in length, US$;

G.3.3. For each episode that is more than sixty (60) minutes in length, US$; and

G.3.4. For each of the first five (5) free television network reruns (as defined in the WGA Theatrical and Television Basic

Agreement) of any such episode, twenty percent (20%) of the applicable royalty for such episode as set forth above;

G.4. If Producer produces a live-action episodic television series that is a so-called "spin-off" of the Series, such spin-off series shall be deemed to be a "Series" for purposes of Paragraph G.3 above, provided that the amounts payable under Paragraph G.3 in connection with a generic spin-off and a planted spin-off shall be reduced by fifty percent (50%) and seventy-five percent (75%), respectively. For purposes hereof, a "generic spin-off" shall mean a live-action episodic television series containing a central character in a continuing role which was created by Seller and appeared in the Motion Picture and which was a central character in a continuing role in the Series; and a "planted spin-off" shall mean a live-action episodic television series containing a central character in a continuing role which was created by Seller and appeared in the Motion Picture but which appeared in only one or a multi-part (continuing story line) episode of the Series;

G.5. If Producer produces a sequel or remake motion picture based upon the Motion Picture which is a movie-of-the-week or mini-series intended for initial release by means of broadcast in the U.S. on a free television network during prime time, and Seller is accorded sole "separated rights" in the Work, provided that Seller is not engaged to render services on such production, the following amount (which amount shall constitute full payment for all runs thereof): US$ for each hour of running time, provided that the aggregate amount payable pursuant to this paragraph shall in no event exceed US$ and the amounts (including the maximum amount) payable pursuant to this paragraph shall be reduced by fifty percent (50%) if such Motion Picture is intended for initial release by means of broadcast in the U.S. on other than a free television network during prime time or Seller is accorded shared "separated rights" in the Work; and

G.6. Except as set forth above, Seller shall not be entitled to receive any additional amounts in connection with the exercise of any rights granted under this Agreement, including without limitation the release, telecast or other use or exploitation of the Motion Picture.

H. *Credit; Separated Rights.* Provided that Seller has not materially breached any representations, warranties or obligations, and subject to any guild or union restrictions, if Producer produces the Motion Picture based upon the Work, Seller shall be entitled to receive "separated rights" for purposes of contingent payments under Paragraph G above and credit on screen and in paid advertising, if any, as determined by Producer in good faith in accordance with the provisions of the WGA Basic Agreement as if such Basic Agreement were applicable hereto.

I. *No Union.* Seller acknowledges and agrees that this Agreement shall not be subject to any union or guild agreement.

J. *Reversion.* Seller shall have a right of reversion in accordance with the terms and conditions of Article 16.A.8 of the WGA Basic Agreement as if such Basic Agreement were applicable hereto (provided that such reversion right shall arise no later than five years after the date on which Producer exercises the Option pursuant to Paragraph E.2 above).

K. *Videocassette.* Provided that Seller has not materially breached any of Seller's representations, warranties or obligations, Producer shall supply each Seller with a VHS videocassette and DVD of the Motion Picture for Seller's private use as soon as such items are made commercially available, subject to any then existing industry-wide practices which may restrict Producer's ability to furnish such items.

L. *Premiere.* If Seller has not materially breached any of Seller's representations, warranties or obligations, each Seller shall be entitled to receive an invitation for himself and a guest to attend one United States celebrity premiere of the Motion Picture held by Producer, if any. If the location of such premiere is more than 50 miles from Seller's principal residence (or then current location if closer), Producer shall use good faith efforts to cause the initial United States distributor of the Motion Picture to provide each Seller with two roundtrip first-class, if available and if used, transportation tickets to the location of such premiere, and to reimburse each Seller for reasonable and documented living expenses incurred while attending such premiere.

M. Future Productions; Restrictions on sequels, etc.

M.1. Provided that Seller has not materially breached any of Seller's representations, warranties or obligations, and that Seller is accorded sole "Written By" or sole "Screenplay By" credit for the Motion Picture, if within seven (7) years after the initial general commercial theatrical release of the Motion Picture in the U.S., if any, Producer or its assignee elects to produce a feature-length prequel, sequel or remake motion picture based upon the Motion Picture intended for initial U.S. theatrical release, a movie-of-the-week or mini-series based upon the Motion Picture intended for initial release by means of television broadcast, or a live-action episodic television series pilot (or initial episode if no pilot) based upon the Motion Picture and the Work intended for initial and primary exhibition by means of television broadcast (collectively, the "Future Productions"), Seller shall be given the first opportunity to negotiate for the right to provide writing services on the first such Future Production. Seller's right of first opportunity shall be exercised as follows: If Producer so elects to produce the first such Future Production, Producer shall so notify Seller in writing. If Seller wishes to provide services on such Future Production, Seller shall so advise Producer in writing within ten (10) business days of Producer's aforesaid notice, which notice from Seller shall state that Seller is then actively engaged as a writer in the theatrical or television motion picture industry, as the case may be, and that Seller is ready, willing and able to provide such services on such Future Production, whereupon Seller and Producer shall negotiate in good faith with respect to the terms and conditions of such engagement for a period of fifteen business days. If the parties are unable to reach an agreement by the expiration of such ten (10) business day period, or if Seller does not notify Producer within the five (5) day period set forth above of a desire to supply Seller's services in connection with the Future Production, Producer shall be free to proceed with such Future Production and shall have no further obligation to Seller with respect to any Future

Productions. Seller's right to furnish the services of Seller on a Future Production intended for television exhibition shall be subject to the approval of the television network or other broadcast entity over which such Future Production is to be initially telecast (provided that Producer shall use good faith reasonable efforts to obtain such approval). If Seller provides services on a Future Production under this Paragraph M.1, Producer shall include in its agreement with Seller for such services a provision substantially similar to this Paragraph M.1.

M.2. Producer shall not authorize the production of a prequel, sequel or remake motion picture based upon the Motion Picture without the participation of Producer in such prequel, sequel or remake.

N. *Additional Insured.* Seller shall be covered under Producer's errors and omissions and general liability insurance policies for the Motion Picture to the extent Producer obtains and maintains such policies, subject to the deductibles, exclusions and limitations set forth therein.

O. *More Than One Seller; Payments.* The word "Seller" whenever used herein shall be deemed to mean "Sellers" and all reference throughout this Agreement to "Seller" shall be deemed to be references to each such person individually and all such persons jointly, it being understood and agreed that all such persons assume and shall be jointly and severally liable for all agreements, covenants, warranties, representations, indemnities, duties and obligations of Seller hereunder and that the breach or failure of any agreement, covenant, warranty, representation, duty or obligation contained herein shall be deemed a breach by each and all such persons. All such persons shall be treated as a single unit for purposes of compensation hereunder and the aggregate compensation payable hereunder shall be payable to each such person as follows, unless Producer is otherwise directed in a writing signed by all such persons, but in all cases shall be subject to the following payment requirements: 50% to DG and 50% to GR. All sums of money due to Seller under this Agreement shall be paid in U.S. Dollars to Seller's authorized agent at the address set forth above for Seller, and the receipt of such sums by such agent shall constitute good and valid discharge of all such indebtedness.

P. *No Double Benefits.* Seller acknowledges that Seller shall not be entitled to duplication of payments or any other benefits (*e.g.,* travel and expenses, premieres, videos) as set forth in this Agreement and any other agreement in connection with the Motion Picture.

Q. *Counterparts.* This Agreement may be executed in one or more counterparts, each of which shall be deemed an original, but all of which taken together shall constitute one and the same document.

R. *Standard Terms.* This Memorandum Agreement consists of these Basic Terms and Conditions and the Standard Terms and Conditions attached hereto and incorporated by reference herein.

IN WITNESS WHEREOF, the parties hereto have entered into this Agreement as of the first date set forth below.

Dated: As of

PRODUCER:

By:

Authorized Representative

SELLER:
Date of Execution:

Standard Terms and Conditions—Option—Screenplay

[Negotiated]

Producer:
  Seller:
  Work: Original screenplay entitled "_____"
These Standard Terms and Conditions, together with the Basic Terms and Conditions, shall constitute the agreement between Producer and Seller with respect to the Work. These Standard Terms and Conditions and such Basic Terms and Conditions shall be collectively referred to herein as the "Agreement." All terms used in these Standard Terms and Conditions shall, unless expressly provided to the contrary herein, have the same respective meanings as set forth in the Basic Terms and Conditions. Unless expressly provided to the contrary herein, to the extent that any provision of these Standard Terms and Conditions conflicts with any provision of the Basic Terms and Conditions, the Basic Terms and Conditions shall control.

1. Grant of Rights.

    1.1. Subject to Paragraph M.2 of the Basic Terms and Conditions, Seller hereby grants to Producer an exclusive and irrevocable option (the "Option") during the Grant Period (as defined in Paragraph E of the Basic Terms and Conditions) to acquire forever in all languages and throughout the universe (exclusively during the current and any renewed or extended term of copyright anywhere in the universe and thereafter non-exclusively) all rights (including without limitation all copyright and any renewals and extensions thereof) of any kind or nature now or hereafter known in and to and derived from the Work and any and all parts thereof, including without limitation the characters contained therein whether as contained therein or otherwise, in all media now or hereafter known throughout the universe, including without limitation all motion picture, television and allied, subsidiary and ancillary rights, including without limitation theatrical motion picture, television motion picture, television series, specials, remakes, sequels, videocassette, videodisc, DVD, floppy and/or hard disk and other electronic and computer-assisted media (whether interactive or otherwise), music, recording, animation, non-theatrical, publication (including novelization), live stage, radio, games, theme parks and other location-based entertainment and merchandising and commercial tie-up rights in and to the Work, and all rights derived therefrom or ancillary thereto. If Producer exercises the Option and thereafter, pursuant to the United States Copyright Act or the laws of any other jurisdiction, Seller (or a successor of Seller) has the right to terminate or recapture the rights granted hereunder, and elects to exercise such right as provided pursuant to such Act or such laws, by giving written notice to Producer of such election to exercise, then, commencing upon the date of Producer's receipt of such written notice (the "Commencement Date"), Producer shall have a right of first negotiation/matching last refusal, as provided in Paragraph 7 below, to arrange for any new license or assignment of the rights granted hereunder.

1.2. Without limiting the generality of the foregoing: Upon exercise of the Option, Seller, on Seller's own behalf and on behalf of Seller's administrators, executors, heirs, successors and assigns, shall be deemed irrevocably to grant and assign exclusively to Producer forever and throughout the universe all rental, lending and other similar rights under national laws (whether implemented pursuant to the EC Rental and Lending Rights Directive or otherwise) to which Seller may now be or hereafter become entitled with respect to the Motion Picture and/or any derivative works derived therefrom. Seller agrees on Seller's own behalf and on behalf of Seller's administrators, executors, heirs, successors and assigns, not to institute, support or maintain any litigation or proceedings instituted, supported or maintained on the ground that Producer's (or its designee's) exercise of the rights granted to Producer in the Work or Motion Picture in any way constitutes an infringement or violation of any such rental, lending or other similar rights as aforesaid. Seller hereby acknowledges and agrees that the consideration to which Seller is entitled pursuant to this Agreement includes full and proper equitable consideration for the assignment of rental, lending and other similar rights provided for in this Paragraph 1.2 and that such consideration is an adequate part of the revenues derived or to be derived by Producer from said rights.

1.3. Seller hereby irrevocably grants to Producer forever and throughout the universe the right to use and to permit others to use Seller's respective names, voices, photographs, likenesses and approved biographies (such approval not to be unreasonably withheld and exercised in accordance with Producer's standard procedures) in connection with the rights granted pursuant to this Agreement, and in advertising, promotion and publicity in connection therewith, provided that no such use shall be as a direct endorsement of any product or service.

1.4. During the Grant Period, as it may be extended, Producer shall have the exclusive right to engage in all customary development and pre-production activities in connection with the Work, including without limitation engaging a writer(s) to revise the Work.

2. *Extension of Grant Period.* If (i) due to an event of *force majeure* (*e.g.,* Act of God, strike, terrorist act, war, failure of technical facilities, failure of Seller to deliver any writing services required by Producer or other material breach by Seller hereunder or under any other agreement between Producer and Seller (if any), or other cause not reasonably within Producer's control) or threat thereof, Producer is materially hampered or delayed in the development and/or production of the Motion Picture or (ii) there is any claim (whether or not such claim results in or is followed by litigation) which if true would involve the breach of any of Seller's representations, warranties or agreements herein contained or under any other agreement between Producer and Seller (if any), the Grant Period shall automatically be extended for a period of time equal to the period of time that the development and/or production of the Motion Picture is so hampered or delayed

due to an event of *force majeure,* and/or a period of time equal to the period of time during which any claim is outstanding and unresolved; provided, however, that with respect to any event of force majeure described in clause (i) above, the Grant Period shall not be extended for a period of more than six (6) months in the aggregate, and with respect to any claim described in clause (ii) above, the Grant Period shall not be extended for a period of more than six (6) months in the aggregate unless such claim results in or is followed by the commencement of litigation within such six (6) months' period, in which event the Grant Period shall be extended until such litigation is resolved by final settlement or court decision not subject to appeal.

3. *Representations and Warranties.* Seller hereby represents and warrants as follows:

  3.1. The Work is entirely fiction and has not been published or registered for copyright anywhere in the universe other than as set forth on Schedule 3.1 attached hereto; except for incidental material in the public domain, the Work is wholly original with Seller, no portion of the Work has been taken from or based on any other work or life story and there has been no claim that the Work or a motion picture or other work based thereon violates, conflicts with, or infringes upon, and the Work does not and will not violate, conflict with or infringe upon, any rights whatsoever (including, without limitation, any copyright, common law or statutory, throughout the universe; any right of publication, performance, or any other right in any work; and, to the best of Seller's knowledge, or that which Seller should have known in the exercise of reasonable prudence, any right against libel, slander, invasion of privacy or similar right) of any person, firm or corporation;

  3.2. Seller has and will continue to have the right to enter into and to perform this Agreement and to grant all rights granted hereunder, and the exercise of such rights will not require the consent of or payment to any third party. Seller is the sole and exclusive owner throughout the universe of the rights herein granted to Producer and has the right to grant such rights exclusively to Producer, and no claim has been made that Seller does not or may not have such right or rights. There is not now valid or outstanding, and Seller will not hereafter grant, any right in connection with the Work which is or would be adverse to, or inconsistent with, or impair, the rights herein granted to Producer;

  3.3. The Work is protected by or subject to protection by copyright in the United States and in those countries which are signatory or adhere to the Universal Copyright Convention and/or the Berne Convention and is not in the public domain anywhere in the universe where copyright protection is available; and

  3.4. The rights granted to Producer hereunder have not been previously sold, licensed or optioned to any third party.

4. *Indemnity.*

  4.1. Seller shall indemnify and save harmless Producer, its successors, licensees and assigns, and any representatives thereof, against any and all claims and expenses (including, without limitation, reasonable outside legal fees and expenses), incurred by any of them by reason of the breach of any warranty, undertaking, representation, agreement or certification made or entered into herein or hereunder by Seller.

4.2. Producer shall indemnify and save harmless Seller against any and all claims and expenses (including, without limitation, reasonable legal fees and expenses), incurred by Seller by reason of any material added by Producer to the Work and not provided by Seller or arising in connection with Producer's development, production, distribution or other exploitation of the Motion Picture or any rights related thereto (other than matters covered by Seller's indemnity of Producer set forth in Paragraph 4.1 above or arising in connection with Seller's willful misconduct or gross negligence).

5. *Credit.* Except as specifically provided in the Basic Terms and Conditions, all aspects of Seller's credit, including without limitation, the position, size, prominence, style, placement and form of any and all credits, shall be determined by Producer in its sole discretion. No casual or inadvertent failure of Producer to comply with, and no failure of any third party to comply with, the credit provisions of this Agreement shall constitute a breach of this Agreement. Producer shall contractually obligate its U.S. theatrical distributor of the Motion Picture to comply with, and advise its other third-party distributors and licensees of, the credit provisions in the Basic Terms and Conditions. Upon Producer's receipt of written notice from Seller of any material failure by Producer to comply with the credit provisions in the Basic Terms and Conditions, Producer shall use good faith efforts (whenever practical to do so) to cure prospectively any such failure to comply with respect to advertising and/or prints created by or under the direct control of Producer after Producer's receipt of such notice.

6. *Producer's Control.* Seller acknowledges the right of Producer to make any changes in the Work in the preparation and exploitation of any productions based upon the Work, and in this connection Seller acknowledges and agrees that Seller will not have any right of approval or consultation with respect to any such changes or with respect to any element (casting, teleplay, screenplay, directing, distribution, etc.) of any productions produced hereunder or the exercise of any other rights hereunder. Without limiting the generality of the foregoing sentence, Producer shall have all artistic control over and the right to cut, edit, add to, subtract from, arrange, rearrange and revise the Work in any manner; Seller hereby waives any rights of *droit moral* or similar rights which Seller may have. Producer shall not be obligated to produce or release the Motion Picture or any other production based upon the Work or to continue such production or release if commenced.

7. *Right of First Negotiation/Matching Last Refusal.* Producer's right of first negotiation/matching last refusal shall be exercised in accordance with the following procedure: Commencing with the applicable Commencement Date, Seller and Producer shall negotiate in good faith for a period of not less than sixty (60) days with respect to mutually

agreeable terms and conditions. If Seller and Producer are unable to agree upon mutually agreeable terms, then Seller shall have the right to offer to third parties the rights which are the subject of the first negotiation/matching last refusal; provided, however, that prior to entering into any agreement with any such third party, Seller shall first submit to Producer the terms and conditions which Seller is then prepared to accept from such third party, and Producer shall thereupon have a right, within ten (10) business days after receipt of such terms and conditions, to notify Seller that Producer elects to enter into an agreement with Seller on all of such material terms and conditions, in which event Seller shall enter into an agreement with Producer on such material terms and conditions. If Producer does not within such ten (10) business days notify Seller that it wishes to enter into such an agreement on such material terms and conditions (with silence being deemed a rejection), Seller shall be free to enter into an agreement with a third party on such material terms and conditions.

8. *Seller's Remedies.* Seller recognizes that in the event of a breach by Producer of its obligations under this Agreement (including, without limitation, breaches of the Agreement arising out of credit obligations, if any), the damage (if any) caused Seller thereby is not irreparable or sufficient to entitle Seller to injunctive or other equitable relief. Seller, therefore, agrees that Seller's rights and remedies shall be limited to the right, if any, to obtain damages at law and that Seller shall not have the right in such event to terminate or rescind this Agreement or to enjoin or restrain the distribution or exhibition of the Motion Picture or any other exploitation of the Work. Any breach by Seller under any other agreement between Producer and Seller ("Other Agreements") shall constitute a breach by Seller under this Agreement, and any breach by Seller under this Agreement shall constitute a breach by Seller under the Other Agreements. Neither the expiration of this Agreement nor any other termination thereof shall affect the ownership by Producer of any rights granted herein to Producer, or alter any of the rights or privileges of Producer, or any warranty or undertaking on the part of Seller.

9. *Assignment.* Producer may assign its rights hereunder to any person, firm or corporation, provided that Producer shall remain liable for its obligations hereunder to Seller unless such assignee assumes such obligations in writing and is (i) a person or entity into which Producer merges or is consolidated or (ii) a person or entity that acquires all or substantially all of Producer's business and assets or (iii) a person or entity that is controlled by, under common control with, or controls Producer or (iv) a so-called "major" or "mini-major" producer or distributor of motion pictures, television network or other financially responsible (at the time of assignment) party, in which event Producer shall be fully released from such obligations; Seller shall not assign any of its rights hereunder, and any such purported assignment shall be void *ab initio* and without force or effect, provided that Seller may, on a one-time only basis and upon written notice to Producer, assign its right to receive payments under Paragraphs G.2 through G.5 of the Basic Terms and Conditions.

10. *Notices.* All payments and notices hereunder shall be given in writing to Seller and Producer at their respective addresses set forth above or to such other address as either party shall specify by notice as herein provided. Copies of all notices to be given to Producer shall be sent to

11. *Additional Documentation.* Seller shall execute, verify, acknowledge and deliver to Producer or shall cause to be executed, verified, acknowledged or delivered to Producer, such assignments, documents or other instruments (including Producer's annotation guide), and shall take such actions (including, without limitation, renewing copyrights and instituting and maintaining actions for infringement of any rights), consistent with this Agreement and as Producer may from time to time reasonably deem necessary or desirable to evidence, establish, maintain, protect, enforce and/or defend any or all of Producer's rights under this Agreement or otherwise to effectuate the purposes of this Agreement. All rights herein granted or agreed to be granted to Producer shall vest in Producer whether or not any such instrument is requested, executed or delivered. If Seller fails to execute and deliver any such instrument or take such action within ten (10) business days (reducible to five (5) days in the event the same is required due to exigencies) following Producer's request therefor, Producer shall have the right to execute said instrument or take such action in Seller's name, place and stead, and Producer is hereby irrevocably appointed Seller's attorney-in-fact for such purposes, which power is coupled with an interest. Producer shall provide to Seller a copy of each document so executed by Producer on behalf of Seller, provided that Producer's casual or inadvertent failure to do so shall not constitute a breach of this Agreement.

12. *Miscellaneous; Arbitration.* Producer shall have the right to deduct all applicable required taxes and similar payments from any amounts payable to Seller hereunder. This Memorandum Agreement shall be deemed made in New York State and shall be construed in accordance with the laws of New York State applicable to contracts entirely made and performed therein, and Seller hereby agrees that any dispute hereunder shall be subject to the exclusive jurisdiction of the federal and state courts located in the City, County and State of New York, and courts with appellate jurisdiction therefrom, to which jurisdiction and venue Seller hereby expressly consents; provided, however, that any dispute regarding credit under Paragraph H of the Basic Terms and Conditions shall be settled by arbitration in the City of New York by a single arbitrator chosen by the parties in accordance with the rules of the American Arbitration Association (which arbitrator shall have at least ten years of experience in the motion picture industry), and judgment upon the award rendered by the arbitrator may be entered in any court having jurisdiction thereof. The cost and expenses of the arbitrator and arbitration shall be shared equally by both parties. Long-form agreements will be entered into if requested by Producer containing other terms and conditions standard in the motion picture and television industries but not inconsistent with the terms hereof (it being understood that, subject to the terms hereof, the rights and obligations of the parties hereto are intended to be governed by industry standards), including, without limitation, relating to conformity to law, payola, etc. Until long-form agreements are

executed, if ever, this Memorandum Agreement constitutes a complete and mutually binding agreement.

Schedule 3.1
Copyright Registrations
Work registered for copyright with the U.S. Copyright Office in the name of Seller under entry number on.

Exhibit E.1

Short-Form Option

Producer:
Seller:
Work: Original screenplay entitled "_____"

Know All Men By These Standards

THIS INSTRUMENT is subject to all the terms and conditions of the Memorandum Agreement dated as of between Producer and Seller relating to the Work.

The undersigned Seller, for One Dollar in hand paid and for other valuable consideration now received, hereby grants to Producer the exclusive and irrevocable option to acquire forever all rights, including all MOTION PICTURE, TELEVISION AND ALLIED, SUBSIDIARY AND ANCILLARY RIGHTS (as more fully described in the Memorandum Agreement), of any kind or nature now or hereafter known in and to and derived from the Work, and all parts thereof, in all media now or hereafter known throughout the universe, and all rights in all copyright thereof (and in any renewals or extensions thereof), together with the sole and exclusive right to use, adapt, change, translate, add to, and take from the Work and the title in connection with the exercise of such rights.

Dated: As of
CITY OF
ss.:
STATE OF
On this _____ day of 2005, before me came, to me known to be the individual described in and who executed the foregoing instrument, and duly acknowledged that he executed the same.

Notary Public

Exhibit E.2

Assignment

Producer:
Seller:
Work: Original screenplay entitled "_____"

Know All Men By These Standards

THIS INSTRUMENT is subject to all the terms and conditions of the Memorandum Agreement dated as of between Producer and Seller relating to the Work.

The undersigned Seller, for One Dollar in hand paid and for other valuable consideration now received, hereby sells to Producer forever, all rights, including all MOTION PICTURE, TELEVISION AND ALLIED, SUBSIDIARY AND ANCILLARY RIGHTS (as more fully described in the Memorandum Agreement) of any kind or nature now or hereafter known in and to and derived from the Work, and all parts thereof, in all media now or hereafter known throughout the universe, and all rights in all copyright thereof (and in any renewals or extensions thereof), together with the sole and exclusive right to use, adapt, change, translate, add to, and take from the Work and the title in the making of motion picture and television productions of every kind or character and to lease, vend, exploit and exhibit (including exhibition on free and pay television) the same throughout the universe and to copyright the same in Producer's name.

The undersigned agrees, insofar as the undersigned now or later may have the power or authority so to do, to cause renewals or extensions of any copyright in the Work duly to be obtained, and the rights herein granted are now assigned to Producer for the renewal or extended term of copyright and after such renewal or extension further or like documents of confirmation of assignment will be given to Producer if requested. If the undersigned fails to do so after Producer's request, the undersigned hereby appoints Producer as irrevocable attorney-in-fact, with the right, but not the obligation, to execute and file all such documents and to do all acts necessary for the obtaining of such extensions or renewals and evidencing the continuation of the same rights in Producer for such renewed or extended terms as are now vested in Producer.

The undersigned further agrees that if, pursuant to the Copyright Law of the United States or the laws of any other jurisdiction, the undersigned (or a successor of the undersigned if the undersigned is deceased) exercises any right of termination or recapture pursuant to such Law or laws of the rights granted to Producer hereunder, Producer shall have a right of first negotiation/matching last refusal with respect to any new license or assignment of the rights now assigned to Producer.

And said Producer, and its successors, licensees and assigns, are hereby empowered to bring, prosecute, defend and appear in suits, actions and proceedings of any kind or nature under or concerning said copyright or its renewals or extensions, or concerning any infringement thereof, and particularly infringement of or interference with any of the rights now granted under said copyright or renewals or extensions, in the name of Producer and/or Seller. Any recovery of costs from infringement or violation of any copyright or its renewals or extensions, so far as it arises from any violation of rights hereby assigned, is now assigned to and shall be paid to said Producer and its successors and assigns.

Dated: As of

CITY OF

ss.:

STATE OF

On this _____ day of 2005, before me came to me known to be the individual described in and who executed the foregoing instrument, and duly acknowledged that he executed the same.

_____

Notary Public

Master Use License

(1) In consideration for the payment of the License Fee promptly following the signing of this agreement, Licensor hereby grants to Licensee, its successors, licensees and assigns the following non-exclusive and irrevocable rights throughout the Territory in perpetuity:

    (a) The right to re-record, reproduce and perform excerpts form the Recording of the type and duration described above in synchronization or timed relation with the Film, to make copies of the Film with the Recording contained therein and to import such copies into and exploit them in each country of the Territory in accordance with the terms, conditions and limitations contained in this license;

(b) The right to distribute, publicly perform, sell, lease, broadcast, transmit, otherwise use and exploit all versions of the Film with the Recording contained therein in any media and by any means now known or hereafter devised (including without limitation in the theatrical, non-theatrical, television (all forms including pay-per-view), on-line, home video media, DVD and CD-Rom);

(c) The right to utilize the Recording on excerpts therefrom in or out of the context in which it is contained in the Film in any media for the purpose of advertising, promoting or publicizing the Film.

(d) The nonexclusive right in each country of the Territory to cause or authorize the inclusion of the Recording on a soundtrack album (the "Album") released in connection with the Film and to manufacture and sell phonorecords of the Album in all configurations now known or hereafter devised. In consideration of the soundtrack album rights herein granted, if the recording is actually utilized in the Album, Licensee will cause to be paid to Licensor a royalty ("basic royalty") based on the retail selling price of the Album equal to ___ % multiplied by a fraction, the numerator of which is one and the denominator of which is the total number of master recordings , including the Recording, contained on the Album. If Licensee is accounted to by the record distributor based on wholesale price then the basic royalty shall be ___ %. Royalties shall be defined, calculated and paid to Licensor on the same number of records, on the same basis and in the same manner that royalties are defined, calculated and paid to Licensee with respect to the Album by the applicable record company and shall be subject to such deductions, reductions and nonpayments as Licensee is subject to. Licensee shall account to Licensor for these royalties in the same manner and at the same time that it is accounted to by the record company. Licensor shall pay any and all recorded royalties (other than mechanical royalties and so-called per record union payments based on record sales) which are payable to the artist, producers and any other third parties in connection with the Album embodying the Recording. Licensee shall not have the right to manufacture or sell phonorecords embodying the Recording as "singles" (i.e. a phonorecord containing not more than three master recordings).

(e) The right to use the name and likeness of Artist in connection with Licensee's references to the Recording in the advertising, promotion and publicity for the Film and the Album.

(2) If any record company receives screen credit with respect to a preexisting master recording utilized in connection with the Film, Licensee shall contractually obligate Licensee's distributor to accord Licensor screen credit with respect to the Recording on the negative and all positive prints of the Film. Other than the position of such credit, the content, form, size, position and other details of such screen credit shall be in the manner no less prominent than that accorded to other record companies.

(3) The Recording may not be used as or in conjunction with the title and/or screen credits of the Film, or as a theme song of the Film without Licensor's prior written consent.

(4) Licensee will obtain in writing all requisite consents and permissions, including, without limitation, those of labor organizations and copyright owners, and will pay all re-use payments, fees, royalties, and other sums required to be paid for such consents and permissions, under applicable collective bargaining agreements, or otherwise in connection with Licensee's use of the Recording.

(5) This License does not authorize or permit any use of the Recording not explicitly set forth herein, all rights not expressly granted herein being reserved to the Licensor.

(6) Licensor warrants and represents that it has the right to grant this License, and that the use of the Recording as herein contemplated will not violate the rights of any person or entity.

(7) In the event of a breach of this agreement by Licensee, Licensor's rights and remedies shall be limited to its right, if any, to recover damages in an action at law and in no event shall Licensor be entitled to injunctive or other equitable relief.

(8) This license shall be binding upon, and shall inure to the benefits of, the parties and their respective successors, licensees and/or assigns.

(9) This license has been entered into in, and shall be interpreted in accordance with the laws of, the State of California, and any action or proceeding concerning the interpretation and/or enforcement of this license shall be heard only in the State or Federal Courts situated in Los Angeles County. The parties hereby submit themselves to the jurisdiction of such courts for such purpose. In any action between the parties to enforce any of the terms of this agreement, the prevailing party shall, in addition to any other award of damages or remedy, be entitled to court costs and reasonable attorneys' fees.

Film Synchronization and Performance License

(1) In consideration for the payment of the License Fee promptly following the signing of this agreement, Licensor hereby grants to Licensee, its successors, licensees and assigns the following non-exclusive and irrevocable rights throughout the Territory in perpetuity:

   (a) The right to record the Composition in synchronization or timed relation with the Film and copies thereof in any manner, medium, form or language, to make copies of such recordings, and to import such recordings and copies into and exploit them in each country of the Territory in accordance with the terms, conditions and limitations contained in this license;

   (b) The right to utilize the Composition, subject to obtaining mechanical licenses therefore (which Licensor agrees to issue at then-customary royalty rates), in soundtrack albums and other soundtrack recordings;

   (c) The right to distribute, publicly perform, sell, lease, broadcast, transmit, exhibit, and otherwise use and exploit all versions and copies of the Film with the now known or hereafter devised (including without limitation in the theatrical, non-theatrical, television (all forms including pay-per-view), on-line, home video, laserdisc, DVD and CD-Rom);

(d) The right to utilize the Composition or excerpts there from, in or out of the context in which the Composition has been recorded in the Film, in any media for the purpose of advertising, promoting or publicizing the Film (including without limitation in trailers, spots and commercials).

(2) Licensee agrees that it shall not authorize the performance of the Composition in the Film in the United States by means of television unless the broadcaster or exhibitor has a valid small performing rights license for the Composition from a performing rights society or from Licensor, unless Licensee has obtained such license directly from Licensor, and with respect to the theatrical or television performance of the Composition in the film in any country outside of the United States where small performing rights licenses are required for such use, unless the performance shall have been cleared by the applicable performing rights society in accordance with such society's customary practice and subject to payment to such society of such society's customary fees for such performance, unless Licensee has otherwise obtained a valid license for such use directly from Licensor.

(3) This license does not authorize or permit any use of the Composition not expressly set forth herein, all rights not expressly granted herein being reserved to the Licensor.

(4) Licensor warrants and represents that it has the right to grant this license, and that the use of the Composition by Licensee as contemplated by this agreement will not violate the rights of any person or entity.

(5) If any music publisher receives screen credit with respect to a musical composition utilized in the Film, Licensor shall similarly be accorded a screen credit with respect to the Composition.

(6) In the event of a breach of this agreement by Licensee, Licensor's rights and remedies shall be limited to its right, if any, to recover damages in action at law and in no event shall Licensor be entitled to injunctive or other equitable relief.

(7) This license shall be binding upon, and shall inure to the benefit of, the parties and their respective successors, licensees and/or assigns.

(8) This license has been entered into in, and shall be interpreted in accordance with the laws of, the State of California, and any action or proceeding concerning the interpretation and/or enforcement of this license shall be heard only in the State or Federal Courts situated in Los Angeles County. The parties hereby submit themselves to the jurisdiction of such courts for such purpose. In any action between the parties to enforce any of the terms of this agreement, the prevailing party shall, in addition to any other award of damages or remedy, be entitled to court costs and reasonable attorneys' fees.

9.2.2.2 The Production/Financing/Distribution Deal

Having secured the necessary rights (and, in some instances, where the producer has a proven track record and/or an ongoing involvement with a studio), the producer is in a position to move ahead to secure a production/finance/distribution agreement—a "PF&D deal"—from one of the studios. In a typical PF&D deal, the studio engages a producer to oversee the development of the script, the recruitment of the director and the lead actors, and, if the studio decides to go forward, to produce the film. The studio agrees to put up funds for development of the script, then to finance production of the film (subject to its approval of the budget, the shooting schedule, and all creative elements), and finally, in its discretion—the studio typically has the right to abandon the project at any time, and reserves total control over all decisions concerning distribution and marketing—to distribute the film. All rights in the film and in the underlying property belong to the studio (unless the studio abandons the project, in which case the producer usually gets a one-year right to re-acquire it—in turnaround—by securing a deal at another studio and repaying the first studio the amount it has paid to the point of abandonment, all of this being subject to the first studio's right to step back in under certain circumstances). The producer is usually nonexclusive from inception until a few weeks prior to the commencement of shooting, but from that point on until well into the post-production period (when the film is scored, edited, etc.), the producer is either exclusive to the studio or on first call to the studio. The bottom line under such an arrangement is, because all important decisions are subject to the complete discretion and control of the studio, that the producer is far from independent.

A producer's fee is usually anywhere between $100,000 and $2,000,000. Less established producers will receive closer to the minimum amounts and proven producers will receive very high amounts, even more than $2,000,000. The average producer receives a fee in the range of $300,000 and $400,000. The producer is usually entitled to 50 percent of some contractually determined net, but—as we shall see below—this is often more concept than reality. Where a producer has a solid track record of success, the producer may receive a share of so-called first dollar gross, gross film rental, adjusted gross, or some other more favorable sharing in the revenues from the film prior to breakeven and as an advance against the producer's share of ultimate net profits.

Assuming that all of this is worked out to the parties' satisfaction, the matter proceeds as follows:

1. Pre-Production. The producer's worst fear is that the film may get lost in the shuffle and left on a shelf. To avoid this, the producer will try to negotiate a "progress to production" schedule in the PF&D deal. This forces the studio to choose to proceed further with development or abandon the project, placing it in a position to be repurchased by the producer. A key step in the pre-production phase is the budget for the film, which is established once the script is essentially finished. In general, most studio executives feel it is necessary to reject the first budget presented. Thus, a producer will often overload the budget in anticipation of extensive negotiations resulting in cuts. Once the budget is set, principal characters have been cast, and a director is on board, the typical PF&D deal accord the producers "pay or play" status. This means that the studio has to pay off the producer whether or not the film is actually

made. During pre-production, the full cast and crew is assembled, locations are scouted, sets are built, costumes and props are made, and actors rehearse scenes.

2. Principal Photography. This is the period (usually 10 to 12 weeks, but sometimes much shorter, e.g., *Smoky and the Bandit:* 18 days; *Wag the Dog:* 29 days) or much longer (*Apocalypse Now:* more than four months) during which the film is actually shot. Preparation of the shooting schedule, once an art form, is now largely computerized, the idea being to cluster scenes in which the same actors appear (and the same sets and/or locations are used) insofar as possible, in order to minimize unproductive time.

3. Post-Production. Once the film is "in the can"—an increasingly quaint celluloid concept as new digital video recording technology evolves—the producer, director, and technical staff perform a wide variety of tasks: re-shoots of scenes where extraneous elements (e.g., the shadow from a boom mike, a distant superhighway in a film about the Old West in the 1870s) appear, overdubs of dialog (perhaps a conversation on a busy street was drowned out by nearby construction noise), creation and/or enhancement of effects in the Foley room (technicians stamping on piles of old film make sounds like autumn leaves crunching), and similar technical enhancements and corrections. In addition, the film will be edited, scored, and titled. At the same time, the studio's distribution department begins its work. It books the film with theatrical exhibitors, and promotes it through "teasers" ("Coming this Summer . . . ") and trailers, billboards, broadcast commercials, press releases, and personal appearances by stars. Then, the studio makes a large number of prints of the final version of the film and delivers them to the exhibitors.

9.2.2.3 Writers, Directors, and Performers Agreements

The main issues in agreements with writers, directors, and performers are usually money, credit, and creative involvement (not necessarily in that order.)

I. The Writer Agreement.

In a writer agreement, a producer is hiring a writer to render writing services on a work for hire basis, so that the producer will own all of the results and proceeds of the writer's services. The basic terms of a writer agreement are as follows:

(a) The writing services to be performed.
(b) Writing and reading periods.
(c) Payments for each writing step and guarantees, if any, of certain steps (i.e., first draft, revisions, etc.).
(d) Sole and shared screenplay credit bonuses, if any.
(e) First opportunity to write on subsequent productions based on the source material.
(f) Passive royalties.
(g) Credit.

One important factor to consider when negotiating a writing deal is whether or not the writer is a member of the Writer's Guild of

America, the labor union for professional writers. Members of the Writer's Guild of America (the "WGA") are prohibited from entering into deals with production entities that are not signatories to the "Writer's Guild of America Basic Agreement"; thus, if representing the producer you must ensure that his or her company affiliates with the guild. If the film is under WGA jurisdiction, the WGA will have the right to determine the writing credits for the film. In this regard, productions must submit a "Notice of Tentative Writing Credits" to the WGA once the film is completed. The WGA has the right to approve of the proposed credits, or to arbitrate them if one or more writers is unsatisfied with his or her credit. More importantly, membership in the WGA entitles the writer to a host of benefits, including minimum payments for specific services, and residuals (royalties?).

II. Life Story Rights Agreements.

The primary question a producer must resolve in bringing a factual story to the screen is what rights are required to be obtained. If the story is based on the life of one or more real people, then it is likely that it will be necessary to obtain at least some rights from such people, to foreclose the risk of lawsuits for defamation, invasion of privacy, and the violation of publicity rights. However, many of these laws differ from state to state, and it is often difficult to assess which rights are necessary to obtain, if any, and whether the production may nevertheless be protected by the First Amendment in its contemplated use of the source material. A general rule of thumb is to err on the side of caution and obtain as many rights as you can from all living persons to be depicted even if you are individually comfortable with your legal position. Distributors are often quite conservative in their evaluation of what releases must be obtained before they will release a picture, and similarly it may be more difficult and/or substantially more expensive to obtain errors and omissions insurance without a conservative number of releases.

Life story rights are very often obtained through an option purchase agreement, but there are different considerations that must be addressed as can be seen from the summary of basic terms below.

(a) The length of the initial option period and any extensions.
(b) The price for the option periods and any extensions, and whether these payments are applicable against the purchase price.
(c) Set up bonuses, if any.
(d) The purchase price for the rights, and if based on a % of the budget, floors and ceilings.
(e) Rights granted. In this instance, the question is more of the scope of the release granted (e.g., some life story rights are limited to specific periods in a person's life, or specific events that occurred to a particular person).
(f) Control over the screenplay, and degree of fictionalization permissible.
(g) Use of copyrighted works created by the subject (such as music, films, comic books).

Of course, only a very small number of writers, directors and performers receive the huge fees we read and hear about. In fact, the sad truth is that the vast majority of the members of the three major talent unions (the Directors' Guild, the Writers' Guild, and the Screen Actors' Guild) cannot earn a living in the film business. Perhaps as many as two-thirds of the members of SAG earn less than $1,000 a year from acting in films.

The labor law aspects of film production are beyond the scope of this book. However, it is important to note the existence of basic agreements between the Directors' Guild, the Screen Actors' Guild, and the Writers' Guild of America and the Association of Motion Picture and Television Producers, the bargaining arm of the studios and other producers, which contain minimum compensation terms (scale), supplementary payments for uses in other markets (residuals), and other requirements and restrictions of general application contained in their collective bargaining agreements. However, anything beyond the basics is open for individual negotiation.

For the screenwriter of a screenplay, the key issues are (1) the grant of rights, (2) representations and warranties, (3) indemnities, (4) producer's control, (5) remedies, (6) suspensions and terminations, (7) insurance, (8) immigration/naturalization, and (9) publicity. The Memorandum Agreement and the Standard Terms and Conditions which are a part of the Memorandum Agreement constitute the entire agreement between the screenwriter and the producer. A representative Memorandum Agreement follows, again subject to negotiation between the contracting parties.

2 *Memorandum Agreement*

Basic Terms and Conditions—Services—Writer—Screenplay

A. Producer.
B. Artist.
C. *Motion Picture.* A possible theatrical motion picture to be produced by Producer tentatively entitled _____.
D. Writing Services.
1. Producer hereby engages the writing services of Artist to write a screenplay (the "Work") for the Motion Picture based on Artist's original idea as previously described to Producer. The Work shall consist of a first draft ("First Draft") and, at Producer's election, a rewrite ("Rewrite") and polish ("Polish"). Artist's writing services hereunder shall be performed as follows:

1. Following Producer's request that Artist commence writing services hereunder, Artist shall complete and deliver the First Draft to Producer within three (3) months after such request;
2. Following delivery of the First Draft, Producer shall have a maximum time of eight (8) weeks to read the First Draft and to discuss possible changes and additions thereto with Artist, and Artist shall be reasonably available at the request of Producer for such consultations. On or before the end of said reading period, Producer shall have the right, but not the obligation, to require Artist to write

the Rewrite, incorporating therein the suggestions of Producer. If Producer exercises such right, Artist shall complete and deliver the Rewrite within six (6) weeks after such request, if any; and

3. Following delivery of the Rewrite, Producer shall have a maximum time of eight (8) weeks to read the Rewrite and to discuss possible changes and additions thereto with Artist, and Artist shall be reasonably available at the request of Producer for such consultations. On or before the end of said reading period, Producer shall have the right, but not the obligation, to require Artist to write the Polish, incorporating therein the suggestions of Producer. If Producer exercises such right, Artist shall complete and deliver the Polish within four (4) weeks after such request, if any.

E. *Compensation.* In full and complete consideration to Artist for entering into this Agreement and performing Artist's obligations hereunder, and for all rights granted hereunder, provided that Artist has not breached any of Artist's material representations, warranties or obligations hereunder, Artist shall be entitled to receive an amount equal to US$15,000, which shall accrue and become payable as follows: (i) fifty percent (50%) upon commencement of Artist's services hereunder; and (ii) fifty percent (50%) upon delivery of the First Draft as required hereunder.

F. *Contingent Payments.* If the following events occur, and provided Artist has not breached any of Artist's material representations, warranties or obligations hereunder, Artist shall be entitled to receive the following contingent payments:

1. If Producer requires Artist to write the Rewrite pursuant to Paragraph D.1.2 above, an amount equal to US$7,500, payable as follows: (i) fifty percent (50%) upon commencement of Artist's services on the Rewrite; and (ii) fifty percent (50%) upon delivery of the Rewrite as required hereunder;

2. If Producer requires Artist to write the Polish pursuant to Paragraph D.1.3 above, an amount equal to US$1,500, payable as follows: (i) fifty percent (50%) upon commencement of Artist's services on the Polish; and (ii) fifty percent (50%) upon delivery of the Polish as required hereunder;

3. If Producer produces the Motion Picture as a feature-length theatrical motion picture based on the Work, and if pursuant to a credit determination under Paragraph G below (such definitive determination of the writing credit in connection with the Motion Picture shall be referred to herein as the "Credit Determination") Artist receives sole "Written By" or "Screenplay By" credit for the Motion Picture, the following amounts (provided that if Artist receives shared "Written By" or "Screenplay By" credit for the Motion Picture, such amounts, including the maximum and minimum amounts, shall be reduced by fifty percent (50%)):

   1. An amount (less any amount paid pursuant to Paragraphs E, F.1 and F.2 above) equal to % of the budgeted cost of the Motion Picture on commencement of principal photography (excluding the contingency, interest and bank charges in connection with financing the Motion Picture, legal fees and expenses, budgeted residual and other guild or union payments, any amounts payable to Artist under

this Agreement or any other agreement with Producer and fees and expenses payable to any completion guarantor) (the "Budget"), provided that the amount paid under this Paragraph F.3.1 (including any amounts paid under Paragraphs E, F.1 and F.2 above) shall be no less than and no greater than . Notwithstanding the foregoing, if at the time any payment is due pursuant to this Paragraph F.3.1, Producer has not finally determined the Budget, Producer shall pay to Artist the minimum amount provided for under this Paragraph F.3.1, and shall pay any additional amounts which may be due Artist pursuant to this Paragraph F.3.1 promptly following the commencement of principal photography of the Motion Picture; and

2. An amount equal to % of Producer's share of the Net Profits, if any, of the Motion Picture, commencing at the point at which Producer is first paid its share of Net Profits. For purposes hereof, "Net Profits" shall be defined, computed and calculated in accordance with the definition of net profits accorded to Producer in the agreement between Producer and the primary financier of the Motion Picture, or if no such definition exists, in accordance with Producer's standard definition of net profits, subject to such changes as may be mutually agreed to after good faith negotiation;

4. If Producer produces a feature-length sequel theatrical motion picture based upon the Motion Picture and the Work, and pursuant to a Credit Determination Artist receives sole "Written By" credit for the Motion Picture, provided Artist is not engaged to render services in connection with such sequel, an amount equal to fifty percent (50%) of the amount paid pursuant to Paragraph F.3.1 above, plus Net Profits, if any, from such sequel at the rate of fifty percent (50%) of the rate used to calculate payments pursuant to Paragraph F.3.2 above, provided that if Artist receives shared "Written By" credit for the Motion Picture, the amounts payable pursuant to this paragraph shall be reduced by fifty percent (50%);

5. If Producer produces a feature-length remake theatrical motion picture based upon the Motion Picture and the Work, and pursuant to a Credit Determination Artist receives sole "Written By" credit for the Motion Picture, provided Artist is not engaged to render services in connection with such remake, an amount equal to thirty-three and one-third percent (33a%) of the amount paid pursuant to Paragraph F.3.1 above, plus Net Profits, if any, from such remake at the rate of thirty-three and one-third percent (33a%) of the rate used to calculate payments pursuant to Paragraph F.3.2 above, provided that if Artist receives shared "Written By" credit for the Motion Picture, the amounts payable pursuant to this paragraph shall be reduced by fifty percent (50%);

6. If Producer produces a live-action episodic television series (the "Series") based upon the Motion Picture and the Work for initial telecast on a free television network (*i.e.*, ABC, CBS, NBC or Fox) during prime time, and pursuant to a Credit Determination Artist receives sole "Written By" credit for the Motion Picture, provided Artist is not engaged to render services in connection with such Series, a first-run royalty in an amount equal to the following for

each episode of such Series so produced and broadcast, depending upon the length of such episode (provided that if Artist receives shared "Written By" credit for the Motion Picture, or if such Series is produced for initial telecast in the U.S. on other than a free television network during prime time, such royalties shall be reduced by fifty percent (50%)):

1. For each episode which is 30 minutes or less in length, $2,000;
2. For each episode which is more than 30 minutes and up to 60 minutes in length, $2,500;
3. For each episode which is more than 60 minutes in length, $3,000; and
4. For each of the first five (5) free television network reruns of any such episode, twenty percent (20%) of the applicable royalty for such episode as set forth above;

7. If Producer produces a sequel or remake motion picture based upon the Motion Picture and the Work which is a movie-of-the-week or mini-series intended for initial release by means of television broadcast on a free television network, and pursuant to a Credit Determination Artist receives sole "Written By" credit for the Picture, provided Artist is not engaged to render services in connection with such sequel or remake, the following amount (which amount shall constitute full payment for all runs thereof), provided that if Artist receives shared "Written By" credit for the Motion Picture, such amount shall be reduced by fifty percent (50%): $10,000 for each hour of running time, provided that the aggregate amount payable pursuant to this Paragraph F.7 shall in no event exceed $80,000; and
8. If Artist does not receive sole or shared "Written By" or "Screenplay By" writing credit for the Motion Picture, Artist shall not be entitled to receive any further compensation in excess of the compensation payable pursuant to Paragraphs E, F.1 or F.2 above, as applicable.

G. *Credit.* Provided Artist has not breached any of Artist's material representations, warranties or obligations hereunder, and subject to any guild or union restrictions, if Producer produces the Motion Picture based on the Work, Artist shall receive writing credit on screen and in paid advertising for the Motion Picture (other than awards, prizes and congratulatory ads and any paid advertising exceptions in agreements between Producer and any distributor(s), licensee(s) or financier(s) of the Motion Picture) issued by or under the direct control of Producer as and to the extent mutually agreed to by the parties in good faith, provided that in the event of a disagreement, the decision of Producer shall control.

H. *Union Agreement.* Artist hereby acknowledges and agrees that this Agreement and Artist's services hereunder are not subject to any guild or union agreement.

I. *Standard Terms.* This Memorandum Agreement consists of these Basic Terms and Conditions and the Standard Terms and Conditions attached hereto and incorporated by reference herein and contains the full and complete understanding between the parties and supersedes all prior and contemporaneous written or oral agreements and understandings pertaining hereto.

Dated: As of
PRODUCER:
By:
Authorized Representative
ARTIST:

Standard Terms and Conditions—Services—Writer—Screenplay

Producer:
  Artist:
  Motion Picture:
  These Standard Terms and Conditions, together with the Basic Terms and Conditions, shall constitute the agreement between Producer and Artist in connection with the Motion Picture. These Standard Terms and Conditions and such Basic Terms and Conditions shall be collectively referred to herein as the "Agreement." Each term used in these Standard Terms and Conditions shall, unless expressly provided to the contrary herein, have the same meaning ascribed thereto in the Basic Terms and Conditions. Unless expressly provided to the contrary herein, to the extent that any provision of these Standard Terms and Conditions conflicts with any provision of the Basic Terms and Conditions, the Basic Terms and Conditions shall control.

I. *Artist's Services.* Artist's services hereunder shall be performed as, when, and where reasonably required by Producer, to the best of Artist's ability and subject to the discretion and control of Producer (including without limitation any requirement by Producer that Artist collaborate with others), on an exclusive basis during all writing periods and on a non-exclusive first-priority basis at all other times. To the extent Producer has not requested the writing services of Artist pursuant to Paragraphs D.1.1, D.1.2 and/or D.1.3 of the Basic Terms and Conditions within the time periods applicable thereto, Producer shall thereafter have the right, but not the obligation, to require Artist to perform such unrequested services for a period not to exceed twenty-four (24) months following the expiration of the last applicable reading period, subject to Artist's prior conflicting professional contractual writing commitments.

II. *Grant of Rights.*

  A. Producer has and shall have exclusively forever and throughout the universe all rights of any kind or nature in and to and derived from the product of Artist's services hereunder in any capacity, and any and all parts thereof and all material contained therein, whether as contained therein or otherwise (collectively, the "Product"), in all languages and media throughout the universe, whether now or hereafter known, including without limitation the characters contained therein whether as contained therein or otherwise, all theatrical motion picture, television motion picture, sequels, remakes, series, miniseries, non-theatrical, merchandising and commercial tie-up, music, videodisc, videocassette, DVD, floppy and/or hard disk, CD-ROM and other electronic, on-line and computer-assisted media (whether interactive, multimedia or otherwise), animation, theme park and other location-based entertainment, live stage, radio, print publication and novelization rights in and to such Product, and all rights derived there from or ancillary thereto, including without limitation the right to obtain copyright thereon and to terminate or extend licenses or assignments there under, as employer-for-hire for copyright purposes, Artist hereby acknowledging and agreeing that Artist is performing Artist's services hereunder as Producer's employee-for-hire, and that all of the Product is a work specially ordered or commissioned for use as part of a motion picture or other audiovisual work and as such is a work-for-hire for Producer for copyright purposes. In the event said work-for-hire status is deemed unenforceable for any reason, Artist hereby acknowledges and agrees that Artist has irrevocably assigned exclusively to Producer forever and throughout the universe, upon its creation, the Product and all copyrights therein, all to the full extent set forth above. Furthermore, Artist hereby irrevocably assigns exclusively to Producer forever and throughout the universe any and all interest Artist may now or hereafter have in and to the copyright of the Motion Picture and any work derived there from or ancillary thereto.

B. Without limiting the generality of the foregoing: Artist, on Artist's own behalf and on behalf of Artist's heirs, executors, administrators, successors and assigns, hereby irrevocably grants and assigns exclusively to Producer forever and throughout the universe all rental, lending and other similar rights under national laws (whether implemented pursuant to the EC Rental and Lending Rights Directive or otherwise) to which Artist may now be or hereafter become entitled with respect to the Product, the Motion Picture and/or any derivative works derived there from. Artist agrees on Artist's own behalf and on behalf of Artist's heirs, executors, administrators, successors and assigns, not to institute, support or maintain any litigation or proceedings instituted or maintained on the ground that Producer's (or its designee's) exercise of the rights granted to Producer in the Product, the Motion Picture or any derivative work in any way constitutes an infringement or violation of any such rental, lending or other similar rights as aforesaid. Artist hereby expressly acknowledges and agrees that the compensation payable to Artist pursuant to the Basic Terms and Conditions of this Agreement includes full and proper equitable remuneration with respect to any right (including Artist's rental, lending and similar rights (if any) with respect to the Motion Picture) to which Artist may now be or hereafter become entitled in connection with the production and/or exploitation of the Motion Picture or any rights therein or related thereto and that such compensation is an adequate part of the revenues derived or to be derived from such rights.

C. Artist hereby irrevocably grants exclusively to Producer forever and throughout the universe the right to use and to permit others to use Artist's name, voice, photograph, likeness, and biography in connection with the rights granted hereunder and in advertising, promotion, and publicity in connection therewith (including, without limitation, in connection with promotional films, including so-called "behind-the-scenes" and "making-of" films, footage and featurettes, merchandising, commercial tie-ups, soundtrack albums and publications relating to or based on the Motion Picture); provided, however, that no such use shall be as a direct endorsement of any product or service, it being agreed that listing Artist's name in credits shall not constitute an endorsement.

III. *Compensation; Additional Payments.* Producer's obligation to pay any compensation or contingent payments to Artist as reflected in the Basic Terms and Conditions shall be subject to Artist's fully complying with all of Artist's material obligations pursuant to this Agreement. Except as specifically provided in the Basic Terms and Conditions, no additional or increased amounts shall be payable to Artist, including with respect to Artist's rendition of services at night, on weekends or holidays, or after the expiration of any particular number of hours on any one day, or for time spent traveling to or from any location where Artist may be required to render services in connection with the Motion Picture, or for so called "forced calls" or meal penalties, or in connection with the exercise of any rights granted under this Agreement, including without limitation the release, telecast or other use, re-use or exploitation of the Motion Picture or any rights therein or related thereto.

IV. *Representations and Warranties.* Artist hereby represents and warrants as follows:

A. All of the Product will be written by and wholly original with Artist and not based on or taken from any other material or life story (except for incidental material in the public domain or material provided to Artist by Producer); and the Product is free and clear of all claims, liens and encumbrances and will not violate, conflict with or infringe upon any rights whatsoever (including, without limitation, any copyright, common law or statutory, throughout the world; any right of publication, performance or any other right in any work; and any right against libel, slander, invasion of privacy or similar right) of any person, firm or corporation; and

B. Artist has and will continue to have the right to enter into and to perform this Agreement and to grant all rights granted hereunder, and the exercise of such rights will not require the consent of or payment to any third party. Artist is the sole and exclusive owner throughout the universe of the rights herein granted to Producer and has the right to grant such rights exclusively to Producer, and no claim has been made that Artist does not or may not have such right or rights. There is not now valid or outstanding, and Artist will not hereafter grant, any right in connection with the Product which is or would be adverse to, or inconsistent with, or impair, the rights herein granted to Producer.

V. *Indemnities.*

A. Artist shall indemnify and save harmless Producer, its successors, licensees and assigns, and any representatives thereof, against any and all claims and expenses (including without limitation reasonable legal fees and expenses) incurred by any of them by reason of the breach or alleged breach of any warranty, undertaking, representation, agreement or certification made or entered into herein or hereunder by Artist.

B. Producer shall indemnify and save harmless Artist against any and all claims and expenses (including without limitation reasonable legal fees and expenses) incurred by Artist by reason of any material added by Producer to the Product.

VI. *Credit.* Except as provided in the Basic Terms and Conditions, all aspects of Artist's credit, including without limitation the position, size, prominence, style, placement and form of all credits, shall be determined by Producer in its sole discretion. No casual or inadvertent failure of Producer to comply with, and no failure of any third party to comply with, the credit provisions of this Agreement shall constitute a breach of this Agreement. Any reference to the title of the Motion Picture in relation to the placement or size of Artist's credit shall be a reference to the so-called "regular" title and not the "artwork" title unless otherwise specified. Any reference to the "size" of credit shall mean only the average height, width, and thickness of the letters used to display such credit.

VII. *Producer's Control.* Artist hereby acknowledges the right of Producer to make any changes in the Product in the preparation and exploitation of any productions based upon or incorporating such Product, and in this connection Artist acknowledges and agrees that Artist will not have any right of approval or consultation with respect to any such changes or with respect to any element (casting, teleplay, screenplay, directing, distribution, etc.) of any productions produced hereunder. Without limiting the generality of the foregoing sentence, Producer shall have all artistic control over and the right to cut, edit, add to, subtract from, arrange, rearrange, and revise the Product in any manner. Artist hereby waives any rights of *droit moral* or similar rights which Artist may have. Artist further acknowledges and agrees that Producer shall have no obligation to make, produce, release, distribute, advertise or exploit the Motion Picture, or to utilize Artist's services, or to commence principal photography on the scheduled starting date, and hereby releases Producer from any liability for any loss or damage Artist may suffer by reason of Producer's failure to make, produce, release, distribute, advertise or exploit the Motion Picture, or utilize Artist's services in connection therewith, or commence principal photography on the scheduled starting date (it being agreed that, in any such event, Producer's obligations under this Agreement shall be fully performed by payment to Artist of any compensation accrued but unpaid prior to the date of such event under Paragraph E of the Basic Terms and Conditions, subject to Producer's rights and remedies (including those under Paragraphs 9, 10 and 11 below)).

VIII. *Artist's Remedies.* Artist hereby recognizes that in the event of a breach by Producer of its obligations under this Agreement (including, without limitation, breaches of the Agreement arising out of credit obligations, if any), the damage (if any) caused Artist thereby is not irreparable or sufficient to entitle Artist to injunctive or other equitable relief. Artist, therefore, agrees that Artist's rights and remedies shall be limited to the right, if any, to obtain damages at law and that Artist shall not have the right in such event to terminate or rescind this Agreement or to enjoin or restrain the production, distribution or exhibition of the Motion Picture or any rights therein or any other exploitation of the Product. Any breach by Artist under any other agreement between Artist and Producer ("Other Agreements") shall constitute a breach by Artist under this Agreement, and any breach by Artist under this Agreement shall constitute a breach by Artist under the Other Agreements. Neither the expiration of this Agreement nor any other termination thereof shall affect the ownership by Producer of the Product or any other rights granted herein to Producer, or alter any of the rights or privileges of Producer, or any warranty, indemnity or undertaking on the part of Artist in connection with such rights. Artist acknowledges that Artist's services are of a unique, extraordinary and intellectual character, the loss of which cannot be adequately compensated in damages in an action at law, and therefore Artist acknowledges and agrees that Producer shall be entitled to injunctive and other equitable relief to prevent or curtail any breach or alleged breach of this Agreement.

IX. *Suspensions and Terminations.* Notwithstanding anything to the contrary contained herein, Artist's employment and compensation hereunder shall automatically be suspended during any and all periods: (i) that Artist does not render services hereunder because of death, illness, incapacity, default or similar matters; (ii) that development or production of the Motion Picture is prevented, interrupted or delayed because of Force Majeure events, including without limitation any labor dispute, fire, war or governmental action, or any event beyond Producer's control; or (iii) that development or production of the Motion Picture is prevented, interrupted or delayed by reason of the death, illness, incapacity or default of any key personnel or a principal member of the cast. Unless this Agreement is terminated as provided in this Paragraph 9, the periods provided for in Paragraph D of the Basic Terms and Conditions shall be deemed extended by a period equivalent to all such periods of suspension. If any matter referred to in clause (i) or (iii) above, other than default on the part of Artist, continues for longer than seven (7) consecutive days or ten (10) days in the aggregate, or if any matter referred to in clause (ii) above continues for more than six (6) consecutive weeks or eight (8) weeks in the aggregate, or in the event of any default on the part of Artist, Producer may terminate this Agreement by written notice. In the event Producer terminates this Agreement pursuant to this Paragraph 9, Producer's only financial obligation to Artist shall be to pay to Artist any compensation accrued but unpaid hereunder prior to such termination, subject to Producer's rights and remedies (including the right of offset in the event of Artist's default). If Artist does not receive compensation due hereunder for any period equal to or greater than six (6) consecutive weeks or eight (8) weeks in the aggregate pursuant to clause (ii) above, Artist may terminate this Agreement by written notice to Producer, provided that Producer may void any such notice of termination given by Artist by resuming payments hereunder to Artist within one (1) week of Producer's receipt of such notice, it being agreed that such resumption shall not limit Producer's rights if another event gives rise to suspension pursuant to this Paragraph 9. In the event Producer so resumes payments, Producer shall have a continuing right to terminate so long as the suspension event continues.

X. *Insurance.* Producer shall have the right, but not the obligation, to secure any type of insurance covering Artist as Producer may desire, and Artist shall not have any interest in any such insurance, but shall assist Producer in obtaining the same and also submit to all examinations in connection therewith. If Producer cannot obtain insurance on Artist at ordinary rates and under customary conditions, or if such insurance is available only at a premium in excess of such ordinary rates, and Artist does not, within five (5) business days of notification by Producer of such excess charges, pay such excess charges, Producer may terminate this Agreement without any further obligation to Artist by written notice to Artist given on or before thirty (30) days after Artist shall have failed to pass such examination or otherwise qualify for such insurance.

XI. *Immigration/Naturalization.* Artist acknowledges that any offer of employment hereunder is subject to and contingent upon Artist's ability to prove Artist's identity and employment eligibility as required by any applicable immigration laws, and Artist hereby agrees to complete, execute and deliver to Producer all documents required by such laws, including documentation of Artist's employment eligibility, prior to the commencement of Artist's services. If Artist fails to verify and deliver such documents as provided above, Producer shall have the right, by notice to such effect given to Artist, to terminate this Agreement, without any further obligation to Artist.

XII. *Publicity.* Artist shall not directly or indirectly issue or authorize the issuance of any publicity or disclose any information concerning this Agreement, Artist's services hereunder, the Motion Picture or Producer's business or production methods without Producer's prior written consent; provided, however, that Artist shall not be deemed in breach of this paragraph if Artist incidentally and nondisparagingly refers to said matters during an interview concerned primarily with Artist rather than any of said matters. Artist shall pose for publicity pictures, appear for such interviews with such persons as Producer may designate and perform such other services as may be required by Producer in connection with publicity and advertising for the Motion Picture without additional compensation, but subject to Artist's other prior conflicting professional contractual commitments in the entertainment industry if after completion of Artist's exclusive services hereunder.

XIII. *Right to Withhold.* Producer shall have the right to deduct and withhold from any sums payable to Artist hereunder any amounts required to be deducted and withheld by Producer pursuant to any present or future law, ordinance or regulation of any country, including, without limitation, any country wherein Artist furnishes any of Artist's services hereunder, or pursuant to any present or future rule or regulation of any union or guild (if any) having jurisdiction over the services to be furnished by Artist hereunder.

XIV. *Assignment.* Producer may assign its rights hereunder to any person, firm or corporation, provided that Producer shall remain secondarily liable for its obligations hereunder to Artist unless such assignee assumes in writing all such obligations, in which event Producer shall be fully released from such obligations. Artist shall not assign any of Artist's rights hereunder, and any such purported assignment shall be void *ab initio* and without force or effect.

XV. *Notices.* Notices hereunder shall be in writing and shall be sent to Artist and Producer at the respective addresses set forth above, or to such other addresses as Producer or Artist may hereafter give notice of in such manner. Copies of all notices to be given to Producer shall be sent to _____.

XVI. *Additional Documentation.* Artist shall execute, verify, acknowledge and deliver to Producer or shall cause to be executed, verified, acknowledged or delivered to Producer, such assignments, documents or other instruments (including certificates of authorship, origin, etc.), and shall take such actions (including, without limitation, renewing copyrights and instituting and maintaining actions for infringement of any rights), as Producer may from time to time reasonably deem necessary or desirable to evidence, establish, maintain, protect, enforce and/or defend any or all of Producer's rights under this Agreement or otherwise to effectuate the purposes of this Agreement. All rights herein granted or agreed to be granted to Producer shall vest in Producer whether or not any such instrument is requested, executed or delivered. If Artist fails to execute and deliver any such instrument within three (3) days following Producer's request therefore, Producer shall have the right to execute said instrument in Artist's name, place and stead, and Producer is hereby irrevocably appointed Artist's attorney-in-fact for such purposes, which power is coupled with an interest.

Miscellaneous. Amounts payable to Artist hereunder shall be payable on Producer's normal payroll date during the week following the week in which such amounts accrued. This Agreement shall be construed in accordance with the laws of New York applicable to contracts entirely made and performed therein, without regard to principles of conflicts of law contained therein. Long-form agreements will be entered into if requested by Producer containing other terms and conditions standard in the motion picture and television industry, but not inconsistent with the terms hereof (it being understood that, subject to the terms hereof, the rights and obligations of the parties hereto shall be governed by industry standards), including, without limitation, relating to completion of services, wage stabilization, conformity to law, payola, worker's compensation, etc. Until long-form agreements are executed, if ever, this Agreement constitutes a complete and mutually binding agreement.

For the director, the key issues are (1) the director's services, (2) the grant of rights, (3) compensation: additional payments, (4) representations and warranties, (5) indemnities, (6) credit, (7) director's cuts, (8) transportation and expenses, (9) premiers, (10) video cassette, (11) additional insured, (12) producer's control, (13) director's remedies, (14) suspensions and terminations, (15) insurance, (16) immigration/naturalization, (17) expenses, (18) compliance with guarantor's instructions, (19) publicity, (20) right to withhold, (21) assignment, and (22) guild membership. The Memorandum Agreement and the Standard Terms and Conditions which are a part of the Memorandum Agreement constitute the entire agreement between the director and the producer. A representative agreement follows, subject to negotiation.

3 *Memorandum Agreement*

Basic Terms and Conditions—Services—Director—Individual

A. Producer.
B. Artist.

C. *Motion Picture.* A possible theatrical motion picture tentatively entitled ".".

D. *Services.* Producer hereby engages from Artist, and Artist hereby agrees to supply, the services of Artist as the director of the Motion Picture, including without limitation all such services reasonably requested by Producer and which are customarily rendered by the director of a first-class theatrical motion picture. Artist's services shall commence on an exclusive basis eight (8) weeks prior to the scheduled commencement of principal photography of the Motion Picture and continue thereafter until delivery of the first cut of the Motion Picture required to be delivered by Artist hereunder. Prior to and after the foregoing period, Artist's services shall be on a non-exclusive, first-priority basis until completion and delivery of the final answer print of the Motion Picture to the primary United States distributor, provided that Artist shall not render services to third parties or on Artist's own behalf which materially interfere with Artist's services hereunder. Artist shall direct the Motion Picture in compliance with the requirements of Producer, including the following: (i) the Motion Picture shall be produced in accordance with the final budget, production and post-production schedules, including being delivered prior to the delivery date specified on the post production schedule (time being of the essence) and final shooting script, all as approved by Producer; (ii) the Motion Picture shall conform to all legal or governmental exhibition requirements, standards and practices, and foreign censorship requirements; (iii) the running time of the Motion Picture shall be between 95 minutes (excluding main and end titles) and 110 minutes (including main and end titles); and (iv) the Motion Picture shall receive an MPAA rating no more restrictive than "PG-13," it being agreed that Artist shall also prepare sufficient alternative scenes and dialogue, as may be requested by Producer, to enable the Motion Picture to be shown on network television in the United States and airlines without impairing the continuity of the Motion Picture. Without limiting the foregoing, Artist shall not make or authorize any changes in the final shooting script (except minor changes required by the exigencies of production), schedule or budget, nor shall Artist make or authorize any commitment for services, rights, facilities or materials for the Motion Picture, without Producer's written approval in each case. All such services, rights, facilities and materials shall be contracted for by Producer in Producer's name.

E. *Compensation.* In full and complete consideration to Artist for entering into this Agreement and performing Artist's material obligations hereunder, and for all rights granted hereunder, provided that Artist has not breached any of Artist's material representations, warranties or obligations hereunder, Artist shall be entitled to receive an amount equal to % of the budgeted cost of the Motion Picture on commencement of principal photography (excluding the contingency and any amounts payable to Artist hereunder or under any other agreement with Producer), which shall accrue and become payable as follows:

E.1. 20% thereof in equal weekly installments commencing eight

(8) weeks prior to the commencement of principal photography;

E.2. 60% thereof in equal weekly installments over the period of principal photography;

E.3. 10% thereof upon delivery of the first cut of the Motion Picture required to be delivered by Artist hereunder; and

E.4. 10% upon delivery of the final answer print of the Motion Picture to the primary United States distributor.

F. *Credit.* Provided Artist has not breached any of Artist's material representations, warranties or obligations hereunder, if the Motion Picture is directed substantially in its entirety (*i.e.,* more that 90%) by Artist, Artist shall be entitled to receive an individual credit, substantially in the form "Directed By " as follows:

F.1 On screen, on all positive prints of the Motion Picture, on a separate card in the main titles (provided that if the credits of all individual producers appear in the end titles, then Artist's credit shall appear only in the end titles) in a size of type no smaller than that of the larger of 50% of the screen title or the credit accorded to the individual producers;

F.2. Subject to Producer's standard exclusions and exceptions as set forth in Producer's Paid Advertising Exhibit attached hereto ("Excluded Advertising"), in the billing block, if any, of all paid advertising issued by or under the direct control of Producer, in a size of type no smaller than that of the larger of 50% of the "regular" title or the credit accorded to the individual producers in such billing block; and

F.3. In the billing block, if any, of all Excluded Advertising issued by or under the direct control of Producer in which any individual producer is accorded billing block credit, other than award, nomination and congratulatory ads in which the only individual accorded credit is the one being awarded, nominated or congratulated, ads announcing a personal appearance, radio ads and audio portion of teasers, trailers and television ads.

G. *Director's Cuts.* Artist shall make and deliver such cuts of and attend such previews for the Motion Picture as required by Producer and in accordance with Producer's instructions, it being understood that Producer shall have the sole right to make any and all cuts, including the so-called "final cut," of the Motion Picture; provided, however, that Artist shall be entitled to one (1) cut and one (1) preview of the Motion Picture, subject to the following:

G.1. Artist has not breached any material representations, warranties or obligations hereunder;

G.2. No Over-Budget Excess (as defined below) has occurred;

G.3. The time and place of the preview shall be mutually determined by Producer and Artist, provided that in the event of a dispute, Producer shall make the final determination in its sole discretion;

G.4. The first cut shall be completed within ten (10) weeks of completion of principal photography of the Motion Picture (unless otherwise specified in the approved production schedule). All previews and subsequent cuts of the Motion Picture (if any are permitted hereunder) shall be completed in accordance with the approved budget and production schedule, but in no event later than five (5) months of completion of principal photography of the Motion Picture;

G.5. Each cut must be within the required running time as provided elsewhere herein;

G.6. The Motion Picture as delivered shall adhere to the approved shooting script, except for minor changes required by the exigencies of production; and

G.7. Upon completion or expiration of Artist's cutting rights, Producer shall have the right to make the final cut of the Motion Picture in its sole discretion. If the actual cost of production of the Motion Picture exceeds an amount equal to one hundred seven and one-half percent (107–1/2%) of the approved direct cost portion of the budget, exclusive of the administrative fee and contingency (if any), then an amount equal to such excess shall be defined for purposes hereof as the "Over-Budget Excess."

H. *Transportation and Expenses.* If Paragraph 12 of the Standard Terms and Conditions attached hereto applies, Artist shall be entitled to receive non-exclusive ground transportation between Artist's accommodations and the set.

I. *Premieres.* Provided that Artist has not breached any of Artist's material representations, warranties, or obligations hereunder, Producer shall use good faith efforts to cause the distributor of the Motion Picture to supply Artist with two (2) invitations to the United States East or West Coast celebrity premiere, if any, of the Motion Picture. With respect to such event at a Distant Location, Producer shall use good faith efforts to cause the distributor to furnish Artist with two (2) business-class roundtrip air (if appropriate) transportation tickets between Artist's principal residence (or then current location, if closer) and the location of such event (if available and used for such purpose) for Artist and his guest, and to reimburse Artist for reasonable expenses in connection with Artist's attendance at such event.

J. *Videocassette.* Provided that Artist has not breached any of Artist's material representations, warranties or obligations hereunder, Producer shall supply Artist with a VHS videocassette and DVD of the Motion Picture for Artist's private home use only promptly after such items are made commercially available in the United States, subject to any then existing industry-wide practices which may restrict Producer's ability to furnish such items.

K. *Additional Insured.* Artist shall be covered under Producer's general liability and errors and omissions insurance policies for the Motion Picture to the extent Producer obtains and maintains such policies, subject to the deductibles, exclusions, and limitations set forth therein.

L. *Standard Terms.* This Memorandum Agreement consists of these Basic Terms and Conditions and the Standard Terms and Conditions attached hereto and incorporated by reference herein and contains the full and complete understanding between the parties and supersedes all prior and contemporaneous written or oral agreements and understandings pertaining hereto.

Dated: As of
PRODUCER:
By:_____
Authorized Representative
ARTIST:

Standard Terms and Conditions—Services—Director—Individual

Producer:
  Artist:
  Motion Picture:

These Standard Terms and Conditions, together with the Basic Terms and Conditions, shall constitute the agreement between Producer and Artist for the services of Artist in connection with the Motion Picture (collectively the "Agreement"). Each term used in these Standard Terms and Conditions shall, unless expressly provided to the contrary herein, have the same meaning ascribed thereto in the Basic Terms and Conditions. Unless expressly provided to the contrary herein, to the extent that any provision of these Standard Terms and Conditions conflicts with any provision of the Basic Terms and Conditions, the Basic Terms and Conditions shall control.

1. *Artist's Services.* Artist's services hereunder shall be performed as when and where reasonably required by Producer, to the best of Artist's ability and in accordance with the direction and control of Producer.
2. *Grant of Rights.*

    1. Producer has and shall have exclusively forever and throughout the universe all rights of any kind or nature in and to and derived from the product of Artist's services hereunder in any capacity, and any and all parts thereof and all material contained therein, whether as contained therein or otherwise (collectively, the "Product"), in all languages and media throughout the universe, whether now or hereafter known, including without limitation the characters contained therein whether as contained therein or otherwise, all theatrical motion picture, television motion picture, sequels, remakes, series, mini-series, non-theatrical, merchandising and commercial tie-up, music (including soundtrack), videodisc, videocassette, floppy and/or hard disk, DVD, CD-ROM and other electronic, on-line and computer-assisted media (whether interactive, multimedia or otherwise), animation, theme park and other location-based entertainment, live stage, radio, print publication, and novelization rights in and to such Product, and all rights derived there from or ancillary thereto, including without limitation the right to obtain copyright thereon and to terminate or extend licenses or assignments thereunder, as employer-for-hire for copyright purposes, Artist hereby acknowledging and agreeing that Artist is performing Artist's services hereunder as Producer's employee-for-hire, and that all of the Product is a work specially ordered or commissioned for use as part of a motion picture or other audiovisual work and as such is a work-for-hire for Producer for copyright purposes. In the event said work-for-hire status is deemed unenforceable for any reason, Artist hereby acknowledges and agrees that Artist has irrevocably granted and assigned exclusively to Producer forever and throughout the universe, upon its creation, the Product and all copyrights therein, all to the full extent set forth above. Furthermore, Artist hereby irrevocably grants and assigns exclusively to Producer forever and throughout the universe any and all interest Artist may now or hereafter have in and to the copyright of the Motion Picture and any work derived therefrom or ancillary thereto (it being agreed that Artist shall not have any right

or interest in any roles or characters contained in the Motion Picture or any derivative or ancillary works, and that Producer is and shall be the exclusive owner forever and throughout the universe of all rights of any kind or nature now or hereafter known, including all the rights described above, in and to the Motion Picture).

2. Without limiting the generality of the foregoing: Artist, on Artist's own behalf and on behalf of Artist's heirs, executors, administrators, successors and assigns, hereby irrevocably grants and assigns exclusively to Producer forever and throughout the universe all rental, lending and other similar rights under national laws (whether implemented pursuant to the EC Rental and Lending Rights Directive or otherwise) to which Artist may now be or hereafter become entitled with respect to the Product, the Motion Picture, and/or any derivative works derived therefrom. Artist agrees on Artist's own behalf and on behalf of Artist's heirs, executors, administrators, successors and assigns, not to institute, support or maintain any litigation or proceedings instituted, supported or maintained on the ground that Producer's (or its designee's) exercise of the rights granted to Producer in the Product, the Motion Picture or any derivative work in any way constitutes an infringement or violation of any such rental, lending or other similar rights as aforesaid. Artist hereby expressly acknowledges and agrees that the compensation payable to Artist pursuant to the Basic Terms and Conditions of this Agreement includes full and proper equitable remuneration with respect to any right (including Artist's rental, lending and similar rights (if any) with respect to the Motion Picture) to which Artist may now be or hereafter become entitled in connection with the production and/or exploitation of the Motion Picture or any rights therein and that such compensation is an adequate part of the revenues derived or to be derived from such rights.

3. Artist hereby irrevocably grants and assigns exclusively to Producer forever and throughout the universe the right to use and to permit others to use Artist's name, voice, photograph, likeness and biography in connection with the rights granted hereunder and in advertising, promotion and publicity in connection therewith (including, without limitation, in connection with promotional films, including so-called "behind-the-scenes" and "making-of" films, footage and featurettes, merchandising, commercial tie-ups, soundtrack albums and publications relating to or based on the Motion Picture); provided, however, that no such use shall be as a direct endorsement of any product or service.

3. *Compensation; No Additional Payments.* Producer's obligation to pay any compensation or contingent payments to Artist as reflected in the Basic Terms and Conditions shall be subject to Artist's fully complying with all Artist's material representations, warranties and obligations pursuant to this Agreement. Except as specifically provided in the Basic Terms and Conditions or required by any applicable guild or union agreement (a "Labor Agreement"), no additional or increased amounts shall be payable to Artist, including with respect to Artist's rendition of services at night, on weekends or holidays, or after the expiration of any particular number of hours on any one day, or for time spent

traveling to or from any location where Artist may be required to render services in connection with the Motion Picture, or for so called "forced calls," meal or other penalties, or in connection with the exercise of any rights granted under this Agreement, including without limitation the release, telecast or other use or re-use of the Motion Picture. If in connection with any services of Artist or the exploitation of any rights granted under this Agreement any additional amounts are required by a Labor Agreement, Artist shall receive such amounts at the minimum rates required by such Labor Agreement; provided, however, that to the maximum extent permitted under such Labor Agreement, any amounts paid to Artist under the Basic Terms and Conditions shall be applied against and shall reduce any such additional amounts to which Artist may become entitled under such Labor Agreement, and vice versa (Artist hereby agreeing that the amounts payable to Artist under the Basic Terms and Conditions include all amounts that may be required by such Labor Agreement). Artist hereby acknowledges that this Agreement is not subject to any Labor Agreement.

4. *Representations and Warranties.* Artist hereby represents and warrants as follows:

   1. All of the Product will be wholly original with Artist and not based on or taken from any other material or life story (except for incidental material in the public domain); and the Product will not violate, conflict with or infringe upon any rights whatsoever (including, without limitation, any copyright, common law or statutory, throughout the world; any right of publication, performance or any other right in any work; and any right against libel, slander, invasion of privacy or similar right) of any person, firm or corporation; and

   2. Artist has and will continue to have the right to enter into and to perform this Agreement, and to grant all rights granted hereunder. Artist is the sole and exclusive owner throughout the universe of the rights herein granted to Producer and has the right to grant such rights exclusively to Producer, no claim has been made that Artist does not or may not have such right or rights and the exercise of such rights will not require any consent of or payment to any third party. There is not now valid or outstanding, and Artist will not hereafter grant, any right in connection with the Product which is or would be adverse to, or inconsistent with, or impair, the rights herein granted to Producer.

5. *Indemnities.*

   1. Artist shall indemnify and save harmless Producer, its successors, licensees and assigns, and any representatives thereof, against any and all claims, liabilities, damages and expenses (including without limitation reasonable legal fees and expenses) incurred by any of them by reason of the breach or alleged breach of any warranty, undertaking, representation, agreement or certification made or entered into herein or hereunder by Artist.

   2. Producer shall indemnify and save harmless Artist against any and all claims, liabilities, damages and expenses (including without limitation reasonable legal fees and expenses) incurred by Artist by reason of any material added by Producer to the Product.

6. *Credit.* Except as provided in the Basic Terms and Conditions, all aspects of Artist's credit, including without limitation the position, size, prominence, style, placement and form of all credits, shall be determined by Producer in its sole discretion. No casual or inadvertent failure of Producer to comply with, and no failure of any third party to comply with, the credit provisions of this Agreement shall constitute a breach of this Agreement. Any reference to the title of the Motion Picture in relation to the placement or size of Artist's credit shall be a reference to the so-called "regular" title and not the "artwork" title unless otherwise specified. Any reference to the "size" of credit shall mean only the average height, width and thickness of the letters used to display such credit. Artist's credit shall in any event be subject to any applicable guild or union requirements.

7. *Producer's Control.* Artist hereby acknowledges the right of Producer to make any changes in the Product in the preparation and exploitation of any productions based upon or incorporating such Product, and in this connection Artist acknowledges and agrees that Artist will not have any right of approval or consultation with respect to any such changes or with respect to any element (casting, teleplay, screenplay, directing, distribution, etc.) of any productions produced hereunder. Without limiting the generality of the foregoing sentence, Producer shall have all artistic control over and the right to cut, edit, add to, subtract from, arrange, rearrange and revise the Product in any manner. Artist hereby waives any rights of *droit moral* or similar rights which Artist may have. Artist further acknowledges and agrees that Producer shall have no obligation to make, produce, release, distribute, advertise or exploit the Motion Picture, or to utilize Artist's services, or to commence principal photography on the scheduled starting date, and hereby releases Producer from any liability for any loss or damage Artist may suffer by reason of Producer's failure to make, produce, release, distribute, advertise or exploit the Motion Picture, or utilize Artist's services in connection therewith, or commence principal photography on the scheduled starting date (it being agreed that, in any such event, Producer's obligations under this Agreement shall be fully performed by payment to Artist of any compensation accrued but unpaid prior to the date of such event under Paragraph E of the Basic Terms and Conditions, subject to Producer's rights and remedies (including those under Paragraphs 9, 10 and 11 below)).

8. *Artist's Remedies.* Artist hereby recognizes that in the event of a breach by Producer of its obligations under this Agreement (including, without limitation, breaches of the Agreement arising out of credit obligations, if any), the damage (if any) caused Artist thereby is not irreparable or sufficient to entitle Artist to injunctive or other equitable relief. Artist, therefore, agrees that Artist's rights and remedies shall be limited to the right, if any, to obtain damages at law and that Artist shall not have the right in such event to terminate or rescind this Agreement or to enjoin or restrain the production, distribution or exhibition of the Motion Picture or any rights therein or any other exploitation of the Product. Neither the expiration of this Agreement nor any other termination thereof shall affect the ownership by Producer of the Product or any other rights granted herein to Producer, or alter any of the rights or privileges of Producer, or any warranty,

indemnity or undertaking on the part of Artist in connection with such rights. Artist acknowledges that Artist's services are of a unique, extraordinary, and intellectual character, the loss of which cannot be adequately compensated in damages in an action at law, and therefore Artist acknowledges and agrees that Producer shall be entitled to injunctive and other equitable relief to prevent or curtail any breach or alleged breach of this Agreement.

9. *Suspensions and Terminations.* Notwithstanding anything to the contrary contained herein, Artist's employment and compensation hereunder shall automatically be suspended during any and all periods: (i) that Artist does not render services hereunder because of death, illness (including physical, mental or emotional disability), incapacity, default or similar matters; (ii) that production of the Motion Picture is prevented, interrupted or delayed because of Force Majeure events, including without limitation any labor dispute, fire, war or governmental action, or any event beyond Producer's control; or (iii) that production of the Motion Picture is prevented, interrupted or delayed by reason of the death, illness (including physical, mental or emotional disability), incapacity or default of the producers or any other key production personnel or a principal member of the cast. Unless this Agreement is terminated as provided in this Paragraph 9, the periods provided for in Paragraph D of the Basic Terms and Conditions shall be deemed extended by a period equivalent to all such periods of suspension. If any matter referred to in clause (i) or (iii) above, other than default on the part of Artist, continues for longer than seven (7) consecutive days or ten (10) days in the aggregate, or if any matter referred to in clause (ii) above continues for more than three (3) consecutive weeks or six (6) weeks in the aggregate, or in the event of any default on the part of Artist, Producer may terminate this Agreement by written notice. In the event Producer terminates this Agreement pursuant to this Paragraph 9 other than for default on the part of Artist, Producer's only obligation to Artist shall be to pay to Artist any compensation accrued but unpaid hereunder prior to such termination, subject to Producer's rights and remedies, provided that if Producer terminates this Agreement for default on the part of Artist, Producer shall have no further obligations to Artist under this Agreement. If Artist does not receive compensation due hereunder for any period equal to or greater than six (6) consecutive weeks or eight (8) weeks in the aggregate pursuant to clause (ii) above, Artist may terminate this Agreement by written notice to Producer, provided that Producer may void any such notice of termination given by Artist by resuming payments hereunder to Artist within one (1) week of Producer's receipt of such notice, it being agreed that such resumption shall not limit Producer's rights if another event gives rise to suspension pursuant to this Paragraph 9. In the event Producer so resumes payments, Producer shall have a continuing right to terminate so long as the suspension event continues.

10. *Insurance.* Producer shall have the right, but not the obligation, to secure any type of insurance covering Artist as Producer may desire, and Artist shall not have any interest in any such insurance, but shall assist Producer in obtaining the same and also submit to all examinations in connection therewith. If Producer cannot obtain insurance

on Artist at ordinary rates and under customary conditions, or if such insurance is available only at a premium in excess of such ordinary rates, and Artist does not, within three (3) days of notification by Producer of such excess charges, pay such excess charges, Producer may terminate this Agreement without any further obligation to Artist by written notice to Artist.

11. *Immigration/Naturalization.* Artist acknowledges that any offer of employment hereunder is subject to and contingent upon Artist's ability to prove Artist's identity and employment eligibility as required by any applicable immigration laws, and Artist hereby agrees to complete, execute and deliver to Producer all documents required by such laws, including documentation of Artist's employment eligibility, prior to the commencement of Artist's services. If Artist fails to verify and deliver such documents as provided above, Producer shall have the right, by notice to such effect given to Artist, to terminate this Agreement, without any further obligation to Artist.

12. *Expenses, etc.* The provisions set forth in Paragraph H of the Basic Terms and Conditions shall apply only if Artist is required by Producer to render services at a place (a "Distant Location") more than seventy-five (75) miles from Artist's principal residence (or from Artist's then current location if closer to such Distant Location). Producer's obligation (if any) to supply accommodations shall extend to the room rate and related taxes only. Such provisions are in lieu of any other obligations which may otherwise apply to Producer with respect to Artist's (or anyone accompanying Artist) transportation, accommodations, meal allowances, and other expenses or perquisites while at such Distant Location.

13. *Compliance with Guarantor's Instructions.* Artist hereby agrees to act in accordance with any completion guarantee agreement with any completion guarantor for the Motion Picture, including without limitation following any instructions in connection with the Motion Picture given by such completion guarantor within the parameters of such guarantee.

14. *Publicity.* Artist shall not directly or indirectly issue or authorize the issuance of any publicity or disclose any information concerning this Agreement, Artist's services hereunder, the Motion Picture or Producer's business or production methods without Producer's prior written consent; provided, however, that Artist shall not be deemed in breach of this paragraph if Artist incidentally and nondisparagingly refers to said matters during an interview concerned primarily with Artist rather than any of said matters. Artist shall pose for publicity pictures, appear for such interviews with such persons as Producer may designate and perform such other services as may be required by Producer in connection with publicity and advertising for the Motion Picture without additional compensation, but subject to Artist's other then prior professional directing contractual commitments in the entertainment industry if after completion of Artist's exclusive services hereunder.

15. *Right to Withhold.* Producer shall have the right to deduct and withhold from any sums payable to Artist hereunder any amounts required to be deducted and withheld by Producer pursuant to any

present or future law, ordinance or regulation of any country or other governmental authority, including, without limitation, any country wherein Artist furnishes any of Artist's services hereunder, or pursuant to any present or future rule or regulation of any union or guild (if any) having jurisdiction over the services to be furnished by Artist hereunder.

16. *Assignment.* Producer may assign this Agreement and/or its rights hereunder to any person, firm or corporation, provided that Producer shall remain secondarily liable for its obligations hereunder to Artist unless such assignee assumes such obligations in writing, in which event Producer shall be fully released from all such obligations. Artist shall not assign any of Artist's rights hereunder, and any such purported assignment shall be void *ab initio* and without force or effect.

17. *Guild Membership.* During the entire term of this Agreement, at such times and during such periods as it may be lawful for Producer to require Artist to do so, Artist shall remain or become and remain a member in good standing of any then properly designated labor organization (as defined and determined under applicable law) representing persons performing services of the type and character that are required to be performed by Artist hereunder. If Artist fails, neglects or refuses to become a member in good standing of any such union(s), Producer shall have the right at Producer's sole election (in addition to Producer's other rights and remedies hereunder) to terminate this Agreement without any further obligation to Artist or to pay on Artist's behalf any required dues, fees or other payments to such union(s), and in the event of any such payment, Producer may deduct the amounts paid by Producer from any compensation otherwise payable to Artist hereunder. Except as expressly provided to the contrary herein, Producer shall be entitled to the maximum rights permitted under any applicable Labor Agreement. In the event of any conflict between any provision hereof and the mandatory terms of any Labor Agreement, the latter shall prevail; provided, however, that in such event the provisions of this Agreement so affected shall be curtailed and limited only to the extent necessary to permit compliance with the minimum mandatory terms and conditions of such Labor Agreement.

18. *Notices.* Notices hereunder shall be in writing and shall be sent to Artist and Producer at the respective addresses set forth above, or to such other addresses as Producer or Artist may hereafter give notice of in such manner. Copies of all notices to be given to Producer shall be sent to _____.

19. *Additional Documentation.* Artist shall execute, verify, acknowledge and deliver to Producer or shall cause to be executed, verified, acknowledged or delivered to Producer, such assignments, documents or other instruments, and shall take such actions (including, without limitation, renewing copyrights and instituting and maintaining actions for infringement of any rights) as Producer may from time to time reasonably deem necessary or desirable to evidence, establish, maintain, protect, enforce and/or defend any or all of Producer's rights under this Agreement or otherwise to effectuate the purposes of this Agreement. All rights herein granted or agreed to be granted

to Producer shall vest in Producer whether or not any such instrument is requested, executed or delivered. If Artist fails to execute and deliver any such instrument within three (3) days following Producer's request therefor, Producer shall have the right to execute said instrument in Artist's name, place and stead, and Producer is hereby irrevocably appointed Artist's attorney-in-fact for such purposes, which power is coupled with an interest.

20. *Miscellaneous.* This Agreement shall be construed in accordance with the laws of New York applicable to contracts entirely made and performed therein, without regard to principles of conflicts of law contained therein, and Artist hereby agrees that any dispute hereunder shall be subject to the non-exclusive jurisdiction of the courts located in New York, and courts with appellate jurisdiction therefrom, to which jurisdiction and venue Artist hereby expressly consents. Long-form agreements will be entered into if requested by Producer containing other terms and conditions standard in the motion picture and television industry, but not inconsistent with the terms hereof (it being understood that, subject to the terms hereof, the rights and obligations of the parties hereto shall be governed by industry standards), including, without limitation, relating to completion of services, wage stabilization, conformity to law, payola, worker's compensation, etc. Until long-form agreements are executed, if ever, this Agreement constitutes a complete and mutually binding agreement.

Paid Advertising Exhibit

Producer's obligation, if any, to accord credit in paid advertising shall be limited to advertising issued by or under the direct control of Producer and shall not include so-called "Excluded Advertising" as follows: (1) group, list or institutional advertising; (2) teaser or special advertising; (3) outdoor advertising; (4) promotional material for exhibitors; (5) publicity, advertising or exploitation relating to the story or literary or dramatic material on which the Motion Picture is based, its title, the authors or writers, the music, the composers or conductor, the director, any members of the cast, or similar matters; (6) any advertising or publicity written in narrative form; (7) a listing in the nature of a cast of characters; (8) trailer or other advertising on the screen; (9) radio or television advertising or exploitation; (10) newspaper or magazine advertising of eight (8) column inches or less; (11) window or lobby displays or advertising; (12) advertising relating to subsidiary or ancillary rights in the Motion Picture (including, without limitation, novelizations, screenplay and other publications, products or merchandising, soundtrack recordings, videocassettes, videodiscs and other home video devices and the covers, packages, containers or jackets therefore); (13) advertising in which no credit is accorded other than credit to one (1) or two (2) stars of the Motion Picture and/or Producer and/or any other company financing or distributing the Motion Picture; (14) advertising, publicity and exploitation relating to by-products or commercial tie-ups; (15) other advertising not relating primarily to the Motion Picture; (16) award, nomination and congratulatory-type ads; and (17) any other exclusions contained in agreements between Producer and any financier, distributor or licensee of the Motion Picture. References in critics' quotes shall not constitute credit for purposes of the Agreement.

For the performer, the key issues are (1) the performer's services, (2) the grant of rights, (3) compensation: additional payments, (4) representations and warranties, (5) indemnities, (6) credit, (7) producer's control, (8) lender's remedies, (9) suspensions and terminations, (10) insurance, (11) immigration/naturalization, (12) expenses, (13) compliance with guarantor's instructions, (14) publicity, (15) right to withhold, (16) assignment, and (17) guild membership. Other issues subject to negotiation are the perks accorded to star talent, such as personal trailers, chauffeur driven limousines, personal assistants, hairdressers, nannies, living allowances, personal trainers and other similar items. The Memorandum Agreement and the Standard Terms and Conditions which are a part of the Memorandum Agreement constitute the entire agreement between the performer and the producer. A representative agreement, subject to negotiation between the contracting parties, follows.

4 *Memorandum Agreement*

Basic Terms and Conditions—Services—Performer—Loanout

A. Producer.
B. *Lender.* , providing the services of ("Artist").
C. *Motion Picture.* A possible theatrical motion picture tentatively entitled " ."
D. *Services.* Producer hereby engages from Lender, and Lender agrees to supply, the acting services of Artist in the role of " " (the "Role") in the Motion Picture, including without limitation any such services requested by Producer and which are customarily rendered by a principal cast member on a first-class theatrical motion picture. Artist's exclusive services to Producer in connection with rehearsal and pre-production of the Motion Picture shall commence on or about two (2) weeks prior to the scheduled commencement of principal photography, and shall continue thereafter until the completion of principal photography. Principal photography is currently scheduled to commence on or about and conclude on or about _____ .
E. *Compensation.* In full and complete consideration to Lender for entering into this Agreement and performing Lender's material obligations hereunder, and for all rights granted hereunder, provided that Lender has not breached any of Lender's material representations, warranties or obligations hereunder, Lender shall be entitled to receive an amount equal to _____ , which shall accrue and be payable in equal weekly installments over the period of principal photography.
F. *Contingent Payments.* If the following events occur, and provided Lender has not breached any of Lender's material representations, warranties or obligations hereunder, Lender shall be entitled to receive the following contingent payments: If Artist's services are required hereunder for more than consecutive "free" weeks for rehearsal or other pre-production services, or for more than consecutive weeks for principal photography services, or for more than not necessarily consecutive "free" days for looping, dubbing, retakes, additional scenes and/or other post-production services, for each additional day for which such services are rendered during rehearsal, pre-production, principal photography or post-production (other than publicity services and travel days, for which no compensation shall be payable), an amount equal to _____ .

G. *Credit.*

    G.1. Subject to Paragraph G.2 below, if Artist appears recognizably in the Role in the Motion Picture during its initial general theatrical release, Artist shall be entitled to receive the following cast credit:

        G.1.1. On screen, on all positive prints of the Motion Picture, on a separate card in position among cast members, in the main titles (provided that if the credits of all other cast members appear only in the end titles, Artist's credit shall appear only in the end titles), in a size of type no smaller than that of the larger of 50% of the screen title or the credit accorded to any other cast member;

        G.1.2. Subject to Producer's standard exclusions and exceptions as set forth in Producer's Paid Advertising Exhibit attached hereto ("Excluded Advertising"), in position among cast members in the billing block, if any, of all paid advertising issued by or under the direct control of Producer, in a size of type no smaller than that of the larger of 50% of the "regular" title or the credit accorded to any other cast member in such billing block; and

        G.1.3. In the billing block, if any, of all Excluded Advertising (or in another similar ad) issued by or under the direct control of Producer in which any cast member is accorded billing block credit, other than award, nomination or congratulatory ads in which the only individual accorded credit is the one being awarded, nominated or congratulated, ads announcing a personal appearance, radio ads and the audio portion of teasers, trailers, and television ads.

    G.2. If any other cast member is accorded credit above the screen title or the "regular" or artwork title of the Motion Picture in any particular item of paid advertising issued by or under the direct control of Producer (other than award, nomination or congratulatory ads in which the only individual accorded such credit is the one being awarded, nominated or congratulated, ads announcing a personal appearance, radio ads and the audio portion of teasers, trailers and television ads), then Artist's credit shall also be accorded above such screen title or "regular" or artwork title in such item of paid advertising (or in another similar ad), as applicable, it being agreed that if Artist receives credit in the artwork portion of any item of paid advertising, then Producer shall not be required to accord Artist credit in the billing block of such item of paid advertising unless any other actor receives credit in both the artwork portion and billing block of such item of paid advertising.

H. *Transportation and Expenses.* If Paragraph 12 of the Standard Terms and Conditions attached hereto applies, Artist shall be entitled to receive the following: (i) one (1) premiere-class roundtrip air (if appropriate) transportation ticket on Aer Lingus (or business class on another airline) between Artist's principal residence (or then current location if closer to the Distant Location (as defined in the Standard Terms and Conditions)) and the Distant Location for use by Artist (if available and used for such purpose); (ii) appropriate accommodations for Artist;

(iii) during principal photography, a non-accountable all-inclusive daily allowance in an amount equal to (which allowance shall be no less than the allowance provided by Producer to any other cast member); (iv) non-exclusive (but shared only with so-called "above-the-line" personnel) ground transportation between Artist's accommodations and the set and exclusive ground transportation to and from airports; and (vii) during principal photography, an exclusive high quality caravan/dressing room (which caravan/dressing room shall be no less favorable than the caravan/dressing room provided by Producer to any other cast member).

I. *Premieres.* Provided that Lender has not breached any of Lender's material representations, warranties or obligations hereunder, Producer shall use reasonable good faith efforts to cause the distributor of the Motion Picture to supply Artist with two (2) invitations to the initial United States East or West Coast celebrity premiere, if any, of the Motion Picture. With respect to such premiere at a Distant Location, Producer shall use good faith reasonable efforts to cause the distributor to furnish Artist with two (2) first-class roundtrip air (if appropriate) transportation tickets between Artist's principal residence (or then current location, if closer) and the location of such event (if available and used for such purpose) for Artist and her guest, and to reimburse Artist for reasonable expenses in connection with Artist's attendance at such event.

J. *Videocassette.* Provided that Lender has not breached any of Lender's material representations, warranties or obligations hereunder, Producer shall supply Artist with a VHS videocassette and DVD of the Motion Picture for Artist's private home use only promptly after such items are made commercially available in the United States, subject to any then existing industry-wide practices which may restrict Producer's ability to furnish such items.

K. *Additional Insured.* Lender and Artist shall be covered under Producer's general liability and errors and omissions insurance policies for the Motion Picture to the extent Producer obtains and maintains such policies, subject to the deductibles, exclusions and limitations set forth therein.

L. *Rest Period.* Producer shall use reasonable efforts to accord Artist a five (5) day work week and a ten (10) hour rest period from the time Artist is dropped off at her accommodations each day until the time she is picked up at her accommodations on the following day (which rest period shall be no less favorable than the rest period accorded to any other adult cast member).

M. *Nudity Rider.* If nudity is required, Lender shall cause Artist to execute a nudity rider in form and substance satisfactory to Producer in connection with her performance of nude scenes in the Picture.

N. *Artist's Consultation Rights.* Artist shall have the following consultation rights with respect to the Motion Picture:

N.1. Artist shall have the right of consultation with respect to Artist's hairdresser, make-up artist and wardrober; and

N.2. Lender acknowledges and agrees that Artist's consultation rights as set forth in this Agreement are personal to Artist and may not be delegated or assigned, and are subject to Artist being available as reasonably required by Producer. Lender agrees that Artist shall exercise such consultation rights in a reasonable manner, on a timely basis and in accordance with the production and post-production schedules, any delivery or guild or union requirements, the requirements of any completion guarantor and the amount allocated for the applicable item in the budget for the Motion Picture approved by Producer. Artist's consultation rights regarding personnel are subject to such individual being available as required by Producer and being able to obtain the necessary work visas and satisfy all applicable governmental requirements to render services, and Producer (or a related company) not having previously experienced a problem with such individual. With respect to such consultation rights, the decision of Producer shall be final and binding upon Artist.

O. *Wardrobe.* Provided that Lender has not breached any of Lender's material representations, warranties, or obligations hereunder, following the delivery of the final answer print of the Motion Picture and subject to the approval of the primary financier, Artist shall be entitled to keep one costume from Artist's wardrobe which was purchased (*i.e.,* not rented or borrowed) by Producer for the Motion Picture.

P. *Standard Terms.* This Memorandum Agreement consists of these Basic Terms and Conditions and the Standard Terms and Conditions attached hereto and incorporated by reference herein and contains the full and complete understanding between the parties and supersedes all prior and contemporaneous written or oral agreements and understandings pertaining hereto.

Dated: As of
PRODUCER:
By:_____
Authorized Representative
LENDER:
By:
Authorized Representative

In order to induce Producer to enter into the foregoing Agreement with Lender, and for other good and valuable consideration, receipt and sufficiency of which are hereby acknowledged, the undersigned hereby represents and warrants that the undersigned is familiar with each term and condition of the foregoing Agreement, and the undersigned hereby consents and agrees to the execution and delivery of said Agreement by Lender and hereby agrees to render all of the services therein provided to be rendered by the undersigned, to grant all of the rights granted therein, and to be bound by and duly perform and observe each and all of the terms and conditions of said Agreement requiring performance or compliance on the part of the undersigned, and hereby joins in all warranties, representations, agreements, and indemnities made by Lender, and further confirms the terms of Paragraph 7 of the Standard Terms and Conditions of the foregoing Agreement and hereby waives any rights of *droit moral* or similar rights which the undersigned may have. The undersigned further represents and warrants that the undersigned is providing services to Lender pursuant to a written agreement (the "Employment Agreement") between the undersigned and Lender and the undersigned agrees to be bound by the terms of the foregoing Agreement notwithstanding the expiration or earlier termination of the Employment Agreement between the undersigned and Lender during the term of the foregoing Agreement. The undersigned further waives any claim against Producer for wages, salary or other compensation of any kind pursuant to said Agreement or in connection with the Motion Picture and the exercise by Producer of rights therein or derived therefrom (provided, however, that such waiver shall not relieve Producer of any of its obligations to Lender under the foregoing Agreement), and the undersigned agrees that the undersigned will look solely to Lender for any and all compensation that the undersigned may become entitled to receive in connection with said Agreement.

Signed:_____

Standard Terms and Conditions—Services—Performer—Loanout

Producer:
Lender:
Artist:
Motion Picture:

These Standard Terms and Conditions, together with the Basic Terms and Conditions, shall constitute the agreement between Producer and Lender for the services of Artist in connection with the Motion Picture (collectively, the "Agreement"). Each term used in these Standard Terms and Conditions shall, unless expressly provided to the contrary herein, have the same meaning ascribed thereto in the Basic Terms and Conditions. Unless expressly provided to the contrary herein, to the extent that any provision of these Standard Terms and Conditions conflicts with any provision of the Basic Terms and Conditions, the Basic Terms and Conditions shall control.

1. *Artist's Services.* Artist's services hereunder shall be performed as, when and where reasonably required by Producer, to the best of Artist's ability and in accordance with the reasonable direction and control of Producer. "On or about" shall mean a date occurring during the period commencing seven (7) days before the date stated and ending seven (7) days after the date stated, as Producer shall designate. Lender shall cause Artist to render services in connection with wardrobe preparation and fittings, rehearsals, pre-recordings, consultations and similar pre-production matters for the Motion Picture as required by Producer without additional compensation; after Artist's period of exclusivity to Producer hereunder and until delivery of the final answer print of the Motion Picture, Lender shall cause Artist to perform post-production services (*e.g.,* retakes, looping, and/or dubbing, added scenes) in connection with the Motion Picture as requested by Producer without additional compensation, but subject to Artist's other then prior professional acting contractual commitments in the entertainment industry in the event such post-production services are not consecutive to Artist's period of exclusivity to Producer hereunder.

2. *Grant of Rights.*

   2.1. Producer has and shall have exclusively forever and throughout the universe all rights of any kind or nature in and to and derived from the product of Artist's services hereunder in any capacity, and any and all parts thereof and all material contained therein, whether as contained therein or otherwise (collectively, the "Product"), in all languages and media throughout the universe, whether now or hereafter known, including without limitation the characters contained therein whether as contained therein or otherwise, all theatrical motion picture, television motion picture, sequels, remakes, series, mini-series, non-theatrical, merchandising and commercial tie-up, music (including soundtrack), videodisc, videocassette, floppy and/or hard disk, DVD, CD-ROM and other electronic, on-line and computer-assisted media (whether interactive, multimedia or otherwise), animation, theme park and other location-based entertainment, live stage, radio, print publication and novelization rights in and to such Product, and all rights derived therefrom or ancillary thereto, including without limitation the right to obtain copyright thereon and to terminate or extend licenses or assignments thereunder, as employer-for-hire for copyright purposes, Lender hereby acknowledging and agreeing that Artist is performing Artist's services hereunder as Producer's employee-for-hire, and that all of the Product is a work specially ordered or commissioned for use as part of a motion picture or other audiovisual work and as such is a work-for-hire for Producer for copyright purposes. In the event said work-for-hire status is deemed unenforceable for any reason, Lender hereby acknowledges and agrees that Lender and Artist have irrevocably granted and assigned exclusively to Producer forever and throughout the universe, upon its creation, the Product and all copyrights therein, all to the full extent set forth above. Furthermore, Lender hereby irrevocably grants and assigns exclusively to Producer forever and throughout the universe any and all interest Lender or Artist may now or hereafter have in and to the copyright of the Motion Picture and any work derived therefrom or ancillary thereto (it being agreed that neither Lender nor Artist shall have any right or interest in the Role or any other characters contained in the Motion Picture or any derivative or ancillary works, and that Producer is and shall be the exclusive owner forever and throughout the universe of all rights of any kind or nature now or hereafter known, including all the rights described above, in and to the Motion Picture).

2.2. Without limiting the generality of the foregoing: Lender, on Lender's and Artist's own behalf and on behalf of their respective heirs, executors, administrators, successors and assigns, hereby irrevocably grants and assigns exclusively to Producer forever and throughout the universe all rental, lending, and other similar rights under national laws (whether implemented pursuant to the EC Rental and Lending Rights Directive or otherwise) to which Lender or Artist may now be or hereafter become entitled with respect to the Product, the Motion Picture, and/or any derivative works derived therefrom. Lender agrees on Lender's and Artist's own behalf and on behalf of their respective heirs, executors, administrators, successors and assigns, not to institute, support or maintain any litigation or proceedings instituted, supported or maintained on the ground that Producer's (or its designee's) exercise of the rights granted to Producer in the Product, the Motion Picture or any derivative work in any way constitutes an infringement or violation of any such rental, lending or other similar rights as aforesaid. Lender hereby expressly acknowledges and agrees that the compensation payable to Lender pursuant to the Basic Terms and Conditions of this Agreement includes full and proper equitable remuneration with respect to any right (including Lender's and Artist's rental, lending and similar rights (if any) with respect to the Motion Picture) to which Lender or Artist may now be or hereafter become entitled in connection with the production and/or exploitation of the Motion Picture or any rights therein and that such compensation is an adequate part of the revenues derived or to be derived from such rights.

2.3. Lender hereby irrevocably grants and assigns exclusively to Producer forever and throughout the universe the right to use and to permit others to use Artist's name, voice, photograph, likeness and biography in connection with the rights granted hereunder and in advertising, promotion and publicity in connection therewith (including, without limitation, in connection with promotional films, including so-called "behind-the-scenes" and "making-of" films, footage and featurettes, merchandising, commercial tie-ups, soundtrack albums and publications relating to or based on the Motion Picture); provided, however, that no such use shall be as a direct endorsement of any product or service.

3. *Compensation; No Additional Payments.* Producer's obligation to pay any compensation or contingent payments to Lender as reflected in the Basic Terms and Conditions shall be subject to Lender's and Artist's fully complying with all their respective material representations, warranties and obligations pursuant to this Agreement. All payments to Lender hereunder shall be payable on Producer's normal payroll date during the week following the week in which such amounts accrued. Except as specifically provided in the Basic Terms and Conditions or required by any applicable guild or union agreement (a "Labor Agreement"), no additional or increased amounts shall be payable to Lender or Artist, including with respect to Artist's rendition of services at night, on weekends or holidays, or after the expiration of any particular number of hours on any one day, or for time spent traveling to or from any location where Artist may be required to render services in connection with the Motion Picture, or for so called "forced calls," meal or other penalties, or in connection with the exercise of any rights granted under this Agreement, including without limitation the release, telecast or other use or re-use of the Motion Picture. If in connection with any services of Artist or the exploitation of any rights granted under this Agreement any additional amounts are required by a Labor Agreement, Lender shall receive such amounts at the minimum rates required by such Labor Agreement; provided, however, that to the maximum extent permitted under such Labor Agreement, any amounts paid to Lender under the Basic Terms and Conditions shall be applied against and shall reduce any such additional amounts to which Lender or Artist may become entitled under such Labor Agreement, and vice versa (Lender hereby agreeing that the amounts payable to Lender under the Basic Terms and Conditions include all amounts that may be required by such Labor Agreement). Lender hereby acknowledges that this Agreement is not subject to any Labor Agreement.

4. *Representations and Warranties.* Lender hereby represents and warrants as follows:

    4.1 All of the Product will be wholly original with Artist and not based on or taken from any other material or life story (except for incidental material in the public domain); and the Product will not violate, conflict with or infringe upon any rights whatsoever (including, without limitation, any copyright, common law or statutory, throughout the world; any right of publication, performance or any other right in any work; and any right against libel, slander, invasion of privacy or similar right) of any person, firm or corporation; and

    4.2 Lender has and will continue to have the right to enter into and to perform this Agreement, and to grant all rights granted hereunder. Lender is the sole and exclusive owner throughout the universe of the rights herein granted to Producer and has the right to grant such rights exclusively to Producer, no claim has been made that Lender does not or may not have such right or rights and the exercise of such rights will not require any consent of or payment to any third party. There is not now valid or outstanding, and Lender will not hereafter grant, any right in connection with the Product which is or would be adverse to, or inconsistent with, or impair, the rights herein granted to Producer.

5. *Indemnities.*

    5.1 Lender shall indemnify and save harmless Producer, its successors, licensees and assigns, and any representatives thereof, against any and all claims, liabilities, damages, and expenses (including without limitation reasonable legal fees and expenses) incurred by any of them by reason of the breach or alleged breach of any warranty, undertaking, representation, agreement or certification made or entered into herein or hereunder by Lender.

    5.2 Producer shall indemnify and save harmless Lender against any and all claims, liabilities, damages and expenses (including without limitation reasonable legal fees and expenses) incurred by Lender by reason of any material added by Producer to the Product.

6. *Credit.* Except as provided in the Basic Terms and Conditions, all aspects of Artist's credit, including without limitation the position, size, prominence, style, placement and form of all credits, shall be determined by Producer in its sole discretion. No casual or inadvertent failure of Producer to comply with, and no failure of any third party to comply with, the credit provisions of this Agreement shall constitute a breach of this Agreement. Any reference to the title of the Motion Picture in relation to the placement or size of Artist's credit shall be a reference to the so-called "regular" title and not the "artwork" title unless otherwise specified. Any reference to the "size" of credit shall mean only the average height, width, and thickness of the letters used to display such credit. Artist's credit shall in any event be subject to any applicable guild or union requirements.

7. *Producer's Control.* Lender hereby acknowledges the right of Producer to make any changes in the Product in the preparation and exploitation of any productions based upon or incorporating such Product,

and in this connection Lender acknowledges and agrees that neither Lender nor Artist will have any right of approval or consultation with respect to any such changes or with respect to any element (casting, teleplay, screenplay, directing, distribution, etc.) of any productions produced hereunder. Without limiting the generality of the foregoing sentence, Producer shall have all artistic control over and the right to cut, edit, add to, subtract from, arrange, rearrange, and revise the Product in any manner. Lender hereby waives any rights of *droit moral* or similar rights which Lender or Artist may have. Lender further acknowledges and agrees that Producer shall have no obligation to make, produce, release, distribute, advertise, or exploit the Motion Picture, or to utilize Artist's services, or to commence principal photography on the scheduled starting date, and hereby releases Producer from any liability for any loss or damage Lender or Artist may suffer by reason of Producer's failure to make, produce, release, distribute, advertise or exploit the Motion Picture, or utilize Artist's services in connection therewith, or commence principal photography on the scheduled starting date (it being agreed that, in any such event, Producer's obligations under this Agreement shall be fully performed by payment to Lender of any compensation accrued but unpaid prior to the date of such event under Paragraph E of the Basic Terms and Conditions, subject to Producer's rights and remedies (including those under Paragraphs 9, 10 and 11 below)).

8. *Lender's Remedies.* Lender hereby recognizes that in the event of a breach by Producer of its obligations under this Agreement (including, without limitation, breaches of the Agreement arising out of credit obligations, if any), the damage (if any) caused Lender or Artist thereby is not irreparable or sufficient to entitle Lender or Artist to injunctive or other equitable relief. Lender, therefore, agrees that Lender's and Artist's rights and remedies shall be limited to the right, if any, to obtain damages at law and that neither Lender nor Artist shall have the right in such event to terminate or rescind this Agreement or to enjoin or restrain the production, distribution or exhibition of the Motion Picture or any rights therein or any other exploitation of the Product. Neither the expiration of this Agreement nor any other termination thereof shall affect the ownership by Producer of the Product or any other rights granted herein to Producer, or alter any of the rights or privileges of Producer, or any warranty, indemnity or undertaking on the part of Lender in connection with such rights. Lender acknowledges that Artist's services are of a unique, extraordinary, and intellectual character, the loss of which cannot be adequately compensated in damages in an action at law, and therefore Lender acknowledges and agrees that Producer shall be entitled to injunctive and other equitable relief to prevent or curtail any breach or alleged breach of this Agreement.

9. *Suspensions and Terminations.* Notwithstanding anything to the contrary contained herein, Lender's and Artist's employment and compensation hereunder shall automatically be suspended during any and all periods: (i) that Artist does not render services hereunder because of death, illness, incapacity, default or similar matters; (ii) that production of the Motion Picture is prevented, interrupted or delayed because of Force Majeure events, including without limitation any

labor dispute, fire, war or governmental action, or any event beyond Producer's control; or (iii) that production of the Motion Picture is prevented, interrupted or delayed by reason of the death, illness, incapacity or default of the producers or any other key production personnel or a principal member of the cast. Unless this Agreement is terminated as provided in this Paragraph 9, the periods provided for in Paragraph D of the Basic Terms and Conditions shall be deemed extended by a period equivalent to all such periods of suspension. If any matter referred to in clause (i) or (iii) above, other than default on the part of Lender or Artist, continues for longer than seven (7) consecutive days or ten (10) days in the aggregate, or if any matter referred to in clause (ii) above continues for more than six (6) consecutive weeks or eight (8) weeks in the aggregate, or in the event of any default on the part of Lender or Artist, Producer may terminate this Agreement by written notice. In the event Producer terminates this Agreement pursuant to this Paragraph 9 other than for default on the part of Lender or Artist, Producer's only obligation to Lender or Artist shall be to pay to Lender any compensation accrued but unpaid hereunder prior to such termination, subject to Producer's rights and remedies, provided that if Producer terminates this Agreement for default on the part of Lender or Artist, Producer shall have no further obligations to Lender or Artist under this Agreement. If Lender does not receive compensation due hereunder for any period equal to or greater than six (6) consecutive weeks or eight (8) weeks in the aggregate pursuant to clause (ii) above, Lender may terminate this Agreement by written notice to Producer, provided that Producer may void any such notice of termination given by Lender by resuming payments hereunder to Lender within one (1) week of Producer's receipt of such notice, it being agreed that such resumption shall not limit Producer's rights if another event gives rise to suspension pursuant to this Paragraph 9. In the event Producer so resumes payments, Producer shall have a continuing right to terminate so long as the suspension event continues.

10. *Insurance.* Producer shall have the right, but not the obligation, to secure any type of insurance covering Artist as Producer may desire, and neither Lender nor Artist shall have any interest in any such insurance, but shall assist Producer in obtaining the same and also submit to all examinations in connection therewith. If Producer cannot obtain insurance on Artist at ordinary rates and under customary conditions, or if such insurance is available only at a premium in excess of such ordinary rates, and Lender does not, within three (3) days of notification by Producer of such excess charges, pay such excess charges, Producer may terminate this Agreement without any further obligation to Lender or Artist by written notice to Lender.

11. *Immigration/Naturalization.* Lender acknowledges that any offer of employment hereunder is subject to and contingent upon Artist's ability to prove Artist's identity and employment eligibility as required by any applicable immigration laws, and Lender hereby agrees to cause Artist to complete, execute, and deliver to Producer all documents required by such laws, including documentation of Artist's employment eligibility, prior to the commencement of Artist's services. If Artist

fails to verify and deliver such documents as provided above, Producer shall have the right, by notice to such effect given to Lender, to terminate this Agreement, without any further obligation to Lender or Artist.

12. *Expenses.* The expense provisions set forth in Paragraph H of the Basic Terms and Conditions shall apply only if Artist is required by Producer to render services at a place (a "Distant Location") more than seventy-five (75) miles from Artist's principal residence (or from Artist's then current location if closer to such Distant Location). Producer's obligation (if any) to supply accommodations shall extend to the room rate and related taxes only. The expense provisions set forth in the Basic Terms and Conditions are in lieu of any other obligations which may otherwise apply to Producer with respect to Artist's (or anyone accompanying Artist) transportation, accommodations, meal allowances, and other expenses or perquisites while at such Distant Location.

13. *Compliance with Guarantor's Instructions.* Lender hereby agrees to cause Artist to act in accordance with any completion guarantee agreement with any completion guarantor for the Motion Picture, including without limitation following any instructions in connection with the Motion Picture given by such completion guarantor within the parameters of such guarantee.

14. *Publicity.* Neither Lender nor Artist shall directly or indirectly issue or authorize the issuance of any publicity or disclose any information concerning this Agreement, Artist's services hereunder, the Motion Picture or Producer's business or production methods without Producer's prior written consent; provided, however, that Artist shall not be deemed in breach of this paragraph if Artist incidentally and non-disparagingly refers to said matters during an interview concerned primarily with Artist rather than any of said matters. Artist shall pose for publicity pictures, appear for such interviews with such persons as Producer may designate and perform such other services as may be required by Producer in connection with publicity and advertising for the Motion Picture without additional compensation, but subject to Artist's other then prior professional acting contractual commitments in the entertainment industry if after Artist's period of exclusivity to Producer hereunder, it being agreed that Producer shall reimburse Artist for reasonable expenses if she is required to perform publicity services at a Distant Location.

15. *Right to Withhold.* Producer shall have the right to deduct and withhold from any sums payable to Lender hereunder any amounts required to be deducted and withheld by Producer pursuant to any present or future law, ordinance or regulation of any country or other governmental authority, including, without limitation, any country wherein Artist furnishes any of Artist's services hereunder, or pursuant to any present or future rule or regulation of any union or guild (if any) having jurisdiction over the services to be furnished by Artist hereunder.

16. *Assignment.* Producer may assign this Agreement and/or its rights hereunder to any person, firm or corporation, provided that Producer shall remain secondarily liable for its obligations hereunder to Lender unless such assignee assumes such obligations in writing, in

which event Producer shall be fully released from such obligations. Neither Lender nor Artist shall assign any of their rights hereunder, and any such purported assignment shall be void *ab initio* and without force or effect.

17. *Guild Membership.* During the entire term of this Agreement, at such times and during such periods as it may be lawful for Producer to require Artist to do so, Artist shall remain or become and remain a member in good standing of any then properly designated labor organization (as defined and determined under applicable law) representing persons performing services of the type and character that are required to be performed by Artist hereunder. If Artist fails, neglects or refuses to become a member in good standing of any such union(s), Producer shall have the right at Producer's sole election (in addition to Producer's other rights and remedies hereunder) to terminate this Agreement without any further obligation to Lender or Artist or to pay on Artist's behalf any required dues, fees or other payments to such union(s), and in the event of any such payment, Producer may deduct the amounts paid by Producer from any compensation otherwise payable to Lender hereunder. Except as expressly provided to the contrary herein, Producer shall be entitled to the maximum rights permitted under any applicable Labor Agreement. In the event of any conflict between any provision hereof and the mandatory terms of any Labor Agreement, the latter shall prevail; provided, however, that in such event the provisions of this Agreement so affected shall be curtailed and limited only to the extent necessary to permit compliance with the minimum mandatory terms and conditions of such Labor Agreement.

18. *Notices.* Notices hereunder shall be in writing and shall be sent to Lender and Producer at the respective addresses set forth above, or to such other addresses as Producer or Lender may hereafter give notice of in such manner. Copies of all notices to be given to Producer shall be sent to_____.

19. *Additional Documentation.* Lender shall execute, verify, acknowledge and deliver to Producer or shall cause to be executed, verified, acknowledged or delivered to Producer, such assignments, documents or other instruments, and shall take such actions (including, without limitation, renewing copyrights and instituting and maintaining actions for infringement of any rights), as Producer may from time to time reasonably deem necessary or desirable to evidence, establish, maintain, protect, enforce, and/or defend any or all of Producer's rights under this Agreement or otherwise to effectuate the purposes of this Agreement. All rights herein granted or agreed to be granted to Producer shall vest in Producer whether or not any such instrument is requested, executed or delivered. If Lender or Artist fails to execute and deliver any such instrument within three (3) days following Producer's request therefor, Producer shall have the right to execute said instrument in Lender's or Artist's name, place and stead, and Producer is hereby irrevocably appointed Lender's and Artist's attorney-in-fact for such purposes, which power is coupled with an interest.

20. *Miscellaneous.* This Agreement shall be construed in accordance with the laws of New York applicable to contracts entirely made

and performed therein, without regard to principles of conflicts of law contained therein, and Lender hereby agrees that any dispute hereunder shall be subject to the exclusive jurisdiction of the courts located in New York, and courts with appellate jurisdiction therefrom, to which jurisdiction and venue Lender hereby expressly consents. Long-form agreements will be entered into if requested by Producer containing other terms and conditions standard in the motion picture and television industry, but not inconsistent with the terms hereof (it being understood that, subject to the terms hereof, the rights and obligations of the parties hereto shall be governed by industry standards), including, without limitation, relating to completion of services, wage stabilization, conformity to law, payola, worker's compensation, etc. Until long-form agreements are executed, if ever, this Agreement constitutes a complete and mutually binding agreement.

Paid Advertising Exhibit

Producer's obligation, if any, to accord credit in paid advertising shall be limited to advertising issued by or under the direct control of Producer and shall not include so-called "Excluded Advertising" as follows: (1) group, list or institutional advertising; (2) teaser or special advertising; (3) outdoor advertising; (4) promotional material for exhibitors; (5) publicity, advertising or exploitation relating to the story or literary or dramatic material on which the Motion Picture is based, its title, the authors or writers, the music, the composers or conductor, the director, any members of the cast, or similar matters; (6) any advertising or publicity written in narrative form; (7) a listing in the nature of a cast of characters; (8) trailer or other advertising on the screen; (9) radio or television advertising or exploitation; (10) newspaper or magazine advertising of eight (8) column inches or less; (11) window or lobby displays or advertising; (12) advertising relating to subsidiary or ancillary rights in the Motion Picture (including, without limitation, novelizations, screenplay and other publications, products or merchandising, soundtrack recordings, videocassettes, videodiscs and other home video devices and the covers, packages, containers or jackets therefore); (13) advertising in which no credit is accorded other than credit to one (1) or two (2) stars of the Motion Picture and/or Producer and/or any other company financing or distributing the Motion Picture; (14) advertising, publicity and exploitation relating to by-products or commercial tie-ups; (15) other advertising not relating primarily to the Motion Picture; (16) award, nomination and congratulatory-type ads; and (17) any other exclusions contained in agreements between Producer and any financier, distributor or licensee of the Motion Picture. References in critics' quotes shall not constitute credit for purposes of the Agreement.

9.2.2.4 Gross Receipts/Net Profits

A major issue in negotiating contracts with "above the line" personnel is the issue of "points." Points are contingent revenue participations in addition to the fixed fee, typically applied to net profits but sometimes (for a very few superstars and major directors) to gross receipts. In either case, the definition of what is *gross* and what is *net* is not determined in accordance with the American Institute of Certified Public Accountants'

Generally Accepted Accounting Principles (GAAP). (Indeed, in the wake of a number of cases in which this was an issue, the studios dropped the terms *gross receipts* and *net profits* and substituted other, less-freighted terms.) The outcome depends on the language of the individual studio's form (there are a number of common themes which run throughout all the studios' forms). Although there are extremely rare situations in which a participant will share from "first dollar" in the vast majority of gross deals and in all net deals, generally the participant receives a fixed fee and contingent compensation that comes into play only after recoupment of the artist's upfront fee and some form of breakeven. For example, for *Coming to America,* Eddie Murphy would have received no contingent compensation until his 15 percent share of the film's gross revenue exceeded his upfront fee of $8 million. For *Captain Hook,* Steven Spielberg, Dustin Hoffman, Robin Williams, and Julia Roberts each received $10 million plus 10 percent of gross; the 10 percent was effective only with respect to monies in excess of $100 million.

How breakeven is calculated is key: Net profits are significantly more complex and contested especially after *Buchwald v. Paramount Pictures Corp.,* 17 Med. L. Rep. 1257 (Cal.Sup.Ct., L.A. County) (*infra*). The basic "getting to net" formula utilized by the studios works as follows (the percentages indicated are typical, but, of course, they may vary from case to case):

- Gross (sometimes called "gross proceeds") will consist of the studio's receipts from theatres, television licensees, and portions of income from various ancillary sources: home video (typically 20 percent of wholesale receipts), soundtrack record sales (5 percent of 90 percent of suggested retail list price), music publishing income (25 percent of the publisher's share of income received by the studio's publishing affiliate), and merchandising (50 percent of the studio's receipts from its merchandising affiliate).
- The first category of deductions will be *distribution fees,* typically 30 percent of film rentals in the U.S. and Canada, 35 percent in the UK, and 40 percent in the rest of the world; 25 percent of U.S. network television fees and 35 percent of other U.S. television fees; and 40 percent of foreign television fees (whether or not the studio will impose distribution fees on ancillary income will vary from studio to studio).
- The second category of deductions will be *distribution costs,* principally the costs of duplicating and handling prints and other distribution materials; advertising, promotion, and publicity expenses; the costs of utilizing the studio's in-house personnel; and an overhead charge of 10 percent of expenditures in the latter category.
- The third category of deductions will be *production costs,* the actual costs of development, pre-production, principal photography, and post-production, plus interest on each item of expenditure at 125 percent of the rolling prime rate charged by the studio's bank, and an overhead charge of 15 percent of the production costs (some studios will charge the overhead fee on the interest, and vice versa).
- The fourth category of deductions will be *deferrals.* In many cases, the budget for a particular film will not support a particular actor's customary fee. However, the actor will not want to reduce his/her fee, because that might

impact his/her ability to command the same (or a higher) fee in the future. So, the actor may agree to defer a portion of his/her fee. For example, the entire budget for a certain early 1980s film was $6 million. The proposed star's regular fee was $2 million (a considerable sum at the time). In order to accommodate the needs of the producer, without lowering his fee, the actor agreed to work for $2 million, to be paid $100,000 per week for the eight weeks of principal photography, and the balance of $1.2 million to be paid to the extent funds were available after the foregoing four categories of deductions had been completed.

If anything remains at that point, the participations kick in. Typically, the studio and the producer split the net 50/50, with the producer's share absorbing all other net participations, subject to a minimum, a "floor," which may be "soft" or "hard." For example, if the director, the two leads, and the writer of a film are each entitled to 10 percent of the net, a total of 40 percent of the producer's 50 percent would be siphoned off, leaving the producer with only 10 percent. Since the producer's fee is so small, the studios have recognized the unfairness of this. Therefore, the studio will agree to one of two forms of relief: the studio will agree to absorb the third party participations to the extent that they would reduce the producer's share below a specific percentage (usually 20 percent [the "hard floor"]), or, more typically, the studio will agree to absorb one-half of the third party participations to the extent that they would reduce the producer's share below the threshold. (In our example, the producer would end up with 15 percent.)

The main rationale for this model is what has been referred to as the "fundamental economic underpinning" of the motion picture business, the theory that a studio must recoup not only its investment in a successful motion picture, but also sufficient additional revenues therefrom to cover the studio's unrecouped investment on its unsuccessful pictures, its ongoing development program, its distribution organization, and to finance its future motion pictures. In short, the winners subsidize the losers. A studio's need to keep revenues in excess of a film's direct cost is the result of three industry norms: (1) most films fail to recover their production costs and distribution expenses during their initial cycle of exploitation in cinemas, home video, and television (although, over time, most studio films finish in the black); (2) the success of a motion picture cannot be predicted; and (3) the studio has no contractual right to ask net profits participants to share the risks attendant to a film. By postponing the point where a studio begins sharing with profit participants until it has recovered a significant return on its investment, the net profit deal assures studios the means to remain viable economic enterprises.

The perception in Hollywood is that net profits are illusory. The studios' accounting techniques will assure that films will always fail to show net profits, even blockbusters. On occasion, some movies do reach net profits. *Pet Cemetery* reached net profits in its theatrical run. *Flashdance, Airplane,* and *Grease* have all earned money for their net profit participants. The screenwriter for *An Officer and a Gentleman* has earned nearly $5 million from his net profit interest.

Buchwald v. Paramount Pictures Corp (see *infra*) rattled the foundations of the entire net profit system. Buchwald sued Paramount Pictures over the movie *Coming to America* and specifically challenged the net profit system. The judge at the district court level found that the studios use of the net profit system was unconscionable. However, it was never decided at the appellate level and was quickly settled. The *Batfilm Productions v. Warner Bros. Inc.* case (see *infra*) came out the opposite way. Thus, a more authoritative decision was never issued and the net profit system is still in effect.

9.3 CONTRACTS OF ADHESION/UNCONSCIONABILITY: THE *BUCHWALD* CASE AND AFTER

Starting more than forty years ago, after the post-World War II collapse of the film studios' "star system," the studios adopted the practice of engaging top talent on a project-by-project basis. To avoid heavy front-end costs, the studios increasingly made deals under which major talents were to participate in net profits. The motion picture studios' net profits formulas went largely unchallenged. Although litigation between actors, directors, writers, and producers, on the one hand, and studios, on the other, has been frequent over the years (see, for example, P. N. Lazarus III, "Ensuring a Fair Cut of a Film's Profits," 5 *Entertainment Law & Finance* (November 1989), there was no serious challenge to the net profits formulas until *Buchwald v. Paramount Pictures Corp.*

The case had two aspects; first, the finding that the Eddie Murphy starring vehicle, *Coming to America,* was based upon Buchwald's story, "King for a Day." The second aspect of the case concerned the manner in which net profits were to be calculated. In the end, Judge Schneider's decision was somewhat Solomonic: Although he invalidated a number of provisions of the studio's standard agreement, he refused to rewrite the parties' agreement and eventually awarded the plaintiffs only an aggregate of $900,000, far less than the millions the plaintiffs had sought. Both sides appealed. According to *The Hollywood Reporter,* the case has been settled (*The Hollywood Reporter,* September 13, 1995, p. 4), but it seems fair to assume that "net profits" litigation will continue. Judge Schneider definitely captured the attention of the entire industry. On the other hand, a subsequent case, *Batfilm Productions v. Warner Bros. Inc.,* has reached a contrary result. While these cases are not precedential, they are very well known in the entertainment industries.

Art Buchwald v. Paramount Pictures Corp., 17 Media L. Rep. 1257 (Cal. Sup. Ct. L. A. County, Dec. 21, 1990)

SCHNEIDER, J.

I. PRELIMINARY STATEMENT

In the first phase of this case, this court ruled that Paramount's film *Coming to America* was "based upon" the screen treatment written by plaintiff Art Buchwald. In the second phase of the case the court has been presented with numerous issues, including whether: (i) The contract between plaintiff Bernheim (a producer) and Paramount is a contract of adhesion; (ii) the contract, or any provision thereof, is unconscionable; (iii) the relationship between Bernheim and Paramount was that of co-venturers; (iv) Paramount owed a fiduciary duty to Bernheim, and (v) conduct on the part of Paramount breached the implied covenant of good faith and fair dealing. The court has also been presented with the task of interpreting other contract provisions, including the so-called "consultation" clause; the "turnaround" provision; and paragraph D.2.b. of the Bernheim Deal Memo.

II. THE CONTRACT

In order to understand the issues presented to the court in this phase of the proceeding, it is important to identify the components of the contract that present those issues. These components are:

1. The February 24, 1983, Deal Memo (consisting of six pages) entered into between Alma Productions, Inc. (Alain Bernheim's loan-out company) and Paramount;
2. The so-called "turnaround" agreement (consisting of three pages);
3. Additional Terms and Conditions (consisting of six pages); and
4. Paramount's standard net profit participation agreement (consisting of 23 pages), with two attachments relating to royalties.

III. DISCUSSION

A. Contract of Adhesion

A "contract of adhesion" "signifies a standardized contract, which, imposed and drafted by the party of superior bargaining strength, relegates to the subscribing party only the opportunity to adhere to the contract or reject it." (Citation omitted.) *Graham v. Scissor-Tail, Inc.*, 28 Cal.3d 807, 817 (1981). As the Court in Graham stated:

Such contracts are, of course, a familiar part of the modern legal landscape, in which the classical model of "free" contracting by parties of equal or near-equal bargaining strength is often found to be unresponsive to the realities brought about by increasing concentrations of economic and other power. They are also an inevitable fact of life for all citizens—businessman and consumer alike. While not lacking in social advantages, they bear within them the clear danger of oppression and overreaching. It is in the context of this tension—between social advantage in the light of modern conditions on the one hand, and the danger of oppression on the other—that courts and legislatures have sometimes acted to prevent perceived abuses. (Id. at 817–818)

In the present case, the court finds that Bernheim's compensation package, as set forth in the Deal Memo, was negotiated by Bernheim's agent and Paramount's representative, as were other provisions of the

Deal Memo not relevant to this case. The court finds, however, that the "boilerplate" language of the Deal Memo was not negotiated.

The court further finds that the "turnaround" provision, the Additional Terms and Conditions, and the net profit participation agreement were not negotiated. With respect to the latter three parts of the Bernheim-Paramount contract, there is not the slightest doubt that they were presented to Bernheim on a "take it or leave it" basis. Indeed, the evidence reveals that Bernheim did not have the "clout" to make a better deal.

It is true Paramount has submitted evidence that it freely negotiates its net profit formula with the talent with which it deals. The court is not impressed with Paramount's evidence. To the contrary, the court concludes plaintiffs have proved by a preponderance of the evidence that Paramount negotiates its net profit formula with only a relatively small number of persons who possess the necessary "clout," and even these negotiations result in changes that are cosmetic, rather than substantive. Indeed, if, as Paramount contends, it freely negotiates with respect to its net profit formula, the court presumes it would have been inundated with examples of contracts where this was done. Succinctly stated, this has not occurred.

The evidence also discloses that the entire contract was drafted by Paramount and that the "turn-around" and net profit participation provisions were standard, form provisions. Indeed, there is evidence in the record that Paramount's net profit formula is standard in the film industry. Further, there is evidence in the record to support the conclusion that essentially the same negotiations are conducted at all studios and that when one studio revises a provision of its net profit formula, that revision is adopted by the other studios.

The above factors lead to the inescapable conclusion that the Bernheim-Paramount contract is a contract of adhesion. The fact that a portion of the contract was negotiated, i.e., Bernheim's compensation package in the Deal Memo, does not require a different conclusion. In Graham, *supra*, the Court held that the contract before it was a contract of adhesion, even though some of the terms were negotiated between the parties. (28 Cal.3d at 807)

B. Unconscionability

In *Graham, supra,* the Court stated:

To describe a contract as adhesive in character is not to indicate its legal effect. It is, rather, "the beginning and not the end of the analysis in so far as enforceability of its terms is concerned." (Citation omitted.) Thus, a contract of adhesion is fully enforceable according to its terms (citations omitted) unless certain other factors are present which, under established legal rules—legislative or judicial—operate to render it otherwise.

Generally speaking, there are two judicially imposed limitations on the enforcement of adhesion contracts or provisions thereof. The first is that such a contract or provision which does not fall within the reasonable expectations of the weaker or 'adhering' party will not be enforced against him. (Citation omitted.) The second—a principle of equity applicable to all contracts generally—is that a contract or provision, even if consistent with the reasonable expectation of the parties, will be denied enforcement if, considered in its context, it is unduly oppressive or "unconscionable." (Citations omitted.) (28 Cal.3d 807 at 819–820)

1. Unconscionability—Sword or Shield

Before addressing the issue of whether the Bernheim-Paramount contract, or any provision thereof, is unconscionable, it is necessary to discuss several contentions advanced by Paramount. First, relying primarily on *Dean Witter Reynolds, Inc. v. Superior Court,* 211 Cal. App. 3d 758 (1989), Paramount argues that plaintiffs are impermissibly using the doctrine of unconscionability as a "sword." Paramount claims that Civil Code section 1670.5, as interpreted by *Dean Witter,* permits the doctrine to be utilized only as a "shield," i.e., by a defendant who has been sued. The Court does not agree. (Civil Code section 1670.5 provides in pertinent part as follows: "(a) If the Court as a matter of law finds the contract or any clause of the contract to have been unconscionable at the time it was made the Court may refuse to enforce the contract, or it may enforce the remainder of the contract without the unconscionable clause, or it may so limit the application of any unconscionable clause as to avoid any unconscionable result.")

In *Dean Witter* the plaintiff brought a class action attacking certain fees charged by Dean Witter. Three of plaintiff's causes of action were the subject of defendant's petition for writ of mandate: The first cause of action for unfair competition; the third cause of action for unconscionability under Civil Code section 1670.5; and the fourth cause of action for unconscionability under the Consumer's Legal Remedy Act (CLRA). Id. at 1631.

In *Dean Witter* the Court of Appeal held, inter alia, that no affirmative cause of action for unconscionability was created by Civil Code section 1670.5. In reaching this conclusion the court found that section 1670.5 merely codified the defense of unconscionability and did not support an affirmative use of action based on that doctrine.

In the present case, plaintiffs have not violated the holding in *Dean Witter* by bringing an affirmative cause of action based on the doctrine of unconscionability. Rather, plaintiffs have raised the doctrine of unconscionability in response to Paramount's reliance on the contract between the parties as written. Several California appellate decisions support the use of the unconscionability doctrine in the manner in which plaintiffs seek to use that doctrine in this case.

In *Graham v. Scissor-Tail, Inc., supra,* plaintiff sued for breach of contract, declaratory relief and rescission. Defendant attempted to invoke the arbitration provision contained in the contract. Plaintiff claimed, however, that this provision was unconscionable. The Court not only permitted the plaintiff to assert the unconscionability doctrine, but found the arbitration provision unconscionable and struck it.

To summarize, in the present case plaintiffs have not attempted to allege a cause of action based on the doctrine of unconscionability. To the contrary, plaintiffs have alleged three causes of action for breach of contract in which they seek damages. Paramount, by contrast, seeks to defend against plaintiffs' contract damage claims by invoking the provisions of the agreement between the parties as written. Plaintiffs, as is permitted by the cases referred to above, have countered by claiming certain contractual provisions are unconscionable. The Court finds that plaintiffs' use of the doctrine of unconscionability comports with the decisions in *Graham, supra; A & M Produce Co., supra*, and *Perdue, supra*.

2. Unconscionability—Surprise

Paramount also argues that the provision of the net profit formula cannot be found to be unconscionable because similar provisions have existed in the film industry for years and that all of the provisions were well known to Bernheim. In other words, Paramount argues the contract provisions, particularly the provisions of the net profit formula, cannot be unconscionable because Bernheim was in no way surprised by them.

It is no doubt true that the prevention of surprise is one of the two principal purposes of the doctrine of unconscionability. *A & M Produce Co., supra*, at 484. "'Surprise' involves the extent to which the supposedly agreed-upon terms of the bargain are hidden in a prolix printed form drafted by the party seeking to enforce the disputed terms." *A & M Produce Co., supra*, at 486. It is equally true that, except perhaps for the amount of gross participation shares given to Murphy and Landis, Bernheim was not surprised by the provisions of the contract in question in this case, i.e., the contract provisions were not contrary to Bernheim's reasonable expectations.

The absence of surprise, however, does not render the doctrine of unconscionability inapplicable. Indeed, in *Graham, supra*, the trial court specifically found that the Plaintiff was not surprised by the contract provision that was being attacked as unconscionable. (28 Cal. 3d at 821) Nevertheless, the trial court found the provision unconscionable, and the California Supreme Court affirmed.

3. Unconscionability—Oppression

The other principal target of the unconscionability doctrine is oppression. *A & M Produce Co., supra*, at 484. "'Oppression' arises from an inequality of bargaining power which results in no real negotiation and 'an absence of meaningful choice.'" *A & M Produce Co., supra*, at 486. This has been referred to as the procedural aspect of unconscionability (*Id.*, at 486).

Unconscionability also has a substantive aspect. In *A & M Produce Co., supra*, the Court stated:

Commercial practicalities dictate that unbargained-for terms only be denied enforcement where they are also substantively unreasonable. (Citations omitted.) No precise definition of substantive unconscionability can be proffered. Cases have talked in terms of "overly harsh" or "one-sided" results. (Citations omitted.) One commentator has pointed out, however, that " . . . unconscionability turns not only on a 'one-sided' result, but also on an absence of 'justification' for it" (citation omitted), which is only to say substantive unconscionability must be evaluated as of the time the contract was made. (Citation omitted.) The most detailed and specific commentaries observed that a contract is largely an allocation of risks between the parties, and therefore that a contractual term is substantively suspect if it reallocates the risks of the bargain in an objectively unreasonable or unexpected manner. (Citations omitted.) But not all unreasonable risk allocations are unconscionable; rather, enforceability of the clause is tied to the procedural aspects of unconscionability (citation omitted) such that the greater the unfair surprise or inequality of bargaining power, the less unreasonable the risk allocation which will be tolerated. (Citation omitted.) (*Id.* at 487)

4. Unconscionability—All or Any Provision of the Contract

There is no question that the law relating to the doctrine of unconscionability permits a court to strike down an entire contract or any provision thereof. Indeed, Civil Code section 1670.5 . . . so provides. See also *Perdue, supra,* at 925–926.

Paramount, while apparently recognizing the above quoted law, argues that it would be impermissible to apply the unconscionability doctrine to this case. As the court understands it, Paramount's argument has two prongs. First, Paramount argues that a court may strike an unconscionable clause of a contract only where that clause is "divisible." (Memorandum of Points and Authorities of Defendant Paramount Pictures Corporation re Phase II hearing on Legal and Contract Interpretation Issues, filed July 24, 1990, at p. 15) (hereinafter referred to as "7/24/90 Memo.") Paramount contends that in the present case, plaintiffs are impermissibly attacking "financially interrelated provisions" and demanding "an individual defense of each" (Id). Second, relying on a number of so-called "price" cases, Paramount argues that "profitability is not relevant to unconscionability" (letter from Paramount's counsel dated October 10, 1990, attached to Notice of Filing Prior Correspondence to Court, filed November 9, 1990).

Addressing the last argument first, it is apparent that the events that occurred at the November 8, 1990, hearing in this case have rendered Paramount's second argument moot. A little discussion of the history of this case is required in order to validate this conclusion.

In many documents filed with the court prior to November 8, 1990, Paramount argued that its net profit formula was justified, and indeed required, in order to permit it to remain in business. For example, in the Response of Defendant Paramount Pictures Corporation to Plaintiffs' Preliminary Statement of Contentions, filed May 21, 1990 (hereinafter referred to as "5/21/90 Memo") Paramount argued:

In agreeing to underwrite what it could thus anticipate to be a $66.5 million investment, Paramount alone bore the risk that the Picture (sic) would not be produced or, if produced, would not commercially succeed and that its investment would be lost. In contrast, Bernheim and Buchwald risked nothing. Not surprisingly, Paramount obtained from Buchwald and Bernheim, as it does in varying degrees of all net participants, the right to attain gross receipts in excess of its direct out-of-pocket costs before it began sharing those receipts with participants. This simply reflects an attempt by the studio to balance the enormous economic risks attendant to motion picture production by insuring that the studio will reap a fair portion of the rewards resulting from a commercial success. As a means for compensating for an allocation of risks in the motion picture industry that places all the uncertainties on the studio, Paramount's contracts with Bernheim and Buchwald are not unconscionable. . . . (at 12).

Similarly, in its 7/24/90 Memo Paramount stated:

"As forty years of studio-talent bargaining has established, a studio is entitled to a return commensurate with the risks of movie-making. Otherwise, it could not remain a viable business." (Citations omitted.) There is nothing unfair or unreasonable about how the "Net Profits" formula strikes this balance.

The level of return allowed to Paramount under its "Net Profits" formula is more than offset by the risks that the studio alone takes. As plaintiffs' experts readily conceded, "Net Profits" participants bear no risk; if a film flops, participants have no obligation to take up the shortfall and their upfront fee is guaranteed. (Citations omitted.)

In contrast, the studio's risks are enormous. When it signed the Buchwald and Bernheim contracts, Paramount assumed the risk that, despite substantial script development costs (nearly $500,000), the picture might never be made and that, even if made, the picture would not make money. Paramount spent $40 million to produce *Coming to America* and committed another $35 million to an advertising and a promotional campaign with no assurance that a single theater admission would be sold. (Citation omitted.)

The risk of failure in the motion picture business is ever-present, immense, and unmitigable. . . . (at 19–21)

The Court interpreted the above quoted statements of Paramount, and many others like them, to mean that Paramount was attempting to justify its net profit formula on the ground that this formula was necessary for Paramount's survival. Indeed, when Paramount's counsel stated, "[o]therwise it could not remain a viable business" (7/24/90 Memo at 19), the Court understood Paramount to mean what its counsel had stated.

It was because Paramount argued that its net profit definition was justified by the exigencies of the film industry that the court decided to appoint its own accounting expert, pursuant to Evidence Code section 730. Indeed, the November 8, 1990, hearing was scheduled for the specific purpose of defining the tasks to be performed by the court's expert. This would have included, of course, an examination of Paramount's books and records to determine the accuracy of Paramount's representation with respect to its profitability, the number of films that make and lose money, and whether it was necessary for successful films to subsidize unsuccessful films. Remarkably, it was at this same hearing that counsel for Paramount abandoned the argument that Paramount's net profit formula was required by the nature of the motion picture business.

Paramount's abandonment of its "justification" argument rendered inquiry into Paramount's profitability moot and the appointment of the court's expert unnecessary. This abandonment also renders inapplicable the so-called "price" cases relied upon by Paramount. These "price" cases were submitted to the Court, according to Paramount, to establish the point that "profitability is not relevant to unconscionability" (October 10, 1990, letter, *supra,* at p. 1). Since Paramount no longer seeks to defend its net profit formula on the ground it is justified by the nature of its business, it is clear Paramount's profitability is irrelevant to the determination of whether the contract involved in this case is unconscionable.

As indicated above, Paramount also argues that the court may not strike down all or any portion of the net profit definition because that definition is part of the entire compensation package between Paramount and Bernheim. Paramount further argues that it would not have paid Bernheim as much "up-front" money if it had known many of the components of the net profit formula would be invalidated, and that Bernheim will reap a windfall if the court finds unconscionable portions of the net profit formula.

Paramount's argument is based on the proposition that the dispute between the parties is one over price. The court is not convinced that this is the case. However, even if Paramount is correct, it is "clear that the price term, like any other term in a contract, may be unconscionable" (*Perdue, supra,* at 926). In fact, in *Perdue* the Court stated:

The courts look to the basis and justification for the price (citation omitted), including "the price actually being paid by . . . other similarly situated consumers in a similar transaction." (Citation omitted.) The cases, however, do not support defendant's contention that a price equal to the market price cannot be held unconscionable. While it is unlikely that a court would find a price set by a freely competitive market to be unconscionable (citation omitted), the market price set by an oligopoly should not be immune from scrutiny. Thus courts consider not only the market price, but also the cost of the goods or services to the seller (citations omitted) the inconvenience imposed on the seller (citation omitted) and the true value of the product or service (citation omitted) (38 Cal.3d at 926–927).

In the present case, the court has already found the Bernheim-Paramount contract to be adhesive. Moreover, it is clear, as the court has already found, that contractual relations between certain talent and studios, at least talent such as Bernheim who lack the "clout" of major stars, do not take place in a freely competitive market. Rather, it is clear that if a talent such as Bernheim wishes to work in the film industry, he must do so on terms substantially dictated by the studio. This is particularly true with respect to the net profit formula contained in the contract involved in this case. As previously indicated, Paramount simply does not negotiate with respect to its net profit formula with talent such as Bernheim.

Additionally, Paramount's argument that it would be unfair if the court found any part of the net profit formula unconscionable is based on the faulty premise that the only thing that mattered to Bernheim was the "up-front" money. While it is true Bernheim's agent, Roger Davis, testified that "up-front" money was important to Bernheim, he also testified that the other important consideration was "to get the project developed into a form where it could be made the basis of a motion picture" (Davis depo. at 54). Presumably, Bernheim wanted to make a picture so that he could profit from it. (See Davis depo. at 33; see also Youngstein depo. at 121–122.)

Moreover, Paramount's argument that net profits represented a relatively insignificant part of Bernheim's total compensation package flies in the face of other evidence in the record. For example, in his Supplemental Declaration, Carmen Desiderio, Paramount's Vice-President of Contract Accounting, testified that Paramount had paid more than $150 million in net profits over the past 15 years, using the net profit formula contained in Bernheim's contract, or one similar to it. Additionally, Paramount itself admitted in its 7/24/90 Memo, at 25, that "'Net Profits' are a valuable form of contingent compensation, not the 'cruel hoax' that plaintiffs insinuate." Indeed, Paramount's "turnaround" provision provides for Paramount to receive net profits in the event Bernheim was successful in convincing another studio to make a film based on Buchwald's treatment (Bernheim Deal Memo, at p. 2).

Further, the doctrine of unconscionability would be rendered nugatory if a contracting party could escape its application by negotiating some monetary provisions, while at the same time imposing unjustifiably onerous provisions with respect to other contract provisions. Yet, that is precisely what Paramount argues is permissible.

Paramount has referred the court to four cases which, it is contended, supports Paramount's position that the court may not strike down certain provisions of its net profit formula while enforcing the remainder of the contract with Bernheim. Paramount's argument is totally refuted by the provisions of Civil Code section 1670.5, which specifically permits the Court to "enforce the remainder of the contract without the unconscionable clause" or to "limit the application of any unconscionable clause as to avoid any unconscionable result." Moreover, none of the four cases relied upon supports Paramount's argument, and at least one refutes it. (These cases are *York v. Georgia-Pacific Corp.*, 58. F. Supp. 1265 [N.D. Miss. 1984]; *Sykes v. Perry*, 162 Kan. 365 [1947]; IMO *Development Corp. v. Dow Corning Corp.*, 135 Cal. App. 3d 451 [1982]; and *Chow v. Levi Strauss*, 49 Cal.App. 3d 315 [1975].)

In *York, Sykes,* and *Chow* the respective courts did not address the question of whether a provision of a contract may be struck as unconscionable, while the balance of the contract is enforced. Indeed, if either of the two out-of-state cases had answered that question in the negative, the result would have been contrary to the express provisions of Civil Code section 1670.5.

Furthermore, the other California case cited by Paramount, *IMO Development*, at least by implication refutes Paramount's argument. In *IMO Development*, the Court specifically held that a contract cannot be partially rescinded, i.e., a party cannot seek to rescind part of a contract and seek enforcement of the remainder. The Court in *IMO Development* never addressed the doctrine of unconscionability because it had never been pled. The language utilized by the Court strongly suggests, however, that if unconscionability had been pled, the result under that doctrine might well have been different than the decision reached on the issue of partial rescission. The Court in *IMO Development* stated:

What *IMO* does allege is that its consent was obtained by economic duress. Business or economic duress exists when threats to business or property interests by way of coercion and/or wrongful compulsion are present. (Citation omitted.) *That, however, is not tantamount to a showing of unconscionability. In other words, the presence of a supposed unconscionable contract provision, such as would admit to differential enforcement, does not logically provide for differential rescission.* (Emphasis in original.) (*Id.* at 460)

In sum, the court concludes that there is nothing about the contract involved in this case, or the circumstances surrounding its execution, which precludes the court from addressing the issue of whether certain component parts of the net profit definition are unconscionable. The next issue that must be addressed is the appropriate manner of applying the doctrine of unconscionability to the contract involved in this case.

5. Unconscionability—The Doctrine Applied

Plaintiffs have challenged as unconscionable a number of provisions of Paramount's net profit formula. The challenged provisions include: 15 percent overhead on Murphy and Landis [profit] participation; 15 percent overhead on Eddie Murphy Productions operational allowance; 10 percent advertising overhead; 15 percent overhead; interest on negative cost balance without credit for distribution fees; interest on overhead; interest on profit participation payments; the interest rate not being in proportion to actual cost of funds; exclusion of 80 percent of video cassette receipts from gross receipts [Typically, the studios distribute home videos through wholly-owned subsidiaries, and only 20 percent of wholesale receipts are included in the gross of the picture—Eds.]; distribution fee on video royalties; charging as distribution costs residuals on 20 percent video royalties; charges for services and facilities in excess of actual costs; no credit to production cost for reusable items retained or sold; charging taxes offset by income tax credit; charging interest in addition to distribution fees; 15 percent overhead in addition to distribution fees; and 10 percent advertising overhead in addition to distribution fees.

Paramount has never argued that any of these provisions are individually fair and reasonable. Rather, as has been indicated, Paramount has argued that the Bernheim-Paramount contract must be considered as a whole, that that contract is fair and reasonable and, therefore, the court is not permitted to focus on individual provisions of the net profit formula to determine if such provisions are unconscionable. As discussed above, the court rejects the argument that it is impermissible for it to focus on individual provisions of the net profit formula.

Plaintiffs, by contrast, have presented evidence which they argue supports their position that each of the challenged provisions are unconscionable. The court is not persuaded that plaintiffs have sustained their burden of proof with respect to each challenged item. In fact, with respect to a number of challenged items it appears plaintiffs would like the court to make a finding of unconscionability based upon the mere description of the item and without supporting evidence. This the court is not prepared to do so. However, with respect to a number of provisions plaintiffs have sustained their burden of proving such revisions are "overly harsh" and "one-sided." *A & M Produce Co., supra,* at 487. Indeed, in light of Paramount's "all or nothing" approach to unconscionability, plaintiffs' evidence stands unrefuted.

The court finds the following provisions of Paramount's net profit formula unconscionable for the reasons indicated:

1. *Fifteen Percent Overhead on Eddie Murphy Productions Operational Allowance.* The court finds this provision unconscionable because an additional 15 percent charge is made for overhead "on top of" this item. In effect, this results in charging overhead on overhead. The court is able to perceive no justification for this obviously one-sided double charge and Paramount has offered none.

2. *Ten Percent Advertising Overhead Not in Proportion to Actual Costs.* This flat overhead charge [The studios typically add 10 percent to the actual costs for in-house advertising personnel and facilities—Eds.], which has no relation to actual costs, adds significantly to the amount that must be recouped by Paramount before the picture will realize net profits. Again, the court is able to discern no justification for this flat charge and Paramount has offered none.

3. *Fifteen Percent Overhead Not in Proportion to Actual Costs.* Paramount's charge of a flat 15 percent for overhead [The studios typically add 15 percent to the "negative cost," the actual costs of preproduction, principal photography, and post production—Eds.] yields huge profits, even though the overhead charges do not even remotely correspond to the actual costs incurred by Paramount. In this connection it should be observed that although Paramount originally contended that this charge was justified because "winners must pay for losers" (Sapsowitz Deposition at 65) this justification was abandoned by Paramount during the November 8, 1990, hearing held in this case.

4. *Charging Interest on Negative Cost Balance Without Credit for Distribution Fees.* Paramount accounts for income on a cash basis, while simultaneously accounting for cost on an accrual basis. This slows down the recoupment of negative costs and inflates the amount of interest charged. The court finds this practice to be "one sided" in the absence of a justification for the practice.

5. *Charging Interest on Overhead.* Paramount receives revenues in the form of distribution fees and overhead charges, neither of which are taken into account in determining whether costs have been recouped. This results in "interest" becoming an additional source of unjustified profit. The court finds this practice to be "overly harsh" and "one sided," and thus unconscionable.

6. *Charging Interest on Profit Participation Payments.* Paramount charges the payments made to gross participants to negative costs. In fact, these payments are not paid until the film has derived receipts. Accordingly, Paramount has not in any real sense advanced this money. Nevertheless, Paramount charges interest on gross participation shares. This is unconscionable.

7. *Charging an Interest Rate Not in Proportion to the Actual Cost of Funds.* Paramount charges an interest rate which can be as much as 20 to 30 percent (Zimbert Deposition at 172), even when no funds have been laid out by Paramount. This is a one-sided, and thus unconscionable, provision.

In sum, the court concludes that the foregoing provisions of Paramount's net profit formula are unconscionable. The conclusion that these provisions are unconscionable is by no means the end of the analytic trail. While this conclusion does actuate the court's powers under Civil Code section 1670.5, it remains to be decided how those powers should be invoked.

As noted in *A & M Produce Co., supra,* "unconscionability is a flexible doctrine designed to allow courts to directly consider numerous factors which may adulterate the contractual process" (135 Cal. App. 3d at 484). Similarly, in *Frostifresh Corporation v. Reynoso,* 274 N.Y.S. 2d 757, 759 (1966) the Court stated that paragraph 2–302 of the Uniform Commercial Code, upon which Civil Code section 1670.5 is based, gives "the courts power 'to police explicitly against the contracts or clauses which they find to be unconscionable.' "

This court interprets the cases dealing with the doctrine of unconscionability as authorizing the court to use its powers under Civil Code section 1670.5 to produce an equitable result. Indeed, "equitable" would appear to be the antithesis of "unconscionable." In *Graham v. Scissor-Tail, Inc., supra,* the court specifically recognized that the doctrine of unconscionability involves "a principle of equity applicable to all contracts generally—. . . that a contract or provision, even if consistent with the reasonable expectation of the parties, will be denied enforcement if, considered in its context, it is unduly oppressive or 'unconscionable'" (28 Cal.3d at 820). See also *Slaughter v. Jefferson Federal Savings and Loan Association,* 361 F. Supp. 590, 602 (D.C.D.C. 1973) in which the court, after concluding the provisions of a contract were unconscionable, stated that in such circumstances "[t]he Court has broad discretion to fashion relief appropriate to the situation presented."

Since it is the task of the court to achieve an equitable result, the question before the court is: What decision is necessary in order to produce such a result? Plaintiffs answer this question by arguing that Bernheim is entitled to receive the compensation provided for in paragraph D.2.b of the Bernheim Deal Memo, after all of the unconscionable provisions are stricken and after permitting Paramount to recoup its actual costs plus a reasonable rate of return on its investment. Counsel for Paramount, although specifically asked by the court during oral argument on December 6, 1990, stated he had no position with respect to this issue in light of his view that the court could not determine that individual provisions of the net profit formula were unconscionable.

After careful consideration, the court has concluded plaintiffs' approach must be rejected because it does not produce an equitable result. There are a number of reasons for the court's conclusion.

If the court were to strike all of the challenged provisions of the net profit formula that it has found to be unconscionable and permit Paramount only to recover its costs, plus a reasonable rate of return, the result would be an inequitable windfall to Bernheim. Stated another way, accepting plaintiffs' argument would result in Bernheim receiving a profit far beyond the contemplation of the parties at the time the contract was entered into and, apparently, far beyond the profit a producer with Bernheim's experience and track record would reasonably have been expected to earn.

The court believes it does not have sufficient facts to fix the amount that Paramount should be required to pay Bernheim in this case. The court intends, therefore, to defer to the third phase of this trial the amount of damages to which Bernheim is entitled and the manner in which such damages should be calculated. The court anticipates that expert testimony may be required. Further, the court desires to hear argument from counsel concerning these issues, particularly with respect to the factors that the court should consider in arriving at an equitable award. Although counsel for Paramount has heretofore declined to take a position with respect to these issues, the court assumes that, in light of the views expressed by the court herein, counsel will now proffer Paramount's position.

The court also desires to emphasize that its focus in the third phase will be on awarding damages to Bernheim which are fair and reasonable, but which will not result in Bernheim receiving a windfall, i.e., an award far beyond the reasonable expectations of the parties when the contract was executed.

The court also intends to defer ruling on the amount to which Buchwald is entitled until after the amount due Bernheim is fixed. The court observes, however, that under the contracts as written, Buchwald was to receive only a fraction of the net profits to which Bernheim would have been entitled (1 1/2 percent for Buchwald; 17 1/2 to 40 percent for Bernheim). The court will in all likelihood be influenced by this fact in setting the amount due Buchwald.

C. The Juxtaposition of Unconscionability and the Consultation Clause

Paragraph D.2.b of the Bernheim Deal Memo contains the so-called "consultation clause." That clause provides that Bernheim "will be consulted on gross and net-profit participations granted by PPC to third parties, but PPC's decision shall be final."

Bernheim contends that Paramount breached the consultation clause by not consulting with him. Paramount argues that the consultation clause is not significant since Paramount retained the right to make the final decision with respect to granting gross and net-profit participations. The court finds it unnecessary to resolve this dispute.

If Bernheim is correct, the result would be that he is entitled to receive 33.5 percent of the net profits on *Coming to America* under the net profit formula contained in the contract as written. This conclusion follows from Bernheim's position that, by reason of Paramount's breach of the "consultation" clause, he is entitled to the highest percentage of net profit permissible under paragraph D.2.b of the Deal Memo and Bernheim's concession that that highest percentage is 33.5 percent. If Paramount is correct, the result would be that [because of the shares of third parties] Bernheim is entitled to receive only 17 1/2 percent of net profits (the floor established in Section D.2.b of the Bernheim Deal Memo) under the net profit formula contained in the contract as written.

In the preceding section of this Tentative Decision, however, the court has concluded that a number of provisions of the net profit formula as written are unconscionable. The court has also determined that it will follow a different path in arriving at equitable compensation for Bernheim and Buchwald in light of such unconscionability. Since, pursuant to the courts ruling, the net profit formula as written no longer exists, it makes no difference whether Bernheim or Paramount is correct with respect to the percentage of net profits to which Bernheim is entitled. This factor also makes Paramount's alleged breach of the consultation clause irrelevant.

D. The "Turnaround" Provision

As indicated above, one of the component parts of the contract between Paramount and Bernheim is the so-called "turnaround" provision. The purpose of the "turnaround" provision is to permit a producer to take his project to another studio if the first studio is no longer interested in pursuing it, while at the same time permitting the first studio to recoup its development costs if the project is undertaken by the second studio. Hahn Declaration, paragraph 19; Sattler Declaration, paragraph 53; Denman 6/28/90 Deposition at 55. Insofar as is pertinent to the present case, the "turnaround" agreement provides:

If, prior to the expiration of the turnaround period, the project is not placed elsewhere and/or if Lender has not complied with the conditions above, including, without limitation, complete reimbursement to Paramount, then at the end of the turnaround period, Lender's rights with respect to the project shall cease and Paramount's ownership thereof and all properties and rights encompassed therein shall be absolute.

The facts with respect to the application of the "turnaround" agreement to the present case are these: In March 1985 Paramount purported to give notice that it was abandoning the project that had been inspired by Buchwald's treatment. In May 1985 Paramount permitted its option with respect to the Buchwald material to expire. Paramount contends that since Bernheim failed to set up the project at another studio within the 12-month period ending in March 1986, the "turnaround" agreement extinguished any obligations Paramount had with respect to Bernheim.

It is true, as Paramount argues, that if the "turnaround" provision is considered in isolation, it would appear Bernheim's rights to compensation ended in March 1986. The vice of Paramount's argument is that the "turnaround" provision cannot be considered in isolation. Paragraph D.1 of the Bernheim Deal Memo provides, in pertinent part, that "[i]f the Picture is produced, Lender will furnish the services of Artist, who shall be employed by PPC to personally render all customary services as producer."

The Court has already concluded that the picture was made, i.e., that *Coming to America* was "based upon" Buchwald's treatment entitled "King for a Day." In light of this conclusion, it is clear Paramount was required to employ Bernheim as producer on *Coming to America* and that Paramount breached its contract with Bernheim by failing to do so. It would make no sense to conclude that Paramount breached the agreement by failing to employ Bernheim, while at the same time concluding Bernheim's right to compensation was terminated by application of the "turnaround" provision.

In reality, and the Court so finds, it was never contemplated that the "turnaround" provision would apply in a situation such as is presented by the facts of this case. Moreover, to the extent that there exists an ambiguity by reason of the existence of paragraph D.1 and the "turnaround" provision, it is clear that such ambiguity must be resolved against Paramount as drafter of the agreement. Civil Code section 1654; *Jacobs v. Freeman,* 104 Cal.App. 3d 177, 189 (1980).

Finally, the Court observes that one of the important purposes, perhaps the most important purpose of the "turnaround" provision, from Paramount's perspective, was to permit it to recoup its costs in the event Bernheim placed the project at another studio. In the present case that purpose has been satisfied since it is too clear to doubt Paramount has recovered all of its costs on *Coming to America.*

E. The Co-venturer and Fiduciary Duty Issues

Bernheim contends that he and Paramount were co-venturers and that Paramount owed a fiduciary duty to him. With one exception to be discussed below, the court is unable to agree with either of these contentions.

Whether or not the relationship between parties is that of co-venturer is essentially a question of fact. *Nelson v. Abraham* 29 Cal.2d 745, 750 (1947). Few, if any, of the features that usually characterize a joint venture are present in this case. Bernheim did not have a right at all times to inspect and copy the purported venture's books and records (*Milton Kauffman v. Superior Court,* 94 Cal. App. 2d 8, 17 (1949)) and Paramount had pervasive control over the purported venture.

Moreover, while there was an agreement between Bernheim and Paramount with respect to the sharing of profits (but not losses) (see *Howard v. Societa Di Unione, etc.* 62 Cal.App. 2d 842, 848 (1944)), Paramount retained the virtually unlimited power to determine whether Bernheim ever received any profit. The factors present in this case do not point to the existence of a joint venture between Bernheim and Paramount.

The Court is also unable to find the existence of a fiduciary relationship between Paramount and Bernheim, except with respect to Paramount's duty to render an accounting. *Waverly Productions v. RKO General, Inc.*, 217 Cal. App. 2d 721 (1963). In fact, the court disposed of Bernheim's fiduciary duty claim in the Statement of Decision that was issued in the first phase of this case. In its Statement of Decision the court stated:

> In addition to their contract claims, plaintiffs have advanced several tort theories of recovery, namely, bad faith denial of existence of contracts, bad faith denial of liability on their contracts, tortious breach of the implied covenant of good faith and fair dealing, breach of fiduciary duty, fraudulent concealment by a fiduciary and constructive trust. The obvious reason plaintiffs have asserted tort causes of action is to recover punitive damages since, absent such damages, the court is able to discern no difference between any tort damages plaintiffs might recover and their contract damages.

The court has concluded, as indicated, that *Coming to America* was based upon Buchwald's treatment. The court is unable to find, however, any tortious conduct on the part of Paramount or any of its representatives. In order to award punitive damages to plaintiffs, the court would be required to find by clear and convincing evidence that defendant was guilty of fraud, oppression or malice, as those terms are defined in Civil Code section 3294. While the court rejects Paramount's contention that *Coming to America* is not "based upon" "King for a Day," the court is unable to conclude that Paramount's conduct was in bad faith, let alone fraudulent, oppressive or malicious. Accordingly, while plaintiffs are entitled to recover on their breach of contract claims, the court finds the defendant is entitled to judgment on plaintiffs' tort claims (Statement of Decision [First Phase] at 33–34).

In light of the court's finding that Paramount's conduct was not tortious, the issue of whether a fiduciary duty existed between Bernheim and Paramount and, if so, whether Paramount breached that duty has been rendered moot. As indicated, however, the court does find that a fiduciary duty exists with respect to Paramount's duty to render an accounting. *Waverly Productions v. RKO General, Inc., supra.*

F. The Covenant of Good Faith and Fair Dealing

Plaintiffs argue that Paramount breached the implied covenant of good faith and fair dealing by improperly or excessively charging a number of different items as costs on *Coming to America*. Paramount has countered by arguing that plaintiffs will be given the opportunity to challenge these costs in the third (damage) phase of this trial.

In a preceding section of this Tentative Decision, the court has ruled that a number of provisions of Paramount's net profit formula are unconscionable. The court also indicated that it intends to fashion relief that will produce an equitable result in this case. In light of the court's ruling, it appears to the court that application of the doctrine of unconscionability will produce damages at least equal to damages that could be awarded for a breach of the covenant. The court finds it unnecessary, therefore, to determine whether a breach of covenant has in fact occurred.

If a statement of decision is requested with respect to this phase of the trial, it shall be prepared by counsel for plaintiffs. This Tentative Decision shall be the statement of decision unless within ten days either party specifies controverted issues or makes proposals not covered in the Tentative Decision (Rule 232. Cal. Rules of Court).

NOTE

In the third phase of the case Judge Schneider awarded Buchwald and Bernheim a total of $900,000 in damages. Pierce O'Donnell, the attorney for the plaintiffs in *Buchwald* [and the author, with Dennis McDougal, of a book about the case, *Fatal Subtraction: How Hollywood Really Does Business* (New York: Doubleday Dell, 1992)], brought a second action, this time on behalf of a number of individuals and corporations who had been involved with the *Batman* project. Like *Coming to America*, the first *Batman* generated revenues in the hundreds of millions of dollars, but apparently no net profits. Like the preceding case, the following decision has not been officially reported.

Batfilm Productions, Inc. v. Warner Bros. Inc., Nos. BC 051653 and BC 051654 (Cal. Super. Ct., L.A. County, March 14, 1994)

YAFFE, JUDGE

[In 1979, plaintiffs Melniker and Uslan obtained an option on the motion picture rights to the *Batman* comic book characters and made a deal with Warner Bros.' predecessors in interest under which they were entitled to receive various forms of fixed and contingent compensation if a film were produced.] . . . In 1988, Mr. Melniker and Mr. Uslan signed a written amendment to the [original agreement] (the "Warner Agreement"). Under the Warner Agreement, Mr. Melniker and Mr. Uslan were entitled to receive $300,000 in fixed compensation for *Batman*, plus a $100,000 "deferment" once the film generated a certain level of receipts, plus 13% of the so-called "Net Profits," as defined in an attachment to the Warner Agreement.

Warner Bros. has paid Messrs. Melniker and Uslan the $300,000 fixed fee and $100,000 deferment. Warner Bros. has also paid Melniker and Uslan an additional $700,000 in fixed fees on two additional motion pictures (*Batman Returns* and *Batman: Mask of the Phantasm*). Warner Bros.

will have similar financial obligations to plaintiffs on each additional Batman motion picture. Although *Batman* has generated more revenue than any other Warner Bros. film, it has not generated any "Net Profits" under plaintiffs' contract. Melniker and Uslan filed suit in 1992 claiming, inter alia, that they were denied their fair "Net Profits" compensation. . . .

. . . In reviewing the evidence, the Court believed that Mr. Melniker and Mr. Uslan had offered evidence to prove that the Warner Agreement was a contract of adhesion that should be strictly interpreted against Warner Bros. and should not be interpreted in a way that would be contrary to the plaintiffs' reasonable expectations.

But a contract of adhesion is a contract, and a contract of adhesion is not the same as an unconscionable contract, which is no contract at all. "Unconscionability" requires a far different level of proof. The plaintiffs did not prove that they are to be relieved of their contract with Warner Bros. on the ground of unconscionability.

Mr. Melniker negotiated the Warner Agreement on his and Mr. Uslan's behalf. No one is less likely to have been coerced against his will into signing a contract like the Warner Agreement than Mr. Melniker. This former general counsel and senior executive of a major motion picture studio (Metro-Goldwyn-Mayer) knew all the tricks of the trade; he knew inside and out how these contracts work, what they mean, and how they are negotiated.

Even with Mr. Melniker's knowledge and experience, plaintiffs complain that Warner Bros. knew when the parties signed the agreement in 1988 that *Batman* would not generate "Net Profits."

At the core of plaintiffs' case is their argument that the contract was not fair to them because Warner Bros. and others earned millions of dollars on *Batman* and plaintiffs did not. The answer to that argument is that ever since the King's Bench decided *Slade's Case* in 1602, right down to today, courts do not refuse to enforce contracts or remake contracts for the parties because the court or the jury thinks that the contract is not fair.

That principle is not some medieval anachronism. This society, this country, this culture operates on the basis of billions of bargains struck willingly every day by people all across the country in all walks of life. And if any one of these people could have their bargain reexamined after the fact on the ground that it was not fair . . . we would have a far different type of society than we have now; we would have one that none of the parties to this case would like very much.

When one talks about a motion picture and the claims of this type that are made, they all have one thing in common: the plaintiff comes in and says, "Without me, they would have had nothing, and look how they treated me." But the process of making a motion picture [involves many parties]. It would not be good for the motion picture business or for the parties to this case if any one of those people on any motion picture could come back and ask a court to remake a bargain that he made on the ground that he now asserts, after the fact, and in light of the success of the picture, that he was not fairly treated in comparison with others.

Whether or not a contract is fair is not the issue. A contract is not unconscionable simply because it is not fair. Plaintiffs claim that the Warner Agreement is unconscionable within the meaning of Civil Code section 1670.5. To be unconscionable, a contract must "shock the conscience" or, as plaintiffs alleged . . . it must be "harsh, oppressive, and unduly one-sided."

After considering all the evidence, the Court finds that the plaintiffs have failed to prove that the Warner Agreement, taken as a whole, is unconscionable.

That, however, is not the end of the inquiry that the Court must make. Under Civil Code section 1670.5, if the evidence shows that any part of a contract is unconscionable, the Court may refuse to enforce that part of the contract.

During the trial, plaintiffs claimed that eight elements of the Warner Agreement's "Net Profits" definition were unconscionable: (1) the 10% advertising overhead charge; (2) Warner Bros.' retention of any economic value of United States tax credits created by the payment of taxes in the foreign territories where *Batman* was distributed; (3) application of the 15% production overhead charge on participation payments to third parties; (4) application of the 15% production overhead charge on the $100,000 deferment; (5) all of the interest charges; (6) the costs charged by Pinewood Studios in England for holding sets and stages after completion of photography; (7) application of the 15% overhead charge to the costs incurred at the Pinewood Studio lot; and (8) the inclusion in "gross receipts" of only 20% of the revenue from videocassettes, less a distribution fee. . . .

In considering Warner Bros.' motion for judgment under Code of Civil Procedure sec. 631.8, the Court had little difficulty in rejecting seven of plaintiffs' claims.

As to all of the items relating to overhead charges (Items One, Three, Four and Seven), the Court granted Warner Bros.' motion for judgment because the plaintiffs failed to prove that historically Warner Bros.' indirect general administrative expenses for motion picture production and advertising—"overhead"—do not equal or exceed the amount charged under the "Net Profits" definition, namely, 15 percent of production costs and 10 percent of advertising expenditures. As a matter of fact, plaintiffs conceded that they could not show that the overhead charges under the "Net Profits" definition exceeded Warner Bros.' actual overhead costs, taken as a whole.

Plaintiffs argued that charging overhead on certain production costs, advertising expenses, gross participations, deferred payments, and payments paid for foreign studios, was unconscionable because the administrative cost of providing those goods or services was less than the contractual 10 or 15 percent overhead surcharge. Plaintiffs did not prove that allegation. And, more important, the test is not whether Warner Bros.' overhead charges on a particular direct cost item exceeded the "actual" administrative or other indirect expenses associated with providing that one item or service to the production or advertising of a movie. As the accounting experts for both sides testified, overhead cannot be assessed with such precision. Under the circumstances, the test must be whether the production and advertising overheads charged by using the percentage allocations are, in total, unconscionably higher than Warner Bros.' actual production and advertising overhead costs on a motion picture. Plaintiffs offered no evidence to support such a finding.

Plaintiffs also failed to show that the advertising costs, gross participations, deferred payments, and payments paid to foreign studios were not historically included in the pool of costs that were compared to Warner Bros.' general and administrative expenses to estimate its rate of overhead. In sum, plaintiffs simply failed to prove that any of the overhead charges are unconscionable.

The Court also granted Warner Bros., motion for judgment as to Item Two, the foreign tax credit. According to plaintiffs, when a motion picture is distributed overseas, many countries impose a tax on the receipts generated. That tax payment gives rise to a credit that can be used under certain circumstances to offset United States income tax obligations. Plaintiffs claimed that, in calculating their "Net Profits," it is unconscionable for Warner Bros. to deduct foreign taxes as a distribution expense without adding something for the value of the foreign tax credits. The plaintiffs failed to prove, however, that Warner Bros. received any foreign tax credits on *Batman,* or the amounts thereof, or that Warner Bros. received any actual financial benefit from those tax credits when calculating and paying its United States tax obligations. Even if such a credit had been received, the plaintiffs failed to prove that they ever asked Warner Bros. to agree that, in computing "Net Profits," Warner Bros. would augment the gross receipts of the picture by the amount of the tax credits. No such provision is contained in plaintiffs' contract and there was no evidence that they ever expected such treatment of the tax credits.

The Court also granted the motion for judgment as to Item Six, the Pinewood Studios sound stage holdover costs, because there was no evidence that the holdover charge is not properly a cost of the first *Batman* movie.

The Court granted the motion for judgment as to Item Eight, videocassette distribution, on the ground that Mr. Melniker knew that a 20 percent royalty was standard in the industry. He never questioned it. He never asked that it be changed. The plaintiffs did not prove that the 20 percent royalty unconscionably exceeded the actual revenues, less expenses, from videocassette distribution. They also offered no evidence that a "distribution fee" on the distribution of videocassettes was unconscionable. Nor did they prove that they could have negotiated a better deal elsewhere at the time this deal was made, in which a higher percentage of video revenue, without deduction of a distribution fee, would be credited to the picture in calculating "Net Profits."

Item Five concerned the "interest" charge on production costs. Under Paragraph 2A of plaintiffs' contract, "Net Profits" become payable once the picture generates enough gross receipts to cover the specified distribution fees, distribution expenses, and production costs. Until then, under Paragraphs 2A and 9 of plaintiffs' "Net Profits" definition, the production costs bear an interest charge. Under the contract, Warner Bros. reduces the interest-bearing balance of production costs with only those gross receipts that remain after deducting the distribution fees and expenses. Plaintiffs claim that [it] is unconscionable for Warner Bros. to not credit the interest-bearing production cost balance with all the gross receipts of the picture. They also claim that because the distribution fee represents a source of "profit" for Warner Bros., this method of calculating interest is unconscionable because it allows Warner Bros. to charge interest on the cost of production after the picture has generated revenues in excess of that amount.

Plaintiffs did present sufficient evidence to require Warner Bros. to defend its method of computing interest under the contract.

After listening to the evidence presented by Warner Bros. and the arguments of counsel, however, the Court finds that Warner Bros. met its burden of showing that the method of calculating interest provided in their contract is not unconscionable. Warner Bros. met its burden in a number of ways.

Warner Bros. showed that the interest provision in the Warner Agreement is really the same provision found in [the underlying agreement] that Warner Bros. did not have anything to do with. Plaintiffs were bound by that contract before they ever dealt with Warner Bros. They cannot complain that they were harmed by being required to abide by a similar provision with the same effect.

Warner Bros. also showed that plaintiffs would not have gotten any better deal on the calculation of interest if they had borrowed the production costs from a third party lender, had produced *Batman* themselves as independent producers, and had hired Warner Bros. (or presumably anybody else) just to distribute it for them. In that case, plaintiffs would not have been able to use all of the gross receipts generated by the film to repay their lender. Just as in their contract with Warner Bros., they would have been able to repay the production financier only with the gross receipts left over after the distributor retained enough to cover the distribution fee and expenses.

And, if there is a "profit" embedded within Warner Bros. distribution fee, plaintiffs did not prove the amount of it or that it prevented the picture from showing a net profit.

All of that evidence is sufficient to overcome the plaintiffs' evidence as to the unconscionability of the method of calculating interest under their "Net Profits" contract.

Separately, plaintiffs argued that the language of their "Net Profits" contract did not permit Warner Bros. to continue charging interest once the gross receipts of the picture—prior to the deduction of distribution fees and expenses—exceed the total production costs. The duty of the Court is to find out what the parties meant by the language of their contract. If the contract is one of adhesion, the Court interprets it so that it does not defeat the reasonable expectations of the party who was forced to adhere to it. But the Court will not substitute its own interpretation of the contract if that is not what the evidence shows the parties intended.

The Court rejects plaintiffs' argument because there was no evidence that plaintiffs ever interpreted the language of the interest provisions in the manner claimed at trial. Mr. Melniker was an old hand at motion picture agreements of this type and had negotiated other "Net Profits" contracts like this himself. He had experience with similar provisions yet he never mentioned the interest issue with anyone at Warner Bros. Plaintiffs offered no evidence that they expected Warner Bros. to compute interest in any other manner. They have thus failed to prove that the contract defeated their reasonable expectations. . . .

NOTES

(1) For an analysis from the New York standpoint, see Paul Bennett Marrow, "Contractual Unconscionability: Identifying and Understanding Its Potential Elements," *N.Y. State Bar J.* Feb. 2000, p. 18.

(2) The following complaint filed by the Estate of Jim Garrison against Warner Bros. provides interesting insight and history on Hollywood's bookkeeping practices and fertile ground for discussion of what "net profit" means to a Hollywood insider.

Complaint

I. Introduction

1. The world of motion pictures is a never-never land of illusion. In the making of a movie, millions of still pictures are strung and spliced together to artfully imitate life, but when each part is disassembled and seen separately each only reflects static, one dimensional and unreal world. This creating of illusions has extended throughout all the facets of the motion picture industry since the days Thomas Alva Edison created and marketed the shuttered lantern projector nearly 90 years ago. Of all the illusions practiced daily in the motion picture world, nothing is more unreal than the promises of "net profits" for movieland's profit participants, a scam that has endured nearly half century, enriching the few at the expense of all the multitudes of talent responsible for actually creating the motion pictures.

2. "Net profits" as defined in Hollywood contracts is an esoteric bookkeeping device that could not be practiced in any other multi-billion dollar industry. The practice, which delays payment of profit sharing often forever, has earned the derisive title "Hollywood accounting." It could only be practiced in company town like Hollywood, where a few major studios control 90 percent of the movie world revenues,

and that enormous economic leverage can be and is used to force the signing and compliance with contract terms no one would sign in any other business or under any other circumstances.

3. From its inception, the moviemaking business has been an uneasy mix of creative talent—the writers, directors, producers and actors whose ideas and skills create the magic on the screen—and the business side—the financiers, marketers and distributors who sell the finished movie to the ticket-buying public. There has never been an equitable accommodation of all creative talents' rights to the profits.

4. "Hollywood accounting" has resulted in a talent caste system where the so-called stars with big, well-established reputations, most often actors or actresses and an occasional producer and director—writers almost never—are given contracts that provide participation in the gross income of motion picture. For creative talent that is less well-established, participation in the "net profits" is used to persuade the creative talent to accept smaller upfront fees with the promise of more later, for their creative work. Yet even the most successful motion pictures seldom, if ever, produce any net profit for creative talent. This law suit then is about the rights of all the moviemaking world's creative talent ("Talent") to participate equitably and in a timely manner in the often huge cash flow that motion pictures generate.

5. This is a class action on behalf of Talent and is brought under the laws of the State of California because of the movie studios' adoption of unconscionable contract terms as part of their standard form contracts, and their refusal to deal with Talent that will not submit to these one-sided terms. This is the result of an illegal conspiracy among the major studios that suppresses competition, fixes prices, and violates the laws of the State of California.

II. The Parties

A. Plaintiffs

6. Jim Garrison was the author of the book *On The Trail of the Assassin.* Mr. Garrison is deceased, and is represented in this action by his estate. During his lifetime, Mr. Garrison was resident and former District Attorney of New Orleans, Louisiana, where his estate is administered by his heirs.

7. The members of the plaintiff class have all either written a book, story or script upon which a motion picture was based, or acted in, directed or produced a motion picture, and, in compensation for those activities, each of the plaintiffs have entered into standard net profit contracts with one or more of the defendants. The representative plaintiffs and Mr. Garrison have engaged in the following transactions with defendants:

> Jim Garrison, during his lifetime, entered into a standard net profit contract dated "As Of January 20, 1989" with Oliver Stone, giving Mr. Stone an option to purchase the motion picture, television and allied rights to Mr. Garrison's best-selling book "On The Trail Of The Assassins." A true and correct copy of that agreement with the standard net profits clause, is attached hereto as Exhibit "B". Oliver Stone assigned his rights in that contract to defendant WARNER BROS and they accepted said contract. This book was an account

of Mr. Garrison's prosecution of an alleged conspiracy in the assassination of President John F. Kennedy. Warner Brothers made this book into a movie entitled "JFK," which has grossed over $150 million to date, and is continuing to earn profits. In spite of the movie's huge financial success, Mr. Garrison and/or his estate have received no payment at all from WARNER BROS. pursuant to the "net profits" clause of the contract as attached. He and now his estate are similar to all the other class members set out hereinafter.

B-E: (Plaintiff named the major film studios as defendants and stated that "At all times relevant to this Complaint, each of the defendants was an agent, employee, joint venturer, co-conspirator and/or partner of each of the remaining defendants, and was at all times acting within the course and scope of such agency, employment, and/or partnership. Each defendant has ratified, approved, and authorized the acts of each of the remaining defendants with full knowledge of those acts.")

III. Definitions

26. For purposes of this Complaint, the following terms shall have the following defined meanings:
27. "Talent" shall mean directors, producers, actors, and authors of books, stories and scripts and all other creative personnel whose efforts are necessary to produce motion pictures throughout the world. The word Talent as used in the motion picture industry is well known and commonly understood, and the words have the same meaning here.
28. "Standard net profits contracts" shall mean the standard form contracts with riders attached which are drafted and utilized by defendants to entice various Talent to render their services in the making of motion pictures and which purport to entitle Talent to a share of the net profits of a motion picture to which the Talent contributes. Representative examples of standard net profits contracts used by the defendants are attached hereto as Exhibits C 1–8.

IV. Class Allegations

29. Plaintiffs bring this action both on behalf of themselves and as a class action on behalf of all Talent (except the defendants and their respective affiliates and co-conspirators) who have entered into standard net profit contracts with one or more of the defendants or their affiliates during the period January 1, 1988 to the present. They are easily ascertainable and are within the knowledge of each defendant named herein.
30. All members of the class were injured in their business or property by reason of the defendants' unlawful conduct as set forth in the Complaint.
31. The defendants entered into standard net profit contracts with numerous Talent purporting to entitle the Talent to share in the "net profits" of motion pictures with which the Talent were connected, making the members of the class so numerous that joinder of all members is impracticable. Since the class members may be identified from records regularly maintained by the defendants and their employees and agents, the number and identity of class members can be easily ascertained through the defendants' own records.

32. Plaintiffs' claims are typical of the claims of each class member. They, like all other class members, sustained damages arising from defendants' violation of the California Laws. Plaintiffs and the members of the class were similarly or identically harmed by the same systematic and pervasive pattern of anticompetitive conduct engaged in by the defendants.

33. Plaintiffs will fairly and adequately represent and protect the interests of the members of the class, and have retained counsel who are both competent and experienced in antitrust and class litigation. There are no material conflicts between the claims of the representative plaintiffs and the members of the class that would make class certification inappropriate. Counsel for the class will vigorously assert the claims of all class members.

34. In this case, a class action is superior to all other methods for the fair and efficient adjudication of this controversy, since joinder of all class members is impracticable. Furthermore, as the damages suffered by individual members of the class may be relatively small, the expense and burden of individual actions makes it impossible for the class members to individually redress the wrongs they have suffered. There will be no difficulty in managing this case as a class action.

35. Common questions of law and fact exist as to all members of the class and predominate over any questions affecting solely individual members of the class. Among the questions of law and fact common to the class are:

   (a) Whether the defendants entered into a conspiracy, contract or combination to fix, lower, maintain or stabilize the prices they paid to Talent for their participation in the making of motion pictures, in violation of State law.

   (b) Whether the defendants entered into a conspiracy, contract or combination to refuse to deal with Talent who would not accept the defendants' standardized contract terms and prices relating to their share of a motion picture's "net profits" for their participation in the making of motion pictures, in violation of State law.

   (c) Whether the plaintiffs and the other members of the class were injured in their business or property by reason of the defendants' unlawful conduct.

   (d) The appropriate class-wide measure of damages.

V. Background Of The Industry

A. History Of The Industry

36. In the late 1890s, the motion picture first developed from the union of still photography with the persistence-of- vision toy, which made drawn figures appear to move. The early films were mostly of still figures and had very little public appeal.

37. On June 19, 1905, the United States public watched The Great Train Robbery, a short silent film, in a theater that was solely devoted to motion pictures. Prior to then, movies had always been shown along with some sort of live entertainment. By 1908 an estimated 10 million Americans were paying their nickels and dimes to see such films.

38. Motion pictures were so popular that thousands of motion picture theaters called nickelodeons sprang up throughout the country. This new industry was very profitable for the founders of the movie picture industry. Young entrepreneurs such as William Fox and Marcus Loewe saw their theaters, which initially cost about $1,600 each, grow into enterprises worth fortunes within a few years. Soon the demand arose for Talent to make the movies to fill the demand of the consuming public.

B. Economic Leverage Over Talent

39. The motion picture industry has a long history of abusing Talent, and in particular of using economic power to deny Talent the rights and earnings to which they are entitled.

40. The early movie studios, for example, as well as their current successors, made every effort to insure that the salaries of the Talent were kept as low as possible. The movie studios began a course of conduct designed to stop Talent from reaping the rewards from a competitive movie system by exerting monopoly power.

41. In the beginning, the names of the actors and actresses in films were kept anonymous so as to keep them from acquiring their own place in a competitive market. As the public's demand for motion pictures increased, however, so did the public's preference for certain actors and actresses. In order to combat fear that public recognition would result in a demand by the players for higher salaries, producers went to great lengths to keep the identity of the actors anonymous by various different means, including demanding the use of pseudonyms. It was not until fan magazines began running stories about the identity of the movie stars that the producers began promoting the names of their actors.

42. Hollywood then embraced the star concept and between 1910 and 1948, movies companies established the star system as a potent business strategy to provide increasing returns on production investments. In 1918, America's two favorite stars, Charlie Chaplin and Mary Pickford, both signed contracts for over $1 million. However, most Talent did not have as much power as Mr. Chaplin and Miss Pickford and earned substantially less.

43. By the 1930s and 1940s, even the major movie stars suffered dramatic reductions in independence and incomes. Due to the advent of talking movies, which destroyed the careers of many silent stars who could not make the transition to sound, and the economic depression of the 1930s, movies studios exercised tremendous control over the actors. An increasing concentration of monopoly power in the hands of the major movie companies left the movie stars at the mercy of studio bosses. While in the 1920s, stars had often received a percentage of net movie profits and substantial artistic control, Talent in the 1930s and 1940s were forced into seven year exclusive contracts which took away net profits and forced the Talent into limited maximum salaries. Talent who objected to an assigned movie role risked being suspended without pay for rejecting a role.

44. This star system allowed movie studios to greatly profit from their movie stars by lending them out to other studios for huge profits. For example, MGM lent out Clark Gable for the making of Gone With the Wind and contributed money towards production costs in exchange for the distribution rights and a sliding scale percentage of the gross

profits starting at 50%. Gable, one of the biggest stars of the era did not want to do the movie, but his contract did not give him the right to turn down parts. Gable received his standard salary per week for playing the part although MGM gave him a small bonus in an act of generosity. By 1967, MGM had earned $75 million in rentals for the movie. This practice highlights the transition of Talent from artist to commodity in the eyes of the movie studios.

45. The first profit participation contract on behalf of Talent was negotiated with Metro Goldwyn Mayer in 1934 on behalf of the Marx Brothers for two movies: "A Day At The Races" and "A Night At The Opera." That contract was a simple straightforward one that netted the brothers 15 percent of all the money the studio received for those movies.

46. Between 1947 and 1953 admissions to movie theaters dropped dramatically. Talent, including many movie stars, suddenly became expendable, and were released from studio contracts to reduce overhead. While some popular stars used this freedom to their economic advantage, the less popular Talent found their incomes and marketability declining rapidly.

47. For some Talent, the results were tragic. In the 1950s, for example, Talent who refused to cooperate with the witch hunts of the House Un-American Activities Committee found themselves blacklisted from the movie industry. However, the studios were not above crediting others for the work that was done by blacklisted artists and reaping the rewards of the blacklisted Talent, further proof of their tremendous economic power.

48. The modern-era of net profit participation in contracts began in 1950 when Jimmy Stewart's agent, Lew Wasserman, was able to negotiate such a provision with Universal for the movie "Harvey." Although such contracts had been executed in the early history of film, this contract was the first one negotiated in the post-war years when the studios were no longer the great forces they had been in the past and the star system was beginning to fall apart.

49. Over the years, the movie industry has refined its use of creative accounting in dealing with Talent. For example, during the 1950s the major studios would put together large numbers of films and sell them as a package in foreign countries. The package might include one or two big hits, but most of the films would be grade B or lower. The hits would play all over the foreign country, while the other movies would not even be shown. But when it came time to divide up the profits, each of the films in the package would get an equal portion. The result was that the net profits participants in the "hits" got little or nothing because their profits were artificially allocated to the unsuccessful films. The participants in the unsuccessful films typically also got nothing. The studios, on the other hand, got the same amount of total return—they just put the money in different columns on their books, offsetting profits, wherever earned, against losses, wherever earned, to make everything come out as close as possible to "zero".

50. In the 1970s, the Securities & Exchange Commission and the Internal Revenue Service investigated alleged tax improprieties of PARAMOUNT and its then parent corporation, Gulf Western. There were serious

questions of the accuracy of the conglomerate's financial reports and other financial improprieties such as expenses assigned to making movies. One company auditor alleged that Gulf & Western altered profit statements to withhold revenues that should have been reported. In 1981, Gulf & Western signed a consent decree with the government to refrain from such practices in the future.

C. Hollywood Accounting Procedures

51. Under the net profit definition used by most of the moviemaking studios, payment of profit participation is delayed by a process of adding fees and costs associated with distribution, production, prints, promotion, advertising and whatever other overhead expenses they wish. Some studio executives admit that they do everything possible to delay payment of net profits, if any survive the interminable deductions.

52. "It is to our benefit to delay paying on profits for as long as possible. We earn interest on the float and the money allows us to finance other ventures," according to a studio executive (referred to as a bean counter) quoted in the June 5, 1995 issue of *Variety*, the entertainment world's leading trade publication.

53. Attached or included in the standard contracts are certain riders that break out the charges and expenses that the studios deduct from gross revenues. Though the amounts of the charges allocated in the net profit contract riders may vary from contract to contract, there are nine categories that are universally included:

    (a) Distribution Fees—this is a set fee that is used by the studios as being necessary to underwrite the costs of maintaining distribution offices and facilities. These are flat rates that range from 30 to 40 percent of a movie's gross receipts (30 percent for domestic distribution, 35 percent for the United Kingdom and 40 percent for foreign distribution).

    (b) Distribution Costs—in addition to the fees that are levied, the actual costs of distribution are also allocated against the income side.

    (c) Advertising—this is the cost of advertising and promotion of the film. This can include all sorts of expense; for example, if a convention is attended by a studio's promotion executives assigned to the picture, those costs can be allocated to the film's expenses under this category. An arbitrary overhead fee, usually a flat 10 percent is added in this category.

    (d) Prints—this is the cost of printing copies of the movie, sometimes thousands of copies are printed, and distributed free to friends of the studio and others on the favored lists.

    (e) Production Costs—these are billed as direct expenses whether there are any out-of-pocket costs or not; these can and do usually include use of studio facilities, cameras, vehicles or other equipment based on a rate card set up for each piece of equipment in the studio inventory. Money paid to Talent receiving gross receipts participation, which can be in the millions of dollars, is also counted as a production cost. Over and above all of this, an overhead charge of 15 percent is also added to the production costs which results in double billing for most equipment.

    (f)   Over-Budget Penalty—for each dollar the film exceeds its budget, an additional $1 ($2 total) is charged as a cost of the film as defined in the Talent net profit contract regardless of whether or not Talent has any direct responsibility for the overage and sometimes whether or not there was an over-budget allocation.

    (g)   Taxes—these are allocated as offsets against income, whether the studio actually pays the taxes or not. As an example, Japan charges a tax of 10 percent for any income taken from Japan to the U.S., but when U.S. taxes are paid, this is a credit against federal taxes.

    (h)   Political Lobbying Expenses—allocated as expenses against Talent's profit participants are dues paid to trade organizations such as the Motion Picture Association of America, which works as the studios' lobbying group.

    (i)   Interest—this is charged from the day production starts and is levied against all budgeted production and promotion costs generally at the rate of 125 percent of the prime rate. Accordingly, over and above charges of every conceivable type—an additional interest is tacked on.

54. The most glaring example of the continuing conspiracy among the defendants is the handling of video revenue from a movie, a source of income that often surpasses 50 percent of the total income. The first studio to license a movie's video rights and then to negotiate a net profit contract for the video income was 20th Century Fox. In that contract, Fox artificially allocated only 20 percent of the video income as revenues to be reported to profit participants, thus preventing Talent from participating in 80 percent of the income received from the film's video contracts. That 20 percent share has become the agreed upon standard for all of the other studios as well from that day forward, and only the star category actors, a few directors and seldom if ever a producer or writer are able to negotiate a higher percentage.

55. At least one court has already ruled that standard net profit contracts are contracts of adhesion; that the studios refuse to negotiate in good faith over the definition of net profits, and that the existing definition was unconscionable because it subtracted numerous costs that were inflated or unjustified.

D. Coercive Effects On Talent

56. The net profit riders attached to Talent's service contracts, which display a startling similarity from studio to studio, usually differ only in exactly the amount of overhead costs that may be added to a film's expenses before those profits can be calculated. This is done through the use of the standard form contract. The studios simply refuse to deal with most creative talent who will not accept these form contracts, which are offered on a "take it or leave it" basis.

57. One of the most recent examples of the effect of the studio practices upon Talent involved the motion picture "Forrest Gump," which had enjoyed the fourth highest gross income in the history of the industry. Winston Groom, author of the book was adapted to the screen, was told that despite a worldwide gross of $660 million as of December of 1994, there had been no net profit. The movie's producer,

Steve Tisch, and the movie's screenwriter Eric Roth, likewise had been coerced into signing contracts with smaller upfront fees with promises of net profit participation; neither had been paid any share of the profits from the picture. This was despite the fact that "Forrest Gump" had been chiefly responsible for its studio, Paramount Pictures, increasing the studio's 1994 box office gross income by 60 percent over the previous year, and boosting it from sixth to third place in market share of the movie business.

58. Even when Talent has a famous name like syndicated columnist Art Buchwald, the court system has been the only recourse. It took Buchwald seven years of litigation to obtain share of profits from "Coming to America," a movie based on an idea and treatment Buchwald had submitted to moviemakers a decade earlier. A settlement finally came for Buchwald.

59. In a coincidental demonstration of the practice's pervasiveness, on Sept. 12, 1995, the day a settlement with Buchwald was announced, another writer made public a Complaint that Paramount had not been paid him any share of profits from "Indecent Proposal," the movie starring Robert Redford and Demi Moore that had grossed $250 million worldwide. Jack Englehard, whose book was adapted for the movie, said Paramount had told him that "Indecent Proposal" still showed a deficit of $37.5 million despite grossing a quarter of a billion dollars.

60. The net profit issue is not limited to one studio; it is an industry-wide system used with little variation from studio to studio. Warner Bros. Inc., the studio that held the largest movie market share four out of the five years of 1989 through 1993, was accused of failing to pay any net profits to two executive producers who worked for 10 years and helped create the hugely popular "Batman" movie that starred Jack Nicholson and Michael Keaton. Benjamin Melniker and Michael Udslan, the complaining producers, were told by Warner Bros. that despite a worldwide gross of $411 million that there had been no net profits.

E. Prior Violations of Antitrust Law—Common Design Plan and Scheme

61. The motion picture industry has a long history of violating the antitrust laws with a similar course and conduct to the acts alleged in the present case. In the 1920s, for example, ten producers and distributors of motion pictures who controlled 60 percent of the motion picture market agreed among themselves that they would only contract with motion picture exhibitors according to the terms of a standard form contract where most of the provisions are favorable to the studios. The United states Government took legal action against the studios, and a court ordered the studios to cease such activities. The matter was appealed to the United states Supreme Court, which in the landmark case of Paramount Famous Lasky Corp. v. United States 282 U.S. 30 (1930) ruled that the studios were engaged in a conspiracy that violated the antitrust laws of the United states.

62. In spite of the warning from both the Justice Department and the Supreme Court, the motion picture industry continued to violate the antitrust laws. In the 1940s, for example, various producers and distributors of motion pictures entered into a wide variety of conspiracies in restraint of competition, including a conspiracy to fix minimum

prices the public had to pay for admission to movie theaters, and a conspiracy to include the same minimum admission price requirements in all of their standard form contracts with movie theaters. The producers and distributors also used standard distribution contracts that discriminated in numerous ways against small independent theaters in favor of large theaters affiliated with the studios and with large groups of theaters. Once again the United states Government had to take legal action, and once again the United states Supreme court in United states v. Paramount Pictures, Inc., et al. 334 U.S. 131 (1948) declared most of the challenged acts and practices illegal under the antitrust laws. The Supreme Court noted that the defendants had "marked proclivity for unlawful conduct" and ordered them to bear the burden of showing that certain future actions came within the law. In spite of these stern warnings from the highest court in the land, the movie industry continues to act in violation of the laws by continuing a common design, plan and scheme to take advantage of the plaintiffs.

F. Fraudulent Concealment

63. Throughout the period set forth in this Complaint, the defendants have fraudulently concealed their unlawful contract, combination and conspiracy from the plaintiffs and the members of the class.

64. In order to fraudulently conceal their contract, combination and conspiracy from the plaintiffs and the members of the class, defendants engaged, among other things, in the following affirmative conduct throughout the period relevant of this Complaint:

   (a) defendants secretly discussed and agreed among themselves, among other things, on the terms of their respective contracts with Talent, and therefore on the prices to be paid to Talent for their ideas and labor, and on their concerted refusal to deal with Talent who would not submit to these unfair terms.

   (b) defendants used communications which they believed to be safe from detection and avoided communication which they believed to be subject to detection.

   (c) defendants used different wording in drafting their standard net profit contracts, while adhering to the same substantive terms that the defendants had secretly agreed upon, in order to conceal their unlawful agreements.

   (d) In recent months, studio legal departments have reacted to court decisions on Talent contracts by attempting to place a new face on the old, discredited system. Studio lawyers have been replacing the term "net profit" with some euphemisms 'like "net proceeds" or other terms designed to hide the fact that the unconscionable practice continues.

65. Because of the active and fraudulent concealment of the conspiracy and the illegal acts in furtherance of that conspiracy that are outlined above, plaintiffs did not know and could not have discovered the antitrust violations alleged in this Complaint until shortly before they initiated this litigation. Therefore, the running of any statute of limitations has been suspended with respect to the claims alleged in this Complaint.

G. Market Power

66. The movie industry is highly concentrated, with only a few major American studios accounting for over 90% of dollar volume of the revenue from the motion pictures made in the United states. The major studios are all located in the same area of Southern California, in and around Los Angeles. Defendants have been able to exercise their market power in dealings with Talent.

H. The Standard Form Contracts

67. Beginning at least as early as January 1, 1988, the exact date being unknown to the plaintiffs, and continuing to the present, pursuant to a conspiracy among themselves and their co- conspirators, the defendants have developed and used standard form contracts for purchasing intellectual property and labor from Talent.

68. Virtually all of these standard form contracts contain provisions for the Talent to receive a percentage of the "net profits" of the motion pictures to which they contribute. Although the contracts use different wording in defining "net profits," the substantive provisions of the contracts, and the substantive definitions of "net profits" contained in each of them, are virtually identical. Among other things, these standard net profit contracts contain nearly identical provisions concerning the deduction of numerous different types of "costs" from a motion picture's profits before the Talent can receive any distributions under the contract. The use of nearly identical net profit definitions by all of the major studios in their form contracts is the result of an illegal agreement among the defendants to use this definition. Attached hereto as Exhibit B is a chart summarizing the net profit definitions of the standard net profit contracts used by each of the defendants.

69. In many instances, the "costs" that are deducted to determine "net profits" are grossly inflated and bear no relation to reality. As a result, no matter how successful the motion picture, there are almost never any "net profits" to be shared with Talent as promised by the contracts. Thus, the true purpose of the defendants' conspiracy is to reduce the price they must pay for the Talent they need to make motion pictures.

70. A small handful of extremely well-known Talent with extremely strong bargaining power can negotiate gross profits clauses to replace the net profits clauses of their contracts with the studios. For the vast majority of Talent, however, the contracts are offered on a take it or leave it basis, and are not subject to negotiation. This is the result of an agreement among the defendants and their co-conspirators to refuse to deal with Talent, except for a small number of extremely well-known Talent, who will not accept the standard net profit contract.

71. From the beginning of the conspiracy to the present, the defendants have continued to discuss and agree upon a common and grossly unfair definition of "net profits," or some euphemistic word with the same meaning, to include that common definition in all of their standard net profit contracts, and to collectively refuse to deal with any Talent (except a handful of very famous Talent) who will not submit

to the oppressive "net profits" clause of the studios 'form contracts. As a result of defendants' ongoing conspiracy, the price paid to Talent for their ideas and services has been kept artificially low, and the Talent has been deprived of their rightful share of the profits of the motion pictures that they made possible.

VI. Effects and Resulting Injury to Plaintiffs and the Class

72. The defendants' illegal combination and conspiracy had the following effects, among others:

(a) Monies paid to plaintiffs and other members of the class for their ideas, labor, and intellectual property were fixed, lowered and maintained at artificial and non-competitive levels .

(b) Talent was deprived of free and open competition for their ideas, labor, and intellectual property.

(c) Competition for Talent among the defendants and their co-conspirators was restrained.

73. During the period covered by this Complaint, plaintiffs and other members of the class sold millions of dollars worth of ideas, labor, and intellectual property to the defendants. By reason of the actions described in this Complaint, plaintiffs and the class members received less for their ideas, labor, and intellectual property than they would have been paid in the absence of the illegal combination and conspiracy and, as a result, have been injured in their business and property and have suffered damages in an amount presently undetermined.

First Cause of Action

(Price Fixing)
(Business & Professions Code Section 16720 et seq.)

74. All foregoing paragraphs of this Complaint are incorporated herein by reference.

75. As set forth above, defendants conspired to fix, depress, maintain and stabilize prices paid to Talent for their ideas, labor, and intellectual property to be used in the making of motion pictures in the United States, in violation of Business & Professions Code Section 16720 et seq. (the Cartwright Act).

76. Plaintiffs and the class have been injured in their business or property by the defendants' antitrust violations as alleged in this Complaint.

77. Plaintiffs and the other members of the class are entitled to recover three times the amount of their actual pursuant to Business & Professions Code 16750(a). damages.

78. Plaintiffs and the class are entitled to recover reasonable attorneys+ fees and litigation, pursuant to Business Professions Code 16750(a).

79. Plaintiffs and the class are entitled to recover pre judgment interest on their actual damages from the date of service of this Complaint until the date of entry of judgment in this case, pursuant to Business & Professions Code Sections 16750(a) and 16761.

WHEREFORE plaintiffs and the other members of the class pray for relief as set forth below.

Second Cause of Action

(Boycott/Concerted Refusal to Deal)

(Business & Professions Code Section 16720 et seq.)

80. All foregoing paragraphs of this Complaint are incorporated herein by reference.

81. As set forth above, defendants conspired and agreed among themselves to refuse to deal with any Talent, except for a small number of very famous Talent, who would not submit to the standardized net profits contract terms that the defendants jointly agreed to impose on Talent, in violation of Business & Professions Code Section 16720 et seq. (the Cartwright Act).

82. One purpose of this boycott and concerted refusal to deal except on particular agreed terms was to facilitate and enforce the defendants ' unlawful agreement to fix, depress, maintain and stabilize prices paid to Talent for their ideas, labor, and intellectual property to be used in the making of motion pictures in the United states, and to force adherence to the terms agreed upon among the defendants and their co-conspirators.

83. Plaintiffs and the class have been injured in their business or property by the defendants' antitrust violations as alleged in this Complaint.

84. Plaintiffs and the other members of the class are entitled to recover three times the amount of their actual damages, pursuant to Business & Professions Code 16750 (a).

85. Plaintiffs and the class are entitled to recover reasonable attorneys' fees and litigation costs upon entry of judgment against any of the defendants, pursuant to Business Professions Code 16750(a).

86. Plaintiffs and the class are entitled to recover pre judgment interest on their actual damages from the date of service of this Complaint until the date of entry of judgment in this case, pursuant to Business & Professions Code 16750(a) and 16761.

WHEREFORE plaintiffs and the other members of the class pray for relief as set forth below.

Third Cause of Action

(For Breach of Contract)

87. All foregoing paragraphs of this Complaint are incorporated herein by reference.

88. By executing the standardized net profit contracts as hereinbefore described and of which representative Agreements are attached hereto as Exhibits Cl to 8, plaintiffs and defendants entered into valid and enforceable written contracts. These contracts are standardized throughout the industry and the substantive provisions of the contracts, and the substantive definitions of "net profits" contained in each of them, are virtually identical.

89. In each of the contracts, defendants agreed to pay plaintiffs a share of the "net profits" of the motion pictures with which the plaintiffs were connected.

90. Plaintiffs have performed fully each and all of the conditions, covenants and obligations imposed upon them under the terms of the Agreements, except to the extent excused therefrom.

91. By reason of the conduct described above, defendants have materially breached the Agreements in numerous respects. Such conduct includes, but is not limited to, failing to pay the net profits of the movie to plaintiffs, but instead in a manner common to all plaintiffs improperly inflating expenses and/or improperly deducting items as expenses.

92. As a direct and proximate result of defendants' material breaches of the Agreements, plaintiffs have suffered monetary damages in an amount that is known by defendants who have concealed said amount from plaintiffs, but which amount exceeds the jurisdictional limits of this Court.

WHEREFORE plaintiffs and the other members of the class pray for relief as set forth below.

Fourth Cause of Action

(For Breach of the Implied Covenant of Good Faith and Fair Dealing)

93. All foregoing paragraphs of this Complaint are incorporated herein by reference.

94. By executing the Agreements alleged herein, plaintiffs and defendants entered into written contracts. Plaintiffs thus reposed trust and confidence in defendants to, among other things, deal with them fairly and in good faith, and not to wrongly deprive them of their contractual compensation, including but not limited to, the right to share in the profits of the movies. Defendants knew of and accepted such trust and confidence at the time they entered into the Agreements.

95. Plaintiffs have performed fully each and all of the conditions, covenants and obligations imposed upon them under the terms of the Agreements, except to the extent excused therefrom.

96. By virtue of the wrongful acts of defendants, and each of them, in failing to pay net profit proceeds to plaintiffs, defendants breached their duties of good faith and fair dealing.

97. As a proximate result of defendants' actions, plaintiffs have suffered monetary damage in an amount within the jurisdiction of this Court, together with interest thereon.

98. At all times herein alleged, defendants acted willfully, wantonly, with oppression, fraud and/or malice, and with a conscious disregard of the rights of others, such that plaintiffs request that the trier of fact, in the exercise of its sound discretion, should award plaintiffs additional damages for the sake of example and in a sufficient amount to punish said defendants for their conduct, in an amount reasonably related to plaintiffs' actual damages and defendants' wealth and sufficiently large to be an example to others and to deter these defendants and others from engaging in similar conduct in the future.

Fifth Cause of Action

(Unjust enrichment)

99. All foregoing paragraphs of this Complaint are incorporated herein by reference.

100. As a result of the wrongful acts of defendants in failing to pay plaintiffs net profits proceeds, defendants have been unjustly enriched at the expense of plaintiffs by keeping monies which should have been paid over to plaintiffs.
101. If defendants are allowed to keep these monies, they will unjustly benefit from their actions and the plaintiffs will unjustly suffer a loss.
102. By virtue of defendants' wrongful acts, and their resulting wrongful gain of the funds to which plaintiffs are entitled, defendants hold these funds as a constructive trustee for the benefit of plaintiffs.

WHEREFORE plaintiffs and the other members of the class pray for relief as set forth below.

Sixth Cause of Action

(Imposition of constructive trust and for an accounting)
103. All foregoing paragraphs of this Complaint are incorporated herein by reference.
104. Based upon the contracts entered into between plaintiffs and defendants, plaintiffs have an interest in funds which, as alleged herein, should have been paid over to them. The specific amount of these funds is unknown to plaintiffs and cannot be ascertained without a full and complete accounting, the means of which are within the knowledge of the defendants. Plaintiffs are informed and believe and on that basis allege that the amounts owed exceed the minimal jurisdictional limits of this Court.
105. Through the breach of their duties to plaintiffs and the wrongful acts which they committed as alleged herein, defendants have wrongfully appropriated and failed to pay to plaintiffs the funds to which plaintiffs are entitled. Plaintiffs have been damaged by their failure to receive the monies.
106. By virtue of defendants' wrongful acts, and their resulting wrongful gain of the funds to which the plaintiffs are entitled, defendants hold these funds as a constructive trustee for the benefit of plaintiffs.

WHEREFORE plaintiffs and the other members of the class pray for relief as set forth below.

Seventh Cause of Action

(For Declaratory Relief)
107. All foregoing paragraphs of this Complaint are incorporated herein by reference.
108. An actual controversy has arisen and now exists between plaintiffs and defendants in that plaintiffs contend and defendants deny that:
    (a) The Agreements entered into by plaintiffs are standardized contracts drafted by defendants, a party with superior bargaining strength, and imposed by defendants on plaintiffs who lacked effective bargaining power and who were given the opportunity only to accept or reject the contract, and the Agreements therefore constitute an unenforceable contract of adhesion.
    (b) That certain provisions of the Agreements as more fully set forth herein were harsh, oppressive and unduly one-sided, and thus

unconscionable at the time the Agreements were entered into and should not be enforced.

(c) The unconscionable provisions of the Agreements taken both in isolation and combined, include, but are not limited to, the following:

(1) charging a fixed percent overhead on operational allowances;

(2) charging a fixed percent advertising overhead not in proportion to actual costs;

(3) charging a fixed rate overhead not in proportion to actual costs;

(4) charging interest on negative cost balance without credit for distribution fees;

(5) charging interest on overhead; and

(6) charging an interest rate not in proportion to the actual cost of finance.

(d) The unconscionable provisions of the Agreements, should be declared illegal and given no legal effect by the Court.

WHEREFORE plaintiffs and the other members of the class pray for relief as set forth below.

Eighth Cause of Action

(For Violation of Business & Professions Code Section 17200 et seq.)

109. All foregoing paragraphs of this Complaint are incorporated herein by reference.

110. The wrongful conduct of defendants, and each of them, constitutes a violation of Business & Professions Code 17200 et seq., which prohibits unfair business practices, including unlawful, unfair or fraudulent business practices. This conduct includes, but is not limited to, unlawfully compelling Talent that lack bargaining power to enter into adhesive agreements containing standardized net profit definitions which are unconscionable in whole or in part.

111. Defendants' primary business involves the production and distribution of theatrical motion pictures, and the Agreements related to and occurred in the course of defendants 'business.

112. As a direct and proximate result of defendants' unfair competition, defendants have acquired and continue to acquire labor, ideas, and intellectual property from plaintiffs.

113. Pursuant to California Business & Professions Code 17204, plaintiffs are entitled to restitution and/or other relief necessary to restore to plaintiffs any money or property, which were acquired by means of the unfair and unlawful conduct alleged herein.

WHEREFORE plaintiffs and the other members of the class pray for relief as set forth below.

Ninth Cause of Action

(For Injunctive Relief)

114. All foregoing paragraphs of this Complaint are incorporated herein by reference.

115. Beginning in or around January, 1988 and continuing to the present time, as described herein above, Defendants have unlawfully and wrongfully engaged in a conspiracy to cheat Talent out of their rightful share of the profits of the motion pictures that they made possible by forcing them to enter into unconscionable contracts and refusing to deal with Talent who refused to agree to such contracts.

116. The Defendants' continuing wrongful conduct against Plaintiffs, unless and until enjoined and restrained by order of this Court, will cause great and irreparable harm to the Plaintiffs in that they will continue to be forced to accept unconscionable terms or will be unable to obtain employment in the motion picture industry.

117. Plaintiffs have no adequate remedy at law for the injuries that are threatened in that pecuniary compensation would not afford adequate relief and/or it would be extremely difficult to ascertain the amount of compensation that would afford adequate relief.

WHEREFORE, plaintiffs and the other members of the class pray for relief as set forth below.

Prayer for Relief

Plaintiffs and the class pray for relief as follows:

(a) That the unlawful combinations and conspiracies alleged in this Complaint be adjudged and decreed to be in unreasonable restraint of trade and commerce and in violation of Business & Professions Code Section 16720 et seq.

(b) That the defendants, and each of them, be enjoined from continuing the conspiracies, and all acts in furtherance of those conspiracies, as alleged in this Complaint, including but not limited to, the use of the standard net profit contracts and definitions and the refusal to deal with Talent who will not submit to those terms.

(c) That the plaintiffs and the class be awarded compensatory and general damages according to proof.

(d) That the plaintiffs and the class be awarded three times their actual damages.

(e) That the plaintiffs and the class be awarded pre judgment interest at the maximum legal rate.

(f) That the plaintiffs and the class be awarded their costs of this suit.

(g) That the plaintiffs and the class be awarded reasonable attorneys fees.

(h) That punitive damage be awarded according to proof.

(i) For a declaration that the terms of the Agreements set forth above are unconscionable as according to proof.

(j) For an order that defendants should hold the funds to which plaintiffs are entitled in trust for plaintiffs.

(k) For an accounting on each of the standard form contracts according to proof.

(l) That the plaintiffs and the class be awarded such other and further relief as the Court deems just and proper.

DATED: November, 1995. It is believed that the case was settled prior to the service of an answer to the complaint.

9.4 PRODUCING FILMS: THE INDEPENDENT MODEL

Independent films constitute a major part of the film industry. One-fourth to one-third of all major studio releases are in fact produced by independents, some under so-called negative pick-up deals (see below), and some without advance studio commitments. A studio may do this to fill in gaps in its release schedule, or it may do so to take advantage of the lower costs that may result if an independent film is shot in a "right to work" state such as Texas, or in a jurisdiction in which local union work rules may be more relaxed than they are in Los Angeles or New York.

Independent films are gaining increasing importance within the industry. Young actors look to star in independent films as a way of becoming known. Known actors look to participate in independent films because they like the story, believe in the film, or want to help the producer or director of the film. The Academy Awards are not the only awards given for films; there are many film festivals that feature independent filmmakers (Sundance, New York Film Festival, Toronto Film Festival, and Seattle Film Festival are examples). Many directors, producers, and writers get discovered at these festivals, such as Steven Soderbergh's *Sex, Lies, and Videotape* and Ed Burns' *The Brothers McMullen*.

Independent producers face the same problems in rights acquisition as do studios and studio-backed independents, but they have considerable problems of their own.

9.4.1 Financing Independent Films

There are many ways to finance an independent film. The following article written by Alison S. Cohen, a partner in the prestigious New York entertainment law firm of Epstein, Levinson, Bodine, Hurwitz and Weinstein, LLP, describes common ways of financing a film outside of the studio system.

1. Independent Film Financing

There are many ways to finance a film outside of the studio system. Producers can mix and match funds from a variety of sources, including the following:

Advances from pre-sales in foreign territories
Advances from foreign sales agents
Private Equity through a private offering
Private Equity from an independent financier
Bank Loans secured by advances payable on domestic and/or foreign distribution deals
Co-production funds
Tax Credits and other "Soft" Money

The simplest way to discuss how to obtain access to these various production funds is by example. Accordingly, set forth below are two ways to finance an independent film. The first transaction illustrated below presents a film financed by a bank loan secured by a "negative pickup agreement" with a domestic distributor and by amounts received from pre-sales. The second presents a film financed through private equity.

2. The Domestic Negative Pickup coupled with Foreign Pre-Sales.

(a) There are five principal components of this transaction.

(i) A "negative pickup" agreement with a domestic distributor, which states that if the film is delivered with a set list of requirements, the domestic distributor will purchase the film for a set price.

(ii) A sales agency agreement with a foreign sales agent that commits the agent to sell the film and lists the sales agents' projected sales of the film upon completion.

(iii) Pre-existing agreements with multiple foreign distributors guaranteeing the payment of certain advances upon the delivery of the film, with a portion of the advance paid upon signature of the agreement.

(iv) A loan agreement, where a bank loans the producers the budget of the film, secured by the producer's rights under each of the agreements above and all of the producer's rights in and to the film.

(v) A completion agreement with a completion company, who upon execution of the agreement gives a guaranty to the bank that the film will be delivered within the budget to each of the distributors.

(vi) Two interparty agreements—one among the domestic distributor, the producer, the bank, and the completion guarantor, and the other among the foreign sales agent, the producer, the bank and the completion guarantor.

The basic premise of this structure is that the bank will be loaning the producer the production funds to make the movie based on two things: (i) the fact that a large portion of the budget will be repaid upon the film's completion, and (ii) the bank's trust in the sales agent to sell the remaining territories in accordance with its projections by the time the film is finished so that the loan can be repaid in a timely manner. The difference between the advances secured by executed distribution agreements and the total amount of the loan is called the "Gap" and will be discussed further below. Each one of the agreements listed above will be discussed in turn.

(b) *The Negative Pickup Agreement.* The Negative Pickup Agreement is, as mentioned above, an agreement between a producer and a distributor which provides for the distributor's purchase of a motion picture upon the delivery of the motion picture to the distributor. It differs from a typical domestic distribution agreement and a foreign distribution agreement in that the distributor is heavily involved in the production of the film, despite its decision not to cash flow the production. The basic points of a negative pickup agreement are as follows:

(i) The Advance paid on delivery, and any contingent compensation paid to the producer once the advance has been recouped.

(ii) The Rights Granted.

   (iii) Who, if any, are "essential elements" to the production. Essential elements are most often directors and/or cast members, but they can also be producers and/or executive producers of a film.

   (iv) The creative approval rights of the distributor. These approval rights include approvals over the selection of the cast, crew, (including the director), locations where the film will be shot, screenplay, and changes to the screenplay.

   (v) The business approval rights of the distributor. These approval rights usually involve approval over the budget, changes to the budget, cashflow schedule, material terms in agreements with the principal cast and key crew, approval over any obligations which will extend beyond the delivery of the film (e.g., credit obligations).

   (vi) The procedures that must be followed during production.

   (vii) The distributor's access to production.

  (viii) The delivery date.

   (ix) The delivery materials.

(c) *The Sales Agency Agreement.* The sales agent has an extremely important role in the financing that is being described here. Not only is the agent responsible for delivering the distribution agreements that will trigger the bank's agreement to loan the producer the production funds, the sales agent is committing to sell enough remaining territories to cover the gap. The basic points of a sales agency agreement are as follows:

   (i) The term.

   (ii) The territory.

   (iii) The rights granted.

   (iv) The ask/take prices.

   (v) Producer's approval rights.

   (vi) The sales commission.

   (vii) The sales agent's expenses, and any "Cap" on such expenses.

  (viii) The allocation of Gross Receipts.

   (xi) The delivery schedule.

(d) *The Foreign Distribution Agreement.* Foreign distribution agreements are usually much more basic than a negative pickup agreement, for the simple fact that a negative pickup usually covers 30% or more of the budget, and a distribution agreement a fraction of that percentage. The terms that are covered are as follows:

   (i) The term.

   (ii) The territory.

   (iii) The minimum guarantee.

   (iv) Authorized Languages.

   (v) The rights granted and the rights reserved. While in negative pickups, the rights granted are usually all rights available, rights granted to foreign distributors are often limited or split among companies. The rights usually for sale are the following:

     (A) Theatrical

     (B) Non-Theatrical

     (C) Home Video

     (D) Pay TV

(E) Free TV
(F) Pay per View

The rights usually reserved are the following:

(A) Merchandising
(B) Soundtrack Album
(C) Music Publishing
(D) Interactive Rights
(E) Print Publication Rights
(F) Ship and Airline Rights

(vi) Overspill.
(vii) Producer's Approvals.

(A) Video and Television Windows
(B) Marketing and Advertising Budgets
(C) Marketing Materials

(viii) The distribution fees taken by the distributor, and/or the royalties paid.

(A) Theatrical and Non-Theatrical
(B) Television
(C) Home Video

(ix) The delivery schedule.

(e) *The Loan Agreement.* The loan agreement for the transaction being discussed has the following deal specific terms included:

(i) The Amount.
(ii) The Maturity Date.
(iii) The Gap.
(iv) The Interest Reserve.
(v) Specifics of the Film Production.
(vi) Bank Approval Rights.
(vii) Bank Takeover Rights.
(viii) The Bank's security interest in the picture.

(f) *The Completion Agreement.* A completion guarantor is a company that will provide a guaranty to the bank that the film will be finished on time and delivered to certain distributors that are covered by the guaranty. To the extent that a film goes over budget, it is the completion guarantor's responsibility to front these additional costs. The completion agreement is the agreement between the producer and the completion bond company that sets forth the terms and conditions upon which the completion guarantor will provide the completion guaranty to the bank, and the basic terms are as follows:

(i) The Completion Guarantor's fee.
(ii) The Completion Guarantor's expenditure of sums in connection with the picture, and the method of recoupment of such sums.
(iii) The Completion Guarantor's approval rights and control of the production.
(iv) The Completion Guarantors' takeover rights.
(v) The Completion Guarantor's security interest in the picture.

(g) *The Interparty Agreements.* As you can see from the scenario above, there are various parties who often have conflicting rights in a motion picture which is bankfinanced. The bank also has an interest in entering into a direct agreement with the negative pickup distributor to ensure that the advance will be timely paid. Accordingly, there are often 1 or 2 interparty agreements amongst the parties, which set forth the following:

   (i) The limited circumstances upon which a negative pickup distributor can reject delivery of a picture.
   (ii) A uniform delivery system, and method for disputing delivery.
   (iii) A prioritization of the parties' security interests in the film, at varying stages of production.

3. Private Equity – a Private Offering.

(a) Private Offerings are typically used for films with smaller budgets (under 5 million dollars). A producer forms a limited liability company, prepares an offering memorandum, and sells units of the LLC to investors, using the investments in the company to fund the production of the picture. The producer in this instance must comply with federal and state securities laws, and therefore these types of financings also involve applying for an appropriate exemption under Regulation D of the Federal Securities Code, and complying with each individual state's blue sky laws (federal securities laws). While an in depth discussion of the securities aspects of these transactions will not be covered here, set forth below are the basic points of the Offering Memorandum which should be supplied to the investors of the film.

(b) Number and Cost of Units.

(c) Allocation of Net Profits. A typical allocation of the gross receipts of a film financed by private equity film is as follows:

   (i) First, to the payment of the actual, out of pocket, costs of production; actual, out of pocket business expenses related directly to the picture; and/or distribution expenses in excess of the approved budget, including, without limitation, sales expenses, sales fees, and residuals to the extent not assumed by any third party distributor of the picture;

   (ii) Second, 100% to the financiers of the picture on a pro-rata, pari passu basis, until distributions to the financiers equal, on a cumulative basis, 100% of the aggregate cash investments in the picture made by such financiers;

   (iii) Third, 100% to the financiers of the picture on a pro-rata, pari passu basis until distributions to the financiers equal, on a cumulative basis (i.e., including the amounts set forth in paragraph (b) above), 120% of the aggregate cash investments in the picture made by such financiers;

   (iv) Fourth, to the payment of any contingent amounts paid, earned or payable to any person or entity engaged to render or furnish services in connection with the picture based upon, or computed in respect of, Gross Receipts (whether payable before or after a breakeven point or other agreed level of receipts) prior to the point, if ever, that "Net Proceeds" are payable in accordance herewith; and

(v) Fifth, after payment of all amounts set forth in paragraph (a) through (e) above, the remaining Gross Receipts should be deemed Net Proceeds, and should be allocated and paid on a pro-rata, pari passu, 50% to the financiers and 50% to the production company. The production company will be responsible for the payment of all third party Net Proceeds participations, to the extent it has contractually agreed to do so.

(d) Information about the Film and the Film Business. An offering memorandum should set forth information about the producers and a synopsis of the film. It is also a good idea to put in some information about the film business in general, to educate your investors on the ways a film can (or cannot) generate income.

(e) Risk Factors. It is very important that the offering memorandum set forth a host of risk factors for investors to review, in order to defend against any 10(b)(5) claims regarding securities fraud, in particular, given the risky nature of film investments.

9.4.2 Insurance

Studios generally have blanket insurance policies that cover all of their films and activities. Independent filmmakers must obtain this insurance on their own for each individual project. Financiers and investors typically will not provide funds without the necessary coverage. Insurance is a very costly aspect of film production and requires a balancing of needs and risks. To control its risk, the insurance company must determine exactly what the risks are. To control the cost, the producer needs to determine how much of a risk it is willing to assume in the form of deductibles, policy limits, and the length of the term of coverage.

Special circumstances involved in the production of a particular movie can necessitate extra forms of insurance, filming overseas for instance, especially in danger zones, such as the Middle East. Sometimes actors have to do their own stunts and that requires special insurance. It may be more cost effective to hire extra stunt people or film the shot differently to avoid this extra cost. Insurance also forces actors to stop doing certain activities during the shooting of a film. This is not because of risks to their physical well-being, but because if the star of the film is hurt or killed, the movie is effectively over or it will cost too much to re-shoot the scenes. For example, during the filming of the last three *Star Trek* movies, Michael Dorn (Worf) was unable to take part in his favorite hobby, flying planes. Typically, there will be so-called cast insurance covering the death or incapacity of principal actors. Additionally, if an actor or director is a key or essential element in a license or pre-sale, then "essential elements" insurance is required.

Several types of insurance are available to film producers: some are required; some are only needed based on the actual movie that is being filmed. Most of the insurance policies deal with things like theft, damage, injury to cast members, workers compensation, or weather insurance.

Others are applicable only in certain situations. Foreign insurance is only needed if any of the filming takes place in a foreign country. Aircraft and water insurance are applicable only if the film involves activities that require the use of such equipment in the shooting.

Errors and omissions insurance is a specialized form of insurance which typically protects film producers (as well as the distributors and exhibitors with whom they deal) from claims such as violation of rights of publicity and privacy, quasi-contractual claims from submitters of ideas, copyright infringements, and violations of Section 43a of the Lanham Act. It does not provide reimbursement for lost profits or for production costs (other than prints and advertising) and it does not cover crimes or intentional torts. E&O insurance carriers require the submission of an extremely detailed application (which sometimes requires the producer's attorney's signature as well as that of the producer, but *always* requires the participation of the attorney) in which the producer must catalogue such matters as whether the film will portray persons living or dead, and, depending on whether such persons are alive or deceased, whether clearances have been obtained from such persons of their legal representatives; whether the title of the production has been cleared; whether the production is based on existing material; and so on.

9.5 THE INTERNATIONAL MARKET

The American film industry dominates the international market. For example, *Titanic* alone accounted for 13 percent of the tickets sold in Europe in 1998. More than half of the total revenue derived by the U.S. studios comes from foreign sources, often bringing domestically unprofitable films into the black. Some movies make far more money in the international market than they do in the domestic film market. In 1998, *Armageddon* made approximately $201.6 million domestically and $306.4 million internationally. The split for *Saving Private Ryan* was $191 million domestically and $242.3 million internationally; *Mission: Impossible* did $180.9 million domestically, $284 million internationally; and *A Perfect World,* starring Clint Eastwood and Kevin Costner at the height of their careers, did only about $37 million domestically, but did almost four times that much in foreign sales. All-time box office champion *Titanic* took in $600.8 million domestically, and $1.2 billion overseas.

Foreign countries, especially in Europe, have been a source of financing for American movies for many years. Though it has long been a regular method for independent films via the pre-sale process, the major studios have also tapped foreign sources as a way to spread risk. Canal Plus, Ciby 2000, Banque Paribas, and FILMS are major European investors in American films. For example, the most aggressive European investor, Canal Plus, has invested in *A Bronx Tale, The Power of One, JFK, Under Siege, Terminator 2: Judgment Day, Basic Instinct, Boiling Point, Stargate, Free Willy 2, Boys on the Side, Sommersby,* and *Murder in the First.* Some other films with European investors are *The Madness of King George, Cliffhanger, Fortress,* and *Man Without a Face.*

However, an increasing number of films by European producers are produced with the assistance of a system of quotas and subsidies. Although the United States does not do so, most European countries give subsidies and quotas to encourage investment in locally produced films. Because of the ethnic and linguistic diversity of the population of Europe, it is very difficult for local producers to create a product with general appeal. Therefore, in order to help European-produced films to compete with American blockbusters, the European Union (EU) and its member states have established local-content quotas for prime-time television and a range of subsidies available to EU-based producers who utilize the requisite proportion of local talent and technical support. While American producers can participate in these productions, they generally must cede control to the local co-venturer.

Each country's subsidy system is different. Some are extensive, while others are very limited. Great Britain and France offer examples of the two extremes. In Britain, subsidies have declined greatly since the 1980s. However, £3 to £5 million are still available every year from British Screen Finance. Approximately 25 percent of British-produced films receive funding from British Screen each year. Furthermore, British Screen provides support for international co-productions. British Screen is owned by Rank, United Artists' Screen Entertainment, Channel Four, and Granada, but also receives approximately £2 million in annual funding from the government. British Screen requires projects to be of high quality (not only from a United Kingdom perspective) and to demonstrate profit potential, and insists on a preferential position for its loans plus 60 percent of the net profits.

Subsidies in France are administered by the French Center for Cinematography through direct payments and tax concessions. They are based on a point system. Points are awarded to a project based on French or European subject matter, director, writer, location of shooting and location of post-production, and other criteria. The subsidy is earned by the track record of an approved production, and is applicable to the producer's next production. In that way, subsidies are linked to success. France funds its subsidy program through a tax on box office receipts of motion picture theaters. It is ironic that most of the box office receipts are from showings of American films.

Another source of financing is from supranational bodies that provide support to international co-productions. These bodies encourage co-productions in order to spread the risk of filmmaking and encourage films to cross international boundaries commercially. The two major bodies are Eurimages and the European Convention on Cinematographic Co-production.

Eurimages gives support to co-production where at least three co-producers are from EU member states. The support is in the form of "advances on receipts" of an amount of up to 20 percent of the budget, with a maximum of 5 million francs per film. Eurimages still provides funding to films even if producers from nonmember states are involved in the film, so long as the participation is under 30 percent. Furthermore, pre-sales to distributors in the United States is not considered participation. Eurimages has invested in over 200 films, the most significant film being *The House of the Spirits*. This film was in English and starred three American actresses: Meryl Streep, Glenn Close, and Wynona Ryder. The budget for this film came mostly from pre-sales, the largest amount being paid by Miramax.

The European Convention on Cinematographic Co-production is intended to simplify co-productions, making access to European national funds and subsidies available to a broader range of co-production structures. The Convention has only been ratified by ten European countries, so it has not proven its effectiveness to the same extent as Eurimages. The Convention applies to co-productions where all producers are nationals of signatory states or where at least three producers are from three states providing at least 70 percent of the financing. As is the case with the Eurimages model, producers from nonsignatory states can participate in the project. There are three major benefits deriving from the Convention. First, multilateral co-productions are able to gain access to national funds. Second, the minimum contribution is 20 percent and there are no specific terms relating to studios, labor, location, filming, and so forth. Third, there is no local language requirement.

International co-financing is a way to spread the risk that is inherent in the film industry. It also allows American producers access to the European system of subsidies. A final important advantage is that it allows some more creative, artistic films to be made that the major studios pass on.

Chapter 10

TELEVISION

10.1 THE TELEVISION BUSINESS

Nothing is as ubiquitous in our lives as television. And, except for the Internet, nothing has changed as rapidly in recent years. Indeed, as we see the emergence of "digital video recorders" (such as TiVo and cable-supplied DVRs) and "Internet appliances" which permit viewers to bypass the home video process, on the one hand, and to perform some computer functions on their TV sets, on the other, it appears that television (albeit highly transformed) will become even more ubiquitous as years pass. For example, Forrester Research has estimated that 14 million homes will have DVRs by 2004, and that by 2009, they will be in 80% of American homes. Further, the impact of Netflix (monthly flat rate unlimited DVD movie rentals through the mail) and DVDs on television viewing patterns continues to change when, how and why we watch and/or use the television screen.

10.1.1 The Changing Face of the Television Industry

No other entertainment industry has seen the same degree of technological innovation over such a short time span as the television industry. In the last few years, more than 26 million consumers have subscribed to the DirectTV (with 15 million subscribers) and Dish Network (with over 11 million) satellite delivery systems. High definition television (HDTV) has arrived, with pictures vastly sharper than anything currently available (although at this writing sets are still on the expensive side and, in the U.S. and many other countries, only limited broadcast service is available in high definition). Television programming can now be delivered via the Internet, with Walt Disney Co.'s ABC-TV planning to deliver later in 2006 selected ABC shows like "Desperate Housewives," "Lost," and "Alias" to 22 million U.S. homes that regularly stream video over the Internet (and as downloads through iTunes for $1.99). See "The Web: Webcasting a 'Viable' Secondary Market," Gene Koprowski, *UPI,* April 26, 2006. Set-top "Internet appliances" permit users to perform some computer operations through their TV sets. The landscape shifts incessantly.

Broadcast television is now dominated by four major networks, the American Broadcasting Corporation (ABC), the National Broadcasting Company (NBC), and the Columbia Broadcasting System (CBS), and Fox (which came along in the mid-1980s, and which has recently ranked first in audience share and revenue). Although their ratings have lagged far behind the big four, the WB Network and United Paramount Network (UPN) will merge and be replaced by the new CW Network in September 2006. CW will be owned equally by Warner Brothers and CBS Corp. and will draw on selective programming from both the old WB and UPN networks. See Jessica Seid, 'Gilmore Girls' meet 'Smackdown," CNNMoney.com, January 24, 2006. Other television broadcast companies listed after the main four networks are Tribune Broadcasting, Gannett, Hearst-Argyle TV, Belo, Univision, and Cox Enterprises. Pax TV and PBS are still relatively minor factors.

Each network is a division of, and owned by, a larger conglomerate. NBC is owned by General Electric; ABC is owned by the Walt Disney Company; CBS and UPN are owned by Viacom; Fox is owned by News Corp; the WB is owned by Time-Warner Inc. In January 2006 it was announced that Viacom will split into two media companies: CBS, Inc. [including CBS Network (gets Katie Couric), CBS Radio (lost Howard Stern), Showtime, Simon & Schuster and KingWorld Syndication]; and the new Viacom [Paramount Pictures, Comedy Central, MTV, VH1, BET, Nickelodeon]. Sumner Redstone will continue to be CEO of both companies with overwhelming shareholder control. Some industry analysts suggest that this may signal a reversal of the prior trend of consolidation and more toward entertainment industry "deconsolidation." See *Newsweek* April 24, 2006 and Will Swarts, "Viacom's Split Personality," *SmartMoney.com Will Swartz,* March 21, 2006.

The broadcast network share of audience has declined by more than a third since the early 1970s, most of the lost viewers having drifted to cable network programming and computers. Cable viewership first exceeded that of the networks in 1997. While cable ad revenues grew rapidly during the 1990s, broadcast network revenues grew by much smaller percentages. Nevertheless, given the audience shrinkage which has befallen the broadcast networks, their rates (measured in "CPM" or cost per thousand viewers) remain high. In 2006, the "upfront market" (in which 80% of prime time ads are sold) is estimated to be approximately $8.8 billion, down 1%-2% over 2005, translating to a loss of $100-$200 million. See "Media Execs on 2006 Upfront: Broadcast Ad Spending To Drop," MediaBuyerPlanner.com, April 26, 2006. Nevertheless, the television broadcast networks are under constant pressure to cut costs and increase profits. In recent years, all four networks have undergone cutbacks in various departments. Furthermore, the networks have ordered fewer pilots from producers than in previous years and have increased the number of "newsmagazines," game shows, and "reality" shows, which are far less expensive to produce that traditional entertainment programming.

In 1995, in response to the erosion of the broadcast networks' domination, the Federal Communications Commission (FCC) eliminated 1970s-era rules which had prohibited network ownership interest in entertainment programming and barred networks from participating in "syndication," i.e., the practice of licensing off-network programming as well as programming specifically created for syndication (so-called first-run syndication) to individual stations. As the off-network syndication deals for such shows as *Cosby, Seinfeld,* and *Home Improvement* and the first-run syndication success of *Rosie* have demonstrated, huge profits are possible in syndication. (For example, the first two cycles of broadcast syndication and cable for *Seinfeld* yielded a reputed $2 billion. *Scott Hetrick, "A Super 'Seinfeld' Deal," The Hollywood Reporter,* Sept. 15–21, 1998, p. 4.) This has created tension between the networks and the studios. In 1998, NBC announced that it would not make deals with any studio unless it was given an ownership interest in the show, a position NBC later dropped. ABC also attempted to extract ownership interests from producers in the late stage of series negotiations, provoking equivalent consternation among the studios.

Recognizing the inevitable, the networks belatedly embraced the cable business. Each broadcast network has an affiliation with one or more cable networks. NBC has CNBC and MSNBC (joint venture with Microsoft). CBS owns Country Music Television (CMT), The Nashville Network (TNN), and MTV. The other networks are linked to various cable networks through their parent companies. For example, FX, Fox News, and the Golf Channel are owned by News Corp., and Time-Warner owns all of the Turner Broadcasting channels such as TNT, TBS, Cartoon Network, and CNN. ABC has linked its sports programming to that of ESPN, since both are owned by Disney, along with ownership interests in The History Channel, A&E and Lifetime.

Each of the major film studios also produces television shows. As is the case with the film, the major studios are Twentieth Century Fox, Universal, Warner Brothers, Paramount, Columbia-Tristar (Sony), and Disney. Emerging "major" Dreamworks SKG is in the television industry as well. Furthermore, there are a significant number of independent producers that have development deals with the larger studios, including Carsey-Werner (Sony), Steven Bochco Productions (Twentieth Century Fox), David E. Kelley Productions (Twentieth Century Fox), and Bright/Kaufman/Crane Productions (Warner Brothers).

10.1.2 Broadcast Television

Even with the erosion of audiences, broadcast network television is still the major player in the television industry. The three original networks plus Fox are organized along similar lines, though minor organizational differences exist. Each network has offices in Los Angeles, where most of their entertainment programming is produced, and in New York City, where the advertisers, news department, sports department, and corporate offices are located. All the networks arc divided into several divisions: entertainment, news, sports (each of these are operated as separate companies) advertising sales, affiliate relations, operations, technical services, administration, personnel, and labor relations. Then each network has its owned and operated affiliates, which are also operated as separate companies.

Although legislative and regulatory changes in recent years have raised the limits on the number of individual stations that a network can own, it is still necessary for the networks to maintain relationships with local stations owned by other companies or individuals in order to reach all 211 markets throughout the country. Under a typical network affiliation agreement with a local station, the network provides a schedule of programs with national or regional commercials and financial compensation for the airtime utilized. The affiliate is allotted a portion of the commercial spots time to sell to local advertisers. In theory, the affiliate does not have to accept all the programming the network provides, though local rejections are rare. If a local affiliate does reject a particular program, the network can license the show to another station in the market.

The amount of money the network has to pay the affiliate, or the "network compensation," depends on a variety of factors. These factors are the number of commercial minutes in the hour, the ratio of commercial time sold nationally versus locally, the relative strength of the station versus other stations in the market, the amount of time that the program occupies, the size and demographic profile of the audience, and the size of the market.

The size of the market is the most important element. The larger the market, the larger the potential audience, and the more advertising dollars the networks can derive from selling "spots" to advertisers. Markets are ranked by the total number of households with television sets that can receive broadcasts from the particular city's principal broadcasters. The top ten markets are New York City, Los Angeles, Chicago, Philadelphia, San Francisco, Boston, Washington D.C., Dallas-Fort Worth, Detroit, and Atlanta. The networks try to own as many affiliates in the top ten markets as possible, which guarantee them clearances for their programs in the major markets. ABC, NBC, and ABC all own their affiliates in New York City, Los Angeles, Chicago, and several other cities in the top ten markets. No network owns all of its affiliates in all of the top ten markets.

Most of the other affiliates not owned by the networks are owned by various station groups. Station groups own several affiliates in different markets and are usually larger conglomerates. Major station groups include the Tribune Corporation, Hearst Corporation, Gannett, and Viacom, each owning several different media outlets in addition to the local stations. Station group ownership is the dominant trend and will have repercussions on the way the FCC operates. The FCC had structured many of its regulations to protect local stations from being overpowered and swallowed up by the networks. However, in light of legislation in recent years which has relaxed limitations on station ownership (leading to the rapid growth of station groups), the old focus on individual local stations seems anachronistic.

10.1.3 Cable and Satellite Television

Cable TV, or community antennae television (CATV), was created in order to boost reception in areas where broadcast television signals were blocked or otherwise weakened, resulting in unavailability or causing poor reception. So, CATV systems were built to boost the signal and subscribers were charged for the service. Since these systems did not have the technical limitations of broadcast television, they could provide multiple channels, including distant network signals as well as independent, non-network-affiliated channels from nearby cities. From a slow start, cable has grown into a multi-billion dollar industry. Cable ad revenues for 2005 were up by 5.6% for Comcast to $1.36 billion and 3.7% for Time Warner to $534 million, together representing about 40% of the U.S. local cable advertising. *Multichannel Newswire, Feb. 7, 2006.*

By 2004, approximately 80 million television households, i.e., 80 percent of American television households, were cable subscribers. However, as satellite delivery systems gain more and more users, the cable business feels the competition. Until recently, municipal governments were solely responsible for controlling and regulating the cable business. Local government's ace in the hole has been the simple fact that cable needs to be hardwired from the source to each household, which, in turn requires use of rights of way, which is usually controlled by local governments. Typically, the local municipality has awarded an exclusive franchise for all or part of its territory to a single cable company based upon a proposal describing the technical capabilities of the system, the channels that would be offered, the channel capacity, the rate schedule, the construction schedule, and the background of the company. In many cases, this local monopoly has led to poor service and attendant consumer dissatisfaction. As a result, the federal government and local authorities are seeking to end cable monopolies. (For example, one of the major issues in the AOL/Time Warner merger was the degree to which the Time Warner fiber optic cable networks would be made available to competing services, and a major problem in the AT&T acquisition of Media One was the FCC regulation, adopted pursuant to the Cable Act of 1992, limiting the reach of any single cable company to 30% of the market.)

Most cable companies are multiple system operators (MSOs). MSOs control dozens or even hundreds of systems in various areas around the country. Most MSOs are owned by larger companies or conglomerates.

The biggest MSOs are Comcast Cable Communications with 21.4 million subscribers, Time Warner Cable with 11 million subscribers, Cox Communications with 6.3 million, Charter Communications with 5.9 million subscribers, Adelphia Communications with 5.1 million subscribers, Cablevision Systems with 3 million subscribers, and Bright House Networks with about 2.2 million subscribers. Some other MSOs are, Mediacom, Insight, and CableOne. See *National Cable & Telecommunications Association at ncta.com.*

The FCC has imposed certain restrictions on the business practices of cable companies. First, cable companies are required to carry all of the broadcast networks, which are shown in their local markets. Second, they are also required to carry public television stations. Third, they must carry a certain number of public access channels. This is all for the purpose of encouraging local broadcasting, which has been the goal of the FCC since its earliest regulation of television. However, cable companies do not possess infinite carrying capacity. There are over 150 cable networks in the United States, but most cable providers only have space for a maximum of 50, and since FCC rules mandate carriage of a certain number of channels, a cable operator may have only limited capacity for carriage of cable networks.

Cable is basically a retail industry. For its "basic" service, a cable operator buys "wholesale" by paying each cable network it carries a monthly fee of 5 to 40 cents per subscriber (depending upon the popularity of the individual cable network). The cable company groups the broadcast channels it retransmits together with a number of (typically) advertiser-supported cable networks into a "basic cable" package. While prices vary depending upon the makeup of the package and the locality, the average price for basic cable is between $25 and $35. This price usually represents a 100 percent markup over the price charged to the MSO. The cable company also derives increasing revenue through advertising sales. The cable company gets a limited number of commercial spots from the various cable programming services which provide advertiser-supported programming to the cable operator, and then sells them to local merchants.

"Pay" cable, on the other hand, usually provides higher-cost programming and is not advertiser-supported. HBO, Cinemax, Starz, and Showtime are typical examples. Cable providers get these channels for approximately $5 to $6 per month per subscriber and mark the fee up 100 percent to the consumer. Due to the significant markup, the typical cable system offers its subscribers a variety of packages at different cost levels. Cable's popularity has risen to such a level that some cable networks are more popular than the traditional broadcast networks, among certain audiences, and others (such as CNN, ESPN, USA, TNT, and TBS) have become just like household appliances. On the other hand, whereas traditional broadcast networks are necessarily dependent upon mass demographics (especially the 18–34 group so sought after by advertisers) the availability of multiple channels on cable (and even more so via satellite) permits niche marketing to more specialized audiences. It would be hard to imagine such services as Lifetime, the Discovery Channel, The Learning Channel (TLC), the Golf Channel, or the History Channel on conventional broadcast television.

Court TV has had an impact of its own, broadcasting entire trials (a la the O.J. Simpson trial) and opening up the court system to viewers. In *Courtroom Television Network LLC v. The State of New York*, 5 N.Y.3d 222, 833 N.E.2d 1197, 800 N.Y.S.2d 522, 2005 N.Y. LEXIS 1260 (2005), Court TV challenged the New York statute barring cameras in courtrooms, arguing that it violated the right of access to courtroom proceedings under the New York State Constitution and the Federal Constitution. (New York is the only state with an almost absolute ban on television cameras in the courtroom). The Court of Appeals rejected Court TV's argument: "Though the public acquires information about trials chiefly through the press and electronic media, the press is not imbued with any special right of access. Rather, the media possesses "the same right of access as the public . . . so that they may report what people in attendance have seen and heard". . . . Thus, the press has "no right to information about a trial superior to that of the general public" . . . , nor any right to information greater than the. . . . Civil Rights Law § 52 does not prevent the press, including television journalists, from attending trials and reporting on the proceedings. What they cannot do under the statute is bring cameras into the courtroom. This is not a restriction on the openness of court proceedings but rather on what means can be used in order to gather news. The media's access is thus guaranteed. But it does not extend to a right to televise those proceedings. . . . The New York State Constitution, similarly, does not provide a right to televise trials. Article I, section 8 states, "Every citizen may freely speak, write and publish his or her sentiments on all subjects, being responsible for the abuse of that right; and no law shall be passed to restrain or abridge the liberty of speech or of the press." Court TV argues that *Civil Rights Law § 52* is an unlawful "restraint on the press. . . ." In *Johnson Newspaper Corp. v Melino*, this Court held that there is no broader protection for the press under the State Constitution article I, section 8, than under the United States Constitution with respect to right of access to judicial proceedings. . . . Johnson also refused to find that there was a greater protection for the press than for the public to have access to the court. . . . We will not circumscribe the authority constitutionally delegated to the Legislature to determine whether audio-visual coverage of courtroom proceedings is in the best interest of the citizens of this state. "A state constitutional rule expanding the rights of the media in New York to include the right to photograph and broadcast court proceedings would derail what is, and always has been a legislative process. . . ."(77 N.Y.2d 1, 8, 564 N.E.2d 1046, 563 N.Y.S.2d 380 [1990]).

Just as they are heavily involved in the creation of programming for traditional broadcasting, the major studios are heavily involved with pay cable networks. In addition to owning Twentieth Century Fox and

Fox Broadcasting Network, News Corp. owns FX (cable network), Fox News (cable network), Fox Family Channel (cable network), and Fox Sports (cable network). In addition to owning Warner Bros., Inc. and Warner Bros. Television, AOL Time Warner owns TNT, TBS, HBO, CNN, Cartoon Network, Cinemax, and parts of several other networks like 2006 start-up, CW Network.

Apart from the facts that satellite delivery (DirectTV and Dish Network) does not require costly cable installation and that the price of acquiring and installing the "dish" has dropped dramatically since the concept was introduced, the fact that satellite systems offer a vastly greater number of channels than cable systems (in some areas, it is possible to receive seven different cycles of HBO) provides additional outlets for niche marketing.

10.2 CREATING AND ACQUIRING PROGRAMMING

Even with all of the changes in the television industry, the goal of any network is to develop its own identity through original programming. Cable programmers are no different from traditional networks in this respect. NBC stresses its "Must See TV" promotion. CBS uses "Come Home to CBS." But cable programmers have the same need as the broadcast networks to establish and maintain their individual identities. Shows like *The Sopranos, Real Time With Bill Maher* and *The Larry Sanders Show* helped create a specific image for HBO, while *South Park, The Daily Show with Jon Stewart,* and *The Colbert Report* have done the same for Comedy Central. In an evolving world in which the sheer number of available channels makes viewer loyalty problematic, product line recognition is of increasing importance throughout the industry. More than 40 cable networks now create at least some of the product they distribute. *Ray Richmond, "Original View," The Hollywood Reporter,* May 5, 2000, p. S-1.

10.2.1 Dealmaking in the Television Industry

Over the past thirty years or so, a customary pattern of deal making evolved in television industry, largely due to the FCC financial interest and syndication rule and various consent decrees entered into with the Justice Department. Though the rules have been dropped and the consent decrees are no longer operative, the pattern (albeit in transition and subject to variation with each deal) still provides a basic blueprint for series deals in the television industry.

Just as with the film industry, everything starts with an idea and the acquisition of rights in that idea. An idea may be pitched by a producer to a studio or a network or the network or studio may ask an established producer or writer to come up with a series (often with only some vague description). This is how the 1998–1999 breakout hit *Providence* was created. NBC went to John Masius (producer of *St. Elsewhere* and creator of *Touched by an Angel*) and asked him to write a "feel good series for thirty-year olds." The unplanned evolution of the hugely successful *Seinfeld* television sit-com by Jerry Seinfeld and Larry David is well documented in the show itself as a "show about nothing."

However, no matter where the idea originates, the first step is almost always writing the overall "treatment" for the series and a treatment for the first episode, called the "pilot." The treatment for a television series is a description of the characters, the central theme of the series, and a brief description of future episodes. The treatment for the pilot is a description of the action that will take place in the first episode of the series. The network or studio, or both, reviews the treatment and if they approve they order a script of the pilot episode and possibly for the second or third episode as well.

When the network or studio approves the script, the next step is the creation of the pilot. This gives the network an idea of what the series will look and feel like, and the appeal it will have to the audience. Many pilots never make it to the air. However, if the network picks up the pilot, the network will then decide whether to order episodes of the series to place on the air.

If the network approves the pilot, it will then usually order between 7 and 13 episodes of the series (for *Seinfeld* NBC ordered only 4 shows, indicating how much they believed in its potential). Based upon the performance of the first episodes ordered, the network may then decide to order additional episodes, up to an aggregate of 22 (the usual number for a television season). Traditionally, if a series started in the Fall, the network would fill out the balance of the twenty-two episode first season order, and then have three annual renewal options of 22 episodes each. If the series was picked up for a mid-season launch, the split-order pattern would apply to the second year as well, and then there would be three 22-order options. After the fourth full year (assuming the network exercised all its options) the producer would have the right to take the show elsewhere, subject to the network's right of first negotiation/right of first refusal (which, in almost all cases, effectively prevents the producer from moving the show to another network.)

The network's rights are limited to the U.S., and the network receives the right to air each show (with some exceptions) twice: one original showing and one rerun. After the end of the network's exclusive term, the producer would have the right to license existing episodes to third parties.

This is still the normal path that a television deal follows.

The writer is extremely important in this process. The current trend among networks is to refuse to make commitments on the basis of just ideas and pitches; they tend to require a completed treatment. The Writer's Guild Basic Agreement prescribes minimum payments for treatments, scripts, and pilots, but higher compensation is negotiable by an experienced and successful writer. The writer will receive partial payments at various stages of the development process, with a lump sum payment on delivery. If the network rejects the pilot script, the writer will have a "turnaround" provision in the contract which will permit the writer to take the series to another network or studio for syndication, usually upon repayment of certain development expenses. If the writer is also the creator of the series, the writer will receive ongoing royalties if the series is produced. John Masius still collects royalties from the series he created *Touched by an Angel,* even though he never worked on any episode past the pilot.

10.2.2 The Development Deal

The goal of any television writer or producer is to get a development deal from one of the major studios or networks or a combination of both. While the movie industry is trying to cut back on these types of deals, television deals are expanding. Every network is afraid to let the next *Seinfeld* get away from them, so they lock up successful writers and producers in long term deals. Steven Bochco obtained a guaranteed minimum $50,000,000 deal to produce ten series for Twentieth Century Fox and ABC. Bochco is the creator of *Hill Street Blues, L.A. Law,* and *NYPD Blue.* David E. Kelley, creator of *Picket Fences, The Practice,* and *Ally McBeal* has a similar deal from Twentieth Century Fox and ABC as well. Bright/Kaufman/Crane Productions (*Friends*) has an agreement with Warner Brothers and Carsey-Werner (*Cosby, A Different World, Roseanne, Third Rock from the Sun*) has an agreement with Sony.

In a typical development deal, the studio pays the writer, producer, or production company a minimum annual payment and provides offices, studio facilities, a development fund, and other essential services. The studio gets first look at anything created under the agreement, typically under the normal pattern described in Section 10.2.1. If the studio gives the green light, it automatically gets the distribution rights and the syndication rights to the new series. The funds spent on development are deducted from the earnings of the creations of the writer or producer generated under the arrangement. When the series is put on a network, the major talent earns fees as an executive producer, even though they may only have superficial duties with the show. Royalties are also collected by the talent from the series for all future broadcasts.

10.2.3 Deficit Funding

Until the early 1980s, television shows were licensed to the networks for an amount that (theoretically) equaled the cost of production. Producers earned their profits from syndication of their series following the end of their network run (see Section 10.3) and the networks earned the revenues from advertising sales. Since the early 1980s production costs have significantly increased, but the networks' licensing fees have not increased in the same proportion (largely due to the audience shrinkage referred to above, which has held down gains in advertising revenue). So, as a result, most television shows operate at a deficit.

This deficit is the difference between actual cost of production and the license fee the network must pay. The producer or studio must absorb this deficit.

The average network license fee generally covers no more than 80 percent of the cost of production. Production costs for a one hour television series average between $1,000,000 and $2,000,000 and $500,000 to $1,500,000 for a half hour television series. On average, television series are licensed for approximately $500,000 per episode for a sitcom and $1 million to $1.2 million for an hourlong dramatic show. Where a show includes costly special effects and/or pricey lead actors (which is especially true as series continue), the network agreement may provide for "breakage," *i.e.*, additional payments not characterized as license fees. However, television series almost always run substantial deficits. (One famous example: *Miami Vice*, which ran a deficit of more than $500,000 a week, a sizeable sum for the period during which the series ran). According to Tom Werner of Carsey/Werner, a 22-episode series season can result in a $15 million deficit. Bernard Weinraub, "On TV, A Loss of Independents," *New York Times*, May 7, 2000, Sec. 2, p. 1. This is why almost all producers work in conjunction with studios. This deficit is a serious problem for major companies and an unmanageable burden for a small company. This is why television production is dominated by the major studios (and, increasingly, by the networks themselves).

Hopefully, the deficit is made back in the syndication market (see Section 10.3). The shows that do make it into syndication have to make a large enough profit so as to make up for the deficit on shows that do not make it into syndication. However, success in syndication is not guaranteed, so for some shows, the deficit is mitigated by co-production agreements with networks or smaller production companies. The studio wants to decrease its costs and the networks and smaller production companies want access to the syndication profits.

In some cases the deficit works the other way, in other words, in favor of the studios instead of the networks. In the case of *ER*, NBC has to pay Warner Brothers $13,000,000 per episode. Thus, *ER* is one of the very few shows that makes a substantial profit in its first run. These are rare cases and are not the norm, but the money involved makes it important to mention.

10.3 SYNDICATION

The broadcast networks do not provide programming for the entire day. So, the affiliates must look elsewhere for programming to fill in the time not programmed by the networks. Also, cable networks have to provide programming for the entire day. In today's society, an entire day usually means 24 hours. The most popular current syndicated programming genres are talk shows, game shows, entertainment and newsmagazines, off-network sitcoms and dramas and some original television shows produced specifically for syndication.

Syndication is simply selling a program individually to the affiliates in local markets or to a cable network. For a series to be attractive in syndication (where programming is customarily "stripped," *e.g.*, shown five nights per week) it is usually necessary to have four years' worth of shows (approximately 88 episodes, which enhances the risks of deficit financing, since most shows do not survive that long on the networks). Syndication is usually done through a straight cash deal, under a barter system, or a combination of the two. Under the straight cash system, the syndicator licenses the shows to each market for as much money as possible. However, this method has gradually fallen out of use. Under a barter system, the local licensee pays no cash; instead, the syndicator gets the right to a specified number of minutes of commercial time, which the syndicator then turns around and sells to advertisers.

The cash-plus-barter system has become the most common method of syndication. This method utilizes a cash payment to the syndicator, but not as much as what would occur under the straight cash method. In exchange for the lower cash payment, the syndicator also gets the right to sell some commercial spots in the program. This has the advantage of limiting a station's cash payment and at the same time providing a potentially greater upside to the syndicator. The amount the station has to pay depends on the popularity of the show and the size of the market. The more popular the show and the larger the market, the more that has to be paid out.

Studios (and now, in some instances, networks as well) look to make up their production deficits in the syndication market. In fact, off-network series (network television programs sold into syndication) get some of the biggest ratings. On average, eight of the top twenty syndicated shows are off-network programs. Some of the most popular syndicated shows at this writing include *Friends, Seinfeld, The X-Files,* and even the weekend edition of *Seinfeld.* Each of these shows gets between 4 and 6 million viewers each night. The deficits these shows have incurred are more than made up in syndication, and the top shows make enormous profits. After all, the cost of producing the show has already been spent, so syndication has only negligible costs. *Friends,* distributed by Warner Brothers, earned $250,000 per episode in New York City and Los Angeles, and gets $200,000 an episode in Chicago. These are the top markets; and overall, the license fees amount to several million dollars per episode. Jerry Seinfeld and Larry David were catapulted into the top ten earning entertainers due to the mega-million dollar syndication deal for their show *Seinfeld.*

With the growing power of cable networks, syndicators are finding it even more profitable to sell to them. The cable networks, especially those that reach over 90 percent of the market, have bought exclusive rights to a number of off-network shows. For example, TNT paid more than $1,000,000 per episode for the exclusive rights to *ER* and the USA Network paid $750,000 per episode for the rights to *Walker, Texas Ranger.* These deals usually extend for three years, but as prices for these shows increase, the length of the contract will also increase.

In many cases, syndicators only sell the weeknight rights to the cable networks. This way, they can sell the weekend rights to other local affiliates under a cash-barter system. This is the case with *ER, The X-Files, NYPD Blue,* and other shows depending on the market.

Many large conglomerates that own studios and cable networks or affiliates try to keep their shows "in the family" so to speak, by licensing their off-network shows to their own cable networks or to their owned and operated broadcast affiliates. For example: 20th Century Fox's cable network FX, televised *The X-Files* and *NYPD Blue* weeknights and also acquired the rights to the hit shows *Ally McBeal* and *The Practice.* All of these shows were produced by Twentieth Century Fox Television Studios. TNT, which bought the syndication rights to *ER,* and Warner Brothers, the producer, are both part of AOL Time Warner Inc., and The WB Network has *Friends* in syndication. In addition to increasing the drawing power (and, hopefully, profits) of an affiliate, this practice also provides outlets for less successful series to make up some of the money the studio has lost in deficit funding.

Original programming for syndication usually involves game shows such as *Wheel of Fortune* and *Jeopardy* or talk shows such as *Ellen* and *Oprah.* These tend to be relatively cheap to produce and are "cleared" (i.e., shown) in nearly all of the 211 markets. There are some original dramatic television series that are produced for syndication. Though not the first original syndicated television series, *Star Trek: The Next Generation* was the first enormously successful original series, becoming the first syndicated show nominated for a primetime Emmy in 1994. *Hercules, Xena,* and *Baywatch* have also enjoyed success. The key to producing these television series is clearance in as many of the markets as possible as well as in international markets. This provides a base of revenue to cover production costs and then, based on the performance of the series, new deals can be worked out.

10.4 THE RATINGS GAME

Ratings are the life blood of television. Television shows live or die based on their ratings. The success of any show depends on a number of factors mostly based on ratings. Its ratings with the total viewing audience, its rating within key demographics, especially the key advertising demographic of the 18 to 49 group, and how it performs compared to other shows in its time slot. All of this information is used by the networks to determine whether to renew or cancel a show.

Advertisers use the ratings to determine where to buy commercial spots. The networks make their money by selling the people who watch their shows to advertisers. Advertisers want to reach the most people for the least amount of money. The advertisers buy spots during the shows based on the specific number it takes to reach one thousand viewers. This is commonly referred to as the cost per thousand or CPT. So, the amount the advertisers have to pay is based on the number of viewers of a particular television show. The advertisers also use the demographic breakdowns to determine where to place commercial spots. Certain products cater to certain audiences. For example, a toy company would much rather advertise on the Cartoon Network than Court TV. Ultimately, the ratings are the biggest factor in determining where to advertise.

The leading company in ratings is the Nielsen Company. The Nielsen Company sends reports to advertising agencies, sponsors, networks, media buyers, rep firms, producers, distributors, and local stations. All of these groups pay a subscription fee for this information. The Nielsen Company compiles the data and computes it into a variety of charts and grids. The information in these charts includes the number of stations carrying the show, the percentage of the country that can see the show, the rating and the share for the total audience, viewers per thousand households, the number of households watching television at that time, and each quarter hour's rating. This information is also broken down by demographics such as age and sex.

The Nielsen Company collects its data by monitoring certain households for their viewing habits. These households are selected based on the statistical rules of sampling. The size and the composition of these households are supposed to represent the national viewership.

Nielsen monitors these households in two ways. The most accurate way is through the PeopleMeter. The PeopleMeter collects minute-by-minute viewing information. It reports whether the set is on, what channel is watched, and how long that channel has been watched. The remote control has special buttons that identify who is watching at that time. The second way is through entries in diaries. Selected households agree to make written entries into a diary noting each time the television is turned on, what channel it is set on, and who is doing the viewing. This system is less accurate because only about half of the selected households actually do the job properly.

The Nielsen Company gathers information on national audiences and local markets. For national audiences, the Nielsen Television Index is used to measure broadcast network audiences. Five thousand households are monitored by PeopleMeters. Monitoring of local markets is normally through the diary system. However, this is changing because of the unreliability of the diary system. Approximately forty markets have been converted to the meter system and this trend will continue. Nielson also monitors cable ratings and syndication ratings, which are more difficult because they appear in different time slots in different markets.

The most important pieces of information provided by the Nielsen Company are the ratings, shares and viewers. The rating of a program is the percentage of total television households whose sets were tuned to that program. The share of a program is the percentage of total viewing households whose televisions were tuned to that program. The difference between these two is that ratings indicate the absolute number of possible viewers, regardless of time period, and the share is based on the number of televisions that are actually turned on. The Nielsen Company also tabulates the gross number of viewers watching a station each quarter hour.

In November, February, May, and some in July, Nielsen measures the viewers in all 211 television markets, sweeping the entire country. These measurements are called "sweeps." The ratings from sweeps time are used to set the advertising rates for the next few months until the next "sweeps" period. These figures are not set in stone, but rather are used as a basis of negotiations. Sweeps time has been criticized since the networks use November, February, May, and to a much smaller degree July, to show high profile movies and much more exciting story lines than normal in order to artificially inflate viewership. It has become a tradition and it now appears that the viewers expect the best story lines and programs to be shown during sweeps. However, in recent years the fifty largest markets, along with the markets with network owned stations, get daily Nielson ratings, so the "sweeps" months have lost some of their emphasis and priority. With about 110,200,000 U.S. television households as of December 2005, a single ratings' point represents about 1.1 million households for the 2005–06 season (1% of 110,200,000 total households). See *National Cable & Telecommunications Association at ncta.com.*

The Nielsen Company has come under major criticism from networks and advertisers, who question the reliability of Nielsen's measurement samples and the way in which the data is collected, and who have engaged Statistical Research, Inc. to develop a new system of audience measurement, called SMART ("Systems for Measuring and Reporting Television") using the existing wiring of viewers' homes, supposedly making measurement easier and more reliable.

10.5 INTERNATIONAL MARKETS

Television studios service foreign networks as well as those in the United States. Each producing studio has an international distribution arm, which maintains offices in the larger market countries and has sales representatives in smaller market countries. Studios not only sell already produced shows, but also sell "format rights." The foreign network or production company is allowed to take the same format and produce it in its own language demonstrating its own culture. (This has also worked in reverse with shows like *All in the Family* and *Who Wants to Be a Millionaire,* and the immensely popular *American Idol,* having all been based on U.K. shows.) This is common with game shows and some other non-fiction shows. The most popular format shows are the "*Idol*" shows, *Family Feud, Wheel of Fortune, Jeopardy,* and *Sesame Street.* Selling to international markets is another way the television production companies are able to operate with deficit funding.

Other countries have many television households. Russia has an estimated 56 million, India has 50 million, and Japan has 44 million.

In Europe, Germany has 34 million, the United Kingdom has 24 million and France has 22 million. U.S. television studios try to license their shows in as many countries as possible. Canada is the largest market for U.S. television shows with active selling going on in Germany, the United Kingdom, France, Italy, and the Benelux and Scandinavian countries. Japan and Australia are only slightly smaller markets, while Brazil and Mexico are right behind them. The Middle East and Africa are of negligible importance due to extreme cultural differences and the lack of technology in many areas.

Many cable networks are international. Nickelodeon, CNN, and the Cartoon Network are among the most successful. These usually involve partnerships, joint ventures, or other related collaborations with local entities. The U.S. program schedule is the basis of the local schedule, with local programs substituted where necessary. All of the U.S. programs are dubbed in the local language. Many countries fear the extent to which U.S. ideas become a part of their culture, and are therefore resistant to U.S. programming. France is notorious for its xenophobic attitudes towards the United States. So, each channel has to maintain the delicate balance between local presence and U.S. exports.

Another important factor in selling shows is the cultural tastes of the country. A show popular in the United States may not be popular in other countries (and the reverse is certainly true) because the issues dealt with are part of American or local culture. The premise or local perspective or humor of a particular show might not be understood or translate well in other countries. Some television shows are produced as joint ventures between European and U.S. companies. They are then shown on European networks and sold into syndication in the United States. One successful example of this was the *Highlander* series.

The U.S. share of foreign television markets is declining. In 1998, only 18% of all new shows launched abroad were U.S.-made, while 78% were made in Europe or Australia. *Daily Variety*, April 13, 1999, p. 1.

10.6 ANCILLARY MARKETS

Ancillary markets are not as significant a factor in the television industry as they are in film, but they can occasionally become a significant source of revenue. For television, the ancillary markets encompass anything except what is seen on television. Possibilities include home videos, soundtracks, books, merchandise and all sorts of other collectibles.

When VCR's first became popular, television shows were never meant to be sold as home videos. Yet, *Star Trek*, the original series, made instant success being sold on home video cassettes. Then, each of the other *Star Trek* series were sold. By the time the last Star Trek series premiered, Columbia House and other home video clubs had entire divisions dedicated just to marketing various television shows. The list is growing and will continue to grow. From the popular hits like *I Love Lucy* and *Mission: Impossible* to cult classics like *The X-Files* and *The Prisoner*, and, of course, the *Seinfeld* series. A positive aspect of selling television series on home video or DVD is that it is not merely one DVD, like with films, but multiple shows with "outtakes" and interviews, etc., and people will want to buy all the episodes. So, if a series only has 30, 40 or 100 episodes, the audience that are the fans usually will have to buy several DVD sets at about $39 a set. It is a very profitable market.

The retail market of merchandise based on television shows also provides major revenue for producers and studios. Coffee cups, toys, board games and video games, posters, T-shirts, lunch boxes and soundtracks are all popular items. The success in this market all depends on the consumer interest generated in the television series. Obviously, cult television shows like *Star Trek, The X-Files* and *Stargate SG-1* have an easier time in this market than shows such as *NYPD Blue, 24* and *The Practice.* However, the studios will take advantage of all possible revenue producing markets.

10.7 FEDERAL COMMUNICATIONS COMMISSION

10.7.1 Licensing

The principal governing body for the television industry is the Federal Communications Commission, an independent regulatory agency created by the Communications Act of 1934 to take over the functions of the Federal Radio Commission and was given regulatory control over the fledgling television industry and interstate telephone and telegraph communication as well. It is a quasi-autonomous commission with elements of all three branches of government: legislative, executive, and judicial.

The main functions of the FCC are rule-making, licensing and registration, adjudication, and enforcement. In its rule-making capacity, the FCC issues new rules and regulations and amends existing ones. It exercises this power through its own internal procedures and under the auspices of federal law and the Administrative Procedure Act. A final order may be appealed for judicial review to the U.S. Court of Appeals for the District of Columbia. Through the licensing and registration function, the FCC controls broadcast television and cable networks. Broadcast licenses must be renewed every five to ten years. However, renewals are rarely a problem. Cable systems are not licensed; they merely have to register with the FCC. In its adjudication function, the FCC settles disputes between private parties or between the FCC and private parties. Hearings are conducted by administrative law judges pursuant to the Administrative Procedure Act. The next steps are appeals to the FCC Review Board, then to the five commissioners, then to the U.S. Court of Appeals, and finally to the U.S. Supreme Court. Under its enforcement power, the FCC can impose penalties ranging from revocation of licenses to simple fines. Obviously, the FCC is in a position to exert informal influence over the industry as well.

10.7.2 Control of Broadcast Television

In addition to its licensing power, the FCC governs broadcast television in three significant ways. First, it is involved in network affiliate relations. Second, it limits the number of stations that one entity can own (although, as indicated, this control has been, and is being, relaxed). Third, it limits the broadcast hours of networks through the prime-time access rule.

The FCC has issued several regulations controlling the relationship between the networks and their affiliates. First, the networks cannot force the affiliate to take their programming. The affiliates may decline to take any program the network offers for a variety of reasons. Second, the affiliate can take programs from any source with which it can reach an agreement. Third, the network may not control the affiliates' advertising inventory by setting rates or by acting as a national sales representative.

The FCC limits the number of affiliates a network, or any other company, may own. The number is 35 percent of the total affiliates linked to each network. However, as noted in Section 10.1.2, the networks have achieved ownership in the key markets. This makes clearance of their shows and various syndicated series easier. Furthermore, since major companies own groupings of most other affiliates, there are very few solely owned affiliates. Thus, the regulatory intent to protect local broadcasting, is largely defeated.

The prime-time access rule limits the network programming to three hours of the four-hour prime-time slot in the top 50 markets. The purpose of this rule was to encourage local programming, public affairs programming, and independent suppliers. However, syndicators have found this hour to be especially profitable. This is the time slot that off-network sitcoms and game shows have become common place on an affiliate station. Kingworld has made a fortune in this time slot with shows like *Wheel of Fortune* and *Jeopardy*.

10.7.3 Controlling Cable Television

Until the 1960s the FCC left the cable television industry alone. At that point, cable emerged as competition for the broadcast networks, so the FCC began to regulate the cable industry, even though it was not given that express authority until the Cable Act of 1984. However, many of the regulations established before the 1984 act were still in effect after the grant of power. Today dramatic changes have taken place in the 1984 Act as revised in the 1992 and the 1996 Acts.

The FCC regulates cable companies in several ways in addition to the registration requirement. The first major regulation is the "must carry" rule. Originally, cable systems were required to carry all local broadcast channels. Due to First Amendment concerns, Congress revised the rule in 1992. A local station was given the choice between granting a free retransmission consent on a "must carry" basis or negotiating an arm's-length retransmission agreement with the cable system ("retransmission consent"). In order to implement this system, the FCC established three groups within the cable systems. The first group is cable providers with less than 12 channels, the second group has between 12 and 36 channels, and the third group has more than 36 channels. The first group must carry in some way at least three local commercial and one public station. The other two groups must carry all the local commercial stations and public stations.

The FCC also regulates rates . . . Without any competition, cable companies became natural monopolies and the rates were increasing far faster than inflation. These increases, compounded with complaints of substandard services, caused Congress to grant to the FCC the power to set rates for cable companies. Rate setting is accomplished by a simple benchmark approach or by a more complicated cost-effectiveness approach. The goal is to keep cable rates in proportion to the general inflation rate. This rate regulation will not apply to systems where effective competition exists.

Some other regulations exist. First, cable companies cannot import a distant signal to circumvent the blackout of a local sporting event. For example, the National Football League black outs games in a certain geographical area if the game is not sold out. This rule prevents a local cable company from importing a signal from a station outside of that geographical area. Second, the Cable Act of 1984 has made it illegal to take signals from a cable system without authorization. Severe penalties exist for distribution of "black boxes" which descrambles the cable signal, thus, allowing people to receive the cable channels for free.

For more information on FCC regulations, a Communications Law Treatise should be reviewed.

10.8 ISSUES IN TELEVISION DISTRIBUTION

10.8.1 Antitrust: Block Booking

We considered antitrust issues arising in the context of film distribution. Similar to antitrust issues in the film industry, such issues have arisen in the television industry as well. For many years, television syndicators have offered films in packages. As the *Loew's, Inc.* case shows, however, it is unlawful to insist that a station license an entire package.

United States v. Loew's, Inc., 371 U.S. 38 (1962)

Mr. Justice Goldberg[nm delivered the opinion of the Court.]

These consolidated appeals present as a key question the validity under 1 of the Sherman Act of block booking of copyrighted feature motion pictures for television exhibition. We hold that the tying agreements here are illegal and in violation of the Act.

. . . [T]he defendants had, in selling to television stations, conditioned the license or sale of one or more [pre-1948] feature films upon the acceptance by the station of a package or block containing one or more unwanted or inferior films. No combination or conspiracy among the distributors was alleged; nor was any monopolization or attempt to monopolize under 2 of the Sherman Act averred. The sole claim of illegality rested on the manner in which each defendant had marketed its product. The successful pressure applied to television station customers to accept inferior films along with desirable pictures was the gravamen of the complaint . . .

[As one of many examples of offending conduct, the Court described the actions of] Associated Artists Productions, Inc., [which] negotiated four contracts that were found to be block booked. Station WTOP was to pay $118,800 for the license of 99 pictures, which were divided into three groups of 33 films, based on differences in quality. To get "Treasure of the Sierra Madre," "Casablanca," "Johnny Belinda," "Sergeant York," and "The Man Who Came to Dinner," among others, WTOP also had to take such films as "Nancy Drew Troubleshooter," "Tugboat Annie Sails Again," "Kid Nightingale," "Gorilla Man," and "Tear Gas Squad." A similar contract for 100 pictures, involving a license fee of $140,000, was entered into by WMAR of Baltimore. Triangle Publications, owner and operator of five stations, was refused the right to select among Associated's packages, and ultimately purchased the entire library of 754 films for a price of $2,262,000 plus 10% of gross receipts. Station WJAR of Providence, which licensed a package of 58 features for a fee of $25,230, had asked first if certain films it considered undesirable could be dropped from the offered packages and was told that the packages could not be split.

Defendant National Telefilm Associates was found to have entered into five block booked contracts. Station WMAR wanted only 10 Selznick films, but was told that it could not have them unless it also bought 24 inferior films from the "TNT" package and 12 unwanted "Fabulous 40's." It bought all of these, for a total of $62,240. Station WBRE, before buying the "Fox 52" package in its entirety for $7,358.50, requested and was refused the right to eliminate undesirable features. Station WWLP of Springfield, Massachusetts, inquired about the possibility of splitting two of the packages, was told this was not possible, and then bought a total of 59 films in two packages for $8,850. A full package contract for National's "Rocket 86" group of 86 films was entered into by KPIX of San Francisco, payments to total $232,200, after KPIX requested and was denied permission to eliminate undesirable films from the package. Station WJAR wanted to drop 10 or 12 British films from this defendant's "Champagne 58" package, was told that none could be deleted, and then bought the block for $31,000 . . .

This case raises the recurring question of whether specific tying arrangements violate 1 of the Sherman Act. This Court has recognized that "[t]ying agreements serve hardly any purpose beyond the suppression of competition," *Standard Oil Co. of California v. United States*, 337 U.S. 293, 305–306. They are an object of antitrust concern for two reasons—they may force buyers into giving up the purchase of substitutes for the tied product, see *Times-Picayune Pub. Co. v. United States,* 345 U.S. 594, 605, and they may destroy the free access of competing suppliers of the tied product to the consuming market, see *International Salt Co. v. United States,* 332 U.S. 392, 396. A tie-in contract may have one or both of these undesirable effects when the seller, by virtue of his position in the market for the tying product, has economic leverage sufficient to induce his customers to take the tied product along with the tying item. The standard of illegality is that the seller must have "sufficient economic power with respect to the tying product to appreciably restrain free competition in the market for the tied product. . . . " *Northern Pacific R. Co. v. United States,* 356 U.S. 1, 6. Market dominance—some power to control price and to exclude competition—is by no means the only test of whether the seller has the requisite economic power. Even absent a showing of market dominance, the crucial economic power may be inferred from the tying product's desirability to consumers or from uniqueness in its attributes.

The requisite economic power is presumed when the tying product is patented or copyrighted. . . . This principle grew out of a long line of patent cases which had eventuated in the doctrine that a patentee who utilized tying arrangements would be denied all relief against infringements of his patent. . . . These cases reflect a hostility to use of the statutorily granted patent monopoly to extend the patentee's economic control to unpatented products. The patentee is protected as to his invention, but may not use his patent rights to exact tribute for other articles.

Since one of the objectives of the patent laws is to reward uniqueness, the principle of these cases was carried over into antitrust law on the theory that the existence of a valid patent on the tying product, without more, establishes a distinctiveness sufficient to conclude that any tying arrangement involving the patented product would have anticompetitive consequences. . . .

A copyrighted feature film does not lose its legal or economic uniqueness because it is shown on a television rather than a movie screen.

The district judge found that each copyrighted film block booked by appellants for television use "was in itself a unique product"; that feature films "varied in theme, in artistic performance, in stars, in audience appeal, etc." and were not fungible; and that since each defendant by reason of its copyright had a "monopolistic" position as to each tying product, "sufficient economic power" to impose an appreciable restraint on free competition in the tied product was present, as demanded by the *Northern Pacific* decision. 189 F. Supp., at 381. We agree. These findings of the district judge, supported by the record, confirm the presumption of uniqueness resulting from the existence of the copyright itself.

Moreover, there can be no question in this case of the adverse effects on free competition resulting from appellants' illegal block booking contracts. Television stations forced by appellants to take unwanted films were denied access to films marketed by other distributors who, in turn, were foreclosed from selling to the stations. Nor can there be any question as to the substantiality of the commerce involved. . . . A substantial portion of the licensing fees represented the cost of the inferior films which the stations were required to accept. These anticompetitive consequences are an apt illustration of the reasons underlying our recognition that the mere presence of competing substitutes for the tying product, here taking the form of other programming material as well as other feature films, is insufficient to destroy the legal, and indeed the economic, distinctiveness of the copyrighted product. . . . By the same token, the distinctiveness of the copyrighted tied product is not inconsistent with the fact of competition, in the form of other programming material and other films, which is suppressed by the tying arrangements.

It is therefore clear that the tying arrangements here both by their "inherent nature" and by their "effect" injuriously restrained trade. . . .

Appellant C & C in its separate appeal raises certain arguments which amount to an attempted business justification for its admitted block booking policy. C & C purchased the telecasting rights in some 742 films known as the "RKO Library." It did so with a bank loan for the total purchase price, and to get the bank loan it needed a guarantor, which it found in the International Latex Corporation. Latex, however, demanded and secured an agreement from C & C that films would not be sold without obtaining in return a commitment from television stations to show a minimum number of Latex spot advertisements in conjunction with the films. Thus, since stations could not feasibly telecast the minimum number of spots without buying a large number of films to spread them over, C & C by requiring the minimum number of advertisements effectively forced block booking on those stations which purchased its films. C & C contends the block booking was merely the by-product of two legitimate business motives—Latex' desire for a saturation advertising campaign, and C & C's wish to buy a large film library. However, the obvious answer to this contention is that the thrust of the antitrust laws cannot be avoided merely by claiming that the otherwise illegal conduct is compelled by contractual obligations. Were it otherwise, the antitrust laws could be nullified. . . .

The United States contends that the relief afforded by the final judgments is inadequate and that to be adequate it must also: (1) require the defendants to price the films individually and offer them on a picture-by-picture basis; (2) prohibit noncost-justified differentials in price between a film when sold individually and when sold as part of a package; (3) proscribe "temporary" refusals by a distributor to deal on less than a block basis while he is negotiating with a competing television station for a package sale. . . .

Under the final judgments entered by the court, a distributor would be free to offer films in a package initially, without stating individual prices. If, however, he delayed at all in producing individual prices upon request, he would subject himself to a possible contempt sanction. The Government's first request would prevent this "first bite" possibility, forcing the offer of the films on an individual basis at the outset (but, as we view it, not precluding a simultaneous package offer . . .).

This is a necessary addition to the decrees, in view of the evidence appearing in the record. Television stations which asked for the individual prices of some of the better pictures "couldn't get any sort of a firm kind of an answer," according to one station official. He stated that they received a "certain form of equivocation, like the price for the better pictures that we wanted was so high that it wouldn't be worth our while to discuss the matter, . . . the implication being that it wouldn't happen." A Screen Gems intracompany memorandum about a Baton Rouge station's price request stated that "I told him that I would be happy to talk to him about it, figuring we could start the old round robin that worked so well in Houston & San Antonio." Without the proposed amendment to the decree, distributors might surreptitiously violate it by allowing or directing their salesmen to be reluctant to produce the individual price list on request. This subtler form of sales pressure, though not accompanied by any observable delay over time, might well result in some television stations buying the block rather than trying to talk the seller into negotiating on an individual basis. Requiring the production of the individual list on first approach will obviate this danger. . . .

The final judgments as entered only prohibit a price differential between a film offered individually and as part of a package which "has the effect of conditioning the sale or license of such film upon the sale or license of one or more other films." The Government contends that this provision appearing by itself is too vague and will lead to unnecessary litigation. Differentials unjustified by cost savings may already be prohibited under the decree as it now appears. Nevertheless, the addition of a specific provision to prevent such differentials will prevent uncertainty in the operation of the decree. To ensure that litigation over the scope and application of the decrees is not left until a contempt proceeding is brought, the second requested modification should be added. The Government, however, seeks to make distribution costs the only saving which can legitimately be the basis of a discount. We would not so limit the relevant cost justifications. To prevent definitional arguments, and to ensure that all proper bases of quantity discount may be used, the modification should be worded in terms of allowing all legitimate cost justifications. . . .

The Government's third request is, like the first, designed to prevent distributors from subjecting prospective purchasers to a "runaround" on the purchase of individual films. No doubt temporary refusal to sell in broken lots to one customer while negotiating to sell the entire block to another is a proper business practice, viewed *in vacuo*, but we think that if permitted here it may tend to force some stations into buying pre-set packages to forestall a competitor's getting the entire group. In recognition of this the Government seeks a blanket prohibition against all temporary refusals to deal. We agree in the main, except that the modification proposed by the Government fails to give full recognition to that part of this Court's holding in *Paramount Pictures* which said,

We do not suggest that films may not be sold in blocks or groups, when there is no requirement, express or implied, for the purchase of more than one film. All we hold to be illegal is a refusal to license one or more copyrights unless another copyright is accepted. 334 U.S., at 159.

We therefore grant the Government's request, but modify it only to the limited degree necessary to permit a seller briefly to defer licensing or selling to a customer pending the expeditious conclusion of bona fide negotiations already being conducted with a competing station on a proposal wherein the distributor has simultaneously offered to license or sell films either individually or in a package.

The modifications we have specified will bring about a greater precision in the operation of the decrees. We have concluded that they will properly protect the interest of the Government in guarding against violations and the interest of the defendants in seeking in good faith to comply. . . .

10.8.2 Antitrust: Geographical Restrictions

Part of the economic power of a television series lies in the ability of a licensee to obtain exclusive rights to show the series within its broadcast area. As the following case indicates, it is not always possible to define markets with sufficient precision to satisfy all concerned.

Ralph C. Wilson Industries, Inc. v. American Broadcasting Companies, Inc., 598 F. Supp. 694 (N.D. Cal. 1984)

CONTI, J.

. . . Plaintiff is the owner of a television station, [in San Jose, California, south of San Francisco. Plaintiff claims] that defendants have violated the antitrust laws because of various practices they follow concerning the licensing of programs and conspiracies to boycott plaintiff. Plaintiff is pursuing three claims against defendants based upon these alleged practices. First, plaintiff claims that all defendants have violated the Sherman Act by unreasonably restraining trade . . . by licensing programs on an exclusive basis as against plaintiff, by making the licenses unreasonably long and by incorporating, implicitly or explicitly, rights of first refusal into those licenses. Secondly, plaintiff claims that the station defendants have committed a *per se* violation of the Sherman Act by a horizontal conspiracy to boycott plaintiff. Plaintiff alleges that these three defendants have conspired, through direct communication, to exercise exclusivity of programming against plaintiff. . .

A. RULE OF REASON CLAIM

Plaintiff's primary claim against the defendants is that they have unreasonably restrained trade through a vertical contract by their combined practices of licensing television programs on an exclusive basis, making the licenses unreasonably long, and by implicitly or explicitly incorporating rights of first refusal into those licenses. . . .

The unreasonable restraint of trade complained of is as follows. The supplier defendants herein are in the business of licensing television programs to television stations. The undisputed practice of these suppliers is to license programs to the stations on an exclusive basis after a competitive bidding process among interested stations. Thus, for example, a supplier would sell an exclusive license for "M*A*S*H" to defendant KTVU, who would then be the only station in that area permitted to air "M*A*S*H" (or specified episodes of "M*A*S*H") for the duration of the license.

It is undisputed that the station defendants herein enforce this exclusivity against all television stations, including plaintiff, which they consider to be located in the "San Francisco" market area. This area includes San Francisco, Oakland and San Jose, as well as most of the area around these cities. . . . The scope of this exclusive licensing area is determined on the basis of the A. C. Nielsen Co. and Arbitron Co. ratings services' categorization of geographic area into market groups, both of which ratings services include San Francisco and San Jose in the same market group.

Plaintiff does not contend that the practice of licensing television programs on an exclusive basis automatically violates the Sherman Act's prohibition of restraints of trade. In fact, plaintiff itself licenses programs on an exclusive basis. All parties agree that exclusive licenses, as such, may further competition by providing an incentive to the station to invest in promotion and development of the program product and do not constitute a *per se* violation of Section 1 . . .

[Instead,] Plaintiff argues that the station defendants are entitled to license programs on an exclusive basis, but that that exclusivity should not apply to plaintiff because it is not in the same "relevant market" as the station defendants. Plaintiff submits that the station defendants are licensed to and operate in the San Francisco-Oakland Bay Area market. Plaintiff argues that it, on the other hand, is located in and operates in the "South Bay." (Plaintiff does not define the area included within the "South Bay," but it apparently covers San Jose and other areas in and around Santa Clara County.) Accordingly, plaintiff contends that it should be placed in a different geographic market than the station defendants for exclusivity purposes . . . Thus, plaintiff argues that the exclusive licenses violate the antitrust laws because they are overbroad in geographic scope, are unreasonably long in duration and incorporate unreasonable rights of first refusal. . . .

The economic motivation for this suit is to enable plaintiff to license quality programming [from the defendant distributor] at a price below that paid by the station defendants, such as KTVU, for their exclusive licenses to such programs. It is uncontested that the level of prices for exclusive licenses for quality programming is primarily determined by the broadcast market of the prospective licensees. Presently, all the station defendants and plaintiff are placed in the same market for purposes of bidding for the supplier defendants' quality programming. Thus, if defendant KTVU bids $150,000 for an exclusive license for "M*A*S*H," plaintiff must better that bid to obtain the license. Plaintiff has made no argument and there is no evidence showing that plaintiff has been excluded from bidding for quality programming at these price levels. In fact, the evidence shows that if plaintiff wished to bid at this "San Francisco" market price, it could obtain quality programming.

Plaintiff contends that, as a small UHF station, it is not commercially feasible for it to bid at the same price levels as the station defendants to obtain quality programming. What plaintiff seeks is to be placed in some market other than that containing the station defendants for purposes of bidding for quality program licenses. If, for example, plaintiff were placed in the Salinas-Monterey market, in which non-party channel 11 is placed, it could bid for quality programming at a much lower price than that paid by the station defendants. The outcome would be, for example, that defendant KTVU would obtain a license for "M*A*S*H," exclusive against the other San Francisco stations, but not plaintiff, for $100,000, while plaintiff could also license "M*A*S*H," exclusive against other South Bay stations, for, say, $15,000. That is the result plaintiff seeks to achieve by means of this antitrust suit. This, then, is the factual basis for plaintiff's rule of reason antitrust claim.

[To win, the plaintiff would have to show injury to competition through an unreasonable restraint, which would, in turn, require plaintiff to show either] that the restraint is unreasonable because it applies to television stations which are not in "substantial competition" with each other [or] that the challenged practices of exclusivity, length of license and rights of first refusal, are "unreasonable" under the circumstances of this case. . . . For the reasons set forth below, the court holds that plaintiff has not, as a matter of law, met its burden of offering evidence sufficient to support a finding that defendants' exclusivity practices unreasonably restrain trade.

1. Injury to Competition

. . . [The] court must first determine what is the "relevant market" in which competition has allegedly been restrained. See *Gough v. Rossmoor*, 585 F.2d at 385–89. This "relevant market" is generally determined by reference to both the relevant product market and the relevant geographic market. See, e.g., *Harris & Jorde, Antitrust Market Definition: An Integrated Approach*, 72 Cal.L.Rev. 1, 46–52 (1984). In this case, the parties agree, and the court accepts, that the relevant product market is quality television programming. The relevant geographic market, however, is more complex. . . .

Plaintiff contends that the relevant geographic market is the "South Bay." . . .

[However,] the commercial realities are so clear that the court holds that the relevant geographic market is the entire San Francisco-Oakland-San Jose Bay Area, as currently defined.

These commercial realities are as follow. First, the Federal Communications Commission (FCC) considers San Jose and San Francisco to be in the same market. See 47 C.F.R. 76.51; Memorandum Opinion, 37 R.R.2d 695, 698 (1976); 40 R.R.2d 473, 477–78 (1977). Secondly, the two recognized national ratings services, A. C. Nielsen Co. and Arbitron Co., consider San Jose and San Francisco to be in the same market. . . . Thirdly, there is a large overlap in the signal coverage of plaintiff's and the station defendants' signals. . . . Finally, plaintiff and the station defendants share a substantial overlap of viewers. . . .

These facts are so clear that a reasonable jury would have to find that the relevant geographic market is the entire San Francisco Bay Area, including San Jose. Accordingly, the court holds that the relevant market in this case is the San Francisco Bay Area quality television programming market. . . .

[I]t is not sufficient for plaintiff to establish an injury to itself or its own competitive position. . . . This is all plaintiff has done. Plaintiff offers no evidence tending to show that it cannot obtain quality programming, that prices are fixed, that program offerings are detrimentally affected, or that program output has in any way been restricted. Some showing of this type is necessary to establish injury to competition. . . .

Plaintiff has offered no evidence showing that any one defendant has market power. The evidence shows that the ten or more Bay Area stations all compete vigorously in both the South Bay and the Bay Area as a whole. The evidence also shows that the supplier defendants actively compete in both areas. . . . There is no evidence showing that any one defendant has the power to significantly affect prices, available programming, or any other important market component. Consequently, plaintiff has not offered evidence sufficient to go to jury on the issue whether a defendant has market power.

. . . Plaintiff has not shown that the exclusivity practices actually injure competition or that any defendant has market power. Accordingly, the court holds that plaintiff cannot prevail on its rule of reason claim. Defendants are consequently entitled to summary judgment . . .

[But even if plaintiff had shown injury to competition,] plaintiff must then show that the exclusivity practices are "unreasonable." The first way plaintiff may establish this is by offering sufficient evidence to show that plaintiff and defendants are not in "substantial competition." If plaintiff is not in substantial competition with defendants, the exclusivity practices are presumptively unreasonable. See *United States v. Paramount Pictures, Inc.*, 334 U.S. at 144–48, 68 S.Ct. at 922–24. If the parties are in substantial competition, plaintiff must then offer evidence showing that the challenged exclusivity practices are unreasonable given the particular circumstances of this case. . . .

[However,] the station defendants actively compete with plaintiff for viewers, quality programming and advertising in both the San Francisco Bay Area and the South Bay markets [and] plaintiff has failed to offer evidence to support a finding that the exclusivity practices herein, consisting of the geographic breadth of the exclusivity, the length of the licenses and the alleged rights of first refusal, are unreasonable under the circumstances of this case.

The court holds that no reasonable jury could find that the practices complained of herein are unreasonable. The parties agree that exclusivity, in itself, is a reasonable practice in the television programming industry. Such exclusivity gives the licensee the incentive to promote and develop the licensed program. Without exclusivity, it is likely that no one licensee would expend the resources necessary to fully develop the program. . . . Plaintiff itself utilizes exclusive licenses similar to those attacked herein. The exclusive licenses used herein promote competition by maximizing the number of available programs and preventing audience fragmentation for a program. . . .

This exclusivity also promotes competition by maximizing the program's value and avoiding overexposure, which can shorten the program's useful life. . . . Exclusivity permits each station to plan programming to compete with another station's programming, with the knowledge that no other station will dilute the value of this competitive programming by airing the same program at the same time. . . .

Exclusive licenses promote competition among suppliers by providing an incentive to maximize the number of programs offered and by maximizing the supplier's revenues from the licenses . . .

B. CONSPIRACY CLAIM AGAINST STATION DEFENDANTS

Plaintiff's second antitrust claim is directed against the station defendants. Plaintiff contends that the station defendants have violated Section 1 of the Sherman Act by a per se horizontal conspiracy to enforce exclusivity against plaintiff. . . .

Plaintiff's first argument is that the defendants' parallel conduct permits an inference of conspiracy. Even if plaintiff could show that the defendants' conduct with respect to exclusivity is parallel, which defendants dispute, such evidence could not, by itself, support plaintiff's conspiracy claim. . . .

Similarly, plaintiff's offered proof of an opportunity to conspire, even if accepted by a fact finder, cannot, even when combined with proof of parallel conduct, support a finding of conspiracy. . . .

In order to go to the jury on its conspiracy claim, plaintiff must submit some sort of proof that the defendants actually conspired—some "conscious commitment to a common scheme"—or other special facts permitting a finding of conspiracy. . . .

Despite extensive discovery, plaintiff offers only one item of evidence to substantiate its claim that the station defendants conspired to enforce exclusivity against it. This one item is telephone calls by KT-VU's Mr. Breen to other stations in the area, in which they discussed exclusivity practices. Defendants do not dispute that these telephone calls occurred. Rather, defendants present convincing and undisputed evidence showing that these calls were made *after* the alleged conspiracy began, on advice of counsel after plaintiff threatened litigation concerning exclusivity, and were undertaken to *discover* the exclusivity practices of other stations in the area. . . . Such overwhelming and uncontested evidence shows that plaintiff's only item of evidence cannot, as a matter of law, substantiate its conspiracy claim. . . .

In addition to their evidence rebutting plaintiff's meager evidence of conspiracy, the defendants have submitted overwhelming evidence that their exclusivity practices were undertaken in the exercise of their independent and sound business judgment. . . . This showing, which makes it more likely than not that defendants' exclusivity practices were the result of independent business judgment, is sufficient to compel summary judgment on plaintiff's conspiracy claim. . . .

The court is confronted with a situation where the [defendants] made independent decisions concerning exclusivity in the exercise of sound business judgment. Under the circumstances of this case, the court holds that summary judgment for the station defendants is appropriate on plaintiff's conspiracy claim. . . .

Accordingly, the court hereby grants defendants' motion for summary judgment on plaintiff's second claim of a horizontal conspiracy.

NOTE

The issue of geography is not limited to programming. In an unreported case, *Marco Island Cable, Inc v. Comcast Cablevision of the South, Inc.* 04CV26 (US M.D. Florida, 2006), plaintiff, a minor cable company, provided cable service to homes in Marco Island via traditional cable and to a small number of homes outside of Marco Island via microwave. Plaintiff brought an anti-trust action against Comcast alleging that Comcast had a virtual monopoly on cable services within the county, and maintained that monopoly by predatory pricing, long-term exclusive contracts with residents, intimidation, threats to remove cable wiring and threats to sue customers. Comcast alleged that plaintiff did not have competitor status outside of Marco Island and did not have standing as an "efficient enforcer" of the antitrust laws. Further, Comcast noted that plaintiff did not have franchise to distribute cable TV via traditional cable outside of Marco Island. Since plaintiff's distribution of traditional cable was limited to geographic areas, it could not be considered a competitor to Comcast outside of Marco Island. The Court found that the geographic limitation did not apply to plaintiff's distribution of cable by microwave technology and that plaintiff was entitled to maintain its antitrust action with respect to its microwave cable service.

10.8.3 Piracy: Unlawful Interception and Retransmission of Signals

Piracy has been a major problem for the entertainment industries for the last forty years. In recent years, the illegal duplication of DVDs and CDs has grown enormously. The Napster and MyMP3.com, iCrave TV, and DeCSS technologies, discussed in Chapter 11, illustrate the problem of various types of piracy on the Internet. The unauthorized interception of radio signals and their retransmission by a background music service was held to violate Section 605 of the Communications Act and to constitute unfair competition under California Civil Code, Section 3369, subd. 3, in *KMLA Broadcasting Corp. v. Twentieth Century Cigarette Vendors Corp.*, 264 F. Supp. 35 (C.D. Cal. 1967).

The following case illustrates one provider's attempt to prevent piracy through private action.

DirecTV Inc. v. Robert F. Pepe, et al, 431 F.3d 162; 2005 U.S. App. LEXIS 27414 (3d cir. 2005)

VAN ANTWERPEN, CIRCUIT JUDGE

In this consolidated appeal, we are asked to determine whether a private right of action under *18 U.S.C. β 2520* exists for violations of *18 U.S.C. β 2511(1)(a)*, which, as a joint civil-criminal provision of the Electronic Communications Privacy Act of 1986 ("ECPA"), *18 U.S.C. β β 2510–2521*, imposes sanctions against anyone who "intentionally intercepts, endeavors to intercept, or procures any other person to intercept or endeavor to intercept, any . . . electronic communication." *Section 2520(a)* provides for civil actions by "any person whose wire, oral, or electronic communication is intercepted, disclosed, or intentionally used in violation of" the ECPA. *18 U.S.C. β 2520(a)*. Specifically at issue are default judgments entered by the United States District Court for the District of New Jersey against the Appellees, who are alleged by Appellant DIRECTV, Inc. to have pirated its encrypted satellite television broadcasts. In those cases, the District Court concluded that *β β 2511(1)(a)* and *2520(a)* of the ECPA did not allow DIRECTV a cause of action. It did allow claims under *β 705* of the Communications Act, *47 U.S.C. β 605*, which proscribes the unauthorized reception of radio or wire signals.

On January 20, 2005, DIRECTV moved to consolidate its appeals in *DeCroce* and *Pepe*, and this Court granted the motion on February 2, 2005. In both cases, we have jurisdiction to review the final orders of the District Court under *28 U.S.C. β 1291*.[n1] For the following reasons, we will reverse the judgment of the District Court that no private right of action exists under *18 U.S.C. β 2520(a)* for violations of *18 U.S.C. β 2511(1)(a)* where the defendant has, without authorization, intercepted a plaintiff's encrypted satellite television broadcast.

---

n1 DIRECTV did not immediately appeal the Order as to defendant Keal in *DeCroce*, but was compelled by *Fed. R. Civ. P. 54(b)* to await the dismissal of the final defendant in the case. Thereupon the Order became final and appealable. This Court requested that DIRECTV clarify the jurisdictional issue of the timeliness of its appeal. Because no final order existed until the last defendant was dismissed, we conclude that the appeal was timely filed, and that there is no jurisdictional defect.

I

These cases arise as part of a program of litigation undertaken by DIRECTV to deter the illegal interception of the company's encrypted satellite broadcasts. Because the cases arise from default judgments, we draw the relevant facts from the two Complaints that initiated each case presently before us. . . . *See Comdyne I, Inc. v. Corbin*, 908 F.2d 1142, 1149 (3d Cir. 1990). The first Complaint named ten defendants, Robert F. Pepe, . . .; DIRECTV filed it on May 23, 2003 ("*Pepe*"). The second Complaint, filed on October 31, 2003, named five: Anthony DeCroce, . . . ("*DeCroce*"). Both complaints allege that the defendants separately purchased devices which could enable them to intercept and decode DIRECTV's satellite transmissions. While DIRECTV refers to these items as "Pirate Access Devices," they consist of different designs and functions, and are variously known as unloopers, bootloaders, emulators, and access card "programmers."

DIRECTV made the same substantive legal claims in both Complaints. It asserted first that the "defendants have received and/or assisted others in receiving DIRECTV's satellite transmissions of television programming without authorization, in violation of *47 U.S.C. ß 605(a)* [ß 705 of the Communications Act]." App. 70 & 83. *Section 605* provides a civil remedy for the unauthorized use or publication of various wire or radio communications, including encrypted satellite broadcasts. *See 47 U.S.C. ß 605.* Second, DIRECTV claimed that "by using Pirate Access Devices to decrypt and view DIRECTV's satellite transmissions of television programming,[n3] defendants intentionally intercepted, endeavored to intercept, or procured other persons to intercept or endeavor to intercept, DIRECTV's satellite transmission of television programming, in violation of *18 U.S.C. ß 2511(1)(a).*" App. 71. As discussed, *ß 2511(1)(a)* prohibits the intentional and unauthorized interception of "electronic communication[s]." Third, DIRECTV alleged that "defendants possessed and used Pirate Access Devices, knowing or having reason to know that the design of such devices render then primarily useful for the purpose of surreptitious interception[n4] of DIRECTV's satellite transmissions of television programming, and that such devices, or any component thereof, have been or will be sent through the mail or transported via interstate or foreign commerce, in violation of *18 U.S.C. ß 2512(1)(b).*" App. 72 & 85. *Section 2512(1)(b)* criminalizes the manufacture, assembly, possession, or sale of so-called "Pirate Access Devices" in interstate or foreign commerce. With each claim, DIRECTV alleged that it suffered lost revenue, breach of its security and accounting systems, infringement of its proprietary information and trade secrets, and interference with business relations. On these bases, it sought damages, attorneys fees, costs, and injunctive relief.

n3 The *Pepe* Complaint refers to these as "satellite television transmissions." The difference is immaterial. App. 84.

n4 *Section 2510(4) of the ECPA* defines "intercept" to mean "the aural or other acquisition of the contents of any wire, electronic, or oral communication through the use of any electronic, mechanical, or other device."

[Defendants in *Pepe* and *DeCroce* defaulted in the District Court proceedings and default judgments were entered against some of them. The district court dismissed the ECPA claims, finding that no private right of action existed under 18 U.S.C.S. ß 2520(a) for violations of 18 U.S.C.S. ß 2511(1)(a) and that the Communications Act supplanted a private cause of action under the ECPA. DIRECTV then appealed the denial of its *ß 2511* claim. . . .]

The Appellees in these cases have not filed briefs with this Court, apparently a continuation of their silence in the District Court. A group of individuals who are defendants in other cases brought by DIRECTV in other district courts of this Circuit have filed a brief as *amici curiae*, observing that our decision in this case will affect their interests in their own cases.

II

The sole issue for review is whether the District Court erred by determining that no private cause of action exists under *18 U.S.C. ß ß 2511* and *2520*.[n8] We exercise plenary review over questions of statutory interpretation. *Fraser v. Nationwide Mut. Ins. Co.*, 352 F.3d 107, 113 (3d Cir. 2003); *Universal Minerals, Inc. v. C.A. Hughes & Co.*, 669 F.2d 98, 103 (3d Cir. 1981). DIRECTV argues that it should be allowed to assert a claim for unauthorized interception of satellite television broadcasts against Appellees under these sections. We agree.

N8 DIRECTV does not appeal the District Court's denials of its claims under *ß 2512*, rooted in defendants' mere purchase or possession of unauthorized interception devices. We express no opinion as to the merits of District Court's denial of the *ß 2512* claims.

The District Court concluded that the legislative history of the ECPA, case law, and a comparison of the damages provisions of *47 U.S.C. ß 605* and *18 U.S.C. ß 2520*, which admittedly overlap, all indicate that private claims cannot arise under *ß 2511(1)(a)*. In the view of the District Court, *47 U.S.C. ß 605*, provided DIRECTV's sole remedy. We find that the plain language of *ß 2511* compels the opposite result, a conclusion that is supported—not contradicted, as the District Court found-by the legislative history. Accordingly, we are constrained to reverse.

A

As a threshold matter, we must decide whether DIRECTV's satellite television transmissions are "electronic communications" within the meaning of the ECPA. We hold that they are. The ECPA defines "electronic communication" as "any transfer of signs, signals, writing, images, sounds, data, or intelligence of any nature transmitted in whole or in part by a wire, radio, electromagnetic, photoelectronic or photo-optical system that affects interstate or foreign commerce." *18 U.S.C. β 2510(12)*. A television broadcast is self-evidently a "transfer of . . . signals," including, at the very least, images and sounds. The means of transmission is by radio wave from the satellite to a ground-based antenna. We conclude, therefore, that DIRECTV's satellite broadcasts are "electronic communications" as defined by the ECPA. Where our sister courts of appeals have considered the issue, they have reached the same conclusion. *See DIRECTV Inc. v. Nicholas*, 403 F.3d 223, 225–26 (4th Cir. 2005. . . .

B

The plain language of *β 2511(1)(a)* and *β 2520(a)* compels us to conclude that private parties can bring a cause of action for damages and injunctive relief where aggrieved by a defendant's violation of *β 2511(1)(a)*. Where we are called upon to interpret a statute, we must always begin with its plain language. *Robinson v. Shell Oil Co.*, 519 U.S. 337, 340, 117 S. Ct. 843, 136 L. Ed. 2d 808 (1997). Where "the statutory language is unambiguous and 'the statutory scheme is coherent and consistent,'" we cannot look further. *Id.* (quoting *United States v. Ron Pair Enters., Inc.*, 489 U.S. 235, 240, 109 S. Ct. 1026, 103 L. Ed. 2d 290 (1989)).

Section 2511 provides in relevant part that "except as otherwise specifically provided in this chapter any person who . . . intentionally intercepts . . . any . . . electronic communication" is subject to criminal penalties or civil suit by the federal government.[9] *18 U.S.C. β 2511(1)(a)*.[10] Appearing later in the same chapter, *β 2520* expressly authorizes private suits by "any person whose . . . electronic communication is intercepted . . . in violation of this chapter." *18 U.S.C. β 2520(a)*.[11] Both sections reference the interception of electronic communications. The linguistic interlock between the two provisions could not be tighter, nor more obviously deliberate: *β 2511(1)(a)* renders unlawful the unauthorized interception of electronic communications, including encrypted satellite television broadcasts, while *β 2520(a)* authorizes private suit against those who have engaged in such activities.

n9 The civil suit provisions in *β 2511(5)* do not concern civil suits brought by private parties; rather, they enable the federal government to bring civil suits and to seek civil penalties for certain activities not at issue here, including the interception of unencrypted "private satellite video communication[s]" for legal, non-tortious purposes. *Section 2520* addresses civil suits by private parties.

n10 *Section 2511(1)(a)* provides:

(1)   Except as otherwise specifically provided in this chapter any person who—

(a)   intentionally intercepts, endeavors to intercept, or procures any other person to intercept or endeavor to intercept, any wire, oral, or electronic communication; . . . .

shall be punished as provided in subsection (4) or shall be subject to suit as provided in subsection (5).

n11 *Section 2520(a)* provides in full:

(a) In general.—Except as provided in *section 2511(2)(a)(ii),* any person whose wire, oral, or electronic communication is intercepted, disclosed, or intentionally used in violation of this chapter may in a civil action recover from the person or entity, other than the United States, which engaged in that violation such relief as may be appropriate.

To illustrate the point, we observe that the ECPA excepts a number of activities from its reach; however, it nowhere provides an exception for the interception of electronic communications in the form of encrypted satellite television broadcasts. For example, another subsection of *β 2511* excludes interception of certain *unencrypted* satellite transmissions from its scope, but is silent on *encrypted* satellite television broadcasts:

Conduct *otherwise an offense* under this subsection that consists of or relates to the interception of *a satellite transmission that is not encrypted or scrambled* and that is transmitted—

(i)   to a broadcasting station for purposes of retransmission to the general public; or

(ii)   as an audio subcarrier intended for redistribution to facilities open to the public, but not including data transmissions or telephone calls,

is *not an offense under this subsection* unless the conduct is for the purposes of direct or indirect commercial advantage or private financial gain.

18 U.S.C. β 2511(4)(b) (emphasis added).

The clear implication, for present purposes, is that *encrypted* satellite transmissions are not excepted from *β 2511.* In *β 2511(4)(b),* Congress made express provision for "conduct otherwise an offense" under *β 2511* relating to *unencrypted,* non-scrambled satellite transmissions to except it out of the general rule that such interceptions would indeed violate *β 2511. See Lande, 968 F.2d at 909–10* (holding that *β 2511(1)* bars unauthorized interception of encrypted satellite television broadcasts because "no exception is 'specifically provided' for the unauthorized viewing of [such] signals").

Furthermore, as DIRECTV correctly observes, *β 2511(1)(a)* cannot be read to exclude the interception of encrypted satellite television broadcasts from its reach without rendering *β 2511(4)(b)* meaningless. When interpreting statutory language, we must, whenever possible, read the statute in such a manner as to give effect to every part of it. *Mountain States Tel. & Tel. Co. v. Santa Ana,* 472 U.S. 237, 249, 105 S. Ct. 2587, 86 L. Ed. 2d 168 (1985) (citing *Reiter v. Sonotone Corp.,* 442 U.S. 330, 339, 99 S. Ct. 2326, 60 L. Ed. 2d 931 (1979)). Here, Congress included *β 2511(4)(b)* to provide a specific exception for the interception of certain unencrypted satellite transmissions where the purpose is neither commercial nor for private financial gain. To read *β 2511(1)(a)* as excluding from its reach the interception of satellite transmissions in general, encrypted or not, would be to obviate the need for a particularized exception for *unencrypted* satellite transmissions.

Our conclusion that *β 2511(1)(a)* supports a civil claim comports with that of every other court of appeals to have considered the question. *See, e.g., DIRECTV Inc. v. Robson*, 420 F.3d 532, 537 (5th Cir. 2005); *Nicholas*, 403 F.3d at 226. Having concluded that *β 2511(1)(a)* renders the interception of encrypted satellite television broadcasts unlawful, it is plain that *β 2520(a)*, as discussed above, authorizes private suit for such activity: "any person whose . . . electronic communication is intercepted . . . in violation of this chapter may in a civil action recover from the person or entity . . . which engaged in that violation such relief as may be appropriate."

C

Relying on the statute's legislative history, case law, and a comparison of the damages provisions in the ECPA and the Communications Act, the District Court concluded that *47 U.S.C. β 605* supplants a private cause of action under the ECPA's provision in *18 U.S.C. β 2511(1)(a)* for the interception of encrypted satellite television broadcasts. As we will discuss, these considerations do not overcome the plain language of the statute, which controls our analysis.

1

The District Court singled out an excerpt from the record of Senate debate on the ECPA to conclude that *β 2511(1)(a)* does not authorize private suit on the present facts:

The private viewing of satellite cable programming, network feeds and certain audio subcarriers will continue to be governed exclusively by section 705 of the Communications Act, as amended, and not by chapter 119 of title 18 of the United States Code [ECPA, *18 U.S.C. β β 2510–2522*].

132 Cong. Rec. S14441 (daily ed. Oct. 1, 1986) (statement of Sen. Leahy). Taken on its face, this statement does state that *47 U.S.C. β 605* would govern exclusive of the ECPA. Notwithstanding, however, that we are bound not by legislative history but by plain statutory language, the balance of the legislative history directly contradicts this view. On the same date, a colloquy between Senators Danforth and Mathias is squarely contrary:

> Mr. DANFORTH. This legislation covers some conduct that also is prohibited under section 705 of the Communications Act of 1934. *Do I understand correctly that the sanctions contained in this legislation would be imposed in addition to, and not instead of, those contained in section 705 of the Communications Act?*
> Mr. MATHIAS. *That is correct.* This legislation is not intended to substitute for any liabilities for conduct that also is covered by section 705 of

the Communications Act. Similarly, it is not intended to authorize any conduct which otherwise would be prohibited by section 705. *The penalties provided for in the Electronic Communications Privacy Act are in addition to those which are provided by section 705 of the Communications Act.*

As a general rule, conduct which is illegal under section 705 of the Communications Act would also be illegal under this bill. . . .

The exception to the general rule is that we do not provide liability for the noncommercial private viewing of unscrambled network feeds to affiliated stations by the owners of home satellite dishes. Accountability for that conduct will be determined solely under section 705 of the Communications Act. *The private viewing of any other video transmissions not otherwise excepted by section 705(b) could be subject to action under both the Communications Act and this legislation.*

132 Cong. Rec. S14441 (daily ed. Oct. 1, 1986) (colloquy of Sens. Danforth & Mathias) (emphasis added). Here, Sen. Mathias took pains to state, several times even, that ß 705 of the Communications Act did not foreclose action under the ECPA. An exchange in the House of Representatives covered similar ground:

Mr. MOORHEAD. This legislation covers conduct that may be prohibited under section 705 of the Communications Act of 1934. *Do I understand correctly that the sanctions contained in this legislation would be imposed in addition to, and not instead of, those contained in section 705 and other sections of the Communications Act?*

Mr. KASTENMEIER. *That is correct.* This legislation is not intended to alter any rights or liabilities for conduct that also is covered by section 705 or other sections of the Communications Act. Similarly, it is not intended to authorize any conduct which otherwise would be prohibited by section 705 or other sections. It should be noted that we do not provide criminal liability for noncommercial, private viewing of unscrambled network feeds to affiliates by the owners of home satellite dishes. Accountability for that conduct will be determined solely under section 705 of the Communications Act. *The private viewing of any other video transmission not otherwise excepted by section 705(b) will be subject to action under both the Communications Act and this legislation.*

132 Cong. Rec. H8977 (daily ed. Oct. 1, 1986) (colloquy of Reps. Moorhead & Kastenmeier) (emphasis added). Like the colloquy cited above, this exchange unequivocally indicates that encrypted satellite transmissions are covered by both *47 U.S.C. ß 605 and* the ECPA, including *18 U.S.C. ß 2511.*

Based on a thorough reading of the legislative history as a whole, we cannot agree with the District Court's view that it supports the conclusion that the Communications Act provides DIRECTV's sole remedy for interception of its encrypted satellite television broadcasts.

2

The District Court also reasoned that the damages provisions of the ECPA and the Communications Act were irreconcilable, and that because damages awards under the Communications Act afford the court more latitude than the ECPA, the latter act did not provide a cause of action for the unauthorized interception of satellite television broadcasts. We cannot agree with this line of reasoning: the only conclusion to be drawn from the differing damages provisions is that courts should generally disallow double recovery. *See E.E.O.C. v. Waffle House, Inc.,* 534 U.S. 279, 297, 122 S. Ct. 754, 151 L. Ed. 2d 755 (2002) (courts should generally disallow double recovery). As we noted in our discussion of the legislative history *supra,* Congress intended that the damage provisions would not be mutually exclusive.

3

In refusing to find a cause of action under *β 2511(1)(a),* the District Court also relied on the pro-privacy policy considerations underlying the ECPA as expressed in our opinion in *Bartnicki v.* Vopper, 200 F.3d 109, 122 (3d Cir. 1999). In adjudicating the *First Amendment* questions at issue in *Bartnicki,* we noted that *β 2511(1)* protected victims from "the surreptitious interception of private communications" and "the dissemination of private information so obtained." 200 F.3d at 122. In this case the District Court took our language in *Bartnicki* to mean that *β 2511(1)* would apply only to wrongs against private persons, and not piracy against a commercial service such as DIRECTV.

Again, the plain language of the ECPA trumps other considerations, and compels an opposite conclusion. *Section 2520(a)* provides that "any *person* whose . . . electronic communication is intercepted . . . " can recover for violations of the ECPA. (Emphasis added.) In turn, *β 2510(6)* defines "person" to include "any individual, partnership, association, joint stock company, trust, or corporation." As a corporation, DIRECTV is a "person" within the meaning of the ECPA, and can therefore bring suit under it.

III

For the foregoing reasons, we conclude that Congress has made a private right of action available under *β β 2511(1)(a) and 2520 of the ECPA* for the unauthorized interception of encrypted satellite television broadcasts. Accordingly, we reverse the District Court's Orders in both cases to the extent that they deny DIRECTV's claims under *18 U.S.C. β β 2511(1)(a)* and *2520(a),* and remand both cases for further proceedings consistent with this opinion.

NOTES _____

1. DirecTV has been particularly vigilant in protecting itself against pirating of its signal. In *DirecTV, Inc. v. Randy Borow,* 2005 U.S. Dist. LEXIS 1328 (ND Ill., Jan. 3, 2005), defendant posted more than 1000 email messages on pirating sites touting his expertise in pirating plaintiff's satellite television broadcasts. Defendant openly subscribed to a piracy magazine and a piracy Internet forum. After commencement of the action by plaintiff, defendant erased all incriminating evidence from his computer. Defendant admitted to helping several people to

pirate DirecTV and to purchasing 24 piracy devices, yet claimed no wrongdoing. In granting plaintiff's motion for summary judgment, the Court cited defendant's repeated admissions, his attempt to destroy evidence and the several satellite software programs still on his computer when it was surrendered. In a subsequent decision, *DirecTV, Inc. v. Borow*, 2006 U.S. Dist. LEXIS 5036 (N.D. Ill., Jan. 24, 2006), the Court assessed damages of $1,000 per violation under *The Federal Communications Act-47 U.S.C. § 605(a)* for a total of $12,000 and awarded attorneys' fees in the amount of $90,000. Noting that DirecTV had requested attorneys' fees in excess of $185,000, the Court stated: "The court finds that attorneys' fees in the amount of $90,000.00 is appropriate given the protracted litigation in this case." The Complaint was filed in April 2003, and now, in 2006, the case is finally reaching a conclusion. Borow's recalcitrant and deceptive attitude resulted in DirecTV's counsel engaging in long, protracted procedural battles. For example, Borow filed a Motion for Extension of Time to respond to the summary judgment motion, DirecTV was required to respond to this motion, which required research, meetings, and several drafts of a response to Borow's Motion. All of this work resulted in a certain number of billable hours to complete a final product. While the court finds that the total number of hours spent on this litigation is excessive, counsel nonetheless exerted a significant number of hours, mostly as the result of Borow's delay, to respond to each filing. After "trimming the fat" off of counsel's excessive fees, the court finds that $90,000.00 is an appropriate fee, giving the constant delaying tactics employed by Borow, and counsel's efforts to respond to each of Borow's pleadings, regardless of his intentions in filing such motions. *See Tomazzoli, 804 F.2d at 98.*" See also, *DirecTV, Inc., v. Pete Schulien*, 401 F. Supp. 2d 906; 2005 U.S. Dist. LEXIS 28912 (E.D. Ill, Nov. 7, 2005) (television viewer admitted pirating plaintiff's satellite broadcast for 34 months and enabled others to do the same; court awarded damages in excess of $153,000 plus attorneys' fees); and similarly, *DirecTV, Inc. v. Michael Chavez*, 2004 U.S. Dist. LEXIS 2960 (N.D. Ill., Feb. 25, 2004); *DirecTV, Inc. v. Hoa Huynh*, 318 F. Supp. 2d 1122; 2004 U.S. Dist. LEXIS 9038 (M.D. Ala., May 19, 2004); and *DirecTV, Inc. v. John Wright*, 350 F. Supp. 2d 1048; 2004 U.S. Dist. LEXIS 25845 (N.D. Ga., 2004).

2. Protection of broadcast rights lie not only with the satellite provider. The content provider also polices the right to broadcast its materials. In *Garden City Boxing Club, Inc. v. Ayisah*, 2004 U.S. Dist. LEXIS 7867 (S.D.N.Y. 2004), plaintiff obtained the rights to distribute the Lennox Lewis/ Mike Tyson fight in 2002 live to establishments in New York that wished to show the fight publicly to customers. Plaintiff hired independent investigators to identify establishments that exhibited the fight without first securing the right to do so from plaintiff. Defendant, a restaurant, exhibited the fight and did not obtain the rights to do so from plaintiff. After a default judgment, the magistrate held a hearing to determine damages. In making its determination, the Court stated: "Defendants' public exhibition of the Lewis/Tyson fight was an unauthorized interception of radio and cable communications under *47 U.S.C. § 605*. That section provides, in pertinent part, that no person not being authorized by the sender shall intercept any radio communication and divulge or publish the . . . contents . . . of such intercepted communication to any person." Further, this section applies to transmissions which originate by radio or satellite, even if said signals are retransmitted by cable. *(citing cases)*. . . . Because it had a proprietary interest in the intercepted communications, Garden City is a "person aggrieved" within the meaning of *47 U.S.C. § 605 (d)(6)*, and is entitled to bring this action. . . . The record merely reflects that Garden City charged residential consumers $54.95 for pay-per-view access to the fight. Accepting Rielly's estimate that 60 patrons were in Olympus when the fight was shown, and then assessing damages at $50 per person (an amount that other courts have used and that approximates the residential customer rate provided by Garden City), would result in an award of $3,000. . . . Garden City further requests that, under

47 U.S.C. § 605(e)(3)(C)(ii), its damages be enhanced, as the defendants' violation of *Section 605* was purportedly both 'willful' and 'committed for financial gain or commercial advantage.' Specifically, Garden City requests that its damages be increased by the statutory maximum of $100,000. . . . Garden City's Complaint and other submissions are silent as to any prior violations by Olympus or Concepcion. Further, although it can be reasonably inferred that these defendants generated some revenue by showing the fight, Garden City makes no allegations that Olympus or Concepcion reaped 'substantial' monetary gains by its unlawful exhibition of the broadcast. Nor does Garden City delineate any actual damages that it suffered, in the form of lost license fees or otherwise. There is also no evidence of these defendants having advertised the broadcast. . . . Garden City does, however, allege that these defendants' display of the fight could not have been accidental. . . . In any event, Garden City argues that the fight in question could not have been 'mistakenly or innocently intercepted,' and therefore the defendants' conduct must have been willful. Other courts, on the basis of similar factual allegations, have awarded enhanced damages for this type of violation. *(internal citation omitted)* On the record presented in this case, I recommend that Garden City be awarded enhanced damages of $5,000 from Olympus and Concepcion, which is the same amount as was awarded in the *DeBlasio* case, on similar facts, to the same plaintiff." See also, *Garden City Boxing Club, Inc. v. Rodriquez et al.*, 2006 U.S. Dist. LEXIS 21537 (E.D.N.Y., 2006).

10.8.4 Infringement: Unaccredited Copying of Uncopyrighted Works

Sometimes trademark law conflicts with copyright law, with unexpected results. When a film producer incorporates a pre-existing film, which has fallen into the public domain, in a current production, what are the legal responsibilities of the producer regarding the previous copyright owners of the public domain film footage? Not much, according to Justice Antonin Scalia in *Dastar v. Twentieth Century Fox Film Corp.* below. The concern of many legal scholars is the subsequent expanded application of *Dastar,* beyond it being limited to just "source" attribution of an uncopyrighted (public domain) work.

Dastar Corporation, v. Twentieth Century Fox Film Corporation, et al., 539 U.S. 23, 123 S.Ct.,2041 (2003).

Justice *SCALIA* delivered the opinion of the Court, delivered the opinion of the Court, in which all other Members joined, except *BREYER*, J., who took no part in the consideration or decision of the case.

In this case, we are asked to decide whether §43(a) of the Lanham Act, *15 U.S.C. §1125(a)*, prevents the unaccredited copying of a work, and if so, whether a court may double a profit award under §1117(a), in order to deter future infringing conduct.

I

In 1948, three and a half years after the German surrender at Reims, General Dwight D. Eisenhower completed *Crusade in Europe,* his written account of the allied campaign in Europe during World War II. Doubleday published the book, registered it with the Copyright Office in 1948, and granted exclusive television rights to an affiliate of respondent Twentieth Century Fox Film Corporation (Fox). Fox, in turn, arranged for Time, Inc., to produce a television series, also called *Crusade in Europe,* based on the book, and Time assigned its copyright in the series to Fox. The television series, consisting of 26 episodes, was first broadcast in 1949. It combined a soundtrack based on a narration of the book with film footage from the United States Army, Navy, and Coast Guard, the British Ministry of Information and War Office, the National Film Board of Canada, and unidentified "Newsreel Pool Cameramen." In 1975, Doubleday renewed the copyright on the book as the " 'proprietor of copyright in a work made for hire.' " App. to Pet. for Cert. 9a. Fox, however, did not renew the copyright on the Crusade television series, which expired in 1977, leaving the television series in the public domain.

In 1988, Fox reacquired the television rights in General Eisenhower's book, including the exclusive right to distribute the Crusade television series on video and to sublicense others to do so. Respondents SFM Entertainment and New Line Home Video, Inc., in turn, acquired from Fox the exclusive rights to distribute Crusade on video. SFM obtained the negatives of the original television series, restored them, and repackaged the series on videotape; New Line distributed the videotapes.

Enter petitioner Dastar. In 1995, Dastar decided to expand its product line from music compact discs to videos. Anticipating renewed interest in World War II on the 50th anniversary of the war's end, Dastar released a video set entitled *World War II Campaigns in Europe.* To make Campaigns, Dastar purchased eight beta cam tapes of the *original* version of the Crusade television series, which is in the public domain, copied them, and then edited the series. Dastar's Campaigns series is slightly more than half as long as the original Crusade television series. Dastar substituted a new opening sequence, credit page, and final closing for those of the Crusade television series; inserted new chapter-title sequences and narrated chapter introductions; moved the "recap" in the Crusade television series to the beginning and retitled it as a "preview"; and removed references to and images of the book. Dastar created new packaging for its Campaigns series and (as already noted) a new title.

Dastar manufactured and sold the Campaigns video set as its own product. The advertising states: "Produced and Distributed by: *Entertainment Distributing*" (which is owned by Dastar), and makes no reference to the Crusade television series. Similarly, the screen credits state "DASTAR CORP presents" and "an ENTERTAINMENT DISTRIBUTING Production," and list as executive producer, producer, and associate producer employees of Dastar. Supp. App. 2–3, 30. The Campaigns videos themselves also make no reference to the Crusade television series, New Line's Crusade videotapes, or the book. Dastar sells its Campaigns videos to Sam's Club, Costco, Best Buy, and other retailers and mail-order companies for $25 per set, substantially less than New Line's video set.

In 1998, respondents Fox, SFM, and New Line brought this action alleging that Dastar's sale of its Campaigns video set infringes Doubleday's copyright in General Eisenhower's book and, thus, their exclusive television rights in the book. Respondents later amended their complaint to add claims that Dastar's sale of Campaigns "without proper credit" to the Crusade television series constitutes "reverse passing off"[N1] in violation of §43(a) of the Lanham Act, 60 Stat. 441, 15 U.S.C. §1125(a), and in violation of state unfair-competition law. App. to Pet. for Cert. 31a. On cross-motions for summary judgment, the District Court found for respondents on all three counts, *id.,* at 54a-55a, treating its resolution of the Lanham Act claim as controlling on the state-law unfair-competition claim because "the ultimate test under both is whether the public is likely to be deceived or confused," *id.,* at 54a. The court awarded Dastar's profits to respondents and doubled them pursuant to §35 of the Lanham Act, 15 U.S.C. §1117(a), to deter future infringing conduct by petitioner.

N1. Passing off (or palming off, as it is sometimes called) occurs when a producer misrepresents his own goods or services as someone else's. See, *e.g., O. & W. Thum Co. v. Dickinson,* 245 F. 609, 621 (C.A.6 1917). "Reverse passing off," as its name implies, is the opposite: The producer misrepresents someone else's goods or services as his own. See, *e.g., Williams v. Curtiss-Wright Corp.,* 691 F.2d 168, 172 (C.A.3 1982).

The Court of Appeals for the Ninth Circuit affirmed the judgment for respondents on the Lanham Act claim, but reversed as to the copyright claim and remanded. 34 Fed.Appx. 312, 316 (2002). (It said nothing with regard to the state-law claim.) With respect to the Lanham Act claim, the Court of Appeals reasoned that "Dastar copied substantially the entire *Crusade in Europe* series created by Twentieth Century Fox, labeled the resulting product with a different name and marketed it without attribution to Fox[, and] therefore committed a 'bodily appropriation' of Fox's series." *Id.,* at 314. It concluded that "Dastar's 'bodily appropriation' of Fox's original [television] series is sufficient to establish the reverse passing off." Ibid. The court also affirmed the District Court's award under the Lanham Act of twice Dastar's profits. We granted certiorari. 537 U.S. 1099, 123 S.Ct. 816, 154 L.Ed.2d 767 (2003).

II

The Lanham Act was intended to make "actionable the deceptive and misleading use of marks," and "to protect persons engaged in . . . commerce against unfair competition." 15 U.S.C. §1127. While much of the Lanham Act addresses the registration, use, and infringement of trademarks and related marks, §43(a), 15 U.S.C. §1125(a) is one of the few provisions that goes beyond trademark protection. As originally enacted, §43(a) created a federal remedy against a person who used in commerce either "a false designation of origin, or any false description or representation" in connection with "any goods or services."

60 Stat. 441. As the Second Circuit accurately observed with regard to the original enactment, however—and as remains true after the 1988 revision—§ 43(a) "does not have boundless application as a remedy for unfair trade practices," *Alfred Dunhill, Ltd. v. Interstate Cigar Co.*, 499 F.2d 232, 237 (C.A.2 1974). "[B]ecause of its inherently limited wording, §43(a) can never be a federal 'codification' of the overall law of 'unfair competition,'" *4 J. McCarthy, Trademarks and Unfair Competition* §27:7, p. 27–14 (4th ed. 2002) (McCarthy), but can apply only to certain unfair trade practices prohibited by its text.

Although a case can be made that a proper reading of §43(a), as originally enacted, would treat the word "origin" as referring only "to the geographic location in which the goods originated," *Two Pesos, Inc. v. Taco Cabana, Inc.*, 505 U.S. 763, 777, 112 S.Ct. 2753, 120 L.Ed.2d 615 (1992) (STEVENS, J., concurring in judgment),[N3] the Courts of Appeals considering the issue, beginning with the Sixth Circuit, unanimously concluded that it "does not merely refer to geographical origin, but also to origin of source or manufacture," *Federal-Mogul-Bower Bearings, Inc. v. Azoff, 313 F.2d 405, 408 (C.A.6 1963)*, thereby creating a federal cause of action for traditional trademark infringement of unregistered marks. *See* 4 McCarthy § 27:14; *Two Pesos, supra,* at 768, 112 S.Ct. 2753. Moreover, every Circuit to consider the issue found §43(a) broad enough to encompass reverse passing off. See, *e.g., Williams v. Curtiss-Wright Corp.*, 691 F.2d 168, 172 (C.A.3 1982); *Arrow United Indus., Inc. v. Hugh Richards, Inc.*, 678 F.2d 410, 415 (C.A.2 1982); *F.E.L. Publications, Ltd. v. Catholic Bishop of Chicago*, 214 USPQ 409, 416, 1982 WL 19198 (C.A.7 1982); *Smith v. Montoro*, 648 F.2d 602, 603 (C.A.9 1981); *Bangor Punta Operations, Inc. v. Universal Marine Co.*, 543 F.2d 1107, 1109 (C.A.5 1976). The Trademark Law Revision Act of 1988 made clear that §43(a) covers origin of production as well as geographic origin.[N4] Its language is amply inclusive, moreover, of reverse passing off—if indeed it does not implicitly adopt the unanimous court-of-appeals jurisprudence on that subject. See, *e.g., ALPO Petfoods, Inc. v. Ralston Purina Co.*, 913 F.2d 958, 963–964, n. 6 (C.A.D.C.1990) (Thomas, J.).

N3. In the original provision, the cause of action for false designation of origin was arguably "available only to a person doing business in the locality falsely indicated as that of origin," 505 U.S., at 778, n. 3, 112 S.Ct. 2753. As adopted in 1946, §43(a) provided in full:

"Any person who shall affix, apply, or annex, or use in connection with any goods or services, or any container or containers for goods, a false designation of origin, or any false description or representation, including words or other symbols tending falsely to describe or represent the same, and shall cause such goods or services to enter into commerce, and any person who shall with knowledge of the falsity of such designation of origin or description or representation cause or procure the same to be transported or used in commerce or deliver the same to any carrier to be transported or used, shall be liable to a civil action by any person doing business in the locality falsely indicated as that of origin or the region in which said locality is situated, or by any person who believes that he is or is likely to be damaged by the use of any such false description or representation." 60 Stat. 441.

N4. Section 43(a) of the Lanham Act now provides:

"Any person who, on or in connection with any goods or services, or any container for goods, uses in commerce any word, term, name, symbol, or device, or any combination thereof, or any false designation of origin, false or misleading description of fact, or false or misleading representation of fact, which–

"(A) is likely to cause confusion, or to cause mistake, or to deceive as to the affiliation, connection, or association of such person with another person, or as to the origin, sponsorship, or approval of his or her goods, services, or commercial activities by another person, or

"(B) in commercial advertising or promotion, misrepresents the nature, characteristics, qualities, or geographic origin of his or her or another person's goods, services, or commercial activities, shall be liable in a civil action by any person who believes that he or she is or is likely to be damaged by such act." 15 U.S.C. §1125(a)(1).

Thus, as it comes to us, the gravamen of respondents' claim is that, in marketing and selling Campaigns as its own product without acknowledging its nearly wholesale reliance on the Crusade television series, Dastar has made a "false designation of origin, false or misleading description of fact, or false or misleading representation of fact, which . . . is likely to cause confusion . . . as to the origin . . . of his or her goods." §43(a). See, *e.g.,* Brief for Respondents 8, 11. That claim would undoubtedly be sustained if Dastar had bought some of New Line's Crusade videotapes and merely repackaged them as its own. Dastar's alleged wrongdoing, however, is vastly different: It took a creative work in the public domain—the Crusade television series—copied it, made modifications (arguably minor), and produced its very own series of videotapes. If "origin" refers only to the manufacturer or producer of the physical "goods" that are made available to the public (in this case the videotapes), Dastar was the origin. If, however, "origin" includes the creator of the underlying work that Dastar copied, then someone else (perhaps Fox) was the origin of Dastar's product. At bottom, we must decide what §43(a)(1)(A) of the Lanham Act means by the "origin" of "goods."

III

The dictionary definition of "origin" is "[t]he fact or process of coming into being from a source," and "[t]hat from which anything primarily proceeds; source." Webster's New International Dictionary 1720–1721 (2d ed.1949). And the dictionary definition of "goods" (as relevant here) is "[w]ares; merchandise." *Id.,* at 1079. We think the most natural understanding of the "origin" of "goods"—the source of wares—is the producer of the tangible product sold in the marketplace, in this case the physical Campaigns videotape sold by Dastar. The concept might be stretched [as it was under the original version of §43(a)] [N5] to include not only the actual producer, but also the trademark owner who commissioned or assumed responsibility for ("stood behind") production of the physical product. But as used in the Lanham Act, the phrase "origin of goods" is in our view incapable of connoting the person or entity that originated the ideas or communications that "goods" embody or contain. Such an extension would not only stretch the text, but it would be out of accord with the history and purpose of the Lanham Act and inconsistent with precedent.

N5. Under the 1946 version of the Act, §43(a) was read as providing a cause of action for trademark infringement even where the trademark owner had not itself produced the goods sold under its mark, but had licensed others to sell under its name goods produced by them-the typical franchise arrangement. See, *e.g., My Pie Int'l, Inc. v. Debould, Inc.,* 687 F.2d 919 (C.A.7 1982). This stretching of the concept "origin of goods" is seemingly no longer needed: The 1988 amendments to §43(a) now expressly prohibit the use of any "word, term, name, symbol, or device," or "false or misleading description of fact" that is likely to cause confusion as to "affiliation, connection, or association . . . with another person," or as to "sponsorship, or approval" of goods. 15 U.S.C. §1125(a).

Section 43(a) of the Lanham Act prohibits actions like trademark infringement that deceive consumers and impair a producer's goodwill. It forbids, for example, the Coca-Cola Company's passing off its product as Pepsi-Cola or reverse passing off Pepsi-Cola as its product. But the brand-loyal consumer who prefers the drink that the Coca-Cola Company or PepsiCo sells, while he believes that that company produced (or at least stands behind the production of) that product, surely does not necessarily believe that that company was the "origin" of the drink in the sense that it was the very first to devise the formula. The consumer who buys a branded product does not automatically assume that the brand-name company is the same entity that came up with the idea for the product, or designed the product—and typically does not care whether it is. The words of the Lanham Act should not be stretched to cover matters that are typically of no consequence to purchasers.

It could be argued, perhaps, that the reality of purchaser concern is different for what might be called a communicative product—one that is valued not primarily for its physical qualities, such as a hammer, but for the intellectual content that it conveys, such as a book or, as here, a video. The purchaser of a novel is interested not merely, if at all, in the identity of the producer of the physical tome (the publisher), but also, and indeed primarily, in the identity of the creator of the story it conveys (the author). And the author, of course, has at least as much interest in avoiding passing off (or reverse passing off) of his creation as does the publisher. For such a communicative product (the argument goes) "origin of goods" in §43(a) must be deemed to include not merely the producer of the physical item (the publishing house Farrar, Straus and Giroux, or the video producer Dastar) but also the creator of the content that the physical item conveys (the author Tom Wolfe, or—assertedly—respondents).

The problem with this argument according special treatment to communicative products is that it causes the Lanham Act to conflict with the law of copyright, which addresses that subject specifically. The right to copy, and to copy without attribution, once a copyright has expired, like "the right to make [an article whose patent has expired]—including the right to make it in precisely the shape it carried when patented—passes to the public." *Sears, Roebuck & Co. v. Stiffel Co.*, 376 U.S. 225, 230, 84 S.Ct. 784, 11 L.Ed.2d 661 (1964); *see also Kellogg Co. v. National Biscuit Co.*, 305 U.S. 111, 121–122, 59 S.Ct. 109, 83 L.Ed. 73 (1938). "In general, unless an intellectual property right such as a patent or copyright protects an item, it will be subject to copying." *TrafFix Devices, Inc. v. Marketing Displays, Inc.*, 532 U.S. 23, 29, 121 S.Ct. 1255, 149 L.Ed.2d 164 (2001). The rights of a patentee or copyright holder are part of a "carefully crafted bargain," *Bonito Boats, Inc. v. Thunder Craft Boats, Inc.*, 489 U.S. 141, 150–151, 109 S.Ct. 971, 103 L.Ed.2d 118 (1989), under which, once the patent or copyright monopoly has expired, the public may use the invention or work at will and without attribution. Thus, in construing the Lanham Act, we have been "careful to caution against misuse or over-extension" of trademark and related protections into areas traditionally occupied by patent or copyright. *TrafFix*, 532 U.S., at 29, 121 S.Ct. 1255. "The Lanham Act," we have said, "does not exist to reward manufacturers for their innovation in creating a particular device; that is the purpose of the patent law and its period of exclusivity." *Id., at 34, 121 S.Ct. 1255.* Federal trademark law "has no necessary relation to invention or discovery," *In re Trade-Mark Cases*, 100 U.S. 82, 94, 25 L.Ed. 550 (1879), but rather, by preventing competitors from copying "a source-identifying mark," "reduce[s] the customer's costs of shopping and making purchasing decisions," and "helps assure a producer that it (and not an imitating competitor) will reap the financial, reputation-related rewards associated with a desirable product," *Qualitex Co. v. Jacobson Products Co.*, 514 U.S. 159, 163–164, 115 S.Ct. 1300, 131 L.Ed.2d 248 (1995) (internal quotation marks and citation omitted). Assuming for the sake of argument that Dastar's representation of itself as the "Producer" of its videos amounted to a representation that it originated the creative work conveyed by the videos, allowing a cause of action under §43(a) for that representation would create a species of mutant copyright law that limits the public's "federal right to 'copy and to use'" expired copyrights, *Bonito Boats, supra*, at 165, 109 S.Ct. 971.

When Congress has wished to create such an addition to the law of copyright, it has done so with much more specificity than the Lanham Act's ambiguous use of "origin." The Visual Artists Rights Act of 1990, §603(a), 104 Stat. 5128, provides that the author of an artistic work "shall have the right . . . to claim authorship of that work." 17 U.S.C. §106A(a)(1)(A). That express right of attribution is carefully limited and focused: It attaches only to specified "work[s] of visual art," §101, is personal to the artist, §§106A(b) and (e), and endures only for "the life of the author," §106A(d)(1). Recognizing in §43(a) a cause of action for misrepresentation of authorship of noncopyrighted works (visual or otherwise) would render these limitations superfluous. A statutory interpretation that renders another statute superfluous is of course to be avoided. *E.g., Mackey v. Lanier Collection Agency & Service, Inc.*, 486 U.S. 825, 837, and n. 11, 108 S.Ct. 2182, 100 L.Ed.2d 836 (1988).

Reading "origin" in §43(a) to require attribution of uncopyrighted materials would pose serious practical problems. Without a copyrighted work as the basepoint, the word "origin" has no discernable limits. A video of the MGM film Carmen Jones, after its copyright has expired, would presumably require attribution not just to MGM, but to Oscar Hammerstein II (who wrote the musical on which the film was based), to Georges Bizet (who wrote the opera on which the musical was based), and to Prosper Merimee (who wrote the novel on which the opera was based). In many cases, figuring out who is in the line of "origin" would be no simple task. Indeed, in the present case it is far from clear that respondents have that status. Neither SFM nor New Line had anything to do with the production of the Crusade television series—they merely were licensed to distribute the video version. While Fox might have a claim to being in the line of origin, its involvement with the creation of the television series was limited at best. Time, Inc., was the principal, if not the exclusive, creator, albeit under arrangement with Fox. And of course it was neither Fox nor Time, Inc., that shot the film used in the Crusade television series. Rather, that footage came from the United States Army, Navy, and Coast Guard, the British Ministry of Information and War Office, the National Film Board of Canada, and unidentified "Newsreel Pool Cameramen." If anyone has a claim to being the *original* creator of the material used in both the Crusade television series and the Campaigns videotapes, it would be those groups, rather than Fox. We do not think the Lanham Act requires this search for the source of the Nile and all its tributaries.

Another practical difficulty of adopting a special definition of "origin" for communicative products is that it places the manufacturers of those products in a difficult position. On the one hand, they would face Lanham Act liability for *failing* to credit the creator of a work on which their lawful copies are based; and on the other hand they could face Lanham Act liability for *crediting* the creator if that should be regarded as implying the creator's "sponsorship or approval" of the copy, 15 U.S.C. §1125(a)(1)(A). In this case, for example, if Dastar had simply "copied [the television series] as Crusade in Europe and sold it as Crusade in Europe," without changing the title or packaging (including the original credits to Fox), it is hard to have confidence in respondents' assurance that they "would not be here on a Lanham Act cause of action," Tr. of Oral Arg. 35.

Finally, reading §43(a) of the Lanham Act as creating a cause of action for, in effect, plagiarism—the use of otherwise unprotected works and inventions without attribution—would be hard to reconcile with our previous decisions. For example, in *Wal-Mart Stores, Inc. v. Samara Brothers, Inc.*, 529 U.S. 205, 120 S.Ct. 1339, 146 L.Ed.2d 182 (2000), we considered whether product-design trade dress can ever be inherently distinctive. Wal-Mart produced "knockoffs" of children's clothes designed and manufactured by Samara Brothers, containing only "minor modifications" of the original designs. *Id., at 208, 120 S.Ct. 1339.* We concluded that the designs could not be protected under § 43(a) without a showing that they had acquired "secondary meaning," *id., at 214,*

120 S.Ct. 1339, so that they " 'identify the source of the product rather than the product itself,' " id., at 211, 120 S.Ct. 1339 (quoting *Inwood Laboratories, Inc. v. Ives Laboratories, Inc.*, 456 U.S. 844, 851, n. 11, 102 S.Ct. 2182, 72 L.Ed.2d 606 (1982)). This carefully considered limitation would be entirely pointless if the "original" producer could turn around and pursue a reverse-passing-off claim under exactly the same provision of the Lanham Act. Samara would merely have had to argue that it was the "origin" of the designs that Wal-Mart was selling as its own line. It was not, because "origin of goods" in the Lanham Act referred to the producer of the clothes, and not the producer of the (potentially) copyrightable or patentable designs that the clothes embodied.

Similarly under respondents' theory, the "origin of goods" provision of §43(a) would have supported the suit that we rejected in *Bonito Boats*, 489 U.S. 141, 109 S.Ct. 971, where the defendants had used molds to duplicate the plaintiff's unpatented boat hulls (apparently without crediting the plaintiff). And it would have supported the suit we rejected in *TrafFix*, 532 U.S. 23, 121 S.Ct. 1255: The plaintiff, whose patents on flexible road signs had expired, and who could not prevail on a trade-dress claim under § 43(a) because the features of the signs were functional, would have had a reverse-passing-off claim for unattributed copying of his design.

In sum, reading the phrase "origin of goods" in the Lanham Act in accordance with the Act's common-law foundations (which were *not* designed to protect originality or creativity), and in light of the copyright and patent laws (which *were*), we conclude that the phrase refers to the producer of the tangible goods that are offered for sale, and not to the author of any idea, concept, or communication embodied in those goods. Cf. 17 U.S.C. §202 (distinguishing between a copyrighted work and "any material object in which the work is embodied"). To hold otherwise would be akin to finding that §43(a) created a species of perpetual patent and copyright, which Congress may not do. See *Eldred v. Ashcroft*, 537 U.S. 186, 208, 123 S.Ct. 769, 154 L.Ed.2d 683 (2003).

The creative talent of the sort that lay behind the Campaigns videos is not left without protection. The original film footage used in the Crusade television series could have been copyrighted, see 17 U.S.C. §102(a)(6), as was copyrighted (as a compilation) the Crusade television series, even though it included material from the public domain, see §103(a). Had Fox renewed the copyright in the Crusade television series, it would have had an easy claim of copyright infringement. And respondents' contention that Campaigns infringes Doubleday's copyright in General Eisenhower's book is still a live question on remand. If, moreover, the producer of a video that substantially copied the Crusade series were, in advertising or promotion, to give purchasers the impression that the video was quite different from that series, then one or more of the respondents might have a cause of action—not for reverse passing off under the "confusion . . . as to the origin" provision of §43(a)(1)(A), but for misrepresentation under the "misrepresents the nature, characteristics [or] qualities" provision of § 43(a)(1)(B). For merely saying it is the producer of the video, however, no Lanham Act liability attaches to Dastar.

* * *

Because we conclude that Dastar was the "origin" of the products it sold as its own, respondents cannot prevail on their Lanham Act claim. We thus have no occasion to consider whether the Lanham Act permitted an award of double petitioner's profits. The judgment of the Court of Appeals for the Ninth Circuit is reversed, and the case is remanded for further proceedings consistent with this opinion.

It is so ordered.

Justice BREYER took no part in the consideration or decision of this case.

Chapter 11

THE INTERNET AND THE DIGITAL WORLD

11.1 INTRODUCTION

In the fourth edition of this book, released in 2001, the authors stated "[t]he main themes of this book find their most poignant expression in the newest—and most rapidly expanding—entertainment industries, the Internet and multimedia technologies. Over 100 million Americans used the Internet in 1999, and the number continues to grow as bandwidth increases and digital subscriber lines become available more widely." At the time of the printing of the fourth edition, the Internet seemed like the California Gold Rush, the dot com "bubble" had yet to burst, and everyone with the merest glimmer of an idea believed they could start a website and become an instant millionaire—thanks to the flood of advertising revenue that would *inevitably* come pouring in. Like the vast majority of gold miners, most of the early web entrepreneurs went bust. Perhaps the signal event of those times was the January 2000 merger of AOL and Time Warner Inc. Many in the media, and in the nation in general, seemed stunned that one of the great, old-line media companies could be gobbled up by a very young "tech" company. In the end, the transaction was a failure; and in October 2003, AOL Time Warner dropped "AOL" from its name. As Penelope Pasturis wrote in Forbes.com January, 24, 2001, "Time Warner got duped by the AOL hype, and the employees of both outfits are going to pay the price." Hindsight would have added that the Time Warner shareholders would pay a heavy price as well.

Since the bursting of the tech bubble, digital companies have made a comeback and are the most exciting growth companies of the entertainment industries. As of December 31, 2005, 68.1% of North Americans, and 15.7% of the world as a whole, use the Internet. "Internet Usage Statistics—The Big Picture," www.internetworldstats.com, 2006. Fourteen million iPods were sold in the fourth quarter of 2005, an increase from

4.5 million in the same period of 2004. Satellite radio providers showed strong subscriber growth in 2005, with XM adding 2.7 million subscribers for a total of 6 million, and Sirius adding 2.1 million for a total of 3.3 million. In the fourth quarter alone, Sirius added 1.1 million subscribers, due to the fact that it inked a well-publicized, multi-million dollar deal with radio's biggest personality, Howard Stern. Katy Bachman, "XM, Sirius Satellite Radios Hit Subscriber Goals," www.mediaweek.com, January 5, 2006. According to the International Federation of the Phonographic Industry (IFPI), globally, there are over 335 legal download sites, while digital downloads via mobile phones and the Internet resulted in sales of $1.1 billion (6% of overall record industry sales), up from $380 million in 2004. Alex Veiga, "U.S. Music Album Sales Down 7 Percent," *Yahoo! News,* December 28, 2005. 420 million paid downloads occurred in 2005, twice the number recorded in 2004 and twenty times the number in 2003. Phil Gallo, "Digital Music Triple Play," *Daily Variety,* January 20, 2006, p.1. In the U.S., legitimate downloads accounted for sales of $332.7 million, as compared to $134.2 million in 2004. iTunes recorded its one billionth download, in less than three years of operation. Antony Bruno, "iTunes Reaches Billion Download Milestone," www.billboard.biz, February 23, 2006. Digital video recorders (DVRs), video iPods, digital radio, increasingly powerful and multi-functional mobile phones, "podcasting," "blogs," and social networking websites like MySpace and Tagworld have people and entities throughout the entertainment industries scrambling for new ways to reach potential consumers with content and advertising. These new formats hold the promise of a level playing field, where musical, video, or other artists may be able to reach a heretofore unimaginably large audience without the muscle and money of the established media companies. Although the "little guy" now has a chance to build a career on his own, the challenge becomes how to actually get attention from all those ears and eyes, when most people are buried under an avalanche of incoming information.

Despite the foregoing exciting developments, all is not rosy in the current media climate: U.S. album sales were down 7% in 2005 (LPs and singles fell 8%) and CDs still represented more than 95% of total sales. See Veiga, *supra.* In 31 countries, sales of pirated compact discs exceeded sales of legitimate compact discs and the IFPI estimates 1.2 billion counterfeit CDs were sold in 2004 alone. "One In Three Music CDs is Stolen," www.cnnmoney.com, June 24, 2005.

CD music sales continue to plummet. At the same time, Big Champagne, a Los Angeles market research firm, says visits to illegal file-swapping sites are hitting new heights with 6.25 million users a month in the United States. . . . On Wednesday, the Business Software Alliance of Washington, D.C., released results of a survey showing how far the music industry has to go: Two-thirds of college and university students surveyed see nothing unethical about swapping or downloading digital copyrighted files—software, music and movies— without paying for them and more than half—52 percent—think it is also acceptable behavior in the workplace.

Mike Langberg, "Piracy unpreventable. Plan B: Just make music free."
www.mercurynews.com, July 1, 2005.

In a relatively short period of time, we have gotten to a place where the public readily accepts that a bottle of water at a sporting event is worth $4.50, but believes music should be free. (It wasn't so long ago that music had value and the idea of paying for water seemed crazy.) Even the videogame business, which boomed between 2000 and 2004 (videogame software and hardware sales increased from $6.7 billion to $9.9 billion) softened in 2005, with sales for gaming consoles like the Microsoft Xbox and Sony PlayStation2 declining by 12 percent. Robert Levine, "Wave of Video Game Fatigue Afflicts Sales, Not Thumbs," www.nytimes.com, February 6, 2006.

The first issue we address in chapter 11 is jurisdiction: As we see in the *Bensusan* and *Zippo* decisions that follow, jurisdiction within the United States has been addressed on numerous occasions and a substantial body of case law has already been established. In addition, at least one case, *Meckler Media Corp. DC Congress GmbH,* High Court (Chancery) (U.K.), March 7, 1997, Ch. 40 [1998] All. E.R. 148 [1997] F.S.R. 627, has upheld jurisdiction in the United Kingdom based on acts in Germany. But what law controls when a French citizen downloads a recording from a website based in the United States, or vice versa? If one music publisher has the rights to a song in the United States and Canada but another publisher has the rights for Europe (a common occurrence), which publisher is entitled to issue (and collect for) the mechanical reproduction license?

Since the publication of the fourth edition, protests against globalization have become commonplace and are a regular occurrence at international trade conferences. In the case of the Internet, there are no borders and globalization is a given, but power struggles have begun as other nations and entities (e.g. the European Union, Brazil and China) struggle with the Unites States over control of the Internet.

The Internet also presents issues of security, over and apart from the threat presented by the peer-to-peer sites. Numerous incidents of private information leaks have surfaced in recent years. The February 2000 DOS (denial of service) attacks on Yahoo, Amazon.com, eBay, CNN.com, Etrade, and Excite, among others was remarkable for a number of reasons, one of which was "how much the hackers had done with so little. The kind of software used for the attack [was] practically public property." Chris Taylor, "Behind the Hack Attack," *Time,* February 21, 2000, p. 45.

The expansion of the digital "universe" has meant a struggle to determine how existing rights would translate into a new paradigm. Questions have been raised regarding the degree to which pre-Internet grants of rights are sufficiently broad to permit those who acquired the rights to exercise them in the new medium. For example, in *Tasini v. The New York Times, Co.*, Sec. 7.4, *supra,* a group of freelance journalists convinced the Second Circuit that their contracts with various newspapers and magazines did not permit the latter to put the writers' articles up piecemeal on the media's websites where they could be accessed individually rather than as part of the editions in which the articles had originally appeared. In an action on behalf of recording artists, who recorded many years ago, challenging the right of their record companies to exploit their recordings via the Internet, was dismissed on the basis of broad contractual grants of rights. *Chambers v. Time Warner, Inc.*, 123 F. Supp. 2d198, 57 U.S.P.Q. 2d 1314 (SDNY 2000). The action was filed shortly after the commencement of the *Napster* action.

Analyzing the Internet provides its own unique challenges. MP3 technology, for example, does not fit neatly into pre-existing legislative pigeonholes, as we see in *RIAA v. Diamond Multimedia Systems, Inc.* (Section 11.5.2), in which the Ninth Circuit held that the Diamond Rio portable player was not only not an infringement of copyright, but it did not even constitute a digital recording device under the Audio Home Recording Act of 1992. Unauthorized hyperlinks via framing can bring liability with them, as we see in Section 11.3.2.

The regulation of content and the continuing push for censorship is evident in the online world, as we see in section 11.3. The booming Chinese economy has attracted many businesses, including web portals like Yahoo! and Google. Both companies faced enormous criticism recently, when it came to light that they were censoring search results on topics such as the Falun Gong movement and democracy. According to human rights groups, Yahoo! has turned over email records to the Chinese government resulting in imprisonment of dissidents. "Human Rights Groups Are Not Yelling 'Yahoo!'," Jake Tapper and Avery Miller, *www.abcnews.com,* February 9, 2006. Chinese government repression may be an easy target for our criticism, but a closer call might be the recent situation where French restrictions on hate speech conflicted with free speech rights protected by the First Amendment: Yahoo! filed a declaratory judgment action in U.S. federal court to protest a French court's order that required Yahoo! to "take all necessary measures to dissuade and render impossible any access via yahoo.com to the Nazi artifact auction service and to any other site or service that may be construed as constituting an apology for Nazism or a contesting of Nazi crimes." "Court Dismisses Yahoo Free Speech Lawsuit," Declan McCullagh, www.c/netnews.com, January 12, 2006. Because of legislators' concern about the ease of access available to minors, there already have been a number of attempts to limit Internet content. In a recent development, Congress enacted the Family Movie Act which allows for development of software to make "objectionable" scenes and language "imperceptible" by viewers. 17 U.S.C. §110 (11).

One area that has been the source of considerable contention is the extent to which Internet Service Providers (ISPs) can be held liable for defamation, copyright infringement, trademark infringement, or other torts committed by those who avail themselves of an ISP's facilities. *Zeran v. America Online* (Section 11.4) is consistent with cases such as *Lerman v. Flynt Distributing Co.*, as is the protection provided by section 202 of the Digital Millennium Copyright Act (Section 11.5.1). Industry insiders watched on the edge of their seats as the *Aimster, Napster,* and finally *Grokster* decisions were handed down. The recording industry hailed the *Grokster* decision as a great victory, but global music piracy remains a significant threat to the continued health of the music (as well as the film) business. According to the BBC, "[t]he level of file sharing has remained the same for two years, despite 20,000 legal cases in 17 countries." www.newsvote.bbc.co.uk, January 20, 2006.

Finally, what of contracts entered into over the Internet? These, after all, are the key to e-commerce. As we see in the section of Jeffrey Neuburger's and Suellen Bergman's article reproduced in Section 11.7, the concept of the "click-wrap" agreement is alive and well, but must be dealt with cautiously. Verisign estimates that 6 percent of all ecommerce transactions are fraudulent. "Internet Commerce Grows 88 Percent By Dollar Value and 39 Percent By Transaction Volume: Fraud Remains A Concern," www.verisign.com, February 28, 2005. This trend presents e-tailers with a problem their "brick & mortar" counterparts do not face: When a transaction is CNP (credit card lingo for "card not present," which is always the case when a transaction occurs on the Internet), the merchant takes the risk that the merchant has been defrauded by the customer. In the traditional retailing world, by contrast, the risk of loss in such a situation falls on the credit card company.

NOTES _____

1. Several treatises are available in this area, all of which are in loose-leaf format and are supplemented on a regular basis.

   (a) Richard Raysman, Peter Brown, Jeffrey D. Neuburger, and William E. Bandon, III, *Emerging Technologies and the Law: Forms and Analysis* (New York: Law Journal-Seminars Press, 1998)
   (b) Michael D. Scott, *Scott on Multimedia Law* (Englewood Cliffs, NJ: Aspen Law & Business, 1993)
   (c) Kent D. Stuckey, *Internet and Online Law* (New York: Law Journal Press 1996)

2. *Internet Law and Strategies* is published by Aspen Law & Business, 7201 McKinney Circle, Frederick, MD 21704. 1–800–638–8437.

11.2 PERSONAL JURISDICTION

Traditionally, in order for a court to exercise personal jurisdiction over a nonresident defendant, the court must ascertain whether the defendant's contacts with the forum state satisfy the requirements of the state's long-arm statute. Additionally, the court must determine whether exercising jurisdiction over the defendant would satisfy traditional notions of "fair play and substantial justice."

With the increased use of the Internet, courts are frequently confronted with the issue of whether the businesses and individuals are subject to personal jurisdiction wherever their website may be accessed. As the Internet becomes an increasingly important commercial marketing tool, courts have attempted to apply the traditional analys to this emerging technology. As the following cases will demonstrate, a court's decision to exercise personal jurisdiction over a defendant depends on how interactive the defendant's website is. Furthermore, the courts are more likely to find personal jurisdiction if the defendant has made a sufficient number of non-Internet contacts with the forum state.

Bensusan Restaurant Corp. v. King, 937 F. Supp. 295 (SDNY 1996), aff'd 126 F.3d 25 (2d Cir. 1997)

Stein, District Judge

Plaintiff Bensusan Restaurant Corp. ("Bensusan") brought this action against defendant Richard King, individually and doing business as The Blue Note, alleging that King is infringing on Bensusan's rights in its trademark "The Blue Note." King has moved to dismiss the complaint for lack of personal jurisdiction pursuant to Fed.R.Civ.P. 12(b)(2). The issue raised by that motion is whether the existence of a "site" on the World Wide Web of the Internet, without anything more, is sufficient to vest this Court with personal jurisdiction over defendant pursuant to New York's long-arm statute and the Due Process Clause of the United States Constitution. For the reasons that follow, the motion to dismiss the complaint is granted.

I. BACKGROUND

Bensusan, a New York corporation, is the creator of a jazz club in New York City known as "The Blue Note." It also operates other jazz clubs around the world. Bensusan owns all right, title and interest in and to the federally registered mark "The Blue Note." King is an individual who lives in Columbia, Missouri, and he owns and operates a "small club" in that city which is also called "The Blue Note."

In April of 1996, King posted a "site" on the World Wide Web of the Internet to promote his club. . . . This Web site, which is located on a computer server in Missouri, allegedly contains "a fanciful logo which is substantially similar to the logo utilized by [Bensusan]." The Web site is a general access site, which means that it requires no authentication or access code for entry, and is accessible to anyone around the world who has access to the Internet. It contains general information about the club in Missouri as well as a calendar of events and ticketing information. The ticketing information includes the names and addresses of ticket outlets in Columbia and a telephone number for charge-by-phone ticket orders, which are available for pick-up on the night of the show at the Blue Note box office in Columbia.

At the time this action was brought, the first page of the Web site contained the following disclaimer: "The Blue Note's Cyberspot should not be confused with one of the world's finest jazz club[s] [the] Blue Note, located in the heart of New York's Greenwich Village. If you should find yourself in the big apple give them a visit." Furthermore, the reference to Bensusan's club in the disclaimer contained a "hyperlink"* which permits Internet users to connect directly to Bensusan's Web site by "clicking" on the link. After Bensusan objected to the Web site, King dropped the sentence "If you should find yourself in the big apple give them a visit" from the disclaimer and removed the hyperlink.

Bensusan brought this action asserting claims for trademark infringement, trademark dilution and unfair competition. King has now moved to dismiss the action for lack of personal jurisdiction pursuant to Fed. R.Civ.P. 12(b)(2).

II. DISCUSSION

... Knowing that personal jurisdiction over a defendant is measured by the law of the jurisdiction in which the federal court sits, Bensusan relies on subdivisions(a)(2) and (a)(3)(ii) of N.Y.C.P.L.R. 302, New York's long-arm statute, to support its position that personal jurisdiction exists over King in this action. Each provision will be addressed in turn.

A. C.P.L.R. 302(A)(2)

C.P.L.R. 302(a)(2) permits a court to exercise personal jurisdiction over any non-domiciliary who "commits a tortious act within the state" as long as the cause of action asserted arises from the tortious act [citations omitted].

In *Vanity Fair Mills, Inc. v. T. Eaton Co.*, 234 F.2d 633, 639 (2d Cir.), *cert .denied*, 352 U.S. 871, 77 S.Ct. 96, 1 L.Ed.2d 76 (1956), the United States Court of Appeals for the Second Circuit held that trademark infringement occurs" where the passing off occurs, i.e., where the deceived customer buys the defendant's product in the belief that he is buying the plaintiff's." Under this standard, courts have found that an offering for sale of even one copy of an infringing product in New York, even if no sale results, is sufficient to vest a court with jurisdiction over the alleged infringer. See *Editorial Musical Latino Americana*, 829 F. Supp. at 64–65; *German Educational Television Network, Ltd. v. Oregon Public Broadcasting Co.*, 569 F. Supp. 1529 (S.D.N.Y. 1983); [other citations omitted]. Accordingly, the issue that arises in this action is whether the creation of a Web site, which exists either in Missouri or in cyberspace—i.e., anywhere the Internet exists—with a telephone number to order the allegedly infringing product, is an offer to sell the product in New York.

Even after construing all allegations in the light most favorable to Bensusan, its allegations are insufficient to support a finding of long-arm jurisdiction over plaintiff. A New York resident with Internet access and either knowledge of King's Web site location or a "search engine" capable of finding it could gain access to the Web site and view information concerning the Blue Note in Missouri.

It takes several affirmative steps by the New York resident, however, to obtain access to the Web site and utilize the information there. First, the New York resident has to access the Web site using his or her computer hardware and software. See *Shea,* 930 F. Supp. at 930. Then, if the user wished to attend a show in defendant's club, he or she would have to telephone the box office in Missouri and reserve tickets. Finally, that user would need to pick up the tickets in Missouri because King does not mail or otherwise transmit tickets to the user. Even assuming that the user was confused about the relationship of the Missouri club to the one in New York, such an act of infringement would have occurred in Missouri, not New York. The mere fact that a person can gain information on the allegedly infringing product is not the equivalent of a person advertising, promoting, selling or otherwise making an effort to target its product in New York. See *Hertz,* 549 F. Supp. at 797. Here, there is simply no allegation or proof that any infringing goods were shipped into New York or that any other infringing activity was directed at New York or caused by King to occur here. Cf. *People v. Concert Connection,* Ltd., 211 A.D.2d. 310, 314, 629 N.Y.S.2d 254, 257 (2d Dep't. 1995), *appeal dismissed,* 86 N.Y.2d 837, 634 N.Y.S.2d 445, 658 N.E.2d 223 (1995) (Table).

According, C.P.L.R. 302(a)(2) does not authorize this Court to exercise jurisdiction over King.

B. C.P.L.R. 302(a)(3)(ii)

Bensusan also contends that personal jurisdiction is established pursuant to C.P.L.R. 302(a)(3)(ii), which permits a court to exercise personal jurisdiction over any non-domiciliary for tortious acts committed outside the state that cause injury in the state if the non-domiciliary "expects or should reasonably expect the act to have consequences in the state and derives substantial revenue from interstate or international commerce." See *American Eutectic Welding Alloys Sales Co. v. Dytron Alloys Corp.,* 439 F.2d 428, 432–35 (2d Cir. 1971) [other citations omitted].

As an initial matter, Bensusan does not allege that King derives substantial revenue from interstate or international commerce. Instead, it relies on arguments that King participates in interstate commerce by hiring and showcasing bands of national stature. Section 302(a)(3)(ii), however, explicitly states that substantial "revenue" is required from interstate commerce, not mere participation in it. King has submitted an affidavit stating that 99% of his patronage and revenue is derived from local residents of Columbia, Missouri (primarily students from the University of Missouri), and that most of the few out-of-state customers have either an existing or a prior connection to the area, such as graduates of the University of Missouri.

Moreover, Bensusan's allegations of foreseeability, which are based solely on the fact that King knew that Bensusan's club is located in New York, is insufficient to satisfy the requirement that a defendant "expects or should reasonably expect the act to have consequences in the state." That prong of the statute requires that a defendant make "a discernable effort . . . to serve, directly or indirectly, a market in the forum state." *Darienzo v. Wise Shoe Stores, Inc.,* 74 A.D.2d 342, 346, 427 N.Y.S.2d 831, 834 (N.V. App. Div. 2d Dep't. 1980).

Finally, Bensusan's conclusory allegation of a loss in New York is nothing more that an allegation of an "indirect financial loss resulting from the fact that the injured person resides or is domiciled in New York," which is not the allegation of a "significant economic injury" required by section 302(a)(3) [citations omitted].

Accordingly, C.P.L.R. 302(a)(3) does not authorize this Court to exercise jurisdiction over King.

Bensusan's primary argument in support of both statutory bases for personal jurisdiction is that, because defendant's Web site is accessible in New York, defendant could have foreseen that the site was able to be viewed in New York and taken steps to restrict access to his site only to users in a certain geographic region, presumably Missouri. Regardless of the technical feasibility of such a procedure, see *Shea,* 930 F. Supp. at 929–30, 933–34, mere foreseeability of an in-state consequence and a failure to avert that consequence is not sufficient to establish personal jurisdiction. See *Fox v. Boucher,* 794 F.2d 34, 37 (2d Cir. 1986); *Taurus Int'l Inc. v. Titan Wheel Int'l Inc.,* 892 F. Supp. 79, 82 (S.D.N.Y. 1995).

C. Due Process

Furthermore, even if jurisdiction were proper under New York's long-arm statute, asserting personal jurisdiction over King in this forum would violate the Due Process Clause of the United States Constitution. See, e.g., *Burger King Corp. v. Rudzewicz,* 471 U.S. 462, 475–76, 105 S.Ct. 2174, 2183–84, 85 L.Ed.2d 528 (1985); *World-Wide Volkswagen Corp. v. Woodson,* 444 U.S. 286, 292, 100 S.Ct. 559, 564, 62 L.Ed.2d 4980 (1980); see also Richard S. Zembek, Comment, Jurisdiction and the Internet: Fundamental Fairness in the Networked World of Cyperspace, 6 Alb. L.J. Sci. & Tech. 339, 367–80 (1996). Due process requires "that the non-resident defendant has purposefully established 'minimum contact' with the forum state such that the 'maintenance of the suit does not offend' traditional notions of fair play and substantial justice" *Darby v. Compagnie Nationale Air France,* 769 F. Supp. 1255, 1262 (S.D.N.Y. 1991) (quoting *International Shoe Co. v. Washington,* 326 U.S. 310, 316, 66 S.Ct. 154, 158, 90 L.Ed. 95 (1945)).

The following factors are relevant to this determination: "(1) whether the defendant purposefully availed himself of the benefits of the forum state; (2)whether the defendant's conduct and connection with the forum state are such that he should reasonably anticipate being hauled into court there; and (3)whether the defendant carries on a continuous and systematic part of its general business within the forum state." *Independent Nat'l Distributors, Inc. v. Black Rain Communications,* Inc., No. 94 Civ. 8464, 1995 WL 571449, at *5–6 (S.D.N.Y. Sept. 28, 1995).

As set forth above, King has done nothing to purposefully avail himself of the benefits of New York. King, like numerous others, simply created a Web site and permitted anyone who could find it to access it. Creating a site, like placing a product into the stream of commerce, may be felt nationwide—or even worldwide—but, without more, it is not an act purposefully directed toward the forum state. See *Asahi Metal Indus. Co. v. Superior Court*, 480 U.S. 102, 112, 107 S.Ct. 1026, 1032, 94 L.Ed.2d 92 (1992) (plurality opinion). There are no allegations that King actively sought to encourage New Yorkers to access his site, or that he conducted any business—let alone a continuous and systematic part of its business—in New York. There is in fact no suggestion that King has any presence of any kind in New York other than the Web site that can be accessed worldwide. Bensusan's argument that King should have foreseen that users could access the site in New York and be confused as to the relationship of the two Blue Note clubs is insufficient to satisfy due process. See *Fox*, 794 F.2d at 37; *Beckett v. Prudential Ins. Co. of Am.*, 893 F. Supp. 234, 239 (SDNY 1995).

Although *CompuServe Inc. v. Patterson*, 89 F.3d 1257 (6th Cir. 1996), a recent decision of the United States Court of Appeals for the Sixth Circuit, reached a different result, it was based on vastly different facts. In that case, the Sixth Circuit found personal jurisdiction proper in Ohio over an Internet user from Texas who subscribed to a network service based in Ohio. The user, however, specifically targeted Ohio by subscribing to the service and entering into a separate agreement with the service to sell his software over the Internet. Furthermore, he advised his software through the service and repeatedly sent his software to the service in Ohio. *Id.* at 1264–65. This led that court to conclude that the Internet user "reached out" from Texas to Ohio and "originated and maintained" contacts with Ohio. *Id.* at 1266.* This action, on the other hand, contains no allegations that King in any way directed any contact to, or had any contact with, New York or intended to avail itself of any of New York's benefits.

Accordingly, the exercise of personal jurisdiction over King in this case would violate the protections of the Due Process Clause.

III. CONCLUSION

For the reasons set forth above, defendant's motion to dismiss the complaint pursuant to Fed.R.Civ.P. 12(b)(2) for lack of personal jurisdiction is granted and the complaint is dismissed.

Zippo Manufacturing Co. v. Zippo Dot Com, Inc. 952 F. Supp. 1119 (W.D. Pa. 1997).

McLaughlin, District Judge

This is an Internet domain name dispute. At this stage of the controversy, we must decide the Constitutionally permissible reach of Pennsylvania's Long Arm Statute, 42 Pa.C.S.A. 5322, through cyberspace. Plaintiff Zippo Manufacturing Corporation ("Manufacturing") has filed a five count complaint against Zippo Dot Com, Inc. ("Dot Com") alleging trademark dilution, infringement, and false designation under the Federal Trademark Act, 15 U.S.C. 1051–1127. In addition, the Complaint alleges causes of action based on state law trademark dilution under 54 Pa.C.S.A. 1124, and seeks equitable accounting and imposition of a constructive trust. Dot Com has moved to dismiss for lack of personal jurisdiction and improper venue pursuant to Fed. R.Civ.P. 12(b)(2) and (3) or, in the alternative, to transfer the case pursuant to 28 U.S.C. 1406(a). For the reasons set forth below, Defendant's motion is denied.

I. BACKGROUND

The facts relevant to this motion are as follows. Manufacturing is a Pennsylvania corporation with its principal place of business in Bradford, Pennsylvania. Manufacturing makes, among other things, well-known "Zippo" tobacco lighters. Dot Com is a California corporation with its principal place of business in Sunnyvale, California. Dot Com operates an Internet Web site and an Internet news service and has obtained the exclusive right to use the domain names "zippo.com", "zippo.net" and "zipponews.com" on the Internet.

Dot Com's Web site contains information about the company, advertisements and an application for its Internet news service. The news service itself consists of three levels of membership—public/free, "Original" and "Super." Each successive level offers access to a greater number of Internet newsgroups. A customer who wants to subscribe to either the "Original" or "Super" level of service, fills out an on-line application that asks for a variety of information including the person's name and address. Payment is made by credit card over the Internet or the telephone. The application is then processed and the subscriber is assigned a password which permits the subscriber to view and/or download Internet newsgroup messages that are stored on the Defendant's server in California.

Dot Com's contacts with Pennsylvania have occurred almost exclusively over the Internet. Dot Com's offices, employees and Internet servers are located in California. Dot Com maintains no offices, employees or agents in Pennsylvania. Dot Com's advertising for its service to Pennsylvania residents involves posting information about its service on its Web page, which is accessible to Pennsylvania residents via the Internet. Defendant has approximately 140,000 paying subscribers worldwide. Approximately two percent (3,000) of those subscribers are Pennsylvania residents. These subscribers have contracted to receive Dot Com's service by visiting its Web site and filling out the application. Additionally, Dot Com has entered into agreements with seven Internet access providers in Pennsylvania to permit their subscribers to access Dot Com's news service. Two of these providers are located in the Western District of Pennsylvania.

The basis of the trademark claims is Dot Com's use of the word "Zippo" in the domain names it holds, in numerous locations in its Web site and in the heading of Internet newsgroup messages that have been posted by Dot Com subscribers. When an Internet user views or downloads a newsgroup message posted by a Dot Com subscriber, the word "Zippo" appears in the "Message-Id" and "Organization" sections of the heading. The news message itself, containing text and/or pictures, follows. Manufacturing points out that some of the messages contain adult oriented, sexually explicit subject matter.

[II]. DISCUSSION

A. Personal Jurisdiction

1. The Traditional Framework

Our authority to exercise personal jurisdiction in this case is conferred by state law. Fed.R.Civ.P. 4(e); *Mellon,* 960 F.2d at 1221. The extent to which we may exercise that authority is governed by the Due Process Clause of the Fourteenth Amendment to the Federal Constitution. *Kulko v. Superior Court of California,* 436 U.S. 84, 91, 98 S.Ct. 1690, 1696, 56 L.Ed.2d 132 (1978).

Pennsylvania's long arm jurisdiction statute is codified at 42 Pa.C.S.A. 5322(a). The portion of the statute authorizing us to exercise jurisdiction here permits the exercise of jurisdiction over non-resident defendants upon: (2) Contracting to supply services or things in this Commonwealth. 42 Pa.C.S.A. 5322(a). It is undisputed that Dot Com contracted to supply Internet news services to approximately 3,000 Pennsylvania residents and also entered into agreements with seven Internet access providers in Pennsylvania. Moreover, even if Dot Com's conduct did not satisfy a specific provision of the statute, we would nevertheless be authorized to exercise jurisdiction to the "fullest extent allowed under the Constitution of the United States." 42 Pa.C.S.A.5322(b).

The Constitutional limitations on the exercise of personal jurisdiction differ depending upon whether a court seeks to exercise general or specific jurisdiction over a non-resident defendant. *Mellon,* 960 F.2d at 1221. General jurisdiction permits a court to exercise personal jurisdiction over a non-resident defendant for non-forum related activities when the defendant has engaged in "systematic and continuous" activities in the forum state. *Helicopteros Nacionales de Colombia, v. S.A. Hall,* 466 U.S. 408, 414–16, 104 S.Ct. 1868, 1872–73, 80 L.Ed.2d 404(1984). In the absence of general jurisdiction, specific jurisdiction permits a court to exercise personal jurisdiction over a non-resident defendant for forum-related activities where the "relationship between the defendant and the forum falls within the 'minimum contacts' framework" of *International Shoe Co. v. Washington,* 326 U.S. 310, 66 S.Ct. 154, 90 L.Ed. 95 (1945) and its progeny. *Mellon,* 960 F.2d at 1221. Manufacturing does not contend that we should exercise general personal jurisdiction over Dot Com. Manufacturing concedes that if personal jurisdiction exists in this case, it must be specific. . . .

2. The Internet and Jurisdiction

In *Hanson v. Denckla,* the Supreme Court noted that "[a]s technological progress has increased the flow of commerce between States, the need for jurisdiction has undergone a similar increase." *Hanson v. Denckla,* 357 U.S. 235, 250–51, 78 S.Ct. 1228, 1237–39, 2 L.Ed.2d 1283 (1958). Twenty-seven years later, the Court observed that jurisdiction could not be avoided "merely because the defendant did not physically enter the forum state." *Burger King,* 471 U.S. at 476, 105 S.Ct. at 2184. The Court observed that:

[I]t is an inescapable fact of modern commercial life that a substantial amount of commercial business is transacted solely by mail and wire communications across state lines, thus obviating the need for physical presence within a State in which business is conducted. *Id.*

Enter the Internet, a global "'super-network' of over 15,000 computer networks used by over 30 million individuals, corporations, organizations, and educational institutions worldwide" *Panavision Intern., L.P. v. Toeppen,* 938 F.Supp. 616 (C.D.Cal. 1996) (citing *American Civil Liberties Union v. Reno,* 929 F.Supp. 824, 830–48 (E.D.Pa. 1996)). "In recent years, businesses have begun to use the Internet to provide information and products to consumers and other businesses." *Id.* The Internet makes it possible to conduct business throughout the world entirely from a desktop. With this global revolution looming on the horizon, the development of the law concerning the permissible scope of personal jurisdiction based on Internet use is in its infant stages. The cases are scant. Nevertheless, our review of the available cases and materials . . . reveals that the likelihood that personal jurisdiction can be constitutionally exercised is directly proportionate to the nature and quality of commercial activity that an entity conducts over the Internet. This sliding scale is consistent with well-developed personal jurisdiction principles. At one end of the spectrum are situations whereas defendant clearly does business over the Internet. If the defendant enters into contracts with residents of a foreign jurisdiction that involve the knowing and repeated transmission of computer files over the Internet, personal jurisdiction is proper. E.g., *CompuServe, Inc. v. Patterson,* 89 F.3d 1257 (6th Cir. 1996). At the opposite end are situations where a defendant has simply posted information on an Internet Web site which is accessible to users in foreign jurisdictions. A passive Web site that does little more than make information available to those who are interested in it is not grounds for the exercise [of] personal jurisdiction. E.g., *Bensusan Restaurant Corp. v. King,* 937 F. Supp. 295 (S.D.N.Y. 1996). The middle ground is occupied by interactive Web sites where a user can exchange information with the host computer. In these cases, the exercise of jurisdiction is determined by examining the level of interactivity and commercial nature of the exchange of information that occurs on the Web site. E.g., *Martiz, Inc. v. Cybergold, Inc.*, 947 F. Supp. 1328 (E.D. Mo. 1996).

Traditionally, when an entity intentionally reaches beyond its boundaries to conduct business with foreign residents, the exercise of specific jurisdiction is proper. *Burger King* [*v. Rudzewicz*], 471 U.S. at 475, 105 S.Ct. at 2183–84. Different results should not be reached simply because business is conducted over the Internet. In *CompuServe, Inc. v. Patterson*, 89 F.3d 1257 (6th Cir. 1996), the Sixth Circuit addressed the significance of doing business over the Internet. In that case, Patterson, a Texas resident, entered into a contract to distribute shareware* through CompuServe's Internet server located in Ohio. *CompuServe*, 89 F.3d at 1260. From Texas, Patterson electronically uploaded thirty-two master software files to CompuServe's server in Ohio via the Internet. *Id.* at 1261. One of Patterson's software products was designed to help people navigate the Internet. *Id.* When CompuServe later began to market a product that Patterson believed to be similar to his own, he threatened to sue. *Id.* CompuServe brought an action in the Southern District of Ohio, seeking a declaratory judgment. *Id.* The District Court granted Patterson's motion to dismiss for lack of personal jurisdiction and CompuServe appealed. *Id.* The Sixth Circuit reversed, reasoning that Patterson had purposefully directed his business activities toward Ohio by knowingly entering into a contract with an Ohio resident and then "deliberately and repeatedly" transmitted files to Ohio. *Id.* at 1264–66.

[The Court then proceeded to summarize the *Bensusan* case]

3. Application to this Case

First, we note that this is not an Internet advertising case in the line of *Inset Systems* and *Bensusan, supra.* Dot Com has not just posted information on a Website that is accessible to Pennsylvania residents who are connected to the Internet. This is not even an interactivity case in the line of *Maritz, supra.* Dot Com has done more than create an interactive Web site through which it exchanges information with Pennsylvania residents in hopes of using that information for commercial gain later. . . . We are being asked to determine whether Dot Com's conducting of electronic commerce with Pennsylvania residents constitutes the purposeful availment of doing business in Pennsylvania. We conclude that it does. Dot Com has contracted with approximately 3,000 individuals and seven Internet access providers in Pennsylvania. The intended object of these transactions has been the downloading of the electronic messages that form the basis of this suit in Pennsylvania.

We find Dot Com's efforts to characterize its conduct as falling short of purposeful availment of doing business in Pennsylvania wholly unpersuasive. . . . Dot Com has done more than advertise on the Internet in Pennsylvania. Defendant has sold passwords to approximately 3,000 subscribers in Pennsylvania and entered into seven contracts with

---

* "Sharware" is software which a user is permitted to download and use for a trial period, after which the user is asked to pay a fee to the author for continued use. Compuserve, 69 F.3d at 1260.

Internet access providers to furnish its services to their customers in Pennsylvania.

Dot Com also contends that its contacts with Pennsylvania residents are "fortuitous" within the meaning of *World-Wide Volkswagen* [*Corp. v. Woodson*], 444 U.S. 286, 100 S.Ct. 559 (1980). Defendant argues that it has not "actively" solicited business in Pennsylvania and that any business it conducts with Pennsylvania residents has resulted from contracts that were initiated by Pennsylvanians who visited the Defendant's Web site. The fact that Dot Com's services have been consumed in Pennsylvania is not "fortuitous" within the meaning of *World-Wide Volkswagen*. In *World-Wide Volkswagen,* a couple that had purchased a vehicle in New York, while they were New York residents, were injured while driving that vehicle through Oklahoma and brought suit in an Oklahoma state court. *World-Wide Volkswagen,* 444 U.S. at 288, 100 S.Ct. at 562–63. The manufacturer did not sell its vehicles in Oklahoma and had not made an effort to establish business relationships in Oklahoma. *Id.* at 295, 100 S.Ct. at 566. The Supreme Court characterized the manufacturer's ties with Oklahoma as fortuitous because they resulted entirely out the fact that the plaintiffs had driven their car into that state. *Id.*

Here, Dot Com argues that its contacts with Pennsylvania residents are fortuitous because Pennsylvanians happened to find its Web site or heard about its news service elsewhere and decided to subscribe. This argument misconstrues the concept of fortuitous contacts embodied in *World-Wide Volkswagen*. Dot Com's contacts with Pennsylvania would be fortuitous within the meaning of *World-Wide Volkswagen* if it had no Pennsylvania subscribers and an Ohio subscriber forwarded a copy of a file he obtained from Dot Com to a friend in Pennsylvania or an Ohio subscriber brought his computer along on a trip to Pennsylvania and used it to access Dot Com's service. That is not the situation here. Dot Com repeatedly and consciously chose to process Pennsylvania residents' applications and to assign them passwords. Dot Com knew that the result of these contracts would be the transmission of electronic messages into Pennsylvania. The transmission of these files was entirely within its control. Dot Com cannot maintain that these contracts are "fortuitous" or "coincidental" within the meaning of *World-Wide Volkswagen*. When a defendant makes a conscious choice to conduct business with the residents of a forum state, "it has clear notice that it is subject to suit there." *World-Wide Volkswagen,* 444 U.S. at 297, 100 S.Ct. at 567. Dot Com was under no obligation to sell its services to Pennsylvania residents. It freely chose to do so, presumably in order to profit from those transactions. If a corporation determines that the risk of being subject to personal jurisdiction in a particular forum is too great, it can choose to sever its connection to the state. *Id.* If Dot Com had not wanted to be amenable to jurisdiction in Pennsylvania, the solution would have been simple—it could have chosen not to sell its services to Pennsylvania residents.

Next, Dot Com argues that its forum-related activities are not numerous or significant enough to create a "substantial connection" with

Pennsylvania. Defendant points to the fact that only two percent of its subscribers are Pennsylvania residents. However, the Supreme Court has made it clear that even a single contact can be sufficient. *McGee* [*v. International Life Ins. Co.*], 355 U.S. [220(1957)] at 223, 78 S.Ct. at 201. The test has always focused on the "nature and quality" of the contacts with the forum and not the quantity of those contacts. *International Shoe* [*v. Washington*], 326 U.S. [310 (1945)] at 320, 66 S.Ct. at 160. The Sixth Circuit also rejected a similar argument in *CompuServe* when it wrote that the contacts were "deliberate and repeated even if they yielded little revenue." *CompuServe*, 89, F.3d at 1265.

We also conclude that the cause of action arises out of Dot Com's forum-related conduct in this case. The Third Circuit has stated that "a cause of action for trademark infringement occurs where the passing off occurs." *Cottman Transmission Systems Inc. v. Martino*, 36 F.3d 291, 294 (citing *Tefal, S.A. v. Products Int'l Co.*, 529 F.2d 495, 456 n. 1 (3d Cir. 1976); *Indianapolis Colts v. Metro. Baltimore Football*, 34 F.3d 410 (7th Cir. 1994)....

In the instant case, both a significant amount of the alleged infringement and dilution, and resulting injury have occurred in Pennsylvania. The object of Dot Com's contracts with Pennsylvania residents is the transmission of the messages that Plaintiff claims dilute and infringe upon its trademark. When these messages are transmitted into Pennsylvania and viewed by Pennsylvania residents on their computers, there can be no question that the alleged infringement and dilution occur in Pennsylvania. Moreover, since Manufacturing is a Pennsylvania corporation, a substantial amount of the injury from the alleged wrongdoing is likely to occur in Pennsylvania, Thus, we conclude that the cause of action arises out of Dot Com's forum-related activities under the authority of both *Tefal* and *Indianapolis Colts, supra.*

Finally, Dot Com argues that the exercise of jurisdiction would be unreasonable in this case. We disagree. There can be no question that Pennsylvania has a strong interest in adjudicating disputes involving the alleged infringement of trademarks owned by resident corporations. We must also give due regard to the Plaintiff's choice to seek relief in Pennsylvania. *Kulko*, 436 U.S. at 92, 98 S.Ct. at 1696–97. These concerns outweigh the burden created by forcing the Defendant to defend the suit in Pennsylvania, especially when Dot Com consciously chose to conduct business in Pennsylvania, pursuing profits from the actions that are now in question. The Due Process Clause is not a "territorial shield to interstate obligations that have been voluntarily assumed." *Burger King* [*v. Rudzewicz*], 471 U.S. [462 (1985)] at 474, 105 S.Ct. at 2183....

[III]. CONCLUSION

We conclude that this Court may appropriately exercise personal jurisdiction over the Defendant and that venue is proper in this judicial district.

NOTES _____

1. See also, *Metro-Goldwyn-Mayer Studios, Inc., et al. v. Grokster, Ltd., et al.*, 243 F. Supp.2d 1073 (C.D. Cal. 2003): Sharman Networks, principal owner of Kazaa, was organized under the laws of Vanuatu. Sharman filed a motion to dismiss, based on a lack of personal jurisdiction. The court dismissed the motion, holding that although general jurisdiction was not available, specific jurisdiction was. "Under prevailing Ninth Circuit doctrine, specific jurisdiction is presumptively reasonable where: 1) a nonresident defendant purposefully avails itself of the privilege of conducting activities in the forum state, thereby invoking the protections of its laws; and 2) the plaintiff's claims arise out of the defendants' forum-related activities. *See Ochoa v. J.B. Martin & Sons Farms,* 287 F.3d at 1189 n. 2; *Ziegler,* 64 F.3d at 473." *Id.* at 1084. In this case, Sharman "purposefully availed" itself in the following ways: An estimated two million of its users were California residents and the distribution of its KMD software to those users was "an essentially commercial act." *Id.* at 1087.

2. A good place to begin research on the area of personal jurisdiction is the Chicago-Kent College of Law "Internet Jurisdiction Hyperlink Guide" found at http://www.kentlaw.edu/cyberlaw/resources/guide.html.

11.3 REGULATING CONTENT AND CONTROLLING DISTRIBUTION OF INFORMATION ONLINE

11.3.1 Censorship

This section is excerpted from Jeffrey D. Neuburger, "*Technology, the Internet and Electronic Commerce—Staying Interactive in the High-Tech Environment*" (February 28, 2006). The publication was kindly provided by Jeffrey Neuburger, a partner in the New York office of Brown Raysman Millstein Felder & Steiner LLP.

The Internet has been described as "the most participatory form of mass speech yet developed."[1] The ability of individuals to transmit information globally in a matter of moments has challenged traditional assumptions underpinning the rules of jurisdiction and liability, both civil and criminal.

Defamation

The law of defamation addresses harm to a party's reputation or good name through the torts of libel and slander.[2] The Internet makes it easier than ever before to disseminate defamatory statements to a wide audience.[3] The risk of liability associated with such statements is an important consideration for parties seeking to communicate with others on the Internet.

---

1. *American Civil Liberties Union v. Reno,* 929 F. Supp. 824, 883 (E.D. Pa. 1996), aff'd, 521 U.S. 844 (1997), available at http://caselaw.lp.findlaw.com/scripts/getcase.pl?court=US&vol=000&invol=96–511.

2. Libel generally involves written communications, while slander is based on oral communications.

3. The ability to disseminate statements virtually instantaneously on a global basis has also raised issues of jurisdiction and the extraterritorial application of law. See discussion infra in the section entitled "Jurisdiction."

- **Bynog v. SL Green Realty Corp.**—The First Amendment precludes the issuance of a preliminary injunction against the posting of allegedly defamatory statements by a former employee on her Web site and related weblog.[4] The employer and union sought injunctive relief in connection with their counterclaims for trade libel and other torts, filed in the discrimination litigation brought by the former employee. The court noted established precedent in the Second Circuit that absent extraordinary circumstances, no injunction should be issued in a defamation case. The court concluded that no extraordinary circumstances had been shown by the employer and the labor union.
- **Franklin Prescriptions Inc. v. The New York Times Co.**—An Internet pharmacy that prevailed on the merits of its defamation claim but was awarded no monetary damages is not entitled to a new trial on the grounds of error in the instructions to the jury.[5] The jury found in favor of the pharmacy on the merits of its claim that it was defamed by the juxtaposition of a screen shot of the pharmacy's Web site with a side bar suggesting that certain Internet pharmacies should be avoided by consumers. The appeals court upheld the lower court ruling that the pharmacy did not properly object to the court's proposed jury instructions on damages during the trial. The court also upheld the lower court ruling that the pharmacy was not entitled to an instruction on presumed damages under Pennsylvania law, nor was it entitled to an instruction on defamation per se.
- **Barrett v. Negrete**—The fact that the defendants in a malicious prosecution action made efforts to widely publish allegedly false allegations about the plaintiff on the Internet supports a finding that the defendants acted with malice in filing defamation claims against him.[6] The appellate court concluded that support for a finding of malice could be found in the "sensational" and "scurrilous nature" of the defendants' numerous allegations of wrongdoing against the plaintiff, and the fact that they withdrew their claims in response to the plaintiff's discovery demands for evidentiary support of their allegations.

Publication on the Internet has also raised issues concerning the applicability of statutes and other legal rules that were developed with print publications in mind, such as the statute of limitations, retraction requirements, and heightened First Amendment standards.

- **Churchill v. State of New Jersey**—The period of limitation for a defamation claim based on items posted on an Internet Web site begins to run when the items are first posted on the Web site, and does not begin to run again each time the Web site is updated.[7] The court followed the nearly unanimous line of cases that have concluded that the "single publication rule" should be applied to Internet publications in the same manner as it applies to "other forms of mass media." The court rejected arguments that Internet publication should be treated differently because of alleged lack of internal editorial controls, propensity for fraud or abuse, or likelihood of being more pervasive or permanent as compared to traditional print media.

4. *Bynog v. SL Green Realty Corp.*, No. 05–0305, 2005 U.S. Dist. LEXIS 34617 (SDNY Dec. 22, 2005).
5. *Franklin Prescriptions Inc. v. The New York Times Co.*, No. 04–34–4 (3d Cir. Sept. 12, 2005).
6. *Barrett v. Negrete*, 2005 U.S.App. LEXIS 4273 (9th Cir. March 14, 2005) (unpublished).
7. *Churchill v. State of New Jersey*, No. A-4804–03T5, 4808–03T5 (N.J. Super. Ct. App. Div. June 23, 2005).

Immunity Under §230 Of The Communications Decency Act

Section 230(c)(1) of the Communications Decency Act of 1996 (CDA) provides that "no provider or user of an interactive computer service shall be treated as the publisher or speaker of any information provided by another information content provider."[8] Section 230(c)(1) immunity has been invoked to bar defamation claims against Internet Service Providers and private individuals,[9] and has been extended to non-speech communications as well.[10]

- **Doe v. Bates**—A civil claim based on allegations that a service provider violated a federal statute prohibiting the distribution of child pornography fall within the immunity provision of Section 230 of the Communications Decency Act (CDA).[11] The plaintiffs alleged that the service provider was responsible for the hosting and operation of the "Candyman" forum on its servers, through which photographs of the plaintiffs' minor child were distributed. The plaintiffs argued that their claim was based upon the civil remedies provision contained in the federal statute criminalizing the distribution of child pornography, and therefore fell within the express exception from immunity in Section 230 for "enforcement" of a "federal criminal statute." Noting that the case was one of first impression, the magistrate concluded that the exception from immunity in Section 230 applies only to criminal prosecutions under federal criminal statutes, not to their civil remedies sections.

- **Austin v. CrystalTech Web Hosting**—Section 230 of the Communications Decency Act, which immunizes a provider or user of an interactive computer service from liability as a "publisher or speaker" of information provided by a third party, also precludes holding a provider or user liable as a distributor of third-party content.[12] The court granted summary judgment dismissing a defamation claim brought against an Internet service provider on the ground that the ISP refused to remove allegedly defamatory statements contained in a Web site hosted on its servers. Citing the leading case of Zeran v. America Online, Inc., 129 F.3d 327 (4th Cir. 1997), the court rejected the plaintiff's argument that Section 230 of the CDA immunizes only publishers of defamatory content, leaving the ISP open to liability as a distributor of the statements that it "knew or had reason to know" were defamatory.

- **Barnes v. Yahoo!, Inc.**—A service provider is entitled to immunity under Section 230(e) of the Communications Decency Act for breach of a promise to remove defamatory online profiles posted by a third party impersonating the plaintiff.[13] The court rejected the plaintiff's argument that her claim was not barred by Section 230 because she was not seeking to hold the service liable as a publisher, but rather was asserting a claim under the Restatement of Torts for failure to exercise reasonable care in

---

8. 47 U.S.C. § 230(c)(1).

9. See, e.g., *Zeran v. America Online, Inc.*, 129 F.3d 327 (4th Cir. 1997).

10. *Green v. America Online* (AOL), 318 F.3d 465 (3d Cir. Jan. 16, 2003), (electronic signal sent through AOL chat room is "information" for purposes of determining § 230(c)(i) immunity).

11. *Doe v. Bates*, No. 5:05CV91 (E.D. Tex. Jan. 18, 2006) (recommendation of Magistrate Judge).

12. *Austin v. CrystalTech Web Hosting*, No. 1 CA-CV 04–0823, 2005 Ariz. App. LEXIS 168 (Ariz. Ct. App., Div. 1, Dec. 22, 2005).

13. *Barnes v. Yahoo!, Inc.*, No. 05–926-AA, 2005 U.S. Dist. LEXIS 28061 (D. Ore. Nov. 8, 2005).

performing an undertaking, i.e., the removal of the defamatory profiles. The court noted that judicial interpretations of Section 230 have generally barred suits "that seek to hold the provider of an interactive computer service liable for [tortious] or unlawful information that someone else disseminates using that service."

- **Associated Bank-Corp. v. Earthlink, Inc.**—An Internet Service Provider (ISP) cannot be held liable for erroneously identifying a legitimate bank Web site as a fraudulent site where the ISP relied upon a list of "phishing" sites provided in anti-phishing software licensed from a third party.[14] The court dismissed a suit brought against the ISP by a bank whose Web site was erroneously identified to the ISP's customers as fraudulent, due to an error in the anti-phishing software. The court concluded that ISP was an "interactive computer service" that was immune under Section 230 of the Communications Decency Act from liability for information provided by an "information content provider." The court noted that the list of phishing sites was input into the software database by the software company, without any alteration of content by the ISP.

A number of courts and individual judges have raised questions about the scope of CDA Section 230 immunity, ruling that immunity does not extend to distributor liability, i.e., the dissemination of a defamatory statement made by another party, with knowledge or the reason to know that it is false.

- **Barrett v. Rosenthal**—The California Supreme Court has agreed to review the controversial Court of Appeals decision in *Barrett v. Rosenthal*.[15] The Court of Appeals ruled in January 2004 that the immunity provided to a "provider or user of an interactive service" by §230(c)(1) of the Communications Decency Act (CDA) does not abrogate the common law principle of distributor or knowledge-based liability. On appeal of an order striking a libel complaint pursuant to California's anti-SLAPP statute, the appeals court held that the trial court erred in finding that §230 of the CDA shielded a newsgroup poster from defamation liability. The poster allegedly distributed to various Internet newsgroups a defamatory e-mail message that she received from another defendant, and then refused to remove and in fact repeatedly reposted the message after being informed of its defamatory nature. Contrary to the trial court (and the leading case of *Zeran v. America Online, Inc.*, 129 F.3d 327 (4th Cir. 1997)), the appeals court held that §230 of the CDA does not restrict distributor liability under the common law, and the plaintiff's defamation claim was not barred by the statute.
- **Grace v. eBay, Inc.**—An online site is not entitled to immunity under §230 of the Communications Decency Act (CDA) for a user's alleged defamation of another user in a "feedback" posting, if the site's publisher "knew or had reason to know" of the alleged defamation and refused to remove the posting.[16] In analyzing the issue, the court focused on §230's immunity from liability as a "publisher or speaker" of information. The court distinguished this potential liability from that of a distributor, and found that the CDA immunity provisions did not shield against distributor

---

14. *Associated Bank-Corp., v. Earthlink, Inc.*, No. 05-C-0233-S (W.D. Wis. Sept. 13, 2005).

15. *Barrett v. Rosenthal*, 14 Cal. App. 4th 1379 (1st Dist. Jan. 21, 2004), judgment vacated, petition for review granted, 12 Cal. Rptr. 3d 48, 87 P.3d 797 (Cal. April 14, 2004).

16. *Grace v. eBay, Inc.*, No. B168765 (Cal. Ct. App. 2d Dist. July 22, 2004).

liability. The court concluded that the auction site nevertheless escaped liability for the allegedly defamatory posting because the site's User Agreement contained a general release of liability for all claims of any kind related to disputes among users of the site.

Net Censorship

Pornography is ubiquitous on the Internet. Lawmakers, community leaders, parents and educators are seeking ways to limit access to obscene and indecent material. Not surprisingly, these efforts at regulating online speech have faced repeated First Amendment challenges by those who oppose any type of "censorship." In general, courts have upheld laws criminalizing the transmission of child pornography but are hesitant to outlaw the transmission of, or limit access to, material deemed "indecent," "harmful to minors," "patently offensive," or "sexually explicit."

Child Pornography

- **Ashcroft v. Free Speech Coalition**—In April 2002, the U.S. Supreme Court held that the Child Pornography Prevention Act of 1996 (CPPA), which extended the federal prohibition against child pornography to sexually explicit images that "appear" to depict minors but are produced without using any real children, is an unconstitutional abridgement of free speech. By a 6–3 margin, the Court affirmed the ruling below from the Ninth Circuit, and held that the CPPA's prohibition against "virtual child pornography" unconstitutionally abridged lawful speech that "records no crime and creates no victims by its production."[17] The CPPA was enacted to address the proliferation of "virtual" child pornography, which uses digital and other techniques to produce images that appear to depict children engaged in sexually explicit activity.

"Indecent" Material

- **The Child Online Protection Act (COPA)** prohibits commercial Web sites from making available to minors material that is "harmful to minors."[18] The Act has been the subject of a sustained constitutional challenge, ACLU v. Reno sub nom. Ashcroft v. ACLU, which is not yet completely resolved and has resulted in several important judicial decisions.

---

17. *Ashcroft v. Free Speech Coalition,* 122 S. Ct. 1389; 152 L. Ed. 2d 403 (U.S., Apr. 16, 2002).

18. 47 U.S.C. § 231. When drafting COPA, Congress tried to avoid the constitutional defects of the CDA by using the "harmful to minors" standard, which has been upheld by the Supreme Court. COPA provides criminal and civil penalties for commercial Web sites that "knowingly" make available to minors material that

"(A) the average person, applying contemporary community standards, would find, taking the material as a whole and with respect to minors, is designed to appeal to, or is designed to pander to, the prurient interest;

(B) depicts, describes, or represents, in a manner patently offensive with respect to minors, an actual or simulated sexual act or sexual contact. . .; and

(C) taken as a whole, lacks serious literary, artistic, political, or scientific value for minors." COPA also provides an affirmative defense to Web sites that restrict access to harmful material by requiring the use of a credit card, debit card, adult access code, or adult personal identification number or "by accepting a digital certificate that verifies age" or by using "other reasonable measures."

In June 2000, the Third Circuit Court of Appeals affirmed a permanent injunction issued by the District Court against the enforcement
of the new law, finding that the "harmful to minors" standard would
require Web site operators—operating in the borderless community
of Cyberspace—to abide by the most restrictive community standards
in the country in order to avoid liability, and that the statute was thus
overbroad.[19] The court noted that "current technology does not permit
a Web publisher to restrict access to its site based on the geographic
locale of each particular Internet user."

In May 2002, a highly fragmented U.S. Supreme Court held that
COPA was wrongly invalidated by the Third Circuit.[20] The Court remanded the case to the Third Circuit to more fully address whether
the statute is unconstitutionally vague and whether it can survive review
under the strict scrutiny standard, but left intact for the time being the
injunction against enforcement of the statute.

In March 2003, the Third Circuit held that COPA was not narrowly
tailored to achieve the Government's interest in protecting children
from harmful content, and would likely deter adults from accessing
restricted but legal content.[21]

In June 2004, the U.S. Supreme Court held that the District Court did
not err in entering a preliminary injunction against the enforcement
of the Act.[22] The Court concluded that the government had failed to
show that the use of blocking and filtering software was a less restrictive alternative means of preventing access to such material by minors
than a content-based speech restriction. The Court also found that the
issuance of the preliminary injunction avoided the extraordinary harm
and a serious chill on protected speech that might result from the application of the statute. However, the Court also ruled that the government could seek to show the efficacy of blocking and filtering at a full
trial on the merits, and remanded for further proceedings.

The case took on a new aspect in January 2006 when the Justice
Department served a third-party subpoena on search engine operator
Google, Inc., seeking the disclosure of a large number of user search requests. The Government sought the data in aid of its attempt to demonstrate the efficacy of blocking and filtering in the pending trial. In March
2006, the District Court in Gonzales v. Google, Inc.,[23] ruled that because
of the potential for the loss of user trust in the privacy of their search
requests, the Government was not entitled to obtain any user search requests. The court did order the disclosure of a sample of 50,000 urls from
the search engine's search index, in order to permit the Government to
conduct a study measuring the effectiveness of filtering software.

---

19. *American Civil Liberties Union v. Reno,* 217 F.3d 162 (3d Cir. 2000).
20. *Ashcroft v. American Civil Liberties Union, et al,* 122 S. Ct. 1700; 152 L. Ed. 2d 771 (U.S. May
13, 2002).
21. *American Civil Liberties Union v. Ashcroft 322 F. 3d 240* (3d Cir. Mar., 6, 2003).
22. *Ashcroft v. American Civil Liberties Union,* No. 03–218, 2004 U.S. LEXIS 4762 (U.S. June
29, 2004).
23. *Gonzales v. Google, Inc.,* No. 5:06-mc-80006-JW (N.D. Cal. Mar. 17, 2006).

- **Reno v. ACLU**—Congress's first attempt to regulate Internet content came in the form of the Communications Decency Act (CDA),[24] which was enacted in February 1996 as Title V of the Telecommunications Act of 1996 (the "Telecom Act").[25] The CDA created criminal liability for the creation, transmission and display of obscene, indecent and patently offensive material to minors over the Internet and commercial online services. In July 1997, the U.S. Supreme Court ruled that the challenged provisions of the statute regulating transmissions and display of "indecent" and "patently offensive" materials are unconstitutional.[26] (The provisions of the CDA that govern the transmission of obscene content may still be enforced.) In reaching its decision, the Court afforded the highest level of First Amendment protection to Internet speech.

NOTES

1. *Reno v. ACLU*, 521 U.S. 844 (1997), noted above, establishes an extremely high bar to Internet censorship, as is evidenced by observations in both the majority and concurring/partially dissenting opinions. There were a variety of constitutional issues with CDA. The challenged provisions had been inserted in the CDA by floor amendment and in conference committee, and were not supported by any legislative history. The CDA was vague; it did not define "indecent transmission" or "patently offensive display," nor did it incorporate references to other statutes defining such terms. It was overbroad (as in many cases involving traditional media) and the Court was especially disturbed by the fact that a statutory defense to criminal penalties required that actions to exclude minors be "good faith, reasonable, effective, and appropriate," instead of merely taken reasonably and in good faith, or that the distributor "restrict[s]access to such communication by requiring use of a verified credit card, debit account, adult access code, or adult personal identification number." Similar fates have befallen other attempts at censorship (as opposed to content-neutral "time, place and manner" regulations). However, it is clear that the Court saw the Internet as unique, requiring special care.

Speaking for the majority, Mr. Justice Stevens stated that:

    . . . In *Ginsberg* [*v. New York*, 390 U.S. 629, 88 S.Ct. 1274, 20 L.Ed.2nd 195 (1968)], we upheld the constitutionality of a New York statute that prohibited selling to minors under 17 years of age material that was considered obscene as to them even if not obscene as to adults. . . .

    . . . In four important respects, the statute upheld in *Ginsberg* was narrower than the CDA. First, we noted in *Ginsberg* that "the prohibition against sales to minors does not bar parents who so desire from purchasing the magazines for their children." . . . Under the CDA, by contrast, neither the parents' consent—nor even their participation—in the communication would avoid the application of the statute. Second, the New York statute applied only to commercial transactions . . . whereas the CDA contains no such limitation. Third, the New York statute cabined its definition of material that is harmful to minors with the requirement that it be "utterly without redeeming social importance for minors." . . . The CDA fails to provide us with any definition of the term "indecent" . . . and, importantly, omits any requirement that the "patently offensive" material . . . lack serious literary, artistic, political, or scientific value. Fourth, the New York statute defined a minor

---

24. 47 U.S.C. § 223(a), (d)-(h) (1996), available at http://www4.law.cornell.edu/uscode/47/223.html.
25. Pub. L. No. 104–104 (codified as amended at 47 U.S.C. §151 et. seq. (1996)).
26. *Reno v. American Civil Liberties Union*, 117 S.Ct. 2329, 138 L.Ed. 2d 874 (1997).

as a person under the age of 17, whereas the CDA, in applying to all those under 18 years, includes an additional year of those nearest majority.

In [*FCC*] *v. Pacifica* [*Foundation,* 438 U.S. 726, 98 S.Ct. 3026, 57 L.Ed.2d 1073 (1978)], we upheld a declaratory order of the Federal Communications Commission, holding that the broadcast of a recording of a 12-minute monologue entitled "Filthy Words" that had previously been delivered to a live audience "could have been the subject of administrative sanctions." . . . [T]he Court concluded that the ease with which children may obtain access to broadcasts, "coupled with the concerns recognized in *Ginsberg,*" justified special treatment of indecent broadcasting. . . .

[Similarly], there are significant differences between the order upheld in *Pacifica* and the CDA. First, the order in *Pacifica,* issued by an agency that had been regulating radio stations for decades, targeted a specific broadcast that represented a rather dramatic departure from traditional program content in order to designate when—rather than whether—it would be permissible to air such a program in that particular medium. The CDA's broad categorical prohibitions are not limited to particular times and are not dependent on any evaluation by an agency familiar with the unique characteristics of the Internet. Second, unlike the CDA, the Commission's declaratory order was not punitive; we expressly refused to decide whether the indecent broadcast "would justify a criminal prosecution." . . . Finally, the Commission's order applied to a medium which as a matter of history had "received the most limited First Amendment protection," . . . in large part because warnings could not adequately protect the listener from unexpected program content. The Internet, however, has no comparable history. Moreover, the District Court found that the risk of encountering indecent material by accident is remote because a series of affirmative steps is required to access specific material.

In *Renton* [*v. Playtime Theaters, Inc.,* 475 U.S. 41, 106 S.Ct. 925, 89 L.Ed.2d 29 (1986)],we upheld a zoning ordinance that kept adult movie theaters out of residential neighborhoods. The ordinance was aimed, not at the content of the films shown in the theaters, but rather at the "secondary effects"—such as crime and deteriorating property values—that these theaters fostered: "It is th[e] secondary effect which these zoning ordinances attempt to avoid, not the dissemination of 'offensive' speech." 475 U.S., at 49, 106 S.Ct., at 930 (quoting *Young v. American Mini Theaters, Inc.,* 427 U.S. 50, 71, n. 34, 96 S.Ct. 2440, 2453, n. 34, 49 L.Ed.2d 310 [1976]). According to the Government, the CDA is constitutional because it constitutes a sort of "cyberzoning" on the Internet. But the CDA applies broadly to the entire universe of cyberspace. And the purpose of the CDA is to protect children from the primary effects of "indecent" and "patently offensive" speech, rather than any "secondary" effect of such speech. Thus, the CDA is a content-based blanket restriction on speech, and, as such, cannot be "properly analyzed as a form of time, place, and manner regulation." . . .

These precedents, then, surely do not require us to uphold the CDA and are fully consistent with the application of the most stringent review of its provisions.

[The factors which have been held to justify FCC broadcast regulation] are not present in cyberspace. Neither before nor after the enactment of the CDA have the vast democratic fora of the Internet been subject to the type of government supervision and regulation that has attended the broadcast industry. Moreover, the Internet is not as "invasive" as radio or television. The District Court specifically found that "[c]ommunications over the Internet do not 'invade' an individual's home or appear on one's computer screen unbidden. Users seldom encounter content 'by accident.'" 929 F. Supp., at 844 (finding 88). It also found that "[a]lmost all sexually explicit images are preceded by warnings as to the content," and cited testimony that "'odds are slim' that a user would come across a sexually explicit sight by accident." . . .

Finally, unlike the conditions that prevailed when Congress first authorized regulation of the broadcast spectrum, the Internet can hardly be considered a "scarce" expressive commodity. It provides relatively unlimited, low-cost capacity for communication of all kinds. . . . We agree with [the District Court's] conclusion that our cases provide no basis for qualifying the level of First Amendment scrutiny that should be applied to this medium.

In arguing that the CDA does not [improperly] diminish adult communication, the Government relies on the incorrect factual premise that prohibiting a transmission whenever it is known that one of its recipients is a minor would not interfere with adult-to-adult communication. [However, g]iven the size of the potential audience for most messages, in the absence of a viable age verification process, the sender must be charged with knowing that one or more minors will likely view it. Knowledge that, for instance, one or more members of a 100-person chat group will be minor—and therefore that it would be a crime to send the group an indecent message—would surely burden communication among adults. . . . The District Court found that at the time of trial existing technology did not include any effective method for a sender to prevent minors from obtaining access to its communications on the Internet without also denying access to adults. The Court found no effective way to determine the age of a user who is accessing material through e-mail, mail exploders, newsgroups, or chat rooms . . . [and] that it would be prohibitively expensive for noncommercial—as well as some commercial—speakers who have Web sites to verify that their users are adults. . . . These limitations must inevitably curtail a significant amount of adult communication on the Internet. By contrast, the District Court found that "[d]espite its limitations, currently available user-based software suggests that a reasonably effective method by which parents can prevent their children from accessing sexually explicit and other material which parents may believe is inappropriate for their children will soon be widely available."

The breadth of the CDA's coverage is wholly unprecedented. Unlike the regulations upheld in *Ginsberg* and *Pacifica,* the scope of the CDA is not limited to commercial speech or commercial entities. Its open-ended prohibitions embrace all nonprofit entities and individuals posting indecent messages or displaying them on their own computers in the presence of minors. . . . Moreover, the "community standards" criterion as applied to the Internet means that any communication available to a nation-wide audience will be judged by the standards of the community most likely to be offended by the message. . . .

[M]ost Internet fora—including chat rooms, newsgroups, mail exploders, and the Web—are open to all comers. The Government's assertion that the knowledge requirement somehow protects the communications of adults is therefore untenable. Even the strongest reading of the "specific person" requirement of 223(d) cannot save the statute. It would confer broad powers of censorship, in the form of a "heckler's veto," upon any opponent of indecent speech who might simply log on and inform the would-be discoursers that his 17-year-old child—a "specific person . . . under 18 years of age," 47 U.S.C.A. 223(d)(1)(A) (Supp. 1997)—would be present. . . .

[Access can be limited] by requiring use of a verified credit card or adult identification. Such verification is not only technologically available but actually is used by commercial providers of sexually explicit material. These providers, therefore, would be protected by the defense. Under the findings of the District Court, however, it is not economically feasible for most noncommercial speakers to employ such verification. Accordingly, this defense would not significantly narrow the statute's burden on noncommercial speech. Even with respect to the commercial pornographers that would be protected by the defense, the Government failed to adduce any evidence that these verification techniques actually preclude minors from posing as adults. . . . The CDA, casting a far darker shadow over free speech, threatens to torch a large segment of the Internet community. . . .

[T]he Government asserts that—in addition to its interest in protecting children—its "[e]qually significant" interest in fostering the growth of the

Internet provides an independent basis for upholding the constitutionality of the CDA. . . . The Government apparently assumes that the unregulated availability of "indecent" and "patently offensive" material on the Internet is driving countless citizens away from the medium because of the risk of exposing themselves or their children to harmful material.

We find this argument singularly unpersuasive. The dramatic expansion of this new marketplace of ideas contradicts the factual basis of this contention. The record demonstrates that the growth of the Internet has been and continues to be phenomenal. As a matter of constitutional tradition, in the absence of evidence to the contrary, we presume that governmental regulation of the content of speech is more likely to interfere with the free exchange of ideas than to encourage it. The interest in encouraging freedom of expression in a democratic society outweighs any theoretical but unproven benefit of censorship.

Justice O'Connor (with whom Chief Justice Rehnquist joined) agreed that

[A] "zoning" law is valid only if adults are still able to obtain the regulated speech. If they cannot, the law does more than simply keep children away from speech they have no right to obtain—it interferes with the rights of adults to obtain constitutionally protected speech and effectively "reduce[s] the adult population. . . . to reading only what is fit for children." *Butler v. Michigan*, 352 U.S. 380, 383, 77 S.Ct. 524, 526, 1 L.Ed.2d 412 (1957). . . . Before today, there was no reason to question this assumption, for the Court has previously only considered laws that operated in the physical world, a world that with two characteristics that make it possible to create "adult zones": geography and identity. See Lessig, "Reading the Constitution in Cyberspace," 45 *Emory L. J.* 869, 886 (1996). . . . [However, t]he electronic world is fundamentally different. Because it is no more than the interconnection of electronic pathways, cyberspace allows speakers and listeners to mask their identities. Cyberspace undeniably reflects some form of geography; chat rooms and Web sites, for example, exist at fixed "locations" on the Internet. Since users can transmit and receive messages on the Internet without revealing anything about their identities or ages, see Lessig, *supra*, at 901, however, it is not currently possible to exclude persons from accessing certain messages on the basis of their identity.

Cyberspace differs from the physical world in another basic way: Cyberspace is malleable. Thus, it is possible to construct barriers in cyberspace and use them to screen for identity, making cyberspace more like the physical world and, consequently, more amenable to zoning laws. . . . Internet speakers (users who post material on the Internet) have begun to zone cyberspace itself through the use of "gateway" technology. Such technology requires Internet users to enter information about themselves—perhaps an adult identification number or a credit card number—before they can access certain areas of cyberspace. . . .

Until gateway technology is available throughout cyberspace, and it is not in 1997, a speaker cannot be reasonably assured that the speech he displays will reach only adults because it is impossible to confine speech to an "adult zone." . . .

[Justice O'Connor, however, would have upheld the statute insofar as its scope could be limited to situations involving a knowing transmission by a single adult to one or more minors.]

2. In contrast to the optimism displayed by the Supreme Court in *Reno,* according to one critic, screening technology, "called software filters by their advocates and censorware by their critics, are not very effective and screen for too much." Charles Marson, "The Great Filter Folly," *California Lawyer,* January 2000, p. 53.

3. It is interesting to speculate how the appointments of conservative judges like Chief Justice John Roberts and Justice Samuel Alito may change the Supreme Court's handling of censorship matters. One of Congress' recent efforts to legislate so-called "family values" was Section 110 of the Copyright Act, The Family

Movie Act, which allows for the creation of software designed to make certain "objectionable" aural and visual film elements "imperceptible." One interesting item to note is that the software *cannot identify the offending material by itself.* An individual must perform the editing function and insert certain cues in the film. This begs the question of who is an appropriate editor.

4. In *American Library Association v. Pataki*, 969 F. Supp. 160 (SDNY 1997), a New York statute modeled on Section 230 of the Communications Decency Act of 1996 was held to be an unconstitutional interference with interstate commerce.

5. However, traditional obscenity prosecutions are still possible. For example, in *United States v. Thomas*, 74. F.3d 701 (6th Cir. 1996), criminal liability under federal statutes prohibiting the distribution of obscene materials in interstate or foreign commerce was upheld based on "community standards" prevalent in Tennessee, where a postal inspector downloaded materials from a California bulletin board in response to a complaint from a Tennessee resident. (The three-part *Miller* test is discussed in the *Skywalker* decision. See Sec. 4.3.3.)

11.3.2 Control of Access: Framing and Linking

Framing allows visitors of Website A to link to Website B while particular information (usually advertisements provided by Website A) remains as a frame around Website B. *See* John F. Delaney & Robert Murphy, "The Law of the Internet: A Summary of U.S. Internet Caselaw and Legal Developments," 570 *Patents, Copyrights, Trademarks, and Literary Property Course Handbook Series* (PLI) 169, 227 (August/September 1999).

Framing can cause confusion as to the source of the information and can allow the framing website to generate advertising revenues solely from the efforts of a third party. In 1997, media giants such as The Washington Post Company and CNN brought an action against Total News, Inc. for framing their websites. The case settled. Although Total News was permitted, under certain circumstances, to link Plaintiff's websites via hyperlinks, Total News agreed "permanently not to directly or indirectly cause any Plaintiff's website to appear on a user's computer screen with any material . . . supplied by or associated with Defendant." The public stipulation and order of settlement and dismissal of the case can be viewed at http://legal.web.aol.com/decisions/dlip/washorde.html.

A "hyperlink" is an electronic connection between a marked place in one Internet document and marked place in another. "Deep linking" is the creation of hyperlinks that take a browser below the level of the target-site's homepage. Deep linking is a convenient way for one website to steer browsers to information, while bypassing the information gathering and, probably more importantly, the advertising present on most home pages.

In *eBay, Inc., vs. Bidder's Edge, Inc.,* 100 F.Supp. 2d 1058 (N.D. Cal. 2000), Plaintiff eBay moved for a preliminary injunction to enjoin defendant Bidder's Edge, Inc. ("BE") from accessing eBay's computer systems by use of any automated querying program without eBay's written authorization. eBay is the largest Internet-based, person-to-person trading site, and one of the Internet's greatest success stories. "BE is an auction aggregation site designed to offer on-line auction buyers the ability to search for items across numerous on-line auctions without having to search each host site individually." *Id.* at 1061. BE's site performed this function through the use of a "software robot." "A software robot is a computer program which operates across the Internet to perform searching, copying and retrieving functions on the web sites of others. A software robot is capable of executing thousands of instructions per minute, far in excess of what a human can accomplish. Robots consume the processing and storage resources of a system, making that portion of the system's capacity unavailable to the system owner or other users. Consumption of sufficient system resources will slow the processing of the overall system and can overload the system such that it will malfunction or 'crash.' A severe malfunction can cause a loss of data and an interruption in services." *Id.* at 1061. Initially eBay gave BE permission to include its information BE's site. Later, eBay withdrew its permission and attempted, on two occasions, to negotiate a license with BE. These negotiations failed. *Id.* at 1062.

As stated by the court:

It appears that the primary dispute was over the method BE uses to search the eBay database. eBay wanted BE to conduct a search of the eBay system only when the BE system was queried by a BE user. This reduces the load on the eBay system and increases the accuracy of the BE data. BE wanted to recursively crawl the eBay system to compile its own auction database. This increases the speed of BE searches and allows BE to track the auctions generally and automatically update its users when activity occurs in particular auctions, categories of auctions, or when new items are added. . . .

Under such circumstances, there is a legitimate claim that the robots would not pose any threat of irreparable harm. However, eBay's right to injunctive relief is also based upon a much stronger argument. . . .

If BE's activity is allowed to continue unchecked, it would encourage other auction aggregators to engage in similar recursive searching of the eBay system such that eBay would suffer irreparable harm from reduced system performance, system unavailability, or data losses. . . . BE does not appear to seriously contest that reduced system performance, system unavailability or data loss would inflict irreparable harm on eBay consisting of lost profits and lost customer goodwill. Harm resulting from lost profits and lost customer goodwill is irreparable because it is neither easily calculable, nor easily compensable and is therefore an appropriate basis for injunctive relief. See, e.g., People of State of California ex rel. Van De Kamp v. Tahoe Reg'l Planning Agency, 766 F.2d 1316, 1319 (9th Cir. 1985). Where, as here, the denial of preliminary injunctive relief would encourage an increase in the complained of activity, and such an increase would present a strong likelihood of irreparable harm, the plaintiff has at least established a possibility of irreparable harm.

The Court went on to issue the following order:

Bidder's Edge, its officers, agents, servants, employees, attorneys and those in active concert or participation with them who receive actual notice of this order by personal service or otherwise, are hereby enjoined pending the trial of this matter, from using any automated query program, robot, web crawler or other similar device, without written authorization, to access eBay's computer systems or networks, for the purpose of copying any part of eBay's auction database. As a condition of the preliminary injunction, eBay is ordered to post a bond in the amount of $ 2,000,000 to secure payment of any damages sustained by defendant if it is later found to have been wrongfully enjoined. This order shall take effect 10 days from the date on which it is filed.

Nothing in this order precludes BE from utilizing information obtained from eBay's site other than by automated query program, robot, web crawler or similar device. The court denies eBay's request for a preliminary injunction barring access to its site based upon BE's alleged trademark infringement, trademark dilution and other claims. This denial is without prejudice to an application for an injunction limiting or conditioning the use of any information obtained on the theory that BE's use violates some protected right of eBay.

NOTES _____

1. See, also, Michael T. Zeller, "How to Combat Attempts to Divert Web Traffic," *The Internet Newsletter,* January 2000, p. 1.
2. In *Intellectual Reserve, Inc. v. Utah Lighthouse Ministry, Inc., et al.,* 75 F. Supp. 2d 1290 (D. Utah 1999), Plaintiff sought a preliminary injunction to prevent the defendant from directly infringing and contributing to the infringement of its copyright in the "Church Handbook of Instructions ("Handbook"). After being ordered to remove the infringing material from its website defendant "placed a notice on their website that the Handbook was online, and gave three website addresses of websites containing the material defendants were ordered to remove from their website." Id. at 1291. Additionally, defendant responded to an email from an individual who had trouble on one of the three sites with instructions on how to view the material. The court found that those who viewed the copyrighted material had made a temporary, but nonetheless infringing copy of the Handbook and that the defendants had encouraged them to do so. Defendants were ordered to, inter alia,

    1. Defendants, their agents and those under their control, shall remove from and not post on defendants' website the material alleged to infringe plaintiff's copyright;
    2. Defendants, their agents and those under their control, shall not reproduce or distribute verbatim, in a tangible medium, material alleged to infringe plaintiff's copyright
    3. Defendants, their agents and those under their control, shall remove from and not post on defendants' website, addresses to websites that defendants know, or have reason to know, contain the material alleged to infringe plaintiff's copyright. . .

Id. at 1294.

11.4 LIABILITY OF INTERNET SERVICE PROVIDERS

11.4.1 Defamation

As more people gain access to the Internet, more defamatory material is posted there. In addition to asserting claims over the individuals who posted the defamatory material, injured parties have attempted to hold liable the Internet Service Providers (ISPs) on which the material appeared. The ISPs have argued that they are more like common carriers than publishers, and therefore should not be responsible for the content of the transmitted messages.

Zeran v. America Online, Inc., 129 F.3d 327 (4th Cir. 1997), cert. denied, 118 S.Ct. 2341 (1998).

WILKINSON, CHIEF JUDGE

Kenneth Zeran brought this action against America Online, Inc. ("AOL"), arguing that AOL unreasonably delayed in removing defamatory messages posted by an unidentified third party, refused to post retractions of those messages, and failed to screen for similar postings thereafter. The district court granted judgment for AOL on the grounds that the Communications Decency Act of 1996 ("CDA")—47 U.S.C. 230—bars Zeran's claims. Zeran appeals, arguing that 230 leaves intact liability for interactive computer service providers who possess notice of defamatory material posted through their services. He also contends that 230 does not apply here because his claims arise from AOL's alleged negligence prior to the CDA's enactment. Section 230, however, plainly immunizes computer service providers like AOL from liability for information that originates with third parties. Furthermore, Congress clearly expressed its intent that 230 apply to lawsuits, like Zeran's, instituted after the CDA's enactment. Accordingly, we affirm the judgment of the district court. . . .

AOL is . . . an interactive computer service. Much of the information transmitted over its network originates with the company's millions of subscribers. They may transmit information privately via electronic mail, or they may communicate publicly by posting messages on AOL bulletin boards, where the messages may be read by any AOL subscriber.

The instant case comes before us on a motion for judgment on the pleadings, see Fed.R.Civ.P. 12(c), so we accept the facts alleged in the complaint as true. *Bruce v. Riddle*, 631 F.2d 272, 273 (4th Cir. 1980). On April 25, 1995, an unidentified person posted a message on an AOL bulletin board advertising "Naughty Oklahoma T-Shirts." The posting described the sale of shirts featuring offensive and tasteless slogans related to the April 19, 1995, bombing of the Alfred P. Murray Federal Building in Oklahoma City. Those interested in purchasing the shirts were instructed to call "Ken" at Zeran's home phone number in Seattle, Washington. As a result of this anonymously perpetrated prank, Zeran received a high volume of calls, comprised primarily of angry and derogatory messages, but also including death threats. Zeran could not change his phone number because he relied on its availability to the public in running his business out of his home. Later that day, Zeran called AOL and informed a company representative of his predicament. The employee assured Zeran that the posting would be removed from AOL's bulletin board but explained that as a matter of policy AOL would not post a retraction. The parties dispute the date that AOL removed this original posting from its bulletin board.

On April 26, the next day, an unknown person posted another message advertising additional shirts with new tasteless slogans related to the Oklahoma City bombing. Again, interested buyers were told to call Zeran's phone number, to ask for "Ken," and to "please call back if busy" due to high demand. The angry, threatening phone calls intensified. Over the next four days, an unidentified party continued to post messages on AOL's bulletin board, advertising additional items including bumper stickers and key chains with still more offensive slogans. During this time period, Zeran called AOL repeatedly and was told by company representatives that the individual account from which the messages were posted would soon be closed. Zeran also reported his case to Seattle FBI agents. By April 30, Zeran was receiving an abusive phone call approximately every two minutes.

Meanwhile, an announcer for Oklahoma City radio station KRXO received a copy of the first AOL posting. On May 1, the announcer related the message's contents on the air, attributed them to "Ken" at Zeran's phone number, and urged the listening audience to call the number. After this radio broadcast, Zeran was inundated with death threats and other violent calls from Oklahoma City residents. Over the next few days, Zeran talked to both KRXO and AOL representatives. He also spoke to his local police, who subsequently surveilled his home to protect his safety. By May 14, after an Oklahoma City newspaper published a story exposing the shirt advertisements as a hoax and after KRXO made an on-air apology, the number of calls of Zeran's residence finally subsided to fifteen per day.

Zeran first filed suit on January 4, 1996, against radio station KRXO in the United States District Court for the Western District of Oklahoma. On April 23,1996, he filed this separate suit against AOL in the same court. Zeran did not bring any action against the party who posted the offensive messages. . . . After Zeran's suit against AOL was transferred to the Eastern District of Virginia pursuant to 28 U.S.C. 1404(a), AOL answered Zeran's complaint and interposed 47 U.S.C. 230 as an affirmative defense. AOL then moved for judgment on the pleadings pursuant to Fed.R.Civ.P. 12(c). The district court granted AOL's motion, and Zeran filed this appeal.

II

A

Because 230 was successfully advanced by AOL in the district court as a defense to Zeran's claims, we shall briefly examine its operation here. Zeran seeks to hold AOL liable for defamatory speech initiated by a third party. He argued to the district court that once he notified AOL of the unidentified third party's hoax, AOL had a duty to remove the defamatory posting promptly, to notify its subscribers of the message's false nature, and to effectively screen future defamatory material. Section 230 entered this litigation as an affirmative defense pled by AOL. The company claimed that Congress immunized interactive computer service providers from claims based on information posted by a third party.

The relevant portion of 230 states: "No provider or user of an interactive computer service shall be treated as the publisher or speaker of any information provided by another information content provider." 47 U.S.C. 230(c)(1).... By its plain language, 230 creates a federal immunity to any cause of action that would make service providers liable for information originating with a third-party user of the service. Specifically, 230 precludes courts from entertaining claims that would place a computer service provider in a publisher's role. Thus, lawsuits seeking to hold a service provider liable for its exercise of a publisher's traditional editorial functions—such as deciding whether to publish, withdraw, postpone or alter content—are barred.

The purpose of this statutory immunity is not difficult to discern. Congress recognized the threat that tort-based lawsuits pose to freedom of speech in the new and burgeoning Internet medium. The imposition of tort liability on service providers for the communications of others represented, for Congress, simply another form of intrusive government regulation of speech. Section 230 was enacted, in part, to maintain the robust nature of Internet communication and, accordingly, to keep government interference in the medium to a minimum. In specific statutory findings, Congress recognized the Internet and interactive computer services as offering "a forum for a true diversity of political discourse, unique opportunities for cultural development, and myriad avenues for intellectual activity." *Id.* 230(a)(3). It also found that the Internet and interactive computer services "have flourished, to the benefit of all Americans, with a minimum of government regulation." *Id.* 230(a)(4). Congress further stated that it is "the policy of the United States . . . to preserve the vibrant and competitive free market that presently exists for the Internet and other interactive computer services, unfettered by Federal or State regulation." *Id.* 230(b)(2).

None of this means, of course, that the original culpable party who posts defamatory messages would escape accountability. While Congress acted to keep government regulation of the Internet to a minimum, it also found it to be the policy of the United States "to ensure vigorous enforcement of Federal criminal laws to deter and punish trafficking in obscenity, stalking, and harassment by means of computer." *Id.* 230(b)(5). Congress made a policy choice, however, not to deter harmful online speech through the separate route of imposing tort liability on companies that serve as intermediaries for other parties' potentially injurious messages.

Congress' purpose in providing the 230 immunity was thus evident. Interactive computer services have millions of users. See *Reno v. ACLU,*—U.S. at—, 117 S.Ct. at 2334 (noting that at time of district court trial, "commercial online services had almost 12 million individual subscribers"). The amount of information communicated via interactive computer services is therefore staggering. The specter of tort liability in an area of such prolific speech would have an obvious chilling effect. It would be impossible for service providers to screen each of their millions of postings for possible problems. Faced with potential liability for each message republished by their services, interactive computer service providers might choose to severely restrict the number and type of messages posted. Congress considered the weight of the speech interests implicated and chose to immunize service providers to avoid any such restrictive effect.

Another important purpose of 230 was to encourage service providers to self-regulate the dissemination of offensive material over their services. In this respect, 230 responded to a New York state court decision, *Stratton Oakmont, Inc. v. Prodigy Servs. Co.*, 1995 WL 323710 (N.Y. Sup. May 24, 1995). There, the plaintiffs sued Prodigy—an interactive computer service like AOL—for defamatory comments made by an unidentified party on one of Prodigy's bulletin boards. The court held Prodigy to the strict liability standard normally applied to original publishers of defamatory statements, rejecting Prodigy's claims that it should be held only to the lower "knowledge" standard usually reserved for distributors. The court reasoned that Prodigy acted more like an original publisher than a distributor both because it advertised its practice of controlling content on its service and because it actively screened and edited messages posted on its bulletin boards.

Congress enacted 230 to remove the disincentives to self regulation created by the *Stratton Oakmont* decision. Under that court's holding, computer service providers who regulated the dissemination of offensive material on their services risked subjecting themselves to liability, because such regulation cast the service provider in the role of a publisher. Fearing that the specter of liability would therefore deter service providers from blocking and screening offensive material, Congress enacted 230's broad immunity "to remove disincentives for the development and utilization of blocking and filtering technologies that empower parents to restrict their children's access to objectionable or inappropriate online material." 47 U.S.C. 230(b)(4). In line with this purpose, 230 forbids the imposition of publisher liability on a service provider for the exercise of its editorial and self-regulatory functions.

B

Zeran argues, however, that the 230 immunity eliminates only publisher liability, leaving distributor liability intact. Publishers can be held liable for defamatory statements contained in their works even absent proof that they had specific knowledge of the statement's inclusion. W. Page Keeton et al., *Prosser and Keeton on the Law of Torts* 113, at 810 (5th ed. 1984). According to Zeran, interactive computer service providers like AOL are normally considered instead to be distributors, like

930 • LAW AND BUSINESS

traditional news vendors or book sellers. Distributors cannot beheld liable for defamatory statements contained in the materials they distribute unless it is proven at a minimum that they have actual knowledge of the defamatory statements upon which liability is predicated. *Id.* at 811 (explaining that distributors are not liable "in the absence of proof that they knew or had reason to know of the existence of defamatory matter contained in matter published"). Zeran contends that he provided AOL with sufficient notice of the defamatory statements appearing on the company's bulletin board. This notice is significant, says Zeran, because AOL could be held liable as a distributor only if it acquired knowledge of the defamatory statements' existence.

Because of the difference between these two forms of liability, Zeran contends that the term "distributor" carries a legally distinct meaning from the term "publisher." Accordingly, he asserts that Congress' use of only the term "publisher" in 230 indicates a purpose to immunize service providers only from publisher liability. He argues that distributors are left unprotected by 230 and, therefore, his suit should be permitted to proceed against AOL. We disagree. Assuming arguendo that Zeran has satisfied the requirements for imposition of distributor liability, this theory of liability is merely a subset, or a species, of publisher liability, and is therefore also foreclosed by 230.

The terms "publisher" and "distributor" derive their legal significance from the context of defamation law. Although Zeran attempts to artfully plead his claims as ones of negligence, they are indistinguishable from a garden variety defamation action. Because the publication of a statement is a necessary element in a defamation action, only one who publishes can be subject to this form of tort liability. Restatement (Second) of Torts 558(b) (1977); Keeton et al., *supra*, 113, at 802. Publication does not only describe the choice by an author to include certain information. In addition, both the negligent communication of a defamatory statement and the failure to remove such a statement when first communicated by another party—each alleged by Zeran here under a negligence label—constitute publication. Restatement (Second) of Torts 577; see also *Tacket v. General Motors Corp.*, 836 F.2d 1042, 1046–47 (7th Cir. 1987). In fact, every repetition of a defamatory statement is considered a publication. Keeton et al., *supra*, 113, at 799.

In this case, AOL is legally considered to be a publisher. "[E]very one who takes part in the publication . . . is charged with publication." *Id.* Even distributors are considered to be publishers for purposes of defamation law:

Those who are in the business of making their facilities available to disseminate the writings composed, the speeches made, and the information gathered by others may also be regarded as participating to such an extent in making the books, newspapers, magazines, and information available to others as to be regarded as publishers. They are intentionally making the contents available to others, sometimes without knowing all of the contents—including the defamatory content—and sometimes without any opportunity to ascertain, in advance, that any defamatory matter was to be included in the matter published. *Id.* at 803.

AOL falls squarely within this traditional definition of a publisher and, therefore, is clearly protected by 230's immunity. . . .

Zeran next contends that interpreting 230 to impose liability on service providers with knowledge of defamatory content on their services is consistent with the statutory purposes outlined in Part IIA. Zeran fails, however, to understand the practical implications of notice liability in the interactive computer service context. Liability upon notice would defeat the dual purposes advanced by 230 of the CDA. Like the strict liability imposed by the *Stratton Oakmont* court, liability upon notice reinforces service providers' incentives to restrict speech and abstain from self-regulation.

If computer service providers were subject to distributor liability, they would face potential liability each time they receive notice of a potentially defamatory statement—from any party, concerning any message. Each notification would require a careful yet rapid investigation of the circumstances surrounding the posted information, a legal judgment concerning the information's defamatory character, and an on-the-spot editorial decision whether to risk liability by allowing the continued publication of that information. Although this might be feasible for the traditional print publisher, the sheer number of postings on interactive computer services would create an impossible burden in the Internet context. Cf. *Auvil v. CBS 60 Minutes,* 800 F. Supp. 928, 931 (E.D. Wash. 1992) (recognizing that it is unrealistic for network affiliates to "monitor incoming transmissions and exercise on-the-spot discretionary calls"). Because service providers would be subject to liability only for the publication of information, and not for its removal, they would have a natural incentive simply to remove messages upon notification, whether the contents were defamatory or not. See *Philadelphia Newspapers, Inc. v. Hepps,* 475 U.S. 767, 777, 106 S. Ct. 1558, 1564, 89 L.Ed.2d 783 (1986) (recognizing that fears of unjustified liability produce a chilling effect antithetical to First Amendment's protection of speech). Thus, like strict liability, liability upon notice has a chilling effect on the freedom of Internet speech.

Similarly, notice-based liability would deter service providers from regulating the dissemination of offensive material over their own services. Any efforts by a service provider to investigate and screen material posted on its service would only lead to notice of potentially defamatory material more frequently and thereby create a stronger basis for liability. Instead of subjecting themselves to further possible lawsuits, service providers would likely eschew any attempts at self-regulation.

More generally, notice-based liability for interactive computer service providers would provide third parties with a no-cost means to create the basis for future lawsuits. Whenever one was displeased with the speech of another party conducted over an interactive computer service, the offended party could simply "notify" the relevant service provider, claiming the information to be legally defamatory. In light of the vast amount of speech communicated through interactive computer services, these notices could produce an impossible burden for service providers, who would be faced with ceaseless choices of suppressing controversial speech or sustaining prohibitive liability. Because the probable effects of distributor liability on the vigor of Internet speech and on service provider self-regulation are directly contrary to 230's statutory purposes, we will not assume that Congress intended to leave liability upon notice intact. . . .

Section 230 represents the approach of Congress to a problem of national and international dimension. The Supreme Court underscored this point in *Reno v. ACLU,* finding that the Internet allows "tens of millions of people to communicate with one another and to access vast amounts of information from around the world. [It] is 'a unique and wholly new medium of worldwide human communication.'"—U.S. at—, 117 S.Ct. at 2334 [citation omitted]. Application of the canon invoked by Zeran here would significantly lessen Congress' power, derived from the Commerce Clause, to act in a field whose international character is apparent. While Congress allowed for the enforcement of "any State law that is consistent with [§ 230]," 47 U.S.C. 230(d)(3), it is equally plain that Congress' desire to promote unfettered speech on the Internet must supersede conflicting common law causes of action. Section 230(d)(3) continues: "No cause of action may be brought and no liability may be imposed under any State or local law that is inconsistent with this section." With respect to federal-state preemption, the Court has advised: "[W]hen Congress has 'unmistakably . . . ordained,' that its enactments alone are to regulate a part of commerce, state laws regulating that aspect of commerce must fall. The result is compelled whether Congress' command is explicitly stated in the statute's language or implicitly contained in its structure and purpose." *Jones v. Rath Packing Co.,* 430 U.S. 519, 525, 97 S.Ct. 1305, 1309, 51 L.Ed.2d 604 (1977) [citations omitted]. Here, Congress' command is explicitly stated. Its exercise of its commerce power is clear and counteracts the caution counseled by the interpretive canon favoring retention of common law principles. . . .

NOTE

1. In *Lunney v. Prodigy Services Company,* 250 A.D.2d 230, 683 N.Y.S.2d 557 (N.Y. App. Div., 2d Dept. 1998), the court held that an ISP cannot be held liable if it does not engage in an editorial function or "at least [in a] participatory function" in the posting of offending and threatening e-mails.

11.4.2 Privacy

11.4.2.1 Consumer Profiles

Highly-publicized leaks and losses of financial and personal data filled the news in 2005. According to The Privacy Clearinghouse, in 2005 more than 52 million individuals had their confidential personal and financial information exposed in more than 25 different incidents. Bob Sullivan, "ChoicePoint to Pay $15 Million Over Data Breach," www. msnbc.com, January 26, 2006. In February, 2005, ChoicePoint revealed that it had provided information to criminals who had created fake businesses to obtain consumers' private information. Consequently, 145,000 U.S. consumers' had their personal information compromised. ChoicePoint agreed to pay a $10 million fine to the Federal Trade Commission and to create a $5 million fund to help those consumers who were victims of identity theft. Id., Robert Lemos, "Data Security Moves Front and Center in 2005, www.securityfocus.com, December 29, 2005. Shortly after, Bank of America disclosed that it had lost computer backup tapes that contained the personal information (including Social Security numbers and account information) of over 1.2 million federal employees, including members of the U.S. Senate. The Associated Press, "Bank of America Loses Customer Data," www.msnbc.com, March 1, 2005. "Topping the year of revelations, MasterCard International told consumers that online attackers managed to compromise a database of third-party credit processor CardSystems Solutions, leaking 40 million accounts encompassing the four major types of credit cards." Lemos, s*upra*. The fact that these serious security breaches came to light is credited to the 2003 enactment of the California data breach disclosure statute, California Civil Code Sections 1798.29, 1798.83 and 1798.84.

NOTE

1. For a running tally of data security breaches since the ChoicePoint incident, see http://www.privacyrights.org/ar/ChronDataBreaches.htm.

11.4.2.2 Spamming

The CAN-SPAM Act of 2003, was enacted to create a uniform response to the efforts to control "spam"—the transmission of unwanted junk mail and other communications. It provides as follows:

15 USCA § 7703

Sec. 4. Prohibition Against Predatory and Abusive Commercial e-Mail.

(a) OFFENSE.
 (1) IN GENERAL. Chapter 47 of title 18, United States Code, is amended by adding at the end the following new section:

 18 USCA § 1037
  "§ 1037. Fraud and related activity in connection with electronic mail
  "(a) IN GENERAL. Whoever, in or affecting interstate or foreign commerce, knowingly—
   "(1) accesses a protected computer without authorization, and intentionally initiates the transmission of multiple commercial electronic mail messages from or through such computer,
   "(2) uses a protected computer to relay or retransmit multiple commercial electronic mail messages, with the intent to deceive or mislead recipients, or any Internet access service, as to the origin of such messages,

"(3) materially falsifies header information in multiple commercial electronic mail messages and intentionally initiates the transmission of such messages,

"(4) registers, using information that materially falsifies the identity of the actual registrant, for five or more electronic mail accounts or online user accounts or two or more domain names, and intentionally initiates the transmission of multiple commercial electronic mail messages from any combination of such accounts or domain names, or

"(5) falsely represents oneself to be the registrant or the legitimate successor in interest to the registrant of 5 or more Internet Protocol addresses, and intentionally initiates the transmission of multiple commercial electronic mail messages from such addresses, or conspires to do so, shall be punished as provided in subsection (b).

"(b) PENALTIES. The punishment for an offense under subsection (a) is—

"(1) a fine under this title, imprisonment for not more than 5 years, or both, if—

"(A) the offense is committed in furtherance of any felony under the laws of the United States or of any State; or

"(B) the defendant has previously been convicted under this section or section 1030, or under the law of any State for conduct involving the transmission of multiple commercial electronic mail messages or unauthorized access to a computer system;

"(2) a fine under this title, imprisonment for not more than 3 years, or both, if—

"(A) the offense is an offense under subsection (a)(1);

"(B) the offense is an offense under subsection (a)(4) and involved 20 or more falsified electronic mail or online user account registrations, or 10 or more falsified domain name registrations;

"(C) the volume of electronic mail messages transmitted in furtherance of the offense exceeded 2,500 during any 24-hour period, 25,000 during any 30- day period, or 250,000 during any 1-year period;

"(D) the offense caused loss to one or more persons aggregating $5,000 or more in value during any 1-year period;

"(E) as a result of the offense any individual committing the offense obtained anything of value aggregating $5,000 or more during any 1-year period; or

"(F) the offense was undertaken by the defendant in concert with three or more other persons with respect to whom the defendant occupied a position of organizer or leader; and

"(3) a fine under this title or imprisonment for not more than 1 year, or both, in any other case.

"(c) FORFEITURE.

"(1) IN GENERAL. The court, in imposing sentence on a person who is convicted of an offense under this section, shall order that the defendant forfeit to the United States—

"(A) any property, real or personal, constituting or traceable to gross proceeds obtained from such offense; and

"(B) any equipment, software, or other technology used or intended to be used to commit or to facilitate the commission of such offense.

"(2) PROCEDURES. The procedures set forth in section 413 of the Controlled Substances Act (21 U.S.C. 853), other than subsection (d) of that section, and in Rule 32.2 of the Federal Rules of Criminal Procedure, shall apply to all stages of a criminal forfeiture proceeding under this section.

"(d) DEFINITIONS. In this section:

"(1) LOSS. The term 'loss' has the meaning given that term in section 1030(e) of this title.

"(2) MATERIALLY. For purposes of paragraphs (3) and (4) of subsection (a), header information or registration information is materially falsified if it is altered or concealed in a manner that would impair the ability of a recipient of the message, an Internet access service processing the message on behalf of a recipient, a person alleging a violation of this section, or a law enforcement agency to identify, locate, or respond to a person who initiated the electronic mail message or to investigate the alleged violation.

"(3) MULTIPLE. The term 'multiple' means more than 100 electronic mail messages during a 24-hour period, more than 1,000 electronic mail messages during a 30-day period, or more than 10,000 electronic mail messages during a 1-year period.

"(4) OTHER TERMS. Any other term has the meaning given that term by section 3 of the CAN-SPAM Act of 2003."

In April 2004, the first criminal complaints under the CAN-SPAM Act were brought against Phoenix Avatar, LLC of Detroit and Global Web Promotions of Australia and New Zealand. "Feds Nab Two Big Spammers," www.consumeraffairs.com, April 29, 2004. Both operations, purveyors of "diet patches," were identified by Spamhaus as among the largest spammers in the world. *Id.* In March 2005, Phoenix Avatar settled with the FTC under a stipulated order for permanent injunction and a final judgment as to the Phoenix principals.

NOTES ———————————————————————————————

1. For general information dealing with the issue of spamming see www.cauce.org.

2. California has recently enacted legislation to protect consumers from identity theft and increase penalties for spamming: SB355 makes the practice of Internet "phishing" a crime in California. "Phishing" is when web surfers are tricked or lured into providing personal information such as Social Security numbers or credit card numbers, which are later used without the consumer's consent. SB97 provides that a person who violates California's anti-spam law has committed a misdemeanor punishable by a fine of not more than $1,000, imprisonment in a county jail for not more than six months, or both. "California Cracks Down On Phishing," www.centralvalleybusinesstimes.com, December 30, 2005.

3. In *Cybersell, Inc. v. Cyber Sell, Inc.*, 130 F.3d 414 (9th Cir. 1997), the court held that mere spamming is not sufficient contact to support the exercise of long-arm jurisdiction over an out-of-state defendant.

11.5 COPYRIGHT INFRINGEMENT

The internet and other digital technologies are affected by the following international treaties and domestic legislation adopted within the last fifteen years.

- The Audio Home Recording Act of 1992, Pub. L. No. 102–563, 106 Stat. 4237, which imposed a surcharge on digital recording equipment and digital "blanks," in recognition of their potential to cut into sales of traditional records.
- The 1994 Uruguay Round of the General Agreement on Tariffs and Trade, incorporating provisions concerning the trade-related aspects of intellectual property rights (the so-called TRIPS provisions), 33 I.L.M. 136 (1994), which added to, and provided for, enforcement via the World Trade Organization of the intellectual property protections previously provided under the Berne Convention and other international agreements.
- The Digital Performance Right in Sound Recordings Act of 1995, Pub. L. No. 104–39, 109Stat. 336 (1995)(amended Pub. L. No. 105–80 (1997), which, for the first time (and to a limited extent), accorded a performance right in sound recordings.
- The World Intellectual Property Organization Treaty on Copyright, CRNR/DC/94(adopted Dec. 20, 1996), which recognized the right of digital distribution.
- The WIPO Treaty on Performances and Phonograms, CRNR/DC/94 (adopted Dec. 20,1996), which broadened the recognition of the rights of broadcasters, performers, and the creators of phonograms.
- The No Electronic Theft Act, Pub. L. No. 105–147, 111 Stat. 2678 (1997), enacted in response to the decision in *United States v. La Macchia*, 871 F. Supp. 535 (D. Mass.1994) (MIT student uploader acquitted of wire fraud charge by reason of lack of profit motive) which made it a crime to willfully upload copyrighted materials to the Internet (with very low minimum thresholds: one or more uploads in a 180-day period of copyrighted works having an aggregate retail value of $1,000 or more can result in a fine and/or imprisonment, which can be up to three years if the retail value exceeds $2,500,with potential imprisonment for up to six years for a second or subsequent offense)regardless of the presence or absence of a profit motive. The first conviction under this statute was recorded in December 1999.

11.5.1 Digital Millennium Copyright Act

The Digital Millennium Copyright Act of 1998, Pub. L. No. 105–304, 112 Stat. 28601(1998) (amended Pub. L. No. 106–113 §1000 (a)(9) (the "DMCA"), among other things, bound the United States to the 1996 World Intellectual Property Organization (WIPO) treaties and expanded the scope of the performance right in sound recordings (while at the same time providing compulsory licensing to "streaming" stations). In addition, the DMCA establishes a potential "safe harbor" for an ISP when copyright infringement is committed by a third party through the use of the ISP's facilities. The DMCA does not change existing law concerning either infringement or defenses to infringement. However, 17 U.S.C. §512 establishes four "safe harbor" situations in which an ISP can be immune:

1. Where the ISP serves as a mere conduit.
2. "System caching," that is, autocopying/retention of copies such as

frequently visited remote websites, to improve network performance and reduce congestion.

3. Where the ISP provides access without receiving a direct financial benefit, is unaware of the infringement, and is unaware of facts and circumstances under which the infringement would be apparent, and has not received notification thereof.

4. Where the ISP serves as a hyperlink to infringing material that appears on another service.

The DMCA sets up a "notice and takedown" procedure under which copyright proprietors can notify an ISP of the presence of infringing material and demand its removal. If the ISP proceeds to remove the material expeditiously, and otherwise meets the foregoing criteria, the ISP will be immune from damages and/or injunctive relief at the behest of either side. Provision is made for notice by the ISP to the uploader, who has the right to send a counter-notice seeking restoration of the material. Again, if the ISP has followed the statutory procedures, the ISP will be immune to damages and/or injunctive relief at the behest of the uploader. To facilitate the foregoing procedures, the ISP is required to designate an official recipient for such notices. Finally, in order to identify uploaders, the act provides an expedited procedure for subpoenas to ISPs.

Recording Industry Association of America, Inc. v. Verizon Internet Services, Inc., 351 F.3rd 1229 (D.C. Cir. 2003) Before: GINSBURG, Chief Judge, and ROBERTS, Circuit Judge, and WILLIAMS, Senior Circuit Judge.

OPINION FOR THE COURT FILED BY CHIEF JUDGE GINSBURG:

This case concerns the Recording Industry Association of America's use of the subpoena provision of the Digital Millennium Copyright Act, *17 U.S.C. § 512(h)*, to identify internet users the RIAA believes are infringing the copyrights of its members. The RIAA served two subpoenas upon Verizon Internet Services in order to discover the names of two Verizon subscribers who appeared to be trading large numbers of .mp3 files of copyrighted music via "peer-to-peer" (P2P) file sharing programs, such as KaZaA. Verizon refused to comply with the subpoenas on various legal grounds.

The district court rejected Verizon's statutory and constitutional challenges to § 512(h) and ordered the internet service provider (ISP) to disclose to the RIAA the names of the two subscribers. On appeal Verizon presents three alternative arguments for reversing the orders of the district court: (1) § 512(h) does not authorize the issuance of a subpoena to an ISP acting solely as a conduit for communications the content of which is determined by others; if the statute does authorize such a subpoena, then the statute is unconstitutional because (2) the district court lacked Article III jurisdiction to issue a subpoena with no underlying "case or controversy" pending before the court; and (3) § 512(h) violates the First Amendment because it lacks sufficient safeguards to protect an internet user's ability to speak and to associate anonymously. Because we agree with Verizon's interpretation of the statute, we reverse the orders of the district court enforcing the subpoenas and do not reach either of Verizon's constitutional arguments.

I. BACKGROUND

Individuals with a personal computer and access to the internet began to offer digital copies of recordings for download by other users, an activity known as file sharing, in the late 1990's using a program called Napster. Although recording companies and music publishers successfully obtained an injunction against Napster's facilitating the sharing of files containing copyrighted recordings, *see* A&M Records, Inc. v. Napster, Inc., 284 F.3d 1091 (9th Cir.2002); *A&M Records, Inc. v. Napster, Inc., 239 F.3d 1004 (9th Cir.2001)*, millions of people in the United States and around the world continue to share digital .mp3 files of copyrighted recordings using P2P computer programs such as KaZaA, Morpheus, Grokster, and eDonkey. *See* John Borland, *File Swapping Shifts Up a Gear* (May 27, 2003), *available at http:// news.com. com/2100–1026–1009742.html* (last visited December 2, 2003). Unlike Napster, which relied upon a centralized communication architecture to identify the .mp3 files available for download, the current generation of P2P file sharing programs allow an internet user to search directly the .mp3 file libraries of other users; no web site is involved. *See* Douglas Lichtman & William Landes, *Indirect Liability for Copyright Infringement: An Economic Perspective,* 16 Harv. J. LawW & Tech. 395, 403, 408–09 (2003). To date, owners of copyrights have not been able to stop the use of these decentralized programs. *See Metro-Goldwyn-Mayer Studios, Inc. v. Grokster, Ltd., 259 F.Supp.2d 1029 (C.D.Cal.2003)* (holding Grokster not contributorily liable for copyright infringement by users of its P2P file sharing program).

The RIAA now has begun to direct its anti-infringement efforts against individual users of P2P file sharing programs. In order to pursue apparent infringers the RIAA needs to be able to identify the individuals who are sharing and trading files using P2P programs. The RIAA can readily obtain the screen name of an individual user, and using the Internet Protocol (IP) address associated with that screen name, can trace the user to his ISP. Only the ISP, however, can link the IP address used to access a P2P program with the name and address of a person—the ISP's customer—who can then be contacted or, if need be, sued by the RIAA.

The RIAA has used the subpoena provisions of § 512(h) of the Digital Millennium Copyright Act (DMCA) to compel ISPs to disclose the

---

FN* The district court's jurisdiction to issue the orders here under review is not drawn into question by Verizon's Article III argument. *See Interstate Commerce Comm'n v. Brimson, 154 U.S. 447, 476–78, 14 S.Ct. 1125, 1132–34, 38 L.Ed. 1047 (1894)* (application of ICC to enforce subpoena issued by agency in furtherance of investigation presents "case or controversy" subject to judicial resolution).

names of subscribers whom the RIAA has reason to believe are infringing its members' copyrights. *See 17 U.S.C. § 512(h)(1)* (copyright owner may "request the clerk of any United States district court to issue a subpoena to [an ISP] for identification of an alleged infringer"). Some ISPs have complied with the RIAA's *§ 512(h)* subpoenas and identified the names of the subscribers sought by the RIAA. The RIAA has sent letters to and filed lawsuits against several hundred such individuals, each of whom allegedly made available for download by other users hundreds or in some cases even thousands of .mp3 files of copyrighted recordings. Verizon refused to comply with and instead has challenged the validity of the two *§ 512(h)* subpoenas it has received.

A copyright owner (or its agent, such as the RIAA) must file three items along with its request that the Clerk of a district court issue a subpoena: (1) a "notification of claimed infringement" identifying the copyrighted work(s) claimed to have been infringed and the infringing material or activity, and providing information reasonably sufficient for the ISP to locate the material, all as further specified in *§ 512(c)(3)(A)*; (2) the proposed subpoena directed to the ISP; and (3) a sworn declaration that the purpose of the subpoena is "to obtain the identity of an alleged infringer and that such information will only be used for the purpose of protecting" rights under the copyright laws of the United States. *17 U.S.C. § § 512(h)(2)(A)-(C).* If the copyright owner's request contains all three items, then the Clerk "shall expeditiously issue and sign the proposed subpoena and return it to the requester for delivery to the [ISP]." *17 U.S.C. § 512(h)(4).* Upon receipt of the subpoena the ISP is "authorize[d] and order[ed]" to disclose to the copyright owner the identity of the alleged infringer. *See 17 U.S.C. § § 512(h)(3), (5).*

On July 24, 2002 the RIAA served Verizon with a subpoena issued pursuant to *§ 512(h)*, seeking the identity of a subscriber whom the RIAA believed to be engaged in infringing activity. The subpoena was for "information sufficient to identify the alleged infringer of the sound recordings described in the attached notification." The "notification of claimed infringement" identified the IP address of the subscriber and about 800 sound files he offered for trading; expressed the RIAA's "good faith belief" the file sharing activity of Verizon's subscriber constituted infringement of its members' copyrights; and asked for Verizon's "immediate assistance in stopping this unauthorized activity." "Specifically, we request that you remove or disable access to the infringing sound files via your system."

When Verizon refused to disclose the name of its subscriber, the RIAA filed a motion to compel production pursuant to *Federal Rule of Civil Procedure 45(c)(2)(B)* and *§ 512(h)(6)* of the Act. In opposition to that motion, Verizon argued *§ 512(h)* does not apply to an ISP acting merely as a conduit for an individual using a P2P file sharing program to exchange files. The district court rejected Verizon's argument based upon "the language and structure of the statute, as confirmed by the purpose and history of the legislation," and ordered Verizon to disclose to the RIAA the name of its subscriber. *In re Verizon Internet Servs., Inc., 240 F.Supp.2d 24, 45 (D.D.C.2003)* (*Verizon I*).

The RIAA then obtained another *§ 512(h)* subpoena directed to Verizon. This time Verizon moved to quash the subpoena, arguing that the district court, acting through the Clerk, lacked jurisdiction under Article III to issue the subpoena and in the alternative that *§ 512(h)* violates the First Amendment. The district court rejected Verizon's constitutional arguments, denied the motion to quash, and again ordered Verizon to disclose the identity of its subscriber. *In re Verizon Internet Servs., Inc., 257 F.Supp.2d 244, 247, 275 (D.D.C.2003)* (*Verizon II*).

Verizon appealed both orders to this Court and we consolidated the two cases. As it did before the district court, the RIAA defends both the applicability of *§ 512(h)* to an ISP acting as a conduit for P2P file sharing and the constitutionality of *§ 512(h)*. The United States has intervened solely to defend the constitutionality of the statute.

II. Analysis

The court ordinarily reviews a district court's grant of a motion to compel or denial of a motion to quash for abuse of discretion. *See, e.g., In re Sealed Case, 121 F.3d 729, 740 (D.C.Cir.1997)*. Here, however, Verizon contends the orders of the district court were based upon errors of law, specifically errors regarding the meaning of § 512(h). Our review is therefore plenary. *See In re Subpoena Served Upon the Comptroller of the Currency, 967 F.2d 630, 633 (D.C.Cir.1992)*.

The issue is whether *§ 512(h)* applies to an ISP acting only as a conduit for data transferred between two internet users, such as persons sending and receiving e-mail or, as in this case, sharing P2P files. Verizon contends *§ 512(h)* does not authorize the issuance of a subpoena to an ISP that transmits infringing material but does not store any such material on its servers. The RIAA argues *§ 512(h)* on its face authorizes the issuance of a subpoena to an "[internet] service provider" without regard to whether the ISP is acting as a conduit for user-directed communications. We conclude from both the terms of *§ 512(h)* and the overall structure of *§ 512* that, as Verizon contends, a subpoena may be issued only to an ISP engaged in storing on its servers material that is infringing or the subject of infringing activity.

A. Subsection 512(h) by its Terms

We begin our analysis, as always, with the text of the statute. *See Barnhart v. Sigmon Coal Co., 534 U.S. 438, 450, 122 S.Ct. 941, 950, 151 L.Ed.2d 908 (2002)*. Verizon's statutory arguments address the meaning of and interaction between *§ § 512(h)* and 512(a)-(d). Having already discussed the general requirements of *§ 512(h)*, we now introduce *§ § 512(a)-(d)*.

Section 512 creates four safe harbors, each of which immunizes ISPs from liability for copyright infringement under certain highly specified conditions. Subsection 512(a), entitled "Transitory digital network communications," provides a safe harbor "for infringement of copyright by reason of the [ISP's] transmitting, routing, or providing connections for" infringing material, subject to certain conditions, including that the transmission is initiated and directed by an internet user. *See 17 U.S.C. § § 512(a)(1)-(5).* Subsection 512(b), "System caching," provides immunity from liability "for infringement of copyright by reason of the intermediate and temporary storage of material on a system or network controlled or operated by or for the [ISP]," *§ 512(b)(1),* as long as certain conditions regarding the transmission and retrieval of the material created by the ISP are met. *See 17 U.S.C. § § 512(b)(2)(A)-(E).* Subsection 512(c). "Information residing on systems or networks at the direction of users," creates a safe harbor from liability "for infringement of copyright by reason of the storage at the direction of a user of material that resides on a system or network controlled or operated by or for the service provider," as long as the ISP meets certain conditions regarding its lack of knowledge concerning, financial benefit from, and expeditious efforts to remove or deny access to, material that is infringing or that is claimed to be the subject of infringing activity. *See 17 U.S.C. § § 512(c)(1)(A)-(C).* Finally, *§ 512(d),* "Information location tools," provides a safe harbor from liability "for infringement of copyright by reason of the provider referring or linking users to an online location containing infringing material or infringing activity, by using information location tools" such as "a directory, index, reference, pointer, or hypertext link," subject to the same conditions as in *§ § 512(c)(1)(A)-(C). See 17 U.S.C. § § 512(d)(1)-(3).*

Notably present in *§ § 512(b)-(d),* and notably absent from *§ 512(a),* is the so-called notice and take-down provision. It makes a condition of the ISP's protection from liability for copyright infringement that "upon notification of claimed infringement as described in [§ 512](c)(3)," the ISP "responds expeditiously to remove, or disable access to, the material that is claimed to be infringing." *See* 17 U.S.C. § § 512(b)(2)(E), 512(c)(1)(C), and 512(d)(3).

Verizon argues that § 512(h) by its terms precludes the Clerk of Court from issuing a subpoena to an ISP acting as a conduit for P2P communications because a § 512(h) subpoena request cannot meet the requirement in § 512(h)(2)(A) that a proposed subpoena contain "a copy of a notification [of claimed infringement, as] described in [§ 512](c)(3)(A)."[n1] In particular, Verizon maintains the two subpoenas obtained by the RIAA fail to meet the requirements of § 512(c)(3)(A)(iii) in that they do not—because Verizon is not storing the infringing material on its server—and can not, identify material "to be removed or access to which is to be disabled" by Verizon. Here Verizon points out that § 512(h)(4) makes satisfaction of the notification requirement of § 512(c)(3)(A) a condition precedent to issuance of a subpoena: "If the notification filed satisfies the provisions of [§ 512](c)(3)(A)" and the other content requirements of § 512(h)(2) are met, then "the clerk shall expeditiously issue and sign the proposed subpoena . . . for delivery" to the ISP.

Infringing material obtained or distributed via P2P file sharing is located in the computer (or in an off-line storage device, such as a compact disc) of an individual user. No matter what information the copyright owner may provide, the ISP can neither "remove" nor "disable access to" the infringing material because that material is not stored on the ISP's servers. Verizon can not remove or disable one user's access to infringing material resident on another user's computer because Verizon does not control the content on its subscribers' computers.

The RIAA contends an ISP can indeed "disable access" to infringing material by terminating the offending subscriber's internet account. This argument is undone by the terms of the Act, however. As Verizon notes, the Congress considered disabling an individual's access to infringing material and disabling access to the internet to be different remedies for the protection of copyright owners, the former blocking access to the infringing material on the offender's computer and the latter more broadly blocking the offender's access to the internet (at least via his chosen ISP). *Compare* 17 U.S.C. § 512(j)(1)(A)(i) (authorizing injunction restraining ISP "from providing access to infringing material") *with* 17 U.S.C. § 512(j)(1)(A)(ii) (authorizing injunction restraining ISP "from providing access to a subscriber or account holder . . . who is engaging in infringing activity . . . by terminating the accounts of the subscriber or account holder"). "[W]here different terms are used in a single piece of legislation, the court must presume that Congress intended the terms have different meanings." Transbrasil S.A. Linhas Aereas v. Dep't of Transp., 791 F.2d 202, 205 (D.C.Cir.1986). These distinct statutory remedies establish that terminating a subscriber's account is not the same as removing or disabling access by others to the infringing material resident on the subscriber's computer.

---

n1 Subsection 512(c)(3)(A) provides that "[t]o be effective under this subsection, a notification of claimed infringement must be a written communication . . . that includes substantially the following":

(i) A physical or electronic signature of a person authorized to act on behalf of the owner of an exclusive right that is allegedly infringed.

(ii) Identification of the copyrighted work claimed to have been infringed, or, if multiple copyrighted works at a single online site are covered by a single notification, a representative list of such works at that site.

(iii) Identification of the material that is claimed to be infringing or to be the subject of infringing activity and that is to be removed or access to which is to be disabled, and information reasonably sufficient to permit the service provider to locate the material.

(iv) Information reasonably sufficient to permit the service provider to contact the complaining party, such as an address, telephone number, and, if available, an electronic mail address at which the complaining party may be contacted.

(v) A statement that the complaining party has a good faith belief that use of the material in the manner complained of is not authorized by the copyright owner, its agent, or the law.

(vi) A statement that the information in the notification is accurate, and under penalty of perjury, that the complaining party is authorized to act on behalf of the owner of an exclusive right that is allegedly infringed.

The RIAA points out that even if, with respect to an ISP functioning as a conduit for user-directed communications, a copyright owner cannot satisfy the requirement of § 512(c)(3)(A)(iii) by identifying material to be removed by the ISP, a notification is effective under § 512(c)(3)(A) if it "includes substantially" the required information; that standard is satisfied, the RIAA maintains, because the ISP can identify the infringer based upon the information provided by the copyright owner pursuant to § § 512(c)(3)(A)(i)-(ii) and (iv)-(vi). According to the RIAA, the purpose of § 512(h) being to identify infringers, a notice should be deemed sufficient so long as the ISP can identify the infringer from the IP address in the subpoena.

Nothing in the Act itself says how we should determine whether a notification "includes substantially" all the required information; both the Senate and House Reports, however, state the term means only that "technical errors . . . such as misspelling a name" or "supplying an outdated area code" will not render ineffective an otherwise complete § 512(c)(3)(A) notification. S.Rep. No. 105–190, at 47 (1998); H.R.Rep. No. 105–551 (II), at 56 (1998). Clearly, however, the defect in the RIAA's notification is not a mere technical error; nor could it be thought "insubstantial" even under a more forgiving standard. The RIAA's notification identifies absolutely no material Verizon could remove or access to which it could disable, which indicates to us that § 512(c)(3)(A) concerns means of infringement other than P2P file sharing.

Finally, the RIAA argues the definition of "[internet] service provider" in § 512(k)(1)(B) makes § 512(h) applicable to an ISP regardless what function it performs with respect to infringing material—transmitting it per § 512(a), caching it per § 512(b), hosting it per § 512(c), or locating it per § 512(d).

This argument borders upon the silly. The details of this argument need not burden the Federal Reporter, for the specific provisions of § 512(h), which we have just rehearsed, make clear that however broadly "[internet] service provider" is defined in § 512(k)(1)(B), a subpoena may issue to an ISP only under the prescribed conditions regarding notification. Define all the world as an ISP if you like, the validity of a § 512(h) subpoena still depends upon the copyright holder having given the ISP, however defined, a notification effective under § 512(c)(3)(A). And as we have seen, any notice to an ISP concerning its activity as a mere conduit does not satisfy the condition of § 512(c)(3)(A)(iii) and is therefore ineffective.

In sum, we agree with Verizon that § 512(h) does not by its terms authorize the subpoenas issued here. A § 512(h) subpoena simply cannot meet the notice requirement of § 512(c)(3)(A)(iii).

B. Structure

Verizon also argues the subpoena provision, § 512(h), relates uniquely to the safe harbor in § 512(c) for ISPs engaged in storing copyrighted material and does not apply to the transmitting function addressed by the safe harbor in § 512(a). Verizon's claim is based upon the "three separate cross-references" in § 512(h) to the notification described in § 512(c)(3)(A). First, as we have seen, § 512(h)(2)(A) requires the copyright owner to file, along with its request for a subpoena, the notification described in § 512(c)(3)(A). Second, and again as we have seen, § 512(h)(4) requires that the notification satisfy "the provisions of [§ 512](c)(3)(A)" as a condition precedent to the Clerk's issuing the requested subpoena. Third, § 512(h)(5) conditions the ISP's obligation to identify the alleged infringer upon "receipt of a notification described in [§ 512](c)(3)(A)." We agree that the presence in § 512(h) of three separate references to § 512(c) and the absence of any reference to § 512(a) suggests the subpoena power of § 512(h) applies only to ISPs engaged in storing copyrighted material and not to those engaged solely in transmitting it on behalf of others.

As the RIAA points out in response, however, because § § 512(b) and (d) also require a copyright owner to provide a "notification . . . as described in [§ 512](c)(3)," the cross-references to § 512(c)(3)(A) in § 512(h) can not confine the operation of § 512(h) solely to the functions described in § 512(c), but must also include, at a minimum, the functions described in § § 512(b) and (d). Therefore, according to the RIAA, because Verizon is mistaken in stating that "the take-down notice described in [§ 512](c)(3)(A) . . . applies exclusively to the particular functions described in [§ 512](c) of the statute," the subpoena power in § 512(h) is not linked exclusively to § 512(c) but rather applies to all the ISP functions, wherever they may be described in § § 512(a)-(d).

Although the RIAA's conclusion is a non-sequitur with respect to § 512(a), we agree with the RIAA that Verizon overreaches by claiming the notification described in § 512(c)(3)(A) applies only to the functions identified in § 512(c). As Verizon correctly notes, however, the ISP activities described in § § 512(b) and (d) are storage functions. As such, they are, like the ISP activities described in § 512(c) and unlike the transmission functions listed in § 512(a), susceptible to the notice and take down regime of § § 512(b)-(d), of which the subpoena power of § 512(h) is an integral part. We think it clear, therefore, that the cross-references to § 512(c)(3) in § § 512(b)-(d) demonstrate that § 512(h) applies to an ISP storing infringing material on its servers in any capacity-whether as a temporary cache of a web page created by the ISP per § 512(b), as a web site stored on the ISP's server per § 512(c), or as an information locating tool hosted by the ISP per § 512(d)—and does not apply to an ISP routing infringing material to or from a personal computer owned and used by a subscriber.

The storage activities described in the safe harbors of § § 512(b)-(d) are subject to § 512(c)(3), including the notification described in § 512(c)(3)(A). By contrast, as we have already seen, an ISP performing a function described in § 512(a), such as transmitting e-mails, instant messages, or files sent by an internet user from his computer to that of another internet user, cannot be sent an effective § 512(c)(3)(A) notification. Therefore, the references to § 512(c)(3) in § § 512(b) and (d) lead inexorably to the conclusion that § 512(h) is structurally linked to the storage functions of an ISP and not to its transmission functions, such as those listed in § 512(a).

C. Legislative History

In support of its claim that § 512(h) can—and should—be read to reach P2P technology, the RIAA points to congressional testimony and news articles available to the Congress prior to passage of the DMCA. These sources document the threat to copyright owners posed by bulletin board services (BBSs) and file transfer protocol (FTP) sites, which the RIAA says were precursors to P2P programs.

We need not, however, resort to investigating what the 105th Congress may have known because the text of § 512(h) and the overall structure of § 512 clearly establish, as we have seen, that § 512(h) does not authorize the issuance of a subpoena to an ISP acting as a mere conduit for the transmission of information sent by others. Legislative history can serve to inform the court's reading of an otherwise ambiguous text; it cannot lead the court to contradict the legislation itself. *See* Ratzlaf v. United States, 510 U.S. 135, 147–48, 114 S.Ct. 655, 662–63, 126 L.Ed.2d 615 (1994) ("[W]e do not resort to legislative history to cloud a statutory text that is clear").

In any event, not only is the statute clear (albeit complex), the legislative history of the DMCA betrays no awareness whatsoever that internet users might be able directly to exchange files containing copyrighted works. That is not surprising; P2P software was "not even a glimmer in anyone's eye when the DMCA was enacted." In re Verizon I, 240 F.Supp.2d at 38. Furthermore, such testimony as was available to the Congress prior to passage of the DMCA concerned "hackers" who established unauthorized FTP or BBS sites on the servers of ISPs, *see Balance of Responsibilities on the Internet and the Online Copyright Liability Limitation Act: Hearing on H.R. 2180 Before the House Subcomm. on Courts and Intellectual Property, Comm. on the Judiciary,* 105th Cong. (1997) (statement of Ken Wasch, President, Software Publishers Ass'n); rogue ISPs that posted FTP sites on their servers, thereby making files of copyrighted musical works available for download, *see* Complaint, *Geffen Records, Inc. v. Arizona Bizness Network,* No. CIV. 98–0794, at ¶ 1 (D. Ariz. May 5, 1998) *available at http:// www.riaa.com/news/newsletter/ pdf/geffencomplaint.pdf,* (last visited December 2, 2003); and BBS subscribers using dial-up technology to connect to a BBS hosted by an ISP. The Congress had no reason to foresee the application of § 512(h) to P2P file sharing, nor did they draft the DMCA broadly enough to reach the new technology when it came along. Had the Congress been aware of P2P technology, or anticipated its development, § 512(h) might have been drafted more generally. Be that as it may, contrary to the RIAA's claim, nothing in the legislative history supports the issuance of a § 512(h) subpoena to an ISP acting as a conduit for P2P file sharing.

D. Purpose of the DMCA

Finally, the RIAA argues Verizon's interpretation of the statute "would defeat the core objectives" of the Act. More specifically, according to the RIAA there is no policy justification for limiting the reach of § 512(h) to situations in which the ISP stores infringing material on its system, considering that many more acts of copyright infringement are committed in the P2P realm, in which the ISP merely transmits the material for others, and that the burden upon an ISP required to identify an infringing subscriber is minimal.

We are not unsympathetic either to the RIAA's concern regarding the widespread infringement of its members' copyrights, or to the need for legal tools to protect those rights. It is not the province of the courts, however, to rewrite the DMCA in order to make it fit a new and unforeseen internet architecture, no matter how damaging that development has been to the music industry or threatens being to the motion picture and software industries. The plight of copyright holders must be addressed in the first instance by the Congress; only the "Congress has the constitutional authority and the institutional ability to accommodate fully the varied permutations of competing interests that are inevitably implicated by such new technology." *See* Sony Corp. v. Universal City Studios, Inc., 464 U.S. 417, 431, 104 S.Ct. 774, 783, 78 L.Ed.2d 574 (1984).

The stakes are large for the music, motion picture, and software industries and their role in fostering technological innovation and our popular culture. It is not surprising, therefore, that even as this case was being argued, committees of the Congress were considering how best to deal with the threat to copyrights posed by P2P file sharing schemes. *See, e.g., Privacy & Piracy: The Paradox of Illegal File Sharing on Peer-to-Peer Networks and the Impact of Technology on the Entertainment Industry: Hearing Before the Senate Comm. On Governmental Affairs,* 108th Congress (Sept. 30, 2003); *Pornography, Technology, and Process: Problems and Solutions on Peer-to-Peer Networks: Hearing Before the Senate Comm. on the Judiciary,* 108th Congress (Sept. 9, 2003).

III. CONCLUSION

For the foregoing reasons, we remand this case to the district court to vacate its order enforcing the July 24 subpoena and to grant Verizon's motion to quash the February 4 subpoena.

So ordered.

NOTES _____

1. In *In re Charter Communications, Inc., 393 F.3d 771* (8th Cir. 2005), Charter sought to quash a subpoena requiring it to provide subscriber information linked to certain IP addresses known to have transmitted infringing files. The ISP argued that §512(h) of the DMCA did not apply to it, as it was only a conduit, as opposed to an ISP that stored infringing material. The Eighth Circuit reversed

the lower court, following the reasoning of the District of Columbia Court of Appeals in *RIAA v. Verizon Internet Services, Inc.,* 351 F.3d 1229 (D.C. Cir. 2003). "Thus, where Charter acted solely as a conduit for the transmission of material by others (its subscribers using P2P file-sharing software to exchange files stored on their personal computers), Charter contends the subpoena was not properly issued. We agree." *Id.* at 777.

2. The *In re Charter* court noted "The RIAA, to our knowledge, has never prevailed in any infringement actions brought against individual downloaders." *Id.* at 772. This situation was remedied by *BMG Music, et al. v. Gonzalez, infra.*

11.5.2 The Impact of Internet-Specific Technologies

11.5.2.1 MP3

No area of the entertainment industries has received more press or been the cause of more hand-wringing than spread of compression and file-sharing technologies and the resulting rise of piracy of intellectual property. As noted in the introduction, there has been explosive growth in the sale of legitimate digital media product in recent years. Nevertheless, according to one market research firm, 6.25 million individuals visit illegal file-sharing sites each month. Lamberg, *supra.* While piracy of intellectual property has existed for many years, digital technology made the threat graver, as the act of copying no longer resulted in a degraded product. In effect, anyone with a CD burner or access to a file-sharing network could distribute product comparable in quality to that distributed by the content owners themselves.

The first battleground was the compression technology known as MP3, and the first of the MP3 cases, *Recording Industry Association of America [RIAA] v. Diamond Multimedia Systems, Inc.,* 180 F.3d 1072 (9th Cir. 1999), reached a result similar to that in *Sony Corp. of America v. Universal City Studios, Inc.,* 464 U.S.417 (1984), the so-called "Betamax" case, which held that since "time shifting" was a primary—and legitimate—reason why consumers used VCRs, the devices were not *per se* instruments of copyright infringement. The court denied the RIAA's motion for preliminary injunction on the ground that the handheld RioPort player was not a "digital audio recording device" within the definition of the Audio Home Recording Act of 1992 (AHRA), 17 U.S.C. 1001 et seq., because it copied from a computer, not from a recording, and the language and legislative history of the AHRA demonstrated an intent to exclude computers from the scope of the act. "The Act does not broadly prohibit digital serial copying of copyright protected audio recordings. Instead, the Act places restrictions only upon a specific type of recording device. . . . The legislative history . . . expressly recognizes that computers (and other devices) have recording functions capable of recording digital musical recordings, and thus implicate the home taping and piracy concerns to which the Act is responsive. . . . [T]he legislative history is consistent with the Act's plain language—computers are not digital audio recording devices." While the court conceded that "the predominant use of MP3 is the trafficking in illicit audio recordings, presumably because MP3 files do not contain codes identifying whether the compressed audio material is copyright protected [and that] various pirate websites offer free downloads of copyrighted material, and a single pirate site on the Internet may contain thousands of pirated audio computer files," the court stated that "the Rio's operation is entirely consistent with the [AHRA's] main purpose—the facilitation of personal use. As the Senate Report explains, [t]he purpose of [the Act] is to ensure the right of consumers to make analog or digital audio recordings of copyrighted music for their private, noncommercial use' S. Rep. 102–294, at *86. The Act does so through its home taping exemption, see 17 U.S.C. 1008, which 'protects all noncommercial copying by consumers of digital and analog musical recordings,' H.R. Rep. 102–873(I), at*59. The Rio merely makes copies in order to render portable, or 'space-shift,' those files that already reside on a user's hard drive." This case demonstrates the limitations of a statute enacted in response to a transient technological improvement.

Set forth below are a series of cases that establish the vicarious or contributory liability of file-sharing services—both those that operate a central database of files available on its system (*MP3.com* and *Napster)* and those that have no central database (*Grokster*). The *Gonzalez* case makes clear that individuals will be held liable as direct infringers.

UMG Recordings, Inc. v. MP3.Com, Inc., 92 F.Supp. 2d 349, 2000 WL 524808 (S.D.N.Y. 2000)

RAKOFF, J.

The complex marvels of cyberspatial communication may create difficult legal issues; but not in this case. Defendant's infringement of plaintiffs' copyrights is clear. Accordingly, on April 28, 2000, the Court granted defendant's motion for partial summary judgment holding defendant liable for copyright infringement. This opinion will state the reasons why. . . .

Utilizing [MP3] technology, defendant MP3.com . . . launched its "My.MP3.com" service, which is advertised as permitting subscribers to store, customize and listen to the recordings contained on their CDs from any place where they have an Internet connection. To make good on this offer, defendant purchased tens of thousands of popular CDs in which plaintiffs held the copyrights, and, without authorization, copied their recordings onto its computer servers so as to be able to replay the recordings for its subscribers. Specifically, in order to first access such a recording, a subscriber to MP3.com must either "prove" that he already owns the CD version of the recording by inserting his copy of the commercial CD into his computer CD-Rom drive for a few seconds (the "Beam-it Service") or must purchase the CD from one of defendant's cooperating online retailers (the "instant Listening Service"). Thereafter, however, the subscriber can access via the Internet from a computer anywhere in the world the copy of plaintiffs' recording made by defendant. Thus, although defendant seeks to portray its service as the "functional equivalent" of storing its subscribers' CDs, in actuality defendant is re-playing for the subscribers converted versions of the recordings it copied, without authorization, from plaintiffs' copyrighted CDs. On its face, this makes out a presumptive case of infringement under the Copyright Act of 1976 ("Copyright Act"), 17 U.S.C. 101 et seq. See, e.g., *Castle Rock Entertainment, Inc. v. Carol Publishing Group, Inc.*, 150 F.3d132, 132, 137 (2d Cir. 1998); *Hasbro Bradley, Inc. v. Sparkle Toys, Inc.*, 780 F.2d189, 192 (2d Cir. 1985).

Defendant argues, however, that such copying is protected by the affirmative defense of "fair use." See 17 U.S.C. 107. In analyzing such a defense, the Copyright Act specifies four factors that must be considered: "(1) the purpose and character of the use, including whether such use is of a commercial nature or is for nonprofit educational purposes; (2) the nature of the copyrighted work; (3) the amount and substantiality of the portion used in relation to the copyrighted work as a whole; and (4) the effect of the use upon the potential market for or value of the copyrighted work." *Id.* Other relevant factors may also be considered, since fair use is an "equitable rule of reason" to be applied in light of the overall purposes of the Copyright Act. *Sony Corporation of America v. Universal City Studios, Inc.*, 464 U.S. 417, 448, 454 (1984); see *Harper & Row, Publishers, Inc. v. Nation Enterprises*, 471 U.S. 539, 549 (1985).

Regarding the first factor—"the purpose and character of the use"—defendant does not dispute that its purpose is commercial, for while subscribers to My.MP3.com are not currently charged a fee, defendant seeks to attract a sufficiently large subscription base to draw advertising and otherwise make a profit. Consideration of the first factor, however, also involves inquiring into whether the new use essentially repeats the old or whether, instead, it "transforms" it by infusing it with new meaning, new understandings, or the like. See, e.g., *Campbell v. Acuff-Rose Music, Inc.*, 510 U.S. 569, 579 (1994); *Castle Rock*, 150 F.3dat 142; see also Pierre N. Leval, "Toward a Fair Use Standard," 103 *Harv. L. Rev.*1105, 111 (1990). Here, although defendant recites that My.MP3.com provides a transformative "space shift" by which subscribers can enjoy the sound recordings contained on their CDs without lugging around the physical discs themselves, this is simply another way of saying that the unauthorized copies are being retransmitted in another medium—an insufficient basis for any legitimate claim of transformation. See, e.g., *Infinity Broadcast Corp. v. Kirkwood*, 150 F.3d 104,108 (2d Cir. 1998) (rejecting the fair use defense by operator of a service that retransmitted copyrighted radio broadcasts over telephone lines); *Los Angeles News Serv. v. Reuters Television Int'l Ltd.*, 149 F.3d 987 (9th Cir. 1998) (rejecting the fair use defense where television news agencies copied copyrighted news footage and retransmitted it to news organizations), *cert. denied*, 525 U.S. 1141(1999); see also *American Geophysical Union v. Texaco Inc.*, 60 F.3d 913, 923(2d Cir.), *cert dismissed*, 516 U.S. 1005 (1995); *Basic Books, Inc. v. Kinko's Graphics Corp.*, 758 F. Supp. 1522, 1530–31

(S.D.N.Y. 1991); see generally Leval, *supra,* at 1111 (repetition of copyrighted material that "merely repackages or republishes the original" is unlikely to be deemed a fair use).

Here, defendant adds no "new aesthetics, new insights and understandings" to the original music recordings it copies, see *Castle Rock,* 150 F.3d at 142(internal quotation marks omitted), but simply repackages those recordings to facilitate their transmission through another medium. While such services maybe innovative, they are not transformative.

Regarding the second factor—"the nature of the copyrighted work"— the creative recordings here being copied are "close[] to the core of intended copyright protection," *Campbell,* 510 U.S. at 586, and, conversely, far removed from the more factual or descriptive work more amenable to "fair use," see *Nihon Keizai Shimbun, Inc. v. Comline Business Data, Inc.* 166 F.3d 65, 72–73 (2d Cir. 1999); See also *Castle Rock,* 150 F.3d at 143–44.

Regarding the third factor—"the amount and substantiality of the portion [of the copyrighted work] used [by the copier] in relation to the copyrighted work as a whole"—it is undisputed that defendant copies, and replays, the entirety of the copyrighted works here in issue, thus again negating any claim of fair use. See *Infinity Broadcast,* 150 F.3d at 109 ("[T]he more of a copyrighted work that is taken, the less likely the use is to be fair . . . "); see generally Leval, *supra,* at1122 ("[T]he larger the volume . . . of what is taken, the greater the affront to the interests of the copyright owner, and the less likely that a taking will qualify as a fair use").

Regarding the fourth factor—"the effect of the use upon the potential market for or value of the copyrighted work"—defendant's activities on their face invade plaintiffs' statutory right to license their copyrighted sound recordings to others for reproduction. See 17 U.S.C. 106. Defendant, however, argues that, so far as the derivative market here involves is concerned, plaintiffs have not shown that such licensing is "traditional, reasonable, or likely to be developed." *American Geophysical,* 60 F.3d at 930 n. 17. Moreover, defendant argues, its activities can only enhance plaintiffs' sales, since subscribers cannot gain access to particular recordings made available by MP3.com unless they have already "purchased"(actually or purportedly), or agreed to purchase, their own CD copies of those recordings.

Such arguments—though dressed in the garb of an expert's "opinion" (that, on inspection, consists almost entirely of speculative and conclusory statements)—are unpersuasive. Any allegedly positive impact of defendant's activities on plaintiff's prior market in no way frees defendant to usurp a further market that directly derives from reproduction of the plaintiffs' copyrighted works. See *Infinity Broadcast,* 150 F.3d at 111. This would be so even if the copyright holder had not yet entered the new market in issue, for a copyright holder's "exclusive" rights, derived from the Constitution and the Copyright Act, include the right, within broad limits, to curb the development of such a derivative market by refusing to license a copyrighted work or by doing so only on terms the copyright owner finds acceptable. See *Castle Rock,* 150 F.3d at 145–46; *Salinger v. Random House, Inc.,* 811 F.2d 90, 99 (2d Cir.), *cert. denied,* 484 U.S. 890 (1987). Here, moreover, plaintiffs have adduced substantial evidence that they have in fact taken steps to enter that market by entering into various licensing agreements. . . .

Finally, regarding defendant's purported reliance on other factors, see *Campbell,* 510 U.S. at 577, this essentially reduces to the claim that My.MP3.comprovides a useful service to consumers that, in its absence, will be served by "pirates." Copyright, however, is not designed to afford consumer protection or convenience but, rather, to protect the copyright holders' property interests. Moreover, as a practical matter, plaintiffs have indicated no objection in principle to licensing their recordings to companies like MP3.com; they simply want to make sure they get the remuneration the law reserves for them as holders of copyrights on creative works. Stripped to its essence, defendant's "consumer protection" argument amounts to nothing more than a bald claim that defendant should be able to misappropriate plaintiffs' property simply because there is a consumer demand for it. This hardly appeals to the conscience of equity.

In sum, on any view, defendant's "fair use" defense is indefensible and must be denied as a matter of law. Defendant's other affirmative defenses, such as copyright misuse, abandonment, unclean hands, and estoppel, are essentially frivolous and may be disposed of briefly. While defendant contends, under the rubric of copyright misuse, that plaintiffs are misusing their "dominant market position to selectively prosecute only certain online music technology companies," . . . the admissible evidence of records shows only that plaintiffs have reasonably exercised their right to determine which infringers to pursue, and in which order to pursue them, cf. *Broadcast Music, Inc. v. Peppermint Club, Inc.,* 1985 WL 6141, at *4 (N.D.Ohio, 1985). The abandonment defense must also fall since defendant has failed to adduce any competent evidence of an overt act indicating that plaintiffs, who filed suit against MP3.com shortly after MP3.com launched its infringing My.MP3.com service, intentionally abandoned their copyrights. See *Richard Feiner & Co., Inc. v. H.R. Indus., Inc.,* 10 F. Supp. 2d 310, 313 (SDNY1998). Similarly, defendant's estoppel defense must be rejected because defendant has failed to provide any competent evidence that it relied on any action by plaintiffs with respect to defendant's My.MP3.com service. Finally, the Court must reject defendant's unclean hands defense given defendant's failure to come forth with any admissible evidence showing bad faith or misconduct on the part of plaintiffs. See generally *Dunlop-McCullen v. Local I-S, AFL-CIO-CLC,* 149F.3d 85, 90 (2d Cir. 1998); *A. H. Emery Co. v. Marcan Prods. Corp.,* 389 F.2d 11, 18n. 4 (2d Cir.) *cert denied,* 393 U.S. 835 (1968). . . . Accordingly, the Court, for the foregoing reasons, has determined that plaintiffs are entitled to partial summary judgment holding defendant to have infringed plaintiffs' copyrights.

A&M Records, Inc. v. Napster, Inc., 239 F.3d 1004 (9th Cir. 2001)

BEEZER, CIRCUIT JUDGE:

Plaintiffs are engaged in the commercial recording, distribution and sale of copyrighted musical compositions and sound recordings. The complaint alleges that Napster, Inc. ("Napster") is a contributory and vicarious copyright infringer. . . . The district court preliminarily enjoined Napster "from engaging in, or facilitating others in copying, downloading, uploading, transmitting, or distributing plaintiffs' copyrighted musical compositions and sound recordings, protected by either federal or state law, without express permission of the rights owner." . . . We entered a temporary stay of the preliminary injunction pending resolution of this appeal. . . . We affirm in part, reverse in part and remand.

I

[I]t appears that Napster has designed and operates a system which permits the transmission and retention of sound recordings employing digital technology. In 1987, the Moving Picture Experts Group set a standard file format for the storage of audio recordings in a digital format called MPEG-3, abbreviated as "MP3."Digital MP3 files are created through a process colloquially called "ripping." Ripping software allows a computer owner to copy an audio compact disk ("audio CD") directly onto a computer's hard drive by compressing the audio information on the CD into the MP3 format. The MP3's compressed format allows for rapid transmission of digital audio files from one computer to another by electronic mail or any other file transfer protocol. Napster facilitates the transmission of MP3 files between and among its users. Through a process commonly called "peer-to-peer" file sharing, Napster allows its users to: (1) make MP3 music files stored on individual computer hard drives available for copying by other Napster users; (2) search for MP3 music files stored on other users' computers; and (3) transfer exact copies of the contents of other users' MP3 files from one computer to another via the Internet. These functions are made possible by Napster's Music Share software, available free of charge from Napster's Internet site, and Napster's network servers and server-side software. Napster provides technical support for the indexing and searching of MP3 files, as well as for its other functions, including a "chat room," where users can meet to discuss music, and a directory where participating artists can provide information about their music. . . .

[The court then went through a detailed description of how one obtained the Napster software, listed the files he or she wanted to share, searched for files she or she wanted to obtain, and transferred files. It

then stated then the standard of review for the grant or denial of preliminary injunctions]

III

Plaintiffs claim Napster users are engaged in the wholesale reproduction and distribution of copyrighted works, all constituting direct
infringement. Secondary liability for copyright infringement does not
exist in the absence of direct infringement by a third party. *Religious
Tech. Ctr. v. Netcom On-Line Communication Servs., Inc.,* 907 F. Supp.
1361, 1371 (N.D. Cal. 1995) ("[T]here can be no contributory infringement by a defendant without direct infringement by another"). It follows that Napster does not facilitate infringement of the copyright laws
in the absence of direct infringement by its users. The district court
agreed. We note that the district court's conclusion that plaintiffs have
presented a prima facie case of direct infringement by Napster users is
not presently appealed by Napster. . . . Plaintiffs have sufficiently demonstrated ownership [of the material copied]. The record supports the
district court's determination that "as much as eighty-seven percent of
the files available on Napster may be copyrighted and more than seventy percent may be owned or administered by plaintiffs [and] that a
majority of Napster users use the service to download and upload copyrighted music. . . . And by doing that, it constitutes—the uses constitute
direct infringement of plaintiffs' musical compositions, recordings."
The district court also noted that "it is pretty much acknowledged . . .
by Napster that this is infringement." *Id.* We agree that plaintiffs have
shown that Napster users infringe at least two of the copyright holders'
exclusive rights: the rights of reproduction, § 106(1); and distribution,
§ 106(3). Napster users who upload file names to the search index for
others to copy violate plaintiffs' distribution rights. Napster users who
download files containing copyrighted music violate plaintiffs' reproduction rights. . . .

B. Fair Use

Napster contends that its users do not directly infringe plaintiffs'
copyrights because the users are engaged in fair use of the material
[within the meaning of 17 U.S.C. § 107, an argument rejected by the
District Court, with which the Ninth Circuit agreed. . . .

[The court then went through the "four factor" fair use analysis and
found no error in the district court's rejection of Napster's fair use
defense.]

We find no error in the district court's determination that plaintiffs
will likely succeed in establishing that Napster users do not have a fair
use defense. Accordingly, we next address whether Napster is secondarily liable for the direct infringement under two doctrines of copyright law: contributory copyright infringement and vicarious copyright
infringement.

IV

We first address plaintiffs' claim that Napster is liable for contributory copyright infringement. Traditionally, "one who, with knowledge of the infringing activity, induces, causes or materially contributes to the infringing conduct of another, may be held liable as a 'contributory' infringer." [Citations omitted.] The district court determined that plaintiffs in all likelihood would establish Napster's liability as a contributory infringer. The district court did not err; Napster, by its conduct, knowingly encourages and assists the infringement of plaintiffs' copyrights.

A. Knowledge

Contributory liability requires that the secondary infringer "know or have reason to know" of direct infringement. [Citations omitted.] The district court found that Napster had both actual and constructive knowledge that its users exchanged copyrighted music. The district court also concluded that the law does not require knowledge of "specific acts of infringement" and rejected Napster's contention that because the company cannot distinguish infringing from non-infringing files, it does not "know" of the direct infringement. . . . It is apparent from the record that Napster has knowledge, both actual and constructive. The district court found actual knowledge because: (1) a document authored by Napster co-founder Sean Parker mentioned "the need to remain ignorant of users' real names and IP addresses 'since they are exchanging pirated music'"; and (2) the Recording Industry Association of America ("RIAA") informed Napster of more than 12,000 infringing files, some of which are still available. . . . The district court found constructive knowledge because: (a) Napster executives have recording industry experience; (b) they have enforced intellectual property rights in other instances; (c) Napster executives have downloaded copyrighted songs from the system; and (d) they have promoted the site with "screen shots listing infringing files." *Id.* at 919. Napster claims that it is nevertheless protected from contributory liability by the teaching of *Sony Corp. v. Universal City Studios, Inc.*, 464 U.S. 417 (1984). We disagree. We observe that Napster's actual, specific knowledge of direct infringement renders Sony's holding of limited assistance to Napster. We are compelled to make a clear distinction between the architecture of the Napster system and Napster's conduct in relation to the operational capacity of the system. The Sony Court refused to hold the manufacturer and retailers of video tape recorders liable for contributory infringement despite evidence that such machines could be and were used to infringe plaintiffs' copyrighted television shows. Sony stated that if liability "is to be imposed on petitioners in this case, it must rest on the fact that they have sold equipment with constructive knowledge of the fact that their customers may use that equipment to make unauthorized copies of copyrighted material." *Id.* at 439. The Sony Court declined to impute the requisite level of knowledge where the defendants made and sold equipment capable of both infringing and "substantial noninfring-ing uses." *Id.* at 442 (adopting a modified "staple article of commerce" doctrine from patent law). See also *Universal City Studios, Inc. v. Sony Corp.*, 480 F. Supp. 429, 459 (C.D. Cal. 1979) ("This court agrees with defendants that their knowledge was insufficient to make them con-tributory infringers."), *rev'd*, 659 F.2d 963 (9th Cir. 1981), *rev'd*, 464 U.S. 417 (1984); Alfred C. Yen, Internet Service Provider Liability for Subscriber Copyright Infringement, Enterprise Liability, and the First Amendment, 88 Geo. L.J. 1833, 1874& 1893 n.210 (2000) (suggest-ing that, after Sony, most Internet service providers lack "the requisite level of knowledge" for the imposition of contributory liability).We are bound to follow Sony, and will not impute the requisite level of knowl-edge to Napster merely because peer-to-peer file sharing technology may be used to infringe plaintiffs' copyrights. See 464 U.S. at 436 (re-jecting argument that merely supplying the "'means' to accomplish an infringing activity" leads to imposition of liability). We depart from the reasoning of the district court that Napster failed to demonstrate that its system is capable of commercially significant noninfringing uses. See *Napster,* 114 F. Supp. 2d at 916, 917–18. The district court improp-erly confined the use analysis to current uses, ignoring the system's capabilities. See generally *Sony,* 464 U.S. at 442–43 (framing inquiry as whether the video tape recorder is "capable of commercially significant noninfringing uses") (emphasis added). Consequently, the district court placed undue weight on the proportion of current infringing use as compared to current and future noninfringing use. See generally *Vault Corp. v. Quaid Software Ltd.*, 847 F.2d 255, 264–67 (5th Cir. 1997) (single noninfringing use implicated Sony). Nonetheless, whether we might arrive at a different result is not the issue here. See *Sports Form, Inc. v. United Press Int'l, Inc.*, 686 F.2d 750, 752 (9th Cir. 1982).The in-stant appeal occurs at an early point in the proceedings and "the fully developed factual record may be materially different from that initially before the district court . . . " *Id.* at 753. Regardless of the number of Napster's infringing versus noninfringing uses, the evidentiary record here supported the district court's finding that plaintiffs would likely prevail in establishing that Napster knew or had reason to know of its users' infringement of plaintiffs' copyrights.

This analysis is similar to that of *Religious Technology Center v. Netcom On-Line Communication Services, Inc.*, which suggests that in an online context, evidence of actual knowledge of specific acts of infringement is required to hold a computer system operator liable for contributory copyright infringement. 907 F. Supp. at 1371. Netcom considered the potential contributory copyright liability of a computer bulletin board operator whose system supported the posting of infringing material. *Id.* at 1374. The court, in denying Netcom's motion for summary judgment of noninfringement and plaintiff's motion for judgment on the pleadings, found that a disputed issue of fact existed as to whether the operator had sufficient knowledge of infringing activity. *Id.* at 1374–75.

The court determined that for the operator to have sufficient knowledge, the copyright holder must "provide the necessary documentation to show there is likely infringement." 907 F. Supp. at 1374. [Additional citation omitted.] If such documentation was provided, the court reasoned that Netcom would be liable for contributory infringement because its failure to remove the material "and thereby stop an infringing copy from being distributed worldwide constitutes substantial participation" in distribution of copyrighted material. *Id.*

We agree that if a computer system operator learns of specific infringing material available on his system and fails to purge such material from the system, the operator knows of and contributes to direct infringement. See *Netcom,* 907F. Supp. at 1374. Conversely, absent any specific information which identifies infringing activity, a computer system operator cannot be liable for contributory infringement merely because the structure of the system allows for the exchange of copyrighted material. See *Sony,* 464 U.S. at 436, 442–43. To enjoin simply because a computer network allows for infringing use would, in our opinion, violate Sony and potentially restrict activity unrelated to infringing use. We nevertheless conclude that sufficient knowledge exists to impose contributory liability when linked to demonstrated infringing use of the Napster system. . . . The record supports the district court's finding that Napster has actual knowledge that specific infringing material is available using its system, that it could block access to the system by suppliers of the infringing material, and that it failed to remove the material. See *Napster,* 114 F. Supp. 2d at 918, 920–21. As stated by the district court:

Plaintiff[s] . . . demonstrate that defendant had actual notice of direct infringement because the RIAA informed it of more than 12,000 infringing files. . . . Although Napster, Inc. purportedly terminated the users offering these files, the songs are still available using the Napster service, as are the copyrighted works which the record company plaintiffs identified. . . .

114 F. Supp. 2d at 918.

B. Material Contribution

Under the facts as found by the district court, Napster materially contributes to the infringing activity. Relying on *Fonovisa, Inc. v. Cherry Auction, Inc.* 76 F.3d 259 (9th Cir. 1996)] the district court concluded that "without the support services defendant provides, Napster users could not find and download the music they want with the ease of which defendant boasts." *Napster,* 114 F. Supp. 2d at 919–20 ("Napster is an integrated service designed to enable users to locate and download MP3 music files."). We agree that Napster provides "the site and facilities" for direct infringement. See *Fonovisa,* 76 F.3d at 264; cf. *Netcom,* 907F. Supp. at 1372 ("Netcom will be liable for contributory infringement since its failure to cancel [a user's] infringing message and thereby stop an infringing copy from being distributed worldwide constitutes substantial participation."). The district court correctly applied the reasoning in *Fonovisa,* and properly found that Napster materially contributes to direct infringement. We affirm the district court's conclusion that plaintiffs have demonstrated a likelihood of success on the merits of the contributory copyright infringement claim. We will address the scope of the injunction in part VIII of this opinion.

V

We turn to the question whether Napster engages in vicarious copyright infringement. Vicarious copyright liability is an "outgrowth" of respondeat superior. *Fonovisa*, 76 F.3d at 262. In the context of copyright law, vicarious liability extends beyond an employer/employee relationship to cases in which a defendant "has the right and ability to supervise the infringing activity and also has a direct financial interest in such activities." *Id.* [Additional citations omitted.] . . . Before moving into this discussion, we note that Sony's "staple article of commerce" analysis has no application to Napster's potential liability for vicarious copyright infringement. See *Sony*, 464 U.S. at 434–435 [Additional citation omitted.] . . .

The issues of Sony's liability under the "doctrines of 'direct infringement' and 'vicarious liability'" were not before the Supreme Court, although the Court recognized that the "lines between direct infringement, contributory infringement, and vicarious liability are not clearly drawn." *Id.* at 435 n.17. Consequently, when the Sony Court used the term "vicarious liability," it did so broadly and outside of a technical analysis of the doctrine of vicarious copyright infringement. *Id.* at 435 . . .

A. Financial Benefit

The district court determined that plaintiffs had demonstrated they would likely succeed in establishing that Napster has a direct financial interest in the infringing activity. . . . We agree. Financial benefit exists where the availability of infringing material "acts as a 'draw' for customers." *Fonovisa*, 76 F.3d at 263–64 (stating that financial benefit may be shown "where infringing performances enhance the attractiveness of a venue"). Ample evidence supports the district court's finding that Napster's future revenue is directly dependent upon "increases in userbase." More users register with the Napster system as the "quality and quantity of available music increases." 114 F. Supp. 2d at 902. We conclude that the district court did not err in determining that Napster financially benefits from the availability of protected works on its system.

B. Supervision

The district court determined that Napster has the right and ability to supervise its users' conduct. Napster . . . We agree in part. The ability to block infringers' access to a particular environment for any reason whatsoever is evidence of the right and ability to supervise. See *Fonovisa*, 76 F.3d at 262 ("Cherry Auction had the right to terminate vendors for any reason whatsoever and through that right had the ability to control the activities of vendors on the premises."). [Additional citation omitted.] Here, plaintiffs have demonstrated that Napster retains the right to control access to its system. Napster has an express reservation of rights policy, stating on its website that it expressly reserves the "right to refuse service and terminate accounts in [its] discretion, including, but not limited to, if Napster believes that user conduct violates applicable law . . . or for any reason in Napster's sole discretion, with or without cause." To escape imposition of vicarious liability, the reserved right to police must be exercised to its fullest extent. Turning a blind eye to detectable acts of infringement for the sake of profit gives rise to liability. See, *e.g.*, *Fonovisa,* 76 F.3d at 261. [Additional citations omitted.] The district court correctly determined that Napster had the right and ability to police its system and failed to exercise that right to prevent the exchange of copyrighted material. The district court, however, failed to recognize that the boundaries of the premises that Napster "controls and patrols" are limited. See, *e.g.*, *Fonovisa,*76 F.2d at 262–63 (in addition to having the right to exclude vendors, defendant" controlled and patrolled" the premises); see also *Polygram,* 855 F. Supp. at1328–29 (in addition to having the contractual right to remove exhibitors, tradeshow operator reserved the right to police during the show and had its "employees walk the aisles to ensure 'rules compliance'"). Put differently, Napster's reserved "right and ability" to police is cabined by the system's current architecture. . . . [T]he Napster system does not "read" the content of indexed files, other than to check that they are in the proper MP3 format. Napster, however, has the ability to locate infringing material listed on its search indices, and the right to terminate users' access to the system. The file name indices, therefore, are within the "premises" that Napster has the ability to police. We recognize that the files are user-named and may not match copyrighted material exactly (for example, the artist or song could be spelled wrong). For Napster to function effectively, however, file names must reasonably or roughly correspond to the material contained in the files, otherwise no user could ever locate any desired music. As a practical matter, Napster, its users and the record company plaintiffs have equal access to infringing material by employing Napster's "search function." Our review of the record requires us to accept the district court's conclusion that plaintiffs have demonstrated a likelihood of success on the merits of the vicarious copyright infringement claim. Napster's failure to police the system's "premises," combined with a showing that Napster financially benefits from the continuing availability of infringing files on its system, leads to the imposition of vicarious liability. We address the scope of the injunction in part VIII of this opinion.

VI

We next address whether Napster has asserted defenses which would preclude the entry of a preliminary injunction. Napster alleges that two statutes insulate it from liability. First, Napster asserts that its users engage in actions protected by § 1008 of the Audio Home Recording Act of 1992, 17 U.S.C. § 1008. Second, Napster argues that its liability for contributory and vicarious infringement is limited by the Digital Millennium Copyright Act, 17 U.S.C. § 512. We address the application of each statute in turn.

A. Audio Home Recording Act

The statute states in part:

No action may be brought under this title alleging infringement of copyright based on the manufacture, importation, or distribution of a digital audio recording device, a digital audio recording medium, an analog recording device, or an analog recording medium, or based on the noncommercial use by a consumer of such a device or medium for making digital musical recordings or analog musical recordings.

17 U.S.C. § 1008. Napster contends that MP3 file exchange is the type of "noncommercial use" protected from infringement actions by the statute. Napster asserts it cannot be secondarily liable for users' nonactionable exchange of copyrighted musical recordings. The district court rejected Napster's argument, stating that the Audio Home Recording Act is "irrelevant" to the action because: (1) plaintiffs did not bring claims under the Audio Home Recording Act; and (2) the Audio Home Recording Act does not cover the downloading of MP3 files. . . .

We agree with the district court that the Audio Home Recording Act does not cover the downloading of MP3 files to computer hard drives. First, "[u]nder the plain meaning of the Act's definition of digital audio recording devices, computers (and their hard drives) are not digital audio recording devices because their' primary purpose' is not to make digital audio copied recordings." *Recording Indus. Ass'n of Am. v. Diamond Multimedia Sys., Inc.*, 180 F.3d 1072, 1078 (9th Cir. 1999). Second, notwithstanding Napster's claim that computers are "digital audio recording devices," computers do not make "digital music recordings" as defined by the Audio Home Recording Act. *Id.* at 1077 (citing S. Rep. 102–294) ("There are simply no grounds in either the plain language of the definition or in the legislative history for interpreting the term 'digital musical recording' to include songs fixed on computer hard drives.").

B. Digital Millennium Copyright Act

Napster also interposes a statutory limitation on liability by asserting the protections of the "safe harbor" from copyright infringement suits for "Internet service providers" contained in the Digital Millennium Copyright Act, 17 U.S.C. § 512. . . .

The district court did not give this statutory limitation any weight favoring a denial of temporary injunctive relief. The court concluded that Napster "has failed to persuade this court that subsection 512(d) shelters contributory infringers." . . . We need not accept a blanket conclusion that § 512 of the Digital Millennium Copyright Act will never protect secondary infringers. . . . We do not agree that Napster's potential liability for contributory and vicarious infringement renders the Digital Millennium Copyright Act inapplicable per se. We instead recognize that this issue will be more fully developed at trial. At this stage of the litigation, plaintiffs raise serious questions regarding Napster's ability to obtain shelter under § 512, and plaintiffs also demonstrate that the balance of hardships tips in their favor. . . . Plaintiffs have raised and continue to raise significant questions under this statute, including: (1) whether Napster is an Internet service provider as defined by 17 U.S.C. § 512(d); (2) whether copyright owners must give a service provider "official" notice of infringing activity in order for it to have knowledge or awareness of infringing activity on its system; and (3) whether Napster complies with § 512(i), which requires a service provider to timely establish a detailed copyright compliance policy. See *A&M Records, Inc. v. Napster, Inc.*, No. 99–05183, 2000 WL 573136 (N.D. Cal. May 12, 2000) (denying summary judgment to Napster under a different subsection of the Digital Millennium Copyright Act, § 512(a)). The district court considered ample evidence to support its determination that the balance of hardships tips in plaintiffs' favor: Any destruction of Napster, Inc. by a preliminary injunction is speculative compared to the statistical evidence of massive, unauthorized downloading and uploading of plaintiffs' copyrighted works—as many as 10,000 files per second by defendant's own admission. . . . The court has every reason to believe that, without a preliminary injunction, these numbers will mushroom as Napster users, and newcomers attracted by the publicity, scramble to obtain as much free music as possible before trial.

VII

Napster contends that even if the district court's preliminary determinations that it is liable for facilitating copyright infringement are correct, the district court improperly rejected valid affirmative defenses of waiver, implied license and copyright misuse. We address the defenses in turn.

A. Waiver

"Waiver is the intentional relinquishment of a known right with knowledge of its existence and the intent to relinquish it." [Citations omitted.] Napster argues that the district court erred in finding that plaintiffs knowingly provided consumers with technology designed to copy and distribute MP3 files over the Internet and, thus, waived any legal authority to exercise exclusive control over creation and distribution of MP3 files. The district court, however, was not convinced" that the record companies created the monster that is now devouring their intellectual property rights." *Napster*, 114 F. Supp. 2d at 924. We find no error in the district court's finding that "in hastening the proliferation of MP3 files, plaintiffs did [nothing] more than seek partners for their commercial downloading ventures and develop music players for files they planned to sell over the Internet." *Id.* Napster additionally asserts that the district court improperly refused to allow additional discovery into affirmative defenses and also erroneously failed to hold an evidentiary hearing. . . . We conclude that the court did not abuse its discretion in denying further discovery and refusing to conduct an evidentiary hearing.

B. Implied License

Napster also argues that plaintiffs granted the company an implied license by encouraging MP3 file exchange over the Internet. Courts have found implied licenses only in "narrow" circumstances where one party "created a work at [the other's] request and handed it over, intending that [the other] copy and distribute it." *SmithKline Beecham Consumer Healthcare, L.P. v. Watson Pharms., Inc.,* 211 F.3d 21, 25 (2d Cir. 2000) (quoting *Effects Assocs., Inc. v. Cohen,* 908 F.2d 555,558 [9th Cir. 1990]), *cert. denied,* 121 S. Ct. 173 (2000). The district court observed that no evidence exists to support this defense: "indeed, the RIAA gave defendant express notice that it objected to the availability of its members' copyrighted music on Napster." *Napster,* 114 F. Supp. 2d at 924–25. The record supports this conclusion.

C. Misuse

The defense of copyright misuse forbids a copyright holder from "secur[ing] an exclusive right or limited monopoly not granted by the Copyright Office." [Citations omitted.] Napster alleges that online distribution is not within the copyright monopoly. According to Napster, plaintiffs have colluded to "use their copyrights to extend their control to online distributions." We find no error in the district court's preliminary rejection of this affirmative defense. The misuse defense prevents copyright holders from leveraging their limited monopoly to allow them control of areas outside the monopoly. [Citations omitted.] The district court correctly stated that "most of the cases" that recognize the affirmative defense of copyright misuse involve unduly restrictive licensing schemes. See *Napster,* 114 F. Supp. 2d at 923 [Additional citations omitted.] . . . There is no evidence here that plaintiffs seek to control areas outside of their grant of monopoly. Rather, plaintiffs seek to control reproduction and distribution of their copyrighted works, exclusive rights of copyright holders. 17 U.S.C. § 106 [Additional citation omitted.] . . . That the copyrighted works are transmitted in another medium—MP3 format rather than audio CD—has no bearing on our analysis. . . .

VIII

The district court correctly recognized that a preliminary injunction against Napster's participation in copyright infringement is not only warranted but required. We believe, however, that the scope of the injunction needs modification in light of our opinion. Specifically, we reiterate that contributory liability may potentially be imposed only to the extent that Napster: (1) receives reasonable knowledge of specific infringing files with copyrighted musical compositions and sound recordings; (2) knows or should know that such files are available on the Napster system; and (3) fails to act to prevent viral distribution of the works. [Citation omitted.] The mere existence of the Napster system, absent actual notice and Napster's demonstrated failure to remove the offending material, is insufficient to impose contributory liability. See *Sony*, 464 U.S. at 442–43. Conversely, Napster may be vicariously liable when it fails to affirmatively use its ability to patrol its system and preclude access to potentially infringing files listed in its search index. Napster has both the ability to use its search function to identify infringing musical recordings and the right to bar participation of users who engage in the transmission of infringing files. The preliminary injunction which we stayed is overbroad because it places on Napster the entire burden of ensuring that no "copying, downloading, uploading, transmitting, or distributing" of plaintiffs' works occur on the system. As stated, we place the burden on plaintiffs to provide notice to Napster of copyrighted works and files containing such works available on the Napster system before Napster has the duty to disable access to the offending content. Napster, however, also bears the burden of policing the system within the limits of the system. Here, we recognize that this is not an exact science in that the files are user named. In crafting the injunction on remand, the district court should recognize that Napster's system does not currently appear to allow Napster access to users' MP3 files. Based on our decision to remand, Napster's additional arguments on appeal going to the scope of the injunction need not be addressed. We, however, briefly address Napster's First Amendment argument so that it is not reasserted on remand. Napster contends that the present injunction violates the First Amendment because it is broader than necessary. The company asserts two distinct free speech rights: (1)its right to publish a "directory" (here, the search index) and (2) its users' right to exchange information. We note that First Amendment concerns in copyright are allayed by the presence of the fair use doctrine. See 17 U.S.C. § 107 [Additional citations omitted.] . . . There was a preliminary determination here that Napster users are not fair users. Uses of copyrighted material that are not fair uses are rightfully enjoined. See *Dr. Seuss Enters. v. Penguin Books USA, Inc.*, 109 F.3d 1394, 1403 (9th Cir. 1997) (rejecting defendants' claim that injunction would constitute a prior restraint in violation of the First Amendment).

IX

[The Court then rejected Napster's argument that the plaintiffs should have been required to post a higher bond, as well as Napster's argument that] the district court should have imposed a monetary penalty by way of a compulsory royalty in place of an injunction. . . . Napster tells us that "where great public injury would be worked by an injunction, the courts might . . . award damages or a continuing royalty instead of an injunction in such special circumstances." *Abend v. MCA, Inc.,* 863 F.2d 1465, 1479 (9th Cir. 1988) (quoting 3 Melville B. Nimmer & David Nimmer, *Nimmer On Copyright* § 14.06 = [B =] (1988)), *aff'd,* 495 U.S. 207(1990). We are at a total loss to find any "special circumstances" simply because this case requires us to apply well-established doctrines of copyright law to a new technology. Neither do we agree with Napster that an injunction would cause "great public injury." Further, we narrowly construe any suggestion that compulsory royalties are appropriate in this context because Congress has arguably limited the application of compulsory royalties to specific circumstances, none of which are present here. See 17 U.S.C. § 115. The Copyright Act provides for various sanctions for infringers. See, *e.g.,* 17 U.S.C. §§ 502 (injunctions); 504 (damages); and 506 (criminal penalties); see also 18 U.S.C. § 2319A (criminal penalties for the unauthorized fixation of and trafficking in sound recordings and music videos of live musical performances). These statutory sanctions represent a more than adequate legislative solution to the problem created by copyright infringement. Imposing a compulsory royalty payment schedule would give Napster an "easy out" of this case. If such royalties were imposed, Napster would avoid penalties for any future violation of an injunction, statutory copyright damages and any possible criminal penalties for continuing infringement. The royalty structure would also grant Napster the luxury of either choosing to continue and pay royalties or shut down. On the other hand, the wronged parties would be forced to do business with a company that profits from the wrongful use of intellectual properties. Plaintiffs would lose the power to control their intellectual property: they could not make a business decision not to license their property to Napster, and, in the event they planned to do business with Napster, compulsory royalties would take away the copyright holders' ability to negotiate the terms of any contractual arrangement.

X

[T]he preliminary injunction . . . shall remain stayed until it is modified by the district court to conform to the requirements of this opinion. [However, e]ven though the preliminary injunction requires modification, appellees have substantially and primarily prevailed on appeal. Appellees shall recover their statutory costs on appeal. See Fed. R. App. P. 39(a)(4) ("[i]f a judgment is affirmed in part, reversed in part, modified, or vacated, costs are taxed only as the court orders.").

AFFIRMED IN PART, REVERSED IN PART AND REMANDED.

NOTE

1. Although issues raised in the *Aimster* decision below were subsequently addressed by the Supreme Court in *Grokster, Aimster* is worth examining, because its author

was renowned economist Judge Richard Posner of the Seventh Circuit. Applying a "cost-benefit" analysis to the Sony doctrine, Posner's analysis sets out the concept of the staple article of commerce doctrine and how it can apply to digital file sharing and communication services. Judge Posner tactfully affirms an injunction against a file-sharing service that uses AOL Instant Messaging to illegally share copyrighted files, without implicating the messaging service itself.

In re: Aimster Copyright Litigation., 334 F.3d 643 (7th Cir. 2003), cert. denied 540 U.S. 1107 (U.S. 2004)

OPINION BY: POSNER, CIRCUIT JUDGE

Owners of copyrighted popular music filed a number of closely related suits, which were consolidated and transferred to the Northern District of Illinois by the Multi-district Litigation Panel, against John Deep and corporations that are controlled by him and need not be discussed separately. The numerous plaintiffs, who among them appear to own most subsisting copyrights on American popular music, claim that Deep's "Aimster" Internet service (recently renamed "Madster") is a contributory and vicarious infringer of these copyrights. The district judge entered a broad preliminary injunction, which had the effect of shutting down the Aimster service until the merits of the suit are finally resolved, from which Deep appeals. Aimster is one of a number of enterprises (the former Napster is the best known) that have been sued for facilitating the swapping of digital copies of popular music, most of it copyrighted, over the Internet [citations omitted]. To simplify exposition, we refer to the appellant as "Aimster" and to the appellees (the plaintiffs) as the recording industry.

Teenagers and young adults who have access to the Internet like to swap computer files containing popular music. If the music is copyrighted, such swapping, which involves making and transmitting a digital copy of the music, infringes copyright. The swappers, who are ignorant or more commonly disdainful of copyright and in any event discount the likelihood of being sued or prosecuted for copyright infringement, are the direct infringers. But firms that facilitate their infringement, even if they are not themselves infringers because they are not making copies of the music that is shared, may be liable to the copyright owners as contributory infringers. Recognizing the impracticability or futility of a copyright owner's suing a multitude of individual infringers ("chasing individual consumers is time consuming and is a teaspoon solution to an ocean problem," Randal C. Picker, "Copyright as Entry Policy: The Case of Digital Distribution," 47 Antitrust Bull. 423, 442 (2002)), the law allows a copyright holder to sue a contributor to the infringement instead, in effect as an aider and abettor. Another analogy is to the tort of intentional interference with contract, that is, inducing a breach of contract. See, e.g., *Sufrin v. Hosier*, 128 F.3d 594, 597 (7th Cir. 1997). If a breach of contract (and a copyright license is just a type of contract) can be prevented most effectively by actions taken by a third party, it makes sense to have a legal mechanism for placing liability for the consequences of the breach on him as well as on the party that broke the contract.

The district judge ruled that the recording industry had demonstrated a likelihood of prevailing on the merits should the case proceed to trial. He so ruled with respect to vicarious as well as contributory infringement; we begin with the latter, the more familiar charge.

The Aimster system has the following essential components: proprietary software that can be downloaded free of charge from Aimster's Web site.

[The court then described in detail the characteristics and uses of the Aimster network.]

. . . .

What we have described so far is a type of Internet file-sharing system that might be created for innocuous purposes such as the expeditious exchange of confidential business data among employees of a business firm. [citations omitted.] The fact that copyrighted materials might sometimes be shared between users of such a system without the authorization of the copyright owner or a fair-use privilege would not make the firm a contributory infringer. Otherwise AOL's instant-messaging system, which Aimster piggybacks on, might be deemed a contributory infringer. For there is no doubt that some of the attachments that AOL's multitudinous subscribers transfer are copyrighted, and such distribution is an infringement unless authorized by the owner of the copyright. The Supreme Court made clear in the Sony decision that the producer of a product that has substantial non-infringing uses is not a contributory infringer merely because some of the uses actually made of the product (in that case a machine, the predecessor of today's videocassette recorders, for recording television programs on tape) are infringing. *Sony Corp. of America, Inc. v. Universal City Studios, Inc.*, 464 U.S. 417, 78 L. Ed. 2d 574, 104 S. Ct. 774 (1984); *see also Vault Corp. v. Quaid Software Ltd.*, 847 F.2d 255, 262–67 (5th Cir. 1988). How much more the Court held is the principal issue that divides the parties; and let us try to resolve it, recognizing of course that the Court must have the last word.

Sony's Betamax video recorder was used for three principal purposes, as Sony was well aware (a fourth, playing home movies, involved no copying). The first, which the majority opinion emphasized, was time shifting, that is, recording a television program that was being shown at a time inconvenient for the owner of the Betamax for later watching at a convenient time. The second was "library building," that is, making copies of programs to retain permanently. The third was skipping commercials by taping a program before watching it and then, while watching the tape, using the fast-forward button on the recorder to skip over the commercials. The first use the Court held was a fair use (and hence not infringing) because it enlarged the audience for the program. The copying involved in the second and third uses was unquestionably infringing to the extent that the programs copied were under copyright and the taping of them was not authorized by the copyright owners— but not all fell in either category. Subject to this qualification, building a library of taped programs was infringing because it was the equivalent of borrowing a copyrighted book from a public library, making a copy of it for one's personal library, then returning the original to the public library. The third use, commercial-skipping, amounted to creating an unauthorized derivative work [citations omitted], namely a commercial-free copy that would reduce the copyright owner's income from his original program, since "free" television programs are financed by the purchase of commercials by advertisers.

Thus the video recorder was being used for a mixture of infringing and noninfringing uses and the Court thought that Sony could not demix them because once Sony sold the recorder it lost all control over its use. *Sony Corp. of America, Inc. v. Universal City Studios, Inc., supra*, 464 U.S at 438. The court ruled that "the sale of copying equipment, like the sale of other articles of commerce, does not constitute contributory infringement if the product is widely used for legitimate, unobjectionable purposes. Indeed, it need merely be capable of substantial noninfringing uses. The question is thus whether the Betamax is capable of commercially significant noninfringing uses. In order to resolve that question, we need not explore all the different potential uses of the machine and determine whether or not they would constitute infringement. Rather, we need only consider whether on the basis of the facts as found by the district court a significant number of them would be non-infringing. Moreover, in order to resolve this case we need not give precise content to the question of how much use is commercially significant. For one potential use of the Betamax plainly satisfies this standard, however it is understood: private, noncommercial time-shifting in the home." *Id.* at 441.

In our case the recording industry, emphasizing the reference to "articles of commerce" in the passage just quoted and elsewhere in the Court's opinion (see *id.* at 440; cf. 35 U.S.C. § 271(c)), and emphasizing as well the Court's evident concern that the copyright holders were trying to lever their copyright monopolies into a monopoly over video recorders, *Sony Corp. of America, Inc. v. Universal City Studios, Inc., supra*, 464 U.S at 441–42 and n. 21, and also remarking Sony's helplessness to prevent infringing uses of its recorders once it sold them, argues that Sony is inapplicable to services. With regard to services, the industry argues, the test is merely whether the provider knows it's being used to infringe copyright. The industry points out that the provider of a service, unlike the seller of a product, has a continuing relation with its customers and therefore should be able to prevent, or at least limit, their infringing copyright by monitoring their use of the service and terminating them when it is discovered that they are infringing. Although Sony could have engineered its video recorder in a way that would have reduced the likelihood of infringement, as by eliminating the fast-forward capability, or, as suggested by the dissent, *id.* at 494, by enabling broadcasters by scrambling their signal to disable the Betamax from recording their programs (for that matter, it could have been engineered to have only a play, not a recording, capability), the majority did not discuss these possibilities and we agree with the recording industry that the ability of a service provider to prevent its customers from infringing is a factor to be considered in determining whether the provider is a contributory infringer. Congress so recognized in the Digital Millennium Copyright Act, which we discuss later in this opinion.

It is not necessarily a controlling factor, however, as the recording industry believes. If a service facilitates both infringing and noninfringing uses, as in the case of AOL's instant-messaging service, and the detection and prevention of the infringing uses would be highly burdensome, the rule for which the recording industry is contending could result in the shutting down of the service or its annexation by the copyright owners (contrary to the clear import of the Sony decision), because the provider might find it impossible to estimate its potential damages liability to the copyright holders and would anyway face the risk of being enjoined. The fact that the recording industry's argument if accepted might endanger AOL's instant-messaging service (though the service might find shelter under the Digital Millennium Copyright Act—a question complicated, however, by AOL's intention, of which more later, of offering an encryption option to the visitors to its chat rooms) is not only alarming; it is paradoxical, since subsidiaries of AOL's parent company (AOL Time Warner), such as Warner Brothers Records and Atlantic Recording Corporation, are among the plaintiffs in this case and music chat rooms are among the facilities offered by AOL's instant-messaging service.

We also reject the industry's argument that Sony provides no defense to a charge of contributory infringement when, in the words of the industry's brief, there is anything "more than a mere showing that a product may be used for infringing purposes." Although the fact was downplayed in the majority opinion, it was apparent that the Betamax was being used for infringing as well as noninfringing purposes—even the majority acknowledged that 25 percent of Betamax users were fast forwarding through commercials, *id.* at 452 n. 36—yet Sony was held not to be a contributory infringer. The Court was unwilling to allow copyright holders to prevent infringement effectuated by means of a new technology at the price of possibly denying noninfringing consumers the benefit of the technology. We therefore agree with Professor Goldstein that the Ninth Circuit erred in *A&M Records, Inc. v. Napster, Inc.*, 239 F.3d 1004, 1020 (9th Cir. 2001), in suggesting that actual knowledge of specific infringing uses is a sufficient condition for deeming a facilitator a contributory infringer. 2 Paul Goldstein, Copyright § 6.1.2, p. 6:12–1 (2d ed. 2003)

The recording industry's hostility to the Sony decision is both understandable, given the amount of Internet-enabled infringement of music copyrights, and manifest—the industry in its brief offers five reasons for confining its holding to its specific facts. But it is being articulated in the wrong forum.

Equally, however, we reject Aimster's argument that to prevail the recording industry must prove it has actually lost money as a result of the copying that its service facilitates. It is true that the Court in Sony emphasized that the plaintiffs had failed to show that they had sustained substantial harm from the Betamax. *Id.* at 450–54, 456. But the Court did so in the context of assessing the argument that time shifting of television programs was fair use rather than infringement. One reason time shifting was fair use, the Court believed, was that it wasn't hurting the copyright owners because it was enlarging the audience for their programs. But a copyright owner who can prove infringement need not show that the infringement caused him a financial loss. Granted, without such a showing he cannot obtain compensatory damages; but he can obtain statutory damages, or an injunction, just as the owner of physical property can obtain an injunction against a trespasser without proving that the trespass has caused him a financial loss.

What is true is that when a supplier is offering a product or service that has noninfringing as well as infringing uses, some estimate of the respective magnitudes of these uses is necessary for a finding of contributory infringement. The Court's action in striking the cost-benefit trade-off in favor of Sony came to seem prescient when it later turned out that the principal use of video recorders was to allow people to watch at home movies that they bought or rented rather than to tape television programs. (In 1984, when Sony was decided, the industry was unsure how great the demand would be for prerecorded tapes compared to time shifting. The original Betamax played one-hour tapes, long enough for most television broadcasts but too short for a feature film. Sony's competitors used the VHS format, which came to market later but with a longer playing time; this contributed to VHS's eventual displacement of Betamax.) An enormous new market thus opened for the movie industry—which by the way gives point to the Court's emphasis on potential as well as actual noninfringing uses. But the balancing of costs and benefits is necessary only in a case in which substantial noninfringing uses, present or prospective, are demonstrated.

We also reject Aimster's argument that because the Court said in Sony that mere "constructive knowledge" of infringing uses is not enough for contributory infringement, 464 U.S. at 439, and the encryption feature of Aimster's service prevented Deep from knowing what songs were being copied by the users of his system, he lacked the knowledge of infringing uses that liability for contributory infringement requires. Willful blindness is knowledge, in copyright law (where indeed it may be enough that the defendant should have known of the direct infringement, *Casella v. Morris*, 820 F.2d 362, 365 (11th Cir. 1987); 2 Goldstein, *supra*, § 6.1, p. 6:6), as it is in the law generally. See, e.g., *Louis Vuitton S.A. v. Lee*, 875 F.2d 584, 590 (7th Cir. 1989) (contributory trademark infringement). One who, knowing or strongly suspecting that he is involved in shady dealings, takes steps to make sure that he does not acquire full or exact knowledge of the nature and extent of those dealings is held to have a criminal intent, *United States v. Giovannetti*, 919 F.2d 1223, 1228 (7th Cir. 1990), because a deliberate effort to avoid guilty knowledge is all that the law requires to establish a guilty state of mind. [citations omitted.] In *United States v. Diaz*, 864 F.2d 544, 550 (7th Cir. 1988), the defendant, a drug trafficker, sought "to insulate himself from the actual drug transaction so that he could deny knowledge of it," which he did sometimes by absenting himself from the scene of the actual delivery and sometimes by pretending to be fussing under the hood of his car. He did not escape liability by this maneuver; no more can Deep by using encryption software to prevent himself from learning what surely he strongly suspects to be the case: that the users of his service—maybe all the users of his service—are copyright infringers.

This is not to say that the provider of an encrypted instant-messaging service or encryption software is ipso factor a contributory infringer should his buyers use the service to infringe copyright, merely because encryption, like secrecy generally, facilitates unlawful transactions. ("Encryption" comes from the Greek word for concealment.) Encryption fosters privacy, and privacy is a social benefit though also a source of social costs. "AOL has begun testing an encrypted version of AIM [AOL Instant Messaging]. Encryption is considered critical for widespread adoption of IM in some industries and federal agencies." Vise, *supra*. Our point is only that a service provider that would otherwise be a contributory infringer does not obtain immunity by using encryption to shield itself from actual knowledge of the unlawful purposes for which the service is being used.

We also do not buy Aimster's argument that since the Supreme Court distinguished, in the long passage from the Sony opinion that we quoted earlier, between actual and potential noninfringing uses, all Aimster has to show in order to escape liability for contributory infringement is that its file-sharing system could be used in noninfringing ways, which obviously it could be. Were that the law, the seller of a product or service used solely to facilitate copyright infringement, though it was capable in principle of noninfringing uses, would be immune from liability for contributory infringement. That would be an extreme result, and one not envisaged by the Sony majority. Otherwise its opinion would have had no occasion to emphasize the fact (at least the majority thought it a fact—the dissent disagreed, 464 U.S. at 458–59) that Sony had not in its advertising encouraged the use of the Betamax to infringe copyright. *Id.* at 438. Nor would the Court have thought it important to say that the Betamax was used "principally" for time shifting, *id.* at 421; see also *id.* at 423, which as we recall the Court deemed a fair use, or to remark that the plaintiffs owned only a small percentage of the total amount of copyrighted television programming and it was unclear how many of the other owners objected to home taping. *Id.* at 443; see also *id.* at 446.

There are analogies in the law of aiding and abetting, the criminal counterpart to contributory infringement. A retailer of slinky dresses is not guilty of aiding and abetting prostitution even if he knows that some of his customers are prostitutes—he may even know which ones are [citations omitted]. The extent to which his activities and those of similar sellers actually promote prostitution is likely to be slight relative to the social costs of imposing a risk of prosecution on him. But the owner of a massage parlor who employs women who are capable of giving massages, but in fact as he knows sell only sex and never massages to their customers, is an aider and abettor of prostitution (as well as being guilty of pimping or operating a brothel) [citations omitted]. The slinky-dress case corresponds to Sony, and, like Sony, is not inconsistent with imposing liability on the seller of a product or service that, as in the massage-parlor case, is capable of noninfringing uses but in fact is used only to infringe. To the recording industry, a single known infringing use brands the facilitator as a contributory infringer. To the Aimsters of this world, a single noninfringing use provides complete immunity from liability. Neither is correct.

To situate Aimster's service between these unacceptable poles, we need to say just a bit more about it. In explaining how to use the Aimster software, the tutorial gives as its only examples of file sharing the sharing of copyrighted music, including copyrighted music that the recording industry had notified Aimster was being infringed by Aimster's users. The tutorial is the invitation to infringement that the Supreme Court found was missing in Sony. In addition, membership in Club Aimster enables the member for a fee of $4.95 a month to download with a single click the music most often shared by Aimster users, which turns out to be music copyrighted by the plaintiffs. Because Aimster's software is made available free of charge and Aimster does not sell paid advertising on its Web site, Club Aimster's monthly fee is the only means by which Aimster is financed and so the club cannot be separated from the provision of the free software. When a member of the club clicks on "play" next to the name of a song on the club's Web site, Aimster's server searches through the computers of the Aimster users who are online until it finds one who has listed the song as available for sharing, and it then effects the transmission of the file to the computer of the club member who selected it. Club Aimster lists only the 40 songs that are currently most popular among its members; invariably these are under copyright.

The evidence that we have summarized does not exclude the possibility of substantial noninfringing uses of the Aimster system, but the evidence is sufficient, especially in a preliminary-injunction proceeding, which is summary in character, to shift the burden of production to Aimster to demonstrate that its service has substantial noninfringing uses. [citations omitted.] As it might:

1. Not all popular music is copyrighted. Apart from music on which the copyright has expired (not much of which, however, is of interest to the teenagers and young adults interested in swapping music), startup bands and performers may waive copyright in the hope that it will encourage

the playing of their music and create a following that they can convert to customers of their subsequent works.

2. A music file-swapping service might increase the value of a recording by enabling it to be used as currency in the music-sharing community, since someone who only downloads and never uploads, thus acting as a pure free rider, will not be very popular.

3. Users of Aimster's software might form select (as distinct from all-comers) "buddy" groups to exchange non-copyrighted information about popular music, or for that matter to exchange ideas and opinions about wholly unrelated matters as the buddies became friendlier. Some of the chat-room messages that accompany the listing of music files offered or requested contain information or opinions concerning the music; to that extent, though unremarked by the parties, some non-infringing use is made of Aimster's service, though it is incidental to the infringement.

4. Aimster's users might appreciate the encryption feature because as their friendship deepened they might decide that they wanted to exchange off-color, but not copyrighted, photographs, or dirty jokes, or other forms of expression that people like to keep private, rather than just copyrighted music.

5. Someone might own a popular-music CD that he was particularly fond of, but he had not downloaded it into his computer and now he finds himself out of town but with his laptop and he wants to listen to the CD, so he uses Aimster's service to download a copy. This might be a fair use rather than a copyright infringement, by analogy to the time shifting approved as fair use in the Sony case. *Recording Industry Ass'n of America v. Diamond Multimedia Systems, Inc.*, 180 F.3d 1072, 1079 (9th Cir. 1999); cf. *Vault Corp. v. Quaid Software Ltd.*, supra, 847 F.2d at 266–67. The analogy was sidestepped in *A&M Records, Inc. v. Napster, Inc.*, supra, 239 F.3d at 1019, because Napster's system did not limit downloading to music on CDs owned by the downloader. The analogy was rejected in *UMG Recordings v. MP3.com, Inc.*, 92 F. Supp. 2d 349 (SDNY 2000), on the ground that the copy on the defendant's server was an unauthorized derivative work; a solider ground, in light of Sony's rejection of the parallel argument with respect to time shifting, would have been that the defendant's method for requiring that its customers "prove" that they owned the CDs containing the music they wanted to download was too lax.

All five of our examples of actually or arguably noninfringing uses of Aimster's service are possibilities, but as should be evident from our earlier discussion the question is how probable they are. It is not enough, as we have said, that a product or service be physically capable, as it were, of a noninfringing use. Aimster has failed to produce any evidence that its service has ever been used for a noninfringing use, let alone evidence concerning the frequency of such uses. In the words of the district judge, "defendants here have provided no evidence whatsoever (besides the unsupported declaration of Deep) that Aimster is actually used for any of the stated non-infringing purposes. Absent is any indication from real-life Aimster users that their primary use of the system is to transfer non-copyrighted files to their friends or identify users of similar interests and share information. Absent is any indication that even a single business without a network administrator uses Aimster to exchange business records as Deep suggests." *In re Aimster Copyright Litigation*, 252 F. Supp. 2d 634, 653 (N.D. Ill. 2002). We have to assume for purposes of deciding this appeal that no such evidence exists; its absence, in combination with the evidence presented by the recording industry, justified the district judge in concluding that the industry would be likely to prevail in a full trial on the issue of contributory infringement. Because Aimster failed to show that its service is ever used for any purpose other than to infringe the plaintiffs' copyrights, the question (as yet unsettled, see *Wu, supra*, at 708 and nn. 95 and 98) of the net effect of Napster-like services on the music industry's income is irrelevant to this case. If the only effect of a service challenged as contributory infringement is to enable copyrights to be infringed, the magnitude of the resulting loss, even whether there is a net loss, becomes irrelevant to liability.

Even when there are noninfringing uses of an Internet file-sharing service, moreover, if the infringing uses are substantial then to avoid liability as a contributory infringer the provider of the service must show that it would have been disproportionately costly for him to eliminate or at least reduce substantially the infringing uses. Aimster failed to make that showing too, by failing to present evidence that the provision of an encryption capability effective against the service provider itself added important value to the service or saved significant cost. Aimster blinded itself in the hope that by doing so it might come within the rule of the Sony decision.

It complains about the district judge's refusal to hold an evidentiary hearing. But his refusal was consistent with our decision in *Ty, Inc. v. GMA Accessories, Inc., supra*, 132 F.3d at 1171 (citations omitted), where we explained that "if genuine issues of material fact are created by the response to a motion for a preliminary injunction, an evidentiary hearing is indeed required. But as in any case in which a party seeks an evidentiary hearing, he must be able to persuade the court that the issue is indeed genuine and material and so a hearing would be productive—he must show in other words that he has and intends to introduce evidence that if believed will so weaken the moving party's case as to affect the judge's decision on whether to issue an injunction." Aimster hampered its search for evidence by providing encryption. It must take responsibility for that self-inflicted wound.

Turning to the second issue presented by the appeal, we are less confident than the district judge was that the recording industry would also be likely to prevail on the issue of vicarious infringement should the case be tried, though we shall not have to resolve our doubts in order to decide the appeal. "Vicarious liability" generally refers to the liability of a principal, such as an employer, for the torts committed by his agent, an employee for example, in the course of the agent's employment. The teenagers and young adults who use Aimster's system to infringe copyright are of course not Aimster's agents. But one of the principal rationales of vicarious liability, namely the difficulty of obtaining effective relief against an agent, who is likely to be impecunious, Alan O. Sykes, "The Economics of Vicarious Liability," 93 *Yale L.J.* 1231, 1241–42, 1272 (1984), has been extended in the copyright area to cases in which the only effective relief is obtainable from someone who bears a relation to the direct infringers that is analogous to the relation of a principal to an agent. The canonical illustration is the owner of a dance hall who hires dance bands that sometimes play copyrighted music without authorization. The bands are not the dance hall's agents, but it may be impossible as a practical matter for the copyright holders to identify and obtain a legal remedy against the infringing bands yet quite feasible for the dance hall to prevent or at least limit infringing performances. And so the dance hall that fails to make reasonable efforts to do this is liable as a vicarious infringer. *Dreamland Ball Room v. Shapiro, Bernstein & Co.,* 36 F.2d 354, 355 (7th Cir. 1929), and other cases cited in *Sony Corp. of America, Inc. v. Universal City Studios, Inc.,* supra, 464 U.S. at 437. The dance hall could perhaps be described as a contributory infringer. But one thinks of a contributory infringer as someone who benefits directly from the infringement that he encourages, and that does not seem an apt description of the dance hall, though it does benefit to the extent that competition will force the dance band to charge the dance hall a smaller fee for performing if the band doesn't pay copyright royalties and so has lower costs than it would otherwise have.

How far the doctrine of vicarious liability extends is uncertain. It could conceivably have been applied in the Sony case itself, on the theory that while it was infeasible for the producers of copyrighted television fare to sue the viewers who used the fast-forward button on Sony's video recorder to delete the commercials and thus reduce the copyright holders' income, Sony could have reduced the likelihood of infringement, as we noted earlier, by a design change. But the Court, treating vicarious and contributory infringement interchangeably, *see* id. at 435 n. 17, held that Sony was not a vicarious infringer either. By eliminating the encryption feature and monitoring the use being made of its system, Aimster could like Sony have limited the amount of infringement. Whether failure to do so made it a vicarious infringer notwithstanding the outcome in Sony is academic, however; its ostrich-like refusal to discover the extent to which its system was being used to infringe copyright is merely another piece of evidence that it was a contributory infringer.

We turn now to Aimster's defenses under the Online Copyright Infringement Liability Limitation Act, Title II of the Digital Millennium Copyright Act (DMCA), 17 U.S.C. § 512; see 2 Goldstein, *Supra,* § 613. The DMCA is an attempt to deal with special problems created by the so-called digital revolution. One of these is the vulnerability of Internet service providers such as AOL to liability for copyright infringement as a result of file swapping among their subscribers. Although the Act was not passed with Napster-type services in mind, the definition of Internet service provider is broad ("a provider of online services or network access, or the operator of facilities therefor," 17 U.S.C. § 512(k)(1)(B)), and, as the district judge ruled, Aimster fits it. [citation omitted.] The Act provides a series of safe harbors for Internet service providers and related entities, but none in which Aimster can moor. The Act does not abolish contributory infringement. The common element of its safe harbors is that the service provider must do what it can reasonably be asked to do to prevent the use of its service by "repeat infringers." 17 U.S.C. § 512(i)(1)(A). Far from doing anything to discourage repeat infringers of the plaintiffs' copyrights, Aimster invited them to do so, showed them how they could do so with ease using its system, and by teaching its users how to encrypt their unlawful distribution of copyrighted materials disabled itself from doing anything to prevent infringement.

This completes our discussion of the merits of Aimster's appeal. But the fact that the recording industry is likely to win this case if it is ever tried is not by itself a sufficient basis for the issuance of a preliminary injunction. A court asked to issue such an injunction must also consider which party will suffer the greater harm as a result of a ruling for or against issuance. Aimster points out that the preliminary injunction has put it out of business; the recording industry ripostes that until it was put out of business Aimster, with an estimated 2 to 3 million users, undoubtedly was facilitating a substantial infringement of music copyrights—and remember that Aimster has presented no evidence of offsetting noninfringing uses. On this record, therefore, the harm to Aimster from the grant of the injunction must be reckoned comparable to the harm that the recording industry would suffer from denial of the preliminary injunction.

The only harm that is relevant to the decision to grant a preliminary injunction is irreparable harm, since if it is reparable by an award of damages at the end of trial there is no need for preliminary relief. The recording industry's harm should the preliminary injunction be dissolved would undoubtedly be irreparable. The industry's damages from Aimster's contributory infringement cannot be reliably estimated and Aimster would in any event be unlikely ever to have the resources to pay them. Aimster's irreparable harm from the grant of the injunction is, if anything, less, because of the injunction bond of $ 500,000 that the industry was required to post and that Aimster does not contend is inadequate. (Even without the bond, the recording industry would undoubtedly be good for any damages that Aimster may have sustained from being temporarily shut down, though, bond or no bond, there is still the measurement problem.) Even if the irreparable harms are deemed the same, since the plaintiffs have a stronger case on the merits than Aimster does the judge was right to grant the injunction.

Aimster objects to the injunction's breadth. But having failed to suggest alternative language either in the district court or in this court, it has waived the objection. We cannot find a case that makes this point expressly, but it is implicit in the general principle that arguments made but not developed do not preserve issues for appellate review. E.g., *Jones Motor Co. v. Holtkamp, Liese*, 197 F.3d 1190, 1192 (7th Cir. 1999). We are not impressed by Aimster's argument that the district court had an independent duty, rooted in the free-speech clause of the First Amendment, to make sure that the impact of the injunction on communications over the Internet is no greater than is absolutely necessary to provide the recording industry with the legal protection to which it is entitled while the case wends its way to a conclusion. Copyright law and the principles of equitable relief are quite complicated enough without the superimposition of First Amendment case law on them; and we have been told recently by the Supreme Court not only that "copyright law contains built-in First Amendment accommodations" but also that, in any event, the First Amendment "bears less heavily when speakers assert the right to make other people's speeches." *Eldred v. Ashcroft*, 537 U.S. 186, 123 S. Ct. 769, 788–89, 154 L. Ed. 2d 683 (2003). Or, we add, to copy, or enable the copying of, other people's music.

AFFIRMED.

Metro-Goldwyn-Mayer Studios Inc., et al., v. Grokster, Ltd., et al., 125 S. Ct. 2764; 162 L. Ed. 2d 781 (2005)

JUDGES: SOUTER, J., delivered the opinion for a unanimous Court. GINSBURG, J., filed a concurring opinion, in which REHNQUIST, C. J., and KENNEDY, J., joined. BREYER, J., filed a concurring opinion, in which STEVENS and O'CONNOR, JJ., joined.

JUSTICE SOUTER DELIVERED THE OPINION OF THE COURT

The question is under what circumstances the distributor of a product capable of both lawful and unlawful use is liable for acts of copyright infringement by third parties using the product. We hold that one who distributes a device with the object of promoting its use to infringe copyright, as shown by clear expression or other affirmative steps taken to foster infringement, is liable for the resulting acts of infringement by third parties.

I

A

Respondents, Grokster, Ltd., and StreamCast Networks, Inc., defendants in the trial court, distribute free software products that allow computer users to share electronic files through peer-to-peer networks, so called because users' computers communicate directly with each other, not through central servers. The advantage of peer-to-peer networks over information networks of other types shows up in their substantial and growing popularity. Because they need no central computer server to mediate the exchange of information or files among users, the high-bandwidth communications capacity for a server may be dispensed with, and the need for costly server storage space is eliminated. Since copies of a file (particularly a popular one) are available on many users' computers, file requests and retrievals may be faster than on other types of networks, and since file exchanges do not travel through a server, communications can take place between any computers that remain connected to the network without risk that a glitch in the server will disable the network in its entirety. Given these benefits in security, cost, and efficiency, peer-to-peer networks are employed to store and distribute electronic files by universities, government agencies, corporations, and libraries, among others. [n1]

n1 Peer-to-peer networks have disadvantages as well. Searches on peer-to-peer networks may not reach and uncover all available files because search requests may not be transmitted to every computer on the network. There may be redundant copies of popular files. The creator of the software has no incentive to minimize storage or bandwidth consumption, the costs of which are borne by every user of the network. Most relevant here, it is more difficult to control the content of files available for retrieval and the behavior of users.

Other users of peer-to-peer networks include individual recipients of Grokster's and StreamCast's software, and although the networks that they enjoy through using the software can be used to share any type of digital file, they have prominently employed those networks in sharing copyrighted music and video files without authorization. A group of copyright holders (MGM for short, but including motion picture studios, recording companies, songwriters, and music publishers) sued Grokster and StreamCast for their users' copyright infringements, alleging that they knowingly and intentionally distributed their software to enable users to reproduce and distribute the copyrighted works in violation of the Copyright Act, 17 U.S.C. § 101 et seq. (2000 ed. and Supp. II). [n2] MGM sought damages and an injunction.

n2 The studios and recording companies and the songwriters and music publishers filed separate suits against the defendants that were consolidated by the District Court.

Discovery during the litigation revealed the way the software worked, the business aims of each defendant company, and the predilections of the users. Grokster's eponymous software employs what is known as FastTrack technology, a protocol developed by others and licensed to Grokster. StreamCast distributes a very similar product except that its software, called Morpheus, relies on what is known as Gnutella technology. [n3] A user who downloads and installs either software possesses the protocol to send requests for files directly to the computers of others using software compatible with FastTrack or Gnutella. On the FastTrack network opened by the Grokster software, the user's request goes to a computer given an indexing capacity by the software and designated a supernode, or to some other computer with comparable power and capacity to collect temporary indexes of the files available on the computers of users connected to it. The supernode (or indexing computer) searches its own index and may communicate the search request to other supernodes. If the file is found, the supernode discloses its location to the computer requesting it, and the requesting user can download the file directly from the computer located. The copied file is placed in a designated sharing folder on the requesting user's computer, where it is available for other users to download in turn, along with any other file in that folder.

n3 Subsequent versions of Morpheus, released after the record was made in this case, apparently rely not on Gnutella but on a technology called Neonet. These developments are not before us.

In the Gnutella network made available by Morpheus, the process is mostly the same, except that in some versions of the Gnutella protocol there are no supernodes. In these versions, peer computers using the protocol communicate directly with each other. When a user enters a search request into the Morpheus software, it sends the request to computers connected with it, which in turn pass the request along to other connected peers. The search results are communicated to the requesting computer, and the user can download desired files directly from peers' computers. As this description indicates, Grokster and StreamCast use no servers to intercept the content of the search requests or to mediate the file transfers conducted by users of the software, there being no central point through which the substance of the communications passes in either direction. [n4]

n4 There is some evidence that both Grokster and StreamCast previously operated supernodes, which compiled indexes of files available on all of the nodes connected to them. This evidence, pertaining to previous versions of the defendants' software, is not before us and would not affect our conclusions in any event.

Although Grokster and StreamCast do not therefore know when particular files are copied, a few searches using their software would show what is available on the networks the software reaches. MGM commissioned a statistician to conduct a systematic search, and his study showed that nearly 90% of the files available for download on the FastTrack system were copyrighted works. [n5] Grokster and StreamCast dispute this figure, raising methodological problems and arguing that free copying even of copyrighted works may be authorized by the rightholders. They also argue that potential noninfringing uses of their software are significant in kind, even if infrequent in practice. Some musical performers, for example, have gained new audiences by distributing their copyrighted works for free across peer-to-peer networks, and some distributors of unprotected content have used peer-to-peer networks to disseminate files, Shakespeare being an example. Indeed, StreamCast has given Morpheus users the opportunity to download the briefs in this very case, though their popularity has not been quantified.

n5 By comparison, evidence introduced by the plaintiffs in *A & M Records, Inc. v. Napster, Inc.,* 239 F.3d 1004 (9ᵗʰ Cir. 2001), showed that 87% of files available on the Napster filesharing network were copyrighted, *id.,* at 1013.

As for quantification, the parties' anecdotal and statistical evidence entered thus far to show the content available on the FastTrack and Gnutella networks does not say much about which files are actually downloaded by users, and no one can say how often the software is used to obtain copies of unprotected material. But MGM's evidence gives reason to think that the vast majority of users' downloads are acts of infringement, and because well over 100 million copies of the software in question are known to have been downloaded, and billions of files are shared across the FastTrack and Gnutella networks each month, the probable scope of copyright infringement is staggering.

Grokster and StreamCast concede the infringement in most downloads, and it is uncontested that they are aware that users employ their software primarily to download copyrighted files, even if the decentralized FastTrack and Gnutella networks fail to reveal which files are being copied, and when. From time to time, moreover, the companies have learned about their users' infringement directly, as from users who have sent e-mail to each company with questions about playing copyrighted movies they had downloaded, to whom the companies have responded with guidance. [n6] App. 559–563, 808–816, 939–954. And MGM notified the companies of 8 million copyrighted files that could be obtained using their software.

n6 The Grokster founder contends that in answering these e-mails he often did not read them fully. App. 77, 769.

Grokster and StreamCast are not, however, merely passive recipients of information about infringing use. The record is replete with evidence that from the moment Grokster and StreamCast began to distribute their free software, each one clearly voiced the objective that recipients use it to download copyrighted works, and each took active steps to encourage infringement.

After the notorious file-sharing service, Napster, was sued by copyright holders for facilitation of copyright infringement, *A & M Records, Inc. v. Napster, Inc.,* 114 F. Supp. 2d 896 (ND Cal. 2000), aff'd in part, rev'd in part, 239 F.3d 1004 (9ᵗʰ Cir. 2001), StreamCast gave away a software program of a kind known as OpenNap, designed as compatible with the Napster program and open to Napster users for downloading files from other Napster and OpenNap users' computers. Evidence indicates that "it was always [StreamCast's] intent to use [its OpenNap network] to be able to capture email addresses of [its] initial target market so that [it] could promote [its] StreamCast Morpheus interface to them," indeed, the OpenNap program was engineered " 'to leverage Napster's 50 million user base,' " *id.,* at 746.

StreamCast monitored both the number of users downloading its OpenNap program and the number of music files they downloaded. *Id.*, at 859, 863, 866. It also used the resulting OpenNap network to distribute copies of the Morpheus software and to encourage users to adopt it. *Id.*, at 861, 867, 1039. Internal company documents indicate that StreamCast hoped to attract large numbers of former Napster users if that company was shut down by court order or otherwise, and that StreamCast planned to be the next Napster. *Id.*, at 861. A kit developed by StreamCast to be delivered to advertisers, for example, contained press articles about StreamCast's potential to capture former Napster users, *id.*, at 568–572, and it introduced itself to some potential advertisers as a company "which is similar to what Napster was," *id.*, at 884. It broadcast banner advertisements to users of other Napster-compatible software, urging them to adopt its OpenNap. *Id.*, at 586. An internal e-mail from a company executive stated: "'We have put this network in place so that when Napster pulls the plug on their free service . . . or if the Court orders them shut down prior to that . . . we will be positioned to capture the flood of their 32 million users that will be actively looking for an alternative.'" *Id.* at 588–589, 861.

Thus, StreamCast developed promotional materials to market its service as the best Napster alternative. One proposed advertisement read: "Napster Inc. has announced that it will soon begin charging you a fee. That's if the courts don't order it shut down first. What will you do to get around it?" *Id.*, at 897. Another proposed ad touted StreamCast's software as the " # 1 alternative to Napster" and asked "when the lights went off at Napster . . . where did the users go?" *Id.*, at 836 (ellipsis in original). [n7] StreamCast even planned to flaunt the illegal uses of its software; when it launched the OpenNap network, the chief technology officer of the company averred that "the goal is to get in trouble with the law and get sued. It's the best way to get in the news." *Id.* at 916.

n7 The record makes clear that StreamCast developed these promotional materials but not whether it released them to the public. Even if these advertisements were not released to the public and do not show encouragement to infringe, they illuminate StreamCast's purposes.

The evidence that Grokster sought to capture the market of former Napster users is sparser but revealing, for Grokster launched its own OpenNap system called Swaptor and inserted digital codes into its Web site so that computer users using Web search engines to look for "Napster" or "free filesharing" would be directed to the Grokster Web site, where they could download the Grokster software. *Id.* at 992–993. And Grokster's name is an apparent derivative of Napster.

StreamCast's executives monitored the number of songs by certain commercial artists available on their networks, and an internal communication indicates they aimed to have a larger number of copyrighted songs available on their networks than other file-sharing networks. *Id.* at 868. The point, of course, would be to attract users of a mind to infringe, just as it would be with their promotional materials developed showing copyrighted songs as examples of the kinds of files available through Morpheus. *Id.*, at 848. Morpheus in fact allowed users to search specifically for "Top 40" songs, *id.*, at 735, which were inevitably copyrighted. Similarly, Grokster sent users a newsletter promoting its ability to provide particular, popular copyrighted materials. Brief for Motion Picture Studio and Recording Company Petitioners 7–8.

In addition to this evidence of express promotion, marketing, and intent to promote further, the business models employed by Grokster and StreamCast confirm that their principal object was use of their software to download copyrighted works. Grokster and StreamCast receive no revenue from users, who obtain the software itself for nothing. Instead, both companies generate income by selling advertising space, and they stream the advertising to Grokster and Morpheus users while they are employing the programs. As the number of users of each program increases, advertising opportunities become worth more. Cf. App. 539, 804. While there is doubtless some demand for free Shakespeare, the evidence shows that substantive volume is a function of free access to copyrighted work. Users seeking Top 40 songs, for example, or the latest release by Modest Mouse, are certain to be far more numerous than those seeking a free Decameron, and Grokster and StreamCast translated that demand into dollars.

Finally, there is no evidence that either company made an effort to filter copyrighted material from users' downloads or otherwise impede the sharing of copyrighted files. Although Grokster appears to have sent e-mails warning users about infringing content when it received threatening notice from the copyright holders, it never blocked anyone from continuing to use its software to share copyrighted files. *Id.*, at 75–76. StreamCast not only rejected another company's offer of help to monitor infringement, id., at 928–929, but blocked the Internet Protocol addresses of entities it believed were trying to engage in such monitoring on its networks. *Id.* at 917–922.

B

After discovery, the parties on each side of the case cross-moved for summary judgment. The District Court limited its consideration to the asserted liability of Grokster and StreamCast for distributing the current versions of their software, leaving aside whether either was liable "for damages arising from past versions of their software, or from other past activities." 259 F. Supp. 2d 1029, 1033 (CD Cal. 2003). The District Court held that those who used the Grokster and Morpheus software to download copyrighted media files directly infringed MGM's copyrights, a conclusion not contested on appeal, but the court nonetheless granted summary judgment in favor of Grokster and StreamCast as to any liability arising from distribution of the then current versions of their software. Distributing that software gave rise to no liability in the court's view, because its use did not provide the distributors with actual knowledge of specific acts of infringement. Case No. CV 01 08541 SVW (PJWx) (CD Cal., June 18, 2003), App. 1213.

The Court of Appeals affirmed. 380 F.3d 1154 (9th Cir. 2004). In the court's analysis, a defendant was liable as a contributory infringer when it had knowledge of direct infringement and materially contributed to the infringement. But the court read *Sony Corp. of America v. Universal City Studios, Inc.*, 464 U.S. 417, 78 L. Ed. 2d 574, 104 S. Ct. 774 (1984), as holding that distribution of a commercial product capable of substantial noninfringing uses could not give rise to contributory liability for infringement unless the distributor had actual knowledge of specific instances of infringement and failed to act on that knowledge. The fact that the software was capable of substantial noninfringing uses in the Ninth Circuit's view meant that Grokster and StreamCast were not liable, because they had no such actual knowledge, owing to the decentralized architecture of their software. The court also held that Grokster and StreamCast did not materially contribute to their users' infringement because it was the users themselves who searched for, retrieved, and stored the infringing files, with no involvement by the defendants beyond providing the software in the first place.

The Ninth Circuit also considered whether Grokster and StreamCast could be liable under a theory of vicarious infringement. The court held against liability because the defendants did not monitor or control the use of the software, had no agreed-upon right or current ability to supervise its use, and had no independent duty to police infringement. We granted certiorari. 543 U.S. ___, 160 L. Ed. 2d 518, 125 S. Ct. 686 (2004).

II

A

MGM and many of the amici fault the Court of Appeals' holding for upsetting a sound balance between the respective values of supporting creative pursuits through copyright protection and promoting innovation in new communication technologies by limiting the incidence of liability for copyright infringement. The more artistic protection is favored, the more technological innovation may be discouraged; the administration of copyright law is an exercise in managing the trade-off. See *Sony Corp. v. Universal City Studios, supra*, at 442, 78 L. Ed. 2d 574, 104 S. Ct. 774; [citations omitted.] The tension between the two values is the subject of this case, with its claim that digital distribution of copyrighted material threatens copyright holders as never before, because every copy is identical to the original, copying is easy, and many people (especially the young) use file-sharing software to download copyrighted works. This very breadth of the software's use may well draw the public directly into the debate over copyright policy, Peters, Brace Memorial Lecture: Copyright Enters the Public Domain, 51 J. Copyright Soc. 701, 705–717 (2004) (address by Register of

Copyrights), and the indications are that the ease of copying songs or movies using software like Grokster's and Napster's is fostering disdain for copyright protection, Wu, When Code Isn't Law, 89 Va. L. Rev. 679, 724–726 (2003). As the case has been presented to us, these fears are said to be offset by the different concern that imposing liability, not only on infringers but on distributors of software based on its potential for unlawful use, could limit further development of beneficial technologies. [citations omitted.]

n8 The mutual exclusivity of these values should not be overstated, however. On the one hand technological innovators, including those writing filesharing computer programs, may wish for effective copyright protections for their work. See, e.g., Wu, When Code Isn't Law, 89 Va. L. Rev. 679, 750 (2003). (StreamCast itself was urged by an associate to "get [its] technology written down and [its intellectual property] protected." App. 866.) On the other hand the widespread distribution of creative works through improved technologies may enable the synthesis of new works or generate audiences for emerging artists. See *Eldred v. Ashcroft*, 537 U.S. 186, 223–226, 154 L. Ed. 2d 683, 123 S. Ct. 769 (2003) (STEVENS, J., dissenting); Van Houweling, Distributive Values in Copyright, 83 *Texas L. Rev.* 1535, 1539–1540, 1562–1564 (2005); Brief for Sovereign Artists et al. as Amici Curiae 11.

The argument for imposing indirect liability in this case is, however, a powerful one, given the number of infringing downloads that occur every day using StreamCast's and Grokster's software. When a widely shared service or product is used to commit infringement, it may be impossible to enforce rights in the protected work effectively against all direct infringers, the only practical alternative being to go against the distributor of the copying device for secondary liability on a theory of contributory or vicarious infringement. See *In re Aimster Copyright Litigation*, 334 F.3d 643, 645–646 (2d Cir. 2003).

One infringes contributorily by intentionally inducing or encouraging direct infringement, see *Gershwin Pub. Corp. v. Columbia Artists Management, Inc.*, 443 F.2d 1159, 1162 (2d Cir. 1971), and infringes vicariously by profiting from direct infringement while declining to exercise a right to stop or limit it, Shapiro, Bernstein & Co. v. H. L. Green Co., 316 F.2d 304, 307 (2d Cir. 1963). [9] Although "the Copyright Act does not expressly render anyone liable for infringement committed by another," *Sony Corp. v. Universal City Studios*, 464 U.S., at 434, 78 L. Ed. 2d 574, 104 S. Ct. 774 these doctrines of secondary liability emerged from common law principles and are well established in the law, id., at 486, 78 L. Ed. 2d 574, 104 S. Ct. 774 (Blackmun, J., dissenting); *Kalem Co. v. Harper Brothers*, 222 U.S. 55, 62–63, 56 L. Ed. 92, 32 S. Ct. 20 (1911); *Gershwin Pub. Corp. v. Columbia Artists Management, supra*, at 1162; 3 M. Nimmer & D. Nimmer, Copyright, § 12.04[A] (2005).

n9 We stated in *Sony Corp. of America v. Universal City Studios, Inc.*, 464 U.S. 417, 78 L. Ed. 2d 574, 104 S. Ct. 774 (1984), that "'the lines between direct infringement, contributory infringement and vicarious liability are not clearly drawn'. . . . Reasoned analysis of [the Sony plaintiffs' contributory infringement claim] necessarily entails consideration of arguments and case law which may also be forwarded under the other labels, and indeed the parties . . . rely upon such arguments and authority in support of their respective positions on the issue of contributory infringement," *id.*, at 435, n. 17, 78 L. Ed. 2d 574, 104 S. Ct. 774 (quoting *Universal City Studios, Inc. v. Sony Corp.*, 480 F. Supp. 429, 457–458 (CD Cal. 1979)). In the present case MGM has argued a vicarious liability theory, which allows imposition of liability when the defendant profits directly from the infringement and has a right and ability to supervise the direct infringer, even if the defendant initially lacks knowledge of the infringement. See, e.g., Shapiro, Bernstein & Co. v. H. L. Green Co., 316 F.2d 304, 308 (CA2 1963); *Dreamland Ball Room, Inc. v. Shapiro, Bernstein & Co.*, 36 F.2d 354, 355 (CA7 1929). Because we resolve the case based on an inducement theory, there is no need to analyze separately MGM's vicarious liability theory.

B

Despite the currency of these principles of secondary liability, this Court has dealt with secondary copyright infringement in only one recent case, and because MGM has tailored its principal claim to our opinion there, a look at our earlier holding is in order. In Sony Corp. v. Universal City Studios, supra, this Court addressed a claim that secondary liability for infringement can arise from the very distribution of a commercial product. There, the product, novel at the time, was what we know today as the videocassette recorder or VCR. Copyright holders sued Sony as the manufacturer, claiming it was contributorily liable for infringement that occurred when VCR owners taped copyrighted programs because it supplied the means used to infringe, and it had constructive knowledge that infringement would occur. At the trial on the merits, the evidence showed that the principal use of the VCR was for "'time-shifting,'" or taping a program for later viewing at a more convenient time, which the Court found to be a fair, not an infringing, use. *Id.*, at 423–424, 78 L. Ed. 2d 574, 104 S. Ct. 774. There was no evidence that Sony had expressed an object of bringing about taping in violation of copyright or had taken active steps to increase its profits from unlawful taping. *Id.*, at 438, 78 L. Ed. 2d 574, 104 S. Ct. 774. Although Sony's advertisements urged consumers to buy the VCR to "'record favorite shows'" or "'build a library'" of recorded programs, *id.*, at 459, 78 L. Ed. 2d 574, 104 S. Ct. 774 (Blackmun, J., dissenting), neither of these uses was necessarily infringing, *id.*, at 424, 454–455, 78 L. Ed. 2d 574, 104 S. Ct. 774.

On those facts, with no evidence of stated or indicated intent to promote infringing uses, the only conceivable basis for imposing liability was on a theory of contributory infringement arising from its sale of VCRs to consumers with knowledge that some would use them to infringe. *Id.*, at 439, 78 L. Ed. 2d 574, 104 S. Ct. 774. But because the VCR was "capable of commercially significant noninfringing uses," we held the manufacturer could not be faulted solely on the basis of its distribution. *Id.*, at 442, 78 L. Ed. 2d 574, 104 S. Ct. 774.

This analysis reflected patent law's traditional staple article of commerce doctrine, now codified, that distribution of a component of a patented device will not violate the patent if it is suitable for use in other ways. [citations omitted.] The doctrine was devised to identify instances in which it may be presumed from distribution of an article in commerce that the distributor intended the article to be used to infringe another's patent, and so may justly be held liable for that infringement. "One who makes and sells articles which are only adapted to be used in a patented combination will be presumed to intend the natural consequences of his acts; he will be presumed to intend that they shall be used in the combination of the patent." [citations omitted.]

In sum, where an article is "good for nothing else" but infringement, *Canda v. Michigan Malleable Iron Co., supra,* at 489, there is no legitimate public interest in its unlicensed availability, and there is no injustice in presuming or imputing an intent to infringe [citations omitted]. Conversely, the doctrine absolves the equivocal conduct of selling an item with substantial lawful as well as unlawful uses, and limits liability to instances of more acute fault than the mere understanding that some of one's products will be misused. It leaves breathing room for innovation and a vigorous commerce. See *Sony Corp. v. Universal City Studios, supra,* at 442 . . . [citations omitted].

The parties and many of the amici in this case think the key to resolving it is the Sony rule and, in particular, what it means for a product to be "capable of commercially significant noninfringing uses." *Sony Corp. v. Universal City Studios, supra,* at 442, 78 L. Ed. 2d 574, 104 S. Ct. 774. MGM advances the argument that granting summary judgment to Grokster and StreamCast as to their current activities gave too much weight to the value of innovative technology, and too little to the copyrights infringed by users of their software, given that 90% of works available on one of the networks was shown to be copyrighted. Assuming the remaining 10% to be its noninfringing use, MGM says this should not qualify as "substantial," and the Court should quantify Sony to the extent of holding that a product used "principally" for infringement does not qualify. See Brief for Motion Picture Studio and Recording Company Petitioners 31. As mentioned before, Grokster and StreamCast reply by citing evidence that their software can be used to reproduce public domain works, and they point to copyright holders who actually encourage copying. Even if infringement is the principal practice with their software today, they argue, the noninfringing uses are significant and will grow.

We agree with MGM that the Court of Appeals misapplied *Sony,* which it read as limiting secondary liability quite beyond the circumstances to which the case applied. *Sony* barred secondary liability based on presuming or imputing intent to cause infringement solely from the design or distribution of a product capable of substantial lawful use, which the distributor knows is in fact used for infringement. The Ninth Circuit has read *Sony's* limitation to mean that whenever a product is capable of substantial lawful use, the producer can never be held contributorily liable for third parties' infringing use of it; it read the rule as being this broad, even when an actual purpose to cause infringing use is shown by evidence independent of design and distribution of the product, unless the distributors had "specific knowledge of infringement at a time at which they contributed to the infringement, and failed to act upon that information." 380 F.3d at 1162 (internal quotation marks and alterations omitted). Because the Circuit found the StreamCast and Grokster software capable of substantial lawful use, it concluded on the basis of its reading of *Sony* that neither company could be held liable, since there was no showing that their software, being without any central server, afforded them knowledge of specific unlawful uses.

This view of *Sony*, however, was error, converting the case from one about liability resting on imputed intent to one about liability on any theory. Because Sony did not displace other theories of secondary liability, and because we find below that it was error to grant summary judgment to the companies on MGM's inducement claim, we do not revisit *Sony* further, as MGM requests, to add a more quantified description of the point of balance between protection and commerce when liability rests solely on distribution with knowledge that unlawful use will occur. It is enough to note that the Ninth Circuit's judgment rested on an erroneous understanding of Sony and to leave further consideration of the *Sony* rule for a day when that may be required.

C

Sony's rule limits imputing culpable intent as a matter of law from the characteristics or uses of a distributed product. But nothing in Sony requires courts to ignore evidence of intent if there is such evidence, and the case was never meant to foreclose rules of fault-based liability derived from the common law. [10] *Sony Corp. v. Universal City Studios*, 464 U.S., at 439, 78 L. Ed. 2d 574, 104 S. Ct. 774 ("If vicarious liability is to be imposed on Sony in this case, it must rest on the fact that it has sold equipment with constructive knowledge" of the potential for infringement). Thus, where evidence goes beyond a product's characteristics or the knowledge that it may be put to infringing uses, and shows statements or actions directed to promoting infringement, Sony's staple-article rule will not preclude liability.

n10 Nor does the Patent Act's exemption from liability for those who distribute a staple article of commerce, 35 U.S.C. § 271(c), extend to those who induce patent infringement, § 271(b).

The classic case of direct evidence of unlawful purpose occurs when one induces commission of infringement by another, or "entices or persuades another" to infringe, Black's Law Dictionary 790 (8th ed. 2004), as by advertising. Thus at common law a copyright or patent defendant who "not only expected but invoked [infringing use] by advertisement" was liable for infringement "on principles recognized in every part of the law." *Kalem Co. v. Harper Brothers*, 222 U.S., at 62–63, 56 L. Ed. 2d 92, 32 S. Ct. 20 (copyright infringement). [citations omitted.]

The rule on inducement of infringement as developed in the early cases is no different today. [11] Evidence of "active steps . . . taken to encourage direct infringement," *Oak Industries, Inc. v. Zenith Electronics Corp.*, 697 F. Supp. 988, 992 (ND Ill. 1988), such as advertising an infringing use or instructing how to engage in an infringing use, show an affirmative intent that the product be used to infringe, and a showing that infringement was encouraged overcomes the law's reluctance to find liability when a defendant merely sells a commercial product suitable for some lawful use, see, e.g., *Water Technologies Corp. v. Calco, Ltd.*, 850 F.2d 660, 668 (Fed Cir. 1988) (liability for inducement where one "actively and knowingly aids and abets another's direct infringement" (emphasis omitted)); *Fromberg, Inc. v. Thornhill*, 315 F.2d 407, 412–413 (5ᵗʰ Cir. 1963) (demonstrations by sales staff of infringing uses supported liability for inducement); *Haworth Inc. v. Herman Miller Inc.*, 37 USPQ 2d 1080, 1090 (W.D. Mich. 1994) (evidence that defendant "demonstrated and recommended infringing configurations" of its product could support inducement liability); *Sims v. Mack Trucks, Inc.*, 459 F. Supp. 1198, 1215 (E.D. Pa. 1978) (finding inducement where the use "depicted by the defendant in its promotional film and brochures infringes the . . . patent"), overruled on other grounds, 608 F.2d 87 (3ʳᵈ Cir. 1979). Cf. W. Keeton, D. Dobbs, R. Keeton, & D. Owen, Prosser and Keeton on Law of Torts 37 (5th ed. 1984) ("There is a definite tendency to impose greater responsibility upon a defendant whose conduct was intended to do harm, or was morally wrong").

n11 Inducement has been codified in patent law. Ibid.

For the same reasons that *Sony* took the staple-article doctrine of patent law as a model for its copyright safe-harbor rule, the inducement rule, too, is a sensible one for copyright. We adopt it here, holding that one who distributes a device with the object of promoting its use to infringe copyright, as shown by clear expression or other affirmative steps taken to foster infringement, is liable for the resulting acts of infringement by third parties. We are, of course, mindful of the need to keep from trenching on regular commerce or discouraging the development of technologies with lawful and unlawful potential. Accordingly, just as Sony did not find intentional inducement despite the knowledge of the VCR manufacturer that its device could be used to infringe, 464 U.S., at 439, n. 19, 78 L. Ed. 2d 574, 104 S. Ct. 774, mere knowledge of infringing potential or of actual infringing uses would not be enough here to subject a distributor to liability. Nor would ordinary acts incident to product distribution, such as offering customers technical support or product updates, support liability in themselves. The inducement rule, instead, premises liability on purposeful, culpable expression and conduct, and thus does nothing to compromise legitimate commerce or discourage innovation having a lawful promise.

III

A

The only apparent question about treating MGM's evidence as sufficient to withstand summary judgment under the theory of inducement goes to the need on MGM's part to adduce evidence that StreamCast and Grokster communicated an inducing message to their software users. The classic instance of inducement is by advertisement or solicitation that broadcasts a message designed to stimulate others to commit violations. MGM claims that such a message is shown here. It is undisputed that StreamCast beamed onto the computer screens of users of Napster-compatible programs ads urging the adoption of its OpenNap program, which was designed, as its name implied, to invite the custom of patrons of Napster, then under attack in the courts for facilitating massive infringement. Those who accepted StreamCast's OpenNap program were offered software to perform the same services, which a factfinder could conclude would readily have been understood in the Napster market as the ability to download copyrighted music files. Grokster distributed an electronic newsletter containing links to articles promoting its software's ability to access popular copyrighted music. And anyone whose Napster or free file-sharing searches turned up a link to Grokster would have understood Grokster to be offering the same file-sharing ability as Napster, and to the same people who probably used Napster for infringing downloads; that would also have been the understanding of anyone offered Grokster's suggestively named Swaptor software, its version of OpenNap. And both companies communicated a clear message by responding affirmatively to requests for help in locating and playing copyrighted materials.

In StreamCast's case, of course, the evidence just described was supplemented by other unequivocal indications of unlawful purpose in the internal communications and advertising designs aimed at Napster users ("When the lights went off at Napster . . . where did the users go?" App. 836 (ellipsis in original)). Whether the messages were communicated is not to the point on this record. The function of the message in the theory of inducement is to prove by a defendant's own statements that his unlawful purpose disqualifies him from claiming protection (and incidentally to point to actual violators likely to be found among those who hear or read the message). See *supra*, at 17–19. Proving that a message was sent out, then, is the preeminent but not exclusive way of showing that active steps were taken with the purpose of bringing about infringing acts, and of showing that infringing acts took place by using the device distributed. Here, the summary judgment record is replete with other evidence that Grokster and StreamCast, unlike the manufacturer and distributor in Sony, acted with a purpose to cause copyright violations by use of software suitable for illegal use. See supra, at 6–9.

Three features of this evidence of intent are particularly notable. First, each company showed itself to be aiming to satisfy a known source of demand for copyright infringement, the market comprising former Napster users. StreamCast's internal documents made constant reference to Napster, it initially distributed its Morpheus software through an OpenNap program compatible with Napster, it advertised its OpenNap program to Napster users, and its Morpheus software functions as Napster did except that it could be used to distribute more kinds of files, including copyrighted movies and software programs. Grokster's name is apparently derived from Napster, it too initially offered an OpenNap program, its software's function is likewise comparable to Napster's, and it attempted to divert queries for Napster onto its own Web site. Grokster and StreamCast's efforts to supply services to former Napster users, deprived of a mechanism to copy and distribute what were overwhelmingly infringing files, indicate a principal, if not exclusive, intent on the part of each to bring about infringement.

Second, this evidence of unlawful objective is given added significance by MGM's showing that neither company attempted to develop filtering tools or other mechanisms to diminish the infringing activity using their software. While the Ninth Circuit treated the defendants' failure to develop such tools as irrelevant because they lacked an independent duty to monitor their users' activity, we think this evidence underscores Grokster's and StreamCast's intentional facilitation of their users' infringement. [12]

n12 Of course, in the absence of other evidence of intent, a court would be unable to find contributory infringement liability merely based on a failure to take affirmative steps to prevent infringement, if the device otherwise was capable of substantial noninfringing uses. Such a holding would tread too close to the Sony safe harbor.

Third, there is a further complement to the direct evidence of unlawful objective. It is useful to recall that StreamCast and Grokster make money by selling advertising space, by directing ads to the screens of computers employing their software. As the record shows, the more the software is used, the more ads are sent out and the greater the advertising revenue becomes. Since the extent of the software's use determines the gain to the distributors, the commercial sense of their enterprise turns on high-volume use, which the record shows is infringing. [13] This evidence alone would not justify an inference of unlawful intent, but viewed in the context of the entire record its import is clear.

n13 Grokster and StreamCast contend that any theory of liability based on their conduct is not properly before this Court because the rulings in the trial and appellate courts dealt only with the present versions of their software, not "past acts . . . that allegedly encouraged infringement or assisted . . . known acts of infringement." Brief for Respondents 14; see also *id.*, at 34. This contention misapprehends the basis for their potential liability. It is not only that encouraging a particular consumer to infringe a copyright can give rise to secondary liability for the infringement that results. Inducement liability goes beyond that, and the distribution of a product can itself give rise to liability where evidence shows that the distributor intended and encouraged the product to be used to infringe. In such a case, the culpable act is not merely the encouragement of infringement but also the distribution of the tool intended for infringing use. [citations omitted.]

The unlawful objective is unmistakable.

B

In addition to intent to bring about infringement and distribution of a device suitable for infringing use, the inducement theory of course requires evidence of actual infringement by recipients of the device, the software in this case. As the account of the facts indicates, there is evidence of infringement on a gigantic scale, and there is no serious issue of the adequacy of MGM's showing on this point in order to survive the companies' summary judgment requests. Although an exact calculation of infringing use, as a basis for a claim of damages, is subject to dispute, there is no question that the summary judgment evidence is at least adequate to entitle MGM to go forward with claims for damages and equitable relief.

. . . .

In sum, this case is significantly different from Sony and reliance on that case to rule in favor of StreamCast and Grokster was error. Sony dealt with a claim of liability based solely on distributing a product with alternative lawful and unlawful uses, with knowledge that some users would follow the unlawful course. The case struck a balance between the interests of protection and innovation by holding that the product's capability of substantial lawful employment should bar the imputation of fault and consequent secondary liability for the unlawful acts of others.

MGM's evidence in this case most obviously addresses a different basis of liability for distributing a product open to alternative uses. Here, evidence of the distributors' words and deeds going beyond distribution as such shows a purpose to cause and profit from third-party acts of copyright infringement. If liability for inducing infringement is ultimately found, it will not be on the basis of presuming or imputing fault, but from inferring a patently illegal objective from statements and actions showing what that objective was.

There is substantial evidence in MGM's favor on all elements of inducement, and summary judgment in favor of Grokster and StreamCast was error. On remand, reconsideration of MGM's motion for summary judgment will be in order.

The judgment of the Court of Appeals is vacated, and the case is remanded for further proceedings consistent with this opinion.

It is so ordered.

CONCUR: JUSTICE GINSBURG, WITH WHOM THE CHIEF JUSTICE AND JUSTICE KENNEDY JOIN, CONCURRING

I concur in the Court's decision, which vacates in full the judgment of the Court of Appeals for the Ninth Circuit, ante, at 24, and write separately to clarify why I conclude that the Court of Appeals misperceived, and hence misapplied, our holding in *Sony Corp. of America v. Universal City Studios, Inc.*, 464 U.S. 417, 78 L. Ed. 2d 574, 104 S. Ct. 774 (1984). There is here at least a "genuine issue as to [a] material fact," Fed. Rule Civ. Proc. 56(c), on the liability of Grokster or StreamCast, not only for actively inducing copyright infringement, but also or alternatively, based on the distribution of their software products, for contributory copyright infringement. On neither score was summary judgment for Grokster and StreamCast warranted.

At bottom, however labeled, the question in this case is whether Grokster and StreamCast are liable for the direct infringing acts of others. Liability under our jurisprudence may be predicated on actively encouraging (or inducing) infringement through specific acts (as the Court's opinion develops) or on distributing a product distributees use to infringe copyrights, if the product is not capable of "substantial" or "commercially significant" noninfringing uses. *Sony*, 464 U.S., at 442, 78 L. Ed. 2d 574, 104 S. Ct. 774; *see also* 3 M. Nimmer & D. Nimmer, Nimmer on Copyright § 12.04[A][2] (2005). While the two categories overlap, they capture different culpable behavior. Long coexisting, both are now codified in patent law. Compare 35 U.S.C. § 271(b) (active inducement liability), with § 271(c) (contributory liability for distribution of a product not "suitable for substantial noninfringing use").

In *Sony*, 464 U.S. 417, 78 L. Ed. 2d 574, 104 S. Ct. 774, the Court considered Sony's liability for selling the Betamax video cassette recorder. It did so enlightened by a full trial record. Drawing an analogy to the staple article of commerce doctrine from patent law, the Sony Court observed that the "sale of an article . . . adapted to [a patent] infringing use" does not suffice "to make the seller a contributory infringer" if the article "is also adapted to other and lawful uses." *Id.*, at 441, 78 L. Ed. 2d 574, 104 S. Ct. 774 (quoting Henry v. A. B. Dick Co., 224 U.S. 1, 48, 56 L. Ed. 645, 32 S. Ct. 364, 1912 Dec. Comm'r Pat. 575 (1912), overruled on other grounds, *Motion Picture Patents Co. v. Universal Film Mfg. Co.*, 243 U.S. 502, 517, 61 L. Ed. 871, 37 S. Ct. 416, 1917 Dec. Comm'r Pat. 391 (1917)).

. . . .

The Ninth Circuit went astray, I will endeavor to explain, when that court granted summary judgment to Grokster and StreamCast on the charge of contributory liability based on distribution of their software products. Relying on its earlier opinion in *A&M Records, Inc. v. Napster, Inc.*, 239 F.3d 1004 (9th Cir. 2001), the Court of Appeals held that "if substantial noninfringing use was shown, the copyright owner would be required to show that the defendant had reasonable knowledge of specific infringing files." 380 F.3d 1154, 1161 (CA9 2004). "A careful examination of the record," the court concluded, "indicates that there is no genuine issue of material fact as to noninfringing use." Ibid. The appeals court pointed to the band Wilco, which made one of its albums available for free downloading, to other recording artists who may have authorized free distribution of their music through the Internet, and to public domain literary works and films available through Grokster's and StreamCast's software. Ibid. Although it acknowledged MGM's assertion that "the vast majority of the software use is for copyright infringement," the court concluded that Grokster's and StreamCast's proffered evidence met Sony's requirement that "a product need only be capable of substantial noninfringing uses." 380 F.3d at 1162. [n2 omitted.]

This case differs markedly from Sony. Cf. Peters, Brace Memorial Lecture: Copyright Enters the Public Domain, 51 J. Copyright Soc. 701, 724 (2004) ("The Grokster panel's reading of Sony is the broadest that any court has given it. . . . "). Here, there has been no finding of any fair use and little beyond anecdotal evidence of noninfringing uses. In finding the Grokster and StreamCast software products capable of substantial noninfringing uses, the District Court and the Court of Appeals appear to have relied largely on declarations submitted by the defendants. These declarations include assertions (some of them hearsay) that a number of copyright owners authorize distribution of their works on the Internet and that some public domain material is available through peer-to-peer networks including those accessed through Grokster's and StreamCast's software. 380 F.3d at 1161; 259 F. Supp. 2d 1029, 1035–1036 (CD Cal. 2003); App. 125–171 [n3 and n4 omitted.].
. . . .

Even if the absolute number of noninfringing files copied using the Grokster and StreamCast software is large, it does not follow that the products are therefore put to substantial noninfringing uses and are thus immune from liability. The number of noninfringing copies may be reflective of, and dwarfed by, the huge total volume of files shared. Further, the District Court and the Court of Appeals did not sharply distinguish between uses of Grokster's and StreamCast's software products (which this case is about) and uses of peer-to-peer technology generally (which this case is not about).

In sum, when the record in this case was developed, there was evidence that Grokster's and StreamCast's products were, and had been for some time, overwhelmingly used to infringe, ante, at 4–6; App. 434–439, 476–481, and that this infringement was the overwhelming source of revenue from the products, ante, at 8–9; 259 F. Supp. 2d, at 1043–1044. Fairly appraised, the evidence was insufficient to demonstrate, beyond genuine debate, a reasonable prospect that substantial or commercially significant noninfringing uses were likely to develop over time. On this record, the District Court should not have ruled dispositively on the contributory infringement charge by granting summary judgment to Grokster and StreamCast. n4

If, on remand, the case is not resolved on summary judgment in favor of MGM based on Grokster and StreamCast actively inducing infringement, the Court of Appeals, I would emphasize, should reconsider, on a fuller record, its interpretation of Sony's product distribution holding.

JUSTICE BREYER, WITH WHOM JUSTICE STEVENS AND JUSTICE O'CONNOR JOIN, CONCURRING.

I agree with the Court that the distributor of a dual-use technology may be liable for the infringing activities of third parties where he or she actively seeks to advance the infringement. Ante, at 1. I further agree that, in light of our holding today, we need not now "revisit" *Sony Corp. of America v. Universal City Studios, Inc.*, 464 U.S. 417, 78 L. Ed. 2d 574, 104 S. Ct. 774 (1984). Ante, at 17. Other Members of the Court, however, take up the Sony question: whether Grokster's product is "capable of 'substantial' or 'commercially significant' noninfringing uses." Ante, at 1 (GINSBURG, J., concurring) (quoting Sony, supra, at 442, 78 L. Ed. 2d 574, 104 S. Ct. 774). And they answer that question by stating that the Court of Appeals was wrong when it granted summary judgment on the issue in Grokster's favor. Ante, at 4. I write to explain why I disagree with them on this matter.

I

The Court's opinion in *Sony* and the record evidence (as described and analyzed in the many briefs before us) together convince me that the Court of Appeals' conclusion has adequate legal support.

A

[Justice Breyer set forth in the Sony standard and discussed the Court's decision in the original *Betamax* case.]

B

When measured against Sony's underlying evidence and analysis, the evidence now before us shows that Grokster passes *Sony's* test—that is, whether the company's product is capable of substantial or commercially significant noninfringing uses. Id., at 442. For one thing, petitioners' (hereinafter MGM) own expert declared that 75% of current files available on Grokster are infringing and 15% are "likely infringing." That leaves some number of files near 10% that apparently are noninfringing, a figure very similar to the 9% or so of authorized time-shifting uses of the VCR that the Court faced in Sony.

As in *Sony*, witnesses here explained the nature of the noninfringing files on Grokster's network without detailed quantification. . . .

Importantly, *Sony* also used the word "capable," asking whether the product is "capable of" substantial noninfringing uses. Its language and analysis suggest that a figure like 10%, if fixed for all time, might well prove insufficient, but that such a figure serves as an adequate foundation where there is a reasonable prospect of expanded legitimate uses over time. See *ibid.* (noting a "significant potential for future authorized copying"). And its language also indicates the appropriateness of looking to potential future uses of the product to determine its "capability."

Here the record reveals a significant future market for noninfringing uses of Grokster-type peer-to-peer software. Such software permits the exchange of any sort of digital file—whether that file does, or does not, contain copyrighted material. As more and more uncopyrighted information is stored in swappable form, it seems a likely inference that lawful peer-to-peer sharing will become increasingly prevalent. See, e.g., App. 142, P20 (Decl. of Brewster Kahle) ("The [Internet Archive] welcomes [the] redistribution [of authorized films] by the

Morpheus-Grokster-KaZaa community of users"); id., at 166, P8 (Decl. of Busher) (sales figures of $ 1,000 to $ 10,000 per month through peer-to-peer networks "will increase in the future as Acoustica's trialware is more widely distributed through these networks"); id., at 156–164, PP21–40 (Decl. of Sinnreich).

. . . .

There may be other now-unforeseen noninfringing uses that develop for peer-to-peer software, just as the home-video rental industry (unmentioned in Sony) developed for the VCR. But the foreseeable development of such uses, when taken together with an estimated 10% noninfringing material, is sufficient to meet Sony's standard. And while Sony considered the record following a trial, there are no facts asserted by MGM in its summary judgment filings that lead me to believe the outcome after a trial here could be any different. The lower courts reached the same conclusion.

Of course, Grokster itself may not want to develop these other noninfringing uses. But Sony's standard seeks to protect not the Groksters of this world (which in any event may well be liable under today's holding), but the development of technology more generally. And Grokster's desires in this respect are beside the point.

II

The real question here, I believe, is not whether the record evidence satisfies Sony. As I have interpreted the standard set forth in that case, it does. And of the Courts of Appeals that have considered the matter, only one has proposed interpreting Sony more strictly than I would do—in a case where the product might have failed under any standard. In re Aimster Copyright Litigation, 334 F.3d 643, 653 (CA7 2003) (defendant "failed to show that its service is ever used for any purpose other than to infringe" copyrights (emphasis added)). . . .

Instead, the real question is whether we should modify the Sony standard, as MGM requests, or interpret Sony more strictly, as I believe JUSTICE GINSBURG's approach would do in practice. Compare ante, at 4–8 (concurring) (insufficient evidence in this case of both present lawful uses and of a reasonable prospect that substantial noninfringing uses would develop over time), with Sony, 464 U.S., at 442–447, 78 L. Ed. 2d 574, 104 S. Ct. 774 (basing conclusion as to the likely existence of a substantial market for authorized copying upon general declarations, some survey data, and common sense).

As I have said, Sony itself sought to "strike a balance between a copyright holder's legitimate demand for effective—not merely symbolic—protection of the statutory monopoly, and the rights of others freely to engage in substantially unrelated areas of commerce." Id., at 442, 78 L. Ed. 2d 574, 104 S. Ct. 774. Thus, to determine whether modification, or a strict interpretation, of Sony is needed, I would ask whether MGM has shown that Sony incorrectly balanced copyright and new-technology interests. In particular: (1) Has Sony (as I interpret it) worked to protect new technology? (2) If so, would modification or strict interpretation significantly weaken that protection? (3) If so, would new or necessary copyright-related benefits outweigh any such weakening?

A

The first question is the easiest to answer. *Sony's* rule, as I interpret it, has provided entrepreneurs with needed assurance that they will be shielded from copyright liability as they bring valuable new technologies to market.

Sony's rule is clear. That clarity allows those who develop new products that are capable of substantial noninfringing uses to know, ex ante, that distribution of their product will not yield massive monetary liability. At the same time, it helps deter them from distributing products that have no other real function than—or that are specifically intended for—copyright infringement, deterrence that the Court's holding today reinforces (by adding a weapon to the copyright holder's legal arsenal).

Sony's rule is strongly technology protecting. The rule deliberately makes it difficult for courts to find secondary liability where new technology is at issue. It establishes that the law will not impose copyright liability upon the distributors of dual-use technologies (who do not themselves engage in unauthorized copying) unless the product in question will be used almost exclusively to infringe copyrights (or unless they actively induce infringements as we today describe). Sony thereby recognizes that the copyright laws are not intended to discourage or to control the emergence of new technologies, including (perhaps especially) those that help disseminate information and ideas more broadly or more efficiently. Thus *Sony's* rule shelters VCRs, typewriters, tape recorders, photocopiers, computers, cassette players, compact disc burners, digital video recorders, MP3 players, Internet search engines, and peer-to-peer software. But Sony's rule does not shelter descramblers, even if one could theoretically use a descrambler in a noninfringing way. 464 U.S., at 441–442, 78 L. Ed. 2d 574, 104 S. Ct. 774; Compare Cable/Home Communication Corp., supra, at 837–850 (developer liable for advertising television signal descrambler), with *Vault Corp.*, supra, at 262 (primary use infringing but a substantial noninfringing use).

Sony's rule is forward looking. It does not confine its scope to a static snapshot of a product's current uses (thereby threatening technologies that have undeveloped future markets). Rather, as the VCR example makes clear, a product's market can evolve dramatically over time. And Sony—by referring to a capacity for substantial noninfringing uses—recognizes that fact. *Sony's* word "capable" refers to a plausible, not simply a theoretical, likelihood that such uses will come to pass, and that fact anchors Sony in practical reality. Cf. Aimster, supra, at 651.

Sony's rule is mindful of the limitations facing judges where matters of technology are concerned. Judges have no specialized

technical ability to answer questions about present or future technological feasibililily or commercial viability where technology professionals, engineers, and venture capitalists themselves may radically
disagree and where answers may differ depending upon whether one
focuses upon the time of product development or the time of distribution. Consider, for example, the question whether devices can be
added to Grokster's software that will filter out infringing files. MGM
tells us this is easy enough to do, as do several amici that produce and
sell the filtering technology. Grokster says it is not at all easy to do,
and not an efficient solution in any event, and several apparently dis-
interested computer science professors agree. Which account should
a judge credit? *Sony* says that the judge will not necessarily have to
decide.

Given the nature of the *Sony* rule, it is not surprising that in the last
20 years, there have been relatively few contributory infringement
suits—based on a product distribution theory—brought against technology providers (a small handful of federal appellate court cases and
perhaps fewer than two dozen District Court cases in the last 20 years).
I have found nothing in the briefs or the record that shows that *Sony*
has failed to achieve its innovation-protecting objective.

B

The second, more difficult, question is whether a modified Sony rule
(or a strict interpretation) would significantly weaken the law's ability to protect new technology. JUSTICE GINSBURG's approach would
require defendants to produce considerably more concrete evidence—
more than was presented here—to earn *Sony's* shelter. That heavier
evidentiary demand, and especially the more dramatic (case-by-case
balancing) modifications that MGM and the Government seek, would,
I believe, undercut the protection that *Sony* now offers.

To require defendants to provide, for example, detailed evidence—
say business plans, profitability estimates, projected technological modifications, and so forth—would doubtless make life easier for copyright
holder plaintiffs. But it would simultaneously increase the legal uncertainty that surrounds the creation or development of a new technology
capable of being put to infringing uses. Inventors and entrepreneurs
(in the garage, the dorm room, the corporate lab, or the boardroom)
would have to fear (and in many cases endure) costly and extensive
trials when they create, produce, or distribute the sort of information technology that can be used for copyright infringement. They
would often be left guessing as to how a court, upon later review of
the product and its uses, would decide when necessarily rough estimates amounted to sufficient evidence. They would have no way to
predict how courts would weigh the respective values of infringing and
noninfringing uses; determine the efficiency and advisability of technological changes; or assess a product's potential future markets. The
price of a wrong guess—even if it involves a good-faith effort to assess

technical and commercial viability—could be large statutory damages (not less than $750 and up to $ 30,000 per infringed work). 17 U.S.C. § 504(c)(1). The additional risk and uncertainty would mean a consequent additional chill of technological development.

C

The third question—whether a positive copyright impact would outweigh any technology-related loss—I find the most difficult of the three. I do not doubt that a more intrusive *Sony* test would generally provide greater revenue security for copyright holders. But it is harder to conclude that the gains on the copyright swings would exceed the losses on the technology roundabouts. . . .

I do not know whether these developments and similar alternatives will prove sufficient, but I am reasonably certain that, given their existence, a strong demonstrated need for modifying *Sony* (or for interpreting Sony's standard more strictly) has not yet been shown. That fact, along with the added risks that modification (or strict interpretation) would impose upon technological innovation, leads me to the conclusion that we should maintain Sony.

. . . .

For these reasons, I disagree with JUSTICE GINSBURG, but I agree with the Court and join its opinion.

NOTE

1. As noted above, the battles between the record labels and music publishers and the ISPs and P2P networks were well underway before a decision was entered against an individual downloader. In *BMG Music, et al. v. Gonzalez*, 430 F3d 888 (7th Cir. 2005), the defendant downloaded more than 1,370 copyrighted songs over the KaZaa network. *Id.* at 899. The defendant maintained that some of the downloaded songs were on compact discs that she had purchased prior to downloading or subsequent to downloading, and that her downloading had been fair use, because she had downloaded the songs to evaluate them for future purchase. As noted by the court however, "[i]nstead of erasing the songs she did not buy, she retained them." *Id.* at 890. As this was a review at a summary judgment motion, the court focused on the 30 songs that Gonzalez admitted she had downloaded, and never purchased, owned, or deleted. In upholding the district court's grant of summary judgment, the Seventh Circuit stated that the defendant was not engaged in the time shifting contemplated by the *Betamax* case. *Id.* at 890. "The premise of the *Betamax* is that the broadcast was licensed for one transmission and thus one viewing. . . . The files that Gonzalez obtained, by contrast, were posted in violation of copyright law; there was no license covering a single transmission or hearing—and, to repeat, Gonzalez kept copies." *Id.* at 890.

11.5.2.2 DeCSS

In an effort to protect the content of films distributed on digital videodisc (DVD), the Motion Picture Association of America (MPAA) and the consumer electronics industry developed a content scrambling system (CSS) code which was inserted into commercially distributed DVDs. However, in January 2000, a Norwegian teenager succeeded in hacking the code (thereby creating the DeCSS).

Two civil actions were brought by the CSS control group, one in the Southern District of New York for copyright infringement and one in the California Superior Court for Santa Clara County for theft of trade secrets. The trial judges issued preliminary injunctions against further distribution of the DeCSS code, and the defendants (represented in each case by the Electronic Frontier Foundation) are appealed. The defense theory in each case was that DeCSS simply permits computer users who employ Linux software to access DVDs they have bought legitimately. *DVD Copy Control Ass'n., Inc. v. McLaughlin,* 2000 WL 48512 (Cal. Superior Court, Santa Clara Co. 2000) and *Universal City Studios, Inc. et al. v. Reimerdes, et al.,* 111 F. Supp 2d 294 (S.D.N.Y. 2000).

In *Reimerdes,* eight major film studios sought an injunction to stop the defendants from posting the DeCSS software [software that allows circumvention of the CSS encryption system included in the plaintiffs' DVDs] on their website and providing hyperlinks to other sites that also posted the DeCSS software. After plaintiffs brought this action under the Digital Millennium Copyright Act, the defendants engaged in "what they termed 'electronic civil disobedience'—increasing their efforts to link their website to a larger number of others that [made] DeCSS available." *Id.* at 294. The defendants argued that their actions did not violate the DMCA and that, in any case, the DMCA, as applied to computer software violates the First Amendment. *Id.* at 294. The *Reimerdes* court rejected this position stating:

There was no serious question that's the defendants' posting of DeCSS violates the DMCA . . . [and] Defendants' constitutional argument ultimately rests on two propositions—that computer code, regardless of its function, is 'speech' entitled to maximum constitutional protection and that computer code therefore essentially is exempt from regulation by government. But their argument is baseless. . . .

Computer code is expressive. To that extent, it is a matter of First Amendment concern. But computer code is not purely expressive any more than the assassination of a political figure is purely a political statement. Code causes computers to perform desired functions. Its expressive element no more immunizes its functional aspects from regulation than the expressive motives of an assassin immunize the assassin's action.

In an era in which the transmission of computer viruses—which, like DeCSS, are simply computer code and thus to some degree expressive—can disable systems upon which the nation depends and in which other computer code also is capable of inflicting other harm, society must be able to regulate the use and dissemination of code in appropriate circumstances. The Constitution, after all, is a framework for building a just and democratic society. It is not a suicide pact

Id. at 304–05.

NOTE _____

1. Additional DeCSS cases include *Paramount Pictures Corporation, et al. v. 321 Studios,* 2004 U.S. Dist. Lexis 3306 (SDNY 2004), (holding the only purpose of DeCSS was to circumvent the CSS copy protection and distributing it violated the anti-trafficking

provisions of the DMCA), *Universal City Studios, Inc. et al. v. Corley*, 273 F.3d 429 (2d Cir. 2001) (computer code has speech and non-speech components, and the injunction was content neutral, and targeted only the non-speech component), and *DVD Copy Control Association, Inc. v. Bunner*, 116 Cal. App. 4th 241 (Ct. App. Ca 6th 2004), (Plaintiff Association sued under the Uniform Trade Secrets Act (UTSA) seeking an injunction to prevent the publishing or use of DeCSS. In reversing the trial court's grant of a preliminary injunction, the court stated, ". . . there is a great deal of evidence to show that . . . DeCSS had been so widely distributed that the CSS technology may have lost its trade secret status. There is no evidence to the contrary."

11.5.2.3 DRM Controversy

In an effort to better control the sale and distribution of their product, and to stem the tide of piracy, content providers have sought to protect their intellectual property with digital rights management ("DRM") software. Many of these efforts have been unsuccessful.

In Fall 2005, a firestorm arose around Sony's use of a "Rootkit" DRM on its audio CDs. Privacy and security experts analyzed the software and charged that it was unnecessarily invasive and exposed consumers to threats from viruses and hackers. Brian Krebs, "Study of Sony Ant-Piracy Software Triggers Uproar," www.washingtonpost.com, November 2, 2005. The DRM (which applied only to computers running Microsoft Windows) ". . . was a basically a form of spyware. Rootkit installed itself surreptitiously, relayed back to the company what consumers were doing with their Sony music, and exposed users' PCs to viruses." Lorraine Woellert, "Sony's Escalating 'Spyware' Fiasco," www.businessweek.com, January 21, 2006. The uproar from fans and press alike resulted in Sony pulling 52 DRM-protected titles from retail stores. *Id.* Class action lawsuits were filed against Sony in New York and California. Texas' Attorney General filed suit as well. At the time of this writing, Judge Buchwald of the United States District Court for the Southern District of New York has tentatively approved a settlement that provides:

The proposed settlement for the six cases in the Southern District of New York would allow consumers who bought CDs with the copy protections made by First 4 Internet to received [sic] $7.50 and a promotional code good for one download selected from more than 200 titles. Alternatively, the consumers could receive no money but download three albums, the Associated Press reported. In both cases, the consumer would receive a replacement for the original CD bought, but without the copy protections, according to the report.

Robert Lemos, "Sony Settlement Gets Judge's Nod,"
Security Focus, January 9, 2006

11.6 AGREEMENTS ENTERED INTO OVER THE INTERNET

Computer software comes packaged in materials that include terms and conditions of use, commonly referred to as "shrinkwrap" agreements.

Websites commonly include so-called "clickwrap" agreements, which require the potential visitor to agree to a specific set of terms and conditions prior to being admitted. The content and enforceability of such agreements is discussed in the following portion of Jeffrey Neuberger article first noted above.

Enforceability of Standard Form Contracts—Shrinkwrap and Online "Wrap" Agreements

Prior to the enactment of the federal Electronic Signatures in Global and Electronic Commerce Act in 2002, 15 U.S.C. § 7001 et seq., and the widespread adoption of the Uniform Electronic Transactions Act,[27] commentators and parties were concerned about the general question of whether electronic transactions would be judicially enforceable. These enactments permit private parties to transact electronically by agreement and authorize government agencies to use electronic records and signatures under specified circumstances.

> *Wells v. Wharton*—The Tennessee Public Records Act does not require a custodian of public records to provide such records to a citizen in the manner that the citizen requests.[28] The plaintiff sought relief when the county government limited the citizen's Web site access to public documents in bulk format because the plaintiff's access overloaded its computer system. The court ruled that a citizen requesting such records is not entitled to receive them in electronic format, and noted further that the statutory provisions concerning maintenance of public records "appear to prohibit providing records in electronic form to the public."

> *The Prudential Insurance Company of America v. Prusky*—An insurance company is not required under the federal Electronic Signatures in Global and National Commerce Act to permit policyholders to transact business with them electronically.[29] The court rejected the plaintiff's claim that the federal Act was violated when the insurance company invoked contractual limitations on its acceptance of investment allocation transfers by fax or electronic means, for the stated purpose of discouraging "market timing" in such transfers. The court referenced language in the Act that expressly provides that use or acceptance of electronic signatures is not mandatory, and that the Act does not require private parties to agree to use or accept electronic records or signatures.

> *Miriam Osborn Memorial Home Association v. Assessor of the City of Rye*—A print-out of data obtained from the online database of property sales information collected and maintained by a state agency is admissible as an electronic record, where the person who downloaded, printed and copied the data testified as to the manner in which the print-out was

---

27. UETA has now been enacted in some form in more than two-thirds of the states. The text is available at http://www.law.upenn.edu/bll/ulc/fnact99/1990s/ueta99.htm.

28. *Wells v. Wharton*, No. W2005–00695-COA-R3-CV, 2005 Tenn. App. LEXIS 762 (Tenn. Ct. App. Dec. 7, 2005).

29. *The Prudential Insurance Company of America v. Prusky*, No. 04-CV-462 (E.D. Pa. July 22, 2005).

created.[30] The court ruled that the print-out was admissible under N.Y. C.P.L.R. sec. 4518 as a public record that is admissible if properly authenticated, and under N.Y. State Tech. Law sec. 306 as a tangible exhibit that is a true and accurate representation of an electronic record.

The United Nations has promulgated a Convention aimed at regularizing international commercial electronic contracting.

UNCITRAL Convention on Electronic Contracting—The United Nations General Assembly adopted a new Convention on the Use of Electronic Communications in International Contracting on November 23, 2005.[31] The Convention was prepared by the United Nations Commission on International Trade (UNCITRAL) during proceedings that commenced in 2002. The Convention is intended to enhance legal certainty and commercial predictability in international electronic transactions. Among other things, the Convention establishes the general principle that a communication or contract shall not be denied validity or enforceability solely on the ground that it is in electronic form. The Convention opens for signature in January 2006.

The enactment of federal and state electronic signature statutes, both of which broadly validate the use of electronic records and signatures, has shifted the focus to the specific question of what kinds of electronic contracts and agreements will be enforceable, and under what circumstances.

Recursion Software, Inc. v. Interactive Intelligence, Inc.—Uncontradicted evidence showing that a user could not install downloaded software without clicking "Yes" upon the presentation of clickwrap license terms supports the entry of summary judgment on the licensor's claim that the defendant, who admitted to using the software, assented to the terms of the license.[32] The court noted that clickwrap licenses are valid and enforceable under applicable Texas law. The court declined, however, to grant summary judgment on the licensor's claims that the defendant breached the license, because there were issues of material fact precluding summary judgment on the defendant's defenses of laches, estoppel and waiver.

CSX Transportation, Inc. v. Recovery Express, Inc.—The fact that an e-mail address contains a corporation's name does not establish the authority of the e-mail sender to act on behalf of the corporation.[33] In granting the corporation's motion for summary judgment dismissing the plaintiff's complaint for breach of contract, the court ruled that the plaintiff had been unreasonable as a matter of law in relying solely on an e-mail domain name in concluding that the sender was acting on the authority of the corporation. The court analogized the e-mail domain name to "low-tech" indicia of authority such as business cards containing a company name and logo or company stationary, noting that no cases were found

---

30. *Miriam Osborn Memorial Home Association v. Assessor of the City of Rye*, No. 1717597 (N.Y. Sup. Ct., App. Term, 1st Dept. Aug. 29, 2005).

31. The press release announcing the adoption of the Convention is available at http://www.un.org/News/Press/docs/2005/ga10424.doc.htm.

32. *Recursion Software, Inc. v. Interactive Intelligence, Inc.*, No. 3:03-cv-271, 2006 U.S. Dist. LEXIS 7314 (N.D. Tex. Feb. 27, 2006).

33. *CSX Transportation, Inc. v. Recovery Express, Inc.* No. 04–12293-WGY, 2006 U.S. Dist. LEXIS 3770 (D. Mass. Feb. 1, 2006).

in which these indicia, by themselves, were held sufficient to sustain a claim of apparent authority. The court commented that if the granting of an e-mail domain name was found to "cloak the recipient with carte blanche authority to act," then "every subordinate employee with a company e-mail address— down to the night watchman—could bind a company to the same contracts as the president."

Lamle v. Mattel, Inc.—An e-mail detailing the terms of a negotiated license agreement and stating that the terms "had been agreed in principle" may satisfy the writing requirement of the California Statute of Frauds.[34] The court noted that the e-mail sent by an employee of the party disputing the agreement did not contain all of the terms that the proponent of the agreement asserted were part of an oral contract memorialized in the e-mail. The court concluded, however, that a jury might reasonably conclude that the missing terms were not material to the agreement and thus their absence would not preclude a finding that all of the material terms of the agreement were contained in the e-mail. The court also concluded that the signature requirement of the statute was met by the typed name of the sender appearing at the end of the e-mail.

While there appears to be a general trend toward the enforcement of clickwrap, shrinkwrap and other kinds of standard form agreements, there have been mixed results in cases involving choice of law, choice of forum, arbitration and other kinds of agreements, particularly with consumer end users.

Aral v. Earthlink, Inc.—The Federal Arbitration Act (FAA) does not preclude a California consumer's class action challenge to an arbitration clause in an online service subscriber agreement based upon alleged unconscionability of the clause under state law.[35] The court ruled that an unconscionability challenge to an arbitration clause is permitted under the FAA because unconscionability is a defense to any contract provision, not merely to an arbitration clause. The court concluded that the clause precluding class actions was both substantively and procedurally unconscionable, because it was presented on a "take it or leave it" basis, and because it would preclude a class action in a case involving small value consumer claims which arose from what was alleged to be deliberate overcharging by the defendant. The court also ruled that the forum selection clause was unconscionable because it required California consumers to arbitrate small value consumer claims in Georgia, a result which "discourages legitimate claims by imposing unreasonable geographical barriers."

Hessel v. Christie's Inc.—An "Important Notice" link at the foot of the Web site of an auction house that lead to information concerning conditions of sale may have given sufficient notice of the conditions to be binding on a bidder.[36] In evaluating the probability of success on the merits of a bidder's claim that the conditions were inapplicable because of insufficient notice, the court noted that the link was not immediately visible and could only be reached by scrolling down the browser window.

---

34. *Lamle v. Mattel, Inc.*, No. 04–1151 (Fed. Cir. Jan 7, 2005).

35. *Aral v. Earthlink, Inc.*, No. B177146, 2005 Cal. App. LEXIS 1847 (Cal. Ct. App. 2d Dist. Nov. 29, 2005).

36. *Hessel v. Christie's Inc.*, No. 05 Civ. 9277, 2005 U.S. Dist. LEXIS 27814 (S.D.N.Y. Nov. 10, 2005).

Nevertheless, the court concluded that the bidder had not demonstrated a likelihood of success on his claim that the conditions were not binding.

Briceno v. Sprint Spectrum, L.P.—A mandatory arbitration provision contained in terms and conditions that were available on a cellular phone provider's Web site and that were referenced in the monthly invoice sent to all subscribers is enforceable in a tort action brought by a subscriber.[37] The subscriber brought the tort action against the provider alleging that its employees obtained password information from her when she brought in her camera-telephone for repair and then used the password information to obtain and disseminate personal photographs of her body to third persons via the Internet. The court found that the terms and conditions of the subscriber contract were not unconscionable because the notice on the invoice gave the subscriber "fair and clear" warning of the terms and conditions, and also permitted the subscriber to reject the terms and terminate the contract if she did not agree with the changes.

Hubbert v. Dell Corp.—An arbitration provision included in terms and conditions of sale that were accessible via a hyperlink during an online transaction is binding and enforceable.[38] The court concluded that the purchasers had sufficient notice that the terms and conditions would be binding upon them because the hyperlink to the terms and conditions appeared on several screens during the online purchasing process, and three of the screens contained the explicit statement that the transaction was subject to the terms and conditions of sale. The court commented that the successive screens presented during the purchasing process "should be treated the same as a multipage written paper contract." Nothing that the transaction involved the purchase of a computer, the court further commented that "[c]ommon sense dictates that because the plaintiffs were purchasing computers online, they were not novices when using computers. A person using a computer quickly learns that more information is available by clicking on a blue hyperlink." The court also concluded that the arbitration clause was neither procedurally nor substantively unconscionable.

Martin v. Snapple—The fact that a Web site had an "I agree" button that required consumers to click in order to obtain goods offered as part of a retailer's product promotion is irrelevant if there is no evidence that the consumers actually clicked on the button.[39] The appeals court ruled that absence such evidence, the trial court had no factual basis for finding that the consumers entered into an agreement with the retailer that contained an arbitration clause. The court noted that the consumer plaintiffs were alleging that they never entered into a transaction on the Web site because the goods they sought to obtain were no longer available at the time they sought to participate in the promotion. Had the plaintiffs actually entered their personal information on the Web site and clicked "I agree" in order to enter into a transaction, the court concluded, the retailer would have been able to produce the required evidence of a transaction.

---

37. *Briceno v. Sprint Spectrum, L.P.*, No. 3D05–144 (Fla. Ct. App. 3d Dist. August 31, 2005).
38. *Hubbert v. Dell Corp.*, No. 5–03–0643 (Ill. App. Ct. 5th Dist. Aug. 12, 2005).
39. *Martin v. Snapple*, B174847 (Cal. Ct. App., 2d Dist. July 7, 2005) (unpublished).

Rogers v. Dell Computer Corp.—Determining the enforceability of an arbitration provision included in a terms and conditions of sale document enclosed with a mail-ordered computer requires fact-finding concerning the "language and circumstances" surrounding the order of the computer.[40] The court remanded the case for fact-finding addressed to whether a contract was formed at the time the order was placed, or whether a contract was formed only after the terms and conditions of sale document was received with the computer. The court ruled that if a contract was formed at the time the order was placed, under Uniform Commercial Code section 2–206, the arbitration term in the conditions of sale document constituted an additional term to which the purchaser did not manifest assent merely by retaining the computer.

NOTES

The Electronic Signatures in Global and National Commerce Act (also known as the "E-Sign Act" and the "Millennium Digital Commerce Act"), gives electronic signatures, contracts, or other records the same legal effect as their written counterparts. Congress specifically intended that this act will provide a uniform national standard and *pre-empt state law*. Therefore, section 102(a) specifies that a state statue, rule, or regulation may only limit, modify, or supersede Section 101 if the state has enacted the Uniform Electronic Transactions Act (UETA) or if the state has adopted alternative procedures or requirements for electronic signatures and records that are consistent with S. 761.

The Electronic Signatures in Global and National Commerce Act contains a very liberal definition of what constitutes an electronic signature: an "electronic sound, symbol or process, attached to or logically associated with a contract or other record and executed or adopted by a person with the intent to sign the record." S. 761, 106(5).

The act provides that an electronic signature will be as legally binding and valid as a handwritten signature; however, some transactions are excluded. Section 103 specifically excludes the following from the scope of the act's coverage: wills, trusts and estate matters; marriage, divorce, adoption, and other family law matters; Uniform Commercial Code(UCC) other than sections 1–107 and 1–1206, Article 2 (Sale of Goods), article 2a (Leases); court documents and filings; notices terminating or canceling utility services (water, power, heat); notices of default, foreclosure, repossession, eviction, etc. regarding a primary residence; notice of cancellation or termination of health insurance or benefits or life insurance benefits; notice of a recall of a product or material failure of a product that affects health or safety; and any document requirement to accompany the transportation or handling of hazardous materials, pesticides or other toxic or dangerous materials. Section 103(c) requires the secretary of commerce to evaluate the exemptions over three years and determine whether the exemptions are still necessary to protect consumers.

---

40. *Rogers v. Dell Computer Corp.*, 2005 OK 51 (June 28, 2005).

TABLE OF CASES

Page numbers set in **boldface type** indicate that the text of the case is given.

INDEX

Fiduciary duties: co-venturers, 816; generally, 396–97, 391–409. *See also* Attorneys

Film industry, 742, 828, 832, 833, 858, 968

Final cut, 431, 742

First Amendment: advertising and promotion, 262–63; defense, 260; generally, 187, 199, 204–8, 215–16, 267–69, 282–90; internet, 900, 914–21, 938–47; limitations, 436–37, 457–59; reproduction, 24

Grant of Rights: entertainment rights, 348, 356–64, 372, 378–80; film, 744, 751, 765, 769, 775–79, 787–91; literary publishing, 623; remedies, 522, 566, 607, 623; sound recordings, 715

Guilds/unions: arbitration, 552–53; generally, 85, 111–12, 151, 191, 317, 327, 427, 567, 602, 605–6, 763–65, 857, 137; regulation of, 28; right to credit, 148–49

Harry Fox Agency, 382, 637, 638, 657, 678, 725–26

Ideas: submission of, 338–39

Indemnification: literary publishing agreement, 616–17; management contract, 75; music publishing, 655; recording agreement, 726–27, 732; screenplay agreement, 754, 772, 781, 794

Injunctions: as a remedy, 483–500; statutes, 128–37, 191

Internet, 897–1003: clickwrap/shrink-wrap contracts, 999–1001; copyright infringement, 935–98; personal jurisdiction, 901–13; privacy concerns, 918, 932–33, 947, 968, 998

Internet Service Providers (ISPs): generally, 900; immunity, 915–17; liability, 925, 938, 944, 955, 959–60, 973–74. *See also RIAA v. Verizon Internet Services, Inc.*

Lanham Act: contract performance, 435; credit disputes, 151; prohibited conduct, 163–69, 173, 178–79; remedies of, 211; violations of, 157–62, 242–47, 260–62, 281–96, 298, 846, 887–91, 896. *See also Allen v. National Video, Inc.; Follett v. Arbor House Publishing Co., Inc.; Gilliam v. American Broadcasting Companies; King v. Innovation Books; New Kids on the Block v. News American Publishing; Rogers v. Grimaldi; Pump, Inc. v. Collins*

Management; Waits v. Frito-Lay; White v. Samsung Electronics

Life Story: agreements, 764, 771, 781, 794. *See also Rosemount Enterprises, Inc. v. Random House Inc.*

Likeness: right to, 218–37, 249, 250–54; statutory provisions, 230–37, 256–58; use of, 146, 181, 186–88, 199, 203–4, 210–12

Literary Publishing: generally, 557–633; industry of, 385

Long playing records (LPs), 68–69, 654, 711, 898

Major labels: generally, 706–13, 723; recording agreements, 387, 487

Malice: actual malice, 207–4, 412; professional responsibility, 20; standard of fault, 205–7. *See also Barrett v. Negrete; Waits v. Frito-Lay*

Market share: movies and film, 830–31; music companies, 638–39

Masters: recorded music, 387–89; remedies, 475–76; sample agreement, 715–24

Mechanical licenses: artist recording agreement, 725–26, 733; issuance of, 650; record companies, 382. *See also Mills Music Inc. v. Snyder*

Merchandising: agreements, 28, 69, 73, 715–17, 723, 728, 751, 769, 779–80, 793

Minors: contracts, 83–92; internet, 900, 917–22; statutory provisions, 42, 85–92

Most favored nations clauses, 181–82

MP3.com, 878, 948–52, 971. *See also UMG Recordings, Inc. v. MP3.com*

Music publishing: agreements, 23–25, 59–61, 69, 126, 363, 386; generally, 386–91, 635–705

Music videos: artist agreement, 59; promotion, 714; sampling settlement agreement, 703; unauthorized fixation, 963. *See also 18 U.S.C. § 2319A*

Negotiation: music publishing, 645–57; recording contracts, 710, 715, 736, 737; talent contracts, 13, 78

New York Civil Rights Law: sections 50 and 51, 84, 177–80, 188–200, 202–4, 247, 255, 264–66, 274–80

Newsworthy: defense or privilege, 200–206, 209; exception, 192–99; First Amendment, 207; public figure, 260

ABOUT THE AUTHORS

DONALD E. BIEDERMAN was Executive Vice President/Legal & Business Affairs and General Counsel, Warner/Chappell Music, Inc., Los Angeles, and Professor of Law and Director, National Institute of Entertainment & Media Law, at Southwestern University School of Law, Los Angeles, CA (now the Donald E. Biederman Entertainment & Media Law Institute).

EDWARD P. PIERSON is Executive Vice President of Legal and Business Affairs and General Counsel of Warner/Chappell Music, Inc., Los Angeles, CA, and Adjunct Professor of Law at Southwestern University School of Law and past Chair of the American Bar Association Forum on the Entertainment and Sports Industries.

MARTIN E. SILFEN is an entertainment attorney and since 1978, has taught Entertainment and Sports Law at several law schools. He is currently a Fulbright Senior Specialist and an Adjunct Professor at the Intellectual Property Summer Institute at Franklin Pierce Law Center. He is a member of the Virginia Bar.

JANNA GLASSER is an entertainment attorney and Vice President and General Counsel of Mona Lisa Sound, Inc. She has served as an Adjunct Professor at Pace University School of Law. She is a member of the New York Bar.

CHARLES J. BIEDERMAN is Counsel with Manatt, Phelps & Phillips in Los Angeles. He has served as Adjunct Professor at Vanderbilt University Law School and Mike Curb College of Entertainment and Music Business. He is a member of the New York, Georgia, and Tennessee Bars.

KENNETH J. ABDO is Vice President of Lommen Abdo Law Firm in Minneapolis, MN. He is also Adjunct Professor at William Mitchell College of Law, St. Paul, Minnesota and past Chair of the American Bar Association Forum on the Entertainment and Sports Industries.

SCOTT D. SANDERS of Scott D. Sanders, P.C., is an entertainment attorney, entertainment litigator, and member of the Georgia Bar. He is an Adjunct Professor of Law at Emory University School of Law in Atlanta, GA, teaching Entertainment Law. In *Jennings* v. *The Black Crowes,* a case based upon a "pie-chart" agreement between a band and their tour manager, he was lead counsel for the plaintiff in the first music industry related trial televised "live" on Court-TV.